THE OXFORD ENCYCLOPEDIA

OF THE

Modern Islamic World

John L. Esposito

EDITOR IN CHIEF

VOLUME 4

OXFORD
UNIVERSITY PRESS

OXFORD
UNIVERSITY PRESS

Oxford New York
Athens Auckland Bangkok Bogotá Buenos Aires Cape Town
Chennai Dar es Salaam Delhi Florence Hong Kong Istanbul Karachi
Kolkata Kuala Lumpur Madrid Melbourne Mexico City Mumbai Nairobi
Paris São Paulo Shanghai Singapore Taipei Tokyo Toronto Warsaw

and associated companies in
Berlin Ibadan

First published by Oxford University Press, Inc., 1995
198 Madison Avenue, New York, New York 10016

First issued as an Oxford University Press paperback, 2001

Oxford is a registered trademark of Oxford University Press

Library of Congress Cataloging-in-Publication Data
The Oxford encyclopedia of the modern Islamic world
John L. Esposito, editor in chief
p. cm.
Includes bibliographic references and index.
1. Islamic countries—Encyclopedias. 2. Islam—Encyclopedias.
I. Esposito, John L.
DS35.53.095 1995 909'.097671'003—dc20 94-30758 CIP

ISBN: 978-0-19-506613-5 (Set)
ISBN: 978-0-19-514906-7 (Volume 4)

Grateful acknowledgment is made to grantors of permission to use the following written and illustrative materials in this volume. Aesthetic Theory: *photographs by Walter B. Denny.* African Languages and Literatures, *article on* West Africa: *permission to reprint translations by Jan Knappert published in the* Journal for Islamic Studies *granted by Jan Knappert.* Architecture, *article on* Traditional Forms: *figure 1 © the Walt Disney Company; figure 5, courtesy of American Institute of Indian Studies, Center for Art & Archaeology; figures 2–4, 6–7, photographs by Irene A. Bierman.* Architecture, *article on* Contemporary Forms: *figures 3–6, courtesy of the Aga Khan Award for Architecture.* Carpets: *photographs by Walter B. Denny.*

EDITORIAL AND PRODUCTION STAFF

SENIOR PROJECT EDITOR: Jeffrey P. Edelstein
DEVELOPMENT EDITOR: Mark D. Cummings
COPYEDITORS AND PROOFREADERS: Jane McGary, Carl D. Rosen,
Philomena Mariani, Karen Fraley, Donald Spanel
BIBLIOGRAPHIC AND TECHNICAL RESEARCHERS: Yaḥyá Monastra, Philomena Mariani
ILLUSTRATIONS COORDINATOR: Paul Arthur
INDEXER: Stephen R. Ingle
PRODUCTION COORDINATOR: Donna Ng
MANUFACTURING CONTROLLER: Sara Connell
BOOK DESIGNER: Joan Greenfield

$315.00 (set)

THE OXFORD ENCYCLOPEDIA

OF THE

Modern Islamic World

S

CONTINUED

SATAN. The name rendered "Satan" (Ar., *shayṭān*) is derived from the Hebrew word for "adversary." It has several meanings in the Islamic traditions. When the word is used as a generic, it refers to a class of *jinn* with exceptional powers; this is the case in stories about Solomon, who uses *jinn* and satans to do his work. Satans are also like familiar spirits who accompany and inspire poets and other talented people. Someone who is possessed by a *jinn* or a satan is thought to be psychologically deviant, but in this sense satans are not necessarily evil. Satans are also said to bring diseases and cause mischief. They are said to be powerless during the fasting month of Ramaḍān except against those who improperly break the fast, and the recitation of the Basmalah will drive them from any room. In the popular culture, prophylactic amulets worn to ward off satans are often fashioned in the shape of a hand with five fingers, five being a powerful magic number. Satans in corporal form are said to be ugly, with hooves for feet, and to dwell in dark places and ruins.

In a more specific sense, a satan is a representative of evil, the chief of the satans being Iblīs, the rebel *jinn* who refused to bow down to Adam when all the angels were commanded to do so by God (Qur'ān, 15.30–34, 17.61), for which he was cast out of heaven and said to be cursed *(rajīm)*. His real punishment is delayed until the day of judgment. In the interval, he is able to lead astray anyone who is not faithful to God. In the story of Adam and Eve, he climbed into the mouth of the serpent to induce them to disobedience; this resulted in the serpent's loss of her feathers and legs. Iblīs is said to have married the serpent afterward, thus linking serpents and Satan. Some traditions hold that the *jinn* are offspring of this union. Iblīs is not the ruler of hell—a job reserved for an angel named Malik—but he will be thrown into hell along with all his host and the rest of the damned on the day of judgment (26.94–95). In post-Qur'ānic speculation there is much discussion about whether Iblīs is an angel or a *jinn*, and whether a *jinn*, a satan, and an angel belong to the same class or are different. Satans and *jinn* are said to have been created from fire and angels from light, but the story of Iblīs's rebellion against God seems to classify him with the angels. Some commentators assert that a *jinn* who is not a Muslim is a satan; if very large and powerful, it is an *ʿifrīt*. The *ʿifrīt*s appear in the *Thousand and One Nights* and other popular tales and, though often evil, are sometimes helpful to humans. Islamic tradition never really settles the issue of the nature of satans, *jinn*, angels, and other similar creatures, although they are all regarded as having been created by God and, in the case of the *jinn* in particular, capable of becoming Muslim and being saved.

In Islamic thought, the satan Iblīs represents the power of evil and is an enemy of God and humanity. Iblīs's disobedience comes from pride, his belief that he was superior to Adam and the other angels. In keeping with Islamic monotheism, however, theologians point out that Iblīs has no real power over humans that they do not themselves grant by being deceived by his trickery. He is always whispering in the ears of humans, but each person can resist the temptation. In popular tradition, he is also the one who instills the propensity to sin into humans at birth; some stories say that Jesus was preserved from sin by his mother's ability to ward off Satan. There is also a popular belief that every human is accompanied by both an angel and a satan offering contradictory inspirations. (Some popular accounts say that Muḥammad had a satan to whom he taught passages of the Qur'ān.) Muslims on pilgrimage are reminded of the existence of Satan through the ritual act of stoning Satan in the form of a stone column, an act that ritually repels the evil in the world and also recalls Abraham's stoning of Satan at Mina.

Within the Ṣūfī tradition, Satan or Iblīs is presented as a complex figure whose initial sin of rebellion against God was not simply evil or pride. Iblīs, according to the mystic al-Ḥusayn ibn Manṣūr al-Ḥallāj, refused to worship Adam because of his absolute commitment to monotheism. This absolute preference for the unity of God, even at the risk of disobeying God, makes Satan an ambiguous figure for the mystic who must ponder the tension between principle and obedience to divine command. Some Ṣūfīs contend that Iblīs will be ultimately forgiven by God at the day of judgment because of his staunch unitarian position. Satan has also been identified with the lower appetites of humans, the so-called *nafs,* and as such has been identified with the serpent. Mystics who have attained spiritual mastery over the *nafs* can convert the base appetite into something useful, just as Moses's rod was transformed into a snake and back again. Such spiritual masters have power over snakes, according to the legends, and can control actual as well as spiritual serpents.

Satan is not only the force of evil leading humans astray, but for some Muslims, particularly in modern times, he can appear in the person of a particular ruler or individual. During the Iranian Islamic Revolution, for example, popular rhetoric identified the Shah and subsequently the United States as the "Great Satan"—a usage paralleling both the Islamic and Jewish use of the term "pharaoh" to represent any evil ruler. In this view, Satan represents the personification of evil and loses some of the nuanced character shown in the Ṣūfī tradition.

[*See also* Angels.]

BIBLIOGRAPHY

Kisā'ī, Muḥammad ibn ᶜAbd Allāh al-. *The Tales of the Prophets of al-Kisā'ī.* Translated by Wheeler M. Thackston. Boston, 1978. Good translation of extra-Qur'ānic stories about prophets, angels, devils, etc.

Macdonald, J. "The Creation of Man and Angels in the Eschatological Literature." *Islamic Studies* 3 (1964): 285–308. Sound discussion of early Muslim ideas about angels.

Newby, Gordon D. *The Making of the Last Prophet.* Columbia, S.C., 1989. Good translation of some of the tales of the prophets mentioned in the Qur'ān.

Schimmel, Annemarie. *Mystical Dimensions of Islam.* Chapel Hill, N.C., 1975. Sensitive treatment of Ṣūfī traditions in Islam.

Schwarzbaum, Haim. *Biblical and Extra-Biblical Legends in Islamic Folk-Literature.* Walldorf-Hessen, 1982. Thorough treatment of Islamic folklore and methodology, with a good bibliography.

Welch, Alford T. "Allah and Other Supernatural Beings: The Emergence of the Qur'anic Doctrine of Tawḥīd." *Journal of the American Academy of Religion* 47.4 (1979): 739, 749, and *passim.*

GORDON D. NEWBY

SAᶜŪD, ᶜABD AL-ᶜAZĪZ IBN ᶜABD AL-RAḤMĀN ĀL (1880–1953), founder of the present Kingdom of Saudi Arabia and its first ruler. His father was the youngest of the three sons of the renowned Imam Fayṣal. A self-defeating family feud enabled the rival Āl Rashīd of Ḥaᶜil to extinguish the second Saudi polity and to establish themselves as rulers of central Arabia. Subsequent paternal involvement in an abortive insurgency against Āl Rashīd forced the Saᶜūd family to flee Riyadh. They eventually accepted asylum in Kuwait and spent ten years there.

Although reared in the stern principles of Unitarianism (a rigorous monotheism, often imprecisely referred to as "Wahhābism," promoted by Muḥammad ibn ᶜAbd al-Wahhāb in the mid-eighteenth century), ᶜAbd al-ᶜAzīz showed scant interest in becoming an *ᶜālim* (religious scholar) like his father. Rather, frequent attendance at the *majlis* (parliament) of successive rulers of Kuwait taught him the intricacies of governance of Arabian tribal societies, inculcated a more cosmopolitan outlook than was generally prevalent among xenophobic Najdī tribesmen, and reinforced his ambition to recover the Āl Saᶜūd patrimony.

In 1901, with help from the ruler of Kuwait, ᶜAbd al-ᶜAzīz led forty companions in a successful attack against the Āl Rashīd governor of Riyadh, thereby enabling the reestablishment of a Saᶜūdī polity. Proclaimed imam by his Unitarian followers, he nevertheless chose to delegate religious authority to his father during the latter's lifetime (d. 1928), as ᶜAbd al-ᶜAzīz devoted himself to consolidating and expanding the Saudi domains.

Al-Ḥasa Province was conquered from the Turks in 1913, the al-ᶜAydh emirate of ᶜAṣīr was annexed in 1919, and the Rashīds were decisively defeated in 1921. The British-supported Hashemite family of the Hejaz (al-Ḥijāz) was forced to abdicate in 1925, leaving ᶜAbd al-ᶜAzīz in possession of the Muslim holy cities of Mecca (Makkah) and Medina (Madinah). Henceforth, the Ḥanbalī interpretation of *sharīᶜah* (the divine law) would dominate the legal structure of the expanded state. In 1932 the Kingdom of Saudi Arabia was formally proclaimed. Two years later, after a successful war against Yemen, a border between them was vaguely arranged. By then ᶜAbd al-ᶜAzīz was widely recognized as the paramount ruler in the Arabian Peninsula.

As the Saudi polity grew, the religio-political legitimacy of ᶜAbd al-ᶜAzīz came to be rooted in the promotion of Unitarian doctrines. As early as 1909, in an attempt to bring the fractious central Arabian tribes under greater control, he began settling the tribes in permanent *hijar* (paramilitary settlements). *Muṭawwaᶜīn* (religious tutors) were sent to instruct the tribesmen in the principles of Unitarianism. Strategically placed, fervidly devoted *ikhwān* ("brethren") tribal forces were now available to further his expansionist goals.

Yet, by the late 1920s, various tribal *ikhwān* had become restive over constraints placed on them by their ruler. Raiding into Transjordan, Kuwait, and Iraq, they killed and looted Sunnīs and Shīᶜīs alike. British military action was needed to expel them. Belatedly realizing the threat they posed, ᶜAbd al-ᶜAzīz managed to mobilize other indigenous forces, defeated his erstwhile tribal allies, and razed their settlements.

The Unitarian seizure of Mecca (Makkah) in 1925 also created widespread concern in the Islamic world lest Muslims of other schools and sects suffer Unitarian harassment when making their obligatory pilgrimage. Efforts by Egyptian, Indian, and other Muslim communities to place the *ḥaramayn* (holy cities of Mecca and Medina) under international Muslim jurisdiction were aborted, following assurances from ᶜAbd al-ᶜAzīz that Muslims from anywhere, regardless of school or sect, could perform their pilgrimage rites without harassment. That commitment was scrupulously honored.

ᶜAbd al-ᶜAzīz was sometimes charged by conservative *ᶜulamā'* (religious scholars) and *ikhwān* with introducing *bidᶜah* (innovation) into the Saudi polity. His assumption of the regnal title, for reasons of external relations, offended their Unitarian sensibilities. As late as the 1940s, they rejected it as inconsistent with Islam and continued to refer to him as imam or, secularly, as *shaykh al-shuyūkh*. Similarly, his introduction of the telephone, telegraph, and various transport improvements initially aroused strong opposition. This was overcome by demonstrating that Qur'ānic passages could be transmitted by these instruments.

A further source of Unitarian misgiving was the award by ᶜAbd al-ᶜAzīz of an oil concession in 1933 to the Standard Oil Company of California, which introduced non-Muslim petroleum engineers to al-Ḥasa Province. It also opened the door to the progressive, if slow, infrastructural modernization of Saudi Arabia. ᶜAbd al-ᶜAzīz's towering leadership abilities were required to surmount such criticisms.

The immediate post–World War II era heard speculation in the emergent Arab world that an Islamic caliphate might be reestablished. ᶜAbd al-ᶜAzīz was prominently mentioned as a putative candidate, but nothing came of the idea. ᶜAbd al-ᶜAzīz's meeting with President Franklin D. Roosevelt aboard the USS *Quincy* in 1945 accorded him international stature.

During his lifetime, ᶜAbd al-ᶜAzīz sired thirty-six sons and at least twenty-one daughters. He died in 1953, before vast oil wealth eroded many traditional social values. His sons continue to rule the Saudi state.

[*See also* Saudi Arabia; Wahhābīyah.]

BIBLIOGRAPHY

Almana, Mohammed. *Arabia Unified: A Portrait of Ibn Saᶜud*. London, 1980.

Benoist-Méchin, Jacques. *Arabian Destiny*. Translated by Denis Weaver. Fair Lawn, N.J., 1958.

Howarth, David. *The Desert King: A Life of Ibn Saud*. London, 1964.

HERMANN FREDERICK EILTS

SAᶜŪD, FAYṢAL IBN ᶜABD AL-ᶜAZĪZ ĀL

(1906–1975), king of Saudi Arabia during the crucial period between its unification and its transformation into one of the world's most influential oil-producing powers. Fayṣal was born on 9 April 1906, at a time when his father, ᶜAbd al-ᶜAzīz ibn ᶜAbd al-Raḥmān Āl Saᶜūd, was unifying the Najdī tribes. Because Fayṣal's mother, Tarfah, died in 1912, the young prince's education was entrusted to his maternal godfather, Shaykh ᶜAbdullāh ibn ᶜAbd al-Laṭīf Āl al-Shaykh. The latter, a grandson of Muḥammad ibn ᶜAbd al-Wahhāb, the founder of the Muwaḥḥidūn (Unitarian) movement that gave religious legitimacy to Saudi rule, was a leading *ᶜalim* (religious scholar) who instilled in Fayṣal strong religious beliefs. At the age of fourteen, Fayṣal commanded his father's forces in ᶜAsīr Province (he also distinguished himself militarily by leading an assault on Yemen in 1933). In 1930, Fayṣal became Saudi Arabia's first foreign minister and held the office until his death in 1975, save for a two-year period during King Saᶜūd's rule. He led the Saudi delegation to the April 1945 San Francisco conference that established the United Nations, and signed the UN Charter on 26 June 1945, making Saudi Arabia a founding member of the world body.

Fayṣal shaped Saudi foreign policy by giving it an ideological base, insisting on a strict balance with internal developments and adopting a level of consistency unparalleled throughout the Arab and Muslim worlds. This consistency was amply visible throughout the 1960s and early 1970s when the kingdom faced the Nasserist challenge. Riyadh responded to the rising wave of

Arab nationalism by emphasizing Islamic values. Rejecting both secularism and socialism, Fayṣal supported Yemeni tribes who favored the monarchy and, in the aftermath of the 1967 Arab-Israeli War, sought a rapprochement with Egypt to end the Arab Cold War (1957–1967). By early 1973, however, Fayṣal perceived the need to link the kingdom's oil power to the unending Arab-Israeli conflict, especially as Washington failed to note Saudi pleas. Following the outbreak of the 1973 war, and the U.S. decision to create a weapons airbridge to Israel, Fayṣal authorized an oil embargo against both the United States and the Netherlands. But ever the astute statesman, the king rescinded his decision when Washington reactivated its moribund peace efforts. However, his lifelong wish to pray at Jerusalem's al-Aqṣā Mosque never materialized.

Although few members of the Āl Saʿūd ruling family challenged Fayṣal on foreign policy questions, his rule was not free from turmoil. The most significant conflict was the rivalry between then Crown Prince Fayṣal and King Saʿūd (r. 1953–1964). The king was inward looking, and chiefly interested in tribal affairs, whereas Fayṣal was outward looking, aiming to enhance the kingdom's position on both the regional as well as world scenes. Fayṣal perceived his brother's accommodation with revolutionary Egypt to be ill advised and, at a time when regional upheavals—including the 1956 Suez crisis, the Egyptian-Syrian union, the overthrow of the Iraqi monarchy, and the civil war in Yemen—threatened the kingdom, he considered Saʿūd's positions to be intolerable. Such policies, coupled with disastrous financial mismanagement, encouraged Fayṣal to take over. In November 1963, the Council of Senior Princes, supported by a *fatwā* (formal legal opinion) from the *ʿulamāʾ*, called on Saʿūd to abdicate in favor of Fayṣal, who acceded to the throne on 2 November 1964. Fayṣal's ten-point reform program to abolish slavery, modernize the administration, reorganize the country's religious and judicial institutions, revamp labor and social laws, utilize natural resources soundly, build efficient infrastructures, and establish consultative as well as local councils, won him widespread praise. Many reforms were gradually introduced and others were implemented by successor rulers. When, for example, the grand *muftī* died in 1970, Fayṣal abolished the post, replacing it with two separate and less-autonomous institutions. The Ministry of Justice was established to integrate the Saudi judiciary into the government, and the Council of Senior ʿUlamāʾ, comprising seventeen members appointed by the king, was created to provide the ruler with appropriate religious opinions and approvals. Significant socioeconomic reforms were embodied in the first five-year development plan, which was followed by a second, more ambitious, plan in 1975. Assassinated by a nephew on 25 March 1975, Fayṣal died before the actual implementation of his second plan, but he left his successors effective institutions to carry on his legacy.

[*See also* Saudi Arabia; *and the biography of the elder Saʿūd.*]

BIBLIOGRAPHY

Beling, Willard A., ed. *King Faisal and the Modernisation of Saudi Arabia.* Boulder, 1980. Thirteen essays covering the creation of the Saudi state, its modernization, currents of social change, and the role of Islam in the conduct of its foreign policy.

Benoist-Méchin, Jacques. *Fayçal, roi d'Arabie: L'homme, le souverain, sa place dans le monde, 1906–1975.* Paris, 1975. Classic work by an "insider."

Bligh, Alexander. *From Prince to King: Royal Succession in the House of Saud in the Twentieth Century.* New York, 1984. Thorough academic examination of political participation in the kingdom's decision-making process.

De Gaury, Gerald. *Faisal, King of Saudi Arabia.* New York and Washington, D.C., 1967. Thought-provoking essay on Fayṣal's remarkable accomplishments.

JOSEPH A. KECHICHIAN

SAUDI ARABIA. The Kingdom of Saudi Arabia was formally proclaimed in 1932 by ʿAbd al-ʿAzīz ibn ʿAbd al-Raḥmān Āl Saʿūd and is ruled by his descendants under a monarchal form of government. The population holding Saudi citizenship, who are all Muslim, were estimated by the Saudi government in 1990 to be nearly 15 million, projected to reach 20 million by the year 2000. Unofficial sources, however, put the 1990 population at the significantly lower figure of 8 to 10 million. In 1990 approximately 5 million foreigners, primarily from other Arabic-speaking countries, were living in the kingdom.

The kingdom occupies 80 percent of the Arabian Peninsula and includes four distinct geographical and cultural regions that were united through conquest by ʿAbd al-ʿAzīz in the first quarter of the twentieth century. The Eastern Province on the Gulf coast, also called al-Ḥasā after the oasis of that name, is one of the kingdom's most fertile areas as well as the site of its oil industry and the home of Saudi Arabia's Shīʿī minority (estimates of the Shīʿī population range from 200,000 to 500,000). The ʿAsīr is an agricultural region in the southwest with cultural ties to Yemen, with which it shares a common border. The Hejaz (Ḥijāz) on the Red Sea contains the holy cities of Mecca and Medina, the focus of pilgrimage for centuries. Its population is ethnically mixed and predominantly Sunnī, with a huge foreign population comprising as much as 70 percent of the people in the port city of Jeddah. Finally, the Najd in central Arabia is bounded on three sides by deserts. It is the homeland of the ruling Āl Saʿūd family and the fount of the Wahhābī movement, which provided the rationale for conquest of the peninsula in the eighteenth century and again in the twentieth and shaped the religious character of government and society under Āl Saʿūd rule.

History. The Wahhābī movement began in the mid-eighteenth century with an alliance between a chieftain of southern Najd named Muḥammad ibn Saʿūd and a religious reformer of Najd, Muḥammad ibn ʿAbd al-Wahhāb. In his teaching Ibn ʿAbd al-Wahhāb stressed the necessity of upholding the essential oneness of God in ritual practice, opposing the practice of praying to saints, which was widespread in the peninsula, especially among Shīʿīs and Ṣūfīs. He opposed saint-worship on the grounds that a worshiper who seeks the intercession of a saint with God is attributing to the saint powers that should only be attributed to God. This, he believed, was polytheism.

Ibn ʿAbd al-Wahhāb also emphasized the necessity behaving in conformity with the laws of the Qur'ān and the practices exemplified in the *sunnah* of the Prophet, as interpreted by the early scholars of Islam. Because, in his view, the ultimate goal of the Muslim community is to become the living embodiment of God's laws on earth, he taught that everyone must be educated in order to understand the laws of God in order to live in conformity with them. Ibn ʿAbd al-Wahhāb's philosophy complemented the political ambitions of Muḥammad ibn Saʿūd: the religious reformer called for obedience to a just Muslim ruler, because the community of believers can fulfill its goal only by submitting an oath of allegiance to a Muslim ruler who, in consultation with *ʿulamā'*, is willing to enforce God's laws. For the Wahhābīs of Najd, the marriage between the *ʿulamā'* and those who hold political power is the hallmark of a true Islamic government.

Ibn ʿAbd al-Wahhāb and Muḥammad ibn Saʿūd propagated Ibn ʿAbd al-Wahhāb's ideas and began a wave of expansion that, by the opening of the nineteenth century, culminated in the conquest of most of the Arabian Peninsula. This first Wahhābī empire was crushed by Egyptian forces in 1818, and its capital at Dirʿīyah was destroyed. Henceforth the territory under the control of the Āl Saʿūd family and the descendants of Ibn ʿAbd al-Wahhāb, who took the name Āl Shaykh, shrank to the area of southern Najd. However, the social, religious, and political agenda set forth in Wahhābī ideology remained firmly rooted throughout Najd, to be revived at the opening of the twentieth century. [*See* Wahhābīyah *and the biography of Ibn ʿAbd al-Wahhāb.*]

In 1902 ʿAbd al-Azīz ibn Saʿūd, a descendant of the first Saudi rulers of Najd, captured the city of Riyadh, which was then under the control of the Āl Rashīd family of northern Najd, and began a wave of conquest that reached a decisive stage in the defeat of the sharīfian Hashemite ruler of the Hejaz in late 1924. Replicating the method of his ancestors, ʿAbd al-ʿAzīz accomplished his goal by promoting Wahhābī ideology on the popular level, sponsoring Qur'ānic education, mosque preaching, and missionary teaching in remote villages and among the bedouin, and by creating a military force, the Ikhwān (Brotherhood), inspired to conquer by religious faith.

The Ikhwān came into being after 1912, when ʿAbd al-ʿAzīz appropriated a movement that had begun among the bedouin to abandon the nomadic way of life and settle in an agricultural community where, the former nomads believed, they could become true Muslims by fulfilling God's laws. The settlements were called *hujar*, (sg., *hujrah*), related to the word for the Prophet's emigration from Mecca to Medina and connoting migration from a land of unbelief to the land of belief. By moving to a *hujrah* the former nomads committed themselves to a narrow and literal interpretation of the *sunnah*, enjoining public prayer, mosque attendance, and sex-segregation while condemning music, smoking, alcohol, and technology unknown at the time of the Prophet. The settlers were zealous followers of Ibn ʿAbd al-Wahhāb's ideas, but, being inexperienced farmers, they were also receptive to the subsidies of food, cash, arms, and agricultural equipment offered by ʿAbd al-ʿAzīz. In return, the former nomads joined the Ikhwān, the brotherhood of fighters who formed the backbone of ʿAbd al-ʿAzīz's army, and the *hujrah* settlements became in effect military cantonments in the service of his expansion.

By 1917, the capital of ʿAbd al-ʿAzīz's empire, Riyadh, was the center of a religious revival. Qur'ānic schools flourished and scholarly achievement was rewarded in official public ceremonies. Attendance was taken at public prayers, and corporal punishment was meted out to those who were absent. Smoking was prohibited, music condemned, and loud laughter taken as a sign of impiety. Life in the capital was characterized by a high degree of conformity in public behavior stemming from the desire of believers and subjects of the new Wahhābī polity to meet Islamic standards as interpreted by the scholars of Najd. The conformity in behavior demanded during the revival era of the 1920s was self-perpetuating. Because conduct was considered a visible expression of inward faith, the Muslim community could judge the quality of the faith of others by observing their outward actions. In this sense, public opinion in Najd became and continues to be a constant regulator of individual behavior.

By reviving the notion of a community of believers, united by their submission to God and a willingness to live in conformity with God's laws, the Wahhābī ideology fostered under ʿAbd al-ʿAzīz forged a sense of national identity among the ethnically and tribally diverse people of the peninsula. By claiming to rule in consultation with the *ʿulamāʾ* ʿAbd al-ʿAzīz made faith in Islam and obedience to himself as the just Islamic ruler the glue that would hold his kingdom together. Since his death in 1953 the Saudi leadership has deemphasized its identity as inheritor of the Wahhābī legacy, and the Āl Shaykh family no longer holds the highest posts in the religious bureaucracy. In society, however, Wahhābī influence remains tangible in a visible conformity in dress, public deportment, and public prayer. Most significantly, the Wahhābī legacy is manifest in the social ethos that assumes government responsibility for the collective moral ordering of society, from the behavior of individuals to that of institutions, businesses, and the government itself.

Institutionalization of Islam. In the 1990s the legitimacy of the monarchy continues to rest on the fragile premise that the house of Saʿūd rules in consultation with the *ʿulamā.*' While pursuing the agenda of a developing nation, the monarchy has also maintained the appearance of serving the interests of religious constituencies, and it does so through specific religious organizations institutionalized within the state power structure.

The most influential religious body in the kingdom is the state-funded Council of Senior ʿUlamāʾ, headed by ʿAbd Allāh ibn ʿAbd al-ʿAzīz ibn Bāz. One of the primary functions of the Council is to provide religious approval for policies determined by the government. For example, education for women, which began in 1960 under King Fayṣal, was approved by the *ʿulamāʾ* in spite of sometimes fierce public opposition, with a determination that female education was acceptable provided that it was compatible with woman's Islamic role as wife and mother. As another example, when the Grand Mosque in Mecca was besieged in 1979 and more than sixty participants were handed death sentences after perfunctory trials, the Council of Senior ʿUlamāʾ sanctioned the mass beheadings. In 1990, when King Fahd decided to invite American forces to defend the Kingdom against a possible attack by Iraqi president Saddam Hussein, the Council was called on to provide Islamic approval for the monarch's decision; the Council subsequently issued a *fatwā* (legal ruling) stating that the Qur'ān allows a ruler to seek assistance in order to defend against outside aggression.

Religious police, known as the Committee for the Promotion of Virtue and Prevention of Vice and funded through the Ministry of the Interior, help to enforce guidelines on public morality issued by the Council, as well as enforcing rules that many regard as arbitrary and capricious. For example, they monitor the closing of shops at prayer time and seek out alcohol and drug offenders, but they also monitor men's and women's dress in public, non-Muslim religious services, and social interaction between men and women in cars, public places, and sometimes even in private homes.

Even though the Saudi monarchy supports a conservative social agenda, the kingdom has still been affected by the rise in Islamic conservatism that has swept the region. This sentiment has been inspired by a number of factors, including a reaction to the cultural incursion of the West brought on by massive development and the resulting breakdown of traditional family structures, the presence of foreigners in the kingdom, disaffection with the West, and the influence of the Islamic Republic of Iran and its call to export Islamic revolution. A particularly important factor influencing the rise in Islamic conservatism has been a downturn in the Saudi economy, combined with an overabundance of educated youth whom the economy cannot absorb. This has brought about widespread unemployment, particularly among university-educated youth.

Unemployed graduates of religious colleges in particular, said to number some 150,000 in 1992, have been attracted to the politics of neo-Wahhābī groups, which are also known as Salafīyah or those who wish to purify the *sharīʿah* from the innovations of scholarship that occurred after the first three centuries of Islam. These groups make the same demands for social justice that Islamist groups in other Arab countries are making: they want jobs, a fairer distribution of wealth, better access to health and education facilities, political participation, and accountability in government. In addition, they want strict enforcement of rules that promote Islamic moral values such as sex-segregation and public modesty, along with the enactment of Qur'ānic punishments (*ḥudūd*) and Islamic banking (to comply with the Islamic ban on usury). [*See* Salafīyah; Ḥudūd; Banks and Banking.]

Gulf War. The war against Iraq in 1990–1991 marked a major turning point in the rise of both Islamist sentiment and opposition to the absolutism of the Saudi monarchy among Western-oriented liberals, religious conservatives, and human-rights and minority-group advocates alike. Many Saudis of different religious and political persuasions opposed the invitation to American forces and instead advocated a nonviolent Arab solution to what was regarded as a regional problem. Opposition voices pointed out the incompetence of the Saudi military in spite of the huge expenditures lavished on sophisticated training and equipment even at a time of cutbacks in funding for social programs. Religious conservatives resented the presence of non-Muslim foreign soldiers on Saudi soil, particularly the presence of women soldiers. Moreover, the Gulf War placed an international spotlight on the absolutism of Saudi rule and exposed the kingdom's shortcomings with respect to human rights. This signaled an opportunity for numerous interest groups with differing political objectives to demand political reform.

The initial response of the government was to allow the more radical Islamist voices to speak out while backing a conservative social agenda. In this way the government was able to intimidate Western-oriented liberals who sought an opening up of the political process while appeasing the broadly based conservative mainstream. For example, in November 1990 a group of Saudi women staged a public demonstration demanding the right to drive cars. In a move that received widespread public approval, the government responded by punishing the participants for promoting what the *ʿulamāʾ* called un-Islamic behavior in the kingdom. The women were labeled sexually promiscuous on posters publicly displayed by the religious police. The head of the Council of Senior ʿUlamāʾ issued a ruling that women should never drive, nor should they ever participate in politics in any way. The women protestors who were university professors were fired from their jobs and their passports were confiscated for one year. Meanwhile, state funding for the activities of the religious police was increased.

Again during the Gulf War period, petitions were sent to the king demanding a constitution, a consultative council, an independent judiciary, and equality among all citizens regardless of ethnic, tribal, sectarian, or social origins. The petition was signed by secular leaders, university professors, and religious leaders; signatories to a follow-up petition asking that the proposed consultative council be empowered to evaluate all laws in light of the *sharīʿah* even included members of the Council of Senior ʿUlamā.' The king's response was to announce that government reform was in the planning stages. A year later, in March 1992, the king announced the establishment of a "Basic Law" of government and a Consultative Council (Majlis al-Shūrā), but the announced changes, called "empty reforms" by the human-rights organization Middle East Watch, fail to open up government decision-making to diverse interest groups; indeed, they actually reinforce the power of the ruling establishment and in particular of the king.

The end of the Gulf War period saw a dramatic rise in the activity of Salafīyah groups and Shīʿīs as well as of human-rights proponents. To counter the rise in opposition from religious groups the government has strengthened the allegiance of the Council of Senior ʿUlamāʾ while increasing repression of dissident voices. In 1993, for example, seven members of the council who had expressed sympathy with some Shīʿī and Salafī demands were replaced by scholars considered more sympathetic to the monarchy. In May of that year, a human-rights organization called the Committee for the Defense of Legitimate Rights was formed to gather information from citizens about human-rights abuses. The committee's declaration, signed by scholars who declared themselves to be *ahl al-sunnah* (people of the *sunnah*) and loyal to the Saudi state, met with criticism from the council, which issued a statement declaring that the organization was superfluous because the *sharīʿah* already provides for human rights, and that it was offensive to the government that upholds the *sharīʿah*. The signatories were subsequently harassed, and some were arrested or had their law licenses revoked.

Similar punishments have been meted out to other

petition-signers and critics of the government. Preachers, religious scholars, and university professors have been dismissed from their posts, imprisoned, or had their passports confiscated, and student activists have been denied admission to the university. A Shīʿī organization, al-Jazīrah al-Arabīyah (The Arabian Peninsula), which became active after the war in seeking an end to discrimination in hiring and educational opportunities, sent a statement of grievances to the king that led to the imprisonment of some of its signatories.

Fearing that its own support for conservative religious causes abroad has fueled conservative opposition at home, the Saudi government banned contributions by private citizens for religious activities outside the kingdom. This indicates a major reversal of long-standing Saudi policy aimed at elevating the House of Saʿūd to a position of undisputed leadership in the Islamic world: in 1986 King Fahd assumed the sobriquet of Custodian of the Two Holy Places, once used by his father and formerly by the Sharīf of Mecca. He and his predecessors, furthermore, had provided generous funding for the building of mosques and the distribution of Qur'āns, emergency aid, and welfare funds to Muslims abroad and established and funded international organizations promoting Muslim solidarity, such as the Muslim World League and Organization of the Islamic Conference. The challenge that lies before the Saudi rulers in the 1990s is to maintain their Islamic identity in the eyes of Saudi Arabia's conservative society, while at the same time satisfying the desire for economic and social justice growing within.

[*See also* King Faisal Foundation; Muslim World League; Organization of the Islamic Conference. *For biographical entries on ʿAbd al-ʿAzīz and Fayṣal, see under Saʿūd.*]

BIBLIOGRAPHY

Al-Yassini, Ayman. *Religion and State in the Kingdom of Saudi Arabia.* Boulder, 1985.

Doumato, Eleanor A. "Women and the Stability of Saudi Arabia." *Middle East Report,* no. 171 (July 1991): 34–37.

Doumato, Eleanor A. "Gender, Monarchy, and National Identity in Saudi Arabia." *British Journal of Middle Eastern Studies* 19.1 (1992): 31–47.

Habib, John S. *Ibn Saʿud's Warriors of Islam.* Leiden, 1978.

Helms, Christine Moss. *The Cohesion of Saudi Arabia: Evolution of Political Identity.* Baltimore, 1981.

Niblock, Tim, ed. *State, Society, and Economy in Saudi Arabia.* New York, 1982.

Ochsenwald, William. "Saudi Arabia." In *The Politics of Islamic Revivalism,* edited by Shireen Hunter, pp. 103–115. Bloomington, 1988.

Piscatori, J. P., ed. *Islamic Fundamentalisms and the Gulf Crisis.* Chicago, 1991.

Rentz, George. "Wahhabism and Saudi Arabia." In *The Arabian Peninsula: Society and Politics,* edited by Derek Hopwood, pp. 54–66. London, 1972.

ELEANOR ABDELLA DOUMATO

ṢAWM. In Islam numerous fasts (*ṣawm,* also *ṣiyām*) are urged on the believer; the Islamic religion is permeated by the piety of fasting. The Islamic fasts reflect Jewish, Christian, and pre-Islamic Arabian influences, although the precise contribution of each of these traditions remains a subject of controversy. An obligatory collective fast occupies the entire month of Ramaḍān. Various traditions also recommend voluntary fasting; examples are the fast of ʿĀshūrā' (the tenth day of the month of Muḥarram, originally in imitation of the Jewish fast of the Day of Atonement), fasting six days in Shawwāl (the month following Ramaḍān), fasting three days of each month, and fasting on Mondays and Thursdays. Expiatory fasting (*kaffārah*) atones for certain transgressions or compensates for omissions of duty; fasts of varying durations may be undertaken for, among other things, failing to fulfill an oath (see the Qur'ān, surahs 5.89 and 58.4) or the accidental killing of a believer (4.92). Some Ṣūfīs also undergo fasts as part of their spiritual exercises.

The great fast of the Muslims is the fast of Ramaḍān, undertaken by the entire community; fasting in this month is the fourth of the five pillars of Islam. The Ramaḍān fast is instituted in the Qur'ān (2.183–187) which begins, "O you who believe, fasting is prescribed for you," and continues by recommending the fast of "a certain number of days," with allowances for the sick and the traveler to fast "an [equal] number of other days," as well as the "ransoming" of the fast by feeding the poor. In these verses the Qur'ān also identifies Ramaḍān as the month in which the Qur'ān was revealed to Muḥammad, restricts sexual intercourse to the hours of darkness when the fast is not in effect, and commands the believers to begin their fast again when "the white thread becomes to you distinct from the black thread of the dawn." Thus in Ramaḍān the believer is obligated strictly to abstain from food, drink, and sexual relations in the daylight hours.

Other provisions concerning the fast come from the traditions of the Prophet (*ḥadīth*) and the legal (*fiqh*) literature. These literatures treat such matters as the regulations for the sighting of the new moon of the Ramaḍān month (which begins the fast), forming the proper intent *(niyah)* to fast, the times for the beginning and breaking of each day's fast, actions that have the effect of breaking the fast, exemptions from the fast, and the making up of missed days.

The Ramaḍān fast, despite the hardships involved (especially in summer when the days are long and the heat intense), has always been widely and strictly kept, and in modern times with the progress of Islamic revivalism observance has become even more general. Only preadolescents and menstruating women are exempt; pregnant and lactating women, the sick, the elderly, travelers, and those engaged in *jihād* may also be excused, subject to certain conditions.

Ramaḍān has nevertheless the character of a festival: a substantial and elaborate meal (*ifṭār*, "breakfast") at the conclusion of each day is a time for family and community gatherings; the local authorities are likely to decorate the streets with lights and ornaments; and at the end of the month there is the ʿĪd al-Fiṭr (festival of the breaking of the fast) in which the faithful gather together for prayer, new clothes are worn, and money and presents are given to children. The *zakāt al-fiṭr* (almstax of the breaking of the fast), a small amount of money used for charitable purposes, is also contributed at this time. During Ramaḍān, gatherings for extra prayer (*tarāwīḥ*) are often held at the mosque at night. The Laylat al-Qadr or Night of Power, said to occur sometime in the last ten days of Ramaḍān—on which it is believed that the Qur'ān was sent down to Muḥammad and events are determined for the coming year—may also be commemorated, for instance by retiring (*iʿtikāf*) to the mosque with one's fellow Muslims for extra devotions.

Various local customs are connected with Ramaḍān. In Egypt the children carry elaborately decorated tin lamps from door to door, asking gifts of money or sweets. In Middle Eastern countries a cannon is sounded to signal the end of the day's fast, sometimes broadcast by radio. In Malaysia around the time of Laylat al-Qadr, small kerosene-lit tin lamps are set outside houses to burn the whole night; these are increasingly being replaced by strings of colored electric lights. In rural areas in Malaysia and Indonesia, the end of the fast is signaled by means of a buffalo-skin drum gong or *beduk*, a function now also being taken over by broadcast announcement.

Legal opinions (*fatwā*s) continue to be issued on the subject of the fast, and they sometimes touch on novel problems arising from the circumstances of modern life. For instance, does an injection break the fast? On this opinions vary. According to the Fatwā Committee of the great Egyptian Islamic university of al-Azhar (Shaykh Khāmis ʿUmar Muḥammad Ṣubḥī, *Namādhij min al-fatwā*, Latakia, Syria, 1391/1971, p. 66), any injection violates the fast, but according to Maḥmūd Shaltūt, a former rector of the same college (*Al-fatāwā*, Cairo, n.d., pp. 117–118), all injections and medication taken other than by mouth are allowed. According to the Egyptian Islamic reformer Muḥammad Rashīd Riḍā (d. 1935), it is not permitted to a believer pursuing his studies at a Christian school to break his fast in order to continue to excel in that difficult environment (*Fatāwā al-Imām Muḥammad Rashīd Riḍā*, Beirut, 1390–1391/1970–1971, vol. 1, pp. 25–26). According to the al-Azhar scholar al-Qaraḍāwī (*Hudā al-Islām, fatāwā muʿāṣirah*, Cairo, 1401/1981, p. 282), it is allowed for a Muslim to watch television during the fast, the medium itself not being forbidden; however, one must while fasting be more careful than ever that what is watched is not corrupting in itself, and the broadcasting authorities must also be more vigilant during Ramaḍān.

In 1960 a series of *fatwā*s was issued in Tunisia under the influence of the secular government, maintaining that those engaged in the economic struggle (*jihād*) to build the country should (on analogy with the exemption granted those engaged in the military *jihād*) be exempt from the fast. The *fatwā*s were directed at a phenomenon observable in many parts of the Muslim world: the slowing down of government and economic activities during the fasting month. This opinion did not, however, find favor.

It has often been asked how the fast is to be carried out in places in the extreme north or south where Muslims may now reside, but where the fasting month and the length of days cannot be determined because the sun is not seen to rise and set in the same way as in the middle latitudes. In the opinion of Rashīd Riḍā (vol. 6, pp. 2077–2078), the fast will depend on an estimation of the extent of the month and days, rather than on the sighting of the moon or the rising and setting of the sun; according to Shaltūt (*Fatāwā*, pp. 124–125), persons in these areas should take the length of the days to be that of the nearest location where night and day can be distinguished. The question has also arisen whether Muslims in modern times can depend on astronomical calculations to fix the time of the birth of the moon, rather than on the apparently less accurate method of sighting the moon with the naked eye. According to Rashīd Riḍā, one must always rely on actual sighting to signal the beginning of the fast, rather than on science: qualified scientists may not be found in every location, and such persons are not in any case religiously competent (vol. 4, pp. 1508–1509). So anxious have Muslims been to establish all possible regulations for the fast that even the instance of fasting on the moon has been considered; in this case the rule is, according to the Lebanese *fatwā* council (*al-Fikr al-Islāmī* 1, no. 2, Shawwāl 1389/October 1969, pp. 122–123), that the sighting of the nearest heavenly body—the earth—should be substituted for that of the moon.

The question of the sighting of the moon in general has given rise to conflict in immigrant Muslim communities in the West. One faction maintains that fasting must be begun upon sighting the moon with the naked eye, while another wishes to follow modern science by consulting observatories or published tables. In addition, members of different national backgrounds have wanted to fast according to the sighting of the moon in their homelands; this has resulted, contrary to the Islamic ideal, in various groups of fasters in one location beginning Ramaḍān and even celebrating ʿĪd al-Fiṭr at different times.

The religious meaning of Ramaḍān has been discerned by modern thinkers to consist not only in obedience to God but also in moral and spiritual discipline—for instance, in purifying one's mind (particularly of bodily desires), strengthening one's will, and sharing in the hardships of the poor. According to this philosophy, fasting consists not only of abstaining from food, drink, and sex, but also of rejecting all illicit things and thoughts of them. It should not be imagined, however, that this view of fasting is exclusively modern. It has been in evidence throughout Islamic history, beginning with the *ḥadīth,* and receives eloquent expression in the *Mysteries of Fasting* (published in English, 1968) of the great mystic and theologian al-Ghazālī (d. 1111). Some contemporary Muslims also emphasize the nonpenitential nature of the Ramaḍān fast, contrasting this with Christian and Jewish traditions.

Some Muslims, seeking a scientific basis for the fast, have pointed to its health benefits. Scholarly commentators, however, while allowing that there may be advantages for the body in the practice of *ṣawm,* prefer to deemphasize these and dwell instead on the spiritual aspects. The medical profession has lately become interested in the effects of the fast and the management of patients keeping Ramaḍān, resulting in scientific studies and a number of articles in professional journals.

Public violation of the fast is abhorred in organized Muslim society. The punishment for deliberately breaking the fast is in the category of *taʿzīr* ("chastisement"). *Taʿzīr* penalties are meant to be exemplary and are left to the discretion of the Islamic judge or other authority; *taʿzīr* may consist of anything from verbal reproach to flogging. The reinstitution of Islamic law in some countries has also meant the reinstatement of *taʿzīr. Taʿzīr* punishment for breaking the fast is imposed in Saudi Arabia and is also valid in the Islamic Republic of Iran, although in both these countries there has been considerable latitude in enforcement and wide variation in the nature of the penalty. In some cases the *taʿzīr* punishments have been codified; thus in Malaysia those violating the fast are subject by law (when it is enforced) to a small fine.

[*See also* ʿĀshūrā; Fatwā; ʿĪd al-Fiṭr; Pillars of Islam; Ramaḍān.]

BIBLIOGRAPHY

Berg, C. C. "Ṣawm." In *First Encyclopaedia of Islam,* vol. 7, pp. 192–199. Leiden, 1913–. Offers a detailed account of the legal rules pertaining to the fast.

Gentz, Jochen. "Tunesische Fatwas ueber Fasten im Ramadan." *Die Welt des Islams,* n.s. 7 (1961): 39–65. Includes the texts of the opinions.

Ghazālī, Abū Ḥamīd al-. *The Mysteries of Fasting (A Translation of the Kitāb asrār al-ṣawm of the Iḥyāʾ ʿulūm al-dīn).* Translated by Nabih A. Faris. Lahore, 1968.

Goitein, S. D. "Ramaḍān, the Muslim Month of Fasting." In *Studies in Islamic History and Institutions,* pp. 90–110. Leiden, 1966. The best overall discussion of the subject; treats the origins of Ramaḍān, especially Jewish origins, and subsequent development.

Jomier, Jacques and Jean Corbon. "Le Ramadan au Caire, en 1956." *Mélanges de l'Institut Dominicain du Caire* 3 (1956): 1–74. Lively and detailed picture of the daily observances and mores of the fasting month.

Morgan, Kenneth W., ed. *Islam, the Straight Path: Islam Interpreted by Muslims.* New York, 1958. Includes short statements on the fast from contemporary authorities.

Von Grunebaum, G. E. "Ramadân." In *Muhammadan Festivals,* pp. 51–66. New York, 1951. Summary discussion of the fasting month, followed by mention of popular customs, with further references supplied.

Wagtendonk, K. *Fasting in the Koran.* Leiden, 1968. Exhaustive review of the scholarly literature and close examination of the Qur'ānic text yields new interpretations of the origins and development of fasting in Islam.

LYNDA CLARKE

SAYYID. An honorific title popularly used for the descendants of the prophet Muḥammad, especially those who descend from his second grandson, Ḥusayn ibn ʿAl'ī, the son of Muḥammad's daughter Fāṭimah, *sayyid* literally means lord, master, prince, or one who possesses glory, honor, dignity, eminence, or exalted position among his people. It was commonly used by the Arabs before Islam for those who possessed these qualities either by birth or by acquiring them through noble deeds and magnanimous acts. In pre-Islamic literature such expressions as "he was or became chief, lord, or master [sayyid] of his people" can be found. Sayyid was even used to refer to animals, for example, "my she-camel left behind all other camels or beasts [sayyids]." Sayyid was also typically the name for the head of a tribe or clan, as in the Qur'ān (33.67), "And they (the unbelievers) would say: 'Our Lord: we obeyed our chiefs [sayyids] and our great ones, and they misled us.' " The Qur'ān also uses sayyid in praise of the prophet Yahya: "God gives you glad tidings of Yahya, verifying the truth of a word from God, and be besides noble [sayyid] chaste and a Prophet of a goodly company of the righteous" (surah 3.39).

In Mecca the ancestors of Muḥammad—Quṣayy, ʿAbd Manāf, Hāshim, and ʿAbd al-Muṭṭalib—being the custodians of the Kaʿbah, the most venerated sanctuary of the Arabian Peninsula, were called "sayyids of their times." The Prophet's grandfather ʿAbd al-Muṭṭalib has been particularly described by the sources as "the leader [sayyid] of the Quraysh until his death." The Prophet, being fully conscious of his lineal distinctions, is reported to have said: "Allāh chose Ismāʿīl from the sons of Ibrāhīm and from the sons of Ismāʿīl the Banū Kinānah, and from Banū Kinānah the Quraysh and from the Quraysh the Banū Hāshim; consequently, I am the best of you as regards family and the best of you as regards geneology." In him, therefore, lineal dignity and personal qualities as the recipient of divine revelation and Apostle of God found their highest manifestation. This was duly recognized by the *ummah* (community), and he was called, in his own lifetime, the sayyid par excellence. Among the most popular epithets with which the Prophet is addressed by the *ummah* are *sayyid al-nās, sayyid al-bashar, sayyid al-ʿArab, sayyid al-mursalīn, sayyid al-anbiyā'*, that is, lord of mankind, humanity, the apostles, the prophets.

It was, therefore, natural that the Prophet's lineal distinctions and his own exalted position as the sayyid should be extended to his family members and descendants. Numerous traditions are recorded by both the Sunnīs and Shīʿīs in which the Prophet reportedly bestowed great distinctions and honors on his daughter Fāṭimah, his son-in-law ʿAlī ibn Abī Ṭālib (d. 661), and his two grandsons Ḥasan (d. 671) and Ḥusayn (d. 680). For example, he declared ʿAlī "sayyid in this world and a sayyid in the next". He also called ʿAlī "Sayyid al-Muslimīn," lord of the Muslims. He exalted the status of his daughter, saying: "Fāṭimah is the *sayyidah* [mistress] of the women of the World [*ʿālamīn*]"; "*sayyidah* of the women of my community"; and "*sayyidah* of the women of the dwellers in Paradise." Similarly, for his grandsons he emphatically declared: "al-Ḥasan and al-Ḥusayn are the sayyids [lords] of young men among the inhabitants of Paradise," and "the two lords of the young men of my community."

Since the Prophet had no offspring from his son, who died in infancy, his grandsons from his daughter were given the unique privilege of being called Ibn Rasūl Allāh, sons of the Prophet of God. In justification of this, Muḥammad said: "All the sons of one mother trace themselves back to an agnate, except the sons of Fāṭimah, for I am their nearest relative and their agnate." In another tradition, the Prophet says: "every bond of relationship and consanguinity [*thabat wa-nasab*] will be severed on the day of resurrection except mine."

It is against this background that the title *sayyid* became an exclusive distinction of the descendants of the Prophet in the male lines of Ḥasan and Ḥusayn. In the early period, however, the title *sharīf* was also used for both grandsons, but gradually *sharīf* came to be more commonly used for the descendants of Ḥasan, while *sayyid* became the title of the descendants of Ḥusayn. [*See* Sharīf.] After ʿAlī and Ḥasan, the first two imams respectively, there were nine imams and their brothers in the male line of Ḥusayn (the twelfth imam went into occultation while still a child). The sayyids are thus mainly those who are in the line of descent from the nine imams and their brothers from Ḥusayn to Ḥasan al-ʿAskarī, the eleventh imam (d. 873).

With the expansion of the Islamic empire and changing sociopolitical conditions from the seven century onward, the descendants of the Prophet moved to various parts of the Islamic world. It was especially during the Umayyad (661–750) and ʿAbbāsid (749–1258) periods that the descendants of the Prophet, considered by the caliphs as a threat to their authority, had to take refuge in far-flung areas. A great number of sayyids migrated initially to Yemen and Iran, where they found conditions more congenial. Later migrations took place mainly from these two countries to other parts of the world. Sindh, in the Indian subcontinent, was another place where the sayyids migrated very early on. In course of time, however, their number multiplied, and in every Muslim country today numerous sayyid families are well established. Wherever they settled, they were treated with extraordinary respect and veneration because of their direct relation to the Prophet. The Muslims of newly conquered areas, being converts from different faiths, thought it their religious duty to pay utmost regard to the progeny of the Prophet. Sentimentally and psychologically, the Muslims' love and respect for the descendants of the Prophet has been, in fact, a natural result of love and respect for the Prophet himself. Socially, the status of the sayyids is so elevated that a non-sayyid would not dare marry a sayyidah, daughter of a sayyid, whereas it would be an honor for a non-sayyid to give his daughter in marriage to a sayyid. Also, one may not sit if a sayyid is standing. In rural Punjab, Sindh, and other parts of the Indian subcontinent, people will not sit beside sayyids but prefer to sit on the floor. Sayyids are also the first to be greeted, even by those in authority. In royal courts and ceremonies sayyids are exempted from paying the usual signs of respect, such as touching the ground or prostrating themselves, or continuing to stand before a king.

Sayyids are also distinguished in a number of other ways, for example, *zakāt* (alms) or other *ṣadaqāt* (charities) cannot be given to them. This is because of the fact that the Prophet is reported to have frequently said of *ṣadaqāt:* "it is the filth of men [also see Quran 9.103] and permitted neither to Muḥammad nor the family of Muḥammad." To save them from financial hardship and to maintain their dignity, a special form of tax, called *khums*, is paid to the sayyids, a tax which was originally meant for the Prophet himself. During Muslim rule in India, as in other Muslim countries, distinguished and learned sayyid families were granted gifts of landed properties and rich stipends. [*See* Zakāt; Khums.]

The sayyids, especially in medieval times, as persons who distinguished themselves by religious learning and pious life, were acknowledged as saints. In fact, most of the Ṣūfī masters or founders of various Ṣūfī orders were the descendants of the Prophet, and it was through their efforts that a majority of non-Muslims converted to Islam. That is particularly the case of the Muslims in the Indian subcontinent. There are a number of tombs in Sindh, Punjab, Delhi, and Rajasthan which are centers of pilgrimage and veneration for the Muslims in the Indian subcontinent. Similarly, in Egypt, Iran, Iraq, and other Muslim countries, tombs of sayyids and sayyidas are frequently visited by the people to invoke their blessings. These saints-sayyids are considered intermediaries between God and the devotees.

To acknowledge their spiritual as well as social supremacy, the sayyids are also called shah (king) in most parts of Pakistan. In Iran and Turkey the title sayyid is sometimes interchangeable with *mir*, and perhaps it is because of Iranian influence that in Sindh *mīr* is also used for sayyids, especially for those who command political authority as well.

In modern times, with changing sociocultural conditions and with rather uncertain pedigrees, the traditional reverance has weakened. Still, the sayyids today constitute a respectable class in Muslim societies.

BIBLIOGRAPHY

For pre-Islamic etymological and semantic usages of the title *Sayyid*, see Ibn Manẓūr, *Lisān al-ʿArab*, vol. 4, pp. 215ff (Cairo, 1882), and Edward W. Lane, *Arabic-English Lexicon*, vol. 4, pp. 1460–1462 (Beirut, 1982). Both works cite references from pre-Islamic literature and the term's subsequent usages in the Islamic period, including references from the Qur'ān and *ḥadīth* literature. Cornelis van Arendonk, "Sharīf," in *E. J. Brill's First Encyclopaedia of Islam*, vol. 7, pp. 324–329 (Leiden, 1987), gives a comprehensive bibliography of *sharīf* and *sayyid* and their use in different regions. Ignácz Goldziher, *Muslim Studies*, vol. 1, pp. 45–98, translated by C. R. Barber and S. M. Stern (London, 1967), is an in-depth study of original sources for the Arab concept of family honor and dignity. Ibn Hishām, *Sīrat Rasūl Allāh*, vol. 1, pp. 131–145 (Cairo, 1936), is the oldest and best original source for the study of the exalted position of the Prophet's ancestry. Standard Sunnī and Shīʿī collections of Prophetic traditions provide examples of assigning the title *Sayyid* to ʿAlī, Fāṭimah, al-Ḥasan, and al-Ḥusayn. For use of the title *sayyid* for the twelve imams from the House of the Prophet and their descendants in different periods and regions, see the following:

Ibn ʿInabah, Jamāl al-Dīn Aḥmad ibn ʿAlī. *ʿUmdat al-Ṭālib fī Ansāb Āl Abī Ṭālib*. Bombay, 1900.

Lane, Edward W. *An Account of the Manners and Customs of the Modern Egyptians*. London, 1842.

Niebuhr, Carsten. *Beschreibung von Arabien aus eigenen beobachtungen und in lande selbst gesammleten nachrichten abgeffasset von Carsten Niebuhr*. Copenhagen, 1772.

Shablanjī, Mu'min ibn Ḥasan Mu'min. *Nūr al-Abṣār fī manāqib Ahl Bayt al-Nabī al-Mukhtār*. Bombay, 1983.

Zabīdī, Aḥmad ibn Aḥmad. *Ṭabaqāt al-khawāṣṣ ahl al-ṣidq wa-al-ikhlāṣ*. Sanʿa, 1986.

SYED HUSAIN M. JAFRI

SCIENCE. Between the ninth and thirteenth centuries Islamic civilization made major original contributions to the development of premodern science and transmitted Greek learning to Europe through extensive translations. The real emergence of modern science and crystallization of the scientific method, however, occurred in the massive revolution that began in sixteenth-century Europe and left in its wake a world transformed both intellectually and materially. Traditional belief systems were challenged by the paradigm of a new culture based on experimentation, prediction, quantification, and control. Power relations between countries became increasingly defined by their mastery of technology, ultimately leading to the colonization by European nations of much of the Islamic world. For many traditional societies, and for some Islamic societies in particular, acceptance of the new scientific paradigm was—and in some cases still is—problematic both for its association with colonialism and for internal cultural reasons. Combined with global inequities in the distribution of power and wealth, this may be an important factor in explaining the disproportionately small representation in science and technology of Muslims, who constitute about 20 percent of the world's population.

Historical Development. The introduction of post-Renaissance science, technology, and thought into Islamic societies was pioneered by several outstanding individuals in the nineteenth century. In Egypt following the Napoleonic occupation, Muḥammad ʿAlī seized state power and ruled from 1805 through 1848; during this period he made bold attempts to transfer French and British technology into the country, relying principally on European expatriates. He introduced the first printing press—a device initially condemned by some of the *ʿulamāʾ* for having a belt of pigskin. This resistance was overcome, and the Būlāq press in Cairo published eighty-one Arabic books on science between 1821 and 1850. Technology for irrigation, textile manufacturing, surveying, prospecting and mining for coal and iron, and military hardware received high priority. Major earthmoving and civil engineering projects were begun. Even more significantly, technical schools with foreign teachers were established with the aim of generating manpower. More than four hundred students were sent to Europe to study various branches of science, including military tactics. However, the success of Muḥammad ʿAlī's industrialization policies was mixed. The quality of domestic products such as textiles was poor. Technical schools provided insufficient exposure to theoretical science and failed to create a base of technicians or engineers of sufficiently high caliber. After Muḥammad ʿAlī's death in 1849 these schools were closed down under the rule of Khedive ʿAbbās and Khedive Saʿīd, and scientific momentum ground to a halt.

Among other nineteenth-century Arab rulers, Sulṭān Saʿīd ibn Sulṭān of Oman (1806–1856) was notable for his interest in acquiring European technology. He made numerous attempts to have sugar refineries installed in Zanzibar, an Omani possession, as well as unsuccessful attempts at shipbuilding. Amīr ʿAbd al-Qādir of Algeria (r. 1832–1847) engaged various experts to build small ordnance factories and appears to have understood the importance of technology for progress.

The Turkish Ottomans established an extensive and magnificent empire in the sixteenth century and soon recognized the utility of military technology, particularly cannons, which they readily borrowed from the West. Strong religious taboos, however, prevented the use of such innovations as the printing press or public clocks. Travelers to Turkey in this period remarked on the lack of interest in matters of science and learning. Sweeping changes in civil administration and education came with Sultan Selim III (1761–1808), the last and the most radical of the Ottoman reformers. Selim established a new military corps armed and organized in the most modern European techniques of warfare. Gunfounding was introduced, printing presses were set up, and the works of Western authors were translated into Turkish. To sustain the modern army the subjects of algebra, trigonometry, mechanics, ballistics, and metallurgy were introduced into the teaching curriculum. Like Muḥammad ʿAlī, Selim had no choice but to import teachers from Europe for these subjects. The importance of theoretical science as a basis for continued development appears not to have been recognized. The major impetus to scientific and industrial development came after the revolution brought about by Mustafa Kemal Atatürk (1881–1938) in 1924. Before this education had been limited to the cities and controlled by religious authorities, but after the secularization of Turkey, control was taken over by the state and curricula revised to include modern science, mathematics, world history, and other secular subjects. Among Muslim countries, Turkey is today the most advanced in scientific research and in terms of the quality of its universities.

On the Indian subcontinent modern scientific ideas and

techniques came in the wake of the English conquest. In preceding decades the rule of the Mughals had produced a civilization known for impressive architecture, literature, and poetry but with few achievements in the realm of scientific knowledge. The Mughals did not set up any universities or centers of learning. Some transmission of Western technology had taken place in the reign of Emperor Akbar (1542–1605), when Europeans came as traders. Notably, ships of large tonnage and forms similar to English ones were built, but they lacked such technology as compasses, gimbals, and navigational charts. Reading glasses were greatly admired by Akbar, but they appear to have been imported from France. After the banishment of the last Mughal emperor, Bahādur Shāh Ẓafar, in 1857, the English consolidated their rule and introduced modern education. A combination of shame, pride, defiance, and conservatism led Muslims to resist Western learning. Consequently, Muslims were at a substantial disadvantage relative to Hindus; for example, between 1876–1877 and 1885–1886, 51 Muslims and 1,338 Hindus took the B.A. degree at Calcutta; in 1870 only two Muslims, both of whom failed, sat for the B.A., while in the same year 151 Hindus took the examination and 56 received the degree.

The resistance of Muslims of the subcontinent to modern ideas motivated Sayyid Aḥmad Khān (1817–1898) to become a forceful proponent of modern science and thought. He was convinced that the subjugation of Muslims to the West was a result of their scientific backwardness, and that this in turn was a consequence of the dominance of superstitious beliefs and of rejection of *maʿqūlāt* (reason) in favor of blind obedience to *manqūlāt* (tradition). He therefore set about the monumental task of reinterpreting Muslim theology, making it compatible with post-Renaissance Western humanistic and scientific ideas. Sayyid Aḥmad Khān founded the Aligarh Muslim University, which provided Muslims of the subcontinent a unique opportunity for higher education. His articles in the periodical *Tahẕīb al-akhlāq*, which included translations and explanations of scientific tracts as well as his interpretations of religious issues, were highly influential among upper-class Muslims. To maintain consistency with science, he argued that miracles like Noah's Flood must be understood in allegorical rather than literal terms. This position brought him widespread condemnation and numerous *fatwā*s against his life. [*See* Aligarh *and the biography of Aḥmad Khān.*]

Jamāl al-Dīn al-Afghānī (1838–1897), also a supporter of Western science and modern ideas but an implacable opponent of Sayyid Aḥmad Khān, was a determined anti-imperialist who inspired Muslims in Turkey, Egypt, Iran, and India. Like his mentor Muḥammad ʿAbduh (1849–1905), Afghānī held that there was no contradiction between Islam and science and that Islam encouraged rational thought and discouraged blind imitation. In 1870, because of pressure from the clergy, Afghānī was expelled from Istanbul for advocating the setting up of a Dār al-Funūn, a new university devoted to the teaching of modern science. He is known for his vitriolic criticism of those *ʿulamā'* who opposed modern ideas and science. [*See the biography of Afghānī.*]

Modernization and the introduction of science have inevitably raised the issue of choosing between traditional and modern education for Muslims or of devising an acceptable synthesis. Traditional Islamic education, with its emphases on teaching of the Qur'ān and *sunnah* and on memorization, had remained essentially unchanged since the Niẓāmīyah curriculum was devised under the rule of Sultan Niẓām al-Mulk in the eleventh century. Ibn Khaldūn, in a comparative study of education in Muslim lands of the fourteenth century, pointed out that only in Muslim Spain and Persia were subjects such as poetry, grammar, and arithmetic included in the syllabi. Elsewhere, subjects unrelated to the Qur'ān were regarded as too secular to teach to children. The Niẓāmīyah curriculum was faithfully passed on to subsequent generations and was adopted unchanged in Mughal India, until somewhat modified by Shāh Walī Allāh (1703–1762) to include arithmetic and logic. However, al-Azhar University in Cairo did have some scientific subjects in its syllabus, including mathematics and astronomy, even before the Napoleonic invasion. These largely reflected knowledge which had long since been superseded: the astronomy taught, for example, was based on a Ptolemaic model in which the sun revolved around the earth. Thus it was a prime goal of Muslim modernists to transfer Western models of universities and schools into their societies.

The spread of science teaching in various Arab countries—such as Egypt, Syria, Iraq, and Lebanon—and on the Indian subcontinent was greatly aided by Christian missionary efforts. Although their purpose was primarily evangelical, they brought considerable intellectual stimulus based on new developments in the West. The first Western scientific institutions in the Arab world were the Syrian Protestant College and the Jesuit St. Joseph's College, both in Beirut.

Scientific Achievements. According to an ISESCO (Islamic Educational and Scientific Organization) report of 1986, there are 628 science and technology research institutes and centers in Muslim countries, of which 173 are engaged in agricultural research. There are four desert institutes, 58 centers of medical research, 47 for veterinary sciences, 45 for energy, and 44 for industrial research. There are nine centers for nuclear studies, eight for space research, seven for biotechnology, nine for oceanography, and four in computer sciences. Pakistan has the largest number of research institutes (142), followed by Indonesia (70), Turkey (58), and Egypt (35). The quality of these institutions, however, is generally below that of those in more advanced countries. Recent and reasonably complete scientometric studies of Muslim scientific productivity appear not to be available. In 1976 a study by Michael Moravcsik counted 352,000 scientific authors of whom only 3,300 were from Muslim countries ("International Conference on Science in Islamic Polities," vol. 1, Islamabad, 1983). A small-scale study conducted in 1989 showed Muslim authorship of physics papers to be 46 out of a sample of 4,168, 53 out of 5,050 in mathematics, and 128 out of 5,375 in chemistry (for this and other quantitative indicators, see Hoodbhoy, 1991, chap. 4). From publications quoted in the scientific citation index of 1988 it appears that Egypt (17) and Turkey (10.5) are relatively advanced among Muslim countries, although much below the level of Israel (72) and India (90).

According to a 1987 report on the status of scientific research in Arab countries authored by the Federation of Arab Scientific Research Councils, there are 82 universities and about 250 independent research institutions in the Arab world. The total number of academic staff is about 52,000, of whom about 55 percent are Ph.D's. About 59 percent of all researchers are in Egypt. Expenditure on scientific research ranges from 0.02 to 0.5 percent of the gross national product, a percentage that is very low compared to that of developed countries. The report cites a survey showing that the number of papers by these researchers in scientific journals was about 20 percent of those published in India, 4 percent of those in the USSR, and less than 1 percent of those in the USA. The number of papers per researcher per year ranges between 0.1 and 0.6. Reasons for this low productivity are stated to include lack of funds, excessive teaching loads, and lack of promotion incentives.

Although the productivity of Muslim scientists residing in their own countries is low, Muslims living abroad in the advanced countries are relatively much more productive, and several have been credited with important scientific discoveries. Mohammed Abdus Salam, together with Steven Weinberg and Sheldon Glashow, received the Nobel Prize for physics in 1979 for fundamental work that unified the weak and electromagnetic interactions. (However, it should be noted that Salam's Aḥmadīyah sect, although it continues to claim adherence to Islam, was officially excommunicated by an act of the Pakistani parliament in 1974.) Salam has been by far the most articulate and effective proponent of Muslim scientific development and is the founder-director of the International Centre for Theoretical Physics (ICTP), which has played an important role in stimulating scientific research in developing countries by inviting thousands of researchers to participate in research conferences and workshops in Trieste, Italy. The Third World Academy of Sciences, an offshoot of the ICTP, is also headed by Salam and receives some financial support from Muslim countries.

The global diffusion of modern technology has profoundly altered lifestyles in Muslim countries. It is not, however, easy to decide on the status of a country in the field of science and technology in a simple quantitative manner. One important indicator of the level of scientific-technological development of a country is the extent to which industry and manufacturing are part of its economy. This in turn is estimated by the "value added" in manufacturing, which includes machinery and transport equipment, chemicals, textiles, and other factors. Data on value added is published yearly in the Development Report of the World Bank. Indonesia and Malaysia are among the fastest-growing economies of the world, partly because of their success in attracting foreign investment and partly because of their own high investments in human-resource development. There has been a steady rise in value added for most Muslim countries, but absolute levels are still low: in 1983, of forty-six Muslim states, only twenty-four produced cement, eleven produced sugar, five had heavy engineering industries, six produced textiles, and five produced light armaments. By and large, Muslim states are consumers of technology and producers of raw materials, oil being the most important.

In the nuclear area, the domain of medium to high technology, Pakistan has the most advanced program among Muslim countries. It has one Canadian-supplied power reactor and a second, Chinese-supplied one in the process of installation in 1994, as well as an extensive uranium-enrichment program using centrifugal technology derived from the Netherlands and Belgium. It is the only Muslim country that has nuclear-weapons capability, and as of 1993 was thought to possess sufficient material to make between six and twelve Hiroshima-size devices. Before the destruction of its nuclear installations after the Gulf War, Iraq was estimated to be only two or three years away from achieving nuclear capability. Iran and Egypt have small, energy-oriented nuclear programs but appear to have no serious intentions of acquiring nuclear weapons.

Reactions to Science. The relatively slow growth of science and modern ideas in most Muslim countries has elicited three types of responses from Muslims. An extreme reaction, exemplified by Sayyid Quṭb of Egypt and Sayyid Abū al-Aʿlā Mawdūdī of Pakistan, has been to claim that this is nothing to regret because modern science is guided not by moral values but by naked materialism and arrogance. Its emphasis on constant change is in contradiction to the immutable values of Islam, and its claims to high achievement and total dependence on human reason amount to worship of humanity. According to this view, scientific development is not possible—nor even desirable—in an Islamic society.

A second reaction has been to reinterpret the faith in order to reconcile the demands of modern science and civilization with the teachings and traditions of Islam. This school of thought has a historical tradition going back to the rationalist Muʿtazilah movement of the ninth century and to the work of Ibn Rushd, particularly his book *Tahāfut al-tahāfut,* in which he refuted the antirationalism of Imam al-Ghazālī. In this "reconstructionist" tradition, it is argued that the world of God cannot be wrong, but also that the truths of science are manifest and real. Therefore the only issue is to arrive at suitable interpretations of the Qur'ān, through careful etymological examination, wherever there is an apparent conflict between revealed truth and physical reality. It is held that Islam in the days of the Prophet and the Khilāfah-yi Rāshidah was revolutionary, progressive, and rational, and that the subsequent slide into stultifying rigidity was due to the triumph of *taqlīd* (tradition) over *ijtihād* (innovation). Muḥammad ʿAbduh, Muḥammad Rashīd Riḍā, and Sayyid Aḥmad Khān were the leading proponents of this point of view.

A third attitude has been to treat the requirements of science and modernity as essentially unrelated to the direct concerns of religion and faith. Its adherents are satisfied with the vague belief that Islam and science are not in conflict but are disinclined to examine such issues too closely. From this point of view, the preoccupation of those who search for Qur'ānic justifications of the facts of modern science appears redundant and arcane. It is probably fair to say that this is the majority point of view among Muslims today.

It is interesting to examine Muslim attitudes toward major developments in science, and Darwin's theory of evolution provides the most contentious example. The first major debate, which pitted traditionalist Muslim and Christian Arabs against rationalists and radicals, was initiated in 1884 following the publication of a work in Arabic by Shiblī Shumayyil (1853–1917) favoring Darwinism. Expectedly, religious conservatives denounced Darwin's theory as amounting to the denial of God and a refutation of the Qur'ānic and biblical theories of creation. Even Afghānī, otherwise a powerful proponent of science, derided Darwinism—although it appears that he had not understood or even read any of Darwin's work. A few Muslims, such as the writer Ismāʿīl Maẓhar (1891–1962), did make serious efforts to understand Darwinian evolution and asserted the need to reinterpret Islamic theology in the light of established facts. Others, such as the theologian Ḥusayn al-Jisr (1845–1909), sought to reconcile elements of Darwin's work with Islam. A comprehensive account of this historical debate may be found in *Western Science in the Arab World: The Impact of Darwinism, 1860–1930* by Adel A. Ziadat (London, 1986). The author concludes that an author's religion—whether Muslim or Christian—was of secondary importance in this debate; Rather, it was largely a debate between religious men and secularists. In the contemporary Muslim world attitudes toward Darwinism are mixed. Teaching of the theory of evolution is allowed in Turkey, Egypt, Iraq, Iran, Indonesia, and several other countries; however, it was removed from the syllabus in Pakistan in the regime of General Zia ul-Haq, and it is expressly forbidden in Saudi Arabia and Sudan.

It is harder to find specific Muslim responses to other major scientific developments such as Einstein's theory of relativity, quantum mechanics, big-bang cosmology, or chaos theory. Following the standard criticisms common earlier in this century in the West—wherein Einstein's relativity was taken to imply moral relativism and quantum mechanical uncertainty as an unacceptable limitation on the power of God—a few Muslim writers have continued to argue that these major ideas of science are in conflict with Qur'ānic teachings. However, these seem to be isolated examples, and the majority attitude has been to ignore such issues or to accept them passively. Unlike the vigorous science-vs.-religion debates in Europe after the scientific revolution, there seems to be little discussion on the philosophical implications of modern scientific issues in Muslim countries, except perhaps in Turkey and Iran. The reason for this relatively low-level interest may be the increasing specialization of science and the difficulty of translating its ideas into ordinary language, as well as the reluctance of the *ʿulamā'* to be drawn into new fields. However, some issues continue to be routinely debated and commented upon. One such issue is whether the new moon that determines the lunar calendar must be visually sighted, or whether its position can be predicted in advance with modern astronomical techniques. This becomes important and contentious especially around the time of ʿĪd al-Fiṭr. In Pakistan a Ruet-i-Hilāl committee has been formed by the government to make final decisions on this matter. Weather prediction is an issue on which there has been a considerable softening of the traditionally hard position that God alone knows and decides when it will rain, and that he has prescribed the *namāz-i istisqā* (prayer for rain) so that believers may supplicate him; presently all Muslim countries maintain some form of meteorological department and provide weather information. Although orthodox *ʿulamā'* maintain their position against the dissection of cadavers for medical training, blood transfusions, and organ transplants, this is now essentially disregarded almost everywhere in Muslim countries.

In recent years the applications, methodology, and epistemology of modern science have been severely criticized by growing numbers of Muslim conservatives. At one level, in close similarity with the radical critiques of science by the German "Greens" as well as European Marxists and anarchists, it is argued that the development and application of a supposedly value-free science is the prime cause of the great problems faced by the world today—weapons of mass destruction, environmental degradation, global inequities in the distribution of wealth and power, and the alienation of the individual among them. Others go a step beyond this and reject the validity of the scientific method as well as the notion of science as knowledge, believing that the goals and techniques of modern science, which are considered distinct from those of medieval science, will inevitably damage the fabric of Islam. Knowledge for the sake of knowledge is declared to be a dangerous and illegitimate goal, and the only form of legitimate knowledge is that which leads to a greater understanding of the divine. The most articulate representative of this point of view is the Iranian-born scholar Seyyed Hossein Nasr, who also argues that the word *ʿilm*, the knowledge whose pursuit is a religious duty, has been willfully distorted to mean science and secular learning by Muslim modernists in an effort to make science more acceptable in Islamic societies. [*See the biography of Nasr.*]

The reaction of Muslim orthodoxy to the teaching of modern science in schools has been to demand basic changes. These include some or all of the following: introduction of all scientific facts with reference to God; dilution of the cause-and-effect relation to accommodate the divine will; rewriting of all science books by people of sound Islamic beliefs; highlighting of the former Muslim supremacy in science; and removal of names associated with specific physical laws (e.g., Boyle's Law or Einstein's Theory). It should be noted, however, that the Iranian clergy has allowed science taught in Iranian schools to maintain its secular character.

Islamic Science. Exponents of "Islamic science" argue that it offers an Islamic alternative to the challenge of modern Western science, which they consider to be reductionist and incapable of accommodating Islamic beliefs. Many individual proposals for creating this alternative science have emerged since the 1970s. However, given the absence of a centralized religious authority—an "Islamic Church"—the validity of these proposals cannot clearly be certified from the religious point of view. One fairly common definition of "Islamic science" is that every scientific fact and phenomenon known today was anticipated fourteen hundred years ago, and that all scientific predictions can and must be based upon study of the Qur'ān. This has been the concern of dozens of conferences in numerous Muslim countries, including Egypt, Pakistan, Malaysia, and Saudi Arabia. A popular author who advocates this version of Islamic science is Maurice Bucaille, a French surgeon who became a spiritualist. His major book, *The Bible, the Qur'an, and Science,* seeks to establish that the Qur'ān correctly anticipated all major discoveries of science while the Bible was flawed in places; it has been translated into several languages and is read widely in Muslim countries.

Another opinion is that Islamic science is knowledge that is based on Islamic values and beliefs such as *tawḥīd* (unity of God), *ʿibādah* (worship), *khilāfah* (trusteeship), and that stands for the rejection of *ẓālim* (tyrannical) science as well as science for the sake of curiosity. Revelation rather than reason ought to be the ultimate guide to valid knowledge. Seyyed Hossein Nasr (1982) asserts that "a truly Islamic science cannot but derive ultimately from the intellect which is Divine and not human reason . . . the seat of the intellect is the heart rather than the head, and reason is no more than its reflection upon the mental plane." He provides no further suggestions as to how the new science should be organized. Other Muslim authors insist that the study of natural disasters, which constitutes Islamic environmental science, must begin with trying to understand God's will, because earthquakes, volcanic eruptions, floods, and so on are events under his direct control and part of a grand scheme. One of the most articulate advocates of the islamization of knowledge, including science, was the late Ismāʿīl al-Fārūqī. [*See* Education, *article on* Islamization of Knowledge; *and the biography of Fārūqī.*]

One should distinguish science practiced by Muslims—whether in the present epoch or in the golden age of Islamic civilization—from "Islamic science," which is supposed to reflect specifically Islamic characteristics. The claim that an Islamic science of the physical world is a meaningful concept can be challenged on at least three grounds. First, decades of efforts to create a specifically Islamic science have failed. The fact is that Islamic science has not led to the building of a single new machine or instrument, the design of a new experiment, or the discovery of a new and testable fact. Only post-facto explanations have been provided, never a prediction. Second, specifying a set of moral and theological principles, no matter how elevated, does not permit one to build a new science from scratch. There are numerous examples of scientists subscribing to very different philosophical assumptions and having very different emotional and psychological dispositions, who have nonetheless arrived at very similar results in their scientific investigations. Although a scientist may be inspired to make a particular discovery as a consequence of his belief, his claims of discovery must be validated by a system of science that relies on experimentation and testing as its basis. Third, there has never existed a definition of Islamic science acceptable to Muslims universally. Many of the great Muslim scholars of medieval times, including al-Kindī, al-Rāzī, Ibn Sīnā, and Ibn Rushd, suffered persecution at the hands of the orthodoxy because of their nontraditional religious and spiritual beliefs. The sectarian divisions among Muslims today would be reflected in any endeavor to establish a common set of rules. It is also worthy of note that all suggestions for creating a new epistemology of science based on ideological or moral principles have proved to be of little value because they have been far too vague and ill-defined.

[*See also* Astronomy; Mathematics; Medicine; Natural Sciences; *and* Technology and Applied Sciences.]

BIBLIOGRAPHY

Gottstein, Klaus, ed. *Islamic Cultural Identity and Scientific-Technological Development.* Baden-Baden, 1986. Collection of papers dealing with questions of cultural diversity and identity, and science and development in Muslim countries.

Hoodbhoy, Pervez. *Islam and Science: Religious Orthodoxy and the Battle for Rationality.* London, 1991. Critical account of the relationship between the scientific spirit and Muslim orthodoxy, covering both present and medieval times.

Islam: Source and Purpose of Knowledge: Proceedings and Selected Papers of the Second Conference on the Islamization of Knowledge. Herndon, Va., 1982. Useful compendium of papers setting out the Islamic perspective on the nature and purpose of knowledge.

Issawi, Charles, ed. *The Economic History of the Middle East, 1800–1914.* Chicago, 1966.

Keddie, Nikki R. *An Islamic Response to Imperialism.* 2d ed. Berkeley, 1983. Authoritative account of Jamāl al-Dīn al-Afghānī's life and thought, and his encounter with the antiscience orthodoxy of his times.

Kumar, Deepak, ed. *Science and Empire: Essays in Indian Context, 1700–1947.* Delhi, 1991. Useful collection detailing the introduction of science in British India.

Lewis, Bernard. *The Muslim Discovery of Europe.* New York, 1982. Details the encounter of Muslims with the modern civilization of the West.

Maryam Jameelah. *Modern Technology and the Dehumanization of Man.* Lahore, 1983. Scathing criticism of science and modernism from an orthodox Muslim perspective.

Mawdūdī, Sayyid Abū al-Aʿlā. *Taʿlīmāt.* 3d ed. Lahore, [1972]. Critique of modern education and sketch of the Islamic alternative, by a leading twentieth-century conservative.

Nasr, Seyyed Hossein. "Islam and Modern Science." In *Islam and Contemporary Society,* edited by Salem Azzam, pp. 177–190. London, 1982. Attack on the foundations of modern science and an appeal for a science based on Islam, by one of the best-known opponents of Western science.

Sāqib, Ghulām Nabī. *Modernization of Muslim Education in Egypt, Pakistan, and Turkey.* Lahore, 1983. Detailed analysis of Islam and modernity from an Islamic modernist's point of view.

Tibawi, A. L. *Islamic Education.* London, 1972.

Troll, Christian W. *Sayyid Ahmad Khan: A Reinterpretation of Muslim Theology.* Karachi, 1978. Traces the evolution of Sayyid Aḥmad Khān from a staunch Muslim conservative into an outstanding exponent of modernism in British India.

Zahlan, A. B. *Science and Science Policy in the Arab World*. New York, 1980. Valuable if somewhat dated work on science and technological levels in Arab countries.

PERVEZ HOODBHOY

SECLUSION. The practice of confining women to the exclusive company of other women in their own home or in separate female living quarters is one mechanism among others—including modest dress, veiling, self-effacing mannerisms, and the separation of men and women in public places—that are employed to undergird sexual morality in Middle Eastern Muslim societies. The practice of women's seclusion is grounded in both religion and social custom. Numerous verses in the Qur'ān enjoin separation and modesty in dress and behavior on women. Surah 33.32–33, for example, states:

> O ye wives of the Prophet! Ye are not like other women. If ye keep your duty (to Allāh) then be not soft of speech, lest he in whose heart is a disease aspire (to you), but utter customary speech, and stay in your houses. Bedizen not yourselves with the bedizenment of the times of ignorance.

Qur'ānic commentators were later to hold up the modesty and confinement enjoined on the Prophet's wives as a model of decorum for all women.

Such practices are also grounded in the idea that women are a source of temptation (*fitnah*) for men, and in the fear that social interaction between unrelated men and women would therefore lead to illicit sexual intercourse and chaos in the community of believers. The importance of controlling women in order to control *fitnah* was elaborated by theologians as a religious imperative and incorporated into law under the influence, most notably, of Imām al-Ghazālī (1050–1111) in his book *The Revivification of the Religious Sciences*.

Although Islam helped to institutionalize and perpetuate modesty and seclusion practices by endowing them with the aura of religious sanctity, these practices did not originate with Islam; they were well established in Byzantine and Syriac Christian and pre-Christian societies of the Mediterranean, Mesopotamia, and Persia before the coming of Islam. Female separation practices encouraged in Islam are also compatible with Middle Eastern tribal patriarchy and with tribal attitudes about maintaining blood purity, which necessitate controls over women's reproductive capacity.

The ultimate expression of female seclusion is the *ḥarīm* (harem) system, *ḥarīm* meaning both the area of the home in which women dwell and the women of the family, the word connoting sacredness and inviolability. The *ḥarīm* system became fully institutionalized during the ʿAbbāsid Caliphate. Under it women of the household, female retainers, and servants lived in complete seclusion from the outside world under the guardianship of eunuchs. Seclusion remained a practice characteristic of nobility and the urban middle and upper classes, among whom the financial ability to allow one's wife to remain at home was a mark of status. However, confinement to the home has also been practiced in some regions, such as the Arabian Peninsula, by very poor families among whom seclusion of women is a great hardship. In general, because most women are agricultural workers, urban poor, or domestic servants, seclusion in the form of confinement to the home has always been economically unrealistic. For women workers and women of wealth alike, the face veil and the *chadūr* or *ʿabāyah* represent a mechanism for extending one's physical seclusion outside the home.

The practice of female seclusion declined precipitously in the early twentieth century as a result of education and increased economic opportunity for women, but it has not entirely disappeared. In rural areas of Afghanistan, for example, and in conservative Gulf states where tribal affiliations remain strong and income is high, a value is still placed on rigid separation of women from unrelated men.

Since the early 1980s female modesty and separation practices have found renewed encouragement in the sermons and *fatwā*s of conservative preachers and theologians who call for use of the *ḥijāb* (Islamic dress), veiling, and limiting women's access to public places. In Saudi Arabia, some radical scholars and political groups call for a return to seclusion and an end to all female employment outside the home.

The positive response of young women, especially well-educated urban women, to the religious revival and its call for women's modesty underscores the fact that seclusion practices reflect social realities as well as religious values. For professional working women, adopting the *ḥijāb* is a way of carving out legitimate space for themselves in the public arena traditionally reserved for men; the *ḥijāb* is a strategy for coping with a social climate in which men are uncomfortable working with women, and which holds women responsible for men's moral behavior. For religious women, some of whom are actually trying to emulate the seclusion practices eschewed by their grandmother's generation, seclusion is an affirmation of religious values in the face of massive westernization and the dilution of what are considered mores and practices ordained by God.

[*See also* Dress; Fitnah; Ḥarām; Ḥijāb; Modesty; Sexuality; Women and Islam, *article on* Role and Status of Women.]

BIBLIOGRAPHY

Abu-Lughod, Lila. *Veiled Sentiments: Honor and Poetry in a Bedouin Society*. Berkeley, 1986. Discusses the values of honor, modesty, and patriarchy in a bedouin community as the fundamental rationale for separation practices.

Ahmed, Leila. *Women and Gender in Islam: Historical Roots of a Modern Debate*. New Haven, 1992. Discusses seclusion in historical perspective.

Doumato, Eleanor A. "Hearing Other Voices: Christian Women and the Coming of Islam." *International Journal of Middle East Studies* 23 (1991): 177–199. Discussion of seclusion practices among pre-Islamic Christian women in the Arabian Peninsula.

Mernissi, Fatima. *Beyond the Veil: Male-Female Dynamics in Modern Muslim Society*. Rev. ed. Bloomington, 1987. Discusses the rationale for seclusion practices in Muslim theology and in Middle Eastern social norms regarding heterosexual relations.

Shaʿrāwī, Hūdā. *Harem Years: The Memoirs of an Egyptian Feminist*. Translated by Margot Badran. London, 1986. Describes growing up in an upper-middle-class "hareem" in Cairo.

ELEANOR ABDELLA DOUMATO

SECULARISM. The term *secularism* signifies that which is not religious. It is rooted in the Latin world *saeculum,* which initially meant "age" or "generations" in the sense of temporal time. It later became associated with matters of this world, as distinct from those of the spirit directed toward attainment of paradise. The French word *laïcité* also signifies secularism but originally designated "lay people," those who were not of the clergy (Berkes, 1964, p. 5).

Historians define the nature or extent of secularism in a society or culture as indicating the "placement" (C. John Sommerville, *The Secularization of Early Modern England,* New York and Oxford, 1992, p. 8) of religion in that society or culture: is the ruling authority religious, either a god-monarch or religious officials administering laws believed divinely inspired?; is the state secular in appearance, governed by people outside a religious hierarchy, but the society and culture religious, with state authority sanctioned by that hierarchy (as often occurred in the Christian Middle Ages and lasted in Spain well into the twentieth century)?; or does the sanction for government and its laws derive from nonreligious legitimation with religion a matter of personal faith?

Secularism or the secularization process derives from the European historical experience. It meant the gradual separation of "almost all aspects of life and thought from religious associations and ecclesiastical direction," a process that developed in England in the sixteenth century with the transfer of political power from the religious arena to the state and legal cases from religious to secular courts (Sommerville, 1992, pp. 112–117). Historians note that preindustrial secularization had the support of Protestantism, which they define as a "secularizing religion," that is, one that approved the separation of religion from state functions in order to purify it by removing it from the realm of worldly corruption. The word *secular* was not used to describe this process until the nineteenth century.

In the European historical experience, which itself varied widely, the secularization process coexisted with an intensification of religiosity on the personal and popular level. Some sociologists argue that these variations indicate a mythology of secularism that assumes a classic religious age existed that then became transformed into a secular age: they argue that aspects of secularism and religiosity always coexisted and still do. Secularization did not mean a necessary erosion of religious belief, either in the preindustrial age or the industrial. Religious belief and practice, as faith, intensified rather than declined during the secularization of the state and later, following the French and Industrial Revolutions, that of society. It served to create emotional, spiritual, and social bonds in the face of a new liberalism perceived as inhuman, and "to develop social and sometimes educational and political institutions in an [often rural, less urbanized] environment which provided none" (E. J. Hobsbawm, *The Age of Revolution, 1789–1948,* New York, 1962, p. 272). Religion today coexists with industrial, technically secular society and has intensified its activities in the United States where in official circles "it is considered an almost essential part of being American" (Glasner, 1977, p. 115).

Islam and the Islamic experience historically have been quite different from Christianity and the West. Roman and Protestant Christianity both acknowledged, albeit with differing interpretations, the distinction between church and state and their differing spheres of authority. Islam did not. Islamic theologians distinguished between matters of *dīn* (religion) and those of *dawlah* (the state) in respect to affairs directed toward attaining salvation and those concerned solely with *dunyā* (material life in this world). Nevertheless, Islam has never defined religious and political matters as the existence of two separate institutions. Neither has Islam possessed ecclesiastical institutions that could be separated from political institutions. Public office existed to serve Islamic needs, to preserve the *ummah* (community) and to ensure the application of *sharīʿah* (Islamic law). This concept has been revived most effectively in the modern era by Abū al-Aʿlā Mawdūdī (d. 1979), a Pakistani, whose writings have had a major influence on Sunnī fundamentalist thought throughout the Muslim World.

Islam has not experienced a Reformation analogous to that of Protestantism in Western Christianity. Islam's reformist movements before the impact of the West sought to purify Islam of worldly or heretical accretions by reinforcing Islamic authority over society and ensuring total adherence to the law, the opposite of the Protestant desire to purify religion by separating it from state affiliation. This distinction reflects historical developments. The rise of the nation-state in western Europe encouraged allegiances to secular authorities and freedom from the overarching claims of the papacy. Muslim allegiance has traditionally been to the *ummah,* a community defined by common adherence to faith, not by political or ethnic boundaries. The idea of the nation-state did not appear in Muslim thought until the late nineteenth century. Its political evolution resulted from the collapse of the Ottoman Empire following World War I and the imposition of state boundaries by European mandatories to suit their imperial requirements.

The secularization process in Europe was gradual, evolving in conjunction with socioeconomic developments. In contrast the Islamic experience has been one of secularism as an ideology imposed from outside by invaders, a product of European imperialism and its extension of a foreign culture initiated at the beginning of the nineteenth century.

No precise word for secularism existed in Arabic. The pejorative *dahrīyah* was used in the nineteenth century. It meant "materialist" or "atheist," one who believed in earthly eternity rather than divine retribution and spiritual life; the root *dahr,* referring to ages or generations, is analogous to the initial meaning of *saeculum.* Today the word more commonly used in Arabic is *ʿilmānīyah,* whose root refers to science and knowledge and whose closest derivation means "the world" or "worldly matters."

The question for Muslims in the modern era, confronted by European imperialism, became one of survival, of preserving an independent existence or regaining it from foreign occupiers. Mastery of European secular culture, especially its science (as the basis of military prowess), seemed the means to achieve modernization. The controversy over this choice and the alternatives selected by various Muslim societies has lasted to the present.

Many areas of the Islamic world have witnessed the intensification of religious faith that accompanied secularization in Europe. This intensification process has led to the rise of popular movements often independent of the official religious hierarchy. Unlike their Western counterparts, these movements have demanded the reassertion of Islam over the state or as the state, the latter successfully achieved in Iran in 1979.

The battle between secularism and religion today is more intense than ever. In most cases the extreme positions are those of secularist attempts to define Islam as a matter of personal belief set against those for whom the reimposition of *sharīʿah* and Islamic political authority is essential. Within this framework there is considerable diversity. Although secular ideologies were openly espoused in the past in certain regions of the Islamic world, secularists today often find themselves in dangerous conflicts. Many argue from within the Islamic tradition against literal application of the *sharīʿah* and might be better defined as Islamic modernists. As in the past, the question of survival remains a key issue, with Islamists arguing that Muslim societies require their own laws and principles if they are to compete with non-Muslim countries.

A key issue with respect to secularization in Muslim societies is the status of women. Modernizing Muslim societies since the late nineteenth century have witnessed the advocacy of greater freedom for women; the removal of the veil has been the most visible step in this. Advocates of women's greater independence, often intellectuals attracted to Western ideals, have found a positive response among educated middle- and upper-class women, but have encountered strong resistance from more traditional male sectors of society.

Using the experience of the West to justify removal of restrictions on women is seen by conservatives as an example of foreign influence. In recent years many women with university educations, often employed in such major urban centers as Cairo, have forsaken Western dress and returned to Muslim garb for reasons ranging from religious belief to a desire to avoid criticism and harassment from men, whether religiously inspired or not. The placement of women in Muslim societies today is often a benchmark for evaluating the placement of Islam itself in the eyes of secular/modernist and conservative groups. [*See* Women and Social Reform.]

Ottoman Empire and Its Legacy. Ottoman Turkey, as a bureaucratic empire, had institutionalized both civil and religious authority in the imperial administration and in the person of the ruler, the sultan/caliph. During the nineteenth century a state-sponsored modernizing reform movement created secular institutions intended to introduce Western educational methods, legal systems, and military techniques. These institutions, and the elite that administered them, did not so much destroy corresponding Muslim organizations as supplant them; the latter remained in existence meeting the needs of the Muslim population. This process of reform, called the Tanzimat or reorganization process, encountered strong resistance throughout the century as Ottoman Turks struggled to confront the question of the empire's survival and how best to achieve it. For avowed secularist reformers, such as a minister of education in the 1870s, Saffat Pasha, survival was the issue: ". . . unless Turkey . . . accept[s] the civilization of Europe in its entirety . . . she will never free herself from the European intervention and tutelage and will lose her prestige, her rights, and even her independence" (Berkes, 1964, p. 185, quoting from a letter written in 1879).

After World War I and the defeat and dismemberment of the Ottoman Empire, the new state of Turkey emerged under the leadership of Mustafa Kemal, later known as Atatürk. He abolished both the political sultanate and religious caliphate. For Muslims generally, this ended a legacy of the prophet Muḥammad, a religiously sanctioned office of political authority. For Mustafa Kemal, it opened the way for a civil state in which Islam would be relegated to the status of personal faith. The Muslim calendar was replaced by the Gregorian, Arabic script by the Latin, and the veil was discouraged.

This secularization from above created a secular state, but it could not erase Islam as a religion followed by the mass of the people. With the advent of a multiparty democratic system after World War II, ostensibly secular politicians won elections by appealing to mass religiosity, appearing to threaten the Atatürk legacy. Military intervention in 1960 and since indicates ongoing political uneasiness in Turkey over the boundaries of Islamic expression within the secular state. The Turkish experience shows that state-sponsored secularization cannot create a mass secular culture and that the introduction of Western democracy encourages the reassertion of Islam as a political factor.

Most Turkish politicans accept a balance between a secular state and personal Islamic expression, but recent fundamentalist activity theatens to undermine this balance. In July 1993 Turkish Islamists burned a hotel where a conference of Turkish secular intellectuals was in session, killing forty, apparently in revenge for critical comments about Islam made at the conference. Murders of secular intellectuals in Egypt and Algeria as well suggest a targeting of advocates of secularism in the growing conflict between secularist and fundamentalist forces.

The Arab World. A wide range of governments exist in the Arab Muslim world, ranging from the Wahhābī-sanctioned Saudi Arabian state to the avowedly secular, socialist regimes in Iraq and Syria. Saudi Arabia, because of the two-centuries-old link of the house of Saʿūd to the Wahhābī reform movement, proclaims itself an Islamic state. Technically, its rulers are secular officials governing in accordance with *sharīʿah* as interpreted by the *ʿulamāʾ*. Islam legitimizes the state which is governed by *sharīʿah*. Saudi officials finance Islamic movements in other states against governments considered secular; the goal is to restore *sharīʿah* as the governing law of these states, returning these countries to the model known in the early Islamic centuries. Nevertheless, the Saudi ruling house has come under attack from more fundamentalist Muslim groups for its supposed deviance from Islamic norms.

At the opposite end of the spectrum are the rival socialist states of Syria and Iraq, each claiming to represent the true ideology of the Baʿth (Renaissance) Party. Although Islam is recognized as the official religion of each state, it is relegated to matters of personal faith in practice. Women are proclaimed equal to men, and many are employed in major urban centers.

Conversely, there exists strong religious opposition in Syria to the regime of Hafez Assad, epitomized by the Muslim Brotherhood, which, like its parent organization in Egypt, seeks the creation of an Islamic state. Such movements have been ruthlessly suppressed: in 1982 Assad ordered the bombardment of Hama, with an estimated twenty thousand casualties, to destroy centers of the Muslim Brotherhood, whose members had infiltrated the ranks of military cadets. Sunnī and Shīʿī clerics in Iraq have been forced to accommodate themselves to the regime of Saddam Hussein. In the aftermath of the Gulf War of 1991 and Shīʿī rebellion against Hussein, Iraqi troops destroyed shrines at Karbala and Najaf central to Shīʿī worship This has probably created a religious opposition to Baʿthism, but more on political than strictly religious grounds. [*See* Baʿth Parties.]

Sustained efforts to create Islamic states and to reject secularism are occuring in Egypt and Algeria, countries that have had very different patterns of modernization and national development.

In Egypt, the creation of a secular state and legal institutions began in the nineteenth century, encouraged by Khedive Ismail (1863–1879) and applied more intensely under the British occupation from 1882 onward. The early twentieth century saw the emergence of an avowedly secular cadre of Muslim intellectuals linked to Aḥmad Luṭfī al-Sayyid and the newspaper *Al-jarīdah,* which advocated the relegation of Islam to matters of personal faith. Following World War I, Egyptian nationalist parties were generally secular, agreeing that Islamic institutions, including the mosque/university of al-Azhar, should be placed under state supervision and that *sharīʿah* should be supplanted by Western law codes in all areas except those of personal status.

Muslim secularists, such as Muḥammad Ḥusayn Haykal and Ṭāhā Ḥusayn, aggressively advocated these ideas and the superiority of Western culture during the 1920s. In 1925, ʿAlī ʿAbd al-Rāziq, a member of the *ʿulamāʾ*, argued that Islam contained no political principles and permitted freedom of opinion and democracy. These declarations caused a backlash which contributed to the creation of a popular movement in 1928, the Muslim Brotherhood, that condemned both the advocates of secularism and al-Azhar as being ineffectual in opposing them. The leader of the brotherhood, Ḥasan al-Bannāʾ, called for the restoration of *sharīʿah* and application of Islamic norms such as *zakāt* or tithing to create a more just society; the Western model was condemned as creating socioeconomic inequality, an argument that has great resonance today.

To avoid political condemnation and to justify secular goals from within Islam, secularists often turned to writing studies of the early Islamic period. Haykal argued that basic Muslim principles supported freedom of opinion and democracy in accordance with modern ideals. He stressed that the Rāshidūn or "rightly guided" caliphs left no organizational model for later generations, but rather a set of principles whose specific application could change according to the needs of the age. This argument was directed against calls for restoration of an Islamic system where *sharīʿah* would be applied. Ṭāhā Ḥusayn distinguished between the suitability of Islam for the masses and the intellectual need for Western guidance, insisting in 1938 that Egypt was really part of western European culture.

Since the 1930s a state of tension has continued in Egypt between the secular state and a strong religious movement calling for a return to an Islamic society. The type of secular government has fluctuated, from parliamentary government under a monarch until 1952, to a military quasi-dictatorship from 1954 to 1970 under Gamal Abdel Nasser, to a more liberal autocracy that opened the door to parliamentary parties, which began under Anwar el-Sadat (in power 1970–1981) and has continued under his successor, Hosni Mubarak. Throughout this period secular culture continued to expand, as did secular education, avowedly socialistic in tone under Nasser, who suppressed the Muslim Brotherhood. The brotherhood survived, however, and intensified its struggle, as seen especially in the writings of Sayyid Quṭb (d. 1966), who condemned "Atatürkism" as the basic secular evil and called for a return to rule under *sharīʿah.* In his search for allies against leftist factions, Sadat permitted the resurgence of the brotherhood and allowed it to publicly declare its goals. However, his corresponding economic opening to the West in the 1970s, the *infitāḥ,* led to increased corruption and resulted in open Muslim condemnation of secularism, contributing to Sadat's assassination in 1981.

Today, outright advocacy of secular culture in Egypt is dangerous, as witnessed by the assassination of the journalist and professor Faraj Fawdah in 1992. Those who call for the restriction of Islam to matters of personal faith do so from within an Islamic context, essentially returning to the tactics of intellectuals in the 1930s. They counter the fundamentalist call for rejection of Western culture by declaring that it was the West that had religious control of the state in the Middle Ages, unlike Sunnī Islam, which had never had the direct imposition of religious authority over the state; they argue for Western values from an ostensibly anti-Western stance (Imara, 1979, 1984). The debate in Egypt between Islamic modernists and fundamentalists is in the public arena. Many of the modernists espouse goals advocated by secularists in the past, but with greater respect for religious sensibilities. The ongoing strength of religious culture in Egypt requires that "the attempt to justify greater intellectual flexibility in approaching religious and social issues must come from within Islam, not against it . . . [defined] within an historical and cultural framework . . . established by Islam itself" (Smith, 1983, p. 198).

Left unanswered by this approach is the question of social equity and social order. The Egyptian secular state seems incapable of addressing socioeconomic crises, whereas religious groups, far better organized at local levels, provide social services, including medical care, that the government apparently cannot. Such organizations, like their European and American counterparts in relatively isolated communities in the nineteenth century, provide cohesion that the state fails to offer; in contemporary societies, these isolated regions might be slums in great cities, not rural hamlets.

Caught amid these conflicts are devout Muslims, many with university educations, who prefer a secular state and culture to a religious one because it can promise democracy and free expression. In Tunisia as well as Egypt, tolerance of the abuses of secular government and hope for greater political freedom might outweigh a desire for a fully religious state and culture. State crackdowns on Islamic groups without concern for legal niceties, however, increases sympathy for fundamentalists.

For many fundamentalists, freedom of opinion exists only within the parameters of Islamic discourse. In their view the Western concept of freedom fosters moral and social corruption. Some Islamist advocates, such as the Muslim Brotherhood in Egypt and Jordan, are sensitive to this question and accept a gradualist approach to power in which parliamentary government is retained and differing views are tolerated. The major Islamic movement in Algeria, the Islamic Salvation Front (FIS), however, sought to come to power by the parliamentary process between 1990 and 1992 but vacillated as to whether parliamentary government tolerating nonreligious opinion would continue.

The Algerian experience illustrates how a secular, in this case socialist, government, while paying obeisance to Islamic values, can lose the allegiance of poor and unemployed citizens who heed the argument that true socioeconomic justice is based on the restoration of a religious state and the rejection of foreign values. It is all the more significant that the secular Algerian state carried the legacy of leading the nationalist resistance to French occupation, a unifying symbol now apparently meaningless to many Algerians.

Although an Ottoman province like Egypt, Algeria was never fully controlled or united territorially, nor was there a central Islamic authority acknowledged by all as was found in al-Azhar in Egypt. The legal authority of the Algerian *ʿulamāʾ* coexisted uneasily with that of the marabouts and Ṣūfī shaykhs, who had great sway among the populace. In addition, Algeria's colonial experience was radically different from Egypt's. Egyptian secular state formation had begun under Muḥammad ʿAlī (1805–1849) well before the British occupation in 1882. Even then an Egyptian government existed in name and form, with British rule imposed through shadow not direct government.

In contrast, the French occupied Algeria in 1831, although their conquest of the desert interior took nearly fifty years. The French created a political unity heretofore nonexistent and governed directly. Unlike other colonies, France made Algeria a province of France and encouraged European colonization and settlement, intending to govern the region forever. Egypt never experienced such direct government or colonization.

Algeria'a lack of political institutions and its heterogenous society, combined with direct French rule, meant that Algerian nationalism developed in the post–World War I period outside of the realm of political parties and represented conceptions derived from vastly different social experiences. Francophone Algerian secular intellectuals, such as Ferhat Abbas, defined an Algerian sociocultural identity based on region with a French political identity. In contrast, ʿAbd al-Ḥamīd ibn Bādīs and others created an Islamic reform movement somewhat modernist in its goals but concerned also with a return to the early Islamic period to purify religion, not unlike the ideas of the Egyptian Muḥammad ʿAbduh (d. 1905) who had had a great influence on Luṭfī al-Sayyid and later Egyptian intellectuals. Beyond this realm, Ibn Bādīs and his colleagues were the first to assert the idea of an Algerian nation. Nevertheless, the reform movement's influence was limited, and it remained for an Algerian movement of workers transplanted to France to found the first true national movement that called for Algerian independence, the Etoile Nord-Africaine. [*See the biography of Ibn Bādīs.*]

This brief survey illustrates the complexity of the Algerian national movement prior to the revolutionary phase that would be led by the National Liberation Front (FLN), an amalgam of nationalist tendencies that subsumed Islamic, socialist, and liberal intellectual trends. With independence in 1962, the FLN, composed of diverse factions, assumed leadership of the country. The mass of the people, still rural, remained profoundly Muslim even when they migrated to the major cities seeking work. In 1963 the nature of the polity was embodied in the Algerian Constitution, which declared Algeria to be a socialist state with Islam as its official religion. Algeria, like Egypt, was a secular state with a secular culture for the urban bourgeoisie and intellectuals, but another culture, that of Islam, dominated the countryside and increasingly the urban slums. With the failure of FLN socialism and authoritarianism in the 1980s came both the demand for greater democracy and the appearance of a mass Islamic movement, the FIS, that galvanized the discontented and played on the apparent impotence of the government.

The FIS and its rival Muslim organizations call for an Islamic state run by *sharīʿah*. They are anti-Western, condemning its secular culture as corrupt and alienating, the antithesis of the concern for society proclaimed by Islam. Secularism as *läicité* is specifically attacked as antireligious, and those who support it are seen as identifying with the French colonial heritage. The FIS thus links itself to Algerian nationalism in the name of Islam. Its leaders, ʿAbbāsī Madanī and ʿAlī Bel Ḥajj, also condemn socialism and communism, as distinct from secularism, as foreign imports. Madanī's position regarding democracy is moderate, while Bel Ḥajj's views are more confrontational. [*See* Islamic Salvation Front *and the biography of Madanī.*]

Significantly, there are many sectors of society, urban especially, that oppose the Islamic movement; workers, urban intellectuals and bureaucrats, and women of the middle and upper classes, even though many of these women are adopting Islamic dress. In Algeria the conflict between secularists and Islamists has been open until the recent violence, which has included assassination of secular intellectuals and police attacks on Islamists. In particular, in the view of one Algerian writer, "the most salient characteristic of this confrontation [before 1992] is that it has principally been channeled through the subject of the status and role of women in Algerian society" (Cheriet, 1992, p. 203). Independent womanhood is viewed as an affront to an Islamic society and Islamic values.

The Algerian government's harsh repression of the Islamic movement generally and the FIS in particular following the abrogation of the 1992 electoral process has created a situation that at times approaches that of civil war. The military has intervened as defender of the Algerian Revolution, attempting to suppress if not destroy the FIS. The Algerian experience is watched warily by Islamic movements and secularists elsewhere, because the FIS's rejection of democracy if elected contradicts the gradualist approach of the Muslim Brotherhood in Egypt and Jordan, which officially includes tolerance of diverging views so long as the state is Islamic. Whether that would occur in practice if the brotherhood's goals were achieved, with *sharīʿah* applied "in the educational, media, political, economic and social fields" remains to be seen (Voll, 1991, vol. 1, p. 387).

Iran. The only Muslim society currently governed by religious officials and Islamic law is Iran; Sudan is in principle an Islamic state, but its government does not control all of territorial Sudan, and there is much opposition to the imposition of *sharīʿah*. The Iranian experience illustrates the weakness of the concept of a secular nation-state in a society where the traditional rulers had not exercised direct control over all of the state. Since 1500 Iran has been a Shīʿī Muslim society. The rulers were legitimized by their protection of Shīʿī Islam as interpreted by Shīʿī clerics. The Qājār dynasty (1794–1925) ruled Iran as Shīʿī Muslims acting on behalf of the religious community. Iran was never a colony of a European power, but its economic life gradually fell under European control at the end of the nineteenth century. This led to the short-lived 1906 Constitutional Revolution in whose vanguard was an alliance of Shīʿī mullahs, merchants, and secular liberals, all seeking to restrict the authority of the shahs; a provision in the constitution called for a committee of mullahs to review all legislation to ensure its compatibility with Islamic principles.

For most Iranians, Iranian nationalism had religious overtones. The failure of the 1906 revolution, undermined by Anglo-Russian intrigue and the shah, did not erase memory of its ideals. Neither did the appearance of the Pahlavi dynasty in 1925 created by the colonel Reza Shah, who sought to emulate Mustafa Kemal Atatürk and create a secular state from the top. The period of the Pahlavi dynasty (1925–1979) was a secular interlude in which efforts to impose state-ordered modernization ultimately aroused mass resistance encouraged by Shīʿī religious officials, whose authority had never been fully quelled. Secularism as a foreign importation was linked to the gradual exertion of American influence over Iran and over the second Pahlavi, Muhammad Reza Shah.

The Iranian Revolution of 1979 brought together mullahs, merchants, and many secular Iranian nationalists including educated women, all whom sought the overthrow of the shah without necessarily expecting a government of mullahs. Secularism as a principle and Atatürk as its Middle Eastern sponsor are condemned in Iran today just as they are by the Egyptian Muslim Brotherhood. The parameters for public ideological debate are restricted to the field of Islamic discourse, although there are significant differences here that remain submerged, in particular the ideas of ʿAlī Sharīʿatī (d. 1977), who opposed the authoritarian secular state created by the shah and the authority of the mullahs; he is considered both to be stagnant and repressive. He encouraged an approach to Islam that permitted application of the principle of *ijtihād* (self-interpretation) that would unite Iranian society under the guidance of modern but still religiously inspired intellectuals. Although Sharīʿatī appealed to many of the younger generation in Iran, his followers were not effectively organized and were easily outflanked by the mullahs. [*See the biography of Sharīʿatī.*]

South and Southeast Asia. The majority of the world's Muslim population lives in South and Southeast Asia, stretching from Pakistan to Indonesia. There exists in this region a great diversity of political and geographic circumstances as well as the existence of other ethnic and religious groups with whom Asian Muslims must accommodate themselves. This is especially true in India and Malaysia and has served to intensify religious as opposed to secular, national identities, most notably in India, where Hindu sectarian movements have increased in assertiveness in recent years.

With independence in 1947, the Indian polity proclaimed itself a democratic secular state with religious identities presumably submerged in the common bond of Indian nationalism. The dominant Congress Party had long claimed to embrace all religious and ethnic groups as Indian. Although still a secular state, India has fallen victim to sectarian passions, Sikh as well as Hindu. Hindu revivalism has focused on a desire to erase India's Islamic past. Hindu sectarianism, encouraged by poverty and illiteracy, has become a political force threatening, for the moment, the basis of Indian citizenship (Sen, 1993). India's Muslim population is estimated at 100 million, which is only 12 percent of the total population. These tensions intensify the long-existing rivalry between India and Pakistan, whose roots lie in the achievement of independence.

Indian independence brought with it the creation of the Muslim state of Pakistan, the result of the determination of Mohammad Ali Jinnah and the Muslim League to preserve a separate Muslim identity. The stage was then set for a battle over what type of Muslim state Pakistan would be. The battle was not between avowed secularists and Islamists but rather between Islamic modernists and fundamentalists. The modernists called for democracy, pluralism, and applications of the basic principles of Islam in accordance with modern needs; the state would be secular and the culture open to Western practices. The fundamentalists, centered around Mawdūdī and the organization known as the Jamāʿat-i Islāmī, called for a democratic Pakistan to be governed by *sharīʿah*.

In principle, Pakistan has always been an Islamic republic. In fact, however, Pakistan was governed for years as a secular state despite the broad statement embodied in the 1949 Objectives Resolution that "sovereignty over the entire universe belongs to God Almighty alone, and the authority which He has delegated to the State of Pakistan through its people for being exercised within the limits prescribed by Him is a sacred trust" (Ahmad, 1991, p. 470). Recognition of God's sovereignty signified that *sharīʿah* should be applied as state law. Despite this preamble, the modernists won, as recognition was given to "the principles of democracy, freedom, equality, tolerance and social justice as enunciated by Islam . . ." (Ahmad, 1991, p. 470). Similarly, the 1956 constitution, though paying obeisance to Islamic thought as its guide, was not bound by Islamic statutes. It contained secular laws creating a parliamentary democracy on the British model with the parliamentary right to ensure that no laws were passed that undermined Islamic legal principles. No mention was made of Islam as the state religion.

The distinction between adherence to Islamic legal principles as opposed to strict application of Islamic law is the classic modernist position. It essentially permits the existence of a secular state and the tolerance of a secular urban culture in a society whose constitutional framework and popular culture would remain Islamic. Whereas this had been argued from a defensive position by Egyptian modernists, it was now the basis of the Pakistani state.

Surprisingly, Mawdūdī and the Jamāʿat-i Islāmī accepted the 1956 constitution as embracing its dual objectives of enshrining Islam and democracy, despite the fact that Mawdūdī's call for a fully Islamic constitution had not been realized. Mawdūdī was not as insistent on the complete application of *sharīʿah* as his followers in the Arab world have been. Pakistan might have continued on this course except for a military coup that brought General Ayub Khan to power in 1958. He abrogated the 1956 constitution and called for a more modern, industrialized nation. Proclaiming himself as defender of modern Islam, he introduced legislation aimed at traditional Islamic practices. He revised laws to limit polygamy, to control more strictly divorce procedures, and to protect women's rights of maintenance; he also ordered government absorption of *awqāf* (religious endowments), whose religious guardians had ties to powerful landowners. These steps, affecting women and the economic bases of important religious institutions, resemble those taken by Muhammad Reza Shah in Iran that intensified Shīʿī Muslim determination to oust him.

In Pakistan, Ayub Khan's policies caused Mawdūdī and the Jamāʿat-i Islāmī to move from support to open opposition. This opposition intensified once Zulfiqar ʿAli Bhutto became prime minister in 1970. Initially, Bhutto publicly espoused socialism including the nationalization of private property. He thus repudiated Islamic principles of the right to private property in the name of a socialist ideology that challenged the Islamic foundation of Pakistan. The Bhutto regime (1970–1977) proved to be a turning point in Pakistani history. Bhutto aroused sufficient opposition to force a compromise with Islamic groups. His 1973 constitution, a concession to them, contained more open acknowledgment of Islam than that of 1956: all existing references were retained, Islam was recognized as the state religion, and it decreed that the president and prime minister had to be Muslims. His socialism, like Nasser's in Egypt during the 1960s, became "Islamic socialism" in an effort to appease public opinion.

However, this victory for the Jamāʿat-i Islāmī in parliamentary maneuvering did not signify a rapprochement with Bhutto or an ongoing commitment to parliamentary democracy. Open elections held in 1970 had led to a resounding defeat for the party. Mawdūdī's belief in Islam and democracy thus shaken, he and the party were quite willing to choose between these alternatives when General Zia ul-Haq staged a military coup in 1977, two years before Mawdūdī's death in 1979. Zia ul-Haq began to impose an Islamic program including the Islamic penal code. Bhutto was later executed for state corruption.

Recent Pakistani history has reflected the tensions inherent in its past struggles between democracy and state enforcement of an Islamic system, as well as between conflicting visions of Islam. Despite the Jamāʿat-i Islāmī's political activism, it has failed to capture more than a fraction of popular electoral support. Despite its earlier advocacy of democracy, it willingly backed Zia ul-Haq's autocracy, but then shifted to opposition in 1988, shortly before Zia's death, and condemned state tyranny and corruption; the party then decided to support Bhutto's daughter Benazir. Though widely known outside Pakistan, the Jamāʿat-i Islāmī, as a popular movement, has failed to supplant groups representing the *ʿulamā'* or to shake traditional adherence to populist Islam in the countryside, as witnessed by its poor showing in elections.

The most notable legacy of the Jamāʿat-i Islāmī lies in the writings of its founder, Mawdūdī, whose call for an Islamic state as the only answer to the modern age was always extranational and, in his view, applicable throughout the Islamic world. His writings have been widely read by members of this Egyptian Muslim Brotherhood and the Algerian FIS. Ironically, Mawdūdī may be revered more outside Pakistan than within it. [*See* Jamāʿat-i Islāmī *and the biography of Mawdūdī.*]

In Pakistan itself, the struggle between Islamic modernism and traditionalism continues, buffeted by external factors such as Afghan resistance to Soviet occupation, which became a Muslim cause and strengthened traditionalist as well as fundamentalist Islam during the 1980s. In Pakistan, like Egypt, secular and modernist interests must be expressed within an Islamic framework; unlike Egypt, that framework had been granted official recognition in Pakistan through the 1956 constitution, opening the door for a possible future compromise.

In sharp contrast to the political activism of the Jamāʿat-i Islāmī and the political implications of Mawdūdī's writings lies the existence of an individualistic Muslim reform movement that eschews political activism. This is the Tablīghī Jamāʿat, founded in 1926 in India. It is an Islamic revivalist movement based on personal preaching and the call to adhere to the Qur'ān and the *sunnah* of the prophet Muḥammad. Like Protestantism, it views politics as corrupting and "as with the eighteenth-century English evangelical Nonconformists, the primary instrument of the Tablīghī Jamāʿat workers is itinerancy" (Ahmad, 1991, p. 515). Espoused by individual missionaries, it has spread throughout the Arab world, Asia, and Africa, seeking a revival of personal morality through adherence to the basic values of Islam and a fostering of communal ties and services to maintain an Islamic society among its members.

Such a movement tolerates a secular government or state for the sake of creating an Islamic social order independent of state support, thus permitting a focus on personal salvation. Conversely, this approach enhances survival in avowedly secular societies by rejecting political activism, a particularly beneficial stance among Indian Muslims, but attractive in Europe and North America as well. On a broader level, Tablīghī practices depoliticize religious activists and have served to weaken institutional or politically inspired religious efforts in Malaysia as well as Pakistan. As Mumtaz Ahmad has shown, the Tablīghī is an authentic international Islamic movement, postulating the authority of the preacher over that of the religious official, in this case represented by the *ʿulamāʾ* but not unlike the evangelical Protestant response to secularism. [*See* Tablīghī Jamāʿat.]

The South Asian experience has provided two resolutions to the question of the place of Islam in regard to society and the state, the Jamāʿat-i Islāmī and Tablīghī Jamāʿat. Their philosophies and strategies are diametrically opposed to each other. On an organizational level, the politically activist Jamāʿat-i Islāmī has succeeded in influencing Islamist reform in Pakistan but has failed to win popular electoral backing; the Tablīghī Jamāʿat rejects political activism, and opts for individual preaching and moral reform. On the ideological level, both movements have become international in scope. The writings of Mawdūdī have served as a basic source of inspiration for the contemporary Muslim Brotherhood and especially for revolutionary fundamentalists, such as the Egyptian Sayyid Quṭb, who expanded Mawdūdī's call for Islamic government to include the conquest of the non-Muslim world. The Tablīghī movement has sent missionaries worldwide and his influenced Muslim communities in North America and Europe as well as in Africa and Asia.

In essence these movements reflect the two poles of Islamic *daʿwah* or propagation of the faith. The first insists on the union of religion and state and strives to recreate in modern form the Islamic system of government believed to exist in early Islam; the second rejects politics for the sake of moral values and principles—to the Tablīghīs, the essence of Islam found in the era of the Prophet—thereby insisting on the separation of religion and the state. The one rejects secularism outright, the other aspects its political manifestation as a necessary evil to be tolerated in order to fulfill personal religious goals. They both return to the same source, early Islam, for their solutions, as have Egyptian secularists, Islamic modernists, and the Muslim Brotherhood.

Analogous differences appear in the two sharply contrasting approaches to Islam and secularism found in Malaysia and Indonesia which result from their different histories and colonial experiences. As Manning Nash has observed, both Malaysia and Indonesia are "Islamic nations but secular states," but their concepts of nationhood are themselves quite different.

The vast archipelago called Indonesia contains more than 160 million people, a population that is nearly 85 percent Muslim. It is the largest Muslim country in the world but the state is officially secular and celebrates a variety of expressions of Islam. Secular and Islamic educational systems are both state sponsored, and secular and *sharīʿah* courts coexist. But this duality does not mean that the products of secular education are antireligious. Many, like their counterparts in Northern Africa, are devout Muslims who accept a secular state as preferable to a religious one so long as it does not impinge on their private lives. Infringement can arouse strong protest, as occurred in the mid-1970s when the government was forced to withdraw a proposed family status/marriage law that would have permitted Muslim women to marry non-Muslim men and granted civil courts final authority in cases regarding divorce or polygamy. Strong public opposition led to a reassertion of Muslim statutes and legal authority in such cases and banned interreligious marriages for Muslim women (Johns, 1987, pp. 217–19). Indonesian tolerance and pluralism regarding manifestations of Islam could easily change if the state were perceived as trying to modernize at the expense of Islam, as occurred under the Ayub Khan regime in Pakistan.

Malaysia is 45 percent Muslim. Unlike Indonesia, Islam is declared the official religion of the country. Islam serves as a source of national identity to Malays in a country with Chinese and Indian minorities amounting to 37 and 11 percent of the population respectively. Nevertheless, Malaysian Islam is itself fragmented. Though there is a national government and Islamic officialdom, there are also thirteen states, nine of which have their own bureaus, legal officials, and religious courts.

With such official fragmentation, Islamic revivalism has taken root in the *dakwah* movement, a version of *daʿwah*. It is evangelical and personally or communally organized. It attracts primarily urban, often university educated youth who reject Western culture and its secular values as corrupt, quite similar to Islam's appeal to many in Egypt for example. Frustrated by the diversity of Muslim groups in the federation, many young Malays of the *dakwah* desire an Islamic state. They are quite close in aspiration to the Muslim Brotherhood. The achievement of their goals would signify the end of the current Malaysian secular state unless explicit guarantees for ethnic minorities were given.

These movements signify discontent with official Islam and its Malaysian leaders. As evangelical groups who seek to isolate themselves from society and its corruptions, they resemble Tablīghī Jamāʿat members, but their ultimate goal, an Islamic state and official rejection of secularism, contradicts Tablīghī perspectives. However, there is also a Tablīghī *dakwah* in Malaysia that eschews political goals. These differences permit the secular political parties and government to tolerate their activities for now, but a spread of Islamic militancy, expressed politically and socially through dress codes as a symbol of frustration with modern values, could threaten the current Malaysian political system.

The historical relationship between secularism and Islam has passed through several stages that have varied according to the particular Islamic society under study. Muslim governing elites often were attracted to Western secular values in the nineteenth century, because western culture had proved superior militarily. Adoption of the scientific products of that culture could provide the means to reject European political dominance. In the early twentieth century a new generation educated usually in Western schools more readily and positively turned to European secular values as an alternative to Islam for their societies. They considered Islam to be backward and a hindrance to modernity. Behind this attitude was another, however, that had been shared by the earlier generation of bureaucrats in the Ottoman government, that the issue was one of survival, of achieving independence from foreign control and achieving equal status with the West.

There always existed Muslim opposition to the exponents of secularism, either centered in major Muslim institutions, such as al-Azhar in Egypt, or in nationalist groups that were often more eager to oust the imperial occupiers than were the secular modernists. From the 1920s onward new forms of Muslim opposition arose, often rooted in popular movements that criticized official Islam as represented by the *ʿulamāʾ* along with the secularists. The Muslim Brotherhood of Egypt is the most obvious example but the reformist movement of Shaykh Ibn Bādīs in Algeria, from within the *ʿulamāʾ*, and the later Jamāʿat-i Islāmī and the postindependence *dakwah* activities in Southeast Asia, reflect the same trend. Most of these groups have originated as both Islamic and nationalist movements, although several have sought to encourage Islamist tendencies elsewhere. The only movement led by religious officials identified with nationalism and Islamic reform that has succeeded is in Iran.

All these movements have seen secularism, whether Western liberal or socialist, as increasing not lessening dependency on foreign powers. In their view, secularism, as an outgrowth of Western culture, has also undermined values indigenous to Islamic societies and, in the secular-nationalist form of Zionism and the state of Israel, taken away territory that had been Muslim for centuries. For the religious opposition, secularism as the basis of newly independent nations after World War II ultimately acquiesced in a new form of colonialism, primarily economic but often political and cultural. The issue, to the opponents of secularism, is the same survival that initially motivated its proponents, but survival is often defined now in cultural rather than scientific terms; Western science and technology are acceptable but the dehumanization identified with secular culture is not.

This sense of dehumanization is not confined to Muslim views of secularism. It exists among all fundamentalist movements that seek to establish the word of God as the basis of social as well as personal action. The Republican candidate for lieutenant governor of Virginia in 1993, a member of the Moral Majority, forcefully espoused education at home instead of at public schools, which he believes to be riddled with "secular humanism," and hoped to establish public policy that would remove books reflecting such values from the public schools (Vest, 1993).

But such efforts are undertaken in a preexisting democratic context that secularists and Islamic modernists strive to attain in their own societies and that Muslim fundamentalist movements often oppose if non-Muslim views are to be tolerated. Open espousal of secularism as a cultural value has become not simply rare but dangerous in many Muslim societies. More likely is a situation where Islamic modernists argue for pluralism and tolerance as reflected in the principles of Islam and as opposed to an Islamic system. That system to them would be no improvement but a deterioration of the already difficult conditions found in the secular, authoritarian states that often prevail.

[*See also* Fundamentalism.]

BIBLIOGRAPHY

Adams, Charles J. "Mawdudi and the Islamic State." In *Voices of Resurgent Islam,* edited by John L. Esposito, pp. 99–133. New York and Oxford, 1983.

Ahmad, Mumtaz. "Islamic Fundamentalism in South Asia: the Jamaat-i Islami and the Tablighi Jamaat of South Asia." In *Fundamentalisms Observed,* edited by Martin E. Marty and R. Scott Appleby, pp. 457–530. Chicago, 1991.

Al-Ahnaf, Mustafa, Bernard Botiveau, and Franck Frégosi. *L'Algérie par ses islamistes.* Paris, 1991.

Ayubi, Nazih. *Political Islam: Religion and Politics in the Arab World.* London, 1991.

Berkes, Niyazi. *The Development of Secularism in Turkey.* Montreal, 1964.

Cheriet, Boutheina. "Islamism and Feminism: Algeria's 'Rites of Passage' to Democracy." In *State and Society in Algeria,* edited by John P. Entelis and Philip C. Naylor, pp. 171–216. Boulder, 1991.

Entelis, John P. "Introduction: State and Society in Transition." In *State and Society in Algeria,* edited by John P. Entelis and Philip C. Naylor, pp. 1–30. Boulder, 1991.

Esposito, John L., ed. *Islam and Development.* Syracuse, 1980.

Esposito, John L., ed. *Islam in Asia: Religion, Politics and Society.* New York and Oxford, 1987.

Federspiel, Howard M. *Muslim Intellectuals and National Development in Indonesia.* Commack, N.Y., 1992.

Ferjani, Mohamed-Chérif. 1991. *Islamisme, laïcité, et droits de l'homme: Un siècle de debat sans cesse reporté au sein de la pensée Arabe contemporaine.* Paris, 1991.

Flores, Alexander. "Secularism, Integralism, and Political Islam." In *Middle East Report* 23.4 (July–August 1993): 32–38. This entire issue, titled *Political Islam,* is worth reading, especially the article by Gudrun Krämer listed below.

Glasner, Peter E. *The Sociology of Secularisation: A Critique of a Concept.* London, 1977.

Goldzihez, Ignácz. [A. M. Goichon]. "Dahriyya." In *Encyclopaedia of Islam,* new ed., vol. 2, pp. 95–97. Leiden, 1960–.

Haddad, Yvonne Yazbeck. "Sayyid Qutb: Ideologue of Islamic Revival." In *Voices of Resurgent Islam,* edited by John L. Esposito, pp. 67–98. New York and Oxford, 1983.

ʿImārah, Muḥammad. *Al-Islām wa-al-sulṭah al-dīnīyah* (Islam and Religious Authority). Cairo, 1979.

ʿImārah, Muḥammad. *Jamāl al-Dīn al-Afghānī, al-muftarā ʿalayhi* (Jamāl al-Dīn al-Afghānī, the Slandered). Cairo, 1984.

Johns, Anthony H. "Indonesia: Islam and Cultural Pluralism." In *Islam in Asia,* edited by John L. Esposito, pp. 202–229. New York and Oxford, 1987.

Kepel, Gilles. *The Prophet and Pharaoh: Muslim Extremism in Egypt.* London, 1985.

Knauss, Peter R. "Algerian Women Since Independence." In *State and Society in Algeria,* edited by John P. Entelis and Philip C. Naylor, pp. 151–170. Boulder, 1991.

Krämer, Gudrun. "Islamist Notions of Democracy." In *Middle East Report* 23.4 (July–August 1993): 2–13.

Mehmet, Ozay. *Islamic Identity and Development: Studies of the Islamic Periphery [Turkey and Malaysia].* New York, 1990.

Mitchell, Richard P. *The Society of the Muslim Brothers.* London and New York, 1969.

Nash, Manning. "Islamic Resurgence in Malaysia and Indonesia." In *Fundamentalisms Observed,* edited by Martin E. Marty and R. Scott Appleby, Chicago, 1991.

Roff, William R., ed. *Islam and the Political Economy of Meaning.* London, 1987.

Ruedy, John. *Modern Algeria: The Origins and Development of a Nation.* Bloomington, 1992.

Sanson, Henri. *Laïcité islamique en Algérie.* Paris, 1983.

Sen, Amartya. 1993. "The Threats to Secular India." In *The New York Review of Books* 40.7 (8 April 1993): 26–32.

Sivan, Emmanuel. *Radical Islam: Medieval Theology and Modern Politics.* New Haven, 1985.

Smith, Charles D. *Islam and the Search for Social Order in Modern Egypt.* Albany, 1983.

Smith, Charles D. "The Intellectual, Islam, and Modernization: Haykal and Shariati." In *Comparing Muslim Societies,* edited by Juan Cole, pp. 163–192. Ann Arbor, 1992.

Toprak, Binnaz. *Islam and Political Development in Turkey.* Leiden, 1981.

Vest, Jason. "Mike Farris, For God's Sake." *Washington Post,* 5 August 1993, section C, pp. 1–2.

Voll, John O. "Fundamentalism in the Sunni Arab World." In *Fundamentalisms Observed,* edited by Martin E. Marty and R. Scott Appleby, pp. 345–402. Chicago, 1991.

Voll, John O. *Islam: Continuity and Change in the Modern World.* Syracuse, 1994.

CHARLES D. SMITH

SELJUK DYNASTY. A Turkish family of Central Asian origin which ruled much of the eastern Islamic world beginning in the mid-eleventh century, the Seljuks (or Saljūqs, 1038–1194) were converted to Islam in the late tenth century, probably by traveling Ṣūfī missionaries, while still living by the Jaxartes River, on the borders of the *dār al-Islām* (Muslim lands). They and their followers were hired as mercenaries by the Sāmānid and Kara-Khanid rulers of Transoxiana, and then moved into the eastern Iranian province of Khurasan in 1035, under the leadership of two brothers, Toghril Beg and Chaghri Beg. They defeated the dominant power in the region, the Ghaznavid sultan Masʿūd, at Dandānqān in 1040. Chaghri was left to hold the east while Toghril marched westward, entering Baghdad in 1055 and bringing to an end the rule of the Shīʿī Būyids.

By the time of Toghril's death (1063), the Seljuk empire included modern Iran and Iraq, as well as parts of

Central Asia. There was later expansion into Syria, and a cadet branch of the family established the Seljuk sultanate of Rūm in Anatolia in the aftermath of the Byzantine defeat at the hands of Toghril's successor, Alp Arslan, at Manzikert in 1071: such was the origin of what ultimately became Turkey. The stability of the empire did not last much longer than the reign of Alp Arslan's son, Malikshāh (r. 1072–1092). Between 1118 and 1157, the overall supremacy of the sultan Sanjar, ruler of the empire's eastern half, was recognized at least in theory; but after Sanjar's death, Seljuk rule in Khurasan ended. In Iraq, there were nine Seljuk sultans between 1118 and 1194. The last, Toghril III, was killed in battle with the Khwārazm-shah, the effective successor to the Seljuks in the east. The Seljuks of Rūm retained their independence until their defeat by the Mongols at Köse-Dagh in 1243.

The lasting significance of the Seljuk period was considerable. Their arrival marked, if it did not necessarily cause, a revival in the fortunes of Sunnī Islam after a period in which Shiism, under the sympathetic rule of the Fāṭimids in Egypt and the Būyids in Iraq and Iran, had seemed triumphant. The ʿAbbāsid caliphate in Baghdad was freed from subservience to the Būyids, and its standing was enhanced, even if relations between the caliphs and the Seljuks were often strained. The title of sultan was conferred on Toghril Beg by the caliph al-Qā'im, thus recognizing, in practice if not in theory, that some kind of distinction between religious and secular power existed. Some of the most notable Sunnī intellectuals, above all Abū Ḥāmid al-Ghazālī (d. 1111), flourished under the Seljuks. Such developments as the encouragement of the foundation of *madrasah*s (religious colleges) by Niẓām al-Mulk, vizier (Ar., *wazīr*) to Alp Arslan and Malikshāh, and others supported the revival of Sunnism. A threat to Sunnism, however, grew with the establishment in the Alburz Mountains of northern Iran and elsewhere of the strongholds of the Nizārī Ismāʿīlīyah, otherwise known as the Assassins, who remained a thorn in the side of Sunnī Islam until their near-extirpation by the Mongols in 1256. [*See* Ismāʿīlīyah.]

Individual Turks had been well known in the Islamic world before the Seljuks, especially in their role as *mamlūk*s (military slaves). But the Seljuks were the first major incursion of Turks as a large, coherent grouping still organized tribally. As such, their arrival marked both the beginning of many centuries of Turkish political and military dominance throughout most of the Middle East and the introduction of a major new ethnic element into the region. It may also have resulted in an increase in the pastoral nomadic sector of the population, especially in Iran. The Seljuks' administrative legacy was also lasting. The governmental system associated especially with Niẓām al-Mulk, which drew on the practice of earlier regimes, nevertheless established a pattern which prevailed in Iran until the nineteenth century.

BIBLIOGRAPHY

Boyle, J. A., ed. *The Cambridge History of Iran*, vol. 5, *The Saljuq and Mongol Periods*. Cambridge, 1968. Standard work on the period, with valuable chapters especially by C. E. Bosworth on political history and Ann K. S. Lambton on administration.

Cahen, Claude. "The Turkish Invasions: The Selchükids." In *A History of the Crusades*, edited by Kenneth M. Setton, vol. 1, pp. 135–176. Madison, Wis., 1969. The best introduction to the Seljuk period.

Humphreys, R. Stephen. *Islamic History: A Framework for Enquiry*. Princeton and London, 1991. Chapter 6, "Ideology and Propaganda: Religion and State in the Early Seljukid Period" (pp. 148–168), is a very useful discussion which provides extensive bibliographical information.

Lambton, Ann K. S. *Continuity and Change in Medieval Persia: Aspects of Administrative, Economic, and Social History, 11th–14th Century*. Albany, N.Y., and London, 1988. Profound analysis with much of importance on the Seljuks.

Morgan, David O. *Medieval Persia, 1040–1797*. London, 1988. Chapters 3–5 (pp. 25–50) are a short survey of the period and its significance.

D. O. MORGAN

SENEGAL. Possessed of a strong regional cohesion and distinct Islamic identity for many centuries, Senegal lies just below the westernmost part of the Sahara, which constitutes today the Islamic Republic of Mauritania. Senegal is circumscribed by the arc of the Senegal River, which begins in the mountains of Futa Jalon in today's Guinea; it flows north before turning increasingly to the west and entering the Atlantic Ocean near the town of St. Louis. The Gambia River arises in the same mountains and cuts through the southern portion of the region; it is partly for this reason that the region is often called Senegambia. The climate is primarily Sahelian, but the increasing rainfall in the south produces a more dense vegetation.

The earliest Islamic communities are identified with Takrur, an area, a state, and possibly also a town that can be correlated with the middle valley of the Senegal River. The term Takrur was eventually applied to West

African pilgrims to Mecca of whatever provenance; it is also the root of the term *Tokolor,* the ethnic label that came to be applied to the inhabitants of the middle valley of the Senegal River in the nineteenth century. Senegalese history was subsequently dominated by a number of states, particularly the Mali empire in the fourteenth and fifteenth centuries, and the Jolof kingdom in the fifteenth and sixteenth. Each of these larger confederations, and the smaller states they comprised, gave encouragement to the practice of Muslim communities at the courts and in the trading centers. Muslim identity was closely tied to the vocation of trade, and Muslim communities lived primarily along the commercial routes and in the political capitals, where they might exercise considerable influence over the courts. Members of the ruling class often claimed to be Muslim, and a few went quite far in their expressions of piety—making the pilgrimage to Mecca, for instance. But more frequently they were "mixers" of religious practices because of the complex roles they played in relation to their subject constituencies.

From time to time some Muslim scholars challenged the coexistence of Muslim and non-Muslim practices and the general weakness of Islamic identity. Sometimes they organized their dissatisfaction in the form of military movements that sought to take power. Setting aside the eleventh-century movement of the Almoravids, whose main influence was just to the north and east of Senegal, the earliest known instance occurred in the late seventeenth century, when the *zwāyā* or Muslims of Berber origin sought to establish an Islamic state in opposition to both the Arab Maʿqil lineages, who had moved in from the northern Sahara, and the dynasties of the black regimes in northwestern Senegal. This movement, called the *toubenan* (probably from the Arabic *tawbah,* "repentance, conversion"), did not succeed for very long, but it did strengthen the more militant Muslim communities in Senegal and lay the groundwork for future protest.

The challenge was picked up in the eighteenth century by sedentary Fulbe scholars. In Futa Jalon, at the headwaters of the Senegal and Gambia rivers, a group of reformers and warriors succeeded over several decades in establishing their control of this very fertile region. They called their regime the Imamate and gave a strong impetus to Islamic education and worship throughout southeastern Senegal and down to Sierra Leone. In the nineteenth century they dominated a very large zone, profited from the capture, sale, and use of slaves, and became an important center for Islamic learning. The scholars of Labe, in particular, established a new pedagogy for writing and teaching in their language, Pular, which they considered second only to Arabic in importance.

Another group of Fulbe reformers came to power at the end of the eighteenth century in Futa Toro, the middle valley and floodplain of the Senegal River and the supposed location of Takrur. They adopted the title of Imamate as well. Although they were not as successful politically or economically as their predecessors in Futa Jalon and could not maintain cohesion after their first imam was killed in the early nineteenth century, the inhabitants of Futa Toro did exercise great influence on Islamic life in Senegal by their example and by the movements of reform they spawned. The best known Futanke leader was ʿUmar Tal, who led a vast mobilization in Senegambia in order to wage war in the area of the old Mali empire in the mid-nineteenth century. Usually known as al-Ḥājj ʿUmar, he was the foremost exponent of the Tijānīyah Ṣūfī order, which spread widely in Senegal and other parts of the Western Sudan under his influence. He has been regarded by many contemporary Senegalese as a hero of Muslim resistance to French rule, even though his main energies were directed against peoples to the east of Senegal. [*See the biography of* ʿ*Umar Tal.*]

Another militant reformer of Futanke origin was Ma Ba Diakho, who was active on the north bank of the Gambia River and in Salum in midcentury; he seriously challenged the traditional dynasties and French interests along the coast. In many ways the sharpest challenge to these forces came in the 1870s from the Madiyanke (sons of the Mahdi, a prophetic figure who had been active in Futa Toro earlier in the century). A coalition of French forces and the armies of Cayor and other Wolof kingdoms destroyed the Madiyanke in 1875.

By this time Islamic identity and practice in many areas had become synonymous with protest against the violence and demands of the traditional courts and the growing intrusion of the French, particularly into the peanut basin of west central Senegal where most of the Wolof and Serer ethnic groups lived. This protest echoed earlier statements against the enslavement of Muslims in conjunction with the Atlantic and trans-Saharan slave trades, but it now took sharper form and singled out the *ceddos* or slave warriors associated with the traditional courts.

Some Muslim scholars, including those cited above, voiced their protest in the form of militant movements that took the form of *jihād*. Others confined themselves to the practice of *hijrah,* of moving away into less populated and less well-controlled zones where they might establish more fully the practice of Islam. These critics of violence, European intervention, and the oppressive status quo usually made little distinction between the so-called traditional dynasties and the supposedly Islamic regimes of Futa Jalon and Futa Toro.

By about 1890 the French had conquered most of the territory of Senegal and the British had established their domination of the slender river valley which constituted colonial Gambia. Recognizing their own military weakness, Muslim leaders and scholars had for some time been exploring ways to survive and nurture the practice of Islam under non-Muslim rule. Some of the pioneers in this process were "white" or Mauritanian scholars who were themselves spiritual descendants of the *zwāyā* movement of the seventeenth century, but who had long since come to work within the confines of Arab warrior power and now French colonial rule. Saʿad Bu, a son of the southeastern Mauritanian scholar Muhammad Fadhil, who had pioneered multiple affiliation to Ṣūfī orders, was one of the foremost exponents of accommodation and the possibilities of enhanced islamization under the auspices of secular colonial rule. He was joined in this approach by Sīdīyā Bābā, a southern Mauritanian scholar best remembered for his assistance to the French in the conquest of Mauritania; he, like Saʿad Bu, exercised considerable influence in Senegal.

By the time of World War I, the principal leadership in Senegalese Islam had passed to a number of Ṣūfī brotherhoods based in western Senegal and tied to the strong French interests in peanut cultivation. The first of these leaders (called *marabouts* in Senegalese French, from the Arabic *murābiṭ*) to settle in the peanut basin and work within the confines of colonial rule was al-Ḥājj Malik Sy, a scholar with impressive links to Futa Toro and to the Umarian movement, but also to Tijānīyah affiliates in Mauritania and Morocco. In about 1902 Malik Sy settled in the town of Tivaouane, a railroad transshipment center in the heart of the old Wolof state of Cayor; there he continued his writing of poetry and treatises on Islamic law and conduct along with the teaching of his community. After 1910 he cooperated more actively with the colonial administration in matters dealing with the conquest of Mauritania and Morocco, the recruitment of troops for World War I, and other issues involving Muslim acceptance of French rule. He had close ties with the communities in the important urban centers of St. Louis, the capital of the colonial territory of Senegal, and Dakar, the capital of the whole French West African Federation. In addition, he helped persuade another Tijānīyah leader of the peanut basin, Abdulaye Niasse, to settle in the Salum town of Kaolack and relate more openly to the colonial administration. Since Sy's death in 1922, the Tivaouane Tijānīyah have been on close terms with the French government and its successors, the independent regimes led by Presidents Leopold Senghor and Abdou Diouf.

The best studied and best known of the "maraboutic" brotherhoods of the peanut basin is the Murīdīyah, which had closer links to the Qādirīyah order and some of its shaykhs in Mauritania. The Murīdīyah leadership, in the person of Amadu Bamba, went through a much more troubled relationship with the French regime in the 1890s and the first decade of the twentieth century. Bamba was exiled on three occasions: to Gabon in Central Africa, to Mauritania and the care of Sīdīyā Bābā, and finally to a remote corner of Jolof in northern Senegal. Nonetheless, well before the eruption of the First World War and the emergence of French needs for loyal West African soldiers, Bamba, his brothers, and his lieutenants and followers had come to terms with the new regime from their headquarters in M'Backe and Touba in the old Wolof province of Baol.

Indeed, like their Tijānīyah counterparts in Tivaouane and Kaolack, the Murīdīyah had become part of the new social and economic order that marked colonial Senegal. The maraboutic leadership, drawn mainly from the M'Backe, Sy, and Niasse families, exercised considerable authority through hierarchies of officials, most of whom were also marabouts; they organized a vast production of peanuts for export, and monopolized the pedagogy of instruction at the brotherhood's various levels of operation. While their bases remained in rural areas, they also maintained property and representatives in the larger cities, especially in Dakar, and kept close if less visible ties with the regime. Although these organizations can certainly be called Ṣūfī brotherhoods, they gave a new meaning of cohesion and economic power to the term. The transformations of these brotherhoods, and the more traditional societies of the rural areas that produced their followers, are well described by the British sociologist Donal Cruise O'Brien in *Saints and Politicians: Essays in the Organisation of a Senegalese Peasant Society* (Cambridge, 1975).

For their part, the French overcame their suspicion of Ṣūfī orders—even the Tijānīyah, which they had demonized in the late nineteenth century when fighting against ʿUmar, Ma Ba Diakho, and the Madiyanke. They realized that they had to come to terms with the overwhelming Muslim identity (perhaps 60 percent in 1900 and closer to 90 percent by independence in 1960) of Senegal and other countries in the Sahelian belt of French West Africa. Under the leadership of the Bureau of Muslim Affairs and the Islamicist Paul Marty, who had initially been trained in Tunisia, they compiled a vast inventory of Senegalese marabouts in the peanut basin and the hinterland to the east, and they checked periodically on their teaching, number of pupils, and political leanings. Gradually they reduced their effort to establish Muslim tribunals, the *medersa* (Ar., *madrasah*) or Franco-Arabic secondary school, mechanisms of Qur'ānic school control, and even some of their supervision of the pilgrimage. This can be partly explained by the successful relationships with the key brotherhoods in the peanut basin by the interwar years, and partly by the general success in isolating what they called the "Black Islam" of French West Africa from the more "orthodox" practices of the Mediterranean heartlands. One of their key Senegalese intermediaries during this period was Seydu Nuru Tal, a grandson of ʿUmar Tal who had been introduced to the French through the auspices of the brotherhood in Tivaouane and who, from his base in Dakar, performed innumerable missions of representation and reconciliation among Muslims of French West Africa during the forty years prior to independence.

The Niasse branch of the Tijānīyah deserves special mention in connection with the ties it developed in northern Nigeria. While Muhammad Niasse succeeded to the leadership of the order in Kaolack on his father's death in 1922, his younger brother Ibrahim Niasse inherited the mantle of spiritual and scholarly leadership. In the 1930s Ibrahim Niasse proclaimed himself the *ghawth al-zaman*, "the nurturer of the age," which in Tijānīyah thinking gave him the same rank as al-Ḥājj ʿUmar and the founder Aḥmad al-Tijāni in previous eras. He made a very strong impression on the Tijānīyah leadership in Fez, where the founder was buried, and then upon Abdullahi Bayero, the emir of Kano in northern Nigeria, in the 1930s. Ibrahim and Abdullahi probably met on the Meccan pilgrimage in 1937, and Ibrahim visited Kano a few years later to a tumultuous reception. He became the dominant spiritual leader of the Tijānīyah of that area, which had its own tradition going back to the visit of al-Ḥājj ʿUmar in the 1830s; from this point onward he began to receive numerous Nigerian disciples at his lodge in Kaolack. Before his death in 1975, Ibrahim Niasse had extended his influence into Niger, Ghana, Chad, and other parts of Africa, and indeed into Europe and North America. Among others, his deputy Shaykh Aliyu Cisse has sustained much of this influence up to the present day. Some of the writing and teaching of the "Niasse school" and of the other principal Muslim scholars of twentieth-century Senegal can be found in Amar Samb's *Essai sur la contribution du Sénégal à la littérature d'expression arabe* (Dakar, 1972).

The secular state that the French established in the early twentieth century and that the independent government of Senegal has maintained, and the great influence that Muslim organizations such as the brotherhoods have exercised for many decades, have made it more difficult for Muslim interests of the Near East to exert influence and to mount serious critical challenges to local patterns in the practice of Islam. It is nonetheless true that petrodollars and other funds have been channeled into Senegal for some time to build mosques, to support schools, and in many ways to challenge the cozy relations of brotherhood and government. Large numbers of Senegalese have made the pilgrimage, and an increasing number have studied in Mediterranean Islamic communities ranging from Morocco to Iran. Some of the brotherhood leaders, however, have been quite alert to the need for renewal and the breakdown of the artificial relations between "Black Islam" and the heartlands, and they have distanced themselves from an increasingly paralyzed government and economy. While it is difficult to see what form solutions to Senegal's considerable dilemmas will take, it seems unlikely that specifically Islamic solutions or political parties will play the crucial role.

[*See also* Murīdīyah; Tijānīyah.]

BIBLIOGRAPHY

Barry, Boubacar. *La Sénégambie du XVe au XIXe siècle: La traite négrière, Islam et conquête coloniale*. Paris, 1988.

Curtin, Philip D. *Economic Change in Pre-Colonial Africa: Senegambia in the Era of the Slave Trade*. 2 vols. Madison, Wis., 1975. The author gives extensive treatment to defining the region of Senegal in this seminal work.

Cruise O'Brien, Donal B. *The Mourides of Senegal: The Political and Economic Organization of an Islamic Brotherhood*. Oxford, 1971.

Cruise O'Brien, Donal B., and Christian Coulon, eds. *Charisma and Brotherhood in African Islam*. Oxford, 1988.

Gray, Christopher. "The Rise of the Niassene Tijaniyya, 1875 to the Present." *Islam et Sociétés au Sud du Sahara* 2 (1988): 34–60. Provides a useful summary of the influence of the Niasse branch of the Tijānīyah.

Harrison, Chris. *France and Islam in West Africa, 1860–1960*. Cambridge, 1968.

Klein, Martin. *Islam and Imperialism in Senegal: Sine-Saloum, 1847–1914*. Stanford, Calif., 1968. Includes information on the militant reformer Ma Ba Diakho.

Klein, Martin. "Social and Economic Factors in the Muslim Revolutions in Senegambia." *Journal of African History* 13 (1972): 419–441.

Levtzion, Nehemia, and Humphrey J. Fisher, eds. *Rural and Urban Islam in West Africa*. London and Boulder, 1987. Also published in *Asian and African Studies* (Haifa) 20 (1986).

Robinson, David. "The Islamic Revolution of Futa Toro." *International Journal of African Historical Sources* 8 (1975): 185–221.

Robinson, David. *The Holy War of Umar Tal: The Western Sudan in the Mid-Nineteenth Century*. Oxford and New York, 1985.

Sow, Alfa Ibrahima. *Le filon du bonheur éternal*. Paris, 1971. Sow is the main source on the development of the new pedagogy for teaching in the Pular language.

DAVID ROBINSON

SEVENERS. *See* Ismāʿīlīyah.

SEXUALITY. In the Muslim world, sexuality is simultaneously more open and more conservative than in other geographic regions. These contradictory aspects result from a confluence of Muslim principles and regional ideologies of gender combined with centuries of cultural modulation. Misrepresentations of Muslim sexuality frequently focus on gender relations.

Islamic law recognizes the sexual nature of believers; sexuality provides a balance to the spiritual, material, and intellectual spheres of life. However, the Freudian critiques of Abdelwahab Bouhdiba (*Sexuality in Islam*, London, 1985) and Fatna Sabbah (*Women in the Muslim Unconscious*, New York, 1984) posit an authoritarian relationship in Islam of God-to-man and man-to-woman. Within this hierarchical formula, with women ranking lowest, it is assumed that men fear the supposedly disruptive potential of women's sexuality *(fitna)*. Thus the need to contain it in a rigidly patriarchal framework. The Freudian interpretation of Muslim sexuality and others drawing on colonial mythology and Orientalism do not fully recognize mainstream Islam's rejection of asceticism, or its vision of the complementary role of the sexes. Muslims understand sexual fulfillment within marriage for both partners to be the ideal state of affairs; sexual needs are understood, satisfied, and allow the couple other forms of communication as well as other pursuits. Licensed sex is neither sinful, nor restricted solely to procreation, but serves as a means of communication and a source of solace. The subordination of women within the marriage institution is considered a degradation, or corruption, of Muslim practice.

Characteristics of the ideal man and woman constitute a flexible masculinity and femininity: strength, stubbornness, bravery, jealousy are found in a man; delicacy, shyness, resourcefulness, patience define a woman. Some Muslims argue that women naturally require male protection, and that a man's sexual needs may exceed a woman's thereby supporting arguments for polygyny. Others refute both claims, holding that women may be physically smaller than men, but not weaker, and that it is impossible to accord multiple wives the equitable treatment demanded by the Qur'ān. Conceptions of gender have traditionally defined sex roles. Women who have experienced expanded sex roles by working in male fields or occupations, are sometimes accused of being masculine, or aggressive. Yet in reality, the range of personal and sexual identities is enormous, limited more in the Muslim ideal than in daily life.

Sexuality may be realized through gender identity and cross-gender interaction. Muslims consider puberty to be the age at which gender identity is fully manifest. As secondary sex traits emerge, the issue of hermaphroditism is resolved one way or the other; either male or female gender identity results. Homosexuality exists in the Muslim world (and was probably encouraged under the system of strict separation of the sexes). It is either considered unlawful, abnormal, and punishable under *sharīʿah*, or tolerated in areas where homosexuals are viewed as a "third sex," neither men nor women.

Although sexual impulses may arise after puberty, virginity is highly valued for girls. Brides are assumed to be virgins when they marry, and may be required to obtain a certificate of virginity from a physician in some countries. Muslim families do not expect or permit teenagers to engage in sexual activity. But, since the age of marriage has risen for economic reasons, and because young people are expected to complete their education, this prohibition on youthful sexuality produces a relatively long period of sexual tension. Separation of the sexes is enforced in social and school networks enhancing same-sex communication and strengthening the notion of spheres for men and women. In urban areas, young couples may date, sometimes chaperoned, sometimes only in groups.

Female circumcision is practiced in Egypt, the Sudan, parts of the Gulf, Libya, Chad, and other Muslim areas of Africa in order to control female sexuality and ensure virginity at marriage. Pre-Islamic in origin, the operation, which may also involve infibulation, serious medical complications, and psychological trauma, is wrongly considered to be Muslim, intended to "purify" or "clean" the circumcised. Although illegal in Egypt, it is nonetheless the rule among more than half the population. [*See* Clitoridectomy.]

Other aspects of female sexuality are affected by popular customs. Kidnapping of brides was a common practice in Lebanon, Jordan, and Syria until a generation ago, as were arranged marriages. Although family involvement in the selection of a marriage partner is part of Muslim tradition, a woman's consent must be obtained. Honor killings continue, mostly in rural areas when a wife, daughter, or sister is suspected of illicit sexual relations. These practices represent specific abuses of Muslim family standards. But more general tensions have developed since the demise of the harem system in the early twentieth century and the integration of women into the workplace and other aspects of public life. These tensions are sometimes overt, as in the case of male harassment in public places, or form the subtext of intellectual and media debates over the proper status of women and the potential danger to societal morality posed by the relaxation of sexual codes.

Education has promoted new ideas concerning family planning and population growth. Birth control is viewed as an aid to managing family resources, and allows married couples the opportunity to enjoy sex for itself. Still, powerful links remain between sexuality and reproduction. Traditional birth control practices reflected social conditions and gender inequities. With less than secure legal protections against divorce, women believed that if they did not bear children they would be repudiated. Men disliked the use of birth control devices, which they considered a mediator (*waṣiṭah*), interfering with their sexual pleasure. The Prophet recommended coitus interruptus to control impregnation (*ʿazl*). (Basim Musallam has written about many other historical forms of reproductive control in *Sex and Society in Medieval Islam*, London, 1983.) Official rulings from religious scholars were needed to legitimize modern forms of birth control. But resistance to certain forms of reproductive control continues.

Some Muslim doctors and scholars have called for a ban on sterilization. Almost all disapprove of abortion. Muslims generally hold that children are divinely created, and fetal rights legitimately restrict a woman's rights over her body. Although life was once considered to begin when the mother could feel fetal movement (at about four months), modern Muslim opinions have found that life begins at fertilization. Abortion has been permitted only when the mother's life is severely medically compromised.

Impotence and infertility or sterility are considered shameful culturally, although the Qur'ān reminds adults that children are a divine gift. Infertility treatments, including *in vitro* fertilization, are permitted by a number of jurists, but not the use of donor sperm, eggs, or surrogate arrangements.

Sexual relations are licensed only within a legal and normative marriage, or among the Shīʿī, in a temporary marriage contracted between an unmarried woman and a married or unmarried man (*mutʿah* in Arabic, *sīgheh* in Farsi). Sexual intercourse is prohibited during menstruation, for forty days after childbirth, during the day hours of Ramaḍān, and on pilgrimage. Women must be chaste for three months after divorcing, and for four months after a man's vow of sexual abstinence and desertion. Legal arguments also allow or oppose specific forms of sexual activity, and mandate women's rights to conjugal pleasure as well as men's.

[*See also* Family; Family Planning; Marriage and Divorce; Mutʿah; Polygyny; Puberty Rites; Seclusion.]

BIBLIOGRAPHY

Ahmed, Leila. *Women and Gender in Islam*. New Haven, 1992. General history of women and gender issues, mainly in the Arab Muslim world with a narrower focus on Egypt in the nineteenth and twentieth centuries.

ʿAẓm, Ṣādiq Jalāl al-. *Fī al-ḥubb wa-al-ḥubb al-ʿudhrī*. 3d ed. Casablanca, 1987. Critique of emotional relations and conceptions of love, including "courtly" or unrequited love in Arabo-Islamic society.

Bauer, Janet L. "Sexuality and the Moral 'Construction' of Women in an Islamic Society." *Anthropological Quarterly* 58.3 (July 1985): 120–129. Presents attitudes imposed under the Islamic Republic.

Bowen, Donna Lee. "Muslim Juridical Opinions Concerning the Status of Women as Demonstrated by the Case of *ʿAzl.*" *Journal of Near Eastern Studies* 40.4 (October 1981): 323–328. Detailed treatment of the topic that also explains distinctions in the status of slave vs. free wives.

Esposito, John L. *Women in Muslim Family Law.* Syracuse, N.Y., 1968. An excellent introduction to specific issues in *sharʿiah* related to gender and stemming from a Muslim perception of sexuality and family.

Malti-Douglas, Fedwa. *Woman's Body, Woman's Word: Gender and Discourse in Arabo-Islamic Writing.* Princeton, N.J., 1991. Analysis of the discourse of gender, woman, and female sexuality through specific classical and modern texts.

Mernissi, Fatima. "Virginity and Patriarchy." *Women's Studies International Forum* 5.2 (1982); 183–192. This issue contains other articles concerning aspects of women's status including al-Saʿdāwī (below).

Sabbah, Fatna (pseud.) *Women in the Muslim Unconscious,* New York, 1984.

Saʿdāwī, Nawāl al-. "Woman and Islam." *Women's Studies International Forum* 5.2 (1982): 193–206.

Sanders, Paula. "Gendering the Ungendered Body: Hermaphrodites in Medieval Islamic Law." In *Women in Middle Eastern History: Shifting Boundaries in Sex and Gender,* edited by Nikki R. Keddie and Beth Baron, pp. 74–95. New Haven and London, 1991.

Toubia, Nahid. "Women and Health in Sudan." In *Women of the Arab World: The Coming Challenge,* edited by Nahid Toubia, pp. 98–109. London, 1988. Discusses social and psychological as well as medical aspects of female circumcision.

Wikan, Unni. *Behind the Veil in Arabia: Women in Oman.* Baltimore, 1982. Covers gender issues as well as homosexual men in Sohari society.

Zuhur, Sherifa. *Revealing Reveiling: Islamist Gender Ideology in Contemporary Egypt.* Albany, N.Y., 1992. Presents the polemics of gender issues and conceptions of femininity since the advent of Islam, and Islamist ideals of cross-gender relations, family interaction, and women's roles.

SHERIFA ZUHUR

SHABAZZ, EL-HAJJ MALIK EL-. *See* Malcolm X.

SHĀDHILĪYAH. Together with the Rifāʿīyah, Qādirīyah, and Aḥmadīyah, the Shādhilīyah is one of the four oldest *ṭarīqahs* (Ṣūfī orders) in the Muslim world. It takes its name from the Moroccan-born Abū al-Ḥasan ʿAlī al-Shādhilī, whose chain of initiation *(silsilah)* is traced through Shaykh ʿAbd al-Salām ibn Mashīsh to Abū Madyan al-Ghawth (d. 1126), the patron saint of Tlemcen. Sīdī Abū al-Ḥasan (as he is generally known) traveled extensively in North Africa—he was for a time imprisoned in Tunis by a jealous *ʿālim*—before establishing a *zāwiyah* in Alexandria. He died at Ḥumaytharah (in the present-day Governorate of Aswan) on his way to the *ḥajj* in AH 656/1258 CE. He left no scholarly works but passed down a number of enduringly popular collects *(aḥzāb)*, one of which, *Ḥizb al-baḥr,* was widely used as a prayer for safety at sea. The *aḥzāb* have been compiled (with transliterations and translations) in volume 1 of *The School of S̲hadhdhuliyyah* by A. N. Durkee (Alexandria, 1991).

It was not until the *ṭarīqah* passed into the hands of its third shaykh, Aḥmad ibn ʿAṭāʾ Allāh, al-Iskandarī (d. 1309) that its doctrines were systematized, and the biographies of Sīdī Abū al-Ḥasan and his successor Sīdī Abū al-ʿAbbās al-Mursī (d. 1287) were recorded. Ibn ʿAṭāʾ Allāh's Aphorisms *(Ḥikam)* guaranteed the popularity of the Shādhilīyah; they are spoken of as "undisputedly the last Ṣūfī miracle performed on the banks of the Nile . . . and . . . one of the instruments for the [Shādhilīyah's] expansion" (P. Nwyia, *Ibn ʿAta' Allah et la naissance de la confrèrie šadilite,* Beirut, 1972, p. 35). An English translation of the *Ḥikam* was published by Victor Danner under the title *Ibn ʿAṭā'illah's Sufi Aphorisms (Kitāb al-ḥikam)* (Leiden, 1973).

The *ṭarīqah,* which represents what Annemarie Schimmel (1986, p. 251) calls the sober "Baghdadian" school of Sufism, is known for a pragmatic approach to worldly comforts; for the Shādhilīs, wealth per se does not exclude one from the community of *fuqarā'* (lit., "the poor in God"). Sīdī Abū al-Ḥasan is also said to have preferred the grateful rich to the patient poor. This subtle distinction informed the discrepancy between the outlooks of the Shādhilīyah and Qādirīyah in seventeenth-century Sudan (Grandin, 1986, pp. 170–171) and is used to explain the *ṭarīqah*'s high profile in contemporary reformist Sufism, particularly in Egypt.

The Shādhilīyah is spread over a large part of the Muslim world. It is represented in North Africa mainly by the Fāsīyah and Darqāwīyah branches and has a large presence in Egypt, where fourteen branches were officially recognized in 1985. It continues to be active in Sudan, where it was overwhelmingly popular (along with the Qādirīyah) between the sixteenth and nineteenth centuries, before the entry of the more reformist Idrīsī orders. It is also represented in sub-Saharan and East Africa, and it is the majority *ṭarīqah* of the Comoro Islands.

During the Ottoman period the Shādhilīyah was active in Turkey and may well have received royal patronage from Sultan Abdülhamid II. The *ṭarīqah* also spread into southeastern Europe, where it was represented in Bulgaria, Romania, and the former Yugoslavia, as well as in Kosovo and Macedonia. The Fāsīyah branch was introduced into Sri Lanka in the mid-twentieth century, and other branches are reported to have been active in parts of China. The *ṭarīqah* was also represented in Yemen in late medieval times and is credited with the introduction of the use of coffee to facilitate long sessions of invocation *(dhikr)*. In the twentieth century, the Fāsīyah Shādhilīyah were persecuted by the Zaydī imams Yaḥyā (1904–1948) and Aḥmad (1948–1962).

The Burhānīyah Disūqīyah branch, which originated in Sudan under Shaykh Muḥammad ʿUthmān ʿAbduh (d. 1983), became widely popular in Egypt in the 1960s and spread to Syria in 1968. The orthodoxy of this branch became the subject of debate in Egypt in the 1970s and 1980s; however, despite the reservations of the *ʿulamāʾ* the Burhānīyah Disūqīyah is today more popular than ever.

Three other branches of the *ṭarīqah* stand out in Egypt. The Ḥāmidīyah, founded by Sīdī Salāmah al-Rāḍī (d. 1939), is credited with being one of the first *ṭarīqahs* to face the problems of anti-Ṣūfī criticism and diminishing membership by compiling a rule *(qānūn)* defining correct behavior for its members (Michael Gilsenan, *Saint and Sufi in Modern Egypt*, Oxford, 1973, pp. 92–128). This branch, whose main *ḥaḍrah* (congregational invocation) is held at the mosque of al-Sayyidah Zaynab in Cairo, has acquired a reputation for the careful organization and control of its public rituals.

The ʿAzamīyah Shādhilīyah was founded in 1915 in the Sudan by Muḥammad Māḍī Abū al-ʿAzāʾim. Currently headed by his grandson ʿIzz al-Dīn, this branch has campaigned actively for reform of Ṣūfī practices. It is also critical of what it views as Jamāʿāt Islāmīyah's Khārijī tendencies and emphasizes the necessarily Ṣūfī nature of any "Islamic solution."

The ʿAshīrah Muḥammadīyah (Muḥammadan Family) is a registered friendly society with a core of initiates known as the Muḥammadīyah Shādhilīyah. The ʿAshīrah was officially recognized in 1951, although its present shaykh, Muḥammad Zakī Ibrāhīm, was ousted from the Ṣūfī Council *(majlis)* for challenging the status quo. He took legal action and was reinstated in January 1956. Since then, this branch of the *ṭarīqah* has devoted itself to reforming Sufism and defending it against hostile critics. It also claims responsibility for the introduction of the 1976 Ṣūfī Ordinance *(lāʾiḥah)*, which regulates the disciplinary and financial matters of the Egyptian *ṭarīqahs*.

BIBLIOGRAPHY

Grandin, Nicole. "Les *turuq* au Soudan, dans la Corne de l'Afrique et en Afrique orientale." In *Les ordres mystiques dan l'Islam: Cheminements et situation actuelle*, edited by Alexandre Popovic and Gilles Veinstein, pp. 165–204. Paris, 1986.

Ibn ʿAṭāʾ Allāh, Aḥmad ibn Muḥammad. *Laṭāʾif al-Minan fī Manāqib Abī al-ʿAbbās al-Mursī wa-Shaykhihi al-Shādhilī Abī al-Ḥasan*. Edited by ʿAbd al-Ḥalīm Maḥmūd. Cairo, 1974.

Luizard, Pierre-Jean. "Le rôle des confrères soufies dans le système politique égyptien." *Monde Arabe Maghreb-Machreq* 131 (January–March 1991): 26–53.

Maḥmūd, ʿAbd al-Ḥalīm. *Al-Madrasah al-Shadhilīyah al-Ḥadīthah wa-Imāmuhā Abū al-Ḥasan al-Shādhilī*. Cairo, c. 1968.

Schimmel, Annemarie. *Mystical Dimensions of Islam*. Chapel Hill, N.C., 1975.

J. E. A. Johansen

SHADOW OF GOD. The ancient Iranians developed an elaborate concept of sacral kingship. Both Achaemenid (559–33 BCE) and Sassanian (224–651 CE) kings were believed to possess *farr-i izadi* (divine grace) and ruled by divine dispensation. A mediator with the divine, the king could bring good fortune to his people. Hence, the perceived omnipotence of the king was derived from his divinity.

This concept of divine kingship found its corollary in Islamic statecraft as well. Muslim caliphs and kings claimed to be the Shadow of God, Vicegerent of God on earth, or descendants of the Prophet and imams. Purporting to be Ẓill Allāh (God's Shadow), many kings considered themselves accountable only to God, thus removing themselves from public scrutiny. Classical Persian texts instruct Muslims that "God has two guardians over the people; his guardians in heaven are the angels, and his guardians on earth are kings" (Niẓām al-Mulk, *The Book of Government or Rules for Kings*, London, 1960, p. 294).

With the adoption of Shiism as the state religion under the Ṣafavid dynasty (1501–1722), the elitist concept of *imāmah* helped to reinforce divine kingship. Ṣafavid tribal leaders, such as Junayd (r. 1447–1460), were regarded as divine incarnations, and Junayd's son, Ḥaydar (r. 1460–1488), was regarded as the son of God. Ismāʿīl, the son of Ḥaydar and the founder of the Ṣafavid dynasty, was considered a forerunner of the Mahdi, or Hidden Imam. Although the Islamic doctrine of *tawḥīd* forbids the idea of divinity or reincarnation, through the effective use of Mahdism and *imāmah*, early Ṣafavid kings claimed divinity and incarnation without any considerable doctrinal challenge.

With Karīm Khān-i Zand (r. 1750–1779), the monarchy lost its divine connotations. Instead, Zand took the title Vakīl-i Raʿaya (Regent of the People) and acted as a patriarchal tribal leader. Zand's subordination of divine kingship to notions of regency proved temporary, as the Qājār dynasty (1796–1925) reinstituted divinity in kingship.

Although some of the Qājār rulers formally carried the title Shadow of God, they no longer claimed to be the representative of the Hidden Imam. In this context, the *mujtahids* (learned clerics) collectively claimed some of the authority of the imams, which in Ṣafavid times had devolved on the kings.

In the Pahlavi dynasty (1926–1979) the monarchy became increasingly secularized, but both Pahlavi monarchs used the myth of divine kingship to bolster their power. Muhammad Reza Shah, for example, believed that the monarchy could not survive without its traditional divine aura. He also believed that monarchy had such deep roots in Iranian culture that if he were not the ruler, another king would replace him. As he stated, kings were expected to be "a symbol of earthly redemption, perhaps, because the king was the linkage with the almighty" (E. A. Bayne, *Persian Kingship in Transition*, New York, 1968, p. 72).

Since Iranian state power historically has been abusive and its institutions corrupt, the people have been loyal to the symbols of state power (the good king) rather than the state itself. The epithet Shadow of God created the image of a divine protector, binding the nation together and validating its mission. In a culture in which politics remains personal and the lines between the sacred and secular are blurred, divine rule of kings personalizes and sacralizes monarchy and personifies the nation-state.

[*See also* Iran; Qājār Dynasty; Ṣafavid Dynasty; Shah; Zand Dynasty.]

BIBLIOGRAPHY

Arjomand, Said Amir. *The Shadow of God and the Hidden Imam*. Chicago, 1984. Penetrating sociological analysis of religion and politics in Iranian history.

Boyce, Mary. *Zoroastrians: Their Religious Beliefs and Practices*. London, 1979. Presents an authoritative account of Zoroastrian religion and its impact on the ancient civilization of Iran.

Dorraj, Manochehr. *From Zarathustra to Khomeini: Populism and Dissent in Iran*. Boulder and London, 1990. Historical study of Iranian populism with emphasis on the impact of pre-Islamic as well as Islamic political traditions.

Meisami, Julie Scott, ed. *The Sea of Precious Virtues: A Medieval Islamic Mirror for Princes*. Salt Lake City, 1991. Very useful collection on medieval Islamic statecraft and kingship.

Wilber, Donald. *Iran: Past and Present*. Princeton, 1955). Good account of ancient and modern history of Iran.

Zaehner, Robert C. *The Dawn and Twilight of Zoroastrianism*. London, 1961. Good analysis on the rise and demise of Zoroastrian religion.

MANOCHEHR DORRAJ

SHĀFIʿĪ. *See* Law, *article on* Legal Thought and Jurisprudence.

SHAFĪQ, DURRĪYAH (Doria Shafik; 1908–1976), Egyptian scholar, teacher, journalist, and feminist activist. The writings and activism of Durrīyah Shafīq followed in the secular, democratic tradition of the Egyptian feminists Hudā Shaʿrāwī and Amīnah al-Saʿīd. Shafīq was educated in Western schools, first in a kindergarten run by Italian nuns and then at a French mission school. She was an admirer of Shaʿrāwī from youth, and it was with Shaʿrāwī's assistance that Shafīq was able to attend the Sorbonne, where she received a doctorate in 1940.

Upon returning to Egypt Shafīq taught at Alexandria College for Girls and at the Sannia School; she then worked for the Ministry of Education as a French-language inspector before beginning her career as a journalist and political activist. In 1945 she founded the magazine *Majallat bint al-Nīl* (Daughter of the Nile Magazine), which included a segment devoted to promoting political rights for women called *Bint al-Nīl al-siyāsīyah* (Political Daughter of the Nile).

In 1948 Shafīq founded the Ittiḥād Bint al-Nīl (Daughter of the Nile Union), a middle-class feminist association with branches in several provincial cities, dedicated to encouraging female literacy and full political rights for women. In a bid to gain international recognition for Egyptian feminism, Shafīq affiliated the Union with the International Council of Women under the name of the National Council for Egyptian Women.

In 1951 a thousand members of Shafīq's Union disrupted the Egyptian parliament in a demonstration calling for the vote and other political rights for women. The demonstration sparked a reaction on the part of religious conservatives, and the Union of Muslim Associations in Egypt, which included the Muslim Brotherhood, demanded that the king abolish all women's organizations that called for participation in politics, that women be encouraged to stay at home, and that the use of the veil be enforced. Shafīq responded with a "White Paper on the Rights of Egyptian Women" *(Al-kitāb al-abyad li-ḥuqūq al-mar'ah al-Miṣrīyah),* in which she argued in the reformist tradition of Muslim feminists that Islam speaks for the equality of women and requires neither the veil nor domesticity.

The following year political opposition groups conducted a series of strikes against foreign interests in a bid to undermine the British occupation, and the paramilitary arm of Shafīq's Union joined in the strike by picketing Barclay's Bank. After the Free Officers came to power in 1952, Shafīq continued to agitate for political rights for women. She founded a short-lived "Daughter of the Nile" political party, which was disbanded with all other political parties in 1953 by the revolutionary government. In 1954, when the constitutional assembly formed by President Gamal Abdel Nasser to adopt or reject a proposed new constitution included no women, Shafīq carried out a much-publicized hunger strike to demand political rights for women, in which she was joined by members of the Bint al-Nīl Union in Cairo and Alexandria. Having sought and gained international recognition for her strike, Shafīq was rewarded when the governor of Cairo agreed to put in writing that the constitution would guarantee full political rights for women. The 1956 constitution did in fact grant women the right to vote, but only to those who formally applied for it, while for men the right to vote was automatic. Consequently, Shafīq filed a legal protest.

The following year marked Shafīq's political undoing. She announced to Nasser and the press that she was going on a hunger strike to protest Nasser's dictatorship, as well as the lingering Israeli occupation of the Sinai in the wake of the Suez invasion, which should have ended with the UN-ordered withdrawal. Shafīq's colleagues at the Bint al-Nīl Union not only failed to support her but asked her to resign, and, along with other women's associations, they denounced her as a traitor. She was placed under house arrest, and the Bint al-Nīl Union and magazine were closed down. In the following years Shafīq experienced repeated emotional breakdowns and eventually committed suicide in 1976.

Shafīq, like her predecessor Hudā Shaʿrāwī, had anticipated erroneously that women's participation in the struggle for national liberation would engender popular support for feminist causes. Shafīq miscalculated on two counts—first on the strength of Islamic conservative reaction, and second on the charisma of Nasser, who in spite of his repression of democracy enjoyed great popularity for having initiated the final evacuation of the British from Egypt.

In addition to her political writings, Shafīq wrote *Al-mar'ah al-Miṣrīyah min al-faraʿīnah ilā al-yawm* (Egyptian Women from the Pharaohs until Today), and, with Ibrāhīm ʿAbduh, *Taṭawwur al-nahḍah al-Miṣrīyah, 1798–1951* (Development of the Women's Renaissance in Egypt), as well as several books of poetry and prose published in France.

[*See also* Feminism; *and the biography of Shaʿrāwī.*]

BIBLIOGRAPHY

Ahmed, Leila. *Women and Gender in Islam: Historical Roots of a Modern Debate.* New Haven, 1992. Excellent discussion of the development of nineteenth- to twentieth-century feminism in the Middle East.

Badran, Margot, and Miriam Cooke, eds. *Opening the Gates: A Century of Arab Feminist Writing.* Bloomington, 1990. Includes a sample of Shafīq's political writing, "White Paper on the Rights of Egyptian Women" (pp. 352–356).

Sullivan, Earl L. *Women in Egyptian Public Life.* Syracuse, N.Y., 1986.

ELEANOR ABDELLA DOUMATO

SHAH. One of the most common titles used by the dynastic rulers of Iran and the Turko-Persian cultural area, shah (Ar. and Pers., *shāh*) when employed by the monarch of a large territory, is often used in a compound form such as *pādishāh* ("emperor") or *shāhānshāh* ("king of kings"). However, it can also appear as part of the title of a regional authority (such as the Kābul-shāh or Shārvān-shāh) or as part of a ruler's personal name (Tūrānshāh, Shāh Jahān, etc.).

Philologists trace this word's origin back to an Old Persian root, *khshay* ("to rule"), from which the Achaemenid kings (559–33 BCE) derived their title, *khshāyathiya.* The subsequent forms *shāh* and *shāhānshāh* were routinely applied to the princes and kings of the Sassanian dynasty (224–651 CE). After the Arab conquest of Persia, the title fell into disuse except by a few petty provincial dynasts; the term *shāhānshāh* in particular acquired a pejorative connotation and was condemned in some *ḥadīths* as blasphemous. As the empire of the caliphs began to break up into provincial polities, some ambitious regional dynasts reportedly aspired to revive the imperial title of *shāhānshāh*. The first Muslim rulers definitely known to have used it were the Būyids of western Iran (perhaps as early as 936), probably to emphasize their independence from the authority of the ʿAbbāsid caliphs and later as a way of ranking authority within the Būyid family hierarchy. Thereafter, it became common for Muslim rulers to include shah as part of their titulature; it appears not only among Iranian dynasties, such as the Khwārazm-shahs but also among various Turko-Mongol rulers from the Seljūks to the Kara-koyunlu, Timurids, and Ottomans, as well as numerous Indian dynasties in Bengal, Kashmir, Jawnpur, Malwa, and elsewhere. However, such rulers generally used the term merely as one of many pompous and high-sounding titles without attaching any special significance to it. This was not the case with Ismāʿīl Ṣafavī, who took the title shah following the conquest of Tabriz and establishment of the Ṣafavid dynasty in 1501. Shah once more became the particular and distinctive title of the dynastic rulers of the Iranian plateau, and it continued to be used in this sense not only by the Ṣafavids but by virtually all the subsequent rulers of Iran. In 1925, Reza Khan, after having briefly flirted with the idea of establishing a republican form of government, also opted to assume the title shah.

The term *shāh* is invariably translated into English as "king," but this does not convey fully all its nuances. Like tsar or kaiser, the title is rich in historical associations and suggests an institution of great antiquity, legitimacy, power, and authority. In its original and most distinctive usage, it is closely linked to the Persian ideal of sacred kingship. The wish to capitalize on this concept of the shah as the possesor of an awesome "kingly glory" who must be respected and obeyed has doubtless been a major factor in the various revivals of the title. A recent and ill-fated example of this may be seen in Muhammad Reza Shah Pahlavi's extreme glorification of the monarchy as the unifying force of the Iranian nation-state, a tradition which was brought to an abrupt end by the Islamic Revolution and the consequent abolition of the office in 1979.

[*See also* Iran; Monarchy.]

BIBLIOGRAPHY

Büchner, V. F. "Shāh." In *Encyclopaedia of Islam*, vol. 4, pp. 256–257. Leiden, 1913–1938. Useful overview of the philological aspects of the term.

Dihkhudā, ʿAlī Akbar., "Shāh." In *Lughatnāmah*. Tehran, 1947–. Lexicographical explication of the term with many references to its usage in literary sources.

Filipani-Ronconi, Pio. "The Tradition of Sacred Kingship in Iran." In *Iran under the Pahlavis*, edited by George Lenczowski, pp. 51–83. Stanford, Calif., 1978. Interesting interpretation of the concept of sacred kingship in Iranian history.

Madelung, Wilferd. "The Assumption of the Title Shāhānshāh by the Būyids and 'The Reign of the Daylam (*Dawlat al-Daylam*).' " *Journal of Near Eastern Studies* 28 (1969): 84–108, 168–183. Important article dealing with the usage of the title in early Islamic times.

ELTON L. DANIEL

SHAHĀDAH. The Islamic witness of faith is, "There is no god but God, and Muḥammad is the Apostle of God" (Arabic, *lā ilāha illā Allāh wa-Muḥammad rasūl Allāh*). Recitation of the *shahādah* (literally, "witness") is the first of the five pillars of Islam. The formula is not in the Qur'ān, although the book speaks often of the "witness" of various articles of faith; the phrase "there is no god but God" is found (37.35, 47.19), as well as the same declaration many other times in similar words; and Muḥammad is constantly referred to as a messenger. The formula is recorded, however, in several different contexts in the prophetic traditions (*ḥadīth*). There it stands as the earliest and simplest form of the articles of faith; some *ḥadīths* have only "There is no god but God."

The traditions indicate that at the beginning of Islam the *shahādah* alone was enough to establish belief and membership in the community. In one report the Prophet states that God has forbidden the fire of Hell to those who recite "There is no god but God," while in another he declares, "I have been ordered [by God] to fight the people until they say, 'There is no god except God,' and the life and property of them who say this are protected from me" (that is, they shall be considered to have confessed faith and may no longer be warred against as non-Muslims). Later, however, several controversies arose. What, it was asked, is the position of one who pronounces the *shahādah* hypocritically? A common answer was that such persons, while their declaration would not be accepted by God, were still to be regarded as members of the community for practical purposes, for example for burial and exemption from the poll-tax (provided they had not otherwise flaunted their unbelief). The question was also raised whether the person who recites the *shahādah* must have a real understanding of what he says in order to gain salvation. In this case it was generally agreed that true understanding of the basic tenets was necessary; sincere and heartfelt faith was also emphasized. The *shahādah* also entered into the controversy over faith and works, with those arguing for the necessity of works along with faith asserting that the witness itself was a work—"the work of the tongue."

The elementary witness finally became merely the nucleus of increasingly elaborate and diverse creeds, reflecting the evolution of the community from a simple unity to ever greater fragmentation. [*See* ʿAqīdah.] The *shahādah* is still, however, accepted as declaration of acceptance of Islam by a convert: the convert has only to repeat it twice in the presence of other Muslims. A more detailed declaration may be required by some institutions, for instance by the Saudi authorities for the purpose of admittance to the Two Holy Sanctuaries and by the great Egyptian Islamic university al-Azhar for the purpose of certification of Muslim status, but the basis of the affirmation is still recitation of the *shahādah*.

[*See also* Pillars of Islam.]

BIBLIOGRAPHY

Ālūsī, Maḥmūd Shukrī al-. *Kanz al-saʿādah fī sharḥ al-shahādah*. Cairo, 1411/1991. Brief elaboration of the meaning of the *shahādah*, largely from a grammatical point of view. Al-Ālūsī died in 1924.

Carra de Vaux, Bernard. "Shahāda." In *First Encyclopaedia of Islam*, vol. 7, p. 259. Leiden, 1913–.

Shaʿrānī, ʿAbd al-Wahhāb ibn Aḥmad al-. *Asrār arkān al-Islām*. Cairo, 1400/1980. Interpretation of the five pillars, including the *shahādah*, from a Ṣūfī perspective. Al-Shaʿrānī died in 1565/6.

LYNDA CLARKE

SHALTŪT, MAḤMŪD. (1893–1963), one of a celebrated number of Azharī shaykhs who undertook the reform of al-Azhar, reversing its decline, which occurred during the nineteenth century, and recapturing its old role as an active participant in Egypt's educational, cultural, and political destiny. Although best known and esteemed for his vast knowledge of Islamic *fiqh* (jurisprudence) and Qur'ānic interpretation, Shaltūt really made his mark as the shaykh of al-Azhar (1958–1963). During his tenure, al-Azhar began to take its modern shape. This transformation was complicated by the Nasser government, which sought direct control of the mosque/university. Although compromising with the state over administrative control, Shaltūt managed to bring about the partial realization of the dreams of past religious reformers of al-Azhar, including Shaykhs Rifāʿah al-Ṭahṭāwī, Muḥammad ʿAbduh, and Muṣṭafā al-Marāghī.

Born in 1893 in the small village of Minyat Banī Manṣūr (Buḥayrah Province), in Lower Egypt, Shaltūt memorized the Qur'ān as a child, entered the Alexandria Religious Institute in 1906, and later joined al-Azhar, where he received the ʿĀlamīyah degree in 1918. After teaching at the Alexandria Religious Institute for a number of years, Shaltūt joined al-Azhar through the auspices of Shaykh Muṣṭafā al-Marāghī. The association between the two shaykhs would be a long-lasting one of cooperation in both the national and Azhari spheres. When al-Marāghī was fired by King Fu'ād in 1930, Shaltūt and seventy other Azharīs who supported his reform plans for al-Azhar were also dismissed. Shaltūt had also supported al-Marāghī's opposition to Fu'ād's efforts to have himself elected the new Islamic caliph following the 1924 Atatürk cancellation of the Ottoman caliphate.

On his return to the leadership of al-Azhar in 1935, al-Marāghī asked Shaltūt, who had turned to practicing law, to rejoin the university. He did so, rising through the hierarchy to become accepted as one of al-Azhar's chief *ʿulamā'* (religious scholars) after presenting a highly acclaimed study, "Civil and Criminal Responsibility in the Islamic *Sharīʿah*" at the International Law Conference at the Hague in 1937. In his study, Shaltūt outlined his vision of a reformed Islam and of a *sharīʿah* that could become one of the sources for modern legislation.

In 1946 he was one of the few intellectuals selected as a member of the newly formed Majmaʿ al-Lughah al-ʿArabīyah (Arab Language Organization). He was also invited to teach *fiqh* and *sunnah* (Prophetic traditions) at Cairo University's Faculty of Law and became general supervisor for Murāqabat al-Buḥūth al-Islāmīyah (Inspectorate/Control of Islamic Research) an office that allowed him to travel widely throughout the Islamic world to promote better relations between Islamic nations. In 1957 he became the secretary general of the Islamic Conference and under secretary of al-Azhar. In the following year he was chosen to be shaykh of al-Azhar, a position he held until his death in 1963.

Shaltūt became the head of al-Azhar during the most radical phase of Egypt's 1952 revolution; most standing institutions were undergoing fundamental reorganization at the time. By 1961 the law reorganizing al-Azhar was passed by an extremely reluctant Majlis al-Ummah. Even though Shaltūt shared credit as architect of the law, he was not entirely happy with it, because it brought al-Azhar under the direct domination of the state. Since 1958, power over al-Azhar had been shared with a secular authority in the shape of a minister of al-Azhar and religious affairs. The 1961 law came at a critical time in Egypt's history, just before the imposition of Nasserist socialist laws and the declaration of the National Charter. It was a time of strong nationalist feelings and revolutionary actions that touched all areas of life. Al-Azhar was to be remolded into an instrument of a new Egyptian-dominated Arab nationalist and socialist order. It was expected to fulfill this role through reorganization, reform, and a wider national and international role.

Shaltūt may have had mixed feelings about the 1961 law, but it should be remembered that he came from the generation that had participated in the 1919 revolution. His 1964 book, *The Azhar in a Thousand Years,* shows that he had long stood for an activist al-Azhar that could play a greater international role in fighting religious fanaticism and uniting the Islamic *ummah* (community) with its various schools of thought. Reorganization, and the budgetary allowances that came with it, meant the partial fulfillment of the goals of his teacher, Shaykh Muḥammad ʿAbduh, and his collaborator, al-Marāghī: reopening the door of *ijtihād* (individual inquiry in legal matters); reforming education at al-Azhar through the introduction of modern subjects; and ending the religious fanaticism that kept the Islamic world divided by narrowing the differences between different Muslim *madhhab*s (legal schools).

The reformed al-Azhar was to graduate *ʿulamāʾ* with an all-around education. Thus to the university's traditional religious education were added modern faculties for graduating doctors, engineers, scientists, and even a college for women. A new division, Idārat al-Thaqāfah wa al-Buʿūth al-Islāmīyah (Department of Culture and Islamic Missions), delegated al-Azhar graduates to teach and preach in Islamic countries and supervised foreign students studying at al-Azhar. Cairo's Madīnat al-Buʿūth al-Islāmīyah (City of Islamic Missions) enabled thousands of students from all over the Islamic world to study at al-Azhar. Primary and secondary *maʿāhid Azhārīyah* (Islamic institutions) became active in graduating *daʿis* (missionaries) to work throughout the Islamic world. Even women graduates of the *maʿāhid* and al-Azhar's Kulliyat al-Banāt (Girl's College) could act as future *dāʿis* among Egyptian and Arab women.

Other achievements of Shaltūt's tenure with a long-term impact on Egypt and the Islamic world included the formation of al-Majlis al-Aʿlā lil-Shu'ūn al-Islāmīyah (High Council for Islamic Affairs), which brought together for the first time representatives of eight Islamic *madhhab*s (Ḥanafī, Mālikī, Shāfiʿī, Ḥanbalī, Jaʿfarī, Zaydī, ʿIbādī, and Ẓāhirī) to meet in Cairo in 1962 for theological discussions. The meeting resulted in the publication of the first encyclopedia to cover the different interpretations of *muʿāmalāt* (acts concerned with human intercourse) according to the eight sects, *Mawsūʿat Nāṣir lil-fiqh al-Islāmī.*

One other institution attributed to Shaltūt, Majmaʿ al-Buḥūth al-Islāmīyah (Islamic Research Center), has had a deep impact on Egyptian intellectual life. Meant as a scholarly center to assure the accuracy of religious works, it has turned into an organ of censorship that monitors the purity of literature, declaring what is heretical, demanding the removal of publications from the market and libraries, as well as calling for the punishment of authors it considers "innovators" and "heretical enemies of Islam." For Shaltūt, a man famous for his innovative ten-volume *Tafsīr al-Qur'ān* (Interpretation of the Qur'ān) and for his resourceful *Al-fatāwah* (Formal Legal Opinion), this would hardly have been acceptable.

[*See also* Azhar, al-; *and the biography of Marāghī.*]

BIBLIOGRAPHY

Shaltūt, Maḥmūd. *Al-Fatawā.* Cairo, 1986.
Shaltūt, Maḥmūd. *Tafsīr al-Qur'ān al-Karīm,* 10 vols. Cairo, 1982.
Shaltūt, Maḥmūd. *Ilā al-Qur'ān al-Karīm.* Cairo, 1978.

Amira El Azhary Sonbol

SHAME. The concept of shame (Ar., *ḥashm;* Pers., *sharm*) is an aspect of social status often paired with honor as contraries of moral evaluation. This is at once too narrow and too broad. Notions of shame draw in religious injunctions to modesty, temperance, and covering that symbolically limit interaction with others. Local, tribal, and class-bound notions are commonly merged with understandings of Islamic concepts, which are used to justify and rationalize specific social constraints, particularly on women and sexuality. The same words gloss a range of experiences from misery to embarrassment, and from bashful to coy behaviors. Rather than being the contrary of honor, shame might be understood better as one of its companions in ensembles of ideas about social status and self-presentation.

The exteriority that makes seclusion, veiling, and segregation of women available to analysis has tended to skew understandings of shame toward an emphasis on extramarital sexual relations. More nuanced accounts of honor as performance have shown the equation to be too narrow; shame gives meaning to such behavior rather than taking meaning from it. The problematic identity attributed to women inheres in their ambiguous status in patrilineally denominated relationships of descent and kinship. Strong concerns with virginity and chastity mark their symbiotic and symbolic relationship to paternity.

Additional grounds for shame are as diverse as experiences of it. Where, as in tribal and peasant societies, land and control of productive resources are important, a person who must exchange labor for livelihood is in a position of social shame as a dependent and should act modestly. Such generic shame is relative; in commercial settings, artisans may have less social honor than traders but more than common laborers. More specific shame arises with bad dealings and social failures, which may be caused by another or self-inflicted. Shame can thus be an aspect of status, performances, and attitudes.

Indigenous understandings of shame are grounded in notions of persons and behaviors as balances of *ʿaql* and *nafs*—or cognitive and affective capacities—that inform a comprehensive social metaphysics. This metaphysics highlights control and self-possession, with shame marking their absence, lapse, or compromise in a problematic moral universe. Shame is involuntary and emotional, but also figures in the responses of shyness and modesty.

Shame can powerfully motivate efforts to overcome or wipe it out. It is the negative motive of *jihād*, the struggle to subordinate one's own life and the social environment to the dictates of religion. Shame is also the harborage of revenge, which both wipes out a shame and at the same time affirms it. Much ritual politeness of Muslim society is a matter of avoiding shame, shaming or calling attention to the shame of another lest these consequences be invoked. Shame unrestrained or unmitigated can lead to violence equally without restraint. Recognition of this power underwrites tendencies to avoid degrading another.

[*See also* Honor; Modesty; Seclusion.]

BIBLIOGRAPHY

Anderson, Jon W. "Social Structures and the Veil: Comportment and the Composition of Interaction in Afghanistan." *Anthropos* 77 (1982): 397–420.

Delaney, Carol. "Seeds of Honor, Fields of Shame." In *Honor and Shame and the Unity of the Mediterranean*, edited by David D. Gilmore, pp. 35–48. Washington, D.C., 1987.

Wikan, Unni. "Shame and Honor: A Contestable Pair." *Man* 19 (1984): 635–652.

JON W. ANDERSON

SHAʿRĀWĪ, HUDĀ (1879–1947), Egyptian feminist leader. Born in Minyā in Upper Egypt to Sulṭān Pāshā, a wealthy landowner and provincial administrator, and Iqbāl Hānim, a young woman of Circassian origin, Nūr al-Hudā Sulṭān (known after her marriage as Hudā Shaʿrāwī) was raised in Cairo. Following her father's death when she was four, Hūdā was raised in a household headed by both her mother and a co-wife. Tutored at home, Hudā became proficient in French (the language of the elite) but, despite efforts to acquire fluency in Arabic, was permitted only enough instruction to memorize the Qur'ān. Through comparisons with her younger brother, Hudā became acutely aware of gender difference, the privileging of males, and the restrictions placed upon females. At thirteen, she reluctantly acquiesced to marriage with her paternal cousin, ʿAlī Shaʿrāwī, her legal guardian and the executor of her father's estate. At fourteen she began a seven-year separation from her husband. During this time (the 1890s), she attended a women's salon, where through discussions with other members, Hudā became aware that veiling the face and female confinement in the home were not Islamic requirements, as women had been led to believe. (Such critical examination of customary practice vis-à-vis religious prescription was part of the Islamic modernist movement initiated by Shaykh Muḥammad ʿAbduh in the nineteenth century.) In 1900 Shaʿrāwī resumed married life. She gave birth to a daughter, Bathna, in 1903 and a son, Muḥammad, in 1905. In 1909 Shaʿrāwī helped found the secular women's philanthropy, the Mabarrat Muḥammad ʿAlī, bringing together Muslim and Christian women to operate a medical dispensary for poor women and children. That same year she helped organize the first "public" lectures for and by women, held at the new Egyptian University and in the offices of the liberal newspaper, *Al-jarīdah.* In 1914 she participated in forming the Women's Refinement Union (al-Ittiḥād al-Nisā'ī al-Tahdībī) and the Ladies Literary Improvement Society (Jamʿīyat al-Raqy al-Adabīyah lil-Sayyidāt al-Miṣrīyāt). Shaʿrāwī was active in the movement for national independence from 1919 to 1922. An organizer of the first women's demonstration in 1919, she became the president of the Women's Central Committee (Lajnat al-Wafd al-Markazīyah lil-Sayyidāt) of the (male) nationalist Wafd party. Shaʿrāwī led militant nationalist women in broadening the popular base of the party, organizing boycotts of British goods and services, and assuming central leadership roles when nationalist men were exiled.

In 1923, the year after independence, Shaʿarāwī spearheaded the creation of the Egyptian Feminist Union (al-Ittiḥād al-Nisā'ī al-Miṣrī; EFU) and, as president, led the first organized feminist movement in Egypt (and in the Arab world). That same year, while returning from the Rome Conference of the International Woman Suffrage Alliance (which she attended as an EFU delegate), she removed her face veil in public in an act of political protest. Shaʿrāwī generously donated her personal wealth to the work of the Egyptian Feminist Union, while also supporting other organizations and individuals. She opened the House of Cooperative Reform (Dār al-Taʿāwun al-Iṣlāḥī), a medical dispensary for poor women and children and a center for crafts training for girls, in 1924 under the aegis of the EFU, and the following year founded *L'Egyptienne,* a monthly journal serving the feminist movement. Several years later, in 1937, she established the Arabic bimonthly *Al-miṣrīyah* (The Egyptian Woman).

The feminist movement of which Shaʿrāwī was a leader brought together Muslim and Christian women of the upper and middle classes who identified as Egyptians. Although a secular movement, its agenda was articulated within the framework of modernist Islam. The feminist movement supported women's right to all levels of education and forms of work, called for full political rights for women, advocated reform of the Personal Status Code, pressured the government to provide basic health and social services to poor women, and demanded an end to state-licensed prostitution. Along with these woman-centered reforms, Shaʿrāwī stressed the nationalist goals of the feminist movement, calling for Egyptian sovereignty, including an end to British military occupation and the termination of the capitulations, which extended privileges and immunities to foreigners. In 1937 she created three dispensaries, a girls' school, and a boys' school in villages in the province of Minyā, and later a short-lived branch of the Egyptian Feminist Union in the city of Minyā. As a nationalist feminist, Shaʿrāwī was active in the international women's movement, serving on the executive board of the International Woman Suffrage Alliance (later called the International Alliance of Women for Suffrage and Equal Citizenship) from 1926 until her death. In 1938 she hosted the Women's Conference for the Defense of Palestine. Shaʿrāwī played a key role in consolidating Pan-Arab feminism, which grew out of Arab women's collective national activism on behalf of Palestine, organizing the Arab Feminist Conference in Cairo in 1944. She was elected president of the Arab Feminist Union (al-Ittiḥād al-Nisā'ī al-ʿArabī), created in 1945. Shortly before her death in 1947, the Egyptian state awarded Shaʿrāwī its highest decoration.

[*See also* Feminism.]

BIBLIOGRAPHY

Works by Hudā Shaʿrāwī

"Discours de Mme. Charaoui Pacha, Presidente de l'Union Feministe Egyptienne." *L'Egyptienne* (December 1933): 10–14. Speech given at a ceremony honoring the first women to graduate from university in Egypt, dealing with the evolution of Egyptian women with a focus on education.

"Asas al-Nahḍah al-Nisā'īyah wa-Taṭawwuratihā fī Miṣr" (The Foundation of the Feminist Renaissance and Its Evolution in Egypt). *Majallat al-Shu'ūn al-Ijtimāʿīyah* (Cairo) (August 1941): 16–24. Broad overview.

Mudhakkirāt Hudā Shaʿrāwī, Rā'idat al-Mar'ah al-ʿArabīyah al-Ḥadīthah (The Memoirs of Hudā Shaʿrāwī, Pioneer of the Modern Arab Woman). Introduction by Amīnah al-Saʿīd. Cairo, 1981.

Harem Years: The Memoirs of an Egyptian Feminist. Translated, edited, and introduced by Margot Badran. London, 1986. English translation of the *Mudhakkirāt.*

Other Sources

Badran, Margot. "Dual Liberation: Feminism and Nationalism in Egypt from the 1870s–1925." *Feminist Issues* 8.1 (Spring 1988): 15–34.

Badran, Margot. "From Consciousness to Activism: Feminist Politics in Early Twentieth-Century Egypt." In *Problems of the Middle East in Historical Perspective,* edited by John P. Spagnolo, pp. 27–48. London, 1992.

Badran, Margot. *Feminists, Islam, and Nation: Gender and the Making of Modern Egypt*. Princeton, 1995.

Subkī, Āmāl al-. *Al-ḥarakāh al-nisāʾīyah fī Miṣr mā bayna al-thawratayn 1919 wa 1952*. Cairo, 1986.

MARGOT BADRAN

SHARĪʿAH. *See* Law.

SHARĪʿATĪ, ʿALĪ (1933–1977), one of the most important social thinkers of twentieth-century Iran. Sharīʿatī's ideas are distinguished more by their practical impact than their intellectual content. In this regard, he can be compared in stature with Jamāl al-Dīn al-Afghānī (1838 or 1839–1897) or the Egyptian writer and activist Sayyid Quṭb (1906–1966).

Life. Born in the village of Mazīnān, near the town of Sabzavār, on the edge of the Dasht-i Kavīr desert in Khurasan province of northeastern Iran, Sharīʿatī's worldview was influenced by his rural upbringing, as the title of his most revealing work, *Kavīr,* indicates. He came from a well-known family whose paternal line included clergymen active in the religious circles of Mashhad, the burial site of the eighth imam, ʿAlī al-Riḍā (d. 818).

Unfortunately, much of Sharīʿatī's life remains obscure. Since his death, annual commemoration volumes have been published in Iran providing data about him, but these are incomplete, contradictory, and hagiographical, making it difficult to sort truth from legend. Outside Iran, scholars have contributed significantly to our understanding of his words and deeds, but these, too, have not settled all the questions that have been raised about this unique figure. We still do not have an authoritative intellectual biography of Sharīʿatī.

Sharīʿatī's grandfather, Ākhūnd Ḥakīm, was a respected *ʿālim* whose fame apparently had extended beyond Iran to Bukhara and Najaf. He had spent some time at Tehran's Sipah Salar mosque but soon returned to his native district, declining the shah's posts and honors. Ākhūnd Ḥakīm's brother, ʿĀdil Nīshābūrī, had also earned a reputation as a scholar in the religious sciences.

Sharīʿatī's own father, Muḥammad Taqī Sharīʿatī, was of the same ilk, but he was also a modernist who had lost patience with the traditional perspectives of the *ʿulamāʾ*, which he saw to be suffused with abstract scholasticism. The father was a reformer who desired to apply new methods to the study of religion. He possessed a large and comprehensive library that ʿAlī Sharīʿatī fondly remembered, regarding it metaphorically as the spring from which he nourished his mind and soul. Sharīʿatī's father not only taught students of the religious sciences in Mashhad (next to that of Qom, the country's most important center for religious studies), but he was the founder of the city's Kānūn-i Nashr-i Ḥaqāyiq-i Islāmī (Society for the Propagation of Islamic Verities). This institution was a lay organization dedicated to the revival of Islam as a religion of social obligation and commitment.

Little is known of Sharīʿatī's early years. He went to government (as opposed to seminary) schools in Mashhad but also took lessons from his father. On graduating from secondary school, apparently in 1949, Sharīʿatī enrolled in a two-year program at Mashhad's Teachers Training College (Dānishsarāy-i Tarbiyat-i Muʿallim).

He seems to have begun teaching at the age of eighteen or nineteen (1951–1952), probably in one of the government village schools near Mashhad. Both he and his father were involved in pro-National Front rallies held by the Mashhad branch of the National Resistance Movement (Nahżat-i Muqāvamat-i Millī) after the royalist coup d'état in August 1953 that overthrew the government of Prime Minister Mohammad Mossadegh (Muḥammad Muṣaddiq). The movement was founded by Mehdi Bāzargān and the social-activist clergyman Sayyid Maḥmud Ṭāleqāni (Ṭāliqānī). [*See the biographies of Bāzargān and Ṭāleqāni.*]

Sharīʿatī was arrested in September 1957 for his role in one such demonstration, and he was jailed at Tehran's Qizil Qalʿah prison until May 1958. He is also said to have affiliated himself with a political movement known as the Movement of Socialist Believers in God (Junbish-i Khudāparastān-i Sūsiyalīst). Apparently, he had entered Mashhad University for the B.A. degree in 1956 and married that same year.

Sharīʿatī was therefore about twenty-seven at the time he received his degree, with honors, in French and Persian literature in 1960. He forthwith left for Paris, stipend in hand, to study at the Sorbonne. Since he later frequently alluded to the French Orientalist Louis Massignon, the sociologist Georges Gurevich, the historian Jacques Berque, and the philosopher Jean-Paul Sartre, many of his supporters believed that he had been formally trained in philosophy and social sciences. However, his doctoral dissertation was a translation of and introduction to a medieval book, *The Notables of Balkh*

(Faẓāʾil-i Balkh). If, therefore, he had received such training, it was not reflected in his research.

During these years abroad, he actively participated in the antishah student movement and came to know Ibrāhīm Yazdī, Ṣādiq Quṭbzādah, Abol-Hasan Bani Sadr (Abū al-Ḥasan Banī Ṣadr), and Muṣṭafā Chamrān, all of whom became principals in Iran's early postrevolutionary government. During the 1962 Wiesbaden (Germany) Congress of the National Front in Europe, Sharīᶜatī was elected editor of the organization's newly established newspaper, *Īrān-i āzād (Free Iran).* He also contributed articles to the Algerian revolutionary resistance newspaper, *Al-mujāhid.* Accordingly, he became familiar with the ideas of Third World liberation thinkers, such as Franz Fanon (d. 1961), Aimé Césaire, and Amilcar Cabral (d. 1973).

Sharīᶜatī returned to Iran in 1964 and was immediately arrested at the Turkish-Iranian frontier and jailed for six months for his political activities in France. After his release, he went back to Mashhad and briefly taught in a regional secondary school before securing an obscure post as an instructor in humanities at Mashhad University's Faculty of Agriculture. Shortly thereafter, he transferred to the Faculty of Arts. Sharīᶜatī's lectures attracted students from outside the university as well and soon became so popular that the government engineered his dismissal. However, he continued to receive invitations to lecture from university student organizations on campuses in various cities.

Meanwhile, in Tehran, a group of religious reformers had established the Ḥusaynīyah-yi Irshād in 1965. This religious institution, like the Kānūn-i Nashr-i Ḥaqāyiq-i Islāmī of Mashhad, granted no degrees but instead sponsored lectures, discussions, seminars, and publications on religious subjects. Sharīᶜatī joined the Ḥusaynīyah-yi Irshād in 1967 and not long after became its most popular instructor. For six years, his lectures were packed with students eager to hear a new interpretation of Islam and its role in society. His activities angered the orthodox clergy, who saw in him an untutored agitator who was undermining respect for the seminary and its teachers. However, the younger generation was enthralled by his innovative approach, so much in contrast to what they believed was the traditional clergy's antediluvian methods, scholastic pedantry, and purely pietistic concerns. He sought to apply Islam to the requirements of the age, to make it relevant, in keeping with the *ḥadīth* (saying attributed to the Prophet): "If it is a matter of religion, then have recourse to me, but if it is a matter of your world, you know better [than I do]." This *ḥadīth* has frequently been interpreted to mean that scripture requires adaptation to changing historical circumstances in certain realms of human endeavor, such as politics.

Because of pervasive censorship, Sharīᶜatī had to couch his discussions in elliptical language. One of the leading intellectuals of the Iranian Revolution of 1979, Ayatollah Murtaẓā Muṭahharī (d. 1979), remarked that he and Sharīᶜatī's other colleagues at the Ḥusaynīyah-yi Irshād believed that his talks were too overtly political in content and feared a government crackdown. By mid-1973, the regime had indeed come to regard Sharīᶜatī as a dangerous radical, and Sharīᶜatī was again arrested and jailed, his father joining him for part of the time. Sharīᶜatī was released on 20 March 1975 only because of the intervention of the Algerian government. The Iranian press then published his essay *Marxism and Other Western Fallacies: A Critique of Marxism from the Perspective of Islam* without his permission in a transparent attempt to suggest that Sharīᶜatī had sold out to the shah and was collaborating with the regime—an effort that failed abysmally.

Under virtual house arrest for about two years, Sharīᶜatī was finally allowed to go abroad in spring 1977. His plans were to meet his wife and family in Europe and then to proceed to the United States, where his son, Iḥsān, was a student. However, the government prevented his family's departure, and Sharīᶜatī, who had already flown to Brussels, went to England to stay with his brother pending developments. On 19 June 1977 his body was discovered at his brother's house in southern England. The official ruling was death from a heart attack, but many believe that he had been assassinated by the shah's secret police.

Sharīᶜatī's body was transferred to Iranian authorities in London, and the Iranian government sought to persuade his wife to go claim the body and return it for burial at state expense. However, she refused to participate in this blatant attempt to exploit Sharīᶜatī's death for the shah's own propaganda purposes, and Sharīᶜatī was buried in Damascus near the tomb of Zaynab, the Prophet's granddaughter and sister of the third imam, Ḥusayn ibn ᶜAlī (d. 680). Officiating at the funeral was Mūsā al-Ṣadr, leader of the Lebanese Shīᶜah.

Thought. Sharīᶜatī was less a disciplined scholar than a social and political activist. By the time of his final arrest, he had given over two hundred lectures at the Ḥusayniyah-yi Irshad, many of which had been prepared for publication and sold thousands of copies in several printings. His early works include *Maktab-i vasāṭah (The Middle School of Thought),* which he wrote while in the Teachers' Training College and which upheld Islam as the virtuous path between capitalism and communism, and *Tārikh-i takāmul-i falsafah (The History of the Perfection of Philosophy),* written in 1955. He was also deeply impressed by the biography *Abū Dharr al-Ghifārī* by Jawdah al-Saḥḥār, whose protagonist, Abū Dharr (d. 657), symbolized Muslim resistance to injustice. In fact, Sharīʿatī's admirers affixed the sobriquet "Abū Dharr-i Zaman" (The Abu Dharr of Our Times) to his name after his death.

As a thinker, Sharīʿatī exhibited a paradoxical sensibility. He was an intensely private thinker engaged in a lifetime search for truth through a mystical, intuitive understanding of the world and God's role in the scheme of things. Yet he took very public stands to promote a collectivist revolutionary course of action to bring about social justice and freedom for the downtrodden. The hallmark of his thought was his conviction that religion must be transformed from a purely private set of ethical injunctions into a revolutionary program to change the world. In this respect, he greatly resembled Ayatollah Ruhollah al-Musavi Khomeini (1902–1989), who repeatedly rejected the idea that Islam was merely a matter of arcane rules and rituals pertaining to such technical problems as ablution, menstruation, parturition, diet, and the like. [*See the biography of Khomeini.*]

Sharīʿatī was always looking for what was fresh and original in Islam and had little patience with traditional formulas and modes of thinking. The system of thought that he constructed was not parsimonious or logically rigorous. He was in too much of a hurry to be able to work out an elaborate, internally consistent social theory. His primary purpose was to exhort people to action in the mold of Imam Ḥusayn, who, Sharīʿatī believed, had consciously sacrificed his life on behalf of the political and social liberation of his followers. In this view of Imam Ḥusayn, Sharīʿatī scandalized the traditional religious establishment, which felt that he had converted their revered imam into a vulgar powerseeker and crude ideologist.

In calling for liberation through a reinterpretation of the faith, Sharīʿatī clearly rejected the fashionable Western revolutionary view that religion was the "opiate of the masses." Religion, in Sharīʿatī's perspective, lends itself to ideological commitment for the emancipation of the individual believer from oppression. In this respect, he shares much in common with the contemporary Egyptian philosopher Ḥasan Ḥanafī. The project of both thinkers is to undertake a fresh reading of Islamic scripture in order to reconstruct Islam's concepts into a modern, autochthonous, and progressive ideology of mobilization to enfranchise and empower the masses. [*See the biography of Ḥanafī.*]

Sharīʿatī's detractors, mainly scripturalists with an ahistorical view of the sacred texts, felt that he had diffused and distilled the Qur'ān and *sunnah* into a mere vulgate, with debasing appeals to "enlightened thinkers" to overturn the existing social arrangements for the sake of an anthropocentric "new order." This view, however, ascribing to Sharīʿatī no more than a merely instrumental approach to the faith, falls to the ground in light of the role he ascribed to religious belief in the total life of the individual. Sharīʿatī never invoked the metaphor of the individual engaged in a saga of epic struggle inevitably ending in his triumph over the forces of evil.

There might be a residual basis for the scripturalists' concerns, however, because Sharīʿatī did invoke a central theme of the humanistic, Enlightenment tradition: the individual's enormous potential for living a life of emancipation, harmony, and well-being through the exercise of right reason. For all of Sharīʿatī's ecstatic paeans to Allāh's majesty and love, his system did seem to imply the vision of those who believed in history's progressive march toward the liberation of mankind from the evils of superstition, obscurantism, and mystification. His scheme did at least imply the possibility that human reason was uniquely capable of achieving mankind's emancipation and enfranchisement. Sharīʿatī critics blamed him for opening the door to the emergence of a human community that would vanquish the forces of evil through dedication to its own confraternity. Even if this community submitted itself to Allāh, Sharīʿatī's critics implied, such submission was suspect because it appeared to be contingent rather than categorical. Whether Sharīʿatī's critics are right in suspecting that in Sharīʿati's worldview Allāh's role appears to be reduced to merely providing comfort from personal doubts, one thing is clear: Sharīʿatī was, perhaps more than anything else, concerned about human injustice and the need to act to eliminate it.

Sharīʿatī evinced a profound revulsion against injustice, which he viewed both as a symptom and, more important, as an integral consequence of a failed human emancipation. He dedicated his life to fighting injustice.

How can Shīʿīs, so devoted to the cause of Imams ʿAlī ibn Abī Ṭālib (d. 661) and Ḥusayn, acquiesce in injustice, Sharīʿatī demanded. Rulers have oppressed the faithful, often in the name of Shiism itself. But the traditional clergy must share the blame, because they have for centuries encouraged stoic acceptance of despotism, some for opportunistic reasons, others in the expectation that the Hidden Imam would one day return to purge all the accumulated wrongs visited on the righteous. In this refusal to wait passively for the redeemer, Sharīʿatī once again had much in common with Ayatollah Khomeini. Nonetheless, Khomeini was not an admirer of Sharīʿatī and doubtless shared his fellow *mujtahids*' views that Sharīʿatī was an ignorant hothead who made gratuitous attacks on the Shīʿī clergy.

Although a controversial figure, almost all agree that Sharīʿatī's was an urgent voice. Despite the prevalence of Shīʿī symbols, his cause was humanity in general, especially the masses of the Third World. He believed that Western imperialism wished to transform the masses into slaves. Islam was, in his view, the answer to both Marxism and capitalism. Some of the key concepts in Sharīʿatī's writings and speeches were *shahadat* (martyrdom); *intiẓār* (anticipation of the return of the Hidden Imam); *ẓulm* (oppression of the Imam's justice); *jihād iʿtirāẓ* (protest); *ijtihād* (independent judgment in adducing a rule of law); *rawshānfikrān* (enlightened thinkers); *tārīkh* ([the movement of] history); *mas'ūlīyat* (responsibility); and *ʿādalat* ([social] justice).

From Marxism, Sharīʿatī borrowed the notion of dialectical conflict and appropriated the term *jabr-i tārīkh* (historical determinism). But he preferred Hegel's primacy of contradictions among ideas along the path to an Absolute Truth to Marx's insistence on the precedence of material contradictions and class conflict. From Western liberal thought, Sharīʿatī adopted the Enlightenment's stress on reason as the corrective for the maladies of society. From all, he seems to have gained an appreciation of the dangers that institutionalized religion can pose.

In this connection, Sharīʿatī believed that *ijtihād* is the purview not merely of the experts but of every individual. All persons have the responsibility to exercise *ijtihād* on substantive, nontechnical matters. He likened the emulation of putative experts—the *mujtahids*—in regard to such basic problems as authority, justice, mobilization, and participation to abdication of individual choice and will. We can see, then, the manifest influence of existentialist and Marxist philosophy on Sharīʿatī. From the former, he adopted the notion that the individual must take responsibility for his or her actions. And from Marx's mediation of the Prometheus legend, Sharīʿatī absorbed the humanistic admonition that religion can be made to serve despots, that the eternal verities represented by religion must be determined by individuals appropriating true knowledge from those seeking to monopolize it for non- or even antihumanistic ends.

It is difficult to summarize Sharīʿatī's overall contributions. Although his ideas have suffered eclipse in official circles in the aftermath of the revolution that he struggled so hard to effect, he has left a legacy that Iranians will not easily forget and which will no doubt continue to be invoked.

[*See also* Iran; Shīʿī Islam, *article on* Modern Shīʿī Thought.]

BIBLIOGRAPHY

For a comprehensive listing of Sharīʿatī's works, see Yann Richard, *Abstracta Iranica* (supplement to *Studia Iranica*), vols. 1–2 (Leuven, Belgium, 1978–1979). For critical evaluations, see the following:

Abrahamian, Ervand. "ʿAli Shariʿati: Ideologue of the Iranian Revolution." *Middle East Research and Information Project Report*, no. 102 (January 1982): 24–28. Depicts Sharīʿatī as a cosmopolitan thinker seeking to synthesize socialism and Shiism and applying revolutionary theories of Third World revolution.

Aḥmadī, Ḥamīd, ed. *Sharīʿatī dar Jahān* (Sharīʿatī in the World). Tehran, 1365/1986. Series of essays on Sharīʿatī's life and thought.

Akhavi, Shahrough. "Shariati's Social Thought." In *Religion and Politics in Iran*, edited by Nikki R. Keddie, pp. 125–144. New Haven, 1983. Examination of the ontology, epistemology, philosophy of history, and political theory of Sharīʿatī's thought.

Algar, Hamid. "Islam bih ʿUnvān-i Yak Īdiyuluzhī" (Islam as an Ideology). In *Sharīʿatī dar Jahān*, edited by Ḥamīd Aḥmadī. Publication of a lecture given at the Muslim Institute in London, focusing on the importance of ideology in Sharīʿatī's outlook.

Bayat, Mangol. "Shiʿism in Contemporary Iranian Politics: The Case of Ali Shariʿati." In *Towards a Modern Iran*, edited by Elie Kedourie and Sylvia G. Haim, pp. 155–168. London, 1980. Views Sharīʿatī as an "embourgeoisé modernist" reflecting the identity crisis of modern intellectuals.

Dabashi, Hamid. "Ali Shariʿati: The Islamic Ideologue Par Excellence." In *Theology of Discontent*, pp. 102–146. New York, 1993. Extended study of Sharīʿatī's ideas, stressing his moral vision as a politically engaged "prophet."

Hanson, Brad. "The 'Westoxication' of Iran: Depictions and Reactions of Behrangi, Āl-e Ahmad, and Shariʿati." *International Journal of Middle East Studies* 15.1 (1983): 1–23. Examines Sharīʿatī's anti-Western polemics.

Hermansen, Marcia K. "Fatimeh as a Role Model in the Works of Ali Shariʿati." In *Women and Revolution in Iran*, edited by Guity Nashat, pp. 87–96. Boulder, 1983. Examines Sharīʿatī's ideal type of Shīʿī woman as faithful, aware, and engaged, and critiques as

utopian his lack of concern for women's institutions and organizations to implement their goals.
ʿIrfānī, Surūsh. "ʿAli Sharʿati, Teacher of Revolution." In *Revolutionary Islam in Iran.* London, 1983. Stresses the revolutionary nature of Sharīʿatī's message.
Malushkov, V. G., and K. A. Khromova. *Poiski Puteĭ Reformatsii v Islame Opyt Irana* (The Search for the Path of Reform in Iran's Experience). Moscow, 1991. Contains several chapters analyzing Sharīʿatī's life and thought.
Sachedina, A. A. "Shariati: Ideologue of the Iranian Revolution." In *Voices of Resurgent Islam,* edited by John L. Esposito, pp. 191–214. New York and Oxford, 1983. Argues that Sharīʿatī was above all the founder of a discipline of "Islamology"—the study of how Islam may be applied to contemporary social problems in the search for solutions.
Sharīʿatī, ʿAlī. *On the Sociology of Islam.* Translated by Hamid Algar. Berkeley, 1979. Contains useful information on Sharīʿatī's life and excerpts from his important work, *Islāmshināsī.*

SHAHROUGH AKHAVI

SHARĪF. The meanings of the Arabic word *sharīf* (pl., *ashrāf, shurafāʾ*) include "noble," "honorable," "highborn," and "highbred" (*Lisān al-ʿArāb,* p. 2241). In most contexts the word *sharīf* is associated with honor, high position, nobility, and distinction. A *sharīf* is a man who claims descent from prominent ancestors, usually the prophet Muḥammad.

Although the Qurʾān and most of the Prophet's sayings emphasized the equality of all believers and allotted distinction on the basis only of devoutness and adherence to religion, there are instances where the lineage of the Prophet is given preference. The influence of Shīʿī views and increased veneration for the Prophet and his family over time made membership in the house of Muḥammad a sign of particular eminence; thus tracing one's ancestry to *ahl al-bayt* (the house of Muḥammad) is a necessary requirement for being a *sharīf.* In other contexts, *sharīf* also means a person of importance and high social status, or a free man as opposed to a slave.

Throughout the Muslim world the *sharīf*s wore turbans, usually green and white, to distinguish them from others. They were also to be revered and respected. They were not subject to the same religious stipulations that apply to other Muslims because their sins will be forgiven by God. In earlier periods a religious official, the *naqīb al-ashrāf,* was responsible for legally ascertaining the validity of the *sharīf*s' lineage, monitoring their conduct, reminding them of their obligations, and keeping them from doing what might injure their prestige.

There is an association and similarity between the *sharīf* and the *sayyid,* which also denotes a free man, lord, or master. The *sayyid* is revered as a saint, especially after his death, when his tomb is likely to become a place of pilgrimage. His blessing confers good fortune, and he acts as an intermediary in popular disputes.

Countless families of *sharīf*s and *sayyid*s can be found throughout the Muslim world. Several of these families were major rulers at different periods. The *sharīf*s ruled in Mecca and the Hejaz (Ḥijāz) from the tenth century until 1924, when *al-sharīf* Ḥusayn, who had proclaimed the Arab revolt against the Ottomans in 1916 and become king of the Hejaz, was defeated by Ibn Saʿūd. The Hashemites, descendants of Meccan *sharīf*s, rule Jordan and ruled Iraq until 1958. King Ḥasan II comes from a sharifian dynasty that has ruled Morocco since the seventeenth century. This genealogical tradition has also survived strongly in western Arabia and the Hadramawt in Yemen. Other such families exercise local influence throughout the Arab and broader Muslim world, although it is noteworthy that while *sharīf*s usually occupy high social status, they are not necessarily wealthy.

[*See also* Ahl al-Bayt; Sayyid.]

BIBLIOGRAPHY

Al-Munjid fī al-lughah wa-al-aʿlām. Dar el-Machreq, Beirut, 1992.

SINAN ANTOON and BASSAM S. A. HADDAD

SHAṬṬĀRĪYAH. A Ṣūfī order of importance in India and Indonesia, the Shaṭṭārīyah is in the Tayfūrī line of Ṣūfī orders that follow the mystical tradition of Abū Yazīd al-Bisṭāmī (d. 874) and was called the Bisṭāmīyah in Ottoman Turkey and ʿIshqīyah in Iran and Central Asia (the principal exponent in Transoxiana was Abū Yazīd al-ʿIshqī). The foundation of the Shaṭṭārī order is attributed to the eponymous ʿAbdullāh Shaṭṭārī (d. 1485), who claimed hereditary descent from Shihāb al-Dīn Suhrawardī (d. 1244). The title *shaṭṭārī* is said to have been given him by his spiritual master, Muḥammad ʿĀrif Tayfūrī, in recognition of the rapidity with which ʿAbdullāh advanced on the Ṣūfī path. As such, the word should probably be read *shuṭṭārī* (from *shuṭṭār,* pl. of *shāṭir,* meaning "skillful," "clever").

ʿAbdullāh Shaṭṭārī is said to have made a theatrical migration to India during the reign of the Timurid sultan Abū Saʿīd (r. 1451–1469), wearing royal robes and accompanied by a retinue of black-gowned mystics beating drums and waving banners. He maintained a close relationship with Sultan G̲h̲iyās̲uddīn Khaljī (r. 1469–1501), dedicating his book *Laṭā'if-i ghaybīyah* to the king and providing him with spiritual aid during the siege of Chitor. The Mughal emperor Humāyūn erected a mausoleum for him at Mandu in Malwa. ʿAbdullāh was succeeded by his son, Abulfatḥ Hadyatullāh Sarmast (d. 1497), and by a much more influential disciple, Muḥammad ibn ʿAlā Qāḍin Tirhūtī (d. 1495). The latter is said to have been initiated into the Shaṭṭārī order during ʿAbdullāh Shaṭṭārī's journey to Bihar around 1475. Muḥammad Qāḍin actively propagated the Shaṭṭārīyah until his death and was the most important figure in its spread in Bihar, which ranks second only to Gujarat as a center of Shaṭṭārī activity in India. He wrote two major works, *Maʿādin al-asrār* and *Awrād-i Qāḍin Shaṭṭārī*. An annual fair is held on the anniversary of his death at a tomb atop a Buddhist stupa in Basharh, Punjab; the date of this festival is reckoned according to the Hindu/Buddhist calendar.

The most important figure in the formation of the Shaṭṭārī order is Muḥammad Ghaus̱ of Gwalior (d. 1562), fourth in line from ʿAbdullāh Shaṭṭārī. Both Muḥammad Ghaus̱ and his brother and fellow Shaṭṭārī Shaykh Bahlūl (also known as Shaykh Phūl, d. 1538) were held in high esteem by Emperor Humāyūn, which caused them much trouble. Shaykh Bahlūl was executed by Humāyūn's brother Hindal, and Muḥammad Ghaus̱ was forced to flee from northern India to Gujarat when Humāyūn was overthrown in 1539 by Sher Shāh Sūrī. While in Gujarat, Muḥammad Ghaus̱ established important Shaṭṭārī centers in Ahmadabad and Bharoch (Broach). He visited Agra briefly in 1558 after Akbar had restored Mughal rule and then returned to Gwalior. Akbar built an imposing tomb over his grave. Tan Sen, the most famous figure in the history of Hindustani classical music, was a devotee of Muḥammad Ghaus̱ and is buried near him.

Muḥammad Ghaus̱ was a rigorous ascetic who spent twelve years in solitary meditation in the Chunar hills near Benares (Varanasi). He was also a productive author to whom the following works are attributed: *Jawāhir-i khamsa, Risāla-yi miʿrājīyah, Baḥr ul-ḥayāt, Kalīd-i makhāzin, Ḍamā'ir, Baṣā'ir, Kanz ul-waḥdat,* and *Awrād-i ghaus̱īyah*. *Jawāhir-i khamsa* is the most important and exists in a popular Arabic version in addition to the Persian original. It deals with Ṣūfī doctrines and practices as well as astrological issues in connection with the divine names. *Risālah-yi miʿrājīyah* describes a spiritual journey and contains some ecstatic utterances; it is reminiscent of a similar work by Abū Yazīd al-Bisṭāmī, from whom the Shaṭṭārīyah is derived. The *Baḥr ul-ḥayāt* is a Persian translation of the Hatha-yoga treatise *Amṛtakuṇḍa* and is probably the first translation of a Hindu religious work undertaken by a Muslim.

Muḥammad Ghaus̱'s heterodox beliefs and active interest in yogic practices earned him the condemnation of the *ʿulamā'* of Gujarat. He was vindicated by one of them, Shāh Wajīhuddīn (d. 1589), a reputable religious scholar who became his main successor. Wajīhuddīn was a prolific author credited with approximately three hundred works. His famous *madrasah* at Ahmadabad attracted such important Ṣūfīs as ʿAbd al-Ḥaqq Muḥaddis Dihlavī (d. 1642) and survived until 1820. His shrine at Khanpur is a major pilgrimage center for Gujarat; his festival is held on the last day of Muḥarram and the first of Ṣafar.

Wajīhuddīn discarded many of the ecstatic and yogic practices of his teacher and forbade his disciples to accept non-Muslims as followers. He promulgated a form of Sufism that subordinated itself to the precepts of Islamic law, bringing the Shaṭṭārīyah much closer to the vastly more popular Qādirī order to which he had originally belonged. A secondary branch of the Shaṭṭārīyah, which continued to emphasize the more heterodox of Muḥammad Ghaus̱'s practices, came to be known as the Ghaus̱īyah.

Wajīhuddīn was succeeded by two disciples, Muḥammad ibn Faḍlullāh Burhānpūrī (whose *At-tuḥfa al-mursala ilā'n-nabī* was influential in spreading Sufism in Indonesia) and Shāh Sibghatullāh of Bharoch (d. 1607). Shāh Sibghatullāh migrated to Medina, where he built a *khānqāh* (Ṣūfī convent), using money given to him either by the rulers of Bijapur and Ahmadnagar, or else by the local representative of the Ottoman sultan. It was largely through his disciple Aḥmad Shinnavī (d. 1619) that the Shaṭṭārīyah spread outside India.

In 1643 ʿAbdurra'ūf ibn ʿAlī (d. about 1693) of Singkep in Sumatra made a pilgrimage to Mecca, where he became a disciple of Aḥmad Qushshāshī (d. about 1661), the successor of Aḥmad Shinnavī. He stayed with Qushshāshī until the latter's death nineteen years later, when ʿAbdurra'ūf returned to Aceh in Sumatra where he actively promoted the Shaṭṭārīyah. He wrote several treatises in Malay, including the first known Malay translation of the Qur'ān with a commentary. The Shaṭṭārīyah was the first Ṣūfī order to establish itself in Java, and ʿAbdurra'ūf's shrine remains an important Sumatran and Javanese pilgrimage site.

A major source of information on the Shaṭṭārīyah is *Gulzār-i abrār,* a biographical work written by a spiritual descendant of Muḥammad Ghauṣ named Muḥammad Ghauṣī (d. after 1633). Descriptions of the sect's beliefs and practices are also found in *As-salsabīl al-mu'īn* by Muḥammad al-Sanūsī and in *Irshādāt al-ʿārifīn* by Muḥammad Ibrāhīm Gazūr-i Ilāhī.

The Shaṭṭārīyah is perhaps the most thoroughly Indian of the Ṣūfī orders, having embraced wholeheartedly the Indian cultural milieu and Hindu—especially yogic—ideas. ʿAbdullāh Shaṭṭārī is said to have studied yoga and composed songs in Indian vernaculars. Later Shaṭṭārī shaykhs went so far as to allow their disciples to use Sanskrit and Hindi formulae in *dhikr* (Ṣūfī prayer). Meditation exercises involving yogic postures and breath control were certainly practiced by Muḥammad Ghauṣ. These have been described by Sanūsī as a *dhikr* exercise called the *jūjīyah* (i.e., yoga). Among the Shaṭṭārīs, mystical practice is directly related to magical and supernatural powers, and many of their shaykhs (including the sober Wajīhuddīn) are remembered as exorcists and healers.

BIBLIOGRAPHY

Ahmad, Qazi Mueenuddin. "History of the Shattārī Silsilah." Ph.d. diss., Aligarh Muslim University, 1963.

Desai, Z. A. "The Major Shrines of Ahmadabad." In *Muslim Shrines in India: Their Character, History, and Significance,* edited by Christian W. Troll, pp. 76–97. Delhi, 1989.

Eaton, Richard M. *Sufis of Bijapur, 1300–1700: Social Roles of Sufis in Medieval India.* Princeton, 1978.

Lawrence, Bruce B. *Notes from a Distant Flute: Sufi Literature in Pre-Mughal India.* Tehran, 1978.

Margoliouth, D. S. "Shaṭṭārīya." In *First Encyclopaedia of Islam, 1913–1936,* vol. 7, p. 339. Leiden, 1987.

Rizvi, S. A. A. *A History of Sufism in India.* 2 vols. New Delhi, 1978. The most encyclopedic source on Sufism in India published to date.

Sanūsī, Muḥammad ibn ʿAlī al-. *Al-salsabīl al-mu'īn fī al-ṭarā'iq al-arbaʿīn.* In the margins of the same author's *Al-masā'il al-ʿashar.* Cairo, 1935. Extremely valuable work on the practices of Ṣūfī orders.

Schimmel, Annemarie. *Mystical Dimensions of Islam.* Chapel Hill, N.C., 1975. Excellent introduction to Sufism; balances readability with exhaustive scholarship.

Schimmel, Annemarie. *Islam in the Indian Subcontinent.* Leiden, 1980.

Subhan, John A. *Sufism: Its Saints and Shrines.* New York, 1970. Valuable introduction to the major Ṣūfī orders and shrines of India.

JAMAL J. ELIAS

SHAYKH. The Arabic term *shaykh* is an honorific title given since pre-Islamic times to men of distinction. Its meaning embraces several concepts expressed by the English words "leader," "patriarch," "notable," "elder," "chief," and "counselor." Throughout the Muslim era the term *shaykh al-dīn* ("leader of the faith") has been applied to men who possess scriptural learning. Heads of religious orders are called shaykhs, as are Ṣūfī adepts, Qur'ānic scholars, jurists, and those who preach and lead prayers in the mosques. Muslim scholars have paid close attention to the careers of prominent religious shaykhs; the intellectual and genealogical pedigrees of these learned men have been accumulating in biographical dictionaries (known as *tarājim* or *ṭabāqat*) for centuries. One would hardly suspect, given the immense weight of this clerical literature, that the majority of shaykhs, both now and in the past, have not been religious functionaries. Instead, they have belonged to a more secular and, historically speaking, much older political elite consisting of clan leaders, village headmen, and tribal chiefs.

The *shaykh al-dīn* is associated with a metropolitan culture of great antiquity and richness, whereas the tribal shaykh has long been associated with the agricultural and pastoral hinterland and particularly with remote areas beyond state control. The contrast is overdrawn. Shaykhs have always been caught up in the political economy of urban society—at times, they have taxed and controlled the trade of cities—and the most powerful shaykhs keep residences in both town and country. The base of the shaykh's power, however, has traditionally been in the countryside, where most tribespeople and peasants have lived even into modern times. The shaykh's influence in outlying regions, which cannot always be easily controlled from the urban center, makes him an important resource to the state. Historically, the most influential shaykhs have acted as middlemen between governed and ungoverned space, and it is their relationship to the latter that has distinguished them over time as a recognizable political type.

The Arab philosopher of history Ibn Khaldūn (1332–1406) argued that tribal shaykhs, because they do not possess "royal authority," are unable to coerce their followers or compel their allegiance. In the absence of "governmental and educational laws," shaykhs can only exercise a "restraining influence," and this they can accomplish only insofar as they are venerated and respected by fellow tribesmen. Such respect is seldom won on the basis of a shaykh's piety or erudition. Indeed, until recent decades, most tribal shaykhs were illiterate, and their understanding of Islam was rarely orthodox. A shaykh's reputation depends instead on four important characteristics: his ability to resolve disputes, which requires a detailed knowledge of customary law (*ʿurf* or *ʿawāyid*), a legal system that is often at odds with Islamic law; his ability to dispense hospitality on a grand scale and to offer gifts and financial support to followers; his ability to lead in times of raiding and warfare; and his ability to deal with state governments in ways that advance his own interests while preserving, as much as possible, the autonomy of the tribespeople he represents.

Since tribal shaykhs do not control the military and administrative apparatus of the state, their capacity to dominate tribal affairs is often attributed to personal charisma. They are commonly (and somewhat romantically) depicted as eloquent, shrewd, persuasive, brave, and wise. Among tribespeople, the title is not inherited by right—ideally, anyone can attain or fall from that rank—and the urge to portray shaykhs as "first among equals" is especially strong in the West. This egalitarian view, though popular, is exaggerated. In many tribes, the shaykhdom has remained in the same family for centuries. Such concentrations of power and influence are not based on charisma alone. Until the establishment of modern nation-states in the twentieth century, tribal shaykhs were able to impose protection taxes (known as *khawa*, or "brotherhood") on peasant communities; they extracted escort fees from caravans that passed through their territories; and in settled areas, they frequently owned sizeable tracts of land. These financial resources gave the shaykhs' families a distinct political advantage over ordinary tribesmen. Moreover, shaykhs exercised this advantage in the contested zones between urban centers. By playing regional governments against each other, shaykhs could generate a reliable flow of stipends from rulers who competed for their loyalty.

In the modern era, as domains of state control have grown to encompass tribal areas, the status of these families has changed. Many of the most powerful shaykhs have been successfully incorporated by national regimes. In Jordan, for instance, tribal leaders sit in legislative assemblies, serve as government ministers, and control the upper ranks of the military. Throughout the Arab world, shaykhs have preserved their role as judges of tribal law, which, although many countries have officially delegitimized it, continues to be practiced in both urban and rural settings. Shaykhs have fared best, however, on the Arabian Peninsula, where they found themselves in possession of vast oil reserves. The emirates and kingdoms of the Gulf region are ruled today by families who in the nineteenth century were known simply as tribal shaykhs. In Yemen, where government control of the hinterland is comparatively weak, shaykhs take an active part in foreign and domestic affairs of state, and their political power has at times rivaled that of the central government.

It is now common for both Middle Eastern and Western intellectuals to identify shaykhs with parochialism and reactionary politics. The conservative social and economic agendas of the Gulf states, for example, are often ascribed to the "traditional mentality" of their ruling shaykhs. Given the value nationalist ideology sets on progress, unity, and allegiance, it was perhaps inevitable that shaykhs would assume the place they now occupy in the political imagination of the region. Long before nationalism arrived, tribal shaykhs were associated with "backward" domains, fratricidal politics, and resistance to the laws of God and the state. This view, so obviously colored by the attitudes of the urban elite, has been slow to change. The shaykhly families themselves, however, have proven remarkably adaptable. Despite confident predictions that they will soon disappear, the shaykhs and the tribes they lead remain prominent features of the political landscape of the Middle East and North Africa.

[*See also* ʿAṣabīyah; Ḥaḍārah; Tribe.]

BIBLIOGRAPHY

Dresch, Paul. *Tribes, Government, and History in Yemen*. Oxford, 1989. Study of Yemeni politics and the role shaykhs have played in it, from the time of the first Zaydī imams to the early decades of the republican era.

Fernea, Robert A. *Shaykh and Effendi: Changing Patterns of Authority among the El Shabana of Southern Iraq*. Cambridge, Mass., 1970. Analysis of changing interactions between shaykhs and government officials during periods of Ottoman, British, and Iraqi administration.

Ibn Khaldūn. *The Muqaddimah*. Princeton, 1969. Franz Rosenthal's translation of Ibn Khaldūn's classic, edited and abridged by N. J. Dawood. The best English version of the Arabic original, completed in 1377 CE, includes a brilliant analysis of tribes and their relationship to the state in North Africa.

Lancaster, William. *The Rwala Bedouin Today*. Cambridge, 1981. Contains several chapters examining the adaptations bedouin shaykhs have made to the policies of the nation-states that, since the 1920s, have steadily grown up around them.

Lavie, Smadar. *The Poetics of Military Occupation: Mzeina Allegories of Bedouin Identity under Israeli and Egyptian Rule*. Berkeley, 1990. Engaging account of the strategies members of a Sinai tribe, shaykhs included, use to maintain their own sense of autonomy and bedouin identity.

Musil, Alois. *The Manners and Customs of the Rwala Bedoiuns.* New York, 1928. Widely considered to be the best ethnography ever written on bedouin life; includes extensive treatment of shaykhs and their status among the North Arabian tribes.

Shryock, Andrew J. "The Rise of Nasir al-Nims: A Tribal Commentary on Being and Becoming a Shaykh." *Journal of Anthropological Research* 46.2 (Summer 1990): 153–176. Analysis of the social and political conditions that give rise to the types of shaykhly authority common among Middle Eastern tribespeople.

ANDREW J. SHRYOCK

SHAYKH AL-ISLĀM. Connected with Islamic religious figures, the title Shaykh al-Islām assumed a more precise and formal meaning during the Ottoman period. The title emerged initially in Khurasan in the latter part of the tenth century; it then spread east to India and Muslim areas of China and west into the Middle East. Apparently it was used early both as an honorific title, for ranking Ṣūfīs among others, and to denote formal office; it has been argued, for example, that, in Khurasan by the eleventh century, it denoted individuals holding key offices within the local educational system (Bulliet, 1972, p. 61). The functions connected to the title appear to have varied, however, from region to region in the pre-Ottoman period. Generally speaking, it seems to have connoted religious preeminence and, specifically, training in the Islamic religious law, the *sharīʿah.*

In the Ottoman system, the Shaykh al-Islām (Tk., şeyhülislam) was the chief *muftī,* or jurisconsult, and head of the state hierarchy of *ʿulamā'.* The development of the office and the influence wielded by several of its later occupants, particularly Ali Efendi (1501–1525) and Mehmet Ebüssu'ûd Efendi (1545–1574), must be seen in their historical context, and, specifically, in the desire of the Ottoman sultans to establish authority over the religious establishment. The appointment of the Shaykh al-Islām allowed the Ottoman state to wrest control over the educational system, until then a key source of influence for the religious elite.

As a *muftī,* the holder of the office was chiefly responsible for issuing *fatwā*s (Tk., *fetwā*) or written legal opinions based on Islamic legal tradition. Although these were nonbinding, they carried the considerable moral and, in many instances, political weight of the office from which they were issued. The *fatwā*s of the Shaykh al-Islām related not only to legal and religious issues but to questions of state policy as well; both Ali Efendi and Mehmet Ebüssu'ûd, for example, issued closely read opinions on the waging of war against rivals of the empire. The Shaykh al-Islām also often served as a key adviser to the sultan's court on important political affairs, and, on a number of occasions, holders of the office issued opinions or adopted positions contrary to those of the sultans. It has also been argued that sitting office holders frequently moderated more militant and arbitrary positions on the part of other religious figures and the court. Only later, by the early seventeenth century does the office appear to have lost much of its independence and authority.

By the nineteenth century, the position of the Shaykh al-Islām, like that of other ranking religious officials of the Ottoman system, increasingly fell victim to a series of secularizing and reformist policies. The creation of new legal and educational institutions meant the steady erosion of the Shaykh al-Islām's influence. In November 1922, the office, along with all remaining institutions of the Ottoman sultanate, was abolished by the new Turkish nationalist regime under Mustafa Kemal Atatürk (1881–1938).

[*See also* Ottoman Empire.]

BIBLIOGRAPHY

Bulliet, Richard W. "The Shaikh al-Islam and the Evolution of Islamic Society." *Studia Islamica* 35 (1972): 53–67.

Kramers, J. H. "Shaikh al-Islām." In *Encyclopaedia of Islam,* vol. 7, pp. 275–279. Leiden, 1913–.

Pixley, Michael M. "The Development and Role of the Şeyhülislam in Early Ottoman History." *Journal of the American Oriental Society* 96 (1976): 89–96.

Zilfi, Madeline C. "Shaykh al-Islām." In *The Encyclopedia of Religion,* edited by Mircea Eliade, vol. 13, pp. 229–230. New York, 1987.

MATTHEW S. GORDON

SHAYKHĪYAH. A branch of Twelver Shiism, Shaykhīyah is named after Shaykh Aḥmad al-Aḥsā'ī (1753–1826), a theologian born in Bahrain. Aḥsā'ī had a predisposition for mystical experiences and spiritual visions. He spent fifteen years in Iran, where he won the esteem of many believers, including the Qājār ruler Fatḥ ʿAlī Shāh. But Aḥsā'ī was eventually anathematized by some *ʿulamā'* (religious scholars) because of his doctrine on the resurrection. He was obliged to retire in Mecca, far from any Shīʿī center of learning. Aḥsā'ī opposed the mainstream of clerical Shiism called Uṣūlīyah. He was influenced by the Akhbārī school (which stresses the importance of the Shīʿī traditions [*akhbār*] coming from the Twelve Imams) and by the theosophical teachings of Mullā Ṣadrā and his disciples. In this doctrine there is an intermediary stage, called *barzakh* or *Hūrqalyā*, between earthly life and celestial spirituality in which the body becomes spirit. The spiritual being's survival in *Hūrqalyā* solves the problem of corporal resurrection after death: only the spiritual corpse remains (as a luminous substance) and is resurrected in a new elemental corpse.

Like the Akhbārīs, the Shaykhīs deny the division of believers in the two categories: *muqallid*s (laymen) and *mujtahid*s (formally trained jurisprudents). According to them, everyone has to understand his faith, and the only accepted religious authority is the Hidden Imam. Thus, leaving *ʿadl* (justice of God) as a mere attribute, the Shaykhīs accept three fundamental principles of Shiism: the unity of God, the prophethood of Muḥammad, and the imamate of ʿAlī and his descendants. To this, they add a "Fourth Pillar" *(rukn-i rābiʿ)*, the vicegerency of the Perfect Shīʿī, also called the *bāb* ("gate"), who, in revelatory meditation, comes into the presence of the Hidden Imam.

Through his visionary experiences, Shaykh Aḥmad al-Aḥsāʾī thought he had received such a mission from the Imam and believed that in each era there is a Nāṭiq Vāḥid (Singular Spokesperson), whose existence is not publicly manifested during Occultation. After the rise of the Bābī doctrine, which took its justification in this theory, the later Shaykhīs tried to minimize the importance of the Fourth Pillar. Aḥsāʾī's disciple, Sayyid Kāẓim Rashtī (d. 1843/44), continued his teaching in Karbala, where he made Shaykhīyah an independent school. Shaykhīs suffered further excommunications, which did not, however, keep the doctrine from spreading in Iran, where there was a climate of exacerbated expectations that the Hidden Imam would appear. Many future Bābīs were Rashtī's disciples, including the Bāb himself. [*See* Bābism.] The later Shaykhīs, starting with Muḥammad Karīm Khān Kirmānī (d. 1871), established in the Iranian town of Kerman, had good relations with the ruling dynasty and emphasized their attachment to orthodox Shiism. Nevertheless, the opposition of the dominant Uṣūlī *ʿulamāʾ* brought renewed persecution after the Iranian Revolution of 1979. The Shaykhīs' leader, Sarkār Āqā ʿAbd al-Riẕā Khān Ibrāhīmī, who wore the frock of mullahs, but was an agronomist as well as a theologian, was assassinated in the first year of the Islamic Republic. Soon before the beginning of the Iran-Iraq War, his successor, Sayyid ʿAlī Mūsawī Baṣrī, moved the community's headquarters to Basra in Iraq, where it would face new difficulties.

[*See also* Akhbārīyah; Imam.]

BIBLIOGRAPHY

Amanat, Abbas. *Resurrection and Renewal: The Making of the Babi Movement in Iran, 1844–1850*. Ithaca, N.Y., 1989.

Bayat, Mangol. *Mysticism and Dissent: Socioreligious Thought in Qajar Iran*. Syracuse, N.Y., 1982.

Corbin, Henry. *En Islam iranien: Aspects spirituels et philosophiques*, vol. 4, *L'École d'Ispahan, l'École Shaykie, le douzième Imâm*. Paris, 1972.

Corbin, Henry. *Corps spirituel et Terre céleste: De l'Iran mazdéen à l'Iran shīʿite*. 2d ed. Paris, 1979.

YANN RICHARD

SHĪʿĪ ISLAM. [*This entry comprises two articles. The first provides a historical overview of the Shīʿah, the partisans of ʿAlī; the second traces the development of Shīʿī thought in the nineteenth and twentieth centuries.*]

Historical Overview

The term *shīʿah* literally means followers, party, group, associate, partisan, or supporters. Expressing these meanings, *shīʿah* occurs a number of times in the Qurʾān, for example, surahs 19.69, 28.15, and 37.83. Technically the term refers to those Muslims who derive their religious code and spiritual inspiration, after the Prophet, from Muḥammad's descendants, the *ahl al-bayt*. The focal point of Shiism is the source of religious guidance after the Prophet; although the Sunnīs accept it from the *ṣaḥābah* (companions) of the Prophet, the Shīʿīs restrict it to the members of the *ahl al-bayt*. This pivotal point, which distinguishes Shīʿī from Sunnī Islam, is based on two important factors: one sociocultural and the other drawn from the Qurʾānic concept of the exalted and virtuous nature of the prophetic families.

To understand the sociocultural factor we must keep in mind the nature and composition of the Muslim community at Medina under the leadership of the prophet Muḥammad. This community was homogeneous neither in its sociocultural background and traditions nor in political-social institutions. The formation of a religions community, the *ummah*, under a new religious-moral impulse, did not eliminate or drastically change some of the deeply rooted tribal values and traditions. It was therefore natural that some of these tribal inclinations would be reflected in certain aspects of the new religious order.

The two main constituent groups of the *ummah* at the time of the Prophet's death at Medina in 632 were the Arabs of northern and central Arabia, of whom the Quraysh of Mecca was the most dominant tribe, and the people of south Arabian origin, whose two major branches, the Aws and Khazraj, had settled at Medina. The Arabs of north and central Arabia developed along different lines from the southern Arabs of Yemen in character, way of life, profession, and sociopolitical and sociocultural institutions. More important, the two groups differed widely from each other in religious sensibility and feelings. Among the people of the south there was a clear predominence of religious ideas, whereas among the people of the north religious sentiments were not so strong.

This difference in religious sentiments was naturally reflected in patterns of tribal leadership. The chief or shaykh in the north had always been elected on a principle of seniority in age and ability in leadership. There might sometimes be some other considerations, such as nobility and lineal prestige, but in the north these were of little importance. The Arabs in the south, on the other hand, were accustomed to succession in leadership based on hereditary sanctity and divine rights. To this we must also add the nature and character of Islam itself as it appeared in seventh-century Arabia. Islam has been both a religious discipline and a sociopolitical movement. Muḥammad, the messenger of God, was also the founder of the new polity in Medina. The Prophet thus left behind a religious heritage and also a political legacy.

The question of succession to the Prophet thus became involved with the vision of the leadership of the Muslim community, with different approaches to and varying degrees of emphasis on its political and religious aspects. To some it was more political than religious; to others it was more religious than political. The majority of Muḥammad's companions, with their north Arabian background, conceived the function of his successor in terms of safeguarding the community's political character and of propagating the message of Islam beyond Arabia. Some others, mainly but not solely of south Arabian origin, however small in number, conceived the succession in terms of Muḥammad's spiritual authority. They believed that the divine guidance had to continue through his successors, who should combine in themselves the Prophet's religious as well as temporal functions. Such leaders were the Imams, who inherited the mantle of the Prophet in providing the revealed guidance for the creation of the Islamic order.

Besides these sociocultural traditions, another factor, derived from the Qur'ānic concept of the exalted position of the prophetic families, also played a significant role in defining the succession. The Qur'ān describes the prophets as having been particularly concerned with ensuring that the special favor of God bestowed on them for the guidance of people be maintained in their families and be inherited by their descendants. Thus, Abraham prays to God to continue God's guidance and special favor in his descendants so that the divine purposes would continue to be fulfilled. Prophetic progeny is expressed in the Qur'ān in several places through four key terms: *dhurrīyah* ("direct descendant"), *āl* ("offspring"), *ahl* ("progeny"), and *qurbā* ("nearest of kin"). When mentioned in relation to the Prophet, the commentators of the Qur'ān have interpreted these terms as referring to Muḥammad's nearest of kin: ʿAlī, his cousin and son-in-law, Fāṭimah, his daughter; and Ḥasan and Ḥusayn, their sons. The Shīʿīs also extend the status of *ahl al-bayt* to the descendants of Ḥasan and Ḥusayn.

Rāshidūn Period. Taking into account the above-mentioned factors the origin of the Shīʿī movement can be traced to the Medinan period of the Prophet's life. Some prominent companions saw the Prophet's cousin ʿAlī ibn Abī Ṭālib as his *waṣī* (legatee) and the Imam to lead the community after him. But soon after the death of the prophet, the beginning of the Rāshidūn period (632–661), this special regard for ʿAlī found an unequivocal expression when he was denied the leadership of the community. The supporters of ʿAlī thus constituted the first nucleus of the Shīʿah. [*See the biography of ʿAlī ibn Abī Ṭālib.*]

However, after the initial defeat of ʿAlī's supporters and his own recognition of Abū Bakr's administration six months later, the circumstances were such that Shīʿī tendencies lost most of their open and active manifestations. The period of the caliphates of Abū Bakr and his successor, ʿUmar (r. 632–644), is thus one of comparative dormancy in the history of Shiism. After the death of ʿUmar, Shīʿī feelings once again found expression in the protest made by ʿAlī's supporters when ʿUthmān was declared the third caliph. It must be noted that the office was first offered to ʿAlī on the condition that he follow the precedents established by the first two caliphs, which he stringently refused and ʿUthmān readily accepted. This refusal of ʿAlī forms the earliest theoretical point which ultimately gave rise to the later development of two different schools of law under the titles of Shīᶜī and Sunnī, the former including the Ithnā ᶜAsharīyah, Ismāᶜīlīyah, and Zaydīyah, the latter comprising the Ḥanafī, Mālikī, Shāfiᶜī, and Hanbalī. If ideological differences between the two schools date back to the election of Abū Bakr, the differences in legal matters, at least theoretically, must be dated from ᶜAlī's refusal to follow the precedents of the first two caliphs. This refusal thus serves as a cornerstone in the development of Shīᶜī legal thought, although, like the Sunnī legal system, it took a long time to be fully distinguishable. [*See* Law, *article on* Shīᶜī Schools of Law.]

Unlike the first two caliphs, ᶜUthmān belonged to the powerful clan of the Umayyads which, in his accession, found an opportunity to regain its past political importance, which it had lost after the emergence of Islam. Within a few years of ᶜUthmān's accession the Umayyad claimed among themselves all the positions of power and advantage and appropriated to themselves the immense wealth of the empire at the expense of the masses. The resulting disequilibrium in the economic and social structure naturally aroused the resentment of various sections of the population and provided ample combustible material for an explosion. The simmering discontent exploded into violent revolt and the caliph was killed by the unruly mob in 656. It is important to note that the hatred against ᶜUthmān and the support of ᶜAlī grew side by side. The pious opposition to the Umayyad aristocracy became eagerly involved with the partisanship for ᶜAlī. He was thus forced by the majority of the people to accept the caliphate, which he did with great reluctance. ᶜAlī's accession was, however, strongly resisted by the Umayyads, represented by Muᶜāwiyah and some of the companions who were aspiring for the caliphate for themselves. This resulted in the first civil wars in Islam and ultimately led to ᶜAlī's assassination in 661.

The sixteen-year period beginning with the caliphate of ᶜUthmān and ending with the assassination of ᶜAlī represents a marked difference from the preceding period in the development of Shiism in many ways. First, it created an atmosphere which encouraged the Shīᶜī tendencies to become more evident and conspicuous. Second, the events which took place gave an active and sometimes violent character to the hitherto inactive Shīᶜī movement. Finally, the circumstances that prevailed involved the Shīᶜī outlook, for the first time, in a number of political, geographical, and economic considerations fused together. This fusion not only provided a new sphere of activity for the Shīᶜī movement, but also widened its circle of influence to those who needed an outlet for their political grievances, especially against the Umayyad aristocracy and Syrian domination. The emergence of the political Shīᶜah at this stage is thus characterized both by the increase in its influence and numbers and by its sudden and rapid growth thereafter.

Umayyad and ᶜAbbāsid Periods. If the Rāshidūn period provided Shiism with its theoretical foundation, the Umayyad period (661–750) proved to be decisive in the formulation of its attitudes, whereas the ᶜAbbāsid era (750–945) witnessed consolidation of the Shīᶜī identity.

During the first twenty years of Umayyad rule under Muᶜāwiyah, Ḥasan, the elder son of ᶜAlī, who was acclaimed caliph by the overwhelming majority of the Muslims, was forced to abdicate. Some of the ardent supporters of the Shīᶜī cause were ruthlessly executed, ᶜAlī was cursed from pulpits all over the empire as an official duty proclaimed by the governors, and the Shīᶜīs were kept in a state of extreme oppression and terror. But the single event which set the seal on the nature of official Shiism was the martyrdom of Ḥusayn in 681 at Karbala. Ḥusayn, the only surviving grandson of the Prophet and the center of Shīᶜī aspirations, along with eighteen male members of his family and many companions, was brutally killed, and the women and children of his caravan were made captives to be humiliated in the markets and courts of Kufa and Damascus.

The tragedy of Karbala became the most effective agent in the propagation and spread of Shiism. It added to Shīᶜī Islam an element of passion, which renders human psychology more receptive to doctrine than anything else. Henceforth the element of passion in expressing the love (*walāyah*) for *ahl al-bayt* became a characteristic feature of Shiism. [*See* Walāyah.] Within a year the tragedy gave rise to a movement known as Tawwābūn (Penitents), three thousand of whom sacrificed their lives fighting the overwhelming force of the Umayyads as a way of repenting for their inability to help Ḥusayn in his hour of trial. Since this passionate act of self-sacrifice took place without a leader from among the *ahl al-bayt*, it gave a new turn to the mode and nature of the Shīᶜī movement, making it an independent and self-sustaining undertaking. [*See* Karbala; Martyrdom; *and the biography of Ḥusayn ibn ᶜAlī.*]

The death of Ḥusayn and the quiescent attitude of his only surviving son, ᶜAlī Zayn al-ᶜĀbidīn, however, marks the first conflict over the leadership of the followers of the *ahl al-bayt,* resulting in their division into various groups. The Shīʿīs in Kufa, especially the *mawālī,* the non-Arabs and the downtrodden masses, wanted an active movement which could relieve them from the oppressive rule of the Syrians. Mukhtār ibn Abī ʿUbaydah al-Thaqafī, a Shīʿī activist who failed to obtain the support of Ḥusayn's son, started projecting ʿAlī's third son, Muḥammad ibn al-Ḥanafīyah, born of a Ḥanafī woman, as the Mahdi. Confused and frustrated, the Shīʿīs saw a ray of hope in the messianic role propagated by Mukhtār for Ibn al-Ḥanafīyah and followed him as their Imam-Mahdi, abandoning Zayn al-ʿĀbidīn. Mukhtār's uprising was put down in 686 and Mukhtār himself was killed, but the propaganda on behalf of Ibn al-Ḥanafīyah continued, and when the latter died in 700 a group of his followers, known as Kaysānīyah, believed that he had not died but had gone into occultation and could return. Mukhtār and the followers of Ibn al-Ḥanafīyah were thus the first to introduce two key ideas that were henceforth to be of great importance in the development of Shīʿī thought; the idea of the Mahdi and the concepts of *ghaybah* (occultation) and *rajʿah* (return).

After Mukhtār's uprising, the first ʿAlid of the Ḥusaynid line who rose against the Umayyad was Zayd, the second son of Zayn al-ʿĀbidīn. Zayd and his followers wanted no quiescent or Hidden Imam, like al-Bāqir and Ibn al-Ḥanafīyah. The imam, in their eyes, although he had to be a descendant of ʿAlī and Fāṭimah, could not claim a allegiance unless he asserted his imamate publicly and, if necessary, fought for it. Zayd's activist policy toward the imamate earned him the support of the majority of the Shīʿī groups, his adoption of the Muʿtazilah's doctrines secured him their support, and his acceptance of the legitimacy of the first two caliphs gained him the full sympathy of the traditionist circles. Zayd's revolt, however, was unsuccessful. He and many of his followers were killed in 740, and his son Yaḥyā, who continued his father's activities for three years, met the same fate in 743.

After the collapse of Zayd's revolt, no serious Shīʿī uprising took place during the Umayyad period except that of the ʿAbbāsids, which began as a manifestation of the Shīʿī cause. The agents of the ʿAbbāsids called the people to rise in the name of an imam to be chosen from among the *ahl al-bayt.* To the extremists of the Kaysānīyah, the followers of Ibn al-Ḥanafīyah and his son Abū Hāshim, the activists of the Zaydīyah, and the other groups of the Shīʿah, this implied an ʿAlid, and they wholeheartedly supported the ʿAbbāsids. The ʿAbbāsids thus succeeded in overthrowing the Umayyad regime. Once in power, they realized that the Shīʿīs would not accept them as legitimate rulers, so they turned toward the *ahl al-ḥadīth* for their religious support and began to persecute the Shīʿīs. The series of Zaydī revolts, particularly among ʿAlids of the Ḥasanid line, which had begun toward the end of the Umayyad era, continued into the ʿAbbāsid period. Muḥammad al-Nafs al-Zakīyah, a great-grandson of Ḥasan who had long coveted the role of Mahdi for himself, rose against the ʿAbbāsids. However, he and his brother Ibrāhīm were defeated and killed in 762. Some of al-Nafs al-Zakīyah's followers believed that he was not dead but went into occultation and would return.

With these movements in the formative phase of Shiism, three major trends of thought—activism, extremism, and legitimism—dominated the Shīʿī perception of the imamate. For the early period, however, it is difficult to identify well-organized groups representing each of these trends, a there was considerable fusion among these ideas. The activists, for example, sometimes adopted extremist ideas, as was the case with the Kaysānīyah. The extremists, known as *ghulāt* (exaggerators) because of their ascription of divinity to the Imams, often resorted to activist methods. It is, however, important to note that the *ghulāt,* identified as Shīʿīs by Sunnī heresiographers, remained a minority that was never accepted by the main body of the Shīʿīs, and their Imams and were vehemently condemned and cursed by them. In the course of history, however, extremists and other small branches died out of were merged into the three main branches which have survived today.

The Zaydīyah, followers of Zayd ibn ʿAlī ibn al-Ḥusayn, are mainly in Yemen and also in small numbers in Iraq and some parts of Africa. They represent the activist groups of the early Shīʿah, as Zayd believed that the Imam ought to be a ruler of the state and therefore must fight for his rights. [*See* Zaydīyah.]

The Ismāʿīlīyah, named after Ismāʿīl, the eldest son of Imam Jaʿfar al-Ṣādiq, who predeceased his father, declared Ismāʿīl's son Muḥammad as their seventh Imam (instead of following Jaʿfar's second son, Mūsa al-Kāẓim). The Ismāʿīlīyah are also known as the Bāṭinīyah, that is, those who maintained the central role of the esoteric aspects of Islamic revelation in their religious system. Ismāʿīlīs rose to great political and religious prominence at times and founded the Fāṭimid Empire (909–1171). [*See* Ismāʿīlīyah.]

The majority of the Shīʿīs belong to the Twelvers, the Ithnā ʿAsharīyah. Their theological position is regarded as relatively moderate. They represent the legitimist or central body of the Shīʿīs who believe in twelve Imams beginning from ʿAlī as the first Imam followed by his two sons, Ḥasan and and Ḥusayn, as the second and the third Imams, respectively. After Ḥusayn, according to the Twelver Shīʿīs, the imamate remained with his descendants until it reached the twelfth Imam, Muḥammad al-Mahdī, who went into occultation to return at the end of time as the messianic Imam to restore justice and equity on earth. [*See* Ithnā ʿAsharīyah.]

The consolidation of the Ithnā ʿAsharī position was owed to the efforts of Imam Jaʿfar al-Ṣādiq, the sixth Imam of the quiescent Ḥusaynid branch, who expounded his theory of the imamate based on *naṣṣ*, that is, by explicit designation by the previous Imam, and the special knowledge of religion coming down in the family from generation to generation. With the efforts of Jaʿfar, the quiescent line of the Ḥusaynid Imams once again achieved prominance, which it had lost after the death of Ḥusayn. Jaʿfar was surrounded by a large number of traditionists, theologians, and jurists who played an important role in establishing the Shīʿī legal and theological system. By the time of Jaʿfar's death in 765, the Shīʿīs (later to become the Twelvers) were fully equipped in all branches of religion and had acquired a distinctive character. The remaining six Imams of the Twelvers' line living under the ʿAbbāsids in varying circumstances further strengthened the Imāmī Shiism until the twelfth Imam, Muḥammad al-Mahdī, went into occultation.

Būyid Period. The Būyids (945–1055) accorded the Shīʿīs the most favorable conditions for elaboration and standardization of their tenets. In this period compilation of the major collections of Shīʿī *ḥadīth* and formulation of Shīʿī law took place. This elaboration began with Muḥammad ibn Yaʿqūb al-Kulaynī (d. 490), author of the monumental *Uṣūl al-kāfī*, and was followed by such figures as Ibn Babuyah, also called Shaykh al-Ṣadūq (d. 991), Shaykh al-Mufīd (d. 1022), and Shaykh al-Ṭā'ifah, or Muḥammad ibn al-Ḥasan al-Ṭūsi (d. 1067), with whom the principle doctrinal works of Shīʿī theology and religious sciences were finally established. This was also the period of a number of other renowned Shīʿī scholars, such as al-Sharīf al-Raḍī (d. 1015), who compiled the sermons and sayings of ʿAlī, and his brother, Murtaḍā ʿĀlam al-Hudā (d. 1044).

These intellectual activities continued after the fall of the Būyids through such Shīʿī scholars as Faḍl al-Ṭabarsī (d. 1153), known for his monumental Qur'ānic commentary; Raḍī al-Dīn ʿAlī ibn al-Ṭā'ūs (d. 1266), theologian and gnostic; Naṣīr al-Dīn al-Ṭūsī (d. 1273); ʿAllamah Ḥillī (d. 1326); and Ḥaydar al-Āmulī (d. after 1385), who set a new trend of systematic rational theology.

It was also in the Būyid period that two popular Shīʿī commemorations were instituted in Baghdad: the martyrdom of Imam Ḥusayn on 10 Muḥarram, which was observed with great religious fervor and zeal; and the festival of Ghadīr al-Khumm, commemorating the Prophet's nomination of ʿAlī as his successor at Ghadir al-Khumm on 18 Dhu al-Ḥijjah. It was also during this period that public mourning ceremonies for Ḥusayn were initiated, shrines were built for the Imams, and the custom of pilgrimage to these shrines was more popularly established. [*See* Shrine; Ziyārah.]

In short, by the close of the Būyid era Shiism's basic formulations were completed, leaving to the following periods only further elaborations, interpretations, rationalizations, and certain adaptations and additions. The list of the scholars who immensely enriched Shīʿī literature in the past eight hundred years in all branches of learning, especially in philosophy, theology, and law during the Mongol, Ṣafavid, and Qājār periods, is too long to be enumerated here. However, mention must be made of such great figures of the Ṣafavid period as Mīr Dāmād (d. 1631) and Mullā Ṣadrā (d. 1640), masters of metaphysics with whom Islamic philosophy reached a new peak; Bahā' al-Dīn al-ʿĀmilī, theologian and mathematician; and finally the two Majlisīs, the second, Muḥammad Baqir, being the author of the most voluminous compendium of the Shīʿī sciences, the *Biḥār al-anwār*. [*See* Ṣafavid Dynasty; Qājār Dynasty; *and the biography of Majlisī.*]

Although Ithna ʿAsharī Shiism attained its final position under the Būyids who ruled over Baghdad and Iran, the Ismāʿīlīyah and the Zaydīyah also consolidated their doctrinal positions almost in the same period. The Ismāʿīlīs controlled Egypt, southern Syria, much of North Africa, and the Hejaz, and the Zaydīs established their rule in northern Iran and Yemen. This political supermacy provided the Ismāʿīlīyah and the Zaydīyah with opportunities to elaborate and standardize their doctrinal positions. Thus by the end of the tenth century, all the three branches of Shiism, were established firmly enough to withstand the vicissitudes of history and the strains and stresses of the sectarian role to which they were pushed by the Sunnī majority.

[*See also* Imam; Imāmah; Mahdi.]

BIBLIOGRAPHY

Classic histories such as Muḥammad ibn Jarīr al-Ṭabarī's *Tārīkh al-rusul wa-al-mlulk* (2d ed., 10 vols., Cairo, 1979), Aḥmad ibn Abī Yaʿqub Yaʿqūbī's *Tārīkh al-Yaʿqūbī* (2 vols., Beirut, 1980), and Abū Ḥanīfah Aḥmad ibn Dāwūd Dīnawarī's *Al-akhbār al-ṭiwāl*, edited by ʿAbd al-Munʿim ʿĀmir (Cairo, 1960) give historical accounts of the political events and religious thought of the first three centuries of Islam. Some heresiographical works of both the Shīʿīs and the Sunnīs are Abū al-Ḥasan ʿAlī ibn Ismāʿīl Ashʿarī's *Maqālāt al-Islāmīyīn wa-ikhtilāf al-muṣallīn*, edited by Muḥammad Muḥyī al-Dīn ʿAbd al-Ḥamīd (2d rev. ed., Cairo, 1969), Muḥammad ibn ʿAbd al-Karīm Shahrastānī's *Al-milal wa-an niḥal*, edited by Muḥammad Sayyid Kīlānī (2 vols., Beirut, 1982), and al-Ḥasan ibn Mūsā Nawbakhtī's *Firaq al-Shīʿah* (2d ed., Beirut, 1984); the first two give the Sunnī account and the third the Shīʿī view of various Shīʿī sects which emerged in the first two centuries of Islam. Theological and creedal works of the Shīʿīs include Shaykh Ṣadūq ibn Bābawayh al-Qummī's *Risālat al-Iʿtiqād* (translated by A. A. A. Fyzee as *A Shīʿite Creed*, London, 1942), Ḥasan ibn Yūsuf al-Ḥillī's *Al-Bāb al-Hādī ʿAshar* (translated by W. M. Miller, London, 1928), Muḥammad Ḥusayn Ṭabāṭabāʾī's *Shīʿah dar Islām* (edited and translated by Seyyed Hossein Nasr as *Shīʿite Islam*, Albany, N.Y., 1975); the first two provide the most authentic Shīʿī creed by scholars of the fourth/tenth century and the last a philosophical exposition by a modern scholar. Two modern studies are my *Origins and Early Development of Shīʿa Islam* (London, 1979), which examines the development of Shīʿī thought in historical perspective until the time of Imam Jaʿfar; and Moojan Momen's *An Introduction to Shīʿī Islam: The History and Doctrines of Twelver Shīʿism* (New Haven, 1985), which mainly gives political and dynastic history until modern times.

SYED HUSAIN M. JAFRI

Modern Shīʿī Thought

The intellectual dimension of Shiism has a long and varied history that includes political, juridical, theological, philosophical, and mystical traditions. Although practically all these branches of Shīʿī learning have continued and flourished to the present time, it is only the political dimension of Shiism that has significantly responded to the issues and problems posed by modernity. The metaphysics of "reason" and "progress," defining the claims of "modernity" on its history, came into direct and radical conflict with the Islamic metaphysics that has doctrinally sustained and legitimized Shiism as a world religion. As a result, even the nonpolitical dimensions of Shiism, for example its juridical and philosophical traditions, responded to modernity with a fire and tenacity indicative of their political and not necessarily juridical or epistemological crisis. Consequently, such issues in Shīʿī juridical and philosophical discourses that do not address their problems in and with modernity remain principally premodern in the terms and dispositions of their engagement. In addressing the political dimension of modern Shīʿī thought, this article thus examines such points of contact and dialogue between Shiism and modernity that have been instrumental in placing it in its contemporary history.

Although the origins of modern Shīʿī political thought can be traced back to the sixteenth century and the rise of the Ṣafavid Empire (Corbin, 1971; Arjomand, 1984), it was not until well into the nineteenth century that the major characteristics of a distinctly Shīʿī political imagination were noticed (see Arjomand, 1984). In fact, a fuller understanding of modern Shīʿī political thought is possible only through a careful tracing of some salient features of Shiism from its earliest roots in the time of Muḥammad (570–632), following the problem of succession to his authority (see Jafri, 1979; Madelung, 1982, 1988; Dabashi, 1989) and particularly after the so-called Ghaybah period (see Modarressi, 1993), to the crucial, even revolutionary, doctrinal changes in modern Shīʿī political dispositions (see Arjomand, "Ideological Revolution in Shīʿīsm," in Arjomand, 1988, pp. 178–209). In fact, radical political change has been a hallmark of Shiism throughout its history (see Lewis, 1967; Arjomand, 1984; Moosa, 1988; Daftari, 1990; Momen, 1985, pp. 1–104).

The centrality of the first and the third Shīʿī Imams, ʿAlī and Ḥusayn, in resuscitating Shīʿī political sentiments are noteworthy. The figure of Ḥusayn in particular has been the subject of much imaginative recreation for specifically political purposes (see *Al-serat*, vol. 12, 1986). The sermons, letters, and sayings attributed to ʿAlī and collected as *Nahj al-balāghah* have also been the subjects of much creative repoliticization (see Sachedina, 1988; English translation of *Nahj al-balāghah*, 1984). The lives of other Shīʿī Imams (see al-Mufīd, 1981; see also Chittick, 1981) have also been the subject of contemporary political renarration. The concept of *ghaybah* (occultation, or "disappearance," of the last Shīʿī Imam) has proven equally conducive to repeated political uses (see Sachedina, 1981). But the Ṣafavid establishment of Shiism as the official state ideology is a defining point in the long and arduous history of this small but significant branch of Islam.

The rapid and effective universalization of Shiism during the Ṣafavid period gave historical expression to the potentialities of the faith, creating what Weber called a world religion (Weber, 1920). The theological, juridical, philosophical, mystical, and literary imagination coalesced during the Ṣafavid period to rejuvenate earlier traits in the Shīʿī sacred imagination.

The whole categorical validity of modern Shīʿī political thought can be understood as the dialogical outcome of the encounter between Shīʿī political, therefore, juridical and philosophical, sensibilities and institutions, on one hand, and the preeminence of such modern forces as rationalism, secularism, constitutional democracy, socialism, and nationalism, on the other. The history of modern Shīʿī political thought is the history of premodern Shīʿī sensibilities and institutions negotiating their relevance and continued validity against the onslaught of modernity (see Enayat, 1982).

Despite the political demise of Shiism after the fall of the Ṣafavids in the eighteenth century, its institutional dimensions had grown so large that it soon became reincarnated in the Qājār body-politic. In both political and doctrinal institutions—from palaces to bazaars and *madrasahs*—Shiism stretched its ideological domains over a vast and pervasive political culture.

As an ideology, Shiism was the most important aspect of Qājār political legitimacy. The Qājār monarchs took full advantage of Shiism in buttressing the ideological foundation of their reign (see Algar, 1969; see also Algar, in Keddie, 1972). By the nineteenth century, the institution of the *ʿulamāʾ* had been established on solid social grounds (see Lambton, 1956; Keddie, 1962 and 1972; Algar, 1969; Cole, in Keddie, 1983; Modarressi, 1984). Rooted in both their juridical learning and popular support (see Amanat, "In Between the Madrasa and the Marketplace: The Designation of Clerical Leadership in Modern Shiʿism," in Arjomand, 1988, pp. 98–132), the *ʿulamāʾ* solidly institutionalized their power of self-legitimation and had a major legitimizing authority in relation to the Qājār dynasty.

The doctrinal legitimacy of the authority of the *ʿulamāʾ* as the principal constitutional cornerstone of modern Shīʿī political thought was challenged by internal strife over the problematic of Akhbārīyah. Amir Arjomand (1984, chap. 5) has offered a solid sociological explanation for the rise of an autonomous clerical class in the Ṣafavid period. But Akhbārīyah, a literalist movement that considerably limited the political power of the *ʿulamāʾ*, lasted until the Constitutional Revolution of 1906–1911 in Iran. Having doctrinally defeated Akhbārī literalism, the Uṣūlī hermeneutics, which put much interpretative power at the disposal of the *ʿulamāʾ*, became the doctrinal basis of *ijtihād* and its practitioners, the *mujtahids*. The ultimate triumph of Uṣūlīyah must thus be considered the institutional success of a politically conscious *ʿulamāʾ*, which had released itself from the fetters of literalist conservatism. [*See* Akhbārīyah; Uṣūlīyah.]

Beyond its institutional bases in the formation of an Uṣūlī-oriented *ʿulamāʾ*, modern Shīʿī political thought emerged in conscious or tacit responses to historical events entirely outside the purview of Shīʿī political culture. Arjomand has warned against the confusion of Shīʿī political culture with the political culture of the Shīʿīs (1988, pp. 10–11). The historically evolving political culture surrounding a nominal or practicing Shīʿī has been a multicultural and multifaceted phenomenon entirely irreducible to particular tenets of Shiism. In fact, "Shiism" is an essentializing term put forward at considerable risk to historical realities. In a permanent dialogical engagement with historical forces beyond their control, the changing sensibilities of Shīʿī authorities have constantly redefined the received symbolics of their faith. The perception of the central drama of Shīʿī faith, the martyrdom of the third Imam, Ḥusayn, has moved from a revolutionary episode to a quietist act of piety only to emerge yet again as a radical event in the changing configuration of the Shīʿī collective imagination. The specific components of that collective imagination have historically responded to political and cultural forces of diverse origin and destination. In the context of specific communities to the east of the Mediterranean world, Shīʿī doctrines, symbolics, sensibilities, and institutions have emerged in interaction with religious, cultural, social, and political forces of Arab, Iranian, Indian, and Turkish origins. Historical communities consciously tracing themselves to such designations as Arab, Iranian, and so forth have been the material space on which Shīʿī doctrines, symbolics, and institutions have been articulated. In both premodern and modern circumstances, Shīʿī political thought has thus been produced in dialogical responses to external material forces.

Having had its institutional bases consolidated in the self-conscious formations of the *ʿulamāʾ*, and having been squarely based on the ideological rhetoric of Uṣūlī hermeneutics, Shīʿī political thought entered the Qājār phase with its classical medieval baggage. In dialogue with Arabic, Persian, Greek, Indian, and other conceptions of legitimate authority, Shīʿī political thought continued in its traditional genre of royal advice to the Qājār princes, thus legitimizing both the princes and the *ʿulamāʾ*. One can detect a gradual increase in the power and authority of the *ʿulamāʾ* during the Qājār period, judged by colorful accounts of prominent clerics given in Tunikābunī's *Qiṣaṣ al-ʿulamāʾ* (for a sample of these accounts, see Arjomand, 1988, chap. 14). It is evident that the relation of power between the political and the religious establishment was a constant struggle of one-upsmanship. The Qājār kings noted a worthy rival in such prominent clerics as Mullā Aḥmad Narāqī and Ḥājjī Sayyid Muḥammad Bāqir Shaftī who matched their wealth with their *sahm-i imām* revenues and their army with their devoted followers. In addition, the *ʿulamāʾ* had the exclusive historical access to the legitimizing rhetorics of the Qur'ān, and claim to the metaphysical presence of God on their side. The dialogical relationship between the Qājār kings and the Shīʿī *ʿulamāʾ* resulted in a clear recognition on the part of the clergy that they were potentially capable of mobilizing considerable political power.

Mullā Aḥmad Narāqī is a crucial figure in the emerging power of the *ʿulamāʾ* during the Qājār period (see Dabashi, in Nasr et al., eds., 1989). He persuasively resuscitated the early Imāmī traditions that claimed sweeping authority of the *ʿulamāʾ* as the legitimate successors of the Prophet. Later, in the course of the 1979 Islamic Revolution in Iran, the ideas of Narāqī would be further elaborated on by Ayatollah Khomeini.

The emerging power of the *ʿulamāʾ* in the Qājār period should not be considered a unilateral phenomenon without resistance and opposition from the political establishment. As evident, for example, from a correspondence between Ḥājj Mullā ʿAlī Kanī and Mīrzā ʿAbd al-Vahhāb Khān ʿĀṣif al-Dawlah (see a translation of this correspondence in Arjomand, 1988, chap. 15), the political establishment was particularly resentful of the rising power of the *ʿulamāʾ* and put up a stiff resistance to it. There are also reports of severe punishments publicly executed against particularly disobedient *ʿulamāʾ* (Qūchānī, 1983).

The institutional and ideological consolidation of the *ʿulamāʾ* during the nineteenth century, as well as their rising political power, were put to a crucial test during the so-called Tobacco Revolt of 1891–1892. But the greatest challenge to both the clerical and the monarchical authority, challenging the very foundation of their legitimate claim to authority appeared in the form of the most radical millenarian Shīʿī movement of the nineteenth century: the Bābī movement led by Sayyid ʿAlī Muḥammad Shīrāzī (1819–1850). Bringing the revolutionary potentials of a crucial Shīʿī tenet to radical fruition, the Bābī movement was the last and most effective social protest launched from within the medieval terms of the Shīʿī political imagination (Amanat, 1989). [*See* Bābism.]

Both the Bābī movement and the Tobacco Revolt fade in comparison, however, to the challenge of the Constitutional Revolution of 1906–1911, in the course of which Shīʿī political thought entered its modern phase. The ambivalence of the clerical class in regard to the Constitutional Revolution marks the conflicting impact of patently secular ideas on the modern turn of Shīʿī political thought. From the late eighteenth century onward there was a gradual rise of a patently secular political discourse that added momentum and change to the classical repertoire of the Arabic, Iranian, Indian, and Turkish political cultures. The construction of and encounter with the idea of "The West," which was concomitant with the rise of European colonialism, added a new, mightily potent, ingredient to these political cultures. In Iran proper, where Shīʿī political thought had its deepest and widest roots, the encounter with the colonial powers generated an efflorescence of secular ideas. The catastrophic results of the Russo-Iranian Wars of 1804–1824, the unanticipated consequences of the dispatch of Iranian students to Europe by ʿAbbās Mīrzā (1787–1833), the presence and rivalry of colonial officers from England and France, the introduction of the printing machine for mass publication, a massive translation movement from European literary and historical sources, publication of newspapers and journals, and, ultimately, the formation of a consciously nationalist political discourse in prose and poetry were among the chief institutional and ideological forces that precipitated the dawn of a new secular imagination in the Iranian political culture. The Shīʿī religious establishment was once again put in a position to respond to a historical event beyond its control. some Shīʿī *ʿulamāʾ* responded positively to the new movement, some negatively, and very few had a clear idea what precisely a constitutional government entailed for the social, cultural, political, and ultimately religious future of the nation. As early as the mid-1880s, Shīʿī men of learning were conscious of and concerned about the rising tide of secularism in the former Ottoman domains. When in 1885 Mīrzā Muḥammad Ḥusayn Farāhānī traveled to the Ottoman Empire, he noted with horror and disgust the changes in the Turks from Islamic habits to European manners: "They [i.e., the Turks] have abolished the rules of Islam [*dīn-e aḥmadī*] and made imperfect civil law in the manner of the Europeans. . . . They act with no regard for this world or the next. Of Islam, there is only the name and nothing more. The customs and ceremonies which they have gradually learned completely from the Europeans are the ways of irreligion and indifference about [matters of] doctrine and religious practice" (Farāhānī, 1990, p. 129).

The two leading religious leaders of Tehran, Ayatollahs Sayyid Muḥammad Ṭabāṭabā'ī (1841–1920) and Sayyid ʿAbd Allāh Bihbahānī (d. 1871), fully participated in the revolutionary mobilization launched toward the foundation of a constitutional monarchy. The active participation of proconstitutional clerics in the revolutionary event should not, however, lead to the designation of the event as a "religious revolution." As Arjomand has noted (1988, p. 15), the active exaggeration of the role of the *ʿulamā'* by such Orientalist historians as Ann Lambton, Nikki Keddie, and Hamid Algar has led to the erroneous assumption that not only did the Shī'ī clergy lead the Constitutional Revolution but did so from within traditional Shī'ī political thought. The view of such Iranian historians as Aḥmad Kasravī, Faraydūn Ādamīyat, A. H. Ḥā'irī, ʿAbd al-Karīn Lāhījī, and Mangol Bayat, who have had a much more extensive access to, and critical intimacy with, the primary sources, reveals a more paradoxical and limited role for the Shī'ī clergy. Indeed, the dominant Orientalist view is a revisionist reading of the Constitutional Revolution very much in line with the exaggeration of the role of Islam in the entire course of Middle Eastern history, a view which the clerical establishment finds conducive to its own class interests. (For the dominant Orientalist view, see Lambton, 1956 and 1970; Keddie, 1962 and 1972; and Algar, 1969. For an alternative view of Iranian historians, see Kirmānī, 1983; Ādamīyat, 1976; Hairi, 1977; Arjomand, 1981; Lāhījī, in Arjomand, 1988; Kasravī, 1984; Bayat, 1991; Fashāhī, 1975; Ashraf, 1980; Maḥmūd, 1974.)

A typical example of a staunchly anticonstitutional attitude is to be found in Shaykh Faẓlullāh Nūrī (1843–1909), who gave full and powerful expression to an antimodern reading of juridical Shiism. Nūrī's opposition to constitutionalism was primarily on legal grounds, rejecting the postulation of a political law that, *ipso facto*, subverted the authority of Shī'ī law. Stripped of the community of its legal tradition, Nūrī thought, Shiism would dwindle into pale reminiscences of a benign religious culture. In brilliant manifestos, written with a remarkable penchant for political rhetoric, Nūrī refuted the legal and ideological validity of a constitutional government in a Shī'ī community. *Kitāb tadhkirat al-ghāfil va irshād al-jāhil* (Book of Admonition to the Heedless and Guidance for the Ignorant) was one such treatise in which Nūrī gave full expression to his rhetorical power in opposing the constitutional government. "Imposing man-made law," he asserted, "is contrary to Islam, and legislation is the prerogative of a Messenger. It is for this reason that every time a messenger appeared, it was to bring a law" (see Arjomand, 1988, p. 355). [*See the biography of Nūrī.*]

A contemporary of Nūrī, ʿAbd al-ʿAẓīm ʿImād al-ʿUlamā' Khalkhālī, however, represents precisely the opposite view of a Shī'ī cleric fully in support of the constitutional government. In Khalkhālī's treatise one sees as much reference to and reliance on a modernist reading of the Shī'ī canonical sources as on abstract notions of reason and progress, thus giving full expression to the rising force of political modernism in Iran. Khalkhālī wrote late in 1907, "Today all European states have established constitutions and treat their nations in accordance with them. Perhaps it can be said that, today, the Europeans are better and more intelligent than we Iranians. If this Constitutionalism is nonsense and useless, why is it that they have adopted it? And if it be beneficial, why should the Iranians abandon it?" (see Arjomand, 1988, p. 340).

As constitutionalism became a key catalyst of Shī'ī political consciousness, leading religious authorities tried to reconcile between their understanding of what constitutionalism was and their selective remembrance of their received faith. Shaykh Mīrzā Muḥammad Ḥusayn Nā'īnī (1860–1936) wrote his famous tract on constitutionalism under such circumstances. *Tanbīh al-ummah va tanzīh al-millah* (Guidance of the Public and Edification of the Nation) was written (in 1909, the year of the public hanging of Nūrī) in a deliberate attempt to propagate the course of the constitutionalist government with particular attention to its compatibility to the Shī'ī faith. This tract reveals Nā'īnī's deep concerns for the future of the political culture and institutions in Iran. Nā'īnī was equally active in the 1920s uprising in Iraq, giving both ideological and political momentum to the rising revolutionary sensibilities of the reconstructed Shiism. Detectable in Nā'īnī's tract is a frustration with depoliticized or compromised Shiism. In his idea dwell one of the earliest and most successful syncratic discourses, wedding elements of Shīᶜī political culture and the rising force of constitutional modernism. [*See the biography of Nāᶜīnī.*]

A careful reading of such conflicting ideas as those of Nūrī, Khalkhālī, and Nāᶜīnī reveals that the Shīᶜī authorities had a much more ambiguous relationship toward constitutionalism than hitherto assumed. Indeed, the work of such scholars as Kasravī, Ādamīyat, Ḥā'irī, Arjomand, Lāhījī, and Bayat points out that the clerical establishment entered into a historical negotiation with the secular revolutionaries, and in return for their support of the constitutional government they secured a prominent position for themselves in the institutional fabric of that constitution (see, in particular, Lāhījī, in Arjomand, 1988, chap. 6).

After the tumultuous period of the constitutional movement, the 1910s was a decade of relative political inaction for Shīᶜī clerics. The occupation of northern Iran by the Russians did not engender much political concern for the clerics in this period. Much of the clerical attention, as is evident in the work of Sayyid Asad Allāh Khāraqānī (d. 1936), was directed against the clerics' declining moral authority, which was concomitant with the rapid rise of secularism.

In 1920, Iraqi Shīᶜī authorities were instrumental in the popular uprising against British colonialism. Mīrzā Muḥammad Taqī Shīrāzī emerged as the leading clerical authority in Iraqi anticolonial struggles (see Nakash, 1994, pp. 66–72). In collaboration with Shaykh al-Sharīᶜah al-Iṣfahānī and other leading Shīᶜī authorities, Shīrāzī called for the establishment of "a theocratic government built upon one of the fundamental principles of the Shīᶜah doctrine" (Nakash, 1994, p. 68). The Irāqī Shīᶜīs were much influenced by proconstitutional Shīᶜī authorities in Iran and wished to emulate that system in Iraq.

Under British pressure, Shaykh Muḥammad Khāliṣī (d. 1963) went to Iran in 1922 and joined forces with Khāraqānī in an incipient war against the rising tide of secularism in which they found both a political and a moral danger. Khāraqānī and Khāliṣī, in fact, saw a link between the rise of secularism and British imperialism, which sought to undermine clerical authority (see Arjomand 1988, p. 187). The secularizing agenda of Reza Shah and the antisecularization anger of the clerical establishment finally came to a head-on collision in the late 1920s, and Khāraqānī and Khāliṣī, among other clerical activists, were severely punished.

The 1930s and 1940s were decades of Shīᶜī polemical responses to the rising power of secularism. Mīrzā Muḥammad Ḥusayn Nā'īnī (d. 1936), Shaykh ʿAbd al-Karīm Ḥā'irī Yazdī (d. 1937), Ḥājj Āqā Ḥusayn Ṭabāṭabā'ī Qummī (d. 1947) were the leading Shīᶜī jurists of these decades, chiefly responsible for elevating Qom to a position of prominence in juridical studies, on the same level as Najaf. It was the collective work of these leading jurists that paved the way for Muḥammad Ḥusayn Ṭabāṭabā'ī Burūjirdī (Moḥammad Ḥosayn Borujerdi, d. 1961), who enjoyed unprecedented power and prestige as a Shīᶜī authority.

The political agenda of the 1940s was chiefly characterized by the continued anger of the clerical establishment against the relentless unfolding of secularism. The enemy of the clerical authority now seemed to have disseminated from the tyrannical absolutism of the state to a widespread and hard-to-grasp diffusion of secular ideas and practices. Khāliṣī's treatise on veiling in Islam (see Arjomand, 1988, p. 188), published in 1948, represents the dominant sentiment of the clerics in this period. In this treatise, Khāliṣī tried to strike a balance between the radical traditionalists who denied women any social presence and status and the rising secularism in which women were actively unveiled and socially present. [*See the biographies of Ḥā'irī Yazdī and Borujerdi.*]

The rising tide of modernity in the 1930s and 1940s, which in political terms ultimately led to the establishment of the Pahlavi state apparatus, also witnessed a contrapuntal mode of reform in Shīᶜī political thought. Mīrzā Riẓā Qulī Sharīᶜat Sangalajī (1890–1944) is the chief representative of a rather radical notion of modernity who tried to advance such subversive ideas as the total discarding of the institution of *taqlīd*, or "emulation of the exemplary conduct of the religious authorities" (see Bīgdilī, 1944; and Richard, in Arjomand, 1988, chap. 7). What is detectable in Sharīᶜat Sangalajī's thought is an almost Wahhābī return to absolute monotheism, a rejection of the Shīᶜī cult of saint that immediately sets Sangalajī next to Kasravī, and a solid streak of rationalism which is meant to rescue the Shīᶜī faith from medieval absolutism, while equipping it for confrontation with the supposed evils of "The West."

The two chief antagonist forces to which Shīᶜī political thought responded actively in the 1940s and 1950s were the Bahā'ī faith and communism. In 1951 Khāliṣī published *Bandits of Right and Truth, or, Those Who Return to Barbarism and Ignorance* in response to the antireligious tract published by the Tudeh Party, *Guardians of Magic and Myth* (see Arjomand, 1988, pp. 188–189).

The 1950s also gave rise to a reemergence of nationalism in Iran, a movement chiefly identified with Mohammad Mossadegh, the champion of the Iranian nationalist resurgence. And it was to nationalism that Shīʿī political thought responded in the 1950s. ʿAlī Akbar Tashayyud was chiefly responsible for an active coordination of Shīʿī doctrines with the dominant themes of nationalism in the 1950s. While Tashayyud tried to assimilate nationalism into Shīʿī political thought, Sayyid Maḥmūd Ṭāliqānī (Ṭāleqāni, 1910–1979) sought to give an active rereading of such key Shīʿī figures as Nā'īnī and Khāraqānī by posing Shiism as an alternative to nationalism (Dabashi, 1993, chap. 4). [*See the biography of Ṭāleqāni.*]

According to Arjomand, "The 1960s was a decade of fateful change in Shīʿīsm" (1988, p. 189). The decade of the 1960s began with the death of Ayatollah Burūjirdī as the last principally apolitical jurist in the tradition of Shaykh ʿAbd al-Karīm Ḥā'irī Yazdī and Abū al-Ḥasan Iṣfahānī. Burūjirdī's passive condoning of Muhammad Reza Shah, very much reminiscent of Ḥā'irī Yazdī's passive acceptance of Reza Shah, had limited Shīʿī political activism to an antisecular, anti-Bahā'ī, anti-Tudeh Party agenda with which the Pahlavi regime in fact had much sympathy. The death of Burūjirdī, however, brought the whole question of supreme political authority in the Shīʿī community to a new critical point (see Dabashi, 1993, pp. 264–265).

At this critical moment the leading Shīʿī authorities gathered in Qom to ponder the future of religious and political authority. The proceedings of this conference were subsequently published in a volume, *Baḥsī dar bārah-yi marjaʿīyat va rūḥānīyat* (A Discussion Concerning the Sources of Exemplary Conduct and the Religious Authorities). Practically all the leading revolutionary ideologues of the late 1970s, with the notable exception of Ayatollah Ruhollah Khomeini, contributed to this volume in which such issues as the range of the *marjaʿ al-taqlīd*'s religious and political authorities, the viability of the notion of following the most learned, the supervision of *sahm-i imām* revenue, and many other related issues were openly discussed and debated.

A major institutional development following the death of Burūjirdī was the emergence of Qur'ānic commentary schools (autonomous religious centers), such as the one established by Ṭāliqānī in Tehran. Muslim student associations on many university campuses, Muslim professional associations of engineers, physicians, teachers, lawyers, and so forth were among the voluntary associations that began to emerge in the 1960s. These organizations provided the institutional bases for the propagation of modern Shīʿī political thought. Informal gatherings, such as those organized by ʿAllāmah Muḥammad Ḥusayn Ṭabāṭabā'ʿi in Qom and those organized by Murtaẕā Muṭahharī in Tehran, added momentum and energy to Shīʿī political thought (see Dabashi, 1993, chaps. 3 and 5). Weekly and monthly journals, such as *Maktab-i tashayyuʿ* and *Guftār-i māh* propagated the ideas of the rising Shīʿī ideologues. But ultimately the establishment of the Ḥusaynīyah Irshād in 1965 in Tehran must be considered the most successful modern institution of radical Shīʿī thought.

The major event of the 1960s was Ayatollah Khomeini's first revolutionary uprising. Since the 1940s, Khomeini had been active in Qom where he was busy pursuing his juridical studies under Hā'irī Yazdī. While such politically conscious and active clerics as Ṭāliqānī and Muṭahharī were busy debating Pahlavi legitimacy, Khomeini seized the moment by publicly calling for the ouster of the shah. The June 1963 uprising was severely crushed, and Khomeini was exiled first to Turkey and then to Iraq (see Dabashi, 1993, chap. 8).

As Arjomand has noted (1988, p. 190), Khomeini's 1963 uprising put clerical reform on hold and gave added momentum to the continued validity of the institution of the *ʿulamā'* (see also Göbel, 1984, chap. 3). At least two high-ranking members of the *ʿulamā'*, Ḥasan Farīd Gulpaygānī and Shaykh ʿAlī Tihrānī, carried forward the theoretical implications of Khomeini's 1963 uprising and in the 1970s wrote treatises in which ideas of supreme collective clerical rule for the Shīʿī *ʿulamā'* were expounded (see Arjomand 1988, p. 191). The result of Khomeini's radical politicization of the institution of the *ʿulamā'* is so drastic that one can indeed speak of "an ideological revolution in Shīʿīsm" (Arjomand, 1984, chap. 10, and 1988, p. 192).

The greatest and most effective challenge to the authority of the *ʿulamā'* as an institution, however, came from ʿAlī Sharīʿatī (1933–1977). In the 1960s and 1970s, Sharīʿatī singlehandedly reimagined a whole new, radically active spectrum for Islam. In a series of effectively delivered public lectures and persuasively written essays, Sharīʿatī generated an unprecedented energy and enthusiasm among politically committed intellectuals with a religious bent (for samples of his works in English, see Sharīʿatī, 1979, 1981, 1986). Educated in Mashhad and Paris, Sharīʿatī mastered an effective repertoire of rhetorical devices and then returned to his homeland, fully committed to transforming Shiism into a full-fledged political ideology. Sharīʿatī considered the institution of the clerical establishment as fundamentally outdated and compromised. He sought to release the Shīʿī sacred imaginations from the authority of the *ʿulamāʾ*. With a barely concealed disdain for clerical quietism or what he considered irrelevant piety, Sharāʿatī wed the sacrosanct memories of Shiism to the most serious problems of his time: cultural colonialism, social injustice, political repression, and the worldwide domination of what he saw as "Western imperialism." Combining his own brand of Jean-Paul Sartre's existentialism and Frantz Fanon's Third Worldism, Sharīʿatī championed an autonomous and independent man fully in charge of his destiny. He also reconstructed outdated figures of Shīʿī collective history, such as Fāṭimah, the Prophet's daughter and the wife of the first Shīʿī imam, ʿAlī, whom he turned into a devoted revolutionary woman to be emulated by his contemporaries (see Dabashi, 1993, chap. 2). Sharīʿatī redefined the role of revolutionary intellectuals, ridiculed and dismissed secular intellectuals, and made faith and belief once again acceptable, even fashionable, among young Shīʿīs. In his major work, *Islāmshināsī* (1972), Sharīʿatī took on himself the stupendous task of redefining what it means to be a Muslim. He went back deep into the most sacrosanct corners of Shīʿī and Islamic memories and brought back to life what he thought was "the true Islam," an Islam which was all but forgotten and yet waiting to mobilize its adherents to an active, radical, and revolutionary commitment in life. He redefined monotheism in classless, repressionless, antityrannical terms. [*See the biography of Sharīʿatī.*]

The person who had facilitated much of what Sharīʿatī accomplished in his radical repolitication of Shīʿī Islam was Jalāl Āl-i Aḥmad (1923–1969), who, in such works as *Gharbzadagī* (Westoxication) and "On the Services and Treasons of Intellectuals," argued vociferously against what he called "Western" culture, including its revolutionary ideologies, and for a local, domestically viable, construction of a revolutionary ideology (see Āl-i Aḥmad, 1984). Āl-i Aḥmad pointed toward recent Iranian and Iraqi history in which the only successful social mobilizations had occurred when the Shīʿī clerics were involved. A disillusioned Marxist, Āl-i Aḥmad sought to rekindle a radical trait in Shiism. What Āl-i Aḥmad had barely noticed, Sharīʿatī took to its fullest potential, persuasively arguing for the revolutionary possibilities of Shīʿī ideology (see Dabashi, 1993, chap. 1).

By far, the most erudite, systematic, and relentless ideologue who carried the revolutionary potential of a repoliticized Shiism to its logical conclusion was Murtaẕā Muṭahharī (1920–1979). On some fundamental issues, particularly on the central role of the *ʿulamāʾ* in politics, Muṭahharī disagreed with Sharīʿatī. Perhaps the unintended consequence of his ideas was the further consolidation of "Islamic ideology" as the most potent revolutionary machinery preceding the events of 1979. Launching his revolutionary zeal from his solid place in the Shīʿī clerical establishment, Muṭahharī mobilized Shīʿī doctrines and institutions to argue against all other (Marxist-materialist and nationalist-liberal) revolutionary alternatives. Islamic philosophy was his principal weapon in a deliberate attempt to dislodge historical materialism (for samples of his writing, see Muṭahharī, 1985, 1986, n.d.). He shifted his attention from a popularization of the recondite language of Islamic philosophy to public lectures to various Muslim associations on a variety of issues, including the renarration of popular religious stories. He severely criticized the clerical establishment for its abandonment of politics, and in such works as *Akhlāq-i jinsī dar Islām va jahān-i gharb*, *ʿIlal-i girāyish bih māddī-garī*, and *Islam va muqtaẕīyat-i zamān*, he confronted all the vital issues of his time, preaching to and preparing a massive audience that ultimately joined him and other clerics in 1979 to topple the Pahlavi monarchy (see Dabashi, 1993, chap. 3). [*See the biography of Muṭahharī.*]

Muṭahharī's philosophical preoccupation with historical materialism and his concerns with popularizing a more readily accessible and politically relevant Islamic philosophy was largely indebted to his close association with ʿAllāmah Sayyid Muḥammad Ḥusayn Ṭabāṭabāʾī (1903–1981), a distinguished Shīʿī scholar who was equally concerned with the erosion of Islamic doctrines and ideas. In his major philosophical contribution to the active engagement with Marxism, and historical materialism, *Uṣūl-i falsafah va rāvish-i riʾālīzm* (1953–1985), Ṭabāṭabāʾī took issue with those pervasive ideas. His concern was primarily for the seminary students in Qom who had apparently been drawn to radical, secular ideas (for a sample of Ṭabāṭabāʾī's writings, see Ṭabāṭabāʾī, 1989). But Muṭahharī's extensive commentaries on these texts made them accessible to more secular students in Tehran University. Throughout his Qurʾānic commentaries and his participation in questions of supreme juridical/political authority among the Shīʿīs and a host of related issues, Ṭabāṭabā'ī actively participated in his generation of high-ranking clerics' concern with the rise of Marxism, historical materialism, secularism, and ultimately the future of the Shīʿī faith and its social and political contexts (see Dabashi, 1993, chap. 5). [*See the biography of Ṭabāṭabā'ī.*]

To address the specifics of those social and political contexts in a language that bore the sacred authority of the Qur'ān, another major political thinker of this period, Sayyid Maḥmūd Ṭāliqānī, used the discourse of Qur'ānic commentary as his preferred narrative. Through a succession of Qur'ānic commentaries, published later as *Partuvī az Qur'ān* (1979–1983), Ṭāliqānī read an actively revolutionary message into the Islamic holy text. In and out of prison for his political activities over an extended period of time, Ṭāliqānī preached his radical, revolutionary reading of the Qur'ān, linking its sacrosanct message to the most immediate and compelling problems of his time. Ṭāliqānī felt equally compelled to battle Marxism, especially its economic theory. He wrote a book, *Islam and Ownership* (1953; for an English translation, see Ṭāleqāni, 1983), in which he countered the Marxist conception of the economic basis of social structure and then assimilated its principal terms and discourse in narrating an Islamic political economy (see Dabashi, 1993, chap. 4). Ṭāliqānī's ideological and political leadership were instrumental in the formation of the Mujāhidīn-i Khalq organization, an urban guerrilla movement that paralyzed the Pahlavi regime, then joined the 1979 revolution but subsequently broke ranks with Ayatollah Khomeini's followers (Abrahamian, 1989). [*See* Mujāhidīn, *article on* Mujāhidīn-i Khalq.]

The economic aspect of "Islamic Ideology," as the Shīʿī ideologues now actively identified their rallying cry, was more extensively elaborated by Sayyid Abol-Hasan Bani Sadr (Abū al-Ḥasan Banī Ṣadr, b. 1933). Long before he attained the distinction of becoming the first president of the Islamic Republic of Iran, Bani Sadr actively participated in anti-Pahlavi movements and wrote extensively on the political economy of oil production in the Middle East in general and Iran in particular (for his political views, see Bani Sadr, 1981). In such works as *Iqtiṣād-i tawḥīdī* (1978) and *Naft va sulṭah* (1977), Bani Sadr argued enthusiastically that the Pahlavi regime was plundering Iranian natural resources and selling them cheaply to the United States and Europe (see Dabashi, 1993, chap. 7).

Mehdi Bāzargān (b. 1907), a quiet revolutionary, with an unending admiration for Mohandas Gandhi, became the link between revolutionary ideologues and their targeted audience. Long before he had the precarious distinction of becoming the first (transitional) prime minister after the fall of the Pahlavi regime in 1979, Bāzargān had been actively involved in the political mobilization of the professional classes. Having received his engineering education in France (he was sent to Europe along with a group of other students by Reza Shah in 1929), Bāzargān returned to his homeland determined to reawaken religious sensibilities against the rising tide of secularism and to activate political mobilization to gain power. In 1961, Bāzargān, Ṭāliqānī, and a number of other Muslim activists established the Liberation Movement of Iran (see Chehabi, 1990). Imprisoned for his political activities, Bāzargān spent much of his time rewriting a history of the Indian independence movement as a disguise to express his own wishes for a similar revolutionary movement in his homeland. Bāzargān used the occasion of his defense at the Pahlavi court to issue a strong condemnation of tyranny and injustice. After his release from prison, Bāzargān wrote and gave public lectures on a variety of issues, all targeted at an active resuscitation of a religious sensitivity conducive to revolutionary changes in the status quo (see Dabashi, 1993, chap. 6). [*See* Liberation Movement of Iran; *and the biography of Bāzargān.*]

By far the most rhetorically successful revolutionary Shīʿī was Ayatollah Khomeini (1902–1989), who ultimately engineered the downfall of the Persian monarchy. Born in the small village of Khomein (Khumayn), near Tehran, Khomeini grew up in the immediate aftermath of the Constitutional Revolution, which ushered in the rapid institutionalization of modernity in Iran. He received his early education in Khomein and Arak and then moved to Qom to pursue his higher scholastic studies, where he was even more aggravated by the rise to power of the Pahlavis and the even more rapid dissemination of politically mandated modernization. Khomeini watched with visceral contempt the shah's absolutist rule in the late 1950s and early 1960s. Khomeini's 1963 uprising against the shah was based on decades of resentful deliberation in religious and political terms. The increasing secularization of Pahlavi society and the American domination of Iranian political, social, economic, and cultural life were the principal points of contention that moved Khomeini to open revolt. After the June 1963 uprising and exile, Khomeini launched a major campaign against the legitimacy of the Pahlavi regime and of the monarch's authority. The principal text that was produced in this period was *Vilāyat-i faqīh* (1970), in which Khomeini defined the principal doctrines of his Islamic government (for a translation, see Algar, 1981). The major thesis of *Vilāyat-i faqīh* is quite simple: The Islamic government established by the prophet Muḥammad and (according to the Shīʿīs) continued by the Imams was not meant to be a transitional government. In the absence of the Twelfth Imam, who is now in occultation, the world is plunging deeply into corruption and despair. The Shīʿīs cannot know exactly when the Twelfth Imam is to appear. In the meantime, the responsibilities of leading Muslim nations cannot be entrusted to corrupt and tyrannical rulers like the shah, who simply aggravate the situation because they are deeply corrupt themselves. At this point, Khomeini accumulates a series of Qur'ānic passages and prophetic traditions that he interprets to mean that the (Shīʿī) jurists are to assume power, because, by virtue of having access to the specifics of the sacred law, they know how to regulate the daily affairs of Muslims that assures their salvation. Other than *Vilāyat-i faqīh,* Khomeini wrote letters incessantly to Muslim student associations in Iran, Europe, the United States, and Canada, inviting and encouraging them to unite and revolt against the Pahlavi regime. Khomeini wrote extensively on other issues—juridical, mystical, and philosophical in particular. Even some of his poetry has been posthumously published. But the main access to his political ideas remains in his letters, in his proclamations, and in *Vilāyat-i faqīh* (Dabashi, 1993, chap. 8). [*See* Wilāyat al-Faqīh; *and the biography of Khomeini.*]

As Khomeini's leadership of the Iranian Revolution was gaining momentum late in 1970, in Lebanon another Iranian cleric, Imam Mūsā al-Ṣadr, gave charismatic expression to the hopes and aspirations of the disenfranchised Shīʿī community in that war-torn country. Mūsā al-Ṣadr was instrumental in turning the Shīʿī minority of Lebanon into a major political force that not only the Sunnīs and Maronite Christians had to take seriously, but that the two occupying powers, the Syrians and the Israelis, had to contend with. In the summer of 1978, Mūsā al-Ṣadr disappeared while on a short visit to Libya (Ajami, 1986). [*See the biography of Ṣadr.*]

In the meantime in Iran, after the success of the Islamic Revolution in February 1979, there followed a period of ideological institutionalization of Shīʿī political ideas. In this respect, the constitution of the Islamic Republic of Iran must be considered the latest document in the saga of modern Shīʿī political thought (for a translation, see Algar, 1980).

The most prominent Shīʿī political theorist after the success of the Islamic Revolution is ʿAbd al-Karīm Surūsh, whose theory of *qabẓ va basṭ-i sharīʿat* ("contraction and expansion of religious law") created much controversy in Iran. In a series of highly effective essays, Surūsh read the ideas of such major ideologues of the Islamic Revolution as Murtaẓā Muṭahharī into a metanarrative of Islamic revolutionary revivalism. With the same stroke he tried to elevate the level of ideological debate in Iran beyond the incessant factionalism of the opposing parties that fought for the immediate fruits of their revolution. The result was of course a typical response to such highly effective propositions: while the entrenched clerical establishment smelled disenchantment and trouble from the writings of Surūsh, a group of young and disenfranchised Muslim intellectuals began to gather around him. Surūsh's serious engagements with the ideological and philosophical consequences of the success of the "Islamic" revolution thus went without any serious critical judgment meeting it on its own terms and turf. But as the most philosophically engaged ideologue of the post–Islamic Revolution, Surūsh will undoubtedly emerge as the future systematizer of yet another master-dialogue of Shiism with its history.

[*See also* Constitutional Revolution; Iran; Iranian Revolution of 1979; Qājār Dynasty; *and* Ṣafavid Dynasty. *For biographies of Reza Shah and Muhamad Reza Shah, see under Pahlavi.*]

BIBLIOGRAPHY

Abrahamian, Ervand. *Radical Islam: The Iranian Mojahedin.* London, 1989.

Ādamīyat, Farīdūn. *Īdi'ūlūzhī-yi Nahẓat-i Mashrūṭīyat-i Īrān.* Tehran, 1355/1976.

Ajami, Fouad. *The Vanished Imam: Musa al Sadr and the Shia of Lebanon.* Ithaca and London; 1986.

Algar, Hamid. *Religion and State in Iran, 1785–1906; The Role of the Ulama in the Qajar Period.* Berkeley, 1969.

Algar, Hamid, trans. *Constitution of the Islamic Republic of Iran.* Berkeley, 1980.

Algar, Hamid, trans. and ed. *Islam and Revolution: Writings and Declarations of Imam Khomeini.* Berkeley, 1981.

Āl-i Aḥmad, Jalāl. *Occidentosis: A Plague from the West.* Translated by R. Campbell. Berkeley, 1984.

ʿAlī ibn Abī Ṭālib. *Nahjul Balaghah: Sermons, Letters and Sayings.* Rome, 1984.

Alserât 12 (Spring–Autumn, 1986). Special issue: The Imam Husayn Conference Number: Papers from the Imam Husayn Conference, London, July 1984.

Amanat, Abbas. *Resurrection and Renewal: The Making of the Babi Movement in Iran, 1844–1850.* Ithaca, N.Y., 1989.

Arjomand, Said Amir. "The ʿ*Ulama*'s Traditionalist Opposition to Parlimentarianism, 1907–1909." *Journal of Middle Eastern Studies* 17 (1981).

Arjomand, Said Amir. *The Shadow of God and the Hidden Imam: Religion, Political Order, and Societal Change in Shi'ite Iran from the Beginning to 1890*. Chicago, 1984.

Arjomand, Said Amir, ed. *Authority and Political Culture in Shi'ism*. Albany, N.Y., 1988.

Ashraf, Aḥmad. *Mavāniʿ-i tārīkhī-i rushd-i sarmāyah-dārī dar Īrān: Dawrah-i Qājār*. Tehran, 1359/1980.

Bani Sadr, Abol-Hasan. *The Fundamental Principles and Precepts of Islamic Government*. Lexington, Ky., 1981.

Bayat, Mangol. *Iran's First Revolution: Shi'ism and the Constitutional Revolution of 1905–1906*. New York and Oxford, 1991.

Bīgdilī, Abū al-Ḥasan, ed. *Bi-munāsabat-i yakumīn sāl-i Riḥlat-i sharīʿat*. Tehran, 1323/1944.

Chehabi, H. E. *Iranian Politics and Religious Modernism: The Liberation Movement of Iran under the Shah and Khomeini*. Ithaca, N.Y., 1990.

Chittick, William C., ed. *A Shi'ite Anthology*. Albany, N.Y., 1981.

Corbin, Henry. *En Islam iranien*. 4 vols. Paris, 1971.

Dabashi, Hamid. *Authority in Islam: From the Rise of Muhammad to the Establishment of the Umayyads*. New Brunswick, N.J., 1989.

Dabashi, Hamid. *Theology of Discontent: The Ideological Foundation of the Islamic Revolution in Iran*. New York, 1993.

Daftari, Farhad. *The Ismāʿīlīs: Their History and Doctrines*. Cambridge, 1990.

Enayat, Hamid. *Modern Islamic Political Thought*. London and Austin, 1982.

Farahānī, Mīrzā Moḥammad Ḥosayn. *A Shi'ite Pilgrimage to Mecca, 1885–1886*. Edited, translated, and annotated by Hafez Farmayan and Elton L. Daniel. Austin, 1990.

Fashāhī, Muḥammad Rizā. *Guzārishī kūtāh az taḥavvulāt-i fikrī va ijtimāʿī dar jāmiʿah-yi fiʾūdālī-i Īrān*. Tehran, 1354/1975.

Göbel, Karl-Heinrich. *Moderne Schiitische Politik und Staatsidee*. Opladen, Germany, 1984.

Hairi, A. H. *Shi'ism and Constitutionalism in Iran: A Study of the Role Played by the Persian Residents of Iraq in Iranian Politics*. Leiden, 1977.

Jafri, S. H. M. *The Origins and Early Development of Shi'a Islam*. London and New York, 1979.

Kasravī, Aḥmad. *Tārīkh-i mashrūṭah-yi Īrān*. Tehran, 1363/1984.

Keddie, Nikki. "Religion and Irreligion in Early Iranian Nationalism," *Comparative Studies in Society and History* 4 (1962).

Keddie, Nikki. "Roots of the ʿUlama's Power in Modern Iran." In *Scholars, Sufis and Saints: Muslim Religious Institutions since 1500*, edited by Nikki Keddie. Berkeley and Los Angeles, 1972.

Keddie, Nikki, ed. *Scholars, Saints, and Sufis: Muslim Religious Institutions in the Middle East since 1500*. Berkeley and Los Angeles, 1972.

Keddie, Nikki. *Religion and Politics in Iran: Shi'ism from Quietism to Revolution*. New Haven and London, 1983.

Kirmānī, Nāẓim al-Islām. *Tārīkh-i bīdārī-i Īrānīyān*. Edited and annotated by ʿAlī Akbar Saʿīdī Sirjānī. Tehran, 1362/1983.

Lambton, Ann K. S. "Quis Custodiet Custodes: Some Reflections on the Persian Theory of Government." *Studia Islamica* 5–6 (1956); reprinted in Ann K. S. Lambton, *Theory and Practice in Medieval Persian Government*. London 1980, pp. 125–148.

Lambton, Ann K. S. "The Persian ʿ*Ulama* and Constitutional Reform." In *Le Shi'ism imamite*. Paris, 1970.

Lewis, Bernard. *The Assassins*. London, 1967.

Madelung, Wilferd, "Authority in Twelver Shi'ism in the Absence of the Imam." In *La Notion d'Authorité au Moyen Age: Islam, Byzance, Occident*, edited by George Makdisi et al. Paris, 1982.

Madelung, Wilferd. *Religious Trends in Early Islamic Iran*. Albany, N.Y., 1988.

Maḥmūd, Maḥmūd. *Tārīkh-i ravābiṭ-i Siyāsī-i Īrān va Inglīstān dar qarn-i nuzdah*. 8 vols. Tehran, 1353/1974.

Modarressi, Hossein. "Rational and Traditional in Shīʿī Jurisprudence: A Preliminary Survey," *Studia Islamica* 59 (1984).

Modarressi, Hosein. *Crisis and Consolidation in the Formative Period of Shi'ite Islam*. Princeton, 1993.

Momen, Moojan. *An Introduction to Shi'i Islam*. New Haven and London, 1985.

Moosa, Matti. *Extremist Shiites: The Ghulat Sects*. Syracuse, N.Y., 1988.

Mufīd, Shaykh al-. *Kitāb al-Irshād: The Book of Guidance*. London, 1981.

Muṭahharī, Murtaẓā. *Fundamentals of Islamic Thought: God, Man, and the Universe*. Translated by R. Campbell. Berkeley, 1985.

Muṭahharī, Murtaẓā. *Social and Historial Change: An Islamic Perspective*. Translated by R. Campbell. Berkeley, 1986.

Muṭahharī, Murtaẓā. *The Islamic Modest Dress*. Translated by Laleh Bakhtiar. Albuquerque, n.d.

Nakash, Yitzhak. *The Shi'ites of Iraq*. Princeton, 1994.

Nasr, S. H., et al., eds. *Expectation of the Millennium: Shi'ism in History*. Albany, N.Y., 1989.

Qūchānī, Āqā Najafī. *Siyāḥat-i Sharq*. Tehran, 1362/1983.

Sachedina, A. A. *Islamic Messianism: The Idea of the Mahdi in Twelver Shi'ism*. Albany, N.Y., 1981.

Sachedina, A. A. *The Just Ruler In Shi'ite Islam: The Comprehensive Authority of the Jurist in Imamite Jurisprudence*. New York and Oxford, 1988.

Sharīʿatī, ʿAlī. *On the Sociology of Islam*. Translated by Hamid Algar. Berkeley, 1979.

Sharīʿatī, ʿAlī. *Man and Islam*. Translated by Fatollah Marjani. Houston, 1981.

Sharīʿatī, ʿAlī. *What Is To Be Done?* Edited and annotated by Farhang Rajaee. Houston, 1986.

Ṭabāṭabāʾī, Muḥammed Ḥusayn. *Islamic Teachings: An Overview*. Translated by R. Campbell. New York, 1989.

Ṭāleqāni, Maḥmud. *Islam and Ownership*. Translated b y Ahman Jabbari and Farhang Rajaee. Lexington, Ky., 1983.

Weber, Max. *Gesammelte Aufsätze zur Religionssoziologie*. 3 vols. Tübingen, 1920.

HAMID DABASHI

SHĪRĀZĪ, SAYYID ʿALĪ MUḤAMMAD AL-. *See* Bāb.

SHIRK. *See* Kufr.

SHRINE. The Arabic term *qubbah* (a tomb surmounted by a dome) refers throughout the Muslim world to saints' shrines and mausoleums and places of special spiritual significance. Shrines are never just buildings, however. They stand for a complex of rituals, symbols, and shifting social and spiritual ties that link believers to Islam and create a sacred geography. Shrines are often associated with natural phenomena—in Indonesia, for example, they are frequently located in elevated spots and have their own sources of water. In North Africa, the shrines of marabouts, or *al-ṣāliḥūn* ("pious ones"), dot the landscape so pervasively that they are rarely out of sight. Some are squat, white-washed buildings. Others are quite elaborate. A visit to one of these shrines is thought to offer spiritual blessings, particularly if ties exist between the client (or client group) and the descendants of the marabout. Every rural settlement has such a shrine, sometimes just a semiderelict, sporadically maintained structure in a cemetery. In western Morocco, there is roughly one shrine for every 6 square kilometers and 150 people. These tombs constitute a framework that concretely symbolizes social groups and their relations. As alliances change, derelict shrines can be restored or new ones constructed to reflect new identities.

In addition to these modest local shrines, there are more elaborate complexes linked to major religious figures. Major shrines have annual *mawsims* (festivals) that draw tens of thousands of pilgrims annually and have full-time caretakers, often descendants of the saint or pious one. Jews in North Africa also have shrines, most of which have been maintained despite the diminution of the Jewish population since the 1950s. Indeed, some Jewish shrines have been "relocated" in Israel as their North African supporters have emigrated there. In Morocco, some shrines attract both Jewish and Muslim pilgrims.

Shīʿī Muslims also have elaborate shrine complexes associated with the principal imams and religious centers, and many of these, such as Qom in Iran and Karbala in southern Iraq, have religious schools associated with them along with bureaucracies to accept donations, support humanitarian works, and administer the endowed properties *(awqāf;* sg., *waqf*) that produce revenue for their upkeep. In Java, in contrast, modernist Muslims discourage visits to shrines, although the texts and oral traditions associated with them offer a vivid view of Java's past and suggest its future directions. Thus shrines for many Javanese spatially represent their history and identity.

The most important shrine complex in the Muslim world is that of the Kaʿbah and the Great Mosque in Mecca. Some Muslims believe that the Kaʿbah (literally, "cube") was brought to Abraham by the angel Gabriel. At first it was white, but it turned black through contact with the impurities of the pre-Islamic period. Others say that the Kaʿbah was built by Adam and that he is buried there. The Kaʿbah is the most sacred space in the Muslim world, the point to which all Muslims turn to pray, and the direction to which their heads point in burial. It is the most important place of *ḥajj* (pilgrimage), and is distinguished from visits to local or regional shrines, known as *ziyārahs*. As the spiritual center of the earth, actions at the Kaʿbah, such as its circumambulation, are duplicated in the heavens and at the throne of God.

Shrines define sacred space, both for the Great Mosque in Mecca and for the local shrines throughout the Muslim world devoted to mythical figures, great scholars imputed with mystical powers, and persons of exceptional piety. Shrines in Indonesia are associated with the coming of Islam and also relate to sacred time. To obtain the most benefit, pilgrims often visit several shrines, calculating their arrival on the day most favorably associated with each shrine in complex, interlocking cycles of five- and seven-day weeks. Major shrines can have ten thousand to fifty thousand visitors on their most auspicious days. Some modernist Muslims have sought to ban visits to shrines, but such visits retain their popularity except in Saudi Arabia, where the Wahhābīs have forced their cessation, allowing only visits to those in Mecca and Medina.

Shrines also separate sacred and secular space. People can seek sanctuary in them and await the intervention of religious intermediaries to negotiate a truce or settlement. Oaths sworn at shrines are especially binding, because their violation incurs the wrath of the shrine's marabout or *walī*. Some are known as centers for healing. Visits to the shrine of Bū Yā ʿUmār, located near Marrakesh, Morocco, are reputed to cure the mentally ill.

Gender divisions are often associated with shrines. The shrine for Lalla Ḥnīya, a daughter of Sīdī Mḥammad al-Sharqī in Boujad, Morocco, is visited almost exclusively by women seeking a remedy for infertility. Visitors tear strips of cloth from their clothing and affix it to the door of the shrine as a *waʿdah* (promise) to offer a gift or sacrifice if they bear a child. Such offerings are not made at Lalla Ḥnīya's tomb, but at the nearby shrine complex of her father. Until recently, women in rural Turkey were largely confined to their homes, except for visits to local shrines on religious and secular festivals. Visits to shrines secure blessings for the household and can be used to signal changes in personal status—marriage, the birth of a child, or mourning. Women say prayers at these shrines and are more conscious than men of local sacred geography. Men occasionally visit shrines with women, but rarely do so on their own.

The sacred geography of shrines is not confined to supposed vestiges of the past, although shrines, such as that at Mecca, had pre-Islamic significance, and other shrines, as in Java, are not associated exclusively with Islamic figures. Instead, they constitute a physical representation of the sacred, defining not only relations of particular social groups and categories with the divine but also the relations among social groups and between genders. Thus they offer a rich means of ordering the religious and social universes, and for many, they serve as a means of aligning one with the other.

[*See also* Ḥajj; Sainthood; Sufism, *article on* Ṣūfī Shrine Culture; *and* Ziyārah.]

BIBLIOGRAPHY

Eickelman, Dale F. *Moroccan Islam: Tradition and Society in a Pilgrimage Center.* Austin, 1976. Describes a major shrine complex in Morocco and the practices associated with it.

Esin, Emil. *Mecca the Blessed, Madinah the Radiant.* London, 1963. Beautifully written and illustrated account of Mecca and Medina as shrine complexes.

Fischer, Michael M. J. *Iran: From Religious Dispute to Revolution.* Cambridge, Mass., 1980. Chapter 4, "Qum: Arena of Conflict," describes religious and political action in a major Shīʿī shrine center.

Fox, James. J. "Ziarah Visits to the Tombs of the Wali, the Founders of Islam on Java." In *Islam in the Indonesian Social Context,* edited by Merle C. Ricklefs, pp. 19–38. Clayton, Australia, 1991.

McChesney, Robert. *Waqf in Central Asia: Four Hundred Years in the History of a Muslim Shrine.* Princeton, 1991. The best account for the historical continuity and changing significance of a major shrine in Central Asia.

Naamouni, Khadija. *Le culte de Bouya Omar.* Casablanca, 1993. Fascinating account by a Moroccan scholar of a shrine center associated with the cure of mental illness in southern Morocco.

Tapper, Nancy. "*Ziyaret:* Gender, Movement, and Exchange in a Turkish Community." In *Muslim Travellers: Pilgrimage, Migration, and the Religious Imagination,* edited by Dale F. Eickelman and J. P. Piscatori, pp. 236–255. Berkeley and Los Angeles. 1990.

Weingrod, Alex. "Saints and Shrines, Politics and Culture: A Morocco-Israel Comparison." In *Muslim Travellers: Pilgrimage, Migration, and the Religious Imagination,* edited by Dale F. Eickelman and J. P. Piscatori, pp. 217–235. Berkeley and Los Angeles. 1990.

DALE F. EICKELMAN

SHŪRĀ. *See* Democracy.

SIBĀʿĪ, MUṢṬAFĀ AL- (1915–1964), Syrian political thinker, educator, and founder of the Muslim Brotherhood in Syria. Born in Homs, al-Sibaʿī came from a prominent family of *ʿulamā'*. His father's nurturance of him in Islamic learning included a strong sense of political activism that later put him on a collision course with the authorities of the French mandate.

When al-Sibāʿī was eighteen years old, he traveled to Egypt, a country that would have a profound impact on his intellectual development and public life. His studies at al-Azhar were accompanied by involvement in political activism, membership in the Egyptian Muslim Brotherhood, and close association with Ḥasan al-Bannā'. In 1934 al-Sibāʿī was jailed for participating in anti-British demonstrations; in 1940 the British charged him with subversion and sent him to the Sarfad camp in Palestine. After his release (1941), he returned to Homs to establish an organization called Shabāb Muḥammad (Muḥammad's Youth). Soon he was arrested and jailed by the French for two and a half years. Despite his deteriorating health brought on by torture, al-Sibāʿī's release from prison in 1943 ushered in two decades of dynamic activity as writer, teacher, and leader of Syria's Islamic movement.

By 1946 al-Sibāʿī had forged a merger between different Islamic *jamʿīyāt* to form the Muslim Brotherhood, and was elected its general supervisor *(al-murāqib al-ʿāmm).* Until the brotherhood's suppression by the Shishāklī regime in 1952, al-Sibāʿī worked to strengthen his movement, which he conceived not as a *jamʿīyah* or political party but as a *rūḥ* (spirit) seeking to raise public consciousness to achieve comprehensive Islamic reform. He was also a distinguished educator and administrator at the University of Damascus.

Al-Sibāʿī's most important contribution to Islamic thought was his book, *Ishtirakīyat al-Islām* (The Socialism of Islam), in which he argued that Islam teaches a unique type of socialism, one distinct from its Western materialistic variants emphasizing class struggle. He saw Islamic Socialism as conforming with human nature, based on five natural rights: life, freedom, knowledge, dignity, and ownership. God is the ultimate owner of all, and man is deputized to make use of property through honest labor. The state plays a regulatory function through nationalization *(taʿmīm)* of essential public services, implementation of Islamic laws on mutual social responsibility *(al-takāful al-ijtimāʿī)*, and sanctions *(muʿayyidāt)*. Al-Sibaʿī's theory created an uproar because of its opposition to capitalism, its association of Islam with socialism, and its ostensible support of Nasser's ideology at a time when the Egyptian Brotherhood was suppressed.

Because of his failing health, in 1957 al-Sibāʿī turned over leadership of the brotherhood to ʿIṣām al-ʿAṭṭār, although he continued to write until his death (1964). In addition to his book on socialism, al-Sibaʿī edited three journals, *Al-manār* (The Lighthouse), *Al-muslimīn* (The Muslims), and *Ḥaḍārat al-Islām* (The Civilization of Islam), and began to compile an *Encyclopedia of Islamic Law*. His other books were *Mar'ah bayna al-fiqh wa-al-qānūn* and *Hākadhā ʿallamatnī al-hayāh*.

[*See also* Muslim Brotherhood, *article on* Muslim Brotherhood in Syria; Socialism and Islam.]

BIBLIOGRAPHY

Abd-Allah, Umar F. *The Islamic Struggle in Syria*. Berkeley, 1983.
Dekmejian, R. Hrair. *Islam in Revolution*. Syracuse, N.Y., 1985.
Donohue, John J., and John L. Esposito, eds. *Islam in Transition*. New York, 1982.
Enayat, Hamid. *Modern Islamic Political Thought*. Austin, 1982.
Ismael, Tareq Y., and Jacqueline S. Ismael. *Government and Politics in Islam*. New York, 1985.

R. Hrair Dekmejian

SIN. In the Qur'ān several words are used for sin, a breach of the laws and norms laid down by a religion, including *dhanb, ithm, khaṭī'ah,* and *sayyi'ah*. A sin may be one of omission or commission; technically, any violation of a religious law or ethical norm would be a sin, but the sin for which one will be held accountable is, as a rule, the one intentionally committed.

If sin is violation, the question arises whether all sins are alike or whether it is possible to grade them. The question is more complex than it appears. The Qur'ān clearly speaks of two types of sins, major and minor. Surah 4.31 says, "If, of the things that have been forbidden to you, you stay away from the major ones [i.e., major sins], We shall forgive you your [minor] sins." In surah 53.31–32, likewise, hope of salvation is held out to those who avoid major sins, though they may have committed minor sins (see also 42.37). In a *ḥadīth* Muḥammad says that the five prayers, two Friday prayers, and two months of Ramaḍān wipe off the sins committed during the intervening periods—that is, sins committed after one prayer are wiped off by the next prayer, and so on. A principal issue arising from this distinction is that of the objectivity of sin: what makes a sin major or minor? The Qur'ān does provide some help in answering this question by labeling certain acts as major sins. Thus setting up peers to God *(shirk)* is the most heinous sin in Islam, the Qur'ān categorically stating that one who commits this sin shall not be forgiven (5.72). Murder and illicit sex are also regarded as major sins (25.69, 5.32). The *sunnah* of the Prophet, embodied in *ḥadīth*, elaborates the subject.

In spite of the help they furnish in identifying a number of major sins, and in spite of the many general warnings they contain against sinful behavior, the Qur'ān and the *sunnah* appear reluctant to identify minor sins. A little reflection suggests why this is so. A religion that attaches great importance to intention as an imbuer and determinant of moral value cannot look with favor on an overly formal or mechanical view of sin. For example, *kufr* (unbelief) is one of the most severely castigated qualities in the Qur'ān, and yet expression of unbelief is allowed to a believer under duress (16.106). Formal similarity of two acts thus may not represent substantive similarity. A related point is that labeling sins as minor might create a tolerance for or even crass indifference toward them. It is probably for this reason that comprehensive lists of major and minor sins are not provided. The absence of such listings might, however, lead one to categorize as major sins what common sense might designate as minor and vice versa. Such a tendency is found, for example, in Muḥammad ibn Aḥmad al-Dhahabī's *Kitāb al-kabā'ir,* where no fewer than seventy sins are identified as major.

The Qur'ān does not take a static view of sin; like other moral categories, sin can grow and diminish. According to a well-known *ḥadīth* of the Prophet, when a man commits a sin, his heart is marked with a black spot. If he keeps committing sins, the heart is fully covered with such spots, so that he loses the capacity to do good: God seals off his heart, rendering him incapable of good acts. By contrast, good actions wash away sins (Qur'ān 11.111).

The notion of inherited sin is foreign to Islam. The Qur'ānic story of Adam, which differs from the Biblical account in several important respects, is crucial to understanding the Islamic view. According to the story, Adam, forbidden to eat of the fruit of a certain tree in Eden, succumbed to the suggestions of Iblīs and ate of the fruit; Eve too ate of it. Realizing their mistake, the two sought forgiveness, were forgiven by God, and then were sent to earth with a clean slate. Since Adam and Eve, as the first parents, represent humanity, the Qur'ānic story has several implications: first, human beings are vulnerable to sin and suggestions of sin; second, they have enough moral sense to distinguish between good and sinful acts, and, having committed a sin, to feel remorse and seek to make atonement; third, forgiveness of sins by God is direct and not vicarious; and finally, there is no such thing as original sin.

Although Islam does not accept the notion of original sin, it does not deny that humans are vulnerable to sin. This is understandable because, in Islamic teaching, the purpose of the creation of humans is to put them to the test, to see whether they take the right or the wrong path—both of which have been shown to them. One of the qualities enabling humans to tell the right from the wrong path is the inner light that may be called conscience, which God has implanted in every human being, and which, like a sensor, gives appropriate signals when man sets out on the right or wrong path; surah 75.2 calls it *al-nafs al-lawwāmah*, the "blaming self." When one repents after committing a sin, God responds by forgiving the sin; and it is God alone who forgives (9.104, 42.25). A distinction, however, is made here between sins that constitute a violation of other human beings' rights *(ḥuqūq al-ʿibād)* and sins that violate the rights of God *(ḥuqūq Allāh)*; the former are forgiven on condition that the forgiveness of the wronged party is obtained first. Finally, since there is no original sin, it follows that neither Adam (or man) nor Eve (or woman) is the source of evil on earth.

But this raises another question about sin: what is the origin of sinful human behavior? Within the context of Qur'ānic thought, the only defensible answer would seem to be that sin, at least sin that calls for reprimand or punishment, arises from a willful misuse by humans of the freedom that has been accorded them.

A notable aspect of the Islamic notion of sin, and one that is based on some of the texts in the fundamental sources of Islam—Qur'ān and *ḥadīth*—but whose details were worked out later, has to do with the possibility of prophetic sin. Since a prophet brings the divine word, one has to assume, the argument goes, that the prophet must be under divine protection in his capacity as prophet, for otherwise how could the integrity of the divine word be guaranteed? At the same time, the prophets are human and therefore vulnerable to sin. Some Sunnī theologians solved this problem by drawing a distinction between a prophet's prophetic and personal capacities. As a mortal human, a prophet may make mistakes and commit lapses, but as a prophet, a carrier of the revelatory message, he is immune to all error—a view that came to be known as the doctrine of *ʿiṣmah* (protection from error, hence "infallibility" or "sinlessness"). A modern writer, Abū al-Aʿlā Mawdūdī (d. 1979), in his commentary on the last two surahs of the Qur'ān, defends the notion of *ʿiṣmah,* arguing that neither physical injury (sustained by Muḥammad during the Battle of Uḥud, AH 4/625 CE) nor influence of magic (a magician is supposed to have cast a spell on Muḥammad) in any way affected Muḥammad's role and performance as prophet. In Shiism sinlessness is ascribed not only to prophets but also to the designated imams.

The essential Islamic statement of sin is found in the Qur'ān, which speaks of sin and its relationship to other moral categories. It is to be kept in mind that, from a philosophical point of view, the Islamic imperative to avoid sin is both religious and moral. On the one hand it is grounded in the idea that God's commands are to be obeyed simply because they are the commands of a being who is omniscient and all-wise (2.216, 232; see also 4.11 where the legislation concerning distribution of inherited property is followed by the terse statement, "You do not know which one of them [inheritors] shall be of greater benefit to you," implying that the divine legislation on this subject is wiser than any that can be devised by humans, who, swayed by emotion or prejudice in favor of one of the inheritors, might arrive at an unfair system of distribution). This is the religious aspect of the subject. On the other hand, the Qur'ān frequently emphasizes that God's commands are just and can be recognized as such by human reason, making an appeal to reason. This is the ethical aspect. Ideally, Islam would achieve a synthesis between the religious and the ethical, but in practice it is difficult to disentangle one strand from the other, and this difficulty led some early Muslim thinkers to take extreme positions.

The Qur'ān speaks of sin not only in the context of individual piety but also in the context of collective behavior and national conduct. Noah's people, we are told, was destroyed on account of its sins, and so were the peoples of Pharaoh, ʿĀd, Thamūd, and others. The Qur'ān alludes to Abraham's "debate" with God concerning the people of Lot (11.74). The conversation, which is reported in detail in the Bible, clearly implies that the people of Lot was destroyed because it had become thoroughly corrupt. The Qur'ānic view seems to be that while individuals will be recompensed for their actions in the next world, nations are recompensed in this world, a *sunnah* ("law") of God that shall not change (17.77, 33.62, 35.43, 48.23). The poet-philosopher Muhammad Iqbal says in a pungent verse that *Fiṭrat* (Nature; here, laws governing existence and survival; from Arabic *fiṭrah*) may forgive the sins of individuals but never forgives the sins committed by nations.

Like the Qur'ān, the *ḥadīths* take a religious-moral approach to sin in explicating the Qur'ānic doctrine. According to one *ḥadīth,* a person who repents of his sins becomes like one who has never committed any sins; another *ḥadīth* attributes the same efficacy to the pilgrimage *(ḥajj).* In one *ḥadīth* a man asks Muḥammad whether the door of repentance is open to one who has committed all kinds of sins—major and minor—and the Prophet responds that if he is a believer and performs good actions, avoiding evil actions, God will turn all his sins into good deeds (cf. Qur'ān 25.70). Still another *ḥadīth,* emphasizing the readiness of God to forgive a sinning person, says that when a person commits a sin, the recording angel waits for several hours before recording it; if the person repents in the meantime, the angel does not record it and the person will not be punished for it on the Last Day. Sometimes a *ḥadīth* glosses the Qur'ān. For example, the Qur'ān says that *shirk* is the most heinous sin. A *ḥadīth* says that hypocritical conduct that is meant to create an impression of piety *(riyā')* is also *shirk,* though of a lesser grade *(al-shirk al-aṣghar).* To take another example, the Qur'ān says that he who kills a believer will never enter paradise (4.93); a *ḥadīth* lays down the same punishment for killing a member of a non-Muslim people with whom Muslims have entered into a pact *(muʿāhad).*

In theology sin is discussed from the standpoint of whether a person who commits certain sins stands inside or outside the fold of the faith. Of relevance in this connection is the question of the relationship of faith and works, and an early discussion among Muslim theologians revolved around this topic. A certain group known as the Khawārij (those who "seceded" from the camp of the caliph ʿAlī during a war with Muʿāwiyah), maintained that one guilty of a major sin no longer remained a Muslim. The Murji'ah, in opposition to this view, attached greater importance to faith.

In law, sin is dealt with from the point of view of religious qualification—to determine, for example, what sins disqualify their perpetrator as a witness in a court of law. A person who makes false accusations of unchastity against innocent women is declared an unreliable witness on the basis of a Qur'ānic injunction, and his testimony is never to be accepted (24.4).

In Sufism sin is discussed with reference to the quality of the interior life. The existence in humans of *al-nafs al-ammārah* (Qur'an 12.54), the "bidding self" that incites one to commit evil, is not merely recognized; a systematic attempt is made to tame this self so that one can walk safely the path leading to spiritual perfection. The novice is asked to begin his spiritual journey by repenting, and he is advised to achieve through repentance a level of inner purification where even the thought of sin disappears.

In modern times concern with political freedom and social justice has led a number of Muslim thinkers to declare *ẓulm* (injustice, oppression) to be a great wrong or sin that the masses must resist and defeat. The oneness of God, it is argued, entails the oneness of humanity. As Fazlur Rahman says, Islamic monotheism cannot be dissociated from Islamic social humanism. The inescapable conclusion is that monotheism would remain an empty concept if its implications were not realized through a program seeking to ensure social justice and welfare. Another conclusion that could be drawn is that people in general have a right, indeed an obligation, to resist tyranny and oppression in any form. Pharaoh of Egypt made light of his people, the Qur'ān says, and the people obeyed him (43.54); the implication is that through their passivity the people of Pharaoh themselves were responsible, at least in part, for allowing him to oppress them. The same is true in the field of international relations. Muhammad Iqbal says in many places that for a nation to be weak or powerless is to commit a sin or crime, adding that the wages of weakness is death and extinction. To fight political oppression or to confront any form of alien intervention in Muslim affairs, therefore, is regarded as *jihād* no less than fighting a war, and to neglect to do so is to commit a gross sin.

[*See also* Kufr; Repentance.]

BIBLIOGRAPHY

Dhahabī, Muḥammad ibn Aḥmad al-. *Kitāb al-kabā'ir.* Cairo, 1978.
Ghazālī, Abū Ḥāmid al-. *Iḥyā' ʿulūm al-dīn.* 5 vols. Beirut, 1991.
Jawzīyah, Ibn Qayyim al-. *Al-Jawāb al-kāfī li-man sa'ala ʿan al-dawā' al-shāfī: Al-dā' wa-al-dawā'.* Edited by Maḥmūd ʿAbd al-Wahhāb Fāyid. Cairo, 1388/1968.
Muḥāsibī, al-Ḥārith ibn Asad al-. *Al-tawbah.* Edited by ʿAbd al-Qādir Aḥmad ʿAṭā. 1977.

MUSTANSIR MIR

ŞINASI, İBRAHIM (1826–1870), Turkish journalist. Şinasi is one of the more enigmatic figures of Turkish intellectual history. Despite his role as the founding father of modern Turkish journalism and his basic contributions to the rise of a Turkish critique of society, information about his life is insufficient to paint a portrait of him as an intellectual.

Şinasi began his career in government during the first years of the Tanzimat, the era of reforms and modernization initiated by the Gülhane Rescript of 1839. Encouraged by a patron of modernization in the Ottoman Empire, he was sent as a government-funded student to Europe in 1849. He remained in France until 1853 and is known to have been acquainted with such personalities as Alphonse de Lamartine. After his return he was appointed to the Educational Committee, which was engaged in redrawing Ottoman educational institutions.

Although quite cautious in his intellectual stance, he seems to have antagonized higher officials and was dismissed. Reinstated and dismissed once more in 1863, he eventually went into self-exile in Paris, where he devoted himself to the study of literature and linguistics. He returned permanently to Istanbul in 1870, where he lived as a recluse in some financial need.

Şinasi's major contribution to Ottoman/Turkish intellectual life was the Journal *Tasvir-i efkâr* (Interpreter of Ideas, founded in 1862). This was not the first newspaper in the Ottoman Empire; an Englishman named Churchill had published an earlier gazette, and in 1861 Şinasi and his friend Agâh Efendi had jointly published the *Terceüman-i ahval* (Interpreter of Events); however, *Tasvir-i efkâr* was the first newspaper that (though careful in its approach) expressed a critique of the state of Ottoman government and society in the modern media. Şinasi's second dismissal from his employment in the central government was due to his timid libertarianism: "mentioning matters of state too often" was the cause of his downfall. An article by Şinasi explaining the principle of "no taxation without representation" appeared in the *Tasvir-i efkâr* the day before the order for his dismissal was drafted and may have been the proximate cause of it.

Şinasi is unanimously considered by historians of Turkish intellectual history to be the first advocate of "europeanization" in the Ottoman Empire, a somewhat different project than that of "modernization" voiced before him. His impact, however, stems from his development of a medium that expressed private views about the state of the empire. Until Şinasi and his use of journalism as a medium for influencing—and, in a way, creating—public opinion, schemes of modernization had been the result of official concern with reform. Şinasi represents a new trend in which government officials concerned with the fate of the empire began to form an intelligentsia often contradicting positions adopted by their superiors. In that sense, he may be seen as having laid the groundwork for the Young Ottomans.

Another of Şinasi's important contributions may be described as "encyclopedism," or the attempt to inform his readers of the new methods and the new branches of knowledge that flourished in Europe in his time. Natural law, the historical method, the history of pre-Ottoman Turkey, and Buffon's *Histoire naturelle* were some of the ideas that he took up in the pages of *Tasvir-i efkâr*. In one of his most celebrated poems Şinasi praised the author of the Gülhane Rescript, Mustafa Reşid Paşa (Mustafa Reshid Pasha), for having brought "the European climate of opinion" to Turkey, and for having reminded the ruler of his responsibilities. In another, the achievements of a later grand vizier were compared to those of Plato and Newton.

Şinasi's mention in the preface of *Tercüman-i ahral* that he was using a language directed to "the people in general" also represents an important watershed. By the nineteenth century Ottoman Turkish as the language of officials had become a complex and flowery idiom difficult for the majority of the population, who used a vernacular called "rough Turkish." One of Şinasi's aims was to transcend officialese; he thus began the trend described by Grand Vizier Said Paşa, himself a writer, as "journalistic Turkish." This trend was further promoted by the Young Ottomans. The celebrated article by Ziya Paşa, "Siir ve Insa' " (Poetry and Prose), is a good example of the further developments that much later, in the 1930s, took a more radical turn toward the "purification" of Turkish by the removal of words with Arabic and Persian roots.

[*See also* Tanzimat.]

BIBLIOGRAPHY

Akyüz, Kenan. "Şinasi'nin Fransadaki Ögrenimi ile ilgili Bazı Belgeler," *Türk Dili* 3 (1954): 379–405.

Dizdaroğlu, Hikmet. *Şinasi-Hayatı ve Eserleri*. Istanbul, 1954.

Iskit, Server N. *Türkiyede Matbuat Idareleri ve Politikaları*. Istanbul, 1943.

Rasim, Ahmad. *Matbuat Tarihimize Methal*. Istanbul, 1927.

ŞERIF MARDIN

SINGAPORE. The geographical position of Singapore defines the history and contemporary position of its Muslim community. Singapore is the northernmost island in the Riau archipelago, which links the east coast of Sumatra with peninsular Malaysia. This territory is the traditional home of the Malay people. Malay history is intimately linked with Islam, and the first Malay-Muslim trading city, Melaka (Malacca), flourished in the fifteenth century. The sacking of Melaka by the Portuguese in 1511 marked the beginning of an era of intrusions by various colonial powers interested in the strategic sea lanes through the Straits of Melaka.

In 1819 Sir Stamford Raffles founded the British colony of Singapore, which quickly flourished as an entrepôt trading center for the region. Singapore remained a British colony until it was granted self-government in 1959. In 1963 it became a state within the Federation of Malaysia, and in 1965 it separated from the Federation to become the independant Republic of Singapore.

In terms of ethnic percentages, Singapore's population has remained relatively stable since the mid-nineteenth century. The major demographic change occurred early in the nineteenth century, when the Chinese gradually overtook the originally predominant Malays. By 1891 Chinese numbered 67.1 percent of the population, Malays 19.7 percent, Indians 8.8 percent, and others (including Europeans) 4.3 percent. A century later in 1990, the resident Singapore population was 2.7 million, with Chinese forming the majority (77.7 percent), followed by Malays (14.1 percent), Indians (7.1 percent), and others (1.1 percent).

Colonial Period. The nineteenth-century Singapore Muslim community was divided into two broad categories: Muslims indigenous to the region (mostly Malays) who formed the majority, and a minority of wealthy and better-educated Indian Muslims, Arabs, and Jawi Peranakans (indigenized Indian Muslims), who formed the social and economic elite. This elite spearheaded the flowering of Singapore as a Muslim publishing and educational center for the region. Arab families such as the Alsagoffs, the Alkaffs and the Aljunieds were prominent contributors to Muslim mosque-building funds, educational institutions, and other charitable Muslim organizations.

From the middle of the nineteenth century, the Dutch took repressive measures to prevent Muslims in the Dutch East Indies from performing the pilgrimage, and so Singapore increasingly became a focal point for such departures. The British reluctantly realized the need to intervene in the affairs of the Muslim community, beginning with quarantine controls on departing and arriving pilgrims.

In 1880 the British government passed the Mahomedan Marriage Ordinance; in 1905 the Mahomedan and Hindu Endowment Board was set up to regulate trusts (*awqāf*; sg., *waqf*); and in 1915 the Muhammedan Advisory Board was constituted to advise the government on matters pertaining to the Muslim community.

Post-independence Period. In August 1966, a year after Singapore's independence, the Singapore parliament passed the Administration of Muslim Law Act (AMLA), ushering in a new phase in the legal and administrative history of Islam in the country. The Singapore Muslim Religious Council (Majlis Ugama Islam Singapura or MUIS) was constituted under the Act and inaugurated in 1968. MUIS is the supreme Islamic religious authority in Singapore and advises the government on matters relating to Islam. MUIS administers the mosque-building program, manages mosques and endowment properties, and coordinates the annual pilgrimage to Mecca.

The Shariah Court and Registry of Muslim Marriages were set up in 1958. In addition to hearing divorce petitions, the Shariah Court also considers applications for inheritance certificates relating to Muslim estates. All appeals to either the Registry or the Shariah Court are channeled to an appeals board formed by MUIS. MUIS, the Shariah Court, and the Registry of Muslim Marriages are administered within the Ministry of Community Development. There is also a Minister in Charge of Muslim Affairs who acts as a liaison between the Muslim community and the political leadership.

The government has attached a great deal of importance to improving the standard of living of the Malay-Muslim minority. Traditionally this community has tended to lag behind the Chinese majority in terms of educational achievement, occupational advancement, and income levels. Government policy has been to emphasize and support self-help groups within the community, such as MENDAKI (Council on Education for Muslim Children) and the AMP (Association of Muslim Professionals).

In sum, Singapore is a Chinese-majority, secular state located in the Malay-Muslim world of Southeast Asia. The Singapore Malay-Muslim community is cognizant of its position as a national minority that is also part of a larger regional Muslim majority.

[*See also* Islam, *article on* Islam in Southeast Asia and the Pacific.]

BIBLIOGRAPHY

Ahmad bin Mohamed Ibrahim. *The Legal Status of the Muslims in Singapore*. Singapore, 1965. The most complete book on the history of Muslim law in pre-independent Singapore.

Djamour, Judith. *The Muslim Matrimonial Court in Singapore*. New York, 1966. Interesting collection of court cases from the 1950s.

Hussin Zoohri, Wan. *The Singapore Malays: The Dilemma of Development*. Singapore, 1990. Serves as a summary of key community developments in the post-independence period.

Roff, William R. *The Origins of Malay Nationalism*. New Haven, 1967. Classic on the development of the nationalist movement in Singapore and British Malaya.

Siddique, Sharon. "The Administration of Islam in Singapore." In *Islam and Society in Southeast Asia*, edited by Taufik Abdullah and Sharon Siddique, pp. 215–331. Singapore, 1987. Discusses the bureaucratization of Islam in independent Singapore.

Yegar, Moshe. *Islam and Islamic Institutions in British Malaya*. Jerusalem, 1979. Well-researched directory of the development of Islamic institutions under colonial rule.

SHARON SIDDIQUE

SIPĀH-I PASDARĀN-I INQILĀB-I ISLĀMĪ.

One of the most interesting aspects of the Iranian Revolution is the institutional arrangement that was negotiated over the shape and structure of the postrevolutionary armed forces. Rather than completely dismantling the prerevolutionary military structure and replacing it with a militia-based organization, as has been done in many other revolutionary situations, the leadership in Iran has combined a systematic purge and islamization of the armed forces with the creation of a parallel military force, the Sipāh-i Pasdarān-i Inqilāb-i Islāmī (Islamic Revolutionary Guards Corps [IRGC]), which now includes its own military command units (army, air force, and navy) as well as a cabinet-level ministry.

The beginnings of this organization can be traced back to the most chaotic days of the Iranian Revolution, when armed groups of local neighborhood committees (*komitehs*) were organized into a paramilitary force to maintain order in major cities. [*See* Komiteh.] During this period, the armed insurrection that led to complete power seizure was accomplished by a tactical grouping of diverse clerical and secular forces leaving many people but especially the more radical groups well armed. Shaul Bakhash argues that the formation of the IRGC reflected the desire of some of the radical clerics to have an organizational counterweight both to the regular army and the parties of the Left, who were suspected of creating their own armed units. Its creation, then, was a clear signal suggesting the radical clerics' determination to protect "their" nascent revolution with an armed institution of their own. As such, the IRGC's history has mirrored the trials and struggles of the Islamic activists in their aspiration to usurp, maintain, and consolidate state power. Restoring order to the cities and dislodging members of opposition groups from government positions in the earliest days of the revolution, suppressing ethnic uprisings throughout the country in the summer and spring of 1979, helping Ayatollah Ruhollah Khomeini's efforts to monopolize power in the middle of intense and violent attacks by the leftist Mujāhidīn in the spring and summer of 1981, and actively participating in a war that Iraq launched to loosen the Islamic activists' grip on power are just some of the more important tasks the IRGC has had to pursue in order to assure the survival of the Islamic regime.

The organization was formally established by a decree issued by Ayatollah Khomeini on 5 May 1979. Its continued existence and role as the guardian of the Islamic Revolution were affirmed in the Islamic Constitution (Article 150). Like the rest of the armed forces, the IRGC is expected to be Islamic, popular, and constituted from those who believe in the goals of the Islamic Revolution and are devoted to their fulfillment (Article 144). In defining the meaning of Islamic armed forces, the constitution uses the term *maktabi* (cleaving to the line of Khomeini) to require training in principles of belief as well as commitment to the defense of Islam. To fight and make peace in accordance with the requirements of Islamic doctrine necessarily entails the defense of the country, since the former views the latter to be a legitimate right.

Since its inception, the IRGC has witnessed phenomenal growth, reportedly numbering as high as 450,000 uniformed personnel by 1987. Most observers agree that much of this growth can be attributed to the war with Iraq. In addition, the war afforded the opportunity for appropriating such additional functions as mobilization of sufficient numbers for the war and coordinating the war activities of its affiliate militia organization, Basīj-i Mustaẓʿafīn (Mobilization of the Oppressed), which was the linchpin of the so-called human-wave attacks against the Iraqi positions.

Throughout this period of growth, the IRGC leadership has shown a remarkable degree of continuity. After an initial and unsuccessful attempt by non-clerical leaders (such as Defense Minister Muṣṭafā Chamrān and President Abol-Hasan Bani Sadr) to control it, the most important positions in the IRGC's command hierarchy have been occupied by men who had either been appointed in the early 1980s or come up through the IRGC's chain of command. The composition of the rank and file, however, reflects subtle changes. Initially, the IRGC drew from both highly educated and politically sophisticated men who had fought in the underground against the shah and religiously minded lower-class families. But with increased size and sophistication, which has entailed the organization of IRGC academies throughout the country, some changes are evident. Sepehr Zabih estimates that the rank and file consists mostly of young men in the 18–26 age group, with a predominantly urban lower-class background. He, nevertheless, admits that kinship and affiliation with clerical leaders continue to play a role in both recruitment and promotion in rank.

With the end of the war, the IRGC, like the Islamic Revolution itself, has had to find ways to adapt itself. Several important concerns have surfaced. The first relates to the size of the armed forces, including the IRGC. However, security concerns and the potentially disastrous political consequences of antagonizing the IRGC by cuts in budget and personnel have prevented the articulation of this concern in coherent ways. A second related concern, regarding the larger Basīj forces, has also not been effectively confronted. In 1991 and 1992, the regime indicated that it would maintain some of these forces in conjunction with the IRGC near major cities as antiriot squads. The political necessity of maintaining a large number of people on the state payroll, however, continues to be a headache for an already bloated state in the middle of economic difficulties.

The final, and conceivably the most important concern, is the relationship between the IRGC and the regular Iranian armed forces. The existing dual structure is costly, detrimental to the creation of a clear decision-making center on defense matters, and potentially explosive. However, attempts to merge the two forces in spring 1991 were effectively resisted by the IRGC. Instead, some exchange of leadership personnel and cooperative activities, such as joint maneuvers and operations, have been promoted. The issue is bound to remain important in the future. As one of the most important institutions born during the revolutionary moment, the IRGC's identity and future remains solidly tied to the shifting power alliances of Iranian postrevolutionary politics. As such, political maneuvers and divisions within the broader polity are bound to be reproduced within the IRGC, itself a highly politicized institution. For now, the IRGC, along with the regular islamized forces, does enjoy a certain amount of legitimacy because of its success in defending the country's territorial integrity. But, it has a considerable way to go before it becomes part of a more integrated and cohesive armed force.

[*See also* Iranian Revolution of 1979.]

BIBLIOGRAPHY

Bakhash, Shaul. *The Reign of the Ayatollahs: Iran and Islamic Revolution.* New York, 1984. The best available commentary on the events surrounding the creation of IRGC.

Entessar, Nader. "The Military and Politics in the Islamic Republic of Iran." In *Post-Revolutionary Iran*, edited by Hooshang Amirahmadi and Manoucher Parvin, pp. 56–74. Boulder, 1988. The most concise analysis of the effects of the Islamic revolution on the structure of the armed forces.

Hunter, Shireen. *Iran after Khomeini.* New York, 1992. Presents an overview of the most recent changes within the dual structure of the military (see chapter 2).

Katzman, Kenneth. *The Warriors of Islam: Iran's Revolutionary Guard.* Boulder, 1993. The most comprehensive discussion of the organization of the IRGC and the ways it has resisted professionalization so far.

Zabih, Sepehr. *The Iranian Military in Revolution and War.* New York, 1988. Effective use of Iranian sources to analyze the conduct and structure of IRGC (see chapter 8).

FARIDEH FARHI

SIRHINDĪ, AḤMAD (1564–1624), eminent Indian Ṣūfī whose ideas shaped the second or Mujaddidī phase of the Naqshbandī order. Sirhindī was born in the town of Sirhind, East Punjab, the son of a Chishtī-Ṣabīrī shaykh, ʿAbdulaḥad. Educated by his father and at Sialkot, he was later invited to the Mughal court where he assisted the chief minister Abu'l-Faḍl. In 1599 he was initiated into the Naqshbandī order by Khoja Bāqī Billāh (1563–1603). Subsequently he devoted his considerable energies to expounding Naqshbandī doctrine. Some of his claims, for instance that he had surpassed Ibn ʿArabī to reach the last divine manifestation, brought him powerful opposition from colleagues. In 1619 the emperor Jahāngīr imprisoned him so that his "confused mind would calm down a little." After a year he was released but was kept under surveillance until he died.

Sirhindī's creative life falls into two periods: his pre-Ṣūfī phase, when he wrote work typical of a scholar of his time, refuting Shiism and proving the necessity of prophecy; and his Ṣūfī phase, when he produced a range of works suffused with spiritual insight. The most important of these was his collection of 534 letters to nearly two hundred recipients, the *Maktūbāt-i imām-i rabbānī*. Nearly seventy of these letters were to Mughal officials whom he was concerned to win to his views—that orthodoxy should be revived, that superstitious Ṣūfī practices should be suppressed, and that infidels should be humiliated. The great majority of the letters were concerned with his exploration of spiritual mysteries. Regarded as a landmark in Indo-Muslim thought, the letters continue to be republished in their original Persian as well as in Arabic, Turkish, and Urdu.

Sirhindī's prime concern was to integrate his ṣūfī ideas within a Sunnī frame, thus achieving the "perfections of prophecy," the highest Ṣūfī achievement. In pursuing his spiritual quest he elevated the concept of *waḥdat al-shuhūd* (unity of witness) over Ibn ʿArabī's *waḥdat al-wujūd* (unity of being) that had dominated Ṣūfī thought for several centuries. Believers had to realize that "Everything is from Him" and not that "Everything is Him." This new emphasis focused attention away from otherworldly contemplation toward worldly action: the Muslim must strive to realize revelation on earth. This was the basis of Sirhindī's involvement with political power and his emphasis on orthodoxy, and the source of ʿAbdulḥakīm Siyālkotī's (d. 1656) title for him, Mujaddid-i Alf-i Ṣānī, the Renewer of the Second Millennium of Islam.

In the twentieth century the significance of Sirhindī has been much debated. He has been seen variously in religio-political roles as the defiant rebel against government, as the savior of Indian Islam from Mughal heresies, and as the progenitor of a narrow-minded Muslim communalism, and in a Ṣūfī role as replacing *waḥdat al-wujūd* with *waḥdat al-shuhūd*. But his impact on seventeenth-century India was not as great as has been claimed; his religious vision was much contested, and Awrangzīb proscribed his *Maktūbāt*. Moreover, his *waḥdat al-shuhūd* did not replace *waḥdat al-wujūd* in Naqshbandī-Mujaddidī thinking. His emphasis, however, on obedience to *sharīʿah* and *sunnah* as a means of achieving spiritual realization was widely accepted by the Naqshbandīyah and was carried by his successors into Central Asia, Turkey, and the Arab lands, where it has been a source of inspiration to the present.

[*See also* Islam, *article on* Islam in South Asia; Mughal Empire; Naqshbandīyah; *and the biography of Ibn al-ʿArabī.*]

BIBLIOGRAPHY

Ansari, Muhammad Abdul Haq. *Sufism and Sharīʿah: A Study of Shaykh Aḥmad Sirhindī's Effort to Reform Sufism*. Leicester, 1986. Synthesis of Sirhindī's main ideas, with some of his letters in English translation.

Faruqi, Burhan Ahmad. *The Mujaddid's Concept of Tawhid*. 2d ed. Lahore, 1943. Argues that Sirhindī replaced *waḥdat al-wujūd* with *waḥdat al-shuhūd*.

Friedmann, Yohanan. *Shaykh Aḥmad Sirhindī: An Outline of His Thought and a Study of His Image in the Eyes of Posterity*. Montreal, 1971. The best analysis of Sirhindī's thought, although the author's judgment is perhaps too influenced by a desire to correct the distortions of others.

Gaborieau, Marc, et al., eds. *Naqshbandis: Historical Developments and Present Situation of a Muslim Mystical Order*. Istanbul and Paris, 1990. Articles by Hamid Algar, Johan ter Haar, Yohanan Friedmann, Charles Adams, Fateh Mohammad Malik, Marc Gaborieau, and David Damrel cover aspects of Sirhindī's thought and influence.

FRANCIS ROBINSON

SLAVERY. A prevalent institution of the Islamic world throughout its history, slavery (*ʿubūdīyah, riqq*) had a crucial influence on societies and cultures of Islam.

Slavery was common in pre-Islamic and contemporary societies in the Mediterranean basin, Asia, and Africa. Early Islamic dogma assumed its existence as part of society and set out to mitigate the conditions of human bondage. Islamic law defined slavery as an intrusive practice: it forbade the enslavement of free members of Islamic society, including *dhimmī*s (non-Muslims) residing in the abode of Islam. The *sharīʿah* (divine law) regarded as legal salves only those non-Muslims who were imprisoned or bought beyond the borders of Islamic rule, or the sons and daughters of slaves already in captivity. Furthermore, Islam's contention that man is basically free (*al-aṣl huwa al-ḥurrīyah*) forbade the enslavement of foundlings and orphans. The manumission of slaves (*ʿitq*) was condoned as a meritorious act. Islamic law offered several procedures of manumission through a declaration, a will, or a grant of enfranchisement.

The legal status of slaves was somewhat obscure. From a legal viewpoint slaves (male slaves were termed *ʿabd, mamlūk, raqīq, asīr*, or *ghulām;* female slaves were usually termed *jāriyagh* or *fatāh*) were both persons and the properties of others. Slaves were not to be mutilated or killed by their master. Yet the master owned the slave's labor and property and was entitled to his or her sexual submission. Slaves could be bought and sold at the owner's will. A slave was not entirely responsible for his or her actions and was not expected to adhere to the same rigid codes of conduct demanded from a free Muslim. In criminal cases slaves were punished less severely than free Muslims, and sometimes the law required that their master be punished in their stead. In practice (though not always according to the letter of the law) slaves had a right to a certain amount of personal property during their lifetime. On their death, however, any such property reverted to the owner.

Under ʿAbbāsid rule (749–1258) these elaborate legal injunctions of the *sharīʿah* developed alongside other state institutions, not always in complete accord. In practice, slavery deviated from the rules laid down by the *sharīʿah*. The introduction of slave soldiers (*mamlūk*) into the retinues of rulers created a new kind of slave, one that was a member of the political elite, more a master than a slave. Military slavery developed into a major institution of the Islamic world and reached its apex in the Mamlūk sultanate (1254–1517), in which slaves became the rulers of the state. [*See* Mamlūk State.] Side by side with the military institution, domestic and agricultural slavery continued to exist.

The Ottoman Empire inherited the entire spectrum of Islamic slavery and adjusted it to its own needs. From the fifteenth century onward the Ottomans modified military slavery, raising periodic levies of Christian youths from villages inside the empire's territory (*devşirme*), formally enslaving and converting them to Islam and finally incorporating them into the sultan's service. After rigorous training and socialization, these recruits (*kul, kapı kulları*) became the Ottoman ruling elite. Although the imperial palace had a monopoly on this unorthodox method of enslavement, other Ottoman officials, imitating the sultan's household, maintained a parallel recruitment pattern of slaves from abroad, and an elaborate hierarchy of slaves: trained *kul* and other *mamlūk*s, concubines, eunuchs (*khādim, khaṣī*), and valets of all kinds. From the sixteenth century to the end of the nineteenth century slaves rose to the most prominent positions in the state. From this time onward, even free Muslims of old families who wished to enter high-level positions would sometimes request to become "slaves of the *pādishāh*."

The majority of slaves were still used in domestic service. Menial workers were to be found in the houses of the upper and middle classes. In the city and the countryside slaves were also used in industry and sometimes in agriculture. They served as oarsmen and pearl divers in the southern seas, and as plantation laborers in Egypt, Iraq, Yemen, or Africa. Such a disparity created by necessity a clear continuum, at the extremes of which were two types of slaves. The *kul* were to become the social and political elite of master-slaves, while at the other extreme chattel slaves, most often termed *köle*, were employed in the most profane tasks and suffered harsh conditions. The same was true for female slaves—from concubines who became the sultans' consorts to slaves used for domestic and agricultural manual labor. Although mobility along the parallel social ladder of slavery was possible, the move from one extreme to the other, hinging as it were on ascribed statuses of color and race, was quite uncommon. Yet all kinds of slavery, regardless of the differences in status, were united by the harshness of the slaves trade, by the abrupt dislocation of the slave from family and society, and by the almost total domination of slave by master. Similar models of slavery on a somewhat smaller scale existed in the other large Islamic empires of the time—the Mughal state in India and the Ṣafavids in Persia. In Islamic Africa chattel slavery, mainly female, was more common.

From the fifteenth to the eighteenth century several thousand slaves reached the Ottoman Empire every year by caravan or boat from Africa, the Caucasus, and eastern Europe. At the beginning of the nineteenth century the slave trade veered southward. The Russian conquest of the Caucasus and the Crimea, along with repeated defeats in the Balkans, compelled the Ottomans to look for new markets in Africa. This trend was emphasized by the policy of Muḥammad ʿAlī, the rebellious pasha of Egypt, who planned to recruit a new slave army based on black Africans. Although Muḥammad ʿAlī's slave army was a failure, the conquest of the Sudan, and the trade routes opened by Egyptian troops, led to an increase in the numbers of slaves imported to and through Egypt. This trend was amplified by the increased supply of slaves in the aftermath of *jihād* wars in Central and West Africa at the beginning of the nineteenth century.

In later decades the growing involvement of European powers, mainly Britain, posed a new challenge to slavery and the slave trade. Having just abolished slavery in Europe itself, British diplomats struggled to reduce the number of slaves brought into the United States and the Ottoman Empire in a series of treaties from the 1840s to the 1880s prohibiting slave trade. These efforts culminated in the Anglo-Egyptian convention for the suppression of the slave trade in 1877, and its Anglo-Ottoman parallel in 1880. In 1890 the Ottoman government signed the Brussels Act against the slave trade, and the maritime trade in African slaves gradually abated.

In a parallel development the status of the institution itself was eroded. Although most senior officials, including avowed reformers, still maintained large slave and *mamlūk* households, later decades of the nineteenth century witnessed a rapid erosion of slavery's legal and moral basis. Laws concerning the legal status of slaves were enacted as part of the changes promised in the Gülhâne rescript of 1839 and the Islâhat Fermanı of 1856. Some of the first decisions by the reformed courts and committees in the Ottoman Empire and Egypt denied slaves the special status of diminished responsibility accorded them by *sharīʿah.* Other verdicts established the legal equality of slaves. When slave-holding Circassian tribes fleeing the Russians sought refuge in the empire in midcentury, Ottoman courts debated the status of their slaves, and decided to accord them Ottoman citizenship. Other decisions further eroded the *sharīʿah* basis of slavery by defining it as a specifically Islamic institution, which can therefore be enforced only on those who have decided to embrace Islam. Thus, from an Islamic point of view, slavery ceased to be a purely intrusive institution. The legality of slavery was finally revoked in a decree of 1887, declaring that "The Imperial government not officially recognizing the state of slavery, considers by law every person living in the empire to be free" (George Young, *Corps de droit Ottoman,* 1905, vol. 2, p. 170).

In spite of these declarations, at the beginning of the twentieth century slavery lived on in the Ottoman Empire and in other parts of the Islamic world. The imperial harem of Abdülhamid II (r. 1876–1909) still contained hundreds of women and eunuchs. Large slave populations continued to exist in Arab lands, in the Indian subcontinent, and in Africa. In most states of the Arabian peninsula slavery was abolished only in the second half of the twentieth century. Since then it is almost extinct in the central lands of Islam but has never entirely disappeared. During the 1980s, as a result of civil wars in Sudan and Somalia, slavery reappeared in these regions. Reports from Sudan reveal that the practice is still widespread in border areas between the northern and southern parts of the country.

BIBLIOGRAPHY

Baer, Gabriel. "Slavery and its Abolition." In *Studies in the Social History of Modern Egypt.* Chicago, 1969. Well-documented research of slavery in Ottoman Egypt to the twentieth century.

Brunschvig, Robert. "ʿAbd." In *Encyclopaedia of Islam,* new ed., vol. 1, pp. 24–40. Leiden, 1960–. Extensive survey of Islamic slavery, focusing on Islamic law and jurisprudence.

Lewis, Bernard. *Race and Slavery in the Middle East.* New York, 1990. Historical inquiry into the question of race and its effect on the status of slaves in the Middle East. Contains much valuable information on the institution.

Pipes, Daniel. *Slave Soldiers and Islam: The Genesis of a Military System.* New Haven, 1981. Informed attempt to explain the propensity toward military slavery in Islamic societies.

Toledano, Ehud R. *The Ottoman Slave Trade and Its Suppression, 1840–1890.* Princeton, 1982. The most comprehensive study of slave trade in the Ottoman Empire to date.

Toledano, Ehud R. "Ottoman Concepts of Slavery in the Period of Reform, 1830s to 1880s." In *Breaking the Chains: Slavery, Bondage, and Emancipation in Africa and Asia,* edited by Martin A. Klein. Madison, Wis., 1992. Discussion of the Ottoman deliberations on the institution and its abolition.

DROR ZE'EVI

SOCIALISM AND ISLAM. Two important currents of social and religious philosophy that have flowed through centuries of Middle Eastern and North African development are socialism and Islam. Although they have often reinforced each other, sometimes they have come into conflict. Both schools of thought have individually and collectively exerted major influences on the political and spiritual direction of the region.

Socialist philosophy and practice, though generally considered to be of European origin, also have roots in the Arab Middle East. One of the earliest references to socialism can be found in the writings of Jamāl al-Dīn al-Afghānī (1838–1897), among the most celebrated Islamic reformers of the late nineteenth century. Al-Afghānī located the concept of *ishtirākīyah* (socialism) in pre-Islamic Arabian bedouin traditions. The framers of the initial Islamic state in the seventh century, according to al-Afghānī, adopted these traditions as the structural basis from which to organize and regulate society. Al-Afghānī contended that socialism was an indigenous Arab doctrine, which explained the Muslim community's historic commitment to the welfare of all its inhabitants.

In Egypt, among the first and most prominent socialist thinkers was Salāmah Mūsā (1887–1958), whose long career as an advocate for social justice began while he was a student in England in the early 1900s. In 1913, on his return to Egypt, he published his groundbreaking essay entitled *Al-ishtirākīyah* (Socialism), a work that introduced the socialist theme to a generation of Arab intellectuals and activists interested in reformist strategies for modernization and development. Deeply influenced by Fabian thought, Mūsā published some fifty books on social, economic, and philosophical subjects which were widely read and profoundly respected.

Salāmah Mūsā also engaged in political organization, and in 1920 he participated in the formation of the short-lived Egyptian Socialist Party, which was recast as the Egyptian Communist Party in 1923 and guided by Marxist ideology. Objecting to the radical ideas of the recast party, Salāmah Mūsā and others of his reformist philosophical inclination dropped out of organized oppositional activity. The Communist Party had marginalized Fabian socialists, who no longer had an organization in which to operate.

In Egypt, secular socialists had organized both legally and clandestinely since World War I, but Islamic reformers did not begin articulating religiously based ideas of social justice until the 1930s and 1940s. The Muslim Brotherhood, for example, founded in 1928, did not adhere to socialist ideology, but throughout its existence it has interacted, often in a confrontational manner, with both secular and religious socialists. Philosophically, the brotherhood embraced the vision of the nineteenth-century Islamic revivalist movement, which supported the establishment of an Islamic system of government based on the Qur'ān and the *sunnah* of the Prophet. The organization opposed the Western penetration of the Islamic world, including socialist thought, which it understood as another form of colonial ideology imposed on Muslim society.

Ḥasan al-Bannā' (1906–1949), supreme guide of the Egyptian Muslim Brotherhood, and others represented a new generation of nationalists who had lost faith in the prevailing liberal, economic, and Western model of development. Calling for national independence, socioeconomic modernization, and Islamic social justice, they advocated society's rebirth through the affirmation of religiously inspired concepts. Asserting Islam's universality and its commitment to comprehensive human and economic justice, Islamic reformers went back to the Qur'ān itself for confirmation of the faith's spiritual and material compatibility with social progress. Identifying relevant passages from the Holy Book and examples from the prophet Muḥammad's life, Islamic thinkers maintained that religious doctrine not only contained prescriptions for the relationship between a believer and the Lord, but also mandated how a society should organize itself and how its people should be ministered to. The Muslim Brotherhood's ideologues went back to the time of the Prophet and his immediate successors in order to produce an appropriate paradigm.

In the post–World War II period, Islamic socialism (a phrase used sometimes interchangeably with Arab socialism) took root in the Middle East and North Africa. Egypt, Syria, Libya, Iraq, Iran, Tunisia, Algeria, and South Yemen separately and at different times have subscribed to variations of Islamic socialism. However, it was Gamal Abdel Nasser (1918–1970) who first capitalized on the intersection between Islam and socialism and used it to consolidate and then to protect his regime.

Nasser's socialist revolution, carried out by junior-level military officers in 1952, paid tribute to the writings of progressive Islamic intellectuals in Egypt. In particular, Shaykh Khālid Muḥammad Khālid (b. 1920), in his book *Min hunā nabda'* (From Here We Start), argued that socialism was sanctioned by Islam and necessary as an alternative to capitalist economic development in the country. Although Khālid's ideas were derived from the European social democratic movement, his interpretation of modern Egypt was firmly grounded in the conditions of the time: British colonial control, economic backwardness, and moral bankruptcy. Egypt, he contended, would not develop spiritually or economically until it improved the lives of its people and provided them with the decent treatment and justice stipulated by the Qur'ān. Khālid believed that the revolution of 1952 could be the beginning of meaningful societal development and Islamic spiritual growth.

A critic of mainstream Islam as taught and practiced at al-Azhar, Khālid argued that the religion of the priesthood was a religion of reaction that strengthened the position of the wealthy and excused the poverty of the majority. For him, true Islam was compassionate, fair, and grounded in a commitment to economic justice. [*See the biography of Khālid.*]

One of the most influential theorists of the Nasser period was Muṣṭafā al-Sibā'ī (1915–1964), dean of the Faculty of Islamic Jurisprudence and the School of Law at the University of Damascus and head of the Syrian branch of the Muslim Brotherhood (known as the Islamic Socialist Front) between 1945 and 1961. An ally of Nasser, al-Sibāʿī dissolved the Syrian branch of the Muslim Brotherhood in 1958 when all Syrian political parties and organizations were abolished in preparation for the establishment of the United Arab Republic.

In 1959, al-Sibāʿī published *Ishtirākīyat al-Islām* (The Socialism of Islam) in which he argued that socialism and Islam were not only compatible, but that the adoption of socialism must be society's goal. According to al-Sibāʿī, socialism was more important than the nationalization of property, more significant than progressive taxation, and more meaningful than setting a limit on personal ownership; socialism as a developmental tool was a means by which society could prosper and mature. Moreover, it was a guarantor against human exploitation and an instrument to be used by the state to supervise economic development. Socialism was al-Sibāʿī's formula for eliminating poverty and for allowing individuals to achieve their potential.

Asserting that it protected the right of ownership, al-Sibāʿī defined Islam as less rigid than communism. In fact, Islamic socialism is different from so-called scientific socialism or communism in that it allows for the private ownership of the means of production and only appropriates property when its advocates deem property owners to be exploitative. Islamic socialism allows the public sector to exist side-by-side with the private sector and advocates harmonious relations between social groups, not class warfare. Society thus allows different occupational groupings to exist and to constitute a division of labor in society, but these groups are envisioned as cooperative and not adversarial.

The basis of social solidarity in the Islamic socialist model was, according to al-Sibāʿī, *al-takāful al-ijtimāʿī*, or a combination of equality, justice, mutuality, and responsibility. When socialist society achieves its goals, he maintained, it will be free of conflict, basing itself on moral principles and collectivism.

Al-Sibāʿī asserted that Islamic socialism rested on five pillars: the right to live protected and healthy; the right to liberty; the right to knowledge; the right to dignity; and the qualified right to property. He stressed that Islam recognized a person's desire to create and amass wealth and to own property. Although al-Sibāʿī believed in the social obligations connected to affluence, such as *zakāt* (giving alms), he also argued that these obligations did not constitute socialism. He was emphatic in his belief that the only way to eliminate hunger, disease, and injustice was through national legislation backed up by the authority of the state. Economic and social development would not be accomplished by means of charity alone. Al-Sibāʿī's ideas were embraced by Nasser and used to defend the Egyptian regime. The National Charter of 1962 was Nasser's attempt to merge nationalism, socialism, and Islam. [*See the biographies of Sibāʿī and Nasser.*]

Although al-Sibāʿī played a profound role in providing the intellectual justification for Islamic socialism, not all Islamic thinkers or activists agreed with this approach. Sayyid Quṭb (1906–1966), for example, the major ideologue of the Muslim Brotherhood of Egypt in the Nasser period, denounced the term Islamic socialism, believing that Islam alone provided for human and economic justice, moral and spiritual values, and equality. Quṭb held that Islam provided the only solution to the social, economic, national, and moral problems created both by capitalism and communism.

For Quṭb, there were only two ideological paths a society could follow: there was the Islamic route or the one he called Jāhilīyah, or pre-Islamic ignorance. Quṭb contended that capitalism, socialism, and communism were similarly part of Jāhilīyah and could never be reconciled with Islam. Islam, on the contrary, was just and would satisfy all human needs. Quṭb's opposition to Nasser's socialism and his militant writings made him an enemy of the regime. He was imprisoned for many years and finally executed in 1966. [*See* Jāhilīyah *and the biography of Quṭb.*]

The creation of an Islamic state based on *sharīʿah* (the divine law) was an imperative for Sayyid Quṭb; any other type of society was illegitimate. In the many books he wrote on Islam, Quṭb argued that all Muslims should give of themselves completely in the effort to achieve the true Islamic society.

Outside Egypt, Baʿthists in both Syria and Iraq adopted the broad features of Islamic socialism. Baʿthist ideology has been consistently anticolonialist, Pan-Arabist, and interventionist in social legislation in the areas of health, education, and workers' rights. It has supported the nationalization of basic industries, banks, and foreign trade and boasted a planned economy. According to Michel ʿAflaq (1910–1989) and Ṣalāḥ al-Dīn al-Bayṭār (b. 1912), Syrian political thinkers and philosophers, Baʿthist ideology celebrates Arab culture and the historical experiences of the prophet Muḥammad. In principle, Baʿthism rejects religious intolerance and promises the greatest human and societal freedom. [*See* Baʿth Parties.]

Consistent with the major revolutionary changes in the Arab world in the 1950s and 1960s, Libya, too, witnessed dramatic upheaval. In 1969, Muʿammar al-Qadhdhāfī (b. 1942) and a group of young army officers overthrew the monarchy of King Idrīs and established a radically new society based on Pan-Arabism, socialism, and Islam.

Qadhdhāfī followed the revolutionary and ideological model set by his mentor, Nasser, and embraced the latter's commitment to Arab unity, economic equality, and antiimperialism. But Qadhdhāfī went beyond Nasser and placed his highly idiosyncratic stamp on Libya by the affirmative islamization of social life. In particular, Qadhdhāfī prohibited the practice of gambling, the use of alcohol, and the presence of nightclubs in an effort to improve public morality. He also introduced Islamic punishments for such crimes as theft, adultery, and usury.

Qadhdhāfī codified his ideas in a three-volume work entitled *The Green Book*. In the first volume, "The Solution to the Problem of Democracy," published in 1975, Qadhdhāfī outlined his Third International theory (also known as The Third Way), which he conceived as an alternative to both capitalism and communism. In *The Green Book*, Qadhdhāfī excoriated both Western colonialism and Soviet domination, arguing that foreign influences have contaminated Muslim societies and led the believers astray morally and theologically.

As a means to resist imperialist forces, Qadhdhāfī produced a doctrine whose inspiration was the Qur'ān and whose natural constituency were to be Muslims and anticolonialists throughout the Middle East and the Third World. In the teachings of the Qur'ān, he indirectly suggested, solutions could be found to all problems of humanity—ranging from personal matters to international relations. For Qadhdhāfī, the application of the Islamic socialist and democratic model would prevent both foreign and domestic exploitation and would lead to the creation of a just society.

The Green Book was written not as a religious text, but rather as a provocative and inspirational pamphlet, accessible to a wide audience. Its influence spread far beyond the borders of Libya into the rest of the Middle East, North Africa, and the Third World. [*See the biography of Qadhdhāfī.*]

Islam also informed national liberation movements in other parts of the Maghrib (known as the Arab West or North Africa), and after nationalism triumphed socialist regimes typically were created. A proliferation of independence movements grew up in reaction to the harsh colonial policies of the French, who had gained control over most of the area in the nineteenth and twentieth centuries. North African Arabs and Berbers deeply resented France's sustained attempts to eradicate local political traditions and to undermine indigenous leaders. Like other colonized peoples at this time, they suffered humiliation in the face of France's prejudicial attitudes, its contempt for local religious customs, and its rejection of indigenous culture. For North Africans a particularly sore spot was the requirement that French be used as the official language of the area.

In the post–World War I period, Islamic reformers in the Maghrib were small in number. They exerted influence, however, when they merged with nationalists who commanded large popular followings. Despite an orientation fundamentally different from secular nationalists, they maintained their focus on the Arab-Islamic heritage, which proved able to unite otherwise disparate political and tribal forces. Islam, in fact, contributed to the identity of the nationalist movement and helped it to triumph over the colonial power.

The longest and bloodiest battle for national liberation was waged in Algeria where colonization lasted from 1847 to 1962. The French strove to impose their culture on the Algerians, and in this crusade hoped to destroy Islam through the systematic closing down of Qur'ānic schools and *madrasahs* (high schools) and by converting mosques into churches. A young generation of educated reformers and nationalists emerged in self-defense, appropriating Islam and using it as a unifying force in society. The reformers argued that Islam was compatible with the modern world and that Algerians would be best served by adapting Islam to their political and social struggles. Islam became an especially important component of the liberation struggle waged by a cross-section of Algerian nationalists.

In Tunisia, where the French had been the colonial masters from 1881 until the grant of formal independence in 1956, recognition of an Arab-Islamic heritage grew in the postindependence period. Tunisia tried to recast its national identity and image under Habib Bourguiba (b. 1903), leader of the Neo-Destour party (renamed in 1959 as the Socialist Destour party) and head of the one-party state until his removal in 1987. [*See* Destour.]

Influenced by the writings of al-Afghānī and Muḥammad ʿAbduh (1849–1905), leaders of the Arab East's Salafīyah movement, Maghrib reformers emphasized the importance of their Islamic heritage. In analyzing their society, they were not only critical of the French, but of equal significance they denounced local Ṣūfī leaders who were seen as reactionary and complicitous with the foreign occupation. Reformers also stressed the importance of understanding the modern world from a religious as well as scientific perspective and appealed for a renaissance in Islamic learning.

A section of the Iranian oppositional movement in the 1960s and 1970s, whose goal was to oust Muhammad Reza Shah from power, also linked Islam with change. Jalāl Āl Aḥmad, who had been a secular intellectual with connections to the Iranian Communist (Tudeh) party, called for reshaping the nation's purpose, its identity, and its destiny. In his highly acclaimed work *Gharbzadegi* (Weststruckness), published in 1962, he decried the westernization of Iranian society, with its destructive glorification of foreign culture and its resulting surrender of true national identity. Jalal Āl Aḥmad came to believe that Islam could inspire the mass of Iranian society to rise up against the shah's rule. His theme of Islam and socialism motivated many to reflect on their society and take action against the status quo.

Among the intellectuals and activists who shared an Islamic vision of change in the 1960s and 1970s were Mehdi Bāzargān (b. 1907), who became the provisional prime minister of the Islamic Republic of Iran in 1979, ʿAlī Sharīʿatī (1933–1977), and the ayatollah Ruhollah Khomeini (1902–1989).

ʿAli Sharīʿatī's influence on Iranian society in the 1970s, particularly among the students and young people who read his work, took his classes, and listened to the provocative lectures he delivered, was profound. Sharīʿatī's followers were galvanized by his stirring calls for social justice and Islamic revivalism. Joining together in religious groups and secular political organizations, they participated in revolutionary activities which altered the direction and orientation of Iranian society.

Sharīʿatī was influenced not only by original religious texts, but also by the interpretive works of al-Afghānī and the Pakistanian Islamic reformer, Muhammad Iqbal. He drew also from the corpus of revolutionary theory articulated by such Third World activists as Frantz Fanon and Che Guevara. Calling for a renaissance within the Islamic community, Sharīʿatī advocated modernization and scientific change informed by Iranian culture and Muslim religious tradition. Sharīʿatī's teachings were anathema to the shah, who imprisoned him, then put him under village arrest. Sharīʿatī was eventually allowed to travel to England, where he died of suspicious causes. Mehdi Bāzargān, on the other hand, appealed to a different audience consisting mainly of merchants, civil servants, and other members of the middle class. He popularized a modernized view of Islam that incorporated the themes of justice, science, and faith. In 1979, Ayatollah Khomeini capitalized on the prevailing revolutionary spirit that had been produced by the initiatives of Jalal al-Aḥmad, Mehdi Bāzargān, and ʿAlī Sharīʿatī and established the Islamic Republic of Iran. [*See the biographies of Bāzargān, Sharīʿatī, and Khomeini.*]

The synthesis of socialist thought with Islamic theology has been complex and irregular. Although often in conflict, the schools of thought have sometimes mutually informed one another. Politically, nationalist movements have been vitalized by Islamic thinking, although the independent governments produced by such movements have regularly relied on socialist principles for the structuring of society. One would expect this fusion and crossfertilization to continue in the Muslim world.

[*See also* Arab Socialism; Communism and Islam.]

BIBLIOGRAPHY

Primary Sources

Āl Aḥmad, Jalāl. *Gharbzadegi: Weststruckness*. Translated by John Green and Ahmad Alizadeh. Lexington, Ky., 1982. Harsh critique of Western influences on Iranian civilization.

Āl Aḥmad, Jalāl. *Iranian Society*. Edited by Michael C. Hillman. Lexington, Ky., 1982. Anthology of Āl Aḥmād's writings.

Mūsā, Salāmah. *Al-ishtirākīyah (Socialism)*. Cairo, 1913. Famed work on socialist thought and practice.

Qadhdhāfī, Muʿammar al-. *The Green Book*. London, 1976.

Sharīʿatī, ʿAlī. *On the Sociology of Islam*. Translated by Hamid Algar. Berkeley, 1979.

Sharīʿatī, ʿAlī. *Marxism and Other Western Fallacies*. Translated by R. Campbell. Berkeley, 1980. Stirring discussion of Islamic accomplishments in twentieth-century Iran, with a critique of leftist dogma.

Sibāʿī, Muṣṭafā al-. "Islamic Socialism." In *Political and Social Thought in the Contemporary Middle East*, edited by Kemal Karpat, pp. 123–126. London, 1968.

Ṭāleqānī, Maḥmud. *Islam and Ownership*. Translated by Ahmad Jabari and Farhang Rajaee. Lexington, Ky., 1983.

Interpretive Works

Binder, Leonard. *Islamic Liberalism*. Chicago, 1988. Wide-ranging discussion of major "development ideologies" in the modern Islamic world.

Donohue, John J., and John L. Esposito, eds. *Islam in Transition*. New York, 1982. Translations of selected Muslim thinkers and their responses to the challenges of modernity.

Esposito, John L. *Islam and Politics*. Syracuse, N.Y., 1984. Concise overview of Islamic thinkers and practitioners in the Middle East, North Africa, and Asia.

Haddad, Yvonne Yazbeck. "Sayyid Qutb: Ideologue of Islamic Revival." In *Voices of Resurgent Islam*, edited by John L. Esposito, pp. 67–98. New York and Oxford, 1983.

Keddie, Nikki R. *Sayyid Jamāl al-Dīn "Al-Afghānī": A Political Biography*. Berkeley, 1972.

Said, Abdel Moghny. *Arab Socialism*. New York, 1972. Good description of the major socialist movements from a sympathetic perspective.

SELMA BOTMAN

SOCIAL SCIENCES. A strong interest in the social order was manifested from the earliest period of Islamic history. Society was to be patterned according to the guidelines laid down in the Qur'ān. The emergence of the schools of law (*madhahabs*) indicated the serious concern with social issues; the interests of the individual were placed within the context of the greater society.

The earliest formulation of the concept of a good society and government containing elements of political and social philosophy was the comprehensive instruction of the fourth righteous caliph, ʿAlī ibn Abī Ṭālib, to the newly appointed governor of Egypt, Mālik al-Ashtar, in 658 CE. It contains many points that are as valid today as they were in the seventh century.

Caliph ʿAlī's other writings, compiled in the *Nahj al-balāghah*, drew attention to history and the problem of oppression. This is the earliest record of one of a prominent Islamic figure attempting to encourage the study of history and society in the universal and enlightened sense. In his advice to his son Ḥasan, ʿAlī stressed the need to study history, the fate of past people. He pondered over their performance and the events surrounding them with great empathy, saying:

> I walked among their ruins till I was regarded one of them. In fact by virtue of their affairs that have become known to me it is as though I have lived with them from the first to the last. I have therefore been able to discern the dirty from the clean and the benefit from the harm" (*Nahjul Balagha: Sermons, Letters and Sayings of Imam Ali*. p. 426).

ʿAlī also stressed the need for a ruler to keep continuous discourse with men of learning in order to understand the causes of prosperity and stability. The interest in inquiring into the conditions of society, prosperity, oppression and tyranny, moral decadence, religious devotion and deviation, the dynamics of conflict between man, and a host of other related themes was first kindled by ʿAlī. It was a result of reflection on what he had to confront in real life. Centuries later many of the themes raised by ʿAlī became apparent and it was left to Ibn Khaldūn to develop them and to link them into a pattern in history.

The passion for history eventually extended toward the study of society, subsequently exemplified by the intellectually revolutionary formulation of historiography and sociology by ʿAbd al-Raḥmān ibn Khaldūn in the fourteenth century. Ibn Khaldūn has been called the founder of the disciplines of history and sociology. In his monumental *Muqaddimah* he introduced the cyclical theory of the rise and fall of dynasties, together with their foundation, the different types of solidarity (*ʿaṣabīyah*). Ibn Khaldūn anticipated many findings of modern social science, including the idea of systemic causation and the principle of interdependence among factors, as well as the general influence of social factors on events and human psychology. [*See the biography of Ibn Khaldūn.*]

Despite his great contribution to the study of society, no succeeding development appeared in this field after Ibn Khaldūn; until the present day there has been no attempt at the historical analysis of Muslim society surpassing Ibn Khaldūn's achievement. Modern Islamic social-science thinking in the nineteenth and twentieth centuries at best raised isolated problems without the foundation of a thorough framework sustained through decades of cumulative research by a community of scholars immersed in the relevant disciplines.

What is meant by Islamic social science? By this we do not mean mere studies of Islamic society and its social problems, or the discussion of Islamic ideas and events in the Muslim community; we mean critical or affirmative discussion of the Islamic religious system, or the application of the social sciences in the study of social phenomena derived from Islamic influence. An analogous Western example is Max Weber's study of the Protestant ethic, which theorizes that Calvinist doctrine conditioned the rise of the capitalist spirit. An analogous study could be that of the way Islam awakened the scientific spirit during the ʿAbbāsid caliphate in the ninth century CE, bringing social-science concepts and methodology to bear on the historical data.

Studies of this kind are rare but have begun to appear in the twentieth century. Far more abundant, however, are discourses on social philosophy and agitation for Islamic reform, exemplified by Jamāl al-Dīn al-Afghānī and Sayyid Aḥmad Khān in the nineteenth century, and in the twentieth by writers such as Said Nursî in Turkey and Muḥammad Bāqir al-Ṣadr in Iraq. Their works did evince greater intellectual acumen than many in their times; Bāqir al-Ṣadr's *Our Philosophy* dealt, among other topics, with the refutation of Marxism, but employed hardly any historical data.

Nearer to the social-science sphere are some of the discussions offered by Murtaẓā Muṭahharī, ʿAlī Sharīʿatī, and Malek Bennabi. A very interesting contribution was made by Edward W. Blyden, a Liberian professor and cabinet minister in 1887, on Islam and the African character. The works of all these thinkers raise significant problems worthy of serious scholarly pursuit.

Certain salient points in their contributions suggest the prospective research scenario for the social sciences in Islamic society. A leading recent thinker is Malek Bennabi, an Algerian engineer, patriot, and reformer appointed Director of Higher Education in 1963. He was noted for his part in the struggle for independence and for numerous public lectures on politics and Islamic reform. The key to the problem of reform is what he described as the "post–al-Muwaḥḥid man," Bennabi's personification of the decadence and backwardness that emerged after the fall of the al-Muwaḥḥid (Almohad) dynasty in the thirteenth century in North Africa. Bennabi attributed the consequent stagnation of Islamic society to the pervasive influence of this human type on the subsequent course of Islamic history. He catalogued a number of psychological traits dominating the post–al-Muwaḥḥid man, a type he believed became dominant around the epoch of Ibn Khaldūn in the fourteenth century.

An important observation of Bennabi is his comparison between the traditionalism of the English conservative and the traditionalism of the post–al-Muwaḥḥid man. Writing about the sociological "heredity" of the two societies, Bennabi said:

> But these two aspects of heredity are not identical: in the one case, it is a question of aptitude, in the other the ineptitude. The Englishman voluntarily inclines towards a certain traditionalism, judged necessary for national equilibrium; but this equilibrium is dynamic. In the Muslim society, on the contrary, it bespeaks of an impotence to surpass that which is given, to go beyond the known, to cross new historical frontiers, to create and assimilate anew. Here it is no more a question of determination but of an insolvency. (1991, p. 12)

Thus Bennabi highlighted the significance of a human type collectively dominating the reaction and attitude of Islamic society toward the problems of the age. Bennabi raises numerous valid and significant problems susceptible to further sociological and historical research. It is this emphasis on a human type, persisting for centuries, that makes Bennabi's contribution most original. Although he did not deal exhaustively with any of the problems he raised, nevertheless he brought them up for discussion.

Another author somewhat similar in sensibility to Bennabi in his concern with the problem of decadence and human type is ʿAlī Sharīʿatī. He directed his attention to martyrdom and its sociology and psychology, a theme that emanates from the Shīʿī religious outlook. Sharīʿatī introduced significant sociological inquiry into the nature, meaning, and function of martyrdom, centering around the tragedy of Karbala (680 CE) in which Ḥusayn ibn ʿAlī, the grandson of the prophet Muḥammad, and seventy-two followers pitted themselves against an overwhelmingly superior force.

Sharīʿatī saw the significance of this event as the expression of revolt against evil when no other means are available: the intention was not to overpower the enemy but to expose him and to awaken the spirit of resistance. He deduced sociological and historical consequences from the martyrdom of Ḥusayn. Two kinds of martyrdom are distinguished by Sharīʿatī—*jihād* and *shahādah*. *Jihād* is the defense of the faith with power and struggle as in a holy war, while *shahādah* is the defense of the faith through dying for it in a conscious manner, as planned by Ḥusayn ibn ʿAlī, to whom the alternative was to pay homage to evil.

Ḥusayn's martyrdom exposed the infamy of the ruling power and influenced the rest of the Muslim world. Even the Sunnī imams became uncompromising in their attitudes toward the Umayyad and ʿAbbāsid dynasties (Sharīʿatī, 1986). Sharīʿatī's thesis on the impact of Ḥusayn's martyrdom offers attractive results from a historical and sociological perspective. Much attention had previously been given to the tragedy in the historical narrative sense, but little to its overall sociological and historical impact, and Sharīʿatī attempted to supply the latter. [*See the biography of Sharīʿatī.*]

Muṭahharī, who was himself assassinated, also wrote about martyrdom to clarify its aims and concepts. Muṭahharī wrote on numerous subjects, but the one of most interest here is his discussion of the historical transformation of Iran through conversion to Islam. He notes, "the arrival of Islam in Iran was an invasion from the viewpoint of the politico-religious forces ruling the country. But it was a revolution in the fullest sense of the word and with all its characteristics from the viewpoint of the masses and the Iranian nation" ("Islam and Iran: A Historical Study of Mutual Services," *Al-tawḥīd* [Tehran] 8.2 [Nov. 1990–Jan. 1991]: 157). Among the significant transformations brought about by Islam was the rise of Iranians to ascendancy in scientific and other cultural domains for the first time in their history, preceded by the first unification of religious faith in Iran. The religious and political boundaries once drawn around Iran were demolished by Islam, and the new interaction with the outside world stimulated the Iranians. Their talents were accepted far and wide, and they became exemplars: in the pre-Islamic period, there were no such Iranian figures as al-Razī, al-Fārābī, and Ibn Sīnā.

There were many other significant changes mentioned by Muṭahharī worthy of sociological research, such as the radical change in class structure. Muṭahharī's treatment of the subject is comprehensive in the sense of raising the awareness of Islamic influence on Iranian society, although its methodology is not entirely sociological.

In yet another work Muṭahharī addresses the differential effect of the Islamic reform movement in the nineteenth and twentieth centuries among the Sunnīs and Shīʿīs. Why did revolutionary movements involving mass action take place among Shīʿīs and not among the Sunnīs? Muṭahharī was referring not to the movement against Western imperialism but to that against injustice and exploitation. He writes:

> In the history of the Sunnī world, we do not come across movements like the anti-tobacco movement led by the religious leaders in Iran as a result of which monopolization was canceled and external colonization and internal absolutism were dealt a severe blow. There was no movement like the uprising in Iraq which liberated that country from the yoke of British colonization. There was no movement like that of constitutionalism against the autocratic regime in Iran resulting in the establishment of constitutionalism. And lastly there has been no movement in the Sunnī world like the one which is led by the religious leaders in Iran today. (1979, p. 51)

The explanation given by Muṭahharī is the differential role and position of the religious leadership in the two communities. In the Sunnī world the religious institution is aligned with and under the control of the ruling power, whereas among the Shīʿīs it is independent of the ruling power. The Shīʿī religious leaders were thus in a better position to exert their influence and lead the masses against an oppressive regime. Hence Muṭahharī opens the subject of the sociology of leadership in the Muslim world as conditioned by the nature of the religious framework creating differential functions and impacts. [*See the biography of Muṭahharī.*]

What is presently lacking is in-depth study of the problems raised by Muṭahharī, Sharīʿatī, Bennabi, and Afghānī. Their thoughts and discourse are Islam-centered, and any research and analysis in this direction would serve to establish the Islamic social-science tradition.

Another interesting work comes from another quarter, not from a Muslim but from an ardent admirer of Islam, Edward W. Blyden (1832–1912), a West Indian black clergyman who became a Liberian national and secretary of state as well as professor of classics at Liberia College. His magnum opus, *Christianity, Islam, and the African Race* (1887; rev. ed. 1992) is strewn with original insights and significant material for sociological and cultural-anthropological research. He discusses the effects of Islam and Christianity on the African people and showed how the nature of each faith patterned different results.

What is most original in Blyden's analysis, of great significance in the sociology of religion, is his distinction between the nature of conversion for Africans drawn to Christianity and those drawn to Islam. He explains the different phenomena by relating them to African cultural and situational background, Western colonialism, and historical contacts with Arabia. According to Blyden, conversion to Christianity made Africans imitators, and conversion to Islam made them disciples. Culturally and sociologically, Islam introduced a superstructure on a permanent indigenous structure. When Arabs met Africans in their own home, the result was amalgamation rather than absorption or undue repression (Blyden, 1992, p. 33). Christianity, on the other hand, introduced the sense of subordination to the white man, his symbols and images, while Islam allowed the flow of African symbols into religious life, because Islam lacked preexisting pictorial representation. In addition, Africans found it easy to blend their identity with Islam because a member of their race, Bilāl, was a companion of the Prophet and assisted at the birth of the religion (p. 400), and an African slave was the mother of the Prophet's ancestor Ismāʿīl.

Blyden's work is rich in sociological insights and causal explanations. An example is the contrasting types of the Arab and European missionary: the Arab missionary married and intermingled with the African converts; the European missionary kept a social distance. Blyden's work offers suggestions for sociological and cultural study of the integration of Islam into African culture, the changes wrought by Islam at the institutional as well as the personal psychological level, and an understanding of the interplay of various historical and social factors in the spread of Islam and the nature of conversion.

This discussion has dealt mainly with the study of social phenomena derived from Islamic institutions and beliefs, a nascent field. It has excluded the large body of work on socioeconomic problems not directly related to Islam. The bulk of modern writing, scholarly and otherwise, has however been in the area of social philosophy rather than in social science proper. A recent example within the confines of social science is Fatima Mernissi's work on the origin of Islamic family institution as conditioned by the Islamic religious system (*Women and Islam: An Historical and Theological Enquiry*, Oxford, 1991). [*See the biography of Mernissi.*]

There is a noticeable growth in social-science research on economic and related social problems, but it can hardly be Islamic in thematic and problematic orientation. Developing Islamic social-science research is a hopeful prospect, but the obstacles are great if cooperation is not forthcoming from authority. For example, in a society attempting to implement the traditional *sharīʿah* law (*ḥudūd*), sociological study of its impact would only be possible with the cooperation of the ruling power and with access to data in official files. This has not yet occurred; instead, what we have are bits and pieces of information filtered through the mass media or other nonscientific sources.

Islamic social science research has yet to emerge as a sustained and collective effort dealing with problems conditioned by the Islamic religious system. In the West social science emerged out of social philosophy, and the present ascendancy of Islamic social philosophy in the Muslim world is bound to give birth to a comparable Islamic social-science tradition. After endless discourse on the perfect social order, one is bound to ask why reality is otherwise. A balanced and reflective mind will seek the aid of the social sciences. Culinary recipes do not satisfy hunger—only the actual dish does. That requires a science of cooking practiced by living cooks, not by those of bygone ages. The dead can only inspire; it is the living who must aspire.

BIBLIOGRAPHY

In addition to the works mentioned above, the following provide a general appreciation of social-science themes that have emerged from various research perspectives on Islamic society.

Alatas, Syed Hussein. *Modernization and Social Change.* Sydney, 1972.

Alatas Syed Hussein. *Intellectuals in Developing Societies.* London, 1977.

Alatas, Syed Hussein. *The Myth of the Lazy Native.* London, 1977.

Alatas, Syed Hussein. *Corruption: Its Nature, Cause, and Functions.* Aldershot, England, 1990.

ʿAlī ibn Abī Ṭālib. *Nahjul Balagha: Sermons, Letters, and Sayings of Imam Ali.* Compiled by Al-Sharīf al-Raḍī. Translated by Jafar Hussein. Qom, 1989. See page 426.

Bennabi, Malek. *Islam in History and Society.* Translated by Asma Rashid. Islamabad, 1988. See page 12.

Berkes, Niyazi. *The Development of Secularism in Turkey.* Montreal, 1964.

Blyden, Edward W. *Christianity, Islam, and the Negro Race.* London, 1887. Reprinted as *Christianity, Islam, and the African Race.* San Francisco, 1992.

Ibn Khaldūn. *The Muqaddimah.* Vols. 1–2. Translated by Franz Rosenthal. New York, 1958.

Keddie, Nikki R. *An Islamic Response to Imperialism.* 2d ed. Berkeley, 1983.

Mernissi, Fatima. *Women and Islam: An Historical and Theological Enquiry.* Translated by Mary Jo Lakeland. Oxford, 1991.

Muṭahharī, Murtaẓā. *Islamic Movements in the Twentieth Century.* Translated by Maktab-e-Qoran (Office of the Qur'ān). Tehran, 1979. See page 41.

Sharīʿatī, ʿAlī. *On the Sociology of Islam.* Translated by Hamid Algar. Berkeley, 1979.

Sharīʿatī, ʿAlī. "Shahādat." In *Jihād and Shahādat: Struggle and Martyrdom in Islam,* edited by Maḥmud Ṭāleqāni and Murtaẓā Muṭahharī, pp. 153–229. Houston, 1986.

Sharīʿatī, ʿAlī. *What Is to Be Done: The Enlightened Thinkers and an Islamic Renaissance.* Edited by Farhang Rajaee. Houston, 1986.

SYED HUSSEIN ALATAS

SOKOTO CALIPHATE. Founded in the early nineteenth century by Usuman Dan Fodio, the Sokoto Caliphate continues to exert strong cultural influence in Nigeria. Three historical phases of the caliphate can be identified: the establishment of the caliphate (1803–1837), its transformation (1837–1960), and the current era (since 1960).

The savannah states of Hausaland in West Africa had been nominally Muslim since the fifteenth or sixteenth century under the impact of the trans-Saharan trade from North Africa. Hausa city-state rulers administered a form of Muslim law, especially in the urban areas, but pre-Islamic culture remained strongly influential in their agrarian hinterlands.

With the migration of Fulani pastoralists from the western savannah, among them many Muslim scholars and teachers, new cultural influences and ideas began to permeate Hausaland. At first some of the Fulani clerics resided in the courts of the Hausa states. Later many became dissatisfied with the syncretism of Hausa society and began to envision a reformation in which Islamic ideals could be implemented in the region.

The Islamic movement of Usuman Dan Fodio was to have profound consequences in West Africa. He united the peoples of Hausaland and many surrounding areas into a single polity. He established a standard of literature, thought, and action that is still a major reference point in northern Nigeria and in many parts of West Africa.

Usuman was born in 1754 and grew up in Degel, where he learned the Islamic classics, including Qur'ān, *ḥadīth,* and history. He also studied Sufism in the Qādirīyah tradition. As he matured his writings became widely known, and he developed a following of intellectuals and clerics; they came to be known as the Jamāʿa and spread across Daura, Katsina, Kano, Birnin Kebbi, Zazzau (Zaria), and Bauchi, as well as Degel. Usuman began to demand that the ruler of Gobir give the Jamāʿa the freedom to preach and to live according to their interpretation of Islamic society. The sultan of Gobir allowed such toleration and the following of Usuman increased, although tensions developed with the upper stratum of Hausa society.

In 1794 Usuman had a dream in which he was given "the sword of truth" to defend his community. Still there was an uneasy truce with the political powers, until 1803 when the ruler of Gobir died, to be succeeded by an ambitious ruler who decided to crack down on the Jamāʿa. Usuman issued letters to his followers setting out the need for a Muslim community with its own leadership and principles. Threats were made on Usuman's life by the rulers, and he fled outside Gobir territory with many of his followers. The armed struggle began shortly thereafter when Usuman (known as the *shehu,* or *shaykh*) issued a formal declaration of *jihād.*

Between 1804 and 1808 the holy war of Usuman Dan Fodio defeated most of the rulers of the Hausa states and established a new capital at Sokoto in 1809, where a "caliphate" was to evolve over the ensuing decades. Simultaneous uprisings throughout Hausaland involving elements of Fulani, Tuareg, and Hausa populations resulted in the largest political community in West Africa since the fall of Songhay (1591). Many of the Hausa rulers fled to establish themselves outside the caliphate; the Zaria rulers, for example, fled to Abuja. The large empire of Borno to the west witnessed a number of uprisings but in the end resisted the *jihād.*

The Sokoto Caliphate was a loose confederation of emirates that recognized the leadership of Usuman as "commander of the faithful." When Usuman died in 1817, he was succeeded by his son Muhammad Bello (d. 1837), although Usuman's brother Abdullahi Dan Fodio was given authority in the "western territories" based in Gwandu. Bello and Abdullahi as well as Usuman's daughter Asma continued his intellectual legacy, and each is associated with dozens of well-known books and letters written in Hausa and Fulfulde as well as in Arabic. (Many of these works have been or are currently being translated into English.)

After the passing of the first generation of reformists, many of the emirates began to fuse the lessons of the reforms with the cultural realities of the prereform period, while keeping the structure and legitimacy of Usuman Dan Fodio's legacy. By the mid-nineteenth century there were about thirty emirates linked to Sokoto, including the large market state of Kano. The caliphate stretched from areas in present Burkina Faso in the west to Cameroon in the east. To the south, the caliphate included the Nupe areas around Bida and the Yoruba areas around Ilorin. Tensions between Sokoto and Yorubaland to the south and Borno to the west continued throughout the nineteenth century.

Meanwhile, British impact on the Sudanic interior of West Africa became more pronounced after the Berlin Conference (1884/85). In 1900 Frederick Lugard became high commissioner of the Protectorate of Northern Nigeria. In 1903 Lugard's troops occupied the two major cities of the caliphate, Kano and Sokoto. Thus began the colonial period within the caliphate, it kept many of the structures of the caliphate in place through a policy of indirect rule. The "sultan of Sokoto" was given centrality within northern Nigeria, and the "emirs and chiefs" became part of the colonial infrastructure.

With Nigerian independence in 1960 many descendants of the founders of the Sokoto Caliphate were among the first generation of national leaders; they included Ahmadu Bello, who became premier of the Northern Region of Nigeria. The sultan of Sokoto has continued to be regarded as a spiritual leader of the Muslim community in Nigeria, although legislative and executive functions of government have passed to local, state, and federal bodies. With the death of Sultan Abubakar III in 1988—he had come to power in 1937—the sultanship passed to a different branch of the families who trace direct lineage to Usuman Dan Fodio. Sultan Ibrahim Dasuki (b. 1923) was installed in March 1990 and plays a central role in the Supreme Council of Islamic Affairs in Nigeria.

The original emirates of the Sokoto Caliphate have been reorganized into various states within the Federation of Nigeria. Of the thirty states created in 1991, twelve have some direct experience in the caliphal/emirate system stemming from the reform movement of Usuman Dan Fodio: Sokoto, Kebbi, Katsina, Kano, Jigawa, Bauchi, Niger, Kaduna (including Zaria), Kwara, Kogi, Adamawa, and Taraba.

[*See also* Nigeria *and the biography of Dan Fodio.*]

BIBLIOGRAPHY

Boyd, Jean (with Hamzat Maishanu). *Sir Siddiq Abubakar III, Sarkin Musulmi*. Kaduna, 1991. Thoughtful biography of Sultan Abubakar, in power 1937–1988, by an Englishwoman who worked in Sokoto for twenty-five years and had access to archival and local literatures.

Khānī, Aḥmad, and Kabir Gandi, eds. *State and Society in the Sokoto Caliphate*. Sokoto, 1990. Conference papers in honor of the sultan of Sokoto, Alhaji Ibrahim Dasuki.

Last, Murray. *The Sokoto Caliphate*. London, 1966. Major scholarly work on the subject.

Paden, John N. *Ahmadu Bello, Sardauna of Sokoto: Values and Leadership in Nigeria*. London, 1986. Biographical coverage of the premier of Northern Region of Nigeria, with a focus on the transition from colonialism to independence.

Sulaiman, Ibraheem. *A Revolution in History: The Jihad of Usman Dan Fodio*. London, 1986. *The Islamic State and the Challenge of History: Ideals, Policies, and Operation of the Sokoto Caliphate*. London, 1987. Sympathetic yet scholarly assessment by the acting director of the Centre for Islamic Legal Studies, Ahmadu Bello University, Zaria.

Usman, Yusufu, B., ed. *Studies in the History of the Sokoto Caliphate: The Sokoto Seminar Papers*. New York, 1979. Collection of papers from a scholarly conference held in Sokoto, January 1965.

JOHN N. PADEN

SOMALIA. The Muslims of Somalia constitute almost 99 percent of an estimated population of eight to ten million. Four Ṣūfī orders—the Qādirīyah, Aḥmadīyah, Ṣāliḥīyah and Rifāʿīyah—have greatly influenced Somali Islamic practices. As in other cultures, Somali Islam has incorporated some pre-Islamic customs, for example, obligatory prayers for rain often involving young children. Somali lore divides society into two main categories, the man of religion *(wadaad)* and the warrior (*waranleh*, literally "spearbearer"). Ideally, a *wadaad* is expected to mediate clan conflicts, thus remaining aloof from politics. Most Somalis belong to one of five clan-families subdivided into clans, subclans, and lineage groups.

Somalia's geography has influenced its history; for centuries the Red Sea and the Indian Ocean have facilitated long-distance trade. The ancient world knew Somalia as the Land of Punt, a source of frankincense and myrrh. The Islamic epoch, starting in the tenth century, accelerated trends toward trade and settlements. City-states such as Zeila, Bulhar, Berbera, Mogadishu, Merca, and Barawa were established. Forms of Islamic administration were adapted to the decentralized pastoral society. Islamic commercial laws and regulations, systems of weights and measures, navigation technologies, and security arrangements facilitated trade.

During the sixteenth century, highland Abyssinian (Ethiopian) rulers invaded the Muslim state of Adal to secure a passage to the sea. The Muslims were avenged by the famed Imam Ahmed Gurey (Aḥmad Grāñ). Pushing deep into the highlands, Imam Gurey turned the defensive wars into an expansionist campaign. He was eventually killed in 1542 when the Abyssinian armies were joined by at least four hundred Portuguese bearing modern firearms.

Contrary to its expansionist phase, Islam in Somalia found itself on the defensive during the nineteenth and twentieth centuries. During the late nineteenth century, the British, French, and Italians and the Abyssinian Emperor Menelik colonized various parts of Somali territory. This led to the emergence of a radical Islamic revivalist movement, led by Sayyid Mohamed Abdille Hassan (Muḥammad ibn ʿAbd Allāh Ḥasan) from 1899 to 1920. His earlier efforts to mediate clan disputes and to preach anticolonialism won him fame and recruits. Sayyid Mohamed was also a great poet in a land of poets. However, his attempts to convert Somalis from the popular Qādirīyah into the puritanical Ṣāliḥīyah sect met stiff resistance, bringing out a fanatical tendency in him. In 1909 the Sayyid was allegedly implicated in the murder of the charismatic Qādirīyah shaykh Uways, who was propagating his order's teachings in the southern interior among nominal Muslims and non-Muslims. In 1920 the British conducted aerial and ground assaults of his fortress at Taleh; the Sayyid escaped, and though defeated, he died peacefully in 1921. Many Somalis have derived one major conclusion from his legacy—the need to separate religious inspiration from secular power.

The fanaticism of the Sayyid was replaced during the 1920s and 1930s by the cautious reformism of two Islamic modernist leaders, Ḥajjī Farah Omar in Somaliland and Maalim Jama in Mogadishu. Ḥajjī Farah formed the Somali Islamic Association, a cultural organization that blended the best in Islamic education with aspects of Western education. However, modern Somali nationalism remained secular in outlook, despite the presence of leaders with religious backgrounds. Among the founders of the main southern nationalist party, the Somali Youth League, were the unassuming Shaykh Abdulkadir Sekhawedin and Ḥajjī Mohamed Hussein, who inclined toward Nasserism and Islamic socialism. Somali nationalism was obsessed with irredentism in the form of unification with Somalis in French Djibouti, Ethiopia's Ogaden region, and northern Kenya.

The Somali Republic operated a multiparty parliamentary system between 1960 and 1969. Islamic issues were secondary, except for the policy of providing a script for Somali: the Latin alphabet was favored by the governments and bureaucratic elite; a chauvinistic group advocated an invented script called Osmania; and a number of educational and cultural leaders preferred the Arabic alphabet. During this period a remarkable group of religious leaders interested in agricultural production emerged and led grassroots voluntary development organizations: Shaykh Mohamed Raghe in the north, and Shaykh Bananey's solidarity cooperative in the south.

In 1969 General Mohamed Siyad Barre carried out a military coup and proclaimed scientific socialism as the official ideology. The Latin script was adopted for writing Somali. The military dictatorship imported Soviet methods of repression and waged campaigns against religion. In 1975, Barre executed ten religious leaders for peacefully protesting his imposition of a new family and marriage law that violated Islamic regulations. In protest against the regime's hostility, many embraced an Islamic renewal: regular prayers and fasting, religious dress, and the public display of rosaries. Students wearing Islamic dress were arrested and often jailed. In 1989 and again in 1990, Barre's troops massacred hundreds of religious leaders and their followers. Islam had fared better under European colonialism than under his dictatorship.

From bases in Ethiopia, clan-based armed oppositions successfully challenged Siyad's forces. On 15 May 1990 more than one hundred former political leaders and administrators issued a public manifesto asking him to resign. A similarly large group of religious leaders issued the "Islamic Call" on 7 October 1990. The Call accepted parliamentary democracy as a general objective but insisted on an Islamic *shūrā* institution. Barre's fall in January 1991 culminated in chaos, civil wars, banditry, and famine leading to a humanitarian intervention by the United Nations under American leadership in December 1992.

An Islamic resurgence, manifested in increased forms of piety, continues among Somalis at home and abroad. There are, however, pockets of Islamic fundamentalists among the clan-based armed movements. For the moment they do not have a charismatic leader, and clanism continues to act as a check against Islamic radicalism. The main Somali fundamentalist movement, al-Ittiḥād al-Islāmī (Islamic Unity), has been more active in the northeast; in June 1992 it seized control of the port of Bosaso but was expelled after heavy losses by the Somali Salvation Democratic Front (SSDF). It retreated to the nearby port of Las Khorey where it retained control as of March 1993, allegedly receiving assistance from the Sudan and Iran. Although Islam will continue to play a critical role in Somali culture and politics, it remains to be seen how much and what kind of Islam are compatible with, or necessary for, Somali political development.

BIBLIOGRAPHY

Adam, Hussein M. "Islam and Politics in Somalia." Unpublished ms., 1991. Contains interview material and documentary sources not available in libraries.

Andrzejewski B. W., and I. M. Lewis. *Somali Poetry*. Oxford, 1964. Contains a useful introduction to Somali practice of Islam, as well as a collection of religious poetry in Arabic.

Cassanelli, Lee V. *The Shaping of Somali Society*. Philadelphia, 1982. Provides an excellent study of Islamic themes in southern Somali history, including saints, practices, and sects; complements I. M. Lewis's studies of Somali Islam in the north.

Esposito, John L., ed. *Islam and Development*. Syracuse, N.Y., 1980. Collection of insightful essays providing critical theoretical constructs.

Lewis, I. M. "Sufism in Somaliland: A Study in Tribal Islam." *Bulletin of the School of Oriental and African Studies* 17.3 (1955): 581–602, and 18.1 (1956): 145–160. Excellent and insightful study of popular forms of Islam in the former British Somaliland.

Lewis, I. M. "Shaikhs and Warriors of Somaliland." In *African Systems of Thought*, edited by Meyer Fortes and Germaine Dieterlen, pp. 204–223. London, 1965. Detailed study of the ironies and ambiguities in Somali notions of religious and secular power.

Lewis, I. M., ed. *Islam in Tropical Africa*. London, 1966. Provides a useful comparative framework and contains Lewis's chapter on conformity and contrast in Somali Islam.

Trimingham, J. Spencer. *Islam in East Africa*. Oxford, 1961. Historical and general overview of Islam in East Africa, including a useful bibliography.

HUSSEIN M. ADAM

SOUTH AFRICA. The 1993 South African apartheid census figures divided the population into four categories: Africans, 32 million; Coloureds, 5 million; Indians, 1 million; and Whites, 5 million. The total number of Muslims is currently more than half a million, of whom 2.5 percent are Africans, 49.8 percent Coloureds, 47 percent Indians, and .7 percent Whites. By the twenty-first century Muslims will probably comprise 2 percent of the total population, as compared to 1 percent in 1993.

Muslims came to South Africa in two groups. The first (1652–1807), brought by the Dutch colonialists, was made up of involuntary immigrants (slaves, political prisoners, and criminals) from West and East Africa and Southeast Asia. They were classified as "Cape Malays" because many hailed from the Malay archipelago. The second group (1860–1914) was brought by the British colonialists from India as indentured laborers and free passengers to Natal and Transvaal. During 1873–1880 a large group of Zanzibaris also went to South Africa.

The Muslim population remained small from the arrival of Shaykh Yūsuf (d. 1699), called "the founder of Islam at the Cape," in 1694 as a political prisoner, until 1789 when Qāḍī ʿAbdussalām ("Tuan Guru," d. 1807) laid the foundations for the first mosque. A sharp increase took place between 1804 and 1834, to the extent that Muslims constituted one-third of the Cape's population (6,435); the institutions of slavery, conversion, marriage, adoption, and education had a direct bearing upon this. Many of these Muslims had Ṣūfī affiliations, so that Ṣūfī practices became an important part of Cape Muslim culture. Leaders of Ṣūfī orders such as the Qādirīyah were buried around Cape Town and are locally believed to constitute a "holy circle of *karāmāh*s." Indian Ṣūfīs such as Ghulām Muḥammad Ḥabībī ("Sufi Sahib," d. 1910) had by the end of the nineteenth century made valuable sociocultural contributions. Ḥabībī's mausoleum in Durban was declared a national monument.

By the nineteenth century the local Malayo-Portuguese Creole in the Cape was replaced by Dutch as the lingua franca. Muslims, who had formerly written their texts in the Arabic script, switched to Dutch to write the Arabic-Afrikaans religious texts. One of the most famous Arabic-Afrikaans texts, *Bayānuddīn,* was written by Shaykh Abū Bakr Effendi (d. 1880), a Turkish Ḥanafī scholar, who came to the Cape in 1863 at the request of the governor to resolve theological disputes. Only recently has the importance of these texts been realized with regard to the genesis of the Afrikaans language.

In Natal the Muslims spoke English and their ancestral Indian languages, including Gujarati and Urdu. The Gujarati Muslims published a weekly religio-political newspaper, *Al-Islām,* between 1907 and 1910. Muslim newspapers such as *Al-qalam* (Durban/Johannesburg founded 1973) and *Muslim News/Views* (Cape Town, 1960–1986) have been important conduits through which the Muslims have expressed their sociopolitical and religious thoughts.

The Cape Muslims were generally seen as a peaceful and law-abiding community. Already in 1806 a Cape Malay artillery unit had demonstrated its loyalty to Dutch colonists in the Battle of Blaauberg, and in 1846 a conscripted "Malay Corps" had fought gallantly on the eastern frontier of the Battle of the Axe. However, Muslims did not remain subservient to the Dutch or British authorities. They protested against the enforcement of vaccination during the 1840 smallpox epidemic; they strongly voiced their opinion against the municipality that banned the Khalifah display in 1856; in 1886 they demonstrated under the leadership of Abdul Burns (d. 1898) against the 1883 Public Health Act; and in 1894 they unsuccessfully contested a seat in the Cape parliament. Shafiʿī-Ḥanafī theological and legal battles continued unabated between 1866 and 1900 in the Cape Supreme Court. Amid these protests and strife, Muslims flourished as artisans, tailors, fishmongers, and hawkers at many levels of Cape society and gradually entered all the professions.

In both the Cape and Natal, many sociocultural organizations emerged during the twentieth century to serve specific ethnic communities. Organizations such as the Cape Malay Association (established in 1920) and the South African Indian Congress (1923) were formed to maintain distinctive ethnic identities—in line with governmental policies—and to negotiate with the government for specific rights. Muḥammad Arshad Gamiet (d. 1935) and ʿAbdullah Kajee (d. 1946) were, respectively, the leading figures of these organizations.

Clerical bodies emerged to serve the religious needs of the communities. In 1923 the Jamʿīyat al-ʿUlamā' of Transvaal was formed, followed by the Cape Muslim

Judicial Council in 1945, and the Natal Jamʿīyat al-ʿUlamā' in 1952; the leading members of these groups were respectively Maulana Sanjalvi, Shaykh Behardien and Maulana Omarjee. These bodies were conservative and did not engage in any activities that might jeopordize their relations with the state. There were, however, individuals like Maulana Cachalia (b. 1919) and Imam Haron (d. 1969) who vociferously protested against such discriminatory laws as the Sabotage Bill and Group Areas Act; the latter died in detention, and the former went into exile and represented the African National Congress in India. During the 1940s and 1950s, social welfare and educational organizations were established: in Cape Town, the Hospital Welfare and Muslim Educational Movement (established in 1943); in Durban, the Arabic Study Circle (1950); and in Johannesburg, the Central Islamic Trust (1952). Numerous others followed in the 1960s and 1970s. At the beginning of the twentieth century, Dr. ʿAbdurahman (d. 1940), a medical doctor and educational reformer, established a number of Muslim state-aided primary schools; similar schools were later established in Durban. Independent colleges such as the Newcastle Dārulʿulūm (Natal), *madrasahs* such as the Lenasia Madaris Association (Transvaal), and Muslim private schools such as Ḥabībīyah Islamic College (Cape) were established to meet Muslims' educational needs.

South African society experienced dramatic sociopolitical changes during the 1970s and 1980s that also affected Muslims. During this period much literature came from the Middle East and Indian subcontinent; the works of the Egyptian Sayyid Quṭb, the Pakistani Mawlānā Abū al-Aʿlā Mawdūdī, and the Iranian ʿAlī Sharīʿatī were circulated among Muslim youth, especially at the universities.

One of the organizations that played a pivotal role in disseminating these ideas was the Durban-based Muslim Youth Movement of South Africa (MYMSA, founded in 1970). The MYMSA and other Muslim organizations brought prominent Muslim scholars such as the Palestinian-American Ismāʿīl al-Fārūqī and the Pakistani Khurshid Aḥmad to share their ideas and guide the Muslim leadership. They also held conventions, conferences, seminars, and camps, and established libraries and bookshops. The MYMSA gave birth to many other organizations, including the Islamic Medical Association, South African Association of Muslim Social Scientists, Jaame, South African National Zakat Fund, Islamic Daʿwah Movement of South Africa, Women's Islamic Movement, Muslim Students Association, and Islamic Relief Agency. Each of these organizations published a newsletter, notably the *JAAME Review* and *IMA Bulletin*. The MYMSA strengthened ties with the World Assembly of Muslim Youth. WAMY's sister organization, the World Muslim Congress, was instrumental in forming the Islamic Council of South Africa in 1975; this body, however, disintegrated after four years because of internal conflicts and personality clashes.

Each of these organizations carved out a niche for itself after splitting off from the MYMSA. The ISRA played an active role during the 1985–1986 South African urban upheavals. It was able to draw on the resources of many other Muslim organizations that did not share MYMSA's ideological positions. The ISRA also served the needs of the Muslims beyond the confines of South Africa, aiding Iranian earthquake victims, starving Somalians, oppressed Palestinians, and victimized Bosnians. SANZF made great strides in pooling Muslim financial resources. In 1988 and 1992 the Islamic and Al-Baraka Banks were opened to draw overseas and local investments. IDMSA has been spreading Islamic literature in indigenous tongues and has established an institute to train African *daʿwah* (missionary) workers. A *daʿwah* organization founded in 1957 by Ahmad Deedat, recipient of the 1986 King Faiṣal Award, is the Durban-based International Islamic Propagation Centre with branches in London and Abu Dhabi. On a different level, the Tablīghī Jamāʿat has also operated under the leadership of Bhai Padia since 1962.

While some Muslims concentrated on *daʿwah*, others felt the need to shift attention to the political arena. The MYMSA was one such organization, particularly after its transformation. Two other organizations, the Qibla Muslim Movement (established in 1980) and the Call of Islam (COI, 1984), played prominent political roles. The latter, an affiliate of the ANC, was in the early 1990s led by Ebrahim Rasool; the former, which has close ties with the Pan Africanist Congress, was then led by Ahmad Cassiem.

In South Africa at present there have been the "Charterist" Muslim groups that supported the ANC as well as the "Africanist" groups that supported the PAC. Conservative groups such as the Jamʿīyat al-ʿUlamā' opted to remain neutral. In 1990 a historic National Muslim Conference took place, following an initiative of the COI. Delegates from Muslim organizations throughout the country came together to consider their response to the new political situation. This resulted in the formation of the Muslim Front and formulation of the Religious Charter by the South African chapter of the World Conference on Religion and Peace in 1992. While the Muslim Front canvassed for the ANC vote for the April 1994 elections, many of the other political parties have been wooing the Muslims to vote for their respective candidates in the various provinces. Some Muslims, however, chose to form Muslim political parties, namely the Africa Muslim Party and the Islamic Party, which failed to win seats in the National Assembly. Moreover, the ANC government appointed ʿAbdullah Omar, a committed Muslim, and minister of justice to its cabinet.

BIBLIOGRAPHY

Argyle, W. J. "Muslims in South Africa: Origins, Development, and Present Economic Status." *Journal Institute of Muslim Minority Affairs* 3.2 (September 1981): 222–254. Excellent study of the Muslims' economic status.

Davids, Achmat. "The Words Cape Slaves Made." *South African Journal of Linguistics*. 8.2 (August 1990): 1–35. Excellent overview of Arabic-Afrikaans literature in the Cape.

Esack, Farid. "Three Islamic Strands in the South African Struggle for Justice." *Third World Quarterly* 10.2 (April 1988): 473–498. Interesting assessment of contemporary progressive Muslim movements.

Hampson, Ruth. *Islam in South Africa: A Bibliography*. Cape Town, 1964. Pioneering bibliographical text on Islam in South Africa.

Haron, Muhammed. "Islamic Education in South Africa." *Muslim Educational Quarterly* 5.2 (July 1988): 41–54. Fairly descriptive overview of South African Muslim educational developments.

Haron, Muhammed. "Theses on Islam at South African Universities." *Islam et Sociétés au Sud du Sahara* 5 (December 1991): 141–163. Bibliographical article reflecting upon research done in the field of Arabic and Islamic studies at South African universities.

Karim, Goolam Mohamed. "The Contribution of Muslims to South African Culture." *Bulletin for Christian-Muslim Relations in Africa* 2.1 (January 1984): 1–10. Useful assessment of the Muslim contribution to South African culture.

Lubbe, Gerrie. "A Bibliography on Islam in South Africa." *Journal for Islamic Studies* 5 (December 1985): 115–133. Important bibliographical essay complementing and updating Hampson's text.

Shell, Robert. "Rites and Rebellion: Islamic Conversion at the Cape, 1808–1915." *Studies in the History of Cape Town* 5 (1984): 1–45. Excellent analysis of the processes and institutions of Islamic coversion during the nineteenth and early twentieth centuries.

MUHAMMED HARON

SPANISH UMAYYADS. *See* Córdoba, Caliphate of.

SPORT. *See* Games and Sport.

STATE. *See* Dawlah.

STEREOTYPES IN MASS MEDIA. Numerous Americans come to know approximately 250 million Arabs and more than one billion Muslims from mainstream mass media, in particular, television programs and motion pictures, which provide virtually most images citizens have of the peoples of the world. Thorough examination of more than 500 feature films and hundreds of television programs, comic books and strips, music recordings, newspapers and magazines (complete with advertisements, crossword puzzles, and editorial cartoons), plus school textbooks, novels and reference works, computer and video games, and scores of graphic images emanating from other communication channels reveals stereotypical portraits of Arab Muslims. Although more than 15 million Arab Christians reside in the Middle East—ranging from Eastern Orthodox to Roman Catholic to Protestant—they are invisible in the media. Thus, the Arab-as-Muslim theme positions itself firmly in peoples' psyches.

Seemingly mindlessly adopted and casually adapted, prominent images present the Muslim as the bogeyman, the quintessential Other. How else to explain the actions taken by a student at the University of Wisconsin who sent this message to an Iranian student: "Death to all Arabs, die, Islamic scumbags" ("College Debate: Free Speech versus Freedom from Bigotry," *Chicago Tribune*, 8 March 1991, p. 2). Often, imagemakers lump together Arab, Iranian, or Turkish Muslims as dark-complexioned people, flaunting beards or moustaches.

Selective media framing makes belittling Islam feasible. Screen scenarios often reinforce audiences' misperceptions by declaring that the Muslim man deceives, suppresses, and abuses white Western females. In *Not without My Daughter* (1990), for example, the Iranian protagonist treats his American wife like chattel; he slaps her face and keeps her prisoner in their home, boasting, "I'm a Muslim." The film contends that Muslims are hypocrites; breaking his oath sworn on the Qur'ān, the husband says, "Islam is the greatest gift I can give my daughter." As his family leaves the mosque, posters of Ayatollah Ruhollah Khomeini are featured, suggesting Muslims and ayatollahs are one and the same.

Rigid and repetitive news images of Iran's Ayatollah Khomeini and Iraq's President Saddam Hussein blend with scores of fictional motion pictures and television programs featuring Muslim terrorists shouting, "Allah be praised," while murdering innocents. Deceptive portraits are mainstays; skewed documentaries are tagged *The Sword of Islam* and *The Islamic Bomb,* books are labeled *The Assassins: Holy Killers of Islam, The Dagger of Islam, The Fire of Islam, Holy Wars, Inflamed Islam,* and *Militant Islam,* and magazine essays are stamped "The Roots of Muslim Rage" (*Atlantic Monthly,* 1991) and "The Muslims Are Coming, The Muslims Are Coming!" (*National Review,* 1991). As a result of these representations, the media's Arab Muslim lacks a human face.

Demonized and delegitimized, the Muslim surfaces as different. In *Under Siege* (1986), a television movie written in part by Bob Woodward, Muslims hailing from Dearborn, Michigan, are presented as anti-American "religious fanatics" willingly sacrificing their lives in "holy wars" for "the cause." They topple the dome of the U.S. Capitol building and kill scores of American civilians. The FBI director explains to his associate that "those people," Arab/Iranian Muslims, are different. The writers and producers, unable to distinguish Arabs from Iranians, portray them as one ethnic group, in spite of the fact that each group has its own distinctive origin, ethnicity, language, and cultural heritage. Subsequently, throughout the film, "Arab" is used interchangablely with "Iranian." Referring to atrocities being committed by Muslims in the United States, the FBI director tells his associate: "It's a whole different ball game. I mean the East and the Middle East. They have their own notion of what's right and what's wrong, what's worth living for and dying for. But we insist on dealing with them as if they're the same as us. We'd better wake up!"

Stereotypical images and statements transmitted by media have a telling effect. In 1990, Iraq invaded Kuwait, leading to the Gulf War. During this time, two prominent Americans, Senator J. J. Exon of Nebraska and former U.S. Ambassador to Iraq Edward Peck offered comparable commentary about Arabs and Muslims. In remarks for which he later apologized (according to Casey Kasem), Exon said, "In the Arab world, life is not as important as in the non-Arab world" (*Omaha World Herald,* 30 August 1990, p. 3). Edward Peck stated on television, "We in the West tend to think of our New Testament heritage, where you turn the other cheek and you let bygones be bygones and forgive and forget. [But] the people of the Middle East are the people of the Old Testament. With Muslims there's much more of an eye for an eye and a tooth for a tooth. You don't forget and you don't forgive; you carry on the vendetta and the struggle long after people in the West would be prepared to say it's all right, it's over, let's not worry about it any longer" (*NBC Nightly News,* 16 January 1991).

To enhance the myth of Muslim otherness, imagemakers clothe him in foreign garb, such as strange "bedsheets." Made up to have dark features, he is unattractive and in need of a shave. Speaking with a "foreign" accent, he poses an economic threat by using oil and/or terrorism as a weapon against developed societies. Most important, he is painted as worshiping a different deity and possessing an unprovoked hatred of "civilized" peoples, notably American Christians and Jews. "These bastards [Muslim hijackers] shot those people in cold blood. They think it's open season on Americans," explains a passenger in the television movie, *Hostage Flight* (1985). Journalist Edward R. Murrow said that what we do not see is as important, if not more important, than what we do see. Seldom do audiences see or read about a devout Muslim caring for his wife or children, writing poetry, or attending the sick.

Children's cartoons, such as *Inspector Gadget* and *Heathcliff,* show Muslims glorifying not God, but idolizing Westerners. In an episode of *Heathcliff,* Egyptians, perceiving Heathcliff to be their ancient ruler, bow before the cat. When, in a *Mr. Gadget* episode, Gadget discovers an ancient relic, Arab hordes worship him. Falling to their knees, they mumble "the chosen one, the chosen one."

Consider how the media paint two holy cities, Mecca and Jerusalem. In 1991, on CBS-TV's top-rated *60 Minutes* program, Teddy Kollek, the mayor of Jerusalem, neglects to mention Jerusalem's Muslim population, stating instead that Jerusalem is a city inhabited by "Christians, Jews, and Arabs."

The city of Mecca is the birthplace of Muḥammad and the site of the Grand Mosque, the most sacred place in the Islamic World. Yet, dream merchants transform Mecca into a corrupt town, where offensive antics govern the moment. In 1966, producers of the successful television series *I Dream of Jeannie* represented Mecca not as a holy city with devout worshipers, but as a topsy-turvy bazaar filled with thieves robbing Western tourists (episode no. 16). The plot focused on Jeannie, a two-thousand-year-old genie, who will soon die unless she visit's Mecca's "thieves market." In the "First National Bank of Mecca," Jeannie's friend performs ridiculous rituals. To save her life, he must "raise his right arm, . . . face the minaret of the rising sun, and repeat the sacred words: 'bottle to genie, genie to master, master to Mecca. Ronda!' "

The dialogue and imagery in *I Dream of Jeannie* is designed to amuse; instead, it narrows our vision and blurs reality. In 1987, *Ishtar,* a $50-million comedy, starring Warren Beatty and Dustin Hoffman continued this trend. Riddled with anti-Arab sentiments—Arab culture is labeled "devious," and Hoffman is told, "Go act like an Arab"—*Ishtar* also lampoons Mecca with "I Look to Mecca," a song concerning a romantic rendezvous under a tree. Islam's holiest city and the pilgrimage to Mecca, a sacred journey that Muslims look forward to making all their lives, are belittled by sexual innuendo. There is a dangerous and cumulative effect when imagemakers continually transmit rigid and repetitive pictures of Muslims. Such imagery does not exist in a vacuum. Teaching viewers and readers whom to fear and whom to hate, the Muslim stereotype affects perceptions and subsequently U.S. public opinion and policy decisions.

Some public figures are recognizing the differences between image and reality. On 8 March 1991, following the Gulf War, General Norman Schwarzkopf made these remarks to departing American troops in Dhahran, Saudi Arabia: "You are going to take back home the fact that 'Islam' is not a word to be feared, a religion to be feared. It's a religion to be respected, just as we respect all other religions. That's the American way." Although the general's comments appeared in the *Washington Post,* his statements about Islam were not widely circulated.

Even imagemakers are gradually addressing negative portraits of Muslims. In the 1990s, producers of documentaries and feature films, print journalists, and others are presenting more accurate and humane portraits. *Islam: A Civilization and Its Art* (1991), is an informative ninety-minute documentary focusing on Islamic civilization, culture, and art. *Legacy* (1992), a PBS television documentary series, points out that Islam is "the true basis" of our culture. Host Michael Wood reveals that "the West's rediscovery of its ancient science and knowledge of the Italian Renaissance was indebted to the Muslims." Revealing scenes of mosques, mosaics and calligraphy, and devout Muslims at prayer underscore his commentary: "When Europe was still in the dark ages, the fertile crescent entered another glorious phase of its culture. Here, in the universities and libraries of Baghdad, Babylonian astronomy, Hindu mathematics, Chinese science and technology were passed on by Arabs. It was one of the great multicultural epochs of all time. The triumph of the modern West was made possible by a flood of ancient learning and science from Islam."

The feature film, *Robin Hood: Prince of Thieves* (1991), introduces Azeem, a Moorish Muslim. He is devout, intelligent, innovative, and Robin's equal, both as a combatant and as a humanist. With Robin in the English countryside, Azeem takes his prayer rug, faces Mecca, and prays. He refuses to drink alcohol, "I must decline, Allah forbids it," and he is tolerant of other faiths, "it is vanity to force other men to our religion." Also, Azeem embraces other races and colors: "Allah loves wondrous variety." Equipped with scimitar, Arab headdress, and robe, he not only manages to deliver a breech baby, but to save Robin's life and the day by introducing the telescope and gunpowder to the British Isles. Robin acknowledges the Moor's humanity, saying, "You truly are a great one."

In *Chicago* magazine, journalist Gretchen Reynolds describes a service at a mosque, calling it "a revelation. Canonical and dignified, moving even if you don't know the language, it evokes deep visceral emotion in Muslims attending. Some of the women start to cry. The people attending stand and kneel, call back to the khatib leading them. Anyone looking to have western preconceptions of Arab religion confirmed would be disappointed: There is no fanaticism here, only faith" (April 1991, p. 26).

Mindful that American Muslims are either dehumanized or neglected in media, on 6 February 1992, for the first time, the U.S. Senate invited an imam, W. Deen Mohammed, to offer the opening prayer. As for the future, the ultimate result should be an image of the Muslim as neither saint nor devil, but as a fellow human being, with all the potentials and frailities that condition implies.

JACK G. SHAHEEN

SUAVI, ALI (1839–1878), a popular reformist figure of the nineteenth-century Ottoman Empire. Suavi exemplifies the ideas of conservative Ottomans who were drawn into a struggle for the expression of the popular will. Although trained in the modern educational system of the *rüşdiye*, the secular postprimary schools established during the Tanzimat reforms, he assumed the role of a spokesperson for a type of popular discontent with the Tanzimat which was expressed in a religious idiom. His ideas acquired a wide audience when he began to contribute to a newspaper published in Istanbul, *Muhbir*.

Suavi joined the Young Ottoman leaders Mehmet Namık Kemal and Mehmet Ziya Paşa when they fled to Europe, and he was the editor of the first newspaper published by these exiles, also titled *Muhbir*. It soon became clear that there were fundamental differences between his political ideals and those of Kemal and Ziya. Suavi was suspicious of parliamentary government, and his idea of democracy was one in which the just ruler dealt directly with his subjects. After leaving the Young Ottomans, Suavi devoted himself to the publication of *Ulûm*, an encyclopedic periodical. This attempt to demonstrate that conservative Muslims like himself could keep abreast of Western scientific knowledge predated that of better-known nineteenth-century Muslim thinkers, such as Jamāl al-Dīn al-Afghānī (1838/39–1897), who wrote in the same vein. Returning from France, where he had established himself after the dethroning of Sultan Abdülaziz (1876), he was made the director of the Galatasary Lyceé, a school for training the Ottoman elite in conformity with a French program of instruction. He was dismissed owing to his incompetence. Abdülaziz's successor, Murad V, had a short reign, having been found mentally unbalanced. In 1878, Suavi attempted to reestablish Murad, but was killed during the coup that he organized.

Suavi's populism was bolstered by an Islamic conception of politics that underscores the differences between his worldview and that of the Young Ottomans. Suavi found Kemal's principle of popular sovereignty to be meaningless. In response to the Young Ottomans' separation of powers, he proposed the "unity of the imamate," referring to all forms of leadership. Suavi also believed that violence was a legitimate means of achieving the just political system; here, too, he was at odds with Kemal. Suavi believed that the natural social hierarchy was one where the *ʿulamāʾ* occupied a position of arbiter of sociopolitical regulations. This type of elitism coexisting with a sincere populism provides us a model of the ideas that were to appear much later in the thought of Ayatollah Ruhollah Khomeini (1902–1989) and underlines the necessity to see Islamic social ideals as incommensurable with those of Western democracy. Suavi's literary style was also a harbinger of "pure" Turkish to be used increasingly in the late nineteenth and twentieth centuries. He was one of the first persons to explore the original identity of Ottomans as "Turks" in a well-known article that appeared in his *Ulûm*, published in Europe after his split with the Young Ottomans.

[*See also* Tanzimat; Young Ottomans; *and the biography of Kemal.*]

BIBLIOGRAPHY

Mardin, Şerif. *The Genesis of Young Ottoman Thought*. Princeton, 1962.

Uzunçarşılı İsmail Hakkı. "Ali Suavi ve Çırağan Sarayı Vak'ası." *Belleten* 8 (1944): 71–118.

ŞERIF MARDIN

SUDAN. Islam entered the region of the Sudan, as it is known today, decisively in the sixteenth century CE. Today approximately 70 percent of Sudan's 22 million people are Muslims, living in the northern two-thirds of Africa's largest country. Non-Muslim minority peoples are found in the Nuba Mountains and southern Sudan where they follow indigenous animist religions, alongside or combined with various Christian denominations introduced during colonial times.

A distinctive cultural pattern of African Islam, grounded in Malikī observance and traditions, is practiced in Sudan. This spread from the west where African kingdoms had been islamized since the twelfth century. Islam also came from Egypt to the north, especially after the fall of Christian kingdoms in Nubia in the fifteenth century. The spread of Islam southward along the Nile had been effectively blocked by these christianized Nubian kingdoms, dating from 350–550. The first Muslim state in Sudan was the Funj Sultanate, established at Sinnar in 1504. [*See* Funj Sultanate.]

Arabization and islamization followed relatively quickly after the fall of the last Nubian Christian kingdom, but a distinctive Sudanese culture and character was retained, with the Nubians maintaining their language and distinctive culture to the present day. Islam spread southward along the Nile and westward into Kordofan and Darfur. In Sinnar the Funj, also known as the "Black Sultanate," attracted holy men from the Hejaz and from Egypt who introduced Islamic theology and jurisprudence and established the first religious courts. Pilgrims traveling across the vast trans-Saharan pilgrimage routes to Mecca were another source of continuous contact and influence of West African Islam on regions to the east, including the Sudan.

By the nineteenth century Islam was well established in the Sudan after three centuries of contact and infusion of religion and culture from West Africa, Egypt, and Arabia. Widely described by historians as the "century of Islamic revolution," the nineteenth century was also the era of greatest imperial adventure in the Sudan, beginning with the Turco-Egyptian invasion in 1821 and culminating in conquest by the British in 1898. These events shaped the nation of Sudan and its modern borders and prepared an important place for Islam in the governance of the country.

Modern Sudanese history is usually said to begin at the time of the Ottoman Turkish-Egyptian invasion of 1821, which resulted in the occupation and control of the Sudan until 1881. Known as the Turkīyah, this rule was a form of Turkish administrative methods and bureaucracy, managed by Egyptian and local officials and enforced by the Turco-Egyptian army. Invasion and occupation of the Sudan was no easy task, with resistance initially mounted by the Shayqīyah and Jaʿalin peoples and kept alive in periodic revolts throughout the Turkīyah. Turkish rule is recalled even today by Sudanese as harsh, with oppressive taxes, forced conscription of soldiers, and slaving expeditions that were imposed on generally egalitarian peoples unacquainted with the notion of a state or its human and material demands. There was no general rising until the sixth decade of Turkish occupation, when Muḥammad Aḥmad of Dongola, known as the Mahdi, unified this resistance and led a successful revolt that ended Turco-Egyptian rule.

Across Sudanic Africa a number of successful *jihād* movements flared in the nineteenth century in response to foreign intervention; they succeeded in establishing the ideal of Islamic government in sultanates among the Fulani and in Sokoto and Kanem-Bornu. The most famous of these was undoubtedly that of the Sudanese Mahdi, whose dramatic resistance not only ended Turkish rule but also prevented the English from becoming their immediate successors, despite the doomed effort of General Charles Gordon. The events that occurred between 1881 and 1898, known as the Mahdīyah, have become a significant part of both British and Sudanese history. From the standpoint of the British, the defeat of Gordon at Khartoum and the reconquest of the Sudan were among the low and high points in their imperial history; they have also captured a lasting place in Western consciousness in its longer historical confrontation with Islam. From the standpoint of Sudanese Muslim history, the Mahdīyah represents the triumph of Islamic resistance over foreign domination.

Muḥammad Aḥmad, the Mahdi, received a traditional religious education in northern Sudan and joined the Sammānīyah order after studying with the grandson of its founder, Muḥammad Sharīf Nūr al-Dā'im. He practiced a vigorous asceticism and strongly criticized the immorality and corruption of the political and social leaders of his day. His own zeal blended with the traditional Islamic concept of an "Expected One" (comparable to the Judaic and Christian idea of a Messiah); this, combined with a society in crisis, led Muḥammad Aḥmad to proclaim himself the Mahdi in May 1881. His divine mission included a calling his people to arms against the Turkish and Egyptian occupiers and purifying society by introducing a comprehensive Islamic governance. He built support rapidly in the northern and western Sudan among diverse ethnic groups by using the idea of Islamic community or *ummah*. By January 1885 the Mahdi's forces seized Khartoum, killing General Charles Gordon, who was serving both Egyptian khedival and British imperial interests in the Sudan; this set the stage for revenge and the conquest of the Mahdist Sudan by the British empire.

Muḥammad Aḥmad al-Mahdī died soon after the fall of Khartoum and was succeeded by Caliph Abdallahi al-Ta'ishi, who governed the nascent Islamic state from Omdurman and based its practice on the idea of a revived Muslim community living in the ways of the earliest converts to Islam in Medina. A puritanical and zealous movement, it continued its military campaigns to extend the *dār al-Islām* southward by attacking and attempting to convert the animist peoples in the Nuba Mountains and Bahr al-Ghazal regions. This period is recalled in the south as the beginning of the intrusion of northern Muslim governments in successive efforts to dominate southern Sudan religiously and politically. In the north the Mahdist state, as the only successful anti-imperialist Islamic republic in Africa at the time, is recalled as a time of glory and early nationalism born in the context of a renewed Islam. More than one observer has noted the early beginnings of modern Islamic revival in Sudanese Mahdism—especially the parallel with the Islamic revolution in Iran almost exactly a century later in 1979. The fall of Mahdism and the military conquest of the Sudan took place in 1898 under the command of General Horatio Herbert Kitchener, whose gunboats and Gatling guns overpowered the swords of the Mahdist Anṣār. The massacre at Karreri battlefield outside Omdurman marked the symbolic and real defeat of Mahdism. [*See also* Mahdi; Mahdīyah.]

The powerful impact of the Mahdist revolution on Sudanese Islam and political life can be seen in the continuing influence of the al-Mahdī family. Muḥammad Aḥmad's son ʿAbd al-Raḥmān al-Mahdī rose to the difficult role of family, religious, and political leader of the Anṣār at the dawn of colonialism in the Anglo-Egyptian Sudan. The British kept him under close surveillance until World War I, when he and other religious leaders declared their allegiance to the Crown and not to Constantinople. The Anṣār political organization developed into one of the nationalist parties, the Ummah Party, which was led by ʿAbd al-Raḥman's son Ṣiddīq. Ṣiddīq's son, Ṣādiq al-Mahdī, has twice served as prime minister of Sudan, demonstrating the persistent influence of this Muslim family. [*See* Anṣār *and the biography of Mahdī, al-Ṣādiq al-*.]

Paralleling and often conflicting with this tradition of state-organized Islam is the Ṣūfī tradition. By the nineteenth century the process of islamization was in its fourth century in the Sudan, with populist Ṣūfī orders acting as its main agents. With their style of religious performance in the form of *dhikr* ("remembrance" of God), and the use of drumming, chanting, and dancing led by a local *shaykh,* the Ṣūfīs blended with and enhanced local traditions without threatening them. The Ṣūfī brotherhoods—the most significant in the Sudan are the Qādirīyah, Sammānīyah, Khatmīyah, Sānusīyah, and Shādhilīyah—are generally egalitarian and decentralized in organization; thus they eschew the formalism of such Islamic institutions as *sharīʿah* courts or state-supported official interpretations issued by the *ʿulamāʾ*. With the introduction of the state, bureaucracy, courts, and the official administration of Islam, the local Ṣūfī leaders were undermined; in response they withheld their support from the state. At times the state further antagonized the orders by declaring them to be outside the boundaries of orthodox Islam because of their veneration of local holy men and unrestrained modes of worship. The Ṣūfī orders are still popular today, and this tension remains a constant feature of the dynamics of the spread of Islam, its institutional establishment in society, and its relationship to the state. [*See also* Qādirīyah; Khatmīyah; Sānusīyah; *and* Shādhilīyah.]

With the reconquest and pacification of Mahdist forces came the creation of a colonialist state, constructed as the Anglo-Egyptian Sudan between 1898 and 1902. The attitude toward Islam in the post-Mahdist Sudan was a careful one, specifically seeking to control the religion without crushing it and to administer Muslims through their own institutions, though under British rule. The task was one of erecting semi-autonomous Islamic institutions and finding reliable agents to govern in the conquerors' behalf. Carefully selected *ʿulamāʾ* were placed strategically within a new structure that was on one hand Muslim and familiar and on the other distinctly foreign and colonial.

A "Mohammedan" legal establishment was developed that was to have its own system of courts, appeals, and jurisdiction separate from the English-derived civil and criminal courts and law. The Sudan Mohammedan Law Courts were made competent to decide matters affecting the personal status of Sudanese Muslims—for example, questions of marriage, divorce, child custody and support, inheritance, wills, and religious bequest or *waqf.* The grand *qāḍī* of the *sharīʿah* courts was appointed by the governor-general of the Sudan and operated under the direct authority of a colonial official, the legal secretary. The grand *qāḍī* was granted the right to issue Judicial Circulars that would regulate decisions and procedures of the courts. In practice, these circulars functioned to determine the course of development of Islamic law in Sudan throughout the twentieth century, until islamization of the law took place in 1983. Significant developments of this period included reform in the law of divorce, permitting judicial divorce for women in instances of proven harm or abuse; expansion of women's rights to maintenance after divorce and custody of children under specified circumstances; confirmation in the 1930s of the right of the marriage guardian (usually the father) to contract a marriage for a woman (however, the sole right of the woman to consent in marriage was ultimately recognized by circulars issued in the 1960s); and the regulation of *waqf*s naming family members so as to avoid favoring particular relations and thus violating Qur'ānic laws of inheritance. (For a complete translation of the Sudanese Judicial Circulars, 1902–1979, see C. Fluehr-Lobban and H. B. Hillawi, 1983.) Analysis of the circulars suggests that the role of the *ʿulamāʾ* under colonialism was not an entirely subordinate one, and that independence of thought and action provided by the mechanism of the Judicial Circulars was in fact pursued by them as the only legitimate class of the guardians of the faith under foreign rule.

Outside this realm of official Islam, the more traditional Muslim organizations continued to exert an influence within their precolonial constituencies, such as the Mahdist followers, the Anṣār, or members of the powerful religious orders like the Khatmīyah sect of the Mirghānī family. Although certainly subdued during the initial decades of imperial rule, these religious orders grew more political and evolved into nationalist parties, notably the Ummah Party of the Mahdist sect and the Unionist Party, many of whose followers were affiliated with the Khatmīyah. The Ummah Party was formed in 1945 and advocated an independent Sudan, while the Unionist Party, founded in 1944, supported union with Egypt. This basic political difference combined with the traditional rivalry between these two most powerful Muslim sects and left them bitter enemies, unable to collaborate and divided on nearly every issue from pre-independence times to the present. [*See* Ummah-Anṣār.]

The Muslim Brotherhood, a new type of politico-religious movement founded in Egypt in 1928, spread its influence to neighboring Sudan in the 1940s, and a branch was established there early in the 1950s. While the two giants of Islamic mobilization, the Ummah and Unionist parties, battled for power at the time of independence in 1956, the Muslim Brotherhood did not begin to exert its influence until the mid-1960s, when its Islamic Charter Front entered electoral politics and attempted to build a mass organization. From the earliest days the leader of the Muslim Brotherhood in Sudan has been Ḥasan al-Turābī, originally from the University of Khartoum's faculty of law and more recently an internationally recognized leader of resurgent Islam. [*See* Muslim Brotherhood, *article on* Muslim Brotherhood in the Sudan; *and the biography of Turābī.*]

For most of its post-independence period Sudan has been governed by secular nationalist and militarist regimes that left the question of Islam and Muslim institutions formally out of the political arena. Nonetheless, the issue of the status and future of Islam was very much part of political agendas, whether of those seeking a secular, multinational, and multireligious state and an end to the civil war between north and south Sudan, which emerged after independence, or of those seeking a greater role for Islamic government and law within what they see as a predominantly Muslim country.

This situation changed decisively during the military regime of Jaʿfar Nimeiri (1969–1985), whose initially secular nationalist policies turned dramatically toward Islamist rule with his 1983 presidential decree that Islamic law would be the sole and comprehensive law for the entire country. Angry and feeling betrayed, southern Sudanese organized as the Sudan People's Liberation Movement (SPLM) and resumed a civil war between north and south that had broken out first in the 1950s. Nimeiri's use of the *sharīʿah* as a weapon of political repression against his enemies resulted in abusive application of the *ḥudūd* ("to the limit") penalties. It is estimated that at least two hundred victims had limbs amputated during the two years (1983–1985) of this punishment. Popular displeasure with the turn of the Nimeiri government was heightened by his regime's execution of Maḥmūd Muḥammad Ṭāhā, the elderly leader of the Republican Brothers. Within a matter of weeks a popular revolution and coup d'état overthrew Nimeiri and restored democracy to the country in 1985. [*See* Republican Brothers.]

After a transitional period Ṣādiq al-Mahdī was elected prime minister a second time and served from 1986 to 1989. However, he failed to settle either of the critical issues facing the country: ending the war in the south and modification of the *sharīʿah* as state law. A second coup d'état in 1989 brought an Islamist regime to power, formally headed by General ʿUmar al-Bashīr but supported by the Islamist leader Ḥasan al-Turābī.

The issue of the proper place of religion, especially Islamic government and law, is central to the future political stability and national unity of Sudan. For a multiethnic, multireligious country the issue of the role of Islam in state and society is crucial. The alternatives of a secular, democratic model or a committed Islamic model stand as two possible outcomes in a time of civil conflict.

BIBLIOGRAPHY

Affendi, Abdelwahab El-. *Turabi's Revolution: Islam and Power in the Sudan*. London, 1991. An insider's view of the ideology and rise to a powerful position in Sudanese politics of the Muslim Brotherhood movement and its chief proponent, Ḥasan al-Turābī. Placing the Sudanese movement within a larger framework of Islamic revival el-Affendi traces the Muslim Brothers from a marginal place in a dominantly secular Sudan after independence to an increasing Islamist tendency that became dominant after islamization of law in 1983 and the 1989 military regime of ʿUmar al-Bashīr. Turābī's role in the latter events is profound.

ʿAbd al-Rahim, Muddathir. *Imperialism and Nationalism in the Sudan: A Study in Constitutional and Political Development, 1899–1956*. Oxford, 1969. A view of the reception of English colonial rule and the development of Sudanese nationalism in response to it from the perspective of an indigenous scholar. Written before the ascendency of the Islamist trend, the volume concentrates on the role of secular nationalism in the road to independence.

Beshir, Mohammed Omer. *Revolution and Nationalism in the Sudan*. New York, 1974. A thematic treatment of the rise of Sudanese nationalism that takes into account the dissatisfaction of the south with the political configuration of the Sudan after independence. Mohammed Omer Beshir is among a handful of northern Muslim scholars to take an early, serious interest in the political concerns of southern Sudanese and the implications for national unity.

Collins, Robert O. *Shadows in the Grass: Britain in the Southern Sudan, 1918–1956*. New Haven, 1983. The definitive study by an American historian of the role of English colonial rule in the southern Sudan, documenting a policy of separation and economic underdevelopment mandating a dependency on the northern merchants and politicians. It is essential reading for understanding the immediate historical background to the current conflict.

Daly, M. W. *Empire on the Nile: The Anglo-Egyptian Sudan, 1898–1934*. Cambridge, 1986. See remarks following next item, below.

Daly, M. W. *Imperial Sudan: The Anglo-Egyptian Condominium, 1934–1956*. Cambridge, 1991. This two-volume series presents a comprehensive survey of the political and economic history of the Anglo-Egyptian Sudan based on extensive archival research in Sudan, the United States, and especially in the Sudan Archive at Durham University. With an obvious dependence upon colonial records, the historical point of view is Anglocentric and might be balanced by reference to histories of the same period written from a Sudanese perspective. Nevertheless, the volumes represent a detailed description of the Condominium years.

Fluehr-Lobban, Carolyn. *Islamic Law and Society in the Sudan*. London, 1987. A historical and legal anthropological study of the *sharīʿah* as applied law in twentieth-century Sudan, with court observations and case material from 1979–1980. Chapters cover the personal status law applied before islamization in 1983 including marriage, divorce, maintence and child custody, the status of women, inheritance, and a chapter on Islamist movements.

Fluehr-Lobban, Carolyn, and Hatim Babiker Hillawi. "Circulars of the Shari'a Courts in the Sudan (Manshurat el-Mahakim el-Shari'a fi Sudan), 1902–1979." *Journal of African Law* 27.2 (1983): 79–140. The Judicial Circulars (Manshurat) were a mechanism introduced by the English to amend or modify the application of *sharīʿah* law in the Sudan. They constitute a unique documentary history of the practice and functioning of Islamic law during colonial times and after independence until islamization of law in 1983. A historical introduction precedes the complete translation and transcription of the Circulars issued by Sudanese grand *qāḍīs* from 1902 to 1979 and cover matters of marriage guardianship and consent, divorce, child custody and inheritance reforms, as well as regulations and procedures of the *sharīʿah* courts.

Voll, John O., ed. *Sudan: State and Society in Crisis*. Bloomington, 1991. One of the best collections of essays to explore the political crisis in the Sudan that was precipitated in the context of islamization of law and state in the 1980s and 1990s. Neglect of the south, failure of economic development plans, and coping with large refugee populations are issues reviewed together with the better known political development of the Islamist trend.

CAROLYN FLUEHR-LOBBAN

SUFISM. [*This entry comprises three articles:*
Ṣūfī Thought and Practice
Ṣūfī Orders
Ṣūfī Shrine Culture
The first provides an overview of the traditional themes, practices, literatures, and institutions of Sufism; the second surveys the development and spread of Ṣūfī orders throughout the Muslim world; and the third treats the spiritual, social, and political significance of Ṣūfī shrines. See also Sufism and Politics.]

Ṣūfī Thought and Practice

In a broad sense, Sufism can be described as the interiorization and intensification of Islamic faith and practice. The Arabic term *ṣūfī*, however, has been used in a wide variety of meanings over the centuries, both by proponents and opponents, and this is reflected in the primary and secondary sources, which offer diverse interpretations of what Sufism entails. Western observers have not helped to clarify the matter by referring to Sufism as "Islamic mysticism" or sometimes "Islamic esotericism." Such terms are vague and often imply a negative value judgment, as well as encouraging people to consider as non-Ṣūfī anything that does not fit into preconceived notions.

The original sense of *ṣūfī* seems to have been "one who wears wool." By the eighth century the word was sometimes applied to Muslims whose ascetic inclinations led them to wear coarse and uncomfortable woolen garments. Gradually it came to designate a group who differentiated themselves from others by emphasis on certain specific teachings and practices of the Qur'ān and the *sunnah*. By the ninth century the gerund form *taṣawwuf*, literally "being a Ṣūfī" or "Sufism," was adopted by representatives of this group as their appropriate designation.

In general, the Ṣūfīs have looked upon themselves as Muslims who take seriously God's call to perceive his presence both in the world and in the self. They tend to stress inwardness over outwardness, contemplation over action, spiritual development over legalism, and cultivation of the soul over social interaction. On the theological level, Ṣūfīs speak of God's mercy, gentleness, and beauty far more than they discuss the wrath, severity, and majesty that play important roles in both *fiqh* (jurisprudence) and *kalām* (dogmatic theology). Sufism has been associated not only with specific institutions and individuals but also with an enormously rich literature, especially poetry. [*See* Fiqh; Theology.]

Given the difficulty of providing an exact definition of Sufism, it is not easy to discern which Muslims have been Ṣūfīs and which have not. Being a Ṣūfī certainly has nothing to do with the Sunnī/Shīʿī split nor with the schools of jurisprudence. It has no special connection with geography, though it has played a greater role in some locations than in others. There is no necessary correlation with family, and it is common to find individuals who profess a Ṣūfī affiliation despite the hostility of family members, or people who have been born into a family of Ṣūfīs yet consider it an unacceptable form of Islam. Both men and (less commonly) women become Ṣūfīs, and even children participate in Ṣūfī ritual activities, though they are seldom accepted as fullfledged members before puberty. Sufism has nothing to do with social class, although some Ṣūfī organizations may be more or less class specific. Sufism is closely associated with popular religion, but it has also produced the most elite expressions of Islamic teachings. It is often seen as opposed to the state-supported jurists, yet jurists have always been counted among its devotees, and Sufism has frequently been supported by the state along with jurisprudence. The characteristic Ṣūfī institutions—the "orders" (*ṭarīqahs*)—do not begin to play a major role in Islamic history until about the twelfth century, but even after that time being a Ṣūfī has not necessarily entailed membership in an order.

Working Description. Specialists in the study of Sufism have reached no consensus as to what they are studying. Those who take seriously the self-understanding of the Ṣūfī authorities usually picture Sufism as an essential component of Islam. Those who are hostile toward Sufism, or hostile toward Islam but sympathetic toward Sufism, or skeptical of any self-understanding by the objects of their study, typically describe Sufism as a movement that was added to Islam after the prophetic period. The diverse theories of Sufism's nature and origins proposed by modern and premodern scholars cannot be summarized here. The best one can do is to suggest that most of Sufism's own theoreticians have understood it to be the living spirit of the Islamic tradition. One of the greatest Ṣūfī teachers, Abū Ḥāmid al-Ghazālī (d. 1111), gives a nutshell description of Sufism's role within Islam in the very title of his magnum opus, *Iḥyāʾ ʿulūm al-dīn* (Giving Life to the Sciences of the Religion).

Understood as Islam's life-giving core, Sufism is coextensive with Islam. Wherever there have been Muslims, there have been Ṣūfīs. If there was no phenomenon called "Sufism" at the time of the Prophet, neither was there anything called "*fiqh*" or "*kalām*" in the later senses of these terms. All these are names that came to be applied to various dimensions of Islam after the tradition became diversified and elaborated. If one wants to call the Ṣūfī dimension "mysticism," then one needs an exceedingly broad description of the role that mysticism plays in religion, such as that provided by Louis Dupré, who writes that religions "retain their vitality only as long as their members continue to believe in a transcendent reality with which they can in some way communicate by direct experience" ("Mysticism," *Encyclopedia of Religion,* edited by Mircea Eliade, New York, 1987, vol. 10, p. 247).

In historical terms, it is helpful to think of Sufism on two levels. On the first level—which is the primary focus of the Ṣūfī authorities themselves—Sufism has no history, because it is the invisible, animating life of the Muslim community. On the second level, which concerns both Muslim authors and modern historians, Sufism's presence is made known through certain observable characteristics of people and society or certain specific institutional forms. Ṣūfī authors who looked at Sufism on the second level wanted to describe how the great Muslims achieved the goal of human life, nearness to God. Hence their typical genre was hagiography, which aims at bringing out the extraordinary human qualities of those who achieve divine nearness. In contrast, Muslim opponents of Sufism have been anxious to show that Sufism is a distortion of Islam, and they have happily seized on any opportunity to associate Sufism with unbelief and moral laxity (see Carl Ernst, *Words of Ecstasy in Sufism,* Albany, 1985, pp. 117ff.).

The attacks on Sufism frequent in Islamic history have many causes. Not least of these has been the social and political influence of Ṣūfī teachers, which often threatened the power and privileges of jurists and even rulers. Although the great Ṣūfī authorities set down many guidelines for keeping Sufism squarely at the heart of the Islamic tradition, popular religious movements that aimed at intensifying religious experience and had little concern for Islamic norms were also associated with Sufism. Whether or not the members of these movements considered themselves Ṣūfīs, opponents of Sufism were happy to claim that their excesses represented Sufism's true nature. The Ṣūfī authorities themselves frequently criticized false Ṣūfīs, and the dangers connected with loss of contact with the ahistorical core of Sufism could only increase when much of Sufism became institutionalized through the Ṣūfī orders (see, for example, the criticisms by the sixteenth century Ṣūfī ʿAbd al-Wahhāb al-Shaʿrānī in Michael Winter, *Society and Religion in Early Ottoman Egypt: Studies in the Writings of ʿAbd al-Wahhāb al-Shaʿrānī*, New Brunswick, N.J., 1982, pp. 102ff.). If Sufism is essentially invisible and ahistorical, the problem faced by those who study specific historical phenomena is how to judge the degree to which these deserve the name Sufism. The Ṣūfī authorities typically answer that the criteria of authentic Sufism are found in correct activity and correct understanding, and these pertain to the very definition of Islam.

In looking for a Qur'ānic name for the phenomenon that later generations came to call Sufism, some authors settled on the term *iḥsān*, "doing what is beautiful," a divine and human quality about which the Qur'ān says a good deal, mentioning in particular that God loves those who possess it. In the famous *ḥadīth* of Gabriel, the Prophet describes *iḥsān* as the innermost dimension of Islam, after *islām* ("submission" or correct activity) and *īmān* ("faith" or correct understanding). *Iḥsān* is a deepened understanding and experience that, in the words of this *ḥadīth*, allows one "to worship God as if you see him." This means that Ṣūfīs strive always to be aware of God's presence in both the world and themselves and to act appropriately. Historically, *islām* became manifest through the *sharīʿah* and jurisprudence, whereas *īmān* became institutionalized through *kalām* and other forms of doctrinal teachings. In the same way, *iḥsān* revealed its presence mainly through Ṣūfī teachings and practices (see W. C. Chittick, *Faith and Practice of Islam: Three Thirteenth Century Sufi Texts*, Albany, 1992, parts 1 and 4). [*See* Īmān.]

By codifying the *sharīʿah* jurisprudence delineates the exact manner in which people should submit their activities to God. *Kalām* defines the contents of Islamic faith while providing a rational defense for the Qur'ān and the *ḥadīth*. For its part, Sufism focuses on giving both submission and faith their full due. Hence it functions on two levels, theory (corresponding to *īmān*) and practice (corresponding to *islām*). On the theoretical level, Sufism explains the rationale for both faith and submission. Its explanations of faith differ from those of *kalām* both in perspective and in focus, but they are no less carefully rooted in the sources of the tradition. On the practical level, Sufism explains the means whereby Muslims can strengthen their understanding and observance of Islam with a view toward finding God's presence in themselves and the world. It intensifies Islamic ritual life through careful attention to the details of the *sunnah* and by focusing on the remembrance of God's name *(dhikr)*, which is commanded by the Qur'ān and the *ḥadīth* and is taken by the Ṣūfī authorities as the raison d'être of all Islamic ritual. *Dhikr* typically takes the form of the methodical repetition of certain names of God or Qur'ānic formulas, such as the first Shahādah. In communal gatherings, Ṣūfīs usually perform *dhikr* aloud, often with musical accompaniment. In some Ṣūfī groups these communal sessions became the basic ritual, with corresponding neglect of various aspects of the *sunnah*. At this point Ṣūfī practice became suspect not only in the eyes of the jurists, but also in the eyes of most Ṣūfī authorities.

Like other branches of Islamic learning, Sufism is passed down from master (typically called a *shaykh*) to disciple. The master's oral teachings give life to the articles of faith, and without his transmission, *dhikr* is considered invalid if not dangerous. As with *ḥadīth*, transmission is traced back through a chain of authorities (called *silsilah*) to the Prophet. The typical initiation rite is modeled on the handclasp known as *bayʿat al-riḍwān* (the oathtaking of God's good pleasure) that the Prophet exacted from his companions at Ḥudaybīyah, referred to in the Qur'ān, surah 48.10 and 48.18. The rite is understood to transmit an invisible spiritual force or blessing *(barakah)* that makes possible the transformation of the disciple's soul. The master's fundamental concern—as in other forms of Islamic learning—is to shape the character *(khuluq)* of the disciple so that it conforms to the prophetic model. [*See* Dhikr; Shaykh; Barakah.]

If molding the character of students and disciples was a universal concern of Islamic teaching, the Ṣūfīs developed a science of human character traits that had no parallels in jurisprudence or theology, though the philosophers knew something similar. Ibn al-ʿArabī (d. 1240), Sufism's greatest theoretician, described Sufism as "assuming the character traits of God" (Chittick, *Sufi Path of Knowledge,* Albany, 1989, p. 283). Since God created human beings in his own image, it is their duty to actualize the divine character traits that are latent in their own souls. This helps explain the great attention that Ṣūfī authorities devote to the "stations" *(maqāmāt)* of spiritual ascent on the path to God and the "states" *(aḥwāl)* or psychological transformations that spiritual travelers undergo in their attempt to pass through the stations.

Ṣūfī theory offered a theological perspective that was far more attractive to the vast majority of Muslims than *kalām,* which was an academic exercise with little practical impact on most people. From the beginning, the *kalām* experts attempted to understand Qur'ānic teachings in rational terms with the help of methods drawn from Greek thought. In keeping with the inherent tendency of reason to discern and differentiate, *kalām* fastened on all those Qur'ānic verses that assert the transcendence and otherness of God. When faced with verses that assert God's immanence and presence, *kalām* explained them away through forced interpretations *(ta'wīl).* As H. A. R. Gibb has pointed out, "The more developed theological systems were largely negative and substituted for the vivid personal relation between God and man presented by the Koran an abstract and depersonalized discussion of logical concepts" (*Mohammedanism,* London, 1961, p. 127). Ibn al-ʿArabī made a similar point when he said that if Muslims had been left only with theological proofs, none of them would ever have loved God (Chittick, *Sufi Path,* p. 180). [*See the biography of Ibn al-ʿArabī.*]

The Qur'ān speaks of God with a wide variety of terminology that can conveniently be summarized as God's "most beautiful names" *(al-asmā' al-ḥusnā).* For the most part, *kalām* stresses those names that assert God's severity, grandeur, distance, and aloofness. Although many early expressions of Sufism went along with the dominant attitudes in *kalām,* another strand of Ṣūfī thinking gradually gained strength and became predominant by the eleventh or twelfth century. This perspective focused on divine names that speak of nearness, sameness, similarity, concern, compassion, and love. The Ṣūfī teachers emphasized the personal dimensions of the divine-human relationship, agreeing with the *kalām* authorities that God was distant, but holding that his simultaneous nearness was the more important consideration. The grand theological theme of the Ṣūfī authors is epitomized in the *ḥadīth qudsī* in which God says, "My mercy takes precedence over my wrath," which is to say that God's nearness is more real than his distance.

If *kalām* and jurisprudence depended on reason to establish categories and distinctions, the Ṣūfī authorities depended on another faculty of the soul to bridge gaps and make connections. Many of them referred to this faculty as imagination *(khayāl)* and considered it the power of the soul that can perceive the presence of God in all things. They read literally the Qur'ānic verse, "Wherever you turn, there is the face of God" (2:115), and they find a reference to imagination's power to perceive this face in the Prophet's definition of *iḥsān:* "It is to worship God *as if* you see him." Through methodical concentration on the face of God as revealed in the Qur'ān, the Ṣūfīs gradually remove the "as if" so that they are left with "unveiling" *(kashf),* the generic term for suprarational vision of God's presence in the world and the soul. Ibn al-ʿArabī asserts that unveiling is a mode of knowledge superior to reason, but he also insists that reason provides the indispensable checks and balances without which it is impossible to differentiate among divine, angelic, psychic, and satanic inrushes of imaginal knowledge.

Spectrums of Ṣūfī Theory and Practice. One way to classify the great variety of phenomena that have been called Sufism in Islamic history is to look at the types of responses they have made to basic Islamic theological teachings. *Tawḥīd,* the fundamental assertion of Islam, declares that God is one, but it also implies that the world is many. The connection between God's oneness and the world's manyness can be found in God's eternal knowledge of all things, on the basis of which he creates an infinitely diverse universe and reveals scriptures that differentiate between true and false, right and wrong, absolute and relative, and all other qualities that have a bearing on human salvation. Oneness and manyness represent two poles not only of reality but also of thought. Imaginal thinking tends to see the oneness and identity of things, while rational thinking focuses on manyness, diversity, and difference. A creative tension has existed between these two basic ways of looking at God and the world throughout Islamic history. By and large, the *kalām* authorities and jurists have emphasized the rational perception of God's distance, while the Ṣūfī authorities have countered with the imaginal perception of God's nearness. On occasion the balance between these two perspectives has been broken by a stern and exclusivist legalism on one hand or an excessively emotional religiosity on the other. In the first case, the understanding of the inner domains of Islamic experience is lost, and nothing is left but legal nit-picking and theological bickering. In the second case, the necessity for the divine guidance provided by the *sharīʿah* is forgotten, and the resulting sectarian movements break off from Islam's mainstream. In modern times these two extremes are represented by certain forms of fundamentalism on one side and deracinated Sufism on the other (for an interesting case study, see Mark Woodward, *Islam in Java,* Tucson, 1989, especially pp. 234ff.).

Within the theory and practice of Sufism itself, a parallel differentiation of perspectives can be found. Many expressions of Sufism vigorously assert the reality of God's omnipresent oneness and the possibility of union with him, while others emphasize the duties of servanthood that arise out of discerning among the many things and discriminating between Creator and creature, absolute and relative, or right and wrong. In order to describe the psychological accompaniments of these two emphases, the Ṣūfīs offer various sets of terms, such as "intoxication" *(sukr)* and "sobriety" *(ṣaḥw)* or "annihilation" *(fanāʾ)* and "subsistence" *(baqāʾ)*. Intoxication follows upon being overcome by the presence of God: the Ṣūfī sees God in all things and loses the ability to discriminate among creatures. Intoxication is associated with intimacy *(uns),* the sense of God's loving nearness, and this in turn is associated with the divine names that assert that God is close and caring. Sobriety is connected with awe *(haybah),* the sense that God is majestic, mighty, wrathful, and distant, far beyond the petty concerns of human beings. God's distance and aloofness allow for a clear view of the difference between servant and Lord, but his nearness blinds the discerning powers of reason. Perfect vision of the nature of things necessitates a balance between reason and imaginal unveiling.

The contrast between sober and drunk, or the vision of oneness and the vision of manyness, reverberates throughout Ṣūfī writing and is reflected in the hagiographical accounts of the Ṣūfī masters. Those who experience intimacy are boldly confident of God's mercy, while those who experience awe remain wary of God's wrath. By and large, drunken Ṣūfīs tend to deemphasize the *sharīʿah* and declare union with God openly, whereas sober Ṣūfīs observe the courtesy *(adab)* that relationships with the Lord demand. The sober fault the drunk for disregarding the *sunnah,* and the drunk fault the sober for forgetting the overriding reality of God's mercy and depending on reason instead of God. Those who, in Ibn al-ʿArabī's terms, "see with both eyes" keep reason and unveiling in perfect balance while acknowledging the rights of both sober and drunk.

Expressions of sobriety and intoxication often have rhetorical purposes. An author who disregards rational norms has not necessarily been overcome by the divine wine—if he had, he would hardly have put pen to paper. So also, sober expressions of Sufism do not mean that the authors know nothing of intoxication; typically, sobriety is described as a station that follows intoxication, since the sobriety that precedes intoxication is in fact the intoxication of forgetfulness. Ṣūfīs always wrote for the purpose of edification, and different teachers attempted to inculcate psychological attitudes reflecting the needs they perceived in their listeners.

Drunken expressions of Sufism predominate in Ṣūfī poetry, which is ideally suited to describe the imaginal realm of unveiled knowledge, the vision of union and oneness. In contrast, reason is locked into theological abstractions that keep the servant distant from the Lord; it is perfectly adapted to the expression of system, order, and rules. If Ṣūfī poetry constantly reminds us of God's presence, Ṣūfī prose tends toward a rational discourse that is ideal for manuals of doctrine and practice—works that always keep one eye on the opinions of the jurists and the *kalām* experts. Poetic licence allowed the Ṣūfī poets to say things that could not be expressed openly in prose. In the best examples, such as Ibn al-Fāriḍ in Arabic, ʿAṭṭār, Rūmī, and Ḥāfiẓ in Persian, and Yunus Emre in Turkish, the poetry gives rise to a marvellous joy and intoxication in the listener and conveys the experience of God's presence in creation. Since this experience flies in the face of juridical and theological discourse, it is sometimes expressed in ways that shock the pious (for a good study of the role of poetry and music in contemporary Sufism, see Earl H. Waugh, *The Munshidīn of Egypt: Their World and Their Song,* Columbia, S.C., 1989). [*See* Devotional Music; Devotional Poetry.]

For many Western observers, whether scholars or would-be practitioners, "real" Sufism has been identified with the drunken manifestations that denigrate the external and practical concerns of "orthodox" Islam. It is seldom noted that many of those who express themselves in the daring poetry of union also employ the respectful prose of separation and servanthood. Drunken

Sufism rarely demonstrates interest in juridical issues or theological debates, whereas sober Sufism offers methodical discussions of these topics that can quickly prove tiring to any but those trained in the Islamic sciences. The poets address the highest concerns of the soul and employ the most delicious and enticing imagery; the theoreticians discuss details of practice, behavior, moral development, Qur'ānic exegesis, and the nature of God and the world. Drunken Sufism has always been popular among Muslims of all classes and persuasions, and even the most literal-minded jurists are likely to enjoy the poetry while condemning the ideas. Sober Sufism has attacted the more educated Ṣūfī practitioners who were willing to devote long hours to studying texts that were no easier than works on jurisprudence, *kalām*, or philosophy.

For Sufism to remain whole, it needs to keep a balance between sobriety and drunkenness, reason and unveiling—that is, between concern for the *sharīʿah* and Islamic doctrine on one hand and for the experience of God's presence on the other. If sobriety is lost, so also is rationality, and along with it the strictures of *islām* and *īmān;* if drunkenness is lost, so also is religious experience, along with love, compassion, and *iḥsān*. Within Sufism's diverse forms, a wide range of perspectives is observable, depending on whether the stress falls on oneness or manyness, love or knowledge, intoxication or sobriety. Too much stress on either side means that Sufism becomes distorted and ceases to be itself, but where the line must be drawn is impossible to say with any precision.

The classic example of the contrast between drunken and sober Sufism is found in the pictures drawn of Ḥallāj (d. 922) and Junayd (d. 910). The first became Sufism's great martyr because of his open avowal of the mysteries of divine union and his disregard for the niceties of shariatic propriety. The second, known as the "master of all the Ṣūfīs" *(shaykh al-ṭā'ifah)*, kept coolly sober despite achieving the highest degree of union with God. Another example can be found in the contrast between the two high points of the whole Ṣūfī tradition, Ibn al-ʿArabī (d. 1240) and Jalāl al-Dīn Rūmī (d. 1273). The former wrote voluminously in Arabic prose and addressed every theoretical and practical issue that arises within the context of Islamic thought and practice. His works are enormously erudite and exceedingly difficult, and only the most learned of Muslims who were already trained in jurisprudence, *kalām*, and other Islamic sciences could hope to read and understand them. In contrast, Rūmī wrote more than seventy thousand verses of intoxicating poetry in a language that every Persian-speaking Muslim could understand. He sings constantly of the trials of separation from the Beloved and the joys of union with him. But the contrast between the two authors should not suggest that Rūmī was irrational or unlearned, or that Ibn al-ʿArabī was not a lover of God and a poet; it is rather a case of rhetorical means and emphasis. Among Western scholars, Henry Corbin argues forcefully that Rūmī and Ibn al-ʿArabī belong to the same group of *fidèles d'amour* (*Creative Imagination in the Ṣūfism of Ibn ʿArabī*, Princeton, 1969, pp. 70–71).

In the classical Ṣūfī texts there are two basic and complementary ways of describing Sufism. If the drunken side of Sufism is stressed, it is contrasted with jurisprudence and *kalām;* if sobriety is stressed, it is viewed as the perfection *(iḥsān)* of right practice *(islām)* and right faith *(īmān)*. The great theoreticians of Sufism, who speak from the viewpoint of sobriety, strive to establish a balance among all dimensions of Islamic thought and practice, with Sufism as the animating spirit of the whole. These thinkers include Sarrāj (d. 988), Kalabādhī (d. 990), Sulamī (d. 1021), Qushayrī (d. 1072), Hujwīrī (d. 1072), Ghazālī, Shihāb al-Dīn ʿUmar Suhrawardī (d. 1234), Ibn al-ʿArabī, Najm al-Dīn Rāzī (d. 1256), and ʿIzz al-Dīn Kāshānī (d. 1334/35). In contrast, the actual everyday practice of Sufism, especially in its popular dimensions, tends to appear antagonistic toward legalistic Islam, even though this is by no means always the case (see, for example, Jonathan Berkey, *The Transmission of Knowledge in Medieval Cairo,* Princeton, 1992, especially chapter 3, which makes clear that Ṣūfīs and jurists have sometimes been indistinguishable).

Sufism in the Modern World. In the modern period many Muslims have sought a revival of authentically Islamic teachings and practices, not least in order to fend off Western hegemony. Some have responded largely in political terms, while others have tried to revive Islam's inner life. Among most of the politically minded, Sufism became the scapegoat through which Islam's "backwardness" could be explained. In this view, Sufism is the religion of the common people and embodies superstition and un-Islamic elements adopted from local cultures; in order for Islam to reclaim its birthright, which includes modern science and technology, Sufism must be eradicated. Until recently most Western observers have considered the modernist reformers to be "Islam's hope to enter the modern age." Nowadays, the dissolution of Western cultural identity and an awareness of the ideological roots of ideas such as progress and development have left the modernists looking naive and sterile. In the meantime, various Ṣūfī teachers have been busy reviving the Islamic heritage by focusing on what they consider the root cause of every disorder—forgetfulness of God. Especially interesting here is the case of the famous Algerian freedom fighter ʿAbd al-Qādir Jazā'irī (d. 1883), who devoted his exile in Syria to reviving the heritage of Ibn al-ʿArabī (see Emir Abd el-Kader, *Ecrits spirituels,* translated by M. Chodkiewicz, Paris, 1982). [*See the biography of ʿAbd al-Qādir.*] Today grassroots Islam is far more likely to be inspired by Ṣūfī teachers than by modernist intellectuals, who are cut off from the masses because of their Western-style academic training. The presence of demagogues who have no qualms about manipulating religious sentiment for their own ends complicates the picture immensely.

Parallel to the resurgence of Sufism in the Islamic world has been the spread of Ṣūfī teachings to the West. In America, drunken Sufism was introduced in the early part of this century by the Chistī *shaykh* and musician Inayat Khan (*The Complete Works,* Tucson, 1988); his teachings have been continued by his son, Pir Vilayet Inayat Khan, a frequent lecturer on the New Age circuit. In Europe, sober Sufism gained a wide audience among intellectuals through the writings of the French metaphysician René Guénon, who died in Cairo in 1951 (*The Symbolism of the Cross,* London, 1958). More recently hundreds of volumes have been published in Western languages that are addressed to Ṣūfī seekers and reflect the range of perspectives found in the original texts, from sobriety to intoxication. Many of these works are written by authentic representatives of Ṣūfī *silsilah*s, but many more are written by people who have adopted Sufism to justify teachings of questionable origin, or who have left the safeguards of right practice and right thought—*islām* and *īmān*—and hence have no access to the *iḥsān* that is built upon the two.

Contemporary representatives of sober Sufism emphasize knowledge, discernment, and differentiation and usually stress the importance of the *sharīʿah.* Best known in this group is Frithjof Schuon (*Islam and the Perennial Philosophy,* London, 1976), who makes no explicit claims in his books to Ṣūfī affiliations but, as reviewers have often remarked, writes with an air of spiritual authority. He is said to be a member of the Shādhilīyah-ʿAlawīyah order of North Africa (G. C. Anawati and L. Gardet, *Mystique musulmane,* Paris, 1968, p. 72). He takes an extreme position on the importance of discernment and offers a rigorous criticism of the roots of modern antireligion. The main thrust of his writings seems to be to offer a theory of world religions based on the idea of a universal esoterism, the Islamic form of which is Sufism. He frequently asserts the necessity for esoterists of all religions to observe the exoteric teachings of their traditions, this being the *sharīʿah* in the case of Islam. Titus Burckhardt (*Fez: City of Islam,* Cambridge, England, 1992) represents a similar perspective, but his works are more explicitly grounded in traditional Ṣūfī teachings. Martin Lings (*What is Sufism?,* Berkeley, 1975), who has also published under the name Abū Bakr Sirāj ed-Dīn (*The Book of Certainty,* London, 1952), presents a picture of Sufism that is intellectually rigorous but firmly grounded in explicit Islamic teachings. The noted Iranian scholar Seyyed Hossein Nasr (*Sufi Essays,* London, 1972) also stresses intellectual discernment more than love, and he repeatedly insists that there is no Sufism without the *sharīʿah.* The books of the Turkish Cerrahi leader Muzaffer Ozak (*The Unveiling of Love,* New York, 1982) present *sharīʿah*-oriented Sufism that is much more focused on love than on intellectual discernment. The Naqshbandī master Nazim al-Qubrusi (*Mercy Ocean's Divine Sources,* London, 1983) offers a warm presentation of desirable human qualities, again rooted in a perspective that stresses love and often discusses the shariatic basis of Sufism. The Iranian Niʿmatullāhī leader Javād Nūrbakhsh (*Sufi Symbolism,* vols. 1–5, London, 1984–1991) has published several anthologies of classic Ṣūfī texts; his own perspective falls on the side of intoxication, with emphasis on oneness of being and union with God. He pays little attention to the *sharīʿah,* but he discusses the importance of Ṣūfī communal activities such as sessions of *dhikr.* Even more to the side of love and intoxication are the works of Guru Bawa Muhaiyaddeen (*Golden Words of A Sufi Sheikh,* Philadelphia, 1982), who presents a synthesis of Sufism and Hindu teachings that is recognizably Islamic only in its terminology.

BIBLIOGRAPHY

Addas, Claude. *Quest for the Red Sulphur: The Life of Ibn ʿArabī.* Cambridge, 1993. Fascinating study of the inner life and historical context of Sufism's greatest theoretician.

Andrae, Tor. *In the Garden of Myrtles: Studies in Early Islamic Mysticism.* Albany, N.Y., 1987. Sympathetic account of trends in early Sufism, with frequent comparisons to Christianity.

Anṣārī al-Harawī, ʿAbd Allāh ibn Muḥammad. *Les étapes des itinérants vers dieu.* Translated by Serge de Laugier de Beaurecueil. Cairo, 1962. French translation of a classic text on the stations of the Ṣūfī path, *Manāzil al-sā'irīn.*

Awn, Peter J. *Satan's Tragedy and Redemption: Iblīs in Sufi Psychology.* Leiden, 1983. Illustrates how Ṣūfīs could offer unusual insight into the human condition by reversing the normal theological perception of things.

Baldick, Julian. *Mystical Islam.* New York and London, 1989. Study of the origins and development of Sufism by perhaps the last specialist to believe that the key to understanding Sufism lies in tracing lines of historical influence.

Böwering, Gerhard. *The Mystical Vision of Existence in Classical Islam: The Quranic Hermeneutics of the Ṣūfī Sahl At-Tustarī (d. 283/896).* New York, 1980. Erudite study of an important early Ṣūfī.

Chittick, William C. *The Sufi Path to Love: The Spiritual Teachings of Rūmī.* Albany, N.Y., 1983. Anthology of Rūmī's poetry, arranged to illustrate the theoretical underpinnings of his worldview.

Chodkiewicz, Michel. *An Ocean without Shore: Ibn ʿArabi, the Book, and the Law.* Albany, N.Y., 1993. Fine exposition of Ibn al-ʿArabī's grounding in the Qur'ān.

Corbin, Henry. *The Man of Light in Iranian Sufism.* Boulder, 1978. Fascinating study of the role of light and imagination in Ṣūfī theoretical teachings.

Farīd al-Dīn ʿAṭṭār. *Muslim Saints and Mystics.* Translated by A. J. Arberry. Chicago, 1966. One of the classics of Ṣūfī hagiography, partially translated by a prolific translator of Ṣūfī texts.

Farīd al-Dīn ʿAṭṭār. *The Conference of the Birds.* Translated by Afkham Darbandi and Dick Davis. New York, 1984. Successful poetic version of a symbolic tale by the Persian poet ʿAṭṭār.

Ghazālī, Abū Ḥamid al-. *Freedom and Fulfillment: An Annotated Translation of al-Ghazālī's al-Munqidh min al-Ḍalāl and Other Relevant Works of al-Ghazālī.* Translated by Richard J. McCarthy. Boston, 1980. The best study of al-Ghazālī's Sufism.

Hujwīrī, ʿAlī ibn ʿUthmān al-. *The Kashf al-Mahjūb: The Oldest Persian Treatise on Sufism.* Translated by Reynold A. Nicholson. Reprint, London, 1970. One of several still useful translations and studies by a great scholar of Sufism.

Lings, Martin. *A Sufi Saint of the Twentieth Century.* 2d ed. London, 1971. Sympathetic account of a contemporary Ṣūfī master of North Africa.

Massignon, Louis. *The Passion of al-Ḥallāj: Mystic and Martyr of Islam.* 4 vols. Princeton, 1982. Monumental study of al-Ḥallāj's historical context and importance in Sufism.

Murata, Sachiko. *The Tao of Islam: A Sourcebook on Gender Relationships in Islamic Thought.* Albany, N.Y., 1992. Broad survey of Ṣūfī and philosophical views on God, the cosmos, and the human soul, with special attention to the Islamic views of male and female.

Najm al-Dīn Rāzī, ʿAbd Allah ibn Muḥammad. *The Path of God's Bondsmen.* Translated by Hamid Algar. Delmar, N.Y., 1982. Readable translation of a classic Persian text that provides one version of Ṣūfī cosmology and psychology and their relevance to a life of devotion to God.

Nasr, Seyyed Hossein. *Islamic Spirituality,* vol. 1, *Foundations;* vol. 2, *Manifestations.* New York, 1987–1990. The best overview of the whole range of Sufism's teachings and historical manifestations.

Schimmel, Annemarie. *Mystical Dimensions of Islam.* Chapel Hill, N.C., 1975. The best overview of the Ṣūfī tradition.

Trimingham, J. Spencer. *The Sufi Orders in Islam.* Oxford, 1971. Good historical survey of the orders, along with descriptions of basic Ṣūfī teachings and practices.

William C. Chittick

Ṣūfī Orders

Ṣūfī orders represent one of the most important forms of personal piety and social organization in the Islamic world. In most areas, an order is called a *ṭarīqah* (pl., *ṭuruq*), which is the Arabic word for "path" or "way." The term *ṭarīqah* is used for both the social organization and the special devotional exercises that are the basis of the order's ritual and structure. As a result, the "Ṣūfī orders" or *ṭarīqahs* include a broad spectrum of activities in Muslim history and society.

Mystical explanations of Islam emerged early in Muslim history, and there were pious mystics who developed their personal spiritual paths involving devotional practices, recitations, and literature of piety. These mystics, or Ṣūfīs, sometimes came into conflict with authorities in the Islamic community and provided an alternative to the more legalistic orientation of many of the *ʿulamā'*. However, Ṣūfīs gradually became important figures in the religious life of the general population and began to gather around themselves groups of followers who were identified and bound together by the special mystic path (*ṭarīqah*) of the teacher. By the twelfth century (the fifth century in the Islamic era), these paths began to provide the basis for more permanent fellowships, and Ṣūfī orders emerged as major social organizations in the Islamic community.

The orders have taken a variety of forms throughout the Islamic world. These range from the simple preservation of the *ṭarīqah* as a set of devotional exercises to vast interregional organizations with carefully defined structures. The orders also include the short-lived organizations that developed around particular individuals and more long-lasting structures with institutional coherence. The orders are not restricted to particular classes, although the orders in which the educated urban elite participated had different perspectives from the orders that reflected a more broadly based popular piety, and specific practices and approaches varied from region to region.

In all Ṣūfī orders there were central prescribed rituals which involved regular group meetings for recitations of prayers, poems, and selections from the Qur'ān. These meetings were usually described as acts of "remembering God" or *dhikr*. In addition, daily devotional exercises for the followers were also set, as were other activities of special meditation, asceticism, and devotion. Some of the special prayers of early Ṣūfīs became widely used, while the structure and format of the ritual was the distinctive character provided by the individual who established the *ṭarīqah*. The founder was the spiritual guide for all followers in the order, who would swear a special oath of obedience to him as their shaykh or teacher. As orders continued, the record of the transmission of the ritual would be preserved in a formal chain of spiritual descent, called a *silsilah,* which stated that the person took the order from a shaykh who took it from another shaykh in a line extending back to the founder, and then usually beyond the founder to the prophet Muḥammad. As orders became firmly established, leadership would pass from one shaykh to the next, sometimes within a family line and sometimes on the basis of spiritual seniority within the *ṭarīqah*. At times, a follower would reach a sufficient degree of special distinction that his prayers would represent a recognized subbranch within a larger order; at other times, such a follower might be seen as initiating a whole new *ṭarīqah*.

Within all this diversity, it is difficult to provide a simple account of the development of Ṣūfī orders, but at least some of the main features of the different types of orders and their development can be noted.

Premodern Foundations. Different types of orders developed in the early centuries of *ṭarīqah*-formation. These provide important foundations for the Ṣūfī orders of the modern era.

Large inclusive traditions. One type of order is the large inclusive *ṭarīqah* tradition with a clearly defined core of devotional literature. In the twelfth and thirteenth centuries, some major figures emerge as the organizers of orders that were to become the largest in the Islamic world. In some cases, the orders may actually have been organized by the immediate followers of the "founders," but these teachers represent the emergence of large-scale orders. The most frequently noted of these early orders is the Qādirīyah, organized around the teachings of ʿAbd al-Qādir al-Jīlānī (d. 1166), which grew rapidly and became the most widespread of the orders. Two other major orders originating in this era are the Suhrawardīyah, based on the teachings and organization of Abū al-Najīb al-Suhrawardī (d. 1168) and his nephew, Shihāb al-Dīn al-Suhrawardī (d. 1234); and the Rifa'īyah, representing the *ṭarīqah* of Aḥmad al-Rifa'ī (d. 1182). By the thirteenth century, increasing numbers of *ṭarīqah*s were being organized in the traditions of great teachers. Many of these were of primarily local or regional influence, but some became as widespread as the earlier orders. Among the most important of these are the Shādhilīyah (established by Abū al-Ḥasan al-Shādhilī, d. 1258) in Egypt and North Africa, and the Chishtīyah (Muʿin al-Dīn Chishtī, d. 1142) in Central and South Asia.

These large *ṭarīqah*s are an important type of order representing a coherent tradition based on a central core of writings by the founder. Within these broad traditions over the centuries, later teachers would arise and create their own particular variants, but these would still maintain an identification with the main tradition. For example, throughout the Islamic world there are distinctive branches of the Qādirīyah, but these are generally identified as part of the Qādirīyah tradition, as is the case with the Bakkā'īyah established by Aḥmad al-Bakkā'ī al-Kuntī (d. 1504) in West Africa, or the various branches of the Ghawthīyah originating with Muḥammad Ghawth (d. 1517) in South Asia. This process of creating independent suborders continues to the present and can be seen in the variety of relatively new *ṭarīqah*s in the traditions of the early orders, often identified with compound names, such as the Ḥāmidīyah Shādhilīyah of contemporary Egypt.

Orders based on "ancient ways." A second major style of Ṣūfī order developed within less clearly defined traditions that appealed to the early Ṣūfīs and utilized some of their prayers and writings but developed distinctive identities of their own. Thus many *ṭarīqah* organizers traced their inspiration back to early Ṣūfīs like Abū al-Qāsim al-Junayd (d. 910) or Abū Yazīd al-Bisṭāmī (d. 874). One may speak of the Junaydī tradition and the "way of Junayd" as insisting on constant ritual purity and fasting (Schimmel, 1975, p. 255) or the more ecstatic mood in the tradition of al-Bisṭāmī. However, the great "Junaydī" or "Bisṭāmī" orders are independent and have their own separate traditions. Among the most important Junaydī orders are the Kubrawīyah and the Mawlawīyah; orders such as the Yasawīyah and Naqshbandīyah are seen as being more in the Bisṭāmī tradition. Within the framework of affirming inspiration and instruction by a chain of teachers that stretches back to the early Ṣūfīs, new orders continue to be created within this broader framework.

Individual-based orders. A third type of major order is the *ṭarīqah* that develops as a result of the initiatives and teachings of a later teacher and has its own clear identity. These teachers usually would affirm their ties to earlier teachers and *ṭarīqah*s, but in some significant ways they would proclaim the unique validity of their particular *ṭarīqah*. Sometimes this would take the form of an affirmation that the new *ṭarīqah* was a synthesis of preceding *ṭarīqah*s; sometimes the claim for authority would be based on direct inspiration from the prophet Muḥammad, in which case the order might be called a *ṭarīqah Muḥammadīyah*, or from some other special agent of God, for example al-Khiḍr. Orders of this type have been very important in the modern Muslim world and include the Tijānīyah, the Khatmīyah, and the Sanūsīyah.

Shrine ṭarīqahs. Local orders centered on particular shrines or families represent another very important type of *ṭarīqah*. Teachers with special reputations for sanctity might develop significant followings during their lifetime, but their writings and work might not provide the basis for a larger order to develop. Tombs of such pious teachers throughout the Muslim world have been important focuses of popular piety, and the rituals surrounding the ceremonies of remembrance and homage become a local *ṭarīqah*. Sometimes these might be indirectly identified with some more general Ṣūfī tradition, but the real impact and identity is local. The special centers of popular piety in North Africa that have developed around the tombs of the "marabouts," or the various centers of pilgrimage that developed in Central Asia and even survived the policies of suppression by the former Soviet regime, provide good examples of this style of *ṭarīqah*.

Foundations of the Modern Orders. Many observers have proclaimed the effective end of the Ṣūfī orders in the modern era. A major French authority on medieval Sufism, for example, announced in the middle of the twentieth century that the orders were "in a state of complete decline" and that they faced "the hostility and contempt of the elite of the modern Muslim world" (Massignon, 1953, p. 574). This reflects both the long historical tension between the Muslim urban intellectual elites and the *ṭarīqah*s and also the specifically modern belief that mystic religious experience and modernity were incompatible. However, by the end of the twentieth century it was clear that Ṣūfī orders remained a dynamic part of the religious life of the Islamic world; moreover, they were at the forefront of the expansion of Islam, not only in "traditional" rural areas but also in modern societies in the West and among the modernized intellectual elites within the Muslim world. These apparently contradictory views reflect the complex history and development of *ṭarīqah*s since the eighteenth century.

There is an underlying continuity of experience in the Ṣūfī orders which provides an important backdrop to specific modern developments. The rituals of popular piety among Muslims—educated and uneducated, rural and urban—cannot be ignored. Although over the past three centuries educated Muslims have paid less attention to the more miraculous and magical elements of saint visitation and other aspects of popular Ṣūfī piety, the intellectual appeal of Islamic mysticism has remained strong, and the sense of social cohesion provided by the Ṣūfī organizations has been important, especially in areas like the Muslim Central Asian societies of the former Soviet Union. Popular participation in regular Ṣūfī gatherings and support for various types of *ṭarīqah*s remain at remarkably high levels throughout the Muslim world. Estimates of membership in Ṣūfī orders in Egypt, for example, are in the millions, in contrast to the hundreds or thousands in the more militant Islamic revivalist organizations.

Popular Islamic piety among all classes of people remains strong throughout the modern era and shows little sign of a decline at the end of the twentieth century. This popular piety frequently is expressed in terms of participation in the activities of *ṭarīqah*s or other groups reflecting Ṣūfī approaches to the faith. However, the activities of the organizations of this popular piety do not usually attract much attention, despite their long-term importance. This situation provides the proper background for examining the specific experiences of the more visible Ṣūfī orders of the modern era.

The history of *ṭarīqah*s in the seventeenth and eighteenth centuries provides an important foundation for understanding the dynamics of the recent development of Ṣūfī orders. Ṣūfī organizations and leadership from this period remain significant in setting the discourse and defining the issues of Islamic piety in the modern era.

Some modern scholars argue that a number of new initiatives can be seen in the development of the Ṣūfī organizations and thought of the early modern era. Among some Ṣūfī teachers there were efforts to remove the more ecstatic and pantheistic elements of the Ṣūfī tradition and to create more reform-oriented Ṣūfī organizations and practices. Fazlur Rahman called this tendency "neo-Sufism" (*Islam*, Chicago, 1979), a term that came to be used by other scholars as well. "Neo-Sufism" referred to a mood rather than making any claim that the term represented a monolithic school of Ṣūfī thought. Other scholars have tended to reject the term because it seemed to ignore important continuities in Ṣūfī traditions and also seemed to assume a greater degree of similarity among movements than might exist.

Regardless of the details of the debate, in the eighteenth century the broad spectrum of Ṣūfī orders and practices extended from the local varieties of popular folk religion to a more sober and sometimes reformist Ṣūfī leadership that did not approve of the popular cultic practices. Whether or not one calls the latter approach "neo-Sufism" is less important than it is to recognize that the less ecstatic and more *sharīʿah*-minded Sufism existed and provided the basis for emerging *ṭarīqahs* important in the modern era. These orders represented a "new organizational phenomenon" of orders that were "relatively more centralized and less prone to fission than their predecessors" (O'Fahey, 1990, p. 4).

In the context of Islamic societies in the eighteenth century, immediately before the major encounter with the modernizing West, Ṣūfī orders were a significant part of the social fabric throughout the Islamic world. They provided vehicles for the expression of the faith of urban elites, served as networks for interregional interaction and travel, acted as an effective inclusive structure for the missionary expansion of Islam, and in some ways shaped the context within which movements of puritanical reform or spiritual revival developed.

Elite ṭarīqahs. In the large urban centers in regions where Islam was the established faith of the overwhelming majority of the population, the orders were vehicles for the expression of piety among both the masses and the elites. New presentations of the old traditions, such as the Qādirīyah, Shādhilīyah, and Khalwatīyah, were important in places like Cairo. By the eighteenth century the larger orders of all types were expanding into many different regions.

The history of the Naqshbandīyah in the Middle East provides an important example of this development. It spread from Central and South Asia into Ottoman lands in at least two different forms—that of Aḥmad Sirhindī (d. 1625), called the Mujaddid or renewer of the second millennium, and the earlier line of ʿUbaydullāh Aḥrār. By the eighteenth century, notables in the *ṭarīqah* were prominent in Istanbul and other major Ottoman cities like Damascus, where the great Ḥanafī *muftī* and historian Muḥammad Khalīl al-Murādī (d. 1791) was a scion of a family associated with the Naqshbandīyah. At the beginning of the nineteenth century, Shaykh Khālid al-Baghdādī (d. 1827) of the Mujaddidī line led a major movement of revival in the lands of the Fertile Crescent; the activities of the Khālidī branch established the Naqshbandīyah as "the paramount order in Turkey" (Hamid Algar, "Nakshbandiyya," *Encyclopaedia of Islam*, new ed., 1960–, vol. 7, p. 936).

Interregional networks. The Naqshbandīyah also presents a good example of how the orders provided structures for interregional networks among the *ʿulamāʾ* and commercial classes. Students, pilgrims, and travelers could move from city to city, finding shelter and instruction in the Naqshbandī centers. One such person was a Chinese scholar, Ma Mingxin (d. 1781), who traveled and studied in major Naqshbandīyah centers in Central Asia, Yemen, and Mecca and Medina. Combined networks of commercial activities and pious instruction can be seen in the activities of family-based *ṭarīqahs* like the ʿAydarusīyah, the order of an important family in the Hadramawt, the ʿAydarus, with branches in the islands of Southeast Asia, India, South Arabia, and Cairo. The lists of teachers of scholars in the eighteenth century show that major intellectual figures often received devotional instruction in broad interregional networks of Ṣūfī masters.

Missionary expansion. Ṣūfī orders had also long been vehicles in the missionary expansion of Islam. The less legalistic approach to the faith of Ṣūfī teachers often involved an adaptation to specific local customs and practices. This helped Islam to become a part of popular religious activity with a minimum of conflict. At the same time, the traditions of the Ṣūfī devotions represented ties to the broad Islamic world that could integrate the newer believers into the identity of the Islamic community as a whole. In this way, orders like the Qādirīyah played a significant role in the expansion of Islam in Africa. In Sudan, for example, its decentralized structure allowed specific regional and tribal leaders to assume roles of leadership within the order. In Southeast Asia, the *ṭarīqahs* were also important in providing a context within which existing religious customs could be combined with more explicitly Islamic activities. Thus orders like the Shaṭṭārīyah became major forces in the Islamic life of peoples in Java and Sumatra. This missionary dimension is visible wherever Islam was expanding in the eighteenth century—in Africa, southeastern Europe, and central, southern and southeastern Asia. [*See* Da^cwah.]

Puritan reformism. Ṣūfī orders also helped to provide concepts of organization for groups actively engaged in efforts to "purify" religious practice and revive the faith. Although the best-known eighteenth century revivalist movement, the Wahhābīs, was vigorously opposed to the Ṣūfī orders, most revivalists in fact had some significant Ṣūfī affiliations. In West Africa, the leaders of movements to establish more explicitly Islamic states in Futa Jallon and Futa Toro, in the areas of modern Senegal and Guinea, were associated with important branches of the Qādirīyah. The great *jihād* at the beginning of the nineteenth century in northern Nigeria and neighboring territories was led by Usuman dan Fodio, a teacher closely identified with the Qādirīyah. At the other end of the Islamic world of the eighteenth century, the "neo-orthodox reformist movement" called the "New Teaching" that "swept Northwest China" in the late eighteenth century was the Naqshbandīyah as presented by Ma Mingxin (A. D. W. Forbes, "Ma Ming-Hsin," *Encyclopaedia of Islam,* new ed., 1960–, vol. 5, p. 850). In many other areas as well, Ṣūfī orders were associated with the development of reformist and jihadist movements of purification.

The developments of the eighteenth century provide important foundations for later events in Islamic life in general and in the history of Ṣūfī orders in particular. It was the Islamic world as it existed in the eighteenth and early nineteenth century, not some classical medieval formulation, that encountered the expanding and modernizing West. In those encounters the Ṣūfī orders played an important role, which sometimes does not receive as much attention as the activities of more radical movements or movements more explicitly shaped and influenced by the West.

Ṣūfī Orders in the Modern Era. In the nineteenth and twentieth centuries the different Ṣūfī traditions were involved in many different ways in helping to shape Muslim responses to the West and also in defining Islamic forms of modernity. At the same time, although in changing contexts, many of the main themes of the older experiences of the orders continue. Among the many aspects of the history of Ṣūfī orders in the modern era, it is important to examine a number more closely: the Ṣūfī orders continued to serve as an important basis for popular devotional life; they were important forces in responding to imperial rule; they helped to provide organizational and intellectual inspiration for Muslim responses to modern challenges to the faith; and they continued to be an important force in the mission of Muslims to non-Muslims.

Popular piety. *Ṭarīqah*s remained very important in the life of popular piety among the masses; however, this important level of popular devotional life is not as visible in the public arena as the more activist roles of the orders. New orders continued to emerge around respected teachers and saintly personalities important in the daily lives of common people. Throughout the nineteenth and twentieth century it is possible to identify such orders in virtually all parts of the Islamic world. It is especially important to observe that these new devotional paths were not simply the products of rural, conservative, or so-called "traditional" people.

An example is the career of Qarīb Allāh Abū Ṣāliḥ (1866–1936), a pious teacher in Omdurman, Sudan, and a member of the Sammānīyah *ṭarīqah,* an order established in the eighteenth century within the Khalwatīyah tradition. He participated in the Mahdist movement in the late nineteenth century and during the early twentieth century attracted disciples from both the poorer people and the emerging modern educated classes in Sudan. His devotional writings and mystic poetry were published and became an important part of the modern literature of Sudan (Ṭāhir Muḥammad ^cAlī al-Bashīr, *Al-adab al-Ṣūfī fī al-Sūdān,* Cairo, 1970). The Qarībīyah was not politically active as an organization, although its members may have been politically involved as individuals.

Across the Islamic world, similar groups have emerged as a pious foundation for devotional life in all levels of society. Similarly, intellectuals and professionals as well as the more general population continued in relatively significant numbers to participate in activities of the older established orders. This phenomenon could be observed, for example, in Cairo during the 1960s at the peak of enthusiasm for Gamal Abdel Nasser's Arab Socialism (Voll, 1992). Although the contexts had changed since the beginning of the nineteenth century, at the end of the twentieth century, new orders which served popular devotional needs continued to be created and to flourish in ways that provide a sense of both great continuity and significant adaptability to changing conditions.

Antiforeign resistance. Ṣūfī orders provided significant organization and support for movements of resistance to foreign rule. This was especially true in the nineteenth century, when many of the major wars against expanding European powers were fought by Muslim organizations that originated with Ṣūfī orders. At the beginning of the nineteenth century in Sumatra, a revivalist movement building on reform activities initiated by the Naqshbandīyah and Shaṭṭārīyah, and possibly inspired by Wahhābī strictness or the teachings of Aḥmad ibn Idrīs, provided major resistance to Dutch expansion in the Padri War of 1821–1838. The strongest opposition to the French conquest of Algeria, which began in 1830, was provided by a Qādirīyah leader, Amīr ʿAbd al-Qādir, whose resistance lasted until 1847. In the Caucasus region, Naqshbandīyah fighters under the leadership of Imam Shāmil maintained a holy war against Russian imperial expansion for twenty-five years, ending in 1859. At the end of the nineteenth century, it was a *ṭarīqah* leader, Muḥammad ʿAbd Allāh Ḥasan (1864–1921) of the Ṣāliḥīyah, who led a major anti-imperialist holy war in Somaliland against the British. Ṣūfī orders provided the basis for many other movements of resistance, but these examples confirm that the phenomenon was significant and widespread.

Some other Ṣūfī orders that came into conflict with expanding European imperialism also reflect the development of distinctive, new *ṭarīqah* traditions. Perhaps the most important of these orders are those established by followers of Aḥmad ibn Idrīs (d. 1837) and others influenced by this Idrīsī tradition. Ibn Idrīs was a north African scholar who taught for a number of years in Mecca; some of his major students established *ṭarīqah*s that became important orders throughout the nineteenth and twentieth centuries. The best-known of these groups is the Sanūsīyah, founded by Muḥammad ibn ʿAlī al-Sanūsī (d. 1859). This order established centers in North Africa and Saharan areas, with special centers in Libya. It provided stability and regional coordination among nomadic tribes and became very influential in a vast area in northern Africa. As a result, expanding French imperial forces in many Saharan areas contacted and eventually came into conflict with the Sanūsīyah in the later nineteenth century. When Italy attempted to conquer Libya in the twentieth century, it was the Sanūsīyah that provided the most effective opposition, both during the Ottoman-Italian war of 1911–1912 and following World War I, when the victorious allied powers decided to create an independent Libya, it was the head of the Sanūsīyah who was proclaimed Idrīs I, the king of independent Libya. The Sanūsīyah as a Ṣūfī order was tied to the newly created tradition of Aḥmad ibn Idrīs rather than being solely associated with older *ṭarīqah* traditions.

Other similarly independent orders which developed in this Idrīsī tradition were the Khatmīyah, which became one of the major Islamic organizations in the modern Sudan; the Ṣāliḥīyah and Rashīdīyah, which were important in east Africa; and the Idrīsīyah, established by the family of the original teacher. These orders, along with the Sanūsīyah, represent a major Ṣūfī tradition in the modern era, especially in Africa. Less directly, teachers influenced by the Idrīsī tradition had some impact in southeastern Europe and South and Southeast Asia.

Another independent Ṣūfī tradition developed as a result of the work of Aḥmad al-Tijānī (d. 1815). The Tijānīyah was an exclusive order that claimed to be a synthesis of major *ṭarīqah* traditions inspired and instructed initially by the prophet Muḥammad himself. The order became an important force in North Africa but did not get involved in opposition to French expansion in the Mediterranean countries. However, the Tijānīyah expanded rapidly into Saharan and sub-Saharan Africa. Al-Ḥajj ʿUmar Tal (d. 1864) organized a major holy war under the Tijānīyah banner in the regions of Guinea, Senegal, and Mali; ultimately his successful movement was restricted and then ended by the consolidation of French imperial control in the region. However, the Tijānīyah was more than an antiforeign movement. It became a major vehicle for intensification of Islamic practice in already Muslim areas and for the expansion of Islam into non-Muslim areas. By the end of the twentieth century, the Tijānīyah had become a major force throughout the Sudanic region.

It is clear that major orders like the Sanūsīyah and Tijānīyah, which were established in the nineteenth century, were not simply anti-imperialist movements in Ṣūfī form. They represented an important style of cohesive social organization based on the traditions of *ṭarīqah* structures. They were not necessarily alternatives to emerging modern state structures but were autonomous within the developing polities defined as sovereign nation-states. This alternative mode is also seen in the developments of distinctive orders whose self-definition was more closely identified with older Ṣūfī traditions. Thus the Naqshbandīyah suborder established by Said Nursî in Turkey in the twentieth century became an important vehicle for the articulation of a revivalist Islamic worldview in the context of an officially secular state. Similarly, a number of orders provided important foundations for the unofficial, "underground" Islam that was so essential for the survival of the Muslim sense of community in Central Asia under Soviet rule.

Responses to modernity. Ṣūfī orders also were important in helping to shape the responses to the challenges to Muslim faith in the modern era. In the nineteenth century this was more in terms of providing organizational bases for opposition to European expansion and in the direct continuation of the traditions of activist reformist movements such as the Naqshbandīyah. In the twentieth century, *ṭarīqahs* reponded to specific needs in a variety of ways. In some countries orders provided the direct organizational basis for modern-style political parties. In Sudan, for example, the Khatmīyah provided the foundation for the National Unionist Party, then the People's Democratic Party; late in the twentieth century the head of the order was also the president of the Democratic Unionist Party. In Senegal, the Murīdīyah provided an organization for the development of cash crops and played an important role in modernizing the agricultural sector of the Senegalese economy. In the days of Soviet communist rule in Central Asia, the popular local *ṭarīqahs* and the established traditional ones like the Naqshbandīyah provided the framework within which Islamic communal identity could be maintained in the face of the official efforts to suppress religion. In the holy war in Afghanistan after the Soviet occupation in 1979, leaders of established orders like the Qādirīyah and Naqshbandīyah Mujaddidīyah were among the most important organizers of *mujāhidīn* groups. These examples affirm the fact that in many different areas, the organizational traditions of the Ṣūfī orders provided important bases for responding to specific challenges.

In the twentieth century, however, the role of the orders was sometimes different. The established *ṭarīqahs* might seem ineffective in meeting particular challenges of modernity, but the basic structures or the general approach might still provide models for new Islamic revivalist and reformist movements.

Sufism and participation in a reform-minded *ṭarīqah* was, for example, an important part of the early experience of Ḥasan al-Bannā' (d. 1949), the founder of one of the major modern Muslim revivalist organizations in the twentieth century, the Muslim Brotherhood in Egypt. As a young man, al-Bannā' was impressed by accounts of the strictness of a Ṣūfī shaykh, Ḥasanayn al-Ḥaṣāfī (d. 1910), and became an active member of the *ṭarīqah* he had founded, the Ḥaṣāfīyah. Al-Bannā' was involved with the *ṭarīqah* for twenty years and maintained a respect for this strict style of Sufism throughout his life. It appears to have influenced his organizational thinking in terms of the methods of instruction in his Muslim Brotherhood and the daily rituals required of its members. Another major Islamic activist movement, the Muslim Brotherhood in Sudan, has some similar aspects. Many of its early organizers came from families strongly identified with *ṭarīqahs* in Sudan. The most prominent of the leaders in the Sudanese Brotherhood in the second half of the twentieth century is Ḥasan al-Turābī, who came from a religiously notable family whose center was a school-tomb complex of a traditional localized Ṣūfī type. One of his ancestors in the eighteenth century had proclaimed himself to be a Mahdi bringing purification to the Muslims. Turābī emphasized the continuing need for humans to reinterpret the implications of the Islamic faith in changing historical circumstances. In this, one active member of Turābī's movement noted that "Turābī's revolution" was a "reaffirmation of the ancient Ṣūfī ethic, with its emphasis on the spirit rather than the letter of Islam" (Abdelwahab El-Affendi, *Turābī's Revolution*, London, 1991). The Ṣūfī organizational traditions thus both provided direct means for meeting challenges in modern situations and also helped to inspire new approaches.

Missionary expansion. The Ṣūfī orders continued in the modern era to serve as important vehicles for the expansion of Islam in basically non-Muslim societies. In many areas, this is simply a direct continuation of past activities. In sub-Saharan Africa, for example, under colonial rule the Ṣūfī orders were among the few types of indigenous social organizations that imperial administrators would allow. As a result, they became very important structures both for the expression of indigenous opinion and for the expansion of Islam. It was under colonial rule in the late nineteenth and twentieth centuries that Islam was able to make significant advances in areas south of the Sudanic savannas.

More remarkably, the Ṣūfī orders have become important vehicles for Islamic expansion in modern Western societies, where the open inclusiveness and the aesthetic dimensions of the great Ṣūfī philosophies have considerable appeal. Ṣūfī thought was important in influencing nineteenth-century Western intellectuals such as Ralph Waldo Emerson; in the later twentieth century, the writings of Idries Shah became very well known and could be found in bookstores that appealed to popular as well as intellectual tastes. Important Western converts to Islam in the twentieth century were often Ṣūfī in orientation and institutional affiliation. The writings of Martin Lings and his description of the *ṭarīqah* of the Tunisian Ṣūfī Shaykh Aḥmad al-ʿAlawī are significant examples.

Ṣūfī orders are active organizationally in Western societies. They provide a clearly satisfying and effective vehicle for the expression of religious life and values in modern Western societies and have an appeal among professionals and the general population. The communities established by orders in western Europe and the Americas have been strengthened in the second half of the twentieth century by the significant growth of the Muslim communities through both immigration and conversion. A good example of this *ṭarīqah* activity is the expansion of the Niʿmatullāhī order, which by 1990 had centers in nine major cities in the United States, published a magazine, *Sufi,* and worked with academic institutions in organizing conferences on Sufism. In ways like this, Ṣūfī orders continue to serve as an important means for the modern expansion of Islam.

Challenges and Future Prospects. Throughout Islamic history there have been strong critics of Ṣūfī teachers and organizations. In one of the most famous instances, a medieval mystic, al-Ḥallāj (d. 922), was executed for proclaiming his mystical union with God in an extreme manner. More literalist and legalist interpreters of Islam have opposed the practices of the Ṣūfī orders as providing vehicles for non-Islamic practices and beliefs. In the eighteenth century, some of the strongest opposition to the *ṭarīqahs* came from the developing Wahhābī movement. In the modern era, modernizing reformers strongly criticized the orders for encouraging and strengthening popular superstitions, and Islamic modernists attempted to reduce the influence of Ṣūfī shaykhs in their societies.

Such modernist opposition can be seen in actions of reformers throughout the Islamic world. Wherever the Salafīyah modernist movement—which emerged with the thought and actions of late nineteenth-century scholars such as Muḥammad ʿAbduh (d. 1905) of Egypt—had influence, there was strong opposition to the popular devotional practices and influence of the Ṣūfī orders. This can be seen in the activities and teachings of ʿAbd Allāh ibn Idrīs al-Sanūsī (d. 1931) in Morocco, the Association of Algerian ʿUlamāʾ organized in the 1930s, the Muhammadiyah in Indonesia throughout the twentieth century, the Jadīdist movement within the old Russian Empire, and many other areas. In addition, more explicitly westernizing reform programs attempted to eliminate the influence of the orders, best illustrated in the reforms of Mustafa Kemal Atatürk during the 1920s and 1930s in the new republic of Turkey.

Many observers also thought that as societies became more modern and industrialized, the social functions of the Ṣūfī teachers and their organizations would decline. In the mid-twentieth century, many analyses painted a picture of reduced and possibly disappearing Ṣūfī orders. Despite the opposition and the predictions, however, Ṣūfī orders continue to be remarkably strong in most of the Islamic world and also in communities of Muslims where they are minorities.

The Ṣūfī orders continue to provide vehicles for articulating an inclusive Islamic identity with a greater emphasis on individual devotional piety and small-group experience. The contrast with the more legalist orientation with its emphasis on the community as a whole is a longstanding polarity in Islamic history. It is clear that the great transformations of the modern era have not destroyed the basis for this polarity.

In the changing contexts of the late twentieth century, the traditions of the Ṣūfī orders have special strengths in situations where there is a high degree of religious pluralism. They allow the believer to maintain an individual Islamic devotional identity in the absence of a national or societywide Muslim majority. These traditions also allow for an articulation of Islam in a form compatible with secularist perspectives. Thus Sufism has importance in the non-Muslim societies of Western Europe and North America. In addition, as it becomes clear that it is not possible simply to transfer institutional copies of Western-style associations such as labor unions, political parties, and other nongovernmental organizations, *ṭarīqah* traditions may provide ways of adapting modern institutions to the needs of emerging civil societies throughout the Islamic world.

[*See also* Chishtīyah; Idrīsīyah; Khalwatīyah; Khatmīyah; Mawlawīyah; Muhammadiyah; Murīdīyah; Naqshbandīyah; Niʾmatullāhīyah; Qādirīyah; Rifāʿīyah; Sanūsīyah; Shādhilīyah; Shaṭṭārīyah; Tijānīyah; *and the biographies of ʿAlawī, Bakkāʾī al-Kuntī, Dan Fodio, Ibn Idrīs, Tijānī, and ʿUmar Tal.*]

BIBLIOGRAPHY

Awn, Peter J. "Sufism." In *The Encyclopedia of Religion,* vol. 14, pp. 104–123. New York, 1987. Good introduction to the medieval foundations of Ṣūfī beliefs and orders.

Baldick, Julian. *Mystical Islam: An Introduction to Sufism.* New York and London, 1989. Broad historical presentation providing critiques of a number of interpretations of Sufism in the modern era as well as a helpful list of major orders.

Bennigsen, Alexandre, and S. Enders Wimbush. *Mystics and Commissars: Sufism in the Soviet Union.* Berkeley, 1985. The best source on the experience of Ṣūfī orders under Soviet rule.

Gilsenan, Michael. *Saint and Sufi in Modern Egypt.* Oxford, 1973. Important analysis of the general issues involved in the development of orders in the modern era, using the Ḥamīdīyah Shādhilīyah as a case study.

Hoffman-Ladd, Valerie. *Sufism, Mystics, and Saints in Modern Egypt.* Charleston, S.C., 1995. Important study showing the continuing vitality of Ṣūfī organizations at the level of popular religion.

Jong, F. de. *Ṭuruq and Ṭuruq-Linked Institutions in Nineteenth-Century Egypt.* Leiden, 1978. Careful and detailed discussion of Egyptian orders and their relations with the state.

Lings, Martin. *A Sufi Saint of the Twentieth Century: Shaykh Aḥmad al-ʿAlawī.* Berkeley, 1973. Sympathetic presentation showing the basis for the continuing appeal of Sufism in the modern era.

Mardin, Şerif. *Religion and Social Change in Modern Turkey: The Case of Bediüzzaman Said Nursi.* Albany, N.Y. 1989. Study of the experience of a revivalist Ṣūfī tradition in the context of official Turkish secularism.

Martin, B. G. *Muslim Brotherhoods in Nineteenth-Century Africa.* Cambridge, 1976. Well-documented study of major African activist orders in their historical context.

Massignon, Louis. "Ṭarīḳa." In *Shorter Encyclopaedia of Islam*, edited by H. A. R. Gibb and J. H. Kramers, pp. 573–578. Leiden, 1953. An old but still useful summary of the development of the orders, with a long descriptive list.

O'Fahey, R. S. *Enigmatic Saint: Ahmad Ibn Idris and the Idrisi Tradition.* London and Evanston, Ill., 1990. Very important study of a major *ṭarīqah* tradition that emerged at the beginning of the modern era.

Schimmel, Annemarie. *Mystical Dimensions of Islam.* Chapel Hill, N.C., 1975. Sound and readable presentation of the full range of issues related to understanding Sufism.

Schimmel, Annemarie. *Islam in the Indian Subcontinent.* Leiden, 1980. Very helpful interpretation giving special attention to the role of the orders in South Asia.

Trimingham, J. Spencer. *The Sufi Orders in Islam.* Oxford, 1971. The single most comprehensive presentation of the origin and development of the orders.

Voll, John Obert. "Traditional and Conservative Orders." *Annals of the American Academy of Political and Social Science* 524 (November 1992): 66–78. Discussion of the more conservative orders and their role in the modern period.

JOHN O. VOLL

Ṣūfī Shrine Culture

In many Muslim countries special shrines have been constructed honoring famous Ṣūfī leaders or "saints" who, it is believed, could work miracles during their lives and even after their death. This kind of shrine may be called *ḍarīḥ, mazār, zāwiyah* or *maqām* in Arabic. In some areas it is called *qubbah* after the cupola that is the most characteristic architectural element in many shrines. The saint's tomb is certainly the essential part of such a shrine; it is a place to which people make visits to receive divine blessing *(barakah)*. Thus it becomes one of the focal points of popular Islam. Consequently, Ṣūfī shrine culture, supported enthusiastically by common Muslims, has occasionally been criticized both by rigorous Muslim scholars *(ʿulamāʾ)* and by some modern reformers as *bidʿah* or heretical innovation added to authentic early Islam.

Historical Origin. Starting as an individual ascetic movement, Sufism had become regarded as a legitimate part of orthodox Islam by the twelfth century. Great Ṣūfī adepts lived according to strict discipline in their training centers or lodges, where disciples followed the way *(ṭarīqah)* of training which their master taught them. These gatherings developed into the Ṣūfī orders (also called *ṭarīqahs*). Drawing recruits mainly from the illiterate masses, which had formerly lacked access to the Islamic teaching that had been largely monopolized by scholars, Ṣūfī orders gradually spread over various parts of the Muslim world and had become very popular with the Muslim masses by the fifteenth or sixteenth century. Among them were the Qādirīyah, the Rifāʿīyah, the Shādhilīyah, the Suhrawardīyah, the Mawlawīyah, and the Aḥmadīyah. The first four established many branches in different countries; the last two were concentrated in particular regions, the Mawlawīyah mainly in Anatolia and the Aḥmadīyah in the Nile Delta.

As the Ṣūfī orders penetrated into common Muslims' lives and influenced their ritual behaviors, some of the Ṣūfī leaders, usually the founders of orders or the heads of branches, began to develop reputations as saints *(awliyāʾ*; sg., *walī)* who had supernatural power or divine blessing *(barakah)* granted by God. Through this power, it was believed, the saint could work miracles *(karāmāt)* such as foretelling the future, mindreading, flying in the air, treating illness, and other extraordinary acts. Devotees from both within and outside the order often visited the saint asking for a small share of divine blessing, so that he gradually began to be venerated as if he were a divine being. When the saint died, it was firmly believed that he would still respond favorably to requests made at his tomb. Therefore followers erected a special building at the site of the tomb.

Two Cases. Ṣūfī-saint shrine culture displays great

variation in factors such as the person enshrined, the social categories of devotees, the architectural structure of the shrine, the rituals performed in and around it, its political and economic significance, and the form and activities of the Ṣūfī order that provides its main support. In order to illustrate its historical development, two examples will be discussed. Although both come from Egypt, they exemplify respectively a traditional, rural-based Ṣūfī-saint cult and a modern, urban-based one.

Sayyid al-Badawī. Aḥmad al-Badawī, also called Sayyid al-Badawī because of his presumed descent from the Prophet, was born in Fez, Morocco, in 1199 and went to Mecca with his family in his childhood. He later visited Iraq, where he was heavily influenced by the thought of two other great Ṣūfīs, Aḥmad Rifāʿī and ʿAbd al-Qādir al-Jīlānī, and by the activities of the Ṣūfī orders that followed these masters, the Rifāʿīyah and the Qādirīyah. Obeying a divine command received in a vision, Aḥmad al-Badawī decided to go to Tanta, a town in the Nile Delta. Situated in the center of a rich agricultural area, Tanta then flourished as a large marketplace for agricultural products, as it still does today. Overcoming challenges from other religious leaders, he won over a great number of followers in and around the town. He was said to have worked many miracles, through one of which his first supporter in the town was able to prosper in his business. He was also paid homage by the great Mamlūk king, Ẓāhir Baybars, and he even fought against the Crusaders.

Sayyid al-Badawī died in 1276. His senior pupil ʿAbd al-ʿĀl assumed responsibility for the Aḥmadīyah and became his successor *(khalīfah).* The saint's followers from every district flocked to Tanta to pledge their loyalty to his successor; this is said to be the origin of the annual festival or *mawlid* of Sayyid al-Badawī. ʿAbd al-ʿĀl commanded that a large building be erected over the Sayyid's tomb, and this has developed into his shrine together with a large mosque called the Masjid al-Badawī.

The mystical power of the saint began to appeal not only to the peasants and townspeople of the Delta but also to the masses in Cairo and some parts of Upper Egypt, and the devotees of his cult increased greatly. The Aḥmadīyah order in due course developed into one of the four largest Ṣūfī orders in Egypt, and his *mawlid* came to be something of a national festival.

Salāma al-Rāḍī. The founder of the Ḥāmidīyah Shādhilīyah order was born in 1867 in a shabby quarter of Cairo and died there in 1939. Unlike traditional-style saints such as Aḥmad al-Badawī, he was born into a modern Egypt which the Western powers had come to dominate politically and economically. Egyptian society and modern European ideas, both religious and secular, gradually infiltrated into Muslims' daily lives. For this reason, the Ṣūfī orders, if they wanted to revitalize their movements and find recruits in the emerging modernist sectors of Egyptian society, had to deal with new problems in accommodating themselves to the rapidly changing social and cultural conditions.

Having memorized the whole of the Qur'ān before he was ten, Salāma found intellectual satisfaction in Ṣūfī scholarship rather than in the formal school system. While working in a government office as an efficient clerk, he led an ascetic life and joined a Ṣūfī order. In response to a divine vision he decided to set up his own *ṭarīqah,* the Ḥāmidīyah Shādhilīyah, which was officially recognized as an independent *ṭarīqah* by the supreme Ṣūfī council in 1926–1927.

He became venerated as a saint as a result of various apparent miracles, which included the excellence of his religious knowledge without a formal education, his ability to defeat other eminent scholars in debate, and his supernatural power to see everything, including things hidden from normal people. Some educated members of the order, however, apparently discredited these stories of miracles, or at least hesitated to accept them as factual.

After Salāma's death, one of his sons, Ibrāhīm, became the head of the order. Unlike his father, who attracted people with his personal charisma, Ibrāhīm tried to extend the order's influence by means of structural reform. He aimed to establish a more centralized, hierarchical organization. This reform led to the Ḥāmidīyah Shādhilīyah's becoming one of the Ṣūfī orders that accommodated most fully to social and cultural changes in modern Egypt; however, it also stirred internal conflicts between the new elite members recruited mainly from a somewhat modernized middle class and the senior leaders who had been attracted by the charisma of the founding saint.

The saint's tomb became one of the focal points in this conflict. Salāma's shrine was first set up in the Būlāq district of Cairo where he was born and where he established the headquarters of his *ṭarīqah.* After his death, a *mawlid* celebration for him was held there every year. Ibrāhīm died in 1975, and the new elite members, who organized a committee to manage and control the *ṭarīqah,* began to build a large new mosque in Muhandisīn district on the opposite side of the Nile from Būlāq, an attractive residential area for the growing upper and upper-middle classes. Ibrāhīm's tomb was set up in this new mosque. Beside it they constructed a fine new tomb for Salāma, though it remained empty in 1987 as the old members refused to move his tomb from Būlāq. Moreover, they recognized Ibrāhīm's younger brother as head of the *ṭarīqah* and carried on celebrating Salāma's *mawlid* separately in Būlāq—the Muhandisīn faction of course held the *mawlid* celebration at the new mosque.

Enshrinement of Non-Ṣūfīs. These two examples have been the cases of great Ṣūfīs who are venerated as saints and were enshrined after their death. These cases have to be distinguished from others in which the enshrined person is not a Ṣūfī in the strict sense.

First, veneration of the prophet Muḥammad must be considered. According to orthodox belief, he is not an equivalent of God but a mere man, though he is deeply respected as the Last Prophet and the ideal human being. However, he has often been venerated as though divine and similar to God by some groups of Muslims, especially among the less-educated masses. Great numbers eagerly visit his tomb in Medina before or after the pilgrimage to Mecca in order to receive divine blessing. The anniversary of his birthday (the twelfth day of Rabīʿ al-Awwal in the Islamic calendar), called Mawlid al-Nabī (the Prophet's Birthday), has been celebrated in many cities and villages since the thirteenth century. Visitation to his tomb and celebration of his birthday have been conducted like those of Ṣūfī saints. Members of the Ṣūfī orders actively participate in events of the Mawlid al-Nabī.

The Prophet's family is also widely respected in Muslim societies, and Shīʿī Muslims have developed especially elaborate cults of the first imam, ʿAlī, and his descendants. Their tombs are centers of folk Shiism, and many Shīʿīs visit them to receive divine blessing. ʿAlī's tomb in Najaf and that of his son, Ḥusayn in Karbala are the most prestigious, and these towns in Iraq have served as Shīʿī sanctuaries. Although much less famous than these, there are a great number of smaller shrines in Shīʿī areas, especially in Iran, which are presumed to belong to one of the imams and are generally called *imāmzādah*. They closely resemble Sunnī Ṣūfī-saint shrines in their social and cultural functions. [*See* Najaf; Karbala; Imāmzādah.]

Sunnī Muslims also revere Muḥammad's descendants and generally refer to them as *sharīf* (noble person) or *sayyid* (lord). Some rulers of states, such as the Moroccan and Jordanian kings, and some saints such as Sayyid al-Badawī claim descent from the Prophet. Some of the Prophet's descendants are venerated as holy in their own right and are celebrated annually in their own *mawlid*s. The Mawlid al-Ḥusayn, for example, is held annually in Cairo, and a large number of his devotees, many of them members of Ṣūfī orders, visit the mosque-shrine where his head is said to be buried.

Also held in Cairo is the *mawlid* of Imām Shāfiʿī (d. 820), the founder of one of the four orthodox schools of Islamic law. His shrine is set up in a shabby district on the eastern periphery of the city. Although he was never a Ṣūfī, people visit his tomb to seek his mystical help, and they hold an annual celebration as they do for a Ṣūfī saint.

Prophets other than Muḥammad, together with some of the warrior heroes of early Islamic history, were also enshrined and celebrated, especially in Palestine, where there were many tombs and shrines that were presumed to belong to them. Such biblical figures as Abraham, Moses, David, Job, and even Jesus had one or more shrines where people came to receive divine blessing. Some of these shrines also held regular celebrations called *mawsim* (the season of visiting). Shrines set up for heroes in battle can be found in Palestine, Jordan, and other areas; usually such heroes are called not *walī* or *Ṣūfī* but *ṣāliḥ*.

There are various types of holy places in which some natural object such as a tree, a stone, or a cave is treated as sacred, although the *ʿulamāʾ* and others have harshly criticized these practices as non-Islamic. Some of them may be related to Ṣūfī-saint shrine culture. In a Moroccan village, for example, a grotto where a great female spirit *(jinnīyah)* named ʿĀʾishah Qandīshah is said to dwell occupies a part of the sanctuary of the Hamdūshīyah order. Two shrines for its founding Ṣūfīs have been built there.

In the Maghrib, a local veneration and ritual surrounding a Muslim saint is generally known as "maraboutism." The word "marabout" means "saint" and is derived from Arabic *murābiṭ*, which in this context means "a person living in a Ṣūfī lodge." Some of the marabouts were evidently renowned Ṣūfīs in their lifetimes, and their shrines have kept a connection with one of the Ṣūfī orders; others, however, have no direct relation to a particular order. Some marabouts inherit their mystical powers *(barakah)* through the agnatic line, which results in the formation of a maraboutic family like those of the Sharqāwah in Boujad and the Ihansalen among the Berbers in the High Atlas.

In Sufism proper, both leadership and sainthood are passed on patrilineally and are consequently kept within one family or lineage in many Ṣūfī orders. The Majādhib family in El-Damer in the Northern Sudan is one of numerous examples. The family has kept the leadership of the Majdhūbīyah Ṣūfī order, which had considerable political and economic influence in the area before the twentieth century, as well as being venerated as a holy lineage. The shrine of their ancestor has been maintained in the custody of the family.

Spatial Composition. Except in a few cases, the tombs of Muslims are generally very simple in form. They usually have no special decoration except for plaques of ceramic or other materials on which are written personal details of the dead or phrases from the Qur'ān. In contrast, the tombs or shrines of saints, Ṣūfī or otherwise, have distinctive architectural features.

A saint's tomb is usually set up inside a building specially constructed for it, and it often has a cupola. Sometimes the building or shrine is situated in a cemetery. Other institutions such as mosques, Ṣūfī training lodges, or facilities for visitors may also be annexed to large shrines.

The tomb itself usually consists of a rectangular box-like structure with a catafalque, a cloth cover, and other elements, with some variation. The catafalque *(tābūt)* is a wooden box or frame set up over the spot where the saint is buried. It is covered completely with a piece of cloth called *kiswah,* which is generally donated by a devotee. In a place on the upper part of the catafalque (on one of the shorter sides, or at the center of the rectangle) an *ʿimmah* is set up, which consists of a wooden post draped in a green cloth, looking like a head with a turban. The *ʿimmah* is supposed to symbolize the saint's authority.

There are other items, however, that are not necessarily found in all shrines. Some tombs, especially those belonging to renowned saints, are enclosed by a cage. A donation box may be set up to receive money offerings from devotees. Other features may include lamps, candles, copies of the Qur'ān, and plaques on which phrases from the Qur'ān are written or on which pictures of sacred places such as the Kaʿbah are drawn. Most of these, like the *kiswah,* are donated by pious devotees. There are of course neither pictures nor statues of the saint anywhere in the shrine.

Some of the items, however, do raise theological problems. In the shrine of Sayyid al-Badawī, for instance, there is a black stone in the corner of the chamber. On it can be seen two footprints, which are said to be those of the Prophet, and many devotees, mostly peasants of the Nile Delta, are eager to touch and rub it. This practice recalls pilgrims' rituals relating to Abraham's footprints and the Black Stone in the Kaʿbah at Mecca, and many scholars and modernist Muslims criticize it severely as a deviation from orthodox Islam.

The shrine and the other facilities are in many cases maintained financially through a *waqf,* an endowment provided by the Ṣūfī order related to the saint enshrined. In the case of a small shrine a custodian, and in the case of a large shrine custodians or a committee, are responsible for the upkeep of the buildings and facilities.

Ritual Activities. The Ṣūfī saint's shrine is one of the focal points of rituals carried out not only by the members of the Ṣūfī order that has a special spiritual relationship with the saint but also by common Muslims who simply admire the mystical power of the saint and venerate him. There are three important types of ritual: visiting the shrine, *dhikr* rituals conducted there, and the annual festival of the saint.

Visitation. Many devotees of a Ṣūfī saint make frequent visits to his shrine to perform such rituals as special prayers to the saint, circumambulation of his tomb, and kissing its cloth cover. Some of them remain there for a longer period. The main aim of their visit, as with ordinary supplication *(duʿāʾ),* is to ask for divine blessing in general, as well as for more specific benefits such as success in business or study, or recovery from an illness. They may make a vow *(nadhr)* to give a suitable donation to the saint if their wishes are satisfactorily realized; many of the items belonging to the shrine are donations from supplicants. If they break the vow and give nothing to the saint as a reward, it is presumed that there will be divine retribution for their negligence.

Visits to some shrines can be regarded as a substitute for the pilgrimage to Mecca. Indeed, a visit to the shrine of Sayyid al-Badawī has been called "the pauper's *ḥajj.*" The shrine of al-Shādhilī (d. 1465), the founder of the widespread Shādhilīyah Ṣūfī order, is in a town on the Red Sea coast in southern Egypt. It is said that five visits to his shrine have an effect similar to that of one *ḥajj.* It is noteworthy, however, that the visit is not called *ḥajj* but *ziyārah.* Visitors apparently make an essential distinction between the two, even though they may think that repeated visits to a shrine may give them almost the same benefits as the pilgrimage to Mecca. [*See* Ḥajj; Ziyārah.]

Dhikr. On the basis of the Qur'ān (surah 33. 41–42), the *dhikr* ritual, in which participants devoutly repeat the names of God or some formula such as "Allāh ḥayy" ("God is the Eternal One") with prescribed gestures, has become one of the fundamental rituals for most Ṣūfīs. A gathering to perform the ritual, usually called *ḥaḍrah,* usually takes place in the afternoon or at night in the court of a private house, in a public square in a neighborhood, at a lodge, or in an open space near a saint's shrine.

In some cases a *dhikr* is conducted after the communal prayers on Friday. For instance, the Hamad al-Nīl Ṣūfī order, a Sudanese branch of the Qādarīyah, regularly holds a *dhikr* gathering on Friday afternoon in an open space in front of the shrine of its founding Ṣūfī in a cemetery in a suburb of Omdurman. After the *ʿaṣr* prayer, members of the order march to the place from their nearby mosque and start to perform the *dhikr* rituals. Repeating the formulas to the rhythm of drums and religious songs, they line up in several rows and move around a pole set up in the center of the space. The ritual lasts until the sunset *(maghrib)* prayer.

Dhikr rituals, like visits to the shrine, can be carried out at any time. They are, however, enthusiastically conducted on a grand scale on the occasion of the annual festival of the saint. [*See* Dhikr.]

Annual Festival. The yearly celebration in honor of a saint has several different names in Arab countries. In Egypt it is called a *mawlid;* the word *mawsim* ("season," i.e., for celebrating a saint) is used for the case of a marabout in Morocco as well as for the festival of the prophet Moses in Palestine. Members of the Ṣūfī orders in the Sudan hold annual celebrations of their founders called *ḥūlīya* in commemoration not of their birthdays but of the anniversaries of their deaths. These festivals vary greatly in the way in which they are held, the number of participants, and the rituals performed; we will concentrate on the Egyptian cases.

Except for the *mawlid* of the Prophet, whose tomb is in Medina, Egyptian *mawlid* feasts for the Ṣūfī or other saints are celebrated in and around their shrines. The time when these rites are held is an interesting issue. Because the word *mawlid* originally meant "time and place of birth," the date of the celebration would appear to be fixed by the birthday of the saint concerned. Many *mawlid*s for famous holy people, including the Prophet and his family, do occur on or about the days of their birth according to the Islamic lunar calendar, although the feasts themselves generally start several days or weeks before the birthday: the Prophet's *mawlid* is on 12 Rabīʿ al-Awwal, Ḥusayn's on a Wednesday in the latter half of Rabīʿ al-Thānī, Zaynab's on the middle Wednesday of Rajab, and Shāfiʿī's on the middle Thursday of Shaʿbān. By contrast, the dates of some *mawlid*s are fixed according to the solar calendar and may change according to historical and social conditions. The *mawlid* of Aḥmad al-Badawī is a typical case.

In the early nineteenth century there were three feasts in honor of al-Badawī. The largest of these was held a month after the summer solstice, which was then the slack season for the peasants in the area. In the second or third decade of the twentieth century, the date of this *mawlid* was moved to the latter half of October. The development of the irrigation system in the intervening period had resulted in fundamental changes in the annual agricultural cycle of the Nile Delta. Thus October in the Gregorian calendar became the slack season for the peasants, many of whom were enthusiastic devotees of the saint. The date of the great *mawlid* of Sayyid al-Badawī, therefore, is based not on his actual birthday but on the convenience of his devotees.

The space around the shrine of the saint being celebrated naturally becomes a center for the feast and is crowded with visitors to the tomb. There are a number of stands for food and drinks, amusements, and sideshows. Clusters of tents are pitched where Ṣūfīs conduct *dhikr* rituals during the feast days. The number of visitors hoping to receive divine blessing increases remarkably during this period.

Besides the *dhikr* rituals, Ṣūfīs of various orders take part in other events during the feast. Members of some orders used to demonstrate their miraculous powers in front of crowds in performances involving eating live serpents or piercing their bodies with spikes. This kind of bizarre performance has often been criticized for deviation from orthodox belief and proper Sufism. Recently they have tended to disappear, especially in the large cities.

The attractions of a festival also include a procession *(mawkib* or *zaffah)* for which various Ṣūfī orders assemble, forming lines and marching around the town or village. They perform *dhikr* and other rituals in their own styles, as a demonstration to the local people. The saint's shrine is often the starting point and/or the destination of these processions.

Political and Economic Functions. Like Sayyid al-

Badawī, said to have led soldiers against Crusaders, a number of leading Ṣūfīs have played the role of military commanders fighting against tyrannical rulers, ignorant heretics, and invading infidels. Among them was the leader of the Sanūsīyah movement, which fought against the Italian invasion of Libya. Founded by Muḥammad al-Sanūsī, the Sanūsīyah successfully propagated its beliefs among the bedouin tribes of Cyrenaica in the early stages of its development, by intentionally setting up lodges in the boundary areas between tribal territories. Thus the Ṣūfīs of the order could play the role of mediators in tribal conflicts, and this gave them great authority.

Saintly families in the High Atlas also arbitrate in disputes among Berber tribesmen. Moreover, a collective oath, which is a customary legal procedure for judging the truth or falsity of an accusation, has to be made at a saint's shrine if it relates to a serious issue. The shrine is also the place where a special ritual alliance between two tribes is contracted. In Boujad in Morocco, al-Sharqāwah, a maraboutic family, plays almost the same role as do the saints of the Atlas.

A number of saint's shrines can function as sites for conflict resolution and judicial decisions, although they seldom have the military power to enforce them. Because of the divine blessing saints have been granted by God, shrines can become holy places where people are subjected to mystical authority. Some of them have become not only asylums where killers involved in tribal feuds can come to ask for relief, but also sanctuaries where all bloodshed is prohibited.

Since people continuously come and go, and the area around the shrine is relatively peaceful, the place may develop as a market center for the area; or, conversely, an existing market may also become a center for religious training, so that a saint's shrine is eventually built there. Such towns as Tanta in Egypt (the Aḥmadīyah order), Boujad in Morocco (the al-Sharqāwah marabout family), and El-Damer in the Sudan (the Majdhūbīyah order) are local centers for production, storage, and marketing. While the regular weekly market held in these towns has prospered, the annual saint's festival has become an occasion on which the town bustles with massive crowds and a large-scale fair is held, so that the festival has considerable economic effect.

The saint and his family may be able to maintain the economic importance of their town by emphasizing their mystical power. In the eighteenth century the Majādhib family was said to escort trading caravans from Shendi to Berber via El-Damer, its home town. They ensured safe travel for the tribesmen and consequently contributed to the prosperity of towns other than their own. Similar cases exist in other areas.

Criticism. As mentioned earlier, criticisms of the Ṣūfī-saint shrine culture, or at least at certain elements of it, have been expressed by theologians and politicians ever since it developed. Ibn Ṭaymīyah (d. 1328), a strict jurist affiliated to the Ḥanbalī school of Islamic law, was one of the most distinguished critics in the premodern era, although he did not condemn all the activities of the Ṣūfī orders. He stressed that the veneration of a saint would probably lead to the worship of a divine being other than God—to loathsome polytheism—and that showy attractions during feasts were definitely contrary to Islamic law and should therefore be prohibited.

Muḥammad ibn ʿAbd al-Wahhāb (d. 1791), one of the theological successors of Ibn Ṭaymīyah, condemned not only the folk customs of saint veneration but the whole of Sufism. The Wahhābī campaign was led militarily by the Saʿūd family, powerful supporters of Ibn ʿAbd al-Wahhāb's doctrines, who started from a small oasis in the Nejd and gradually expanded their influence in the Arabian Peninsula. In the end they conquered the Hejaz and gained control of Mecca and Medina by 1804. During this campaign, whenever they encountered Ṣūfī saints' shrines or other holy places they did not hesitate to demolish them. Even the dome erected on the spot where the Prophet was born was destroyed. This strong hostility toward saints and Ṣūfīs has been maintained by the contemporary regime in Saudi Arabia, which follows Wahhābism as its state doctrine; officially, no Ṣūfī activity is permitted there.

Exponents of the Salafīyah movement such as Muḥammad ʿAbduh and Muḥammad Rashīd Riḍā openly criticized many elements of Ṣūfī saint culture. They insisted that a saint could not intercede with God for people in earthly matters and therefore did not have the mystical power to grant good fortune. Riḍā sternly rebuked participants in the *mawlid* of Sayyid al-Badawī for committing *bidʿah* (heretical innovation) through activities such as prayers to the saint's tomb and circumambulation of it, asking for worldly benefits, whistling, clapping, fortune-telling, selling charms and amulets, noisy music, the assembly of both sexes, and the practice of transvestism; however, he recognized the *mawlid* itself as legal.

The hostile attitude toward Ṣūfī saint shrine culture

has been taken over by Islamic reformist movements, including so-called fundamentalist groups like the Muslim Brothers. Not only strict fundamentalists but also secular modernists have intensified their opposition to it. Generally speaking, the more widespread public education has become, the more general has been the criticism of shrine cults as mere superstition. Most contemporary devotees of the cult of saints are recruited from the less-educated urban and rural masses. It is noteworthy that some Ṣūfīs, especially those advocating neo-Ṣūfī trends, actively criticize some elements of popular Sufism as *bidʿah,* just as Islamic scholars from outside Ṣūfī circles do.

[*See also* Mawlid; Popular Religion; Sainthood; Shrine.]

BIBLIOGRAPHY

Blackman, W. S. *The Fellahīn of Upper Egypt.* London, 1927. Detailed ethnography of the Upper Egyptian peasants in the early decades of the twentieth century, with special reference to their folk beliefs and practices. Descriptions of Muslim saints as well as those of the Copts and *mawlid* feasts are included.

Canaan, Tewfik. *Mohammedan Saints and Sanctuaries in Palestine.* Jerusalem, 1927. Detailed reports on the folk practices of the veneration of Muslim saints in Palestine before the establishment of Israel.

Crapanzano, Vincent. *The Hamadsha: A Study in Moroccan Ethnopsychiatry.* Berkeley and Los Angeles, 1973. Study of one of the popular religious brotherhoods in Morocco, the Ḥamādishah, with reference to its history and rituals. In the sanctuary of this brotherhood is a grotto where a powerful female spirit, ʿA'ishah Qandīshah, is said to dwell.

Daly, M. W., ed. *Al-Majdhubiyya and al-Mikashfiyya: Two Sufi Tariqas in the Sudan.* Khartoum and London, 1985. Includes two articles on the Sudanese Ṣūfī orders. One of them is a historical study on the Majdhūbīyah Ṣūfī order of al-Damir written by ʿAwaḍ al-Karsani.

Eickelman, Dale F. *Moroccan Islam.* Austin and London, 1976. One of the best anthropological works on maraboutism. Based on field research conducted by the author with the al-Sharqāwah family in Boujad, Central Morocco. His *Knowledge and Power in Morocco* (Princeton, 1985) contains a case study of the critical attitude of a reform-minded student to traditional maraboutism in the first half of the twentieth century.

Geertz, Clifford. *Islam Observed.* New Haven and London, 1968. Compact but informative book on Moroccan maraboutism and Indonesian mysticism in their historical, sociological, and ideological contexts.

Gellner, Ernest. *Saints of the Atlas.* Chicago, 1969. Standard monograph on the saintly families of the High Atlas, Morocco. For his more comprehensive studies of Islam, including maraboutism and fundamentalism, as well as his methodological stance, see his collection of papers entitled *Muslim Society* (Cambridge, 1981).

Gilsenan, Michael. *Saint and Sufi in Modern Egypt.* Oxford, 1973. Sociological study of the Ḥāmidīyah Shādhilīyah Ṣūfī order from its origin to the 1960s. On the internal conflict in the order after the death of the second shaykh in the 1970s, see his *Recognizing Islam* (New York, 1982), which includes information on the saint and/or Ṣūfī cultures in Yemen, Lebanon, and other areas.

Goldziher, Ignácz. *Muslim Studies.* Vol. 2. London, 1971. Collection of papers written by one of the greatest orientalist scholars in the latter half of the nineteenth century, which includes a classic and standard work on the veneration of saints, though its methodological stance could be criticized by today's criteria.

Hourani, Albert. *Arabic Thought in the Liberal Age, 1798–1939.* 2d ed. Cambridge, 1983. Standard study on the sociopolitical thought of great Muslim reformists, whether modernist or fundamentalist, in the modern age. Includes chapters on Muḥammad ibn ʿAbd al-Wahhāb, Muḥammad ʿAbduh, and Muḥammad Rashīd Riḍā who rebuked harshly some, or all, of the elements of Ṣūfī-saint culture.

Lane, E. W. *An Account of the Manners and Customs of the Modern Egyptians* (1836). London, 1978. Invaluable encyclopedic ethnography of everyday life mainly in Cairo, in the first decades of the nineteenth century. It is noteworthy that Lane describes the veneration of saints and the *mawlid* feasts, not in the chapter on "Religion," but in those on "Superstitions" and "Periodical Public Festivals."

Ohtsuka, Kazuo. "Toward a Typology of Benefit-Granting in Islam." *Orient* 24 (1988): 141–152. In this paper, published in the English bulletin of the Japanese Society of the Near Eastern Society, I propose four types of benefit-granting practices in Islam, using exchange theory as the frame of analysis, and locates the practice by which Muslim saints confer benefits within this typology.

Ohtsuka, Kazuo. "How Is Islamic Knowledge Acquired in Modern Egypt? ʿUlama, Sufis, Fundamentalists and Common People." In *Japanese Civilization in the Modern World,* vol. 5, *Culturedness,* edited by Tadeo Umesao et al. Osaka, 1990. My examination of various ways of acquiring "proper" Islamic knowledge in modern Egyptian contexts.

Reeves, E. B. *The Hidden Government: Ritual, Clientelism, and Legitimation in Northern Egypt.* Salt Lake City, 1990. An anthropological study of Sayyid Aḥmad al-Badawī and other Muslim saints in Tanta. It includes valuable information about the historical development of the cult of al-Badawī, contemporary saint veneration in the area, and the actual conditions of *mawlid* and other rituals.

Schimmel, Annemarie. *And Muhammad is His Messenger: The Veneration of the Prophet in Islamic Piety.* Chapel Hill, N.C., and London, 1985. Numerous cases of popular veneration of the Prophet are provided mainly from historical and literary sources, although most of them come from Turkey, Persia, and the Indian Subcontinent.

Trimingham, J. Spencer. *The Sufi Orders in Islam.* Oxford, 1971. Thorough, classic study of Ṣūfī orders, and an encyclopedic text on their history, thought, organization, and ritual.

Westermarck, Edward. *Rituals and Belief in Morocco.* 2 vols. London, 1926. Encyclopedic account of Moroccan folk beliefs and rituals written by a Finnish anthropologist working in London. Westermarck conducted field research in Morocco at the turn of the century and devotes three chapters of his book to describing and analyzing actual cases of the concept of *barakah,* which he translated as "holiness" or "blessed virtue."

KAZUO OHTSUKA

SUFISM AND POLITICS. Traditional Sufism is an interiorization of Sunnī quietism, articulating the pre-Islamic Pahlavi vision of monarchic government by religious principles, as echoed by al-Ghazālī (d. 1111) in his *Naṣīḥat al-mulūk*. A more systematic order found expression in the thirteenth century in the form of the "inner government" (*ḥukūmah bāṭiniyah*), which envisaged the temporal authorities as being subordinate to the spiritual *khalīfah*, who carried out the real tasks of government, aided by a hierarchy of deputies behind the figurehead of the sultan. This idea may may have derived from the patronizing of ascetics at court, where their presence provided moral legitimization for the regime.

The rise of the Western colonial threat in the eighteenth and nineteenth centuries faced Muslim societies with territorial and intellectual challenges. This coincided with the first Wahhābī conquest of Mecca (1804), which had a strong politicizing effect on the Muslim world, with pilgrims returning from the *ḥajj* to spread a new Pan-Islamic awareness as far as West Africa and Indonesia. Some of the more popular and cohesive Ṣūfī orders (*ṭarīqahs*) proved efficient channels for these ideas and were politicized accordingly. Ṣūfī activism continued well into the twentieth century, often providing the inspiration for more overtly secular political movements.

Egypt. Arguably the longest history of institutionalized and politically active ṣūfī orders is in Egypt. The Bakrīyah *ṭarīqah* (established in the sixteenth century) took its name from the Bakrī family, whose senior member was the *naqīb al-ashrāf*, the head of the Prophet's descendants in Egypt. When Muḥammad ʿAlī Pāshā officially recognized the *ṭarīqahs* in 1812, it was Muḥammad al-Bakrī who was authorized to intervene in their affairs.

In 1872 ʿAlī al-Bakrī supported Khedive Ismāʿīl against European intervention in Egypt and campaigned to keep him on the throne. The khedive's successor Tawfīq also relied on al-Bakrī to implement reforms in the *ṭarīqahs*. The youthful ʿAbd al-Bāqī al-Bakrī, who assumed responsibility for the *ṭarīqahs* in 1880, was unable to resist European consular pressure for reform, and various Ṣūfī ceremonies were banned or restricted. During the ʿUrābī insurrection of 1881, ʿAbd al-Bāqī supported the Khedive against the insurgents and entertained the commander of the British occupying forces. By contrast, the Khalwatīyah, a *ṭarīqah* outside al-Bakrī's jurisdiction, supported the rebels, as did the founding shaykhs of the Muḥammadīyah Shādhilīyah.

ʿAbd al-Bāqī was succeeded in 1892 by Muḥammad Tawfīq al-Bakrī, who reasserted the authority of establishment Sufism as the head of the new Ṣūfī Council (al-Majilis al-Ṣūfī) set up in 1895. In 1903 he amended the regulations in an attempt to reduce government involvement in the elections of the Majilis and the appointment of mosque functionaries, but he was opposed by Prime Minister Muṣṭafā Fahmī. The result was that many Ṣūfī shaykhs still owed their status and livelihood directly to the government. Muḥammad Tawfīq also came under pressure from Egyptian reformists and was criticized (notably by Rashīd Riḍā) for failing to outlaw Ṣūfī "innovations." The last Bakrī *shaykh al-sajjādah* was removed by King Fārūq in 1946 for supporting the Sudanese separatists.

From the turn of twentieth century, the *ṭarīqahs* became increasingly influenced by the climate of reformist activism as non-Ṣūfī groups gained political prominence, but most orders retained their traditional outlook. Their structure, if not their doctrines, even provided inspiration for non-Ṣūfī political organizations such as the Muslim Brotherhood (al-Ikhwān al-Muslimūn, founded 1928), which developed as an offshoot of the Ḥaṣāfīyah Shādhilīyah. Two *ṭarīqahs*, however, stand out for their expressly reformist and politically active character. The Azamīyah Shādhilīyah was founded in 1915 in the Sudan by Muḥammad Māḍī Abū al-ʿAzā'im. Currently headed by his grandson ʿIzz al-Dīn, the *ṭarīqah* has campaigned actively for reform of Ṣūfī practices. It is also critical of the Jamāʿāt Islāmīyah's "Kharijī tendencies" and emphasizes the necessarily Ṣūfī nature of any "Islamic solution."

The Ashīrah Muḥammadīyah (Muḥammadan Family) is a registered friendly society which contains a core of initiates known as the Muḥammadīyah Shādhilīyah. The ʿAshīrah was officially recognized in 1951 and has devoted itself to reforming Sufism and defending it against hostile critics. It also claims responsibility for the introduction of the 1976 Ṣūfī Ordinance (*lā'iḥah*). The present shaykh, Muḥammad Zakī Ibrāhīm, has been decorated by presidents Nasser, Sadat, and Mubarak.

The political aspect of Sufism in Egypt has recently been confined to matters of doctrine or internal discipline. One of the most conspicuous events occurred on 15 February 1979, when the People's Assembly (Majlis al-Shaʿb) passed a resolution banning the writings of the Andalusian Ṣūfī Muḥyī al-Dīn Ibn ʿArabī (d. 1240). This was felt by many to be an affront to intellectual and religious freedom; pressure was exerted on the government, which backed down at a meeting (5 March) in which Ibn ʿArabī was praised by Dr. Abū al-Wafāʾ al-Taftāzānī, the present *shaykh al-mashāyikh.*

Another crisis concerned the Burhānīyah order, which was anathematized by al-Azhar on the grounds that the writings of its shaykh, Muḥammad ʿUthmān ʿAbduh, contained numerous heresies. Resolutions were passed by the Majlis urging the *ṭarīqah* to adhere to the *sharīʿah* and withdraw the controversial literature, and an uneasy diplomatic "rehabilitation" was effected.

The Hejaz. As the spiritual center of the Muslim world, Mecca has always attracted a broad ethnic mix of pilgrims, providing a point for both the gathering and dissemination of ideas. A combination of Wahhābī reformism and a growing awareness of Western political and territorial ambitions stimulated this process, which manifested itself in an upsurge of traditional *ḥadīth* scholarship and what Fazlur Rahman (*Islam,* Chicago, 1979, p. 195) calls "neo-Sufism." This brand of Sufism laid more emphasis on political activism than on metaphysics and ecstasy and its *ṭarīqah*s provided ready vehicles for the transmission and implementation of ideas. Reformist *ṭarīqah*s became known increasingly by the name "Muḥammadīyah" in deference to renewed emphasis on the sunnah; this name was applied to the Sanūsīyah, Khatmīyah, and Tijānīyah orders, and even to the Wahhābī movement. Aḥmad Barelwī's Ṭarīqah-i Muḥammadīyah in India is also said to have been founded as a direct result of this Meccan influence.

Muḥammad ʿAlī gave the Hejazi *ṭarīqah*s the same recognition that he had afforded to those in Egypt, giving jurisdiction over those in Mecca and Jeddah to the head of the Khalwatīyah. This made the Khalwatīyah of the Hejaz more amenable to the Ottoman government than their Egyptian branches, and lowered the political profile of other Hejazi *ṭarīqah*s. The exception to this was the Sanūsīyah, who exerted considerable influence from their *zāwiyah*s (lodges) in Mecca, Medina, al-Ṭāʾif, Badr, al-Ḥamrāʾ, Yanbūʿ and Jeddah. Their power was such that the Turks were reluctant to use force against them and preferred to seek their cooperation. However, this did not prevent al-Sanūsī's being expelled from the region by the *ʿulamāʾ* (1840), and it is quite possible that the Ottoman government exerted covert influence to that end.

Syria. The Naqshbandīs enjoyed considerable influence in Syria in the early 20th century; prominent among them was Aḥmad Jiznawī (Kurdish, Ehmedē Ẍizneve), who came to the Jazīrah from Turkey during the time of Atatürk and established a *zāwiyah* at Tall Maʿrūf. Also influential were the Rifāʿīs, who were subjected to a campaign of repression in the 1970s. The *zāwiyah* of shaykh Maḥmūd ʿAbd al-Raḥmān al-Shaqfah in Hama (Ḥamāh) was closed in 1979 and the shaykh killed by the security forces in a campaign of "cleansing."

Iraq and Kurdistan. Naqshbandīs and Qādirīs are distributed in Iraq and Kurdistan according to tribal affiliation. Bitter feuding from the 1920s to the 1960s frequently pitted tribes such as the antiauthoritarian Barzānīs and the broadly pro-government Baradost against each other, with conflict even arising between branches of the same *ṭarīqah.* As was the practice in Cyrenaica and Morocco, a number of shaykhs undertook a mediatory role on tribal boundaries.

The Naqshbandīyah acquired political influence early, with Shaykh Muḥammad Saʿīd (d. 1920) forming a clandestine political party (Ḥizb al-ʿAhd) in 1914 and agitating against the British presence in Iraq. During the period of the monarchy, Shaykh Bahāʾ al-Dīn Bamarnī rose to prominence, counting Prime Minister Nūrī Saʿīd, (d. 1958) as one of his *murīd*s (disciples). The shaykh's son Masʿūd was something of a tyrant, and the inhabitants of Bamarnī and the surrounding villages revolted against him. The government intervened militarily at the end of 1960, whereupon Masʿūd withdrew to Mosul. When the Kurdish war for independence began in 1961, he actively supported the government against Barzānī guerrillas.

Yemen. Yemen was traditionally a stronghold of the Fāsīyah Shādhilīyah under Shaykh Muḥammad Hisān. The shaykh's son was taken hostage by the Zaydī Imām Yaḥyā (r. 1904–1948) after the retreat of the Ottomans; this repressive policy continued under Imām Aḥmad (1948–1962) with the imprisonment and death of the shaykh himself.

In the coastal regions, the Qādirī and Idrīsī *ṭarīqah*s were active. The latter aligned themselves with non-Marxist nationalists against the British, where they remained active in Aden.

Turkey. Perhaps the most politically significant Turkish *ṭarīqah* was the Bektāshīyah, founded by the thirteenth-century Haçi Bektāsh. Its political importance derives from its exclusive links with the Janissaries, with whom Bektāshīs participated in rebellions against the Ottomans, notably the revolt of Kalenderoğlu in 1526/27.

In 1812, Sultan Maḥmūd II centralized control of the Saʿdīyah in one of its *tekke*s (lodges) in Istanbul. In 1826, he took more drastic action to control the *ṭarīqah*s and forcibly disbanded the Janissaries, destroying many Bektāshī *tekke*s at the same time. By 1836, the dervishes of Adrianople (Edirne) were required to possess certificates bearing the seal of their local shaykh, and the Şeyhülislam was authorized to confirm the elections of shaykhs in the same year.

Government involvement in Sufism took a more personal turn in 1875, when Muḥammad Ẓāfir al-Madanī (d. 1903) met the future Sultan Abdülhamid II (r. 1876–1909). He acted as the sultan's adviser for some thirty years and attempted to use his influence to denigrate the Sanūsīyah and promote the Madanīyah.

Turkish Sufism enjoyed something of a literary revival at the turn of the century, and two Ṣūfī journals, *Ceride-i Sufiye* (1910–1920) and *Muḥibbān* (1909–1919), worked to unite the efforts of disparate *ṭarīqah*s. The editors of *Muḥibbān* called for the creation of a unified Ṣūfī league *(cem'iyet-i sufiye-i ittihadiye)* and published a detailed constitution. Although this was never put into effect, it is a valuable source for the concerns of Ṣūfī leaders at the threshold of a new Turkey.

The Naqshbandī Shaykh Saʿīd's Kurdish revolt of 1923 was used by Atatürk as a pretext to eradicate what he considered a subversive political movement, and all *tekke*s were commanded to close "voluntarily" in December 1925. The Havletī-Cerrāhī *ṭarīqah* was the only one to defy the ban and was tolerated as a "folkloric center." It appears that many of the other orders were only forced underground, as by 1952 Turkish Bektāshīs alone were said to number 30,000.

The unanticipated result of the official closure of the *tekke*s was that Ṣūfī energy was channelled to more overtly political ends. Bediüzzaman Said Nursî's Nurculuk movement was more of a "voluntary membership association" than a *ṭarīqah* in the classical sense, although its roots are firmly in the Naqshbandī tradition. This is illustrated by Nursî's incorporating mystical vocabulary from the works of Ibn ʿArabī into a framework of political activity, in an attempt to appeal to the literary and doctrinal tastes of his readership. The movement acquired some influence in Turkish politics from 1950 onward as the governing Democratic Party adopted a more favorable attitude toward Islam. The Naqshbandīs themselves also benefited from this change, with the Adalet Partisi fielding a former Naqshbandī functionary as its presidential candidate in the elections of 1980.

Iran. Premodern Iran provides us with a conspicuous example of Sufism as a vehicle for dissent which later came to personify the establishment. Shāh Ismāʿīl Ṣafavī, the founder of the Ṣafavid Dynasty, came from a Ṣūfī family with considerable influence as spiritual teachers in Ardabil. Under his leadership the Ṣafavī order spread to Shirvan, Azerbaijan, Iraq, and the rest of present-day Iran. In 1501 Ismāʿīl established the Ṣafavid dynasty after a long and intense campaign of religious propaganda, and Sunnism virtually disappeared from Iran.

Tension later developed between the Shīʿī mujtahids and the Ṣūfīs, who objected to the imposition of ʿUṣūlī scholasticism. Two *mujtahid*s rose to fame in this respect at the end of the eighteenth century: Muḥammad Bāqir Bihbahānī (d. 1780/81) and his son ʿAlī (d. 1801/02), who was named "Ṣufī-killer" for his cruel persecution of anti-*mujtahidī* dissent.

However, a dissenting tradition of Sufic and philosophical leanings persisted through the mid-nineteenth century. The Shaykhī school, which looked to the examples of Shaykh Aḥmad Aḥṣā'i (d. 1826) and Kāẓim Rashtī (d. 1844), tried to penetrate the establishment and succeeded in obtaining patronage from the ruling Qājārs. They rejected orthodox millenarian eschatology in favor of a humanistic adaptation of the evolution toward "perfect man" *(al-insān al-kāmil)*, originally a Ṣūfī-Ismāʿīlī concept.

The Shaykhī movement coalesced around Muḥammad Karīm Khān Kirmānī (d. 1871), a Qājār prince and a disciple of Rashtī. Although it was not a Ṣūfī movement in the strictest sense, it did formalize metaphysical and eschatological tenets which had previously been esoterically concealed by Aḥṣā'ī and Rashtī. Muḥammad Karīm Khān accused the *mujtahids* of governing by force and offered an alternative hierarchical schema which placed them just above the common people and beneath the *nujabā'* ("those who call to God") and the *nuqabā'* ("those with perfect knowledge"). The only distinguishing feature of this expression of the *ḥukūmah bāṭiniyah* is that Muḥammad Karīm Khān placed himself at the top of the hierarchy as "the Qājār prince turned philosopher-king" (Mangol Bayat, *Mysticism and Dissent: Socioreligious Thought in Qajar Iran,* Syracuse, 1982, p. 78).

North Caucasus. The Naqshbandīyah and Qādirīyah

have traditionally been strong and politically active in this region, providing a point of unity for local populations and coordinating resistance to colonial incursions. The Naqshbandīyah spread into Daghestan and the Chechen region at the end of the eighteenth century, while the Qādirīyah appeared in the second half of the nineteenth. Each has a distinctive social and political profile, and some branches act as clandestine political parties.

The North Caucasian Naqshbandīyah traces its spiritual genealogy through the Kurdish Mawlānā Khālid of Süleymaniye (d. 1827) back to the Indian Naqshbandī tradition, the political activism of which was inspired by Shaykh Aḥmad Sirhindī (d. 1641). the fist Naqshbandī to have waged *jihād* against the Russians (1782–1791) is said to have been Shaykh Manṣūr Ushurma, who was apparently initiated into the *ṭarīqah* by a Bukharan Naqshbandī traveling to Mecca. He defeated a Russian force on the river Sunzha in 1785 and gained support in Chechnya, North Daghestan, and Kuban, but he was captured at Anapa in 1791 and died in the fortress of Schlüsselburg in 1793.

After a twenty-five-year interregnum, the Naqshbandīyah became active once more, rising up in Shirvan in the 1820s under the Ottoman Shaykh Muḥammad Efendi. This was the beginning of a fierce and drawn-out *jihād* known as the "Mürid Movement" in Russian sources. This war was sustained mainly by two of Muḥammad Efendi's *murīds*, Ghāzī Muḥammad and Imām Shāmil, who coordinated the formidable Caucasian mountaineers against the Russians. After Imām Shāmil surrendered in 1856 and his last stronghold was taken in 1859, the *ṭarīqah* went back underground.

After this defeat, the Qādiriyah appeared and quickly gained popularity. Introduced by the Daghestani Kunta Haji Kishiev (d. 1867), it initially preached mystical detachment but developed an ideology of resistance nonetheless. Outlawed by the authorities in the 1860s, the *ṭarīqah* played a prominent part (with the Naqshbandīs, many of whom were initiated into it) in the anti-Russian revolt in Daghestan and Chechnya (1877–1878). More uprisings followed after the Bolshevik Revolution: the Naqshbandīs, under Imām Najmal-Dīn of Gotzo and Shaykh Uzun Ḥajjī, fought first against the White armies of General Denikin in 1918–1920 and subsequently against the Red Army before being defeated in 1925. Some remained loyal to the Soviets, such as shaykhs Ḥasan and Ḥabīb Allāh Ḥajjī, but many partisan leaders were killed in Stalin's purges. Other Naqshbandī and Qādirī uprisings occurred in the region in 1928, 1934, and 1940–1942.

The Naqshbandīs have also been active in northern Azerbaijan, eastern and southern Turkmenistan, the Karakalpak Republic, and the Ferghana Valley, especially Kyrghyzstan. The Ferghana Valley saw the rise of the Naqshbandī Basmachi Movement in 1918, which was crushed in 1928 by the Red Army. One significant consequence of this defeat was the politicization of the Yasawīyah *ṭarīqah,* which had led a largely apolitical existence in southern Kazakhstan since the twelfth century. A highly political organization called the "Hairy Ishans" (Chachtun Eshander), a branch of the Yasawīyah, was formed by Abumutalib Satybaldyev in the 1920s. Centered in Chilgazy in the Kirghiz SSR and also active in the Osh region and Uzbekistan, the brotherhood quickly acquired a reputation in Soviet intelligence circles for terrorist activity. Thirty-two members were executed in 1936, after which the movement went underground. The organization is said to have been impervious to Soviet agents, while itself succeeding in infiltrating Communist Party organizations.

At the end of the nineteenth century, the modern-reformist Jadīdī movement spread northward from Turkey into Russia, where it was represented by Naqshbandīs such as Ālimjān Barūdī (d. 1921). Barūdī founded the Ittifāq al-Muslimīn party in 1905 and was *muftī* of Orenburg from 1920–1021. In 1943 the Naqshbandī Jadīdst ʿAbd al-Raḥmān Rasūlī signed an agreement with Stalin normalizing relations between the Soviet Muslim establishment and the government. State-sponsored Islam, represented by the Spiritual Boards of Central Asia and Kazakhstan and the North Caucasus and Daghestan, was used thereafter as a propaganda weapon against Ṣūfī or "parallel" Islam. *Fatwās* were pronounced against pilgrimages of holy sites, combining Soviet political expediency with Wahhābī religious doctrine. However, both the official and parallel wings of Islam faced the same materialist threat, and the fact that the official *muftīs* were often from Naqshbandī families prevented direct attacks on Sufism itself. Consequently, Soviet control of the *ṭarīqahs* was not conspicuously successful; generally, the farther away from Moscow, the less likely it was that officials would implement government policies, perhaps even themselves being members of a *ṭarīqah*. In Central Asia in 1979 there were at least 500,000 Ṣūfīs out of a total population of

27 million, and in Daghestan and Chechen-Ingush there were some 200,000 adepts.

China. Ṣūfī influence in China dates back to the Mongols, by whom shaykhs were given positions of influence in government. Their standing was reduced after the eclipse of Mongol power in 1368, which obliged the Muslims to integrate themselves more fully into Chinese society. However, the *ṭarīqah*s remained operational, if not conspicuous.

In 1644 the Manchus established the Qing dynasty, expanding the Chinese empire and effectively annexing one-third of Muslim Central Asia. They attempted to keep the various ethnic elements of the empire separate but were only partially successful. The problem was exacerbated by the activist Naqshbandī tradition, which was established in Xinjiang by Isḥāq Walī (d. 1599). The Qing were thus poorly placed to contain the wave of reformist preaching which began to reach the region in the eighteenth and nineteenth centuries.

The Naqshbandī Shaykh Ma Mingxin (d. 1781) performed the *ḥajj* and studied in Bukhara and Yemen before returning to China in 1761. Ma Mingxin was of the Jahrīyah school of Naqshbandīs, who favored the vocal *dhikr*. He composed a poem celebrating the birth of the Prophet which won him fame at the expense of the Khūfīyah, who preferred silent invocation. The Khūfīyah accused the Jahrīyah of sedition and helped the Qing government put down the "rebels" in 1781, collaborating again with the authorities in an attempt to exterminate them in 1784. However, the Jahrīyah survived, developing a hereditary succession and modifying their reformist tendencies.

A liberation movement developed in Xinjiang under the leadership of the Naqshbandī Shaykh Jahāngīr, who launched a *jihād* against Qing domination in 1817. The Kashgarīs joined the rebellion a few years later, which failed when Jahāngīr was captured in 1828. Internal feuding split the Naqshbandīs thereafter, with the Isḥāqīs and Āfāqīs losing influence to the Mujaddidīs, who inherited the tradition of Aḥmad Sirhindī. The British made use of a Naqshbandī, Aḥmad Shāh, as an informer on political affairs in Xinjiang at this time.

Rebellions broke out once again in Shanxi and Gansu in 1862. The Qing authorities accepted the surrender of the faction led by Ma Zhan'ao, who seems to have been a Khūfī Naqshbandī. However, the government saw the Jahrī leader Ma Hualong as its main enemy, and used his "rebellion" as an excuse to commit atrocities against those who had put themselves under government protection. Ma Hualong was executed in 1871; the last pockets of resistance were eliminated in 1873, and a large part of the population was forcibly relocated.

Naqshbandī *jihād*s were launched by Rāshidīn Khān Khawājah in Kucha and by the Mujaddidī ʿAbd al-Raḥmān Haḍrah in Yarkand (1864). The Naqshbandīs probably also inspired the revolts of Jin Xiangyin and the Kirghiz chief Ṣiddīq Beg in Kashgar, as well as that of Tuo Ming in Urumchi in the same year. As before, internal rivalry hindered the rebels; the rebellions of Rāshidīn Khān Khawājah and ʿAbd al-Raḥmān Haḍrah were put down by Ya'qūb Beg at the instigation of Jin Xiangjin and Ṣiddīq Beg. Ya'qūb went on to establish his own sultanate, but the Qing reconquered southern Xinjiang in 1877.

In twentieth-century China the political influence of the *ṭarīqah*s has declined, although the effect of the Cultural Revolution on Islam in general is not yet known. The Naqshbandīs at least retained enough influence for the Jahrī chief Ma Zhenwu to be denounced by the government for "exploitation" in 1958.

Indian Subcontinent. Ṣūfī activity in India dates back to the early years of Muslim rule in the subcontinent, where Ṣūfīs had a high profile as teachers and mediators between their followers and the government and between political rivals. Although they were to become somewhat eclipsed by the *ʿulamā'* in the Mūghal period (1526–1739), they continued to exert a degree of influence over their political masters and those jurists who were sympathetic to their outlook. The Chishtīyah had long seen themselves as the patron saints of Muslim rulers in India; during the reign of Shāh Jihān (d. 1659), ʿAbd al-Raḥmān Chishtī evoked the *ḥukūmah bāṭiniyah* in speaking of the Chishtīyah as sole protectors of the emperor's life, with responsibility for the very survival of the kingdom.

It was the Naqshbandī *ṭarīqah,* however, which acquired the greatest reputation for political activity during this period. The early example of ʿUbaydullāh Aḥrār (d. 1490), who was closely connected to the Timurid prince Abū Saʿīd and exerted great political influence on Central Asian politics, set a precedent for the Indian Naqshbandīs' attempts to guide their rulers. The would-be kingmaker Shaykh Jalāl al-Dīn Khawajījī provides a vivid example of this, telling the skeptical Emperor Bābur (d. 1530) that "outstanding Ṣūfīs who were responsible for the maintenance of the world" had elected one ʿUbaydullāh Khān as the Uzbek *khalīfah.* Not surprisingly, Babur ignored their decision.

Perhaps the most controversial figure in this respect is the Naqshbandī Aḥmad Sirhindī (d. 1624). The conventional opinion has been that he struggled successfully to reverse the syncretic trends of the court of Akbar, and that Awrangzīb's favoring a more orthodox Islamic policy than his predecessors was a result of Sirhindī's political campaigning. Opponents of this view reason that the numerous letters written by Sirhindī to the political figures of his day are proof of commitment but not necessarily of influence. It should also be pointed out that Sirhindī's activities caused concern in high places; he was imprisoned (1619–1620) by Jahāngīr, and the study of his *Maktūbāt* was prohibited by Awrangzīb in 1679. It is possible that this ban, together with the negative *fatwā*s of various Indian Ṣūfīs and *ʿulamāʾ*, was also the result of Sirhindī's claim to being the *Qayyūm*, the maintainer of the cosmic order. Three of his successors claimed this status—Muḥammad Maʿṣūm (d. 1668), Ḥujjat Allāh Naqshband (d. 1702), and Muḥammad Zubayr (d. 1740).

The death of Awrangzīb in 1707 left a vacuum in the Mughal empire, and some landed Ṣūfīs began to exert themselves against regional authorities which lacked royal support. This period saw the rising profile of the Niẓāmī Chishtī *ṭarīqah,* whose leader Khvājah Nūr Muḥammad (d. 1790) exerted considerable influence over Bahāʾ al-Ḥaqq, the ruler of Bahawalpur, and fought against the Sikhs in the Punjab.

Also influential was the activity of Khvājah Mīr Dard (d. 1785), who combined a stern Naqshbandī ascetism with a love of poetry and music, for which he was criticized by some of his contemporaries. He founded the Ṭarīqah-i Muḥammadiyah whose members he advised to assist the temporal authorities with prayers, dubbing them *lashkar-i duʿā* or "the army of prayer."

The Naqshbandī Shāh Walī Allāh Dihlawī (d. 1763) was also influential. He is credited with completing the reformist work of Sirhindī, and he wrote many letter to the emperor and government officials urging political and financial reforms. He also appealed to the Afghan king Aḥmād Shāh Abdālī to save India from the depredations of Nādir Shāh, who had invaded in 1739; Abdālī did so, but looted and left. The political element of Shāh Walī Allāh's work survives to this day in the school of Deoband, but without his specifically Ṣūfī perspective.

The *jihād* against the Sikhs was continued by Sayyid Aḥmad (d. 1831), who founded his own Ṭarīqah-i Muḥammadīyah, an organization which opposed the "superstition" of the traditional Ṣūfī orders and paved the way for a more openly reformist Islam. The orders thereafter became less conspicuous in nationalist political affairs.

Indonesia. Premodern Islam in Indonesia had a deeply mystical quality. As elsewhere, Ṣūfī orders played a part in legitimating political authority. Ṣūfī ideas also made their mark on historiography, as shown by the *Tambo,* the Minangkabau chronicle which derives creation from the Muḥammadan Light and posits the ideal of harmony between the individual and society and the cosmic order, expressed as *adat.*

However, a growing awareness of Pan-Islamic and Wahhābī ideas began to polarize Indonesian Muslim society, giving rise to the anti-Ṣūfī Padri movement, which was started by three Minangkabau pilgrims returning from Mecca in 1821. War ensued (1825–1830) between the Padris and the traditionalist supporters of *adat,* with the Dutch entering on the *adat* side; the Padris took advantage of inter-*ṭarīqah* rivalry, exploiting the rivalry between the Naqshbandīyah and Qādirīyah and the Shaṭṭārīyah. (Datuk Sutan Maharadja, writing in 1912, highlighted the Ṣūfī-Padri gulf by identifying Sufism with natural law and the Muḥammadan Light with "original *adat,*" reinforcing the link between Sufism and Maningkabau patriotism.)

Anti-Dutch feeling manifested itself in the form of messianic revolts led by Ahmad Ngisa (1871), Kasan Mukmin (1904), Dermadjaja (1907), Dietz (1918), and the Madhist Murakat (1923). However, by this stage it had become increasingly difficult to distinguish among reformist Islamic, traditional Ṣūfī, and even anti-Islamic revolts in this diverse and often syncretistic religious environment. In the 1920s, the Islamic Communism movement was led partly by Ṣūfīs, and even the modern political Sarekat Islam retained a mystical-millenarian image at the popular level.

North Africa. The Sanūsīyah provides one of the clearest examples of a *ṭarīqah* developing along political lines. Founded by Muḥammad ibn ʿAlī al-Sanūsī (d. 1859), a *murīd* of Aḥmad ibn Idrīs (d. 1837), the order had its first *zāwiyah* near Mecca in 1838, but it was forced to leave in 1840 because of local disapproval of Sufism. A *zāwiyah* was founded at the Jabal Akhḍar (Cyrenaica) in 1843, before the center of the *ṭarīqah* was moved south to Jaghbūb in 1856, to avoid Turkish interference and to strengthen its influence in the central Sahara. A comprehensive network of *zāwiyah*s developed, forming a self-sufficient Muslim community. These *zāwiyah*s became centers of tribal unity for the nomads, as well as providing buffer zones between tribes and a sacred space in which disputes could be discussed.

When the Italians invaded Crenaica in 1911 they met fierce resistance from the Sanūsīyah under the leadership of Sīdī Aḥmad al-Sharīf, who had fought the French in the Sahara (1902–1912). It was only in the face of this foreign threat that the Sanūsīs moved closer to the Turks, who provided limited material assistance but withdrew in 1912. In 1916 the Sanūsīyah, led by the young Muḥammad Idrīs al-Sanūsī (later king of Libya) opened negotiations with the Italians and British. Resistance was resumed in the second Italo-Sanūsī war (1923–1932) by ʿUmar al-Mukhtār, who was captured and executed in 1931.

In Algeria, the Darqāwī ʿAbd al-Qādir ibn al-Sharīf agitated in the Turkish province of Oran (1803–1809) and "but for the moderation of the sultan Mawlāy Sulaymān (1792–1822) this . . . might have ended in the annexation of western Algeria by Morocco" (R. Le Tourneau, "Darḳāwa," in *Encyclopaedia of Islam*, new ed. 1960–, vol. 2, p. 160). Ibn al-Sharīf also marched unsuccessfully against the Turks during the English bombardment of Algiers in 1816.

French forces arrived in the summer of 1830; by 1832 their intentions had become clear to the Algerians, who organized a resistance movement. Command was given to Amīr ʿAbd al-Qādir, a young Qādirī shaykh. He was also initiated into the Naqshbandīyah, the Shādhilīyah, and the Tijānīyah. ʿAbd al-Qādir's immense energy and tactical brilliance frustrated the French for fifteen years, during which period he had to contend with the uncertain loyalties of the tribes as well as the opposition of the Darqāwīs, who suspected him of making common cause with the French after the treaties of Desmichels (1834) and Tafna (1837). He was imprisoned in France (1847–1852) and then exiled to Damascus, where he died in 1883. He was buried next to the tomb of Ibn ʿArabī, and his body was repatriated after Algerian independence.

It seems that some of the Qādirīyah modified their oppositional stance after the defeat of the amīr. In 1879, Muḥammad ibn ʿAbbās supported the French in the insurrection at Aurès, and the *ṭarīqah* helped to extend French influence into the Sahara at Wargla and al-Wad. Their *nā'ib*, Muḥammad ibn al-Ṭayyib, fell on the French side at the battle of Charouin in 1901.

Moroccan *ṭarīqah*s have a long history of involvement at all levels of society. The Darqāwīs supported the authorities in return for Mawlāy Sulaymān's encouragement of their shaykh, Mawlāy al-ʿArabī (d. 1823), who was, however, imprisoned later by the suspicious sultan. He was freed after Mawlāy Sulaymān's death in 1822. The *ṭarīqah* also opposed French ambitions in eastern Morocco and accused its own government of appeasement in 1887. In the northeast in 1907, the Banū Snassen rose against the French, who had occupied their lands. This was followed in 1910 by the attempt of Mā'al-ʿAynayn, the twelfth son of the great Mauritanian Qādirī Shaykh Muḥammad Faḍl (d. 1869), to force his own accession to the Moroccan throne.

The Rīf War (1925–1930) was a larger-scale revolt. Although its leader Abd el-Krim (more properly, ʿAbd al-Karīm al-Khaṭṭābī) and many of his followers were Ṣūfīs, it was more of a national liberation struggle than a Ṣūfī movement.

West Africa. By the end of the eighteenth century the new enthusiasm for Islamic unity and reform reached West Africa through the Qādirīyah, exemplified by the leadership of Sidi al-Mukhtār al-Kuntī (d. 1811) and Shaykh Usuman dan Fodio (d. 1817). A revivalist campaign was conducted in Gobir, Zamfara, Katsina, and Kebbi (1774–1804), with a *jihād* against the Haɓe kings in 1797. By 1812, a Muslim Fulani empire had come into being, ruled by Shaykh Usuman's brother ʿAbd Allāh ibn Muḥammad and his second son, Muhammadu Bello (d. 1837), with Shaykh Usuman enjoying overall command as caliph. The momentum of conquest was maintained by one of Shaykh Usuman's disciples, Aḥmad ibn Muḥammad ibn Abī Bakr, who launched a *jihād* in Masina (1810 or 1818), claiming to be the Renewer *(mujaddid)* of the thirteenth lunar century. Another Qādirī *jihād* followed in 1850 under al-Ḥājj Maḥmūd, who had renewed his Qādirī affiliation in Syria, pledging to conquer his own country and build a mosque in every town he took. However, his ambitions clashed with local interests, as the Dyula Muslims had long-established trade links with non-Muslims, and al-Ḥājj Maḥmūd met with limited success.

The nineteenth century also saw the introduction into West Africa of the Tijānīyah. Named after Shaykh Aḥmad al-Tijānī (d. 1815), the *ṭarīqah* was championed by al-Ḥājj ʿUmar Tal (d. 1864) and received early support from Muhammadu Bello. However, the Qādirī establishment of Sokoto became more rigid after Bello's death, and the Tijānīyah acquired the unofficial status of political opposition. This tension remains in present-day Nigeria.

The predominant figure in the history of Mauritanian Sufism is the Qādirī Shaykh Sidiyah al-Kabīr (d. 1868), who attracted a large nomadic following. He founded a central *zāwiyah* at Bontilimit for administrative and political reasons, while remaining mindful of his community's migratory needs. He was a skilled political mediator, acting as a kingmaker among the warrior Ḥassānī. He was taught by Sidi al-Mukhtār al-Kuntī and taught Aḥmad Bamba.

The *ṭarīqahs* arrived in Senegal from North Africa in the late eighteenth and early nineteenth centuries. Many assumed a mediatory role between the French colonists and the rural inhabitants, thus enjoying the political advantage of French support. However, not all enjoyed the confidence of the French; Aḥmad Bamba, the founder of the Murīdīyah order (who had refused the post of *qāḍī* in Kayor in 1882), was considered subversive and was exiled to Gabon (1895–1902) and Mauritania (1903–1907). His release from Gabon was obtained by Shaykh Ibra Fall by using the influence of Senegal's parliamentary deputy.

In 1966 Abdou Lahat M'Backé inherited the *khilāfah*. Although he wished to seem aloof from politics, appearances were maintained; the government continued to be represented at Murīdīyah celebrations, and the *ṭarīqah* was still expected to support rural development programs. Government assistance was given for the development of Touba, the Murīd capital, in return for which Abdou Lahat agreed to the closure of the Murīd-controlled black market, which had grown as a result of economic hardship and urban migration after world War II. The black marketeers defied both government and shaykh; soon afterward, the attempted murder of the imam of the great mosque (Serigne ʿAbd al-Qādir M'backé, Aḥmad Bamba's son) resulted in the posting of gendarmes to Touba for the first time since independence in 1960.

The government was also present at major festivals of the Tijānīyah and gave material support to the Layenne *ṭarīqah,* in spite of its opposition to government legal reforms. The Murīds, meanwhile, hardened their attitudes to other *ṭarīqahs* in the late 1970s, while the Tijāniyah took a reformist line in criticizing controversial aspects of Murīdīyah. Relations remained tense between the order's leadership and the Murīd traders of Touba, as indicated by their lukewarm response to M'backé's instructions to vote for Abdou Diouf in the 1983 general election.

Sudan. The Qādirīyah and Shādhilīyah dominated Sudanese Sufism from the sixteenth century, giving some ground to reformist *ṭarīqahs* in the eighteenth and nineteenth centuries. Sudan also came under foreign influence form the north with the Turco-Egyptian conquest of 1821, which contributed to the politicization of the *ṭarīqahs*, some of which (e.g., the Rāshidīyah and Majdhūbīyah) actively resisted the invaders. Others were used as mediators, such as the Khatmīyah, which supported government intervention in the rebellion of Kassala (1865).

The Sammānīyah, founded in the Hijaz by Muḥammad ibn ʿAbd al-Karīm al-Sammān (d. 1775), enjoyed considerable success in the Sudan. Its two main branches in the Jazīrah were dominated by al-Sammān's descendants of the Ṭayyib family (hence the *ṭarīqahs* other name, al-Ṭayyibīyah) and the family of al-Qurashī Wad al-Zayn, who considered his line to be closer to the founder despite its lacking a family connection. The rivalry between these two branches developed into a schism in 1878 when Muḥammad Aḥmad (the future Mahdī) criticized his shaykh, Muḥammad Sharīf Nūr al-Dā'im, for laxity. Muḥammad Aḥmad transferred his allegiance to the Qurashī branch, which later supported him in his Mahdist campaign (1881–1885); the hereditary branch took sides with the Turks and Egyptians, as did the Khatmīyah. The Mahdīyah were also supported by the Majdhūbīyah, who had been violently opposed to the Turco-Egyptian government since 1821, and whose traditions spoke of a Mahdī appearing in the west.

In establishing the Mahdist state, Muḥammad Aḥmad aimed to supersede the *ṭarīqahs* and even went so far as to suppress them. However, his devotional manual (*rātib*), which was banned by the governor-general, provides evidence for a Ṣūfī perspective underlying his millenarian and reformist ambitions.

After the fall of the Madhī in 1898 and the establishment of the Anglo-Egyptian Condominium (1898–1956), the *ṭarīqahs* regained some of their influence; although the British never formally recognized them, they discovered a convenient anti-Mahdist bulwark in the Khatmīyah. However, during World War I the British feared that Mahdist sympathizers might support the Turks and decided to encourage a "controlled reconstruction" of the Mahdīyah.

The *ṭarīqahs* became increasingly politicized up to and after independence (1956), with the Khatmīyah/Mahdīyah rift remaining contentious. The Khatmīyah remained loyal to the government but politically aloof and maintained privileged links with Egypt. The Hindīyah (originally a pro-Madhist *ṭarīqah*) developed a highly centralized structure and radical political commitment; Sayyid Ṣiddīq Yūsuf al-Hindī (d. 1982) was a staunch opponent of the Nimeiri regime.

Horn of Africa and East Africa. By the nineteenth century the Qādirīyah had become firmly established in the rural Ethiopia and Somalia, forming a barrier against the reformist Idrīsī *ṭarīqahs*. Only the Ṣāliḥīyah (founded by Muḥammad ibn Ṣāliḥ, d. 1917) achieved any significant penetration. A resistance campaign was fought against the Italians and the British (1899–1920) under the leadership of Muḥammad ʿAbd Allāh Ḥasan, who was also hostile to nonaligned brotherhoods such as the Aḥmadīyah and the Qādirīyah. One of his followers assassinated a leading Qādirī shaykh, Uways ibn Muḥammad al-Barawī, in 1909.

Sufism was generally tolerated in German and then British East Africa, although the *dhikr* was first banned (1909–1911) and later restricted (1922–1933) because of its supposedly subversive connotations. Many Ṣūfī founders of the Muslim Association of Tanganyika became leaders of the Tanganyika African Association (founded c. 1929), which formed the basis of a later independence movements. The ʿAskarīyah, Aḥmadīyah-Dandarawīyah, and Shādhilīyah were especially active in this regard.

[*See also* Sufism, *article on* Ṣūfī orders. *In addition many of the specific orders and their founders are the subject of independent entries. For overviews of Islam in the various regions covered, see under* Islam; *see also the entries on individual countries.*]

BIBLIOGRAPHY

ʿAbd al-Qādir ibn Muḥyī al-Dīn. *Écrits spirituels.* Translated by Michel Chodkiewicz. Paris, 1982. Contains a succinct biography of Amīr ʿAbd al-Qādir in the introduction.

Ansari, Muhammad Abdul Haq. *Sufism and Sharīʿah: A Study of Shaykh Ahmad Sirhindi's Efforts to Reform Sufism.* London, 1986.

Benningsen, Alexandre, and Marie Broxup. *The Islamic Threat to the Soviet State.* London, 1983.

Bennigsen, Alexandre, and Marie Broxup, eds. *The North Caucasus Border: The Russian Advance towards the Muslim World.* London, 1992.

Bennigsen, Alexandre, and S. Enders Wimbush. *Mystics and Commissars: Sufism in the Soviet Union.* Berkeley, 1985.

Brelvi, Mahmud. *Islam in Africa.* Lahore, 1964.

Clancy-Smith, Julia. "Saints, Madhis, and Arms: Religion and Resistance in Nineteenth-Century North Africa." In *Islam, Politics, and Social Movements,* edited by Edmund Burke and Ira Lapidus, pp. 60–80. Berkeley and Los Angeles, 1988.

Cour, Auguste. "Darḳāwa." In *Encyclopaedia of Islam,* new ed., vol. 2, p. 160. Leiden, 1960–.

Cruise O'Brien, Donal B. *The Mourides of Senegal: The Political and Economic Organization of an Islamic Brotherhood.* Oxford, 1971.

Cruise O'Brien, Donal B. *Saints and Politicians.* Cambridge, 1975.

Cruise O'Brien, Donal B., and Christian Coulon, eds. *Charisma and Brotherhood in African Islam.* Oxford, 1988.

Dermenghem, Émile. *Le culte des saints dans l'Islam maghrébin.* 4th ed. Paris, 1954.

Esposito, John L., ed. *Islam and Development: Religion and Sociopolitical Change.* Syracuse, N.Y., 1982.

Esposito, John L., ed. *Islam in Asia: Religion, Politics, and Society.* New York, 1987.,

Evans-Pritchard, E. E. *The Sanusi of Cyrenaica.* Oxford, 1949.

Friedmann, Yohanan. *Shaykh Aḥmad Sirhindī: An Outline of His Thought and a Study of His Image in the Eyes of Posterity.* Montreal and London, 1971.

Haig, Thomas W. "Ṣafawids." In *E. J. Brill's First Encyclopaedia of Islam,* vol. 7, pp. 54–55. Leiden, 1987.

Hiskett, Mervyn. *The Development of Islam in West Africa.* London and New York, 1984.

Holt, P. M. *The Mahdist State in the Sudan, 1881–1898).* Oxford, 1958.

Homerin, Th. Emil. "Ibn Arabi in the People's Assembly: Religion, Press, and Politics in Sadat's Egypt." *Middle East Journal* 40.3 (Summer 1986): 462–477.

Hourani, Albert. *The Emergence of the Modern Middle East.* London, 1981.

Jong, F. de. *Ṭuruq and Ṭuruq-Linked Institutions in Nineteenth-Century Egypt.* Leiden, 1978.

Kartodirdjo, Sartono. *Protest Movements in Rural Java: A Study of Agrarian Unrest in the Nineteenth and Early Twentieth Centuries.* Singapore, 1973.

Le Chatelier, Alfred. *Les confréries musulmanes du Hedjaz.* Paris, 1887.

Luizard, Pierre-Jean. "Le rôle des confréries soufies dans le système politique égyptien." *Monde Arabe Maghreb Machrek,* no. 131 (January–March 1991): 26–53.

Mardin, Şerif. *Religion and Social Change in Modern Turkey: The Case of Bediüzzaman Said Nursi.* Albany, N.Y., 1989.

Nimtz, August H., Jr. *Islam and Politics in East Africa: The Sufi Order in Tanzania.* Minneapolis, 1980.

O'Fahey, R. S. *Enigmatic Saint: Ahmad Ibn Idris and the Idrisi Tradition.* London and Evanston, Ill., 1990.

Paden, John N. *Religion and Political Culture in Kano.* Berkeley, 1973.

Paden, John N. *Ahmadu Bello, Sardauna of Sokoto.* London, 1986.

Popovic, Alexandre, and Gilles Veinstein, eds. *Les ordres mystiques dans l'Islam: Cheminements et situation actuelle.* Paris, 1986.

Ricklefs, Merle C. *A History of Modern Indonesia.* London, 1981.

Rizvi, S. A. A. *A History of Sufism in India.* 2 vols. New Delhi, 1978–1981.

Stewart, C. C., and E. K. Stewart. *Islam and Social Order in Mauritania.* Oxford, 1973.

Taufik, Abdullah. "Modernization in the Minangkabau World." In *Culture and Politics in Indonesia,* edited by Claire Holt et al., pp. 179–245. Ithaca, N.Y., and London, 1972.

Trimingham, J. Spencer. *A History of Islam in West Africa.* London, 1962.

Trimingham, J. Spencer. *Islam in the Sudan.* London, 1965.
Trimingham, J. Spencer. *The Sufi Orders in Islam.* Oxford, 1971.
Voll, John Obert. "Hadith Scholars and *tariqahs*: An Ulama Group in the Eighteenth-Century Haramayn and Their Impact on the Islamic World." *Journal of Asian and African Studies.* 15.3–4 (July–October 1980): 264–273.

J. E. A. JOHANSEN

SUICIDE. *Qatl al-nafs,* literally "self-murder," is the term used to denote suicide in classical Islamic texts. *Intiḥār,* originally meaning "cutting of the throat," is the common word in modern Arabic speech.

There is only one phrase in the Qur'ān relevant to the subject of suicide: "O you who believe! Do not consume your wealth in the wrong way—rather only through trade mutually agreed to, and do not kill yourselves. Surely God is Merciful toward you" (4.29). The connection with suicide of even these few words of the revelation is however rather tenuous, as the key phrase (Ar., *wa-lā taqtulū anfusakum*), despite the coincidence with the Arabic term for suicide *(qatl al-nafs),* may also be understood as meaning "do not kill each other." This is the interpretation favored by Muslim exegetes both classical and modern, ultimately on the grounds that it best fits the context of the verse; consequently, the subject of suicide is also little discussed in the exegetical literature.

The prophetic tradition *(ḥadīth),* on the other hand, frequently, clearly, and absolutely prohibits suicide. These traditions are the basis for subsequent discussion of the subject. The most frequently reported tradition on suicide is the following: the Prophet said, "Who throws himself from a mountain and kills himself shall be in the Fire of Hell, there ever falling [that is just as he caused his own fall from the mountain] eternally and forever; and he who drinks poison and kills himself shall stand drinking poison from his own hand, eternally and forever; and he who kills himself with a sharp blade shall stab himself in his stomach with a blade held by his own hand, in the Fire of Hell eternally and forever." Another *ḥadīth* condemns to eternal torment those who "strangle themselves"; still others mention falling on one's sword, piercing oneself with an arrow in order to bleed to death, and cutting one's throat. Such reports suggest frequent and varied occurrence of suicide in the early Arabian environment, a tendency the prophet Muḥammad may have sought to overcome.

The traditions agree that suicides shall be in hell forever, and the heinousness of self-murder is emphasized by description of their tortures in that place. Punishment consists (as in the *ḥadīth* quoted above) of unending repetition of the act by which the suicide delivered himself to death. "Those who kill themselves with a thing," the Prophet is reported as saying, "shall be tormented with that thing on the Day of Judgment."

Commentators on the *ḥadīth,* however, have been reluctant to admit that the suicide is condemned eternally to hell. They maintain that suicides—like murderers and other sinners—are still to be regarded as believers despite their sins. This is because the orthodox are reluctant to accept that believing Muslims can be eternally in the fire; they hold instead that they are tormented only for a time. Similarly, although it is reported in tradition that the Prophet told the people not to pray over a man who had killed himself by cutting his throat with a razor, almost all authorities have permitted suicides the funeral prayer, for to do otherwise would imply exclusion of the deceased from the Muslim community. (The opposite opinion has sometimes prevailed, however, and instances are recorded of suicides having been refused the final prayer.) Apart from the question of the funeral prayer, suicide is very rarely mentioned in the legal literature. Where it appears, it is incidental to discussion of other subjects such as inheritance and marriage. There seems to be no idea, as in Christianity, that the corpse of the suicide is to be roughly treated as punishment for self-murder, nor is there a special penalty for the parasuicide. Thus the attitude of classical Islam to suicide is less rigid than suggested by the *ḥadīth*s.

The prohibition of suicide reflects the Islamic ethic of forbearance and patient acceptance of hardship, joined with reverence for life as a gift from God. Hence it is forbidden by the tradition even to wish for death, let alone inflict it on oneself. Nor is suicide permitted, according to the tradition, to those in extreme conditions such as severe and painful illness or grievous wounding. Suicide is finally not to be contemplated because it is God, not humankind, who has absolute power over human affairs and the term of human life; it is recorded that when a man who was mortally wounded in war killed himself, the Prophet reported God as saying, "My servant has attempted to preempt me; thus have I forbidden Paradise to him."

Religious suicide in search of transfiguration (the type of suicide found, for instance, in Jainism and Catharism) is unknown in Islam. Nor has there been any history of collective suicide, perhaps because Islam has not often been in the position of a persecuted minority. Religious suicide in the sense of self-sacrifice for a religious cause is restrained by the ethic of *taqīyah* ("caution"), according to which the beliefs of an individual must remain concealed or even dissimulated in order to avoid danger and ensure individual and community survival. This ethic is current in both Shīʿī and Sunnī Islam, each of which accepts the well-known tradition, "*Taqīyah* is the shield of the believer." In Shīʿī Islam, however, *taqīyah* is elevated to a cardinal virtue, the result of a sometimes precarious minority position. Thus—despite the example furnished by the passion of Ḥusayn ibn ʿAlī, the grandson of the Prophet and one of the most prominent of the Shīʿī imams—the Shīʿīs in particular have disapproved of sacrificial religious suicide. [*See* Taqīyah.] A significant exception to the prohibition of sacrificial religious suicide is the sect of the Nizārī Ismāʿīlīs, who in the twelfth century became notorious for sending suicidal assassins against their enemies.

Notwithstanding this disapprobation, Muslims, especially Shīʿī Muslims, have recently become known for carrying out "suicidal" military missions. Such incidents have taken place in this century not only in the Middle East but also elsewhere in the Muslim world, for instance in Islamic Southeast Asia and have invariably been a response to the overwhelming force of Western hegemony. Many Muslims, however, have perceived these actions as a necessary part of active armed struggle and the death that results as martyrdom *(shahādah)* rather than suicide. The phenomenon is therefore best considered under that heading. Cases in which there is a pure idealization of death sanctioned by religious authority (as happened to a degree in Iran during the Iran-Iraq war) are more difficult to classify. [*See* Martyrdom.]

The rate of suicide among Muslims in modern times appears to be remarkably low. It is a fraction of the rate in Western countries, and also much lower than that of most non-Muslim developing countries. Moreover, in mixed populations Muslims consistently demonstrate a lower rate of suicide than non-Muslims (although the rate may be dramatically higher among emigrants in Western settings, as has been shown to be the case in France). These conclusions, however, have been questioned on the grounds that there are few reliable statistics for Islamic nations. In particular, it is likely that the rate of suicide and parasuicide has been underreported, since concealment of suicide is thought to occur more frequently in traditional societies, in which it may involve greater social consequences. Finally, there is the suspicion that a low incidence of suicide is correlated with the factor of traditional society, with which Islam still largely coincides, rather than with a particular religion. Nevertheless, a recent crossnational statistical study (Miles E. Simpson and George H. Conklin, "Socio-economic Development, Suicide and Religion: A Test of Durkheim's Theory of Religion and Suicide," *Social Forces* 64.4 [June 1989]: 945–964) finds the percentage of Muslims in the population to be in significant negative relation to a nation's suicide rate, a result that holds even when controlling for economic, social, and demographic modernity. Sociological, medical, and other scientific studies on Muslim suicide have not, however, inquired specifically into the nature of religious beliefs or other religious factors inhibiting self-inflicted violence.

Modern Muslim thinkers have shown little interest in the question of *intiḥār*. This is very different from the case of the Western world, where vigorous debate on suicide began in the seventeenth century as a protest of secular humanism against the rigid attitudes of Christianity and was intensified in the centuries following owing to an exploding rate of suicide. In the Islamic world, in contrast, there has been no great wave of secularism or humanism nor any rapid rise in the suicide rate to force the question. Furthermore, Islam does not stipulate, as Christianity does, gruesome temporal punishments for the parasuicide and the body of the suicide, practices that helped spark the debate in the West.

Contemporary Islamic discussion of suicide proceeds along the lines of the traditions and classical interpretation. The familiar themes are present: suicide is a sin because only God has the right to take the life he has granted; it is forbidden for Muslims to wish for death, no matter what their condition; and the suicide may receive the funeral prayer. It is also sometimes asserted by modern Muslim thinkers that suicide indicates a decrease in faith, since religion tends to alleviate mental depression and the pain of life's tragedies, and that atheism is a prime cause of the spread of suicide. This may indicate an awareness of the conclusions of Western research into the subject of suicide and religion.

[*See also* Funerary Rites; Sin.]

BIBLIOGRAPHY

Headley, Lee A., ed. *Suicide in Asia and the Near East*. Berkeley, 1983. Includes medical/statistical studies on Singapore, Sri Lanka, Iran, Pakistan, Kuwait, Iraq, Syria, Jordan, and Egypt, but neglects religious factors.

Mahmood, Tahir, et al. "Symposium: Organ Transplant—Euthanasia—Right to Die: Indian and Islamic Legal Responses." *Islamic and Comparative Law Quarterly* 7.2 (1987): 111–164. Rare discussion of suicide and "the right to die" from the perspective of Islamic law and Islamic medical ethics.

Rosenthal, Franz. "On Suicide in Islam." *Journal of the American Oriental Society* 66 (1946): 239–259. Consideration of the Qur'ān and *ḥadīth* material, followed by discussion of nontheological opinions, including those influenced by Greek thought. The standard study, with copious references. Notes occurrences of suicide in classical times, but does not cover the modern period.

Rosenthal, Franz. "Intiḥār." In *Encyclopaedia of Islam*, new ed., vol. 3, pp. 1246–1248. Leiden, 1960–. Contains some material additional to the earlier article by Rosenthal listed above.

The *ḥadīths* referred to are recorded, in different versions, in the standard collections. They may be found in the following "books": Funerals (*Janā'iz*), Sickness or Medicine (*Maraḍ; Ṭibb*), *Jihād*, and Faith (*Īmān*). The collections of al-Bukhārī, Muslim, and Abū Dāwūd have been translated into English.

A small number of scientific studies on suicide in individual Islamic countries and Muslim populations have been published in various disciplines; refer to the appropriate indexes. Reliable statistics are scarce. A starting point useful for comparison of suicide rates is the *World Health Statistics Annual* (Geneva, 1962–) of the World Health Organization (United Nations).

LYNDA CLARKE

SULTAN. The Arabic word *sulṭān* is used to denote power, might, and authority, or the possessor of such power, a ruler. In the Qur'ān it refers to divinely vouchsafed authority or a divine mandate, usually in the context of prophecy (7.71, 23.45). In later *ḥadīth* literature, it is often used to denote worldly power or the possessor of governmental authority (Ibn Ḥanbal 6.128–129, 452; 3.404; and Ibn Mājah, 2766–2768).

The term first appears as the official title of a ruler under the Seljuks of Baghdad (1055–1157), under whom governmental power and coercive force were monopolized by the sultan and his agent the vizier (*wazīr*), while authority remained vested in the ʿAbbāsid caliph as imam of the Muslim community. The lack of articulation between loci of power and authority led to the composition of treatises that theoretically defined the roles of sultan and imam. Al-Māwardī (d. 1058), a jurist from Baghdad and author of one of the most influential treatises, emphasized the authority of the caliph over the sultan in order to strengthen the former's hand against the military commanders who held power behind the throne. His views were opposed by the theologian al-Juwaynī (d. 1085), a protegé of the Seljuk vizier Niẓām al-Mulk (d. 1092), who implied that a sultan or an *amīr* was even more necessary than the caliph. The duties of al-Juwaynī's *amīr* mirrored those of the Seljuk sultan: prosecuting *jihād*, appointing officials and judges, and maintaining a standing army. To aid in these tasks, a vizier could be appointed to administer the state bureaucracy and raise revenues for the army. Many of al-Juwaynī's ideas were endorsed by his student al-Ghazālī (d. 1111), who conceived of the sultanate as a bridge between religion (*dīn*) and the state (*dawlah*). Since public policy in Islam is based on the *sharīʿah*, temporal power owes its legitimacy to the fact that it preserves religion. Because maintaining God's laws demands a powerful executive, the sultan—as upholder of the *sharīʿah*—is as necessary as the caliph himself. The ideal Islamic state is thus a triangle of complementarity, in which the caliph guarantees the *sharīʿah*, the sultan preserves it, and the *ʿulamā'* (religious scholars) interpret it.

In subsequent centuries, various combinations of al-Māwardī's, al-Juwaynī's, and al-Ghazālī's theories of the sultanate were used as ideological justifications for authoritarian regimes. The Ottomans (c. 1324–1924) combined al-Juwaynī's and al-Ghazālī's models to justify their claims of universal legitimacy in the absence of the ʿAbbāsid caliph. The Saʿdian and ʿAlawī sharifs of Morocco (1510–) drew more heavily on the writings of al-Māwardī and conceived of their state as a sultanate and imamate combined. Consequently, they were not averse to appropriating caliphal titles, such as *amīr al-mu'minīn* (commander of the believers), which remains an official designation of the king of Morocco today. [*See* Amīr al-Mu'minīn; Morocco.]

Since the king of Morocco no longer holds the official title of *sulṭān*, the only meaningful heirs to the Seljuk heritage in the modern world are the rulers of Oman and Brunei and the Yang Di-Pertuan Agong of Malaysia. The Omani example is the closest to the classical model. Since Oman has no constitution, absolute power is vested in the sultan, who retains executive, legislative, judicial, and military authority. The country is governed through eight national councils and a council of ministers, headed by a prime minister who is appointed by the sultan himself. The *sharīʿah*, as interpreted by the Ibāḍī school of the Khārijī sect, serves as the basis of sultanic authority. [*See* Ibāḍī Dynasty; Oman.] Malaysia, by contrast, is a fully constitutional sultanate headed by the Yang Di-Pertuan Agong. Elected from among the rulers of the nine peninsular Malay states, he serves a term of five years, after which the electors select a successor from among themselves. The main responsibilities of the Yang Di-Pertuan Agong are to symbolize the unity of the Federation, to safeguard the position of Malays in Malaysian society, and to act as head of the Islamic religion for his own state as well as Melaka, Penang, the Federal Territory, Sabah, and Sarawak. Although he may appoint a prime minister at his own discretion, he can act only with the advice of a cabinet drawn from the majority party in parliament. Most of the Yang Di-Pertuan Agong's official duties are commensurate with those of constitutional monarchs in Europe.

[*See also* Amīr; Caliph; Imam; Vizier.]

BIBLIOGRAPHY

Allen, Calvin H., Jr. *Oman: The Modernization of the Sultanate*. Boulder, 1987. Introduction to the development of modern Oman, particularly good for the general reader.

Hallaq, Wael B. "Caliphs, Jurists, and the Saljūqs in the Political Thought of Juwaynī." *Muslim World* 74 (January 1984): 26–41. Detailed examination of Juwaynī's treatise on the state.

Lambton, Ann K. S. *State and Government in Medieval Islam*. Oxford, 1981. The best overall introduction to classical Islamic political theory, stressing the contributions of jurists.

Suffian, Tun Mohamed, et al., eds. *The Constitution of Malaysia: Its Development; 1957–1977*. Kuala Lumpur, 1978. Critical study of the separation of powers in the Malaysian constitution.

Waterbury, John. *The Commander of the Faithful: The Moroccan Political Elite; a Study in Segmented Politics*. New York, 1970. The standard work on Islamic political theory and the modern Moroccan state.

VINCENT J. CORNELL

SUNNAH. The Arabic term *sunnah* since pre-Islamic times has signified established custom, precedent, the conduct of life, and cumulative tradition. In a general sense, such tradition encompasses knowledge and practices believed to have been passed down from previous generations and representing an authoritative, valued, and continuing corpus of beliefs and customs. In the context of early Muslim juridical and theological development, the word *sunnah* came to connote a more specific notion: that the actions and sayings of the prophet Muḥammad complemented the divinely revealed message of the Qur'ān and embodied a paradigm and a model, constituting a source for establishing norms for Muslim conduct.

In the Qur'ān the term *sunnah* occurs in several contexts. It is used with reference to the established practice of earlier peoples and of the Arabs (8.38); it is also associated with previous messengers of God and more specifically identified as the *sunnah* of God, characterized as continuous and unchanging (17.76–77, 33.62, 48.22–23). It is this latter emphasis, grounded in a notion of continuous revelation, that is used in the Qur'ān to challenge the idea of an outmoded or collective sense of tradition, valued simply because of its ancestral or local roots. The *sunnah* of God had primacy over other versions because it was being revealed through Muḥammad, who was to be obeyed as the recipient, mediator, and exemplar of this version of the authentic tradition.

Early Muslim scholars further developed and elaborated the concept of the *sunnat al-Nabī* in their search to recapture as complete a picture of the Prophet's exemplary life as they could authenticate on the basis of the *ḥadīth,* accounts of his words and deeds transmitted by his companions and others from the first generation of Muslims. This quest to memorialize the life of the Prophet and ground it in a historically verifiable process also led to a type of literary reconstruction of the narrative of the Prophet's life called *sīrah*. All these forms of enactment acted as reference points that would subsequently inform and inspire various Muslim communities of interpretation as they sought to ground their own juridical, doctrinal, and historical identities in what they perceive to be the normative *sunnah*.

In this earlier period of Muslim history and thought, the oral nature of the transmission of *ḥadīth,* as well as attempts to document it, through *isnād* (a chain of transmitters) gave rise to several competing versions of the elements that constituted the valid *sunnah*. The methodology and dialectical mode of argument that shaped the debates and discussion, however, provided a common frame of reference that looked to the Prophet's example to substantiate a given point of view. Thus the whole process by which thinkers arrived at various forms of understanding and definition of the *sunnah* must be seen as a dynamic one. It mirrored the diversity and difference prevalent in the intellectual life of the early Muslim community. The concept of the *sunnah,* however, always retained its overarching importance in shaping Muslim religious discourse, providing a wider field of discussion in which the Qur'ān and the Prophet's paradigmatic behavior were always central to the quest for meaning and certainty in practice and doctrine.

Modern academic studies of the development of Muslim law and jurisprudence have come to focus on how the concept of the *sunnah* of the Prophet originated and became normative. One of the central theses, emerging from the work of earlier scholars such as Goldziher and Schacht, maintained that the sources of juristic development lay in the practices of the early Muslim community, several generations after the death of the Prophet. This living tradition, the accepted practice of these communities, was systematized by the discursive and consensual experience of Muslim scholars who gave intellectual leadership to a number of such local communities in the expanding Muslim world. The idea of the *sunnah* of the Prophet, particularly in Schacht's view, was developed by such Muslim scholars, who in their quest to justify and authenticate existing practices equated the living tradition with the supposed practice of the Prophet and his companions. This theory questions the assumption of the Muslim scholarly tradition that there was a direct and valid link between existing practice and the words and practices of the Prophet. In fact, Schacht argued, much of the *ḥadīth* tradition related to jurisprudence was invented, and the *sunnah* of the Prophet was a concept retrospectively imposed on an older idea of *sunnah*. This thesis has been widely contested by later Western and Muslim scholars alike on methodological and textual grounds. Although details regarding the crystallization of the concept of the *sunnah* and the reliability of elements of the *ḥadīth* are still in dispute, consensus has emerged in current scholarship that an emphasis on the merely positivistic aspects of the origin of the *ḥadīth* unduly reduces the concept of the *sunnah* to a formal and legal construct and severely limits its wider meaning in Muslim thought and practice.

Recent scholars, building on epistemological and hermeneutical stances prevalent in current comparative studies, have attempted to widen the basis for studying *sunnah*. They tend to emphasize questions of how oral traditions and written texts are produced, transmitted, and interpreted, and they have further attempted to relate these interpretations to specific communities of scholars, social boundaries, and political contexts. In this wider view the *sunnah* appears as a multivalent concept, illustrating how different kinds of Muslim orientations and institutions have found literary formulation, expression, and codification in law, ethics, theology, and mysticism. The *sunnah* serves as a common template for all these Muslim groups and individuals, permitting them to represent a connection with the beginnings of Islam and acting as a common referent in the religious discourse of community formation and identity.

Role and Function in Islamic Thought and Practice. The formative period of Muslim legal thought and practice is marked by pluralism, reflected in the different schools and communities of legal interpretation. The earliest texts that survive from this period also suggest that the development of a discursive and hermeneutic style embraced debate and reflected divergence. However, the expansion of Muslim territory and administrative control, the presence of local tradition and practice in these areas, and the need to create an integrated framework for dealing with emerging legal and administrative problems provided a context for Muslim rulers and scholars to reconcile and synthesize this diversity. One such synthesis, developed in the second century of Islam by al-Shāfiʿī, reflects the formal incorporation of *sunnah* as a primary source within a coherent theory of jurisprudence. Dealing with the *uṣūl al-fiqh*, the foundations of jurisprudence, Shāfiʿī argued for a much stricter definition of *sunnah* in order to establish legislative authority. He regarded it as a source as binding as the Qur'ān, with the status of indirect revelation—because obedience to the Prophet had been decreed by God. The *sunnah* complemented and stood alongside the Qur'ān, giving precision to its precepts. Its definition thus required greater scrutiny and documentation. Shāfiʿī's insistence on this principle led to a sharp distinction between the authoritative *sunnah* that was scrupulously documented on the basis of proper *isnād* (transmission) and less authoritative versions of the *sunnah* that could not be traced back through a reliable textual link to the Prophet.

In terms of its impact on Muslim jurisprudence and legal practice, Shāfiʿī's definition of the *sunnah*—with its relation to the Qur'ān and to other derivative sources such as *qiyās* (analogical reasoning) and *ijmāʿ* (consensus)—created a more formal, rigorous, and arguably more coherent and textually grounded framework. This is not to suggest that previous or contemporaneous Muslim scholars and the legal schools associated with them gave no importance to the overriding role of the Qur'ān and *sunnah*. They are equally emphasized in the traditions traced back to Abū Ḥanīfah (702–767), Mālik ibn Anās (715–795) and Aḥmad ibn Ḥanbal (780–855), who together with Shāfiʿī' are regarded as the founders of the four established Sunnī schools of law (*madhhabs*). Shāfiʿī's critique did, however, indicate differences pertaining to the question of the authority of individual *ḥadīth* and to issues of the appropriate textual basis and documentation of the *sunnah* in deriving legal rules. The four major Sunnī schools in time agreed in insisting that the *sunnah* of the Prophet was best preserved through a legal methodology based on *uṣūl al-fiqh* and sustained in the custody of learned scholars and jurists.

According to the other major branch of Islam, Shiism, the ideals embodied in the Prophet's life could best be implemented through loyalty, devotion, and obedience to the divinely guided and properly designated imams, descended from the Prophet through his son-in-law ʿAlī and his daughter Fāṭimah. The imams taught, confirmed, and further interpreted the Qur'ān and *sunnah*. Their authoritative role ensured consistency and continuity, and their guidance and teaching were regarded as congruent and coextensive with the *sunnah* of the Prophet. These commonly held beliefs, however, was developed and implemented differently among the Shīʿī groups that emerged subsequently, such as the Ithnā ʿAsharī, Ismāʿīlī and Zaydī sects.

In addition to its significance in legal and theological writings, the *sunnah* also provided a means for a broader interpretation of the teaching and life of the prophet in the philosophical and spiritual sense. For early Muslim philosophers like al-Kindī (d. 870), al-Fārābī (d. 950), and Ibn Sīnā (d. 1037), the *sunnah* had profound philosophical implications. Prophecy represented the most perfect activity of which the human representative faculty was capable. The Prophet's soul was purified and inspired and was not in need of philosophical training. As the perfect ruler, the Prophet was also a lawgiver and the head of a polity, whose goal it was to enable those living in that society to attain happiness in this world and hereafter. The *sunnah* embraced the practical workings of society as set out by an authoritative legal system, but it also offered the possibility of disciplined intellectual inquiry. Intellectual and theoretical contemplation were to be regarded as an integral part of prophecy. A very similar philosophical conception of *sunnah* is evident among the esoteric schools of Shiism, for whom the *sunnah* encompassed the exoteric as well as esoteric pattern reflected in the teachings of the Prophet and imams. This teaching made possible a fuller unfolding of the rational capacity, permitting an integrated understanding of the totality of knowledge in Islam.

In Ṣūfī writings, which reflect an emphasis on the mystical dimension of Muslim thought and practice, the *sunnah* includes the Prophet's spirituality and the presence in his life of values such as self-transcendence and the act of personal remembrance of God in the heart. These values and their practice were believed to have been taught by the Prophet and transmitted through an unbroken line (*silsilah*) of Ṣūfī teachers. Such a spiritual paradigm provided a concrete example of how Muslims might emulate the Prophet's night vigils and be inspired to embark upon the path of spiritual self-perfection that had led the Prophet to the divine presence (Qur'ān, 17.1). Among the Ṣūfīs, the *ḥadīth* or *qudsī*, narratives of the Prophet containing divine sayings, had special significance in highlighting the mystical dimension of the *sunnah* and its role in promoting piety, devotion, and spiritual understanding.

Changing Interpretations. The dynamics of Muslim history since the late eighteenth century, including an extended period of interaction, influence, and colonization by European powers, have created dramatically different conditions for the maintenance of inherited Muslim institutions and ideals. In many societies the authoritative role and shared sense of significance associated with the concept of the *sunnah,* and by the legal and ethical behavior and norms inspired by it, was curtailed or marginalized. New codes appropriated from European models and systems assumed a more prominent role, particularly in the areas of law, public administration, and governance.

This pattern of erosion was challenged by several Muslim intellectual reformers across the Muslim world. Muḥammad ʿAbduh (1849–1905), for instance, in his role as teacher at al-Azhar and *muftī* of Egypt, challenged the view that Islam could not be reconciled with progress and a scientific worldview. He argued for the renewal of *ijtihād* (independent interpretation) and criticized *taqlīd* (unthinking acceptance of received tradition). He distinguished between essentials and nonessentials in the body of law and belief and urged Muslims to apply reason to the primary sources of Islam. Such a view influenced scholars in other parts of the Muslim world who were led to develop ideas that related the sources of Islam to changes in society and a newly emerging spirit of nationalism.

Among those whose views have been labeled literalist or fundamentalist, the normative character of the *sunnah* and its authority were regarded as unchanging and not subject to the vicissitudes of human thought or manipulation. It could only be mediated through the existing system of traditional juristic practice. Others, while according the sources primacy, contended that the vitality of the concept of *sunnah* was reflected in the historical role it had played as a tool in effecting change for the general benefit of society. Its role was not simply restrictive, but rather enabling.

In the later part of the twentieth century this issue has taken on greater significance because many Muslim countries, as part of policies aimed at islamization, wish to recover and define a role for tradition in sanctioning their codified legal systems. Such has been the case in Egypt, Iran, Libya, Pakistan, Saudi Arabia, the Sudan, and the United Arab Emirates, among others. There is in all these instances an increasing recognition of the historical diversity that has existed and the need to reconcile the many strands of influence that have constituted past practice and inherited custom, within the paradigm of the *sunnah*. As in the past, the narrative force of the *sunnah* continues to transcend the public and rhetorical uses to which it may be put, fostering self-identity and enhancing the private moral lives of Muslims wherever they live.

[See also Ḥadīth; *and* Muḥammad, *articles on* Life of the Prophet *and* Biographies.]

BIBLIOGRAPHY

Azami, Muhammad Mustafa. *On Schacht's Origins of Muhammadan Jurisprudence*. New York, 1985. Critique of the standard thesis in Western scholarship on the origin of concepts such as *sunnah*, as appropriated in Sunnī Muslim jurisprudence.

Burton, John. *The Sources of Islamic Law: Islamic Theories of Abrogation*. Edinburgh, 1990. Study of early sources dealing with the development of rules pertaining to abrogation in Muslim juristic interpretation as applied to injunctions based on the Qur'ān and *sunnah*.

Calder, Norman. *Studies in Early Muslim Jurisprudence*. Oxford, 1993. Well-documented study that presents an alternative thesis on the constituent elements reflected in the works of early Muslim jurisprudents.

Coulson, Noel. J. *Conflicts and Tensions in Islamic Jurisprudence*. Chicago, 1969. Analysis of how conflicting views and situations arise in Muslim practice, past and present, and how they are dealt with in jurisprudence practice.

Graham, William A. *Divine Word and Prophetic Word in Early Islam*. The Hague, 1977. Building on sound scholarship and a broader understanding of the meaning of foundational religious discourse, this work traces the complex and early relationship between the Qur'ānic revelation and Prophetic sayings.

Juynboll, G. H. A. *Muslim Tradition: Studies in Chronology, Provenance, and Authorship of Early Ḥadīth*. Cambridge, 1983. Mildly revisionist attempt to establish the basis for the authenticity of some of the early *ḥadīths*.

Khadduri, Majid, and Herbert J. Liebesny, eds. *Law in the Middle East*. 2 vols. Washington, D.C., 1955. Though dated in some respects, this work contains a good selection of representative articles on different schools and periods of Muslim law.

Messick, Brinkley. *The Calligraphic State: Textual Domination and History in a Muslim Society*. Berkeley, 1993. Though focused on Yemen, the work contains many insights into how legal ideals are textualized and institutionalized.

Naʿīm, ʿAbd Allāh Aḥmad. *Towards an Islamic Reformation: Civil Liberties, Human Rights, and International Law*. Syracuse, N.Y., 1990. Sudanese Muslim scholar's attempt to reinterpret Muslim principles such as *sunnah*, in the context of human rights issues and international law.

Powers, David S. *Studies in Qur'an and Ḥadīth: The Formation of the Islamic Law of Inheritance*. Berkeley, 1990. Using one facet of Muslim law, the author traces the interaction between Qur'ānic requirements and subsequent developments.

Rahman, Fazlur. *Islam and Modernity: Transformation of an Intellectual Tradition*. Chicago, 1982. The late noted scholar's contribution to how modern Muslim thought can revitalize itself, based on the Qur'ān and past intellectual tradition.

Sachedina, A. A. *The Just Ruler (al-Sulṭan al-ʿĀdil) in Shīʿite Islam*. New York, 1988. Comprehensive treatment of the history of Shīʿī jurisprudence and the doctrine of custodial authority of the jurist-theologians.

Schacht, Joseph. *Origins of Muhammadan Jurisprudence*. Oxford, 1950. Still regarded by many as the standard work of Western scholarship on the origin and legal development of concepts such as *sunnah*.

Shāfiʿī, Muḥammad ibn Idrīs al-. *Islamic Jurisprudence: Al-Shāfiʿī's Risāla*. Translated by Majid Khadduri. Baltimore, 1961. Pioneering work on jurisprudence by the ninth-century founder of one of the Sunnī schools of law.

Waldman, Marilyn Robinson. "Sunnah." In *The Encyclopedia of Religion*, vol. 14, pp. 149–153. New York, 1987. Excellent and nuanced summation.

Weiss, Bernard G. *The Search for God's Law: Islamic Jurisprudence in the Writings of Sayf al-Din al-Amidi*. Salt Lake City, 1993. Helpful study, focusing on the work of a thirteenth-century scholar.

Azim A. Nanji

SUNNĪ ISLAM. [*This entry comprises two articles. The first provides a historical overview of the major branch of the worldwide Muslim community; the second traces the development of Sunnī thought in the nineteenth and twentieth centuries.*]

Historical Overview

Practiced by the majority of Muslims, Sunnī Islam refers primarily to the customary practice of the prophet Muḥammad. The term *Sunnī* (sometimes rendered "Sunnite") derives from *sunnah* and has the general meaning of "customary practice." This practice, this *sunnah*, is preserved in the *ḥadīth*, the Tradition, which consists of the accounts of what the Prophet said or did and sometimes of his tacit approval of an action. The Tradition, in addition to the Qur'ān is one of the sources of Sunnī religious law. Another source is the consensus of religious scholars, *al-ijmāʿ*. This concept of consensus reflects the emphasis in Sunnī Islam on community and its collective wisdom, guided by the Qur'ān and the *sunnah*. Thus, Sunnī Muslims have referred to themselves as *ahl al-sunna wa al-jamāʿah* ("people of the *sunnah* and the community").

Sunnī Islam, however, is not monolithic. It is comprised of different theological schools and legal schools, as well as a variety of attitudes and outlooks conditioned by historical setting, by locale, and by cultural circumstances. Sunnī Muslims do share, however, certain distinctive beliefs. They differ the the Shīʿah, "the party of ʿAlī" (the Prophet's cousin and son-in-law) in denying that the Prophet designated ʿAlī to succeed him as leader of the Islamic community: ʿAlī, the fourth of the rightly guided caliphs, *al-khulafā' al-Rāshidūn,* like the first three, became a legitimate caliph through a form of public acclamation. They also distinguish themselves from other Islamic sects whose views, they maintain, constitute *bidaʿ* (sg., *bidʿah;* "innovations"), departures from what the community at large holds.

Sunnī Islam developed as a result of political and religious struggles within Islam that began very early in its history. The history of these struggles is complex, but certain historical facts stand out. A key event was an army mutiny in 656 CE. It resulted in the murder of the third caliph, ʿUthmān, a member of the Umayyad clan of the Meccan Quraysh. ʿAlī was acclaimed caliph, but ʿUthmān's kinsman, the Umayyad Muʿāwiyah, governor of Syria, demanded that ʿAlī bring to justice the murderers of ʿUthmān and refused to acknowledge him as caliph. During the ensuing inconclusive civil war between them, part of ʿAlī's army withdrew its support from him but remained opposed to Muʿāwiyah. This group was the basis of the sect of "the Seceders," (al-Khawārij) with their various divisions, who rejected both ʿUthmān and ʿAlī as legitimate caliphs and who confronted Muslims with pivotal theological questions that conditioned the development of sectarian thought. In 661, after a Khārijī assassinated ʿAlī, Muʿāwiyah was acknowledged caliph, initiating a dynastic caliphate, the Umayyad, which lasted until 750.

This period witnessed the polarization of political and religious attitudes that became formalized doctrine. Disputes arose over such questions as the definition of true belief, the status of those who profess Islam but commit a great sin, freedom, and determinism. These remained basic questions discussed by later Sunnī thinkers who sought to formulate theologies consistent with the Qur'ān and the *sunnah.* In 750 the Umayyad Caliphate was toppled by the ʿAbbāsids, descendants of the Prophet's uncle al-ʿAbbās. During the ensuing ʿAbbāsid Caliphate (750–1258), Sunnī Islam came into its own. The four schools of Sunnī law, initiated by Abū Ḥanīfah (d. 767), Mālik ibn Anas (d. 795), al-Shāfiʿī (d. 820), and Ibn Ḥanbal (d. 855) became firmly established. The history of Sunnī Islam in this period is marked by the reaction of Muslims to two things: excessive rationalism in theology and developments in Shiism. [*See* Law, *article on* Sunnī Schools of Law.]

The rationalist school of speculative theology *(kalām),* the Muʿtazilah, which had its roots in the late Umayyad period, alienated the more conventional Muslims, for whom Muʿtazilī intellectualism missed the spirit and intention of the Qur'ān. Things came to a head when the caliph al-Maʿmūn (r. 813–833) espoused Muʿtazilah and attempted to impose its doctrine of the created Qur'ān. This attempt, which continued with his two successors, saw the persecution of dissenters, including Ibn Ḥanbal. A reaction to Muʿtazilah set in. It lost its political power as well as its position of dominance as a school of *kalām* and was superseded by the school of al-Ashʿarī (d. 935), who used the method of the *kalām* to defend traditional Islamic belief. This does not mean that all Sunnīs are Ashʿarīyah. Some subscribe to another school of Sunnī *kalām,* that of al-Māturīdī (d. 944); others totally disavow *kalām.*

Shiism in the ʿAbāssid period was dominated by two related groups, the Ismāʿīlīyah, or Seveners, and the Ithnā ʿAsharīyah, or Twelvers. Both maintained that the rightful Islamic leader, the *imām,* must be a descendant of al-Ḥusayn, son of ʿAlī and Fāṭimah, the Prophet's daughter, and that this *imām* was endowed with special knowledge. They disagreed, however, on who was the rightful seventh *imām.* The Twelvers gained prestige and influence when the Shīʿī Būyid dynasty became the effective ruler in Baghdad (945–1055) although it continued to acknowledge the ʿAbbāsid caliph. The Ismāʿīlīyah established in 910 a countercaliphate, the Fāṭimid, in North Africa, conquered Egypt in 969, and made it their base. The tenth century witnessed a veritable growth of Shīʿī power. In the eleventh century, however, Sunnī power revived when the Seljuk Turks, who were Sunnīs, conquered Baghdad in 1055. They provided effective military opposition to the Fāṭimids in Syria and ideological opposition through the writings of such prominent Sunnī thinkers as Abū

Ḥamīd al-Ghazālī (d. 1111). Islam's great countercrusader, the Sunnī Saladin (Ṣalāḥ al-Dīn; d. 1193), brought an end to the Fāṭimid caliphate in 1171. Twelver Shiism fared better when Shah Ismāʿīl (d. 1523), founder of the Ṣafavid Persian state, espoused it; this strong base in Iran still exists today. The larger Ottoman Empire, however, the rival of the Ṣafavid, was Sunnī. In the late twentieth century the great majority of Muslims continue to be Sunnī.

[*See also* ʿAbbāsid Caliphate; Islam, *overview article;* Ismāʿīlīyah; Ithnā ʿAsharīyah; Khawārij; Shīʿī Islam, *historical overview article;* and Umayyad Caliphate.]

BIBLIOGRAPHY

Coulson, Noel J. *A History of Islamic Law.* Edinburgh, 1964. Readable and comprehensive general introduction that also contains very helpful bibliographical guidance.

Macdonald, D. B. *Development of Muslim Theology, Jurisprudence and Constitutional Theory* (1906). Reprint, Beirut, 1965. At one time a standard study, but now somewhat outdated; nonetheless, still very useful.

Rahman, Fazlur. *Islam.* London, 1966. Although this book assumes some background knowledge of Islam, it is rich in content and discusses issues essential to Sunnism and its development.

Watt, W. Montgomery. *The Formative Period of Islamic Thought.* Edinburgh, 1973. Standard study, excellent in every way; analytic, readable, comprehensive. Offers thought-provoking interpretive hypotheses.

Wensinck, A. J. *The Muslim Creed.* Leiden, 1932. Remains a very valuable study, though somewhat dated and not without a goodly share of "Western" assumptions.

MICHAEL E. MARMURA

Modern Sunnī Thought

Any consideration of modern Sunnī thought has to take into account new interpretations of the Qur'ān, which started to appear at the end of the nineteenth century in the works of reformers who wanted to go back to scripture and early tradition in order to renew Islamic thought. Because any innovating thought that wants to carry weight for a Muslim audience has to refer to the Qur'ān, the reformers Muḥammad ʿAbduh (1849–1905) and Muḥammad Rashīd Riḍā (1865–1935) presented their ideas in the form of a new commentary on the Qur'ān, which was published in the monthly issues of the Egyptian journal *Al-manār* between 1903 and 1935 (later published separately in twelve volumes). A number of such *tafsīrs* (exegetical studies) produced in twentieth-century Egypt have been studied by Jacques Jomier, J. J. G. Jansen, and I. M. al-Sharqāwī; those by ʿĀ'ishah ʿAbd al-Raḥmān (Bint al-Shāṭi') and Sayyid Quṭb deserve to be mentioned here. In the Indo-Pakistan subcontinent, Sayyid Aḥmad Khān's (1817–1898) commentary on the first seventeen surahs of the Qur'ān (seven vols., 1880–1907) was the first modern reformist commentary. Together with subsequent commentaries, the two most noteworthy of which are those by Abū al-Kalām Āzād (1888–1958) and Ghulām Aḥmad Parwez (b. 1903), it has been studied by J. M. S. Baljon. In the 1940s, the Egyptian scholar Amīn al-Khūlī at the University of Cairo, along with his students Muḥammad Aḥmad Khalafallāh and ʿĀ'ishah ʿAbd al-Raḥmān, initiated a new approach to the study of the Qur'ān, regarding it as a literary document to be studied by literary methods without the interference of theological doctrine. In 1947, Khalafallāh submitted his doctoral dissertation on the art of narration in the Qur'ān (in Arabic) in which he proved that the Qur'ān contains reinterpretations of earlier versions of scriptural stories. It met with strong resistance from al-Azhar authorities and could only be published in 1951, in a revised version. More recently, research has been carried out on the Qur'ān by Ḥamad Naṣr Abū Zayd at the University of Cairo. [*See the biographies of ʿAbduh, Rashīd Riḍā, ʿAbd al-Raḥmān, Quṭb, Aḥmad Khān, Āzād, and Khalafallāh.*]

Besides his Qur'ānic research and other publications on Islam, Sayyid Aḥmad Khān carried out extensive studies on Christianity that resulted in a commentary on the first chapters of Genesis and Matthew (1862, 1865, 1887), and the Egyptian scholar Muḥammad Kāmil Ḥusayn also paid considerable attention to the study of Christianity in addition to his work on the Qur'ān.

Two Algerian scholars have also developed new approaches to the Qur'ān. One scholar, Malek Bennabi, has concentrated on how to understand the Qur'ān as revelation and how to account for Muḥammad's subjectivity in the revelatory process. Published in France in 1946, his book *The Qur'ānic Phenomena* appeared in English translation in 1988. The other scholar, Mohammed Arkoun (b. 1928), in his publications pays attention to "reading" the Qur'ān in the light of modern semiotic theory. The problem of interpreting scriptural texts in general is redefined by Arkoun in modern terms in his book *Lectures du Coran* (1982) and other publications in French, still to be translated into English. Especially Arkoun's publications distinguish themselves from the thousands of nineteenth- and twentieth-century Sunnī publications on the Qur'ān by the new questions they ask about the literary and historical aspects of the Qur'ān and its hermeneutics. [*See the biography of Arkoun.*]

In recent years, renewed attention has been paid to the *sīrah* literature, which deals with the biography of Muḥammad. Quite a few literary biographies of the person of Muḥammad have seen the light since World War I; the main Egyptian ones were studied by E. S. Sabanegh in his book *Muhammad: Le prophète* (Paris and Rome, 1983). Al-Qummānī has studied the sociopolitical conditions of ancient Mecca in search of historical causes for the rise of the Islamic state under Muḥammad's leadership. The question of the reliability of *ḥadīth*s on the subject is part of the broader field of Muslim work on *ḥadīth* literature. Western scholarship has denied the historical authenticity of at least part of this literature. Several Muslim scholars recognize the historical problems involved, and Muslim scholarship on the question of the historical authenticity of these texts has been studied by G. H. A. Juynboll.

Another field of major concern in nineteenth- and twentieth-century Sunnī thought is *sharīʿah* (the divine law). Whereas the writings of the great medieval *fuqahā'* (jurisprudents) continue to enjoy high prestige and are considered to be authoritative, Fazlur Rahman and other twentieth-century modernist reformers recognize that the *fiqh* (jurisprudence) treatises remain human formulations of what is considered divine law. Such formulations from the past have to be checked over and over again, on the one hand, against scriptural data, interpreted with the help of reason, and, on the other, against present-day life situations and problems. Formulating *sharīʿah* in human terms, consequently, is an ongoing enterprise. Uniquely, Muʿammar al-Qadhdhāfī contends that *sharīʿah* should be based on the Qur'ān only. Much thought has been given to matters related to *sharīʿah*, as distinct from the civil codes enacted in nearly all Muslim countries in the course of the twentieth century.

At the end of the nineteenth century, Muḥammad ʿAbduh had admitted that *fuqahā'* can draw on the four recognized *fiqh* schools (*madhhab*s) for the study of what *sharīʿah* implies in specific cases. Around sixty years later, Maḥmūd Shaltūt added the Shīʿī Ithnā ʿAsharī *madhhab*. By thus combining not only different Qur'ānic texts but also opinions drawn from different law schools, it turned out to be possible to "modernize" or liberalize certain traditionally valid rules about polygamy, repudiation, and divorce.

No less spectacular has been the development of thought about the implications of *sharīʿah* for constitutional law and the organization of the state. The immediate cause of the revision of traditional doctrine was the formal abolition of the caliphate (which had already been reduced to a largely titular post) by the Turkish National Assembly first in November 1922 and definitively in March 1924. In 1922–1923, Muḥammad Rashīd Riḍā had already proposed a new concept of the caliphate as a parallel religious and political structure which would encompass all Muslim countries. In 1925, the Egyptian scholar ʿAlī ʿAbd al-Rāziq published a study on Islam and the fundamentals of government (in Arabic); he used powerful arguments to deny that the institution of the caliphate has a Qur'ānic and Islamic foundation, as well as to combat the traditional idea that Islam requires a particular form of state and government. He asserted that Muslims are free to choose the form of government they prefer in their countries, since political authority does not constitute a fundamental principle of Islam. This was, of course, meant to give Muslims responsibility for the particular ways in which they wanted to build their states. Since the author made a distinction between Muḥammad as a prophet and religious teacher of eternal truth and as a statesman in historical circumstances, he asserted that the religious character of Islam is distinct from its political character, implying a separation between religion and state. This went against established tradition and doctrine, and ʿAbd al-Rāziq's book was banned by al-Azhar. It should be realized that in the 1920s the question of the caliphate and the implications of its abolition by the Turkish government led to discussions all over the Muslim world, but in particular in the Near East and India. In Turkey, the USSR, and a few other countries, there were jurists who favored a separation between *sharīʿah* and the state, that is, between state and religion. At present this position is defended by Muḥammad Saʿīd al-ʿAshmāwī in Egypt, in his *Al-Islām al-siyāsī* (Political Islam; Cairo, 1987). [*See the biography of ʿAbd al-Rāziq.*]

The reaction came not only from al-Azhar, bastion of established Islam, but also from the circle of the Muslim Brotherhood, founded in Egypt in 1928 and spread to Syria, Palestine, and elsewhere over the next twenty years. It was held in these quarters that Islam prescribes an Islamic social order (*al-niẓām al-islāmī*), and the idea developed that such an Islamic social order could only be developed in an Islamic state (*al-dawlah al-*

islāmīyah). Under the circumstances of the time (foreign rule, World War II, the establishment of the state of Israel), the vision of an Islamic state, if necessary to be established by force, gained ground among the Muslim Brothers. The Muslim Brotherhood's structural parallel in Pakistan was the Jamāʿat-i Islāmī, founded by Abū al-Aʿlā Mawdūdī (1903–1979), who was intent on turning Pakistan into an Islamic state based on *sharīʿah*. More than his Egyptian counterparts, who were persecuted under the Nasser regime between 1954 and 1970, Mawdūdī described in detail the encompassing Islamic order to be realized in the hoped-for Islamic state. To achieve it, an Islamic "revolution," not necessarily of a violent nature, was required, and this would guarantee the fundamental transformation of society, its islamization. Even under Zia ul-Haq, who imposed this kind of islamization in Pakistan, the hoped-for realization of *sharīʿah* in an Islamic social order did not take place. The various Islamic states apply *sharīʿah* in widely differing ways. [*See* Muslim Brotherhood, *article on* Muslim Brotherhood in Egypt; Jamāʿat-i Islāmī; *and the biography of Mawdūdī*.]

A different kind of Sunnī thought developed when the attempt was made not to oppose Islam to things Western (as in the idea of an Islamic order and an Islamic state) but to reconcile some prominent Western ideologies with Islam. Was nationalism compatible with Islam? Until the Egyptian Revolution of 1952 al-Azhar scorned all nationalist divisions among Muslims, maintaining the ideal of the political unity of all Muslims, notwithstanding the fact that a number of new nation-states with Muslim majorities had been and were being founded. Insofar as Islamic sentiment had supported the struggle for independence, there was no conflict; the problem arose, however, when the nationalist leaders created secular rather than Islamic states. Was democracy compatible with Islam? Its proponents argued that Islam possesses an embryonic democracy in the Qur'ānic concept of *shūrā*, as an advisory council to the head of the state. It was also felt that democracy, with its insistence on the responsibility of the citizens and its legitimation of the state as representative of responsible citizens, was a necessity for the development of Muslim societies. But most Muslim societies had been governed on the lines of "Oriental despotism," religion in fact legitimizing the use of power from above. The adherents of an Islamic state affirm that the democracy which Islam brings about is different from the Western model of democracy. [*See* Democracy.]

Most discussions, however, have been carried on about the relationship between socialism and Islam; this also had an immediate political relevance, since some Muslim countries had an open market economy according to the capitalist model, whereas other Muslim countries have at times followed varieties of the socialist model. The Syrian thinker Muṣṭafā al-Sibāʿī's fervent plea for an Islamic socialism, in his 1959 book on the socialism of Islam, was welcomed by Nasser and others at the time when Egypt and other Arab countries were moving to the left. But there turned out to be several versions of Islamic socialism, one being proposed by Sayyid Quṭb, who took a critical distance to the state. There were also different versions of Arab socialism; even the Baʿth variety of the latter developed differently in Syria and Iraq. And if a revolution was to take place, should it be a socialist or an Islamic revolution? [*See also* Socialism and Islam *and the biography of Sibāʿī*.]

In any case, most Muslim thinkers stressed the idea of justice and particularly social justice in Islam. The status of women in Islam continued to be a subject of debate.

A different area of thought cherished in Muslim circles is the more speculative realm of metaphysics and theology, for instance, the problem of the relationship between reason and revelation. Traditional doctrine held that the use and domain of reason is circumscribed by the data of revelation: in the end, reason is subordinated to revelation. The modernist Sunnī reformers Sayyid Aḥmad Khān and Muḥammad ʿAbduh, however, assumed a basic parallelism of reason and revelation, in the visible as well as in the invisible sphere. Both men were inspired by the Muslim philosophical heritage and impressed by the achievements of Western science and thought. Both gave reason a higher place than it occupied in traditional *kalām* (metaphysical theology); for both there is an essential harmony among reason, revelation, and moral conscience; both accepted *sharīʿah* as basically identical with natural law; and for both Islam was a religion of progress. Both, too, acknowledged that human beings have great freedom as the authors of their actions, and both gave much attention to education in the broad sense of the word.

Muḥammad Rashīd Riḍā, too, accepted a parallelism between reason and revelation, but he accorded the former a somewhat lesser status than did ʿAbduh. In his *Islamic Reform* (Berkeley, 1966), Malcolm Kerr recognizes in ʿAbduh's attempt at a rational reform of Islam, based on its sources, a visionary character and a moral purpose. He calls Rashīd Riḍā, however, an ideologist who tried to give a revivalist interpretation of Islam, restating old doctrines in modern terms.

In recent times, the need for rationality and intellectual rigor is increasingly felt as a counterweight to the irrationalisms of modern times. In Egypt Muḥammad ʿImārah has tried to reawaken the rationality of al-Afghānī, ʿAbduh, and Rashīd Riḍā, whose works he has reedited. He has become well known through his study *Al-Islām wa-al-sulṭa al-dīnīyah* (Islam and Religious Authority; 2d ed., Beirut, 1980). Similar rational concerns are alive with present-day thinkers, such as Ḥasan Ḥanafī, who works for a new *tanwīr* (Enlightenment) in Arab-Muslim thought and wants to replace theology by anthropology. Other Muslim countries too, have their champions of rational thought, such as Muḥammad Abū Jābirī in Morocco and ʿAbd al-Majīd Sharfī in Tunisia. These thinkers have often studied in the West and are open to dialogue and to a common struggle for the causes of humanity. Throughout the twentieth century Muslim thought has been stressing the responsibility of man and woman as persons, and much more attention has been given to the problem of human freedom than in earlier times. [*See the biography of Ḥanafī.*]

Another field of modern Muslim thought is that of history. As far as the Middle East is concerned, European imperialism, Western neocolonialism and exploitation by socialist bloc countries, the World Wars and the following Cold War, the establishment of Israel, mutual rivalries, petrodollars, and other factors have made it one of the crisis areas of twentieth-century history. Some Muslim authors are fascinated by the rise and fall of nations and civilizations, with the lurking question of whether the West or Islam will dominate the world of the future. In a similar vein, authors, such as ʿAbbās Maḥmūd al-ʿAqqād and Muḥammad Kamāl Ibrāhīm Jaʿfar in Egypt, have discussed the place of Islam in the ongoing history of religions. Here and there a scholarly interest in religions other than Islam is visible, as distinct from the apologetic and polemical spirit that pervades so much writing on this subject and prevents true dialogue between cultures and religions. Such a dialogue requires, as a first condition, a free development of thought in Muslim countries, and this, unfortunately, is under constant threat. Certain trends of thought have scope to develop among Muslims living in the West and not in Muslim countries. The tragic end of the Sudanese independent thinker Maḥmūd Muḥammad Ṭāhā (d. 1985) is a warning signal.

One of the striking features of late twentieth-century Muslim societies is the increasing "conscientization" of Islam and Islamic norms and values. Against Western secular history, economics, education, and thought, calls can increasingly be heard for an Islamic view and methodology, just as an Islamic Declaration of Human Rights has been proposed besides the United Nations' one. The growing concern with Islamic specificities, norms, and values has led, at least in the Arab-Muslim world, to an increasing concentration on Islamic subjects: *jihād* and religious tolerance, *dhimmah* and religious freedom, the status of woman in Islam as opposed to that in the West, and so forth.

Under the manifold pressures of the present, traditional concerns with Islam as a distinctive entity have apparently developed into what Yvonne Haddad calls "neonormativist" thinking, as opposed to what she calls "acculturationist" thinking, which is open to historical and social forces and willing to change. Typical for neonormativist thinking is the exclusive concern with Islam as a total system embracing all aspects of life, religious as well as worldly *(dīn wa-dunyā)*. Man is seen as vicegerent of God on earth, the Muslim community as fulfilling God's plan with the world.

In this view, the Western world, its culture and religion, is seen as the historical enemy of the Muslim world and a threat to Islam. The Islamic identity itself is threatened by Western secular scholarship, secular methodology, secular education, and ongoing Western cultural and intellectual imperialism, which is seen as incapable of dialogue and of discerning any spiritual quality in things Islamic. Against this sombre image and perception of the West, Islam is seen as eternal and perfect, and Muslims can appropriate it, by zeal and commitment, through orienting themselves to the Qur'ānic view of reality. In this line of thought, Islam is presented as the sole subject of reflection, the absolute religion, accessible either through specific scriptural texts (as held by the fundamentalists) or through the coherent system of a rationalized Islam (as held by the ideologists). The versions of this absolute Islam vary according to political regimes and their oppositions, and on closer analysis they are largely conditioned by political forces.

Yet there are other ways of thinking about Islam as well, where Islam is a domain of personal experience, of communal norms and values, of creative effort in the sense of Muhammad Iqbal (1875–1938), or enlightenment in the sense of Mohammed Arkoun, who wants to free Muslim thought from political conditioning. [*See the biographies of Iqbal and Arkoun.*] Reading the expressions of modern Sunnī thought and also some works of literature, one becomes aware of an immense variety among Muslim thinkers and of the multiple interpretations permitted by Islam. And if more Muslims could express their thinking freely, this variety in Muslim thought would be still more visible than it is today.

All these thinkers work under great political, economic, and social pressures. Under the same pressures states in Muslim lands tend to become authoritarian while the deprived population finds an outlet for its misery in protest movements appealing to Islam.

[*See also* Revival and Renewal.]

BIBLIOGRAPHY

ʿAbduh, Muḥammad. *The Theology of Unity*. Translated from the Arabic by Ishaq Musaʿad and Kenneth Cragg. London, 1966. Modern theological treatise written by an outstanding Muslim modernist reformer, first published in Arabic in 1897.

Abraham, Midhat David. "Maḥmūd Shaltūt (1893–1963), a Muslim Reformist: His Life, Works and Religious Thought." Ph.D. diss., Hartford Seminary, 1976. Important study of a well-known rector of al-Azhar University (1958–1963).

Adams, Charles C. *Islam and Modernism in Egypt*. London, 1933. Classic introduction to the rise of Islamic modernist reform thought in Egypt.

Ahmad, Aziz. *Islamic Modernism in India and Pakistan, 1857–1964*. London, 1967. Excellent survey of Islamic modernist reform thought in the Indo-Pakistani subcontinent.

Ahmad, Aziz, and G. E. Von Grunebaum, eds. *Muslim Self-Statement in India and Pakistan, 1857–1968*. Wiesbaden, 1970. English translations of important texts that provide insight into modern Muslim thinking on Islam in the context of the Indo-Pakistani subcontinent.

Ahmad, Khurshid, and Zafar Ishaq Ansari, eds. *Islamic Perspectives: Studies in Honour of Mawlānā Sayyid Abu Aʿlā Mawdūdī*. Leicester, 1979. Essays on different aspects of the islamization of thought, society, and the state, written by thinkers concerned with a revitalization of Islam.

Anderson, J. N. D. *Law Reform in the Muslim World*. London, 1976. Insightful survey of juridical thought and the relation between modern law and religious law *(sharīʿah)* in a number of Muslim countries.

Arkoun, Mohammed. *Lectures du Coran*. Paris, 1982. Essays on new ways of reading the Qur'ān with the tools of modern semiotics.

Arkoun, Mohammed. *Pour une critique de la raison islamique*. Paris, 1984. Thought-provoking analysis of classical and traditional Muslim thinking, and an urgent plea for its liberation from past political and other conditioning.

Baljon, J. M. S. *Modern Muslim Koran Interpretation, 1880–1960*. Leiden, 1968. Introduction to modern Qur'ān interpretations, in particular in the Indo-Pakistani subcontinent.

Boullata, Issa J. *Trends and Issues in Contemporary Arab Thought*. Albany, N.Y., 1990. Excellent survey of intellectual trends in the present-day Arab world, including thinking on Islam.

Cragg, Kenneth. *The Pen and the Faith: Eight Modern Muslim Writers and the Qur'ān*. London, 1985. Good introduction to the way in which some prominent authors relate themselves to the Qur'ān.

Donohue, John J., and John L. Esposito, eds. *Islam in Transition: Muslim Perspectives*. New York, 1982. Presentation in English translation of important texts from the last hundred years which provide insight into the broad range of modern Muslim thinking.

Enayat, Hamid. *Modern Islamic Political Thought*. Austin and London, 1982. Excellent introduction to both Sunnī and Shīʿī political thinking in the nineteenth and twentieth century.

Gibb, H. A. R. *Modern Trends in Islam*. Chicago, 1947. Classic work on Muslim reformist thought up to World War II.

Haddad, Yvonne Yazbeck. *Contemporary Islam and the Challenge of History*. Albany, N.Y., 1982. Insightful treatment of the various ways in which Muslim thought has responded to the impact of modernism.

Hourani, Albert. *Arabic Thought in the Liberal Age, 1798–1939*. London, 1962. Classic study of many aspects of Arab thought up to World War II.

Iqbal, Muhammad. *Six Lectures on the Reconstruction of Religious Thought in Islam*. Lahore, 1930. Vision of the famous philosopher-poet of the Indo-Pakistani subcontinent on the future of Islam.

Juynboll, G. H. A. *The Authenticity of the Tradition Literature: Discussions in Modern Egypt*. Leiden, 1969. Thorough study of Muslim responses to Western critical scholarship on the historical authenticity of *ḥadīth* literature.

Keddie, Nikki R. *An Islamic Response to Imperialism: Political and Religious Writings of Sayyid Jamāl ad-Dīn "al-Afghānī."* Berkeley, 1968. Texts of one of the first modern Muslim reformers in English translation, with an introduction to the life and thought of al-Afghānī.

McDonough, Sheila. *The Authority of the Past: A Study of Three Muslim Modernists*. Chambersburg, Pa., 1970.

McDonough, Sheila. *Muslim Ethics and Modernity: A Comparative Study of the Ethical Thought of Sayyid Ahmad Khan and Mawlana Mawdudi*. Waterloo, Ont., 1984. Good introduction to the ethical thought of two very different Muslim reformers in the Indo-Pakistani subcontinent.

Na'im, Abdullahi Ahmed An-. *Toward an Islamic Reformation: Civil Liberties, Human Rights, and International Law*. Syracuse, N.Y., 1990. Important study by a prominent Sudanese thinker.

Rahman, Fazlur. *Islam and Modernity: Transformation of an Intellectual Tradition*. Chicago, 1982. Excellent introduction to various trends of thought with regard to renewal of education and thought in Islam.

Sardar, Ziauddin. *Islamic Futures: The Shape of Ideas to Come*. London and New York, 1985. Vision of the future of Muslim thought in response to the demands of the times.

Smith, Wilfred Cantwell. *Modern Islam in India: Social Analysis*. Rev. ed. London, 1946. Masterly study of Muslim thought in nineteenth- and twentieth-century India and its social conditionings.

Ṭāhā, Maḥmūd Muḥammad. *The Second Message of Islam*. Translation and introduction by ʿAbd Allāh Aḥmad Naʿīm. Syracuse, N.Y., 1987. English translation of an important text written by the famous Sudanese Muslim reformer, with a new vision of individual and communal responsibilities in Islam.

Vogelaar, Harold S. "The Religious and Philosophical Thought of Dr. M. Kamel Hussein, an Egyptian Humanist." Ph.D. diss., Columbia University, 1978. Good introduction to the thought of an outstanding Egyptian intellectual, on both Islam and Christianity.

Waardenberg, Jacques. "The Rise of Islamic States Today." *Orient* (Hamburg) 28.2 (1987): 194–215.

JACQUES WAARDENBURG

SŪQ. *See* Bazaar.

SURINAME. A higher percentage of Muslims live in Suriname—a former Dutch colony on South America's northeastern shoulder—than in any other country in the Western Hemisphere. An estimated 25 percent of Suriname's 400,000 citizens profess Islam, according to officials of the country's largest Muslim organization, the Surinaamse Islamitische Vereniging. Some 50,000 Muslims, however, have emigrated to the Netherlands since independence in 1975. Ethnic strife among the country's other minorities—Creoles, Amerindians and so-called Bush Negroes— has further bankrupted the once-strong Surinamese economy.

Throughout most of its history this 163,000-square-kilometer territory, one of the world's largest bauxite producers, was a Dutch colony and was noted for religious tolerance. In the 1630s, Sephardic Jews who had been expelled from Brazil arrived in Suriname, where in 1665 they built South America's first synagogue at a jungle settlement known as Jodensavanna. In 1667 England ceded Suriname to the Dutch in exchange for New York, and the colony began to prosper from exports of coffee, cacao, sugar, and bananas to Holland.

As is the case with Trinidad and Guyana, which also have sizable Islamic minorities, Muslims first came to Suriname as indentured servants. In 1873 the *Lala Rookh* arrived in Paramaribo carrying indentured Indian Muslims. Suriname also has a much larger contingent of Indonesian Muslims descended from Javanese rice farmers who settled here between 1902 and 1935. Indonesian Muslims now comprise some 65 percent of the Surinamese Muslim community, with Indian Muslims making up 30 percent and African converts to Islam the remainder.

Some 150 mosques are scattered around Paramaribo and throughout Suriname's sparsely populated interior. Indonesian Muslims, however, rarely pray at Indian mosques because of language difficulties—Indian services are conducted in Urdu. During Ramaḍān, when the two groups sometimes pray together, services are conducted mainly in Dutch.

In the mid-1980s the East Indians inaugurated Suriname's largest, most elaborate mosque, the Jama Masjid, in the heart of downtown Paramaribo. The building, dominated by four 30-meter minarets, seats eight hundred people; it is adjacent to Congregation Neve Shalom, an eighteenth-century Ashkenazic synagogue recently restored by the country's tiny Jewish community. Muslim and Jewish leaders have long been guests of honor in each other's houses of worship.

Such harmony has not been seen among Suriname's other ethnic groups in recent years. During most of the 1980s, jungle-dwellers descended from escaped African slaves fought a low-level guerrilla war against military strongman Desi Bouterse. Hundreds of people died in the fighting, which affected mostly eastern Suriname near the French Guiana border. Among Bouterse's suspected backers was Libyan leader Muʿammar Qadhdhāfī, who set up a Libyan People's Bureau in Paramaribo in the late 1980s. As a result of Suriname's civil war the Dutch government suspended its $1.5-billion development aid program. In 1990 a bloodless coup led by Bouterse toppled the government. Civilian rule was restored in 1991 with the election of Ronald Venetiaan, and in August 1992 a peace agreement was signed between the government and Suriname's two guerrilla groups.

Since 1970, ʿĪd al-Fiṭr has been celebrated as a national holiday, and Muslims—like all religious groups—enjoy full religious freedom. Besides Surinaamse Islamitische Vereniging, seven other groups supervise Muslim affairs in Suriname, the most important being the Surinaamse Moeslim Associatie, Stichting Islamitische Gemeenten Suriname, and Federatie Islamitische Gemeenten in Suriname. Yet Islamic life is stagnating because of a decline in religious education. Less than 3 percent of the Muslim population speaks or reads Arabic; some teachers have recently arrived from Pakistan and Indonesia to give lessons in Arabic and the fundamentals of Islam. Community leaders cite a lack of Islamic literature in Dutch and English and a dearth of qualified personnel, along with the community's relatively low socioeconomic level and the "brain drain" to the Netherlands and other countries.

BIBLIOGRAPHY

French, Howard W. "In Suriname's Racial Jungle, a Quest for Identity." *New York Times*, 23 October 1990.

Luxner, Larry. "Muslims in the Caribbean." *Aramco World Magazine* 38 (November–December 1987): 2–11.

Meijer, J. *Pioneers of Pauroma: Contribution to the Earliest History of the Jewish Colonization of America*. Paramaribo, 1954.

Treaster, Joseph B. "Suriname's Fall from Paradise: Guerrilla War, Economic Ruin." *New York Times*, 13 July 1987.

LARRY LUXNER

SURROGATE MOTHERHOOD. Surrogate motherhood is a contractual agreement whereby a woman agrees to be impregnated by a man, or implanted with a prefertilized embryo, and then surrenders the resulting baby to the man and his wife after its birth. Gestational surrogacy is the term used when the fertilized egg of a legally married couple is implanted in another woman's uterus. She also bears the child and surrenders it to its biological parents. The surrogate mother may or may not be financially compensated or have grounds to contest custody or visitation of the child. Such arrangements and related issues of *in vitro* fertilization and fertility treatments have been considered by Muslim medical and religious authorities. Muslim scholars and doctors have treated these issues as a comprehensive ethical, religious, and legal concern, whereas in the West, they make up an area of health ethics regulated thus far by federal or state laws. Various schools of Islamic jurisprudence are producing distinct orientations toward issues of sexuality and fertility.

Since women are not encouraged to enter surgery, obstetrics, and gynecology in the same numbers as men, few Muslim women have participated in the debates on fertility and surrogate motherhood. Muslim states and jurists have accepted or rejected various methods of fertility control, allowing certain forms of contraception while generally rejecting abortion. Many Muslims, however, have challenged the underlying assumption that their nations must limit births to enhance the quality of life, arguing that a redistribution of resources is necessary. Nevertheless, a large number of Muslims consider infertility to be a serious problem and seek medical intervention. Faced by the technological developments in the field, Muslim medical personnel are now confronted with complex ethical questions regarding the validity of courses of treatment.

Three legal and historical barriers confront any argument for legalized contractual surrogate motherhood. The Qur'ān distinctly states that children are the gift of God.

> To God belongs the dominion of the heavens and the earth. He creates what He wills [and plans]. He bestows [children] male or female according to His Will [and Plan]. Or He bestows both males and females and he leaves barren whom He will. For he is full of knowledge and power.
>
> (surah *Shūrah* 42.49–50)

On this basis scholars have argued that infertility, or female children, should be accepted by parents. A strict interpretation of this verse was altered with the medical and religious acceptance of fertility treatments (usually ineffective) and then in the 1980s with permission for two methods of in vitro fertilization. These were argued to be permissible as they could succeed only with the will of God and do not involve sperm or egg donation. Because men have the alternative of taking another wife who might be fertile, polygamy serves as a second impediment to the pursuit of fertility alternatives.

The third legal problem concerns the Muslim approach to adoption. The Qur'ān forbids formal adoption and calls for children to carry their own names (surah *Aḥzāb*, 33.4–5). (After revelation of this verse, the Prophet's own adopted son, Zayd, retook his own name, Zayd ibn Ḥārith.) Adopted children could not legally inherit. However, informal adoption exists, known as "embracing" a child, and Muslims may bestow monetary gifts upon such a child during their lifetime.

A form of surrogate motherhood in which a child is nurtured, breast-fed, and disciplined by a woman other than its mother has been practiced for centuries in the Middle East. This surrogate mother is termed a "milk-mother." The prophet Muḥammad was first raised by his milk-mother, Ḥalīmah of the Saʿd bin Bakr tribe. The milk relationship is equivalent to a blood relationship with regard to loyalty and prohibitions of incest. Children who are suckled together may not marry. Muḥammad honored this tie by intercession on behalf of his milk-sister, al-Shaymā, and the women of the Saʿd bin Bakr. This custom has continued into the twentieth century for the convenience of parents, when a man was widowed or divorced, when a woman could or would not nurse, and to encourage familiarity with tribal life in some regions. The Qur'ān sanctions the practice and the monetary compensation given to a milk-mother, or to a nurse (or surrogate) even if a child is older, and could be taken as a precedent for payment of a surrogate contract if formal adoption were not involved. However, a child born of a surrogate mother could not inherit from its genetic father and adoptive mother unless the father had legally married the surrogate mother. In states permitting polygamy he could do so, acknowledged a conservative Sunnī authority recently (Zuhur, 1993, p. 16).

Earlier opinions held that as Islam guards legal sexual relations and requires that a child know its origins, donor insemination could not be allowed. Following this argument, surrogate motherhood involved a donated gamete and/or uterus and so represented an adulterous relationship. Some still consider *in vitro* techniques to be suspect, though not adulterous, as contact between egg and sperm takes place outside its normal environment. Others conceded that even sperm or egg donation involved a medical rather than a sexual act and could not be adulterous, but nonetheless removed parental responsibilities, violated inheritance laws, and increased the risk of unintended incest within the community (Hathout, *Islamic Concepts and Bioethics*, London, 1991). An opponent of all fertility intervention has argued that a surrogate mother's separation from parenting responsibilities also invalidates Muslim conceptions of parenthood, dividing realms of motherhood into conception, childbearing, and parenting (Tahmaz, 1987).

With gestational surrogacy, the problem of legitimacy does not exist, but the above argument has resonance, for the separated functions of motherhood could easily be fulfilled by different women. Although many contemporary parenting responsibilities are assumed by nurses, baby-sitters, and teachers, and the role of the traditional milk-mother implied the possible division of the functions of motherhood, many other Muslims would object to a monetary value being assigned to the act of giving birth. It turns the birth experience into a commercial transaction and could, as some feminists propose, reinforce socioeconomic divisions among women, creating one class of breeders and carriers, and another privileged parent class who could afford their services.

On the other hand, infertile Muslim women have been subjected to cultural if not religious discrimination; women often feared replacement, whether through polygamy or via the temporary marriage *(mutʿah)* permitted to Shīʿī men. It is conceivable that women determined to be mothers might support the acceptance of a modified form of surrogate motherhood. Muslim opinion has truly shifted when some of its most conservative jurists recognize the technological achievement of the test-tube baby, albeit "facilitated by God" (Members of the Sharīʿah Council of the Muslim World Association; [President of the Council, ʿAbd al-ʿAzīz ibn ʿAbd Allāh ibn Baz] "Second Opinion on the Matter of Artificial Insemination and Test-tube Babies," Mecca, 1989). Therefore, a gestational surrogate arrangement conducted without payment, perhaps granting the birth mother visitation rights on an ongoing basis, may one day be seriously considered as well.

[*See also* Abortion; Family Law; *Mutʿah*.]

BIBLIOGRAPHY

Qurʾān; Al-Baqarah 20.220; *Al-Nisāʾ* 4.2, 4.6. 4.10. 4.24. and 4.27; *Banū Isrāʾīl* 17.34; and *Aḥzāb* 33.4–5.

Members of the Sharīʿah Council of the Muslim World Association. "Second Opinion on the Matter of Artificial Insemination and Test-tube Babies." Mecca, 1989. *Fatwā* covering the various forms of reproductive intervention, probably representing more conservative opinion in this matter. Signers indicate some dissension on the decisions.

Gindi, A. R. al-, ed. *Human Reproduction in Islam*. Translated by A. Asbahi. Kuwait, 1989.

Hathout, Hasan. "Islamic Concepts and Bioethics." In *Bioethic Yearbook,* edited by the Center for Ethics, Medicine, and Public Issues, vol. 1. London, 1991. Contains medical and scholarly consensus on organ transplants, and sterilization as well as new reproductive technologies. The author has elsewhere represented Muslim opinion as being opposed to abortion and homosexuality.

International Conference on Islamic Medicine. *Proceedings of the First International Conference on Islamic Medicine*. Edited by Abdul Rahman Abdullah al-Awadi. Kuwait, 1981.

Tahmaz, ʿAbd al-Hamid Mahmud. *al-Ansab wa al-Awlad: Dirāsah limawqif al-sharīʿah al-islamīyah min al-talqih al-sinaʿī wa ma yusama bi atfal al-anabīb*. Beirut and Damascus, 1987.

Zuhur, Sherifa. "Of Milk-Mothers and Sacred Bonds: Islam, Patriarchy, and New Reproductive Technologies." *Creighton Law Review* 25.5 (November, 1992): 1725–1738.

Zuhur, Sherifa. "New Reproductive Technologies: Rulings vs. Meanings." Paper presented to the Middle East Studies Association. Research Triangle Park, N.C., 1993.

If surrogate motherhood is unfamiliar territory, the reader may also wish to glance at some Western sources on surrogacy, law and ethics, including:

Johnson vs. Calvert. 20 May 1993. California Supreme Court. (Panelli, Justice Edward). Twenty-eight-page opinion upholding surrogate mother contracts, and denying legal custody to the gestational surrogate mother of Chris Calvert.

Gimenez, Martha. "The Mode of Reproduction in Transition: A Marxist-Feminist Analysis of Reproductive Technologies." *Gender and Society* 5.3 (September 1991): 334–350.

Mor, Menachem, Charles Dougherty, Martha Field, Barbara Katz Rothman, et. al. *Creighton Law Review*. Symposium Issue: Reproductive Rights. 25.5 (November 1992). Includes perspectives of other religions and communities on the issue of surrogate motherhood.

Stark, Barbara. "Constitutional Analysis of the Baby M Decision." *Harvard Women's Law Journal* 11 (Spring): 19–52.

SHERIFA ZUHUR

SYNCRETISM. Syncretism is the phenomenon by which the practices and beliefs of one religion fuse with those of another to create a new and distinctive tradition. By the terms of this definition, all religions, and most certainly all those that have come to be known as world religions, can be regarded as syncretic in their origins, since each was shaped in dialogue with other faiths. In modern scholarship, however, the concept of syncretism is usually restricted to those religious syntheses that take shape after the initial consolidation of a religion; syncretisms thus diverge from the parent religion's core or ideal expression. Equally important, however, even as they diverge from normative ideals, syncretisms in believers' eyes maintain a residual identification with the parent faith. The actual degree of identification varies widely, however, with the result that it is often difficult to distinguish syncretism from simple religious innovation. These analytic problems suggest that the concept of syncretism is closely linked to that of "normative" religion and to the standards of belief and practice whereby believers determine what is and what is not allowable within the faith.

As with all other world religions, Muslim understandings of the normative core of their religion have varied over time and place. This means that any effort to delineate that which is truly Islamic from that which is syncretistic inevitably raises delicate problems of value and judgment. What some believers regard as syncretistic others may hold to be suitably Islamic. This controversy has been a recurring source of debate in nineteenth- and twentieth-century Islam, as standards as to what is and what is not properly Islamic have changed.

In the face of these analytic difficulties, it is useful to distinguish two different variants of syncretism within modern Islam: those whose followers still identify themselves as Muslim and those who so thoroughly distance themselves from normative Islam as to embrace an extra-Islamic identity. For analytic purposes, the second of these two variants is most easily distinguished as syncretic, while the first type is syncretic only in light of an orthodox ideal that syncretists themselves may reject.

In modern times, some of the most dramatic examples of openly syncretic movements have been found in West Africa, South Asia, Southeast Asia, and other parts of the world where Muslims have lived alongside non-Muslims in a social environment strongly influenced by non-Muslim ideals. In West Africa, for example, the expansion of Islam was associated with the development of trade networks and, later, the rise of powerful trading states under the influence of Berber and non-Arabic African rulers. Caravan routes in the region had already been established by the tenth century CE, and the movement of goods and people facilitated the diffusion of elements of Muslim culture well in advance of any full-scale islamization. In the tropical forest and coastal regions of what are today Ghana, Benin, and Nigeria, non-Muslim peoples looked to Muslim traders and craftspeople to provide religious amulets, antiwitchcraft spells, fertility treatments, and a host of other services loosely based on Muslim magical prototypes. In using these items non-Muslims acknowledged Islam's spiritual power, but regarded it as just one among an array of available spiritual resources.

In nineteenth-century Ghana, the pagan king of Ashanti depended on Muslim traders to serve as intermediaries in the caravan trade and as experts in the manufacture of powerful talismans. The talismans consisted of sentences from the Qur'ān inscribed on paper and wrapped in fine cloth. They were worn around the body for everything from treating illness and warding off the evil eye to deflecting the blows of enemies in combat. During times of drought, warfare, and other afflictions, the pagan king called on local Muslims to offer prayers to their God, whom he recognized as the most powerful of deities, alongside the sacrifices to native divinities performed by the king's own priests. Among the pagan tribes of the southern Sudan, circumcision—elsewhere identified as a symbol of adherence to Islam—appears to have been adopted owing to its high esteem among neighboring Muslim populations. Though an important ritual of male passage, for these practitioners the rite did not imply a commitment to Islam.

In these and other instances, the syncretism at issue is of the most nominal sort, involving little or no identification with Islam. Nonetheless, historical and ethnographic studies have shown that in many parts of Africa this syncretistic diffusion contributed to the perception of Islam as a source of mystical power. By acclimating people to the rituals and habits of Islam, it also prepared the way for the conversion of some to Islam.

Syncretistic preadaptations appear to have played a similarly important role in the conversion of South Asian Hindus to Islam. A significant proportion of the Muslim population of premodern India consisted of Muslim immigrants from Persia, Afghanistan, and other northern portions of the Indian subcontinent. In a few areas, most notably Bengali-speaking regions of what is today Bangladesh and the Indian state of West Bengal, however, the great majority of Muslims are comprised not of the descendants of invaders, but of Hindu converts, primarily from the lower classes, peaceably converted to Islam in the seventeenth to nineteenth centuries.

In the deltaic frontier of the Ganges River basin, local society was characterized by considerable geographic and socioeconomic mobility, all of which rendered the effective development of Hinduism's caste hierarchies problematic. In this only partially hinduized context, Islam penetrated through the efforts of wandering Muslim (usually Ṣūfī) pioneers. Like their Hindu counterparts, these settlers first came to engage in trade and open the jungle to cultivation; in an area lacking established lines of authority, however, some eventually assumed leadership roles as pirs (spiritual guides) in a loose network of Ṣūfī believers spreading across the delta frontier. As Asim Roy has explained in his book *The Islamic Syncretistic Tradition in Bengal* (Princeton, 1983), eventually the tombs of pir leaders became the nerve centers of Bengali Islam and the institutional foundation for one of the Muslim world's most remarkable syncretistic traditions.

Though drawing heavily on the symbolism of South Asian Sufism, the cult of pir worship and supplication came to include shrines not only to Muslim saints, but to non-Islamic pioneers, local divinities, and other old and new objects of religious veneration. Though preceded by an Islamic salutation, the propitiation at the heart of pir worship bore a strong resemblance to a popular Hindu rite, known as the *vrata,* performed to request favors from Hindu divinities. In some areas this syncretic blending was also apparent in Muslim participation in worship of non-Islamic pirs. Conversely, in nearby Assam and Burma, shrines to some of the most celebrated Muslim pirs attracted Chinese Confucians, Burmese Buddhists, and Bengali Hindus. Despite such remarkable syncretism, it is clear that for the most part pirism played a positive role in the conversion of Bengali Hindus to Islam. The theme of an evil Hindu *raja* defeated by a pious Muslim pir figured prominently in pir mythology; pir shrines were open to low castes and untouchables denied access to Hindu temples or their Brahman priests. In the unsettled circumstances of frontier Bengal, such antihierarchical inexclusivity gave pirist Islam broad appeal.

The great literary traditions of Bengali Islam also displayed a syncretic countenance. Some Muslim writers reacted to the divide between the pious elite and the syncretist populace by repudiating their Bengali identity, claiming Arab or Persian ancestry, and refusing to utilize Bengali in religious writings. Others, mostly of Ṣūfī background, rejected such cultural segregation, however, and acted as cultural brokers, adopting Bengali as their language of proselytization and adapting Bengali myths and narrative styles to Muslim ends. The resulting narrative tradition projected Muslim historical figures into a landscape of fantasy and miracles intelligible to the Bengali populace because closely modeled on Hindu poetic forms. Though Persian and Arabic characters were also drawn into such narratives, the mythic geography in which they were represented was strongly influenced by Hindu ideals. Muslim saints did battle with deities from Hindu cosmology, although other *devas* were said to be prophets from the time before Muḥammad. Similarly, while affirming the importance of conformity to *sharīʿah,* divinity was often presented in immanent and monist terms in a fashion consistent with Hindu mysticism. In the twentieth century, Muslim reformers railed against such syncretistic concessions to Bengali culture, with the result that little of this syncretistic literature has survived to this day.

Islam in modern Southeast Asia has experienced a similar push-and-pull between syncretizing concessions to local sensibilities, on one hand, and reformist efforts to maintain the purity of the message, on the other. As in South Asia, Islam in Southeast Asia at first confronted an already established political and aesthetic tradition. The indigenous aesthetic tradition had been strongly influenced by Southeast Asian variants of the Hindu *Ramayana* and *Mahabharata,* and the *raja*-centered political system owed much of its pomp and ceremony to Indian precedents. In most cases, however, the islamization of states in this part of the world did not involve the overthrow of existing dynasties. Islamization most commonly occurred through the ruler's conversion and the gentle reshaping of the structures and idioms of rajaship. The institution preserved many of the symbols and institutions of the pre-Islamic past, although it identified them in terms compatible with Ṣūfī mysticism and Persian-influenced models of rulership.

As with South Asian Islam, however, the development of Islam in this region was also characterized by bitter disputes over the question of to just what lengths Muslims could go in accommodating local customs. Rather than denouncing them as polytheism, most nineteenth-century Javanese and Malays reinterpreted the Hindu deities of the *Rāmāyaṇa* and *Mahābhārata* within a flexibly syncretic cosmology. Bhatara Guru, Brahma, and Iswara were lowered out of the Hindu firmament and reconceptualized either as distinctive Muslim *jinn* or as prophets who had lived prior to Muḥammad. Islamized in this fashion, the Hindu *dewa* were also made accessible to human appeal and came to figure prominently in village-based healing cults of exorcism and soul-purification. Though some pious Muslims rejected these practices as polytheistic, others—probably the majority of Malay and Javanese Muslims in the nineteenth century and early twentieth century—continued to regard appeals to *deva*s as fully compatible with Islam.

Throughout the Malay world during this same period, the majority of village communities institutionalized the Islamic requirement for almsgiving not as charity for the poor, but as an annual rite of invocation and offering to guardian and ancestral spirits. Presented with *sadaga* ("alms") of festive foods, dance, and other entertainments (in which villagers shared), the spirits of the village were enjoined to watch over the fertility and well-being of the community for one more year. Allāh was regarded as a transcendent and unapproachable being; village spirits, by contrast, were seen as spirit-familiars easily susceptible to ritual and moral appeal.

As in Africa and the Indian subcontinent, some natives of Southeast Asia interpreted these syncretistic traditions in such a way as to refuse outright affiliation with Islam. In nineteenth-century Java, for example, there were still a few pockets of Buda (the term used for the religion of pre-Islamic Java) settlement, where local ritual and mythology sought to incorporate Islamic influences but resisted full-scale conversion to Islam. One influential tradition identified Ajisaka, the much-loved culture hero of Javanese folklore, as Muḥammad's equal, and insisted that the two figures had reached an agreement to allow Buda and Islam to live as one. In a model of dualistic complementarity owing much to pre-Islamic concepts of cosmological harmony, Muḥammad and Ajisaka were related to each other, it was said, as male is to female, day is to night, sun is to moon, and earth is to sky. Both religions would prosper, it was implied, by respecting this fertile duality. With the development of movements of Islamic reform in the late nineteenth century, such notions of syncretic harmony are today widely rejected. Elements of their syncretizing vision survive, however, in the sheltered meeting-halls of mystical sects *(kebatinan)* popular among a portion of the urban middle class.

As these examples illustrate, it would be wrong to assume that syncretism primarily consists of non-Islamic survivals, although this is the preferred explanation of the phenomenon among Islamic fundamentalists. In some instances, such as the Bengali pir or the Javanese cult of Ajisaka, it is clear that elements of the syncretic tradition draw on pre-Islamic prototypes. But many syncretic movements are best regarded not as survivals, but as new, dynamic efforts to reshape local traditions in the face of Muslim reformists' efforts to narrow the range of allowable beliefs by introducing new criteria as to what Islam comprises. In India, Java, and West Africa, some of the boldest syncretic movements in the modern era emerged as responses to Muslim reformists' repudiation of local understandings of Islam. These reforms jeopardized social relations with non-Muslims and delegitimized customs long regarded as compatible with the faith.

This same tension appears to have played a role in the development of new forms of religious expression not only at the periphery of the Muslim world, but in its heartland. Since the first decades of the nineteenth century, numerous spirit cults, the most famous being the so-called *zar*, have spread through Ethiopia, Sudan, Egypt, Somalia, East Africa, and even the Arabian peninsula and southern Iraq; similar cults of spirit possession (the *holey* and the *bori*) have spread from West Africa into North Africa.

Whatever its precedence in pre-Islamic religion or contemporary African possession cults, in most of the areas to which it has spread the *zar* cult is an intrusive institution, having developed over the past century and a half. The cult's diffusion has thus been more or less contemporaneous with the rise of modern Islamic reform. Most commonly, *zar* possession afflicts married women.

Though opposed by Muslim leaders as an unacceptable innovation, the *zar* has survived in part because, in many people's eyes, it can be rationalized in Islamic terms. Thus the *zar* spirits are said to be a special category of Islamic *jinn*, capricious in their behavior, hedonistic in their tastes, and predatory (though never life-threatening) on their human hosts. Diagnosis of the affliction requires the services of a female curer (the *shaykhah*), who in urban areas operates a full-time *zar* business but in rural settings usually performs only as demand requires. Once afflicted by a *zar*, a woman can never fully sever the relationship. At best, she is obliged to sponsor intermittent ceremonies in which the spirit (or spirits, since *zar* possession may involve several spirits) is invoked and, speaking through the mouth of its female host, its wishes are voiced and then satisfied. Affliction is thought most common during times of physical or mental hardship, when a woman's spiritual guard is lowered and the afflicting spirit can more easily invade its host. In this roundabout way, the cult mobilizes social and material resources for women during periods of stress. It also allows women to make forceful, if oblique, appeals for attention, in a manner that would be otherwise unthinkable in a male-dominated environment.

The spread of *zar* cults contemporaneous with Islamic reform has led many observers to see in them an assertion of feminine dignity and authority in the face of social trends that have greatly restricted women's public activities and excluded them from prestigious religious roles. Whatever their complex social-psychology, the cults are a reminder that Islamization often involves not only the diffusion of Qur'ānic piety and *sharīʿah*-mindedness, but an extensive assortment of magical, astrological, and spirit-cult lore. These spirit cults also testify to the ability of Muslims to develop new forms of religious expression in the face of changing needs and social circumstances. This same dynamic has motivated the development of intra-Islamic syncretic movements throughout Islamic history.

The modern popularity of the *zar* cult is also a cautionary reminder that judgments as to the syncretism of different beliefs or practices are often deeply value laden. Application of the term to specific practices and beliefs must be done with great care and, more specifically, with an understanding of the varied, and sometimes contradictory, ideals through which Muslims in different times and places have given shape to their vision of the faith.

[*See also* Popular Religion.]

BIBLIOGRAPHY

Boddy, Janice. *Wombs and Alien Spirits: Women, Men, and the Zar Cult in Northern Sudan*. Madison, Wis., 1989. Rich ethnographic study of the *zār* and its implications for men and women's divergent understanding of spirits, Islam, and gender.

Golomb, Louis. *An Anthropology of Curing in Multiethnic Thailand*. Urbana and Chicago, 1985. Insightful ethnographic study of syncretic healing cults among Buddhists and Muslims in southern Thailand.

Hefner, Robert W. *Hindu Javanese: Tengger Tradition and Islam*. Princeton, 1985. A historical and ethnographic study of syncretism and islamization in modern Java.

Holý, Ladislav. *Religion and Custom in a Muslim Society: The Berti of Sudan*. Cambridge, 1991. Detailed ethnography of the tensions between Islam and customary tradition in the northern Sudan.

Hooker, M. B., ed. *Islam in South-East Asia*. Leiden, 1983. Collection rich with insights into the interaction of Islamic traditions with Southeast Asian literature, philosophy, law, and politics.

Laderman, Carol. *Taming the Wind of Desire: Psychology, Medicine, and Aesthetics in Malay Shamanistic Performance*. Berkeley and Los Angeles, 1991. Beautifully evocative ethnography of a syncretistic shamanistic tradition in modern Malaysia.

Lewis, I. M., ed. *Islam in Tropical Africa*. 2d ed. Bloomington and London, 1980. Excellent sourcebook on the dynamics of Islam and local tradition in Africa.

Lombard, Denys. *Le Carrefour Javanais*. Paris, 1990. Exhaustive study of the interaction between Islamic, local, and occidental influences in Java and the Indonesian archipelago.

Nadel, S. F. *Nupe Religion: Traditional Belief and the Influence of Islam in a West African Chiefdom* (1954). New York, 1970. Classic study of a traditional African religion on the eve of its islamization.

Roy, Asim. *The Islamic Syncretistic Tradition in Bengal*. Princeton, 1983. Richly detailed historical study of popular and literary syncretism in premodern and modern Bengal.

ROBERT W. HEFNER

SYNDICATES. Professional syndicates—like labor unions (which are not treated here)—have arisen in the Islamic world in the past century in new or significantly altered occupations which emerged in response to far-reaching socioeconomic change. Although loosely influenced by earlier guild practices (such as calling their leader "*naqīb*"), the syndicates took their main models from the West. Often subsumed in the "bourgeoisie" or "new middle class," professionals have received scant study, and comparative crossnational study of them has hardly begun.

Professionalization is here taken to mean the emergence in an occupation of a significant number of full-time practitioners—other than the clergy, one of the classic "liberal" or "free" professions in the West—trained mainly through higher education. Establishing a higher professional school is usually a first step. Other indicators include the emergence of a critical mass of practitioners, self-consciousness as a profession, external recognition, recognized standards, specialized journals, and a code of ethics. Either the state—pursuing standardization and control—or practitioners themselves can take the lead in founding a syndicate.

In Islamic lands with large European colonies or protracted colonial domination, professions often developed separate branches for Europeans, indigenous Western-style practitioners, and traditional practitioners. Egypt had three lawyers' syndicates (bar associations)—for the Mixed, the National (Ahlīyah or "Native" to the British), and the Sharīʿah Courts. The closing of the Mixed Courts (1949) and the merger of the Sharīʿah and National Courts (1956) finally unified the lawyers in one syndicate.

Higher Professional Schools. Usually, Western practitioners introduced professions they considered "modern" into the Islamic world. Indigenous practitioners educated in Europe followed their example, and then graduates of local professional schools took over. Table 1 lists founding dates for selected professional schools. In Istanbul and Cairo, rulers facing Western challenges founded medical and engineering schools early on to service their reformed armies and, later, civilian needs as well. British India and French Algeria also set up medical schools early. Modern law schools—to bypass the traditional schools of sharīʿah (the divine law)—emerged only after 1850, as European economic penetration, imported Western laws, new mixed and national courts, parliaments, and constitutions created a need for Western-style lawyers.

The Indian universities established at Calcutta, Bombay, and Madras in 1857—examining bodies on the University of London model—awarded degrees in law, medicine, and engineering as well as arts. For some decades, however, few Muslims joined the Hindus in taking advantage of these opportunities.

Ottoman Istanbul competed with Cairo in opening professional schools; both founded medical schools in 1827. American and French missionaries founded the first higher professional schools in the Ottoman Fertile Crescent—colleges of medicine and pharmacy in Beirut. The Ottomans followed after 1900 with medical and law schools in Damascus and a law school in Baghdad. The professional schools of Algiers served mainly *colons*.

Where colonial rulers were absent, arrived late, or hesitated on higher education, modern professional education came later. Modern higher education took root in heavily tribal Libya and the Arabian peninsula only after 1950.

After the Ottoman collapse in 1918, Egypt furnished the main professionalization model for the Arabs. In their Fertile Crescent mandates, Britain and France contented themselves between the world wars with law and medical schools.

Founding the Syndicates. Ignoring unofficial societies and false starts, Table 2 lists founding dates of selected syndicates. The sequence of syndicate foundation in Egypt—lawyers, doctors, engineers, teachers—was fairly usual in other countries. It also reflects the prestige hierarchy among the professions in the first half of the twentieth century.

The syndicate European lawyers founded in Istanbul in 1876 did not last, and Ottoman advocacy went largely unregulated until World War I. In contrast, the syndicate which European Mixed Courts lawyers founded in Egypt in 1876 on the French model became a prototype for later syndicates. It obtained a monopoly on Mixed Courts practice, oversaw lawyers' qualifications and fees, regulated apprenticeships, elected officers and a board, aided needy colleagues, and issued a journal. The National Courts lawyers syndicate of 1912 followed its precedents, and sharīʿah lawyers syndicate of 1916 in turn copied the National Courts syndicate.

Because Europeans skimmed off the wealthier clients and few could afford professional services, indigenous

TABLE 1. *Founding Dates of Professional Higher Schools*

	ISTANBUL	EGYPT	SYRIA	LEBANON	IRAQ	ALGERIA	TUNISIA	IRAN	INDIA	AFGHANISTAN	NIGERIA	INDONESIA
Law	1878	1868	1914	1912	1908	1879	1922	1921	1855	1938		1924
Medic.	1827	1827	1901	1867	1927	1859	1964	★★ᵇ	1835	1932	1947	1927
Engin.	1773	1820	1944	1913	1942	1925		★★ᵇ	1847			1920
Teach.		1880ᵃ	1946		1923						1918	1925

ᵃ1872, if one counts Dar al-ʿUlūm.   ᵇIran's Darolfunun polytechnic school graduated a few engineers and doctors between 1851 and the 1890s.

TABLE 2. *Founding Dates of Professional Syndicates*

	EGYPT	LEBANON	SYRIA	JORDAN	IRAQ
Lawyers	1912	1921	1921	1950	1933
Doctors	1942[a]	1946		1958	1953
Journalists	1941			1953	1958?
Engineers	1946	1951		1958	1958?
Teachers	1955[b]	1957			1958?
Agronomists	1949				
Accountants	1955[c]				

[a]Decreed in 1940. [b]Decreed in 1951. [c]Changed to Business Administration, 1973.

practitioners hesitated to leave state jobs for private practice. Lawyers were the first to do so in significant numbers, with doctors following, and engineers some way behind.

As in the West, internal divisions and a weak professional consciousness made it harder to organize journalists and teachers. Not until 1937 did the American University at Cairo offer the first journalism program in the Arab world. Newspaper owners and employees, printers and reporters, and writers and editors all had different interests. So did private and public school teachers and teachers on the university, secondary-school, and primary-school levels. Low-status press workers, teachers, and health workers often felt more at home in labor unions than in professional syndicates.

Women who wanted to share in these new professional opportunities had an uphill struggle, fighting successively for admission to professional schools, for syndicate membership, and for jobs. Women entered the lawyers syndicates in Lebanon and Egypt in the 1930s, in Iraq in 1943. Even in the mid 1980s there were only six women among 508 Palestinian lawyers in the West Bank.

Syndicates and Independence Struggles. The prestige of advocacy and its affinity for politics in the West carried over into the Islamic world. Lawyers seemed best suited to press the case for independence in the twilight of the colonial age; they were at home with parliamentary debate, parties, constitutions, capitalism, courts, and law codes. Many a national hero was a lawyer: Saʿd Zaghlūl (Egypt), Bishārah al-Khūrī (Lebanon), Habib Bourguiba (Tunisia), Shukrī Qūwatlī (Syria), Mohammad Mossadeq (Iran), and Mohammad Ali Jinnah (Pakistan), not to mention Mohandas Gandhi and Jawaharlal Nehru among the Hindus.

Not just individual lawyers but lawyers syndicates were in the forefront of independence struggles. In Egypt the strike of the National Courts lawyers during the 1919 national revolt derailed the courts for weeks, and the nationalist Wafd party obtained a grip on the syndicate it would keep for over thirty years. British officials no doubt remembered this when they prevented Iraqi lawyers from forming a syndicate until after independence in 1932. National and professional issues intertwined in the lawyers' strikes of 1925–1926 in Damascus during the Syrian national revolt. The strikers protested the French judges who inspected Syrian courts and presided over cases involving foreigners. In 1967 Palestinian lawyers in the West Bank began a strike to protest the Israeli occupation. The Jordanian lawyers syndicate paid them compensation and expelled those who broke ranks to return to work several years later.

Postindependence Syndical Politics. When authoritarian rule—colonial, monarchical, military, or Islamist—suppressed the press, parties, and parliaments, politics resurfaced in such institutions as syndicates, universities, chambers of commerce, and mosques.

In 1952 and 1961–1962 the failure of the mainly Maronite lawyers syndicate of Beirut to win two long strikes pointed up the fragility of Maronite dominance in Lebanon. In 1952 the strikers opposed expanding the power of Christian clerical courts, which Maronite clerics and Muslims mostly favored. The nine-month strike of 1961–1962 tried to close the Arab University of Beirut's new law school. The strikers feared that the profession would be swamped with ill-trained lawyers, many of them Muslim. The Tripoli lawyers syndicate, more Muslim and Greek Orthodox, opposed both strikes.

In Egypt the lawyers syndicate became a source of cabinet ministers when the Wafd party was in, a Wafdist refuge when it was out. Nūrī al-Saʿīd's inability to keep the lawyers syndicate in friendly hands during the 1950s was perhaps a harbinger of the 1958 revolution. Many officers of the Jordanian lawyers syndicate, founded in 1950, were West Bankers and opponents of the regime. In Turkey, Süleyman Demirel's Justice party drove the syndicates toward the opposition Republican People's party by undercutting the architecture and engineering syndicates and relying heavily on foreign experts.

Syndical Politics under Military Regimes. From 1949 onward, military coups in the Arab world and Pakistan overthrew many of the regimes under which lawyers and landlords had flourished. Although few syndicate leaders wept for Iraq's Nūrī al-Saʿīd or Egypt's King Fārūq, they soon clashed with the new military regimes. Nasser purged the Wafdist *naqīb*s of the lawyers, engineers, and agronomists and brought key syndicates to heel with army officers and cabinet ministers who doubled as *naqīb*s.

In Iraq, procommunists took 81 percent of the teachers syndicate vote in January 1959. President ʿAbd al-Karīm Qāsim broke with the communists thereafter, and by 1962 his pressure on state school teachers dropped the figure to 29 percent. The lawyers syndicate was more conservative and Arab nationalist, but in 1965 the ʿArīf regime purged it as well. In Syria the Baʿthist government purged the teachers syndicate in 1964, doubtless remembering the spell their own party's teacher-founders had once cast over students.

Government rewards for cooperative syndicates could include pension funds, health and housing coops (Muhandisīn ["Engineers City"] is now a major Cairo suburb), and paid vacations. Syndicate office was also a good place to cultivate patron-client political ties which might open the way to public-sector posts and lucrative government contracts.

Seeking increased legitimacy and faster economic development, military regimes recruited engineers, economists, and doctors into their cabinets. The three prominent medical doctors of the Syrian Baʿthist regime in 1966–1970 provided a useful facade for its military strongmen. Engineers and doctors displaced lawyers at the top of the civilian professional prestige ladder from the 1950s on, but military rulers often ignored their expert recommendations for political reasons.

As the League of Arab States was taking shape, a Pan-Arab conference of lawyers met in Damascus in 1944 and one of engineers in Alexandria in 1945. Nasser picked up the Arab banner a decade later. A Union of Arab Lawyers was founded in Cairo in 1956. Other professions soon followed with Pan-Arab unions, but interstate rivalries undercut progress toward unified standards and procedures.

As Arab socialism also came into vogue in the 1960s, leftists wanted to abolish professional syndicates or merge them with labor unions. Military regimes tightened their control by swamping syndicates with state employees and higher and technical school graduates. Egyptian syndicate officers had to belong to the Arab Socialist Union. The agronomists syndicate had to admit technical secondary graduates. Half the teachers syndicate board had to be primary school teachers, and only the 1967 war derailed plans to admit school janitors. The doctors and engineers successfully kept technical secondary school graduates out, and journalists survived Gamal Abdel Nasser without admitting state broadcasting and information service employees.

Syndicates could also help topple military regimes, as the Damascus lawyers syndicate did in attacking Adīb al-Shīshaklī in 1954. Protests from the Pakistani lawyers, doctors, and engineers syndicates contributed to Muhammad Ayub Khan's fall in 1969. The Iraqi lawyers, doctors, and engineers syndicates cheered on student demonstrators celebrating Qāsim's fall in 1963.

Most syndicates struggled in vain against overcrowding and lowered standards in their professions. No matter how grim the job prospects, few governments could resist pressures to expand educational opportunities. Egypt's lawyers syndicate began with 582 lawyers in 1912 and reached 7000 in 1967, when the engineers syndicate had 22,000 and the teachers 140,000.

Syndicates and Islamism. In 1977 in Iran, the Writers Association, the National Organization of Physicians, the Association of Iranian Journalists, the National Organization of University Professors, and the teachers syndicate suddenly emerged from long repression to challenge the shah. Mehdi Bāzargān's Association of Engineers (founded in 1941) also played its part. Although Paris-educated, Bāzargān had insisted on the Islamic character of both the Association of Engineers and his Liberation Movement of Iran (1961). An ally of Ayatollah Ruhollah Khomeini, he became the first prime minister of the Islamic Republic when the shah fell. Rejoicing among syndicate leaders was short-lived. Khomeini and Bāzargān fell out, and the Islamists crushed their erstwhile secular allies. [*See* Liberation Movement of Iran *and the biography of Bāzargān.*]

Iran's Islamic Revolution, led by Shiʿi *ʿulamāʾ* from the top, was unique. In Pakistan it was the military under Muhammad Zia ul-Haq which implemented islamizing measures. Standing in for political parties Zia had banned, the lawyers syndicate protested authoritarian rule, and professional women were in the forefront of protests against his islamization program.

In Syria, Hafez al-Assad's secular military regime struggled to contain Islamist challenges. The Muslim Brotherhood had their base among urban Sunnīs hostile to the once peripheral ʿAlawī minority who now dominated the party, the army, and the country. In 1980 Assad purged the lawyers and engineers syndicates for joining the Islamists in protesting his rule. Having a poorer and more provincial clientele, the teachers and agronomists syndicates were more supportive of the regime.

In 1984 Hosni Mubarak loosened the political lid Anwar el-Sadat had clamped on Egypt just before his assassination by Islamists in 1981. The Islamist heirs of Ḥasan al-Bannā's (d. 1949) Muslim Brotherhood surged into parliament (under the banner of other parties), student groups, faculty clubs, and syndicates. Islamists did best in the academically elite scientific and technical faculties, where they honed the organizing skills they later took into syndicate politics. Frustration with career prospects among bright lower-middle-class youth helped fuel the movement. With little organized opposition and only a fraction of those eligible voting, Islamists increasingly carried student, faculty, and syndicate elections. In 1990 they won board elections at the doctors syndicate for the third time, and in 1991 they swept elections in the engineering syndicate. In 1992 they even captured a majority of the seats on the board of the lawyers syndicate, the Wafd's old stronghold.

In the occupied West Bank and Gaza Strip, syndicate and chamber of commerce elections offered rare tests of support for the Palestine Liberation Organization, PLO dissidents, and Islamists. The Gaza Strip syndicate elections of 1992, for example, reversed the gains Islamists of the Ḥamās movement had made in 1990 in the engineers, lawyers, and doctors syndicates. The challenge of Islamism might well overshadow other political and professional issues in syndicates in much of the Islamic world for some time to come.

[*See also* Guilds.]

BIBLIOGRAPHY

Abrahamian, Ervand. *Iran between Two Revolutions*. Princeton, 1982. Example of the general works from which one must glean references on this topic for countries other than Egypt.

Bisharat, George Emile. *Palestinian Lawyers and Israeli Rule: Law and Disorder in the West Bank*. Austin, 1989.

Misra, B. B. *The Indian Middle Classes: Their Growth in Modern Times*. London, 1961. Contains considerable material on professional people, but little on their syndicates.

Moore, Clement Henry. "Professional Syndicates in Contemporary Egypt." *American Journal of Arabic Studies* 3 (1975): 60–82. Compares the politics of various professions within Egypt, picking up in time roughly where Reid ("Rise of Professions") leaves off.

Moore, Clement Henry. *Images of Development: Egyptian Engineers in Search of Industry*. Cambridge, Mass., 1980. Excellent study of the Egyptian engineering profession and its politics.

Reid, Donald M. "The Rise of Professions and Professional Organization in Modern Egypt." *Comparative Studies in Society and History* 16.1 (1974): 24–57. Compares the professionalization of lawyers, doctors, engineers, journalists, and teachers in Egypt through the 1950s.

Reid, Donald M. *Lawyers and Politics in the Arab World, 1880–1960*. Minneapolis, 1981. Basic study of the pioneering modern profession and its politics.

Springborg, Robert. "Professional Syndicates in Egyptian Politics, 1952–1970." *International Journal of Middle East Studies* 9.3 (1978): 275–295. Comparison of professions and their politics in Egypt, picking up in time where Reid ("Rise of Professions") leaves off.

Waardenburg, Jean-Jacques. *Les universités dans le monde arabe actuel*. 2 vols. Paris, 1966. Statistics-packed, basic study of Arab universities.

Ziadeh, Farhat. *Lawyers, the Rule of Law, and Liberalism in Modern Egypt*. Stanford, Calif., 1968. Pioneering study of lawyers and politics in Egypt.

DONALD MALCOLM REID

SYRIA. The Muslim population of Syria is composed of a Sunnī majority and four minority Shīʿī sects. Exact figures are unavailable, but informed estimates place the Sunnī population, found throughout the country, at roughly 70 percent. The largest Shīʿī sect, the ʿAlawīs, is concentrated in the northwestern province of Latakia and comprises around 12 percent of the population. The Druzes are only 3 percent of the population but form a dominant majority in the southwestern province of Suwayda. Ismāʿīlīs in central Syria near Hama and Homs and a small number of Twelver Shīʿīs in the vicinity of Aleppo together account for 1 percent of the population.

Islam's place in Syrian society has changed fundamentally in modern times. At the beginning of the nineteenth century, the Ottoman Empire's political and social elite incorporated Islamic institutions, symbols, and religious scholars (*ʿulamāʾ*). By the second half of the twentieth century, secular tendencies dominated Syria, and movements for restoring Islam's primacy had become the platform for political dissent.

During the Ottoman era (1517–1918), sultans legitimized their authority by claiming to rule in accord with Islam. This religious legitimation accorded with the preeminent place of the *ʿulamāʾ* in Syria's urban elite, which mediated relations between province and capital. Among the religious notables the highest offices were jurisconsult (*muftī*) and doyen of the Prophet's descendants (*naqīb al-ashrāf*). Other high-status dignitaries included law court judges, assistants to the jurisconsult, teachers at endowed schools, and preachers and prayer leaders at prestigious mosques. Thus Ottoman authority and local religious institutions reinforced each other's authority.

The religious institution also incorporated scholars and mosque officials outside the provincial elite. Indeed, stratification according to wealth and status among the *ʿulamāʾ* mirrored that in urban society at large. High status *ʿulamāʾ* enjoyed imperial patronage in the form of rights to farm taxes on rural lands, whose revenues they frequently invested in urban real estate. They also received stipends from the revenues of pious endowments (*waqfs*). Middle-status *ʿulamāʾ* taught at schools and presided at mosques with modest endowments. They often earned the main portion of their livelihood as tradesmen and artisans. The poorest members of the religious institution were petty traders and artisans associated with minor mosques and popular Ṣūfī orders.

The affiliation of the Syrian *ʿulamāʾ* with legal schools and Ṣūfī orders manifested their participation in a cosmopolitan learned culture tolerant of diversity. Of the major Islamic legal schools, the Shāfiʿī had deep roots in Syria, but the Ḥanafī became more widely accepted among high status *ʿulamāʾ* in the eighteenth and nineteenth centuries because of its status as the official legal school of the Ottoman Empire. An ancient though modest Ḥanbalī tradition persisted as well. A religious student normally studied with scholars of each legal school. This diversity and tolerance also characterized affiliations with Ṣūfī orders. A Muslim might cultivate ties to several cosmopolitan orders, such as the Qādirī, Naqshbandī, Rifaʿī, and Khalwatī orders. Local Ṣūfī orders and minor branches of cosmopolitan orders also attracted their own followings.

In the early decades of the nineteenth century, Syria's religious establishment demonstrated its loyalty to the Ottoman sultan by rejecting the call to revolt issued by propagandists of the religious reformist Wahhābī movement in central Arabia. In addition to this political dimension, the Wahhābīs' anathematization of fellow Muslims clashed with the spirit of tolerance that marked relations among Muslims of different legal schools and Ṣūfī orders. By contrast, Syrian *ʿulamāʾ* proved more receptive to the reformist Sufism of Shaykh Khālid, who revived the Naqshbandī order when he settled in Damascus in the 1820s.

In 1831 an Egyptian army invaded and occupied Syria, bringing it under Cairo's rule until 1840. Religious dignitaries received a rude shock when Egyptian authorities sharply reduced their role in governing provincial affairs. The restoration of Ottoman rule in 1841 brought relief, but during the next two decades the rise of a secularizing bureaucratic elite in Istanbul and the growing European commercial and missionary presence alarmed Syrian *ʿulamāʾ*. Anti-European sentiment exploded in 1850 when an anti-Christian outbreak occurred in Aleppo and in 1860 when Muslim mobs massacred Christians in Damascus. Ottoman investigators of the Damascus disturbance accused leading *ʿulamāʾ* of inciting the mob and dealt them severe punishments of prison and exile. The Ottoman response marked a turning point in the historical posture of Syria's *ʿulamāʾ*, who would never regain their central position of influence. Instead, the Ottomans cultivated a new bureaucratic elite nearly devoid of *ʿulamāʾ* participation and more attuned to the secular outlook of Istanbul's bureaucrats and ministers.

In the last decades of Ottoman rule, the religious establishment received one last boost from Sultan Abdülhamid II (r. 1876–1909). This ruler countered European encroachment and internal political dissent with a policy stressing his religious standing as caliph of all Muslims. In Syria, this allowed the sultan to depict his political opponents, mostly partisans of constitutional government, as enemies of Islam. In addition to emphasizing the duty of Muslims to obey their caliph, Abdülhamid financed a revival of religious institutions, primarily mosques and Ṣūfī lodges. Indeed, one of his chief religious advisers for a time was a Syrian Ṣūfī shaykh, Abū al-Huda al-Sayyādī (1849–1909) of the Rifāʿī order, and that order became a mainstay of support for the sultan. [*See* Rifāʿīyah.]

A religious reform movement arose, however, that would oppose Abdülhamid's despotic rule, his claims to legitimacy as caliph of the Muslims, and his patronage for popular Ṣūfī orders. Reformist scholars such as Ṭāhir al-Jazāʾirī (1852–1920) and Jamāl al-Dīn al-Qāsimī (1866–1914) also supported the restoration of constitutional government, which Abdülhamid had suspended in 1878. In the early 1900s, a bitter controversy erupted between reformers, known as Salafīs, and loyalists over religious practices such as visiting saints' tombs for intercessionary prayers, and also over Islamic legal theory, particularly the validity of following the opinions of medieval jurists (*taqlīd*) rather than using independent reasoning (*ijtihād*) to derive rulings from the Qurʾān and the *sunnah*. These religious disputes overlapped with political conflicts both before and after the 1908 restoration of the Ottoman constitution and Sultan Abdülhamid's deposition the following year. Because of the Salafī reformers' identification with liberalizing tendencies, they attracted the younger generation of educated Syrians who were sowing the seeds of Arab nationalism. In the last decade of Ottoman rule, religious reformers and advocates of autonomy for Arab provinces contended for power with civil and religious dignitaries who sided with whatever faction prevailed in Istanbul. The Ottoman Empire's destruction at the end of World War I abruptly terminated this rivalry by altering the grounds of Syrian politics.

First, an independent Arab kingdom under Amīr Fayṣal of the Meccan Hashemite clan struggled to maintain Syrian independence against French pressure. Then in July 1920 French forces invaded Syria, expelled Fayṣal, abolished his government, and under a League of Nations mandate established direct rule that would last until 1946. During that quarter-century, Arab nationalism emerged as the leading ideology of opposition to foreign rule.

This ideology allowed Syrians of all religions—Sunnī, Druze, ʿAlawī, Shīʿī, and Christian—to unite against the European power. Nonetheless, Islam had an important part in the nationalist struggle. Even though Syria's political leaders shared a secular outlook and included no religious dignitaries, the slogans and symbols they used often played on Muslim religious sentiment. Likewise, leading Syrian politicians mobilized religious institutions for the nationalist struggle in order to draw grassroots support from the towns' popular quarters. The politicians succeeded in large part because of their ability to gain the backing of local mosque preachers, religious teachers, and other *ʿulamā'*.

In the sensitive sphere of law, the French left untouched existing criminal, civil, and commercial codes and courts. When the French attempted to implement revisions in the personal status laws based on Islamic law, Muslim judges successfully resisted. As for education, Ottoman reforms had already largely diluted the influence of the *ʿulamā'*, and during the Mandate era modern Western education continued to develop. The most dramatic confrontation between French authorities and Syria's religious institution arose over the administration of religious endowments. The French brought greater regularity to their administration and eventually took control over them, an act that triggered Muslim outrage.

Apart from Islam's place in the nationalist struggle, the Mandate period witnessed the spread of novel grassroots Islamic associations and cultural institutions in Syria's cities. Islamic benevolent associations *(jamʿīyat)* appeared in Damascus, Aleppo, and Hama in the 1920s and 1930s. These societies propagated moral and religious reform along lines drawn by the earlier Salafī trend, established schools for religious education, and published periodicals cultivating proper religious culture. Islamic associations combated what they considered the immoral effects of foreign influence represented by nightclubs, casinos, gambling, and alcohol. Moreover, they agitated against the westernization of women's status and conduct, such as wearing European fashions and appearing at public functions.

On the political front, Islamic associations led opposition to a French proposal in the draft of the 1928 constitution to establish religious equality for all citizens. They also resisted moves to legalize Muslim conversions to other religions and the marriage of Muslim women to non-Muslim men. In the broader Arab arena, religious organizations pressed the Syrian government to support the 1936–1939 Arab revolt in Palestine, and they raised funds to aid their Muslim brethren there.

During the Mandate era Syrian society changed in several respects, including the more effective integration of the Druze and ʿAlawī communities into the mainstream of national politics. Whereas during the Ottoman era these communities' geographical isolation kept them apart from the power structure dominated by Sunnī townsmen, in colonial and independent Syria the extension of central authority to remote areas brought them into national politics. A religiously diverse population made the inclusive ideology of secular Arab nationalism more attractive to political figures seeking to appeal to the entire Syrian nation. Conversely, a political program based on Islam would alienate the country's large non-Sunnī minority.

The secular thrust of independent Syria became apparent in 1949 when it adopted a new civil code enacted in Egypt that same year. Previously, the *Mecelle*, an Ottoman code derived from Ḥanafī law, had regulated civil affairs. By borrowing from Egypt, the Syrian government was inching away from Islamic law. On the other hand, in 1953 the government confirmed Islam's sway over family life with a new Law of Personal Status governing marriage, divorce, and other family matters. This law applies Islamic law to Sunnīs, ʿAlawīs, and Ismāʿīlīs, but the Druze, Christians, and Jews each have their own special codes. Another important reform affecting religious interests was the 1949 initiative to take the administration of religious endowments out of private hands altogether and place them under direct government control.

From independence in 1946 until 1963, Syrian politics consisted of a tumultuous series of military coups, ephemeral civilian cabinets, and a brief period of union with Egypt. The most dynamic political forces were secular Arab nationalist parties such as the Baʿth and leftist parties. The Muslim Brotherhood, first established in Syria in 1946, represented religious sentiment alarmed at the dominant secular tendencies, but it did not achieve great influence in Syrian politics during this period. The brotherhood's leader, Muṣṭafā al-Sibāʿī (1915–1964), placed the organization in Syria's political mainstream with his calls for neutrality in the cold war, armed struggle against Israel, an Islamic version of socialism, and limited private property rights. His fundamental difference with other political forces lay in his opposition to secularism. Sibāʿī left the scene in 1957 because of poor health, and leadership passed on to ʿIṣām al-ʿAṭṭār, an advocate of political moderation. [*See the biography of Sibāʿī.*]

On 8 March 1963, a military coup inaugurated the era of Baʿthist rule. Because of this party's highly minoritarian composition, secularism, and socialist agenda, the political reaction against it took a sectarian hue. Consequently, the most intractable challenge to Baʿthist rule has come from Islamic groups, most notably the Muslim Brothers. The first Islamic rising took place in 1964 in Hama, and other sectarian disturbances followed in 1967. Further protests erupted in 1973 when a new constitution omitted mention of Islam as the state religion. The regime attempted a compromise by adding provisions that the head of state be a Muslim and that Islamic law provide the principal source of legislation, but these points did not satisfy Islamic critics, especially since President Ḥāfiẓ al-Asad (Hafez al-Assad) belongs to the minority ʿAlawī sect, which many Muslims regard as heretical.

By the late 1970s the Baʿthist regime had suppressed or coopted its most threatening secular political rivals. Popular dissatisfaction with the regime's dictatorial rule, its economic policies, and its management of foreign relations therefore coalesced around the Islamic groups. Significantly, this discontent was centered in Syria's major cities and did not spread to the regime's bastion of support in the rural areas. The latter regions historically had been the poorest and most backward parts of Syria, but during Baʿthist rule they witnessed unprecedented progress. Moreover, Syria's religious minorities—Druze, ʿAlawīs, Christians, and Ismāʿīlīs—are concentrated in rural areas and have no sympathy for Islamic aspirations. Hence the insurrection conducted by Islamic groups between 1979 and 1982 did not spread to the countryside, and with a ruthless campaign of repression the regime quelled the insurrection. Another element in the revolt's failure lay in the divisions that plagued the Islamic movement. In 1970 the Muslim Brothers alone split into three groups. The Damascus branch followed the moderate line of ʿIṣām al-ʿAṭṭār. In the northern towns of Aleppo, Homs, and Latakia, branches adopted the strategy of armed struggle to overthrow the regime. A third faction based in Hama also embraced armed struggle but maintained its own independent leadership and organization.

The Syrian regime continues to insist on a strict separation of religion from politics, but otherwise it does not seek to undermine the place of religion in Syrian culture and society. Damascus University has a flourishing faculty of Islamic law, and its Arabic language department teaches courses on early Arab Islamic literature. In 1967 the Baʿthist regime nationalized all private Muslim and Christian schools, but instruction in both religions is still provided in public schools, Muslims studying Islam and Christians studying Christianity. Religious periodicals and literature, including children's books, are published and widely available. Television and radio broadcasts promote the country's Arab-Islamic heritage with historical dramas and highbrow cultural programs. Moreover, customary patterns of social intercourse within the bounds of one's religious community are persistent. Although modern national institutions such as the army and universities contribute to weakening primordial ties of religion and locality, and Syrians commonly socialize across sectarian boundaries, it is still unusual for marriage to take place across them. Broadly speaking, the regime encourages the dissolution of sectarian divisions and promotes a nonpolitical interpretation of Islam wherein the state is responsible for providing the conditions for citizens to fulfill their religious duties, but not for enforcing religious conformity.

[*See also* ʿAlawīyah; Baʿth Parties; Druze; Muslim Brotherhood, *article on* Muslim Brotherhood in Syria; *and* Salafīyah.]

BIBLIOGRAPHY

Abd-Allah, Umar F. *The Islamic Struggle in Syria*. Berkeley, 1983. The fullest account of Syria's Islamic movements from the 1940s to the early 1980s, by a highly sympathetic observer.

Commins, David. *Islamic Reform: Politics and Social Change in Late Ottoman Syria*. New York and Oxford, 1990. Study of the social, intellectual, and political dynamics of the Salafī trend in Damascus between 1885 and 1914.

Hinnebusch, Raymond A. *Authoritarian Power and State Formation in Baʿthist Syria*. Boulder, 1990. Important study of the historical roots of the Baʿthist regime and the mechanisms for its endurance. Contains a chapter on the Islamic opposition to the regime that incorporates the author's findings published in several articles.

Khoury, Philip S. *Urban Notables and Arab Nationalism: The Politics of Damascus, 1860–1920*. Cambridge, 1983. Describes the high status enjoyed by the *ʿulamāʾ* in Ottoman Damascus before 1860 and the process of their exclusion from the notable elite by 1920.

Khoury, Philip S. *Syria and the French Mandate: The Politics of Arab Nationalism, 1920–1945*. Princeton, 1987. Definitive study of Syria during this period, focusing on the secular nationalist leadership, but containing as well information on Islam and religious institutions.

Marcus, Abraham. *The Middle East on the Eye of Modernity: Aleppo in the Eighteenth Century*. New York, 1989. Splendid survey of the city's social history, containing information on religious life and the religious establishment that shows their similarity to those in Damascus.

Schilcher, Linda S. *Families in Politics: Damascene Factions and Estates of the Eighteenth and Nineteenth Centuries*. Stuttgart, 1985. Detailed examination of Damascus' society, economy, and political dynamics, including a wealth of information on the city's leading families of religious dignitaries.

DAVID COMMINS

T

ṬABĀṬABĀ'Ī, MUḤAMMAD ḤUSAYN (1903–1981), known to his contemporaries as ʿAllāmah Ṭabāṭabā'ī, one of the foremost Qur'ānic commentators and traditional Persian philosophers of the twentieth century. Born to a well-known family of Shīʿī scholars of Tabriz in AH 1321/1903 CE, he carried out his early studies in the city of his birth, and when some twenty years old, he set out for Najaf, Iraq, to pursue more advanced studies in the juridical as well as philosophical sciences, reaching the highest level of *ijtihād* in both domains. It was also at this time that he underwent spiritual training and was initiated into the inner dimension of Islam associated in Shīʿī circles with *ʿirfān* ("gnosis"). In 1934 he returned to Tabriz, where he began to teach, but he did not become nationally known until the communist domination of the Iranian province of Azerbaijan forced him to come to Tehran and Qom at the end of World War II. He spent the rest of his life in Qom with some days of each month being spent in Tehran. He devoted his time completely to teaching and writing and died in Qom in 1981.

At once a great teacher, saintly presence, and prolific writer, Ṭabāṭabā'ī wrote a large number of works (see Ṭabāṭabā'ī, 1975, introduction, for his bibliography). Some of his works, some written in Arabic and others in Persian, deal with the Qur'ān and specifically religious matters, the most important of which is the voluminous *Al-mīzān,* written originally in Arabic and translated into Persian mostly under Ṭabāṭabā'ī's direction. Among his religious works are *Qur'ān dar Islām* (The Quran in Islam) and *Shīʿah dar Islām* (Shiʿite Islam), both of which have been translated into English. A second category includes his numerous philosophical works, ranging from his major philosophical opus, *Uṣūl-i falsafah-yi ri'ālīsm,* to his last philosophical writings, *Bidāyat al-ḥikmah* and *Nihāyat al-ḥikmah.* Finally, there are the works dealing with current religious and philosophical debates, of which the most significant is *Muṣāḥabāt bā Ustād Kurbān,* containing some of his discussions with the French Islamist and philosopher, Henry Corbin.

Among Ṭabāṭabā'ī's purely religious writing, the most influential is *Al-mīzān,* in which he used the method of commenting on a particular Qur'ānic verse with the aid of other Qur'ānic verses, while taking into full consideration classical as well as recent Qur'ānic commentaries written by Sunnīs and Shīʿīs alike.

Ṭabāṭabā'ī's philosophical contributions include his refutation of Marxist dialectic on the basis of traditional Islamic philosophy, the revival of the teachings of Mullā Ṣadrā, whose *Asfar* he edited with his own commentary, and his response to various Western philosophical and theological questions, which were usually discussed between him and Corbin in weekly sessions in Tehran during the autumn between 1958 and 1977 that drew many eminent scholars to their midst, the translation and commentary between Persian and French being made by Seyyed Hossein Nasr.

A person of great saintly countenance and piety, Ṭabāṭabā'ī was able to resuscitate Islamic philosophy despite the opposition of many *ʿulamā'.* He taught the philosophy of Ibn Sīnā and Mullā Ṣadrā and gnosis and also gave spiritual direction to a small number of disciples. His students in the field of Islamic philosophy, among the class of *ʿulamā',* included Murtaẓā Muṭahharī, Sayyid Jalāl al-Dīn Āshtiyānī, and Ḥasan Ḥasanzādah Āmulī. Although he shunned politics, some of his students, such as Muṭahharī, became political activists, and many reached positions of prominence after the Iranian Revolution of 1979. Ṭabāṭabā'ī also had students associated with university circles who extended his influence among those who attended Western-style institutions of learning and who were at the same time attracted to traditional Islamic thought.

Since his death, ʿAllāmah Ṭabāṭabā'ī has been greatly honored in Iran. A university has been named after him, and his works continue to enjoy great popularity. His writings are also being translated to an ever greater extent into English, and he is becoming known throughout the Islamic world as one of the major intellectual and spiritual figures not only of Shiism but of Islam as a whole during this century.

[*See also the biographies of Muṭahharī and Nasr.*]

BIBLIOGRAPHY

ʿAllāmah Ṭabāṭabāʾī Commemoration Volume. Tehran, 1983.

Ṭabāṭabāʾī, Muḥammad Ḥusayn. *Shīʿite Islam*. Translated and edited with an introduction by Seyyed Hossein Nasr. Albany, N.Y., 1975. Includes the author's biography and bibliography.

Ṭabāṭabāʾī, Muḥammad Ḥusayn. *The Quran in Islam: Its Impact and Influence in the Life of Muslims*. Translated by A. Yates. London, 1987.

Ṭabāṭabāʾī, Muḥammad Ḥusayn. *Islamic Teachings: An Overview*. Translated by R. Campbell. New York, 1989. Includes a translation of the author's brief autobiography.

Ṭabāṭabāʾī, Muḥammad Ḥusayn. *Bidāyat al-ḥikmah*. Translated by A. Q. Qara'i in *Al-tawḥīd* 8.3 (February 1991): 93–108; 8.4 (May 1991): 97–108; 9.2 (November 1991): 68–82; and 9.3 (April 1992): 92–111.

SEYYED HOSSEIN NASR

ṬABĀṬABĀ'Ī AL-ḤAKĪM, MUḤSIN IBN MAHDĪ. *See* Ḥakīm, Muḥsin al-.

TABLĪGH. Qāẓī Muḥammad Sulaimān Manṣūrpūrī (d. 1930), an Indian scholar known for several works defending Islam against criticism by non-Muslims, defined *tablīgh* in *Tablīgh al-Islām* (Simla, 1928, p. 4) as "a call toward one's religion by one nation to another." He argued that Islam was the only religion whose scriptures obliged its followers to proselytize others. Manṣūrpurī's definition was a rebuttal to Christian missionaries who contended that Islam was not a missionary religion. Max Müller included Islam among the missionary religions when, in a lecture in 1873, he suggested a wider redefinition of the term "mission." He described a missionary religion as one whose founder raises the work of converting unbelievers to the level of a sacred duty, and stated that the spirit of truth in the hearts of believers in a missionary religion impels them to manifest it in thought, word, and deed. This spirit is not satisfied until it has carried its message to every human soul. Mansūrpūrī's definition refers to the common usage of the word *tablīgh* in the nineteenth century, which developed in response to the debate over missionary activity.

The word *tablīgh* is derived from the root *b-l-gh*, meaning to reach one's destination, to achieve an objective, to come to hear, or to come of age. *Tablīgh* is the transitive verbal form, meaning to make someone reach, to communicate, or to report. Muḥammad Aʿlā Thānvī, an eighteenth-century lexicographer in India, treated it as a term in the science of rhetoric, in which it is defined as a literary claim that is physically as well as logically possible. Accordingly, in literary usage *tablīgh* is primarily a function of language; thus the science of rhetoric is called *ʿilm al-balāghah*. The elements of communication, reasonable claim, maturity, and attainment of an objective are significant components of the semantic field of *tablīgh*. The transitivity of the verb *tablīgh* requires an object, for example, *risālah* ("message," frequent in the Qur'ān) or *daʿwah* ("call," as in *tablīgh al-daʿwah*, a commonly used modern phrase). The words *tablīgh* and *daʿwah* are interchangeable in modern usage; the connotation of "claim" in both *balāghah* and *daʿwah* is implicit in Qur'ānic references to prophecy and miracle.

The word *tablīgh* does not occur in the Qur'ān, but its verbal forms have frequently been used in conjunction with prophecy or mission *(risālah)* to mean "to communicate a message or revelation" or "to fulfill a mission" (e.g., surah 5.87). The Qur'ān instead uses the verbal noun *balāgh*, which according to the lexicographer al-Rāghib al-Iṣfahānī (d. 1108) is synonymous with *tablīgh* (*Al-mufradāt fī gharīb al-Qur'ān*, Cairo, 1961).

The Qur'ānic usage of *balāgh* signifies that the mere proclamation of the message is sufficient for the fulfillment of the mission; a preacher is not responsible for conversion. The Qur'ān says, "And say to the People of the Book and to those who are unlearned: 'Do you submit yourselves?' If they do, they are in right guidance. But if they turn back, your duty is only to convey the message" (3.20). Moreover, "Had God willed, they had not been idolatrous. We have not set you as a keeper over them, nor are you responsible for them" (6.106).

According to the Qur'ān, "There is no compulsion in religion. Truth is henceforth distinct from falsehood" (2.256). A preacher's duty is to communicate, warn, and remind others to follow the truth. *Tablīgh* in this sense implies an association with the concept of miracle as God's sign in support of a prophet's claim. Max L. Stackhouse (*Encyclopedia of Religion*, New York, 1987, vol. 9, p. 563) explains that missionary activity is rooted in the fundamental assumption that once people are exposed to the proclaimed truth, they will choose this truth; therefore they should be free to encounter and choose even a foreign truth. The Qur'ānic statement about the completion of mission by mere proclamation of the truth refers to a similar trust in human reason. The Qur'ān further distinguishes the "People of the

Book" *(ahl al-kitāb)* from other human beings because they are the recipients of earlier revelation, which should prepare them to accept the truth more quickly.

The Qur'ān stresses that Islam confirms previous revelations, and since it is the last of them, the duty of *tablīgh* is now assigned to the Muslim *ummah* as a whole: "You are the best community that has been raised up for humankind. You enjoin right conduct and forbid evil; and believe in God. If the people of the Book had believed it had been better for them. Some of them are believers but most of them are evil-livers" (3.110). The doctrine of *al-amr bi-al-maᶜrūf wa-al-nahy ᶜan al-munkar* (enjoining good and forbidding evil) evolved from these verses and forms an essential component of the concept of *tablīgh.*

Commenting on the Qur'ānic verses dealing with *tablīgh* and *amr bi-al-maᶜrūf,* modern scholars have discussed the addressees, methods, and objectives of *tablīgh.* Muḥammad Rashīd Riḍā (d. 1935), an Egyptian reformer, made it clear that Islam is a universal mission; hence all humankind, including believers in other revealed religions, are its addressees, and *tablīgh* is a duty of every Muslim. Muftī Muḥammad Shafīᶜ (d. 1978), a prominent Deobandī scholar in Pakistan, asserted that since *tablīgh* addresses the question of salvation, belief in Muḥammad's prophecy is essential. He refuted the argument of some scholars who, referring to surah 2.62, argued that those who faithfully practiced the religions revealed before Muḥammad were on the right path, implying that they were not required to convert to Islam. Mawlānā ᶜUbaidullāh Sindhī (d. 1945), a Sikh converted to Islam, raised the question of the salvation of those whom the message of Islam had not reached and argued that their salvation did not depend on accepting Islam. Manāẓir Aḥsan Gīlānī, a twentieth-century scholar and author, stated the rule that punishment of individuals after death is always commensurate with their access to *tablīgh* in life.

Abū al-Aᶜlā Mawdūdī (d. 1979), the founder of Jamāᶜat Islāmī, addressed the question of method in *tablīgh.* He stressed that human beings are free to choose between truth and falsehood; *tablīgh* does not require coercion.

These debates echo the discussions between the Muᶜtazilah, a sect stressing human reason as a basis even of revealed laws, and their opponents the Ashᶜarīyah. The Muᶜtazilah believed that humans, as rational beings, were obliged to do good and to avoid evil even in the absence of revelation. Accordingly, those whom *tablīgh* has not reached will be judged by God on the basis of their rational understanding of good and evil. The Ashᶜarīs advocated that good and evil were defined and made known only by revelation; human beings would be pardoned by God if they had not received revelation. The Ashᶜarī theologians found it impossible to conceive of a contemporary human community ignorant of Islam. The only occasion that called for *tablīgh,* therefore, was before the waging of a war. Views on this issue were discussed in the doctrine of *bulūgh al-daᶜwah* (inviting the opponent to Islam).

Wahbah al-Zuḥaylī, a contemporary Syrian jurist, in *Al-fiqh al-Islāmī wa-adillatuh* (Damascus, 1989), explains that juristic opinion is divided on the question of whether *tablīgh* to the opponent is obligatory before waging war. Mālikī jurists consider it obligatory, whereas Ḥanbalīs do not. Most other jurists, including al-Māwardī, a medieval author on constitutional and administrative laws, hold that *tablīgh* is obligatory if the opponent has not previously heard about Islam; it is only commendable in other cases.

Against this background, the doctrine of *amr bi-al-maᶜrūf* received increased emphasis and became almost synonymous with *tablīgh* and *daᶜwah.* As mentioned, the doctrine was derived from the Qur'ānic verses that describe enjoining good as a duty of the Muslim *ummah* (9.72). These verses are read along with a *ḥadīth,* reported by Muslim in his *Ṣaḥīḥ* (Cairo, 1954, vol. 1, p. 69), that says a believer must correct evil by hand or tongue, depending on his ability, or should at least condemn it in his heart. These three levels of action may be compared with *jihād, tablīgh,* and *hijrah* (withdrawal), respectively. The level of action is determined by the ability of the actor. In *jihād,* ability refers to physical fitness and military skills; in *tablīgh,* it includes command of language and knowledge of divine laws. Accordingly, only the *ᶜulamā'* are qualified for this duty. Like *jihād,* therefore, *tablīgh* was deemed *farḍ kifāyah,* an obligation not incumbent on every Muslim.

ᶜAbd al-Qādir ᶜAwdah, a twentieth-century expert on Islamic international and criminal law, explains that only a person with the following qualifications is allowed to perform this duty: maturity, legal capacity, adherence to Islam, physical capacity, and intellectual and moral integrity. ᶜAwdah adds that most jurists stipulate permission from the government as a condition, but he disagrees with this view. However, this stipulation points to the political role of *tablīgh,* and the condition was probably added by Sunnī jurist against the Ismāᶜīlīs and other sects whose *tablīgh* efforts were aimed at the establishment of states of their own.

This cautious permission for *tablīgh* activity was probably also prompted by the fact that *tablīgh,* especially the doctrine of *nahy ʿan al-munkar* (prohibition of the objectionable), could encourage criticism and opposition against a regime that did not abide by Islamic teachings. The Sunnī jurists justified rebellion against a Muslim ruler only in cases of open violation of the *sharīʿah,* but this justification was actually available only in extreme cases. Generally they recommended obedience even to morally corrupt rulers, because their rule was better than anarchy. Such considerations led *tablīgh* to be closely associated with politics. It may also explain why Muslim rulers usually paid no attention to the establishment of formally organized institutions for *tablīgh;* rather, they tried to control individual *tablīgh* efforts.

The issue of *tablīgh* became crucial in politics when Christian missions came to the Muslim world with Western colonial governments, introducing missionary schools and hospitals. Muslims viewed these missions as efforts to subjugate the East to Western colonialism, using education, medicine, nationalism, and economic aid as missionary instruments. *Tablīgh* thus emerged as a weapon of religious and political defense against Christianity and colonialism. *Tablīgh* also became an expression of Muslim identity. In India, for instance, *tablīgh* appeared as a crucial issue in the Hindu-Muslim politics of conflict, and in the mobilization of the Muslim masses as a political entity. *Tablīgh* also urged Muslims to realize that their past glory was based on their adherence to Islamic teachings and that future success also depended on abiding by their religion.

Close encounters with Christian missionaries provided Muslims with the opportunity to study and adapt new missionary methods. Missionary organizations like the Aḥmadīyah Mission founded by Ghulām Aḥmad (d. 1908) in India illustrated the impact of this encounter. Rashīd Riḍā founded Jamʿīyat al-ʿUrwah al-Wuthqā (Society of the Reliable Bond) and al-Daʿwah wa-al-Irshād (Daʿwah and Guidance) for similar purposes.

Muslims have also used education for the purpose of *tablīgh,* and a number of organizations were founded with this objective in mind. Some, like Anjuman-i Ḥimāyat-i Islām (Association for the Defense of Islam) in Lahore and Peshawar in British India, combined *tablīgh* with education as their objectives. Others, such as the Muhammadan Literary Society (founded in 1863), and the Bengal Muhammadan Educational Conference in Calcutta, strove for the modernization of Muslim societies. They founded institutions on European models and published literature in defense of Islam against Christianity. The Muhammadan Anglo-Oriental College, founded in 1875 by Sir Sayyid Aḥmad Khān (1817–1898) in Aligarh, is another such example.

Institutions like Dār al-ʿUlūm Deoband, established in 1867 in India, promoted traditional religious education and took an anti-British stance. This and other religious *madrasahs* produced persons qualified for *tablīgh.* They wrote in defense of Islam, refuting non-Muslim polemics, and participated in dialogues and public debates among Christian, Hindu, and Muslim missionaries. They traveled to towns and villages, preaching among both Muslims and non-Muslims.

In the twentieth century participation of the masses in politics gained significance, especially after the introduction of democratic institutions. Conversion through missionary activities may well have helped to increase the number of politically active individuals. Additionally, modernity and democracy promoted secularism, posing a threat to traditional religious values. Muslims thus felt the need to focus on *tablīgh* among Muslims. Mawlānā Muḥammad Ilyās (d. 1944), the founder of Tablīghī Jamāʿat in 1927, observed that education alone was not sufficient to achieve the objectives of *tablīgh.* Rather than establishing *madrasahs,* he stressed organized and formal travel from place to place for the purpose of *tablīgh* among Muslims. He emphasized that its purpose was not to convert non-Muslims or to preach to others. Iḥtishāmul Ḥasan Kāndhalavī (d. 1971), an ideologue of the Tablīghī Jamāʿat, also defined *tablīgh* without reference to conversion. He said that *tablīgh* was "to convey, and educate others in, the teachings of the true religion" (*Payām-i ḥaqq,* Delhi, 1959). It was, in the words of Mawlānā Muḥammad Yūsuf, the second *amīr* of the Jamāʿat, "an effort to adapt oneself to Islamic practices by inviting others to them." Tablīghī Jamāʿat has been one of the most successful modern Islamist movements.

Political movements and parties in the Muslim world—for example, the Muslim Brotherhood and Jamāʿat Islāmī—generally disagree with the form of *tablīgh* that requires avoiding participation in politics. According to them, the formation of an Islamic state is essential for the reform of Muslim society and the revival of Islam. This argument, which became popular during the struggle for independence against colonialism, is still advocated by those who call for the islamization of modern westernized states in Muslim countries. The conservative religious view expressed by scholars like Qārī Muḥammad Ṭayyib, the former rector of Dār al-ʿUlūm Deoband, holds that *tablīgh* is essential for building a Muslim society, which in turn is necessary for the establishment of an Islamic state.

[*See also* Daʿwah *and* Tablīghī Jamāʿat.]

BIBLIOGRAPHY

Anwarul Haq, M. *The Faith Movement of Mawlānā Muḥammad Ilyās.* London, 1972. Indispensable study of the Tablīghī Jamāʿat founded by Mawlānā Muḥammad Ilyās in 1927 in India. The book discusses the Indian Ṣūfī background to the movement and compares its lexical and operational techniques with those of Ṣūfīs in India.

Arnold, Thomas W. *The Preaching of Islam: A History of the Propagation of the Muslim Faith* (1896). 2d rev. ed. London, 1913. Excellent introduction to the issues concerning *tablīgh,* analyzing the missionary nature of Islam and describing the history of the spread of Islam in different parts of the world.

Arnold, Thomas W. "Missions (Muhammadan)." In *Encyclopaedia of Religion and Ethics,* vol. 8, pp. 745–749. Edinburgh, 1958. Comprehensive theoretical discussion of the Muslim understanding of *tablīgh.*

Kāndhalavī, Iḥtishāmul Ḥasan. "Muslim Degeneration and Its Only Remedy." In *Teachings of Islam,* by Muḥammad Zakarīyā. Des Plaines, Ill., [1983]. Argues that the neglect of the duty of *tablīgh* led to Muslim decline.

Khālidī, Muṣṭafā. *Al-Tabshīr wa-al-istiʿmār fī al-bilād al-ʿArabīyah: ʿArḍ li-Juhūd al-Mubasshirīn allatī tarmā ilā ikhḍāʿ al-Sharq lil-istiʿmār al-Gharbī.* Beirut, 1964. Muslim view of Christian missionary work in the Arab world, which, the author argues, paved the way for the colonization of Muslim countries. The author analyzes how educational institutions, hospitals, literary organs, and political parties were used to influence the Arab mind in favor of Christianity and the West.

Muḥammad Zakarīyā. *Faẓāʾil-i Aʿmāl.* Lahore, [198?]. Revised edition of *Tablīghī Niṣāb* (Islamic Teachings). English translation of a collection of treatises by the author, a patron and close relative of the founder of the Tablīghī Jamāʿat movement. The book is part of the instruction readings of the Jamāʿat. The tract on *tablīgh* provides Islamic teachings about the concept, its merits, and methods.

MUHAMMAD KHALID MASUD

TABLĪGHĪ JAMĀʿAT. The Tablīghī Jamāʿat of the Indo-Pakistan subcontinent, also variously called the Jamāʿat (Party), Taḥrīk (Movement), Niẓam (System), Tanẓīm (Organization), and Taḥrīk-i Īmān (Faith Movement), is one of the most important grassroots Islamic movements in the contemporary Muslim world. From a modest beginning in 1926 with *daʿwah* (missionary) work in Mewat near Delhi under the leadership of the Ṣūfī scholar Maulānā Muḥammad Ilyās (1885–1944), the Jamāʿat today has followers all over the Muslim world and the West. Its 1993 annual international conference in Raiwind near Lahore, Pakistan was attended by more than one million Muslims from ninety-four countries. In fact, in recent years the Raiwind annual conference has become the second largest religious congregation of the Muslim World after the *ḥajj.* Its annual conference in North America normally attracts about ten thousand, probably the largest gathering of Muslims in the West.

The emergence of the Tablīghī Jamāʿat as a movement for the reawakening of faith and reaffirmation of Muslim religio-cultural identity can be seen as a continuation of the broader trend of Islamic revival in North India in the wake of the collapse of Muslim political power and consolidation of the British rule in India in the mid-nineteenth century. In the strictly religious sphere one manifestation of this trend was the rapid growth of the *madrasahs* (religious educational institutions) in North India, which sought to reassert the authority of Islamic orthodoxy and to relink the Muslim masses with Islamic institutions. The pietistic and devotional aspects of the Tablīghī Jamāʿat owe their origin to the Ṣūfī teachings and practices of Shaykh Aḥmad Sirhindī, Shāh Walī Allāh, and the founder of the Mujāhidīn movement, Sayyid Aḥmad Shahīd (1786–1831). These Ṣūfīs, who belonged to the Naqshbandīyah order, considered the observance of the *sharīʿah* integral to their practices. It is in this sense that the Tablīghī Jamāʿat has been described, at least in its initial phase, both as a reinvigorated form of Islamic orthodoxy and as a reformed Sufism.

The emergence of the Tablīghī Jamāʿat was also a direct response to the rise of such aggressive Hindu proselytizing movements as the Shuddhi (Purification) and Sangathan (Consolidation), which launched massive efforts in the early twentieth century to "reclaim" those "fallen-away" Hindus who had converted to Islam in the past. The special target of these revivalist movements were the so-called "borderline" Muslims who had retained most of the religious practices and social customs of their Hindu ancestors. Maulānā Ilyās, the founder of the Tablīghī Jamāʿat, believed that only a grassroots Islamic religious movement could counter the efforts of the Shuddhi and Sangathan, purify the borderline Muslims from their Hindu accretions, and educate them about their beliefs and rituals in order to save them from becoming easy prey to the Hindu proselytizers.

The Tablīghī Jamāʿat originated in Mewat, a Gangetic plateau in North India inhabited by Rajput tribes known as Meos. Historical accounts differ as to the exact time of their conversion to Islam, but most historians place it between the twelfth and thirteenth centuries, the formative phase of Muslim rule in India. There is also evidence to suggest, however, that there were several Meo conversions to Islam, followed by reconversion to Hinduism whenever Muslim political power declined in the region. When Ilyās started his religious movement in Mewat, most Meos were Muslims in name only. They retained many Hindu socioreligious practices; many kept their old Hindu names and even worshiped Hindu deities in their homes and celebrated Hindu religious festivals. Most could not even correctly recite the one-line *shahādah* (the Muslim profession of faith) or say their daily ritual prayers. Very few villages in Mewat had mosques of *madrasahs*. Their birth, marriage, and death rituals were all based on Hindu customs.

Maulānā Ilyās, an Islamic religious scholar in the tradition of the orthodox Deoband seminary in the United Province and a follower of the Naqshbandīyah, learned of the "dismal Islamic situation" in Mewat first through his disciples and later through his own several missionary trips there. His initial efforts toward reislamization of Mewati Muslims were essentially to establish a network of mosque-based religious schools to educate local Muslims about correct Islamic beliefs and practices. Although he was able to establish more than one hundred religious schools in a short time in the Mewat region, he soon became disillusioned with this approach, realizing that these institutions were producing "religious functionaries" but not preachers who were willing to go door to door and remind people of their religious duties. Recognizing the futility of the *madrasah* approach as a basis for reawakening religious consciousness and educating ordinary Muslims about their religion, Maulānā Ilyās decided to quit his teaching position at Madrasah Maẓharul ʿUlūm in Saharanpur and moved to Bastī Niẓāmuddīn in the old quarters of Delhi to begin his missionary work through itinerant preaching. The Tablīghī movement was formally launched in 1926 from this place, which later became the movement's international headquarters. After the partition of India in 1947, however, Raiwind, a small railroad town near Lahore, Pakistan, replaced Bastī Niẓāmuddīn as a major center of the Jamāʿat's organizational and missionary activities.

Physically frail and intellectually unassuming, Maulānā Ilyās possessed none of the qualities attributed to many other prominent leaders of twentieth-century Islam. Neither an outstanding religious scholar and author nor a good public speaker nor a charismatic leader, Maulānā Ilyās was nevertheless imbued with the enormous zeal of a dedicated missionary. His singleminded devotion and determination to reach out to the Muslim masses and touch them with the message of the Qur'ān and *sunnah* took precedence over everything else. He was persistent, untiring, and wholeheartedly devoted to what he described as "the mission of the prophets"—to call people to the path of God. His message to his coreligionists was simple and straightforward: "Ai Musalmāno Musalmān bano" (O Muslims, become good Muslims!).

The method adopted by Maulānā Ilyās to call people to Islam was equally simple. It was to organize units of at least ten persons and send them to various villages. These *tablīghī* units, known as *jamāʿats* (groups), would visit a village, invite the local Muslims to assemble in the mosque or some other meetingplace, and present their message in the form of the following six demands. First, every Muslim must be able to recite the *shahādah* ("There is no God but Allāh and Muḥammad is His Prophet") correctly in Arabic and know its meaning; this asserts the unity of God, rejects all other deities, and emphasizes obedience to the prophet Muḥammad. Second, a Muslim must also learn how to say the *ṣalāt* (obligatory ritual prayer) correctly and in accordance with its prescribed rituals; this not only emphasizes the need for the ritual performance of prayer in its external form but also encourages the believer to strive for complete submission to God by bowing before him in humility and God-consciousness.

Third, a Muslim cannot claim to be a true believer unless he is knowledgeable about the fundamental beliefs and practices of Islam; he must also perform *dhikr* (ritual remembrance of God) frequently. For basic religious knowledge, Tablīghī workers are required to read seven essays written by Maulānā Muḥammed Zakarīyā, a reputable scholar of *ḥadīth* at Saharanpur *madrasah* and an early supporter of the movement. These essays, now compiled in a single volume under the title *Tablīghī niṣāb* (Tablighi Curriculum) deal with life stories of the companions of the Prophet, and the virtues of *ṣalāt*, *dhikr*, charity, *ḥajj*, ritual salutation to the Prophet, and the Qur'ān. Written in simple and lucid Urdu and based mostly on inspirational but historically suspect traditions and anecdotes, these essays also constitute, with little change, the basic source material for the formulaic speech delivered by the Tablīghī missionaries throughout the world. In addition, every Muslim is also encouraged to learn how to read the Qur'ān in Arabic, with correct pronunciation.

Fourth, every Muslim must be respectful and polite toward fellow Muslims and show deference toward them. This idea of *ikrām-i Muslim* (respect for Muslims) is not only a religious obligation but also a basic prerequisite for effective *daᶜwah* work. Included in this principle is also an obligation to recognize and respect the rights of others: the rights of elders to be treated respectfully; the rights of young ones to be treated with love, care, and affection; the rights of the poor to be helped in their needs; the rights of neighbors to be shown consideration; and the rights of those with whom we may have differences. Fifth, a Muslim must always inculcate honesty and sincerity in all endeavors. Everything is to be done for the sake of seeking the pleasure of God and serving his cause, and not for any worldly benefit.

The final demand, which constitutes the most distinctive innovative aspect of the Jamāᶜat's approach to Islamic *daᶜwah* work, deals with the formation of small groups of volunteer preachers willing to donate time and travel from place to place spreading the word of God. For Maulānā Ilyās preaching is not the work of only the professional *ᶜulamā';* it is the duty of every Muslim. People are usually asked to volunteer for a *chillah* (forty days of itinerant preaching), which is considered the maximum stint of outdoor missionary activity for new members. Those who cannot spare forty days may undertake forty one-day retreats in a year. Every member must preach at least four months during his lifetime. Maulānā Ilyās believed that this preaching would prepare people to endure hardships and strengthen their moral and spiritual qualities.

These six principles are the cornerstone of the Tablīghī Jamāᶜat ideology and are to be strictly observed by all members. Maulānā Ilyās later added another rule asking members to abstain from wasting time in idle talk and aimless activities and protect themselves from sinful and prohibited *(ḥaram)* deeds.

The new movement met with spectacular success in a relatively short period. Thousands of Muslims joined Maulānā Ilyās to propagate the message of Islam throughout Mewat. Hundreds of new mosques were built and dozens of new *madrasahs* established for both children and adults. People began to observe obligatory rituals such as saying *ṣalāt,* paying *zākat,* fasting during Ramaḍān, and performing the *ḥajj.* The most visible change was in dress and in the customs associated with birth, marriage, and burial rituals. There were signs of Islamic religious revival everywhere in the area.

By the time Maulānā Ilyās died in 1944 Mewat had come to be seen as the great success of this new approach to Islamic *daᶜwah.* The Jamāᶜat now started extending its activities into other parts of India. Since the Tablīghī method of preaching did not require any degree of religious scholarship, formal training, or lengthy preparation, everyone who joined the Jamāᶜat became an instant preacher on the basis of his familiarity with the six simple principles of *daᶜwah.* Thus the number of itinerant preachers multiplied quickly, and the Jamāᶜat was able to send its Tablīghī missions all over India, from Peshawar in the Northwest Frontier Province to Noakhali in East Bengal.

It is interesting that this Islamic revivalist upsurge was taking place precisely at a time when its political counterpart, the Muslim nationalist movement of the All-India Muslim League with its demand for a separate homeland for Indian Muslims, was also gaining great momentum. The fact that the Tablīghī Jamāᶜat was able to withstand the intense pressures of the Muslim politics of the 1940s and maintain its purely religious course throughout this period of turmoil, communal riots, and eventual partition of the subcontinent emphasizes not only its firm ideological commitment and methodological rigidity but also its ability to operate in isolation from its political environment.

After the death of Maulānā Ilyās, his son Maulānā Yūsuf (1917–1965) was selected as his successor by the elders of the Jamāᶜat. Maulānā Yūsuf was a great organizer and an untiring worker. He spent most of his adult life traveling with preaching groups throughout the subcontinent. He extended the movement's operations beyond the northern provinces and mobilized thousands of groups to tour all over India. It was also during, his tenure that the Jamāᶜat's activities spread to countries of Southeast Asia, the Middle East, Africa, Europe, and North America. Since Maulānā Yūsuf's death in 1965, Maulānā Inᶜāmul Ḥasan has led the Jamāᶜat and has expanded its international operations enormously. Today the Jamāᶜat has become a truly global Islamic movement. Its influence has grown significantly over the past two decades, especially in South and Southeast Asia but also in Africa and among Muslim communities in the West; however, it has not been able to attract any significant following among Arabic-speaking Muslims. The majority of its followers in the Middle East are South Asian immigrant workers.

The success of the Jamāʿat owes much to the dedicated missionary work of its members and followers, its simple, noncontroversial and nonsectarian message, and its direct, personal appeal to and contacts with individual Muslims. Instead of publishing books or addressing large gatherings, Jamāʿat members go door to door and invite people to join their ranks and spread the word of God. Their program of asking Muslims to leave their families, jobs, and home towns for a time and join in a system of communal learning, worship, preaching, and other devotional activities has proved enormously effective in building a community-type structure with close personal relationships and mutual moral-psychological support. Because the basic message of the Jamāʿat is simple enough to be imparted by anyone willing to volunteer, it is ideally suited for ordinary Muslims with little or no previous Islamic education. The Jamāʿat's reliance on lay preachers, rather than on *ʿulamā'*, has helped it greatly to reach and attract the Muslim masses in rural communities and small towns.

Despite its enormous expansion over the past sixty-eight years, the Jamāʿat remains an informal association with no written constitution, standardized organizational rules and procedures, hierarchy of leadership, network of branches and departments, or even office records and membership registry. The *amīr* (chief) is selected for life through informal consultation among the "elders" of the Jamāʿat; he in turn appoints a *shūrā* (consultative body) to advise him on important matters.

In matters of religious beliefs and practices, the Tablīghī Jamāʿat has consistently followed the orthodox Deoband tradition and has emphasized *taqlīd* (following the established schools of Islamic law) over *ijtihād* (independent reasoning). It rejects such popular expressions of religion as veneration of saints, visiting shrines, and observing the syncretic rituals associated with popular Sufism. The Jamāʿat can thus be considered an heir to the reformist-fundamentalist tradition of Shāh Walī Allāh, with its emphasis on reformed Sufism and strict observation of the *sunnah* of the Prophet. Jamāʿat workers are rigid in following orthodox rituals and practices and in observing the rules of the *sharīʿah*. Unlike modernists and neofundamentalists, Tablīghī workers emphasize both the form and the spirit of religious rules and practices.

From its inception the Tablīghī Jamāʿat has deliberately stayed away from politics and political controversies. Maulānā Ilyās believed that the Jamāʿat would not be able to achieve its goals if it got embroiled in partisan politics. Reforming individuals for him was more important than reforming social and political institutions—a process that, he believed, could gradually come about as more and more people joined his movement and became good Muslims. His later years coincided with a great schism in the Indian Muslim religious circles: most of the Deoband *ʿulamā'* opposed the idea of a separate homeland for Muslims and supported the All-India National Congress in calling for a united India; other *ʿulamā'* joined with the Muslim League in its demand for Pakistan. Maulānā Ilyās asked his followers not to take sides with either camp and to continue their essentially nonpolitical *daʿwah* work among Muslims of all political persuasions.

The Jamāʿat has rigidly maintained this nonpolitical posture since. In Pakistan, India, Malaysia, Indonesia, and elsewhere in its operations, it has scrupulously observed its founder's ban on political activities and has refused to take positions on political issues. Thus, in Pakistan, the Jamāʿat remained noncommittal on major national controversies involving the relationship between Islam and the state. In India too the Jamāʿat has never been involved in so-called "Muslim issues" such as communal riots, Muslim family laws, the Shah Bano case, and the Babri mosque. This nonpolitical stance has helped it greatly to operate freely in societies where politically oriented religious activities are viewed with suspicion and fear by the government.

In India, Pakistan, Malaysia, Indonesia, Turkey, and, to a certain extent in the Muslim areas of Thailand and the Philippines, the Tablīghī Jamāʿat has been an important movement in nonpolitical Islamic revivalism and has attracted a large following from rural communities and small towns. Although members do not participate in partisan politics, they do nevertheless constitute a solid vote bank for *ʿulamā'*-based religio-political parties. In Pakistan they have consistently voted for the orthodox, Deobandī-oriented Jamʿiyatul ʿUlāmā'-i Islām. In Malaysia, Tablīghī Jamāʿat followers have been a major source of support for the *ʿulamā'*-based Partai Islam Se-Malaysia in federal and provincial elections. [*See* Jamʿīyatul ʿUlamā'-i Islām; Partai Islam Se-Malaysia.]

In Europe and North America the Tablīghī Jamāʿat has been working among the immigrant Muslim communities, especially among Muslims of South Asian origin, for more than three decades and has established a large following among them. In addition to the propagation of its standard six-point program, the Jamāʿat in the West has also been concerned with the preservation of the religious and cultural identity of Muslims in a non-Islamic environment. Thus it has been active in building mosques and Islamic centers, establishing Islamic Sunday schools for Muslim children and adults, providing *dhabīḥah* (ritually slaughtered) meat to Muslim families, and organizing Islamic training camps and retreats for Muslim youth. In North America the Jamāʿat has also met with some success in gaining converts among African-Americans and Caribbean immigrants. Chicago, Detroit, Los Angeles, Philadelphia, Atlanta, New York, and Washington, D.C., are the major centers of the Jamāʿat's activities in the United States.

Most followers of the Tablīghī Jamāʿat in South Asia come from the lower middle class with minimum exposure to modern Western education and from semiurban areas. It has also attracted a considerable following among lower-level government employees, paraprofessionals and schoolteachers. Its influence on college and university campuses has been minimal. Because of its nonpolitical orientation it has been easy to spread its message in the armed forces of Pakistan, where it has a considerable following among noncommissioned personnel. The Jamāʿat received a great boost during the government of President Zia ul-Haq, who was concerned to develop Islamic spirit among the Pakistani military; an active member of the Jamāʿat rose to the sensitive position of chief of Pakistan Military Intelligence during 1991–1993 and reportedly directed Pakistan's Afghan operation both through conventional intelligence techniques and through holding *dhikr* assemblies.

In Malaysia and Indonesia the social bases of the Jamāʿat's support are more diverse than in South Asia. Its initial followers in these countries were immigrant Muslims from South Asia, but during the past two decades it has penetrated the Malay Muslim community, especially in rural areas. Today the bulk of its support comes from urban-based, well-educated youth. In Indonesia, where the Jamāʿat has worked in close collaboration with such nonpolitical Islamic reform movements as the Muhammadiyah and the Nahdatul Ulama, its activities have focused on converting *abangan* (syncretic, Indic-oriented) Muslims into *santri* (purist) Muslims. Thus the Tablīghī Jamāʿat in Indonesia, unlike India and Pakistan, has been associated both with the ʿulamā' and with urban-based, modern-educated Muslim youth.

BIBLIOGRAPHY

Except for brief references, the Tablīghī Jamāʿat has not received adequate attention from scholars of modern Islamic movements. Only recently have some scholars of South Asian and Southeast Asian Islam begun to study the ideology and program of the Jamāʿat in the context of contemporary Islamic revival. The available literature on Tablīghī Jamāʿat is mostly in Urdu and that, too, consists mainly of inspirational words by its leaders and devotional writings by its followers and admirers. There are also several polemical tracts written by its opponents belonging to the Barelwī school of thought, who regard the Jamāʿat essentially as an offshoot of the militant reformist movement of Sayyid Aḥmad Shahīd and Shāh Ismāʿīl Shahīd.

Aḥmad, Mumtāz. "Islamic Fundamentalism in South Asia: The Jamaat-i-Islami and the Tablighi Jamaat." In *Fundamentalisms Observed*, edited by Martin E. Marty and R. Scott Appleby, pp. 457–530. Chicago, 1991. Discusses the specific circumstances of the Jamāʿat's origin and growth, the nature and methodology of its work, and the religio-political consequences of its ideology.

Anwarul Haq, M. *The Faith Movement of Mawlānā Muḥammad Ilyās*. London, 1972. Sympathetic study of the life, work, and thought of the founder of the Tablīghī Jamāʿat, with an exclusive focus on its Ṣūfī origins.

Mahdī, Tābish. *Tablīghī Jamāʿat apne bānī ke malfūẓāt ke ā'īne men* (Tablīghī Jamāʿat in the Mirror of Its Founder's Utterances). Deoband, 1985. Harshly worded critique of the Jamāʿat by a Barelwī polemicist who argues that the real purpose of the Jamāʿat is not to preach Islam but to propagate Deobandī sectarianism.

Marwa, I. S. "Tabligh Movement among the Meos of Mewat." In *Social Movements in India*, vol. 2, edited by M. S. A. Rao. New Delhi, 1978. Sociological study of the rise and impact of the Tablīghī Jamāʿat in Mewat, where it originated.

Muḥammad Zakarīyā. *Tablīghī Niṣāb* (Tablīghī Curriculum). Lahore, [198–]. Translated as *Teachings of Islam*. Des Plaines, Ill., [1983]. Compilation of Maulānā Zakarīyā's seven essays on the basic teachings of Islam, which constitute the prescribed program of study for Jamāʿat members and followers.

Nadvī, Abulḥasan ʿAlī. *Hazrat Maulānā Muḥammad Ilyās aur unkī dīnī daʿvat* (Revered Maulānā Muḥammad Ilyās and His Call to the Religious Renewal). Lucknow, 1960. Translated by M. A. Kidwai as *Life and Mission of Maulana Mohammad Ilyas*. Lucknow, 1979. Very sympathetic, insightful description of the life and work of Maulānā Ilyās by an ardent admirer.

Qādrī, Muḥammad Ayyūb. *Tablīghī Jamāʿat kā tārīkhī jā'iza* (A Historical Analysis of the Tablīghī Jamāʿat). Karachi, 1971. Excellent work by a meticulous historian, situating the rise of the Tablīghī Jamāʿat in the context of other movements of religious revival that came before it and their impact on its ideology and program.

MUMTAZ AHMAD

TAFSĪR. Exegesis of the Qur'ān is known as *tafsīr*. The focus in this article will be on Sunnī *tafsīr*, but Shīʿī *tafsīr* will also be discussed.

The Qur'ān, regarded as the word of God, needed

tafsīr—elucidation, explanation, interpretation, or commentary—for an obvious reason: it had to be understood clearly and fully so that its commandments could be carried out with the conviction that the will of God had been done. Equally, however, as God's word the Qur'ān seemed to discourage attempts at *tafsīr*, for two different but complementary reasons. First, coming as it did from God, the Qur'ān must be assumed to be clear in its import, thus obviating the need for exposition. Second, how could finite human intelligence claim to be able to discover the true meanings of the texts of a book that emanated from the possessor of infinite wisdom? The case of the prophet Muḥammad was different: he had brought the Qur'ān, and, having been appointed by God as prophet, he could explain the sacred text authoritatively. For these reasons there was in the very early years of Islam a reluctance on the part of Muslims to interpret the Qur'ān but at the same time an eagerness to know and transmit the interpretations attributed to the Prophet in the first instance and to his companions in the second—the assumption being that these latter interpretations too went back directly or indirectly to the Prophet himself.

Only a very small amount of *tafsīr* is ascribed to the Prophet and his companions, and that usually in the form of brief explanations in response to questions asked. But this was hardly sufficient to satisfy the needs of a community that was not only growing apace in numbers but also was coming into contact with culture and traditions very different from those of Arabia. A host of new problems, both conceptual and practical, were arising and calling for solution. Since the Qur'ān was the fundamental text of Islam, it was natural for Muslims to look in it for answers to new problems; thus a need for more comprehensive *tafsīr* was felt.

Soon after the age of the companions, in the age of the successors (those who are said to have met the companions), the so-called schools—Meccan, Medinan, and Iraqi—of *tafsīr* came into existence. As in jurisprudence, so in *tafsīr* Iraq, as against Mecca and Medina, came to be known for a *ra'y*-based approach, that is, an approach that relied on considered personal judgment and not simply on reports transmitted from the Prophet and his companions through dependable channels. The spread of Jewish apocryphal reports was distinctive of the age of the successors. Until then, *tafsīr* on the whole had been transmitted orally and had not been compiled and written down. Furthermore, the discipline of *tafsīr* was not yet clearly distinguishable from that of *ḥadīth* (prophetic tradition) but was rather a special domain within *ḥadīth*. In fact, it was the *muḥaddithūn* ("scholars of *ḥadīth*"; sg., *muḥaddith*) whose collections of *aḥādīth* (pl. of *ḥadīth*, "report"), which included *tafsīr* reports, paved the way for the development of an independent discipline of *tafsīr*. This development led to the emergence of major *mufassirūn* (pl. of *mufassir*, "*tafsīr* scholar") and their works, a topic we shall take up later. The scope of *tafsīr* meanwhile continued to widen as new problems and issues arose. At this point it will be useful to take a synoptic view of the issues and problems that have arisen in the history of *tafsīr*.

Typology of Issues. Three broad areas can be distinguished: linguistic, juristic, and theological. A few points should be noted before going into detail. First, the following typology does not imply that the different categories are historically sequential. Second, not all the problems within any single category arose at one time, although the questions become noticeably more complex over time. Third, several issues fall into more than one category.

In the beginning, questions of vocabulary and syntax are raised: What is the meaning of a given Qur'ānic word? Which of the several possible meanings of a word is intended in a given context? What is the case-ending of a word? Is there any preposing (*taqdīm*) or postposing (*ta'khīr*) in a sentence? Then questions involving rhetoric are asked: Does the imperative always signify a command or does it sometimes signify permission or option as well? How is repetition to be explained in a perfect book from a perfect God? The issue of literal and nonliteral meanings also receives attention.

The law early acquired a prominent position in the hierarchy of Islamic sciences, and the preoccupation of scholars with legal issues had its impact on *tafsīr*. Among the first issues to be raised was that of abrogation (*naskh*). Since the Qur'ān is made up of revelations that came to Muḥammad over a period of about twenty-three years, certain injunctions were understandably meant to be temporary and were repealed by subsequent ones. The abrogated (*mansūkh*) and the abrogating (*nāsikh*) verses thus had to be identified. Then a distinction was made between the general (*ʿāmm*) and the specific *khāṣṣ*) application of an injunction or command. For example, surah 3.97 says that it is incumbent on "people" to perform the pilgrimage to the Kaʿbah. While "people" is general, obviously Muslims are meant; more specifically, only those adult Muslims are meant who are physically able to perform the pilgrimage and have the financial means to undertake the journey. A sophisticated basis for interpreting the Qur'ān from a legal viewpoint was laid down through a fourfold division of the meanings of the text into significative *(ʿibārah),* implicative *(ishārah),* analogical *(dalālah),* and assumptive *(iqtiḍā'),* discussed below.

Several Qur'ānic verses speak of God's hand and face and of his being seated on his throne. Interpreting these verses literally smacked of anthropomorphism, but interpreting them nonliterally seemed to constitute a departure from the Qur'ānic text. A solution considered plausible by many was to interpret the verses literally but with the addition of the rider, "it is not known precisely in what manner." Another issue dealt with was that of the sinlessness or infallibility *(ʿiṣmah)* of the prophets; verses involving certain acts of some prophets were explained with reference to this notion. One such instance is Joseph's relations with Potiphar's wife, for surah 12.24 seems to indicate that Joseph and Potiphar's wife both "made for each other," but that Joseph, upon seeing a sign from God, stopped short of committing adultery. A fundamental issue was that of free will and determinism: different verses seemed to support either the predestinarian or the libertarian view, and reconciling the two possible interpretations was a major preoccupation of the *mufassirūn.*

Principles. The multiplicity and diversity of issues, and the variety of perspectives and approaches brought to bear on them, led to the systematization of the discipline of *tafsīr.* Again it must be emphasized that the systematization did not wait until after all issues had arisen but occurred over a period of time, beginning quite early and leading to the formulation of the principles of *tafsīr* among other developments. A convenient way to cover this subject is by glancing at the medieval scholar Ibn Taymīyah's *Muqaddimah fī uṣūl al-tafsīr* (Introduction to the Principles of *Tafsīr*). Ibn Taymīyah (d. 1328) lists the following as the *uṣūl* ("sources" or "principles," translated here by the latter):

tafsīr of the Qur'ān by the Qur'ān
tafsīr of the Qur'ān by the *sunnah* of Muḥammad
tafsīr of the Qur'ān by reports from the companions of Muḥammad
tafsīr of the Qur'ān by the successors

It is obvious that Ibn Taymīyah puts a high premium on *tafsīr* that is provided by the Prophet himself or in some sense goes back to him, for *tafsīr* by the companions (the "occasions of revelation," *asbāb al-nuzūl,* are apparently subsumed by Ibn Taymīyah under *tafsīr* by the companions) or the successors acquires its authority through its putative connection with the Prophet. Knowledge of the Arabic language—including grammar, rhetoric, and the literary (especially pre-Islamic) tradition—is assumed by Ibn Taymīyah. This approach is heavily weighted in favor of what is known as *tafsīr bi-al-ma'thūr* ("received *tafsīr,*" transmitted from the early times of Islam, beginning with the Prophet's age). It evinces a profound distrust of *tafsīr bi-al-ra'y* ("*tafsīr* by opinion," arrived at through personal reflection or independent rational thinking), and a number of reports attributed to the Prophet or other early authorities condemn the latter. Ibn Taymīyah too rejects *tafsīr bi-al-ra'y* out of hand.

We shall have more to say about *tafsīr bi-al-ra'y* later. Here it should be pointed out that although the traditionally listed principles of *tafsīr* appear to be rather simplistic, the application of these principles in practice not infrequently takes a sophisticated form. Two examples, one from the theological realm and the other (in fact a set of examples) from the juristic, are helpful. In both examples (more exclusively in the first) the principle of interpretation of the Qur'ān by the Qur'ān is employed.

Surah 12.24, as noted above, speaks of Joseph and Potiphar's wife in a certain situation. The text seems to suggest that, like Potiphar's wife, Joseph too was sexually aroused. Coming to the defense of the notion of prophetic *ʿismah,* Fakhr al-Dīn al-Rāzī (1150–1210) constructs an elaborate argument to prove that this is impossible, basing it on an analysis of all those Qur'ānic texts that, in his view, are relevant to the issue. He shows that not only does Joseph claim his innocence (12.26) and prefer to go to prison rather than succumb to temptation (12.33), but Potiphar's wife admits in front of other Egyptian noblewomen (12.32) and then in front of the king (12.51) that Joseph refused to comply with her demands; Potiphar himself accuses his wife, exonerating Joseph (28); an independent witness supports Joseph (2.26); God himself declares that Joseph was one of his chosen men and that he warded off evil from Joseph (24); and Iblīs (Satan) admits that he has no control over the chosen men of God (15.40). In view of such overwhelming evidence from within the Qur'ān, Rāzī concludes, it is impossible to interpret the words, "and he [Joseph], too, made for her" (12.24), to mean that Joseph too had become sexually excited.

The conceptual apparatus developed by Muslim legal

scholars for the interpretation of Islamic texts included the fourfold division of meanings mentioned above. The purpose of this division, which was made by the Ḥanafī school and to which there is a Shāfiʿī counterpart, was to extend the application of the texts through logical deduction. The significative meaning of a Qur'ānic verse is the obvious and primarily intended meaning. The implicative meaning is that which may not be primarily intended but which, reflection will show, is implied by the text. For example, surah 46.15 says that the combined period of pregnancy and weaning is thirty months. Since surah 31.14 says that the period of weaning is two years, it follows, as Ibn ʿAbbās is said to have argued, that the minimum period of pregnancy (determination of which would have a bearing on issues of legitimacy and paternity) is six months. In analogical meaning, the obvious meaning can be extended to cover cases that are either similar or admit of a readier application of the rule. Surah 17.22 forbids one to say *uff* (an Arabic interjection signifying impatience or anger) to one's parents; it follows quite obviously that they may not be manhandled or killed. The assumptive meaning is that which, in order to be complete, requires the assumption of certain words. For example, surah 5.4 says that certain things are forbidden, the meaning being that it is forbidden to eat them, "eating" being assumed to be the act forbidden.

Because of its relative paucity, *tafsīr bi-al-ma'thūr* could not become the basis for interpreting the Qur'ān in its entirety. The attempts to widen the scope of such *tafsīr* necessarily resulted in the inclusion in works on the subject of many reports of doubtful authenticity. Jalāl al-Dīn al-Suyūṭī's (1445–1505) *Al-durr al-manthūr*, a major source of *tafsīr bi-al-ma'thūr*, testifies to this. Not only was there a practical necessity to augment *tafsīr* material through independent study of the Qur'ānic text, there was also sanction for such activity in the Qur'ān itself. Surah 38.29 reads, "A Blessed Book which We have revealed to you so that they may reflect (*li-yatadabbarū*) on its verses, and so that intelligent people may take remembrance." Surah 47.2 asks curtly, "Don't they reflect on the Qur'ān (*a-fa-lā yatadabbarūna al-Qur'ān*)?" The fact that *tafsīr bi-al-ra'y* was given a bad name does not mean that the essential activity it represented lacked warrant or justification. What deserved censure was irresponsible interpretation by unqualified people. Responsible interpretation by competent scholars could not be impugned through an indiscriminate use of the label of *tafsīr bi-al-ra'y*. That is why *tafsīr bi-al-ra'y*, despite opposition, earned itself a respectable place in the tradition, and the advocates of *tafsīr bi-al-ma'thūr* were forced to concede ground in that they came to distinguish between *tafsīr bi-al-ra'y* that was desirable and acceptable (*maḥmūd*) and *tafsīr bi-al-ra'y* that was condemnable (*madhmūm*). Eventually a middle ground between *tafsīr bi-al-ra'y* and *tafsīr bi-al-ma'thur* was reached, the rather pointless semantic quarrel giving way to a sound, practical compromise.

Major *Mufassirūn*. We have seen that only a small amount of *tafsīr* was transmitted from the Prophet and his companions. Perhaps the two distinguishing features of that *tafsīr* are selectiveness and brevity: as a rule, only certain words or phrases in certain verses are explained, and that through citation of synonymous words or phrases. This is the method used in the *tafsīr* attributed to the companion Ibn ʿAbbās, who was Muḥammad's cousin and is known as the "interpreter of the Qur'ān." The same method is used by the successor Sufyān al-Thawrī.

The first activities of compilers of *tafsīr* consisted of attempts to collect reports that were supposed to have originated with the Prophet and his companions or the successors. Ibn Jarīr al-Ṭabarī (839–923) is generally regarded as the most important figure in the formally established classical tradition of *tafsīr*. His *Jāmiʿ al-bayān* is an encyclopedia of *tafsīr* comments and opinions that had come into existence up to his time. As such, it is an indispensable source of traditionist *tafsīr*, which is made up of reports transmitted from early authorities. Ibn Jarīr aims at being comprehensive rather than selective, which makes his book a treasure-house of information, enabling later *mufassirūn* to select data on their own principles. He provides the names of authorities for the reports he cites but generally does not evaluate the chains of transmission, although he does often give his opinion on the reports themselves, without putting any constraints on the reader. In this too he helps later scholars to form their own judgment. These features give Ibn Jarīr's book an objectivity that has earned it deserved distinction.

Ibn Jarīr's work is typical of *tafsīr bi-al-ma'thūr*. Several *mufassirūn* with different points of emphasis compiled works in this category. Suyūṭī's *Al-durr al-manthūr* has already been mentioned. Abū Muḥammad al-Baghawī's (d. 1122) *Maʿālim al-tanzīl*, an abridgement of Abū Isḥāq al-Thaʿlabī's (d. 1035) *Al-kashf wa al-bayān ʿan tafsīr al-Qur'ān*, is unlike the latter in that it excludes Jewish apocrypha and fabricated *ḥadīth*s. The *tafsīr* of Ibn Kathīr (d. 1373) may be called an abridgement of Ibn Jarīr's work; it is much more selective, evaluates the chains of transmission, and pronounces on the authenticity of reports. Ibn Kathīr is essentially a *muḥaddith,* however, and his approach to the subject reflects the viewpoint of one, much more geared to advancing the established orthodox viewpoint.

Alongside traditionist *tafsīr* there developed what may be called literary *tafsīr*. At a basic level this consisted in citing Arabic poetry to support an interpretation of a Qur'ānic word or expression, and at an advanced level in making a rigorous analysis of the language of the Qur'ān. Literary *tafsīr* begins quite early. ʿUmar is reported to have enjoined Muslims to stick to the works of Arabic poetry *(dīwān al-ʿArab)* because it contained *tafsīr* of the Qur'ān. A similar statement is attributed to Ibn ʿAbbās, who may be called the progenitor of this *tafsīr*. According to a report, in a dialogue between Ibn ʿAbbās and the Khārijī Nāfiʿ ibn al-Azraq, the latter put about two hundred questions to Ibn ʿAbbās about the meanings of certain Qur'ānic words, and Ibn ʿAbbās in each case supported his answer by citing Arabic poetry. Whatever authenticity such reports may have, they definitely indicate the crystallization of the general view of the exegetes regarding the usefulness of Arabic poetry in expounding the Qur'ān. Literary *tafsīr* reaches its zenith in Maḥmūd ibn ʿUmar al-Zamakhsharī (1075–1144). Despite his nonorthodox views in theology, Zamakhsharī's *Al-kashshāf* is regarded by all as an invaluable source of linguistic and literary insights. Bayḍāwī's (d. 1286) *Anwār al-tanzīl* is more or less an "expurgated" edition of Zamakhsharī's work, for Bayḍāwī seeks to purge the latter work of theological views considered objectionable by the Sunnīs. Abū al-Barakāt al-Nasafī's (d. 1310) *Madārik al-ta'wīl* is an abridgement of the works of Zamakhsharī and Bayḍāwī taken together, although he also deals with legal issues. Another *tafsīr* with emphasis on language and literature, and one that is important in its own rights, is Abū Ḥayyān's (1256–1344) *Al-baḥr al-muḥīṭ*.

Fakhr al-Dīn al-Rāzī's *Al-tafsīr al-kabīr* represents the dialectical and theological type of *tafsīr*. Study of this commentary provides a full view of the range of Muslim theological debates and differences, especially those between the traditional Ashʿarīs and the so-called rationalist Muʿtazilīs. While Rāzī defends the Ashʿarī doctrine, al-Qāḍī ʿAbd al-Jabbār (d. 1025) in his *Tanzīh al-Qur'ān ʿan al-maṭāʿin* argues for the Muʿtazilī viewpoint.

Juristic *tafsīr* is represented by the *Aḥkām al-Qur'ān* of the Ḥanafī Abū Bakr al-Jaṣṣāṣ (917–981) and *Al-jāmiʿ li-aḥkām al-Qur'ān* of the Mālikī Abū ʿAbd Allāh al-Qurṭubī (d. 1273). Ibn al-Jawzī's (d. 1200) *Zād al-masīr,* although it casts its net much wider, may be regarded as representing the Ḥanbalī viewpoint in this field.

It should be noted that many of these *tafsīr* works would fit into more than one category. Zamakhsharī's *Al-kashshāf*, for example, deals not only with the rhetorical aspects of the Qur'ān but also with theological issues, and Qurṭubī's *Al-Jāmiʿ li-aḥkām al-Qur'ān* is not only juristic *tafsīr* but also discusses linguistic and literary issues. A number of *tafsīr* works were in fact expressly meant to be composite in nature, a good example being the nineteenth-century *tafsīr, Rūḥ al-maʿānī,* by Shihāb al-Dīn Maḥmūd al-Ālūsī (1802–1854).

Ṣūfī *Tafsīr*. Establishing a close personal relationship with God is, generally speaking, the principal aim of Ṣūfīs or Muslim mystics. The focus of their attention is those Qur'ānic verses that speak of God's magnificent attributes and exhort believers to love and fear God. "Acquire the qualities of God" is a well-known Ṣūfī motto, interpreted mainly in ethical and behavioral terms.

Ṣūfī *tafsīr* is notable first for the near absence in it of grammatical, rhetorical, legal, and theological discussions, and second for its attempt to go beyond the apparent meaning of the Qur'ānic text in order to derive deeper, hidden meanings through intuitive perception. Although it is possible to speak of major themes and preoccupations of Ṣūfī *tafsīr*, it would be difficult to say that the Ṣūfī *mufassirūn* employ a certain method of interpretation. The interpretations offered do not always challenge those reached through the use of orthodox methods. Not infrequently, however, the Qur'ānic text is used as a springboard for presenting views that have a very tenuous basis in the text and may even be irrelevant in the context or incompatible with the text. Among the well-known Ṣūfī *mufassirūn* are Sahl ibn ʿAbd Allāh al-Tustarī (d. 986; *Tafsīr al-Tustarī*), Abū ʿAbd al-Raḥmān al-Sulamī (936–1021; *Ḥaqā'iq al-tafsīr*), and Abū al-Qāsim al-Qushayrī (d. 1072; *Laṭā'if al-ishārāt*).

Shīʿī *Tafsīr*. Imāmī Shīʿī *tafsīr* differs from Sunnī not so much in methodology as in respect of its assumptions, sources, and motifs. The distinctive concept of a divinely ordained imamate is expounded and defended, and the verses believed to establish the successorship to Muḥammad within the Prophet's family (beginning with ʿAlī, the first in a series of twelve infallible imams) are treated at length, often polemically. Because the interpretations attributed to the twelve imams are regarded as authoritative beyond question, the traditions reporting these interpretations carry the greatest weight. A distinction is made between the exoteric and the esoteric meanings of the Qur'ānic texts, with the esoteric meaning that goes back to an imam (and believed to have reached the imam from the Prophet through the chain of imams) taking precedence over the exoteric meaning.

On several theological issues—such as the possibility of the beatific vision, guidance and misguidance by God, and the reality of magic—Shīʿī *tafsīr* reflects the influence of Muʿtazilī thought. In the legal sphere, Shīʿī *tafsīr*, besides expounding Shīʿī law, dwells on issues on which basic disagreements with the Sunnīs exist. Among the major Imāmī *mufassirūn* are Abū Jaʿfar al-Ṭūsī (d. 1067; *Al-tibyān*), Abū al-Faḍl al-Ṭabarsī (d. 1153; *Majmaʿ al-bayān*), and Mullā Muḥsin Fayḍ al-Kāshānī (d. 1777; *Al-ṣāfī*). Muḥammad Ḥusayn al-Ṭabāṭabāʾī (1903–1981; *Al-mīzān*) is a distinguished modern Imāmī exegete.

Zaydī *tafsīr*, judged from the work of Muḥammad ibn ʿAlī al-Shawkānī, a nineteenth-century Yemenite scholar, is not very different from Sunnī. His *tafsīr*, *Fatḥ al-Qadīr*, is in fact very popular with Sunnīs. As is well known, of all the Shīʿī sects the Zaydīs are the closest to the Sunnīs in respect of doctrine and interpretation of the crucial period of early Islamic history.

Modern *Tafsīr*. For our purposes modern *tafsīr* is chiefly, though not exclusively, that of the twentieth century. Modern *tafsīr* seeks to address a much wider audience—not only the scholars, but the common people as well. The spread of education and the rise of such political institutions as democracy have led to a heightened awareness of the importance of the man in the street, which has in turn led to the use of an idiom comprehensible to the common people. The need to address the populace in various parts of the Muslim world has also led to the writing of *tafsīr* works in regions other than the central lands of Islam. Particularly important in this respect is the Indo-Pakistan subcontinent, where a number of major works in Urdu have been produced. Some *tafsīr* work has also been produced in the Maghrib and in Southeast Asia.

A change in points of emphasis is notable in modern *tafsīr*. There is in some cases diminished emphasis and in others an almost total neglect with regard to such aspects of classical *tafsīr* as grammar, rhetoric, and theology. By contrast, there is an increased emphasis on the discussion of problems faced by society at large; the *mufassirūn* dwell on verses that bear on issues in the economic, social, moral, and political spheres. In fact, *tafsīr* today has become an important vehicle for advancing ideas in these spheres, and quite a few *mufassirūn* have used it for purposes of reform and revival. The *tafsīr* works of Muḥammad Rashīd Riḍā of Syria (*Al-manār*), Sayyid Quṭb of Egypt (*Fī ẓilāl al-Qurʾān*), Abū al-Aʿlā Mawdūdī of Pakistan (*Tafhīm al-Qurʾān*), and Ibn Bādīs of Algeria (*Tafsīr al-shihāb*, so called because it was published in the journal *Al-shihāb*), are cases in point. Shawkānī uses the medium of *tafsīr* to make a severe criticism of *taqlīd* (unquestioning acceptance of authority). *Tafsīr* remains an important avenue for expressing dissident opinion in closed or repressive societies, and Muslim scholars are not afraid to exploit its potential.

A notable feature of modern *tafsīr* is the assumption it makes of the Qur'ānic surahs as unities. The surahs in their received arrangement are believed to possess *naẓm* (order, coherence, or unity), and this *naẓm* is regarded as hermeneutically significant. Thus in many cases a *naẓm*-based interpretation overrides an interpretation based on a certain "occasion of revelation." Perhaps the most successful attempt made in this area is that by Amīn Aḥsan Iṣlāḥī of Pakistan in his multi-volume Urdu work *Tadabbur-i Qurʾān*.

A word may be said about scientific *tafsīr*. The need to demonstrate the harmony between science and Islamic religion has led certain Muslim writers to argue that all scientific and technological developments were foretold or alluded to in the Qur'ān fourteen centuries ago. The Egyptian scholar ʿAlī Jawharī al-Ṭanṭāwī, in the several volumes of his *Jawāhir al-Qurʾān*, takes this approach to extreme lengths; needless to say, whole sciences are made to hang on tiny pegs.

The differences between classical and modern *tafsīr* are certainly important; still, it is a moot question whether modern *tafsīr*, taken as a whole, is radically different from classical. The declared aims of the modern exegetes are not very different from those of the classical—to make the divine word accessible to believers in a manner that is authentic and also faithful to the tradition of pristine Islam. Moreover, most of the modern *mufassirūn* are by training not very different from the classical. As such, it may be asked whether the break between classical and modern *tafsīr* is fundamental and will become permanent. Here it may not be out of place to look at the views of the late Fazlur Rahman.

Although he was not a *mufassir* as such, Fazlur Rahman was deeply interested in Qur'ānic studies, as shown by his several publications on the subject. He was convinced of the need to develop a new approach to Qur'ānic interpretation, and in his *Islam and Modernity* he proposed what he regarded as the *tafsīr* methodology suitable for modern times. Although he stated the methodology briefly and in general terms and did not expound or support it with actual examples, it nevertheless deserves to be considered. After criticizing the hitherto popular piecemeal approach to the Qur'ān, he stated his premises: the Qur'ān was revealed against a specific sociohistorical background and embedded in its specific pronouncements are *rationes legis* that may or may not be explicit. In order to interpret the Qur'ān meaningfully for present times, therefore, a double movement of thought is needed (pp. 5–7):

> The process of interpretation proposed here consists of a double movement, from the present situation to Qur'ānic times, then back to the present. The Qur'ān is the divine response, through the Prophet's mind, to the moral-social situation of the Prophet's Arabia, particularly to the problems of the commercial Meccan society of his day. . . . The first step of the first movement, then, consists of understanding the meaning of the Qur'ān as a whole as well as in terms of the specific tenets that constitute responses to specific situations. The second step is to generalize those specific answers and enunciate them as statements of general moral-social objectives that can be "distilled" from specific texts of the sociohistorical background and the often-quoted *rationes legis*. . . . [T]he second [movement] is to be from this general view to the specific view that is to be formulated and realized *now*. That is, the general has to be embodied in the present concrete sociohistorical context. This once again requires the careful study of the present situation and the analysis of its various component elements so we can assess the current situation and change the present to whatever extent necessary, and so we can determine priorities afresh in order to implement the Qur'ānic values afresh.

On this view, as Fazlur Rahman himself notes, the historical tradition of *tafsīr*, instead of serving as a criterion of the validity of, or even as an aid to, "the new understanding," will itself become subject to scrutiny and "an object of judgment" (pp. 6–7).

Fazlur Rahman's approach, though challenging, is unlikely to find ready acceptance among the religious scholars of the Muslim world, for two reasons. First, it calls into question in a fundamental way the value of the historical tradition of *tafsīr;* and modern *tafsīr*, for all its distinctive features, is in respect of ethos, inspiration, and structure still dependent on the latter and perhaps not ready to strike out on a totally new path. Second, as Fazlur Rahman himself observes, in order to be successful this approach requires the concerted efforts of the historian, the social scientist, and the ethicist. Modern *mufassirūn*, in spite of their acute consciousness of the changed needs of present-day Muslim societies, continue to be—by training and orientation as well as in their tastes and predilections—theologians and legists in the classical tradition. The role of the social scientist is one that they are particularly ill-equipped to play. [*See the biography of Rahman.*]

Conclusion. The primacy of the Qur'ān in Muslim religious life has always been accepted. In modern times, renewed emphasis has been placed by Muslim scholars on the Qur'ān as a source of guidance. Often implicit in this emphasis is a challenge to many facets of the accepted tradition, in the theological, legal, or other spheres. This being the case, it is likely that *tafsīr* will gain in importance not only as a discipline of Islamic learning but also as a carrier of new ideas and as a medium scholars can use to initiate change or reform. This is borne out by the ever-growing number of *tafsīr* works (sometimes translations or abridgements of existing works) in the Muslim world, not only in Arabic but also in many regional and local languages. The ultimate test of the efficacy of this literature will of course be whether it succeeds in providing satisfactory solutions to the questions it claims to be able to answer.

[*See also* Qur'ān, *article on* The Qur'ān as Scripture.]

BIBLIOGRAPHY

Ayoub, Mahmoud M. *The Qur'an and Its Interpreters.* 2 vols. to date. New York, 1984–.

Baljon, J. M. S. *Modern Muslim Koran Interpretation (1880–1960).* Leiden, 1961.

Böwering, Gerhard. *The Mystical Vision of Existence in Classical Times: The Quranic Hermeneutics of the Ṣūfī At-Tustarī (d. 283/896).* New York, 1980.

Dhahabī, Muḥammad Ḥusayn al-. *Al-tafsīr wa-al-mufassirūn.* 2 vols. 2d ed. Cairo, 1976.

Gätje, Helmut. *The Qur'ān and Its Exegesis: Selected Texts with Classical and Modern Muslim Interpretations.* Translated and edited by Alford T. Welch. Berkeley, 1976.

Goldziher, Ignácz. *Die Richtungen der islamischen Koranauslegung.* Leiden, 1920.

Hawting, G. R., and Abdul-Kader A. Shareef, eds. *Approaches to the Qur'ān.* London and New York, 1993.

Jansen, J. J. G. *The Interpretation of the Koran in Modern Egypt.* Leiden, 1974.

Jullandri, Rashid Ahmad. "Qur'ānic Exegesis and Classical Tafsīr." *Islamic Quarterly* 12 (1968): 71–119.
Lichtenstadler, Ilse. "Qur'ān and Qur'ān Exegesis." *Humaniora Islamica* 2 (1974): 3–28.
Merad, Ali. *Ibn Bādīs, commentateur du Coran.* Paris, 1971.
Mir, Mustansir. *Coherence in the Qur'ān: A Study of Iṣlāḥī's Concept of Naẓm in Tadabbur-i Qur'ān.* Indianapolis, 1986.
Nöldeke, Theodor, et al. *Geschichte des Qorans.* 3 vols. 2d. ed. Leipzig, 1909–1938.
Nwyia, Paul. *Exégèse coranique et langage mystique.* Beirut, 1970.
Rahman, Fazlur. *Islam and Modernity: Transformation of an Intellectual Tradition.* Chicago, 1982.
Rippin, Andrew. "Tafsīr." In *The Encyclopedia of Religion,* vol. 14, pp. 236–244. New York, 1987.
Rippin, Andrew. *Approaches to the History of the Interpretation of the Qur'ān.* Oxford, 1988.
Rippin, Andrew. "Present Status of *Tafsīr* Studies." *Muslim World* 72 (1982): 224–238.
Ṭabāṭabā'ī, Muḥammad Ḥusayn. *The Qur'ān in Islam: Its Impact and Influence on the Life of Muslims.* London, 1987.
Zarkashī, Badr al-Dīn al-. *Al-burhān fī ʿulūm al-Qur'ān.* 4 vols. Edited by Muḥammad Abū al-Faḍl Ibrāhīm. Cairo, 1957–1958.

MUSTANSIR MIR

ṬĀGHŪT. The term *ṭāghūt,* from the root *ṭghy* ("to rebel, transgress, or overstep the mark"), occurs eight times in the Qur'ān, where it denotes a focus of worship other than God and so is often translated as "idols" or "Satan." But its meaning is wider than this: surah 4.60 refers to taking cases for judgment before *ṭāghūt,* implying earthly authorities that have taken the place of God.

The modern Islamic ideologue Abū al-Aʿlā Mawdūdī defines *ṭāghūt* in his Qur'ān commentary as a creature who exceeds the limits of creatureliness and arrogates to himself godhead and lordship—one who not only rebels against God, but imposes his will on others in disregard of God's will (Mawdūdī, 1988, vol. 1, pp. 199–200). In Shīʿī Islam, *ṭāghūt* and the associated word *ṭāghiyān* refer to those who have opposed the rightful imam (see, for example, Ḥusayn ʿAlī Muntaẓirī, *Mabānī-yi fiqhī-i ḥukūmat-i Islāmī,* Tehran, AH 1367/1988 CE, pp. 238, 376), and they were therefore often applied to the Sunnī authorities.

Because of these associations, the word *ṭāghūt* became a general appellation for any person or group accused of being anti-Islamic, in particular those thought to be leading people away from Islam. The modern Shīʿī scholar Muḥammad Ḥusayn Ṭabāṭabā'ī, for example, in his twenty-volume Qur'ānic commentary, *Mīzān al-ḥaqq,* along with the usual definitions of idols, satans, and jinn, defines *ṭāghūt* as "those leaders who lead mankind astray and are obeyed despite God's displeasure" (Beirut, n.d., vol. 2, p. 344).

In particular, *ṭāghūt* was used during and after the Iranian Revolution of 1979 by Ayatollah Ruhollah Khomeini to designate the shah and what Khomeini identified as the illegitimacy, false values, and corruption of his regime; the United States of America ("the accursed Satan," *shayṭān-i rajīm*) and its *ṭāghūtī* agents, the shah and his supporters, were accused of trying to lead people away from Islam and toward false gods.

Khomeini was himself accused of being *ṭāghūt* by his principal religious rivals, the Ḥujjatīyah. This group was founded to oppose the Bahā'ī faith, and consequently one of its main principles is that any claim to leadership before the advent of the Hidden Twelfth Imam usurps the rights of the imam. Since the Hidden Imam will, according to the *ḥadīth,* bring justice to a world filled with injustice, Khomeini's claim that he was establishing a more just society was also considered by the Ḥujjatīyyah as an attempt to usurp the functions of the imam. In Shiism, anyone who usurps the rights of the imams is *ṭāghūt,* which explains why the Ḥujjatīyah accused Khomeini of this. [*See also* Ḥujjatīyah.]

Since the 1979 Iranian Revolution, the term *ṭāghūt* has entered into political discourse in both Iran and the Sunnī world, referring to any person, group, or government who is portrayed as being anti-Islamic and a supporter of the materialism and irreligious values of the West. It is used to refer to those who are seen as agents of Western cultural imperialism and are trying to import these values into the Islamic world.

[*See also* Satan.]

BIBLIOGRAPHY

There has been no extensive study of the word *ṭāghūt* in relation to modern discourse. The Qur'ānic references to *ṭāghūt* include surahs 2.256, 2.257, 4.60, 4.76, 5.60, 16.36, and 39.17. Associated words from the same root also occur in the Qur'ān, but the derivative adjective *ṭāghūtī,* which frequently occurs in modern political discourse, is not found in the Qur'ān. See also Sayyid Abū al-Aʿlā Mawdūdī, *Towards Understanding the Qur'ān,* a translation of Mawdūdī's *Tafhīm al-Qur'ān* by Zafar Ishaq Ansari (Leicester, 1988; 4 vols. to date); and Maḥmud Ṭāleqāni, "Jihād and Shahādat," in *Jihād and Shahādat: Struggle and Martyrdom in Islam,* edited by Mehdi Abedi and Gary Legenhausen, pp. 51–53 (Houston, 1986), an analysis of the term by a modern Shīʿī political cleric. Said Amir Arjomand, in his work *The Turban for the Crown* (New York and Oxford, 1988), discusses the term as applied to the Pahlavi regime on pages 103–105.

MOOJAN MOMEN

TAJDĪD. *See* Revival and Renewal.

TAJIKISTAN. An independent state in Central Asia as of December 1991, Tajikistan was formerly a constituent republic of the Soviet Union. In the nineteenth century the area was divided between the emirate of Bukhara and the khanate of Kokand; in the late nineteenth century, Kokand was annexed by the Russian Empire.

By the beginning of the 1990s, the overwhelming majority of Tajikistan's population of more than five million belonged to nationalities that were historically Muslim. Tajiks (and eastern Iranian peoples counted as Tajiks in Soviet censuses) comprised roughly 60 percent of the population, Uzbeks more than 20 percent, and Tatars, Kirghizes, and Türkmens each less than five percent. The remainder of the population was comprised of historically non-Muslim nationalities. A large majority of the Muslim peoples of Tajikistan are Sunnī and follow the Ḥanafī school of law. A small minority is traditionally Ismāʿīlī Shīʿī; it includes certain eastern Iranian peoples and some Tajiks living in the mountainous southeast of the republic in Badakhshan. Sufism, especially the Naqshbandīyah order, has strong historic roots in Tajikistan and adjoining republics, especially in the Ferghana valley.

During the nineteenth and early twentieth centuries, most Muslims in what later became Tajikistan continued to practice their faith as they had traditionally done. Mosques, *maktab*s, *madrasah*s, and popularly venerated holy places were numerous. There was a high degree of conformity with the standard obligations of Islamic observance.

Despite major changes during the Soviet era, there was significant continuity in the practice of Islam in Tajikistan. Except for a period of relative tolerance in the early and mid-1920s, the Soviet regime sharply restricted the practice of Islam, and, under Stalin and Khrushchev, launched campaigns to destroy it along with other religions. Religious figures were arrested, religious books destroyed, religious schools abolished, and religious instruction of minors made a crime. Mosques and other holy places were closed, converted to secular use, or allowed to fall into ruin. The number of legally recognized religious figures (the "official clergy" in Soviet parlance) was limited to far too few to meet the needs of the Muslim population. By 1989 Tajikistan had only seventeen legally registered Muslim congregations.

Tajikistani Muslims adapted by drawing on the traditional practices of ordinary believers from pre-Soviet times. Religious instruction of children continued in the home and in de facto but illegal local *maktab*s. The main life-cycle rituals and major holidays were still observed. People made pilgrimages to tombs of holy men and to many natural sites associated with the miraculous. Numerous mullahs, Ṣūfīs, fortunetellers, and pious individuals served the needs of believers in ways the "official clergy" could not.

Yet Soviet policies did produce changes. Many people became less observant or nonobservant, although a large proportion of them still considered Islam an important part of their national heritage. By the end of the Soviet era, a number of religious leaders and Islamic activists were criticizing their fellow Muslims for knowing little about the religion beyond the major rituals.

The status of Islam changed in the late Soviet and early independence periods (since 1989); official anti-Islamic measures virtually disappeared, and citizens became openly assertive of the importance of Islam to them not only as religion, but also as a system of worldly values (in contrast to Soviet ideology) and as a part of their cultural and national heritage. Positive treatments of Islamic subjects were published. People organized Islamic study groups and, in a broader sense, reexamined the role they wanted Islam to play in their society. Political parties representing a range of ideologies (even the Communist Party) declared their respect for Islam and an explicitly Muslim party, the Islamic Renaissance or Revival Party (also called the Islamic Movement Party), was established. A new *madrasah* opened in Dushanbe, the capital of the republic. By 1991 Tajikistan had nearly three thousand legally functioning mosques. The old distinctions between "official" and "unofficial" Islam collapsed in the face of the rapid expansion of open observance.

Tajikistan's Muslims have ethnic and cultural as well as religious links to peoples beyond the republic's borders. All the larger Muslim nationalities represented in Tajikistan have members living elsewhere in the former Soviet Union, mostly in adjoining Central Asian republics. Contacts between Tajikistanis and members of the same nationalities in China's Xinjiang Autonomous Region appear to be extremely limited.

Tajik interest in the Tajiks of Afghanistan seems to focus primarily on repudiation of the Soviet war there and on ways to use Tajik cultural development in Afghanistan to enrich Tajikistan's culture after years of

Soviet manipulation. Religious propaganda from various sources and personal contacts have crossed the border between Tajikistan and Afghanistan.

Tajik interest in Iran includes a similar concern with culture. Iran also has some appeal as a country that has gone from self-described dependency on a foreign power to self-reliance. Some Tajikistanis have been adamant that Iran's Islamic Republic could not be a model for Tajikistan because the differences between the Twelver Shiism of Iran and the Sunnism of Tajikistan are too great. Apart from religious or ethnic ties, newly independent Tajikistan is concerned to develop relations with a variety of foreign countries as it seeks the technology and investment funds it urgently needs to address its massive economic problems.

[*See also* Islamic Renaissance Party.]

BIBLIOGRAPHY

Atkin, Muriel. *The Subtlest Battle: Islam in Soviet Tajikistan.* Philadelphia, 1989. Examines the social context of continued Islamic practice and the ways the Soviet regime tried to undermine Islam's influence from the 1970s to the mid-1980s.

Atkin, Muriel. "The Survival of Islam in Soviet Tajikistan." *Middle East Journal* 43.4 (Autumn 1989): 605–618. Explains how Muslims in Tajikistan were able to preserve and disseminate knowledge of Islam, despite the Soviet regime's efforts to prevent that from happening.

Atkin, Muriel. "Religious, National, and Other Identities in Central Asia." In *Muslims in Central Asia: Questions of Identity and Change,* edited by Jo-Ann Gross, pp. 46–72. Durham, N.C., 1992. Discusses the way the theoretically supranational Islamic identity coexists with a strong sense of Tajik national identity and local loyalties in contemporary Central Asia.

Bennigsen, Alexandre, and Chantal Lemercier-Quelquejay. *Islam in the Soviet Union* (1968). Translated by Geoffrey E. Wheeler and Hubert Evans. New York, 1967. Classic history of the problematic political relations between Muslims and the Russian empire and Soviet regime from the late imperial period to the mid-twentieth century.

Carrère d'Encausse, Hélène. *Islam and the Russian Empire: Reform and Revolution in Central Asia* (1966). Translated by Quintin Hoare. Berkeley and London, 1988. Seminal study of the way, in the late nineteenth and early twentieth centuries, some Muslim intellectuals in Central Asia—primarily Uzbeks and Tajiks—sought alternatives to traditionalist Islamic conservatism without repudiating their identity.

Dupree, Louis. "Tajik." In *Muslim Peoples: A World Ethnographic Survey,* edited by Richard V. Weekes, vol. 2, pp. 739–745. Westport, Conn., 1984. Noted anthropologist's introduction to the religion and general way of life of Tajiks living in the Soviet Union, Afghanistan, and elsewhere.

MURIEL ATKIN

TAKFĪR. Literally "pronouncement of unbelief against someone," or, loosely, excommunication, *takfīr* is a controversial concept in Islamist discourse. For militant Islamist groups, current leaders in the Muslim world are in a state of apostasy. They are seen to have become tools of cultural contamination on exposure to the ideas of the Crusaders, Communists, or Zionists. Having defected from Islam, they are believed to use the state machinery to de-islamize society, turning true Muslims into a tiny minority. By rejecting the *ḥakīmīyah* (sovereignty) of God they seem to be guilty of *riddah* (apostasy). Their modern secular *jāhilīyah* (ignorance of Islam) is deemed more resourceful and hence more dangerous than the pre-Islamic *jāhilīyah,* which was primitive. These rulers are considered worse than the nonbelievers, because they have had an opportunity to abide by Islam's principles but have turned their backs on Islam. They have corrupted the moral fiber of society, secularized religious institutions, manipulated the people by nationalist symbols, and used subservient *ʿulamāʾ* (religious scholars) to legitimize their blasphemous actions. Militant Islamists hold that the Islamic response to the deviation of rulers from the path of Allāh is not to appease them or to believe their promises to implement gradually *sharīʿah* (the divine law). Rather, their *takfīr* is necessary to make many allegiance to them un-Islamic, and to identify the "infidels within" as the first targets of a *jihād* (war against nonbelievers) that eliminates *ṭāghūt* (earthly tyrannical power). Accordingly, the priorities of Islamist movements must be reordered. The fight against the enemy at home to capture the state should take precedence over the fight against the enemy farther away.

This concept of *takfīr* is used for sanctioning violence against state leaders on the premise that *bayān* (quietist discourse) is not the Islamic prescription or dealing with Muslims who renounce their faith. Sayyid Quṭb (1906–1966), perhaps the most forceful advocate of *takfīr,* contributed significantly to the formulation of this position. He was influenced by the ideas of Abū al-Aʿlā Mawdūdī (1903–1979) of Pakistan on *ḥakīmīyah* as the only legitimate system. For Quṭb, *jāhilīyah* is a condition that is repeated whenever a society veers from the Islamic principle, "lā ḥukm wa lā siyādah ilā lillāh" ("rule and sovereignty belong only to God"). The yoke of the contemporary *jāhilīyah* has to be broken and *sharīʿah* has to be implemented in its totality and without delay. The society that does not do that is *jāhilī* even if its members perform religious rituals. Nominal confession of faith and mere performance of the five pillars of Islam do not invalidate classifications of present societies as belonging to the *jāhilīyah*.

Takfīr has become a central concept in the ideology of militant groups, such as those in Egypt known as the Jihād, the Soldiers of God, the Fighting Vanguard, and the Islamic Liberation Party, who reflect the ideas of Quṭb, Mawdūdī, Ibn Taymīyah, and Ibn Kathīr. Their belief in *takfīr* has also been influenced by their ordeals in prisons. These ordeals made it possible for them to conclude that those who inflicted ruthless torture on them could not be Muslims. Although some have concealed their belief in *takfīr* owing to their political weakness, others have gone public with it. The scope of *takfīr* has varied. The Jihād, for example, applies it only to the "infidel rulers," as advocated in Muḥammad ʿAbd al-Salām Faraj's monograph *The Neglected Duty* (1981). The Jihād resorts to the assassination of such rulers and the seizure of political power as a basic religious obligation. Other groups, such as the one known as al-Takfīr wa-al-Hijrah, apply *takfīr* to the society at large, and they practice withdrawal and separation from the *jāhilī* society through migration to prepare for an eventual *jihād*. They believe that Muslims who receive the group's call and do not join it are infidels. A third set of groups, including al-Jamāʿat al-Islāmīyah, apply *takfīr* to state and societal systems but not to individual Muslims.

The concept of *takfīr* is opposed by some Islamic groups, such as the Muslim Brotherhood. For them, it represents a "doctrinal deviation" that leads to "deviation in action." Many of their leaders, such as Ḥasan al-Huḍaybī (d. 1977), Yūsuf al-ʿAẓm, and Yūsuf al-Qaraḍāwī, reject *takfīr* of Muslims as a notion inherently marked by *ghulūw* (exaggeration), bigotry, and zealotry. Others, such as Sālim al-Bahnasāwī, argue that militant Islamists have misread Quṭb's approach and failed to take note of the strong appeal of Islamic norms in existing Muslim societies. In this view, the militants' sense of urgency regarding threats to Islam from within has been exaggerated, and their resort to violence has been found to be futile. For the Muslim Brothers, the excommunication of Muslims threatens *fitnah* (strife) that can tear the *ummah* (Islamic community) apart, benefiting only Islam's enemies. The Muslim Brotherhood believes that state and society are morally deficient and should be reformed to rejuvenate Islam, but they do not merit *takfīr*.

The religious establishment has also opposed *takfīr* as a concept and as a rationale for violence. Its leaders believe that the concept smacks of heresy and destabilizes Muslim societies. They also believe that theorists of the "twentieth-century *jāhilīyah*" are in essence "twentieth-century Khawārij," (i.e., contemporary versions of seventh-century sectarian extremists). Islam does not sanction excommunicating Muslims who profess their Islamic faith and perform the ritual pillars of religion, in the view of the official clergy. They also stress that the consequences of *takfīr* are very serious, since they entail killing the person, confiscating his or her property, and denying him or her a Muslim burial. In light of this, the *ʿulamāʾ* raise three main objections to *takfīr* in the form of rhetorical questions. First, who can claim the right to brand a person professing faith in Islam as an infidel? Second, on what religious criteria should the *takfīr* be based? Third, what level of specialized knowledge in *fiqh* (Islamic jurisprudence) is necessary to qualify one for determining whether another Muslim has crossed the line between religious belief and disbelief? Nevertheless, the controversy over *takfīr* is far from over.

[*See also* Jāhilīyah; Jamāʿat al-Islāmīyah, al-; Jihād Organizations; Muslim Brotherhood; Takfīr wa al-Hijrah, Jamāʿat al-; *and the biographies of Mawdūdī and Quṭb.*]

BIBLIOGRAPHY

Kepel, Gilles. *Muslim Extremism in Egypt*. Berkeley, 1986.

Qaraḍāwī, Yūsuf al-. *Islamic Awakening between Rejection and Extremism*. Herndon, Va., 1981.

Quṭb, Sayyid. *Milestones*. Beirut, 1978.

Sivan, Emmanuel. *Radical Islam*. New Haven, 1985.

IBRAHIM A. KARAWAN

TAKFĪR WA AL-HIJRAH, JAMĀʿAT AL-.

After a group of radical Muslims in Cairo abducted and assassinated Shaykh Muḥammad Ḥusayn al-Dhahabī, a former Egyptian minister of *awqāf* and Azhar affairs, in July 1977, the Egyptian media referred to this group as Jamāʿat al-Takfīr wa al-Hijrah. The term defies simple definition, but the meaning is clear: the society "which accuses [nominal Muslims] of unbelief" *(takfīr)* and urges [true Muslims] to "emigrate" *(hijrah)* from the paganism of modern Egypt.

This, however, was not a name that the group had

chosen for itself. Created for it by the Egyptian authorities, the name drew attention to the two tenets of the group that were bound to be the least attractive to the Egyptian public: true Muslims must emigrate to Muslim-controlled political communities, away from the day-to-day unbelief of secular Egypt; and people who do not live according to the Qur'ān are not Muslims, but unbelievers.

The self-appellation of the group appears to have been Jamāʿat al-Muslimīn, the Society of Muslims. This name suggests a certain zeal for religious exclusiveness. The group, so it appears, regarded itself as the real and only community of Muslims. Whoever refused to become a member of the group or wanted to leave it, declared himself to be an enemy of God and was to be treated accordingly. One of the group's surviving ex-members reports that members who considered leaving the group were threatened with death, the traditional punishment for apostasy and desertion from Islam. Such would-be defectors came to fear their fellow-members and so became easy prey for agents of the Egyptian secret services. It follows that in this way the group became the center of a complicated game of information and disinformation that cannot be unraveled by the uninitiated. Every crime supposedly perpetrated by members of the group may have been committed by, or at the instigation of, government provocateurs.

The group was led by Shukrī Aḥmad Muṣṭafā (b. 1942), who was executed 29 March 1978, together with the actual perpetrators of the murder of Shaykh al-Dhahabī. Shukrī taught that all present societies are un-Islamic; that only members of his group are true Muslims; and that the classical system of Islamic law must be rejected because it is not the word of God but only the work of men: "We do not accept the words ascribed to the Prophet's contemporaries, or the opinions of those versed in Islamic Law, the *fuqahā'*. We do not accept the opinions of the early jurists, or their consensus *(ijmāʿ)*, or the other idols *(aṣnām)* like analogy *(qiyās)*. How can words of mere humans be a source of divine guidance?" (Abū al-Khayr, 1980, pp. 9, 139).

Such statements imply an almost complete rejection of *fiqh* (jurisprudence) and *ḥadīth,* hence a rejection of Islam as we know it, with the exception of the Qur'ān. With regard even to the Qur'ān, Shukrī admitted, under questioning in court, that he was not certain about the infallibility of its transmission. What is known of Islamic history Shukrī regarded as "stories of dubious authenticity." The difference from the teachings of modern Muslim mainstream fundamentalists, who want to implement traditional Islamic law in its entirety, both in public and in private life, could not be greater. Indeed, this movement differed markedly from the other, more conventional, Islamic fundamentalist movements in the 1970s and 1980s. Whereas mainstream Islamic radicalism wanted to apply Islamic Law in its totality at whatever cost, the Shukrī movement wanted to do away with Islamic law in its traditional form.

It is ironic that, nevertheless, it was the Shukrī movement that was used by the Egyptian authorities to organize the general suppression of the Islamic fundamentalist revival in Egypt in the late 1970s. In the summer of 1977, the Egyptian authorities were convinced that they had no alternative but to curb the Islamic movement in its entirety. No matter how poorly organized this movement was, by insisting on the application of Islamic law, it challenged the authority of the government, propagated revolution, and demanded the establishment of a nonsecular Islamic state. Shukrī's group could be used by the secret services precisely because its inflexible condemnation of apostates drove into the arms of the authorities those members who contemplated renouncing its ideas. These men concluded that as long as they had to remain in the group, service as government informers or *agents provocateurs* could be profitable. This, one has to conclude, is the larger significance of the Takfīr wa al-Hijrah, a movement that has not lasted.

Like Shukrī's movement, Islamic fundamentalism is a natural response to the secularization of the ruling elites in the Muslim world. Islamic fundamentalists, like Shukrī and his followers, want to put the power of the omnipotent modern state into the hands of the best possible Muslims. It is this obsession with the power of the state that makes them so dangerous in the eyes of the authorities. Yet it is clear in retrospect that Shukrī Muṣṭafā never attracted a mass following and that Takfīr wa al-Hijrah represented a case of cult formation rather than a true revivalist movement.

[*See also* Egypt *and the biography of Muṣṭafā.*]

BIBLIOGRAPHY

Abū al-Khayr, ʿAbd al-Raḥmān (pseudonym?). *Dhikrayātī maʿa Jamāʿat al-Muslimīn "Al-Takfīr wa-al-Hijrah."* Kuwait, 1980. Memoirs of a survivor of the group.

Aḥmad, Rifʿat Sayyid, ed. *Al-rāfiḍūn.* London, 1991. Contains transcripts of the court proceedings against Shukrī Muṣṭafā. See pages 53–109.

Aḥmad, Rif'at Sayyid, ed. *Al-thā'irūn*. London, 1991. Publication of parts of Shukrī's own text, *Kitāb al-khilāfah* (The Book of the Caliphate). See pages 115–160.

Ḥassān Ḥāmid, Muḥammad ʿAbd al-ʿAẓīm ʿAlī, and ʿAbd al-Fattāḥ Yaḥyā Kāmil Aḥmad. *Muwājahat al-fikr al-mutaṭarrif fī al-Islām*. N.p. [Cairo], 1980. Discusses the Shukrī group from the viewpoint of the ruling elite, and contains quotations from the proceedings of Shukrī's trial.

Jansen, J. J. G. "De betekenis van het Islamitisch fundamentalisme: De lotgevallen van de Shukri-groep in Egypte." In *Naar de letter: Beschouwingen over fundamentalisme,* edited by P. Boele et al., pp. 185–202. Utrecht, 1991. Discusses the tenets of the Shukrī group and the way in which the group distinguished itself from mainstream fundamentalism.

Kepel, Gilles. *The Prophet and Pharaoh*. London, 1985. Describes the Shukrī movement and its intellectual links to Sayyid Quṭb. See especially pages 70–102.

Munson, Henry, Jr. *Islam and Revolution in the Middle East*. New Haven, 1988. Standard account of the tragic events in which Shukrī and Shaykh al-Dhahabī played a role. See pages 79–80.

Al-tawḥīd: Majallah Islāmīyah thaqāfīyah shahrīyah (Cairo) 5.10 (September 1977). Discusses the Shukrī group from the viewpoint of mainstream fundamentalism.

JOHANNES J. G. JANSEN

ṬĀLEQĀNI, MAḤMUD (1910–1979), Iranian cleric and political activist, a key ideologue of the Islamic Revolution of 1978–1979. Ṭāleqāni (or Ṭāliqānī) was born into a family of *ʿulamā'* (religious scholars) in the Ṭāleqān Valley northwest of Tehran and spent his childhood in the capital, where his father was prayer leader of a mosque. After extensive studies at the seminaries of Qom and Najaf, he settled in Tehran in 1939. His opposition to royal dictatorship was deepened when in that same year he was jailed for three months for not carrying with him a government-issued license exempting *ʿulamā'* from Reza Shah's European dress code. Disappointed with the *ʿulamā's* preoccupation with matters of faith and indifference to the country's sociopolitical conditions, he sought refuge in the sources of religion, chiefly the Qur'ān. Beginning in 1939 he organized Qur'ān interpretation sessions, in which he attempted to draw exemplary significance from the holy book in a language nonscholars could understand. His main preoccupation after Reza Shah's abdication in 1941 was the rapid spread of communist influence among the youth. Since neither repression nor traditional religion could stop the flow of ideas, the formulation of an attractive ideological alternative was the only solution. Ṭāleqāni collaborated with Mehdi Bāzargān in its elaboration.

In the years of relative political freedom between 1941 and 1953, Ṭāleqāni engaged in public activity on a scale far beyond what was customary for the *ʿulamā'*. In 1946 he accompanied Iranian troops reoccupying Azerbaijan, in 1947 he gave radio talks in which he analyzed social issues in light of religion, and in 1948 he became prayer leader at the Hidāyat Mosque in central Tehran. After the founding of the National Front in 1949, this mosque became a focal point for religiously oriented Mossadeghists, who attended meetings organized by Ṭāleqāni. An early supporter of the nationalist prime minister, Mohammad Mossadegh, Ṭāleqāni was a candidate in the parliamentary elections of 1952, but the voting in his northern constituency was canceled. After his fellow clerical activist Abol-Qāsem Kāshāni broke with Mossadegh, Ṭāleqāni remained loyal to the latter and became active in the National Resistance Movement after the coup of 1953. In 1961 he cofounded the Liberation Movement of Iran (LMI) with Mehdi Bāzargān, and he was arrested in 1963.

During the shah's dictatorship, Ṭāleqāni spent many years in prison or internal exile and was freed only in late 1978. Shortly thereafter he led the gigantic antiregime demonstrations of 10 and 11 December in Tehran that heralded the end of the shah's regime. A charismatic and popular leader in his own right, Ṭāleqāni at no point challenged Ayatollah Ruhollah Khomeini, whose position in the clerical hierarchy was far above his own. Ṭāleqāni did not rejoin the LMI in 1978, so as to be able to work for the unity of all revolutionary forces. Having been elected to the Assembly of Experts from Tehran with the highest number of votes, he died on 9 September 1979 before the final version of the constitution was passed.

As an ideologue, Ṭāleqāni's heritage is claimed by groups as disparate as leaders of the Islamic republic, its radical opponents in the Mujāhidīn-i Khalq, and the liberal Islamists of the LMI. The pervasiveness of his influence makes him one of the key figures in the Islamic Revolution. In 1955 Ṭāleqāni edited and published the book *Tanbīh al-millah wa-tanzīh al-ummah*. Written in 1905 on the basis of Shīʿī doctrine by Ayatollah Muḥammad Ḥusayn Nā'īnī (d. 1936) to defend constitutional government against the supporters of both royal and clerical rule after the Constitutional Revolution of 1905–1909, it acquired new significance for the religiously oriented sectors of the opposition against the shah.

In the early 1960s agrarian reform became a major

issue in Iranian politics with the shah's land-reform program. As a populist, Ṭāleqāni did not share many of his fellow clerics' outright opposition to land reform, but he could not support the regime's self-serving handling of the matter. To solve this problem, he concentrated on the question of ownership and concluded that unlike socialism, Islam accepted the principle of private ownership of land—but unlike capitalism, this acceptance was not absolute and was contingent on the owners using the land productively.

Between 1963 and 1978 Ṭāleqāni worked on a Qur'ānic commentary, which he called "A Ray from the Qur'ān." It differed from traditional exegetical works in that it adopted a simple language accessible to the laity. From the Qur'ān, he deduced an evolutionary view of history in which societies move from a bad to a better condition and advocated "free will" as opposed to "predestination." From these premises Ṭāleqāni concluded that Muslims had to take their destiny into their own hands and strive against their internal and external enemies to improve their condition and achieve justice. By attempting to show the relevance of the Qur'ān to the problems faced by Iranians, he invented an ideological discourse whose lingering attractiveness is testified to by the variety of groups that claim his legacy. This legacy, however, is viewed with skepticism by the more traditional *ʿulamā'*, who criticize his reductionist reading of the Qurān.

[*See also* Iranian Revolution of 1979; Liberation Movement of Iran; *and the biographies of Bāzargān, Kāshāni, Khomeini, and Nā'īnī.*]

BIBLIOGRAPHY

Chehabi, H. E. *Iranian Politics and Religious Modernism: The Liberation Movement of Iran under the Shah and Khomeini*. Ithaca, N.Y., and London, 1990. Contains biographical material and an analysis of Ṭāleqāni's socioeconomic writings.

Dabashi, Hamid. "Taliqani's Qur'anic Exegesis: Elements of a Revolutionary Discourse." In *Modern Capitalism and Islamic Ideology in Iran*, edited by Cyrus Bina and Hamid Zanganeh, pp. 51–81. London, 1992. Excellent discussion and critique of the methodology and content of Ṭāleqāni's interpretation of the Qur'ān.

Dabashi, Hamid. *Theology of Discontent: The Ideological Foundation of the Islamic Republic of Iran*. New York, 1993. See chapter 4 for an exhaustive treatment of Ṭāleqāni's thought.

Taleqani, Seyyed Mahmood (Ṭāleqāni, Maḥmud). *Islam and Ownership*. Translated by Ahmad Jabari and Farhang Rajaee. Lexington, Ky., 1983. Final version of Ṭāleqāni's thought on the forms of ownership according to Islam, published in Persian in 1965.

H. E. CHEHABI

TANZANIA. Although Islam was practiced in East African coastal enclaves and off-shore islands such as Zanzibar (that are now part of Tanzania) as early as the twelfth century CE, only at the end of the nineteenth century did it become a truly popular religion. Its spread from the coast to surrounding areas was linked to trade, and people along the three major routes from the coast to the interior became the most likely converts. These routes were nominally under the control of the ruling Zanzibari oligarchs, who were adherents of the Kharījī Ibāḍī sect, the Muslims who plied them and played a key role in Islam's dissemination, mainly Arab or part-Arab, were usually Sunnī of the Shāfiʿī school—as the majority of Tanzanian Muslims are today. (Less than two percent, mainly of Indian origin, belong to various Shīʿī sects.)

The coming of European rule—first the Germans in 1891 and then the British in 1916—resulted in major gains for Islam. German government policies inadvertently fostered its growth; a subsequent vacuum of political and administrative leadership in the transition from German to effective British rule reinforced it. The period from 1916 to 1924 was in fact when Islam made its greatest gains ever in East Africa. As was true with earlier periods of expansion, upheaval, uncertainty, and crisis fostered Islam's growth. From pre–World War I estimates of about 3 percent of the population, Muslims by 1925 estimates constituted about 25 percent. Although the percentage of Muslims has continued to grow, to about one-third of the population today, the rate of increase has never surpassed the post–World War I period.

Islam's growth after World War I was primarily led by African missionaries, almost exclusively Sunnī. Until the imposition of European colonial rule, the *ʿulamā'* class based in Zanzibar and under the tutelage of the sultanate exercised authority and influence on the mainland. Ethnically, this community consisted mostly of Arabs of Hadrami origin. Arabs of southern Somali Barawi origin also figured significantly within the *ʿulamā'*. The end of Zanzibar's regional rule created opportunities for a learned class on the mainland, and Africans began to emerge as key leaders. Although Arabs disproportionately occupied such posts throughout the twentieth century, African Sunnī leaders increasingly emerged, especially beyond the coastal enclaves.

The chief agent for Islam's growth in the twentieth century was the Ṣūfī order or brotherhood, the *ṭarīqah.*

Although exact figures do not exist, today up to 70 percent of Tanzanian Sunnīs are estimated to be affiliated with Ṣūfī orders. The largest of these is the Qādirīyah, comprised of three major branches whose adherents account for about three-fourths of all brotherhood followers. Other brotherhoods present in Tanzania, ranked in importance, are the Shādhilīyah, the ʿAskarīyah, the Aḥmadīyah–Dandarawīyah, and the Rifāʿīyah. [*See* Qādirīyah; Shādhilīyah; Aḥmadīyah; *and* Rifāʿīyah.]

Islam was africanized primarily through the brotherhoods. The historical hegemony that Arab elites exercised within the Sunnī community was challenged with the advent of the orders at the end of the nineteenth century and their spread in the twentieth. Their emphasis on piety as opposed to the book-learning of the *ʿulamāʾ* made it possible for the first time for Africans to assume positions of authority as *ṭarīqah* heads. The *dhikr* rituals that involved singing and dancing were often looked on with disapproval by the *ʿulamāʾ*, who tended to regard such practices as *bidʿah*. The combination of African leadership and ritual practices made the brotherhoods the key agent in recruiting the African masses to Islam.

African Muslims were particularly active in the struggle for independence. The challenge from the brotherhoods to the traditional *ʿulamāʾ*, manifested mainly at the local level, in fact represented a nascent expression of African nationalism. African Muslims were most active in the Tanganyika African National Union (founded in 1954), the party that led the independence struggle. *Ṭarīqah* leaders mobilized support for the party before and after independence in 1961. Their hope was that independence would redress the inequities of British colonial rule, under which Christians—also about one-third of the population—had relatively better educational and thus economic opportunities.

On both the mainland and Zanzibar, which united with the former in 1965, the ruling parties took steps—at times coercive—to ensure Muslim support in the postcolonial period. However, with the dismantling in the late 1980s of Tanzania's version of African socialism, *ujamaa*, and the adoption of more explicit procapitalist and pro-Western policies by the government, there are now signs of growing discontent among some elements of the African Muslim population. It is likely that free-market policies will exacerbate the inequalities that *ujamaa* never fully overcame and thus that such sentiment will increase. The fact that Islamic fundamentalism is getting a hearing today, which entails more aggressive proselytizing, may also indicate what is on the agenda. Historically, periods of uncertainty and instability have accompanied significant growth of Islam; whether this is the reality today in Tanzania remains to be seen.

BIBLIOGRAPHY

Caplan, Ann Patricia. *Choice and Constraint in a Swahili Community.* London and New York, 1975. Detailed anthropological look at a community on Mafia Island, with some attention to Islam.

Iliffe, John. *A Modern History of Tanganyika.* Cambridge, 1979. The best overview for understanding the twentieth-century social and political context of the Muslim community.

Martin, B. G. "Notes on Some Members of the Learned Classes of Zanzibar and East Africa in the Nineteenth Century." *African Historical Studies* 3 (1971): 525–545. Biographical data on the leading *ʿulamāʾ*, particularly the Ḥaḍramī Arabs.

Nimtz, August H., Jr. "Islam in Tanzania: An Annotated Bibliography." *Tanzania Notes and Records* 72 (1972): 53–74. The only annotated listing and the most comprehensive to 1970.

Nimtz, August H., Jr. *Islam and Politics in East Africa: The Sufi Order in Tanzania.* Minneapolis, 1980. Still regarded as the best overview and introduction. In addition to a regional and national view, provides an in-depth analysis of the coastal town of Bagamoyo.

Prins, A. H. J. *The Swahili-Speaking Peoples of Zanzibar and the East African Coast.* London, 1961. The most comprehensive ethnographic survey, with some reference to Islam. Contains an extensive bibliography.

Trimingham, J. Spencer. *Islam in East Africa.* Oxford, 1964. Still useful introduction to the region, although some of its claims have been refuted by more recent research. Contains a useful glossary.

Westerlund, David. *Ujamaa na Dini: A Study of Some Aspects of Society and Religion in Tanzania, 1961–1977.* Stockholm, 1980. Argues that the country's socialist course has both political and ideological roots in Islam.

AUGUST H. NIMTZ, JR.

TANZIMAT. The Turkish term *Tanzimat* ("regulation") denotes a period of social and political reform that transformed the Ottoman Empire by integrating into it institutions deliberately copied from those of western Europe. The period is generally agreed to begin with the proclamation of the quasi-constitutional Charter of Gülhane in 1839, but its terminal date is harder to determine. Its impetus was halted in 1877 by Sultan Abdülhamid II's suspension of the Ottoman Constitution of 1876, but the sultan continued elements of the Tanzimat's social program. Another endpoint sometimes proposed, the granting of special privileges to Ottoman Christians in 1856, overemphasizes the importance of external pressures on a movement that was in fact driven by internal concerns.

The origins of the Tanzimat lie in the latter half of the eighteenth century, which saw successive efforts to modernize the Ottoman Empire. The most important aspects of this were the modernization of the military, particularly the establishment of a school of military engineering (1776–1794), and a trend among the bureaucratic elite toward imitating the lifestyle of the Western upper classes. The first printing press in the empire was installed in 1729, and translations of Western scientific texts on medicine, botany, astronomy, and mathematics appeared over the rest of the century. Along with increasing appreciation of the material aspects of Western culture, there arose among the elite an interest in what may be called Western civil society. The ideas of the French Revolution, however, had little influence among the Ottoman elite, although it clearly affected the empire's Christian educated classes. The political theory that most noticeably underlay later Ottoman reforms is a variation on the idea of enlightened despotism known as Cameralism.

The reform movement was at once an attempt at modernization and an effort to prevent the disintegration of a multiethnic, multireligious empire. At the inception of the Tanzimat the Ottoman Empire embraced or effectively controlled the present territories of Albania, northern and eastern Greece, Crete, Serbia, Bosnia, Bulgaria, Rumania, Syria, Iraq, Jordan, Saudi Arabia, Egypt, and Libya, and had loose ties with Tunisia.

Sultan Mahmud II (r. 1808–1839) had already linked these two goals of Ottoman policy in his efforts to quell rebellions by ambitious provincial dynasties like the Kurdish Babans or by regional Ottoman notables like Ali Pasha of Janina and Muḥammad ʿAlī of Egypt. On the advice of some of his younger councilors, in 1837 the sultan established two new bodies: an embryonic Council of Ministers (Dâr-i Şurâ-yı Bâb-ı Âli) and the Council of Judicial Ordinances (Meclis-i Vâlâ-yı Akam-ı Adliye). The evolution of these bodies during the nineteenth century eventually led to the separation of the executive from the judiciary. (The Assembly of Provincial Notables convened in Istanbul in 1845 did not, however, much affect the administration of the empire.)

The charter known as the Gülhane Rescript of 1839 was authored primarily by Minister of Foreign Affairs Mustafa Reşid Paşa, who wrote that it was "only intended to introduce a complete security of life, property and honor of individuals and regulate the internal and military expenditures of the Porte." In fact, it has been argued that the Rescript was framed to protect the advantages of Ottoman bureaucrats who resented the sultan's power over them (Mardin, 1962).

Foreign conflicts marked the first years of the Tanzimat period. The first was the attempt by Muḥammad ʿAlī to detach Egypt and Syria from the empire, resolved by a European-driven compromise in 1841 that established Muḥammad ʿAlī and his heirs in possession of Egypt but forced him out of Syria. [*See* Muḥammad ʿAlī Dynasty.] The second was the Crimean War, which had complex origins involving Russian assertions of the right to protect Ottoman Orthodox Christians as well as the interests of European alliances. In 1856 Britain, France, and their allies forced Russia to accept preliminary peace terms.

In February 1856 the Ottoman government proclaimed the second important document of the Tanzimat, the Edict of Reforms (Islâhat Fermanı). This document guaranteed under the law that Muslims and non-Muslims would have equal rights and obligations in regard to military service, the administration of justice, taxation, admission to educational institutions, and public employment. The edict removed the civil powers formerly held by the heads of Christian congregations under the *millet* system, which had provided for separate administration in certain minority communities. Instead, the churches were to be governed by a synod of clergy and a national council of laymen. These features, which were widely resented in both Muslim and Christian communities, were made public by the Ottomans in the days preceding the impending Congress of Paris of 1856, which confirmed this engagement. The Congress also resulted in Turkey's admission to the European alliance and in guarantees of its territorial status.

The first generation of Tanzimat reformers, the supporters of Reşid Paşa, were succeeded by a second generation after 1856. The leading officials of the new era, Âli Paşa and Fuad Paşa, held the highest offices in alternation and continued efforts to erode the sultan's powers and transfer them to the higher bureaucracy. They in turn were accused of autocratic malfeasance by a new movement, the Young Ottomans, who promoted constitutionalism and parliamentary government.

The Young Ottomans rose out of newly established institutions such as the Bureau of Translation and the Ministry of Foreign Affairs, where they had constant contact with Western institutions and publications.

They came to adulthood during a period when the new Turkish journalism was opening windows on current events and scientific advances in the West. The foundation for the movement was laid by the Istanbul journalist and bureaucrat İbrahim Şinasi, who founded the successful periodical *Tasvir-i efkâr* (Herald of Ideas) in 1862. This was the first journal to address not merely the elite, but the wider audience of readers from all the educated classes—an appeal parallel to that of the European Enlightenment. It and its successors subtly transformed Turkish opinion, preparing the way for the Young Ottomans. That organization apparently originated in intellectual, primarily bureaucratic circles in the 1860s; the group's first formal meeting was held in 1865 under the leadership of Mehmet Namık Kemal, a young official who was also a poet and a contributor to *Tasvir-i efkâr*. The Young Ottomans later founded their own journal, *Hürriyet* (Liberty).

At the same time as bureaucratic reformers were interesting themselves in representative government, there was religious ferment among the *ʿulamāʾ*. They realized that the Tanzimat reforms were undermining their role as social arbiters and that the secular schools founded under the Tanzimat were having a similar effect on their control of education. In particular, the Rüşdiye, a primary and middle school on the Western model, was gaining popularity; it replaced the traditional religious curriculum with such new subjects as arithmetic, geography, composition, and secular history. The extended course of theological study in *madrasah*s (Tk., *medrese*) was giving way to a shorter, more practically oriented form of education. The concerns of the *ʿulamāʾ* were voiced most forcefully by Ali Suavi, a seminarian with a bureaucratic career who was also preaching at the Şehzade Mosque, and who wrote for the journal *Muhbir*. He approached the Young Ottomans when he was forced to join some of their leaders in exile in Europe, but they found little common ground with Suavi and the alliance was short-lived. [*See the biography of Suavi.*]

The core of the Young Ottomans were forced by the regime into exile in Europe, where the movement tended to disintegrate. The ideas of Namık Kemal appear in retrospect to be its most cogent and influential results. He was inspired by both Enlightenment contractual theories and nineteenth-century European constitutional currents, and perhaps by French thought under the "liberal empire." Whether out of respect for the ferment among the conservative *ʿulamāʾ* or out of a more general consciousness of the Islamic nature of Ottoman culture, Kemal combined his Western influences with an Islamic foundation. From the West he took the idea of a representative government—a novel concept in the Islamic world—but he proposed that such a body be based on Islamic values. Also novel was the idea of Ottoman patriotism, which inspired some of Kemal's most trenchant articles and his most moving poems. There were serious practical obstacles to both Kemal's innovations: he did not clarify how Islam was to inspire the legislators, nor how Ottoman patriotism could take hold in an empire characterized by deep ethnic and religious divisions. Nevertheless, during his bumpy career (he returned to Turkey to be alternately employed by the government and jailed) he appears to have had some influence in the process leading up the Ottoman constitution of 1876. [*See* Young Ottomans *and the biography of Kemal.*]

The major factor leading to the 1876 constitution, however, was the general setting of the Tanzimat. It established a series of reforms that set the stage, notably the evolution of consultative and judicial bodies, the codification of civil law (the *Mecelle*) based on *şerʾi* (Ar., *sharʿī*; religious) logic, the modernization of education, and the application of the Law on the Administration of the Provinces (1864–1871). The *Mecelle* represented the only concession granted by the Tanzimat to religion. [*See* Mecelle.] The Law on the Administration of the Provinces was based on the French administrative system; it rationalized central administration by dividing the empire into vilayets (departments) and sub-vilayets or *kaza*. Mithat Paşa, the Ottoman governor of the Danube province, elaborated this legislation by strengthening government in the provinces at the same time as he expanded local representative institutions.

The revolutionary movement of 1876 originated among Islamic seminary students protesting the submissive policies of Grand Vizier Mahmud Nedim toward Russia. The agitation enabled a group of ministers, including Minister of Military Education Süleyman Paşa, to depose Sultan Abdülaziz and enthrone Prince Murad, who was known to support liberal ideas. When it became obvious that Murad V was mentally incompetent, the young Prince Abdülhamid was installed as Sultan Abdülhamid II (r. 1876–1909).

With the empire facing dual crises of war with Russia and massive foreign debt, a committee was formed to work on a draft constitution. It included Mithat Paşa, now grand vizier, as well as leading Young Ottomans and members of the deposing junta. Working quickly under the pressures from the war and Western debtor nations, they proclaimed the Ottoman Constitution on 3 December 1876. The newly constituted parliament met for five months in 1877, but the sultan then dismissed Mithat Paşa and suspended the constitution. The resolutions of the Congress of Berlin convened in 1878 to settle the outcome of the war parceled out the peripheral territories of the Ottoman Empire among the new Balkan states, with Russia acquiring Kars, Ardahan, and Batum. Most of the architects of the constitution were soon exiled; Süleyman Paşa was tried for treason and involvement in the death of Sultan Abdülaziz, and Mithat Paşa was murdered in exile. [*See the biography of Abdülhamid II.*]

The rule of Sultan Abdülhamid II has generally been characterized as despotic, and only recently have scholars noted his support for the main reforms of the Tanzimat. Although the democratic thrust of the 1860s was extinguished after 1878, the modernization of Turkey under the Young Turks (1908–1918) and the Republic (1923) can be seen as an uninterrupted movement proceeding from the Tanzimat, facilitated by the internal policy of the sultan. [*See* Young Turks.]

The foreign policy of the Tanzimat and its architects proved less successful. They were unable to precent the empire from being broken up into a number of successor states. The policy that united the subjects of the empire under a law applying equally to them all was unsuccessful. This was due partly to the slow pace of reform, but this slowness was unavoidable in the immense and ultimately intractable task of unifying an extremely diverse society.

[*See also* Ottoman Empire *and* Turkey.]

BIBLIOGRAPHY

Ahmet Cevdet Paşa. *Tezâkir* 1–29, 40. Edited by Cavid Baysun. Ankara, 1953–1967.

Karal, Enver Ziya. *Osmanlı Tarihi VI: Islahat Fermanı Devri 1856–1861*. Ankara, 1954.

Karal, Enver Ziya. *Osmanlı Tarihi VII: Islahat Fermanı Devri 1861–1876*. Ankara, 1956.

Lewis, Bernard. *The Emergence of Modern Turkey*. 2d ed. New York and Oxford, 1968.

Mardin, Şerif. *The Genesis of Young Ottoman Thought*. Princeton, 1962.

Shaw, Stanford J., and Ezel Kural Shaw. *History of the Ottoman Empire and Modern Turkey*, volume 2, *Reform, Revolution and the Republic*. Cambridge, 1977.

Şerif Mardin

TAQĪYAH is the precautionary dissimulation of religious belief and practice in the face of persecution. All Muslims recognize the personal duty of affirming right and forbidding wrong, but they also admit that, when confronted by an overwhelming injustice that threatens the well-being of an individual, this obligation can be fulfilled secretly in the heart rather than overtly. Among Shīʿī Muslims, who from the death of the Prophet onward considered themselves subject to persistent religious persecution by the Sunnī majority and the holders of political power, a further extension of this principle allowed not merely passive or silent resistance, but an active dissimulation of true beliefs when required to protect life, property, and religion itself.

The classic case defining the practice of *taqīyah* is that of ʿAlī ibn Abī Ṭālib, prophet Muḥammad's cousin, whom the Shīʿah hold to have been his sole, chosen successor. Instead of insisting immediately on his God-given right to lead the Muslim community, ʿAlī temporarily acquiesced to the rule of his numerous opponents in the interest of preserving himself and his cause for eventual restoration. ʿAlī swore loyalty to false leaders whom the Shīʿah have otherwise condemned as heretics. Qur'ānic support for such *taqīyah* is given by surah 3.28: "Believers should not accept as protecting friends unbelievers rather than believers . . . unless [it is done] as a precaution in order to guard yourselves from them [or, out of fear of them]." The phrase "as a precaution," as used in this verse, yields the term *taqīyah*. A further Qur'ānic example is surah 16.106: "Whoever expresses disbelief in God after once believing [will suffer greatly], unless that person is under compulsion while yet remaining at peace in belief in the heart." This second verse refers to the case of a Muslim whose parents, rather than renouncing their faith as did the son, accepted martyrdom. The son's temporary act of coerced apostasy was, nonetheless, subsequently forgiven. The Shīʿah see this as further justification for the practice of *taqīyah*.

By the time of the sixth imam, Jaʿfar al-Ṣādiq (d. 765), widespread, clandestine pro-Shīʿi movements had adopted *taqīyah* to hide revolutionary activities. Imam Jaʿfar, in contrast, urged his followers to accept their minority status peacefully and, in place of revolt, to practice a form of permanent *taqīyah* that became, instead, a doctrine of religious quietism. The Shīʿah began to interpret surah 49.13, "the most noble among you in the eyes of God is the most God-fearing," as a recommendation for *taqīyah*. The verb "to fear God," which has the same root as the term *taqīyah,* conveys the latter meaning only secondarily. The Shīʿah under Imam Jaʿfar, however, began to interpret this verse as signifying that "the most noble . . . is the one who practices *taqīyah* most."

Subsequent to Imam Jaʿfar's time, the conditions of persecution, apparent and otherwise, promoted an increasing reliance on this concept, leading eventually to the disappearance of the final imam of the Twelvers—an act that some Shīʿah regard as the ultimate imposition of *taqīyah,* the idea being that, until the imam's own reappearance, all later periods belong to an age of *taqīyah.* One of the most prominent authorities of the tenth century, Ibn Bābawayh (d. 991) insisted that "until the Imam appears *taqīyah* is obligatory and it is not permissible to dispense with it."

Many scholars, such as the great Shaykh al-Mufīd (d. 1022), however, saw in this absolute declaration a dangerous tendency, which they sought to modify. Having once declared that all future statements will be under the rule of *taqīyah,* no later statement, even those concerning *taqīyah* itself, can be accepted at face value. Opponents of the Shīʿah, then and now, fully understand this paradox; the practice of *taqīyah* allows the Shīʿah to say anything and make any claim; no utterance of theirs is to be trusted. To counter this, those like al-Mufīd attempted to set more precise rules for the use of *taqīyah,* readily admitting that the duty of *taqīyah* is not the same for all people or all situations. It is not, therefore, an absolute obligation.

Nevertheless, *taqīyah* was and is practiced broadly by the Shīʿah and other minorities, and it continues to be recognized as a characteristic doctrine of the Shīʿah in general. In more modern times, especially after the Ṣafavids (1501–1722) made Twelver Shiism the state religion of Iran, the necessity of a doctrine of universal *taqīyah* has diminished. The Shīʿah, moveover, have been sensitive to the charge of always dissimulating their true beliefs and have accordingly, like al-Mufīd, rejected unrestricted *taqīyah* in favor of a more limited application. Modern discussions of *taqīyah* thus revolve around the issue of what conditions require it as a religious obligation or merely permit its use without incurring blame. A tendency to claim that the nobler course is to abstain from practicing it, if at all possible, is nearly always present. The modern consensus, which is based on a continuous tradition in juridical literature, is as follows: *taqīyah* may never be employed if it will result directly in the death of another Muslim; it is obligatory only when there is a definite danger that cannot be avoided and against which there is no hope; and it is permitted (discretionary) in the face of a danger to one's own life, that of a family member, the loss of virtue of a female family member, or the serious deprivation of livelihood. Some allow certain conditions of expediency, but the general attitude is that these are areas where, although *taqīyah* may be practiced without blame, it would be preferable (and more noble) not to.

Even so, in those areas where Shīʿīs, and as another example, the Druze, continue to confront dangerous opposition, *taqīyah* persists as an important factor in religious belief and practice. The Shīʿīs for example, still insist that their numbers are systematically undercounted in the censuses of several countries, because adherents there observe *taqīyah.* The Druze, in line with their distant Shīʿī origins and continued minority status, preserve the doctrine of *taqīyah* even where current governments in their regions have tried to promote free expression.

[*See also* Shīʿī Islam.]

BIBLIOGRAPHY

Ibn Bābūyah. *A Shīʿite Creed.* Translated by Asaf A. A. Fyzee. London, 1942. *Taqīyah* is covered in chapter 39 (pp. 110–112).

Kohlberg, Etan. "Some Imāmī-Shīʿī Views on *Taqiyya.*" *Journal of the American Oriental Society* 95 (1975): 395–402. Highly useful article on *taqīyah* in Twelver Shīʿī thought.

Layish, Aharon. "Taqiyya among the Druzes." *Asian and African Studies* 19 (1985): 245–281.

McDermott, Martin J. *The Theology of al-Shaikh al-Mufīd.* Beirut, 1978. Good study of al-Mufīd's thought; note entries in the index under "dissimulation."

Strothmann, Rudolf. "Taḳīya." In *E. J. Brill's First Encyclopaedia of Islam, 1913–1936,* vol. 8, pp. 628–629. Leiden, 1987. Remains an excellent general outline of the subject.

Ṭabāṭabāʾī, Muḥammad Ḥusayn. *Shīʿite Islam.* Translated by Seyyed Hossein Nasr. Albany, N.Y., 1975. See Appendix 1 (pp. 223–225) for a discussion of *taqīyah.*

PAUL E. WALKER

TAQLĪD. Discussions of reform movements in modern Islam frequently depict these movements as aimed primarily at the eradication of a frame of mind called *taqlīd* in Arabic. Often this term is translated as "blind imitation," meaning unquestioning and uncritical conformity to the patterns of behavior and doctrines inherited from past generations. Many writers on modern Islamic reform, as well as its proponents, juxtapose *taqlīd* and *ijtihād* as opposites. The latter term designates the development of doctrine and rules of behavior on the basis of interpretation of the sacred sources of Islam, the Qur'ān and the *sunnah,* whereas the former designates a conscious avoidance of such interpretation in favor of deference to inherited teachings and norms worked out by generations of religious scholars subsequent to the period of original revelation. The rationale for *taqlīd* is the belief that earlier scholars were unsurpassed in their knowledge of the sacred sources, and that they accomplished the interpretative work underlying inherited doctrine in a manner that exceeds the capacities of later generations.

In classical Islamic usage the term *taqlīd* has two different though related meanings. The proper meaning was generally considered to be the *unjustified* conformity of one person to the teaching (whether expressed verbally or implied in behavior) of another person. Whether conformity was justified or not depended on the position of the two parties within a two-tiered hierarchy consisting of those qualified to engage in *ijtihād* and those not so qualified. Those in the first category were known as *mujtahid*s and the second as *ʿāmmīs*, which may be translated here simply as non-*mujtahids*. Conformity was unjustified if the two parties were peers, that is, if both parties were *mujtahids* or both were non-*mujtahids*. Similarly, it was unjustified for a *mujtahid* to conform to the teaching of a non-*mujtahid*. All these kinds of conformity constituted *taqlīd*. What remained outside the realm of *taqlīd,* thus constituting *justified* conformity, was the conformity of a non-*mujtahid* to the teaching of a *mujtahid*.

Alongside this somewhat specialized meaning of *taqlīd,* there emerged in classical usage a broader meaning that included all four types of conformity mentioned above. This more inclusive usage made it possible to refer to justified conformity as *taqlīd,* and it is in fact this sort of conformity that very often is meant by the term. There thus exists a dichotomy of usage in classical Islamic texts involving a definitely pejorative sense of the term on the one hand and a nonpejorative sense on the other. The nonpejorative sense reigns among Twelver Shīʿīs, who divide Muslims into *mujtahid*s and *muqallids*. Every *mujtahid* is presumed to have followers called *muqallid*s and is often designated their *marjaʿ al-taqlīd*. Ambivalence in the usage of the term *taqlīd* is thus more a feature of Sunnī than of Shīʿī discourse. [*See* Marjaʿ al-Taqlīd.]

Conformity of non-*mujtahid*s to the teaching of *mujtahid*s is universally recognized by Muslim religious scholars as a *sine qua non* of Muslim society. It is unthinkable, given the divinely established economy of human interrelationships, that all Muslims should ever be *mujtahid*s. The world needs its merchants, artisans, bankers, soldiers, administrators, farmers, and so on, and none of these can afford the time necessary to become qualified for *ijtihād*. In order to lead a full Muslim life, they must therefore conform to the teachings of those who are so qualified. It is generally anticipated that the non-*mujtahid*s will be many and *mujtahid*s few. Among those willing to call this conformity *taqlīd*, it may thus be said that *taqlīd* is essential to the vitality of Muslim society.

Even religious scholars may deem themselves non-*mujtahid*s. The very existence of four different Sunnī schools of law presupposes that this is so. A Mālikī scholar, for example, is a non-*mujtahid* to the extent that he adheres to the doctrine handed down in the Mālikī school, not subjecting this doctrine to critical review based on his own primary interpretation of the sacred sources. Sunnī thought made it possible to exercise *ijtihād* within the doctrinal confines of a particular school, but only regarding those matters that the traditional doctrine left unresolved, and not those it had definitely settled. One practiced *taqlīd* (in the nonpejorative sense) with respect to the fundamental doctrines of one's school and attempted *ijtihād* only with respect to matters tangential to that doctrine. *Taqlīd* thus supplies the *raison d'être* of the four Sunnī schools.

Reformist attacks on *taqlīd* in modern times have sometimes transformed the term into a broad designation for cultural and intellectual stagnation and unwillingness to experiment with new ideas. More often than not, however, it has been a perceived mindset of the religious intelligentsia of Islam that has been under attack—the *taqlīd* of the schools. Without denying that the masses must always have guidance from a spiritual and intellectual leadership, reformist thought has generally focused its criticism on the leadership itself, which it has seen as too locked into inherited doctrine. This reformist criticism has taken both fundamentalist and modernist directions. The unifying concern is to clear away centuries of doctrinal accretion and facilitate a return to a pristine Islam that will liberate Islamic society from the chains of tradition. Where this liberation permits a greater reconciliation with modernity as defined along the lines of Western rationalism and liberalism, the result is modernism; where it does not, the result is fundamentalism.

Reformist thought among Muslims has varied in the degree to which it has sought to reject traditional doctrine in its battle against *taqlīd*. The most radical approach—complete dissociation from the historic schools—has not prevailed, and the majority of reformists have acknowledged that there is much in the tradition that is worth preserving, provided the proper critical sifting takes place. Future dialogue among Muslim thinkers is thus likely to focus as much on issues relating to the selective appropriation of traditional teaching as on issues relating to the fresh interpretation of the sacred sources.

[*See also* Ijtihād; Law, *article on* Legal Thought and Jurisprudence.]

BIBLIOGRAPHY

Coulson, Noel J. *A History of Islamic Law*. Edinburgh, 1964. See pages 182–201.

Hourani, Albert. *Arabic Thought in the Liberal Age, 1798–1939*. London, 1962. See pages 127–128, 150, and 235.

Rahman, Fazlur. *Islam*. London, 1966. See pages 196–201.

Weiss, Bernard G. *The Search for God's Law: Islamic Jurisprudence in the Writings of Sayf al-Dīn al-Āmidī*. Salt Lake City, 1992. See pages 717–718.

BERNARD G. WEISS

TAQWĀ. A crucial Islamic concept, *taqwā* essentially signifies "god-consciousness" and "godfearing" and, by extension, "piety," with which it seems to have a partially comparable semantic history. *Taqwā* and its derivatives occur more than 250 times in the Qur'ān; it has been rendered variously as: fear, godfearing, godliness, piety, right conduct, righteousness, virtue, warding-off-evil, wariness. A survey of its usage in the Qur'ān indicates that *taqwā* is often paired with faith, goodness, justice, fairness, equity, guidance, truthfulness, perseverance, sincerity, purity, reliance on God, obedience to God, fulfillment of promises, generosity. It is contrasted with *fujūr* (perversity), *fisq* (deviation), and *ẓulm* (oppression).

In addition to its significance in Ṣūfī spiritual thought and practice, and in moral, juristic, and theological discussion, *taqwā* has an important function in Islamic political discourse, particularly in the contemporary period. It is true that most early modern political reformist thinkers, particularly in the Arab world, have either taken it for granted or concentrated on other concepts, such as unity, freedom, justice, and progress. However, three important twentieth-century Muslim thinkers have paid particular attention to *taqwā* within the context of the need to regenerate Islam in the modern world: two prominent fundamentalists, the Indian-Pakistani Abū al-Aʿlā Mawdūdī and the Egyptian Sayyid Quṭb; and the modernist Pakistani academic, Fazlur Rahman of the University of Chicago.

Mawdūdī (d. 1979), founder of the Jamāʿat-i Islāmī, identified *taqwā* as the basic Islamic principle of God-consciousness, together with brotherhood, equality, fairness, and justice, on which the true Islamic society of the future is to be based, provided an Islamic state is established. Sayyid Quṭb (d. 1966), the celebrated ideologue of the Muslim Brotherhood, systematically elaborates the significance of *taqwā* in the context of his commentary on the Qur'ān, which is characterized by an emphasis on political activism. For both activists, *taqwā* is a dynamic concept, not a simple, docile "piety" in the Ṣūfī sense, and it occupies a central place in their articulation of God's *ḥākimīyah* (sovereignty) and *rubūbīyah* (lordship) in the political sense.

Fazlur Rahman (1919–1988) described *taqwā* as "perhaps the most important single term in the Qur'ān." He argued that, owing to inherent inner tensions within the human being, who is a blend of opposites, *taqwā* provides that "inner torch" or "inner vision" to enable humans to overcome their weakness. He considered it the Qur'ān's central endeavor to develop this "keen insight" in humans "here and now where there is opportunity for action and progress." As such, *taqwā* involves a strong sense of moral responsibility, signifying a coalescence of public and private life, and it can be "meaningful only within a social context." The Qur'ān's declaration that "the noblest of you in the sight of God is the one possessed of *taqwā*" (surah 49.13) is highlighted by Rahman, as by Mawdūdī, Quṭb, and others, in the context of human equality.

[*See the biographies of Mawdūdī, Quṭb, and Rahman.*]

BIBLIOGRAPHY

Ahmad, Mumtaz. "Islamic Fundamentalism in South Asia: The Jamaat-i-Islami and the Tablighi Jamaat." In *Fundamentalisms Observed*, edited by Martin E. Marty and R. Scott Appleby, pp. 457–530. Chicago, 1991.

Izutsu, Toshihiko. *Ethico-Religious Concepts in the Qur'ān*. Rev. ed. Montreal, 1966. Semantic but limited study, with emphasis on the negative aspects of *taqwā*.

Kassis, Hanan El. *A Concordance of the Qur'ān*. Berkeley, 1983. Provides the context for each occurrence of *taqwā* in the Qur'ān, using A. J. Arberry's translation. For *taqwā*, see under WQY.

Quṭb, Sayyid. *Fī Ẓilāl al-Qur'ān.* 6 vols. 5th ed. Beirut, 1977. A portion has been translated by M. Adil Salahi and Ashur A. Shamis as *In the Shade of the Qur'ān.* Vol. 30. London, 1979.

Rahman, Fazlur. *Major Themes of the Qur'ān.* Minneapolis, 1980. Important for an insightful appreciation of *taqwā* and other concepts in the Qur'ān.

Rahman, Fazlur. *Islam and Modernity: Transformation of the Intellectual Tradition.* Chicago, 1982. See especially chapter 4.

AHMAD SHBOUL

ṬARĪQAH. *See* Sufism, *article on* Ṣūfī Orders.

TAWḤĪD. An Arabic term meaning literally "making one" or "unifying," is considered by many twentieth-century Islamic activists to be the axial or defining doctrine of Islam.

Although *tawḥīd* has traditionally been recognized as a fundamental doctrine of Islam, its popularity as Islam's defining characteristic is a modern development. Indeed, the term is not mentioned in the Qur'ān. Early theologians used it in their interpretations of the relationship between divine essence and divine attributes, as well as in their defense of divine unity against dualists and trinitarians. In the thirteenth century, renowned Ḥanbalī jurist Ibn Taymīyah rehearsed and clarified the early theologians' positions, adding his own interpretation and shifting the emphasis on *tawḥīd* from theology to sociomoral issues. In the nineteenth century, *tawḥīd* gained some attention with the renewed popularity of Ibn Taymīyah among the Wahhābīyah. The modern importance of *tawḥīd* did not begin to emerge, however, until 1897, when Egyptian reformer Shaykh Muḥammad ʿAbduh published a full discussion of its implications, *Risālat al-tawḥīd* (translated as *Theology of Unity;* London, 1966). Although ʿAbduh's epistle was for the most part an effort to reintroduce the classic issues of Islamic theology, by the mid- to late twentieth century *tawḥīd,* as an organizing principle of human society, had become a rallying cry of many Islamic reformers. In the 1960s Sayyid Quṭb proclaimed *tawḥīd* the underlying principle of all true religion, and in 1982 Ismāʿīl al-Fārūqī claimed that *tawḥīd* was the core of all Islamic religious knowledge, as well as its history, metaphysics, esthetics, ethics, social order, economic order, and indeed the entire Islamic world order. The term has even been adopted by activist organizations, such as the Shīʿī Dār al-Tawḥīd ("Abode of Tawḥīd") in the Gulf region, and the Sunnī Ḥarakat al-Tawḥīd ("Tawḥīd Movement") in Palestine. Thus, the meaning and implications of *tawḥīd* have undergone continuous revision, most dramatically so in the contemporary era.

***Tawḥīd* in Classical References.** The classical religious science of *ʿilm al-kalām,* usually translated as "theology," is also known as *ʿilm al-tawḥīd wa-al-ṣifāt* (science of [divine] unity and the attributes) or simply *ʿilm al-tawḥīd.* As distinguishied from the speculative science of *fiqh* (jurisprudence), *ʿilm al-kalām* was considered traditional knowledge (revealed or transmitted through recognized authorities), presented with rational explanations and refutations of contradictory opinions (e.g., al-Jurjānī, 1977, pp. i, 2). Its synonymy with *ʿilm al-tawḥīd* occurred because of the centrality of the question of divine unity in the early disputes among believers.

The early emphasis on divine unity among Muslim rationalists appears to have resulted from the perceived influence of Manichaean dualism on some groups of Shīʿīs. But rational arguments for divine unity were more fully developed in the context of arguments over the status of a sinner, made famous by the Qadarīyah, Khawārij, and Murjiʿah, and particularly in debates regarding the status of the Qur'ān as created or not created, and how the multiplicity evident in the world could have proceeded from a creator who is essentially one.

The Muʿtazilah, among the earliest groups of thinkers identified by their rationalist approach to Islamic doctrines, held that the Qur'ān was created. As such, it is to be distinguished from the divine essence, which is unitary (simple), eternal, and unchanging. The Qur'ān is the word of God, created in time for humanity. Opponents of the Muʿtazilah held that the Qur'ān was uncreated, part of the essence of God. To the Muʿtazilah, this position appeared to compromise divine immutability, and thus divine simplicity, and ultimately divine unity itself. Indeed, divine unity *(tawḥīd)* became, with divine justice, the Muʿtazilah's first principle. They were known as "the people of justice [*ʿadl*] and unity [*tawḥīd*]."

Ninth-century ʿAbbāsid caliph al-Ma'mūn (r. 813–833) gave official sanction to the Muʿtazilī position; belief that the Qur'ān was created was proclaimed an article of faith. However, that position was perceived as a threat to the traditionalists' position. The divine essence, according to the Muʿtazilah, is beyond human comprehension, whereas the Qur'ān, the divine word, is accessible to human reason. Therefore, the anthropomorphic references to God in the Qur'ān must be considered allegorically. The traditionalists, however, favored a literal interpretation of the Qur'ān and reliance on the practice of the early Islamic community—both without rationalist interpretation—as the model for community leadership. Al-Ma'mūn's position, therefore, sparked a rebellion of sorts among their ranks. Traditionalist Aḥmad ibn Ḥanbal (780–855) was imprisoned, both for his vocal opposition to the doctrine of the created Qur'ān and for his insistence that human reason and authority are to be resorted to only in the rare instances where the Qur'ān is silent on a subject and there is no precedent to be derived from early Muslim practice.

By the middle of the ninth century, the caliph's authority was severely weakened, and the traditionalists gained dominance in positions of doctrine and jurisprudence. The traditionalists' position was eventually systematized under the influence and name of its main thinker (who had actually begun his career as a Muᶜtazilī), Abū al-Ḥasan al-Ashᶜarī (d. about 936). According to the Ashᶜarī interpretation, the Qur'ān is the uncreated word of God, coeternal with God. But, as noted above, the createdness of the Qur'ān had been asserted in order to protect the unity of God. Therefore, the Ashᶜarī thinkers were compelled to demonstrate that their position did not compromise divine unity.

It was for this reason that Ashᶜarī thinkers became insistent on divine unity and transcendence. God is one, unique and eternal, and there is no god but the almighty God. They believed that divine unity could be preserved by viewing the divine attributes, including speech and action (or will, power, and knowledge), as additional *(zā'idah)* to the divine essence. In this context, they argued that if the divine will is an attribute and is identical with the divine essence, as in the Muᶜtazilī position, then God's freedom of choice is called into question. God would be compelled by his very nature (essence) to act. The Muᶜtazilah, however, believed that their assertion that the divine will is created would preclude such a conclusion.

Yet ultimately, for the Ashᶜarīyah, the divine essence is inaccessible to human reason. God is known to human beings only through revelation; indeed, the verses of the Qur'ān are called *āyāt* ("signs") of God, and revelation should be accepted at face value. Ashᶜarī doctrine holds, for example, that God is truly on his throne (according to Qur'ān 20.5) and that God has hands (Qur'ān 38.75 and 5.64). Likewise, God created everything and nothing that God did not want was created. Thus, not only does God create all human actions, allowing only the occasion for the actions to human beings, but God created even the evil deeds that people do. This position was taken in response to the Muᶜtazilī position that God creates with a purpose and that purpose is good. That view, combined with the Muᶜtazilī insistence that people have free will (that we create our own acts by virtue of a contingent power created by God within us) allows the Muᶜtazilah to make sense of the Qur'ānic promise of reward and threat of punishment. The Ashᶜarī position, by contrast, insists that human beings do not have free will and that things are good or evil because God does them as such, not vice versa. However, the Ashᶜarī interpretation continues, in none of these cases (i.e., on the questions of apparent anthropomorphization of God, the lack of free will, and God's creation of evil) are humans to question the modality, or how it is that these things are true. All revelation is to be accepted literally but *bi-lā kayf* ("without [asking] how").

Later Ashᶜari thinkers allowed that some things about God are accessible to human reason *(ᶜaqlīyāt)*, such as that God's attributes do not compromise divine unity *(tawḥīd)*, but regarding the nature of those attributes, we know only what the prophets taught *(samᶜiyāt)*. In this way, Ashᶜarism, which dominated Sunnī Islamic orthodoxy from the tenth to the nineteenth century, insisted on divine unity, but it rejected interpretations of revelation that would make that unity accessible to human reason in favor of assertions of ultimate divine transcendence. Other thinkers approached the question of divine unity from different directions. For example, Abū Manṣūr Muḥammad al-Māturīdī of Samarkand (d. 944), in his *kalām* compendium *Kitāb al-tawḥīd;* places relatively greater emphasis on creation and free will than on the issue of divine attributes. This approach effectively constitutes a parallel tendency or school of theology.

The Philosophers and Tawḥīd. The subject of divine unity was addressed by the classical philosophers of the Islamic world in accordance with their rationalist orientation and frequently under the influence of Platonic, Aristotelian, and Neoplatonic influences, particularly in the area of metaphysics. Al-Kindī (d. about 866), for example, rejects the idea that the attributes superadded to God's essence in order to insist on the absolute oneness of God. In answer to the question of how the One could be responsible for the multiplicity of the world, he claims that indeed, multiplicity could not exist without the One. For him the existence of the One is logically prior to, and necessary to account for, the existence of multiplicity, since the multiplicity (or plurality) is simply a combination of unities.

Al-Fārābī (d. about 950) describes God as pure intellect, superseding the problem of the potential duality of essence and attributes. Yet like al-Kindī, he is then left with the challenge of explaining how the One can be responsible for the multiplicity which characterizes creation. Like many philosophers faced with this problem, al-Kindī and al-Fārābī both rely on versions of the Neoplatonic theory of emanation. Al-Kindī refers to a kind of universal radiation, while al-Fārābī makes use of the more familiar formula wherein the entire universe emanates from God through a succession of nine intellects along with their celestial spheres. The process begins as existence outflows from God, creating the first intelligence, a composite of being (existence) and knowledge (essence). For from the one, only one can come, thus protecting divine simplicity/unity. The emanation proceeds through the ninth intellect, from which emanates a tenth, which is the active intellect that comprises human reason. Accordingly, multiplicity in the universe is only apparent; all existence is unified in God, the source of all.

Ibn Sīnā (980–1037) attacks the problem of the potential duality of essence (attributes) and existence by affirming it in all existents except God. All creatures' existence is superadded to their essence; they are composite creatures. But God's very essence is to exist. God, therefore, is the only simple existent. As with al-Fārābī, other existents result from emanation.

The Spanish philosopher Ibn Rushd (1126–1198) rejects the emanationists' doctrine, particularly its fundamental principle that the one can only give rise to one. He stresses that God is ultimately transcendent and therefore should not be described in human terms. There is no basis for assuming that God's creation is anything like the human act of making, or that the divine will is anything like the human act of willing. Ibn Rushd, therefore, rejects the idea that claiming the multiplicity of the universe was created by God compromises God's unity. He likewise rejects the distinction between essence and existence, claiming it is only an analytic tool. In reality, he claims, with Aristotle, that essences (ideas of things) can only come from things that exist; existence must necessarily precede essence. There is, however, such a thing as potentiality, he claims, and the difference between potentiality and actuality is God. God actuates the potential. Thus God is truly the agent of creation, rather than, as in Ibn Sīnā's scheme, the source of automatic emanation.

***Tawḥīd* in Ṣūfī Thought.** Yet even in the case of Ibn Rushd, the philosophers found themselves caught between the teaching of the Qur'ān, that God created the universe at some point in time, and the results of rational processes. In the case of Neoplatonic emanationists and Aristotelian philosophers alike, the conclusion that the universe is somehow eternal was inevitable, since creation in time implied movement or change in God. Because change or movement is defined philosophically as transition from potentiality to actuality, and potentiality is considered a lack of actuality, change or movement is considered incompatible with divine perfection. Yet the idea of the universe being coeternal with God did not accord with revelation. Ṣūfī thought sought to affirm the unity and primacy of God in a way that transcends such logical conundrums.

As with the theologians and philosophers, the most general meaning of *tawḥīd* for Ṣūfīs is affirmation of the essential oneness of God. Beyond that, however, *tawḥīd* reflects the mystical belief in ascending levels of knowledge or proximity to divine unity. Ordinary believers accept divine unity as a matter of faith; intellectuals might accept it as a matter of reason. But true recognition of divine unity in the Ṣūfī context is not accessible to reason alone. Contemplation of the illusory dichotomies in the universe will produce the ultimate goal of Ṣūfī practice; a realization of the ultimate unity of existence that is quite beyond discursive or rational inquiry.

Accordingly, a Ṣūfī interpretation of the first pillar of Islam, the *shahādah* (bearing witness that there is no god but the One God, Allāh), is that it affirm the ultimate paradox: it first denies divinity and then affirms it in a way that defies categorization and thus knowability by means of the rational faculties. In a non-Ṣūfī context, God's defiance of categorization is known as divine incomparability, as affirmed by the Qur'ān. The implication is thus God's ultimate transcendence: God cannot be known except insofar as he reveals himself. That revelation is contained in *sharīʿah* (Islamic law); therefore, the proper human response to God is obedience to God alone. In the Ṣūfī context, God's incomparability implies as well God's imminence.

God's imminence was expressed definitively by the Spanish-born mystic Ibn ʿArabī (1165–1240) in the phrase *waḥdat al-wujūd* (the unity of all being). Ibn ʿArabī claims that there is only one Reality, also known by various other names, such as the one Real, the one

Truth, and the one Essence. There is only one Real, by virtue of participation in which everything else exists. Thus God is in all creation, but is not identified with creation. No part contains the totality, nor is the totality simply a sum of the parts. Creation is God's self-manifestation. Employing the Neoplatonic emanationist scheme, Ibn ʿArabī claims the First Intelligence represents the perfect individual *(al-insān al-kāmil)*, identified with the inner reality of the prophet Muḥammad. This individual, aware of both divine uniqueness and creaturely multiplicity, is the pivot between the one and the many, between God and creation. The mystic aspires to the sort of awareness represented by *al-insān al-kāmil.* Similarly, the great Ṣūfī poet Jalāl al-Dīn Rūmī (c. 1207–1273) expresses the belief that the Ṣūfī adept can achieve the level of awareness of God represented by the First Intelligence. He must first, however, transcend the confines of his own limited existence—in effect, passing out of existence—in order to affirm the existence of God.

Certain aspects of these themes, echoed throughout Ṣūfī thought, are also evident in philosophical works. Ibn Sīnā, for example, believes there is a level of knowledge beyond the discursive. For just as creatures' existence results from an outflowing from God, so there is the possibility of ascent of levels of knowledge. Al-Ghazālī (1058–1111) is given credit for reconciling mystical and logical claims with revealed doctrine and condemning those conclusions at odds with true belief. He retains belief in the mystic's journey but denies that the adept achieves direct recognition of God. For him, the adept draws near to the divine attributes, which, as an Ashʿarī, he believes are not identical with the divine essence. [*See the biographies of Ghazālī and Ibn al-ʿArabī.*]

Ibn Taymīyah. Even this effort to avoid compromising God's transcendence was considered insufficient by Hanbalī jurisprudent Taqī al-Dīn Aḥmad Ibn Taymīyah (1263–1328). He believed the key issue was *tawḥīd* and attempted to settle the question once and for all. Ibn Taymiyya was convinced that the efforts of Muslim thinkers influenced by Greek philosophy (Islamic philosophy [*falsafah*] and rational theology [*kalām*]) were as misguided as those of the Ṣūfīs, who blurred the distinction between the divine and the mundane, in Ibn Taymīyah's view. Ibn Taymīyah rejected the rationalists' denial of the attributes' reality *(tanzīh* and *taʿṭīl)*, positions taken in efforts to preserve divine simplicity and therefore unity. He also rejected the method of considering the divine attributes allegorically and the traditionalists' literalist or anthropomorphic interpretation of the attributes *(tashbīh)*. His approach to the divine essence and attributes was to simply accept them and leave their true meaning a mystery *(tafwīḍ)*. Likewise, he rejected the philosophers' distinction between the divine essence and existence, and their efforts to demonstrate God's necessary existence.

Ibn Taymīyah believed that God's self-characterization in revelation was sufficient and, indeed, the only understanding of God accessible to humans. That self-characterization, he believed, was epitomized in the brief passage in the Qur'ān, surah 62, entitled "Al-ikhlāṣ" ("The Sincere [Faith]" or "The Pure [Faith]": "In the name of Allāh, the compassionate, the merciful, Say Allāh is one, the eternal God. He begot none, nor was he begotten. None is equal to him.") Beyond that we need not and should not seek. It was in this context that Ibn Taymīyah focused his insistence on the absolute unity of God *(tawḥīd)*. People are created with a natural or instinctive recognition *(fiṭrah)* of God, Ibn Taymīyah believed. Moreover, God's existence is everywhere reflected in creation. The world is full of testimony *(āyāt)* to God's existence. These realities themselves are an aspect of *tawḥīd* for Ibn Taymīyah: God as sole creator, ruler, and judge of the world is everywhere reflected in creation.

However, by the time of Ibn Taymīyah, the controversy over the metaphysical status of the divine attributes had lost their implications for political authority. Indeed, by the thirteenth century, the caliphate as the single, central religio-political power in Islam was a thing of the past. For Ibn Taymīyah, the critical issue was no longer the validity of the caliphate but the nature of faith. Accordingly, having established absolute divine unity *(tawḥīd)* as the cornerstone of Islam, albeit incomprehensible, Ibn Taymīyah went on to focus on what actually was within the scope of human activity, and that, he believed, was the response to *tawḥīd:* submission *(taslīm)* to the will of God as revealed in the Qur'ān and *sunnah*. For Ibn Taymīyah this is the essence of faith. It was not mere intellectual assent but included as well expression through religious practice or ritual and, most importantly, actions. True faith is expressed in virtuous behavior, he believed, both on the individual and the collective levels. Indeed, the two levels (personal and public, or religious and political) were inextricably linked. Human beings require social organization, and that organization must be guided by religion. Furthermore, he shifted emphasis from community leadership to individual piety, stressing that everyone must contribute to the well-being of the state.

Thus, for Ibn Taymīyah *tawḥīd* remains central in Islam but for reasons different from those of the early commentators. *Tawḥīd* precludes both rational understanding of God (the focus of Ashʿarī arguments) and the kind of mystical awareness of God that had become popular among Ṣūfī expositors by the time of Ibn Taymīyah. He believed that rather than attempting to prove the existence of God, or describe God, or to achieve mystical awareness of or communion with the divine, the sole obligation of human beings is to submit to God's revealed will and participate in carrying it out. This is the orientation toward *tawḥīd*'s importance, rather than that of the Muʿtazilah or Ashʿarīyah, that forms the legacy for the early modern and modern commentators. [*See the biography of Ibn Taymīyah.*]

The Wahhābīyah. In the eighteenth century, Arabian reformer Muḥammad ibn ʿAbd al-Wahhāb (1703–1792) drew inspiration from Ibn Taymīyah. In the face of what he considered spiritual stagnation and continuing Ṣūfī excesses, he sought to reassert the radical oneness of God. As with Ibn Taymīyah, God is simply one and beyond comparison, as proclaimed in revelation. It is innovation (*bidʿah;* both unnecessary and irreligious) to attempt to determine the modality of *tawḥīd*. A Ḥanbalī, he denounced those schools of thought traditionally criticized by Ḥanābilah as compromising Islamic unity, including the Shīʿah and Muʿtazilah, as well as what he considered excessive rationalism on the part of the *mutakallimūn* (scholastic theologians) and excessive spirituality on the part of the Ṣūfīs. In particular he denounced the Ṣūfī and Shīʿī practice of praying to saints. Only God, he asserted, is worthy of praise and to God is due all praise. He considered the belief that saints or angels or even prophets could intercede with God sheer polytheism. Moreover, he believed it utter heresy to claim knowledge based on any source beyond the Qur'ān, the *sunnah,* and the results of logical processes.

Furthermore, Islamic unity is a central feature of *tawḥīd* for ʿAbd al-Wahhāb. He therefore rejected sectarianism of any kind and even sought to establish a state based on divine and Islamic unity. In the mid-eighteenth century he formed an alliance with Muḥammad ibn Saʿūd (d. 1765) devoted to the task of purifying Islamic practice and making God's word prevail. Basing themselves on what they considered the prophet Muḥammad's model, they sought to replace tribal solidarity with religious solidarity, purifying the religion from what they considered extraneous practices. When ʿAbd al-Wahhāb and Ibn Saʿūd died, their movement continued and gained strength under Ibn Saʿūd's grandson, Saʿūd ibn ʿAbd al-ʿAzīz (r. 1803–1814). Wahhābī-Saʿūdī influence was eventually spread as far as Karbala, Mecca, and Medina, accompanied by the destruction of saints' tombs and imposition of strict Ḥanbalī-based order. Although the movement was repulsed when it spread into Syria and Iraq, it survived and became the basis of the modern state of Saudi Arabia. [*See* Wahhabīyah *and the biography of Ibn ʿAbd al-Wahhāb.*]

Muḥammad ʿAbduh. Popular Egyptian reformer Muḥammad ʿAbduh (1849–1905) transmits to the modern era both the early theological discussions of *tawḥīd* and the later refocusing of its importance toward the ethical imperative, human responsibility to obey the revealed word of God. In the process, he effectively, though subtly, modifies some key positions of the formerly dominant Ashʿarī position, particularly with regard to the role of free will and reason. He begins his *Risālat al-tawḥīd* (Epistle on Divine Unity; 1897) by noting that the study of *tawḥīd* is the study of "the being and attributes of God, the essential and the possible affirmations about Him, as well as the negations that are necessary to make relating to Him," although he also claims that Islamic theology is named for the most important of its parts, "namely the demonstration of the unity of God in Himself and in the act of creation" (*The Theology of Unity,* translated by I. Musaʿad and K. Cragg, London, 1966, p. 29). He believes it is beyond question that God is omnipotent and omniscient, but that it is likewise self-evident that people have free will (in contradistinction to the Ashʿarī position). Attempts at rational explanation of these seemingly conflicting truths are not only doomed to failure but misguided in the first place. Revealing the influence of Ibn Taymīyah, ʿAbduh asserts that people should occupy themselves with responding to God through obedience rather than intellectual inquiry into matters beyond their ability to grasp.

ʿAbduh asserts that although the Qur'ān gives all the information about God that is permitted to human beings, it does not ask us to believe blindly. On the contrary, it validates reason and thus gave rise to the earliest schools of theology. ʿAbduh outlines the development of early Islamic rationalism, noting that it was experimental at first. This is how he explains Ashʿarism; it was a compromise among extremist interpretations and must be considered in historical context. The same holds true for the work of the later philosophers who criticized al-Ashʿarī's apparent anti-intellectualism. The upshot of the early efforts to meet the intellectual challenge raised by the Qur'ān yet at the same time protect God's transcendence, ʿAbduh concludes, was such confusion that further rational inquiry was effectively precluded, and the Islamic world forfeited its position at the forefront of significant human inquiry. For that reason he takes it on himself to resurrect the rationality of religion.

Formulating the approach that will become popular in twentieth-century Islamic activism, ʿAbduh justifies his own rational inquiries through *tawḥīd*. Islam "is a religion of unity throughout," he explains (ʿAbduh, 1966, p. 39). There can be no conflict between reason and revelation, otherwise God would have created rationality in people in vain. Indeed, ʿAbduh goes on to place *tawḥīd* squarely at the center of the prophet Muḥammad's mission. The most important knowledge for Muslims, he says, is that God is one in himself and that creation was a single act. Then, in perhaps his most direct attack on traditionalism, ʿAbduh concludes, "The purpose of this discipline, theology, is . . . to know God most high and His attributes . . . to acknowledge His messengers . . . , relying therein upon proof and not taking things merely upon tradition" (p. 39). Returning to the traditional assertion of *tawḥīd*, affirming that God is therefore simple or noncomposite, the sole necessary existent on which all other beings are contingent, ʿAbduh affirms that both our reason and revelation tell us that God exists. Nevertheless, now echoing Ibn Taymīyah, ʿAbduh asserts that the nature of God's existence is beyond our comprehension.

Accordingly, ʿAbduh establishes three traditionally recognized aspects of *tawḥīd*. There is only one God, God is essentially one and noncomposite, and God is unique in the sense of being totally transcendent and beyond human comprehension. He then proceeds to direct *tawḥīd* to a modern issue, religious pluralism. At the time ʿAbduh worked, Egypt was facing the challenge of reorganizing as a state independent of both Turkish and European overlords. In that context, the question of the basis of citizenship became central. Thus ʿAbduh developed a fourth dimension of *tawḥīd*, the unity of religion. Relying on Qur'ānic references (surahs 3.67 and 42.13), he claims that diversity in religion, even in the true religion, is not in itself troublesome. God chose to reveal incrementally, "to proceed by stages in the nurture" of humanity (ʿAbduh, 1966, p. 130). "Islam taught that the sole aim of outward forms of worship was to renew the inward recollection of God and that God looks not on the form but on the heart" (p. 134).

Another dimension of *tawḥīd* for ʿAbduh has to do with God's work, creation. Just as perfection must be predicated of God, so must it be of what God has done. Therefore, not only must truth be attributed to God's threats and promises, resulting in the necessity of free will, but purpose must be attributed to God's will. Again, ʿAbduh quotes the Qur'ān affirming that everything was created with a purpose, a goal, of perfection in accordance with God's will (surah 21.16–18). ʿAbduh thus rejects both the traditionally accepted fatalism of predestination and complete freedom of human beings. Instead, he claims that people have free will, but it does not compromise divine omnipotence. He concludes by returning to the two themes of his work that influence subsequent twentieth-century commentators on *tawḥīd*-centered Islamic activism. First, to believe human behavior is predetermined, he says, is to fall into "the disease" of *taqlīd*, blind adherence to precedent or failure to exercise the proper role of the human intellect. Recognition of *tawḥīd* thus requires revival of the spirit of intelligent initiative (*ijtihād*) after centuries of dormancy. Second, rather than focusing on the nature of the divine essence and attributes, as did early *kalām*, that initiative must be directed toward the pursuit of practical Islamic goals, the creation of an Islamic society. [*See the biography of ʿAbduh.*]

***Tawḥīd* as the Focus of Contemporary Activism.** ʿAbduh's orientation toward the centrality of *tawḥīd* in directing human pursuits became more important as the Islamic world continued to suffer political setbacks. It is reflected, for example, in the work of Sayyid Quṭb (1909–1966), ideologue of the Muslim Brotherhood. Quṭb's viewpoint reflects the frustration felt by many Egyptians who were disappointed by Gamal Abdel Nasser's 1952 revolution. Continued European control in the Islamic world, despite Allied victory over former Ottoman suzerains, had created the conditions that prompted enthusiastic support for the military coup among secularists and Muslim Brothers alike. But when Nasser's government failed to achieve its lofty goals of independence, prosperity, and unity throughout the Arab-Islamic world, Sayyid Quṭb's strident and seemingly definitive articulation of a uniquely righteous Islamic worldview (in clear distinction from the weakness of either the Western capitalist or Eastern socialist models), struck a responsive chord.

Tawḥīd is the central feature of this worldview, and the central feature of *tawḥīd* is human response to God. As in previous formulations, *tawḥīd* is the ultimate basis of Islam for Sayyid Quṭb. "The unity of God is such that there is no reality and no true and permanent existence except His. . . . This is the belief that should be entrenched in us. It is a full explanation of human existence" (Sayyid Quṭb, *In the Shade of the Qur'ān*, translated by M. A. Salahi and A. A. Shamis, London, 1979, vol. 30, p. 350). The erstwhile concern for the metaphysical status of divine attributes has been replaced by the insistence that society reflect divine unity through unanimous submission to God's revealed will. Gone also is the tolerance of religious diversity expressed by ʿAbduh. For Quṭb, *tawḥīd* implies that only specifically Islamic revelation is legitimate, earlier forms of revelation having been corrupted by their followers. And all of those deviations are the result of deviation from the doctrine of *tawḥīd*. The uniquely Islamic insistence on the absolute unity of God is expressed in "its being considered a foundation for the realistic and practical system of human life with its effects clearly appearing in legislation as well as in belief" (p. 353). Thus, for Quṭb, *tawḥīd* implies not merely that people should submit to the will of God, but that governments should be based on Islamic law (Sayyid Quṭb, *Khaṣāiṣ al-taṣawwur al-islāmī wa muqawwimātuhu*, Cairo, 1962, p. 45). [*See the biography of Quṭb.*]

This insistence on unanimous submission to God's revealed will is likewise reflected in the work of Palestinian scholar Ismāʿīl Rājī al-Fārūqī (1921–1986). In *Al-Tawḥīd: Its Implications for Thought and Life* (Herndon, Va., 1982), following Sayyid Qutb's approach, al-Fārūqī devotes his entire treatment of *tawḥīd* to its practical implications. Indeed, he ignores completely the metaphysical aspects of divine unity so prevalent in traditional *kalām* and instead declares that the traditional meaning of Islam is that there is only one God. But, he continues, the implications of this assertion include every aspect of human life.

Al-Fārūqī's lengthy discussion of the practical implications of *tawḥīd* begins with the principle of tolerance. For al-Fārūqī, however, it is not the same kind of tolerance reflected in ʿAbduh's support for pluralism in Egypt; the implications of *tawḥīd* are much broader. Muslims, as beneficiaries of the perfect and complete revelation concerning *tawḥīd*, are responsible for all humanity and for the entire cosmos. This universal or cosmic responsibility shared by all Muslims to fashion the world according to the will of God is the essence of *sharīʿah*. The purpose of Islamic law, based on revelation, is to order human life in the service of God. Since *tawḥīd* dictates that all life must be ordered according to divine will, then Islamic law must both legislate concerning every aspect of life and be the dominant legal system throughout the world. It need not be the only legal system, since *tawḥīd* also dictates respect for other religions, including their legal systems. Indeed, protection of other religions is itself part of *tawḥīd*-based Islamic law. This is part of the Islamic world order. Yet it must ultimately prevail.

Of paramount importance in al-Fārūqī's discussion of the implications of *tawḥīd* is the public nature of human responsibility, which characterizes the Islamic world order, or *pax Islamica*, as he calls it. Whereas Christianity, according to al-Fārūqī, had to stress spirituality in its capacity as a corrective to Judaism's excessive materialism and legalism, Islam places human activity squarely in the public sphere of social action. This means, first of all, that the Islamic community is a single community, wherein all believers are equal and subject to Islamic law. "In Islam all this is worship: the actual transformation of the earth and men for the sake of which the Qur'ān itself was revealed, the concrete service of the tenant-farmer in the manor of God which is the earth." (1982, pp. 147–148). [*See the biography of Fārūqī.*]

***Tawḥīd* in Shīʿī Discourse.** The modern emphasis on practical *tawḥīd* so evident in the work of the above-mentioned Sunnī writers is evident in the Shīʿī community as well. Iranian ideologue of the Islamic resurgence, ʿAlī Sharīʿatī (1933–1977), popularized the theme in his lecturing to Iran's disaffected youth. Sharīʿatī criticized those Iranians educated in the Western mode for their spiritual shallowness. Human beings are two dimensional, he believed, both spiritual and material. But both are directed toward the singular human purpose of *khilāfah* (vicegerency). Just as in the work of Pakistani philosopher and poet Muhammad Iqbal (1877–1938), and that of al-Fārūqī, Sharīʿatī stresses the purposefulness of human existence, tracing it to a primordial agreement (or "trust" [*amānah*]) between God and creation. That agreement gives human beings superiority over all other creatures but, at the same time, responsibility for them. Indeed, human beings are responsible for perfecting their environment.

This special relationship between God and humanity

is at the core of *tawḥīd* for Sharīʿatī. Although al-Fārūqī believes that *tawḥīd* is the unique contribution of Islam to the monotheistic tradition, Sharīʿatī believes that it has been in the tradition from the beginning of human existence. Islam simply perfected our understanding of *tawḥīd,* showing it to be the foundation of all other values. Thus, all social organization should be based on *tawḥīd (niẓām-i tawḥīd).* Again, like al-Fārūqī, Sharīʿatī believes that only Islam and its social organization enables people to carry out their sacred trust. Islam's teaching on God's unity and the unity of the universe as a reflection of God's unity is a worldview essential to human perfection. It is a "universal philosophy of sociology" (ʿAlī Sharīʿatī, *On the Sociology of Islam,* translated by Hamid Algar, Berkeley, 1979, p. 33). Reflecting a distinctively Shīʿī orientation, Sharīʿatī explains this universalism by defining *tawḥīd* as "regarding the whole of existence as a single form, a single living and conscious organism, possessing will, intelligence, feeling and purpose," for the relationship between God and creation is "the same as that of light with the lamp that emits it." Yet he warns against monism or the pantheism of the Ṣūfīs: "It is not a question of *waḥdat al-wujūd* [unity of existence] of the Sufis, but a *tawḥīd al-wujūd,* scientific and analytical" (pp. 82–85). That is, all creation must be oriented toward the Creator, and this conviction becomes the basis of social action. A *tawḥīd*-based worldview rejects "legal, class, social, political, racial, national, territorial, genetic or even economic contradictions" and therefore requires believers to work for justice in all its forms. *Tawḥīd,* therefore, transforms "the religion of deceit, stupefaction and justification of the status quo" into the "religion of awareness, activism and revolution" (p. 109). [*See the biography of Sharīʿatī.*]

Similarly, Iran's Ayatollah Ruhollah Khomeini (1902–1989) places *tawḥīd* at the center of Islamic spiritual and material life. Islam, he says, is indeed the school of *tawḥīd,* which calls for the unity of all Muslims. Stressing political unity more than Sharīʿatī did, he claims, "The ultimate reason for all the troubles that afflict the Muslim countries is their disunity and lack of harmony. . . . I beseech God Almighty that He exalt Islam and the Muslims and grant unity to all Muslims in the world" (Imam Khomeini, *Islam and Revolution,* translated by Hamid Algar, London, 1985, p. 277). Indeed, *tawḥīd* was at the root of Ayatollah Khomeini's political views. The "Great Satan" of Westernism is trying to control the Islamic world by sowing disunity among them, he warned. Islamic Iran therefore had to wage "a determined struggle to ensure the unity of all Muslims in the world on the basis of *tawḥīd* and true Islam" (p. 301)

In the work of Ayatollah Khomeini, therefore, *tawḥīd* came to represent revolutionary Islam. His calls for the elimination of specific leaders in the name of true Islam understandably engendered political insecurity among other Muslim leaders in the Middle East. His inflammatory speeches were received negatively in the Arab press. Indeed, in 1987 the Arab League issued a statement to the effect that the greatest source of instability in their region was the threat of Islamic revolution emanating from Iran. The ayatollah's supporters, however, found inspiration to organize and act against what they considered the undue influence of the United States and European political powers among them. [*See the biography of Khomeini.*]

Even by 1936 the modern popularity of *tawḥīd* was not sufficiently developed to warrant more than a scant few paragraphs in the *Encyclopedia of Islam* (Leiden, 1913). In the new edition of the *Encyclopedia of Islam* (Leiden, 1960–), Louis Gardet pondered the demise of *ʿilm al-kalām* or *ʿilm al-tawḥīd.* Even by the twentieth century, he noted, Muḥammad ʿAbduh for the most part simply reiterated classical theories in his *Risālat al-tawḥīd.* He suggests that the reason for the dearth of original thinking on the subject since the time of the controversies over divine essence and attributes is that the arguments of such disputants as the Muʿtazilah were so successfully refuted that the question of God's unity is no longer an issue. The major issues of today, he observed, lay elsewhere. Indeed, he closes his comments wondering if anything more practical than the intensely speculative kind of thinking that characterized discussions of *tawḥīd* until the twentieth century would again gain Muslim thinkers' attention. It appears that the modern development of concern with *ʿilm al-tawḥīd* answers Gardet's question. It seems true, as he noted, that "Ashʿarism no longer appears to be necessitated by the demands of the faith" (" ʿIlm al-kalām," *Encyclopedia of Islam,* new ed., Leiden, 1960–, vol. 3, p. 1150). Concern with the practical manifestations of Islamic unity in a world fragmented by colonialism and nationalism has become today's central issue. As the fragmentation resulting from the colonial period continues throughout the postcolonial era, *tawḥīd* has emerged as a powerful symbol of unity—divine, spiritual, and sociopolitical.

[*See also* Theology.]

BIBLIOGRAPHY

Ashʿarī, Abū al-Ḥasan al-. *The Theology of al-Ashʿarī.* Translated by Richard J. McCarthy. Beirut, 1953.

Averroës [Ibn Rushd]. *Averroes' Tahafut al-Tahafut (The Incoherence of the Incoherence).* 2 vols. Translated by Simon van den Bergh. London, 1969.

Ghazālī, Abū Ḥāmid al-. *The Faith and Practice of al-Ghazālī.* Translated by W. Montgomery Watt. London, 1953.

Goichon, Amélie-Marie. *La distinction de l'essence et de l'existence d'après Ibn Sīnā (Avicenne).* Paris, 1937.

Jurjānī, ʿAlī ibn Muḥammad al-. *Sharḥ al-Mawāqif fī ʿilm al-kalām.* Cairo, 1977. Last third of the work deals with the divine essence and *tawḥīd.*

Kindī, Yaʿqūb ibn Isḥāq al-. *Al-Kindi's Metaphysics.* Translated by Alfred L. Ivry. Albany, N.Y., 1974.

Laoust, Henri. *Essai sur les doctrines sociales et politiques de Takī-d-Dīn Aḥmad b. Taimīya.* Cairo, 1939.

Marmura, Michael E., and J. M. Rist. "Al-Kindi's Discussion of Divine Existence and Oneness." *Medieval Studies* 25 (1963): 338–354.

Māturīdī, Muḥammad ibn Muḥammad al-. *Kitāb al-Tawḥīd.* Edited by Fatḥ Allāh Khulayf. Beirut, 1970.

Sharīʿatī, ʿAlī. *Islām'shināsī.* Mashhad, 1347/1978.

Sharīʿatī, ʿAlī. *On the Sociology of Islam.* Berkeley, 1979.

TAMARA SONN

TAXATION. Islam makes specific provision for taxation, the payment of which is viewed as a religious duty. The most important tax is *zakāt,* a tax based on wealth, which is paid annually at a rate of one-fortieth of the value of personal or business liquid assets. Property and equipment are excluded, but cash holdings and inventories are subject to the tax at the standard rate of 2.5 percent.

There has been considerable debate among Islamic economists and lawyers about what assets are "zakatable," given the changes in the nature and range of economic activity since the time of the Prophet. The type of tax structure which is appropriate for agricultural economies with only simple trading businesses is clearly rather different from one which is suitable for industrializing economies with businesses organized on a corporate basis. It is only during the past decade that Islamic scholars have addressed modern accounting issues, and there remains much work to be done in this field.

There is general agreement that the income from asset disposals should be subject to *zakāt,* although there is some debate whether it is the disposable income at the end of the accounting period which matters or the income as it accrues. The treatment of debt has also been considered in detail. Debt is allowable against *zakāt,* but what counts as debt is not always a simple matter, as there are many forms of business liability.

Zakāt is a transfer payment, as it is designed to be paid by those with surplus liquid wealth for the benefit of the poor and needy. The essential purpose is redistribution, and the funds raised are earmarked for social and humanitarian spending. The proceeds cannot merely be paid into the treasury and used to finance such commitments as expenditure on defense or even infrastructure investment. The collection is usually organized separately from other taxes, with a religious ministry involved. The receipts are often not even counted with fiscal revenue, and balances are accounted for independently.

Although there have been some Muslim economists who have suggested that *zakāt* could be used as an instrument of demand management, there is a general consensus that this would conflict with the social objectives of the tax. However it can be argued that there are more needy people in a recession, so *zakāt* expenditure should be increased, and in a boom period, receipts will be higher. Running surpluses with *zakāt* funds and borrowing to cover deficits raises other problems, including that of *ribā* (interest earnings and payments). This is of course unacceptable from the Islamic point of view. *Zakāt* is in any case a wealth rather than an income tax, so its suitability for Keynesian short-term demand management must be open to question, even when considered from a narrow economic perspective.

The issue of whether taxation should be limited to *zakāt* obligations has been debated since the time of the Prophet by Muslim scholars. In the early years of Islam, a tax called *jizyah* was imposed on non-Muslims. This was justified on the grounds that non-Muslims did not pay *zakāt,* yet they received government protection if they resided in a Muslim state. *Jizyah* was not therefore a punishment on the conquered who refused to convert to Islam, rather it was to ensure that all residents of an Islamic state contributed to its maintenance on a nondiscriminatory basis.

Unlike *zakāt,* the Islamic land tax *(kharāj)* is applied to both Muslims and non-Muslims. The tax is levied according to the acreage of the land, but the rate depends on the output potential. Higher rates apply on irrigated lands, better soils, and fields suitable for higher-value crops. The maximum rate is half the value of the crop. In the event of crop failure owing to climatic factors, the tax is not applied. If low yields are the result of negligence, then the owner will still be obliged to pay. In such circumstances the land may be sold to another farmer, who, it is hoped, will make better use of it. *Kharāj* means that landowners have a responsibility to use their land effectively and realize its potential, as land is a gift from God and should not be wasted.

In the Ottoman Empire land taxes were a major source of state revenue, and all land was registered so that an accurate assessment could be made. This land registration proved very useful, as uncertainties were removed about boundary demarcation, and the security of tenure with land title encouraged productive investment by landowners in irrigation and other farm improvements. State-owned land was auctioned to private operators under the *muqaṭṭaʿah* system, with successful bidders given the right to farm the land for a three-year period. This system was extended to mining, the minting of coinage, and even the collection of customs revenue. This franchising out to private operators of former government-run activities resembled in many respects the privatization methods increasingly adopted by Western governments.

In the nineteenth century the European imperial powers tended to undermine traditional Islamic methods of tax collection. Secular taxes were introduced as Ottoman control weakened, customs duties being a major source of revenue. Income tax was also introduced in many parts of the Islamic world, although this never proved popular, and in practice often only government employees paid the tax. In such countries as Iran tax evasion was widespread under the secular regimes of the shahs, although *zakāt* was administered independently by the mullahs through the mosques. There were frequent attempts at government interference, but these were resisted by the clerics, who had little faith in state social-welfare provision.

Recent years have witnessed a resurgence of interest in Islamic taxation. In Saudi Arabia *zakāt* is the main form of taxation, and although contributions are voluntary, most Muslims willingly pay. In Sudan most domestic social-welfare expenditure is financed from *zakāt* funds, the government spending most of its unearmarked budget on military commitments. In Pakistan Islamic taxation is increasingly important, although much remains to be done if the economic system is to be islamized as the government appears to want.

As with Islamic banking, *zakāt* in most Muslim countries exists in parallel with conventional tax structures. The latter often function ineffectively owing to the reluctance of businesses and individuals to pay. There is little doubt that Islamic taxation could aid development, as the faithful are more than willing to contribute. *Zakāt* and other Islamic taxes can effectively widen the tax base, harnessing hoarded funds in the interests of development, and because the revenue is earmarked, it is likely to improve social welfare rather than procure armaments.

[*See also* Economics, *article on* Economic Theory; Jizyah; Kharāj; Property; Zakāt.]

BIBLIOGRAPHY

Abdul Mannan, Muḥammad. *Abstracts of Researches in Islamic Economics*. Jeddah, 1984. Summary of important work on taxation by Muslim economists in the 1970s and early 1980s.

Abdul Mannan, Muḥammad. *Islamic Economics: Theory and Practice*. Cambridge, 1986. Examines tax structures in the early Islamic period, including taxes on non-Muslims and land taxes.

Chapra, Mohammad Umer. *Islam and the Economic Challenge*. Leicester, 1992. Considers *zakāt*, income distribution, and economic development.

Chapra, Mohammed Umer. "Reforming the Public Finances in Muslim Countries to Realise Growth with Equity." In *Financing Economic Development: Islamic and Mainstream Approaches*, edited by A. M. Sadeq, pp. 125–141. Kuala Lumpur, 1992. Applies Islamic thinking on public finance, using a Western framework.

Kahf, Monzer. "Fiscal and Monetary Policies in an Islamic Economy." In *Monetary and Fiscal Economics of Islam*, edited by Mohammad Ariff, pp. 125–137. Jeddah, 1982. Concise outline of Islamic taxation for those with some knowledge of public finance.

Kahf, Monzer. "*Zakat:* Unresolved Issues in Contemporary *fiqh*." In *Development and Finance in Islam*, edited by A. M. Sadeq et al., pp. 173–190. Selangor, 1991. Considers some of the debates among modern writers on Islamic taxation.

Morad, Munir. "Current Thought on Islamic Taxation: A Critical Synthesis." In *Islamic Law and Finance*, edited by Chibli Mallat, pp. 117–127. London, 1988. A rather personal view which tries to bring together the different strands of thought on Islamic taxation.

Nienhaus, Volker. "Les biens public et la politique financière dans une économie islamique." In *Les capitaux de l'Islam*, edited by Gilbert Beauge, pp. 123–134. Paris, 1990. Excellent French-language summary of the essentials of Islamic public finance.

Tabakoğlu, Ahmed. "Role of Finance in Development: The Ottoman Experience." In *Proceedings of the Third International Conference on Islamic Economics*, edited by A. H. Ajunaid, pp. 2–16. Kuala Lumpur, 1992. Useful account of nineteenth-century Ottoman tax structures.

Wilson, Rodney. "Macroeconomic Policy and the Islamic State." Chapter seven of the author's study *Islamic Business: Theory and Practice*. London, 1985. Examines fiscal policy objectives and the role of *zakāt* as a wealth tax.

RODNEY WILSON

TAʿZĪR. *See* Criminal Law.

TAʿZIYAH. The Shīʿī passion play called *taʿziyah* is the only serious drama ever developed in the Islamic world, except for contemporary Western theater. *Taʿziyah* (from the Arabic word *ʿazāʾ*, "mourning") is mainly performed in Iran. It reenacts the passion and death of Ḥusayn, the beloved grandson of the prophet Muḥammad and the third imam of the Shīʿīs. He was brutally murdered along with his male children and companions while contesting his right to the caliphate in battle on the sun-baked wastes known as the Plain of Karbala (in present Iraq) in 680 CE (AH 61). This tragic massacre became a vicarious martyrdom mourned ever since by Shīʿīs worldwide. In Iran, the mourning for Ḥusayn received royal patronage when Shīʿī Islam was established as the state religion in the sixteenth century.

The mourning for Ḥusayn manifests itself in stationary and ambulatory rituals. The *taʿziyah* as a dramatic theatrical form is a result of the mid-eighteenth-century fusion of ambulatory and stationary rituals that had coexisted for more than a millennium. At first *taʿziyah* plays were performed at crossroads, in marketplaces and town squares, and later in the courtyards of inns and private houses. Finally, special structures called *takīyah* or *Ḥusaynīyah* were built for them, some by well-to-do persons as a pious public service and others with contributions from the citizens of a borough. Some were large, seating thousands of spectators, while others accommodated several hundred. Many *takīyah* structures were temporary, put up by members of a community especially for the Muḥarram/Ṣafar observances. The most famous *taʿziyah* theater was Takīyah Dawlat, the Royal Theater in Tehran, built in the 1870s by Naṣr al-Dīn Shāh. Its dazzling splendor and the intensity of its dramatic action overshadowed, according to many Western visitors, even the opera houses of Western capitals. The building was torn down in 1946.

Although in the second half of the nineteenth century *takīyah* buildings became a major feature in Iranian towns, a distinctly recognizable *takīyah* architecture did not emerge. There are, however, common characteristics of almost all *takīyah* that preserve and enhance the dramatic interplay between actors and spectators. This is theater-in-the-round. The main performing space is a stark, curtainless, raised platform in the center of the building or a courtyard. This central stage can be of various shapes and is surrounded by a circular strip usually covered by sand. This space is used for equestrian and foot battles and for subplots and action indicating journeys, the passage of time, and changes. The scenes are changed by rotation of the stage; the performers jump off the stage and circumambulate it. The actor may now announce that he is going to a certain place; by climbing back onto the stage, he may announce that he has arrived there. The action extends from the main stage to the sand-covered circular band and into the auditorium. Skirmishes often take place behind the audience in unwalled *takīyah*. This centrifugal movement of the action, from the centrally situated stage out to the *takīyah* periphery and back, engulfs the audience and makes it part of the play. In many situations the audience actually participates physically in the play. (Some Western directors and producers have looked recently to the *taʿziyah* for devices to break down barriers between actors and audience.)

The stage decor is almost nonexistent, as the minimalist setting is supposed to evoke the desolate, bleak desert of Karbala. Most of the props are symbolic as well; a basin of water, for example, represents the Euphrates River, and a branch of a tree, a palm grove.

In Takīyah Dawlat Theater during the reign of Naṣr al-Dīn Shāh the costumes were rich and splendid, though no attention was paid to their historicity. Even today the costumes are supposed to help the audience to recognize the characters. The protagonists dress predominantly in green, and the villains wear red. Green symbolizes paradise and the family of the Prophet, and therefore Islam; red symbolizes blood, suffering, and cruelty. Actors playing women are dressed in baggy black garments covering them from head to toe, with faces veiled; thus even bearded men can play female roles as long as their voices do not give them away. When a protagonist puts a white sheet of cloth on his shoulders representing a burial shroud, this indicates that he is ready to sacrifice his life and will be killed shortly. This in turn creates a cathartic state in the audience.

In addition to the colors, there is another clear division between the protagonists and antagonists in the *taʿziyah*. The protagonists sing their parts, and the antagonists recite theirs. In the past, the actors were chosen according to their physical suitability for a role, but a good singing voice had to complement the physical stature of the protagonist actor. The amateur actors used to read their lines from little folded scripts held in the palms of their hands, though the professional actors knew their lines by heart. Holding a script in one's hand indicated that the actor was only a role-carrier; in other words, that he was not the character he portrayed. At present, actors of professional troupes know most of their lines by heart; if not, they pretend to know them and avoid referring conspicuously to their notes. The antagonists declaim their lines, often in violent shrieking voices. Frequently the antagonists are made to appear as ridiculous buffoons, overplayed and overacted. The traditional attempts to distance the actors from the characters they portray are often swept away in the modern productions of the *taʿziyah*. Under the influence of movies and television, the actors identify with the personages they represent to such a degree that they are carried away by the situations. The emotions of the actors are increased by the receptiveness of the audience as it meets the actor halfway. The influence of film and television is noticeable also among the contemporary audience.

A *taʿziyah* director is at the same time a producer, music director, stage director, public relations coordinator, and prompter. He is responsible not only for the play's direction and production, music and *mise-en-scène*, but also for all props, arrangements with the local authorities, and financial returns. The director is always on hand during the performance, regulating the movement of actors, musicians, and audience. He remains constantly on the playing ground, giving actors their cues. His presence on the stage, however, is not disturbing to the audience as he is an integral part of the *taʿziyah* production.

The core of the *taʿziyah* repertory is the plays devoted to the Karbala tragedy and the events surrounding it. The Karbala massacre is divided into many separate episodes performed on separate days. The passage of Ḥusayn from Medina via Mecca to his death at Karbala is represented in some ten plays in as many days. In these plays, a hero singlehandedly fights the entire enemy army, allowing the rest of the protagonists, grouped on the central stage, to muse about their condition and to make comments of a philosophical and religious nature. There is only one fixed day and play in the Muḥarram repertory—the martyrdom of Ḥusayn on the tenth; the others can be performed in varying order. Usually the sequence starts on the first day of the month of Muḥarram with a play dedicated to the death of Ḥusayn's emissary to Kufa, Muslim ibn ʿAqīl. This is followed in daily sequence by the martyrdom of two of Muslim's children, and then by plays about the martyrdom of various members of Ḥusayn's family and companions. Most commonly, on the sixth of Muḥarram the *Martyrdom of Ḥurr* is performed; on the seventh, the *Martyrdom of Qāsim the Bridegroom;* on the eighth, the *Martyrdom of ʿAlī Akbar,* the oldest and favorite son of Ḥusayn; and on the ninth, the *Martyrdom of ʿAbbās,* a half-brother of Ḥusayn and his standardbearer. The basic repertory of the *taʿziyah* does not necessarily end with Ḥusayn's death. The performances may continue after the ʿĀshūrā' day to show the tragic lot of Ḥusayn's women, who were taken as captives to Damascus.

The Shīʿī cult of martyrology brought into the *taʿziyah* fold new plays about other Shīʿī martyrs before and after Karbala. Since the mid-nineteenth century, plays based on the Qur'ān, *ḥadīth,* and even current events have been written and performed. They are connected, however, to the Karbala tragedy through the employment of *gurīz,* a direct verbal reference or the staging of a short scene from Ḥusayn's passion. The expansion of the repertory was followed by the expansion of performing time from the month of Muḥarram to the entire year.

The *taʿziyah* troupes of today are often family businesses, although they depend only partially on the income from performances. Professional troupes today usually stay in one place for ten days to two weeks, giving a different play every day. Sometimes there are two performances a day, one in the evening. A play can last from two to five hours.

In the 1930s Reza Shah's government, considering the *taʿziyah* a backward ritual, imposed restrictions on its performance in urban areas, and it retreated to rural areas. Ayatollah Ruhollah Khomeini, however, used *taʿziyah* and other popular Shīʿī rituals and beliefs into a means of mass mobilization for the Islamic Revolution. During the eight years of war with Iraq, the heroism depicted in the *taʿziyah* was employed to increase the fighting spirit of Iranian combatants and to bring solace to those who had lost their loved ones.

In 1991, *taʿziyah* was staged at the Avignon Arts Festival in southern France, where it received a tumultuous reception. The *taʿziyah*'s popularity continues unabated in Iran. Many articles on the *taʿziyah* form have appeared in recent Iranian journals.

[*See also* ʿĀshūrā'; Ḥusayn ibn ʿAlī; Ḥusaynīyah;

Karbala; Martyrdom; Muḥarram; *and* Shīʿī Islam, *historical overview article.*]

BIBLIOGRAPHY

Alserat 12 (Spring–Autumn 1986). Special issue of the journal containing papers from the Imam Husayn Conference, London, July 1984, and providing important coverage of the Karbala tragedy.

Chelkowski, Peter, ed. *Taʿziyeh: Ritual and Drama in Iran.* New York, 1979. Traces the historical development and flourishing of *taʿziyah* into its full-fledged dramatic form today, including essays on theatrical, anthropological, musical, artistic, and other aspects of the ritual by scholars from many countries in Asia, Europe, and America. Based on the proceedings of the international symposium held during the Shiraz (Iran) Festival of the Arts in August 1976.

Pelly, Lewis. *The Miracle Play of Hasan and Husain.* 2 vols. London, 1879. Contains translations of thirty-seven *taʿziyah* plays, written in an ornate Victorian English.

Riggio, Milla Cozart, ed. *Taʿziyeh: Ritual and Popular Beliefs in Iran.* Hartford, Conn., 1988. Short book containing essays prepared for a drama festival and conference held at Trinity College in the spring of 1988.

Rossi, Ettore, and Alessio Bombaci. *Elenco di drami religiosi persiani.* Vatican, 1961. Catalog of the collection of original *taʿziyah* plays (1,055 manuscripts) housed at the Biblioteca Apostolica Vaticana.

PETER CHELKOWSKI

TECHNOLOGY AND APPLIED SCIENCES.

Between 900 and 1300 CE, the "golden age of science," the Arab and greater Islamic world excelled in scientific activity and many fields of technology, such as civil engineering and optics. This edge disappeared with the invasion and destruction of urban Islamic life by the Mongols, the decline of agriculture and irrigation, the manifestations of religious and intellectual intolerance, and other factors. While science and scholarship thrived in Renaissance Europe, they withered in the Ottoman Empire. The historian Albert Hourani observes that "during the centuries of Ottoman rule there had been no advance in technology and a decline in the level of scientific knowledge" (*A History of the Arab Peoples*, Cambridge, 1991, p. 259). The lack of knowledge of Western languages blocked the flow of ideas.

Napoleon's invasion of Egypt in 1798 with its additional mission of knowledge-gathering and entourage of scholars dramatized the science and technology gap. It resulted in initial efforts in Egypt and Iran to send students to Europe as well as the recruitment of European technicians. Although most of these early efforts at technology transfer failed, they set in motion other forces. The Ottoman sultans began importing military technology and specialists. Armenians, Greeks, Jews, Copts, and other minorities came forward to translate technical manuals and to serve as intermediaries for imported knowledge.

As commerce grew, disease vectors were transported and major epidemics of cholera and plague occurred. Although European therapies (with the exception of smallpox inoculation) were little better than traditional Islamic medicine, European medical techniques were oriented toward research. The majority of the population continued to rely on traditional Islamic healers, but rulers by 1840 had brought European physicians to Tunis and Istanbul. One of the first innovations to be imposed on their advice was quarantine to close ports and commerce to epidemics.

The period between 1850 and the onset of World War I in 1914 was marked by the extraordinarily rapid diffusion of Western technologies throughout most of the Middle East from Morocco to Iran. These included railways, telegraphs, steamships and steam engines, automobiles, and telephones. The opening of the Suez Canal (1868), the major engineering feat of the nineteenth century, reduced shipping time and distance and generated new trade. Much of the technology transfer took the form of government monopoly concessions to European firms. Often members of minority communities provided clerical and skilled labor. There was little or no concern for the development of indigenous capabilities in technology adaptation, design, or maintenance.

Similarly, it was minorities who took the lead in establishing the first Western educational institutions in the region, with engineering figuring prominently in the curriculum. The Syrian Protestant College was founded in Beirut in 1868, soon to be followed by the Jesuits' St. Joseph College. While some elite Muslim families sent their children to these and similar schools in Istanbul, Tunis, Teheran, Algiers, and elsewhere, they primarily served European expatriates and settlers and minority communities. However, one of their major contributions was the translation and publishing in Arabic of major scientific works. Although Charles Darwin's *Origin of the Species* was not published in full in Arabic until 1918, excerpts had appeared in new Arabic science education periodicals by 1876. Scientific societies were also founded in Beirut, Cairo, Damascus, and Istanbul in the late nineteenth century to support the first embryonic scientific communities.

Throughout the period 1800–1914 there was minimal formal Islamic resistance to the gradual spread of western technologies and scientific ideas. The major opposition to Darwinian ideas of evolution came from Christian fundamentalist scholars rather than from Muslims. The medical discoveries of Pasteur, Koch, and others concerning microbes and bacteria were quickly accepted and taught in Middle Eastern medical schools. Public health measures to contain cholera, malaria, and other diseases were imposed by European authorities in North Africa and approved elsewhere by local elites. Where resentment occurred, it was often directed not at imported technologies but at the local minorities who were using them to their own advantage.

The period 1914–1945 was characterized by slow and often frustrating attempts to strengthen indigenous versus imported science and technology. New universities with an emphasis on engineering and medicine were established in Egypt, Turkey, Syria, and the Sudan. However, the depression years reduced employment for graduates and increased discontent over the dominant role of expatriates and minorities.

There were faltering attempts at industrialization for small local markets in Egypt, Iran, Iraq, and Syria. Most technologies were imported, maintenance was a persistent problem, and there was limited shop-floor learning. The one exception was the petroleum industry, which after 1914 assumed major proportions in Iran, Iraq, and Saudi Arabia. The practices of multinational firms varied, but there was everywhere some local subcontracting as well as maintenance engineering. Although local contractors lacked the resources to compete on major petroleum industry contracts, they did participate to some extent.

The nationalism that emerged at the end of World War I in the region did not put mastery of science and technology high on its agenda. The objective of the nationalists was to remove the colonial powers and their minority collaborators. The one exception was Turkey, where Mustafa Kemal Atatürk after 1922 launched an ambitious program of industrialization and expansion of engineering education.

The aftermath of World War II was quite different, with the partition of India and the creation of Pakistan, the 1948 Israeli war for independence, and the pursuit of independence and national sovereignty virtually everywhere. The war had underlined the importance of logistics, communications, mass public health programs, and transport. Governments were expected to do far more than they had in the past, with technology a key instrument.

The results from 1945 to the present have been sometimes impressive and sometimes disappointing. During this period more than sixty new universities and technical schools opened. Enrollment in science and engineering multiplied, with hundreds of thousands of graduates. Several hundred thousand students have gone abroad to North America, Europe, and the former Soviet Union for advanced study. Some have stayed abroad, but the majority have returned. There has, however, been a pronounced brain-drain to the oil-exporting countries from Egypt, the Sudan, Pakistan, and elsewhere. Although female enrollment in science and engineering remains very low, there has been overall impressive growth in human resources.

The problem remains though that universities remain oriented toward teaching rather than research. There are few strong doctoral programs or research centers of academic excellence. Engineering students often lack management training and hands-on experience. In spite of massive financial investment and importation of foreign models, universities in Saudi Arabia, Kuwait and the other Gulf states cannot match their state-of-the-art facilities with research. Universities in the non-oil-exporting countries lack funds and equipment as well as incentives for research.

Language continues to be a problem. The Arab League has systematically promoted scientific translations into Arabic and the creation of new vocabulary, but the available literature continues to be inadequate. At North African universities science and engineering instruction continues to be in French; in Saudi Arabia it is in English. Research on computerizing Arabic progresses, but it is not yet a working language for keeping up with current research in many fields.

The lack of institutionalized research in universities is reflected across many Islamic societies. Applied research units have been established in government ministries of agriculture, health, and public works; however, with limited budgets, patronage appointments, and few linkages to the private sector or to universities, few of these units are productive.

The state-owned enterprises that are pervasive in countries such as Algeria and Syria also have internal research units. These are plagued by poor management, lack of funds and continuity, an inability to disseminate research, and personnel problems. The record of research by state-owned firms in the region is dismal, and the diffusion of research is even worse. Lack of accountability has characterized many of these operations.

Local private firms prefer to import technology rather than to conduct in-house research or to collaborate with universities or government ministries. Industrial import-substitution continues to rely on foreign construction and maintenance. In spite of the massive construction spending in the oil-exporting countries since 1973, only two regional firms compete for major contracts, both founded in Lebanon and receiving no government support. Elsewhere private construction and consulting firms concentrate on national markets where they enjoy preference and do little of their own design work. While the oil-exporters like Saudi Arabia import capital-intensive state-of-the-art technology with minimal adaptation, local private firms in other countries often import used machinery. Only in Turkey and Pakistan is there evidence of significant in-house informal learning to adapt used equipment.

Multinational firms active in the region prefer to conduct research at European or North American sites. There is some adaptive research in the petroleum and petrochemical industries, mostly on a small scale. The nationalization of the oil industry throughout the region has resulted in multinationals operating on contracts and/or concessions; this provides no incentives for joint ventures in research with state-owned companies.

The other institutional outlets for research are relatively minor. There are national and regional professional societies of physicists, dentists, engineers, and other disciplines. At best they provide professional journals and meetings but no structures for research. In several countries, such as Syria, these professional societies have also been decimated by government repression. Researchers who attempt to travel abroad, to maintain overseas contacts, and to read European languages have been targets of suspicion.

Several attempts have been made to anchor research in financially solvent, automomous foundations. One of the most successful is the Institute for Theoretical Physics in Trieste, a multinational research center for third-world scholars. The International Center for Dry Lands Agriculture at Aleppo, Syria, part of the World Bank agricultural research consortium, is a similar institution.

The small size, limited resources and scarce professional personnel of many Islamic countries make regional cooperation in science and technology imperative. This has been discussed since the 1976 CASTARAB conference and a number of schemes proposed, but lack of funding, commitment, and interest have frustrated these efforts. Instead, science and technology policies continue to be pursued mostly at national levels. Pakistan is in the lead with a comprehensive, government-directed research effort including a nuclear energy program. Indonesia has directed its policy at high technology, including a national aerospace industry. Turkey has achieved modest research cooperation between the private and public sectors, especially in hydrology, textiles and agriculture. Egypt has a cumbersome, centralized research bureaucracy with few visible accomplishments. Saudi Arabia and Kuwait have poured vast amounts of money into science and technology, but the mentality remains that of buying rather than developing indigenous capabilities. Algeria, Morocco, and Tunisia maintain modest French-style centralized research policies; lack of linkages and diffusion limits their productivity. Iran and Iraq have concentrated on indigenous petroleum and weapons capabilities to the detriment of other sectors. Other countries like the Sudan or Yemen lack a nucleus of researchers, many of whom have emigrated.

These enormous disparities in resources and capabilities do not preclude cooperation. There is consensus on the research priorities for most of the region. These include solar energy, desalination, arid-lands agriculture, irrigation, animal sciences, and petrochemicals. Although major research on these subjects is taking place outside the region, there are a number of modest regional projects as well as some expensive technology transfers, for instance solar energy in Saudi Arabia. Agreement on priorities, long-term funding, and shared projects is feasible.

The principal obstacles to indigenous science and technology in the Islamic world do not stem from Islam itself. While there are a few advocates of "Islamic science" in Pakistan and elsewhere, most Muslim scientists believe in a universal science. Abdus Salam, the Nobel Prize–winning physicist, declares that "there truly is no disconsonance between Islam and modern science" (1987, p. 212). Instead, the obstacles are repressive governments that arrest researchers and stifle freedom of inquiry, cultural practices that discourage women from studying science and engineering, deficient science education at all levels of instruction, failure to create research institutions with effective linkages, and a preference for buying science and technology.

[See also Mathematics; Science.]

BIBLIOGRAPHY

Butterworth, Charles E., and I. William Zartman, eds. *Political Islam.* New York, 1992. Special issue of the *Annals of the American*

Academy of Political and Social Science, with excellent discussions of Islam and democracy.

Gallagher, Nancy E. *Medicine and Power in Tunisia, 1780–1900*. Cambridge, 1983. Covers the introduction of and reaction to European medicine.

Gallagher, Nancy E. *Egypt's Other Wars: Epidemics and the Politics of Public Health*. Syracuse, N.Y., 1990. Insightful history of anticholera and -malaria campaigns in the 1940s.

Hassan, Ahmad Y. al-, and Donald R. Hill. *Islamic Technology: An Illustrated History*. London, 1992. Splendid account of the Islamic golden age of science and technology.

Hoodbhoy, Pervez. *Islam and Science: Religious Orthodoxy and the Battle for Rationality*. London, 1991. A Pakistani physicist forcefully rejects Islam in favor of a universal science.

Hourani, Albert. *A History of the Arab Peoples*. Cambridge, 1992. Monumental study, excellent on the golden age of science.

Issawi, Charles. *Economic History of the Middle East and North Africa*. New York, 1984. Detailed account of the nineteenth-century growth in trade and the introduction of innovations.

National Academy of Sciences. *Scientists and Human Rights in Syria*. Washington, D.C., 1993. Published by the Committee on Human Rights, this is a searing account of the plight of Syrian scientists.

Salam, Abdus. *Ideals and Realities: Selected Essays*. Philadelphia, 1987. Reflections by a Nobel Prize–winning Pakistani physicist on Islam and science, among other topics.

Sardar, Ziauddin. *Science and Technology in the Middle East*. London, 1982. Country-by-country survey.

Selin, Helaine. *Science across Cultures: An Annotated Bibliography of Books on Non-Western Science, Technology, and Medicine*. New York, 1992.

Zahlan, Anthony. *Acquiring Technological Capacity: A Study of Arab Consulting and Contracting Firms*. New York, 1991.

Ziadat, Adel A. *Western Science in the Arab World: The Impact of Darwinism, 1861–1930*. London, 1986. History of the debate over Darwinism.

AARON SEGAL

TEKKE. *See* Sufism, *article on* Ṣūfī Shrine Culture; Zāwiyah.

TELEVISION. *See* Radio and Television.

TEMPORARY MARRIAGE. *See* Mutʿah.

TERRORISM is the deliberate, unjustifiable, and random use of violence for political ends against protected persons. Obviously, there is no inextricable connection between Islam, or any other great religion, and terrorism. In fact, there is often a great confusion between the phenomenon of political violence and terrorism. The term *terrorism* applies to a special category of opprobrious acts rather than to all acts of politically inspired violence. Muslims have engaged in terrorism in the modern era, and, just as Jews and Christians engaging in terrorism, they have sometimes claimed a justification based in religion. In point of fact, however, *sharīʿah* (the divine law) does not condone the use of violence except to combat injustice, and noncombatant immunity is a prominent feature of Islamic thinking on *jihād* (religiously sanctioned warfare). In warfare, necessity might justify putting noncombatants at risk, but harm to innocents should neither be intentional nor excessive. Thus, phrases such as "Islamic terrorism" significantly misrepresent the religious roots of violence committed by Muslims.

More than any other part of the *ummah*, the Middle East has, since World War II, become infamous as a cockpit for terrorism, although many of the perpetrators have not purported to act in the name of Islam. Arguably, the first modern act of political terrorism in the region was the bombing of the King David Hotel in 1947, which was carried out by Jewish terrorists led by Menachem Begin, then leader of the Irgun. Following the creation of the state of Israel in 1948, Begin became leader of the political opposition, and in 1977 he became prime minister of Israel. In the 1960s and 1970s, Palestinian *fidāʾīyin* (guerrillas) launched dozens of horrendous acts of violence against innocent bystanders, all in the name of gaining recognition for Palestinian nationalism. These acts included the slaughter of Israeli athletes at the Munich Olympics in 1972, a long series of skyjackings, including four in 1970 that helped precipitate the civil war in Jordan, and several bloody attacks on air travelers both inside Israel and in Europe. Significantly, the Palestinian perpetrators were inspired by a secular irredentist ideology, not by religion. The same can be said for Kurdish guerrillas who, in the 1980s and early 1990s, committed a number of vicious acts of violence in Turkey as part of their quest to win an independent Kurdistan.

Muslims, claiming an Islamic rationale for their violence, are also noteworthy. In Egypt, in 1954, the Ikhwān al-Muslimūn (Muslim Brotherhood) attempted to assassinate Gamal Abdel Nasser, who then accelerated his suppression of the organization. More recently, President Anwar el-Sadat was assassinated by extremist Muslim conspirators in 1981. Muslim revolutionaries, intent on toppling the regime of Hosni Mubarak have, since the late 1980s, engaged in escalating acts of violence including terrorism to destabilize further the

Egyptian government. Many of these acts have been egregiously indiscriminate, targeting innocent foreign tourists, in addition to state officials, soldiers, and police officers. These acts illustrate the scope of activities that constitute contemporary political violence; whether they all constitute acts of terrorism is another question.

Terrorism is notoriously difficult to define, since the term is often used to refer to generic acts of violence committed by political adversaries. Terrorism is a marvelous epithet with which to bludgeon or tar one's adversaries. But the moral indictment is often debased, because there is a tendency to apply the label selectively to foes, while turning a blind eye to equally contemptible acts carried out by friends or allies pursuing congenial goals.

The quest for a definition of terrorism has bedeviled diplomats and international lawyers, and there is no internationally accepted definition of terrorism. Although terrorism is frequently decried, the standard practice in international law has been to proceed inductively, criminalizing specific acts such as air piracy, attacks on diplomats, or the theft of nuclear materials. Thus, there is general agreement that hijacking of commercial aircraft or vessels constitutes a form of terrorism when carried out by nonstate perpetrators.

Acts of violence carried out within the borders of a state are more problematic to characterize, since illegal acts of violence might be legitimate, especially when the state authorities harshly repress dissent and when the illegal acts do not target protected persons. To argue that an act of political violence is unlawful (a factual statement) is not the same as arguing that it is illegitimate (a normative conclusion). It is important to distinguish between those political systems where citizens can effectively voice their demands and those where whole categories of citizens are disenfranchised. In the second category of states, those where the state is deaf to its citizens and residents, violence might be justifiable and legitimate even though it is deemed illegal by the authorities. In contrast, in the first category of states, political violence is both illegal and illegitimate, because the enfranchised citizen need not resort to violence to be heard or to enjoy the protection of the state.

Of course, legality and legitimacy are not always easy to disentangle, as the case of Algeria illustrates. The Islamic Salvation Front, often referred to by its French acronym, FIS, was on the verge of attaining an overwhelming parliamentary majority following its impressive victory in the first stage of a two-stage set of elections. Instead of allowing FIS to enjoy the fruits of its electoral victory, the Algerian army, fearful of the Islamists' intentions and supported by about half of Algeria's population seized power in January 1992. Understandably, the membership of FIS reacted with fury to the army's action, and a civil war ensued, with thousands of FIS adherents arrested and detained under martial-law conditions. Moderate leaders in FIS were thoroughly discredited, and the Islamists launched a campaign of insurrection and violence that respected few moral boundaries and targeted not only government officials but also intellectuals deemed unsympathetic to the Islamists and individuals who favored western dress or styles of behavior. In a striking throwback to the Algerian Revolution of the 1950s and early 1960s, when French rule was overthrown, terrorism has again become the coin of the realm for both sides in Algeria, thoroughly polarizing Algerian society. [*See* Islamic Salvation Front.]

The right of a people to resist foreign occupation is widely, if somewhat erratically, upheld. A clear majority of world governments—including Egypt, France, Iran, Saudi Arabia, and the United States—supported Afghan Muslims struggling violently against Soviet occupation. Relatively few observers outside the Soviet Union described the Afghani *mujāhidīn* as terrorists, even though their attacks were often condemned as terrorism by the USSR. So long as the *mujāhidīn* directed their efforts against the Soviet presence in Afghanistan, right was literally on their side. [*See* Mujāhidīn, *article on* Afghan Mujāhidīn.] By the same token, though agreement is less general, the resistance by Lebanese Muslims (as well as Lebanese Christians) to the Israeli occupation of a portion of souther Lebanon, which it has occupied since 1978, would be similarly sanctioned, despite Israel's understandable penchant for describing those that attack its soldiers and client-militiamen as terrorists.

A sounder test addresses the moral legitimacy of the means rather than the technical legality of the ends. If the Afghan or the Lebanese resistance forces broaden their campaigns to encompass protected categories of noncombatants, their actions tend to lose privileged status. Whatever the politics of the observer, distinguishing between attacks on soldiers occupying foreign lands and attacks on persons in universally accepted protected categories, such as children, or, more broadly, noncombatants, is not difficult. So long as a resistance force is discriminate in its methods and targets, it is not objectively justified to affix the terrorism label.

Deliberate and random uses of violence for political ends against protected groups constitutes terrorism. This is a functional and nonpolemical definition that has the merit of parsimony and universality. The perpetrators can be states, agents of states, or individuals acting independently. Indeed, the Iraqi government's al-Anfāl campaign in the 1980s to intimidate and exterminate major segments of its Kurdish population clearly constituted an act of state terrorism. The record shows, however sadly, that states have been often able to commit murderous acts that dwarf the acts of horror committed by nonstate terrorists with impunity. Within the *ummah,* there are many examples, including the following: Indonesia's bloody suppression of East Timor in the early 1960s; Syria's annihilation of more than a thousand people in Hama in 1982; and Sudan's savage campaign in the south to squash resistance to islamization in the 1990s.

In general, militant opposition movements of Muslims have focused their violence domestically on the authoritarian state, which is typically characterized as thwarting the imposition of *sharīʿah* as the sole legitimate source of law. The writings of Sayyid Quṭb (executed in 1966 by the Egyptian government) and his rejuvenation of *jāhilīyah* (literally, a state of ignorance of the truths of Islam) as a description of contemporary Muslim societies has provided, for some contemporary groups, a rationale for acts of violence rationalized as part of a *jihād* to reestablish Islamic society.

Although most militant movements of Muslims have concentrated on domestic goals, the revolution in Iran spawned an ideology that has been used to justify the use of violence on the international stage in the late 1980s. Not only has the Iranian government been implicated in widespread assassinations and plots against political and intellectual opponents, but it has also lent material support to militant Islamist groups. This can be observed in the case of the Lebanese Shīʿī group Ḥizbullāh (Party of God).

Ḥizbullāh is an Iranian-funded party that came to light following the Israeli invasion of Lebanon in 1982. Ḥizbullāh has proven to be a competent, dedicated, and well-led challenger to the more moderate Amal movement of the early 1970s. Although Ḥizbullāh spokespersons were keen to dissociate the party from acts such as the kidnappings of Westerners in the 1980s, it became known that the Islamic Jihād organization that claimed credit for some of the kidnappings was using a flag of convenience masking Ḥizbullāh involvement. Ḥizbullāh played a major role in inflicting a chain of humiliations on the United States: precipitating the 1984 departure of the American marines from Lebanon with the truck bombing of the marine barracks, while also helping to scuttle the U.S.-brokered 17 May agreement between Lebanon and Israel and holding the world in thrall over the fate of foreign hostages (including Terry Waite, the personal envoy of the archbishop of Canterbury). Equally impressive was the success of the Islamic Resistance (al-Muqāwamah al-Islāmīyah) in forcing an Israeli withdrawal from most of Lebanese territory in January 1985.

In effect, the Islamic Revolution in Iran provided the substance for a new ideological framework that served to explain the causes of deprivation and suffering among the Muslim masses. The ideological framework legitimized and commended the use of violence against the enemies of Islam, particularly the West. This comes through quite clearly in the remarkable "Open Letter" of Ḥizbullāh (reproduced in Norton, 1987). This revealing document was released by Ḥizbullāh in February 1985 to mark the anniversary of the assassination of Shaykh Rāghib Ḥarb, the bright young cleric of Jibshīt in southern Lebanon, who was assassinated twelve months earlier.

One of the burdens of the letter is to explain and justify the use of violence by Ḥizbullāh, which, it is argued, has been trivialized in the West as "a handful of fanatics and terrorists who are only concerned with blowing up drinking, gambling, and entertainment spots. . . . Each of us is a combat soldier when the call of jihad demands it and each of us undertakes his task in the battle in accordance with his lawful assignment within the framework of action under the guardianship of the leader jurisprudent."

The letter emphasizes that the 1978–1979 revolution in Iran was an inspiration to action, a proof of all that can be accomplished when the faithful gather under the banner of Islam. "We address all the Arab and Islamic peoples to declare to them that the Muslim's experience in Islamic Iran left no one any excuse since it proved beyond all doubt that bare chests motivated by faith are capable, with God's help, of breaking the iron and oppression of tyrannical regimes." The letter described a world in which "the countries of the arrogant world" and especially the United States and the Soviet Union struggle for influence at the expense of the Third World. As a commentator in *Al-ʿahd,* the Ḥizbullāh newspaper, noted: "The Soviets are not one iota different from the Americans in terms of political danger, indeed are more dangerous than them in terms of ideological considerations as well, and this requires that light be shed on this fact and that the Soviets be assigned their proper place in the . . . forces striving to strike at the interests of the Moslem people and arrogate their political present and future" (9 May 1987, p. 12). Nonetheless, pride of place belonged to the Untied States, which directly, or indirectly through its "spearhead," Israel, has inflicted suffering on the Muslims of Lebanon: "Imam Khomeini, the leader, has repeatedly stressed that America is the reason for all our catastrophes and the source of all malice. By fighting it, we are only exercising our legitimate right to defend our Islam and the dignity of our nation." The French were also been singled out for attack, largely because of their longstanding sympathy for Christians in Lebanon, and for their arms sales to Iraq.

Ḥizbullāh positioned itself as a force resisting the designs and games of Israel and the superpowers, whose jockeying for power, in its view, has led to subjugation and oppression throughout the Third World. "Thus, we have seen that aggression can be repelled only with the sacrifice of blood, and that freedom is not given but regained with the sacrifice of both heart and soul." The objective is to free Lebanon from the manipulation and chicanery of the malevolent outside powers in order to achieve "the final departure of America, France, and their allies from Lebanon and the termination of the influence of any imperialist power in the country." The Christian Phalange, who have, according to Ḥizbullāh, unjustly enjoyed privilege at the expense of the Muslims, must be pummeled into submission. Virtually unnoticed outside of Lebanon, Ḥizbullāh has been especially intolerant of competitors for Shīʿī recruits. In this regard the Communist party, an especially appealing target given its alien and atheistic ideology, has been singled out for attacks. Dozens, if not hundreds, of party members were killed in a brutal, bloody campaign of suppression and assassination in 1984 and 1985. [*See also* Ḥizbullāh, *article on* Ḥizbullāh in Lebanon.]

The cost of terrorism is obviously most severe for its immediate victims, but there are heavy costs for the perpetrators' society as well. The use of terrorism stereotypes a community, thereby reducing rather than enhancing international support for its claims. The heavy moral baggage of past outrages can be a burden. Not surprisingly, many Lebanese Shīʿīs have come to resent the kidnapping of foreigners, sometimes on moral grounds, but often simply on practical grounds. Many acts of terrorism are patently counterproductive. Rather than weakening the resolve of the target population, terrorists—whether agents of a state or acting independently—supply the argument, and all too often the means for their own eradication.

Scholars are wont to emphasize that terrorism is the weapon of the weak. Although there is some truth in this observation, as illustrated by the bombing of the World Trade Center in New York City by a band of militant Muslims, the major perpetrators are not individuals or nonstate actors inspired by a vision of Islam, but strong, authoritarian governments intent on maintaining or extending their power, or punishing their adversaries.

[*See also* Hostages; Revolution.]

BIBLIOGRAPHY

Cole, Juan R. I., and Nikki R. Keddie, eds. *Shīʿism and Social Protest*. New Haven, 1986. This important collection of articles probes the significance of the revolution in Iran for inspiring activism among Muslims outside Iran. A number of the authors stress that local conditions were often more important than the events in Iran for explaining the appeal of radical Islamist movements, including Shīʿī movements in Iraq, Lebanon, and Saudi Arabia.

Esposito, John L. *The Islamic Threat: Myth or Reality*. New York and Oxford, 1992. One of the leading experts on Islam and politics explores and often debunks sensationalist perspectives on the Islamist phenomenon. Esposito distinguishes clear acts of terrorism from other forms of political violence and activism.

Faḍlallāh, Muḥammad Ḥusayn. *Al-Islām wa-manṭiq al-qūwah* (Islam and the Logic of Power). 2d ed. Beirut, 1981. The author is a leading Shīʿī cleric in Lebanon whose writings reach well beyond Lebanon and whose *khuṭbahs* and *fatwās* are widely influential in Lebanon. This book provides an Islamist argument for the use of violence to overturn injustice and to confront the enemies of Islam.

Kepel, Gilles. *Muslim Extremism in Egypt: The Prophet and Pharaoh*. Berkeley, 1986. Kepel, a French scholar, offers a seminal analysis of the Islamist movement during the 1970s and early 1980s including the assassins of Anwar Sadat. His discussion of the importance of the writings of Sayyid Quṭb is particularly noteworthy.

Martin, David C., and John Walcott. *Best Laid Plans: The Inside Story of America's War against Terrorism*. New York, 1988. The authors benefited from many off-the-record interviews with high-level figures in the U.S. government. This book focuses on the U.S. response to Middle East terrorism, but the authors also glean fairly from a number of reliable accounts on "radical" Islamist movements.

Mohaddessin, Mohammad. *Islamic Fundamentalism: The New Global Threat*. Washington, D.C., 1993. The author is associated with the *mujāhidīn-i khalq*, which staunchly opposes the regime of the Islamic Republic of Iran. Although the book is sometimes polemical, it also provides a wealth of reasonably reliable information on Iran's role in planning, fostering, and directing acts of political violence and terrorism.

Norton, Augustus Richard. *Amal and the Shiʿa: A Struggle for the Soul of Lebanon*. Austin, 1987. An account of the political emergence of the Shīʿah of Lebanon. The book includes programmatic documents of the two leading Shīʿī movements.

Quṭb, Sayyid. *Milestones (Maʿālim fī al-ṭarīq)*. Beirut, 1978. The author is arguably the single most important ideologist for radical Islamists in Egypt, and he is also read widely outside of Egypt. He emphasizes the corruption of Egyptian society, which he depicts as *jāhilīyah*, and argues for the organization of an Islamist vanguard.

Sivan, Emmanuel. *Radical Islam: Medieval Theology and Modern Politics*. New Haven, 1985. The author is a leading Israeli scholar, and he offers a readable and competent introduction to the leading thinkers who underlie contemporary radical Islamist politics, including Ibn Taymīyah, Mawdūdī, and Quṭb. Sivan argues that the radical trend will necessarily dominate more conservative or moderate trends in Islamism with clear ramifications for further intersectarian and antisecularist violence in the Middle East in particular.

Tāleqāni, Maḥmud, Murtaẓā Muṭahharī, and ʿAlī Sharīʿatī. *Jihād and Shahādat: Struggle and Martyrdom in Islam*. Edited by Mehdi Abedi and Gary Legenhausen. Houston, 1986. In addition to important articles by Muṭahharī and Sharīʿatī on *jihād* and martyrdom, the authors provide a capable introduction.

Walzer, Michael. *Just and Unjust Wars: A Moral Argument with Historical Illustrations*. New York, 1977. Although this book does not deal with the Islamic world at all, it is an important assessment of the limits that define justifiable versus unjustifiable acts of violence.

Wilkinson, Paul. *Terrorism and the Liberal State*. New York, 1977. This book is commended for its useful development of the distinction between political violence and terrorism.

Wright, Robin. *Sacred Rage: The Wrath of Militant Islam*. Rev. ed. New York, 1986. First-rate reportage by a leading journalist who provides gripping accounts of a potpourri of hijackings, kidnappings, and other acts of violence.

AUGUSTUS RICHARD NORTON

TEXTILES. The achievements of the weavers, dyers, embroiderers, and pattern designers in the lands of Islam have been acclaimed for more than fifteen hundred years. Textiles were the mainstay of many premodern societies, and they continue to be important in many modern ones. They are woven into the workings of societies in complex ways, distinguishing groups within areas and linking the practice of specific groups across significant geographical expanses. The textile culture of the Islamic world emerges as we view the influences of three strata of society—the official, the mercantile, and the local—on the products of the loom. Differences in materials and techniques, in patterns, and in palette are dictated by group needs and desires. International trade, especially with Western buyers and manufacturers, shaped the output of the premodern loom and influenced the modern one in significant ways.

Textiles in the Islamic world are first of all weavings. Products of the loom, they share the basic principles and techniques with weaving all over the world. Fibers, dyes, and patterning techniques vary over time and place, as do the social functions of the textiles. That textiles from the lands of Islam range from exquisite silk and gold velvets, to nomad wool and animal-hair bags, to sheer embroidered muslin, is not only an indication of the diversity of the loom's production—a sign of how the loom served various groups within Islamic societies—but is also evidence of how central the art and craft of weaving has always been in the civilization of Islam.

Official society, primarily court society in the premodern period, demanded from the loom not only textiles for daily use but also weavings for magnificent display within the court, for gift-giving, and for ritual processions. One official use of textiles found at all premodern Islamic courts, as well as in the traditions of some modern governments such as Morocco, is the tradition of the *khilʿah*, commonly understood as a "robe of honor." Usually more than simply a robe, the *khilʿah* often included whole outfits of appropriate court clothing. ʿAbbāsid and Fāṭimid caliphs, Ottoman sultans, and Mughal shahs alike honored favorite courtiers and visiting dignitaries with gifts of textiles. Elaborate silks with gold and silver threads, and richly embroidered belts, sashes and bands usually constituted the *khilʿah*. However, *khilʿah* practice varied by court and according to the recipient; medieval sources indicate that finely woven black wool garments were given to judges at the ʿAbbāsid court, where black was the official court color. Closely associated with *khilʿah* was the tribute of clothing that governors of provinces often gave to the central court, a practice continued in India into the eighteenth century. The governor of Bengal, for example, sent yearly gifts of clothing and textiles to the Mughal emperor Awrangzīb.

In addition to draping reception rooms, sumptuous textiles were hung along the routes of official processions in most Islamic courts. In Fāṭimid practice in the eleventh and twelfth centuries, white textiles, the official Fāṭimid color, were displayed along the route from the royal city of Cairo to Fustat for the caliphal ritual procession during Ramaḍān. Likewise, elaborate multicolored silks were hung along the route between Córdoba and Medinat al-Zahra for the Umayyad caliph in the tenth century, between Fatehpur-Sikri and Agra in the sixteenth century for the Mughal emperor Akbar, and in the sixteenth and seventeenth centuries along the main ceremonial street in Istanbul for the Ottoman sultans. Magnificence was the norm, and while contemporary writers often described such elegant display in general words of praise, they took care to describe the unique in specific terms, such as the kites carried by soldiers in twelfth-century Fāṭimid processions, shaped like lions and made of yellow and red textiles, puffed out by the wind through devices inserted into the lion's mouth. Colors such as saffron yellow and *qirmiz* red were often distinguished because of their costliness, and fibers such as silk, fine linen, and gold and silver filament, as well as techniques such as velvet and shot silk, were singled out for the way they emphasized the sumptuous bounty of the court.

Another use of textiles shared by almost all groups, especially in the premodern period, was the fabrication of textile tents for official functions. Often very elaborate, such tents were used as mobile residences, headquarters for army commanders, and temporary retreats. Starting in the fifteenth century, rulers in the eastern lands of Islam held court in elaborate, large-scale tents set up in gardens. Timur's tent court in Samarkand is well known, and the Mughal emperor Akbar lived in a tent city in the later period of his rule. This court "city" moved from place to place, a practice facilitated by the employment of two complete and identical tent cities, one being assembled at a new location while the other was in use. At each location, the residences of the emperor, his generals and court officials, as well as assembly halls, were placed according to a well-established protocol of spatial relationships. In the Mughal and Ottoman courtly practice, the ruler's tent was further distinguished from those of the members of his court by a textile fence completely surrounding it. Tents used on ceremonial occasions were sometimes fabulously ornamented: for example, in the tent of the tenth century Fāṭimid caliph al-Mustanṣir, the known regions of the world were depicted in emeralds, rubies, diamonds, and seas of sapphires stitched onto the interior walls. Most official tents were woven of heavy fabric and ornamented on the inside with walls of specially woven, appliquéed or embroidered fabric. The largest collection of such official tents, in the Military Museum in Istanbul, displays tents of varying design used by members of the Ottoman court from the sixteenth to the nineteenth century.

The extensive demand courts placed on the looms for specific types of textiles led most imperial courts to formalize arrangements for the production of textiles. Known variously as private embroidery shops, treasuries, or ateliers, these official production centers consisted of weavers, designers, dyers, spinners, embroiderers, and printers who worked to supply the court with textiles in the materials, palette, and design required. Such textile production at the Ottoman and Ṣafavid courts in the sixteenth and seventeenth centuries is the most thoroughly researched to date. Of course, courts in the premodern period purchased favored textiles in the marketplace, often by commissioning special designs or quality. For example, *malmal khāṣṣ*, a special, fine-quality patterned muslin woven in Bangladesh, was made to the order of the sixteenth-century Mughal court. In the modern period, textiles for official use are produced in the marketplace, where the quality of material, design, and workmanship distinguishes the level of use and user.

The *kiswah*, the name given to the textile covering of the Kaʿbah in Mecca, as well as to the textile coverings of the tombs of holy people, is both a traditional and a contemporary official use of textiles. Traditionally, supplying the annual textile covering of the Kaʿbah was the privilege of the government ruling the city of Mecca. In the Middle Ages, it was customary for the rulers of large empires to place on the Kaʿbah several textile covers, one on top of the other, each representing a characteristic cloth from a different area of the empire. Some of these textiles were striped, others patterned or plain, but most displayed verses from the Qur'ān embroidered in gold. In the twentieth century the Saudi Arabian government supplies the *kiswah* for the Kaʿbah, commissioning the embroidery in Egypt. Similarly, textile covers for the tombs of holy people—for example, in Morocco—are also embroidered, often in gold. Men execute the gold embroidery on the *kiswah* for the Kaʿōbah, as well as for the tombs in Morocco.

The mercantile strata of society served the urban populations both by directing the production of the woven textiles and also by making textiles from the various weaving areas generally accessible. Merchants also began to make the products of the looms available to western Europe and later to the United States. In return, these merchants made cheap foreign imports available to various textile economies. In the nineteenth century especially, these imports destroyed the livelihood of weavers and printers, especially where the East India Company participated in the market.

Textiles represented wealth in the premodern period.

not only were they traded for cash, they were used as cash within the marketplace as well as in general social practice. Resist-dyed prints from India were bought in Egypt in the ninth century and stored in treasuries; velvets woven in fifteenth-century Bursa were readily bought in western Europe and given in payment for services; and China and Mamlūk Egypt exchanged patterned silks, which were in turn given as gifts. All of the textile centers that participated in the long-distance trade modified the production of their looms according to the taste of the various markets. On the luxury side, textiles were woven to order by color, pattern, and fineness of weave. Many written sources from the medieval and premodern period attest to the thoroughgoing textile knowledge of the individual consumer, who commonly ordered textiles by the specific content of the warp and weft, their coarseness of fineness, patterning, and color.

Printed and painted cottons made in Iran, Afghanistan, and India for a broadly based market likewise responded to changing demand. high-quality textiles of this type—known as "chintzes" and characterized by all-over small repeat patterning of flowers, birds or plants—were made for European and local consumption from the seventeenth to the nineteenth century. In the late nineteenth century, as cheap, printed machine-made cotton cloth, especially from Manchester, came into those regions, local weavers and printers responded to the loss of the quality market by making only coarser prints. Such quality, unsuitable for the export market, was used domestically only to line clothing and bedding.

In the late twentieth century various modern nations have revived some of the older forms of pattern-making and regional design elements as part of their support for visual linkages with the past. Embroidery in Morocco, Egypt, Turkey, and Palestine, and stamping in Iran and India are but a few examples of the revived textile activity. Many of these patterning techniques are applied to synthetic and imported cloth. For example, the wool used for the outer robes worn by men in Saudi Arabia is woven in England; that fabric is cut and sewn, and neck and front detailing applied in the local area. In some areas the continuation of social traditions, such as tea-drinking in Morocco, supports highly specialized textiles such as the Fez-stitched embroidered circular cover for the tea tray. In Bangladesh, richly embroidered *kanṭhās* are still made by Muslim women for use as wraps, cushions, and Qur'ān holders. In Cairo, tents with appliquéed designs are used for funeral receptions for Muslim leaders. In many other places, traditional weaving and patterning techniques are used to fashion new kinds of objects for contemporary use.

No such wide-ranging influences are found among the products of local looms until very recent times, when nomadic tribes became settled and took on some aspects of the mercantile function, and electronic media assured a global audience. Before recent times, daily use demands of the family, the village, or the nomadic tribe dictated that the energy of the loom be used primarily to produce items whose size and shape reflected not official or trade needs but the need to store and carry bedding, food, and clothing. For the nomad, the need for light, flexible, multipurpose weaving and the demands of daily life fostered the use of woven techniques for the patterning of textiles. Floor and wall coverings, pillow covers, bags and sacks of all shapes and sizes, and animal trappings are woven on the loom. Patterns are produced in flat weaves, such as kilim or tapestry, in knotted pile, and in combinations of these, often with embroidery. Until recent times, the patterns reflected the traditions and experiences of the tribal and village groups, often distinguishing among them. The choice of fibers related to the circumstances of the group. Many groups were sheep- and goatherders and thus had ready access to wool and animal fibers, but they had little access to larger markets where cotton and silk fibers were sold. In such circumstances household textile and clothing fabric was made of wool, and cotton items were bought or traded in the market. Still other groups lived in agrarian areas where cotton was harvested, and local looms made cotton cloth for household use, with heavier weaves serving as bags, containers, and draperies, and finer weaves for clothing. If used at all, gold, silver, and silk threads were reserved for ceremonial clothing. Textiles from local looms rarely display the control and complexity of techniques and the luxury of fibers found in the weavings affected by the official and mercantile strata of society, but they are a sign of how the loom served all groups within Islamic society.

[*See also* Carpets.]

BIBLIOGRAPHY

Bacharach, Jere L., and Irene A. Bierman. *The Warp and Weft of Islam.* Seattle, 1978. Catalog with scholarly essays about the role of weavings in Islamic society and the West.

Baldry, John. *Textiles in the Yemen.* British Museum Occasional Paper no. 27. London, 1982. Scholarly ethnography of dye stuffs and textile making in Yemen.

Gittinger, Mattiebelle. *Master Dyers to the World*. Washington, D.C., 1982. Excellent catalog of Indian dyed textiles with scholarly essays about historical and market issues, and investigations into techniques and dyestuffs.

Goitein, S. D. *A Mediterranean Society: The Jewish Communities of the Arab World as Portrayed in the Documents of the Cairo Geniza*. 6 vols. Berkeley, 1967–1983. See especially vol. 1, *Economic Foundations*, and vol. 4, *Daily Life*, which are particularly rich in detail about the textile industry and the role of textiles in the life of the medieval Mediterranean.

Rogers, J. M., trans. *The Topkapi Saray Museum: Costumes, Embroideries and Other Textiles*. Exp. ed. Boston, 1986. Excellent study of the textiles as well as the written sources concerning the holdings of the Topkapı Sarayı Museum. Exceptionally fine plates.

Stone, Caroline. *The Embroideries of North Africa*. Essex, 1985. Thorough study of embroidery focusing mainly on the traditions of Morocco and Tunisia. Richly illustrated.

Wearden, Jennifer Mary. *Persian Printed Cottons*. London, 1989. A small book with short but insightful introduction to chintzes.

Woven Air: The Muslin and Kantha Tradition of Bangladesh. Exhibition at the Whitechapel Art Gallery, London, 1988. Multiply authored, this scholarly work investigates the most prominent weaving and embroidery traditions of Bangladesh.

IRENE A. BIERMAN

THAILAND. About 90 percent of the Thai population of approximately 54 million adheres to the Theravada Buddhist faith. The second-largest religious affiliation is Islamic. Approximately four million people in Thailand profess the Islamic faith and maintain about 2,300 mosques. The Muslims in Thailand comprise two broad, self-defined categories consisting of Malay Muslims residing primarily in southern Thailand, and Thai Muslims residing in central and northern Thailand.

The approximately three million Malay-speaking Muslims are mostly concentrated in the southern provinces of Narathiwat, Pattani, Satun, and Yala; they were incorporated into the Thai polity during the latter part of the eighteenth century. Despite active assimilationist policies promoted by Thai authorities, the vast majority of Malay Muslims maintain strong ethnic and cultural affinities with neighboring Malaysian Muslims to the south. Thai government assimilationist policies have resulted largely in irredentist and separatist ethnic and religious movements among the Malay Muslims of Thailand.

The Thai Muslim population is a much more heterogeneous group than the Malay Muslim populace of Thailand. The Thai Muslims include descendants of Iranians, Chams, Indonesians, Indians, Pakistanis, Chinese, and Malay Muslims who reside in the predominantly Thai Buddhist regions of central and northern Thailand. Though aware of their own distinctive ethnic heritage and retaining their own religious traditions, the vast majority of these Muslims speak Thai and have assimilated into the mainstream of Thai society. Most of the descendants of Iranians, Chams, Indonesians, Indians, Pakistanis, and Malay Muslims reside in Bangkok and surrounding communities of central Thailand. The population of Bangkok Muslims alone is approximately three hundred thousand. Smaller communities of Chinese, Indian, and Pakistani Muslims reside in the northern provinces of Chiangmai, Chiangrai, and Lamphun. All these Thai Muslims in the central and northern provinces have been exposed to uniform socialization processes through education, the media, the marketplace, and other Thai institutions. Generally, aside from religious belief and practice, these Muslims have internalized many Thai cultural norms and practices, have intermarried among the Thai Buddhist population, and have not identified with the separatist or irredentist activities of the Malay Muslims in the south.

With the exception of a small number Iranian descendants who maintain Shīʿī traditions, all other Muslims in Thailand are Sunnī. However, there have been recent reports of Iranian Shīʿī influence and conversions in southern Thailand. Traditionally Islamic thought, beliefs, and practices in both the Malay Muslim and Thai Muslim communities of Thailand were suffused with Hindu-Buddhist and folk-animistic accretions. Charms, amulets, magical beliefs, and some aspects of Hindu-Buddhist teachings regarding merit-making were interwoven with Islam in both the rural and urban regions of Thailand.

Beginning in the early part of the twentieth century, a reformist, *shariʿah*-minded form of Islam stemming from the renowned Salafīyah movement associated with Muḥammad ʿAbduh of Cairo (1849–1905) had influence on the urban Muslim intellectuals, primarily in Bangkok. Islamic reformism reached Bangkok in the 1920s through an Indonesian political refugee, Ahmad Wahab, who had spent considerable time in Mecca imbibing current Islamic orthodoxy and practice. Through Thai Muslim intellectuals, Wahab established organized centers of reformism that encouraged more orthodox Islamic beliefs and campaigned against popular forms of Islam in Thailand. These reformists viewed many of the popular Islamic beliefs as *shirk*, the association of other beings with the power of Allah, and emphasized the use of *akal* (Ar., *ʿaql*), rational thought, and *ijtihād* (independent judgment) rather than a reliance upon *taqlīd* (authoritative teachings).

Along with increases in education, printing technology and literacy, urbanization, economic development, and more opportunities to travel to the Middle East, the reformist movement has had a substantial influence on Islamic belief and practice in Thailand. One of the principal leaders of the contemporary reform movement is Ibrahim Qureshi (Direk Kulsriswasd), who has translated the Qur'ān, much of the *ḥadīth,* and many other Islamic texts into Thai. In cooperation with the Ministry of Education, Ibrahim Qureshi has sponsored the education of Muslims and non-Muslims regarding Islamic beliefs and practices. His influence has been significant in the decline of rurally based popular forms of Islam.

More recently, since the emergence of Islamic resurgence movements in the Middle East and elsewhere, some Muslims in Thailand have participated in *dakwah* (Ar., *daʿwah*) movements similar to those that have influenced Malaysia and Indonesia. The *dakwah* movement is a response to secularizing processes that have had an effect on Islamic culture and institutions. Many of the *dakwah* leaders are former reformists such as Ibrahim Qureshi who support the reinforcement of Islamic values and institutions in an era of rapid secularization and change. Although the *dakwah* leadership maintains that the movement is apolitical, many Thai government officials view this movement as divisive. Thai officials have therefore actively tried to manage the resources and direction of the *dakwah* movement through certain Islamic leaders. [*See also* Daʿwah.]

The Muslim communities of Thailand interact with the Thai government through a religious bureaucracy headed by the Office of the Chularajmontri, the Central Islamic Committee, and the representatives of the Provincial Islamic Committee that is constitutionally established within the Ministry of the Interior. These representative institutions regulate and manage mosque and educational affairs at the local level. The mosque and Islamic school *(pondok),* are the key institutions of socialization in Muslim communities. They are the center of Ramaḍān activities, ʿĪd prayers, weekly *khuṭbāh* sermons, Qur'ānic recitations, and other religious activities. A mosque committee manages its *waqf,* or endowed property, and acquires legal recognition and government subsidies through the Islamic bureaucracy and Ministry of Interior.

A major challenge facing both the Buddhist majority and Muslim minority population in Thailand is whether the nation can become a truly pluralistic society that recognizes the equality of all religious faiths and ethnic minorities. If that outcome is not foreseen, Buddhist-Muslim tensions will undoubtedly increase. Muslims increasingly participate in the political, educational, and cultural activities of Thailand to help develop the basis for a more open, tolerant, and pluralistic society.

[*See also* Islam, *article on* Islam in Southeast Asia and the Pacific; Patani United Liberation Organization.]

BIBLIOGRAPHY

Che Man, W. K. *Muslim Separatism: The Moros of Southern Philippines and the Malays of Southern Thailand.* Singapore and New York, 1990. Comprehensive comparative analysis of the cultural, political, and religious movements of the minority Muslims of the southern Philippines and Malay-speaking Muslims of South Thailand in a broad international context.

Forbes, Andrew D. W., ed. "The Muslims of Thailand: Historical and Cultural Studies." *South East Asian Review* 13.1–2 (January–December 1988): 1–167; and "The Muslims of Thailand: Politics of the Malay-Speaking South." *South East Asian Review* 14.1–2 (January–December 1989): 1–200. These two volumes contain thorough essays by all Western and non-Western authorities on Muslims in Thailand.

Fraser, Thomas. *Fisherman of Southern Thailand.* New York, 1966. Classic ethnography of a coastal Malay Muslim population residing in southern Thailand.

Golomb, Louis. *An Anthropology of Curing in Multiethnic Thailand.* Urbana and Chicago, 1985. Ethnographic account of popular religious beliefs and magical healing practices that have been an aspect of both Buddhist and Islamic communities in Thailand.

Pitsuwan, Surin. *Islam and Malay Nationalism: A Case Study of the Malay-Muslims of Southern Thailand.* Bangkok, 1985. The most comprehensive treatment of the Malay-Muslim condition in southern Thailand; written by an insider.

Scupin, Raymond, ed. *Aspects of Development: Education and Political Integration for Muslims in Thailand and Malaysia.* Selangor, 1989. Collection of essays focusing on the relationship between education and political development within the various Muslim communities in Thailand and Malaysia.

Suhrke, Astri, and Lela Garner Noble, eds. *Ethnic Conflict in International Relations.* New York, 1977. Essays devoted to the examination of ethnic relations and politics in an international context. Suhrke is a well-known specialist of southern Thailand Muslims.

Thomas, Ladd. *Political Violence in the Muslim Provinces of Southern Thailand.* Singapore, 1975. Thorough monograph depicting the political situation of the Muslim minority in southern Thailand in the 1970s.

Wyatt, David K., and Andries Teeuw. *Hikayat Patani.* The Hague, 1970. Translation and account of the early indigenous narratives regarding the religious center of Pattani in southern Thailand.

RAYMOND SCUPIN

THEOLOGY. Commonly taught Muslim creed differs from the highly technical scholarship found in theological works composed under the religious discipline of *kalām* (lit., "the speech"), which also includes philosophical and mystical theology. The common creed includes the sources of authority, the minimal and essential articles of faith, and the prominent differences among the major Muslim schools of thought.

Formal authority in Islam lies in the Qur'ān and the *sunnah*. In practice, religious leaders, imams, and jurists *(fuqahā')* guide the faithful to live in conformity with the divinely ordained Islamic law *(sharīʿah)*.

All Muslims affirm in speech and in their hearts the Islamic principles *(usūl al-dīn)* of the unity of God *(tawḥīd)*, the necessity of prophets *(nubūwah)*, and the day of resurrection *(qiyāmah)*, to which the Shīʿīs add the necessity of the imamate and the justice of God. The secondary or derivative doctrines held by all Muslims, and known in the West as the "pillars of Islam," are: (1) testimony in being a witness to an absolute monotheistic God, to Muḥammad as his prophet (and for the Shīʿīs, ʿAlī as the friend or *walī* of God); (2) performance of the daily prayers (Qur'ān, 9.114); (3) fasting during the month of Ramaḍān (2.185); (4) pilgrimage to Mecca (11.158, 196–203); (5) paying the *zakāt* or alms (2.43)—and for the Shīʿīs, financial support of the descendants of the Prophet through donation of *khums* (one-fifth); and (6) being in a state of "struggle" *(jihād)* to spread Islam (9.20).

The majority of Muslims, 85 percent, belong to the Sunnī tradition, which adheres to the consensus *(ijmāʿ)* of the community as an important source of authority. On the basis of this consensus the Sunnīs uphold the succession of the first four caliphs—Abū Bakr (r. 632–634), ʿUmar (634–644), ʿUthmān (644–656), and ʿAlī (656–661). The Shīʿīs (the "partisans" of ʿAlī), who constitute 15 percent of Muslims, believe that ʿAlī was explicitly designated by the Prophet to succeed him at a site named Ghadīr Khumm, when he was returning to Medina from his farewell pilgrimage. The Shīʿīs assert that a special class of "infallible" individuals such as the prophet Muḥammad, his daughter Fāṭimah (d. 632), his cousin and son-in-law ʿAlī, and their direct descendants (including the Mahdī, the last hidden imam) are the ultimate religious-moral authorities in Islam.

Contents of Theology Proper. Theological controversies in Islam, focus on seven major issues: (1) the analysis of the concept of God; (2) the ontological and the cosmological proofs of God's existence; (3) the cosmology of the relationship between God and the world; (4) the ethics of the theodicy of God's order with respect to free will, determinism, fate, good, evil, punishment, and reward; (5) the pragmatics of the language of religions, and the peculiar function of the faculty of imagination special to prophets, mystics, and prophet-statesmen; (6) the relationship between reason and revelation; and finally, (7) the politics of the application of divine rule to the community.

History. Islamic theology begins during the reign of the last two "rightly guided" *(rāshidūn)* caliphs, ʿUthmān and ʿAlī (644–661). Salient features of the tradition as developed in various schools of thought are outlined in this section.

Khawārij (the secessionists). Initially this group followed ʿAlī, but when he allowed an arbitration following the battle between him and Muʿāwiyah in 657 at Ṣiffīn, they protested and "seceded" from the party of ʿAlī. The Khawārij rejected the Sunnī view that the ruler must belong to the tribe of Quraysh as well as the Shīʿī claim that he must be a descendant of the Prophet. Instead, they held that right action and faith are the only essential attributes of a true Muslim, including a leader among them. Thus they viewed the caliph as a virtuous authority of Islam, who called for *jihād* and tried to kill whoever they regarded as being outside their egalitarian community.

Murji'ah. This school was developed by Jahm ibn Ṣafwān (d. 745), Abū Ḥanīfah (d. 767), and others as a reaction and even corrective to the extreme puritanism of the Khawārij. Their views were shared by many other Muslims, such as Ibn Karrām (d. 973), the founder of the Karrāmīyah school (see below). The salient doctrine of the Murji'ah was to postpone judgment on believers who committed a grave sin; moreover, they emphasized the promise *(al-waʿd)*, hope *(irja')*, and respite granted by God rather than threat and punishment. They also opposed the doctrine of eternal punishment of sinners and emphasized the goodness of God and his love for human beings. Politically their position opposed the Khārijī view that advocated punishment of believers who committed sins and supported rebellion against Muslim rulers whom the Khawārij considered corrupt or deviating from true Islam. In contrast, the Murji'ah held that one should obey a Muslim ruler even if one disagreed with his policies or questioned his character. The controversy was a politically sensitive one: some Muslims disagreed strongly with the perceived sinful deviation of the third caliph ʿUthmān and the

Umayyad rulers; others criticized the fourth caliph ʿAlī for his submission to arbitration with Muʿāwiyah. The practical side of the theoretical controversy was translated into the practical question of whether or not a Muslim should obey a ruler with whom he disagrees.

Pointing to the Qur'ān (9.106), the Murji'ī doctrines evolved into three important theological theses. First was the primary authoritative and epistemic status given to the intention of faith *(īmān)*. Here they rejected the utilitarian formula that ethical imports are ultimately derivable from consequences of an action. Instead, in accord with the ethical views held by the jurists, they maintained that the intention of the agent—specifically, the state of his or her belief—is the sole criterion for instituting punishment on him or her. Faith became closely associated with both gnosis *(maʿrifah)* and the open proclamation *(iqrār)* of God, with the tendency to equate being a Muslim with having faith. Second, the adherents of this group achieved a pragmatically convenient political posture; it followed from their views that caliphs like ʿUthmān and ʿAlī should be obeyed even if they had committed a sin; consequently this perspective justified and rationalized the moral status of early Islamic history. In addition, their principles justified their obedience to rulers of the Umayyad dynasty with whose policies they disagreed. Third, unlike the Khawārij, they preached tolerance toward other Muslims and supported the spirit of unity within the community of the faithful. In this tenor, followers of Abū Ḥanīfah—for example, Abū Muṭīʿ al-Balkhī, as indicated in his *Al-fiqh al-absaṭ*—held views sympathetic to non-Arabs who embraced the faith of Islam and held no descent or only indirect descent from the original Quraysh family. This perspective was very favorable to the Umayyads, who made extensive use of Christians and non-Arabs in their administration.

Qadarīyah. The major doctrines of this school are discussed in the works of Maʿbad al-Juhānī (d. 699), Abū Marwān Ghaylān ibn Marwān al-Dimashqī al-Qubṭī (d. 730), and others listed by Ḥasan al-Baṣrī (d. 728) in his *Risālah.* The Qadarīyah recognize a power *(qudrah)* in the human agent that makes her/him responsible for acts performed; in this sense human action is different from all other events. They held that only by asserting human freedom can one justify God's power to blame or to punish man. They also agreed with the later Muʿtazilī position of Wāṣil ibn ʿAṭā' that persons intuitively are self-conscious of their capacity to make choices and that this conscious awareness and intention will make persons responsible for the outcome of their acts. The assertion of human free will is a standard argument to absolve God from responsibility for evil in the world. The doctrine of free will is compatible with two distinct views. First was the position that no act can be an effect of two different powers. Therefore if God empowers persons, he cannot exert any subsequent power over their resulting acts; otherwise, he will and will not empower persons, which implies an impossibility and a contradiction. The other alternative was formulated by making the following distinction: God's powers are necessary due to himself, while human powers are derived by acquisition *(kasb)* from God. Eventually the latter position gained more support among the Sunnī theologians, who did not wish to deny that God is a remote cause of all events or that he wills order in the cosmos. Another doctrine accepted by the Qadarīyah was the principle of continuous creation. The practical import of the Qadarī position on human responsibility was politically significant; it held each Umayyad caliph responsible for his acts. Being suspected of having brought secularism into the Islamic state, the Umayyad caliphs were challenged by the Qadarīyah. As a result, al-Juhānī and al-Dimashqī were executed by the Umayyad rulers ʿAbd al-Malik (d. 705) and Hishām (d. 743) respectively. This inquisition *(miḥnah)* was officially in support of the Muʿtazilī position that the Qur'ān is created. The persecutions ended in 848 when Caliph Mutawakkil (r. 847–861) came to power. Many of the positive doctrines of the Qadarīyah were utilized later by the Muʿtazilah, who adapted them to their own system. For example, al-ʿAllāf advocated the Qadarī position in this world, whereas they happen by necessity in the other world.

Muʿtazilah. This group of theologians chose a middle position on the question of whether or not those who are Muslim by faith but commit sin are still Muslims. In addition, this group, supposedly initiated by Wāṣil ibn ʿAṭā' (d. 748), held that in spite of some Qur'ānic passages that speak about God's omnipotence at the expense of God's justice (7.178, 32.13, 3:154, for example), God is basically just. More importantly, God's uniqueness and unity is absolute: the so-called divine "attributes" are all dimensions of the divine essence. They refused to apply anthropomorphic attributions to God, hence their belief that the Qur'ān, as part of divine speech, is created in time and is not eternal. The promises for both rewards and punishments are fulfilled on the Judgment Day. For them good and evil are not irrational or blind byproducts of fate as part of a deterministic theodicy applied to humans. On the contrary, a person has free will, can construe a rational depiction for both good and evil, and is thus responsible for his or her acts. Human reason harmonizes with revelation.

Major Muʿtazilī theologians include Abū al-Hudhayl al-ʿAllāf (d. 849/850), his nephew al-Naẓẓām (d. c.435/445), and the celebrated jurist ʿAbd al-Jabbār (d. 1204/1205). In addition to upholding standard Muʿtazilī doctrines, al-ʿAllāf proposed that there were bodies something like atoms, that were mathematical points created by God, who combined them into different substances and objects, some inert and some alive. Thus life becomes an "accident (al property)" that God adds to the aggregate of atoms that constitute the human body; God can of course destroy a person at will. Later Naṣīr al-Dīn Ṭūsī (d. 1274) criticized this doctrine by pointing out that a mathematical point and a physical body are ontologically two different types of entities; thus embedded in this Muʿtazilī theory is a categorical mistake.

Al-Naẓẓām held that God's acts—including creation—are necessary. God makes the world of infinitely divisible atoms, including human souls, which are a subtle type of body. A body is characterized by qualities such as coldness and sound. The living body, the soul-spirit, permeates aggregates of atoms and is endowed with free will. Several later thinkers, such as Shaykh al-Mufīd (d. 1022) and Naṣīr al-Dīn Ṭūsī, singled out al-Naẓẓām's crude materialism in order to ridicule Muʿtazililī doctrines.

Another major Muʿtazilī was ʿAbd al-Jabbār, the celebrated jurist. Recent studies by George F. Hourani (*Islamic Rationalism: The Ethics of ʿAbd al-Jabbār,* Oxford, 1971) have thrown much light on his theology. ʿAbd al-Jabbār held that God's acts are not necessary; if they were necessary, they could not be classified as "acts" but would be called compulsive responses. One cannot claim, he points out, that God's words are truthful only on the basis of revelation, for that would beg the question and constitute circular reasoning. That must be deduced from rationalistic theology by appeal to God's wisdom. His rationalistic epistemology distinguishes between the semantics of the correspondence of a thought to its designatum, which is an external object, and the pragmatics of the intentional state of satisfaction and tranquility in the subject. He held that ultimately the subjective dimension is affected by the objective correspondence ground. A paradigm of a noncognitive and subjective judgment is an aesthetic judgment, being based primarily on the approval and disapproval of the agent. By contrast, while not innate, ethical judgments are objective because they are received by direct comprehension in the context of empirical experiences. In this sense ethics is analogous to geometry, where instances are used to illustrate principles. ʿAbd al-Jabbār strongly criticized the theistic subjectivism of the Ashʿarīyah, which asserts that God's command is the sole criterion for determining the correctness of an act. A command as a "command-*qua*-command" cannot be the sole source obligating an agent to act; instead, there must be additional factors such as the nature of the agent issuing the command and the consequences of the act for the receiver of the command. Moreover, there could be a plurality of commanders, which implies that the receiver of the command must use at least one criterion different from the mere fact of "having been commanded" to carry out one command and refuse another. The goodness of God is similar to the goodness of persons. But while persons because of the limits of their knowledge may do evil, God is never in a state in which he can make a mistake, and thus all his acts are good by his own free will. The use of logical arguments by Muʿtazilīs, their materialism, and their rationalistic ethics contributed extensively to the development of philosophical methodology in Islamic theology.

Ẓāhirīyah and Ibn Ḥazm. A central conflict in Islamic theology lies in the interpretation of sacred texts. On one extreme there are the so-called Bāṭinīyah, who claim that in many cases the observable exoteric or apparent *(ẓāhir)* signifies an internal *(bāṭin)* meaning often associated with an esoteric, mystic, iconic significance of the outward expression. The doctrines of the Bāṭinīyah school became an important element of Islamic mysticism and central tenets of the Ismāʿīlīs. A group of theologians reacted against this trend by advocating the literal interpretation of texts. The Ẓāhirī school was founded by Dāwūd ibn ʿAlī al-Ẓāhirī (d. 817), a jurist who objected to the views of Shāfiʿī school of jurisprudence, and occupies the other extreme. Dāwūd ibn ʿAlī took the Qur'ān, the *ḥadīth,* and the consensus of Muḥammad's companions to be the only acceptable sources of authority. Although Ibn al-Nadīm (d. 995) lists more than 150 books attributed to Dāwūd ibn ʿAlī, he does not mention the Ẓāhirī movement. The Ẓāhirī school was popularized by ʿAlī ibn Ḥazm (d. 1064), who more than other theologians emphasized syntactic analyses to support his theological position. For example, he distinguishes between two senses of modal "necessity" *(wājib),* which means either a syntactical necessity implied by the rules of grammar or a moral obligation rooted in revelation. In the context of his critique of both the Muʿtazilī and Ashʿarī theologians, as well as of non-Muslim philosophers, Ibn Ḥazm made some original contributions to Islamic epistemology. For example, he granted cognitive legitimacy only to revelation and sensation, because revelation is based on religious authority and sensation is immutable. Since a pattern of deductive reason used in a proof *(burhān)* by itself, according to his analysis, is an abstract schema without content, it cannot provide any content for theology or ethics without an essential normative content acquired from revelation. Another misuse of reasoning is to extend legal knowledge by certain illegitimate techniques that had been adopted by Muslim legal experts.

Ibn Ḥazm's theory of observation includes the notion of a "sixth" sense, a primary type of intelligence *(awwal al-ʿaql)* similar to categories of understanding, from which derive such intuitive principles as those that a part is less than the whole, or that no two bodies can simultaneously occupy the same space. Hourani labels Ibn Ḥazm a "subjective theist" who—against the rationalistic ethics of the Muʿtazilah—argues that all values depend on the will of God, who is totally free from any moral code. Space and time are limited and are created by God, who is himself unlimited; God can even perform infinite division of bodies, and thus for him there are no atoms. Following Dāwūd ibn ʿAlī, he held that the consensus of the community was restricted to the community of the companions of the Prophet; in doing so, he denied legitimacy to the essential thought of the contemporary progressive vehicles of Islamic legal reasoning. Following a literal *(ẓāhir)* reading of the sacred texts, Ibn Ḥazm advocated a return to reliance on tradition *(ḥadīth),* opposing also the principles of imitative following *(taqlīd),* analogy *(qiyās),* good judgment *(istiḥsān),* and giving reason *(taʿaqqul).* For example, in case of analogy, Ibn Ḥazm argues that there is no textual support for this method. Following the Ẓāhirī literal interpretation of texts, he strongly opposed the Shīʿī view of allegorical interpretation *(ta'wīl)* in the same spirit that he rejected the analogical reasoning used by many Sunnī schools. He advocated a grammatical and syntactic interpretation of the Qur'ānic account of God. God's names in the Qur'ān are to be taken literally as names applied to him by himself; they are not adjectives attributed to a substance. We have no right to infer ontological attributes from these names—neither anthropomorphic attributes nor attributes implying duality—because these expressions are merely signs by which we name God. God is an incorporeal, eternal unity unlike any other entity. Psychologically, human happiness lies in a desire for pleasure and a repulsion from care; this state of bliss can be achieved only through salvation. The help of the Prophet and revelation play a key role in human salvation, but the means to achieve salvation is through a proper use of reason, philology, and observational evidence. Ibn Ḥazm's school of thought influenced future theologians as well as mystics, as indicated by the works of Ibn ʿArābī, who investigates the divine names and makes a distinction between God as he is revealed to us and God as absolute reality.

Karrāmīyah. This school is named after its founder, Abū ʿAbd Allāh Muḥammad ibn Karrām (d. 973). Its creeds gained popularity in Khorasan province in Iran and had the patronage of Sultan Maḥmud Ghaznawī, whose court welcomed mystics such as Rūmī, scientists such as Bīrūnī, and philosophers such as Ibn Sīnā. More linked to the Murji'īs and Ḥanbalīs, the Karrāmīyah were accused of anthropomorphism because they advocated the most literal interpretation of the Qur'ān on passages such as surahs 7.55 and 10.3, where physical references are made in the context of the nature of God. According to some of the Karrāmīyah, spatiotemporal dimensions are applicable to God, who literally sits on a throne. Several original and nonstandard doctrines of the Karrāmīyah set them apart from most Muslim thinkers. For example, unlike most Muslim philosophers, this school advocates that God is in fact a substance *(jawhar);* some went so far as to identify God as a body. Most other Muslim theologians take mental intentional belief and/or correct moral behavior to be a criterion for being a faithful believer. The Karrāmī emphasis on verbal expression extended to God and his creation. Supposedly entities are created when God commands with the word "be" *(kun).* In their cosmogony they attempted a synthesis between monotheistic creationism and the doctrine of the eternity of the world by assigning to God a temporal dimension different from that of created existents. When hundreds of thousands of people were massacred by Chinggis Khan in the province of Khorasan, many Karrāmīs were among them. Like the Qadarīyah and the Murji'ah, the Karrāmīyah died as a living movement, and some of its doctrines were integrated by the later Ẓāhirīs and other schools.

Ashᶜarīyah. This school of classical Sunnī thought led by Abū al-Ḥasan al-Ashᶜarī (d. 935) was one of the pioneers of "occasionalism," which depicts the world as a series of occasions that are effects of God's will. This view has several important theological implications. First, against the Muᶜtazilah, al-Ashᶜarī rejects rationalist ethics and holds that man is incapable of understanding the logic of good and evil because these are derived from God. God relates to the world owing to his generosity. Al-Ashᶜarī's system attempts to solve the problem of a need to epistemically justify, for example, the existence of unobserved contingent causal laws between events. Concerning the proof of God's existence, al-Ashᶜarī held that God is the necessary existent, because a series of contingent existents for their actualization need one member to be necessary; otherwise, a vicious infinite regress is implied. God as a creature of temporal entity must be atemporal and unchanging; otherwise he would have been temporally produced and thus not be God. God must be a unity, for if there were multiple gods, there would be a possibility of conflict of will among gods, and one god among many could not be the cause of the set of contingents dependent on a single will. God is alive (2.255), omnipotent (2.284), and omniscient (3.5). His willing an entity implies creating the entity in question. Against the Muᶜtazilah, al-Ashᶜarī argues that God also sees and hears without an implication of either temporality, anthropomorphism, or injustice to God. The Qur'ān as God's speech is eternal. When God asserts for X, "Be!" then X is created (16.40). If the Qur'ān were created—as the Muᶜtazilīs argue—then God would need to have spoken to his own speech, which is absurd. God has eternal speech and eternal will and cannot do evil for the following reasons: God who produces the good is better than the good itself, in the same manner that if there were positive agents of evil, they would have been better than evil; but the evil that is created by God is for another entity and not for himself.

Māturīdīyah. Another key figure in Sunnī theology was Abū Manṣūr Muḥammad al-Māturīdī (d. 956). He presented new methodological schemes to test theological disputes. In terms of content he took a middle position between the Muᶜtazilah and the Ashᶜarīyah on the question of free will as well as on divine justice. With regard to the divine attributes he held that divine justice and grace are interconnected with divine wisdom. For him the notion of an unjust God is meaningless. Consequently, divine justice follows syntactically and ontologically from the nature and the essence of God without limiting God's freedom. With respect to human freedom, he holds that unlike other animals, the human being is endowed with an intellect, a moral sense, and an awareness of freedom. This conscious awareness of freedom is an essential mental constituent of being a living human being. Evidently God, the creator, treats human beings differently from purely physical substances because He has sent them a prophet, a guide. Since the Qur'ān has dictated moral responsibility to persons, persons are necessarily free. Persons intend actions, and God freely realizes these intended actions. This formula preserves both God's omniscience and human freedom.

Māturīdī's method of Qur'ānic interpretation is based on two presuppositions: first, the Qur'an cannot be tested by any other source; and second, a problem does not lie in the text but in our own confused reading of the text. Consequently, when we do not understand a passage, we should attempt to decipher it by comparing it with passages that are clearer to us. It follows from Māturīdī's view that our reactions to the Qur'ānic passages are pragmatic icons to their intended meaning. For example, some passages that do not correlate with a large body of other passages should not be taken in their literal sense, while the meaning of others should be left to God's knowledge. This ingenious method allows Māturīdīs to apply a method analogous to contemporary statistical dimensions of inductive logic to give different "weights of interpretation" to each set of interrelated passages in the entire field of Qur'ānic texts, with the clearer passages being used to comprehend other passages. These problems with understanding the Qur'ān signify the inner complexity of the texts in question. They signal the presence of allegorical, literal, iconic, and other types of intended meanings. They also reveal our capacity, and the transcendental categories by which a finite being attempts to know God.

In the same manner, the problem of divine attributes and the question of their eternity must be solved in the context of religious worship. To begin with, Māturīdī argues, it would be impossible to talk about God without mentioning some attributes. Moreover, if these attributes were not eternal, then God would have been ephemeral, and that contradicts our notion of his omniscience. Consequently we make a distinction between our use of attributes to approach God as we can know Him and the actual nature of God in himself. For example, if we assert that God is wise, we mean that he is aware of all events in the world; we do not mean that the sense of wisdom attributed to God is like the wisdom of human beings. With respect to God, we hold the principles of unity, the denial of similarity *(tanzīh)*, and the absolute difference between him and created entities. This solution permits discourse about God without losing the principle of unity.

Māturīdī preserves the primacy and incorrigibility of the Qur'ān without accepting its literal interpretation. Against the Ẓāhirīs he succeeded in preserving the unity of the concept of God as well as the primal authority of the Qur'ān, while rejecting anthropomorphism. He holds that both morality and reality are open to reason—however, to a limit. The existence of the limit is proven by the contradictions, antinomies, and paradoxes of reason. Because reason has limits, it needs a spiritual guide, a prophet, who by revelation can help us in all secular and religious problems.

Māturīdī's epistemology is directed against skepticism. It takes reports *(al-akhbār)* to be a legitimate source of knowledge in addition to sensation and theoretical thinking. Māturīdī's attribution of cognitive value to reports is in line with ordinary-language analysts in Anglo-American philosophy, who emphasize the ordinary use of language as a significant basis and criterion for a theory of meaning. If we ask, how do we in fact know certain facts, the answer often lies in historical reports and in the accounts we receive from previous generations. To deny this source is to misuse the very meaning of experience and knowledge. Among these reports, some claim, are the sayings of the prophets. Special attention should be paid to these by examining the evidence, such as the chain of narrators and the texts in question.

Māturīdī's clever use of philosophical arguments and new perspectives on Sunnī theology invigorated the Sunnī theological tradition. Later, modern thinkers such as Muḥammad ʿAbduh were able to go back and reinterpret the tradition.

Ibn Taymīyah. Aḥmad ibn Taymīyah (1262–1327), another creative Sunnī theologian, focused on criticism not only of Jews and Christians but also of other Muslims, including al-Ghazālī's criticisms of fellow theologians. He criticized the Ashʿarīs for their denial of free will because such a view, Ibn Taymīyah claimed, negates the usefulness of religious prescriptions and dismisses religion as the foundation of ethics; man for him is a genuine agent with free will. He objected to the Muʿtazilah's identification of God with his essence; this maxim negates the most significant dimension of religious experience, which is the personal aspiration to the relation of love between God and persons. Islam for him is primarily a prophetic religion with an emphasis on revelation to guide mankind; the method of natural religion or natural theology, which sets human reason as the source of truth, is totally mistaken in religious contexts. Ibn Taymīyah held that God is absolutely eternal and self-caused, as he is the efficient cause of the world and the only source of moral command for persons. There is no knowledge of God as he is revealed to us except God's revelations; at most, we should focus on textual exegesis of God's revelation. The Peripatetic philosophers, using logical and causal analyses, mistakenly treat God as an impersonal principle, who has not created the world and has no knowledge of its particulars. These doctrines flatly contradict the only source of truth we have, the revelations. In addition, philosophical methodology, restricted to logic—that is, to clarification of concepts and valid construction of arguments—is inapplicable to theology for the following reasons. Conceptual analyses and definitions at best are merely formal and syntactic constructions of the belief of the logicians, and as definitions *qua* definitions they have no informative or factual content; in the same manner, deductions are useless for establishing facts. Valid deductive schemata are of logical forms; they indulge in the game of manipulation of universal and abstract concepts without any specific existential import.

Ibn Taymīyah extends his criticism to the theoreticians of Sufism, such as Ibn ʿArābī, who advocated monistic mysticism. For Ibn Taymīyah Ṣūfīs are especially guilty because they write against the absolute transcendence of God. For example, Ibn ʿArābī places universals in God, which implies that God's perfection needs the concretion of the universals. Thus he, and other theoreticians of mysticism emphasizing similarity, mistakenly identify God—who is perfect, transcendent, and totally dissimilar—with the created, either in the realm of total nature or with the mind-dependent phenomena of humans' existential intentional experiences. This spiritualization of a psychological phenomenon is wrong both logically and morally. The depiction of unity of being violates the total independence of God from the universe, sacrificing God's transcendence at the expense of his immanence.

Ibn Taymīyah proceeds to criticize the Shīʿīs; he considers them to be like the Jews in claiming special status for themselves, because the Shīʿīs indulge in the myth of the uniqueness of the imam, his infallibility, and his special tie with God, a position Ibn Taymīyah grants only to the prophet Muḥammad (5.20, 9.30–31). Christians are accused of the same folly in their belief in the Trinity, their modification of the Bible, and their antimonotheistic practices.

Philosophical Theology. Islamic theology extends beyond the traditional theological schools to more independent Islamic philosophers and mystics. It is often difficult, indeed, to distinguish the theologian from the philosopher. Many Muslim philosophical writers, such as Abū ʿAlī ibn Sīnā, known to the West as Avicenna (980–1035), Naṣīr al-Dīn al-Ṭūsī (1201–1274), and Shihāb al-Dīn al-Suhrawardī (d. 1191), also wrote on many other disciplines including mathematics, music, linguistics, medicine, and theology. Moreover, the standard Muslim philosophical texts began with a definition of philosophy, an analysis of concepts, the proposal of contingent existents (bodies, souls, and intelligence), and finally the necessary existent, which is God. Islamic metaphysics *(ilāhīyāt)* is equivalent to theology, much as Aristotle's theology is found in book Lambda of his *Metaphysics*, the prototype of all monotheistic metaphysics and theologies.

The most influential and original philosophical theology is found in the works of Ibn Sīnā, who wrote about 250 works that have been translated into dozens of languages; St. Thomas Aquinas used many of his central themes and quoted him more than five hundred times. Ibn Sīnā's major contribution to medieval theology is that as the philosopher of "being," he places the study of being logically prior to the study of God. Instead of "God," Ibn Sīnā initiates his metaphysics on "being" as the primary notion in the soul, and on the set of logical modalities (necessity, impossibility, and contingency) as the primary structures of being. Thus the realm of entities consists of impossible beings (which have no existence), contingent beings (which exist if they are caused), and finally the necessary being (which is the unique necessary existent, God). This deduction of necessary existent from necessary being is the second version of the ontological argument repeated later by St. Anselm (1033–1109), René Descartes, and others. Ibn Sīnā's careful cosmological depiction of God, outside Aristotle's categorical schema, provided a theoretical model for later monistic Ṣūfīs. If God were a substance, and the only substantial changes are generation and destruction, then mystics could not depict a union or a connection between human and God. In this tenor Ibn Sīnā, unlike Aristotle, holds that God is not an individual substance because a substance is a composite of a substratum and an essence; the constituents of the composite are the material causes of the composite; thus, if God were a composite, then it would not be self-caused and thus not a necessary existent. It is, instead, the beholder of the world and the ground of other existents, which are contingent owing to the following account: since the necessary being is absolutely perfect *(fawq al-tāmm)*, it is not only the source of itself, but the source of all other entities; thus the world is emanated from it.

In addition to the analytic features of the necessary existent, Ibn Sīnā reflects on the moral and pragmatic dimensions of God. He explains why a union *(payvand)* with the necessary existent is the highest happiness and the greatest pleasure. Physical pleasures like food and lust have their limits, whereas a person encounters unlimited pleasure in his spiritual search. It is in this relation that a finite being encounters not only the unlimited but also her/his own remote final cause, and in a sense the essence of himself/herself. This desire for imitation of a higher being is an inborn cosmic love; thus the love of the absolute good is embedded by nature in the human being in her/his search for perfection. In examining Ibn Sīnā's cryptic *Treatise on Destiny*, Hourani shows that Ibn Sīnā implies that hell and heaven are in fact intentional states experienced in this life based on one's own spiritual and moral perspectives. In an attempt to solve the problem of evil, he differentiates between a primary function of an entity—for example, sunshine as the source of energy—and the secondary side effects—for example, the sun burning the head of a bald man. God's will applies to the good received in the primary function of entities; their secondary effects are necessary accidents of their own nature. Owing to its nature as the absolute good *(al-khayr al-maḥḍ)*, the necessary existent is not even "free" to create the world. He is the only existent that is categorically necessary; all others are conditionally necessary—that is, the necessary existent is the ultimate cause of realization of all other existents.

Another major Muslim philosophic theologian is Naṣīr al-Dīn Ṭūsī, also known as Khvājah, who developed the refinements of Ibn Sīnā's theology in the context of Shīʿī thought. Without doubt Ṭūsī is the most versatile of all Muslim thinkers. He is the author of approximately one hundred works, including commentaries on Euclid, comprehensive texts on logic, astronomy, mathematics, practical ethics, philosophy, theology, mysticism, and extensive commentaries on Ibn Sīnā's theodicy. He was also an official in the court of Hülegü Khan (1217–1265) and used his influence to oust the last Sunnī caliph in Baghdad. Ṭūsī advocated an early if not the first version of so-called "soft determinism" in accordance with the Shīʿī *ḥadīth* that there is neither an absolute determinism (as maintained by the Ashʿarīs) nor pure free will (as held by the Muʿtazilīs). Accordingly, the universe is the best of all possible worlds, which could not have been otherwise. Every entity has an assigned "rule" in it as its "destiny." For persons, the self-conscious belief in free will means that the will of the human agent is used as a factor when we explain a set of causes that collectively determine its proper effect. Persons are often ignorant of the mechanism that determines their own will and other causes; psychologically, they feel that they are free or that there are accidents. In principle, however, there are always laws that could have been employed to predict future events. Ṭūsī follows Ibn Sīnā in avoiding controversial topics. For example, he notes that if God knows future events, then these events are determined and man is not free; Ṭūsī remarks that God, if omniscient, would also know what he wills and does not will in the future. Thus whatever answer one gives to this puzzle applies to God as well as to men.

As a mathematician, Ṭūsī adds refinements to the problem of infinite regress used in standard forms of cosmological arguments and arguments about the possible division of matter into atoms. He makes a distinction between syntactic series (for example natural numbers) in which members are defined recursively, and series applied to concrete entities, which could be called "ontic" series. In a manner similar to Aristotle's acceptance of "potential" but not "actual" infinity, he labels syntactic infinity permissible and ontic infinity vicious. He uses the argument against vicious infinite regress of ontic series to prove God's existence, while he upholds the infinity of syntactic series to reject the doctrine of atomic substance. Like Ibn Sīnā, he notes that "matter as experienced" is open to a series of divisions that terminate owing to our finite ability to divide indefinitely; however, a mathematical mapping of matter, which is only a syntactic entity, can be divided indefinitely. There is no actual infinite (vicious) regress in either of these divisions. Thus the position of the atomistic theologians is totally mistaken. Ṭūsī holds that an absolute syntactic existence is a mental notion, not a reality external to mind. God in itself as the necessary existent is for him an absolute unity from any perspective, to which no attribute can be added. A remarkable similarity exists between his views and the theodicy of the German philosopher and mathematician Gottfried Leibniz (1646–1716) on both the topic of free will and the impossibility of material substances.

Another philosophical theologian is Suhrawardī, who modified Ibn Sīnā's system by expressing it in illuminationistic terms, where the divine is the "light of lights." He rejected the Aristotelian substance-event language and proposed a new non-Aristotelian terminology. The final destruction of Aristotelian types of philosophy in Islam, however, came with the existent philosophy of Ṣadr al-Dīn al-Shīrāzī, also known as Mullā Ṣadrā (d. 1641). He finally broke the influence of the Peripatetics on Shīʿī theology and established a philosophy that gives primacy to actual existents.

The systems of Mullā Ṣadrā and the Iranian philosopher Hādī ibn Mahdī Sabzavārī (1797/98–1878) have been the subject of commentaries by recent Shīʿī scholars in Iran, notably Ruhollah Khomeini and Jalāl al-Dīn Āshtiyānī. Here Islamic philosophical theology finds no conflict with either the aims of those who study mysticism or of those who focus on the study of Qur'ān, *ḥadīth,* and Islamic law. All these disciplines are taught as required curriculum in the training of Shīʿī jurists, who often employ them for an interdisciplinary perspective on Islamic studies. In recent Shīʿī orthodoxy philosophy has been accepted as the major core of theological analyses.

Mystical Theology. An original dimension of the Islamic contribution to theology is constituted by the mystical writings of philosophers and poets, among them al-Ḥusayn ibn al-Manṣūr al-Ḥallāj (d. 922) Abū Yazīd Bisṭāmī (d. 874), Abū Ḥāmid al-Ghazālī (d. 1111), Muḥyī al-Dīn ibn al-ʿArabī (1165–1240), Farīd al-Dīn ʿAṭṭār (d. 1229), and Jalāl al-Dīn Rūmī (d. 1273). The salient features of Islamic mystical theology include the epistemic priority placed on the immediate experience of a sense of unity of being *(al-waḥdat al-wujūd),* emphasis on allegorical and iconic language to express mystical themes, and often an advocacy of the ethics of the incarnation of the divine.

Ṣūfīs appeal to the mystical passages in the Qur'ān to support their theology. God is held to be thoroughly immanent in all the world (4.132), including in human beings, to whom God is described as being closer than the jugular vein (50.16). All entities return to God as their source (96.9); human beings were created by the very breath of God (15.29). The Qur'ānic texts are used to justify the Ṣūfī claim that an intimacy with God can be reached in the state of mystical union. Some, such as Ibn al-ʿArabī, depict the world in different stages or layers of divine presence. For them there is no possibility of experiencing the noumenal God, God as he is in himself. God in this sense is the primary ontological entity, a reality-truth *(al-ḥaqq)*. He is not a personal God, but is rather analogous to Ibn Sīnā's concept of "being-*qua*-being" *(hastī)*, a primordial reality in himself. This is different from God as he is manifested to persons. For some mystics nature is a theophany, signaling God as he can be experienced in our monadic perspective: by knowing herself/himself and receiving nature, a person can have a gnosis of God as manifested. Worship is a reception of immanent presence and is the mystical interpretation of "testimony," a major pillar of Islam. Because the world exists by the grace of God (7.57), each entity, whether a substance like a leaf, an event like the blossoming of flowers, or a light like that of the sun, is an icon of divine grace. God in himself, from the perspective of a noumenon, is not knowable, but God reveals himself in the world relative to the perspective of each mystic. Texts in Islamic mystical theology have been written by some of its most systematic thinkers, such as Ibn Sīnā, and such acute mathematicians as Naṣīr al-Dīn Ṭūsī. Far from being on the fringe of the theological arena, Islamic mystical theology belongs to its very center.

As a prime example of this tradition one notes Abū Ḥāmid al-Ghazālī, a prominent figure in Islamic theology. The core of his original philosophy has until recently been ignored in the West; most literature on al-Ghazālī focuses on his criticism of what he took to be the Islamic Aristotelian school of al-Fārābī and Ibn Sīnā. Let us begin with a brief sketch of his doctrines. Al-Ghazālī's system may be introduced by a Cartesian skeptical search for certainty, which begins by showing that sense perception and conceptual analyses can be doubted. He rejects the former on the basis of standard arguments from illusion, and the latter by proving that the criteria of self-evidence are psychological and can change with experience. His argument is analogous to the views of Ludwig Wittgenstein, who points out the fallacy of self-reference and notes that one cannot see one's eyes directly or measure a ruler by itself. In the same manner, al-Ghazālī argues that one's own private notion of certainty cannot be the criterion of the correctness of analytical judgments such as mathematical statements or deductive logic schemata. His ultimate epistemological choice is based on an existential phenomenology of voluntarism in the following sense. The primary marks of God and the soul as ultimate realities are not static attributes. Both God and the soul are without any quality or any quantity. Their main mark is dynamic will, such as God's will to create the world or the intentional urge of the soul seeking personal salvation. In his mystical theism al-Ghazālī equates ethical insights with nonanalytical types of knowledge. Accordingly, the noblest states of mind are not the contemplation of atemporal concepts but rather immediate experiences such as exuberance *(dhawq)*, urgency *(shawq)*, and intimacy *(uns)*. Like contemporary existentialists and phenomenologists, he takes only authentic experiences that dynamically transform persons to be paradigmatic cases of cognitive states; his system adopts a normative epistemology in a voluntaristic phenomenology.

For his criticism of other thinkers, al-Ghazālī classified four types of approaches to Islam: the theologians, the philosophers, the so-called Batinīyah (the Ismāʿīlī sects), and the Ṣūfīs (Islamic mystics). His criticisms of the theologians and the Batinīyah are not so intensive as his objections to the philosophers. He accepts the Ṣūfīs and reserves his uncompromising criticisms for the theology of philosophers.

Al-Ghazālī claims that theologians do not begin with a truly open attitude in their inquiry; instead, they are apologists and defenders of orthodoxy instead of being concerned with the existential reality of religious experience. Often they assume a variation of the premises they wish to prove; many of them naively followed the premises of their opponents. Some follow their own mistaken methods so blindly that they end up with the absurd conclusion that God is a body. His attack on the Batinīyah's views of the imam had two major arguments. Al-Ghazālī held that only the Prophet was the true mediator figure, and that the essence of religious experience was the immediate phenomenological will for an intimacy with God, rather than a transference of learned *(taʿlīm)* tradition as taught by the Batinīyah.

In his criticism of the philosophers' theological findings, al-Ghazālī begins by rejecting the materialists and the naturalists, who are obviously irreligious and cannot offer a theology. Ultimately he focuses on the works of philosophers who consider themselves to be theists. Al-Ghazālī finds no problem when these philosophers attend to mathematics, logic, or natural sciences; he finds little problem with their ethics and political philosophy; his main concern is with their theology. Here he shows that some of their theses are contrary to religion; these include the denial of the resurrection of bodies, the denial of God's knowledge of particular events, and the belief in the eternity of the world. Next al-Ghazālī attacks the logic of philosophers' arguments on many theological topics, showing the invalidity of their deductions as well as the weakness of their premises. These include theses such as the denial of God's attributes, God's knowledge through his essence, our claim to the legitimacy of cause-and-effect relationships, and the substantiality of the human soul.

An important topic in the scholarship of Islamic theology is the assessment of al-Ghazālī's influence and importance. We note that Islamic philosophy flourished with vigor after al-Ghazālī in the West in the works of Ibn Ṭufayl and Ibn Rushd (Averroes), who rebutted him on every issue. In the East there was a strong renaissance of philosophy in the works of Suhrawardi, Mullā Ṣadrā, Sabzavārī, and others. The only possible influence that al-Ghazālī might have had on the development of Islamic philosophy was to show the weakness of the Aristotelian system: none of the later systems were Aristotelian. Ibn Rushd commented on Aristotelian philosophy, but his system includes topics such as the pragmatics of religious language that were totally absent from Aristotle's work.

Nonetheless, Muslim philosophers continued to write on theological topics. In fact, philosophical theology became part of the curriculum of both Sunnī schools, such as al-Azhar in Egypt, and Shīʿī *madrasahs* such as those in Mashhad and Qom. Al-Ghazālī's major influence was to provide a legitimate bond between Sunnī orthodoxy and Sufism that strengthened both traditions. In addition, al-Ghazālī stands as a giant, a major master of both the theory and praxis of Islam; he is the creative thinker who embodied the best of what is universal in Islam and in being a Muslim. After al-Ghazālī mysticism continued to develop both in philosophy and in metaphysical poetry. Mystics' attention to and analyses of the intentional and experiential dimensions of religious experience have been among the most original contributions of Islam to civilization.

Recent Theological Movements. Islam is a communitarian religion with a political agenda. Consequently, far from having a fossilized theology, it contains many mechanisms for reform, innovation, and adaptation. Recent theological movements reflect the nature of Islam in the light of modern events. These include the confrontation of classical Islam with Western colonial powers (a parallel to the time of the Crusaders), modern technology (especially military hardware), and fundamental challenges to the core of religious law expressed in changes in family structure, dress codes, and anti-monotheistic literature and movements. Important among these modern thinkers are Jamāl al-Dīn al-Asadābādī (also known as al-Afghānī, 1839–1897), Muḥammad ʿAbduh (1849–1905), Muhammad Iqbal (1878–1938), and Muḥammad Ḥusayn Ṭabāṭabāʾī (1903–1989). The first three thinkers were Muslims with European education who had firsthand experience of the Western world with its science, technology, and social problems. Their attitude depicts a politico-theological confrontation with the West on the basis of Islamic rationalism.

In its true classical Islamic spirit, al-Afghānī's theology is integrated with his political response to the challenge of European Christian civilization. Analyzing European development in its historical setting, he offers on theological grounds a Pan-Islamic movement that revives the caliphate and establishes the Islamic force as a world power. Coming from a political realist, this grand plan in practice is transformed into a call for an Islamic nationalism capable of standing independent of Western economic domination. He supports this program by three appeals: first, to realize the urgency of immediate political and economic independence; second, to recognize the ultimate superiority of Islam over other religions—which as the Muʿtazilah assert, lies in its rationality; and third, to believe in the pragmatic result, a religious life that includes not only the spiritual dimension and the special status of the religious community, but also special inner qualities necessary for achieving bliss. The latter include modesty, honesty, and truthfulness, which free man from the consequences of hedonism and materialism. Like many other modern reformers, al-Afghānī was a major organizer of a group of reform movements represented by Egypt's Salafīyah and the Muslim Brotherhood.

Al-Afghānī had many followers, among them his protegé Muḥammad ʿAbduh, a philosopher, scholar (*ʿālim*), professor at al-Azhar University, journalist, and *muftī* (chief judge); he proposed large-scale social programs for long-term social reform. He taught theology, the science of unity, and wrote a number of works, including legal opinions, on matters such as permitting the consumption of animals slaughtered by Jews and Christians, legalizing loans for interest, and introducing reforms granting rights to women. His theology focused on a close connection between reason and revelation. The latter, according to him, was intuitive knowledge given by God to the prophet primarily to educate the masses rather than to enlighten the elite through exegesis. Following the Muʿtazilah, ʿAbduh believed that the Qur'ān was created in time, and that theology is a rational science. Also, like al-Afghānī, he objected to passive mysticism and invited Muslims to hold fast to the principles of their religion while focusing on reform; he supported the innovation of practices open to learned reexamination and modernization.

Muḥammad Iqbal considered Islam as an intellectual, moral, and experiential phenomenon that draws man as a dynamic instrument of God into the realization of the open, infinite possibilities of the world. Iqbal held that the Islamic intellectual tradition transforms Greek models of abstract knowledge into an empirical investigation of concrete facts, as is illustrated by the Qur'ān's attention to actual specifics. True worship implies an awareness of the factual reality of concrete existents using the empiricist inductive mode of knowledge. Thus the natural knowledge of how God reveals himself in the world is compatible with the idea of a transcendent God.

The next thinker, Ṭabāṭabā'ī, representative of the Iranian Shīʿī religious class, was trained and remained in Iran. During this century, the theological schools of Qom and Mashhad have been the most active centers educating analytic Shīʿī theologians grounded especially in the philosophy of Mullā Ṣadrā as well as in Western classical and contemporary thought. Ṭabāṭabā'ī distinguishes three Shīʿī perspectives: the formal (the extensional and the intentional study), the intellectual (logical arguments on theology and cosmology), and the mystical aspects (for example, gnosis and the method of unveiling). People should realize that even though objects giving them nonspiritual pleasure are made for them, they as humans are not made for the objects. A person's uniqueness as a human person is to reflect on the true meaning of Islam, which means a gnostic submission to one God by imitating the model of the paradigmatic sage, who is the Shīʿī imam, and the perfect human of all time *(al-insān al-kāmil)*. Because this unique feature is the essence of a person differentiating her/him from other creatures, submission to one God—that is, being a Muslim—is the essence of a person. The word "essence" is used here to signify "the cause of completion (Greek, *telos*) of an entity." The knowledge of Islam, for Ṭabāṭabā'ī, in accordance with Shīʿī theology, begins with the knowledge of God (for example , his essence and theodicy), proceeds to knowledge of the Prophet, moves from these to the eschatological return of a person, and finally to the knowledge of the imam. In spite of its status as a minority creed and its concentration in Iran, Pakistan, and Iraq, the present schools of Shīʿī theology possess spiritual and political influence beyond its minority status.

[*See also* Philosophy; Sufism, *article on* Ṣūfī Thought and Practice; *and the biographies of ʿAbduh, Afghānī, Ghazālī, Ibn al-ʿArabī, Ibn Taymīyah, Iqbal, and Ṭabāṭabā'ī.*]

BIBLIOGRAPHY

Excellent summaries of the subject may be found in the following:

Anawati, Georges C. "Kalām." In *The Encyclopedia of Religion*, vol. 8, pp. 231–242. New York, 1987.

Esposito, John L. *Islam: The Straight Path*. Exp. ed. New York, 1991.

Fakhry, Majid. *A History of Islamic Philosophy*. New York, 1970.

Mahdi, Muhsin. "Islām. The New Wisdom: Synthesis of Philosophy and Mysticism." In *The New Encyclopaedia Britannica*, 15th ed., vol. 22, pp. 28–31. Chicago, 1992.

Rahman, Fazlur. *Islam*. London, 1966.

Sharif, M. M., ed. *A History of Muslim Philosophy*. 2 vols. Wiesbaden, 1963–1966.

PARVIZ MOREWEDGE

ṬIBB. *See* Medicine.

TIJĀNĪ, AḤMAD AL- (1737–1815), founder of the Tijānīyah Ṣūfī order. Abū al-ʿAbbās Aḥmad ibn Muḥammad al-Tijānī was born at ʿAyn Māḍī in southern Algeria. At the age of twenty he visited Fez, where he successively experimented with the litanies of several Ṣūfī orders and was disappointed with all of them. Ten years later, in 1767, during his residence in Tlemcen, he had his first spiritual realization *(fatḥ)*.

In 1772–1773 he set out to perform the *ḥajj*. At Azwāwī near Algiers he was initiated by ʿAbd al-Raḥman al-Azharī (d. 1793) into the Khalwatīyah order, which had experienced a revival in Egypt a few decades earlier. Al-Tijānī ardently followed this course; he learned the secrets of the Khalwatīyah from Maḥmūd al-Kurdī (d. 1780) in Cairo and from Muḥammad ibn ʿAbd al-Karīm al-Sammān (d. 1775) in Medina. His attachment to the Khalwatīyah contrasted with his earlier discontent with other Ṣūfī orders. On his return to the Maghrib in 1774–1775 he initiated his first disciples into the Khalwatīyah. The introduction of the revived Khalwatīyah to the Maghrib was a departure from the Ṣūfī tradition of the Shādhilīyah to which most Maghribī orders belonged.

In 1782 al-Tijānī returned to the desert edge in southern Algeria, where he had a visionary encounter in which the prophet Muḥammad taught him a litany (*wird*) enunciating a new independent *ṭarīqah* and instructed him to sever relations with other orders and *shaykhs*. In spite of the break, elements of the revived Khalwatīyah remained more embedded in the doctrines and rituals of the Tijānīyah than the founder and later Tijānīs would admit. Indeed, one of the most unusual features of the Tijānīyah, the exclusivity of the order, was an elaboration of a principle advocated by Muṣṭafā al-Bakrī and applied to some extent in the Egyptian Khalwatīyah.

As his fame as a saint grew, al-Tijānī was compelled by the Ottoman authorities to leave Algeria. He arrived in Fez in 1798, and lived there until his death in 1815. The reformist Moroccan sultan Mawlāy Sulaymān (1792–1822), who sought to eradicate popular Sufism, warmly received al-Tijānī because his Sufism combined strict observance of Islamic law with the rejection of asceticism and withdrawal from the world.

Al-Tijānī claimed the rank of *khātim al-awliyā'* (the seal of the saints), which implied that he was the link between the Prophet and all past and future saints. His adherents therefore had higher spiritual rank as well and were promised access to paradise without the need for giving up their possessions, provided they observed the precepts of Islam as well as they could. In this way he attracted to his order rich merchants and senior officials. Some of the most senior *ʿulamā'* in Fez were hostile to al-Tijānī and rejected his claim to superior status, but other prominent scholars joined the order.

In its adherence to Islamic law and to orthodox practices, as well as its positive attitude toward worldly affairs, the Tijānīyah was one of a group of new Ṣūfī orders that emerged out of trends of renewal and reform in the eighteenth century. The dynamism of the Tijānīyah found expression in its nineteenth-century expansion, both militant and peaceful, mainly in West Africa.

[*See also* Khalwatīyah; Sufism, *article on* Ṣūfī Orders; Tijānīyah.]

BIBLIOGRAPHY

The major source for al-Tijānī's life and teaching is *Kitāb Jawāhir al-maʿānī wa-bulūgh al-amānī fī fayḍ Sīdī Abī al-ʿAbbās al-Tijānī* (Cairo, 1977), written by his disciple, ʿAlī Ḥarāzim ibn al-ʿArabī Barādah, and approved by al-Tijānī himself. The two important modern studies are: Jamil M. Abun-Nasr, *The Tijaniyya: A Sufi Order in the Modern World* (London, 1965), and B. G. Martin, "Notes sur l'origine de la *ṭarīqa* des Tiğāniyya et sur les débuts d'al-Ḥağğ ʿUmar." *Revue des Études Islamiques* 37.2 (1969): 267–290.

NEHEMIA LEVTZION

TIJĀNĪYAH. The Tijānīyah movement was reared out of controversy. From its very inception (c.1782), its members brought challenge to the accepted notions of monastic order. Abū al-ʿAbbās Aḥmad ibn Muḥammad ibn al-Mukhtār al-Tijānī (born AH 1150/1737 CE) at Ayn Māḍī, southern Algeria), the founder of the brotherhood, proclaimed himself the "pole of poles" (*quṭb al-aqṭāb*) and the "seal of sanctity" (*khatm al-wilāyah*), as the Prophet, Muḥammad, had averred himself the "seal of prophecy." The leaders of the Tijānīyah were accused of prohibiting associates from visiting the tombs of the deceased virtuous (*walīs*) from other orders and of disturbing the conviction that spiritual benefit (*barakah*) could be obtained from *walīs* outside the brotherhood. Moreover, Tijānīs were condemned for alleged attempts, against the grain of accepted practice, to prevent their members from affiliating with other Ṣūfī organizations. Finally, at least in their North African context, Tijānīs stood accused of favoring wealth over asceticism (*zuhd*) and became noted for their abjuration of mysticism in place of which they encouraged a simplicity of belief and practice in their daily devotions.

Aḥmad al-Tijānī, as he came to be called, began life in the normal Ṣūfī pattern. Traveling throughout the Maghrib in the familiar peripatetic manner, he sought out learned men for knowledge, embraced *walīs* famed for their *barakah*, and affiliated himself with several religious orders, notably the Wazzanīyah, Darqāwīyah, Nāṣirīyah, and Khalwatīyah, and also espoused many of the tenets of the Shādhilīyah. It was a pattern he was to renounce dramatically around 1782, when he broke the old *silsilah* (chain) of authority and linked piety and belief to his own powers of intercession.

The rapid proliferation of the orders posed an intractable problem to established authority in the Maghrib. Scores of religious brotherhoods had appeared, based on ethnic and occupational affinities. In Morocco, where the prophet Muḥammad and his descendants (*sharīfs*) were held in the highest favor, the organization of the orders came to be drawn tightly round their spiritual influence. By the middle of the nineteenth century, we find many of the educated affiliating with the Darqāwīyah (the chief competitors of the Tijānīyah for this constituency), artisans inclining toward the Kattānīyah, for example, the shoemakers of Fez and the flaxweavers of Tangier, while many butchers and practitioners of unclean professions embraced the Ḥamadshah (Ḥamdūshīyah) and the ʿIsāwīyah. Finally, the residue of merchants and proprietors not attracted to the Tijānīyah joined the Ṭayyibīyah *ṭarīqah*.

Coming as it did in the wake of the anti-Ṣūfī Wahhābī movement in the Hejaz, the proclamation of Aḥmad al-Tijānī arrived at an auspicious moment. The sovereign of Morocco, Mawlāy Sulaymān, became his patron and saw merit in his revolutionary message. The abundance of *ṭarīqah*s in Morocco and the high prestige of sharīfian *zāwiyah*s (lodges) had compromised the authority of the Moroccan ruler, and he perceived in alliance with the Tijānīyah a means of tightening his rein on political and economic affairs. The order received encouragement and was allowed to develop its retreat structure under Mawlāy Sulaymān's procective hand. Despite claims to the contrary, Aḥmad al-Tijānī was not ranked among the illustrious *sharīf*s, and the appeal of the Tijānīyah drew the attention of wealthy non-sharīfians of the urban governmental class (including many converted Jews whom Mawlāy Sulaymān retained as advisers and financiers). These individuals, together with *makhzan* (government) officials, merchants, and influential families, held a considerable share of economic power, especially in Fez.

From the outset, the Tijānīyah espoused a much simplified corpus of ritual and system of organization, in contrast to the requirements of prayer which tied their rivals to the rigors of convention. Tijānīs set much store by their epithet, "the way of Muḥammad" *(al-ṭarīqat al-Muḥammadiyah* or *al-ṭarīqat al-Aḥmadīyah)*, and prided themselves in their devotion to Sunnī practice. Both the *wird*s (collected prayers) and the *waẓīfāh* (daily office) of the order were characterized by a streamlined simplicity, sharply reducing the number of prayers required and the pattern of recitation. The old rigor of progression through the Ṣūfī stages of perfection retained only a faint echo of past tradition. The most efficacious prayers and rituals commended by the founder were entrusted to those who comprised the inner circle.

The claim advanced by Aḥmad al-Tijānī that he was the "seal of sanctity"—that he inhabited the eminence of light that lay between Muḥammad and the saints of Islam—was to rankle relations with rival orders and excite them to ridicule the Tijānīyah. This merit had its ancestry in the teachings of Ibn al-ʿArabī (d. 1240), who, it was suggested, had declined the dignity and left open the door for Aḥmad al-Tijānī to seize hold of it. Such distinctions had allowed the founder to trumpet his merit and abolish the line of virtuous teachers whose blessings sustained the spiritual nourishment of other orders. Moreover, such distinctions had enabled al-Tijānī to cut the power of the Qādirīyah, the oldest Ṣūfī organization, and one fueled on the *barakah* of its ancient affiliations. Another charge uniting its rivals in disdain was that the Tijānīyah discouraged its members from associating with other orders and from frequenting the tombs of their *walī*s. Tijānī spokesman often defended this practice by declaring that a disciple could not hope to receive spiritual sustenance from two shaykhs simultaneously, any more than a woman could serve faithfully two husbands.

Before the rise of Aḥmad al-Tijānī, the most notable feature of the Shādhili-Jazūlī tradition could be seen in the way in which charismatic power was harnessed and accessed *fī sabīl Allāh*, in the path of Allāh. Even the simplest adept could link with the spiritual past and feel the flow of *barakah* that charged his spiritual energy and gave shape and significance to his interior life. The recitation of the *wird* and other assigned prayers served to recharge his spiritual apparatus and redirect his energy in the path of Allāh. Thus, the *ḥizb al-baḥr* and the *dalā'il al-khayrāt* ("proofs of blessings") of al-Jazūlī must be understood as strong currents of charismatic power linked to overt action *fī sabīl Allāh:* prayer for the success of Islam, pilgrimage to the Muslim holy places, *hijrah* from Islam's enemies, and *jihād*.

Aḥmad al-Tijānī streamlined the charismatic "switchboard"—condensed the currents of *barakah* into one powerful "microchip," discarding, as it were, all the bulky "hardware" of past generations. The Wahhābī movement fueled this revolution as it sought to concentrate veneration in the person of Muḥammad. It was a tendancy that Aḥmad al-Tijānī was to recast in his own mold. Yet several other features of the Shādhilī-Jazūlī tradition were absorbed into the teachings of the Tijānīyah. There is danger in placing too much stress on the differences among the *ṭarīqah*s at the expense of realizing the essential eclecticism and sharing of basic tenets that characterized the religious brotherhoods. Aḥmad al-Tijānī drank unabashedly from the font of the Shādhilīyah. Indeed, even in the Tijānīyah, there is a strong compulsion to link with individuals of the Ṣūfī past and imbibe their *barakah.* Al-Shādhilī's *ḥizb al-baḥr* (a powerful incantation of the ninety-nine names of Allāh) became a touchstone of the Tijānī canon, and his relentless pursuit of the person of the Quṭb found a strong echo in al-Tijānī's fixation on this theme. In the Tijānī view, the old *silsilah,* with its long chain of intermediaries, generated a feeble if permanent current. Aḥmad al-Tijānī closed the circuit of charisma as he concentrated power between Muḥammad and himself. It was his claim that the Prophet was near him always, even in waking, allowing for a close and continuous discharge of spiritual grace and an increase in its velocity.

As it began to take root in the Maghrib, the Tijānīyah emerged as a force for stability and preservation of the status quo, at least during the lifetime of the founder. The Shādhilī-Jazūlī tradition, in retrospect, bequeathed a legacy of radical activity, forged on an anvil of opposition to the government of the day. Aḥmad al-Tijānī broke the mold of this radicalism and encouraged his followers to side with established authority. It was this shrewd an pragmatic policy that allowed the Tijānīyah, in the face of sharīfian hostility, to spread and prosper under the protection of the *makhzan.* The sharīfian tradition set much store by nobility of descent: al-Jazūlī had staked his claim on the strength of a pure and noble lineage. Aḥmad al-Tijānī could not hope to stand level with his rivals and post a claim in this direction, he was constrained to stake his claim elsewhere—on a higher level—as he sought to outreach his rivals. Thus, during the founder's time, adherence to authority became the watchword of Tijānī political philosophy. With the passing of al-Tijānī in 1815, and the overthrow of Mawlāy Sulaymān, this policy took on greater flexibility.

There has been a tendancy in past accounts of the Tijānīyah to read into their policies in the Maghrib a pro-French sentiment, but one must demote this view as these activities actually reflected a careful pragmatism not always favorable to French intentions. While it is true that the Tijānīyah managed to ride with success the vicissitudes of the post-Sulaymān era and welcomed the French in the Maghrib with a greater liberality of temper than did many other religious organizations, its policies did not always maintain the coherence sustained under the founder. As the Tijānīyah shunned the extremes of militant *jihād* and renounced "monkery" in favor of a more active inolvement in daily life, a strong element of revenge crept into their pragmatism. Indeed, claimants to the succession did not hesitate to cultivate support wherever it could be found. Dissident Berber groups (a rich quarry for the order), forever at odds with established authority generally, were summoned frequently in support of these claims. After the death of al-Tijānī in 1815, and as the French succeeded in seizing power from the Turks, no one pattern can be said to typify Tijānī policy toward the various players in the Maghribian struggle for power. Even the attitude toward the Turks, steadfast in its contempt, displayed some flexibility. While the Turks on more than one occasion had laid siege to Ayn Māḍī (the mother *zāwiyah*), Turkish support for the order in other areas (notably Tunisia) could not be ignored. Indeed, on several occasions prominent Turkish officials affiliated with the Tijānīyah and supplied funds amply to its coffers. Still, Tijānīs came to endow with great significance Turkish attempts to impose authority by force and extract tribute from religious establishments (Turkish indignation was brought to a flame when Ayn Māḍī repeatedly withheld payment). Yet the Turks were not alone in their attempts to diminish the influence of the *ṭarīqah*s when the occasion demanded, and all political powers rallied to their support when events seemed favorable.

The period of French overmastery offers an object lesson in Tijānī pragmatism as it illustrates the unevenness of the order's policies. When the French wrested hegemony from the Turks in the Maghrib during the nineteenth century and the brotherhoods declared their resentment, the Tijānīyah responded with cautious optimism. According to the founder, succession to power was to alternate between Ayn Māḍī and Tamalhat (on the Tunisian border). The rotation, however, did not always proceed smoothly., and the occasional roughness of the transition (or the retention of power by Ayn Māḍī) accounts for much of the intrigue and variation in policy among the principals of the succession and those who supported their claim. From 1877 until 1911, the *zāwiyah* at Ayn Māḍī maintained a fairly firm grip over Tijānī affairs owing to the role played by a Frenchwoman, Aurèlie Picard, who had married Sīdī Aḥmad, the head of the order, and feigned a commitment to Islam. The French lavished subsidies on their Tijānī subordinates and thus compromised any claims to independence. Nevertheless, it was a period when all religious orders were being drawn into the pockets of the French and placed under surveillance, and when real or imagined movements by Tijānī and other dissidents intensified the paranoia of French imperial policy.

The Tijānīyah's strong association with the government of Morocco persisted until 1912 with the declaration of the Protectorate. By the end of the nineteenth century every large town in Morocco could boast at least one Tijānī *zāwiyah* (there were twelve in Marrakesh alone). The order in Morocco was much more "national" in outlook than its counterparts in Tunisia and Algeria, and much more consonant with the culture in which it was reared. Following the split between Ayn Māḍī and Tamalhat in the 1870s over the succession, intense rivalry ensued into the 1930s when Ayn Māḍī attempted to revive its claims and initiated active campaigns for support in Senegal, Mauritania, Guinea, and Gambia. The order had already achieved significant inroads in these lands and in Mali owing to the prosyletization of the celebrated Moroccan *ʿālim*, Muḥammad ibn Aḥmad al-Kanṣūsī (d. 1877), and the great Senegalese *mujāhid*, al-Ḥājj ʿUmar ibn Saʿīd (ʿUmar Tal, d. 1864). By the beginning of the twentieth century, Tijānīs could claim more than half a million devotees in the Sudan.

The independence movement in the Maghrib produced the ultimate brotherhoods, absorbing to its purpose all the tone and rhetoric of the old organizations that had met their demise as we have described them. One result of the Istiqlāl (independence) movement was to drive the *ṭarīqah*s underground, where their activities, severely circumscribed in the public arena retain only a semblance of their previous importance.

[*See also* Istiqlāl; Morocco; *and the biographies of Tijānī and ʿUmar Tal.*]

BIBLIOGRAPHY

Two works (difficult of access) form the principal sources for the study of the Tijānīyah: Abū al-Ḥasan ʿAlī Ḥarāzimī's *Jawāhir al-maʿānī wa bulūgh al-amānī fi faid Abi al-ʿAbbās Aḥmad al-Tijānī* (Cairo, 1927) concentrates on the persona of the founder and the principal teachings of the order (written by the leading disciple of the founder, the Jawāhir, though authorized by al-Tijānī himself, draws unabashedly from other biographies without acknowledgement). Published on its margin is, ʿUmar ibn Saʿīd's *Rimaḥ ḥizb al-Raḥīm ʿala nuhūr ḥizb al-rajīm* (composed 1261/1845 by the leading disciple of the order outside the Maghrib, the *Rimaḥ* defends the Tijānīyah against its detractors and serves as a guide to conduct for its members). Of the early printed works in European languages, and a basis for much of the analysis done in successive years, are Louis Rinn's *Marabouts et Khouan. Étude sur l'Islam en Algérie* (Algiers, 1884), again difficult of access as is O. Depont and X. Coppolani's *Les Confréries religieuses musulmanes* (Algiers, 1897). Neither of these, with their emphasis on major figures and salient doctrinal features, has been entirely superseded by J. Spencer Trimingham's *The Sufi Orders in Islam* (Oxford, 1971), concerned with the development of the brotherhoods through the centuries and the specific phases through which they passed during this evolution, and J. Abun Nasr's *The Tijaniyya, A Sufi Order in the Modern World* (London, 1965). This work is to be used with caution as the author's translations from French and Arabic are not always trustworthy, and some of his interpretations extremely misleading. See my review article, *Research Bulletin, Centre of Arabic Documentation, University of Ibadan, Institute of African Studies* 2.1 (January 1966): 39–47. Very useful for the modern period and for its general overview is Dale Eickelman's *Moroccan Islam* (Austin, 1976), and Mohammed El Mansour's *Morocco in the Reign of Mawlay Sulayman* (Cambridgeshire, 1990), the most insightful analysis of the historical period in which the brotherhood flourished.

JOHN RALPH WILLIS

TRADE. Three complications arise in assessing trade by Islamic countries in the modern period. First, the identification of countries as Islamic is a recent development, dating back to 1969 and the establishment of the Organization of the Islamic Conference (OIC). Second, there is a dearth of data on Islamic countries for most of the modern period. Third, until the mid-twentieth century most of the Islamic countries were under the direct or indirect influence of non-Islamic foreign powers. The Arab countries were parts of the Ottoman Empire before they came under Western, non-Islamic influence in the early nineteenth century. Pakistan was a part of the Indian subcontinent ruled by Britain until after World War II. Indonesia was under Dutch influence, and Algeria was ruled by France from 1832 to 1962. A similar fate characterized the histories of most of the other OIC members.

In addition to having a lasting impact on the economic and trade policies of Islamic countries, Western influence has had two important results. First, data relating to the present national boundaries of OIC members are recent in origin. Second, the trade policy of these countries was rarely influenced by Islamic thought or principles. Trade policy in the Ottoman period, for example, was influenced by capitulation agreements and colonial interests, which tended to undermine Ottoman authority and Islamic rules.

The capitulations were agreements that awarded concessions to citizens of Western, non-Islamic countries trading or residing within the Ottoman Empire. These concessions protected foreigners against discrimination or restrictions emanating from the Islamic civil laws of the empire. The agreements also gave Westerners more freedom of trade and travel and better terms of trade than enjoyed by natives of the empire. For example, export duties paid by natives were higher than import duties, which proved advantageous for foreigners. These benefits were sometimes extended to native residents who were non-Muslim and had a religious affinity with a particular foreign power. Thus, Catholics enjoyed the protection of France and the Vatican; Protestants, Britain; and Orthodox Christians, Russia. As a result, Greeks, Armenians, Lebanese and Syrian Christians, Egyptian Copts, and similar minorities, such as British, French, and Italian residents, were predominant in both foreign trade and the commerce of the Islamic countries in which they resided. [*See* Capitulations.]

The direction and composition of trade were little effected by Islam and were evidently determined by economic complementarity rather than by the religious identity or doctrine of the trading parties. The impact of colonialism on trade was best demonstrated by the high percentage of trade with non-Islamic foreign countries. Islamic countries traded mostly with the colonial powers to which they were subjected in compliance with the interests of the dominant countries. This situation continues in the 1990s.

This pattern of trade was reinforced by the economic underdevelopment and poverty of the Islamic countries and by the relatively low complementarity between Islamic economies. Trade with non-Islamic Western countries was based on exchanging primary and natural products for manufactured goods that Islamic countries did not produce. Ottoman trade with Europe and the United States constituted 93 percent of all exports and imports in the late nineteenth century. Exports from Islamic countries included wheat, barley, fruits, hides, silks, and other raw material. Imports centered on processed and manufactured goods and machinery.

A number of modifications in trade policy have been enacted since the end of World War II. After the war national interests and increasing the relative share of intra-Islamic trade were emphasized. However, little change has been effected in trade composition or direction or the relation of trade to Islamic principles or doctrines. The OIC charter specifies areas of economic cooperation among the members, including expanded trade and the eventual creation of an Islamic common market. To facilitate trade, Islamic financial institutions have been established, promotional and administrative committees have been formed, and much political rhetoric has been broadcasted. Nevertheless, the direction, volume, and composition of trade among members of the OIC have only slightly been effected. Exports of primary goods, mainly to other Islamic and Third World countries, have continued to dominate, while imports have been dominated mainly by manufactured goods from developed non-Islamic countries. Oil as a major raw-material trade item has reinforced the traditional colonial pattern. The traditional pattern and direction of trade have been reinforced also by the relative poverty and economic and technological underdevelopment of the OIC members. Economic complementarity among OIC members has tended to be lower than it is among the developed non-Islamic countries and OIC members. The OIC members have also tended to be more concerned with political unity than with economic cooperation, and therefore they have been rather slow in creating the conditions for expanded trade among themselves. Furthermore, the pattern of trade has been sustained by tradition and relatively strong ties with former colonial powers, which would be too costly to break. Finally, that pattern of trade is not in contradiction with Islamic principles and doctrines, and therefore the OIC members can hardly argue for its change on religious grounds. It is notable that commercial laws of the Islamic countries of the Middle East reflect no influence of Islamic thought or doctrine. To avoid any potential conflict with nationalistic or religious principles, some Islamic countries, such as Bahrain, Egypt, and Turkey, resort to such neutralizing measures as offshore banking units and free trade zones.

Major task forces have been created and many recommendations have been made to promote economic cooperation and trade among Islamic countries. However, intra-Islamic trade has remained relatively small and the pattern established in preindependence and pre-OIC times has continued because it has a rationality of its own. It is neither contradictory with Islam nor has it been politically feasible to alter. Its rationality is augmented further by the economic conditions within the OIC economies, which include relative poverty, relative underdevelopment, and traditional dependence on the highly developed non-Islamic countries of the West with which they share a high degree of complementarity. The OIC has tried to promote complementarity and trade by establishing the Islamic Chamber of Commerce; the fruits are yet to come.

[*See also* Economics, *article on* Economic Institutions; Islamic Chamber of Commerce; Organization of the Islamic Conference.]

BIBLIOGRAPHY

Aḥsan, ʿAbdullāh al-. *OIC: The Organization of the Islamic Conference.* Herndon, Va., 1988.

"Food Security Situation in the Islamic Countries." *Journal of Economic Cooperation among Islamic Countries* 9 (1988): 1–43.

International Bar Association. *Proceedings of the Seminar on Middle East Law with Reference to Bahrein, Egypt, Iran, Kuwait, Oman, Qatar, Saudi Arabia, U.A.E.* London, 1981.

Issawi, Charles. *The Fertile Crescent: A Documentary History, 1800–1914.* New York, 1988. See pages 141–147.

Pirzada, Syed Sharifuddin. *Speeches and Statements of His Excellency Syed Sharifuddin Pirzada, OIC.* Jeddah, 1987.

Shaw, Stanford J., and Ezel Kural Shaw. *History of the Ottoman Empire and Modern Turkey,* vol. 2, *Reform, Revolution, and Republic: The Rise of Modern Turkey, 1808–1975.* Cambridge, 1977. See pages 122–125, 236–238.

Thornburg, Max Weston. *Turkey: An Economic Appraisal.* New York, 1968. See pages 164–175.

Tignor, Robert. *State, Private Enterprise, and Economic Change in Egypt, 1918–1952.* Princeton, 1984. See pages 20–22, 60–61.

Tuma, Elias H. "The Economic Impact of the Capitulations: The Middle East and Europe, a Reinterpretation." *Journal of European Economic History* 18.3 (1989): 663–682.

United Nations Industrial Development Organization. *Industrial Development of the Islamic Countries: Progress, Present Status, and Prospects.* New York, 1982.

ELIAS H. TUMA

TRADITIONS. *See* Ḥadīth.

TRIBE. In both historical and contemporary times tribes have played important roles in the Islamic world. The English term "tribe" is one that specialists and others have used confusingly to depict what they perceive as actual groups of people, political entities, forms of social organization, structural types, modes of behavior, cultural systems, and ideologies. It is often a translation, not always accurate, of indigenous terms whose use and meaning can vary according to context. Although many scholars and others equate tribalism with nomadism and pastoralism, not all nomads and pastoralists are tribal, and more tribal peoples have been settled than nomadic.

Tribal people, governmental officials, and social scientists hold different ideas concerning what is represented by the term "tribe" and its local equivalents. The analytical constructs of outsiders do not duplicate indigenous concepts; popular discourse is not the same as the official terminology used by governments. People have invoked the notion and acted on their perception of its representations for their own differing purposes.

Many settled people viewed tribes they feared as synonymous with thieves and outlaws; on their part, tribespeople feared the loss of autonomy and thought of themselves as fiercely independent and loyal to their own groups. Settled people often viewed tribal society as inferior to urban society (*ḥaḍārah*), the so-called civilized Islamic ideal. [*See* Ḥaḍārah.] They saw cities as centers of government and order and tribes as rebellious and destructive. From an urban perspective, "tribe" often meant nomads or other rural people beyond the government's reach. Government officials tended to reify the concept of tribe in order to facilitate their own administration, declaring tribes to be identifiable corporate bodies with fixed memberships and territories; they produced lists of the tribes under their supposed authority and acted in terms of them. Such attitudes and the resulting policies both created and fortified social, political, and physical boundaries.

For tribal people themselves, the issue was not so problematic. Within their societies, their own tribal identities and those of others were clear and important ways of classifying people. Outsiders need to understand what being tribal meant for people in different contexts and to discern the patterns underlying the political, social, and symbolic expressions of people who proclaimed themselves members of tribes.

It is often more appropriate to speak of tribal or tribally organized society than of tribe because drawing boundaries around a single group may be difficult. Many Kurds, for example, are tribally organized and hold tribal identities, but we cannot speak of the Kurds as a tribe or even a group of tribes; rather, Kurdish society has tribal components.

Tribal identities are not exclusive or fixed, because tribal people also demonstrate varied linguistic, ethnic, religious, regional, class, residential, and occupational categories and traits. These crosscutting and overlapping elements make it impossible to speak of tribes as bounded, clear-cut entities. Tribal people could be urban, middle-class, white-collar workers as well as nomadic pastoralists or settled agriculturalists.

Tribal identity, like ethnic and national identity, is an "imagined" identity based on continually revised conceptions of history and tradition. Tribal groups, like modern nation-states, were "imagined communities." In constructing their identity tribal people invented and reinvented traditions according to changing sociopolitical conditions. Many tribal groups were composed of people of diverse ethnolinguistic origins, yet each group forged its own "unique" customs and created origin legends that appeared ancient to outsiders. Symbols of group identity—such as the rituals, dwellings, apparel, and notions of honor that group members considered distinctive—emerged out of a political context and served political ends.

Tribes were formed out of the conjunction of people using resources (land for pastoralism and agriculture, water, migratory routes, trade routes, markets), external powers and pressures, and mediating agents (tribal leaders, governmental officials, regional elites, foreign agents, and outside analysts). This was a useful way of organizing people so that the people so organized, their leaders, and external powers could all benefit. The local ties of tribally organized people were created voluntarily according to principles and processes of kinship, marriage, coresidence, economics, and political association.

Tribes were formed when individuals and groups affiliated politically to local and in some cases higher-level groups and leaders. The extent of supralocal, wider tribal ties is in large part explained by the geopolitical and strategic setting, the value placed internally and especially externally on local resources and labor, the extent of external pressures (especially government intervention and influence), the ability of groups to organize and act in terms of their own interests, and the level of military expertise and power. As each of these circumstances altered, so too did the characteristics of tribal groups, leadership systems, and identities. From before the dawn of Islam until the present, tribal people have associated with more complexly organized society, in particular the state, the market, and urban-centered religious institutions; no local group has remained isolated. The main stimulus for tribal formation related to this wider association, and tribal leaders and/or government officials were the principal mediating agents. Tribal leaders were representatives of state power to tribal members, while at the same time they were spokesmen of the interests of the tribal polity to the state.

Some scholars identify tribes as socially egalitarian units, while others see greater complexity. Tribes were not static entities, however, but were historically and situationally dynamic and had decentralizing and egalitarian as well as centralizing and hierarchical tendencies. Rather than defining tribes rigidly, it is necessary to discover the conditions under which a decentralizing or centralizing tendency was dominant within a society at a given time and then to trace its transformations through time. A continuum of possibilities may range from decentralized to centralized society (inegalitarian, hierarchical, and perhaps class-based). Groups at one end of the continuum lacked leaders beyond the level of local elders; those at the other end had powerful, wealthy leaders who formed part of a wider elite and participated in provincial and national politics. Tribal groups expanded and contracted. Small tribal groups joined larger ones when, for example, the state attempted to restrict access to resources or a foreign power sent troops to attack them. Large tribal groups divided into small groups in order to be less visible to the state and escape its reach. Intertribal mobility was a common pattern and was part of the process of tribal formation and dissolution.

A state is characterized by territorial borders (not necessarily secure or clearly delineated), a bureaucratic apparatus, some success at monopolizing physical coercion (especially for suppression), some degree of legitimacy, extraction of resources (especially taxes), maintenance of order associated with distribution of goods and services (such as roads), and a socioeconomically stratified population. Having centralizing goals, state rulers tried to control the territories they claimed and to subordinate and subjugate or pacify any autonomous groups within them. They were not always successful; because of problems with legitimacy and rules of succession, they were vulnerable to competitors, especially those with independent military resources, such as tribal leaders.

Many definitions and models of the state do not apply to the early Islamic world. Few states could claim recognized, legitimized power, for example, and claims to such achievements as territorial control were sometimes limited. Premodern and modern states must be distinguished, although certain so-called traditional or premodern elements have persisted in modern times. Modern nation-states are legal and international entities to be defined, as well, in these terms. When modern rulers came to power, they did so on the basis of a modern, Western-style military and bureaucracy, with state centralization aimed to bring about changes in government and society, including a nationalist ideology, economic development and control, modernization, westernization, and some secularization.

States in history have ranged from fragmented polities lacking autonomous structures of authority, to decentralized polities with rudimentary institutions, to centralized states maintained by a bureaucracy and standing army and claiming a monopoly of the legitimate use of power. The form, organization, and leadership of tribal groups reflected their relationship with states, and thus they have ranged from small, loosely organized, diffuse, noncentralized groups, to fragmented and ephemeral tribal confederacies, to large state-like confederacies with centralized hierarchical leadership systems. From before Islam until the mid-twentieth century, challengers to state rule as well as founders of states often required the military and technological prowess of tribal groups, while established state rulers required tribal support for levies, revenue, and regional security. Tribes were a constant in that they offered a reservoir of military force. State rulers often had to share power with tribes, and their ability to penetrate the countryside often depended on their ties to its tribal elite.

Tribal formations were ways of integrating people into state structures, while at the same time preventing these peoples' subordination to or assimilation into the state. Tribal structures emerged as components of state rule while simultaneously enabling people to resist certain forms of state encroachment. A loosely organized, noncentralized tribal group was as much a response to external pressures as was a complexly organized, centralized one: both were adaptive strategies. A loosely organized group, protected by the diffuseness of its structure and organization, offered little to state agents to manipulate; a centralized group was able to use its complex organization to resist state pressure as well as to benefit from being an instrument of state control.

As a result of these formative and functional relationships, tribes and states through history have been interdependent and have maintained each other as a single system; they have not functioned as two separate, opposing systems. Tribes and states represented alternative polities, each creating and solving political problems for the other. State rulers especially depended on tribes for military power, revenue, and regional security. They exploited and strengthened the structures and systems they encountered, which required little effort on their part and provided order and security. Tribal people in turn sometimes depended on state intervention in regional competition and conflict, and their leaders drew power, authority, and wealth from their connections with states. At certain periods a weak state allowed and facilitated the emergence of strong tribes; strong tribes in turn helped to ensure a weak state. At other periods strong states and strong tribes coexisted, with tolerance or antagonism. Many states began as tribal dynasties from which emerged state-like confederacies and eventually empires, such as the Ottoman Empire. At any time up to the early or mid-twentieth century, what was "tribe" and what was "state" depended upon prevailing political circumstances; some complex polities were characterized by both tribal and state features, for example Swat and the Kalat Khanate of southwestern Asia. The term "state," therefore, is best used to refer to a higher level of political, economic, and social complexity than usually found in tribes and tribal confederacies.

Albert Hourani's discussion ("Conclusion: Tribes and States in Islamic History," in *Tribes and State Formation,* edited by Philip Khoury and Joseph Kostiner, pp. 303–311, Berkeley, 1990) of three spheres of radiation from cities helps to explain the emergence of different kinds of tribes. The first sphere, the city and its dependent hinterland, was an area of direct administration. The second sphere, the intermediate areas where the city and its government could exercise control only through intermediate powers, contained organized and permanent tribes with effective leaders. The third sphere, the mountains and deserts and distant agricultural lands where a city-based ruler might have had some influence but where administration was weak or nonexistent, contained a different kind of tribal entity. Here "tribalism" was a system of ideas, symbols, and rituals that was sometimes dormant and only periodically activated. Tribal leaders in the third sphere held intermittent authority and no effective or permanent power.

Islamic beliefs and institutions were sometimes a mechanism for integrating tribes into the state. Particularly in the Arabian Peninsula and North Africa, close connections existed between tribal society and Islam in its more orthodox institutions and its popular forms such as Ṣūfī orders and saintly lineages. Urban-based religious and legal scholars sometimes held some authority over tribal groups, but they could also polarize tribal society and the state.

Some scholars define tribes in terms of kinship, by which they usually mean descent. Notions of kinship, another symbolic system of classification, were important in relationships among tribal people at the local level, but kinship ties alone did not form tribes or tribal polities. Hence a definition of a tribe as a kinship or kinship-based group is not sufficient or accurate, because it places too much weight on the factor of kinship and neglects other, more significant factors. Kinship principles were often important in giving tribal people a sense of solidarity, especially at the local level, but they were also important in nontribal societies, both rural and urban. In addition, all tribal polities contained people whose ties to local and wider groups were not defined by actual or fictive kinship ties. In the larger tribal polities, no kinship system was elaborate enough to encompass all members. If tribal people asserted connections to a genealogy or common ancestor, they were making a political statement; such genealogies were charters of organization and not maps of actual kinship ties. People also conceptualized political relationships within and between tribal societies in terms of kinship bonds. By these strategies, which should not be glossed simply as "kinship," people aimed to create a political context and operate within it. Finally, for all tribal people, it is important to distinguish among their residential and socioterritorial groups (which recruited members on a voluntary basis), kinship groups (which were defined on the basis of descent—actual or fictive—and marriage), and sociopolitical or "tribal" groups (which recruited members on the basis of political allegiance).

Tribal leaders emerged from local, regional, and state relationships and processes. High-level tribal leaders drew sources of power and authority from their contacts with the state and other external forces, but they also needed support and allegiance at the local level. Their legitimacy was often based on ideologies and systems of values that they shared (or claimed to share) with their political supporters. Various symbolic systems linked tribal leaders of all levels with supporters. They include notions of a shared history, genealogies (political charters), rituals, language, notions of territory, tribal names, sentiments of honor, and conventions of residence, migration, dwellings, apparel, and expressive arts. Tribal people recognized and supported leaders more because of shared cultural beliefs than because of threats of physical coercion. Leaders were often limited in their ability to apply force because tribespeople could "vote with their feet," deny allegiance to leaders, and form ties with other groups and leaders. High-level tribal leaders also played economic roles in a regional, often nontribal context and developed a base of power there as well; the most successful ones simultaneously cultivated the support of their political followers and their regional and governmental contacts.

Tribal leaders who wanted to expand their power and authority beyond immediate tribal boundaries often needed to invoke wider ethnic, Islamic, and/or state and national notions. Thus the Bakhtiyārī khans in the eighteenth and nineteenth centuries shared Iranian, Shīʿī values and notions of kingship with many urban Iranians. Kurdish leaders, to transcend local tribal sources of authority, utilized the institutions and ideologies of Sunnī Islam, particularly religious brotherhoods. In the 1950s the paramount Qashqāʾī khans helped to form the National Front, an Iranian political grouping with liberal, democratic, and nationalist goals.

Members of tribes are sometimes considered also to be part of ethnic groups, especially if their groups are large and complexly organized. Like tribal identities, ethnic identities involve symbolic systems of classification invoked for political reasons under changing circumstances. Ethnicity is a wider, more inclusive construct than that of tribe. As part of the processes of socioeconomic change in the twentieth century, tribal groups were sometimes transformed into ethnic groups, especially when the people were increasingly drawn under state control. When key tribal (sociopolitical) organizations and institutions were undermined or eliminated, usually under state pressure, people formerly encompassed by these systems sometimes adopted or enhanced other traits associated with ethnic groups, particularly a self-conscious sense of distinctiveness. Some tribally organized ethnic populations can also be considered national minorities or parts of them, groups united by a shared political consciousness—a sense of "nation"—and by an interest in achieving political and cultural self-expression.

The tribal peoples of the Islamic world have historically been protected through their membership in these polities and gained advantage over many others in the countryside, especially peasants, who lacked such organizations and leadership systems. Through tribal membership people could maintain political autonomy and defend and expand their economic and territorial interests, sometimes avoiding state manipulation through diffuse structure and sometimes resisting or using it through centralization. Tribespeople also received prestige and support from tribal membership. They were aware of the benefits tribal membership often conferred, and their allegiance to and support of leaders were important elements in tribal formation. Tribal structures, organizations, and ideologies offered long-term survival value because of their highly adaptive and flexible nature; state structures, organizations, and ideologies did not offer them such advantages. Tribal ties and identities were more permanent and enduring for tribal people than the affiliations and loyalties sought, sometimes demanded, by states. States came and went for tribespeople; tribes remained a constant.

[*See also* Ethnicity; Nation.]

BIBLIOGRAPHY

Abu-Lughod, Lila. *Veiled Sentiments: Honor and Poetry in a Bedouin Society*. Berkeley, 1986. Study of the role of ideology and oral poetry, with a focus on women, in a settled Arab tribal community in rural western Egypt.

Barfield, Thomas J. *The Nomadic Alternative*. Englewood Cliffs, N.J., 1993. Ethnographic and historical examination of tribally organized nomadic pastoral societies in the Middle East, Central Asia, and East Africa.

Beck, Lois. *The Qashqa'i of Iran*. New Haven, 1986. Sociohistorical study of the formation of the Qashqā'ī tribal confederacy of southwestern Iran over a two-hundred-year period, concluding with an account of the Qashqā'ī insurgency following the 1978–1979 revolution.

Beck, Lois. *Nomad: A Year in the Life of a Qashqa'i Tribesman in Iran*. Berkeley, 1991. Intimate account of daily and seasonal activity for the nomadic pastoralists of one of Iran's most important tribal confederacies.

Caton, Steven C. *"Peaks of Yemen I Summon": Poetry as Cultural Practice in a North Yemeni Tribe*. Berkeley, 1990. Anthropological study of the role of oral poetry in Yemeni tribal society.

Davis, John. *Libyan Politics: Tribe and Revolution*. Berkeley, 1987. Discussion of how Libya's government works through tribal structures.

Dresch, Paul. *Tribes, Government, and History in Yemen*. Oxford, 1989. Historically based anthropological analysis of the structure and function of tribes of Yemen.

Eickelman, Dale F. *The Middle East: An Anthropological Approach*. 2d ed. Englewood Cliffs, N.J., 1989. Useful text containing a review of the literature on tribal society and nomadic pastoralism.

Evans-Pritchard, E. E. *The Sanusi of Cyrenaica*. Oxford, 1949. Classic study of the mediating role of Islamic institutions in North African tribal society.

Friedl, Erika. *Women of Deh Koh: Lives in an Iranian Village*. Washington, D.C., 1989. Personal stories of tribal women in a small Lur village in the mountains of southwestern Iran.

Harrison, Selig S. *In Afghanistan's Shadow: Baluch Nationalism and Soviet Temptations*. New York, 1981. In-depth assessment of Baluch tribal organization in southwestern Asia and the significance of an emerging Baluch nationalist movement in regional ethnic conflict.

Khoury, Philip S., and Joseph Kostiner, eds. *Tribes and State Formation in the Middle East*. Berkeley, 1990. Excellent collection of theoretical and regional case studies covering historical and contemporary times.

Lavie, Smadar. *The Poetics of Military Occupation: Mzeina Allegories of Bedouin Identity under Israeli and Egyptian Rule*. Berkeley, 1990. Postmodernist exposition concerning tribal people in the Sinai Desert under shifting military rule.

Layne, Linda L. *Home and Homeland: The Dialogics of Tribal and National Identities in Jordan*. Princeton, 1994. Study of the interplay of local, tribal, and national political processes as they affect the formation of collective identities in Jordan.

Tapper, Richard. *Pasture and Politics: Economics, Conflict, and Ritual among Shahsevan Nomads of Northwestern Iran*. London, 1979. Anthropological study of economic, political, and social processes among nomadic pastoralists of the Shahsevan tribal confederacy.

Tapper, Richard, ed. *The Conflict of Tribe and State in Iran and Afghanistan*. London, 1983. Illuminating collection of case studies by authorities on tribal and state forms in these two areas in historical and contemporary times.

Lois Beck

TRINIDAD AND TOBAGO. Muslims make up only 8 percent of the population of Trinidad and Tobago, yet their influence in this twin-island Caribbean nation extends far beyond their numbers. The country's ceremonial president, Noor Mohammed Hassanali, is Muslim, as are many members of parliament and other officials. Many businesses are Muslim-owned. In 1990 Trinidad was thrust briefly into the world spotlight when an obscure Black Muslim group attempted to overthrow Trinidad's democratically elected government by force.

Historians believe Trinidad's first Muslims were not East Indians but black slaves from the Mandingo tribe of West Africa, many of whose members embraced Islam in the 1740s. According to Omar Hasan Kasule's 1978 report "Muslims in Trinidad and Tobago," slaves were first brought to work Trinidad's sugar plantations around 1777, and by 1802 they numbered nearly twenty thousand. Kasule writes, "In the 1830s, a community of Mandingo Muslims who had been captured from Senegal lived in Port of Spain. They were literate in Arabic and organized themselves under a forceful leader named Muhammad Beth, who had purchased his freedom from slavery. They kept their Islamic identity and always yearned to go back to Africa."

The Africans eventually lost contact with their homeland, unlike the later East Indian arrivals, who did maintain links with India and were thus able to sustain their Islamic beliefs. Trinidad's first East Indians came as indentured servants. On 31 May 1845 (an anniversary observed here every year), the *Fatel Razeck* arrived in Port of Spain, carrying 225 Hindu and Muslim laborers from the Indian state of Uttar Pradesh. The indenture system, introduced by Trinidad's British colonial masters shortly after slavery was abolished in 1834, was a form of unpaid servitude that required peasants to work the sugar plantations for a specified period—usually five years—in order to pay off their debts. Inhumane living conditions were often accompanied by efforts to impose

Christianity on the newcomers, regardless of their existing religious beliefs.

For most of the nineteenth century Trinidad's economy depended heavily on sugar exports; during World War II the colony served as an important strategic asset for Great Britain. In 1962 Trinidad received its long-awaited independence, and the country's economic emphasis began shifting from sugar to petroleum. Oil exports soon made Trinidad one of the wealthiest and most industrialized nations in the Caribbean. Yet the country's relatively high standard of living has not guaranteed social equality or even stability.

On 27 July 1990 members of a radical Black Muslim group, the Jamaat al-Muslimeen, stormed the parliament building in Port of Spain, threatening to kill Prime Minister A. N. R. Robinson and other officials unless Robinson resigned and made way for a new government sympathetic to their demands. Although the prime minister survived by agreeing to the radicals' conditions, twenty-four others died in the six-day ordeal, which was marked by widespread looting and fires that gutted downtown Port of Spain.

Most blacks and East Indian Muslims distanced themselves from the Jamaat's leader, Yasin Abu Bakr, whose activities were rumored to have been financed by Libyan leader Muʿammar Qadhdhāfī. Yet despite public outrage, Abu Bakr and his 113 followers were never punished, since the courts later ruled that the amnesty granted to the Black Muslims was legally binding.

According to the 1990 census, 36 percent of Trinidad's 1.2 million inhabitants are Roman Catholic, 23 percent Hindu, 13 percent Protestant and 8 percent Muslim. Most of the country's 100,000 Muslims are of East Indian rather than African origin, and they live mainly in and around Port of Spain. The communities are mixed; mosques often share the same street with white clapboard Baptist churches and elaborate Hindu temples.

There are about eighty-five mosques on the main island of Trinidad. One or two mosques can also be found on Trinidad's sister island Tobago, home to a few dozen African Muslims. One of the largest in the country is the Jinnah Memorial Mosque in St. Joseph. Built in 1954 and named after Pakistan's first governor-general, the structure is easily recognized by its two towering minarets and can accommodate one thousand worshipers. Large mosques are also located in Tunapuna, Curepe, San Fernando, and Rio Claro.

Several Muslim organizations flourish in Trinidad, the largest being the Anjuman Sunnat-ul-Jamaat Association, which was founded in the 1930s and represents some 80 percent of the nation's Muslims. In addition, the Trinidad Muslim League, the Islamic Trust, and the Islamic Missionaries Guild of South America and the Caribbean all have significant followings. Recently the community celebrated the opening of a spacious Islamic Center in Kelly Village, containing classrooms, a library, a bookshop, and meeting rooms for religious functions.

The Trinidadian government officially recognizes several Muslim holidays, including ʿĪd al-Fiṭr, which marks the end of the fast month of Ramaḍān. Thousands of Muslims attend the annual government-sponsored ʿĪd al-Fiṭr gathering at the national stadium in Port of Spain. In addition, more than a hundred Trinidadian Muslims make the annual pilgrimmage to Mecca.

There are increasing ecumenical efforts to combat social problems. Islamic leaders have begun to join their Christian and Hindu brethren in calling attention to Trinidad's growing problems with alcoholism, drug abuse, violent crime, and AIDS, and in denouncing what they see as an erosion of traditional values brought on by the annual Carnival.

BIBLIOGRAPHY

Kasule, Omar Hasan. *Muslims in Trinidad and Tobago*. Pamphlet, Port of Spain, 1978.

Luxner, Larry. "Muslims in the Caribbean." *Aramco World Magazine* 38 (November–December 1987): 2–11.

Trinidad under Siege: The Muslimeen Uprising. Port of Spain, 1990.

LARRY LUXNER

TUNISIA. From almost the introduction of Islam in Tunisia, most Tunisians of the Muslim faith, like most other people of the Maghrib, have been Sunnīs of the Mālikī rite dating back to the eighth-century scholar Mālik ibn ʿAbbās. However, many of the various dynasties that have ruled Tunisia, both of foreign and of Tunisian origin, have been of different persuasion. A Shīʿī dynasty, the Fāṭimids, overthrew the Aghlabid state between 905 and 909 and ruled Tunisia for most of the tenth century until it moved to Cairo in 1073. However, even then the Shīʿīs were a small minority, and there is no Shīʿī community in Tunisia today. The Ḥanafīs form a small but privileged minority of Tunisians, including the last dynasty of beys. Almost all of them are (or claim to be) descendants of the Turks who brought the Ḥanafīyah to Tunisia and who—at first through direct rule and later through a system of suzerainty—exercised substantial influence in the country from the early sixteenth century until the advent of the French protectorate.

During the course of the Ottoman Empire's influence in Tunisia, the Zaytūnah Mosque gradually became the center of all religious teaching, until it finally secured a virtual monopoly of it. According to rules established by Aḥmad Bey in 1842, which lasted well into the twentieth century, half the teachers were to be Malikī and the other half Ḥanafī.

In much of rural Tunisia, especially in the northwest, popular Islam has been widespread for centuries. It fuses the teachings of the Qur'ān with ancient North African rituals such as saint worship and ecstatic cults.

The French Protectorate. While it is impossible to give definite figures about the size of Muslim religious brotherhoods in Tunisia in the early twentieth century, the membership was certainly much greater than the total of 58,143 reported at the time. The four biggest orders were the Qādirīyah, the Raḥmānīyah, the ʿĪsāwā, and the Tijānīyah; the ʿArūsīyah were also quite numerous. However, the political role of these organizations was practically nil, and even their religious influence was gradually declining. This trend has continued and, unlike the situation in Egypt, the recent Islamist revival movement in Tunisia has not taken the form of a brotherhood. The French, in accepting only formal Islam, forced many Krumirs (northwestern Tunisians) to adopt formal Islamic elements in place of their native popular Islam.

When the French protectorate was formally established in 1883 by the Treaty of La Marsa, the Zaytūnah Mosque's school had long been regarded as one of the leading centers of classical Islamic studies. Under the influence of French culture, both Zaytūnah and Khayr al-Dīn Pasha's Sadiki College, founded in 1875 with the intent of introducing modern education to Tunisia, became the heart of the growing nationalist movement in Tunisia, which was rooted in the schools rather than in a popular mass movement. Two early leaders of the movement at Sadiki College, ʿAlī Bāsh Hambak and Bāshir Sfar, who later reconciled and went on to found the Young Tunisians, split over the issue of how much of western rationalism and French culture should be adopted. Sfar then established the revivalist Khaldūnīyah Institute in 1896, named after Ibn Khaldūn, in order to restrict the influence of French culture and restore Arab-Islamic culture in its pure traditional form.

At the beginning of the French protectorate both the Ḥanafī and the Malikī schools of Islamic law were well established in Tunisia. Throughout the period of the Protectorate the French left matters of personal status, such as marriage, divorce, inheritance, and land ownership, to the jurisdiction of *sharīʿah* courts headed by Malikī and Ḥanafī judges. However, through usage, principles of the French legal code were gradually imposed on Islamic law. There also were rabbinical courts for Jewish residents of Tunisia, as well as a separate, secular legal system staffed by French judges with jurisdiction over all cases involving non-Tunisians, as well as commercial matters and crimes.

The French administration discriminated against Tunisian Muslims in many ways, but it made it especially hard to remain a traditional Muslim and also participate in the advantages of the French sector of society. Often, this meant a choice between traditional Islam and socioeconomic advancement. Throughout the period of the French protectorate, there was a ubiquitous dualism of the traditional Tunisian and the French-assimilated or influenced sectors in Tunisia, which pervaded all aspects of life, including the educational and legal systems and the civil service.

That Islam should play a role in politics is not a new theme in Tunisian history. During the struggle for independence against France, Islam provided the moral, cultural, and ideological symbols needed to formulate popular resistance. Such leading nationalist personalities as Thaʿālibī, Sfar, Khiḍr Ḥusayn, and Ṭāhir Ḥaddād called for the defense of Islamic values. Even Habib Bourguiba, the "father of his country," insisted in 1929 on the retention of the veil as a symbol of Tunisian identity. But, following World War II, it was Ṣalāḥ ibn Yūsuf—a rival of Bourguiba—who wielded Islamic symbols and allied himself with organizations based around the university mosque of the Zaytūnah in Tunis.

Independence. On 20 March 1956 France formally recognized Tunisia's independence. In the same year the new president, Habib Bourguiba, pushed through a controversial measure called the Personal Status Code, which replaced Qur'ānic law in the areas of marriage, divorce, and child care, not merely challenging some traditional Muslim practices but confronting them head on, in a way the French never did. Tunisia became the first Arab country to outlaw polygamy. A skillful statesman and a hero of the independence movement, Bourguiba even managed to get partial support for the controversial Personal Status Code reform from influential circles in the *ʿulamā'*, thus taking a less radical approach to reform than Kemal Atatürk of Turkey.

In September of the same year, *sharīʿah* courts were abolished. By nationalizing the *ḥubūs* (religiously endowed) lands, Bourguiba deprived the *ʿulamā'* of an important material source of independence, bringing the religious establishment financially further under the control of the government. Bourguiba's educational reform effectively neutralized Zaytūnah, at least temporarily, by integrating it into the University of Tunis. This was, in fact, part of a broad strategy of weakening independent sources of potential political power within the traditional religious establishment: Islamic officials exercising independent influence through *sharīʿah* courts, schools and *ḥubūs* lands lost their power base as a result of legal and educational reforms.

The strategy of the government did not end with the weakening or eliminating potential competitors. The religious apparatus became an administrative body and an ideological intermediary of a central power eager constantly to increase its intervention in the religious sphere. Bourguiba actively sought to use the Islamic institutions now controlled by the state as a means to push for modernization and economic development. The reactivation of Islam as a state religion meant the use of religion to further goals determined by the state or, more accurately, the political elite in the ruling Neo-Destour Party.

The government actually increased the number of mosques in Tunisia from 810 in 1960 to 2,500 in 1987, and set aside prayer spaces in universities and government ministries. Yet since independence all Tunisian governments, in their quest for modernization, have opposed popular Islam. In the early years after independence permissions for saintly festivals were refused, and a number of shrines were even demolished by the authorities. Certain elements of ritual practice were prohibited, and the orders were severely criticized. Yet, while popular Islam has been weakening in a religious sense, it also has developed into a major symbol of growing peasant consciousness.

After his ascent to power Bourguiba did not openly advocate secular reforms. Rather, his ostensible aim was to reform Islam in Tunisia by putting its activities under the control of his new state apparatus and by correcting decadent practices that no longer accorded with their religious source. Instead of attacking what he believed to be fundamental tenets of Islam, he tried to project himself as a great Muslim reformer in the tradition of Muḥammad ʿAbduh. Whether Bourguiba was seen as opposed to the tenets of Islam depended, of course, on one's perspective. For some, neither Bourguiba nor Bourguibism have ever been hostile to Islam; rather, Bourguiba merely opposed the insistence of fundamentalists that Islam should comprise the central axis of Tunisian identity. Suppressing the traditional educational system at Zaytūnah and reinterpreting the basic tenets of Islam so as to make them more compatible with modernization was required in order to defend Islam from "western contamination" through a selected borrowing of western values in the context of a modern state system, and merely continued the legacy of earlier reformers such as Khayr al-Dīn.

On 5 February 1960, more than three weeks before Ramaḍān began that year, Bourguiba launched an attack on the core Muslim practice of fasting observed by most Tunisians. Asserting that it was his *fatwā* (legal Islamic edict) that economic development was a *jihād* or holy war—which would have, if accepted as true, permitted the temporary suspension of fasting—the president openly defied the fast and called upon Tunisians to do likewise. The policy proved unacceptable to most Tunisians, who defied the order, and it caused substantial unrest. Bourguiba's continuing attempts in the following years to eliminate the practice only made things worse, and eventually he capitulated.

Despite controversy and opposition, Bourguiba's policies had a determinative impact on Islam's role in modern Tunisia. Islam has been made subservient to a secular state, and its role in society has been progressively circumscribed. Although the constitution declares Islam the state religion, *sharīʿah* courts have been abolished, the state prepares the sermons to be preached in the mosques, the Code of Personal Status is based on a liberal interpretation of Islamic law, and religious education itself has been secularized with the establishment of a faculty of theology to replace the Zaytūnah Mosque as the center of Islamic learning.

Despite the apparent victory of secular policies, three modes of Islamic practice continue to be important in Tunisian state and society: traditional practices including the participation in religious brotherhoods, conduct influenced by the Salafī movement and the ideology of Egypt's Muslim Brotherhood, and rational religious behavior that gives precedence to reason in the interpretation of holy texts.

It appears that until about 1970 the government had reason to believe that it had eliminated all religious opposition through emasculation of the traditional religious establishment and neutralization of conservative fundamentalist forces. Except for a demonstration in Kairouan in 1961, there had not been any serious criticism of a religious nature until 1970.

Rise of the Opposition and Current Configuration. Like most of the region's Islamic revivalist groups, Tunisia's Islamic Tendency Movement (known by its French initials MTI) predates the revolution in Iran. Indeed, Iran's 1979 revolution can be seen as only the most visible example of a trend that can be traced to the aftermath of the 1967 Six Day War, when many Muslims felt that their devastating losses were tied to their abandonment of Islam. MTI members and supporters of other Islamist movements are not drawn from the traditional religious elites whose power and prestige was destroyed in the process of modernization, but rather from the urban petite bourgeoisie and the jobless, who felt that Bourguiba's secular state had failed to deliver on its promise of sociopolitical advancement and mobility.

The radicalization and politicization in the late 1970s of Rāshid al-Ghannoūshī and others in the Islamist movement, who had initially been more concerned with religious and moral issues, are attributed to three factors: the exposure of militant Islamic secondary-school students to Marxist thought once they began university-level studies, the conflict between the Tunisian government and the labor federation, and the example of the Iranian revolution of 1978–1979. Feelings of dislocation and alienation turned an essentially apolitical group into an activist organization. There are a number of interesting parallels between the early nationalist movement and today's Islamic revivalists. Both started out almost exclusively as student movements; adjusting for socioeconomic development, both appealed essentially to the same strata in society and were strongest in the same regions; and both used the symbolism of Islam as a unifying rallying point against the existing government, which they portrayed as lacking legitimacy largely because of its insufficient commitment to Islam.

As in most other countries that experienced Islamic revivalism, the movement in Tunisia was independent of the established *ʿulamāʾ*. The first attempt to organize an Islamist movement in Tunisia was made during the early 1960s, without much success, by a Pakistan-based movement called Group of the Call and Communication or simply Daʿwah. The Islamic groups that emerged in Tunisia had distinctly different focuses. The Daʿwah's focus was on the individual rather than on Islamic society as a whole or on Islamic thought, which were characteristic of the MTI and the later Progressive Islamicists. The eventual goal of the Daʿwah was the building of an Islamic society, but its approach was bottom-up: as the building block of society, the individual had to be reformed before society could be. Their key reformist concept is *taṣlīḥ* (restore, fix, make right or righteous), and their goal is to create *ṣāliḥ* (righteous, virtuous, godly) individuals as a means to achieve a true Muslim society. The main reason the Daʿwah failed to catch on may have been its incongruence with Islamic practice in Tunisia.

In 1971, in one of history's ironies, the government actually helped the budding fundamentalist movement by giving the educational curriculum a more conservative cast and by supporting the creation of an Islamic group at the University of Tunis, in an effort to capture the growing Islamist sentiment and at the same time contain the influence of leftist university intellectuals. The organization, the Association for the Safeguarding of the Qur'ān, succeeded in wresting control of the university campuses from the left and supplanted it as the predominant force among the student body. Soon the association's publication *Al-maʿrifah*, founded in 1972, carried a number of articles by Rāshid al-Ghannūshī, a Tunis University professor, and ʿAbd al-Fattāḥ Mūrū, a lawyer, which conveyed a distinctly political message. There was, however not yet any hint of the later politicization of the movement and of Ghannūshī's thought. Ghannūshī's early writings were not very original, often restating the ideas of those he had studied closely in Tunisia and Syria: al-Afghānī, Sayyid Quṭb, Ḥasan al-Bannā', Mawdūdī, and the Ayatollah Khomeini. They shared a profound mistrust of Western secular ideologies and an idealized depiction of Islamic societies.

In 1981, in recognition of its greater focus on political and social activism and after two years of developing local and regional structures, the Islamic Group officially renamed itself Movement of the Islamic Way, more popularly known as the Islamic Tendency Movement (MTI), mentioned above. The MTI was officially founded in June 1981, with Mūrū and Ghannūshī as its leaders. It once again changed its name in 1988, this time to Ḥizb al-Nahḍah (Renaissance Party), in order to accede to government demands that no political party seeking legal recognition have the word "Islam" in its name. Until Ben Ali's regime took a hardline, no-nonsense approach to al-Nahḍah, it remained not only the most active but by far the largest of the Islamist movements in Tunisia, with a platform calling for the reconstruction of economic life on a more equitable basis, the end of single-party politics, the acceptance of political pluralism and democracy, and a return to conservative moral and religious values. Al-Nahḍah did not consider itself the sole representative of Islam in Tunisia, as the government charged; rather, it claimed to represent a religious and political alternative to official Tunisian Islam. From the mid-1970s to the mid-1980s, the Islamists succeeded in creating a parallel society, highly antisecular and antistate in its orientation.

In an attempt to appease, coopt or integrate the Islamist opposition, or at least to remove Islam as a symbol of opposition, President Zine el Abidine Ben Ali ordered various policy changes designed to give Islam a more prominent role in public life and to portray the state as a protector of Islam. The *adhān* and prayers were broadcast on television, Hijrah dates appeared on official documents, and the Zaytūnah was given the status of a university; the president's pilgrimage to Mecca was also made a part of this strategy. Ben Ali also increased the Higher Islamic Council in both size and budget and announced the revival of the virtually dormant Committee of Reflection on Religious Affairs.

When his attempts proved unsuccessful in withdrawing the base of support from the Islamist opposition, Ben Ali's stance hardened. The army and police were purged of Islamic sympathizers, and hundreds of people were arrested. After the 1989 local elections, al-Nahḍah was again refused recognition; Ghannūshī went into voluntary exile in Paris, and his deputy ʿAbd al-Fattāḥ Mūrū assumed leadership of the party. Although al-Nahḍah was permitted to publish a weekly journal, *Al-fajr*, their journal *Mustaqbal* was closed down. Tensions between the government and the Islamic opposition continued to escalate, culminating in an all-out "war" that had effectively destroyed all public vestiges of al-Nahḍah by early 1993.

[*See also* Destour; Ḥizb al-Nahḍah; Zaytūnah; *and the biography of Ghannūshī.*]

BIBLIOGRAPHY

Allman, James. *Social Mobility, Education, and Development in Tunisia*. Leiden, 1979. Thorough social science study of the relationship between social mobility, educational levels, and development potential.

Anderson, Lisa. *The State and Social Transformation in Tunisia and Libya, 1830–1980*. Princeton, 1986. Well-grounded historical analysis explaining the differing developmental pathways taken by Tunisia and Libya, using the state as the instrument of change.

Binsbergen, Wim van. "The Cult of Saints in North-Western Tunisia: An Analysis of Contemporary Pilgrimage Structures." In *Islamic Dilemmas: Reformers, Nationalists, and Industrialization; The Southern Shore of the Mediterranean*, edited by Ernest Gellner, pp. 199–239. Amsterdam, 1985. Clear presentation of the principles and practices of saintly worship in Northwest Tunisia.

Brown, L. Carl. "The Islamic Reformist Movement in North Africa." *Journal of Modern African Studies* 2.1 (1964): 55–63. Craftsmanlike comparative historical survey of Islamic reformism in Tunisia and the Maghrib.

Brown, L. Carl. "The Role of Islam in Modern North Africa." In *State and Society in Independent North Africa*, edited by L. Carl Brown, pp. 97–122. Washington, D.C., 1966. Among the earliest formulations of Islam's political potential in the Maghrib.

Brown, L. Carl. "Islam's Role in North Africa." In *Man, State, and Society in the Contemporary Maghrib*, edited by I. William Zartman, pp. 31–36. New York, 1973.

Brown, L. Carl. "Tunisia: Education, 'Cultural Identity,' and the Future." In *Man, State, and Society in the Contemporary Maghrib*, edited by I. William Zartman, pp. 365–379. New York, 1973.

Brown, L. Carl. *The Tunisia of Ahmad Bey, 1837–1855*. Princeton, 1974. Superb historical treatment of the beginning of nativist modernization in Tunisia.

Burgat, François. *L'Islamisme au Maghreb: La voix du Sud*. Paris, 1988. Insightful portrait of political Islam as an expression of ideological discontent coming from the "South." Extensive discussion of Tunisia's Nahḍah movement and its leader, Rāshid al-Ghannūshī.

Entelis, John P. "Ideological Change and an Emerging Counter-Culture in Tunisian Politics." *Journal of Modern African Studies* 12.4 (December 1974): 543–568. The first social science survey of Tunisian university students to determine the level of support for nativist ideology over Western-inspired Bourguibism among a critical segment of incipient elites.

Entelis, John P. "Reformist Ideology in the Arab World: The Cases of Tunisia and Lebanon." *Review of Politics* 37.4 (October 1975): 513–546.

Entelis, John P., and Mark A. Tessler. "Republic of Tunisia." In *The Government and Politics of the Middle East and North Africa*, edited by David E. Long and Bernard Reich, pp. 435–458. Boulder, 1986.

Faure, Adolphe. "Islam in North-West Africa (Maghrib)." In *Religion in the Middle East: Three Religions in Concord and Conflict*, Vol. 2, *Islam*, edited by C. F. Beckingham and A. J. Arberry, pp. 171–186. Cambridge, 1969.

Gallagher, Charles F. *Contemporary Islam: The Path of Pragmatism; The Human Modernization of Tunisia*. American Universities Field Staff Report Service, North Africa Series, vol. 12, no. 3. Hanover, N.H., 1966. Perceptive analysis by a keen observer of North African cultural life.

Green, Arnold H. *The Tunisian Ulama, 1873–1915: Social Structure and Response to Ideological Currents*. Leiden, 1978.

Hermassi, Elbaki. *Leadership and National Development in North Africa: A Comparative Study*. Berkeley, 1972. Insightful comparative study of Maghribi political development, using competing ideological frameworks.

Hermassi, Elbaki. "The Islamicist Movement and November 7." In *Tunisia: The Political Economy of Reform*, edited by I. William Zartman, pp. 193–204. Boulder, 1991. Finely detailed presentation of the Islamist movement in the Ben Ali period by a close student of the subject currently heading Tunisia's delegation to UNESCO in Paris.

Knapp, Wilfrid. *Tunisia*. London, 1970.

Magnuson, Douglas K. "Islamic Reform in Contemporary Tunisia: Unity and Diversity." In *Tunisia: The Political Economy of Reform*, edited by I. William Zartman, pp. 169–192. Boulder, 1991. Comprehensive survey of the Islamist phenomenon in Tunisia by an American anthropologist who spent three years among Tunisian Islamists researching the subject.

Marshall, Susan E. "Islamic Revival in the Maghreb: The Utility of Tradition for Modernizing Elites." *Studies in Comparative International Development*, no. 14 (1979): 95–108. Somewhat simplistic presentation lacking in direct research experience in the area and overly influenced by modernization theory.

Micaud, Charles, et al. *Tunisia: The Politics of Modernization*. New York, 1964. Overly optimistic portrayal of Tunisian modernization along the Bourguibist model by three of America's leading scholars of the subject, Micaud, Brown, and Moore.

Moore, Clement Henry. *Tunisia since Independence: The Dynamics of One-Party Government*. Berkeley and Los Angeles, 1965. The best single study of Tunisian political development, although overly optimistic in its conclusions.

Moore, Clement Henry. *Politics in North Africa: Algeria, Morocco, and Tunisia*. Boston, 1970. Although out of print for years, this remains the single best study of the comparative politics of North Africa. Treatment of Islamic politics, however, is virtually absent.

Munson, Henry, Jr. "Islamic Revivalism in Morocco and Tunisia." *Muslim World* 76.3–4 (July–October 1986): 203–218. Provides useful empirical details about the leadership, organization, and political orientation of Tunisia's Islamic tendency movement.

Rudebeck, Lars. *Party and People: A Study of Political Change in Tunisia*. New York, 1969. Although poorly organized and written, numerous important factual details of Tunisian political party life are presented.

Stone, Russell A. "Religious Ethic and Capitalism in Tunisia." *International Journal of Middle East Studies* 5.3 (June 1974): 260–273.

Stone, Russell A. "Tunisia: A Single Party System Holds Change in Abeyance." In *Political Elites in Arab North Africa: Morocco, Algeria, Tunisia, Libya, and Egypt*, edited by I. William Zartman et al., pp. 144–176. New York, 1982. Evenhanded presentation of Tunisian political development through a survey of the relevant literature on the subject.

Tessler, Mark A. "Political Change and the Islamic Revival in Tunisia." *Maghrib Review* 5.1 (January–February 1980): 8–19. Carefully argued and persuasively defended presentation of the relationship between political change and the rise of Islamism, by a longtime student of Tunisia.

Tessler, Mark A., William O'Barr, and David Spain. *Tradition and Identity in Changing Africa*. New York, 1973.

Waltz, Susan. "The Islamist Challenge in Tunisia." *Journal of Arab Affairs* 3.1 (Spring 1984): 99–114. Useful complement to article below.

Waltz, Susan. "The Islamist Appeal in Tunisia." *Middle East Journal* 40.4 (Autumn 1986): 651–671. Sensitive and perceptive analysis of the socioeconomic and cultural forces explaining the rise of Islamist movements in Tunisia. Very useful.

Zghal, Abdelkader. "The Reactivation of Tradition in a Post-Traditional Society." *Daedalus* 102.1 (Winter 1973): 225–237. Original assessment by Tunisia's leading sociologist on the importance of traditional beliefs, symbols, and practices for an otherwise "modernizing" polity.

Zghal, Abdelkader. "The New Strategy of the Movement of the Islamic Way: Manipulation or Expression of Political Culture?" In *Tunisia: The Political Economy of Reform*, edited by I. William Zartman, pp. 205–217. Boulder, 1991. Objectively presented evaluation of Islam's competing images, grounded in a thorough understanding of Tunisian culture, society, and polity.

Ziadeh, Nicola A. *Origins of Nationalism in Tunisia*. Beirut, 1969. Remains the most thorough historical presentation on the rise of modern Tunisian nationalism.

JOHN P. ENTELIS

TURĀBĪ, ḤASAN AL- (b. 1932), Sudanese Islamist and political leader. Ḥasan al-Turābī was born in central Sudan and grew up in a particularly devout Muslim family. He received an Islamic education from his father as well as a standard modern education, going on to study law at the universities of Khartoum, London, and the Sorbonne. He joined Sudan's Muslim Brotherhood as a student in the early 1950s and came to prominence during the popular uprising of October 1964. The brotherhood subsequently founded a small but vociferous party, the Islamic Charter Front, through which al-Turābī pushed for an Islamic constitution.

The military coup of 1969 was a setback, and al-Turābī later went into exile, but in 1977 President Jaʿfar Nimeiri sought reconciliation with al-Turābī and his brother-in-law Ṣādiq al-Mahdī. Al-Turābī became attorney general and encouraged the Muslim Brothers to move into many areas of public life, including the new Islamic banks and the armed forces. Many Sudanese believed al-Turābī was behind Nimeiri's introduction of Islamic law in September 1983; however, Nimeiri broke with al-Turābī and imprisoned him shortly before the popular uprising of 1985 in which Nimeiri was overthrown.

In the 1986 elections al-Turābī's party, now known as the National Islamic Front (NIF), came third, but it was clearly the rising force in Sudanese politics. For the next three years the NIF was in and out of Ṣādiq al-Mahdī's weak coalition governments, but the party remained determined to develop Sudan as an Islamic state, even at the expense of perpetuating the civil war in the south. It was widely believed that it was the prospect of a secularizing compromise with the south which precipitated the NIF-backed coup of 30 June 1989 (although al-Turābī was briefly imprisoned along with other leaders of the officially banned parties). Since 1989 he has been seen as the mastermind behind Sudan's effort to establish an Islamic state, even though he has held no formal position in the government.

Al-Turābī has never published a comprehensive account of his thought, but his various writings and pronouncements present a relatively liberal interpretation of Islam, including a belief in democracy and pluralism. He has not repudiated this line of thought; however, the regime for which he regularly speaks, both in Sudan and abroad, has been widely seen as the most restrictive since independence in 1956. Parliamentary democracy was abolished by the military, which has forcibly repressed not only political parties but also many independent groups in civil society in promoting its Islamic revolution. The Muslim Brotherhood has become dominant not only in government but also in the civil service, the professions, and the economy. Feared by neighboring Arab states as a promoter of radical Islamic activism, the new regime has cooperated in turn with Libya, Iraq, and Iran; and the latter connection in particular supported government victories in the civil war in the south in 1992.

Al-Turābī has thus won a reputation for pragmatism and flexibility in the pursuit of resurgent Islam, which he seeks to see expand not only in Sudan but also in neighboring African and Arab countries. His success in building the Muslim Brotherhood in Sudan before 1989 enabled the military regime to pursue its islamizing policies. These actions have entrenched the brotherhood within the country and made it a wider force for the promotion of radical Islamic fundamentalism throughout North and East Africa.

[*See also* Muslim Brotherhood, *article on* Muslim Brotherhood in the Sudan; Sudan.]

BIBLIOGRAPHY

El-Effendi, Abdelwahab. *Turabi's Revolution: Islam and Power in Sudan.* London, 1991. Fullest account of al-Turābī's work and thought.

Turābī, Ḥasan al-. "The Islamic State." In *Voices of Resurgent Islam,* edited by John L. Esposito, pp. 241–251. New York and Oxford, 1983. Personal interpretation.

PETER WOODWARD

TURKEY. One of the successor states created from the ruins of the Ottoman Empire after World War I, Turkey became the first secular state in the Muslim world. The new state in Asia Minor (or Anatolia) was declared a republic in October 1923 after the defeat of the Greek army and the sultan's forces in a bitter civil war. The abandonment of the *sharīʿah* and the adoption of a secular legal system based on Western codes of law, as well as the declaration of a secular republic in 1928, were radical departures from tradition. The new Turkey was predominantly Muslim, with non-Muslims accounting for only 2.6 percent of the population in 1927. There were many who argued that retaining such Islamic symbols as the caliphate would provide legitimacy for the new regime. Until 1924 Turkey had been the seat of the caliphate, and from the very genesis of the Ottoman Empire, the Turkish state and society had been deeply influenced by Islamic traditions and culture, especially the tradition of the *gazi* (Ar., *ghāzī*) warrior. Not surprisingly, Kemal Atatürk, the founder of the republic, enjoyed the honorific "Gazi" into the 1930s.

Asia Minor had been penetrated by Turks and Muslims in the eleventh century, although the conquest of the region came only after the Seljuks defeated the Byzantines in 1071. By the thirteenth century, when the Ottoman state was created, Islam was well established under the influence of such Ṣūfī dervish orders as the Naqshbandīyah, Mawlawīyah, Malamīyah, and Bektāshīyah (Tk., Nakşibendi, Mevlevî, Melami, and Bektaşi). Not only were these orders influential among the people, but many sultans too were followers of their *shaykh*s. Even under a strong state with its own ideology based on Sunnī Islam of the Ḥanafī school, the influence of Ṣūfī orders and the *ʿulamā* (Tk., *ulema*), the guardians of state Islam, remained considerable. The heterodox Bektāshīyah order was particularly influential because of its intimate connection with the Janissary corps, the heart of the Ottoman army. They retained their influence until the destruction of the Janissaries in 1826, when the order was abolished and driven underground; other orders, especially the Naqshbandīyah, were allowed to flourish throughout the empire. [*See* Janissaries.]

The balance between the official Islam of the *ulema* and the popular, folk Islam of the Ṣūfīs began to turn in favor of the *ulema* in the eighteenth century. This was part of the process of centralizing power and modernizing the state in order to meet the challenge of the

West. The Ṣūfī orders were viewed as a conservative force in society and an obstacle to westernization. The orders, as well as the *ulema*, had been able to maintain a certain autonomy vis-à-vis the state thanks to the revenues of religious foundations or *awqāf* (Tk., *evkaf;* sg., *vakf*). But the sultans began to restore their authority over these foundations, and finally Mahmud II (r. 1808–1839) brought them under the control of the newly created Inspectorate (later Ministry) of Evkaf. He also incorporated the *ulema* into his remodeled state by creating an official office for the Shaykh al-Islām known as the Bab-i Mashihat or Fetvahane. The Shaykh al-Islām was transformed into a civil servant with advisory and consultative functions; later he became a member of the cabinet appointed by the sultan.

The process of rationalizing and secularizing the state—and to a lesser extent the society—continued until the founding of the republic in 1923. The Tanzimat reforms (1839–1876) accelerated this trend, and an 1869 law established the right to Ottoman citizenship regardless of religious affiliation. The opening of modern schools like Robert College (1863) and Galatasaray (1868) introduced education in a foreign language, marking an important stage toward religious desegregation. [*See* Tanzimat.]

Meanwhile, however, the Ottoman regime stressed the Islamic character of state and society as a response to the growing nationalism of its Christian subjects and increasing imperialist encroachments on Muslim lands in Asia and Africa. The sultans, especially Abdülhamid II, emphasized Islamic solidarity and their own role as the caliphs of all Muslims. This trend continued throughout the Young Turk period, and even the Kemalists fought the war of liberation mainly on the plank of a religious ideology. Mustafa Kemal (later known as Atatürk) was quite emphatic about this, noting on 1 May 1920 that the "nation whose preservation and defense we have undertaken is composed not only of one ethnic element [i.e., the Turks]. It is composed of various Islamic elements," which he described as Circassians, Kurds, and Lazes. [*See* Young Turks *and the biographies of Abdülhamid II and Atatürk.*]

The Islamic component of Turkish nationalism was bound to be strong because the majority of the new nation's people were Muslims. The composition of the population within the borders of the new republic had changed dramatically between 1914 and the census of 1927; the non-Muslim population had declined from 20 to 2.6 percent and continued to decline thereafter. But secularization may not have been so radical or so swift had the conservatives not used Islam to challenge Kemalist leadership. After dissolving the sultanate in 1922, the Kemalists toyed with the idea of retaining the caliph as a symbolic figurehead; however, the ambitions of Caliph Abdülmecid, supported by Mustafa Kemal's opponents, forced the government to act swiftly and abolish the caliphate on 3 March 1924. All educational institutions were placed under the jurisdiction of the Ministry of Public Instructions, and a Directorate of Religious Affairs under the prime minister was given charge of "all cases and concerns of the exalted Islamic faith which relate to dogma and ritual." [*See* Caliph.]

The Kurdish rebellion of February 1925 led by the Naqshbandī Shaykh Saʿīd prompted the creation of an extraordinary regime that lasted until 4 March 1929. The Kemalists utilized these four years to launch a program of reforms that effectively removed Islam from political life and secularized society. The dervish orders and sacred tombs were closed down in November 1925, and practices such as fortunetelling, magic, and cures by breathing performed by *shaykh*s, *baba*s, *seyyid*s, *murshid*s, *dede*s, and *çelebi*s became illegal. The wearing of the fez, a symbol of Muslim identity, was outlawed, and men were required to wear hats. The Gregorian calendar was adopted along with the twenty-four-hour clock. The Swiss civil code, adapted to Turkey's conditions, replaced the *sharīʿah* on 17 January 1926, depriving the *ulema* of their traditional source of influence. Later, in April 1928, the Assembly voted to remove the words "The religion of the Turkish state is Islam" from Article 2 of the constitution, completing the process of disestablishing Islam. Meanwhile, a committee set up to study the implementation of an "Islamic reformation" presented its findings. It recommended, among other things, introducing pews into mosques and sacred instrumental music into the service. These proposals were too radical, and the committee was quickly disbanded, suggesting that the government had no intention of alienating Muslim opinion. However, the committee's proposal to replace Arabic with Turkish as the liturgical language of Islam was adopted a few years later.

The purpose of these radical reforms was not anti-Islamic but political: to remove from the jurisdiction of religious leaders and their political allies all legal, social, and educational institutions and place them in the hands of the Directorate of Religious Affairs. The state would then direct religious energy toward its own socioeconomic program. One of the reformers defined a secular government as "one which transfers the leadership in religious affairs from the ignorant to the enlightened," and the Kemalist daily *Hakimiyet-i Milliye* (30 December 1925) editorialized, "We can sincerely claim that our Revolution has more of a religious than an irreligious character as it has saved consciences from harmful tyranny and domination. . . . To think that a nation can live without any religion is nothing less than denying humanity, sociology, and history."

Islam became an instrument of government policy. It was recognized as a vital component of the nation's cultural constitution and mobilized to enhance national unity and instill civic virtues. Prayers, especially Friday prayers in the mosque, were encouraged because they instilled discipline and a sense of community; fasting "builds endurance and patience," while giving *zakāt* (Tk., *zekat,* "alms") "stimulates one's sense of generosity." The Friday sermon was specially written to educate the mosque-going public (especially the illiterate) in civic duties. They were told that their religious obligations *(farz)* included paying taxes, doing military service, cooperating with the government, and being loyal and obedient citizens. Islam was presented as a rational and scientific religion ("our Prophet informs us that science is essential for a Believer'); it was open to innovation ("Muslims do not hesitate to accept new movements") and national ("every nation addresses God in its own tongue"). Specially trained military chaplains were assigned to the army and religious instruction made a part of the military routine.

This pragmatic attitude toward Islam might have continued had not circumstances in the early 1930s convinced the regime of the need for a more aggressive ideology. The world economic crisis and the appeal of Italian fascism and Soviet communism in these difficult times were two contributing factors. The more immediate stimulus was the failure of the multiparty experiment of August–November 1930; political liberalization and the formation of the Free Party encouraged an Islamist reaction against the secular regime. Even more traumatic was the Menemen Incident of December 1930, in which Dervish Mehmed, a Naqshbandī devotee, called on the people to destroy the impious regime. He beheaded an officer sent to quell the disturbance, yet no one in the crowd intervened to defend the state. The Kemalist elite was shocked that citizens of the republic had stood by and even applauded Dervish Mehmed. The people had failed to understand the reforms, and that had to be rectified.

The ideology known as Kemalism was launched in May 1931 and written into the constitution in 1937. Its core was the six "fundamental and unchanging principles of Republicanism, Nationalism, Populism, Statism, Secularism, and Revolutionism." Islam was "nationalized" in January 1932, with the Qur'ān being read in Turkish, followed by the Turkish call to prayer in 1933. Although the regime became more consciously secular, Islam was still mobilized for civic ends. Mosques continued to disseminate propaganda in favor of the national economy, and mosques and churches were told to urge their congregations to contribute generously to the Turkish Aviation Society. [*See* Kemalism.]

There were signs of liberalization following the death of President Atatürk in November 1938. His successor, İsmet İnönü, wanted to build a consensus and therefore permitted members of the old opposition, more sympathetic to Islam, to enter politics. A real relaxation of militant secularism, however, came only after the introduction of multiparty politics in 1945, when the ruling Cumhuriyet Halk Partisi (Republican People's Party, CHP) recognized that the competition for votes against the Demokrat Parti (Democrat Party, DP) required the manipulation of Islam. Islam also became an important weapon in the cold war against Moscow as well as against left-wing dissidents at home. Consequently the CHP, the party of secularism, began to undo some of its earlier reforms. In 1948 pilgrims were permitted to visit Mecca. The following year, courses to train prayer-leaders and preachers were set up, and a Faculty of Theology (İlahiyat) was opened in Ankara in October. Also in 1949 religious education was restored to the classroom, and sacred tombs that had been closed down in 1925 were reopened.

Despite these concessions, the Republicans lost the election in 1950. The Democrats continued the policy of liberalization and gained great popularity, especially by restoring the Arabic *ezan* (call to prayer) in June 1950 and lifting the ban on religious radio broadcasts. Turkish voters, however, responded not so much to these religious concessions but to the DP's development policies, which transformed Turkish society by opening up the country with roads, mechanized agriculture, and provided farm subsidies, bringing a level of prosperity peasants had never known. As election results have consistently shown, voters supported the parties they thought would improve their material life. [*See* Cumhuriyet Halk Partisi *and* Demokrat Parti.]

With political liberalization, the Islamic sentiment

that had gone underground reemerged and became vocal. More people attended mosques, and new ones were built throughout the land. There was a growing demand for religious literature that was met by writers who had been biding their time. These developments exposed the fundamental weakness of the Kemalist reforms—their failure to reach deeply into society. Only the cities and large towns benefited under Kemalism and developed a small class committed to it. The countryside remained virtually untouched by the benefits of modern education, and literacy grew only slowly. Thus, even though the social institutions associated with the dervish orders were destroyed, their influence remained strong and began to reassert itself by 1950. Nonetheless, there was no question of going back to an Islamist order under the *sharīʿah* or permitting the Ṣūfī orders to stand in the way of change. Both the DP and the CHP were committed to change; when some Ṣūfī orders attempted to regain their influence, their leaders were prosecuted with the full force of the law—the Tijānīs, Naqshbandīs, and Mevlevîs in 1950, and the Qādirīs in 1951, all by the supposedly pro-Islamist DP. In time the religious orders became appendages of certain parties, exercising influence and patronage through them. The Democrats began to exploit Islam for political ends only after 1957 when their power waned as a result of economic setbacks. A political deadlock with the opposition triggered the military coup of May 1960, which opened a new chapter in the political life of modern Turkey.

The military regime accelerated Turkey's transformation to an industrial society by introducing new institutions, including a liberal constitution that guaranteed, among other things, social justice, the right to strike, and freedom of expression. As a result a Workers' Party (Türkiye İşçi Partisi) was formed and challenged the policies of the ruling classes from the left. The establishment responded by mobilizing "Islam as the antidote to communism," the catchword for any criticism aimed at rectifying the socioeconomic problems in Turkish society. The polarization between left and right soon assumed a religious character. As a result Turkey's Alevis (Ar., ʿAlawīyah), a heterodox offshoot of Shiism who make up an estimated 8 million out of the current (1992) population of 52 million, came under attack from the right. They were accused of being leftists even though their only sin was to be longtime supporters of the secular CHP. Finding that the CHP no longer satisfied their political needs, they formed the Unity Party (Birlik Partisi) in October 1966, though they have never identified it as an Alevi party.

A major consequence of the rapid economic growth of the 1960s—about 7 percent a year between 1963 and 1973—was the concentration of economic power in a few large conglomerates. This process undermined the small producers and merchants of Anatolia, who responded by withdrawing their political support from the principal party of the right, the Justice Party (Adalet Partisi), the DP's successor. They formed splinter parties like the conservative Democratic Party (Demokratik Partisi), the neofascist Nationalist Action Party (Milliyetçi Harekit Partisi), and the National Order Party (Milli Nizam Partisi, MNP), the first openly Islamist party of the republic.

The MNP was led by Necmettin Erbakan, an engineer trained in Germany, who also enjoyed the support of the Naqshbandīs. He was a new politician who emerged in the 1960s to fill the vacuum left by the Democrats, disqualified from political life by the junta. He was provincial rather than cosmopolitan in outlook and had nothing in common with the old elite except the ambition to develop the country. Such people were willing to adopt Western technology to create a modern, capitalist economy, but they were at home in the culture they associated with Islam and were contemptuous of the imported Western culture they identified with loose morals and decadence. The MNP never called for the restoration of the *sharīʿah;* they campaigned only for a national economy independent of foreign control and a national culture based on Ottoman-Islamic traditions and free of corrupting fashions imported from the West.

The party was banned by the military regime in 1971 but regrouped as the National Salvation Party (Milli Sēlamet Partisi, MSP) in 1973. In the next general election the MSP garnered 11 percent of the vote and became the coalition partner of the social democratic CHP, as both shared a similar economic program. When the coalition broke up, Erbakan continued to play a significant role in new coalition governments led by the Justice Party. This gave him considerable powers of patronage, which he exercised on behalf of his supporters, especially the Naqshbandīs. As a result Islamists were soon entrenched throughout the bureaucracy, posing a threat to secular education.

The MSP was banned again by the military junta that seized power in September 1980. When political activity was partially restored in 1983, the Motherland Party (Anavatan Partisi) led by Turgut Özal, a former member of the MSP, assumed the mantle of political Islam. But Muslim opinion in Turkey, radicalized by the Iranian revolution, wanted a more militant party to support. Initially the Welfare Party (Refâh Partisi, RP), the MSP reincarnated, attempted but failed to meet these radical expectations. After failure in the 1987 election the party changed its strategy and emphasized "the struggle against feudalism, imperialism, and fascism." The strategy paid off, and the RP, in coalition with the neofascist Nationalist Labor Party (Milliyetçi Çalişma Partisi), won 17.2 percent of the vote in 1991. It also fared well in local elections in 1993, winning municipalities in squatter and working-class areas, but it was still far from winning power throughout the country. [*See* Refâh Partisi; Anavatan Partisi; *and the biographies of Erbakan and Özal.*]

Generally speaking, Turkey in the 1990s is a country that feels comfortable with Islamic political and cultural discourse. It has become part of the Islamic world and participates in most of its activities, often playing a leadership role. It sees itself as a bridge between the West and the Islamic world and takes its Islamic identity seriously. This trend is likely to continue, although there is one alarming development that may impede further progress. A spate of political assassinations of prominent secularist intellectuals and journalists, allegedly by pro-Iranian groups, threatens to bring about repression against Islamist organizations, just as similar crimes led to repression of the left in the 1970s and 1980s.

[*See also* Bektāshīyah; Mevlevî; Naqshbandīyah; *and* Ottoman Empire.]

BIBLIOGRAPHY

Allen, Henry Elisha. *The Turkish Transformation* (1935). New York, 1968. Perceptive account of social and religious developments in Kemalist Turkey.

Barnes, John Robert, *An Introduction to Religious Foundations in the Ottoman Empire*. Leiden, 1986. Excellent source for information on the rise and fall of the *vakf*s.

Berkes, Niyazi. *The Development of Secularism in Turkey*. Montreal, 1964. The best book on the subject for the eighteenth and nineteenth centuries and the early republic.

Birge, John Kingsley. *The Bektashi Order of Dervishes* (1937). New York, 1982. Fine scholarly study of a neglected subject.

Gibb, H. A. R., and Harold Bowen. *Islamic Society and the West*. Vol. 1, parts 1–2. London and New York, 1950–1957. Somewhat dated but most informative about Ottoman society and institutions in the eighteenth century.

Lewis, Bernard. *The Emergence of Modern Turkey*. 2d ed. London and New York, 1968. Authoritative account of reforms in the Kemalist period up to the early fifties.

Rustow, Dankwart A. "Politics and Islam in Turkey, 1920–1935." In *Islam and the West*, edited by Richard N. Frye, pp. 69–107. The Hague, 1957. Stimulating and full of original ideas.

Smith, Wilfred Cantwell. *Islam in Modern History*. Princeton, 1957. A most stimulating chapter on "Turkey: Islamic Reformation?"

Tapper, Richard, ed. *Islam in Modern Turkey: Religion, Politics, and Literature in a Secular State*. London and New York, 1991. Some excellent articles on a variety of topics by a new generation of Turkish scholars.

Toprak, Binnaz. *Islam and Political Development in Turkey*. Leiden, 1981. Important book on religion and politics.

FEROZ AHMAD

TURKISH LITERATURE. The articulation of Islamic themes and values in Turkish literature of the nineteenth and twentieth centuries differs from that of the preceding era, for it occurs in the context of a struggle for survival and redefinition of selfhood and state. Turkish-speaking Muslims of a weakened and shrinking Ottoman Empire (c. 1300–1918) undertook the westernizing restructurings of the Tanzimat reform period (1839–1876) only to witness the rise of nationalism among non-Turkish groups, whose relatively harmonious coexistence over five centuries came to a close in the debacle of the Balkan Wars (1911–1913) and the ultimate defeat and dismemberment of the Ottoman Empire by the allied powers at the end World War I. Out of the ruins of this multiethnic Islamic empire emerged a small Turkish nation-state established as a secular republic in 1923. This period of radical social transformation and devastating upheaval provoked profound changes in the function and forms of Turkish literature. Prior to the westernizing innovations of the nineteenth century, Ottoman Turkish literature had been dominated by poetry as the favored means of artistic expression throughout all layers of society. Whether that of the erudite Ottoman court *(divan)* poets writing in the Arabo-Persian quantitative *(aruz)* meter or that of the illiterate folk minstrels *(âşık)* reciting extemporaneously in the traditional Turkish syllabic *(hece)* meter, this premodern poetry was suffused with the values of Islamic mysticism; the anguish of separation from the Beloved, whether divine or human, constituted one of its primary aesthetic impulses. Both the *divan* poetry of the Ottoman elite and the more humble poetry of the minstrel *(âşık)* and folk *(halk)* traditions are to be distinguished, however, from the religiously inspired devotional poetry of the *tekke* (dervish lodge) tradition, which reached out to all social classes.

When disruptive changes began to occur in Ottoman society during the period of the Tanzimat reforms, the emphasis in poetry began to shift away from inward probing of the human soul in philosophical-religious contexts toward a preoccupation with external social and political realities. Genres new to Ottoman literature began to appear and were used as effective vehicles for the expression of views on contemporary issues such as constitutionalism, slavery, patriotism, women's rights, tyranny, Islamic unity, individual liberty, arranged marriages, and the effects of westernizing cultural change on value systems and lifestyles in Ottoman Istanbul. The first example of the novel available to readers of Ottoman Turkish, Yusuf Kâmil Paşa's 1859 translation of Abbé Fénelon's didactic adventure story *Télémaque*, underwent numerous reprintings throughout the 1860s and 1870s, in part because of its political theme emphasizing that rulers exist for the sake of their subjects and not the reverse. The first actual Ottoman experimentation in European prose genres was undertaken not by individuals devoted primarily to the literary arts, but rather by influential journalists, political thinkers, and social educators, many of whom served in the Ottoman bureaucracy. Major figures of the Tanzimat era such as İbrahim Şinasi Efendi (1826–1871), Ziya Paşa, (1825–1880), Namık Kemal (1840–1888), and Ahmet Mithat Efendi (1844–1912) saw in literature an effective means of communicating unfamiliar political concepts and social values in a convincing fashion to the widest possible audience. The first play for the legitimate theatre written in Ottoman Turkish, *Şair evlenmesi* (The Marriage of a Poet), a one-act farce mocking the corruptibility of clerics and criticizing marriage ceremonies performed in the absence of the bride, was serialized in 1860 by its author, Şinasi, in the newspaper which he edited, *Tercüman-ı ahval* (Interpreter of Events). Literature and journalism were in fact close associates throughout the Tanzimat period in creating, expanding, and informing public opinion.

If authors and poets themselves tended to see the role of literature as one of reaching and instructing or swaying the people, literature in turn functioned as a forum for the ideological debates of the intelligentsia. As the noted historian of nineteenth-century Turkish literature, Ahmet Hamdi Tanpınar (1901–1962), himself a poet and novelist, has pointed out, it is the struggle among various ideologies, each corresponding to a separate social reality, that in a real sense constitutes the fundamental history of modern Turkish literature. It is in the context of the emergence of these ideological struggles that Islamic themes came to be articulated as a matter of political and social concern, arising in concert with a host of new themes reflecting the outlooks of a diversity of intellectual-political-literary movements. These conflicting aspects are standardly summarized under four labels, each associated with one or more major literary figures: "Ottomanism" with Namık Kemal (1840–1888), "Westernism" with Tevfik Fikret (1867–1915); "Islamism" with Mehmet Âkif Ersoy (1873–1936); and "Turkism" with Ziya Gökalp (1876–1924). In the works of the first generation of Tanzimatists, however, Islamic themes do not appear as a conspicuous feature, although Islamic values may of course occur as one of the givens of a text, and the religious subjects of traditional poetic genres are not abandoned abruptly. For example, the collected poems *(Müntehabât-ı es'arım)* of İbrahim Şinasi—who with the founding in 1862 of his second newspaper, *Tasvir-i Efkâr* (The Depictor of Ideas), set the directions for the development of a modern press and a modern expository prose based on spoken Turkish—lacks a traditional *na*ʿ*t* (eulogy for the prophet Muḥammad) but does contain a *münâcât* (supplication to God); the content of the latter, however, reflects a stance new to Ottoman literature, with the poet seeking a reasoned proof of God's existence through contemplation of the order and beauty of the created universe before falling back on a more conventional expression of blind faith in God's power and mercy. Islamic themes are not, however, part of the primary thrust of Şinasi's life work, which anticipates the dual orientation, "toward the West" *(batıya doğru)* and "toward the people" *(halka doğru)*, that came to undergird the ideology of the Turkish Republic and to serve as the initial mainspring of modern Turkish literature. Şinasi's *The Marriage of a Poet* exemplifies this dual orientation in its affinity with Molière's comedy of manners, *Le mariage forcé*, and its skillful exploitation of indigenous comic techniques and language use characteristic of the traditional shadow-puppet theater *(karagöz)*, the popular theater in the round *(orta oyunu)*, and the professional storytelling of the coffeehouse *meddah*.

The importance of İbrahim Şinasi's role as harbinger of subsequent main directions in Turkish literature requires that attention be paid to the nature of his response to the racialist paradigms of French Orientalist thought, in which he was immersed during two sojourns in Paris in 1849–1854 and 1865–1870. Introduced into Orientalist circles, both literary and academic, by his friend Samuel de Sacy, the son of the famous Orientalist Silvestre de Sacy, Şinasi interacted with such prominent figures as Ernest Renan, Lamartine, Littré, and Pavet de Courteille, whose 1870 *Dictionnaire Turk-Oriental* acknowledges the contribution of his "learned teacher and friend" Şinasi. At a time when more politically active Young Ottoman writers—including the famous novelist, playwright, journalist, and poet Namık Kemal—were thinking in terms of the union and progress of all Ottoman subjects under a constitutional monarchy with equal rights regardless of race, ethnicity, language, or religion, İbrahim Şinasi's interest was turned toward defining the characteristics of a specifically Turkish identity. This he attempted through the collection of proverbs *Durub-u emsâl-i osmaniye,* compiled in Paris in 1851 and published in Istanbul in 1863 as a source revealing "the wisdom of the common populace *(avam)*" and "the character of the thought of a people *(millet),*" as well as through the preparation of an ambitious etymological dictionary that aimed to cover the origins and development of the Turkic languages. Despite his adoption of the racialist bent of an incipient nationalism fostered by his Orientalist milieu, Şinasi included equivalent French and Arabic proverbs in his *Durub-u emsâl-i osmaniye.* This may indicate an attempt to rebuff what Edward Said *(Orientalism,* New York, 1978) has called "the notorious race prejudice directed against Semites (i.e., Muslims and Jews)" of Şinasi's close acquaintance, Ernest Renan. By presenting proverbial evidence of shared values inherent in the cultures of Europeans and Orientals alike, Şinasi could protest the putatively unbridgeable gap separating an unregenerate Muslim East from the Christian West; by emphasizing the non-Semitic origins of Turkish-speaking Muslims through his etymological work, Şinasi was able to provide an immediate escape hatch for himself and other native speakers of Turkish from the racist attitudes of his Parisian friends in a period when the term "Turk" was often used indiscriminately by Europeans for any Muslim subject of the Ottoman sultan.

Although Şinasi's encounter with the anti-Islamic sentiment of his European circle of acquaintances did not provoke the appearance of specifically Islamic themes in his literary output, the reverse would sometimes appear to be the case with the somewhat younger but equally important literary revolutionary of the Tanzimat period, Namık Kemal, whose biographies of successful Muslim military leaders—Saladin (c. 1137–1193), Mehmet the Conqueror (1429–1481), and Sultan Selim I (1467–1520)—appear to have been written expressly in response to his readings of French historians. In an 1872 article published in *İbret* (Admonition), the Young Ottoman newspaper established after his return to Istanbul from political exile in Paris and London, Namık Kemal criticized the bias he perceived in European scholarship under the headline, "Avrupa şarkı bilmez" (Europe Does Not Know the East); and in 1883, while in internal political exile, he wrote a refutation *(Renan müdafaanamesi)* of Renan's widely publicized lecture "Science and Islam," which held Islam to be inherently incompatible with scientific progress. This is not to say, however, that a reactive spirit underlies the Islamic themes running through major literary works of Namık Kemal, or that such themes form the primary focus of this fervent Muslim's literary output. Namık Kemal is perhaps best known for his *Hürriyet kasidesi* (Ode to Freedom), reflecting his dedication to the European Enlightenment ideal of individual liberty, and for his play *Vatan yahut Silistre* (Native Land or Silistre), whose theme emphasizing patriotic love for an Ottoman homeland *(vatan)* rather than devotion to the Ottoman dynasty *(Al-i Osman)* proved such a popular success when performed in 1873 that it earned him exile at the hands of Sultan Abdülaziz (r. 1861–1876) and closure of both the play and his newspaper. The patriotic hero of *Vatan* may be named İslam Bey, but the term of group identity used by his volunteer soldiers at the siege of Silistre in the Balkans is "Ottoman" rather than "Muslim" or "Turk." "We are Ottomans" is the refrain of their patriotic *türkü* (a genre of folksong) as they express their willingness to give up their lives for love of country and the glory of death in battle. An indication that Namık Kemal was not simply offering his audience an intellectual's artificial Ottomanist ideology may be found in the existence of a grassroots equivalent idea of self-identity from the same period in the stirring *'93 Koçaklaması* (Heroic Song of AH 1293, 1877) by the minstrel poet Âşık Şenlik (1854–1914) of Kars in northeastern Turkey; the poet-musician, utilizing the refrain "We shall not give up the homeland *(yurt)* to the enemy so long as we live," calls on Muslims to bring greater glory to the Ottoman dynasty in their defense of the fortress of Kars and resistance to the Russian invasion of eastern Anatolia.

Others of Namık Kemal's major works do treat specifically Islamic subjects; for example, his fifteen-act drama *Celalettin harzemsah,* like his unfinished novel *Cezmî,* presents a theme of Islamic unity attained between Shīʿī and Sunnī Muslims through the royal marriage of the hero. Moreover, allusions to early Islamic history appear as some of the most dramatic imagery of Namık Kemal's poetry even as it presents new political and social content. Like his close associate and fellow Young Ottoman, Ziya Paşa (1825–1880), Namık Kemal, even while advocating the use of Turkish folk meters and verse forms as the basis for a new poetry, remains dependent in his own work on the traditional *aruz* prosody and classical verse forms of *divan* poetry, particularly the *kaside* (eulogy), *gazel* (lyric poem), *murabba* (quatrain), *şarkı* (quatrain), *tarih* (chronogram), *kıta* (independent stanza), and *terkib-i bend* (long poem with refrain couplets rhyming among themselves). This dependence on the meters and forms of classical *divan* poetry did not , however, prevent Namık Kemal from writing a scathing criticism, *Tahrib-i harabat* (Destruction of the Ruins), when his Young Ottoman companion in exile, Ziya Paşa—perhaps inspired by the literary anthologies of Orientalist friends met during two years in London (1868–1870)—published *Harabat* (Wine Shop of the Poets, 1874), a three-volume anthology of Arabic, Persian, Chagatay, and Ottoman *divan* poetry. Namık Kemal considered his friend's presentation of Ottoman *divan* poetry in its classical Islamic context a betrayal of all their ideals as forgers of new directions for Ottoman Turkish literature. Yet—as several scholars including Ahmet Evin have pointed out (*Origins and Development of the Turkish Novel,* Minneapolis, 1983)—Namık Kemal's best-known novel and one of the first to be written in Turkish, *İntibah: Sergüzest-i Ali Bey* (Awakening: The Misadventures of Ali Bey, 1876) bears the imprint of traditional conventions of Ottoman poetry and prose, even if its theme of romantic tragedy, highly popular in Turkish novels of the 1870s and 1880s, displays close similarities to Alexandre Dumas *fils' La dame aux camélias.* A moralizing work critical of the foppery of the half-Europeanized spendthrift sons of well-to-do Ottoman families, this novel, like much of Namık Kemal's work, does not reflect specifically Islamic themes.

As a novelist Namık Kemal is overshadowed by his prolific contemporary Ahmet Mithat Efendi, most of whose journalistic essays and works of fiction, including twenty-nine novels, were published after the abrogation of the Young Ottomanist constitution of 1876 by Sultan Abdülhamid II and the imposition of a severely repressive system of censorship. This censorship did not prevent Ahmet Mithat from taking up the role of social critic or from aiming to educate his readers in all branches of contemporary European science and philosophy. A man of encyclopedic interests, Ahmet Mithat took on the role of fatherly teacher of the people in a period prior to the opening of the first modern Turkish university. Considered a conservative supporter of the Hamidian regime, he believed in accomplishing progressive change gradually though public education rather than through the imposition of revolutionary measures. He owned his own printing presses, and as the son of a small shop-owner who had once worked as an apprentice in Istanbul's Spice Market, he knew how to captivate a far broader audience than any other writer of the period and thus became wealthy through his writing. Although Islamic themes cannot be said to constitute a major aspect of his work, Ahmet Mithat was a dedicated Muslim of strong convictions who did undertake an explicit defense of Islam (*Müdafaa*, Istanbul, 1882) against European assertions that it fostered an intractable resistence to social change and scientific progress. As pointed out by A. H. Tanpınar, Ahmet Mithat even went so far as to attempt to reconcile Lamarck's data from the fossil record with the Qur'ānic account of creation. Aware that the allegedly degraded status of Muslim women was used by Europeans to denigrate Islamic cultural values, he raised his voice in defense of the rights of women, arguing especially for equal rights in education. As pointed out initially by Pertev Naili Boratav and then again by Niyazi Berkes in his *Development of Secularism in Turkey* (Montreal, 1964), Ahmet Mithat even anticipated the day when women would enter all professions. However, it is difficult to count him among early Muslim feminists, as his fiction often reflects implicit values and attitudes that contradict the explicitly feminist themes of his essays—for example, his well-known novel of 1875, *Felâtun Beyle Rakım Efendi.* This work, which contrasts the frivolous and foolish infatuation with all things European of Felâtun Bey with the more measured European interests of the studious and industrious Rakim Efendi, presents the latter as an exemplary type even though he is made a father by his French mistress just as he marries the docile and devoted slave he has educated since childhood.

The first prominent Ottoman Muslim female feminist was the novelist Fatma Aliye Hanım (1864–1936), who presented her views on women's issues not only through her novels *Muhazarat* (Disputations, Istanbul, 1892), *Refet* (Clemency, Istanbul, 1897), and *Udî* (The Lutist, Istanbul, 1899), but also through the new medium of magazines and women's periodicals. In segments from

Women of Islam (*Nisvan-ı İslam*, Istanbul, 1891) available in English translation in Berkes (1964), she argues effectively as a devout Muslim against the position taken by some Islamist intellectuals and members of the *ulema* Ar., *ʿulamāʾ*) on the controversial subject of polygamy. Her early years and education are described in Ahmet Mithat Efendi's biography *Fatma Âliye Hanım or the Emergence of an Ottoman Authoress* (*Fatma Aliye Hanım, yahut bir muharrire-i Osmaniyenin neş'eti*, Istanbul, 1893).

Although women's issues were taken up by virtually all Ottoman male novelists of the last three decades of the nineteenth century, their fiction tended to focus on matters of equal consequence for the condition of men, such as the custom of arranged marriage and the institution of slavery. The egregious transgression of the values underlying the arrangement of marriages by parents for the benefit of their children became one of the most prominent themes of the period. Şemseddin Sami's (1850–1904) *Taaşşuk-i Talât ve Fitnat* (The Love of Talat and Fitnat) of 1872, which some regard as the first Ottoman novel despite its similarities to the romance (*hikâye*) of the Turkish minstrel-tale tradition, ends in the tragic death of the two young lovers because the heroine has been married off against her will to a wealthy man. Refusing to consummate the marriage, she commits suicide, her beloved follows suit, and the husband, upon learning from a note discovered in his young wife's locket that she was actually his own long-lost daughter, suffers a nervous breakdown and dies of grief.

A second major topic for social condemnation was the institution of slavery, which although already declared illegal continued to receive sharp criticism in the novels of the last quarter of the century as in Samipaşazade Sezai's (1858–1936) *Sergüzeşt*, (Misadventure) of 1889. In this work the tension between romantic love and financial security and social status, played out in the conflict between two generations of a wealthy Ottoman household, may contribute to the death of the young gentleman and the tragic suicide of the beloved slave heroine, but the tragedy is at root attributed to the abomination of slavery. A third prominent theme of the Ottoman novel is exemplified by Recaizade Mahmud Ekrem's (1847–1915) *Araba Sevdası* (Carriage Crazy), one of the best-known novels of the 1880s. Like Namık Kemal's *Misadventures of Ali Bey* and Ahmet Mithat's *Felâtun Beyle Rakım Efendi*, this novel mocks the behavior of a generation awash in European fads and fashions. The adventures of the spendthrift hero of *Carriage Crazy*, however, are presented as amusing rather than tragic. Bihruz Bey may lose his fancy carriage to his creditors and suffer a ridiculous disillusionment in love, but in the end he is able to return home to the comfort of his mother's unfashionable mansion in a respectable old neighborhood of Istanbul.

Just as Recaizade's novel epitomizes a main theme of the fiction of this period, his poetry reflects in intensified form the sentimentality often said to mar literary production during the thirty-three-year reign of Sultan Abdülhamid II (r. 1876–1908). In *Tahassür* (Grievous Loss) Recaizade grieves for a daughter who died at birth and laments his inability to locate the exact site of her grave after the passage of fifteen years. In *Ah Nejad!* the poet mourns the death of a son, his anguish quickened by the sight of a child's small footprints along a garden path. Both these melancholy *kindertotenlieder* dwell in dismay on the physical decay of mortal remains and signal a spiritual disquietude in the face of scientific materialism; this must be distinguished from earlier poetic expressions of spiritual anguish over separation from the beloved or metaphysical complaint over the transitory nature of all things mortal.

In its Ottoman Turkish context, the metaphysical anxiety that Alfred North Whitehead (*Science and the Modern World*, New York, 1925) considered characteristic of the nineteenth century and defined in the case of English Romantic poetry as "the intuitive refusal seriously to accept the abstract materialism of science," finds its most compelling example in the works of the prolific poet and dramatist Abülhak Hamid Tarhan (1852–1937). Like many of his generation, he had been raised on the literary classics of two civilizations and thus was as conversant in the traditions of French and British Romanticism as in those of Persian and Turkish mysticism. In one of the most famous poems of the period, *Makber* (The Tomb, 1885), he departs from the classical Ottoman elegiac (*mersiye*) tradition to frame his own private agony over the death of his wife in terms of an anguished questioning of the metaphysical foundations of human existence.

The participation of Abülhak Hamid Tarhan and an entire segment of the Ottoman literary elite in what Masao Miyoshi (*The Divided Self: A Perspective on the Literature of the Victorians*, New York, 1969) has termed "the nineteenth-century literature of spiritual distress" remained, however, entirely one-sided; although Ottoman novelists and poets read widely in French and to a lesser degree in English, as the literary influences spawned by

German Romanticism and French Symbolism crossed continents, European men and women of letters had little opportunity and no inclination to avail themselves of the Ottoman Turkish manifestations of an otherwise truly crosscultural phenomenon—despite the fact that a fascination with the Orient constituted an important element of the Romantic movement in France. The incorporation of European thought and literary practice into the Ottoman Turkish context during the latter part of the nineteenth century was no doubt facilitated by the fact that the metaphysical orientations of Romanticism and Symbolism were, like the scientific interests of Ahmet Mithat Efendi, safe directions for literature in a period of severe political repression, as the last powerful Ottoman sultan strove to maintain the territorial integrity of an empire that had already lost effective control of its financial system and customs regulation. As the eminent scholar of Turkish literature Mehmet Kaplan has pointed out, Abdülhak Hamid's *Makber* marked not only the death of the poet's beloved Fatma Hanım but also the death of the literature of social idealism and political commitment initiated during the Tanzimat era by Şinasi and Namık Kemal. It ushered in the profound pessimism and melancholy of the Edebiyat-ı Cedide (New Literature) movement, whose illustrated literary magazine *Servet-i fünun* (Treasury of Arts and Science), was published under the direction of the leading experimenter in modern European verse forms, Tevfik Fikret (1867–1915), from 1896 until its closure by the Sultan's censors in 1901—for mentioning the year of the French Revolution. Although the *Servet-i fünun* group was effectively silenced as a public forum, literary discussion continued at the Tuesday salons of the poet Nigâr Hanım (1856–1918), whose pensive love poetry had appeared in *Servet-i Fünun* under her pen name Uryan Kalb (Bare Heart); major works by Tevfik Fikret, reflecting a vehement cultural self-hatred and a newly found social concern—exemplified in *Sis* (Mist, 1901), a loathing depiction of Istanbul as a veiled whore in a tyrant's grip, and *Tarih-i kadim* (Ancient History, 1905), a contemptuous castigation of the bloody role of religion in human history—were circulated widely without publication. The elitist and cosmopolitan European orientation of the *Servet-i fünun* circle is particularly evident in the works of the master novelist Halit Ziya Uşaklıgil (1866–1945), whose *Mai ve siyah* (*The Blue and the Black*, 1897) depicts a young poet's intellectual and aesthetic struggles; *Aşk-ı memnu* (Forbidden Love, 1901), a triumph in the literary techniques of realism, paints a detailed portrait of the psychological causes and emotional consequences of adultery set in the lavish world of Ottoman villas on the Bosphorus. The prominence of the short-lived *Servet-i fünun* school and its successor, the *Fecr-i âti* (Dawn of the Future) literary group (1909–1911), augurs the importance of a recurrent, fundamental tension in the history of Turkish literature of the twentieth century between the literature of social commitment and that of aestheticism.

The Young Turk Revolution and the opening of the second constitional period (1908–1918) made room for the resurgence in literature of political themes, with debates over issues of cultural identity and social organzation now crystallizing around the positions identified as Westernist, Islamist, and Turkist. The Ottomanist position of the Tanzimat idealist Namık Kemal, who had called for the union of all Ottoman subjects under a constitutional monarchy, had been rendered nonviable by the emergence of nationalist separatist movements among the non-Muslim groups (*millets*) of the Empire; moreover, the territorial loss and atrocities inflicted on the civilian Muslim population of the Balkans in 1911 and 1912 lent urgency to the debate over the possibilities remaining for the survival of Turkish-speaking Muslims as a political or even social entity.

It is this context that explains the sudden emergence of politically motivated Islamic themes in literature and the vehemence of the dispute that arose between the most prominent of the Westernist poets, Tevfik Fikret, and the leading Islamist poet, Mehmet Âkif. Fikret, an Anglophile idealist, appeared ready to jettison the entire religious and cultural heritage of his forebears the better to embrace his vision of Western civilization as the embodiment of the high moral values of liberty and individual freedom of conscience from institutional restraints, whether governmental or religious. The more pragmatic Mehmet Âkif pointed to the colonialist designs and unprincipled behavior of the European powers in the Balkans, the Middle East, North Africa, and India. In his view, only the scientific and technological aspects of Western civilization were worthy of emulation. Material progress for the Muslim peoples of the world would be attained not through the inculcation of a Western mentality, but rather by a return to the originally progressive values of an authentic Islam, which could blossom again only by maintaining its roots and evolving from them.

The didactic tenor of the poetry in which such arguments were cast is well illustrated by Mehmet Âkif's

Address from the Pulpit of the Suleymaniye Mosque (Süleymaniye Kürsüsünde), a singularly important Islamist narrative of one thousand and two lines in rhyming couplets, employing the classical *aruz* meter yet maintaining a cadence close to that of everyday speech and a vocabulary accessible to the general populace. First published in 1912, this passionate exhortation to Ottoman Muslims to come to their senses is worth close consideration; not only does it provide vivid insights into the Islamist point of view at this criticial juncture, it also sets forth the essentials of an argument that reappears decades later in social-scientific critiques of modernization theories based on a Western model of development. The highlights of Âkif's argument will be paraphrased in some detail.

The setting for the address is established as the poet invites his reader to enter the massive sixteenth-century mosque of Süleyman the Magnificent and points out the structural features that make it an awe-inspiring testament to God's glory and to the engineering genius of its architect. Fortified by this reminder of past technological and artistic accomplishment, the poet and reader join a congregation of three thousand in hearing the prominent Muslim Tatar intellectual Abdürreşid İ brahim (1853–1943) deliver a blistering account of the conditions he had observed during travels throughout the Muslim world following the suppression of his underground printing press by Russian authorities. Degradation, stagnation, superstition, reactionary fanaticism, and brutal subjugation by foreign powers were to be matched only by the irresponsibility and incompetence of the Muslims' own educated elites, the Russified thinkers of Central Asia, and the Westernist intellectuals of Ottoman Istanbul. In Central Asia he found that the once great Islamic centers of scientific learning and discovery—Bukhara, home to the physician and philosopher Ibn Sīnā (980–1037), and Samarkand, site of the famous astronomical observatory of Uluğ Bey (1394–1449)—were now mired in such superstitious ignorance that an eclipse of the moon had brought forth thousands beating on drums in an effort to drive the devil away. More appalling still was the buffoonery and bigotry of local religious fanatics: whatever one might say would be damaging to religion; whatever one might think for the good of the people would be heretical innovation. Among the Muslims of China and Manchuria the speaker found that religion had been reduced to the sterile repetition of superstitious custom; surely the Qur'ān had not been revealed by God for use in the telling of fortunes! His travels offered several points of hope, however. Japan presented a model of successful adaptation of the technology of the West without compromise of cultural integrity. And in India, although his travels had been curtailed by colonial authorities, he was able to see that Muslim youth sent abroad to England received a fine education yet returned with their original values intact; such people would certainly regain their freedom one day.

It is important to note that the criticism of religious fanaticism and backwardness presented by Mehmet Âkif from an Islamist perspective coincides with the criticisms of Islamic practice characteristic of the Westernist stance championed by Tevfik Fikret. For the Islamists, however, instances of present degradation called for reform and recovery, whereas for the Westernists they rationalized rejection of religion as a mainstay of social life. It should also be noted that although both Mehmet Âkif and Abdürreşid İbrahim are regarded as major exponents of the Pan-Islamist movement, this monumental poem makes no call for the political union of Muslims worldwide. The emphasis is on Islamic unity within an Ottoman context, with the poet vehemently rejecting the newly emergent politics of national and ethnic division among the Ottoman Albanians, Arabs, and Turks: Muslims were members of the same family, and ethnic and nationalist divisions would undermine the very foundations of Islam. Weakened by internal division, they would lose their lands to foreign occupation and domination just as had Morocco, Tunisia, Algeria, and even Iran. The civilized West had closed its eyes to the brutal oppression of Muslim peoples and the persecution of Muslim intellectuals in Russia; would it hesitate to move in and swallow up the Ottoman lands in three bites?

This Islamist survey of conditions in Central, South, and East Asia is presented as an admonition, then, to Ottoman Muslims to remedy their own social ills before the last remaining independent Islamic homeland, their own, is trampled under foot. These ills are laid out for examination in the second half of the poem, which opens with an adage that would appear to reflect the poet's own background in veterinary medicine: "Get the diagnosis right and the remedy is easy!" Maintaining the guise of an outside expert in Islamic affairs speaking from the pulpit of the Süleymaniye Mosque, the poet asserts that the paralysis of the body politic has been caused by an estrangement between the intellectuals and the common people. The intellectuals think there is only one path of development—that of the West, which must be followed exactly: the West must be imitated in all social affairs and literary matters, or all is in vain. As for religion, it is the main obstacle to progress, and its fetters must be broken.

Âkif's recapitulation of the Westernist position, however blunt and angry, does capture an essential truth in indicating the degree to which Western-oriented Turkish intellectuals of the day had embraced the notion that a total transformation of their society on a Western model was in order, and that Islam was a primary obstacle to progress. This represents a significant departure from the stance of earlier Western-oriented Ottoman reformers such as Namık Kemal, who had refuted European characterizations of their religion as an inherently retrograde force in society. That Mehmet Âkif placed great value on education in the sciences and did not suffer the anguished sense of conflict between reason and faith, science and religion, that plagued so many of his contemporaries becomes clear as the poem continues. The speaker in the mosque pulpit asserts that the masses have become as reactionary as the intellectuals are rootless. "What is more," he declares, "the excesses of these would-be intellectuals have given the study of science and technology a bad name! They have provoked public opinion against it, and no real scientists are being produced! The few that have emerged are either feeble imitators who try to advance their careers with sophomoric attacks on religion or vague thinkers who get lost in theoretical speculation when it is the practical application of scientific knowledge that is urgently needed!"

The speaker's harshest criticism, however, is reserved for the cosmopolitan poets and novelists of the *Servet-i Fünun* and Fecr-i Âti circles, whom he finds not suitable to lead and guide the people. Had he the strength, he would kick them all out of the country and import Russian authors under contract—despite his emnity toward them—to write for the sake of society. Mehmet Âkif singles out Tevfik Fikret, for a particularly nasty swipe, deriding him, though without mention of his name, as a poet who "denounces God yet takes money as sexton for the Protestants." The gibe refers to the fact that Fikret lived in the Presbyterian missionary milieu of Robert College (the present Bosphorus University), where he had a position teaching Turkish and a comfortable residence close to campus. It reflects Âkif's estimation of Fikret as a hypocrite who could denounce religion in *Tarih-i kadim* (Ancient History) and scorn the need for religious dogma and ritual in *Halûk'un amentüsü* (Credo for My Son), yet accept a position at an educational institution run by men of the cloth. In calling Fikret a sexton, he implies that this genteel poet, whose condescension toward the poor is discernible in works such as *Ramazan sadakası* (Alms in the Month of Fasting), was himself looked down on by the foreigners whose society he kept and whose civilization he so admired.

Fikret's retort to this Islamist attack came in a poem of 1914, *Tarih-i kadim'e zeyl* (Addendum to Ancient History). In it he sets out the tenets of his own deist spirituality, casting aspersions on Âkif's orthodoxy but not providing a substantive rejoiner to the societal issues he raised in the *Address from the Pulpit,* the concluding sections of which reiterate that the path of progress must take different forms in different societies, and that the secret to a people's advancement lies within themselves. Just as Islam had fostered progressive change for the betterment of society in ages past, Âkif argues, so too could it now evolve in step with the attainments of the present century, though not without attending to the health of its roots. Fikret's failure to respond to the essential points of Âkif's argument is perhaps indicative of the fact that the Westernist-Islamist debate could end only in polarized deadlock as long as progress was taken to mean remaking society in the image of the Christian West.

It was left to the advocates of the Turkist position to bring the debate toward constructive resolution by forging the kinds of syntheses that were proposed by the social theoretician and poet Ziya Gökalp, in *Türkleşmek, İslamlaşmak, muasırlaşmak* (Turkification, Islamization, Modernization, 1918) and in *Türkçülüğün esasları* (The Principles of Turkism) published in 1923, the year the Turkish Republic was founded. In the latter work Gökalp addresses the issues of technological progress, cultural authenticity, and the alienation of social classes that had been raised from an Islamist perspective by Mehmet Âkif. He proposes their resolution through the concept of a reciprocal motion "toward the West" and "toward the people" within the framework of a dichotomy posited between civilization and culture, whereby a Western-educated elite would transmit modern civilization to the folk masses and in turn draw from them its own distinctively Turkish culture. In this formulation of a new Turkish social identity Islam takes its place as an element in the social fabric of a westernizing society. Religious knowledge, as an important ingredient of culture, was to be made directly accessible to all citizens through the translation of the Qur'ān into Turkish; this undertaking was accepted by Mehmet Âkif, but it was not brought to fruition.

The importance attached to the use of Turkish rather than Arabic in religious contexts was underscored by Gökalp in the opening lines of his poem *Vatan* (Homeland), which expresses longing for a country in which the call to prayer is made from the minaret in Turkish and in which the words of the daily ritual prayers can be understood by every villager. Gökalp's interest in encouraging the sense of a distinctively Turkish Islam finds expression in the poem *Din* (Religion), in which the basis of his own religious faith is declared in terms of the values of traditional Turkish mysticism as exemplified in the works of such *tekke* poets as Yunus Emre (d. 1320), who sought God as love within the human heart without the incentive hope of heaven and fear of hell. In seeking a Turkish grounding for Islam Gökalp pointed to the central importance in Turkish religious culture of the great fifteenth-century poem, the *Mevlid-i şerif* (Nativity Poem) by Süleyman Çelebi, a work exalting the birth and life of the Prophet Muḥammad; its performance *(mevlût)* in great mosques and ordinary homes has been shared by women and men over the centuries both at major holidays and in memory of the deceased, making it one of the most familiar and best-loved artistic expressions of Islamic faith in the Turkish language. The poem is of special significance for women because of the importance of the role played by Emine, the mother of the prophet Muḥammad, who describes in her own words the miracle of childbirth. It is possible that this inspirational poem, which includes Eve among those holy figures whose forehead is touched by the light of prophetic succession, both reflects and reinforces the profound respect for women and women's own sense of self-worth which many find characteristic of Turkish culture, despite the constraints of the gender subordination that the major monotheisms have legitimized.

Gökalp's interest in interpreting Islam as a religion stressing love of God rather than fear of divine retribution was shared by the prominent novelist, patriot, and feminist Halide Edib Adıvar (1884–1964); it both colored her speeches at the massive street demonstrations before the Mosques of Sultan Ahmet and Fatih during the Allied occupation of Istanbul and informed her novel *Sinekli bakkal* (The Clown and His Daughter, 1935–1936). The novel's main character, the granddaughter of an intolerant fire-and-brimstone imam, develops under the tutelage of a gentle dervish of the Mevlevî order from a talented reciter of the Qur'ān into an inspired and well-paid reciter of the *Mevlid-i şerif*.

Halide Edib's positive view of the values embodied in the Turkish traditions of Islamic mysticism was not, however, taken up by subsequent authors of major consequence. They instead followed the example set by Yakup Kadri Karaosmanoğlu (1889–1974) in his novel, *Nur Baba* (Father Divine, 1922) which depicts an urban Bektaşi (Ar., Bektāshī) dervish lodge as the site of unmitigated debauchery. Karaosmanoğlu's powerful image of Bektaşi decadence was in consonance with the secularist ideology of Turkey's charismatic leader Mustafa Kemal Atatürk (1880–1938), which resulted in the abolition of the caliphate (1924), the suppression of religious orders (1925), and the rejection of Islam as a state religion (1928). Karaosmanoğlu's negative characterization of an urban Bektaşi dervish was followed by equally forceful and repugnant depictions of religious figures in the rural context of his landmark novel *Yaban* (The Strange One, 1932), a work that signaled the emergence of anti-Islamic themes as a prominent feature of twentieth-century fiction and poetry as the competing ideologies of Kemalism and Marxism took control of a Turkish literary scene at odds politically, but at heart united in a value that is profoundly Islamic—a commitment to social justice.

[*See also* Ottoman Empire; Turkey; *and the biographies of Ersoy, Gökalp, Kemal, and Şinasi.*]

BIBLIOGRAPHY

Adıvar, Halide Edib. *The Turkish Ordeal: Being the Further Memoirs of Halide Edib*. New York and London, 1928. Intriguing literary work by a participant in the critical events between the end of World War I and the foundation of the Turkish Republic.

Adıvar, Halide Edib. *Memoirs of Halide Edib*. New York, 1972. Reprint edition of an important historical source covering the years 1885–1919, by a major novelist, nationalist, and feminist strongly influenced by her Muslim upbringing and American girls' school education.

Akyüz, Kenan. *Batı Tesirinde Türk Şiiri Antolojisi*. Ankara, 1970. Outstanding critical anthology of nineteenth- and twentieth-century poetry.

Andrews, Walter G. *Poetry's Voice, Society's Song: Ottoman Lyric Poetry*. Seattle, 1985. Analytic overview of an important Ottoman genre.

Atis, Sarah Moment. *Semantic Structuring in the Modern Turkish Short Story: An Analysis of the Dreams of Abdullah Efendi and Other Short Stories by Ahmet Hamdi Tanpınar*. Leiden, 1983. A concise overview of the history of twentieth-century Turkish literature is provided in the introduction.

Halman, Talat S. "Turkish Poetry." In *Princeton Encyclopedia of Po-*

etry and Poetics, edited by Alex Preminger et al., pp. 872–876. Princeton, 1974. The best general English-language survey of ancient, medieval, and modern Turkish poetry.

Halman, Talat S., ed. *Contemporary Turkish Literature: Fiction and Poetry*. London and Toronto, 1982. Important anthology that includes many previously translated but no longer accessible works.

Kaplan, Mehmet, et al. *Yeni Türk Edebiyatı Antolojisi*. Istanbul, 1988–. Multivolume series projected in ten volumes, the initial three of which provide a wealth of important literary materials culled from inaccessible contemporary periodicals from 1839 onward.

Meeker, Michael E. "The New Muslim Intellectuals in the Republic of Turkey." In *Islam in Modern Turkey: Religion, Politics, and Literature in a Secular State*, edited by Richard Tapper, pp. 189–219. London, 1991. Insightful discussion of three Islamist newspaper columnists and essayists.

Tanpınar, Ahmet Hamdi. *XIX. Asır Türk Edebiyatı Tarihi*. Istanbul, 1976. Remains the best basic survey of nineteenth-century Turkish literature.

SARAH G. MOMENT ATIS

TURKMENISTAN. The Turkmen tribes that converted to Islam during the period of the Seljuks have remained nominally Sunnī Muslims; however, many of their religious practices are strongly influenced by tribal and regional elements, which in turn reflect remnants of pre-Islamic beliefs. These elements—cults associated with holy places (*mukaddes yerleri*) and Ṣūfī saints (pirs), are characteristic of Turkmen Islam and inseparable from it. The Muslim reform movement that surfaced in Bukhara and other parts of the Ferghana Valley at the end of the nineteenth century wrought no changes in Turkmen Islam, nor, apparently, did the determined anti-Muslim efforts of more than seventy years of Soviet rule.

In the nineteenth century much of the region of present-day Turkmenistan was nominally subject to the Emirate of Bukhara; thus Turkmen Islamic institutions, especially the *sharīʿah courts*, were also under the administration of the *qazi-kalon*, who controlled all such courts in the emirate. In Bukhara's western *vilayets* (provincial administrations), including those regions of Turkmenistan under Bukhara's control, the highest religious authority was the *qazi*, who was subordinate to the *shaykh al-Islām;* the latter was second only to the *qazi-kalon*. On the local level, prayers and other functions were under the supervision of the mullah. In actuality, the lines of authority were not that clear: the Turkmens had, and have retained, a strong tribal-regional tradition, and the tribal structure and the Muslim structure on the local level had often coalesced. It is very common to find religious functionaries, such as the *mujavurs* (grave guardians), who are responsible for the maintenance of shrines specific to one or another tribe.

In addition to Bukhara's formalistic Islamic administration, Muslim Ṣūfī movements also carried authority. It is not uncommon for actual decisionmaking to be in the hands of Muslim religious orders such as the Yasawīyah and its offshoot the Khojagon, the Naqshbandīyah, or, further to the north, the Kubrawīyah. The Ṣūfī communities were under the control of an *ishan*, and their members are called *murids*. At present, the Naqshbandīyah is the most widespread in Turkmenistan; its practitioners are referred to colloquially as *kalandars*.

The Russian conquest of the Turkmens at Göktepe in 1880–1881 had no impact on Muslim practices in Turkmenistan. It was not until the imposition of Soviet authority in the mid-1920s that Turkmen Islam began to be affected. Soviet policy was then directed at separating church and state, nationalizing *waqf* holdings, and breaking Islam's financial power. The increasing effectiveness of Soviet atheistic and anti-Islamic propaganda also took a heavy toll; a seeming *coup de grâce* was administered during the Stalinist purges of the late 1930s, when almost the entire Muslim clergy was liquidated.

Until 1943–1944 Soviet Islam was nominally under the administrative and financial control of the Central Muslim Spiritual Administration in Ufa. In 1944, however, its functions were divided among four newly created spiritual administrations. Official Islam in Turkmenistan then became subject to the Spiritual Administration for Muslims of Central Asia, based in Tashkent, Uzbekistan. Subordinate to the Spiritual Administration was a council responsible for all administrative matters concerning official Islam. In addition, Religious Affairs Councils were established in each republic; these oversaw the adherence of all religious organs to party and state policy. In 1965 a Council of Religious Affairs was formed under the aegis of the USSR Council of Ministers. It had the same functions as the councils in the republics. One consequence of Soviet control over Islam was that by 1985 there were only four official mosques in all of Turkmenistan.

Muslim life in Turkmenistan, however, had little contact with official Soviet Islam; it centered around the tombs of Ṣūfī saints, Muslim graveyards, and holy places. An unofficial Muslim clergyman was referred to as a *mollasumak*, a derogatory term meaning "pseudo-mullah." Many of them were itinerant, traveling from village to village and from shrine to shrine. Muslim pirs, or saints, often had a number of shrines devoted to them. Among the active shrines are those dedicated to Agishan (sometimes called Zengi Baba), who is reputedly an ancestor of a clan of the Tekke federation; one is marked by a grave in Archman village in Krasnovodsk oblast and in Goymat village, near Göktepe, where he is identified with the Bekdash clan of the Yomut tribal federation. Shrines to Zengi Baba include a fortress near Sarygamysh and a number of medieval mausoleums in Bakherden Rayon, as well as shrines in Kopetdag and Bekdash. As a remnant of pre-Islamic tradition, Zengi Baba is also known as the patron saint of cattle. Other examples of the eclectic nature of the Turkmen shrines are those dedicated to Babagammar (sometimes Gammarbaba), including one near Kopetdag and another near Yolöten. According to folk tradition, Babagammar is also considered to be the pir of the *saz* and *dutar,* traditional musical instruments probably because of the presence at the shrines, present or past, of a sacred tree, the wood of which was used in making them. Other notable shrines and pilgrimage points at the present time include shrines surrounding the graves of Chopanata, Garababa, Gözlibaba, and Saragtbaba. As in the case of Zengibaba and Gammarbaba, these pirs often have multiple places said to be their burial sties.

After the Iranian Revolution the anti-Muslim campaign conducted by the Soviet authorities became more rigorous, though no more effective, than in the past. Since the Soviet Constitution guaranteed freedom of conscience, sanctions were generally applied primarily to alleged members of the Ṣūfī hierarchies: *murīd*s, dervishes, *kalendar*s, *walī*s, pirs, and *ishan*s. Soviet authorities, to avoid giving the impression that they were acting against Islam itself, punished these individuals for crimes unrelated to Islam, such as parasitism, drunkenness, and wife-beating. After 1981 *mollasumak*s and Ṣūfīs were sentenced to corrective labor in a camp established for that purpose near Neftezavodsk.

In the late 1980s the official attitude regarding all forms of religious belief in the USSR changed. Greater freedom of religious expression was permitted, and mosque construction or rehabilitation resumed. By June 1991 more than seventy mosques had opened in Turkmenistan. Hajji Nasrullah ibn Ibadullah, who had originally been appointed kazi-imam of Turkmenistan by the Spiritual Administration for Muslims of Central Asia in Tashkent, discussed in the mass media the advantages of integrating the *mollasumak*s into the official religious hierarchy, similar to processes already taking place in neighboring Uzbekistan. With the collapse of the Soviet Union, and thus the collapse of Soviet institutions such as the Spiritual Administrations, Hajji Nasrullah ibn Ibadullah, on 1 June 1992, registered the Kaziate Administration of the Muslims of Turkmenistan with the Turkmen Ministry of Justice. It received full juridical powers, in exchange for which law enforcement officials of the Ministry of Justice "maintain a working relationship with the religious representatives" (*Türkmenistan* [Ashkhabad], 3 June 1992, p. 3). At the same time, it is forbidden for a religious organization to register as a political party; hence, the influence in Turkmenistan or nongovernmental Muslim organizations, such as the Islamic Renaissance Party, is unknown.

BIBLIOGRAPHY

Atanyiazov, Soltansha. *Türkmenistanyng geografik atlarynyng düshündirishli sözlügi.* Ashgabat, 1980.

Nissman, David. "Iran and Soviet Islam." *Central Asian Survey* 2.4 (December 1983): 45–60.

DAVID NISSMAN

TWELVERS. *See* Ithnā ʿAsharīyah.

U

UGANDA. Islam entered what is today the small, landlocked Republic of Uganda in the nineteenth century from two directions: from the east through the present republic of Kenya, and from the north through Egypt and the Sudan. However, the boundaries of present-day Uganda were not stabilized until 1914. Since then Islam has remained one of the realities of the sociocultural life of this eastern African nation.

The precise date of Islam's introduction by Swahili and Arab traders from the east is in dispute. Some observers claim that Islam was introduced in the mid-nineteenth century, while others believe it came in the last quarter of the century. It is clear, however, that as early as 1930 there were already thousands of Muslims in Buganda. Their chief leader and patron was a former king of Buganda, Nuhu Mbogo. Today up to half of all the Muslims in Uganda are to be found in the central region of Buganda alone. In this part of Uganda the Shāfiʿī legal school predominates.

The entry of Islam into Uganda from the north occurred in the 1860s, when Khedive Ismāʿīl of Egypt sent a force, basically Muslim in composition, to occupy what is today northern Uganda as part of the Turco-Egyptian empire. The Mālikī legal school predominates among the Muslims in the north. Whatever the precise dates, Islam was virtually unknown in Uganda before the nineteenth century.

Islamization in Uganda was not accompanied by arabization like what occurred in North Africa. Very few Ugandan Muslims speak classical Arabic (although their formal prayers are uttered in that language), and none identify themselves as Arabs. However, the Islam that came via the Sudan was accompanied by an Arabic creole called Nubi, a language that was politically significant in the 1970s and is still spoken in many parts of Uganda.

Virtually all indigenous Ugandan Muslims are Sunnī, although in the period prior to 1972 there was a tiny community of non-Sunnīs, mostly from Muslim communities in South Asia. A few Ugandans have converted to the unorthodox Aḥmadīyah sect founded by Mirzā Ghulām Aḥmad in British colonial India.

Dependable statistical information about the various religious communities in Uganda remains elusive. According to the first national census, taken in 1959, the population of Muslims in Uganda was less than 6 percent of the nation. Unofficially, however, many believed and continue to believe that the actual number of Muslims in Uganda was larger than the 1959 and subsequent official censuses suggested. Nonetheless, it is clear that whether Muslims in that country comprised 5, 10, or even 15 percent of the population, they were obviously vastly outnumbered by Ugandan Christians. According to the United Nations, by 1987 Uganda's population stood at 16 million; it was projected to reach 24 million by the year 2000.

Like many other African countries, Uganda has a triple religious heritage of indigenous African religions, Islam, and Christianity. Islam was the first to arrive of the two major immigrant Semitic monotheistic religions. The introduction of Christianity with British colonial rule in Buganda early in the twentieth century presented Islam with a serious rival. British rule naturally favored and facilitated the spread of Christianity; since colonial days political power has resided in Christian hands. Independent since 1962, postcolonial Uganda has consistently been ruled by Christians—almost all Protestants rather than Catholics—except for the Idi Amin years (1971–1979).

In Amin's Uganda Islam was clearly on the ascendant. In this period many non-Muslims in the country converted to Islam, partly because the Islamic card promised greater access to influence and affluence. Amin surrounded himself increasingly with fellow Muslims, thus substantiating the belief that it paid to be a Muslim. For example, in 1971 Amin and a veteran Muganda politician, Abubaker Mayanja, were the only Muslims in his first cabinet. This contrasted sharply with the fourteen

Muslims in a cabinet of twenty-one ministers in 1977, two years before Amin's overthrow.

Uganda joined the Organization of the Islamic Conference (OIC) in the early 1970s and was fully represented at the OIC Summit Conference in Lahore, Pakistan, in 1974 [*see* Organization of the Islamic Conference]. The 1970s generally were a period when Islam was politically significant in Uganda. Since then it has been on the defensive, but there are several Muslims who remain politically conspicuous and influential. The Uganda Muslim Supreme Council headed by a chief *kadhi* (Ar., *qāḍī*) and established in the 1970s still exists. It is Uganda's main link with the worldwide *ummah* (Islamic community). The Uganda Muslim Students Association (UMSA) was also created in the 1970s to coordinate the activities of Muslim youths.

There are hundreds of mosques scattered across the country. The Qurʾān is widely read and is available in translation in at least two indigenous African languages, Kiswahili and Luganda.

Hundreds of Ugandan Muslims participate in the *ḥajj* to Mecca and Medina annually. The other major tenets of Islam are also widely followed, although not all Muslims perform the five daily prayers obligatory for practicing believers. The Islamic rules of diet and abstinence from alcohol are kept, as is fasting during the holy month of Ramaḍān, and afterward, ʿĪd al-Fiṭr. Over the years many Ugandan Muslims have adopted Muslim dress, culture, and cuisine. Male circumcision is almost universal. *Sharīʿah* is followed selectively and primarily in the private domain (marriage, divorce, inheritance, etc.). Islamic education is carried out in mosques and in a variety of Muslim institutions in the country. Today Uganda boasts a Muslim university funded by the Islamic Development Bank in Jeddah, an affiliate of the OIC. Located in the eastern city of Mbale not far from the border with Kenya, the university is still in its infancy but is likely to make a major contribution to Islamic life and the general education of Ugandan Muslims in the years ahead.

Fridays are no longer a holiday in post-Amin Uganda, but many Muslims perform the Jumuʿah prayer and both ʿĪd al-Fiṭr and ʿĪd al-Ḥajj remain national holidays.

BIBLIOGRAPHY

Conn, Harvie M. "Islam in East Africa: An Overview." *Islamic Studies* 17 (1978): 75–91.

Harries, Lyndon. *Islam in East Africa*. London, 1954.

Kasozi, A. B. K. *The Spread of Islam in Uganda*. Nairobi, 1986.

Kettani, M. Ali. "Muslim East Africa: An Over-View." *Journal Institute of Muslim Minority Affairs* (Jeddah) 14.1–2 (1982): 104–119.

Kiggundu, Suleiman I., and Isa K. K. Lukwago. "The Status of the Muslim Community in Uganda." *Journal Institute of Muslim Minority Affairs* (Jeddah) 14.1–2 (1982): 120–132.

King, N., A. B. K. Kasozi, and Arye Oded. *Islam and the Confluence of Religions in Uganda, 1840–1966*. Tallahassee, 1973.

Kokole, Omari H. "The 'Nubians' of East Africa: Muslim Club or African 'Tribe'? The View from Within." *Journal Institute of Muslim Minority Affairs* (Jeddah) 6.2 (July 1985): 420–448.

Kyewalyanga, Francis-Xavier S. *Traditional Religion, Custom, and Christianity in East Africa as Illustrated by the Ganda, with Reference to other African Cultures (Acholi, Banyarwanda, Chagga, Gikuyu, Luo, Masai, Sukuma, Tharaka, etc. . . .) and Reference to Islam.* Hohenschaftlarn, Germany, 1976.

Oded, Arye. *Islam in Uganda: Islamization through a Centralized State in Pre-Colonial Africa*. New York and Jerusalem, 1974.

Oded, Arye. "A Bibliographic Essay on the History of Islam in Uganda." *Current Bibliography on African Affairs* 8.1 (1975): 54–63.

Owusu-Ansah, D. "The State and Islamization in Nineteenth-Century Africa: Buganda Absolutism versus Asante Constitutionalism." *Journal Institute of Muslim Minority Affairs* 8 (1987): 132–143.

Prunier, Gérard. "L'Islam ougandais depuis l'indépendance, 1962–1986." *Islam et Sociétés au Sud du Sahara* 1 (1987): 49–54.

Rowe, John A. "Islam under Idi Amin: A Case of Déjà Vu?" In *Uganda Now: Between Decay and Development*, edited by Holger Bernt Hansen and Michael Twaddle, pp. 267–279. Athens, Ohio, 1988.

Soghayroun, Ibrahim El-Zein. *The Sudanese Muslim Factor in Uganda*. Khartoum, 1981.

Twaddle, Michael. "The Emergence of Politico-Religious Groupings in Late Nineteenth-Century Buganda." *Journal of African History* 29.1 (1988): 81–92.

OMARI H. KOKOLE

ʿULAMĀʾ. [*This entry comprises articles on religious scholars in the two main branches of Islam.*]

Sunnī ʿUlamāʾ

The Arabic word *ʿulamāʾ* is the plural of *ʿālim,* literally "man of knowledge." The opposite of *ʿilm* ("knowledge") is *jahl* ("ignorance"). In the Qurʾān both terms are frequently used in connection with knowledge of that which was revealed to the Prophet, or knowledge of God. Belief in God is *ʿilm,* so that the *ʿālim* is the believer; disbelief is *jahl,* so that the truly ignorant person is the one who does not believe in God. By implication, one is an *ʿālim* on account of knowledge of particular religious knowledge (the Qurʾān, the *ḥadīth,* and *fiqh* or religious law); and it has always been expected that the *ʿālim* embody the qualities expected of one who believes in God and practices Islam.

This textual background has always lent the term connotations of specifically religious knowledge, either in the sense of gnosis or in the sense of knowledge of exoteric religious law. In the earliest periods of Islamic history, *ʿulamāʾ* were those who had knowledge of specifically religious sciences. Auxiliary sciences, such as knowledge of pre-Islamic Arabic poetry, were seen as important but only as an aid to understanding the Qurʾān. The translation of works of Greek scholarship during Maʾmūn al-Rashīd's reign (813–833) accorded a serious challenge to this unified conception of knowledge. However, despite heated initial debate about the utility of this knowledge, it was the *ʿulamāʾ* who ended up becoming its guardians.

Thus, on the eve of the period of colonial domination of much of the Islamic world in the nineteenth century, a single set of institutions provided basic education in Islamic societies. One could assume a basic course of study including the Qurʾān, Qurʾānic exegesis *(tafsīr)*, *ḥadīth*, religious law, and disciplines like medicine, astronomy, geometry, natural philosophy, rhetoric, and logic for anyone who claimed to be educated. Beyond this, the specialist in Islamic jurisprudence, the teacher of Qurʾānic exegesis, the physician, the astronomer, or the geometrician would each have some additional specialist knowledge. The title *ʿālim*, however, would be applied to one who had specialized in the religious sciences.

Colonial domination constructed a parallel meaning for education. Knowledge of the colonizer's language became a prerequisite for one sense in which the word "educated" could be used. This split in meaning is reflected in modern Arabic, where the word "scientist" is also translated as *ʿālim*. Ironically, it now becomes possible for the word *ʿālim* to be applied to someone who does not even know of the religion of Islam, much less have a knowledge of the religious disciplines.

The colonial reorganization of society introduced a similar discontinuity in the function of the *ʿulamāʾ* in Muslim communities. For example, Western medicine, legal institutions, and administrative structures became an alternative to indigenous systems of medical treatment, legal redress, and governance. A class of professional physicians, lawyers, and administrators emerged who had no effective allegiance or connection to the classical system of education and its personnel. From the perspective of the colonized, the legal system was as much a "religious" institution as was a school for teaching Qurʾānic exegesis. For the colonizing powers, however, the replacement of indigenous institutions had to stop when it came to what was peculiarly "religious" in their own eyes. Thus during colonial rule the domain of operation of the *ʿulamāʾ* became confined to the mosque and the *madrasah*.

The Mosque. Although there is no custom or ritual within Islamic practice for which one needs any particular set of credentials, it is a general rule that the most knowledgeable among a group of people should lead the prayers. Thus a typical function that an *ʿālim* would perform today is that of imam of a mosque. As imam he leads daily prayers, delivers the Friday sermon, and teaches the children in the neighborhood the basics of Islamic law along with Qurʾānic recitation and sometimes writing and calligraphy. He may also be called upon on occasions of birth, death, and marriage for prayers or for help in the performance of the rituals involved.

The more rural the setting, the more likely it is that these functions would be seen rigidly as the functions of the imam of the mosque; in more urban areas or where there is more awareness of Islamic law, it is not uncommon for any individual familiar with a ritual to perform it. Similarly, the more rural the setting, the more likely it is that the imam is *not* an *ʿālim* in the sense of having completed the usual course of study. Nevertheless, he would be perceived as the only person in the area with sufficient familiarity with the rituals, or with sufficient authority in the eyes of the audience, to be able to perform these rituals.

The Madrasah. The two common modes of study in the precolonial period were tutelage with individual scholars, or attendance at a *madrasah* such as the Mustanṣirīyah in Baghdad, the Niẓāmīyah in Baghdad, or al-Azhar in Cairo. The funding of such institutions and their degree of dependence on the state (or on other donors) has varied over time and place. A typical arrangement would involve a grant of land or other income-yielding property to the *madrasah* in perpetuity *(waqf)*. Such an arrangement would yield maximum freedom. On the other end of the scale would be a situation where the state or a nobleman would directly assume the responsibility of meeting the expenses of a *madrasah*.

In modern times too the patronage of *madrasah*s has taken different courses. The colonizers had been diffident in interfering with what they saw as local religious institutions; the new rulers were Muslim and had no such qualms. Thus in some Muslim countries many *madrasahs* ended up being completely state-funded; some even underwent radical curricular changes under government intervention. In other areas, during the colonial period some *madrasahs* had been able to find alternative funding in the form of small private donations from the public at large. Such *madrasahs* clung strongly to the freedom they had been able to achieve even when the colonial rulers left and were replaced with Muslim ones.

As with funding, the nature of the curriculum varies from region to region. In some places the classical curriculum has been modified to the degree that it is almost indistinguishable from the curriculum of a modern Western university. At the other end of the spectrum are the *madrasahs* that have tried to maintain the classical curriculum as much as possible. As indigenous social institutions have been replaced by imported ones, the curricula of these *madrasahs* have become more and more focused on particularly religious sciences. Medicine, astronomy, and geometry are studied only superficially if at all. Logic and natural philosophy have fared only a little better. The literary sciences receive better coverage because they are aids to understanding and interpreting the Qurʾān and the *ḥadīth*. The focus of study has become the Qurʾān, the *ḥadīth*, Islamic jurisprudence *(fiqh)*, and other disciplines necessary for their understanding.

Along with teaching, larger *madrasahs* also typically provide a service of *fatwā*—responsa to individuals who would like to know their religious obligation regarding specific situations in which they find themselves in their daily life. *Fatwā* is applied law: everyone can read the rules, but only a *muftī* is qualified to examine a situation and identify which rules apply and how much weight potentially conflicting rules should be accorded. Again, the ability to offer *fatwā* is a matter of training and not a result of any esoteric knowledge. Thus it is quite acceptable to obtain a *fatwā* from one *mufti* and forward it to a second *muftī* for his comments.

The redefinition of "education" discussed above has provided Islamic societies a course of intellectual discipline very different from that of the traditional *ʿulamāʾ*. In addition, because of the political ascendancy of those who subscribe to this new style of intellectual discipline, it has not been possible for the *ʿulamāʾ* simply to ignore it. In the past few decades educational institutions have developed in Muslim countries that base themselves quite consciously on Western models but take upon themselves the teaching and study of the specifically religious sciences. These are precisely the domains the colonizers had been hesitant to approach. Thus a group of people has emerged who have not gone through the educational institutions and disciplines of the classical *ʿulamāʾ*, but who also lay claim to knowledge of the Qurʾān, *ḥadīth*, and Islamic law. Much of the sometimes bewildering array of opinion on Islam and on what is Islamic results from the attempts of this new group of so-called *ʿulamāʾ* to wrest interpretative authority from the traditional *ʿulamāʾ*.

Despite the changed circumstances and the variety of approaches to knowledge in Muslim communities, the authority of the traditional *ʿulamāʾ* remains quite strong. Particularly in issues relating to the textual sources of Islam, the *ʿulamāʾ* are recognized as the final arbiters. And since there are many places in the Islamic world where the control of the government has never really been complete, the local *ʿālim* continues to be sought out as judge, arbiter, and administrator.

[*See also* Fatwā; Ḥadīth; Madrasah; Mosque, *article on* The Mosque in Education; Muftī.]

BIBLIOGRAPHY

I have described the *ʿulamāʾ* in the context of a struggle in Muslim countries over the definition of knowledge and what it means to be educated. The works in Western languages listed below implicitly refuse to acknowledge that the *ʿulamāʾ* as a phenomenon of Muslim societies represent a complete indigenous vision of knowledge and of what it means to be educated which is an alternative to the vision of knowledge and education of the Western colonizer. As such, these studies participate in the struggle over the definition of knowledge and education on the side of the colonizers. One would want to round out the picture by presenting some of the polemical works written by *ʿulamāʾ* in this struggle. Unfortunately the *ʿulamāʾ* write either in Arabic or their indigenous languages. I cite the following single Urdu work as an example of the perspective of the *ʿulamāʾ* on this redefinition: Manāẓir Aḥsan Gīlānī, *Pāk va Hind Men̲ Musalmānon̲ kā niẓām-e taʿlīm va tarbiyat* (Lahore, n.d.), two vols. in one.

Ahmed, Al-Haj Moinuddin. *Ulama: The Boon and Bane of Islamic Society*. New Delhi, 1990. Criticism of the failures of the *ʿulamāʾ* to lead Muslim societies into modernization.

Antoun, Richard T. *Muslim Preacher in the Modern World: A Jordanian Case Study in Comparative Perspective*. Princeton, 1989. Insightful study of the political roles of the *ʿulamāʾ* in Jordan, with particular reference to the mosque sermons they deliver.

Baer, Gabriel, ed. "The ʿUlamaʾ in Modern History," special issue, *Asian and African Studies* (Jerusalem) 7 (1971). Deals with Sunnī authorities in the Ottoman Empire, Syria, Sudan, Palestine, India, Egypt, and the Maghrib.

Boulares, Habib. *Islam: The Fear and the Hope*. London, 1990. Former Tunisian minister of culture offers a polemic, distinguishing between "the power of the *ʿulamāʾ*" and "the *ʿulamāʾ* of power."

Hassan, Muhammad Kamal. *Muslim Intellectual Responses to 'New Order' Modernization in Indonesia*. Kuala Lumpur, 1982. Focuses on the attitudes of the Indonesian *ʿulamāʾ* to political developments.

Keddie, Nikki R., ed. *Scholars, Saints, and Sufis: Muslim Religious Institutions Since 1500*. Berkeley, 1972. Classic work, which, in Part I, treats various roles of the *ʿulamāʾ* from the Ottoman period to mid-twentieth-century Egypt and Pakistan.

Kepel, Gilles and Yann Richard, eds. *Intellectuels et militants de l'Islam contemporain*. Paris, 1990. In Part I, a useful discussion of the *ʿulamāʾ* in Morocco and Oman.

Levtzion, Nehemia. "Sociopolitical Roles of Muslim Clerics and Scholars in West Africa," in *Comparative Social Dynamics*, edited by Erik Cohen, Moshe Lissak, and Uri Almagor, pp. 95–107. Boulder, 1985.

Qureshi, M. Naeem. "The ʿUlamaʾ of British India and the Hijrat of 1920." *Modern Asian Studies*, 13.1 (1979): 41–59. Analyses importance of religious officials at time of Khilāfat movement agitation in South Asia and the migration of thousands of Indian Muslims to Afghanistan.

Rahman, Fazlur. *Islam and Modernity: Transformation of an Intellectual Tradition*. Chicago, 1982. Modernist Muslim views of how Islamic traditions, and their guardians, may evolve over time.

Roy, Olivier. "Intellectuels et Ulema dans La Resistance Afghane," issue on "L'Islamisme en effervescence," *Peuples Meditérranéens* 21 (October–December 1982): 129–151.

IFTIKHAR ZAMAN

Shīʿī ʿUlamāʾ

Although the Shīʿī *ʿulamāʾ* (professional clergy) have performed many of the same functions undertaken by their Sunnī counterparts, their political impact on society in the modern period has been more direct and incisive. The Iranian Revolution of 1979 is but the latest example of the assertiveness of the Shīʿī *ʿulamāʾ* in the sociopolitical domain during the past two centuries. The reasons for this clerical activism are complex, being related partly to doctrinal issues of juristic authority in Shiism and partly to the set of relationships established by Shīʿī clergymen with their followers independent of doctrinal matters. Recent research on the long-term political quietism of Shīʿī clergymen until the late nineteenth century has stressed that when clerical activism occurred, it was motivated by a variety of different, even conflicting, impulses. It is a mistake, therefore, to suggest a direct correspondence between Shiism and radical or revolutionary behavior.

Dating the rise of the Shīʿī *ʿulamāʾ* as a corporate stratum in a Weberian sense is not easy to do. We know that Shiism, or the veneration of ʿAlī ibn Abī Ṭālib (d. 661) and the family of the Prophet, arose in Kufa, Iraq. It spread to Iran in the lifetime or shortly thereafter of ʿAlī's son, Muḥammad ibn al-Ḥanafīyah (d. 700). Manifested in the Kaysānīyah and Hāshimīyah movements, early Shiism in Iraq and Iran was radically sectarian. When Shīʿī movements ascended under the banner of Abū Muslim (d. 753), a leader of the ʿAbbāsid rebellion against the Umayyads, it appeared that Shiism would triumph throughout the Islamic territories. However, the ʿAbbāsid rulers murdered Abū Muslim and embraced Sunnism, thus limiting Shiism to a heterodox tendency.

The founder of Shīʿī law was the fifth imam, Muḥammad al-Bāqir (d. 733), a grandson of Imam Ḥusayn ibn ʿAlī (d. 680), to whom Kufans had turned increasingly for rulings on religious matters. However, it was al-Bāqir's son, the sixth imam, Jaʿfar al-Ṣādiq (d. 765), who systematized Shīʿī law, and it is perhaps by his time that an appreciable body of *rāwī*s ("transmitters") of the sayings of the Shīʿī imams emerged. Still, one could hardly speak of the Shīʿī *ʿulamāʾ* as a genuine clerical estate at this time, exhibiting the common social customs, behavior, discourse, and occupational traits necessary for such a sodality.

The town of Qom (Qumm) became the center of Iranian Shiism in the half-century after the ʿAbbāsid conquest of 749. It arose to special prominence as the center of Twelver Shiism (Ithnā ʿAsharīyah). Its status was secured by the fact that so many transmitters of the imams' sayings, as cited by the authoritative codices of Muḥammad ibn Yaʿqūb al-Kulaynī (d. 941) and Abū Jaʿfar Muḥammad ibn Bābawayh (d. 991), were men from Qom. Later compilers of Shīʿī *ḥadīth*s, scholars of the school of Baghdad such as Shaykh al-Mufīd (d. 1022), his student, Sharif al-Murtaḍā ʿAlam al-Hudā (d. 1044), and Shaykh al-Ṭāʾifah Ṭūsī (d. 1067), were to break with the Qom traditionists by embracing forms of rationalism known as Muʿtazilah. The Baghdad school of Shīʿī *ʿulamāʾ* (for a body of scholars with identifiable professional characteristics had emerged by the tenth century) condemned the traditionism of Qom and, in the case of the sharif al-Murtaḍā, went as far as to hold that only reason could discover the principles of faith. Increasingly, the traditionists were seen as defending anthropomorphic interpretations of Allāh and predestinarianism, while the Baghdad scholars championed free will. The Baghdad school held that Allāh did not have knowledge of the actions of human beings before they acted; they maintained that Allāh does not know a thing before he wills or creates it; and they stressed that Allāh's knowledge of the universe as well as the universe itself are mutable.

Acting as a bridge between the Baghdad school and modern doctrine are the works of the medieval scholars Naṣīr al-Dīn Ṭūsī (1201–1274); his student, ʿAllāmah ibn al-Muṭahhar al-Ḥillī (1250–1325), author of numerous works on Shīʿī dogma and practice, including *Al-bāb al-ḥādī ʿashar* [*see the biography of Ḥillī*]; and Nadīm al-Dīn Abū al-Qāsim Jaʿfar ibn al-Ḥasan ibn Yaḥyā al-Muḥaqqiq al-Ḥillī (1240–1326), whose *Sharāʾiʿ al-Islām* is perhaps to this day the authoritative work on Shīʿī law. In general, one can say that the Shīʿī *ʿulamāʾ* continued to adhere firmly to Muʿtazilī notions of the role of human reason in matters of belief.

With the victory of the Ṣafavids in 1501, the Shīʿī *ʿulamāʾ* achieved greater stature than before. The Ṣafavid shahs, state centralizers who were determined to establish Shiism in Iran in place of the prevailing Sunnī doctrines, found it necessary to import Shīʿī *mujtahids* from Lebanon and Bahrain. [*See* Ṣafavid Dynasty.] Qom was not a source of supply for the Ṣafavids, since the center at Qom had pretty much disintegrated in the eleventh century in the wake of repeated attacks by the Baghdad school, and it had never really recovered. Some of these *mujtahids* accepted important posts in the state administration, although others maintained an aloofness from political matters. The important *ʿulamāʾ* in this period are too numerous to mention individually, although Muḥammad Bāqir al-Majlisī (d. 1699) stands out for his attack on certain mystical and theosophic tendencies in Shiism that he considered elitist. He was, however, careful to uphold the veneration of the imams, which in many respects is the basis for those mystical tendencies. [*See the biography of Majlisī.*]

Around the time of al-Majlisī's death, a furious doctrinal struggle occurred among the Shīʿī *ʿulamāʾ*, reminiscent of the conflicts of the Qom and Baghdad schools centuries earlier, over the relative importance of the traditions and of human reason. Known as the Akhbārī-Uṣūlī dispute, it was resolved in the defeat of the traditionists and the upholding of the principle of *ijtihād* (independent reasoning to ascertain a legal rule). This important doctrinal victory eventually served those who advocated clerical engagement in social issues. Arguing that the clergy as a body were *al-wakālah al-ʿāmmah* ("general agents") of the Hidden Imam, the jurists seemed to imply that they had been bequeathed a certain residue of the imam's *wilāyah* (authority). [*See* Akhbārīyah; Uṣūlīyah; Wakālah al-ʿĀmmah, al-.]

These doctrinal innovations are important in the light of the achievement of Imam Jaʿfar al-Sadiq generations earlier. According to the doctrine of the imamate, central to Shiism, the imams alone are the legitimate rulers. However, Jaʿfar had directed his followers to desist from any revolutionary activity aimed at restoring legitimate rule to their imams, insisting that at some point an imam would "rise up" *(al-qāʾim)* and reestablish rightful rule. Indeed, so committed was Jaʿfar to this position that he insisted his followers engage in *taqīyah* (pious dissimulation) to protect the Shīʿī community from being destroyed by the Sunnī rulers. Accordingly, the Uṣūlī victory should be seen as a step away from Jaʿfar's quietism, but not yet toward the revolutionary clericalism of Ayatollah Ruhollah al-Musavi Khomeini (1902–1989) two centuries later.

As European imperialism became pervasive in nineteenth-century Iran, the clergy began to participate in society as an autonomous social force. Whereas the Ṣafavid rulers had basically coopted the *ʿulamāʾ*, or else managed to ignore them, the Qājār shahs (1785/97–1925) found themselves subject to the clergy's criticism over foreign concessions, tax policies, loans, territorial losses, and, at times, autocratic conduct. [*See* Qājār Dynasty.]

Perhaps the most important nineteenth-century clergymen were Shaykh Murtaḍā Anṣārī (d. 1864) and Mīrzā Ḥasan Shīrāzī (d. 1896). Anṣārī's strong vindication of Uṣūlī doctrine found its manifestation in the principle that the clergy as a group were vested with a modicum of the imam's authority *(vilāyat-i iʿtibārī)*. This privileged them to be custodians of the infirm, the needy, widows, and orphans and to supervise expenditures on religious matters, including the upkeep of the *sayyids* (Muslims of noble lineage), mosques, shrines, and *waqfs* (mortmain bequests). Beyond this, a new institution known as *marjaʿīyat al-taqlīd* (source or repository of emulation) had come into existence. Shīʿīs were called on to identify a distinguished clergyman, a *marjaʿ al-taqlīd,* whose teachings in matters of ritual they would follow. Such a development institutionalized a special relationship between the highest-ranking clergymen and their followers and was to provide the basis for social mobilization and novel collective protest. The establishment of the principle of *marjaʿīyat al-taqlīd* followed closely on the victory of the advocates of *ijtihād* in the late eighteenth century. Because the boundary line between ritual and sociopolitical matters was not always clear, these twin occurrences manifestly enhanced the top clergy's influence.

A clear example of this is provided by the *fatwā* (religious opinion) associated with Mīrzā Ḥasan al-Shīrāzī against the shah's grant of the tobacco monopoly to a British subject in the early 1890s. Although argued on narrow grounds that tobacco is a personal item whose handling by an infidel renders it ritually unclean, the *fatwā* had enormous political significance, because it mobilized thousands in protest, led to the cancellation of the concession, and led to a crisis between the British and Iranian governments.

For all their increasing activism, the Shiᶜi *ᶜulamā'* did not then possess an institutional church in the Western sense. There was no curia, no ecclesiastical body, no pope, no college of cardinals, no mechanism to select the leadership, no machinery of decision making, rule, or enforcement. Yet, it is clear that by the end of the nineteenth century, the Shīᶜī clergy in Iran were becoming confident that their organization, *sāzmān-i rūḥānīyat* (the religious institution), was a credible force on the stage of national politics. Adding to their power was the fact the several *marjaᶜ al-taqlīd*s were financially independent of the government. Although the amount of funds they received from their supporters in the population varied from year to year, this autonomy permitted them to stake out independent positions and insulated them from government control.

The Shīᶜī *ᶜulamā'* in the modern period did not, of course, have identical or even similar views on such matters as government, administration, public policies, social stratification, or a whole range of issues in the realm of *al-dunyā* (worldly matters). Even in some of the most spirited undertakings by the clergy in modern Iranian history—such as the Constitutional Revolution of 1905–1909, the oil crisis of 1951–1953, the civil disturbances of 1960–1963, and the Iranian Revolution of 1979—clergymen spoke with a variety of voices and behaved in highly variegated ways. In short, the Shīᶜī *ᶜulamā'* are not a monolithic stratum, and its members embody a variety of ideal and material interests.

The doctrinal innovations of Ayatollah Khomeini altered the basic understandings of the role of the clergy. Building on the achievements of Anṣārī regarding the *wilāyah* of the imams and clergy prerogatives, Khomeini argued in his book *The Mandate of the Jurist* (1970) that the clergy was entitled to rule. This radical interpretation meant that clergymen should not content themselves with giving advice to rulers, a position with which he had publicly identified in his book *Kashf al-asrār* (Revealing the Secrets, 1941). His new line was that jurists had the duty not only to give their advice but actually to rule. Since such rule was merely a matter of implementing *sharīᶜah* (holy law), this line of thinking did not appear to him to break with classical teachings. But a number of his colleagues rejected his reinterpretation of the doctrine of the imamate, seeing in it unacceptable encroachments on the substantive *wilāyah* of the imams.

It might be that Khomeini's achievement in reinterpreting the doctrine, as well as leading the revolutionary forces in the Iranian Revolution of 1979, has led to the creation of something resembling a Shīᶜī "church." For the centralization that has occurred in the religious institution in Iran is unprecedented, and actions have been undertaken that resemble patterns in the ecclesiastical church tradition familiar in the West. For example, in 1982, Khomeini encouraged the "defrocking" and "excommunication" of his chief rival, Ayatollah Muḥammad Kāẓim Sharīᶜatmadārī (d. 1986), although no machinery for this has ever existed in Islam. Other trends, such as centralized control over budgets, appointments in the professoriate, curricula in the seminaries, the creation of religious militias, monopolizing the representation of interests, and mounting a *Kulturkampf* in the realm of the arts, the family, and other social issues tell of the growing tendency to create an "Islamic episcopacy" in Iran.

The Iranian Constitution of 1979 specifically mentions Khomeini several times, as the *faqīh* (top jurist) endowed with the imam's *wilāyah,* thereby extending to him extraordinary powers. Moreover, Khomeini's practice of issuing authoritative *fatwā*s, obedience to which is made compulsory, comes close to endowing the top jurist with powers not dissimilar to those of the pope of the Catholic church. After all, compliance with a particular cleric's *fatwā*s in the past had not been mandatory. In late 1987 and early 1988 Khomeini wrote two *fatwā*s in which he declared that everyone had to obey the commands of the state, because it was now an Islamic system. Even if the state commanded a halt to prayer and suspended the pilgrimage, two cardinal features of Islam, he wrote, its orders required unhesitating obedience. These *fatwā*s perhaps represented the furthest elaboration of clerical "caesaropapism."

After Khomeini's death in 1989, the Iranian regime retreated slightly from these trends by emphasizing the position of *rahbar* (leader) and declaring that the leader did not have to be a *marjaᶜ al-taqlīd*. Khomeini's successor as *rahbar,* Sayyid ᶜAli Khamene'i, who was not even an ayatollah at the time of his appointment, could not pretend to have the status of *marjaᶜ al-taqlīd,* although the press tried in a short-lived and desultory campaign to endow him with it. Hence, the regime declared that it was not even necessary for the political system in Iran to be led by an individual of such high rank, preference being given for a leader with the requisite politico-administrative skills. Although this development created the possibility of a reversion to a situation in which power is diffused among several duly acknowledged *marjaᶜ al-taqlīds* in the Shīᶜī community, developments toward centralization have proceeded too far in Iran for them to suddenly lapse with Khomeini's death. Moreover, with the deaths in 1992–1993 of three grand ayatollahs (Abū al-Qāsim Khūʼī, Shihāb al-Dīn Marᶜashī Najafī, and Muḥammad Riẕā Gulpaygānī) the leader of the judicial branch of government, Ayatollah Muḥammad Yazdī, made several speeches in December 1993 in which he tried once again to advance Khameneʼi's candidacy as *marjaᶜ al-taqlīd*. If he succeeds, it will set a precedent, since heretofore individuals have attained this status only through acclamation of the people.

In other countries with large Shīᶜī populations, such as Pakistan, Afghanistan, Lebanon, Kuwait, and Iraq, the trends are less clear-cut. Nowhere outside Iran have the implications of the eighteenth- and nineteenth-century developments in Ithnā ᶜAsharī Shiism been followed through to the conclusions that were reached in Iran after the 1979 Revolution. The official Shīᶜī clergy is under siege in Iraq, whereas in the other countries it must either accommodate itself to the demands of other confessional groups (as in Lebanon) or acknowledge its minoritarian status in the larger Sunnī world in which it finds itself. But even in these countries, ruling regimes will likely face continuing challenges at the hands of the Shīᶜī *ᶜulamāʼ*, who will no longer be as quietist as they have been in the past.

[*See also* Ayatollah; Fatwā, *article on* Modern Usage; Iran; Ithnā ᶜAsharīyah; Marjaᶜ al-Taqlīd; Shīᶜī Islam; *and* Wilāyat al-Faqīh.]

BIBLIOGRAPHY

Akhavi, Shahrough. *Religion and Politics in Contemporary Iran: Clergy-State Relations in the Pahlavī Period*. Albany, N.Y., 1980. Political history of the clergy and the relationship to the modernizing Pahlavi state.

Algar, Hamid. *Religion and State in Iran, 1785–1906*. Berkeley, 1969. Detailed discussion of historical and doctrinal trends in Shiism in the Qājār era, with emphasis on the clergy as defenders against the despotism of the rulers.

Arjomand, Said Amir. *The Shadow of God and the Hidden Imam*. Chicago and London, 1984. Comprehensive discussion of Ithnā ᶜAsharī Shiism in the context of the Weberian sociology of religion. Begins with the classical period and continues up to the 1890s.

Arjomand, Said Amir. *The Turban for the Crown*. New York, 1988. Sociological explanation of the Iranian Revolution of 1979, emphasizing political-cultural variables.

Bayat, Mangol. *Iran's First Revolution*. New York, 1991. Stresses the divergent motivations of the clergy in the Constitutional Revolution of Iran and argues for the primary role of lower-ranking clerics whose actions were often inspired by sectarian ideas and socialist notions.

Eliash, Joseph. "Misconceptions Regarding the Juridical Status of the Iranian *ᶜUlamāʼ*." *International Journal of Middle East Studies* 10.1 (February 1979): 9–25. Reviews the doctrinal bases for clerical activism in Shīᶜī Islam and argues that no categorical warrant for it exists.

Enayat, Hamid. *Modern Islamic Political Thought*. Austin, 1982. General discussion of various problems in Muslim social thought pertaining to rule, authority, representation, justice, and the like.

Enayat, Hamid. "Iran: Khumayni's Concept of the 'Guardianship of the Jurisconsult.' " In *Islam in the Political Process*, edited by J. P. Piscatori, pp. 160–180. Cambridge, 1983. Traces the doctrinal roots of *wilāyah* and argues that *wilāyat al-faqīh* is a concept going no further back than the mid-nineteenth century.

Fischer, Michael M. J. *Iran: From Religious Dispute to Revolution*. Cambridge, Mass., 1980. Anthropological study of the Iranian clergy in the Pahlavi period, with a focus on clerical educational discourse and social behavior in the city of Qom.

Floor, Willem. "The Revolutionary Character of the Iranian *ᶜUlamāʼ*: Wishful Thinking or Reality?" *International Journal of Middle East Studies* 12.4 (December 1980): 501–524. Examination of the Shīᶜī clergy's role in the Iranian protests of 1960–1963, concluding that Shīᶜī Islam does not provide the clergy with inherently revolutionary motivations.

Keddie, Nikki R. "The Roots of the *ᶜUlamāʼ*'s Power in Modern Iran." *Studia Islamica* 29 (1969): 31–53. Traces the doctrinal and historical factors behind the assertiveness of the Shīᶜī clergy in the modern period.

Khomeini, Ruhollah al-Musavi. *Islam and Revolution: Writings and Declarations of Imam Khomeini*. Translated and edited by Hamid Algar. Berkeley, 1981. Important English-language source for Khomeini's writings, including his book, *Islamic Government* (also translated variously elsewhere as *The Mandate of the Jurist* and *The Guardianship of the Jurisconsult*).

Lambton, Ann K. S. "Quis Custodiet Custodes: Some Reflections on the Persian Theory of Government." *Studia Islamica* 5 (1956): 125–148, and 6 (1956): 125–146. Classic exploration and critique of Shīᶜī juristic theory of authority, stressing its blending of ancient Iranian notions of kingship and Islamic concepts of leadership. Emphasizes the illegitimacy of rule not exercised by the imam.

Madelung, Wilferd. *Religious Trends in Early Islamic Iran*. Albany, N.Y., 1988. Clarifies the complexities of early Shiism by tracing the ideas of the early sects as well as the concepts of medieval jurists.

Mallat, Chibli. *Shiᶜi Thought from the South of Lebanon*. Oxford, 1988. An occasional paper of the Centre for Lebanese Studies containing valuable comparisons of the ideas of the Shīᶜī clergy in Lebanon with one another and with their colleagues in Iran. Especially enlightening in regard to differences between certain Lebanese ᶜ*ulamā'* and Ayatollah Khomeini on the matter of *wilāyat al-faqīh (vilāyat-i faqīh).*

Mallat, Chibli. *The Renewal of Islamic Law: Muhammad Baqer as-Sadr, Najaf and the Shīᶜi International.* Cambridge and New York, 1993. Intellectual biography of a leading Shīᶜī clergyman of the second half of the twentieth century, whose ideas in the areas of education, law, and economics have had important resonances in the Shīᶜī world.

Moaddel, Mansoor. *Class, Politics, and Ideology in the Iranian Revolution.* New York, 1993. Examines the Iranian Revolution of 1979 through the prism of contemporary collective protest literature and stresses the importance of ideology as its constitutive feature.

Momen, Moojan. *An Introduction to Shīᶜi Islam.* New Haven, 1985. Comprehensive survey of developments in Shiism, focusing on doctrinal as well as historical trends.

Mottahedeh, Roy P. *The Mantle of the Prophet.* New York, 1985. Iranian Revolution of 1979 as captured by an illuminating exploration of the world of the Shīᶜī seminary, blending fiction, historical analysis, and philosophical analysis to follow the lives of one religious and one secular student.

Shahrough Akhavi

ᶜUMAR AL-MUKHTĀR. *See* Mukhtār, ᶜUmar al-.

ᶜUMAR TAL (c.1794–1864), more fully al-Ḥājj ᶜUmar ibn Saᶜīd, Senegalese Islamic militant leader and thinker. Al-Ḥājj ᶜUmar ibn Saᶜīd deserves recognition as one of the towering figures of West African history in the latter part of the nineteenth century. It is to his efforts that we can ascribe the success of the Tijānīyah brotherhood which, with the ᶜUmarian brand of militant Islam, swept like a flame over much of modern-day Mali, Senegal, Guinea, and Mauritania—an area of some 150,000 square miles at its widest geographic extent. Never before and never again did so much territory in this region submit to a single Islamic authority.

For al-Ḥājj ᶜUmar, the model of Muḥammad presented the perfect frame in which to pattern his *jihād* fervor. The peaks and valleys of the Prophet's life were imitated with pious frequency in the career of Shaykh ᶜUmar. He broke off relations with his kinsmen around 1849/50 and referred to this action as *hijrah* in imitation of the Prophet's move under similar circumstances. In 1852, he launched his *jihād* at the same age at which Muḥammad had commenced his struggle for the diffusion of Islam. Indeed, the shaykh was to state explicitly:

> I was faced with enmity as he [Muḥammad] was faced by it during his difficulty at al-Ḥudaybīyah. . . . I had suffered harm in Allāh's way, and yet I had stood patiently—the same way that the Prophet had suffered harm and had stood patiently in the face of it. . . . Religion, in its infancy, begins as a stranger; and during this phase it will be maintained by *hijrah,* as had happened before. For in most cases no prophet has been supported by his people.

Even in a century of so many great individualists as the nineteenth, ᶜUmar Tal was no ordinary figure. Indeed, the western Sudan of this period was profoundly stirred by his views. As the Qādirī movement of the first quarter of this period failed to clothe its senile form with any new attraction, excitement passed to the Tijānīyah brotherhood. Coming as it did between the *jihād* of Shehu Usuman dan Fodio in northern Nigeria and that of Muḥammad Aḥmad (the Mahdi) in the Anglo-Egyptian Sudan, the movement of al-Ḥājj ᶜUmar maintained its rank absolutely. The mystic shaykh was the peer of the Sudanese Mahdi in his capacity to raise controversy. For his detractors, his struggle in the path of God was a pretext to sanctify political and economic expediencies: *jihād* and the excessive claims of charisma made dangerous allies. The reputation of al-Ḥājj ᶜUmar gained in scope what it had lost in definition as he assumed the guise of an apocalyptic figure. Through a primary inspiration the mystic shaykh became the momentum of Islamic revival, leaving the path of an edifying *imitatio nabī* (imitation of Muḥammad) as the guidance of his mission was subsumed under a beatifying principle. Having lifted himself onto this exalted plane, the shaykh, perceptibly, was in a position to create the taste by which he was to be relished—to rule not by the *sharīᶜah* alone, but by divine inspiration.

The Senegalese militant is no less regarded for his role as a writer and thinker, as one who shaped the content and direction of Tijānī thought during his lifetime and left on it an indelible imprint for posterity. His *Rimāḥ ḥizb al-Raḥīm ᶜala nuhūr ḥizb al-rajīm* (composed in AH 1261/1845 CE) stands in near parity to the *Jawāhir al-maᶜanī* (Cairo, 1927), and together these two great works constitute a complete body of laws for the order and a guide to conduct for its members.

Al-Ḥājj ᶜUmar brought to his writings a perspective rich in experience gained from travel throughout much of the Muslim world and study in many of the leading centers of Islamic thought. He made the pilgrimage to the Muslim holy places in 1825, remaining away from his homeland until the late 1830s. On his return, his preaching and teaching culminated in a *jihād* effort, the effects of which are still evident in his theater of operations.

[*See also* Senegal; Tijānīyah.]

BIBLIOGRAPHY

For literature on this subject, see my epic, *In the Path of Allāh: The Passion of al-Ḥājj ʿUmar, an Essay into the Nature of Charisma in Islam* (London, 1989). For a highly detailed account, consult David Robinson, *The Holy War of ʿUmar Tal: The Western Sudan in the Mid-Nineteenth Century* (Oxford, 1985).

JOHN RALPH WILLIS

UMAYYAD CALIPHATE. The Umayyad dynasty ruled the Islamic caliphate from the death of the fourth caliph, ʿAlī, in 661 until 750. The founder of the dynasty was Muʿāwiyah, son of Abū Sufyān, of the Meccan clan of Umayyah. He had been appointed governor of Syria by the second caliph, ʿUmar; after 656 an attempt by ʿAlī as caliph to replace him led to intermittent hostilities between the two. After the assassination of ʿAlī in 661, Muʿāwiyah gained control of the whole caliphate, and was recognized as caliph. By the time of his death in 680, he had established, with Damascus as the capital, a system of administration for the caliphate that gave it a degree of stability.

Muʿāwiyah's successor, his son Yazīd I, defeated at Karbala an attempt by ʿAlī's son Ḥusayn to become caliph. When Yazīd died in 683, leaving only a young son, Muʿāwiyah II, ʿAbd Allāh ibn al-Zubayr in Mecca claimed the caliphate. Another Umayyad, Marwān, recovered Syria and became caliph in 684; his son ʿAbd al-Malik (r. 685–705) restored Umayyad rule over the whole caliphate, though it was not until 692 that ʿAbd-Allāh ibn al-Zubayr was defeated and this second civil war ended. ʿAbd al-Malik strengthened the organization of the empire. Up to this time, administrators from the previous Byzantine and Sassanian regimes had continued to work for the caliphs, but he now made Arabic the official language of government and replaced the Byzantine and Sassanian coinage with one with Arabic inscriptions.

Although the caliphate of al-Walīd (r. 705–715) was a period of continuing prosperity, continuing rivalry between two groups of Arab tribes known as Qays and Kalb threatened the unity of the empire. ʿUmar ibn ʿAbd al-Azīz or ʿUmar II (r. 717–720) introduced measures that countered this threat, but, after his death, tensions increased again, not only between these two groups but also between the Arabs and the *mawālī* (non-Arab Muslims). When the ʿAbbāsids, descendants of Muḥammad's uncle al-ʿAbbās, raised an army in Khurasan in Iran, which included many *mawālī*, the Umayyads were unable to offer effective resistance. The last Umayyad caliph, Marwān II (r. 744–750) was killed in Egypt in 750. One member of the Umayyad family escaped and in 755 founded in Spain the Umayyad emirate of al-Andalus, which was never incorporated into the ʿAbbāsid empire.

The Umayyads were responsible for a great expansion of the Islamic state. By 661 the Arabs had occupied Egypt, Syria, Iraq, and most of Iran. The Umayyads continued the westward advance through North Africa until they reached the Atlantic. In 711 they crossed into Spain and rapidly conquered most of the country, establishing a forward base at Narbonne in southern France. In 732 their defeat by Charles Martel between Tours and Poitiers checked the advance, but Narbonne remained in Arab hands until 759. Eastward the Umayyads pressed on from Iran into Central Asia (Bukhara and Samarkand) and into northwest India. In the north, however, despite frequent expeditions, little progress was made because of the strength of the Byzantine empire. A long unsuccessful siege of Constantinople began in 672; when Sulaymān (r. 715–717) attacked that city, the Arabs were repulsed and lost almost all of their fleet and army.

This great expansion was primarily military and political, not religious. Indeed, there was a short period when conversion to Islam was discouraged because it reduced the amount collected in taxes. Non-Arabs who became Muslims were also required to become *mawālī* of an Arab tribe; the *mawālī*, who are often called clients, were persons incorporated into the tribe and reckoned as belonging to it, but without all the rights of those who were members by birth. Christians and Jews who kept their religion normally became *dhimmīs* (protected minorities with limited autonomy). In the conquered provinces the center of government was sometimes a city, such as Kairouan (Qayrawān) which had first been a forward army base, then a garrison-town, which increased in size as many of the local population settled around it to serve the needs of the army. Originally the armies were exclusively Arab and Muslim, but in time numerous *mawālī* were added, mostly of Iranian and Berber origin.

Later Muslim historians, writing under the ʿAbbāsids, accused the Umayyads of transforming the Islamic state into an Arab kingdom. In organizing the growing empire the Umayyads did in fact rely largely on the traditional political ideas of the Arabs, but they also claimed to be upholders of Islam, as demonstrated in the works of contemporary court poets. The caliphs realized that Islam was becoming the significant factor that bound the parts of the empire together, especially after the great increase in the numbers of *mawālī*.

[*See also* ʿAbbāsid Caliphate; Caliphate.]

BIBLIOGRAPHY

Brockelmann, Carl. *History of the Islamic Peoples*. London and New York, 1944.

Donner, F. M. *The Early Islamic Conquests*. Princeton, 1981.

Hitti, Philip K. *History of the Arabs*. London, 1937.

Holt, P. M., et al., eds. *The Cambridge History of Islam*, vol. 1. Cambridge, 1970.

Lewis, Bernard. *The Arabs in History*. London, 1950.

Shaban, M. A. *Islamic History: A New Interpretation*, vol. 1, *A.D. 600–750 (A.H. 132)*. Cambridge, 1971.

Wellhausen, Julius. *The Arab Kingdom and Its Fall*. Translated by Margaret G. Weir. Calcutta, 1927; reprint, Beirut, 1963. Deals with the Umayyad period in detail.

William Montgomery Watt

UMMAH. Often translated "Muslim community," the term *ummah* designates a fundamental concept in Islam. Although its meaning has constantly developed through history, it has often been used to express the essential unity of Muslims in *diverse* cultural settings.

Use in Qur'ān and Ḥadīth. The term *ummah* occurs sixty-four times in the Qur'ān. Most studies of the Qur'ānic concept of *ummah* assert that the term designates a people to whom God sends a prophet, or a people who are objects of a divine plan of salvation. According to these studies, the term *ummah* refers to a single group sharing some common religious orientation. In Qur'ānic usage, however, the connotations of community and religion do not always converge, and the word has multiple and diverse meanings.

In several instances *ummah* refers to an unrestricted group of people. Surah 28.23, for example, reads, "And when he [Moses] came to the water of Madyan, he found on it a group of men *(ummah min al-nās)* watering." The term can also mean a specific religion or the beliefs of a certain group of people (43.22–23), or an exemplar or model of faith, as in the reference to Abraham as an "*ummah*, obedient to God" (16.120). *Ummah* also refers to the followers of prophets ("For every *ummah* there is an apostle," 10.47); to a group of people adhering to a specific religion ("To each one of you We have appointed a law and a pattern of life. If God had pleased He could surely have made you all a single *ummah*," 5.48); to a smaller group within the larger community of adherents ("They are not all alike; among the people of the Book is an upright *ummah*, 3.113); to the followers of Muḥammad who are charged with a special responsibility ("And thus We have made you a medium *ummah* that you may be the bearers of witness to the people and that the Apostle may be a bearer of witness to you," 2.143); or to a subgroup of these followers ("So let there be an *ummah* among you who may call to good, enjoin what is right and forbid the wrong, and these it is that shall be successful," 3.104).

Ummah often denotes a misguided group of people ("Were it not that all people would be a single *ummah*, We would certainly have allocated to those who disbelieve in the Beneficent God [to make] of silver the roofs of their houses and the stairs by which they ascend," 43.33), or a misguided party from among the followers of a prophet ("And on the day when We will gather from every *ummah* a party from among those who rejected Our communications, then they shall be formed into groups," 27.83, or "Then We sent Our apostles one after the other; whenever there came to an *ummah* their apostle, they called him a liar, so We made one follow the other [to its dooms], and We turned them into bygone tales," 23.44). Finally, *ummah* could mean a period of time ("And if We hold back from them the punishment until a stated *ummah*/period of time, they will say," 11.8); it can also mean an order of being ("And there is no animal that walks upon the earth nor a bird that flies with its two wings but they are an *ummah* like yourself," 6.38).

The occasional rift between the civil and religious notions of *ummah* in Qur'ānic usage has parallels in *ḥadīth* literature. In several traditions Muḥammad is said to use "my *ummah*" to mean the group related to him by lineage rather than by religion. It is the *ḥadīth* literature, however, that provides the concept of *ummah* with its precise and focused meaning. Besides the Qur'ān, the earliest extant source available is a set of documents written by Muḥammad shortly after his arrival at Medina. These documents, commonly referred to in modern scholarship as the "Constitution of Medina," comprise several practical provisions designed to regulate social and political life in Medina under Islam. Most scholars agree that the main purport of the Constitution is political and not religious. It defines treaty relations between the different groups inhabiting Medina and its environs, including the Muslim tribes of Medina, Muslims who emigrated from Mecca, and Jews.

The "constitution" starts with the pronouncement that all these groups constitute "one distinct community (*ummah*) apart from other people." In the forty-seven clauses of the Constitution the term *ummah* appears in only one other instance, when the Jews of Banū ʿAwf are said to constitute "an *ummah* with the believers." The same clause goes on to state that the Jews have their religion and the Muslims have theirs. The meaning of the term *ummah* in the Constitution is clearly not synonymous with religion. The Constitution also delineates relations of mutual aid among the different constituent tribal groups, actions to be taken against those who violate the terms of the agreement, and actions to be taken against criminals belonging to the incipient community in Medina. Rather than supplanting or abolishing tribal bonds, the Constitution regulates relations among tribes, and between them and the outside world, on the basis of the higher order of the *ummah. Ummah* here is a concept of daily life that also stands for a certain kind of identity and defines a social unit.

While the Constitution of Medina seems to sanction diversity within the Islamic *ummah,* the Qur'ān sanctions differentiation among various *ummah*s as a norm decreed by God. Surah 10.19 reads, "People were once a single *ummah;* but they differed (and followed different ways). Had it not been for the word proclaimed by your lord before, their differences would have been resolved" (see also 2.213, 5.48, 11.118, 16.93, and 42.8). There is a sense, therefore, in which the concept of the *ummah* refers to an ideal state, an original all-encompassing unity that is always invoked but never completely recovered.

This rudimentary concept of the *ummah,* however, is complemented by the narrower concept of the *ummah* of believers. This is the "medium *ummah*" (2.143), which is further qualified in the Qur'ān as: "the best *ummah* evolved for mankind, enjoining what is good, forbidding what is wrong, and believing in God" (3.110; see also 4.41 and 16.89). This specific *ummah,* or the followers of Muḥammad, is further differentiated from the followers of earlier messengers and prophets; whereas the latter's sphere of influence is restricted to particular peoples, the former's scope is all of humanity. When referring to prophets before Muḥammad, the Qur'ān says, "To every *ummah* We have sent an apostle [saying:] Worship God" (16.36; see also 10.47). In reference to Muḥammad, however, the Qur'ān adds, "Say: O men, I am verily the apostle of God to you all" (7.158). The universality of Muḥammad's mission was thereby asserted, and the "medium *ummah*" shouldered the central role in the fulfillment of this mission after him.

Development in Legal and Political Thought. The concept of *ummah* underwent important developments immediately after Muḥammad's death. Different circumstances accompanied the selection of each of the first four caliphs after Muḥammad, yet in each case the appointment was conferred by the majority of the *ummah,* thereby investing ultimate political authority in the *ummah* and its consensus. It was argued that to preserve its unity, the *ummah* needs leadership consolidated in the person of one imam. The second caliph, ʿUmar, relinquished the distribution of conquered land to Muslim conquerors, considering it public property, the property of the whole *ummah.* The idealization of the period of the first four "rightly guided" caliphs is not a mere creation of the historical imagination of later generations of Muslims: it was a period in which important Islamic ideals were actually conceived. These include the principles of the unity of the *ummah,* the *ummah* as the ultimate source of political authority, and the related principles of the unity of political leadership and the unity of the land of Islam.

Under Umayyad rule the need for a unified political authority was overemphasized and used to justify exclusive Arab dynastic rule at the expense of the Islamic ideal of the unity of the *ummah.* Under the ʿAbbāsids the inclusive Qur'ānic notion of the *ummah* was revived, and the political dominance of the ʿAbbāsid family did not preclude the participation of other ethnic groups. This participation, however, eventually led to the gradual loosening of political centralization. As the ʿAbbāsid caliphs wielded less control over an increasingly decentralized state, they continued to function as symbols of the unity of its *ummah.* This unity was corroborated by an Islamic cultural tradition that was well developed by the end of the second century of Islam.

Traditionalists and *ḥadīth* scholars argued that Islam could only be preserved by safeguarding the unity of the *ummah.* The standard legal formulations of the classical period defined it as a spiritual, nonterritorial community distinguished by the shared beliefs of its members. This concept was not a mere abstraction; it had legal consequences. The distinction in Islamic international law between the "land of Islam" *(dār al-Islām)* and the "land of war" *(dār al-ḥarb)* was based on the conceptual division of people into believers and nonbelievers. Nonbelievers were further classified on the basis of their relation to the *ummah* of believers. There were no formal conditions or ritual requirements for joining the *ummah* aside from being born to Muslim parents or freely choosing to become a Muslim. Membership in this *ummah* can thus be viewed as a sort of citizenship that guarantees, at least theoretically, equality among all Muslims. One expression of the treatment of the *ummah* as a legal entity is the distinction in Islamic jurisprudence between religious obligations that fall on individuals and other obligations that the *ummah* shoulders collectively as one unit. As late as the early twentieth century, French courts, for example, had to deal with the implications of a Muslim's membership in the *ummah* as a reality with substantive legal consequences.

In legal theory—for example, in Shāfiʿī's (d. 820) work on the principles of jurisprudence—the consensus of the community was elevated into the status of a source of law second only to the Qur'ān and the traditions of Muḥammad. The *ḥadīth* stating "my *ummah* would never agree on an error" *(lā tajtamiʿu ummatī ʿalā ḍalālah)* was perceived in the legal classics as evidence of the infallibility of the *ummah* and its unrivaled authority. The literature of the classical period thus viewed the *ummah* as a socioreligious reality with legal and political import.

Beginning with the third century of Islam, some writings suggested a distinction between religious forms of human association, or *millah,* and sociopolitical forms, termed "*ummah*" (for example, al-Farābī, d. 950). A more significant distinction was promoted by political theoreticians working during periods of political fragmentation. The celebrated al-Māwardī (d. 1058), for example, conceded the possibility of having more than one executive organ of political power, but he insisted on the unity of the *ummah* and on the symbolic unity of the office of the caliph.

From the third century AH Islamic literature also conferred a distinguished status on the Arabs within the larger *ummah* of Muslims. This literature emphasized the centrality of the Arabs and their language to Islam, in response to the Shuʿūbīyah movement, which denigrated the Arabs in favor of other ethnic identities. Al-Shāfiʿī, for example, lists in his *Risālah fī uṣūl al-fiqh* (Treatise on the Principles of Jurisprudence) the Qur'ānic references to Arabic and its prominence, while Aḥmad ibn Ḥanbal (d. 855) collects numerous *ḥadīths* that enumerate the virtues of Arabs and reprimand their foes. In different genres of writing, including jurisprudence, philosophy, histories, poetry, and prose, the Arabs are said to be privileged by speaking the language of the Qur'ān and of paradise, and by being the core community to whom Muḥammad was sent. As the political hegemony of the Arabs receded, so did the cultural tensions between them and other ethnic groups. The tradition of praising the Arabs, however, did not subside; rather, the initial reactive defense gave way to independent self-conscious reflections on Arabness as a cultural identity, and on its unique and organic link to the religious, political, and social identity of the Islamic *ummah.*

Era of Nationalism. The social reality of the unified *ummah,* and the related concept of *dār al-Islām,* were not undermined by political decentralization in the Islamic world. However, under the pressure of European colonial encroachment on Muslim domains, this social identity was seriously challenged. Islamic resistance movements defending the *ummah* against European intrusions emerged throughout the Islamic world. The attempts of the Ottoman sultan Abdülhamid II (r. 1876–1909) to redeem Islamic unity by reviving the idea of *ummah* were extremely popular among Muslims from India to Morocco. Equally popular was the call by Jamāl al-Dīn al-Afghānī (1839–1897) for Islamic solidarity to reinvigorate the *ummah.* On the other side of the confrontation, European powers were making progress both at the military front and in the form of concessions imposed on the Ottoman Empire. Moreover, the European idea of the secular nation-state had some appeal among Muslim elites.

The earliest forms of nationalism in the Islamic world, however, conceived of Islam as a central component of the nationalist project. With very few exceptions, the early nationalists, including the non-Muslims among them, appropriated the Islamic concept of *ummah.* Although nationalist movements in the guise of Islamic reform often disrupted the actual political unity of the *ummah,* they did not challenge the theoretical authority of the concept. Moreover, the symbols of Arab nationalism retained their religious weight, in contrast to the Turkish nationalism of Mustafa Kemal (Atatürk), who dissociated Turkey from its Islamic tradition.

In reaction to the political vacuum created by Kemal's elimination of the caliphate in 1924, a number of Islamic conferences were held to discuss the political situation of the Muslim *ummah*. These conferences failed to achieve any significant results owing to the conflicting loyalties between the sovereign secular nation-states and the religious *ummah*. These competing loyalties eventually led to greater separation between Islam and nationalism. Beginning in the 1960s, even Arab nationalists began to speak in favor of a complete separation of religious and national identities. In reaction, many Islamists argued that loyalty to the Islamic *ummah* negates any other loyalty to ethnic, linguistic, or geographical entities. Still, the idea of the Islamic *ummah,* as it is used in contemporary political discourse, carries the imprint of the nation-state with which it is competing. The gradual secularization of public life has curtailed political and legal expressions of the idea of the *ummah,* but its significance as a source of social identity persists in the Islamic world.

[*See also* Dār al-Islām; Islamic State; Nation; Pan-Islam.]

BIBLIOGRAPHY

Aḥsan, ʿAbdullāh al-. *Ummah or Nation? Identity Crisis in Contemporary Muslim Society*. Leicester, 1992.

Berkes, Niyazi. *The Development of Secularism in Turkey*. Montreal, 1964. Especially useful for discussions of Turkish nationalism.

Darrow, William R. "Ummah." In *The Encyclopedia of Religion*, vol. 15, pp. 123–125. New York, 1987.

Denny, Frederick Mathewson. "The Meaning of *Ummah* in the Qur'ān." *History of Religions* 15.1 (1975): 35–70.

Denny, Frederick Mathewson. "Ummah in the Constitution of Medina." *Journal of Near Eastern Studies* 36.1 (1977): 39–47.

Giannakis, Elias. "The Concept of Ummah." *Graeco-Arabica* 2 (1983): 99–111.

Gibb, H. A. R. "The Islamic Congress at Jerusalem in December 1931." In *Survey of International Affairs, 1934,* edited by A. J. Toynbee, pp. 99–109. London, 1935.

Gibb, H. A. R. "The Community in Islamic History." *Proceedings of the American Philosophical Society* 107.2 (1963): 173–176.

Hamidullah, Muhammad. *Majmūʿat al-wathāʾiq al-siyāsīyah lil-ʿahd al-nabawī wal-khilāfah al-rāshidah*. Cairo, 1956. Includes the Arabic text of the "constitution of Medina" (pp. 15–21).

Hourani, Albert. *Arabic Thought in the Liberal Age, 1798–1939*. London, 1962. Especially useful for discussions of Arab nationalism.

Kramer, Martin. *Islam Assembled: The Advent of the Muslim Congresses*. New York, 1986.

Kruse, Hans. "The Development of the Concept of Nationality in Islam." *Studies in Islam* 2.1 (1965): 7–16.

Massignon, Louis. "L'umma et ses synonumes: Notion de 'communauté sociale' en Islam." *Revue des Études Islamiques, 1941–1946*, pp. 151–157. Paris, 1959.

Naṣṣār, Naṣīf. *Mafhūm al-ummah bayna al-dīn wa-al-tārīkh*. Beirut, 1978. Useful study of the concept of *ummah* in the Qur'ān, in the "constitution of Medina," and in later philosophical and historical writings.

Naṣṣār, Naṣīf. *Taṣawwurāt al-ummah al-muʿāṣirah*. Al-Kuwayt, 1986. Useful survey of the various conceptions of *ummah* in modern and contemporary Arabic thought.

Nieuwenhuijze, C. A. O. van. "The Ummah: An Analytic Approach." *Studia Islamica* 10 (1959): 5–22.

Paret, Rudi. "Umma." In *Encyclopaedia of Islam*, new ed., vol. 4, pp. 1015–1016. Leiden, 1960–.

Qureshi, Ishtiaq Husain. *The Struggle for Pakistan*. Karachi, 1969. Includes references to the intellectual debates regarding the national identity of Pakistan and its relation to Islam.

Rahman, Fazlur. "The Principle of Shura and the Role of the Umma in Islam." *American Journal of Islamic Studies* 1.1 (1984): 1–9.

Rubin, Uri. "The 'Constitution of Medina': Some Notes." *Studia Islamica* 62 (1985): 5–23.

Sayyid, Riḍwān al-. *Al-ummah wa-al-jamāʿah wa-al-sulṭah: Dirāsāt fī al-fikr al-siyāsī al-ʿArabī al-Islāmī*. Beirut, 1984. By far the best and most comprehensive study of the historical development of the concept of *ummah*. See especially pages 17–87.

Sayyid, Riḍwān al-. "Dār al-Islām wa-al-Niẓām al-Duwalī wa-al-Ummah al-ʿArabīyah." *Mustaqbal al-ʿĀlam al-Islāmī* 1.1 (1991): 37–70. Comparative study of the question of national identity in the modern Islamic world.

Sayyid, Riḍwān al-. *Mafāhīm al-Jamāʿāt fī al-Islām*. Beirut, 1993. Chapter 5 is especially good on the Arabs in Islamic thought.

Serjeant, R. B. "The Constitution of Madinah." *Islamic Quarterly* 8 (June 1964): 3–16.

ʿUmarī, Akram Ḍiyāʾ al-. *Al-Mujtamaʿ al-Madanī fī ʿAhd al-Nubūwah*. Medina, 1983. Meticulous study employing traditional methods of *ḥadīth* criticism to establish the authenticity of the "constitution of Medina" (pp. 107–136).

Von Grunebaum, G. E. "Nationalism and Cultural Trends in the Arab Near East." *Studia Islamica* 14 (1961): 121–153.

Von Grunebaum, G. E. *Modern Islam: The Search for Cultural Identity*. Berkeley, 1962.

Watt, W. Montgomery. *Muhammad at Medina*. Oxford, 1953. Includes a translation of the "constitution of Medina" (pp. 221–225).

AHMAD S. DALLAL

UMMAH-ANṢĀR. The Sudanese Ummah ("community") Party was formed in February 1945 by pro-independence nationalists, most of whom were supporters of Sayyid ʿAbd al-Raḥmān al-Mahdī, the posthumous son of Muḥammad Aḥmad ibn ʿAbd Allāh (d. 1885) who founded the Mahdist movement in that country. The nearly 4 million followers of this movement, known as Anṣār, constitute the bulk of the party's membership. Although Ummah often gained the greatest number of seats voted to a single party in general elections, it was never in a position to form an independent government and was forced to participate in coalitions.

Three main factors contributed to the formation of the Ummah Party. The first was the reemergence of the

Anṣār as an influential religio-political organization under Sayyid ʿAbd al-Raḥmān after World War I. Its sectarian followers provided the mass basis of the Ummah Party and their hierarchical structure of command subsequently served as its backbone. Second, following the rift created between the Graduates' Congress and the Condominium government in 1942, political control of this nationalist organization gradually passed to a militant, and later pro-unionist, faction headed by Ismāʿīl al-Azharī (d. 1969). This development led ʿAbd al-Raḥmān to discard the Congress as an instrument for advancing Sudanese independence and to promote the Ummah Party as a substitute. Third, whereas Congress in 1944 boycotted the establishment of an Advisory Council for the Sudan, ʿAbd al-Raḥmān realized its political significance and was determined to participate in its deliberations. Such participation, however, presupposed the formation of a political organization distinct from the Congress.

ʿAbd al-Raḥmān al-Mahdī, imam of the Anṣār, was the new party's patron, while its leadership initially rested with one of his sons, Ṣiddīq. In October 1955, in order to secure the commitment of his sectarian rival to full independence for the Sudan, ʿAbd al-Raḥmān accepted Sayyid ʿAlī al-Mirghanī's proposal that they pledge themselves and members of their families to refrain from seeking public office. This measure shifted control of the party to the secular wing, then led by ʿAbd Allāh Khalīl. However, the military regime established by General Ibrahim ʿAbbūd in November 1958 disbanded all political parties, thereby neutralizing the secularists and restoring the Ummah's leadership to al-Ṣiddīq al-Mahdī.

Sayyid ʿAbd al-Raḥmān died in March 1959, and al-Ṣiddīq succeeded him as imam. Almost immediately the latter integrated the party's hierarchy of institution with the Anṣār movement. When al-Ṣiddīq himself died in October 1961, his brother al-Hādī was elected as the new imam and his own Oxford-educated son al-Ṣādiq was designated as leader of the Ummah Party. Thus, the party's leadership, though retained by the Mahdī family, became essentially divided along functional lines.

This division proved crucial, for al-Hādī was conservative while al-Ṣādiq was liberal. By 1963 the latter had grown critical of his uncle's tolerance of ʿAbbūd's regime, and he began to advocate that the Ummah should adopt a more democratic structure and a modern political program. With the restoration of democratic rule in October 1964, the struggle between the conservative and liberal wings intensified and in July 1966 precipitated a split within the party. In April 1969, however, dissatisfied with their reduced political role, al-Hādī and al-Ṣādiq came to an agreement that reunified the party and prepared it to head a new coalition government. A few weeks thereafter, and partly in reaction to this development, a second military regime was established under Colonel Jaʿfar al-Nimeiri (or al-Numayrī).

From the outset the Ummah-Anṣār leaders were unequivocably opposed to the leftist orientation of the new junta and, failing to change it by persuasion, they resisted it forcibly. The confrontation led to a military attack on Aba Island in March 1970, in which Imam al-Hādī and thousands of his followers were killed. Al-Ṣādiq was first exiled to Egypt but was later returned to Sudan and kept under house arrest until his release in December 1972.

The Ummah Party participated in setting up the Sudanese National Front in exile to oppose the military regime, and in July 1976 it spearheaded an abortive coup. A year later, al-Ṣādiq negotiated a reconciliation agreement with Nimeiri, following which the Front was dissolved. This agreement created dissension within the Ummah-Anṣār from followers of al-Hādī who were vehemently opposed to Nimeiri and who had not forgotten the bitter split of 1966. Soon, however, al-Ṣādiq became disillusioned with Nimeiri's domestic and foreign policies; in 1978 he led his wing of the Ummah Party again into opposition.

In April 1985 Nimeiri's regime was overthrown and the Ummah joined other parties in forming a transitional regime pending general elections. By March 1986 its various wings were effectively reunited, and al-Ṣādiq was formally reelected as its leader. In the elections held a month later, Ummah was able to gain 100 of the the 260 contested seats and to head the new coalition government formed with the Democratic Union Party and others. In May 1987 al-Ṣādiq was elected imam of the Anṣār to succeed his uncle al-Hādī, thereby unifying in his person the leadership of the Ummah-Anṣār movement.

The instability created by differences over the repeal of Nimeiri's Islamic legal code and the resolution of conflict in the southern Sudan opened the way for the establishment, in June 1989, of a third military regime under General ʿUmar Ḥasan Aḥmad al-Bashīr. Its fundamentalist orientation and its close association with the Muslim Brotherhood drove the Ummah and other parties to form the National Democratic Alliance to oppose it.

Ideologically, the Ummah Party draws its orientation from Sudanese Mahdist thought. Like the Ṣūfī orders and the Muslim Brothers, it believes that Islam plays a major role in the sociopolitical life of Muslims. But unlike the former, it is strongly committed to political activism; and unlike the latter, it believes that a just social order can only be achieved on the basis of the widest popular participation. Accordingly, it supports the establishment of a modern Islamic state, but one that is based on a constitution that recognizes the *ummah* as the source of political authority and the possessor of sovereignty. Believing that the institutions of the modern state are new political phenomena with no resemblance to those of the original Islamic polity, the Ummah Party seeks to restore the functions rather than the traditional patterns of ancient Medinese society. Hence, like the Ṣūfī orders but unlike the Muslim Brothers, it recognizes the *sharīʿah* as the main—but not the sole—source for legislation. In this connection it advocates the establishment of a *shūrā* (advisory) council vested with adequate legislative powers not only to reenact provisions of the *sharīʿah* in the light of modern conditions, but also to validate existing modern legislation for which no precedent can be found in Islamic law. The application of such an Islamic legal system would be restricted to the Muslim population, and other religious faiths would be formally recognized rather than suppressed or simply tolerated, and their members would be guaranteed full freedom of religious conscience and practice. In this way, Ummah believes, Sudanese national unity and territorial integrity can be preserved.

[*See also* Anṣār; Mahdīyah; Sudan; *and the biography of (al-Ṣādiq al-)Mahdī.*]

BIBLIOGRAPHY

Bechtold, Peter K. *Politics in the Sudan: Parliamentary and Military Rule in an Emerging African Nation.* New York, 1976. Overview of political developments up to 1975, based mainly on an evaluation of the general election results.

Cudsi, Alexander S. "Islam and Politics in the Sudan." In *Islam in the Political Process,* edited by J. P. Piscatori, pp. 36–55. Cambridge, 1983. Analysis of the process of islamization in the Sudan under Nimeiri's regime, including a comparison of policies advocated by the major religio-political organizations.

Niblock, Tim. *Class and Power in Sudan: The Dynamics of Sudanese Politics, 1898–1985.* Albany, N.Y., 1987. Insightful overview of the socioeconomic basis of politics in the Sudan that makes constructive use of unpublished postgraduate dissertations and theses on Sudan submitted at British and Sudanese universities. Sections dealing with the reemergence of the Anṣār and sectarian rivalry within the Graduates' Congress provide valuable background material.

Warburg, Gabriel R. *Islam, Nationalism, and Communism in a Traditional Society: The Case of Sudan.* London, 1978. Collection of three papers dealing with the reemergence of the Anṣār, the transition to independence, and Sudanese communism. Regretfully, the paper on the Anṣār is based primarily on British intelligence reports and does not consider records in Sudanese archives.

ALEXANDER S. CUDSI

UNION DES ORGANISATIONS ISLAMIQUES DE FRANCE. Created in 1983, the Union des Organisations Islamiques de France (UOIF) is a federation of Islamic local associations. Although its seat is in Paris, it is especially active in the east and the center of France. Thirty local associations are full adherents of the UOIF, each of which pays 10 percent of its own resources to the organization. There are also about fifty affiliate associations, which contribute 5 percent of their resources. Each category of association has the right to vote for the administrative council and the governing board of the federation. The board is composed of twelve persons of various nationalities; in 1990 the members of the board were Moroccan, Tunisian, Lebanese, Iraqi, and French. In addition to the contributions of the local associations, the UOIF receives financial help from the Muslim World League and from private individuals from Saudi Arabia, Kuwait, and the United Arab Emirates.

Although the leaders of this organization are influenced by the ideology of the Egyptian and Tunisian fundamentalist movements, they have not engaged in any political activities in France. Rather, the main goal of the UOIF is to enhance Islamic culture by legal means and to help Muslims practice their religion in France. Its leaders seek to support the Islamic local associations in managing religious and educational activities. For example, an educational commission gives books to the local associations for the teaching of the Qur'ān and Arabic. Moreover, they have developed educational methods that relate specifically to the needs of Muslim children living in France; they want to protect these children from the temptations of the Western way of life by bringing them up in the Islamic religion. To this end, each year they organize children's holiday camps where there is Qur'ānic teaching; about six hundred families are normally involved in this activity. At the end of 1991, the UOIF created, with funds from Saudi Arabia, the first Muslim seminary in

France for the training of imams. In its first years of operation the seminary had few students and only seven who were not French.

The Union also supports the cause of Islam in France by improving the knowledge of this religion in the country generally. It sought, for instance, the authorization of the French Home Office for Muslim women to sit for their identity card photographs with their *ḥijāb*s (the Islamic headscarf) and supports allowing of Muslim girls to wear their *ḥijāb*s in the classrooms of the state schools. In addition, it organizes a conference on Islam in Paris, where an average of five thousand participants gather and discuss the various forms of Islam in France and in the world.

The UOIF is one of the many federations of Islamic associations in France, testifying to the diversity of French Muslims. These also point to the beginning of institutional answers to Muslim demands for an authentic "Islam of France," at the same time as their activities become substitutes for direct social and political participation.

[*See also* France.]

BIBLIOGRAPHY

Cesari, Jocelyne. *How to Be Muslim in France*. Paris, 1994.

Etienne, Bruno, ed. *L'Islam en France*. Paris, 1991. Excellent collection of articles on the various approaches of Islam in France.

"L'Islam en France." *Les Cahiers de l'Orient* 16–17 (1990): 3–113. Field surveys of Islamic communities during the headscarf affair of 1989.

Kepel, Gilles. *Les banlieues de l'Islam*. Paris, 1987. Analysis of an emerging political and social force in the French suburbs.

Leveau, Rémy. "Musulmans en France: Les enjeux." *Études* 374, no. 3 (March 1991): 323–332. The main stakes experienced by Muslims in France.

Leveau, Rémy, and Gilles Kepel, eds. *Les Musulmans dans la société française*. Paris, 1988. Several surveys on the sociopolitical behavior of French Muslim groups.

"Musulmans de France." *Migrations Société* 5–6 (October–December 1989): 5–80. Various forms of Islam in France according to area of immigrant origin and place of settlement.

Wihtol de Wenden, Catherine. "L'Islam en France." *Regards sur l'Actualité* 158 (February 1990): 23–36. Sociological analysis of the organization and diversity of Islam in France.

CATHERINE WIHTOL DE WENDEN and JOCELYNE CESARI

UNITED ARAB EMIRATES. *See* Gulf States.

UNITED KINGDOM. *See* Great Britain.

UNITED KINGDOM ISLAMIC MISSION. Founded in 1962 in small rented premises in London, and moved to its present head office in North Gower Street around 1980, the United Kingdom Islamic Mission has the express purpose of performing *daʿwah* (missionary activity) work in Britain. Its philosophy, expressed in 1984, is that "Islam as a way of life should be incorporated in all spheres of human life and should be passed on to others as an eternal source of guidance" (United Kingdom Islamic Mission, *Annual Report 1984*).

The policy of the mission is to bring the message of Islam to the United Kingdom's majority non-Muslim population through lectures and hospitality at the mission's various offices and mosques, as well as through distribution of copies of the Qur'ān and by running Islamic bookshops. From the beginning of its existence, however, the mission has concentrated its *daʿwah* program on the strengthening of Islam among immigrants of Muslim background. The main activity of the mission has consequently been the organization of classes in Qur'ān and basic Islamic teachings and practices for children of Muslim families. Several of the mission's centers also provide Urdu teaching. Regular lectures and short courses on Islamic subjects are organized for adults. During the 1980s the mission also started to offer legal advice, and in 1981 it established a marriage bureau. Training camps and activities are organized for young people, and when resources have been available, local branches of the mission organize pastoral visits to prisons.

The mission clearly comes out of the heritage of the Jamāʿat-i Islāmī of Pakistan. It works closely with the Islamic Foundation, which owns some of the buildings in which the mission works, for example, the large Islamic Centre in Sparkbrook, Birmingham. Some of the employees of the foundation are also members of the mission. A few years after the establishment of Bangladesh in 1971, a separate organization, Dawatul Islam, was established for members of Bangladeshi origin; cooperation between the two organizations remains close.

The mission has a three-tier structure of adherents on much the same lines as the Jamāʿat-i Islāmī. Full members commit themselves in their private and public lives to the rules of the mission. They are, for example, not allowed to take interest-bearing mortgages. During the 1980s full membership increased from just under 100 to about 150. Associated members carry a less onerous level of commitment and numbered upward of 500 by the end of the 1980s. Depending on personal circumstances, there is regular movement of individuals between the two categories. The third category is that of sympathizer, of which about 12,000 were claimed in 1985.

For most of the 1980s the mission had about forty branches, circles, and units, depending on the size and level of activity, across the United Kingdom. The largest groupings were to be found in Birmingham, Manchester, and Glasgow. Together, they reported an enrollment of nearly 4,000 children in classes in 1985, employing approximately 120 teachers and 30 imams or *khaṭībs*.

The number of sympathizers claimed by the mission is small compared to the total number of adult Muslims in Britain, and it is clear that many families see the mission's centers primarily as places to send their children for Islamic instruction and as their local mosques. The larger centers have made a significant impact in local communities by cultivating positive relations with the various branches of local government, schools, police, and the churches. In fact, the mission has been one of the most active Muslim organizations in cultivating good relations with churches across the United Kingdom.

[*See also* Great Britain; Islamic Foundation; Jamāʿat-i Islāmī.]

BIBLIOGRAPHY

The United Kingdom Islamic Mission publishes an *Annual Report*, available from the Mission at 202 North Gower Street, London NW1 2LY.

JØRGEN S. NIELSEN

UNITED MALAYS NATIONAL ORGANIZATION. An ethnic Malay party, the United Malays National Organization (UMNO) has been the dominant political force in multiethnic Malaya/Malaysia since the party's inception. UMNO's raison d'être has always been to protect and promote Malay political, sociocultural, religious, and economic interests. Its early goals as a secular political party led by westernized aristocrats were directed to unifying and channeling Malay nationalism and to gaining independence from the British, and later to maintaining political dominance while making compromises necessary in a multiethnic coalition.

Since the ethnic riots of 1969 and their political aftermath, the UMNO-led Malays have asserted their political hegemony, as can be seen in the party's economic policies, which are designed to uplift the Malays through extensive ethnic preferences. With hegemony and increasing cultural security, and with the Malay language no longer an effective ethnic marker, the one remaining significant cultural symbol of Malay ethnic distinctiveness is Islam.

The global Islamic resurgence that swept through Malaysia coincided with the coming to power inside UMNO in 1981 of a new type of UMNO Malay leadership under Prime Minister Dr. Mahathir Mohamed; this was nonaristocratic, locally educated, and somewhat anti-West, and it has been more comfortable than the previous leadership with mixing Islam and politics in a multiethnic and multireligious setting. As a result, the UMNO-dominated government has responded to the Malay opposition Islamic challenge posed by Partai Islam Se-Malaysia (PAS) by promoting an islamization program that, while it has rather alarmed non-Muslims, has so far enabled UMNO to "out-Islam" PAS [*see* Partai Islam Se-Malaysia].

Origins and History. Shortly before World War II, there was a limited and conservative awakening of Malay nationalism, concerned mainly with increasing Malay educational and economic opportunities. There was some mention of creating a national organization, but the war intervened.

After the war, the British inadvertently provided a catalyst to Malay nationalism by announcing a new political arrangement, the Malayan Union, that stripped away most of the powers of the Malay rulers of the various states and offered liberal citizenship regulations for non-Malays. Two months after a White Paper on the Malayan Union was made public, in March 1946, three hundred delegates from forty-one Malay associations from all parts of the peninsula met as a congress in Kuala Lumpur to discuss forming a national organization to ward off "the ignominy of racial extinction." The congress agreed to form a United Malays National Organization, and a committee was set up to draft a constitution. In May 1946 in Johor Bahru, UMNO was formally inaugurated, and Dato Onn bin Ja'afar was elected its first president.

After some Malay mass demonstrations, noncooperation in the bureaucracy, and a boycott of the Malayan Union inaugural ceremonies, the British quickly capitulated. It was announced in July 1946 that the Malayan Union would be replaced, and UMNO was invited to draft formal proposals for an alternative system of government. The alternative was the Federation of Malaya, which was promulgated in February 1948. The new constitutional arrangement represented a phenomenal victory for UNMO and the Malays. The powers of the Malay rulers were restored, special rights for Malays were instituted, and citizenship for non-Malays was tightly restricted. The party remained a rather loose alliance of diverse groups in its early years; it was not until 1949 that direct, rather than organizational, membership was instituted.

Having successfully accomplished its first major goal and having emerged as the dominant indigenous political force in the country, UMNO came almost naturally into its role in promoting independence, although its leaders stressed that the process should be slow and gradual. The British, for their part, made it abundantly clear to the leaders of the respective ethnic communities that they would only be granted independence when it was demonstrated that the various communities could live together peacefully. To this end, Dato Onn came to believe that independence required multiethnic cooperation and that the obvious vehicle for this would be a multiethnic party. In 1951, however, he resigned when the UMNO rank-and-file flatly refused to accept his proposal to open the party's membership to all ethnic groups.

Ironically, the electoral challenge posed by Dato Onn's newly formed multiethnic party in the 1952 Kuala Lumpur Municipal Election led to an informal alliance between the local chapters of UMNO and the Malayan Chinese Association. The success of the ad hoc alliance in this election and subsequent local elections led to the establishment of a formal Alliance party, also including the Malayan Indian Congress, which swept fifty-one of fifty-two seats in the first Legislative Council elections in 1955. The elites of the three ethnic parties comprising the Alliance then worked out and sold to the British and their respective communities a set of constitutional compromises and unwritten understandings known as "the Bargain." The essence of this understanding was that Malays would dominate politically, but the economic interests of non-Malays would be unhindered. The 1957 independence constitution gave the non-Malays revisions in citizenship regulations and the provision of *jus soli* in return for accepting Malay special rights, Islam as the state religion (but with freedom of religion guaranteed), Malay as the sole official language in ten years' time (if parliament approved), and the maintenance of the position of the state rulers. With independence, Tunku Abdul Rahman, a prince of the Kedah royal house and a Cambridge graduate, became the first prime minister. Although publicly UMNO proclaimed that it was merely "first among equals" in the Alliance, it was clearly understood by the partners that UMNO was to dominate.

Despite the saliency of ethnicity and the problems it posed, this arrangement of elite agreement within the Alliance worked well for more than a decade, through the creation of Malaysia in 1963 (by adding Singapore and the Bornean states of Sabah and Sarawak to Malaya), several years of armed confrontation instigated by Indonesia, and the expulsion of Singapore in 1965 because of ethnic conflict. During the 1969 election campaign, however, conflicting ethnic demands escalated. In an atmosphere of heightened ethnic antagonism, riots broke out, mayhem ensued, and a state of emergency was declared.

By the time parliamentary rule was reconvened in 1971, the political system had been altered to entrench certain sensitive ethnic provisions in the constitution and to make the questioning of these provisions illegal. Further, a coalition-building strategy was undertaken by the new prime minister, Tun Razak, to broaden the government's base of support, and in 1974 a nine-party Barisan Nasional coalition replaced the Alliance. It was made bluntly clear in the new coalition that while some ethnic compromises were still possible, and certain protections would continue to be afforded to the non-Malay community, UMNO intended on the whole to exercise its dominance to uplift the Malay community.

Technically, UMNO no longer exists. Following very closely contested UMNO party elections in April 1987, in which Dr. Mahathir and his deputy were barely re-elected, an appeal was made to the High Court to nullify the party elections because unregistered branches had illegally participated in the voting. In February 1988, the High Court judge stunned the nation by declaring that because unregistered branches had participated, in accordance with the law under the Societies Act, UMNO was an illegal organization that must be deregistered. Subsequently Dr. Mahathir registered a new party called UMNO Baru (New UMNO). After the Supreme Court eventually dismissed an appeal in August 1988 to relegalize the old UMNO, the government and press began dropping the "new" from the party name, and the party claimed not only the old UMNO's assets but also its history. Today the party exists, albeit considerably more authoritarian in its structure, for all intents and purposes as if it were the original party.

Ideological Foundations. UMNO was formed by a number of diverse Malay associations and organizations; however, the first leaders were uniformly westernized aristocrats, and the model they adopted for the party was that of a fully secular Western-style party. But because the aim was to unite all Malays, an effort was made to made to create an umbrella organization under which all Malays could fit. Hence, in 1950 a religious wing (or department) was created, known as Persatuan Ulama-ulama Sa-Malaya (Pan-Malayan Union of the Religiously Learned), under the leadership of Haji Ahmad Fuad. When this organization broke away in 1951 and helped form UMNO's archrival, PAS, no new Islamic wing was contemplated.

Before the Islamic wing left the party, the religious department successfully sponsored a number of rather conservative resolutions, such as fixing a date for the commencement of the fasting month, setting up Islamic studies scholarships for Malays wishing to study abroad, and fully implementing Islamic laws against prostitution and related evils. The department also urged the establishment of Islamic councils in states that were without them and urged that work be undertaken to establish nationally uniform Islamic laws and forms of administration.

UMNO's leaders wanted to retain the support of Islamic leaders, and certainly UMNO's policy was to propagate, enhance, and uplift "the excellence of the Religion of Islam." To this end, the UMNO/Alliance government was willing to channel money to build and repair mosques and *suraus* (prayer houses), to sponsor national and international Islamic conferences and Qur'ān-reading competitions, and to support Islamic education. UMNO also stressed Islamic moral virtues and took pains to convince followers that it was not "un-Islamic" for the government to run lotteries, for banks to allow interest on savings, or for peasants to use their *zakat* (tithes) contribution for economic investment.

Nonetheless, UMNO's specific commitment to Islam was limited. Constitutionally, Islam was primarily the prerogative of the rulers of each state, who jealously protected this power. The rulers in turn were guided by Islamic Councils of *ʿulamāʾ*. Hence, the apex of the formal structure of authority and administration of Islamic affairs was (and largely remains) at the state level, where the UMNO leaders were happy to leave it. Further, UMNO's leaders did not believe that the establishment of an Islamic state in Malaysia was either practical or desirable. They were interested in creating a modern, developed secular state adhering to the principles of parliamentary democracy. As Funston points out (1980, p. 146), their outlook was neither traditional nor modernist. They were practicing Muslims but also dedicated political secularists, and they believed that most religious decisions should be left to the individual. To this end, an Islamic state (especially if theocratic) was not seen as a suitable model. Indeed, many of the top UMNO leaders shared a concern that some of the traditional rural Islamic practices and observances might actually retard efforts to achieve economic development. The UMNO rank-and-file seemed to agree with the leaders, which was not too surprising given the feudal nature of Malay society at that time. In 1951 they overwhelmingly rejected a proposal by the Singapore Malay Union that UMNO should have as a goal the establishment of an Islamic state. The first noticeable change in this consistent attitude of keeping Islam at arm's length occurred in 1968, when the Tunku finally relented under pressure from Islamic activists and allowed the formation of a National Council for Islamic Affairs to guide the king—the symbolic leader of Islam at the federal level—in administering national Islamic affairs.

In the 1970s, Islamic affairs assumed a much more prominent role in UMNO, partly because of the Islamic revival and competition against PAS, partly because of different personalities leading UMNO and rank-and-file pressure, and partly because after May 1969 UMNO no longer felt that it needed to muzzle sectarian sentiments. In general, however, the change was symbolic in nature. UMNO leaders started wearing the *songkok* (an Indonesian-style Islamic cap) and attending more conscientiously, at least publicly, to the devotional duties of Islam, such as being seen regularly at Friday prayers. Rock concerts and X-rated movies were banned and other movies noticeably censored as a more puritanical official policy was implemented. Symbolically, the name of the Red Cross was changed to the Red Crescent.

Since mid-1981, when Dr. Mahathir became prime minister, the UMNO-led government has sought to contain the resurgence with its own islamization program and simultaneously to assert more direct leadership and control over Islamic affairs, which can be seen in a number of actions. In 1982 it wooed and coopted Anwar Ibrahim, the charismatic leader of the Muslim Youth Movement of Malaysia (known as ABIM), the most important politicized fundamentalist organization in the country [*see* ABIM]; it established a larger federal bureaucratic Islamic infrastructure and increased the powers of the National Council for Islamic Affairs; it tightened the Societies Act governing associations and amended the penal code in 1983 to give the federal government the absolute right to interpret the Qur'ān, *syariah* (Ar., *sharīʿah*) law, and Islamic teachings (so that those responsible for "deviant" teachings and "incorrect" interpretations could be held liable to prosecution); and it sponsored *daʿwah* (missionary) programs and conferences. Further, in 1982 Dr. Mahathir claimed that Malaysia was already an Islamic state, though not a theocracy, and UMNO started describing itself as the "the world's oldest and third largest Muslim political party" (an admitted guess by a minister that is now stated as fact).

The islamization process also is evident in the establishment of a number of new institutions: an Islamic bank (Bank Islam Malaysia), followed by Islamic insurance companies and pawnshops; an International Islamic University; a Malaysian Islamic Development Foundation; and an Islamic Teachers Training College. Further, the government decided to upgrade the position of *kadis* (Ar., *qāḍī;* Islamic judges) and *syariah* courts to the level of magistrates and civil courts. More symbolically, bans were placed on the importation of non-*ḥalāl* beef (beef not slaughtered in accordance with Islamic ritual), and on smoking in all government offices; the government introduced increased instruction in and use of Jawi (Arabic script); the traditional moon-sighting method for determining Ramadan was reestablished; and the supplementary meal program in all national primary schools was ordered suspended during the fasting month, even for non-Muslim students. The tone of the islamization program has been to show that Islam is dynamic and adaptable to present-day needs, and that a disciplined and morally upright society can modernize without sacrificing Islamic values.

The steps taken by Dr. Mahathir have served to upgrade UMNO's credentials as an Islamic party and have helped UMNO electorally to "out-Islam" its rival, PAS. However, it is not clear that the extensive islamization that has taken place so far has lessened the determination of the fundamentalists to see the constitution altered to allow the imposition of Islamic laws and administration federally. If UMNO feels it must—or chooses to—proceed further with islamization, this may present problems. Inevitably the rights of non-Muslims will be impinged on if Islamic morality laws are implemented and replace civil law, as was suggested briefly at one point, or if Islamic laws in the PAS-controlled state of Kelantan are allowed to apply to non-Muslims, as the prime minister in 1992 stated he would allow them to be.

[*See also* Malaysia.]

BIBLIOGRAPHY

Fan Yew Teng. *The UMNO Drama: Power Struggles in Malaysia.* Kuala Lumpur, 1989. Chronicles the events surrounding the major UMNO split in 1987.

Funston, N. J. *Malay Politics in Malaysia.* Kuala Lumpur, 1980. Detailed study of the origins and development of the two major Malay political parties.

Mauzy, Diane K. *Barisan Nasional.* Kuala Lumpur, 1983. Account of Tun Razak's coalition-building strategy that led to the creation of the ruling nine-party Barisan Nasional under UMNO's domination.

Mauzy, Diane K., and R. S. Milne. "The Mahathir Administration in Malaysia: Discipline Through Islam." *Pacific Affairs* 56.4 (Winter 1983–1984): 617–648. Concerned with early Mahathir policies, particularly his policy of islamization.

Means, Gordon P. *Malaysian Politics: The Second Generation.* Singapore, 1991. Comprehensive and well-done modern political history.

Milne, R. S., and Diane K. Mauzy. *Politics and Government in Malaysia.* 2d ed., rev. Singapore and Vancouver, B.C., 1980. Includes detailed discussion of postindependence party politics and the political process.

Pillay, Chandrasekaran. "Protection of the Malay Community: A Study of UMNO's Position and Opposition Attitudes." Master's Thesis, Universiti Sains Malaysia, 1974. Perceptive study by one of Malaysia's leading intellectuals and social reformers (now known since his conversion to Islam as Chandra Muzaffar).

Ratnam, K. J. *Communalism and the Political Process in Malaya.* Kuala Lumpur, 1965. Indispensable reading for the ethnic agreements worked out at the time of independence; a classic.

Stockwell, A. J. "The Formation and First Years of the United Malays National Organization (U.M.N.O.), 1946–1948." *Modern Asian Studies* 2.4 (October 1977): 481–513. Solid account of the origins of UMNO.

von der Mehden, Fred R. "Malaysia: Islam and Multiethnic Politics." In *Islam in Asia: Religion, Politics, and Society,* edited by John L. Esposito, pp. 177–201. New York and Oxford, 1987. Sophisticated discussion of the political impact of Islam by a leading expert on the subject.

DIANE K. MAUZY

UNITED STATES OF AMERICA. With some three to four million adherents in the United States today, and with numerous Islamic institutions—mosques, centers, and schools—located across the continent, Islam is clearly an American religion. The community is made up of immigrants, African American and white converts, and sojourners (students, diplomats, visitors, and business people). Some two-thirds have either recently arrived from overseas or are second and third generation Americans. Most of the rest are African Americans, belonging to Sunnī Islam or any of a number of sectarian movements.

The Muslim community in North America is growing through immigration, conversion, and procreation, and by early in the next century there might well be more Muslims than Jews in the United States. Most of the major cities of the United States have Muslim populations, with the largest concentrations located in New York City, Chicago, Los Angeles, and Houston. The majority of Muslims in America (about 90 percent) are not associated with organized religious institutions. They continue to identify themselves as Muslims, however, and often come together to celebrate special occasions, such as festivals and observances. They also share with their coreligionists many of the general concerns related to life in American society.

Early History. Increasing evidence is being uncovered by Muslims to suggest that there is a long history of Muslim activity in America. A few scholars have argued for a pre-Columbian presence, as well as for early West African explorations in the Caribbean. It seems fairly certain that Spanish Muslim sailors acted as guides for discoverers from Spain and Portugal and that perhaps thousands of Moriscos (Spaniards who clandestinely retained their Muslim identity after 1492) came to the Americas in the 1500s, most of whom subsequently disappeared through persecution and assimilation.

From the seventeenth to the nineteenth century a major transfer of Muslim population to America took place. Perhaps as much as one-fifth of the Africans brought in the slave trade were Muslim. At first they might have attempted to practice their religion, but most were forced into conversion to Christianity. Little remains of the records of these Muslim slaves aside from a few narratives and a Qur'ān apparently written down from memory. We do hear of some Muslim revolts, such as that in 1758 in Haiti and the brief establishment of a Muslim state in Brazil. The virtual disappearance of earlier African Muslims in America because of intense persecution has been reversed in the twentieth century by the growth of African American Islam and the increase in immigration from continental Africa.

Immigration to America. Regular Muslim emigration to America from various parts of the Islamic world began in the late nineteenth century, with Arabs from the Ottoman Empire comprising the majority. The first wave of immigrants came around 1875 from what was then Syria and was later divided into the countries of Syria, Lebanon, Jordan, and Palestine. They were mainly unskilled and uneducated, peasants who hoped to become financially successful in America, at least in relative terms, and then to return to their homeland. Opportunities were limited, however, and most were forced to become migrant, factory, or mine workers or peddlers, while others became grocers, shopkeepers, and petty merchants. Some decided to homestead in areas of the Midwest, while others ended up serving as cheap labor on work gangs. Many never realized their dreams either of earning a fortune in the new land or of returning home, but those who made it became an impetus for further emigration of their compatriots. The flow of this immigration was interrupted by the end of World War I. A second wave followed in the twenties only to be stopped by World War II. Immigration laws of this period allowed only persons who were negroid or caucasian; Arabs were considered to belong to neither category.

A third wave between the mid-1940s and the mid-1960s was initiated by very different circumstances abroad. Many of those who came were much better educated than the earlier immigrants, often leaving to escape political oppression. The largest contingent were Palestinians leaving after the creation of the state of Israel, Egyptians whose property had been confiscated in the nationalization policies of Gamal Abdel Nasser, Iraqis who wanted to leave after the revolution of 1948, and Muslims from Eastern Europe trying to escape the ravages of World War II or of communist rule.

Changes in immigration policies of the United States in the 1960s placed the needs of the labor market and the potential of immigrants to fulfill those needs over racial or ethnic restrictions. The fourth wave, still in progress, began around 1967. Those arriving in this last influx for the most part have been well educated, westernized, and generally fluent in English. Coming for reasons such as professional advancement and in many cases the desire to escape oppressive regimes, they are clear in their desire to settle in America and to achieve economic and social status. Exceptions to this general trend are the less well educated, often illiterate and unskilled, workers from Yemen and Palestine and some Shīʿīs from Lebanon. Increased numbers of Muslims have come to Canada from the former British colonies of Uganda and Rhodesia (Zimbabwe). Many Indo-Pakistanis and some Africans have moved to Canada, some of whom subsequently have settled in the United States.

Since the 1970s immigrants have reflected the growing Islamic consciousness that has developed as a result of American foreign policy in Muslim nations. There are significant numbers of immigrants and sojourners who have come to escape difficult social and political circumstances in their home countries, including Iranians leaving as a result of the overthrow of the shah; Kurds, Kuwaitis, and Palestinians fleeing after the Gulf War; and Afghans and Somalis, among others, escaping from civil war or famine.

In the mid-twentieth century immigrant Muslims from the Middle East generally were committed to Arab socialism or nationalism and were more secular than religious in orientation. More recently, however, commitments have changed dramatically. Far greater numbers of immigrants from such areas as Southeast Asia and the Arab world are Islamically committed. These Muslims, the majority of whom are well-educated professionals, are interested in establishing a solid religious community in their adopted country. Mosque building has increased substantially, owing both to the commitments of the members of the Islamic community and to the donations coming from oil-rich Gulf countries for the construction of religious establishments in America.

Over the past several decades a number of factors have led to a rapid growth in Islamic institutions and organizations in America. The Muslim population itself has increased markedly, the community is searching for ways in which to establish roots and provide instruction for its children. A series of events, however, have created an atmosphere in which Islam has been criticized and defiled. The Iranian Revolution of 1979, the Israeli invasion of Lebanon, the bombing of Libya, the controversy surrounding the publication of Salman Rushdie's novel, *The Satanic Verses,* and the bombing of the World Trade Center have led to sharp critiques of Islam on the part of the media and the American public. Despite this, the number of Muslim institutions in the United States has risen to more than 2,300, of which more than 1,300 are mosques and Islamic centers.

Islamic Organizations. The earliest immigrants to continental America were often single, young, and usually not well informed about Islamic practices or doctrines. Busy with their economic pursuits and often seeing their stay in America as only temporary, they did not attempt to locate religious communities or identify structures for worship. Gradually, however, small groups gathered for prayer, often led by someone in the community not educated in the essentials of the faith. A number of communities began to consider the importance of establishing a mosque in their area, and soon new structures were built as they began to develop Islamic organizations and institutions. Finding or erecting buildings to serve as mosques or Islamic centers began in the 1920s and 1930s; by 1952 more than twenty mosques formed the Federation of Islamic Associations (FIA) in the United States and Canada. At its peak about fifty mosques were part of the FIA.

Immigrants of the 1960s committed to an Islamist perspective found the FIA to be too americanized. When their efforts to islamize these mosques and make them conform to institutions in Pakistan and Egypt failed, they initiated their own organizations to meet their own specific needs. [*See* Federation of Islamic Associations.]

The Muslim Student Association in the U.S.A. and Canada (MSA) was founded in 1963 by a small group of students to provide service to the hundreds of thousands of Muslim students from overseas enrolled on American campuses, many of whom would return to play major leadership roles in national and international Islamic movements. The MSA regularly sponsors Friday and other prayers on college campuses and establishes Islamic libraries and other services for students. The organization is international in perspective and advocates an Islam that transcends all linguistic, ethnic, and racial distinctions.

Particular needs of students from specific countries initiated nation-specific groups, such as the Muslim Student Association, Persian Speaking Group, founded in the late 1970s by a group of Iranian students. There are now several other linguistically oriented student organizations which cater to specific ethnic identities, including the Muslim Arab Youth Association and a group for Malaysian students.

The Islamic Medical Association was formed by alumni of the MSA in 1967 as a locus for Muslim health professionals to meet, exchange information, and provide services to others in the community. Similar organizations are the Association of Muslim Scientists and Engineers, begun in 1969 for the promotion of scientific research based on Islamic principles, and the Association of Muslim Social Scientists, started in 1972 as a professional, academic, educational, and cultural organization to promote Islamic thought. All of these associations sponsor annual publications and conferences.

In 1978 the Council of Masajid of the United States was established by representatives of the Muslim World

League with a membership of twenty mosques. It has now been consolidated with the Council of Masajid of Canada, formed in 1983, as the Continental Council of Masajid of North America, with the goals of aiding local mosques in their educational and outreach programs, helping them acquire permanent buildings for mosques, perpetuating Islamic culture, and facilitating communications with non-Muslims. By 1985, 151 mosques in the United States and Canada were affiliates. Its sponsorship by a Saudi-based organization, the Muslim World League, has led some to be concerned about foreign intervention in American Muslim affairs.

The Islamic Society of North America (ISNA) is an umbrella organization created in 1982 by the board and alumni of MSA who decided to settle in North America; they were interested in addressing the needs of the Muslim community in the United States. The MSA became a subsidiary group focusing primarily on the needs of students. Headquartered in Plainfield, Indiana, the ISNA provides assistance to students and other Muslims living in America through meetings and conferences, publication of a journal, and helping to negotiate an authentic Islamic presence in North America. More than 350 mosques and Islamic centers are affiliated. [*See* Islamic Society of North America.]

Shīʿī Muslims. Although most of the Muslims who emigrate to America are Sunnī, there is also a sizable community of Shīʿīs who are beginning to gain greater recognition as a separate and identifiable segment of the Islamic population with major mosques in New York, Detroit, Washington, Los Angeles, and Chicago, as well as several major cities in Canada. Until fairly recently little attention was paid to the Shīʿī presence, in part because of the attempt by Muslims themselves to present Islam as a unified whole and in part because there were relatively few Shīʿīs among the immigrant population. That situation changed noticeably since the 1979 revolution in Iran. As a result of the revolution and of the costly war between Iran and Iraq, a large number of Iranians have left the Middle East to come to the United States. The Lebanese civil war and the Israeli invasion of Lebanon in 1982 also displaced many Shīʿīs who now have settled in such areas as Dearborn, Michigan.

Shīʿī immigrants in the late nineteenth and early twentieth centuries tended to be uneducated and relatively impoverished workers, as was true of Sunnīs emigrating at that time, and many of the more recent arrivals from Iran are from the better-educated middle and upper-middle classes. Most are members of the Ithnā ʿAshari (Twelver) branch of Islam, who believe that the twelfth imam disappeared in the tenth century and will return at the end of time to establish justice in the world. In the meantime Twelvers acknowledge the authority of their religious scholars in Iran and Iraq. Substantial numbers of Iranian Shīʿīs have settled in areas of Texas and southern California where they await the time when Prince Reza Pahlavi, son of the late shah, will be restored to power in Iran. The Twelver Shīʿīs have the only operating Islamic seminary in the Americas, located in Medina, New York. It provides a four-year course of Islamic instruction for male students (studying to be imams) at the Jamiʿa Wali al-ʿAsr and for female students (who want to have a teaching career) at Madrasah al-Khadija al-Kubra.

Among other Shīʿī groups in America are the Ismāʿīlīyah (Seveners), who believe that Prince Karim Aga Khan (b. 1936) is the forty-ninth hereditary imam. They have established a thriving community of more than eighty thousand in Canada, especially in Vancouver and Toronto, and have small communities scattered throughout the United States, especially in New York and California. Ismāʿīlīs place a very high premium on education. They have a strong organizational structure and have been able to replicate their institutions effectively in the United States. There are also small pockets of ʿAlawīyūn from Syria, Lebanon, and Turkey and Zaydīyah from Yemen. [*See* Aga Khan; Ismāʿīlīyah; ʿAlawīyah.]

African American Muslims. Roughly a third of the Muslims in continental America are African Americans who have decided to join either mainstream Islam or one of the sectarian movements directly or loosely identified with Islamic doctrines. The earliest to claim a Muslim connection were the followers of Timothy Drew (1886–1929), who changed his name to Noble Drew Ali and began to preach that Christianity is the religion of whites and that the true religion for "Asiatics" (blacks) is Islam. In 1913, in Newark, New Jersey, he founded the Moorish American Science Temple, whose *Koran* is entirely different from the Holy Qur'ān of Islam. The movement spread to such major cities as Detroit and Philadelphia, eventually weakening after the death of its founder; remnants of the community remain today in over seventy major cities.

Islam as a truly American phenomenon first caught the attention of the United States with the rise of the Nation of Islam. In 1929 a person probably of either Turkish or Iranian origin by the name of W. D. Fard began to preach in Detroit on the theme of Islam as the true identity for African Americans. Calling them real Muslims who in this country have been separated from their homeland, he became the first spokesperson for what came to be known as "The Lost-Found Nation of Islam in the Wilderness of North America," or simply the Nation of Islam. Fard's preaching was heard by one Elijah Poole, born in Georgia in 1897, who assumed the name Elijah Muhammad and soon became the leader of the movement and its "Messenger of God." After the disappearance of Fard, Elijah Muhammad preached the necessity of bringing blacks in America to an understanding of their true nature as Muslims and of helping the community regain its self-respect, ethical integrity, and economic independence from whites.

Nation of Islam doctrines were in many ways antithetical to Islam. Elijah taught that the white man is the devil and the black man is good, and that the only way to success for blacks is to separate themselves from their longtime oppressors. His emphasis on ethical responsibility, hard work, and moral uprightness, as well as identification of the root causes of the suffering of blacks, was extremely appealing to many in the African American community. Many of the former followers of Noble Drew Ali, as well as some of the followers of Marcus Garvey, rallied to the call of the Nation of Islam to assume their identity as Muslims.

Although the center of Nation of Islam activity has been in Chicago, temples were established in depressed black areas of a number of metropolitan cities. The message appealed to those needing a way out of their difficult circumstances, including some blacks incarcerated in large urban prisons. Prison ministry has been and continues to be one of the most effective means of recruiting African Americans to Islam. The Nation was also attractive to a number of persons who occupied leadership positions in the African American community, including the educated and professional elite. Several branches were established in the Caribbean and Canada.

By the 1960s internal difficulties began to disrupt the community. Malcolm X (1925–1965), the most prominent and articulate of the Nation of Islam leaders, had converted to Islam in prison and become a deeply committed follower of Elijah Muhammad. A combination of personal disillusionment with his leader and his experience on the pilgrimage of a universal Islam inclusive of all persons and races led Malcolm X to a final break with the Nation of Islam. He was assassinated at a religious rally in 1965; two Nation of Islam members were convicted of the murder. [*See* Nation of Islam *and the biographies of Elijah Muhammad and Malcolm X.*]

With the death of Elijah Muhammad in 1975, the leadership of the movement was assumed by his son Wallace, under the name Warith Deen Muhammad. He began to lead the community away from the separatist teachings of his father and closer to the egalitarian understanding of Sunnī Islam. He preached that Elijah Muhammad's message had been essential to the recovery of the black community in America at the time, a necessary transitional step in their movement from slave mentality toward accepting true Islam. Having received a classical Islamic education, Warith Deen Muhammad assumed the title of *mujaddid* (renewer of faith) and immediately led the movement through a number of name changes, from "Nation of Islam" to "The American Bilalian Community" after the first black convert to Islam under the prophet Muḥammad, to "The World Community of Islam in the West" in 1976, to "The American Muslim Mission" in 1980. Eventually in 1985 the community was urged to integrate into mainstream Sunnī Islam. Warith Deen Muhammad's broadcasts are heard every weekend on more than thirty radio stations across the country.

Elijah Muhammad's Nation of Islam instituted a nationwide system of education known as the University of Islam, later restructured under his son as the Sister Clara Muhammad Schools. Today it includes more than fifty academically certified institutions across the country. These schools offer a curriculum of Islamic studies as well as basic instruction for elementary and sometimes high school students. The individual schools are not responsible to any central authority, but they generally offer a fairly uniform curriculum.

The Nation of Islam as a separate group continues under the leadership of Minister Louis Farrakhan. Concerted efforts are being made to establish a strong black economic system in which members can be free of the dominant white structures. Nation of Islam members also have taken active leadership roles in local community efforts to keep neighborhoods free of drugs and drug-related crime. Farrakhan's movement is based in Chicago, but three other groups lay claim to being the authentic Nation of Islam under different leaders in Baltimore, Detroit, and Atlanta.

Other Muslim groups have attracted African Americans to Sunnī Islam. One that drew considerable attention in the 1960s was known as the Darul Islam movement. Initially formed in the late 1940s and early 1950s, the group established the first Darul Islam mosque in Brooklyn in 1962. It grew fairly rapidly, disbanded because of internal disagreements, and reformed in the early 1970s under the leadership of Imam Yahya. Darul Islam members have had occasional problems with local police; the brotherhood developed what was called a ministry of defense and a parliamentary force called Ra'd (Thunder). By the middle of the 1970s, thirty-one mosque-based Sunnī African American communities had chosen to affiliate with the Darul Islam movement, mainly in the larger cities of the East Coast and a few in the Caribbean. In 1980 Imam Yahya abdicated his leadership of the group; many of his former followers have started local groups and some have come under the influence of a Ṣūfī organization. Other African American Sunnī organizations include the Ḥanafī movement, the Islamic party of North America, the Union of Brothers, and the Islamic People's Movement, centered in the Caribbean and with a mosque in Washington, D.C.

African American and immigrant Muslims for the most part have maintained separate communities in the United States, although there are increasing efforts at cooperation, conversation, and some common worship and social activities. With the return of most of the former members of the Nation of Islam to the fold of Sunnī Islam under Warith Deen Muhammad, significant issues remain to be resolved between the two communities. Some African Americans believe that they are more diligent than their immigrant brothers and sisters in observing the strict codes of diet, dress, and other forms of observance. Immigrants, however, often tend to think that as lifelong Muslims they have a better understanding of Islam than do those who have recently converted. African Americans are a product of American society and are looking for ways to function as equals in the American context; they often feel that they are the most appropriate ones to interpret Islam to non-Muslims. Many immigrant Muslims acknowledge that they might not yet understand American society, but they are nonetheless reluctant to delegate the negotiation of the place of Islam in America to African Americans.

White Converts to Islam. Leaders in the Islamic community estimate that there are some 45,000 to 80,000 white converts in America. Among the earliest was Alexander Russell Webb (d. 1916), U.S. consul to the Philippines at the end of the nineteenth century. Disenchanted with Christianity, Webb began a correspondence with Mirzā Ghulām Aḥmad, leader of the Aḥmadīyah in Lahore, and eventually became an articulate spokesperson for Islam in America. He published a journal called *The Moslem World* as well as several texts about Islam.

The majority of white converts to Islam are women who have married Muslim men and decided to adopt the faith themselves. In some cases women convert before finding a marriage partner out of the conviction that women are held in higher esteem in Islam than in American society in general. A number of Americans who have found themselves at odds either with their own religious tradition or denomination or with the prevailing norms of American culture have looked to Islam to provide alternatives. Often they choose to affiliate with established Ṣūfī or mystical schools of thought operating in the American context.

Sectarian Movements. The Aḥmadīyah movement, an Indo-Pakistani missionary community which for many years has been active in translating the Qur'ān into the world's major languages, began sending agents to America for the express purpose of converting the West to its version of Islam. Failing in early efforts to convert the white population and Sunnī Muslims to their doctrines, the Aḥmadīyah began to target the African American community. Considered a heretical movement by most Muslims, Aḥmadī groups are found in a number of the larger cities of the United States. Since the 1960s both the Qadiani (with headquarters in Washington, D.C.) and the Lahori (with headquarters in California) groups have established several mosques in the United States. [*See* Aḥmadīyah.]

There is also a small Druze community in the United States, the majority of whose members are of Lebanese origin with a few individuals from Syria, Palestine, and Jordan. The Druze originally grew out of Ismāʿīlī Shiism. Some Druze in America today identify themselves as Muslims, although others reject that association. The largest Druze concentration is in Los Angeles, with chapters of the American Druze Society in a number of other cities. Another offshoot of Islam found in America is the Bahā'ī religion. Founded by Bahā' Allāh in Iran in the mid-nineteenth century, Bahā'ī faith was first brought to the United States in 1892. The largest community is in the Chicago area, with the temple and national Bahā'ī archives found in Wilmette, Illinois. Like other immigrant groups, Bahā'īs struggle to determine their distinctive identity in the American context. [*See* Druze; Bahā'ī.]

Among the growing number of African American sectarian movements calling themselves Islamic is that identified as the Five Percenters. A splinter group from the Nation of Islam formed in 1964 under Clarence "Pudding" 13X, they believe that they are the chosen 5 percent of humanity. They see 85 percent of humankind as doomed to self-destruction; another 10 percent has right knowledge and power but use it to deceive the majority. It is the 5 percent who are living a truly righteous Islamic life, manifesting the divine nature of the black man, that are identified with Allāh. The headquarters of the group continues to be in Harlem, although the Five Percenters have branches in major U.S. cities and in many prisons. Five Percenters are highly visible in the rap music industry, using the quick and complicated form of rap lyrics to spread the 5 percent ideology, called the Science of Supreme Mathematics.

The sectarian Ansaru Allah Community was founded in 1970 by Isa Muhammad, born York and known variously as Isa al Haadi al-Mahdi and As Sayyid al Imam Isa al-Mahdi. Isa Muhammad was influenced by the black power movements of the 1960s and his teachings reflect a disenchantment with the culture of the United States, which he considers to be racist. A prolific writer, Isa consistently has presented himself as the divinely inspired interpreter of the true message of the Qur'ān and in the direct lineage of the Sudanese Mahdi, Muḥammad Aḥmad ibn ʿAbd Allāh. Since the founding of the Ansaru Allah in 1970, Isa Muhammad has moved from doctrines of black supremacy to a much closer affiliation with the egalitarian teachings of Islam and back to the original teachings on race with special invective against "pale Arab" Muslims. More recently he has become identified as Rabboni: Yashuʿa. The official headquarters of the group is in Brooklyn, with branches in a number of major cities, including Philadelphia and Los Angeles. Members maintain an active ministry in the penal system. Isa Muhammad's followers can be seen selling his publications in such prominent places as Times Square in New York City.

Ṣūfī Movements. Although many of the Ṣūfī sects are not recognized by Sunnī Muslims as legitimate, others are an acknowledged part of the complex fabric of Muslim life in America. The resurgence of interest among young Americans in religions of the east, most prevalent in the 1960s, contributed to the popularity of these Ṣūfī movements, some of whose members have relatively little knowledge of or even interest in classical Islamic doctrines and practices. Some members do not even realize that Sufism has any connection with Islam.

Among the most influential Ṣūfī orders are the Qādirīyah, which is embodied in the Bawa Muhaiyaddeen Fellowship located in Philadelphia. The fellowship has more than two thousand converts, primarily from the highly educated middle- and upper-middle classes. Members engage in Ṣūfī sessions and listen to taped teachings of the now-deceased Bawa Muhaiyaddeen, whose burial site is considered by some immigrants as a *walī* (saint) shrine.

Ṣūfī convert groups are also found in Upstate New York, California, Texas, Michigan and New Mexico. Some immigrants have perpetuated the Ṣūfī *ṭarīqahs* (lit., "ways") of their countries of origin. These include the Bektashīs, the most thriving of which is the Albanian *tekke* (building for Ṣūfī activities) in Detroit (with a resident Ṣūfī shaykh), the Shādhilīyah, the Ishrāqīyah (among Iranians), and the Naqshbandīyah (among Syrians and Turks).

Islamic Concerns. Among the issues of deep concern to Muslims in America today are the continuing and heightening instances of prejudice in North America against Islam, Arabs, and Muslims. This has encouraged many Muslims over the years to keep a low profile. More recently, concerned with the distorted and inaccurate picture of Islam presented by the media and in the biased treatment of Muslims in textbooks, news coverage, and entertainment programming, Muslims have begun to organize to provide more reliable information. Several Muslim groups have developed television programs on Muslim faith and practice that are aired in the United States and are also distributed worldwide. They also publish numerous magazines, books, and audio- and videotapes on the Muslim experience. More consistent efforts are being put forth to consciously develop mutual systems of support, including political action committees, to combat anti-Muslim views. Some Muslims have initiated conversations with members of Christian and Jewish religious communities for the purpose of providing more accurate data about the nature of Islam in this country and abroad. [*See* Muslim-Christian Dialogue; Muslim-Jewish Dialogue.]

Whether or not to try to assimilate into American society, or in what degree, has been a continuing issue for each wave of immigrants as well as each generation of Muslims in America. Muslims want to be acknowledged as full members of American society, whether as representatives of their respective national groupings, as members of the community of Islam, or simply as American citizens. At the same time some Muslims are recognizing that the prevailing culture often is inimical to their own understanding of Islam; in order to be true to their beliefs it may be necessary not only to maintain social practice and observance in line with the dictates of Islam but also to develop alternative forms of economics and education.

The Social Security system in the United States, for example, has raised questions concerning the necessity of paying the *zakāt* (alms). The fact that Islam does not allow interest on loans causes problems for Muslims using the American banking system. Observing dietary restrictions tends to set Muslims apart, hindering the social integration considered important by Americans for professional advancement. A number of efforts have been made by Islamic organizations to acquaint Americans with Islamic contributions to art, science, and culture. Muslims in general continue to enjoy the context of freedom of association and expression in America, at the same time that they are concerned over the discrimination that nonetheless exists, the fact that Muslims often have difficulty finding employment, and certain aspects of American foreign policy in the Middle East.

A number of particular problems face Muslims in America, among them the need for trained religious leadership, opportunities for observing requirements of the faith, such as prayer and fasting, and matters related to social interactions. Of particular concern to both mainstream and sectarian groups is the education of children. Not all Muslims agree that parochial education is the right answer, but around a hundred Islamic day schools have been established, and others are being planned. Hundreds of Sunday schools function to instruct youth in the basics of the Islamic faith. Often national ties and the bond of a common language seem to unite Muslims in America more than specific religious affiliation, making the establishment of religious associations and organizations difficult. In some areas there are tensions between conservative groups and those who wish to accommodate more flexibly to American customs, as well as between those who strive to be more strictly Islamic, and thus uniform in practice, and others who want to maintain the variations of their own particular cultures.

BIBLIOGRAPHY

Austin, Allan D., ed. *African Muslims in Antebellum America: A Sourcebook*. New York and London, 1984.

Haddad, Yvonne Yazbeck. *A Century of Islam in America*. Washington, D.C., 1986.

Haddad, Yvonne Yazbeck, ed. *The Muslims of America*. New York and Oxford, 1991.

Haddad, Yvonne Yazbeck, and Adair T. Lummis. *Islamic Values in the United States: A Comparative Study*. New York and Oxford, 1987.

Haddad, Yvonne Yazbeck, and Jane I. Smith. *Mission to America: Five Islamic Sectarian Communities in North America*. Gainesville, Fla., 1993.

Haddad, Yvonne Yazbeck, and Jane I. Smith, eds. *Muslim Communities in North America*. Albany, N.Y., 1994.

Turner, Richard Brent. "Islam in the United States in the 1920s: The Quest for a New Vision in Afro-American Religion." Ph.D. diss., Princeton University, 1986.

Waugh, Earle H., Baha Abu-Laban, and Regula B. Qureshi, eds. *The Muslim Community in North America*. Edmonton, Alberta, 1983.

Waugh, Earle H., Sharon McIrvin Abu-Laban, and Regula B. Qureshi, eds. *Muslim Families in North America*. Edmonton, Alberta, 1991.

Williams, Raymond Brady. *Religions of Immigrants from India and Pakistan*. Cambridge and New York, 1988.

YVONNE YAZBECK HADDAD and JANE I. SMITH

UNIVERSITIES. In the classical Islamic world the primary educational institution was the *madrasah*, established by an individual founder through a *waqf* (endowment), the founder was allowed to designate beneficiaries and successors and even to impose his will on the administration. The colleges of late medieval Europe were established in a similar manner. Between 1100 and 1200 there was an influx of new knowledge into western Europe, much of it through the Arab scholars of Spain. In order to explore this knowledge and to free scientific investigation from the control of the church, new universities were formed. By the thirteenth century this secular orientation and dependence on science rather than on revealed truth had become the basis of educational principles in these institutions.

In Muslim education there had never been any dissociation between secular learning and divinely revealed knowledge. With the expansion of the Muslim empire, Muslim scholars came into contact with the Hellenistic tradition of knowledge in Syria and Alexandria; but instead of becoming secularized, they assimilated and islamized this philosophy and thus expanded the sphere of Islamic educational activity. This was possible because the Muslims believed that God is the source of all knowledge. Muslim scholars therefore considered all knowledge to be a basic trust (*amānah*, Qur'ān 33.72) given to humankind. Thus it is a duty to explore, learn, understand, and teach all kinds of knowledge.

Muslim educationalists, however, maintained a dual hierarchy of knowledge. Revealed knowledge was directly transmitted from the divine source to the prophet Muḥammad through whom this message was transmitted to humanity. Acquired knowledge was gained by means of human beings' God-given intellect and reason. The former category was known as "transmitted sciences" (*al-ʿulūm al naqlīyah*) and the latter as "intellectual sciences" (*al-ʿulūm al-aqlīyah*). Wisdom acquired through vision (*kashf*) and the direct perception of truth (*dhawq*) but tested with reference to the Qur'ān was also regarded as a form of knowledge that could be acquired and transmitted to others. The first and second categories of knowledge were taught in the *madrasah*s; the last category was taught mainly in *khanqah*s and *zāwiyah*s.

Muslims brought the Hellenistic sciences into Islamic parameters in order to harmonize reason and revelation. Al-Kindī's *Fī aqsām al-ʿulūm* (On the Types of the Sciences) and al-Fārābī's *Iḥṣā' al-ʿulūm* (The Enumeration of the Sciences) are two works that integrate religion and science. Al-Ghazālī, in volume 2 of his *Iḥyā' ʿulūm al-Dīn*, had by this time simplified the classification of knowledge. According to him, basic knowledge of the *sharīʿah* must be regarded as obligatory (*farḍ al-ʿayn*) for all Muslims; the rest of knowledge was optional for individuals but obligatory for a society, which ensured that other knowledge would be pursued by at least some (*farḍ al-kifāyah*). The new and existing forms of science that were developing in the Islamic world, as well as the sciences acquired from other civilizations, were fitted into the hierarchy based on Islamic concepts drawn from the Qur'ān and *sunnah*. These concepts were metaphysically, philosophically, and rationally justified with reference to the order of life and the universe enunciated by God.

In the Western world by contrast there developed a rift between the theological and secular approaches, a rift characterized by T. S. Eliot as "the dissociation of sensibilities." Western universities, established with the intention of keeping the quest for knowledge free from the control of the church, emphasized a secular scientific approach to external nature and internal human nature. The formulations of philosophers further strengthened scientific thinking along pragmatic and empirical lines. Scientific activity and its mode of operation acquired credibility, prestige, and power. Religious thinkers had not developed new intellectual tools to combat the enthronement of reason as the only means of gaining truth and knowledge, to show the limits of scientific knowledge, or to demonstrate the moral and spiritual needs that faith can fulfil.

The secularist educational system based on this approach entered the Muslim world in earnest early in the nineteenth century. The Muslim world from Morocco to Indonesia became conscious of their lack of modern knowledge when they were colonized. The colonial powers followed a policy of transforming society through the establishment of modern secular schools, colleges, and universities. Resistance from the Muslim *ʿulamā'* and other traditional elements was ignored or suppressed. The colonial governments set up universities to create a new elite who could control, guide, and modernize society. The British established the first university in Calcutta in 1850, but only a few Muslims were admitted.

Perceiving the advancement of Hindu university graduates in India, Sir Sayyid Aḥmad Khān founded Aligarh Muslim College in 1875; it became Aligarh Muslim University in 1920, with the goal of generating a modern elite who would be able to compete successfully with Hindus and to assume new leadership in politics and economics. Sir Sayyid Aḥmad had been influenced by the reformer Jamāl al-Dīn al-Afghānī, and he applied a Western scientific, rational, and empirical approach to the interpretation of the Qur'ān. Although his influence was resisted by the *ʿulamā'*, some of whom were teaching at Aligarh, the new elite that emerged were less conversant with Islam but had gained more secular knowledge. In order to bring about some sort of synthesis, the British government in Bengal introduced the "New Scheme Madrasah," where modern subjects such as history, geography, and mathematics—but not the natural sciences—were taught along with traditional religious subjects. Their students could be directly admitted to universities like Dhaka University, which started taking such students in 1918, without taking the examination in English usually required of *madrasah* students seeking entrance to universities. The educational policy of the British colonial power in India was otherwise entirely secular. Religion was not taught in government schools, but by allowing the Calcutta Alia Madrasah to be run along Islamic orthodox lines, they maintained a dual education system, and Muslims had to choose one system or the other. A clearcut division arose in the

Muslim community of India: one group, basically traditional and orthodox in attitude, had little knowledge of modern education or modern science; the other, more or less secularist, had little in-depth knowledge of their own Islamic faith.

When Pakistan came into existence the subject of Islamic Studies was introduced into all secondary schools. In Karachi Federal University it became an obligatory subject for all Muslim undergraduates, and for non-Muslim students "moral education" was introduced. In other subjects the secular philosophical basis remained unchallenged. As a result, the course in Islamic Studies could not offset the secularization of minds as had been hoped.

From Morocco to Iran modern secular school systems had been introduced in the nineteenth century, although modern universities were not established until the twentieth. This modernization started with military schools in Turkey in the early eighteenth century, but it received a national color after Napoleon's conquest of Egypt and his attempt to remodel the education and legal systems after those of France.

In method and substance Cairo's al-Azhar—established as a mosque in AH 359/970 CE and declared a *jāmiʿah* in 378/988—retained its original *madrasah* character in spite of the influence of al-Afghānī and later of Muḥammad ʿAbduh. The addition of modern sections and the attempt to modernize the curricula to some extent took place under Gamal Abdel Nasser. It then gained faculties of education, medicine, and engineering. Although English was listed in the curriculum in 1901, the first course that was actually offered was in 1958 after Nasser's drastic reform. Al-Azhar did not attempt to produce Islamic analogies for modern branches of knowledge in order to islamize the modern education system; it simply resisted all attempts to modernize its own system. The government in Egypt initiated modern primary and secondary education, and private and foreign-supported schools acquired prestige. A College of Arts was established in 1909. Other higher institutions of law, medicine, engineering, agriculture, and commerce were all incorporated into the University of Cairo in 1925. A second university was opened in Alexandria in 1942, and a third in Ain Shams in 1950. Conflict between al-Azhar and these universities and the government-backed education system resulted in conflict between their graduates in terms of both thought and action. The transformation of the administration of the university and the introduction of faculties beyond the traditional trio of jurisprudence, theology, and Arabic studies did expand the role of al-Azhar graduates; however, the new faculties and the new Institute of Languages and Translation were purely modern, and there was no attempt to islamize the basic philosophical concepts of these different branches of knowledge. Hence this university did not contribute to resolution of the conflict between traditionalism and modernism in Egypt or abroad.

Besides the conflict between tradition and modernity and between orthodox religious consciousness and modern secularist ideas, there was also the politically influential contribution that modern higher education, including university education, made in giving birth to Arab nationalism. Foreign missionary schools and universities in the Levant—Syria, Jerusalem, Lebanon, and Jordan—led to an Arabic cultural revival. By the end of the nineteenth century the philosophy of Arab nationalism had repercussions throughout the region. The Jesuit University of St. Joseph (1897) at Ghazir and the American University of Beirut (first opened as the Syrian Protestant College in 1866) contributed immensely to the modernization process and later to the propagation of Arab nationalism and anti-imperialism.

The dismemberment of the Ottoman Empire after World War I was attended by the growth of nationalism in various Muslim countries; this was especially true in Turkey, where modern Western education had been especially influential. In Turkey higher educational institutions produced an elitist generation that supported Mustafa Kemal (Atatürk)'s Turkish nationalism. As in Egypt, Turkey also had private schools, missionary schools, and foreign schools that contributed to the generation of nationalist sentiment and served as channels for the transmission of Western educational and cultural principles. The first Ottoman University was established by Sultan Abdülhamid in 1900 and reopened in 1908 after the Young Turk revolution; it became Istanbul University in 1923 after Mustafa Kemal took power. Ankara University was established in 1933.

Mustafa Kemal banned all traditional *madrasah*s. In 1948, after his death, the Democratic party came to power, and courses in Islamic studies were initiated in ten provinces. The University of Ankara started teaching Islamic Studies in 1949, and the University of Istanbul established the Islamic Research Institute in 1954. In 1971 Erzurum Atatürk University opened a Faculty of Islamic Studies. Religious education was introduced into elementary schools in 1949, and Qur'ānic courses were being actively organized by the government education system by 1971. Secondary-school textbooks had also been thoroughly revised by that time.

Modern Western education generated a narrow nationalistic spirit in other Islamic communities. An example is the Young Bengal Movement in Calcutta University in the nineteenth century, which became the precursor of a Hindu nationalist movement and later a Muslim nationalist movement in India.

In Iran Reza Shah tried to follow Kemal's secularizing policy. Iran's modernization of higher education dates from 1921. The same pattern seen in Turkey and in Egypt was repeated. Established colleges were integrated into the University of Tehran, and the universities were considered to reinforce the process of secularization. Religious instruction was abolished in schools in 1941. Reza Shah abdicated in 1941 under pressure from the British and Russians. During the reign of his son four more universities were established, but they soon became centers of political unrest. What was seen as an anti-Islamic educational and social policy was modified. The *ʿulamāʾ* came to power in Iran in 1979 after the shah was overthrown by Ayatollah Ruhollah Khomeini's revolutionary movement. Since the revolution a process of islamizing curricula and textbooks has taken place, and the universities have been divided into religious and secular institutions.

In South and Southeast Asia there has been a repetition of the same pattern. Until 1977 most of the universities were those that had been established during the colonial period and hence were liberal and secular in approach. In Malaysia and Indonesia an Islamic education system—the *pesantrens*—coexisted with secular universities. In Indonesia there were private Islamic institutions that have evolved into Islamic universities.

The move to establish Islamic universities in Malaysia and Pakistan began in earnest after the World Conference on Islamic Economics (Jeddah, 1976) and the First World Conference on Muslim Education (Makkah [Mecca], 1977). At the latter, S. A. Ashraf's theory of formulating Islamic concepts for all branches of knowledge as substitutes for secular theories was unanimously accepted. Ismāʿīl al-Fārūqī later suggested certain methods to achieve this end in his 1982 book *Islamization of Knowledge*. Ashraf's Islamic education theory and revision of the university curriculum, especially in the field of teacher education, has been the source for the revision of teacher education and teaching methodology at the International Islamic University of Kuala Lumpur. Brunei Darussalam has declared the gradual islamization of knowledge as their education policy. In Pakistan the Islamic University is experimenting with islamizing the whole area of jurisprudence and the legal system. Other Islamic universities in Bangladesh and Niger are also at the experimental stage.

In Saudi Arabia traditional *madrasah*s have been almost entirely replaced by modern schools with islamized curricula and texts, especially in literature and history, and with intensive teaching of Islam at the primary and secondary levels. At the university level four courses in Islamic culture are taught over the four years to reinforce the Islamic approach to life and knowledge. The deep religious ethos of the society counteracts the secularist tendencies and ideas acquired through modern subjects such as economics and natural sciences. In addition there is the Islamic University of Medina, which is mainly a theological school where the teaching methodology is modern, but the subjects are the same as in the old *madrasah*s.

Jordan and the Gulf states have modern universities, but they have also introduced Islamic culture courses. The same is true of universities in Morocco, Algeria, Tunisia, and Libya.

The five World Conferences on Muslim Education (Makkah [Mecca], 1977; Islamabad, 1980; Dhaka, 1981; Jakarta, 1982; Cairo, 1987) have given Muslim educationalists a new method of solving the conflict between the knowledge to be acquired and the theories to be formulated. Unless Muslim scholars meet the challenge of secular philosophies—as al-Ghazālī did in his *Tahāfut al-falāsifah* (Destruction of Philosophy)—and establish Islamic concepts, producing textbooks in different branches of knowledge based on those concepts, it will not be possible to counteract the secularization process. Many Muslim scholars in both Western and Eastern universities have become conscious of this fact, and attempts are being made.

[*See also* Azhar, al-; Education; International Islamic University at Islamabad; International Islamic University at Kuala Lumpur; Madrasah; Mosque, *article on* The Mosque in Education; Pesantren; *and the biographies of ʿAbduh, Afghānī, Aḥmad Khān, and Fārūqī.*]

BIBLIOGRAPHY

Ashraf, Syed Ali. *New Horizons in Muslim Education*. London, 1985. Criticizes the secularist philosophy of education and suggests Islamic principles for the design of curriculum, textbook preparation, and teaching methodology at all levels.

Bilgrami, H. H., and Syed Ali Ashraf. *The Concept of an Islamic University*. Cambridge, 1985. Historical survey followed by suggestions for the present and future.

Banani, Amin. *The Modernization of Iran, 1921–1941*. Stanford, Calif., 1961. Critical analysis of the condition of Iran under Reza Shah.

Makdisi, George. *The Rise of Colleges*. Edinburgh, 1981. Valuable historical survey that contains a detailed description of the principles and methods of establishing universities and other educational institutions in both Islamic countries and the West.

Naguib al-Attas, Syed, ed. *Aims and Objectives of Islamic Education*. Jeddah, 1979. Publication of the First World Conference on Muslim Education, held at Makkah (Mecca), 1977, containing articles dealing with the conflict between the Western secularist approach and the Islamic approach, with suggestions for resolving them through education.

Nasr, Seyyed Hossein. *Islamic Science*. London, 1976. Contains chapters on Islam and the rise of sciences and the Islamic educational system, along with essays on the early contribution of Muslims to the natural sciences.

Rosenthal, Franz. *Knowledge Triumphant*. Leiden, 1970. Authoritative analysis of the meaning of *ʿilm* (knowledge).

Szyliowicz, Joseph S. *Education and Modernization in the Middle East*. Ithaca, N.Y., 1973. Thorough analysis of the growth of modern Western education in the Middle East, fully supportive of secularist education.

Tritton, A. S. *Materials on Muslim Education in the Middle Ages*. London, 1957. Historical survey of Muslim education.

SYED ALI ASHRAF

URBAN PLANNING. The Islamic world contains both peoples of varying ethnic and cultural origin, and nations with different economic systems and geographic and climatic conditions. Indeed, the range of variation is so great that the notion of a universal Islamic urban form has been the subject of legitimate criticism. Nevertheless, many scholars and practicing planners in the Islamic world today recognize that the cities of the Islamic world, as spaces of social interactions, reflect certain common values, and as built environments, feature unifying symbolic systems that distinguish them from cities elsewhere.

Urban form is generally considered the physical manifestation of an urbanization process. Urban planning consists of both the methods for making decisions about urban form and the specific procedures that result in a physical arrangement of urban activities. Defined this way, one can identify three historical periods of urban planning in the Islamic world: a medieval phase, a premodern colonial phase, and a modern phase.

The medieval phase is best illustrated by the early garrison towns of Basra and Kufa in Iraq, and Fustat in Egypt. The original physical forms of these planned communities, referred to as *amṣār*, represented some of the earliest decision-making processes in Islam. A variety of Islamic principles calling for modesty and simplicity, derived from general tradition, or *ʿurf*, and jurisprudence, or *fiqh*, had an important impact on the allocation of urban functions, the placement of institutional buildings, and the configuration of urban spaces. With time, however, the cities of the vast medieval Muslim world were shaped less by religious ideals than by administrative formulations and the individual will and initiative of powerful rulers. This led to the development of the irregular, labyrinthine patterns that are normally associated with the Islamic city today. Janet Abu-Lughod (1983) has summarized the basic principles that constitute the "deep grammar" of Islamic urbanism as follows: the residential block with its semipublic space; a process-derived, ad hoc circulation system; a close, self-policing relationship between neighbors; and a complex system of property rights that allowed differential responsibility between individuals who shared common facilities. These general principles constituted the basic system of Islamic urban planning until the eighteenth century.

During the nineteenth century the Muslim world witnessed a second period of urban restructuring, owing to the rise of modern capitalism and the emergence of organized political and economic colonialism. During this period, the majority of Muslim peoples and lands came under the control of European colonial empires, particularly those of the British and French. The traditional cities of the Islamic world were transformed by these colonial powers primarily through the addition of dual cities. The development of these planned urban entities, initially for the colonizing elite, is well illustrated in such cities as Algiers and Casablanca in North Africa. In planning the foreign districts, colonial administrators followed specific European models, including the use of geometric grids and a hierarchical ordering of urban functions and spaces. In some instances, as in Cairo, the new urban expansion followed the French planning tradition of Haussmann, by which squares were constructed as urban nodes, and then connected diagonally to penetrate the older, irregular fabric.

By the early 1960s, most peoples of the Islamic world had regained independence. New Islamic nation-states in Africa, Asia, and the Middle East emerged both from international deals struck at the close of World War II, and from successful revolutionary movements. These countries initially had little to cling to as they attempted to fashion new governmental structures. Most had to rely on institutions inherited from the colonial order. The activities and professional practices of urban policy were among those services that had been institutionalized by preindependence colonial governments. Following independence, departments of planning, housing, and urban development were set up as cabinet-level ministries to implement an agenda of modernization.

As a result, the grid plan, with its principal and secondary streets, repetitive housing blocks, and unprotected, unsupervised open spaces, became a dominant feature of cities in the Islamic world. New development strategies favoring large-scale projects and the imitation of Western zoning practices distorted an already fragile system of urban values. New building codes, based on Western norms and requiring setbacks in residential lots, forced the traditional courtyard house out of existence, and replaced it with characterless single-family dwelling units or public housing blocks that were not socially, culturally, or climatically suitable. Today, anyone walking in the streets of cities in the Muslim world cannot help but be surprised by the excessive amount of infringement on public space and a general lack of respect for planning codes. In traditional Islamic culture, people were accustomed to a more fluid relationship with the public realm, which allowed them to appropriate parts of it without necessarily violating it. The new codes have denied them this traditional freedom. In the process, respect for both the new codes and the innovative traditions of Islamic urbanism have been compromised.

Furthermore, an obsession with modernity became a characteristic of most new Islamic nation-states. The Western pattern of urban development continued to serve as the reference for those—particularly among the new elite—who inherited the structures of colonial government. Cut off from established tradition, their new urban planning efforts were not adequately rooted in the culture of the people they intended to serve. This was especially true in relation to the high-rise urban blocks and mid-rise public housing schemes of the 1950s and 1960s. By the early 1980s, however, many architects and planners in the Islamic world had begun to rethink this distorted value system, particularly in light of the evolution of a vibrant urban informal sector that generated its own rules. Some even called for a fundamental rejection of Western norms, forgetting that the Western model will continue to shape their cities through inherited values and regulations.

Currently, the story of Islamic urban planning is incomplete. New chapters are being written by innovative planners and local government administrators in a variety of contexts. These people are discovering that the principles which generated the great Islamic cities of the Middle Ages are not archaic, and that many planners in the West itself are trying to humanize the residential block, differentiate the circulation system, and devise more flexible systems of private and public property rights. All of these were once paradigms of practice within the traditional Islamic city. A new era of authentic regionalism in urban planning may have already begun in the Islamic world.

[*See also* Architecture.]

BIBLIOGRAPHY

Abu-Lughod, Janet. "Preserving the Living Heritage of Islamic Cities." In *Toward an Architecture in the Spirit of Islam,* pp. 27–35. Philadelphia, 1978. Excellent introduction to the issue of preserving and revising traditional planning practices.

Abu-Lughod, Janet. "Contemporary Relevance of Islamic Urban Principles." In *Islamic Architecture and Urbanism,* edited by Aydin Germen, pp. 64–70. Dammam, 1983. Insightful overview of the relevance of some traditional urban planning practices.

Akbar, Jamel. *Crisis in the Built Environment: The Case of the Muslim City.* Singapore, 1988. Good analysis of the distortions that occurred in the traditional planning value system.

AlSayyad, Nezar. *Cities and Caliphs.* Westport, Conn., 1991. Survey of the earliest planning schemes in the Arab Middle East.

AlSayyad, Nezar, ed. *Forms of Dominance: On the Architecture and Urbanism of the Colonial Enterprise.* London, 1992. Contains several chapters on colonial planning projects in countries of the Islamic world.

Brown, L. Carl, ed. *From Madina to Metropolis: Heritage and Change in the Near Eastern City.* Princeton, 1973. Collection of essays on the changing structure of Arab Muslim cities.

Hakim, Besim S. *Arabic-Islamic Cities.* New York, 1986. Includes examples of how Islamic *sharī'ah* values shaped city form.

Serageldin, Ismail, et al. *The Arab City.* Arlington, Va., 1982. Proceedings of a good symposium, held in Medina, on the past and present Arab city.

NEZAR ALSAYYAD

URDU LITERATURE. The articulation of Islamic themes and values in nineteenth- and twentieth-century Urdu literature was in response to two factors: the loss of Muslim political power in the subcontinent to the British, and a deeply felt need to cure Indian Muslims of their spiritual and religious malaise. This second factor was a consequence of a widespread perception among Muslims that as a community they needed to reinvigorate their relationship with Islam in the context of rapid change.

The first attempts to advocate sociopolitical reform of the Indo-Muslim community using Islam as a basis can be traced to Shāh Walī Allāh (d. 1762), the great theologian of Delhi, who believed himself to be a renovator (*mujaddid*) of Islam. Although the most important work in which he expressed his reformist teaching was in Arabic (the *Ḥujjat Allāh al-bālighah*), Shāh Walī Allāh's ideas had a deep impact on later generations of reformist writers in Urdu, ranging from conservatives to modernists and including such luminaries as Sir Sayyid Aḥmad Khān and Muhammad Iqbal. Shāh Walī Allāh felt strongly that Muslims would be better able to live in accordance with the precepts of their faith and to begin resolving their socioreligious problems if they could understand the Qur'ān for themselves without relying on the secondary interpretations of commentaries. Hence he translated the Qur'ān into Persian, the language of belles lettres, historiography, and administration in early modern India, paving the way for his two sons Rafīʿuddīn (d. 1818) and ʿAbdulqādir (d. 1813) to translate it into Urdu; the latter appropriately called his Urdu translation *Mūḍiḥ al-Qur'ān* (Explainer of the Qur'ān). [*See the biography of Walī Allāh.*]

No doubt inspired by Shāh Walī Allāh's activism, his grandson Ismāʿīl Shahīd (d. 1831) became the theoretician for the energetic *mujāhidīn* reformist movement of the early nineteenth century initiated by Sayyid Aḥmad of Rae Bareilly (Sayyid Aḥmad Barelwī), a charismatic preacher who wanted to purge Islam of its accretions and corruptions. Ismāʿīl Shahīd's work *Taqwiyat al-īmān* (Strengthening of the Faith) summarizes the basic ideas of the movement, which called Muslims to *ʿamal ṣāliḥ* (righteous action) according to God's command to improve their situation in this world and the next. Although both reformers lost their lives in a futile attempt to overthrow Sikh rule and establish an Islamic state in the Punjab, their disciples organized themselves into a large-scale popular movement and produced a vast number of religious tracts in simple but vigorous Urdu; these called on the Muslim masses, especially in rural areas, to abandon syncretistic practices in favor of "pure" Islam. [*See the biography of Barelwī.*] Prominent among these reformers in Bengal was the indefatigable Karāmat ʿAlī of Jaunpur (d. 1873) who, despite his affiliations with the reform movement, argued that India under British rule was still part of *dār al-Islām*, making rebellion against the British unlawful. Ismāʿīl Shahīd, like his grandfather, was affiliated to a branch of the activist Naqshbandī Ṣūfī order known as the Ṭarīqah Muḥammadīyah (Muḥammadan Path). As its name suggests, this movement placed strong emphasis on the figure of the prophet Muḥammad as a true and stable paradigm for the Muslim community in a period of political and social flux, a theme that recurs frequently in later Urdu literature. The ideology of the Ṭarīqah Muḥammadīyah influenced many prominent Urdu poets, including the so-called "pillars of Urdu"—the stern Maẓhar Jānjānān (d. 1781) and the mystic poet Mīr Dard (d. 1785). Mu'min (d. 1851), a nineteenth-century writer famous for his exquisite Urdu love poetry, was also connected to this movement and wrote short epic poems in support of the revivalist *mujāhidīn*.

In the aftermath of the 1857 military rebellion, the Muslim community was forced to come to terms not only with British political supremacy in South Asia but also with the growing presence of Western cultural institutions, particularly churches, schools, and colleges. The most influential response to this situation came from Sir Sayyid Aḥmad Khān (d. 1898) and his circle of colleagues. As a young man, Sir Sayyid was well trained in theology in the tradition of Shāh Walī Allāh as well as in Muʿtazilah rationalism; he was also affiliated to the Ṭarīqah Muḥammadīyah. In keeping with the spirit of this Prophet-oriented movement, he wrote in his early years a study intended to help Muslims examine Muḥammad's exemplary life and conduct without such customary hagiographic elements as miracles. In *Khuṭbat-i Aḥmadīyah*, an Urdu biography of the Prophet, he also defended Muḥammad against derogatory attacks by Western scholars. Sir Sayyid was keenly interested in history and authored and edited several historical studies, including *Āṣār as-Sanādīd*, a valuable account of the historical buildings and personalities of Delhi.

After the traumatic events of 1857, Sir Sayyid was convinced that the best path for the Muslim community to follow was that of absolute and unwavering loyalty to the British. In support of his position he cited traditional Muslim authorities on the duties of subjects toward their rulers. Furthermore, he felt that Muslims should participate fully in the Western-style educational system being established by the British in India so that they would not become a social and economic underclass. Western thought, he believed, was not in fundamental conflict with Islam, nor was studying the natural sciences, for there was no conflict between the Qur'ān, the word of God, and nature, the work of God. In this regard he advocated a rational approach to the Qur'ān based on fresh *ijtihād*, because Islam, in his interpretation, accommodates historical change. The mandates of the *sharīʿah*, as interpreted by generations of medieval religious scholars, needed to be reexamined to determine whether they were in fact the essential mandates of the faith. To promote his ideas and provide young Muslims with Western-style higher education, he fought for and eventually founded the Anglo-Muhammadan College, which later became Aligarh Muslim University. Sayyid Aḥmad Khān was a prolific writer in Urdu and hoped to influence Muslims through his books and journals. The most significant of the latter was the monthly Urdu periodical *Tahẕīb al-akhlāq* (The Polishing of Morals), also known as the *Mohamedan Social Reformer,* which revolutionized Urdu journalism. Its pages contained articles in clear and simple prose reflecting Sir Sayyid's modernist views on a wide range of issues, from public hygiene to rational speculation on religious dogma. [*See* Aligarh *and the biography of Aḥmad Khān.*]

Sayyid Aḥmad Khān's approach enjoyed the support of several important personalities in Indo-Muslim society and formed the basis for the so-called Aligarh Movement. Among its members were several important literati who wrote Urdu poetry and prose to disseminate its ideas. Most prominent among these was Altāf Ḥusayn Ḥālī (d. 1914), the founder of Urdu literary criticism. Trained in a strict theological tradition, Ḥālī was an employee of the Government Book Depot in Lahore, where he translated works of English literature into Urdu. He first became famous for the unusual themes of the poems he recited at poetical meetings (*mushāʿirah*) in Lahore. In 1874 Ḥālī moved to Delhi and was drawn into Sir Sayyid's circle. In 1879 he published his *Madd va gazr-i Islām* (The Ebb and Flow of Islam), an epic poem considered to be the Aligarh movement's most enduring literary monument. Popularly known as the *Musaddas* after its six-line stanzas, it contrasts the past glories and achievements of Islamic civilization with the miserable status of the Muslims of Ḥālī's time. The poem, which was recited aloud at conferences and boldly calligraphed in journals and newspapers, sharply attacked the evils prevalent in all segments of the Indian Muslim community. It marked the beginning of a new period in the history of Urdu poetry in which themes of revivalism and political romanticism became dominant. A generation later, we see the same spirit alive in Muhammad Iqbal's *Shikvā* and *Javāb-i shikvā* (The Complaint, Answer to the Complaint) which record the Muslim community's laments to God about seeing wealth and glory everywhere except in the Islamic world.

Some of Ḥālī's poems, such as *Ek bīvī kī munājāt* (A Woman's Petition), focus on the plight of women in Muslim society. This theme was taken up by several reformist writers, including Naẕīr Aḥmad (d. 1912), a pioneer in the development of the Urdu novel. By profession a teacher and a translator of English legal texts into Urdu, Naẕīr Aḥmad had also published a good Urdu translation of the Qur'ān, unusual in that it did not include the Arabic original. He was a firm believer in the importance of educating young people, particularly young women. Most of his novels therefore illustrated social or moral themes, showing the need for reform and change. His most famous book, *Mir'āt al-ʿarūs* (The Bride's Mirror), emphasized the need for female education by highlighting the miseries of an uneducated Muslim bride. In other works he addresses the evils of polygamy and attacks the Indian taboo against the remarriage of widows, which he felt was contrary to the spirit of Islam. Notwithstanding their didactic and moralistic tone, his works were tremendously popular for their realistic descriptions of middle-class Muslim life. They also inspired similar works in other languages such as Sindhi—so much so that a school for girls was a standard feature of Indo-Muslim reformist novels of the late nineteenth century. Other members of Sir Sayyid's circle, particularly Mumtāz ʿAlī, were equally concerned about improving the status of women. He seems to have devoted all his energies to this important issue and even published a special journal, *Tahẕīb al-niswān,* containing articles on women's issues. In his major work *Ḥuqūq al-niswān* (The Rights of Women) he advocates complete equality between men and women.

Perhaps the most radical of Sir Sayyid's collaborators was Chirāgh ʿAlī (d. 1895), who served as finance secretary for the nizam of Hyderabad. Like Sir Sayyid, he advocated a modernist interpretation of the Qur'ān, which he regarded as not containing all the civil and political codes necessary for the regulation of modern society. He dismissed traditional Islamic jurisprudence, claiming that it took little from the Qur'ān. In many instances he was more daring than Sir Sayyid in his Qur'ānic interpretations. For example, he demonstrated that the Qur'ān was actually intended to ameliorate the position of women and implicitly prohibited polygamy, a theme repeated in the works of numerous later reformists. His most controversial stance, however, was in regard to the *ḥadīth* literature, which he considered entirely fabricated and therefore unworthy as a basis for Islamic jurisprudence. [*See the biography of Chirāgh ʿAlī.*] A more conservative and moderate colleague of Sir Sayyid was Muḥsin al-Mulk (d. 1907), a regular contributor to the journal *Tahẕīb al-akhlāq* on a variety of theological issues. It was mainly his advocacy of a balance between religion and science in education that lessened the opposition of conservative religious scholars to the Western-style Aligarh University. Muḥsin al-Mulk played an active role in the Hindi-Urdu controversy in 1900 by founding the Urdu Defence Association; he was also instrumental in establishing Urdu as the official language of Hyderabad state.

Sir Sayyid and the Aligarh Movement represented a pragmatic pro-Western response to the encroachment of Western ideas and customs into Muslim India, but there were a variety of other responses. Interestingly, almost every response (including Sir Sayyid's) based interpretations on and drew inspiration from the work of Shāh Walī Allāh. His writings had placed a renewed emphasis on the *ḥadīth* as a source of authority and guidance for Muslims. In the nineteenth century this emphasis formed the focal point of a group called the Ahl-i Ḥadīth. In an attempt to make the Muslim community conscious of the true heritage of the Prophet, this group stressed the exclusive primacy of the Qur'ān and the *ḥadīth* as fundamental guides in life. One of its most important leaders was Ṣiddīq Ḥasan Khān (d. 1890), whose father had participated in the *jihād* movement of Sayyid Aḥmad of Bareilly and Ismāʿīl Shahīd. A prolific writer of innumerable Urdu works on religious topics, especially *ḥadīth* literature, Ṣiddīq Ḥasan Khān married, amidst great controversy, the widowed princess of Bhopal. He and his colleagues in the Ahl-i Ḥadīth rejected the authority of the founders of the four Sunnī schools of law as interpreters of the *sharīʿah* and thus aroused the hostility of the conservative religious establishment. Since the latter group accepted the entire corpus of classical *ḥadīth* as genuine, they were also extremely critical of the scepticism displayed by some the Aligarh modernists toward the prophetic traditions. For them Sayyid Aḥmad Khān, whom they called "the modern prophet of nature-worshippers," was just the latest instigator of anarchic evils in Muslim society. With their extreme emphasis on the *ḥadīth* as a form of "concealed" revelation, the Ahl-i Ḥadīth became involved in a vitriolic polemical war with a counter-group led by ʿAbdullāh Chakrālavī, called the Ahl al-Qur'ān. As its name suggests, this movement advocated total reliance on the Qur'ān as the most perfect source of guidance; the Qur'ān, according to them, contained all the basic injunctions for Muslims and left them free to decide on other matters.

More influential among the conservatives than these two groups was the theological school of Deoband, founded in 1867 by Rashīd Aḥmad Gangohī (d. 1905) and Maulānā Muḥammad Qāsim Nanotavī (d. 1880). The latter was a charismatic theologian who settled in Mecca after the 1857 rebellion and wrote several Urdu works on *jihād* and Islamic mysticism, and of Rashīd Aḥmad Gangohī. Deoband became a bastion of conservative Sunnī Islam, and its theologians prided themselves on upholding the authority of the four traditional schools of law. In time it acquired a reputation as an outstanding theological school, enrolling students from many parts of the Islamic world. Its curriculum, with Urdu as the medium of instruction, was strictly traditional, excluding English and modern sciences. In their works Deobandī theologians vigorously defended the need to accept the interpretations and consensus of the earlier Sunnī scholars and jurists and attacked all dissenting voices in the Muslim community. Rashid Aḥmad Gangohī, for example, dismissed Sir Sayyid's approach as a "deadly poison." In addition, Maulānā Muḥammad Qāsim acquired a stellar reputation for his polemical disputations with Hindu and Christian missionaries, authoring the book *Taqrīr-i dil pāzīr* on the subject. A later Deobandī scholar, Ashraf ʿAlī Thānvī (d. 1943), who attempted to popularize Islamic values among the less-educated, achieved fame for his ten-volume Urdu work *Bihishtī zevar,* a conservative guidebook for the life and education of Muslim women. [*See* Deobandīs.]

The prestige of Deoband as guardian of Sunnī Islam was enhanced in the late nineteenth and early twentieth centuries when its scholars took a leading role in refuting the claims of Mirzā Ghulām Aḥmad (d. 1908), the founder of the Aḥmadīyah movement. The orthodox were particularly enraged at what they perceived as Ghulām Aḥmad's challenge to the finality of Muḥammad's prophethood. The Aḥmadīyah controversy produced a voluminous stream of pamphlet literature and booklets in Urdu as well as Punjabi, both attacking and defending the movement and its doctrines; after considerable loss of life in riots, the Aḥmadīyah were declared non-Muslim in 1975. [*See* Aḥmadīyah.]

Between Deoband's rigid conservatism and Aligarh's pro-Western stance were a group of religious scholars who founded in 1894 at Lucknow the Nadvat al-ʿUlamāʾ, the second great theological institution of Muslim India. The Nadvat al-ʿUlamāʾ was conceived as an institution to bridge the gap between religious scholars of all shades of opinion and modern educated Muslims. Playing a key role in the establishment of this institution was Muḥammad Shiblī Nuʿmānī (d. 1914), a professor at Aligarh University and the founder of historiography in Urdu. He wrote several biographies of the heroes of Islam, including the caliph ʿUmar, the medieval theologian al-Ghazālī, and the mystic poet Jalāl al-Dīn Rūmī. His biography of the prophet Muḥammad, *Sīrat al-nabī,* partially intended as a response to polemical works by Christian missionaries, was posthumously completed by his disciple Maulānā Sulaymān Nadvī (d. 1953). A prolific writer, Shiblī also achieved renown for his history of Persian literature. Shiblī's interest in Islamic history stemmed primarily from his convictions that Islam needed to be revived from within and that the Muslims of his time could learn valuable lessons from the heroes of the past. His writings show a keen awareness of the social problems facing the Muslim community, not only in India but elsewhere. In this regard Shiblī had established contacts with Muḥammad ʿAbduh in Cairo, a connection that aroused British suspicion that Shiblī was a Pan-Islamist. Toward the end of his life Shiblī established the Dār al-Muṣannifīn or Shibli Academy at Azamgarh, with a view to organizing a school of writers who would engage in the highest traditions of Islamic scholarship. Its journal, *Maʿārif,* contains interesting articles of a theological nature.

Aside from theologians and religious scholars, the burgeoning Urdu press was also active in expressing its views on the challenges faced by the subcontinent's Muslim community. The papers and periodicals varied widely in their positions on various issues, so we cite only a few examples. Extremely popular for its satire was *Avadh Punch,* founded in 1877 by Munshī Sajjād Ḥusayn and modeled after the British *Punch.* Narrow in outlook and conservative on reform, it singled out the reformist Aligarh Movement for its biting sarcasm. Akbar Allāhābādī (d. 1921), a government civil servant and High Court judge, was among its most noted contributors; a poet trained in the Lucknow style, he had a marvelous command of Urdu vocabulary that permitted him to engage in ingenious wordplays, puns, and rhymes. His conservatism led him to write satirical verses that mocked everything Western, particularly Muslims who aped the West. Not surprisingly, Sir Sayyid was an obvious target. Akbar's witty observations on contemporary Muslim life reinvigorated satire in Urdu poetry.

Another periodical given to satire was *Zamīndār;* its editor, after 1909, was Maulānā Ẓafar ʿAlī, who was renowned for his satirical skills and extremely firm in his commitment to Islam. His vehemently anti-British poems had a profound impact in agitating the Muslims of northern India. As Ẓafar ʿAlī satirized everything and everyone he disliked, several of his Muslim compatriots also became targets. Very different in character were Abū al-Kalām Āzād's *Al-hilāl* (founded in 1912) and *Al-balāgh* (1915). Though by training a traditional theologian, Āzād (d. 1958) was unusual in his politics and theology. Pan-Islamic in his views, he was one of the leading thinkers behind the Khilāfat movement that hoped to rally Indian Muslims around the Ottoman Caliph as head of the world Muslim community. His journals took a definite stance against the British and the pro-British loyalties of the Aligarh group. During the independence movement he was firmly against the creation of a separate Muslim country, because he felt that the concept of a nation-state was a Western one, contradicting the models prescribed by God and his prophet Muḥammad. Both his journals had a deep impact on their Muslim readership, but Āzād's main fame in modern Urdu literature rests on his *Tarjumān al-Qurʾān,* a translation and commentary on the Qurʾān begun in 1931 and never completed. This masterpiece of beautiful Urdu reveals the author's mystically tinged theology, stressing God's compassion, love, and beauty. His liberal and humanitarian interpretation of Islam and his theory of divine providence *(rubūbīyah)* have had considerable influence in recent Indo-Muslim thought. [*See the biography of Āzād.*]

The events of the first half of the twentieth century, which eventually led to the establishment of Pakistan as a separate Islamic state, influenced many Urdu writers to produce an interesting diversity of works in which they addressed pressing political, social, and religious issues. The figure that towers over all these writers and whose work had the most profound impact on the Muslim community was Muhammad Iqbal (d. 1938), the philosopher whose reformist poetry achieved such an impact that he is counted among the most significant thinkers of modern Islam. Since Iqbal was the first to advocate the idea of a separate Muslim homeland, he is also widely perceived as the spiritual founder of Pakistan. A huge number of books, articles, and pamphlets have been written in Urdu and English to explain and interpret his ideas on virtually every subject. Every religious, political, and social movement in contemporary Indo-Muslim thought has turned to Iqbal's poetry and prose to find justification for its position.

Iqbal lived in a period of great change during which both Muslim and non-Muslim leaders in several countries were actively advocating revolutionary changes in the nature of their societies. It was the age of Lenin, Ziya Gökalp, Atatürk, and Gandhi. Iqbal received his early education in Lahore, influenced in his thought by Sir Sayyid Aḥmad Khān, the historian Shiblī, and Sir Thomas Arnold, an Orientalist who was attempting to revive a less polemical and more sympathetic understanding of Islam in Western scholarship. In many ways Iqbal was also the inheritor of the ideas of Shāh Walī Allāh and Ḥālī, whose poetic style he followed. At the turn of the century he had already become well known for his Urdu poems expressing nationalist ideas, Hindu-Muslim solidarity, and freedom for India. One of his poems from this period, *Tarānah-yi Hind,* praised the glories of Hindustan and is still popular in India today. In 1905 Iqbal went to Cambridge, where he studied Hegelian philosophy; in 1907 he also received a doctorate from Munich for a thesis entitled *The Development of Metaphysics in Persia.* Iqbal's stay in the West was instrumental in the further evolution of his reformist ideas: it allowed him to become familiar with European philosophy—especially that of Nietzsche and Bergson, whose influence can be detected in his writings; it gave him the opportunity to reflect on the strengths and weaknesses of Muslim societies; and it enabled him to observe firsthand the positive and negative aspects of Western civilization.

On his return to India Iqbal was offered a position at Aligarh but chose to practice law. At heart, however, he was primarily a poet and used his poetry to articulate his thought in a manner unprecedented in modern Islamic history. In his first major reformist Urdu poem, *Shikvā* (The Complaint), written in 1911, he complains that God is fickle and has abandoned the faithful Muslims in favor of the infidels. A year later he composed God's reply in the form of *Javāb-i shikvā* (Answer to the Complaint); here God points out the defects in the way Muslims practice and understand their faith. Both poems were clearly inspired by Ḥālī's *Musaddas.* During the war, Iqbal composed two major works—*Asrār-i khūdī* (Secrets of the Self) and *Rumūz-i bīkhūdī* (Mysteries of Selflessness). These, like all his major philosophical poems, he chose to write in Persian because he intended his ideas for an audience beyond the subcontinent. Here he reinterpreted the Persian mystical concept of *khūdī* (ego) in a positive sense, criticizing traditional Islamic mystical concepts and articulating the dynamic role of the individual in society. His emphasis here and his other Urdu and Persian poems was on activity and dynamism at both the individual and communal levels. He believed that each human, as the vicegerent of God on earth, had a duty actively to develop himself or herself to the highest potential. In 1924 Iqbal published a major collection of Urdu poems under the title *Bang-i darā* (The Call of the Caravan Bell). The title is significant in that it reflects Iqbal's perception of his role and his message: he is the bell at the head of the caravan that rouses the sleeping and erring Muslims of India to activity, leading them to the center of Islam, the Kaʿbah in Mecca. By this time his poetry had garnered so much attention that he was knighted in 1922 by the British monarch.

For more than ten years after this period Iqbal published most of his significant writing either in English (*Reconstruction of Religious Thought in Islam*) or in Persian (*Zabūr-i ʿajam,* Persian Psalms; *Javīdnāmah*). In all these works Iqbal reveals his unique way of interpreting and expressing Islamic concepts and ideas through a skillful combination of Western and Eastern intellectual and literary tools. His next two Urdu works were *Bāl-i Jibrīl* (Gabriel's Wing, 1936) and *Ẕarb-i Kalīm* (The Stroke of Moses, 1937). The former contains some of the finest of Iqbal's Urdu poems, including a renowned piece on the Mosque of Cordoba that recalls the past glory of Muslims. The poems of the latter work are mainly critiques of the existing political and social order, attacking both the British and Muslims who ape Western ways blindly.

Notwithstanding his tremendous literary output in Urdu, Persian, and English, Iqbal was not a systematic thinker. There are many contradictions in his works, a fact that explains why liberals, conservatives, reactionaries, and progressives were all able to interpret them according to their own inclinations. Nor does he seem to have thought through the practical application of his ideas. Some of them, such as the call to return to "pristine" Islam free from the fetters of tradition, the interpretations of the religious scholars, and the demand for *ijtihād*, were typical of the Islamic reformers of his time. His reinterpretation of the active participation of human beings within a dynamic creation, his call for individual action and responsibility, and his conception of the Qur'ān as a revelation that unfolds in time and eternity, were unusual and for some controversial. Yet Iqbal's Urdu verse, with its direct style devoid of the traditional flowery language and literary acrobatics, had tremendous appeal for the Indian Muslims who were searching for leaders with an intellectual and political vision. [*See the biography of Iqbal.*]

Although Iqbal far outshines other twentieth-century Urdu authors writing on Islamic themes, there are several other individuals who should be mentioned either for the uniqueness of their ideas or for the popularity of their works. An interesting contemporary of Iqbal is ʿUbaidullāh Sindhī (d. 1941), a Sikh convert to Islam. Initially trained at Deoband, he regarded himself as a disciple of Shāh Walī Allāh but interpreted his works with a strong revolutionary bias. Islam, in his estimation, preached social revolution and the overthrow of imperialism and feudalism. *Jihād,* the basis of this Islamic revolution, need not be violent; it could be the peaceful work of the pen and heart. The Ṣūfī concept of *waḥdat al-wujūd* or oneness of being formed the foundation for his ideas on Hindu-Muslim unity. Not surprisingly, the British exiled this "firebrand agitator" for more than twenty years.

Socialist ideas also influenced the writings of a few traditionally trained *ʿulamā'*, notably Ḥifẓ al-Raḥmān Sihvārvī of the Deoband school. In his book *Islām kā iqtiṣādī niẓām* he attempts to interprete socialism within an Islamic framework by claiming that the concentration of wealth in the hands of an elite was against Qur'ānic teachings. The Qur'ān, in his interpretation, prescribes *zakāt* (the alms tax) on a Muslim's income as a means of ensuring that wealth was equally distributed among all segments of society. Those whom God has blessed with wealth, intelligence, and skills have an obligation to share with the less privileged. Similar in orientation to ʿUbaidullāh Sindhī and Sihvārvī was Ḥasrat Mūhānī (d. 1951), an unusually talented poet responsible for introducing sociopolitical subjects into the *ghazal,* a poetic genre usually reserved for expressing the tragedies of unfulfilled love. His *ghazal*s, considered by many to be literary masterpieces (he has been honored with the title "prince of *ghazal* writers"), have a powerful socialist message: Islam was socialistic in its essence. In recent times, the poet perhaps most renowned for his biting criticism of the social system, especially in Pakistan, was Faiẓ Aḥmad Faiẓ (d. 1984); however, like many contemporary Urdu members of the Progressive Writers Movement, he did not explicitly deal with Islam or Islamic reform.

Rather different was the versatile Ḥasan Niẓāmī (d. 1955), a prolific writer with more than one hundred books and articles on an astonishing range of topics to his credit. The majority of these were in simple, smooth-flowing, and attractive Urdu, which partially explains their enormous popularity. Ḥasan Niẓāmī was active in the Tablīgh, an Islamic movement intended to counteract the attempts of Hindu reformists to reconvert former Hindus. Through its literature and eloquent preachers, the Tablīgh called for stronger Islamic religious education, especially for the uneducated masses who still observed many Hindu customs. In a rather different context, the call for a total islamization of Muslim life was also the central theme in the right-wing ideology of Sayyid Abu al-ʿAlā Mawdūdī (d. 1979). Mawdūdī and his activist organization, the Jamāʿat-i Islāmī, launched the most serious challenge to liberal and modernist interpretations of Islam in recent times, disseminating their ideas through the Urdu journal *Tarjumān al-Qur'ān*. Mawdūdī's writings, which have been translated into many languages, were especially critical of the secular leadership of Pakistan and the Western values prevalent among the Muslim elite. Instead, Mawdūdī advocated the establishment of a theocracy governed by a highly elaborated and codified *sharīʿah* interpreted by qualified religious scholars. [*See the biography of Mawdūdī.*]

Antithetical to Mawdūdī was Ghulām Aḥmad Parvez, a civil servant associated with a journal named after one of Iqbal's poems urging Muslims to seek new forms of creativity—*Ṭulūʿ-i Islām* (The Rise of Islam). Parvez and his small group of followers proposed a rather daring interpretation of Qur'ānic vocabulary and concepts in a special four-volume dictionary; they also dismissed the validity of *ḥadīth* as a basis for building an Islamic society. According to Parvez, the precarious state of Islam in modern times was the result of the suppression of the open and simple original religion by the traditional legalistic interpretations of the *ʿulamā'*. Not surprisingly, several religious scholars countered by declaring him an apostate.

In summary, Urdu literature in the nineteenth and twentieth centuries has witnessed a blossoming of work in both poetry and prose dealing with Islamic themes. The writers surveyed here reflect different strands within Indo-Muslim society as it has continued attempts to define itself in a changing sociopolitical environment. In giving literary expression to these strands, Urdu writers differed not only in the genres they chose but also in the traditions that inspired them. They have varied greatly in their interpretations of the role of Islam and the duties of a believing Muslim in modern society. Although collectively they represent an entire spectrum of opinions and views, each would agree in his own way with the Qur'ānic verse, "God changes not what is in a people until they change what is in themselves" (surah 13.11).

[*See also* Islam, *article on* Islam in South Asia.]

BIBLIOGRAPHY

Ahmad, Aziz. *Islamic Modernism in India and Pakistan, 1857–1964*. London, 1967.

Ahmad, Aziz, and G. E. Von Grunebaum, eds. *Muslim Self-Statement in India and Pakistan, 1857–1968*. Wiesbaden, 1970.

Baljon, J. M. S. *The Reforms and Religious Ideas of Sir Sayyid Ahmad Khan*. Leiden, 1949.

Hardy, Peter. *The Muslims of British India*. Cambridge, 1972.

Matthews, D. J., Christopher Shackle, and Shahrukh Husain. *Urdu Literature*. London, 1985.

McDonough, Sheila. *The Authority of the Past: A Study of Three Muslim Modernists*. Chambersburg, Pa., 1970.

Sadiq, Muhammad. *A History of Urdu Literature*. 2d ed. Delhi, 1984.

Schimmel, Annemarie. *Gabriel's Wing: A Study into the Religious Ideas of Sir Muhammad Iqbal*. Leiden, 1963.

Schimmel, Annemarie. *Classical Urdu Literature from the Beginning to Iqbāl*. Wiesbaden, 1975.

Schimmel, Annemarie. *Islam in the Indian Subcontinent*. Leiden, 1980.

Smith, Wilfred Cantwell. *Modern Islam in India*. Rev. ed. London, 1946.

Troll, Christian W. *Sayyid Ahmad Khan: A Reinterpretation of Muslim Theology*. Delhi, 1978.

ALI S. ASANI

ʿURF. The Arabic term *ʿurf* (from the root *ʿ-r-f*, "to know, to be aware of, to be acquainted with") is perhaps best translated as "what is commonly known and accepted." In the central Islamic countries it is the common name for unwritten customary law, in contrast to written holy law (*sharīʿah*) or other legal canons. *ʿAdāt* is a synonym used in other parts of the Islamic world, especially in Indonesia.

In the beginning of the Islamic era *ʿurf* was regarded as complementary to *sharīʿah*, which did not contain all the regulations needed to make an increasingly complex society function. Customary handling of legal matters that did not clearly contradict the spirit of *sharīʿah* was accepted. Attempts were even made to treat *ʿurf* as another legitimate foundation of Islamic law, alongside the Qur'ān, the traditions *(ḥadīth)*, analogic reasoning *(qiyās)*, and the consensus of the religious community *(ijmāʿ)*. But because *sharīʿah* in principle covers everything, and above all because it is God-given and not man-made like *ʿurf*, these attempts were never successful. It could be argued, of course, that elements of customary legal practice entered into *sharīʿah* by means of *ḥadīth, qiyās*, and *ijmāʿ*, which all relied on human reasoning. Already the acceptance of sources of *sharīʿah* other than the Qur'ān was a tacit recognition of contributions that are not divine in origin. This was an unavoidable measure, since in its revealed state the holy law was neither complete nor detailed enough. Its general character and selective prescriptions forced succeeding generations of Muslims to develop it into a complete legal system.

ʿUrf has been used to designate three different types of jurisdiction: the way common people maintain order locally, for instance in the marketplace; the legal decisions made by a ruler and his secular representatives; and finally, the practices of local courts. In the first sense, *ʿurf* has often been used for larger political purposes. Imām Yaḥyā (1918–1948) of Yemen tried to impose *sharīʿah* all over the country as a means of centralization. One judge appointed by the government was to replace several local arbitrators chosen by the people themselves. At the same time, *ʿurf* was actually practiced by the members of the state apparatus themselves. In Indonesia, customary law *(adat)* was sponsored by Dutch colonialists in order to counterbalance the Islamic threat and later by native nationalists in order to build the state.

In the second sense, opposition to *ʿurf* has been a motive for rebellion by Muslim revivalists who have reacted against un-Islamic decrees made by a sultan, shah, or president. The most noteworthy example in modern times is Iran.

In the third sense, *ʿurf* appears as a malleable legal practice of the Islamic law courts that is closely related to social and cultural features of the wider society and that may sometimes depart from strict Islamic doctrine. It is reminiscent of case law in contrast to statute law.

Also known under the name of *ʿamal* (judicial practice), this phenomenon is especially prevalent in Morocco.

[See also Adat; Consensus; Law, *article on* Legal Thought and Jurisprudence.]

BIBLIOGRAPHY

Coulson, Noel J. *A History of Islamic Law*. Edinburgh, 1964. Detailed discussion of the growth of Islamic law and its relation to *ʿurf*.

Dresch, Paul. *Tribes, Government, and History in Yemen*. Oxford, 1989. Innovative case study of the relation between tribal and Islamic law in Yemen.

Lev, Daniel S. *Islamic Courts in Indonesia*. Berkeley, 1972. Good case study of legal pluralism and the relation between law and politics.

Levy, Reuben. *The Social Structure of Islam*. Cambridge, 1957. Erudite and comprehensive presentation of Islam as a social system.

Rosen, Lawrence. *The Anthropology of Justice: Law as Culture in Islamic Society*. Cambridge, 1989. Brief account of Islamic law courts in Morocco showing the close relationship between legal operations and local culture.

TOMAS GERHOLM

ʿUSHR. Literally "tithe" or "tenth," *ʿushr* is the land tax levied on the produce of agricultural land owned by Muslims. The term *ʿushr,* which is not mentioned in the Qur'ān, bears some resemblance to the names of pre-Islamic land taxes, including biblical references to tithe; but whereas the pre-Islamic tithe was paid to priests or kings, the Islamic *ʿushr* is defined as a kind of alms tax levied by the state for the public interest. The amount of the tax varies, so that land watered by artificial irrigation will pay half the tax levied on land watered by rain.

ʿUshr, as well as the *kharāj* (land tax), are discussed in legal sources in conjunction with the question of landownership. During the first few years of Islam, the conquered lands were considered *fay'*, or spoils of war, and they were distributed among Muslim individuals. Such lands became *ʿushrī* lands, and their yield was subject to the *ʿushr*. The second caliph, ʿUmar, changed this practice and stipulated that the conquered Sawad lands of Iraq stay in the hands of their original non-Muslim owners, who had the right to cultivate the land in return for paying the *kharāj*. In effect, the ownership of the land passed to the Muslim community and by extension to the state, which represents this community. ʿUmar's laws were designed to guarantee a stable source of public revenue in a state whose subjects were largely non-Muslim. As more people converted to Islam, the *kharāj* was replaced by the considerably smaller *ʿushr,* thus depriving the state of one of its major financial resources. The Umayyad caliph ʿUmar ibn ʿAbd al-ʿAzīz addressed this problem by introducing new laws to prevent the transformation of *kharāj* land into *ʿushrī* land. Before him, both the *jizyah* (poll tax), levied on the persons of non-Muslims, and the *kharāj,* levied on their lands, were dropped on conversion to Islam. ʿUmar Ibn ʿAbd al-ʿAzīz reclassified *kharāj* land based on the way it was conquered, so that the *kharāj* tax remained a burden on the land irrespective of the religion of the owner.

After these changes, the *ʿushrī* lands included all lands privately owned by Muslims if it were: conquered by Muslims and distributed among those who captured it; land whose owners converted to Islam before it was conquered; land apportioned to Muslims by the rulers; dead land revived by Muslims, on the condition that it was not conquered by force; or land which was bought by Muslims before it became *kharāj* land through conquest or peace treaty. The payment of *ʿushr* was considered by all legal schools as proof of property rights, whereas the payment of *kharāj* was considered by all schools except the Ḥanafī as a proof of the public ownership of the land.

The legal codes of contemporary Muslim countries make no use of the concepts of *ʿushr* and *kharāj.* In the contemporary discussions of social justice in Islam, and of alternative Islamic economic systems, however, Muslim thinkers, such as Sayyid Quṭb and Muḥammad Bāqir al-Ṣadr, often gauge their discussions in readings of the theoretical and historical roles of these fiscal Islamic institutions.

[*See also* Kharāj; Taxation.]

BIBLIOGRAPHY

Dennett, Daniel C., Jr. *Conversion and the Poll Tax in Early Islam*. Cambridge, 1950. In contrast to Shemesh and Lökkegaard, the author recognizes the genuine nature of the legal debates on taxation, and their link to actual historical developments.

Ibn al-Farrā', Abū Yaʿlā Muḥammad. *Al-aḥkām al-sulṭānīyah*. Cairo, 1938. Contains an elaborate exposition of the Ḥanbalī laws on taxation.

Ibn Rajab al-Ḥanbalī, ʿAbd al-Raḥmān. *Al-istikhrāj li-aḥkām al-kharāj*. Cairo, 1934. Fourteenth-century digest of the different legal opinions on land taxes.

Ibn Sallām, Abū ʿUbayd al-Qāsim. *Kitāb al-Amwāl*. Cairo, 1935. One of the earliest systematic legal works on taxation.

Lökkegaard, Frede. *Islamic Taxation in the Classical Period*. Copenhagen, 1950. Maintains that the discussions of taxation in the legal sources do not provide a picture of the real state of affairs, and that they are mere exercises in classification.

Māwardī, Abū al-Ḥasan ʿAlī ibn Muḥammad al-. *Al-aḥkām al-sulṭānīyah wa-al-wilāyāt al-dīnīyah*. Al-Manṣūrah, 1989. Translated into French by Edmond Fagnan as *Les statuts gouvernementaux, ou, Règles de droit public et administratif*. Paris, 1982. Contains an elaborate exposition of the Shāfiʿī laws on taxation.

Quṭb, Sayyid. *Social Justice in Islam*. Translated by John B. Hardie. Washington, D.C., 1953. Contains discussions of the legitimate kinds of landownership and of the Islamic notions of communal wealth.

Ṣadr, Muḥammad Bāqir al-. *Iqtiṣāadunā*. New rev. ed. Beirut, 1977. English translation: *Our Economics*. Tehran, 1982. Discusses *kharāj* and *ʿushr* land in the context of comparing the Islamic economic system with socialism and capitalism.

Shemesh, Aharon Ben. *Taxation in Islam*, vol. 1, *Translation of Yaḥyā Ben Ādam's Kitāb al-Kharāj;* vol. 2, *Translation of Qudāma b. JaʿK-itāb al-Kharāj*. Leiden, 1958–1969. Useful translations of some of the most important legal texts on taxation. In his introductions to the translations, however, the author maintains that these legal debates were theoretical and detached from reality, and that the real fiscal policies were completely taken over from Jewish, Byzantine, and Sassanian governments.

Ṭabāṭabāʾī, Ḥusayn Mudarrisī. *Kharāj in Islamic Law*. London, 1983. Points out the similarities between Shīʿī and Sunnī debates on questions of landownership and taxation.

AHMAD S. DALLAL

UṢŪL AL-FIQH. Muslim jurists generally define *uṣūl al-fiqh* ("roots of law") as the body of principles and the investigative methodology through which practical legal rules are derived from their particular sources. Its scope of interest may be likened to the field of jurisprudence in English law as discussed by John Austin or Carleton Allen, as well as to the field of interpretation of statutes. Of prime importance in its inquiry is the question of the legitimacy of rules and whether such rules depend on a certain or a probable base. Rules of probable legitimacy, according to most jurists, are binding in law, whereas in theology beliefs must depend on bases that are certain.

The primary base or source, certain as to its being the word of God that came down to us in a concurrent transmission *(tawātur)*, is the Qur'ān. The second source for legal rules is *sunnah*, the reports about the sayings, actions, or tacit approvals of the Prophet. Depending upon the probity and number of the transmitters, these reports can be considered certain or probable. Those of many concurrent transmissions *(mutawātir)* are considered certain; those that are well known and of slightly lesser standing of authenticity *(mashhūr)* are also considered by Ḥanafī jurists as certain; but those that depend upon one or a few transmitters *(āḥādī)* are considered of probable authenticity *(ẓannī)*.

The third source is the consensus of all Muslim interpretive scholars in a specific age on a legal rule about a new happening not covered in the Qur'ān or *sunnah*. Most Sunnī scholars consider such consensus binding for all times; other scholars, including Shīʿī scholars, say this consensus is impossible. Jurists also differ on the value of consensus by silence *(sukūtī)*, a situation in which some scholars would not give an opinion on a happening or a measure, and are presumed to have agreed with the expressed opinion of other scholars. Most jurists would not accept such a consensus as binding, but Ḥanafī scholars accept it as such.

The fourth source is analogy, which has been defined as making a situation with no textual provision as to its rule follow the rule of another situation with such a textual provision, because both situations share in the cause *(ʿillah)* of such rule. The classic example is the making of all intoxicants follow the rule of wine, which was specifically prohibited in the Qur'ān (5.90), because the cause of the prohibition is intoxication, common to all of them. Jurists make a distinction between the cause and the underlying reason *(ḥikmah)* of the rule. The latter, which is deemed either to bring a benefit to people or ward off a harm from them, is often not apparent or, at least, too indefinite to be the basis for the rule. On the other hand, the cause *(ʿillah)* must be apparent and definite for it to be the basis for the rule. Analogy, therefore, operates when the cause, not the underlying reason, is the same in both situations.

In addition to these four basic sources, several principles and presumptions aid the interpretive jurist in arriving at a rule. One such principle is preference *(istiḥsān);* using this principle a jurist would abandon the result of a clear analogy for a latent analogy or would reject a general rule for an exceptional rule, because of "an indication that sparks in his mind." For example, despite the general rule that the subject of a contract must be in existence, the contract of rent (the subject of which is a future benefit) was allowed by preference because of the peoples' need for it. Ḥanafī jurists were prominent in the articulation of this principle.

Another principle is that of unregulated interest *(al-maṣlaḥah al-mursalah)*, which serves as a basis for a rule. It is an interest that no legal provision has approved or disapproved; examples are the establishment of prisons and the coinage of money. The interest to be served must be real, of a general nature, and not in conflict with a principle established by a legal provision or consensus.

A third principle is the presumption of continuity (*istiṣḥāb*): a situation subsisting previously is presumed to be continuing at present until the contrary is proven. Accordingly, a person is presumed to be free from liability (his original situation at birth) until the contrary is proven.

In interpreting the Qur'ān and the *sunnah*, jurists dealt with the workings of language in detail in an attempt to arrive at the intended meaning. They dealt with such questions as the ways in which words indicate meanings, what is general and what is specific, how the specific limits the general, whether the imperative signifies an obligation and the prohibitive signifies forbiddenness, what is capable of a hidden meaning and what is not, and so forth. These questions are similar to those dealt with by the field of interpretation of statutes.

The rudiments of this science started to appear in the second century AH. The *Fihrist* of Ibn al-Nadīm mentions that the Ḥanafī jurist Abū Yūsuf (d. AH 182/798 CE) collected its principles in a separate volume, but that volume must have been lost. The earliest book that has come down to us is *Al-risālah* of Muḥammad ibn Idrīs al-Shāfiʿī (d. 204/820); therefore, its author has been reputed as the founder of this science, which was later named *uṣūl al-fiqh*. Subsequent jurists followed two distinct methodologies in their expositions. One group, made up mostly of Mālikīs and Shāfiʿīs, followed a theological and logical methodology and paid scant attention to the concrete rules of the particular law school. These men included Abū Ḥāmid al-Ghazālī (d. 505/1111) in *Al-mustaṣfā* and al-Āmidī (d. 631/1233) in *Al-iḥkām*. The other, made up of Ḥanafīs, deduced the principles from the concrete rules of their school. Hence, they often cite the rules to exemplify the principles; these men included al-Dabūsī (d. 430/1039) in *Taqwīm*, al-Bazdawī (d. 482/1089) in *Uṣūl al-fiqh*, and al-Nasafī (d. 710/1310) in *Al-manār*. Later jurists combined the two methodologies.

In modern times jurists who have written about the subject have, in the main, adopted a progressive approach to accommodate this science to the changing times. Muḥammad al-Shawkānī (d. 1250/1834), a Yemeni jurist, railed against those who stick to imitating the established schools (*taqlīd*) and called for interpretation (*ijtihād*) with due consideration given to public interest (*maṣlaḥah*). The modern reformer Muḥammad ʿAbduh (d. 1323/1905) and his student Muḥammad Rashīd Riḍā (d. 1354/1935) found support in his writings for their progressive ideas. Several other writers and jurists also supported in varying ways the principle of public interest (*maṣlaḥah*) as a factor for modernization. These include ʿAbd al-Wahhāb Khallāf (d. 1375/1956), Muḥammad al-Khuḍarī (d. 1354/1927), Muṣṭafā Zayd, Ṣubḥī Maḥmaṣānī, Maʿrūf Dawālībī, Muṣṭafā al-Shalabī, Aḥmad Zakī Yamānī, Kemal Faruki, and Khālid Masʿūd. Some harked back to Najm al-Dīn al-Ṭūfī (d. 716/1316), a Ḥanbalī jurist who had held that the principle of *maṣlaḥah* could restrict (*takhṣīṣ*) the application of consensus as well as that of the Qur'ān and *sunnah* if such application were harmful to public interest. Others invoked the Andalusian jurist al-Shāṭibī (d. 790/1316) for similar views. Most seemed to widen the doctrine of *maṣlaḥah* from the confined field of an unregulated interest (*maṣlaḥah mursalah*) to an independent principle for the interpretation of law; thereby it could prevail over precise rules or over contradictory regulations provided it remained faithful to the higher objectives of law, which aim at preserving religion, physical well-being, progeny, property, and mental faculty. Many also expanded the restricted principle that rules change with changing times to become a cardinal principle of interpretation, or, at least, called for an eclectic approach whereby rules could be drawn from any Islamic school of law if they better conform to the requirements of modern life. Jurists who have written in a more traditional vein include Muḥammad Abū Zahrah, Saʿīd Ramaḍān al-Būṭī, and the Shīʿī jurist Muḥammad Bāqir al-Ṣadr. [*See the biography of Ṣadr.*]

The jurists mentioned above as being progressive managed to stay within the main stream of Muslims, although some of them were subject to criticism by traditional elements. Two highly progressive jurists, however, may be considered nonconformist in calling for the reinterpretation of basic Islamic rules. One is the Indian Fāṭimid jurist A. A. A. Fyzee, who called for a "Protestant" Islam that would separate the church and state, would question the authority of "ancient scholars and *imāms*," and would reinterpret the Qur'ān according to modern exigencies. [*See the biography of Fyzee.*] The other is ʿAbd Allāh al-Naʿīm, the Sudanese student of the late Maḥmūd Muḥammad Ṭāhā who was killed by the Sudanese President Jaʿfar Nimeiri in 1985 for "heresy." Al-Naʿīm, following his master, would distinguish Qur'ānic verses meant to apply in the early stages of the Islamic community from those that were meant to have permanent validity, and so derive rules more consonant with modern life.

[*See also* Law, *articles on* Legal Thought and Jurisprudence *and* Modern Legal Reform.]

BIBLIOGRAPHY

The following works and/or authors have been discussed in the article. Additional annotation has been provided when appropriate.

Abū Zahrah, Muḥammad. *Mālik.* Cairo, 1946.

Āmidī, ʿAlī ibn Muḥammad al-. *Al-Iḥkām fī uṣūl al-aḥkām.* 4 vols. Cairo, 1967. For an appreciation of this work, see Weiss, below.

Bazdawī, ʿAlī ibn Muḥammad al-. *Uṣūl al-fiqh.* On the margin of ʿAbd al-ʿAzīz al-Bukhārī. *Kashf al-asrār ʿan uṣūl Fakhr al-Islām al-Bazdawī,* 4 vols. (Istanbul, AH 1308).

Dabūsī, ʿAbd Allah ibn ʿUmar al-. *Taqwīm al-adillah fī uṣūl al-fiqh.* Dublin, Chester Beatty MS 3343.

Dawālībī, Maʿrūf. *Al-Madkhal ila ʿilm uṣūl al-fiqh.* Damascus, 1959. Textbook for law schools.

Faruki, Kemal A. *Islam Today and Tomorrow.* Karachi, 1974.

Fyzee, Asaf A. A. *A Modern Approach to Islam.* New York, 1963.

Ghazālī, Abū Ḥāmid al-. *Al-Mustaṣfā min ʿilm al-uṣūl.* Edited by Muḥammad Muṣṭafā Abū al-ʿAlā'. Cairo, 1971.

Khadduri, Majid. *Islamic Jurisprudence: Shāfiʿī's Risāla.* Baltimore, 1961. Masterful translation of the first extant work on *uṣūl al-fiqh.*

Khallāf, ʿAbd al-Wahhāb. *ʿIlm uṣūl al-fiqh.* Kuwait, 1972. Very lucid introduction to the subject, with examples from the *sharīʿah* and positive law.

Khuḍarī, Muḥammad al-. *Uṣūl al-fiqh.* Cairo, 1933.

Maḥmaṣānī, Ṣubḥī. *Falsafat al-tashrīʿ fī al-Islām.* Translated by Farhat Ziadeh as *Philosophy of Jurisprudence in Islam.* Leiden, 1961. Excellent introduction by a liberal jurist who is also familiar with Western jurisprudence.

Masud, Muhammad Khalid. *Islamic Legal Philosophy: A Study of Abū Isḥāq al-Shāṭibī's Life and Thought.* Islamabad, 1977. Study of the most original jurist of Andalusia.

Naim, ʿAbd Allah Ahmad. *Toward an Islamic Reformation: Civil Liberties, Human Rights, and International Law.* Syracuse, N.Y., 1990.

Nasafī, ʿAbd Allah ibn Aḥmad al-. *Kashf al-asrār fī sharḥ al-manār.* 2 vols. Cairo, 1898.

Ṣadr, Muḥammad Bāqir al-. *A Short History of ʿIlmul Uṣūl.* Accra, London, and New York, 1984. Shīʿī work by an ayatollah who was liquidated by the Iraqi regime in 1980. The translation into English is especially good.

Shalabī, Muṣṭafā al-. *Al-Fiqh al-Islāmī bayna al-mithālīyah wa-al-wāqiʿīyah.* Beirut, 1982.

Shawkānī, Muḥammad ibn ʿAlī al-. *Al-Qawl al-mufīd fī adillat al-ijtihād wa-al-taqlīd.* Cairo, 1934.

Shawkānī, Muḥammad ibn ʿAlī al-. *Irshād al-fuḥūl ilā taḥqīq al-ḥaqq min ʿilm al-uṣūl.* Cairo, 1937.

Weiss, Bernard G. *The Search for God's Law: Islamic Jurisprudence in the Writing of Sayf al-Dīn al-Āmidī.* Salt Lake City, 1992.

Yamānī, Aḥmad Zakī. *Al-Sharīʿah al-khālidah wa-mushkilāt al-ʿaṣr.* Jiddah, 1983.

Zayd, Muṣṭafā. *Al-Maslaḥah fī al-tashrīʿ al-Islāmī wa-Najm al-Dīn al-Ṭūfī.* Cairo, 1954.

Zysow, Aron. *The Economy of Certainty: An Introduction to the Typology of Islamic Legal Theory.* Forthcoming.

FARHAT J. ZIADEH

UṢŪLĪYAH. A school of law relying on a series of rational processes, the Uṣūlīyah has been almost universally accepted by Shīʿī Muslims for the past two centuries. Its designation "Uṣūlīyah," derived from the expression *uṣūl al-fiqh* ("principles of jurisprudence"), is not encountered before the mid-twelfth century, but there can be little doubt that the application of rational methods to the deduction of the specific ordinances of the law from its sources was known already during the lifetime of the imams. Clearly rationalist in tendency was Shaykh al-Mufīd (d. 1022), who rejected with great polemical vigor the view of his traditionist opponents (the forerunners of the Akhbārīyah) that traditions narrated by only one line of transmission were acceptable sources of law. His positions were developed, with some modification, by Shaykh al-Ṭā'ifah al-Ṭūsī (d. 1067), Muḥaqqiq al-Ḥillī (d. 1277), and ʿAllāmah al-Ḥillī (d. 1326). The last took the crucial step of recognizing the principle of *ijtihād* (disciplined reasoning based on the *sharīʿah*) that was to become central to the Uṣūlīyah; he is therefore sometimes regarded as the first Uṣūlī *sensu stricto.* This gradual clarification of the bases of rationalist jurisprudence in Shiism owed much to earlier developments in Sunnī law, something that did not go unnoticed by the Akhbārī adversaries of the Uṣūlī doctrine.

When the Ṣafavids set about propagating Shiism in Iran, creating for the first time the conditions for the application of Shīʿī law in a major Islamic society, representatives of the Uṣūlī position—such as ʿAlī al-Karakī (d. 1534) and Muḥaqqiq Ardabīlī (d. 1585)—were initially in the ascendant. In the mid-seventeenth century, however, there was a late blossoming of the Akhbārī school under the auspices of Mullah Muḥammad Amīn Akhbārī (d. 1624). It succeeded in gaining the loyalty of many of the major intellectual figures of the day and came to enjoy nearly complete control of the *ʿatabāt* in Iraq by the mid-eighteenth century. The supremacy of the Uṣūlīyah was definitively reestablished toward the end of the century by Āqā Muḥammad Bāqir Bihbahānī (d. 1791) by means of both vigorous public debate in the *madrasahs* of Karbala and the composition of treatises on *uṣūl al-fiqh.* His numerous associates and students consolidated this triumph in both Iraq and Iran, and the Uṣūlī positions were from that time virtually coterminous with Shīʿī law as such.

Bihbahānī not only reasserted the legitimate or even obligatory nature of *ijtihād* but also made it incumbent on all who had not attained the qualifications for *ijtihād* to follow, in matters of religious law, those who had. This process is known as *taqlīd* ("imitation"), and the scholar practicing *ijtihād* who is selected for imitation is called the *marjaᶜ al-taqlīd* ("source of imitation"). The structuring of the Shīᶜī community that this implied, with obedience to a practitioner of *ijtihād* made a matter of religious duty, greatly elevated the status of the religious jurists and had a profound impact on Iranian history and society; it paved the way for the political activism of the Shīᶜī *ᶜulamā'* throughout the nineteenth and twentieth centuries and may even be regarded as an ancestor of the Islamic Revolution of 1978–1979.

The principles of the Uṣūlī school were further refined by Shaykh Murtaḍā Anṣārī (d. 1864), who laid stress on the necessity of choosing as *marjaᶜ al-taqlīd* the most learned jurist available, and by Ākhūnd Muḥammad Kāẓim Khurāsānī (d. 1911). The doctrine of *wilāyat al-faqīh* ("the viceregency of the jurist"), according to which a jurist may claim full governmental powers, may be regarded as a radical but nonetheless logical working out of the implications of Uṣūlī doctrine; in elaborating it, Ayatollah Ruhollah Khomeini (d. 1989) was able to cite indications scattered in the works of earlier Uṣūlī scholars.

[*See also* Akhbārīyah; ᶜAtabāt; Ijtihād; Marjaᶜ al-Taqlīd; Taqlīd; ᶜUlamā'; Uṣūl al-Fiqh; Wilāyat al-Faqīh; *and the biography of Ḥillī.*]

BIBLIOGRAPHY

Algar, Hamid. "Religious Forces in Eighteenth- and Nineteenth-Century Iran." In *The Cambridge History of Iran*, vol. 7, *From Nadir Shah to the Islamic Republic*, ed. Peter Avery et al., pp. 710–714. Cambridge, 1991.

Cole, Juan R. I. "Shīᶜī Clerics in Iraq and Iran, 1722–1780: The Akhbārī-Uṣūlī Conflict Reconsidered." *Iranian Studies* 28.1 (Winter 1985): 3–34.

Gurjī, Abū al-Qāsim. "Nigāhī bā taḥavvul-i ᶜilm-i uṣūl." In *Maqālāt va bar'rasīhā*, pp. 13–16. N.p., 1973.

Scarcia, Gianroberto. "Intorno alle controversie tra Ahbārī e Uṣūlī presso gli Imamiti di Persia." *Rivista degli Studi Orientali* 33 (1958): 211–250.

Ṭabāṭabā'ī, Mudarrisī (Tabatabai, Hossein Modarressi). *An Introduction to Shii Law*. London, 1984. See pages 40–58.

HAMID ALGAR

UZBEKISTAN. Within the territory of Uzbekistan lie the most prestigious centers of Islamic culture and influence in Central Asia: the ancient cities of Bukhara, Samarkand, and Khiva, where the religion took root in the seventh century CE. With European colonial expansion and the spread of European ideas to other Islamic realms in Asia and North Africa, "holy" Bukhara (*Bukhārā-yi sharīf*)—which retained a quasi-independent status under its emirs even after Russian conquest of Turkestan in the nineteenth century—was an object of special veneration in Muslim eyes as a locus of uncontaminated belief. Bukharan *madrasahs* attracted students from other Muslim areas of the Russian Empire and beyond. Baymirza Hayit, an Uzbek Muslim who reached the West during World War II, described (1956) his homeland prior to 1917 as "a land of Islamic dervishes" and superstition, with four active Ṣūfī orders (the Naqshbandīyah, Qādirīyah, Kubrawīyah, and Qalandārīyah).

Tashkent, the capital of modern Uzbekistan, was the dominant political center of the whole region during both the tsarist and Soviet periods. Following establishment of Soviet rule after 1917, anti-Islamic policies prevailed, despite initial resistance to them even from within the ranks of Uzbek and other Central Asian Communists. At a 1923 party meeting in Tashkent (described in Ramiz, 1928), indigenous members openly jeered a speaker who condemned Islam. A few years later, however, party discipline had been restored. Yet despite harsh measures against Islam, official media attacks on Islamic "survivals" throughout the Soviet period revealed that a substantial number of Uzbek Muslims were continuing to defy or circumvent strictures by continuing to observe religious life-cycle rituals and making forbidden pilgrimages to the graves of holy men.

During World War II a Muslim "Spiritual Board" under a *muftī* was created in Tashkent with official sanction and along the lines of Russian Orthodox hierarchical structures. Its jurisdiction extended throughout the four Central Asian republics and Kazakhstan (always regarded by Soviet officials as a separate geographic entity). Any hope that this was a step toward legitimation of Islam was soon dashed, however, when the persecution of religion resumed at the end of the war. The Spiritual Board emerged in its true role as an official instrument for controlling Islamic activity within Central Asia, and as a handmaiden of the regime for foreign political purposes. Tashkent became a showcase used in attempts to impress foreign Muslims with the supposed superiority of the Soviet system for members of their religion.

With some fluctuation, anti-Islamic policies remained in force after Joseph Stalin's death in 1953, but erosion of Moscow's control over the republics in the period of "stagnation" under Brezhnev was marked by a de facto softening. In the new milder climate it became possible for Uzbek social scientists to collect and publish data on the extent of Islamic practice. The Uzbek researcher Talib S. Saidbaev published a book (*Islam i obshchestvo*, Moscow, 1982) showing that in traditional Muslim areas of the Soviet Union religion was far more pervasive, especially among the young and the educated, than in Christian parts of the country. Saidbaev found that the structure of society, with tightly knit extended families that cut across socioeconomic lines and remained loyal to age-old tribal and clan affiliations, led to increased social pressures to conform to religious obligations. Officials charged by the Communist Party with responsibility for "atheist indoctrination" warned that their work was being frustrated by a widespread public tendency to identify Islamic rituals with national tradition, thus cementing their popularity even among nonbelievers.

Members of Uzbekistan's Soviet-educated professional elite joined in global efforts to reform Islam to make it more acceptable. The Uzbek Encyclopedia (*Ozbek Sovet Entsiklopediyasi*, vol. 5, Tashkent, 1974) listed some of the aspects of "Islamic modernism," among them portrayal of Muḥammad as a democrat and reformer, identification of Islam with socialism and communism, equation of religious and communist morality, and modernization of *sharīʿah* rules governing women, the family, and daily life.

When Mikhail Gorbachev first came to power in Moscow in 1985 he viewed elimination of religion as an essential ingredient of his own program of reform. This was manifested in especially brutal fashion in Uzbekistan, where in Tashkent in 1986 Gorbachev made an anti-Islamic speech so harsh that it was never published. His visit was followed by mass expulsions from the Uzbek Communist Party of members accused of participation in religious events. Ironically, relaxation of central controls over the Soviet republics produced an effect opposite to that he had intended. In February 1989 the *muftī* of Tashkent, Shamsuddin Baba Khan (Shams al-Dīn Bābā Khān), a mainstay of the regime and grandson of the original *muftī* appointed in 1943, was ousted from office following a demonstration by members of the *ummah* who accused him of alcoholism and womanizing, apparently with the connivance of the local authorities. In June 1989 a new Uzbek Communist Party chief, Islam A. Karimov (subsequently president of independent Uzbekistan), came to power and presided over the inception of a much more tolerant policy toward Islam.

The new *muftī*, Muḥammad Ṣādiq Muḥammad Yūsuf, became a highly visible public figure, appearing on state-controlled television. He also published articles containing liberal advice on such matters as family relations and the treatment of women; the newspaper that carried these, *Ozbekistan adabiyati va san"ati*, had until recently been a vehicle of systematic attacks on Islam. As part of his new public role, the *muftī* scrupulously refrained from appearing as spokesman for the aspirations and grievances of the rank-and-file *ummah* or of Uzbeks in general, avoiding any criticism of the secular power. This led to discontent among some segments of the *ʿulamāʾ* and *ummah*, who repeatedly attempted to depose him. On one occasion he managed to hold onto office in the face of accusations that he had enriched himself unjustly through the sale of Qur'āns donated by Saudi Arabia.

Uzbekistan's declaration of independence on 31 August 1991 removed the remaining impediment to such manifestations of spiritual life as public worship and religious education. In ancient mosques newly restored to religious control, and in new ones, Qur'ān classes began for adults of both sexes as well as for children. Once-forbidden religious publications now appeared on sale at kiosks, and there were advertisements for bus tours to take Uzbeks on pilgrimages to religious shrines. (In the wider context, the independence of other Central Asian republics led to the Tashkent *muftī*'s loss of authority and the emergence of rival leaders on their territories.)

At the same time, increased religious leverage and visits by emissaries of such conservative Muslim countries as Iran and Saudi Arabia led many Uzbeks, including believers, to fear that the tyranny of Soviet rule might be replaced by the tyranny of "Islamic fundamentalism," a phrase that was soon on everyone's lips. Muslims welcomed toleration of their religion after so many decades of persecution, but some, especially the better-educated who make up a significant part of the population, were alarmed by the perceived danger of an "Islamic republic" in which public power would be governed by the *sharīʿah* in its more conservative interpretation. Such fears were fed by grass-roots religious ferment—especially in the Ferghana Valley, where Muslim activists seized a public building—and above all by the turmoil in neighboring

Tajikistan, in which Islamic elements appeared to be a major force. The government of Uzbekistan acquiesced in the deployment of Russian troops to help control the situation, and many Uzbeks spoke approvingly of the secular Turkish model.

To contain Muslim ferment, the civil government of President Karimov adopted a dual policy. On the one hand, the loyal official clergy was supported in various ways as a counterweight to unauthorized activity, replicating the pattern set in the Soviet period. On the other, secular power was wielded where the influence of the official clergy was insufficient.

With Islam now elevated to the position of a virtual state religion, however, the official clergy was no longer quite the tame instrument it had once been. Its base had been expanded by accretion of restored religious properties and by enormous growth in the scope and scale of sanctioned religious activity. Symbolic of its new status was a new deference on the part of the civil power; for example, the government conceded to the clergy a de facto veto of any official effort to deal with the pressing problem of population growth, which every year was creating a half-million new mouths to feed in an economy where unemployment was rife.

Muslims seeking to act outside permissible limits were confronted, as in Soviet times, by the coercive power of the state. Force has been used to break up unauthorized manifestations, at times with brutal consequences. With the Mufti's blessing, the Karimov government has prohibited organized political activity by Muslims, denying legal registration to the Islamic Revival Party (as it has to secular opposition parties). Against a backdrop of unsolved social and economic problems, the climate of repression has enhanced the potential of Islam as champion of the poor and downtrodden and has increased the leverage of radical elements seeking to destabilize the secular institutions. The 1993 flight to Saudi Arabia of the Tashkent *muftī* suggested that even loyalist Islamic elements were finding it difficult to accommodate the Karimov regime.

[*See also* Islam, *article on* Islam in Central Asia and the Caucasus.]

BIBLIOGRAPHY

Barthold, V. V. *Istoriia kul'turnoĭ zhizni Turkestana*. Leningrad, 1927.

Bennigsen, Alexandre, and Chantal Lemercier-Quelquejay. *Islam in the Soviet Union*. New York, 1967.

Critchlow, James. "Islam and Nationalism in Central Asia." In *Religion and Nationalism in Soviet and East European Politics*, edited by Pedro Ramet, pp. 196–217. 2d ed. Durham, N.C., 1989.

Critchlow, James. "Islam in Soviet Central Asia: Renaissance or Revolution?" *Religion in Communist Dominated Areas* 29 (Autumn 1990): 196–211.

Critchlow, James. *Nationalism in Uzbekistan: A Soviet Republic's Road to Sovereignty*. Boulder, 1991. See "The Islamic Factor."

Hayit, Baymirza. *Turkestan im XX. Jahrhundert*. Darmstadt, 1956.

Ramiz, Mannan. *Khayaldan Haqiqatqha*. Tashkent-Samarkand, 1928. Uncataloged manuscript in the Near East Division, Library of Congress, described in James Critchlow, "Religious-Nationalist Dissent in the Turkestan Communist Party: An Old Document Resurfaces," *Report on the USSR*, 19 January 1990.

Schuyler, Eugene. *Turkistan: Notes of a Journey in Russian Turkistan, Khokand, Bukhara, and Kuldja* (1878). New York, 1966.

JAMES CRITCHLOW

V

VEIL. *See* Ḥijāb.

VICEGERENT. One appointed by a ruler to exercise his or her power and authority is called a "vicegerent." According to the teachings of Islam, all human beings are commanded to fulfill their individual roles as vicegerents to God. Because they are aware of this injunction, Muslims must strive to adhere to and advance God's word by establishing something like a divine society on earth; that is, they serve as "agents" or "vicegerents" of God by carrying out his moral laws. Accordingly, human beings have been given the necessary mental intelligence and physical strength to study nature and its order so that they may then use their faculties, in accordance with nature and the moral guidelines ordained by God, to benefit humanity.

The Qur'ānic term for "vicegerent" is *khalīfah,* and that for "vicegerency" is *khilāfah.* On two occasions in the Qur'ān, specific human beings are identified as vicegerents. Adam is the first to be referred to in this manner. In Surat al-Baqara (2.30), God announces to the angels that he "will create a vicegerent on earth," namely, Adam. When they express fear that this vicegerent will "make mischief there and shed blood," God replies, "I know what you do not know." This latter verse is generally understood as indicating God's trust that his vicegerent will obey his commands. In A. Yusuf Ali's commentary on this verse, for example, it is noted that "the perfect vicegerent is he who has the power of initiative himself, but whose independent action always reflects perfectly the will of his Principal" (1983, p. 24).

The second person to be identified as a vicegerent in the Qur'ān is King David. Indeed, in surah 38.26, he is urged to avoid the temptations of the heart and to adhere to the path of God. Here, too, the verse seems to point to the need for God's vicegerent to model his actions on God's commands and especially his moral laws.

There is agreement among scholars that these references to Adam and King David are not meant to identify them as the exclusive possessors of the responsibility to fulfill God's commands on earth. On the contrary, since Adam is the father of all humankind, the reference to him as a vicegerent shows that this role defers upon the human race as a whole. Muhammad Fazl-ur-Rahman Ansari, for example, cites surah 2.30 to urge that the vicegerency of God "has been bestowed on humanity as a whole by its Creator" (n.d., p. 122). Similarly, Sayyid Maḥmud Ṭāleqāni insists that the species of Adam, and not just Adam himself, is the vicegerent of God. Thus, "although in his thought and behavior he [i.e., every human being] is free and independent, and has discretionary powers, in accordance with the title of vicegerent he is restricted to carrying out the will and attaining the object of Allāh" (1982, p. 53).

As vicegerents, therefore, human beings must fulfill the destiny assigned to them by God. Muslims do not view this as absolute determinism, however. As Ansari notes, although God is "the real architect of man's destiny . . . God and man both participate in the making of" it (n.d., p. 165).

[*See also* Caliph.]

BIBLIOGRAPHY

ʿAli, ʿAbdallāh Yūsuf. *The Holy Qur'ān: Translation and Commentary.* Brentwood, Md., 1983.

Ansari, Muhammad Fazl-ur-Rahman. *The Qur'anic Foundations and Structure of Muslim Society.* Karachi, n.d.

Ṭāleqāni, Maḥmud. *Society and Economics in Islam.* Berkeley, 1982.

CHARLES E. BUTTERWORTH and SANA ABED-KOTOB

VILĀYAT-I FAQĪH. *See* Wilāyat al-Faqīh.

VIZIER. The word "vizier" (from the Arabic and Persian *wazīr, vazīr,* and Turkish *vezîr*) is thought to have passed from the Old Persian word for "judge" into Arabic, where it denoted "bearer of burdens" or "minister," then back into pre-Islamic Persian, and finally from that language into general Islamic usage. In the ʿAbbāsid caliphal era (750–1258 CE) the position acquired its characteristic definition as the sovereign's chief minister or deputy. As deputy, the vizier acted for the caliph in military and civil matters when the press of business became too great and as the office of caliph took on a more exalted and remote aspect. Under the first ʿAbbāsids the office was conferred upon successive members of the Barmakid family to recognize formally the special place of the Barmakids (the "Barmecides" of *Arabian Nights* fame) as royal confidants and to acknowledge the caliph's practical need for a mediating deputy. Among the other medieval Islamic dynasties, notably the Seljuks of Iran and Anatolia (eleventh through thirteenth centuries CE) and the Mamlūks of Egypt and Syria (1250–1517) the institution was similarly ambiguous, serving sometimes as a reward for royal intimates and at other times as the capstone position in the developing government hierarchy.

Under the Ottoman Empire (1300–1923), especially after the conquest of Constantinople in 1453, it was the practice to confer the rank and title of vizier upon several officials simultaneously. Normally the most senior of these became the sultan's absolute deputy, the grand vizier *(vezîr-i aʿzam)*. In addition to his traditional functions, the grand vizier came to preside over the Imperial Divan (Dîvân-i Hümâyûn), which was comprised of the ordinary viziers as well as other officers of state. The grand vizier's responsibilities grew with the empire, which, from its capital at Istanbul, controlled sizable territories in western Asia, North Africa and Europe. Although the grand vizier was often the effective ruler, it was only in the mid-seventeenth century that a permanent residence, separate from the sultan's palace, was established to house him and the numerous departments under him. As the new center of government, the "Sublime Porte" (Bâb-i Âlî), as the residence was called, quickly become synonymous with the state itself.

After a series of military setbacks and internal rebellions in the eighteenth and early nineteenth centuries, Sultan Mahmud II (r. 1808–1839), as a part of efforts to restructure the state along Western lines and preserve the empire from further dismantling, sought to transform the grand vizierate into an office approximating that of a prime minister. Mahmud organized the ministries of foreign affairs, interior, justice, finance, admiralty, and trade out of the bureaus that had been subordinate to the grand vizier as the sultan's absolute deputy. The grand vizier, often called the "chief minister" *(baş vekîl)* in the nineteenth century, was to chair the new Supreme Council of Ministers (Meclis-i Hâss-i Vükelâ) and coordinate its policymaking activities. In practice, however, the nineteenth-century sultans' desire to preserve their own power prevailed over the vision of a Western-style cabinet, and each minister reported directly to the sultan. Although the Supreme Council's central part in drafting reform legislation and the civil bureaucracy's expanded role in society assured the grand vizier of power second only to that of the sultan, it was a power that he could exercise only to the degree that the sovereign permitted. The autocracy of Sultan Abdülhamid II (1877–1909) demonstrated both the precariousness of the grand viziers' independence of action and the shallowness of many of the century's political reforms.

[*See also* Caliph; Ottoman Empire.]

BIBLIOGRAPHY

Findley, Carter Vaughn. *Ottoman Civil Officialdom*. Princeton, 1989. Important study of the changing nature of the Ottoman bureaucracy and its personnel in the last Ottoman century.

Shaw, Stanford J., and Ezel Kural Shaw. *History of the Ottoman Empire and Modern Turkey*. 2 vols. Cambridge, 1977.

MADELINE C. ZILFI

W

WAHHĀBĪYAH. The religious movement known as the Wahhābīyah, sometimes anglicized as "Wahhabism," is founded on the teachings of Muḥammad Ibn ʿAbd al-Wahhāb (1703–1791), who wrote on a variety of Islamic subjects such as theology, exegesis, jurisprudence, and the life of the prophet Muḥammad. A set of issues dominated the teachings of Muḥammad Ibn ʿAbd al-Wahhāb and distinguished the Wahhābīyah from other Islamic movements. These include *tawḥīd* (the unity of God), *tawassul* (intercession), *ziyārat al-qubūr* (visitation of graves and erection of tombs), *takfīr* (charge of unbelief), *bidʿah* (innovation), and *ijtihād* and *taqlīd* (original juristic opinions and imitation of tradition).

Tawḥīd is the central theme in the Wahhābī doctrine; Ibn ʿAbd al-Wahhāb considered it the religion of Islam in itself. He maintained that the unity of God reveals itself in three distinct manners. The first is *tawḥīd al-rubūbīyah,* the assertion of the unity of God and his action: God alone is the creator, provider, and disposer of the universe. The second is *tawḥīd al-asmāʾ wa-al-ṣifāt* (unity of names and attributes), which deals with God's characteristics. "God is the Beneficent, the Merciful, . . . the Knowledgeable. He is established on the Throne, and unto Him belongeth whatsoever is in the heavens and whatsoever is in the earth, and whatsoever is between them, and whatsoever is beneath the sod" (Qur'ān, surah 20.6). The third aspect, *tawḥīd al-Ilāhīyah,* prescribes that worship should be to God alone. The assertion that "there is no god but Allāh and Muḥammad is the Prophet of God" means that all forms of worship should be devoted solely to God; Muḥammad is not to be worshiped, but, as an apostle, he should be obeyed and followed.

The Wahhābīs strongly disagreed with their opponents on the question of *tawassul* (intercession). For Muḥammad Ibn ʿAbd al-Wahhāb, *ʿibādah* (worship) refers to all the utterances and actions—inward as well as outward—that God desires and commands. He wrote that to seek protection from trees, stones, and the like is polytheistic, nor are aid, protection, or refuge to be sought from anyone except God. Intercession cannot be granted without God's permission and his satisfaction with the one for whom it is asked, who must be a true monotheist. The common practice of seeking intercession from dead saints is prohibited, as is excessive devotion at their tombs. Invoking the Prophet to intercede for individuals before God is also unacceptable, because the Prophet was neither able to guide those he liked to Islam without the will of God nor was he allowed to ask forgiveness from God for polytheists.

The doctrine of intercession led the Wahhābīs to denounce vehemently the widely followed practice of visitation of tombs and the building of domes near them. Initially Ibn ʿAbd al-Wahhāb had considered visitation, if performed in the true spirit of Islam, a pious and praiseworthy act. However, Wahhābīs believe that people have transformed the prayers for the dead into prayers *to* the dead; gravesites became places of assembly for worshipers. The excessive veneration of the deceased who enjoyed a holy reputation was a first step that had led people to idol-worship in the past. To avoid polytheism, the Wahhābīs consider it an obligation to destroy all such existing tombs. They insist that burial sites should be level with the ground and that inscriptions, decoration, or illumination of graves should be avoided. The Wahhābīs also believe that mere affiliation with Islam is not sufficient in itself to prevent a Muslim from becoming a polytheist. The person who utters the Shahādah and still practices polytheism (as defined by the Wahhābīs) should be denounced as an infidel and killed.

Innovation *(bidʿah)* is another Wahhābī concern. It is defined as any doctrine or action not based on the Qur'ān, the traditions, or the authority of the Prophet's companions. Ibn ʿAbd al-Wahhāb condemned all forms of innovation and rejected the views of those who maintained that an innovation could be good or praiseworthy. He invoked the authority of the Qur'ān and the traditions of Muḥammad to support his views. The Wahhābīs rejected as *bidᶜah* such acts as celebrating the Prophet's birthday, seeking intercession from saints, reciting the Fatīḥah on behalf of the founders of Ṣūfī orders after the five daily prayers, and repeating the five daily prayers after the final Friday prayer in the month of Ramaḍān.

The conflict of *ijtihād* and *taqlīd* is the sixth principal concern. According to Ibn ᶜAbd al-Wahhāb and his followers, God commanded people to obey him alone and to follow the teachings of the Prophet. This complete adherence to the Qur'ān and the traditions that Wahhābīs demanded of Muslims also entailed a rejection of all interpretations offered by the four schools of Islamic jurisprudence—including the Wahhābīs' own Ḥanbalī school where it is not in accordance with the two prime sources.

The Wahhābīs developed strict procedures to direct the discussion of doctrinal issues. To judge religious questions, they first search the texts of the Qur'ān and the *ḥadīth*s and define their views accordingly. If reference is not found in these texts, they look for the consensus of the "Virtuous Ancestors," particularly the companions and their successors, and the *ijmāᶜ* (consensus) of scholars; *ijmāᶜ*, however, is restricted to those who follow the Qur'ān and the traditions.

The Wahhābīs reject the idea that the doors of *ijtihād* are closed. Although they follow the Ḥanbalī school, they do not accept its precepts as final. If any Ḥanbalī interpretation can be proven wrong, then it must be abandoned. In support of their argument, the Wahhābīs quote Qur'ānic verses that imply that the Qur'an and the traditions constitute the only bases of Islamic law.

The Wahhābīyah became the dominant religious and political force in the Arabian Peninsula around 1746, when the Āl Saᶜūd combined their political force with Wahhābī teachings. One principality after another fell under the attacks of the Saudi forces. In 1773 the Principality of Riyadh fell and its properties were incorporated by the treasury of al-Dirᶜīyah, the seat of the Āl Saᶜūd and the Wahhābīs. With the fall of Riyadh a new order was established in the peninsula, ushering the period of the first Saudi state and establishing the Wahhābīyah as the strongest religio-political force in the Arabian Peninsula during the nineteenth and early twentieth centuries. Today many of the Wahhābī principles guide the legal and social life of the Kingdom of Saudi Arabia.

[*See also* Bidᶜah; Ijtihād; Saudi Arabia; Takfīr; Tawḥīd; Ziyārah; *and the biography of* Ibn ᶜAbd al-Wahhāb.]

BIBLIOGRAPHY

Wahhābīyah

Al-Yassini, Ayman. *Religion and State in the Kingdom of Saudi Arabia.* Boulder, 1985.

Armstrong, H. C. *Lord of Arabia, Ibn Saud.* London, 1934.

Asad, Muhammad. *The Road to Mecca.* New York, 1954.

Benoist-Méchin, Jacques. *Arabian Destiny.* Fair Lawn, N.J., 1958.

De Gaury, Gerald. *Rulers of Mecca.* London, 1951.

Muḥammad Ibn ᶜAbd al-Wahhāb

Lebkicher, Roy, et al. *The Arabia of Ibn Saud.* New York, 1952.

Philby, H. St. John. *Arabian Highlands.* Ithaca, N.Y., 1952.

Schacht, Joseph, ed. *The Legacy of Islam.* 2d ed. Oxford, 1974.

Smith, Wilfred Cantwell. *Islam in Modern History.* Princeton, 1957.

AYMAN AL-YASSINI

WAKĀLAH AL-ᶜĀMMAH, AL-. The concept in Ithnā ᶜAsharī Shīᶜī Islam that justifies the assumption by the *ᶜulamā'* of the leadership role and prerogatives of the Hidden Twelfth Imam as his collective deputy is called *al-wakālah al-ᶜāmmah* ("general vicegerency or agency"). In Ithnā ᶜĀsharī Shīᶜī Islam, all political and spiritual authority rests with the imam. The legitimacy of any political or judicial position must therefore derive from the imam, and all revenues from the religious taxes go to him. When the Twelfth Imam went into occultation *(ghaybah)* and the period of the four successive deputies of the Hidden Imam (*al-wikālah al-khāṣṣah*) ended in 941 CE., a vacuum was left at the head of Shiism. At first, the Shīᶜī *ᶜulamā'* (community of religious scholars) considered that all of the functions of the imam had lapsed. This, however, left the Ithnā ᶜAsharī community with no leadership, organization, or financial structure. Over the course of the next four centuries, the *ᶜulamā'* gradually evolved a theoretical justification for their assumption of the religious functions of the imam. This justification was based on a small number of *ḥadīth* from the imams indicating that faithful Shīᶜīs should not take their disputes to a Sunnī court but rather to a competent Shīᶜī jurist who was thus set in the position of judge. The Shīᶜī *ᶜulamā'* argued that this legitimized their assumption of a judicial role, and this was later extended to justify their collection of the religious taxes of *khums* and *zakāt*.

The concept of the general vicegerency of the *ᶜulamā'* put the Shīᶜī *ᶜulamā'* in a strong independent position in regard to the secular authorities; it gave them a legitimacy and a source of income that was independent of any secular appointment or state support. By the time of the Qājār dynasty in nineteenth-century Iran, the *ᶜulamā'* had been able to build this into a separate basis of power from which they could challenge the secular authorities whenever they felt their interests were threatened. Having established their own legitimacy on the basis of this concept, they were then able to challenge the legitimacy of the secular authorities (since political authority also derives from the imam). In nineteenth-century Iran, the Bāb posed a major threat to the *ᶜulamā'*, and his movement was severely persecuted by them, precisely because his claim to be the Hidden Twelfth Imam threatened an end to their general vicegerency. [*See the biography of the Bāb.*]

More recently, the concept of *al-wakālah al-ᶜammah* formed the basis of Ayatollah Ruhollah Khomeini's derivation of the concept of *wilāyat al-faqīh*. Indeed, Khomeini's ideas can be considered a logical extension of *al-wakālah al-ᶜāmmah*, although they were nevertheless a definite departure from the ethos of the Shīᶜī religious leadership, which had previously disdained political involvement.

In modern political discourse (i.e., since the Iranian Revolution of 1979), the two concepts of al-*wakālah al-ᶜāmmah* and *wilāyat al-faqīh* have become merged under the name of the latter, and recent works, such as Ayatollah Ḥusayn ᶜAlī Muntaẓirī's *Mabānī-yi fiqhī-i ḥukūmat-i Islāmī* (Tehran, AH 1367/1988 CE), make no distinction between the two. The two merged concepts have become enshrined in the Constitution of the Islamic Republic of Iran in the Preamble and in Articles 4 and 5.

[*See also* Ghaybah; Imam; Wikālah al-Khāṣṣah, al-; Wilāyat al-Faqīh.]

BIBLIOGRAPHY

Calder, Norman. "The Structure of Authority in Imāmī Shīᶜī Jurisprudence." Ph.D. diss., School of Oriental and African Studies, 1980. Contains the best description of the gradual historical evolution of the concept of *al-wakālah al-ᶜāmmah*.

Enayat, Hamid. "Khumayni's Concept of the 'Guardianship of the Jurisconsult.' " In *Islam in the Political Process*, edited by J. P. Piscatori, pp. 160–180. Cambridge, 1983. Most modern works discuss *al-wakālah al-ᶜāmmah* in the context of the *wilāyat al-faqīh*.

Fischer, Michael. *Iran: From Religious Dispute to Revolution*. Cambridge, Mass., 1980. See pages 151–154. (See comment under Enayat, above.)

Khomeini, Ruhollah. *Writings and Declarations of Imam Khomeini*. Translated by Hamid Algar. Berkeley, 1981. Contains a translation of Khomeini's *Wilāyat-i faqīh dar khuṣūṣ-i ḥukūmat-i islāmī*, which is the source for Khomeini's derivation of *wilāyat al-faqīh* from *al-wakālah al-ᶜāmmah*.

Momen, Moojan. *Introduction to Shīᶜī Islam: The History and Doctrines of Twelver Shīᶜism*. New Haven, 1984. See pages 189–199.

Mottahedeh, Roy. *The Mantle of the Prophet*. London, 1986. See pages 243–247. (See comment under Enayat, above.)

Sachedina, Abdulaziz A. *The Just Ruler (al-Sulṭān al-ᶜĀdil) in Shīᶜite Islam: The Comprehensive Authority of the Jurist in Imamite Jurisprudence*. New York, 1988. The best discussion of *al-wakālah al-ᶜāmmah*.

MOOJAN MOMEN

WAKĀLAH AL-KHĀṢṢAH, AL-. In Ithnā ᶜAsharī Shiism, the designation of four successive persons to act as deputies of the Hidden Twelfth Imam is termed *al-wakālah al-khāṣṣah* ("special vicegerency or agency"). Although this authority lapsed in 941 CE, it contains millennialist potential, and certain overtones of it play a part even in orthodox modern Shiism. When the Twelfth Imam of the Ithnā ᶜAsharī Shīᶜīs went into occultation (*ghaybah*) in 873–874 CE, there followed a period called the lesser occultation in which four successive persons claimed to be the deputies of the Hidden Imam. These four were each called *bāb* ("gate") or *na'ib* ("deputy") and were said to hold *al-wakālah al-khāṣṣah*. Then in 941 the last *bāb* declared that there would be no more specific representatives until the Hidden Imam returned, and thus Shīᶜīs entered the greater occultation. The Shīᶜī *ᶜulamā'* (community of religious scholars) over the next few centuries, however, developed the concept of a general vicegerency delegated to them by the imams, known as *al-wakālah al-ᶜāmmah*.

Since 941, no one within orthodox Ithnā ᶜAsharī Shiism has been able overtly to claim the special vicegerency, but there have been a number of movements and trends that have echoes of this concept. The nineteenth-century Shaykhī movement held the concept of a spiritual hierarchy at the head of which was al-Shīᶜī al-Kāmil ("the perfect Shīᶜī"), who must exist in every age. Although the Shaykhī leaders did not specifically link this Perfect Shīᶜī to the concept of *al-wakālah al-khāṣṣah* or claim to be this figure, at least some of their followers appear to have made both of these connections; thus we find the first two Shaykhī leaders referred to as *bābs*.

The only figure to make an overt claim to be the specific vicegerent of the Hidden Imam was Sayyid ᶜAlī Muḥammad the Bāb, the founder of Bābism in nineteenth-century Iran. In the opening chapter of his first prophetic book, the *Qayyūm al-asmā'*, there is a sentence that amounts to a claim to *al-wakālah al-khāṣṣah*. Both Sunnī and Shīʿī *ʿulamā'* saw, however, that the text of even this first book presaged much higher claims, which were to become explicit some four years later when the Bāb claimed to be the Hidden Imam (see Momen, 1982, pp. 141–142). [*See also* Bābism *and the biography of the Bāb*.]

Shortly after the start of the Shaykhī movement, a movement began within orthodox Ithnā ʿAsharī Shiism toward a focal leader, the concept of the sole *marjaʿ al-taqlīd*. This reached a peak with Ayatollah Ruhollah Khomeini, who, during the height of the 1979 Iranian Revolution, was referred to as Nā'ib al-Imām ("deputy of the Imam") and was undoubtedly seen in the popular imagination as the representative of the Hidden Imam.

The Constitution of the Islamic Republic of Iran confines what had been the collective responsibility of the *ʿulamā'* in the general vicegerency to one person, *al-faqīh* ("the jurist"), that is, Khomeini (although it does allow for a council of jurists in place of the single jurist). Thus by concentrating the function of the general vicegerency in one man, Khomeini became de facto if not de jure the specific vicegerent of the Hidden Imam.

[*See also* Ghaybah; Imam; Marjaʿ al-Taqlīd; Shaykīyah; Wakālah al-ʿĀmmah, al-.]

BIBLIOGRAPHY

Amanat, Abbas. *Resurrection and Renewal: The Making of the Bābī Movement in Iran, 1844–1850*. Ithaca, 1989. See pages 149–151, 171–173, and 199–200 for a discussion of the *bāb*'s claims.

Hussain, Jassim. *The Occultation of the Twelfth Imam*. London, 1982. Gives the history of the original four *bābs*.

Lambton, Ann K. S. "A Reconsideration of the Position of *Marjaʿ at-taqlīd* and the Religious Institution." *Studia Islamica* 5 (1964): 115–135. A discussion of the *Baḥṣīdar bārah-'i marjaʿīyat va rūḥānīyat* (Tehran, 1963), a work of discussions among the *ʿulamā'* concerning the concentration of leadership in one person, the sole *marjaʿ al-taqlīd*.

Momen, Moojan. "The Trial of Mullā ʿAlī Basṭāmī: A Combined Sunnī-Shīʿī *fatwā* against the Bāb." *Iran* 20 (1982): 113–143. Discusses the *bāb*'s claims.

Momen, Moojan. *Introduction to Shīʿī Islam: The History and Doctrines of Twelver Shīʿism*. New Haven, 1984. See pages 161–165, 289.

MOOJAN MOMEN

WALĀYAH. Sometimes translated "sainthood," *walāyah* is the term denoting the characteristics required for succession in Shiism. Shīʿīs do not believe that the prophet Muḥammad died without appointing a successor—as was his custom even for a short absence. That successor is said to have been ʿAlī ibn Abī Ṭalib, a cousin of the Prophet and the earliest male convert to Islam.

While returning from his farewell pilgrimage, the Prophet gave a speech at the oasis of Ghadīr Khumm, saying, "For whomever I am the master *(mawlā)* and authority whom he obeys, ʿAlī will be his master." The Feast of Ghadīr celebrates the formal transfer of political power from the Prophet to ʿAlī. The Qur'ānic passage, "Your *walī* can only be Allāh, and His messenger and those who believe, who establish worship while paying the poor due" (5.58), is said to be further evidence of the Prophet's preference for ʿAlī as the *walī* or guardian of believers. The term *walāyah* originates with ʿAlī, and the line of succession continues through those appointed based on their esoteric knowledge. Such successors must also trace their ancestry to the Prophet's household in order to fulfill Muḥammad's deathbed statement, "I leave two great and precious things among you: the Book of Allāh and my household." The descendants of the Prophet's daughter Fāṭimah, the wife of ʿAlī, thus become the rightful guardians of the pure tradition of Islam.

Their guardianship requires not only political leadership and active involvement in upholding religious law, but also special knowledge of the esoteric dimension of Qur'ānic revelation. Such a rightful imam leads in both external action and inward or esoteric guidance. In both Sunnī and Shīʿī Islam the imam is the one who leads the prayer. In Shiism the imam is also seen as the rightful inheritor of esoteric leadership. Shīʿīs believe that the imperfection of men is reflected in their political system, and the perfect government is that of the imam. The imam's duty is to fulfill the function of *walāyah*, and thus the *walī* and the imam are one and the same.

When the cycle of prophecy *(dā'irat al-nubūwah)* ended with seal of the prophets, Muḥammad, the cycle of initiation *(dā'irat al-walāyah)* began. This is a chain of authority in esoteric interpretation extending directly from the Prophet, which will continue until the day of judgment. The prophet brings the divine laws, then leaves; but the imam is always present, even if hidden or unknown. Like the prophet, the imam also has *ʿiṣmah* (inerrancy in religious and spiritual matters) because he carries *al-nūr al-Muḥammadī* (the Muḥammadan light). He is also an intermediary between man and God.

God chooses the person who bears the duty of interpreting the inner meaning of revelation to men and of preserving the link between humankind and divine revelation. He is the *walī* of Allāh, the friend of God. He is given divine protection against error, like the prophets, in order to preserve God's religion intact.

[*See also* Guardianship; Imam; Wilāyah; *and the biography of ʿAlī ibn Abī Ṭalib.*]

BIBLIOGRAPHY

Nasr, Seyyed Hossein. *Ideals and Realities of Islam.* Boston, 1975. Provides a brief overview of key concepts in Islamic thought, including the distinctive Shīʿī understanding of some concepts.

Ṭabāṭabāʾī, Muḥammad Ḥusayn. *Shīʿite Islam.* 2d ed. Translated and edited by Seyyed Hossein Nasr. Albany, N.Y., 1977. Comprehensive overview of the history, doctrine, and ideology of Shiism and Shīʿī perspectives on issues of shared concern between Shīʿī and Sunnī Muslims.

ĀMINA WADŪD-MUḤSIN

WALĪ. *See* Sufism, *article on* Ṣūfī Shrine Culture.

WALĪ ALLĀH, SHĀH (1703–1762), the most prominent Muslim intellectual of eighteenth-century India and a prolific writer on a wide range of Islamic topics in Arabic and Persian. Shāh Walī Allāh's formal name was Quṭb al-Dīn Aḥmad Abū al-Fayyāḍ. Biographical material and anecdotes concerning his life and family may be found in his brief Persian autobiography, *Al-juzʾ al-laṭīf fī tarjamat al-ʿabd al-ḍaʿīf* and in his Persian work *Anfas al-ʿārifīn.* Some additional material on his life appears in the hagiographic account *Al-qawl al-jalī,* written by his close disciple Muḥammad ʿĀshiq (1773).

Shāh Walī Allāh's father and spiritual guide, Shāh ʿAbd al-Raḥīm (d. 1719), was a well-known scholar in charge of his own *madrasah* in Delhi and also a practicing mystic. Shāh ʿAbd al-Raḥīm devoted considerable attention to the education of his precocious son: besides religious subjects, his studies included astronomy, mathematics, Arabic and Persian language and grammar, and medical science (*ṭibb*), from which many concepts and theories influence his works.

He was married at fourteen to the daughter of his maternal uncle. When he was fifteen years old, his father accepted him as a disciple in the Naqshbandīyah order, and he began to perform its practices. He also completed his course in Islamic studies in that year and was permitted by his father to teach others. For twelve years after his father's death Shāh Walī Allāh taught and studied the religious sciences and continued in meditative discipline. Then, in 1731, he left India to perform the pilgrimage to Mecca and Medina, where he stayed for some fourteen months.

This stay in the Hejaz was an important formative influence on his thought and subsequent life. There he studied *ḥadīth, fiqh,* and Sufism with various eminent teachers, the most important influence being Shaykh Abū Ṭāhir al-Kurdī al-Madanī (d. 1733). These teachers in Mecca exposed Shāh Walī Allāh to the trend of increased cosmopolitanism in *ḥadīth* scholarship that began to emerge there in the eighteen century from a blending of the North African, Hejazi, and Indian traditions of study and evaluation (Voll, 1980). While in the holy cities Shāh Walī Allāh developed a particular respect for Mālik's work, the *Muwaṭṭaʾ,* on which he later wrote two commentaries, *Musawwā* (Arabic) and *Muṣaffā* (Persian).

Shāh Walī Allāh's writing career began in earnest on his return from pilgrimage. His most important and influential work, *Ḥujjat Allāh al-bālighah* (in Arabic), in which he aimed to restore the Islamic sciences through *ḥadīth* studies, was composed sometime during the decade after his return. This is the most readily available and best-known of his works; even today it is considered important by the present generation of Islamic reformers, whether Islamists or modernists, and it is studied in the Arab Middle East and Southeast Asia as well as in Muslim South Asia.

Shāh Walī Allāh's activities after his return to India included teaching in his *madrasah,* acting as a guide in Sufism, and writing on a wide range of Islamic subjects. In 1744, having been widowed, he made a second marriage from which four sons and one daughter were born; he had a son and a daughter from his first marriage.

His works are often characterized by a historical, systematic approach coupled with an attempt to explain and mediate divisive tendencies. Among his other important writings are: *Al-budūr al-bāzighah,* an Arabic work outlining his theory of social and religious development in human history, closely parallel to some sections of *Ḥujjat Allāh al-bālighah; Fatḥ al-Raḥmān fī tarjamat al-Qurʾān* (completed in 1738), a pioneering annotated Persian translation of the Qurʾān; *Al-fawz al-kabīr fī uṣūl al-tafsīr* (Persian), a study of the principles of Qurʾānic interpretation (*tafsīr*); and *Al-tafhīmāt al-*

ilāhīyah, a two-volume collection of shorter mystical reflections in Arabic and Persian. In addition, he wrote two works in Persian supporting the Sunnī position on the issue of succession to the caliphate, *Qurrat al-ʿaynayn fī tafḍīl al-shaykhayn* and *Izālat al-khafa' ʿan khilāfat al-khulafā'*.

After Shāh Walī Allāh's death in 1762, his teachings were carried on by his descendants, in particular his sons, Shāh ʿAbd al-ʿAzīz (do. 1824) and Shāh Rafīʿ al-Dīn (d. 1818), and his grandson Shāh Ismāʿīl Shahīd (d. 1831). The influence of this notable family was termed the "Walī Allāhī movement" by ʿUbayd Allāh Sindhī (d. 1944), a South Asian activist who wrote extensively in Urdu interpreting Shāh Walī Allāh's thought and emphasizing its reformist, progressive tendencies. With the creation of Pakistan, Shāh Walī Allāh began to be characterized by certain historians and by the popular imagination as an early nationalist hero and political activist, in much the same way as the role of the seventeenth-century mystic Shaykh Aḥmad Sirhindī had been reenvisioned. [*See the biography* of *Sirhindī.*]

Today all major religious movements in Muslim South Asia claim Shāh Walī Allāh as an intellectual progenitor. One such group, the Deobandīs, trace their inspiration through his son Shāh ʿAbd al-ʿAzīz, a noted scholar and teacher with a wide circle of pupils, some of whom were directly associated with the establishment of the Deoband *madrasah.* This institution came to symbolize a particular mode of thought among South Asian Muslims that can be characterized as an acceptance of the mystical elements of the Islamic intellectual and practical tradition combined with a rejection of those practices more associated with local customs and the less-educated masses (Metcalf, 1984). [*See* Deobandīs *and the biography of ʿAbd al-ʿAzīz.*]

Movements characterized by a more anti-Ṣūfī, puritan outlook, such as the Ahl-i Ḥadīth and even the followers of Mawlānā Mawdūdī, find in Shāh Walī Allāh's return to the fundamentals of *sharīʿah* and political rejection of alien influences a precursor of their own reformist beliefs. Walī Allāh's grandson Shāh Ismāʿīl Shahīd, who advocated the elimination of local practices and a *jihād* against non-Muslim forces, would seem to be the closest intellectual link to such movements, if one overlooks the fact that he also composed works of theosophical mysticism in the style of Ibn al-ʿArābī. Yet another group of his successors, best exemplified by his closest disciple and cousin Muḥammad ʿĀshiq (1773), seems to have practically pursued his mystical inclinations, for there is some indication that Walī Allāh attempted to establish his own eclectic Ṣūfī order and a theory and repertoire of mystical practices (see *Al-tafhīmāt al-ilāhīyah* 2, 5–98). Finally, South Asian Islamic modernists such as Muhammad Iqbal (d. 1938) and Fazlur Rahman (d. 1988) have seen in Shāh Walī Allāh a thinker who responded to the crisis of his time by accommodating diverse legal and ideological opinions, calling for a renewed *ijtihād* and searching for the spirit behind the tradition. [*See the biographies of Iqbal and Rahman.*]

BIBLIOGRAPHY

General Works

Baljon, J. M. S. *Religion and Thought of Shāh Walī Allāh Dihlawī, 1703–1762.* Leiden, 1986. The most complete and readable study of major themes of Shāh Walī Allāh's thought; with an annotated list of his works (pp. 8–14).

Metcalf, Barbara D. *Islamic Revival in British India: Deoband, 1800–1900.* Berkeley, 1984.

Rahman, Fazlur. "Revival and Reform in Islam." In *The Cambridge History of Islam,* edited by P. M. Holt et al., vol. 2, pp. 632–656. Cambridge, 1978.

Rizvi, S. A. A. *Shāh Walī-Allāh and His Times.* Canberra, 1980. Detailed study of the historical environment as well as Walī Allāh's works. Notable for its extensive use of manuscript sources.

Voll, John Obert. "Hadith Scholars and Tarīqahs: An ʿUlema' Group." *Journal of Asian and African Studies* 15 (July–October 1980): 264–273. Interprets his activities as part of a wider reformist Ṣūfī network.

Translations

Published English translations of Shāh Walī Allāh's works up to this point have generally lacked a scholarly critical apparatus. This lack is particularly crucial since he uses a highly technical, often idiosyncratic, vocabulary.

A Mystical Interpretation of Prophetic Tales by an Indian Muslim: Shāh Walī Allāh's Ta'wīl al-Aḥādīth. Translated by J. M. S. Baljon. Leiden, 1973. Abridged and annotated translation.

Al-Khair al-Kathīr. Translated by G. N. Jalbani. Hyderabad, 1974.

The Sacred Knowledge of the Higher Functions of the Mind (Alṭāf al-quds fī maʿrifat laṭā'if al-nafs). Translated by G. N. Jalbani and D. Pendelberry. London, 1984.

The Principles of Qur'ān Commentary (Al-fauz al-kabīr fī uṣūl al-taksīr). Translated by G. N. Jalbani. Islamabad, 1985.

Sufism and the Islamic Tradition: The Lamahat and Sataʿat of Shah Waliullah. Translated by G. N. Jalbani. London, 1986.

Full Moon Rising on the Horizon (Al-budūr al-bāzighah). Translated by J. M. S. Baljon. Lahore, 1988. Unannotated but readable translation.

Marcia K. Hermansen

WAQF. Literally "confinement" or "prohibition," the Arabic word *waqf* (pl., *awqāf*) is used in Islam to mean "the holding and preservation of a certain property for the confined benefit of a certain philanthropy with the intention of prohibiting any use or disposition of the property outside that specific purpose." The definition indicates the perpetual nature of *waqf;* in other words, the term applies to nonperishable property whose benefit can be extracted without consuming the property itself. Therefore, *waqf* widely relates to land and buildings, although there is also *waqf* of books, agricultural machinery, cattle, shares and stocks, and cash money. In North and West Africa, *waqf* is called *habs,* which literally means "confinement."

***Waqf* in History.** The idea of *waqf* is as old as the human race. Muslim jurists argue that the first *waqf* is the sacred building of the Kaʿbah in Mecca, which the Qur'ān (3.96) mentions as being the first house of worship set aside for the people. Virtually all societies have set aside certain lots of land and buildings as places of worship. For ages, temples, churches, and other forms of construction have been built and devoted to religious practices. Moreover, the pharaohs of Egypt assigned land for the benefit of monks, and ancient Greeks and Romans dedicated properties exclusively for libraries and education. Today, the idea of *awqāf* is known and practiced all over the world. It exists in North America under the name of foundations, especially religious and charitable foundations. There are tens of thousands of foundations in the United States alone.

***Waqf* in Islamic History.** In the history of Islam, the first religious *waqf* was the mosque of Qubā' in Medina. This mosque was built on the arrival of the prophet Muḥammad in 622. It exists today on the same site with a new and enlarged structure. Six months after it was raised, the Qubā' mosque was followed by the mosque of the Prophet in the center of Medina. Mosques, as well as real estate that exclusively provides revenues for mosque maintenance and service expenses, are in the category of religious *waqf.*

Philanthropic *waqf* is the second kind of *waqf.* It aims at supporting the poor segments of society and the public interest at large by funding such institutions and activities as libraries, scientific research, education, health services, and care of animals and the environment. It can also be used for loans to small businesses and the construction and maintenance of parks, roads, bridges, and dams. Philanthropic *waqf* also began in the time of the prophet Muḥammad. A man called Mukhayriq specified in his will that his seven orchards in Medina be given after his death to Muḥammad. In 626, Mukhayriq died and the Prophet acquired the orchards and made them a charitable *waqf* for the benefit of the poor and needy. This practice was followed by the companion of the Prophet and his second successor, ʿUmar. When he asked the Prophet what to do with a palm orchard that he had acquired in the northern Arabian city of Khaibar, the Prophet said, "If you like, you may hold the property as *waqf* and give its fruits as charity." By the time of the Prophet's death in 632, many other charitable *awqāf* had been made.

A third kind of *waqf* was initiated shortly after the death of the Prophet during the caliphate of ʿUmar (635–645). When ʿUmar decided to make a written document of his *waqf* in Khaibar, he invited some of the companions of the Prophet to witness the document. Jaber, another companion, says that when the document was released, many real estate owners made *awqāf.* Some of them added a condition to the *waqf* to ensure that its fruits and revenues first be given to their own children and their descendants and only the surplus, if any, should be given to the poor. This kind of *waqf* is called posterity or family *waqf.* Unlike foundations in America, which are restricted to religious or philanthropic purposes, *waqf* in Islamic society can also be for one's own family and descendants.

Main Characteristics of *Waqf*. From a legal point of view, the ownership of *waqf* property lies outside the person who created the *waqf.* Some Muslim jurists argue that the right of ownership of *waqf* belongs to God. Others believe that it belongs to the beneficiaries, although their ownership is not complete in the sense that they are not permitted to dispose of the property or use it in a way different from what was decreed by the founder of *waqf.* In this regard, *waqf* differs from a foundation, since the management of a foundation is usually able to sell its property. This implies that perpetuity is stronger in *waqf* than in foundations.

Perpetuity means that once a property, often real estate, is assigned as *waqf* it remains *waqf* forever. Elimination of the *waqf* character of a property involves a difficult and lengthy procedure. A *waqf* property can only be exchanged for another property of equivalent value. This exchange requires the approval of the local court. Upon completion of such an exchange, the new property immediately becomes *waqf* for the same purpose and beneficiaries as the former one. Hence, in theory, perpetuity implies that *waqf* properties should not decrease. Because of this characteristic, many Muslim jurists maintain that *waqf* should apply to real estate only. There are jurists who accept the idea of durability or long life of a property as an approximation of perpetuity. Accordingly, books, weapons, machinery, cattle, and money can be made *waqf*.

To preserve *waqf* properties, both founders and courts took extra precautions in documenting and preserving *waqf* deeds. They often insisted on recording these deeds in courts and having them witnessed by renowned people. Courts in many cities and towns kept detailed records of *waqf* properties as early as the fifteenth and sixteenth centuries. Many of these records are still preserved and historians study them in Istanbul, Cairo, Fez, Damascus, Jerusalem, Isfahan, and other ancient cities.

Since *waqf* is a voluntary act of benevolence, conditions specified by the founder must be fulfilled to their letter as long as they do not contradict or violate any *sharīʿah* (Islamic law) rulings. This implies that revenues of *waqf* should exclusively be used for the purpose for which the *waqf* was established and that this purpose cannot be changed by management or supervisory courts as long as it is compatible with *sharīʿah* on the one hand and is still achievable on the other. If a *waqf* purpose becomes impossible to achieve, the revenue should be spent on the closest possible purpose; otherwise, it goes to the poor and needy. The condition of permanence covers all the founder's stipulations whether they relate to purpose, distribution of revenues, management, supervisory authority, or some other element.

Waqf creation requires certain conditions, of which the most important are listed below.

1. The property must be real estate or a durable thing. Muslim societies have *waqf* land, buildings, herds of camels, cows, and sheep, books, jewelry, swords and other weapons, and agricultural tools.

2. The property should be given on a permanent basis. Some jurists approve temporary *awqāf* only in the case of family *awqāf*.

3. The *waqf* founder should be legally fit and able to take such an action. A child, an insane person, or a person who does not own the property cannot create a *waqf*.

4. The purpose of the *waqf* must, in the ultimate analysis, be an act of charity from the viewpoints both of *sharīʿah* and the founder. Hence, *waqf* for the rich alone is not permissible, because it is not charity.

5. Finally, beneficiaries must be alive and legitimate. *Waqf* for the dead is not permissible.

Management of *Waqf*. In principle, the founder determines the type of management of his or her *waqf*. The *waqf* manager is usually called *mutawallī* or *nāẓir*. The manager's responsibility is to administer the *waqf* property in the best interest of the beneficiaries. The first duty of the *mutawallī* is to preserve the property, then to maximize the revenues of the beneficiaries. The *waqf* document usually mentions how the *mutawallī* is compensated for this effort, but if the document does not mention compensation, the *mutawallī* either volunteers the work or seeks assignment of a compensation from the court.

The judicial system, that is, the court, is the authority of reference with regard to all matters and disputes related to *waqf*. In the early part of the eighth century, a judge in Egypt established a special register and office to record and supervise *awqāf* in his area. This culminated in the establishment of an *awqāf* office for registration and control which was linked to the chief justice, who used to be called the "judge of judges."

With the decline of Islamic civilization, corruption reached the *waqf* properties. This called for more governmental interference. Hence, in the early nineteenth century, a special ministry was established for *awqāf* in the Ottoman Empire and laws of *awqāf* were enacted. The most important of these was the Law of Awqāf of 29 November 1863. This law regulated the management and supervision of *awqāf*. It remained in application in several countries (Turkey, Syria, Iraq, Lebanon, Palestine, and Saudi Arabia) for many years after the dismemberment of the Ottoman Empire in 1918. Presently, most Muslim countries have either ministries or departments of *awqāf* and religious affairs combined. These ministries control the *waqf* properties and use their revenues for financing the construction and maintenance of mosques.

Muslim communities in non-Muslim countries have organized their *awqāf* in accordance with Islamic *sharīʿah* within the limits of prevailing laws and regulations. For instance, in India, where there is a relatively large Muslim minority, a *waqf* act was adopted at the federal level in 1954 and the Indian minister of law was made the supervisory authority on *waqf*. Each state in India has a *waqf* board which consists of eleven Muslim members.

In the United States and Canada, Muslim communities administer their *waqf* properties in accordance with the acts and regulations pertaining to foundations. The usual practice is that each Muslim community establishes a nonprofit organization that in turn owns the *waqf* property, which consists in most cases of the local mosque or Islamic center. In 1975, the North American Islamic Trust (NAIT) was registered in the state of Indiana. One of the main objectives of this nonprofit Islamic organization is to own and promote the *waqf* of Muslims in North America. A few years later, a sister organization under the same name was registered in the province of Ontario in Canada. NAIT and its Canadian counterpart own and maintain many mosques, Islamic centers, and Islamic schools in North America.

Sociopolitical Role of *Waqf*. The permanent nature of *waqf* resulted in the accumulation of *waqf* properties all over the Muslim lands, and the variety of its objectives provides support for widespread religious and philanthropic activities. The size of *waqf* and its objectives play an important role in the sociopolitical life of Muslim societies and communities.

Information extracted from the registers of *awqāf* in Istanbul, Jerusalem, Cairo, and other cities indicates that *waqf* lands cover a considerable proportion of total cultivated area. For instance, in the years 1812 and 1813, a survey of land in Egypt showed that *waqf* represents 600,000 *feddan* (570,000 acres) out of a total of 2.5 million feddan (2.375 million acres; Ramaḍan, 1983, p. 128); in 1841, in Algiers, Algeria, the number of lots of *awqāf* land whose revenues were assigned for the grand mosque was 543 (Abū al-Ajfān, 1985, p. 326); in Turkey, about one-third of its land was *awqāf* at the turn of the twentieth century (Armagan, 1989, p. 339); and finally, in Palestine the number of *waqf* deeds recorded up to middle of the sixteenth century is 233 containing 890 properties, in comparison with 92 deeds of private ownership containing 108 properties (IRCICA, 1982, p. L).

Waqf revenues are most frequently spent on mosques. This includes salaries of the imam (prayer leader who delivers the Friday religious sermon), teachers of Islamic studies, and preachers. With the help of this independent source of financing, religious leaders and teachers have often been able to take social and political positions independent of those of the ruling class. For example, when French troops occupied Algeria in 1831, the colonial authority took control of the *waqf* property in order to suppress religious leaders who fought against them (Abū al-Ajfān, 1985, p. 325).

Although religious education is usually covered by *awqāf* on mosques, education in general has been the second largest recipient of *waqf* revenues. Since the beginning of Islam in the early seventh century, education has been financed by *waqf* and voluntary contributions. Even government financing of education used to take the form of constructing a school and assigning certain property as *waqf* for its running expenses. *Awqāf* of the Ayyūbid (1171–1249) and the Mamlūk (1250–1517) dynasties in Palestine and Egypt are good examples. According to historical sources, Jerusalem had sixty-four schools at the beginning of the twentieth century, all of them are *awqāf*. They are also supported by *waqf* properties in Palestine, Turkey, and Syria. Of these schools, forty were made *awqāf* by Ayyūbid and Mamlūk rulers and governors (al-ʿAsalī, 1983, pp. 95–111). The University of al-Azhar is another example. It was founded in Cairo in 972 and was financed by its *waqf* revenues until the government of Muḥammad ʿAlī in Egypt took control over the *awqāf* in 1812 (Ramaḍan, 1983, p. 135).

Waqf financing of education usually covers libraries, books, salaries of teachers and other staff, and stipends to students. Financing was not restricted to religious studies, especially during the rise of Islam. In addition to providing freedom of education, this financing approach helped create a learned class not derived from the rich and ruling classes. At times, the majority of Muslim scholars were from poor and slave segments of the society, and very often they strongly opposed the policies of the rulers (al-Sayyid, 1989, pp. 237–258).

The third big beneficiary of *waqf* is the poor, the needy, orphans, persons in prison, and so on. Other recipients of *waqf* revenues include health services, which cover construction of hospitals and funding for physicians, apprentices, and patients. One of the examples of a health *waqf* is the Shīshlī Children's Hospital in Istanbul, founded in 1898 (al-Sayyid, 1989, p. 287).

There is also *waqf* for animals. An example is the *waqf* for cats and the *waqf* for unwanted riding animals, both in Damascus (al-Sibāʿī, 1969). There are *awqāf* for helping people go to Mecca for pilgrimage and for helping girls get married and for many other philanthropic purposes.

***Waqf* in the Twentieth Century.** During the colonial period of the nineteenth century and a good part of the twentieth century, the management of *waqf* continued to follow inherited patterns in most Muslim countries and communities which were subjected to colonial rule, with a few exceptions, such as Algeria and Indonesia. However, the general atmosphere of underdevelopment and backwardness prevalent in the Muslim world also enveloped the *waqf* properties. In addition, the Western system of education that was introduced by colonial authorities and supported by newly created economic opportunities was a strong blow to traditional education, which was financed by an already debilitated *waqf* system.

With the independence of most Islamic countries in the middle of the twentieth century came the establishment of national states. The new leadership took various, often negative, stands toward *waqf*. For instance, many *waqf* properties in Syria, Egypt, Turkey, Tunis, and Algeria were added to the public property of the government and were distributed through land reforms and other means, although governments in those countries took responsibility for the funding of mosques and some religious schools, including al-Azhar University in Cairo. Many Muslim countries established departments for *awqāf* and religious affairs for this limited purpose. After being stripped of its developmental and productive content, the word *waqf* is now used mostly to refer to mosques only.

However, some countries including Lebanon, Turkey, Jordan, and recently, Algeria, started to revive and develop the properties of *waqf*. They enacted new laws of *awqāf* that are helping to recover, preserve, and develop these properties, as well as to encourage their people to create new *awqāf*.

[*See also* Economics, *article on* Economic Institutions; Property.]

BIBLIOGRAPHY

Abū al-Ajfān, Muḥammad. "Al-Waqf ʿalā al-masjid fī al-Maghrib wa-al-Andalus" (*Waqf* on Mosques in Northwest Africa and Andalusia). In *Dirāsāt fī al-Iqtiṣād al-Islāmī*, pp. 315–342. Jeddah, 1985.

Armagan, Servet. "Lamḥah ʿan ḥālat al-awqāf fī Turkiyā" (A Glance at the State of *awqāf* in Turkey). In *Idārat wa-Tathmīr Mumtalakāt al-awqāf*, edited by Ḥasan ʿAbd Allāh al-Amīn, pp. 335–344. Jeddah, 1989.

ʿAsalī, Kāmil Jamīl al-. "Mu'assasat al-awqāf wa-madāris Bayt al-Maqdis" (*Awqāf* Institution and the Schools of Jersalem). In *Symposium on Awqaf Institutions in the Arab and Islamic World*, pp. 93–112. Baghdad, 1983.

Baṣar, Haṣmat, ed. *Management and Development of Awqaf Properties*. Jeddah, 1987.

Islamic Research Center for History, Culture, and Arts (IRCICA). *The Muslim Pious Foundations [awqāf] and Real Estates in Palestine*. Istanbul, 1982.

Janssens, G. Bussan De. *Les Wakfs dan l'Islam contemporain*. Paris, 1954.

Qureshi, M. A. *Waqf in India*. New Delhi, 1989.

Ramaḍan, Muṣṭafā Muḥammad. "Dawr al-awqāf fī daʿm al-Azhar." In *Symposium on Awqaf Institutions in the Arab and Islamic World*, pp. 125–148. Baghdad, 1983.

Sayyid, ʿAbd al-Malik al-. "Al-waqf al-Islāmī wa-al-dawr alladhī laʿibahu fī al-numūw al-Ijtimāʿī fī al-Islām" (Islamic *waqf* and the Role It Played in Social Development in Islam). In *Idārat wa-Tathmīr Mumtalakāt al-awqāf*, edited by Ḥasan ʿAbd Allāh al-Amīn, pp. 225–304. Jeddah, 1989.

Sibāʿī, Muṣṭafā al-. *Min rawā'iʿ ḥaḍāratinā*. Beirut, 1969.

Zarqā, Muṣṭafā. *Aḥkām al-awqāf*. Damascus, 1947.

MONZER KAHF

WAR. *See* Fitnah; Ghazw; Jihād; Military Forces.

WAṬAN. Traditional Islamic culture uses the term *waṭan* to indicate a person's place of birth or residence. The word was redefined in the nineteenth century to embrace the meaning attached to the concept of "patrie" or "fatherland" in European languages.

Thus, in the vocabulary of modern Islam *waṭan* denotes one's fatherland as a political entity with definite boundaries, territorial integrity, and a distinct national identity. This new definition was gradually introduced into the political and literary culture of various Islamic countries as a result of ideas and reforms associated with the Tanzimat reforms (1839–1876) in the Ottoman Empire.

Although Ottoman officials and writers referred to the whole territory of their empire as one single *waṭan*, particularly between 1839 and 1914, educated elites of other non-Turkish provinces, such as Syria, Tunisia, and Egypt, preferred to bestow the title of *waṭan* on their respective autonomous units.

The modern adoption of the term by Muslim elites and intellectuals triggered an association of ideas that amounted to an ideological commitment. *Waṭan* became a well-defined entity to be loved and cherished in its own right. It was, moreover, incorporated into the mainstream culture of Islam by invoking a saying attributed to the Prophet Muḥammad: "The love of the fatherland is an article of faith." This adage gained such widespread popularity in the second half of the nineteenth century that numerous literary societies, magazines, and newspapers adopted it as a motto or title. Hence, *waṭan* conjoined the twin ideas of the rule of law and cultural integration, superseding arbitrary regulations or undefined networks of kinship and tribal affiliations. Its mere invocation denoted a conscious and rational endeavor undertaken to create a new form of human organization.

In this sense, an Islamic *waṭan* acquired, for the first time in its existence, an intelligible pattern of historical development. After 1860, history books were written dealing with one particular Islamic *waṭan*. This practice expressed deeper patriotic allegiances, which emerged in the Ottoman provinces and slowly established themselves after World War I in almost all Islamic countries. To Islamic modernists and reformists, such as the Ottoman Namık Kemal (1840–1888) and the Egyptian Muḥammad ʿAbduh (1849–1905), the love of one's country occupied a central position in their program for political, economic, and social renewal. It conveyed meaningful messages and created a fruitful dialogue with the new spirit of scientific and industrial progress. Writing in the 1930s, ʿAbd al-Ḥamīd ibn Bādīs (1889–1940), the Algerian religious leader, argued that "individuals are affiliated to the fatherland *(al-waṭan)* by the memories of the past, the interests of the present and the aspirations of the future." [*See the biographies of Kemal, ʿAbduh, and Ibn Bādīs.*]

In the second half of the twentieth century, the concept of *waṭan* became associated with nationalism and the active participation of a country's citizens in their general well-being. In the era of independence, one's *waṭan* and one's state were merged and rendered synonymous, regardless of widely divergent political cultures. However, certain pan-movements, such as Arab nationalism and Islamism, continue to use *waṭan* in their ideology to encompass either all the Arab countries or the whole Islamic world.

[*See also* Arab Nationalism; Nation.]

BIBLIOGRAPHY

Berkes, Niyazi. *The Development of Secularism in Turkey*. Montreal, 1964. Essential text that covers modern Ottoman and Turkish notions of patriotism, the state, and Western culture.

Choueiri, Youssef M. *Arab History and the Nation-State, 1820–1980*. London and New York, 1989. Introduction to the concepts of the fatherland and the nation in modern Arab historiography.

Cleveland, William L. *The Making of an Arab Nationalist: Ottomanism and Arabism in the Life and Thought of Satiʿ al-Husri*. Princeton, 1971. Exhaustive and articulate study of the nationalist thought of one of the most influential Arab intellectuals.

Ibn Bādīs, ʿAbd al-Ḥamīd. *Kitāb āthār Ibn Bādīs*. Vol. 1, part 1. Algiers, 1968. Useful collection of essays and speeches by a reformist religious leader.

Piscatori, James P. *Islam in a World of Nation-States*. Cambridge, 1986. Analytical study of the accommodation of Islam to the modern international order.

YOUSSEF M. CHOUEIRI

WAẒĪFAH. Something which is assigned or appointed, *waẓīfah,* in its principal meaning, refers to the apportioning of sections of the Qur'ān for orderly recitation. The injunction that the Qur'ān should be read "in a slow and distinct manner" (surah 73.4) was a reminder to the prophet Muḥammad and his companions that recitation of the Word of God should not be precipitate. The Prophet is quoted as saying, "One who reads the Qur'ān in less than three days has not understood it." Early Muslim authorities impugn as false piety the temptation to rush the recitation of the 114 surahs (chapters) of the Qur'ān. To guard against this danger Muḥammad approved an apportioning of the scripture for purposes of intelligent recitation.

The simplest mode of division arranges the reading of the Qur'ān into seven *manāzil* ("stages") so that the entire scripture can be recited in a week (Friday to Thursday). An alternative way of recitation divides the Qur'ān into thirty *ajzā'* ("parts") equivalent to the number of days in a (lunar) month—this being of particular blessing during the month of Ramaḍān, when it is believed that the revelation of the Qur'ān began (surah 2.184). These divisions do not correspond to the chapter divisions of the Qur'ān, nor are they indicated within the actual text of scripture. As Qur'ānic calligraphy developed, they were shown by marginal markings on the pages where they occur in recitation, either by a simple dot of the pen, or the insertion of the word *ḥizb* (section), or by stylized florations. "It is praiseworthy," wrote Imam al-Ghazālī (d. 1111), "to make the writing of the Qur'ān beautiful and to make its [letters] clear and distinct. There is no sin in dotting letters and writing different marks with red and other colors, because these colors adorn the Qur'ān, make its (letters) distinct, and avert the reader from making mistakes and incorrect reading." He wished to assure pious Muslims that these additions to the Qur'ānic page, as distinct from text, were *bidʿah ḥasanah* ("a good innovation") which should be considered within the Prophet's intention.

A second meaning of *waẓīfah* unrelated to the first applies to the apportioning of monies in Islamic administration. Here we find the word used in two ways. Most commonly it refers to the system of *waqf* (pious endowment) by which a devout Muslim gives personal funds for the creation and upkeep of an institution of religious nature, for example, a mosque. In this context, *waẓīfah* denotes the portion of the financial provision which is to be assigned for the maintenance of religious functionaries, such as the imam and the muezzin (Ar., *mu'adhdhin*). In the earliest development of mosques, legal scholars expressed misgivings about the principle of such payments. But with the institutional growth of these offices, their incumbents' need for financial support was met by a determination on the part of the originator of the *waqf* as to the terms and amount of remuneration.

Waẓīfah also occurs in the language of Islamic taxation. A major source of public revenue in the history of Islamic government has been land, deemed to be the commonwealth of the Muslim community. So the owners of land were required under Islamic law to pay *kharāj* (land tax) to the central treasury. The tax was assessed in one of two ways: on the basis of the actual produce of a piece of land *(mukasamah)*, or its potential for production, whether or not it was actually cultivated *(waẓīfah)*. Where this second form of taxation prevailed, the term *waẓifah* came to be used as a synonym of *kharāj*.

[*See also* Economics, *article on* Economic Institutions; Kharāj; Qur'ānic Recitation; *and* Waqf.]

BIBLIOGRAPHY

Antoun, Richard. *Muslim Preacher in the Modern World: A Jordanian Case Study in Comparative Perspective*. Princeton, 1989.

Gardet, Louis. *La cité musulmane: Vie sociale et politique*. 4th ed., Paris, 1976.

Quasem, Muhammad A., *The Recitation and Interpretation of the Qur'an: Al-Ghazālī's Theory*, Bangi, Selangor, Malaysia, 1979.

DAVID A. KERR

WAZĪR. *See* Vizier.

WEST BANK AND GAZA. The territories west of the Jordan River, lost by Jordan in the 1967 war with Israel, are known as the West Bank; the Gaza Strip, lost to Israel by Egypt in the same war, is a narrow strip of land on the Mediterranean coast. These territories have been the subject of dispute between Israel and the Palestinians, the majority population of both areas. Islamic tradition has considered Palestine central to the faith. The prophet Muḥammad ordained Jerusalem the site of the first *(qiblah)*. The city is also the location of the "Farthest Temple" appearing in the Vision of the Ascension of the Prophet (surah 17.1), which details a mystical night journey by the Prophet to Jerusalem. Muslim leaders throughout the history of Islam have fought against any power threatening Muslim rulership of the holy city. Thus, the nature of Islamic life in the territories of the West Bank and Gaza Strip is inextricably linked to the symbolism of Palestine to the Muslim faith. This link has meant that the Muslim community of the world feels a special affinity to the city of Jerusalem and feels compelled to protest and defend it when the Islamic sanctity of the shrines associated with the prophet Muḥammad is threatened by rulership that is non-Islamic.

The links between religion, war, and politics were reinforced in the early decades of the twentieth century, following the defeat of the Ottoman Empire in World War I and the end of the caliphate. Palestine's Muslim leaders assumed new roles under the mandate of the British colonial authorities (1917–1948). The most senior religious figure, al-Ḥājj Amīn al-Ḥusaynī, *muftī* of Jerusalem and a British appointee, faced challenges from the growth of a secular and nationalist Palestinian movement, foreign authority, and the Zionist movement. Within the Palestinian Islamic movement he was confronted by the rise of a populist Islamic movement led by Syrian-born and Egyptian-educated Shaykh ʿIzz al-Dīn al-Qassām (d. 1935).

Such developments were new to Islam in Palestine and threatened to undermine traditional Islamic rule in Jerusalem, the third most holy site of Islam. Palestinian Islamic thinkers during this period were influenced by Islamic thinkers in Cairo, in particular Muḥammad Rashīd Riḍā (1865–1935), a follower of Muḥammad ʿAbduh (1849–1905). ʿAbduh and Riḍā were the leaders of the Islamic modernist movement, which sought to combine the essentials of the Islamic faith with the modern political context of Middle Eastern society under Western influences.

Within the Palestinian context both al-Ḥusaynī and al-Qassām were disciples of the modernist movement. Yet these leaders employed radically different approaches to the political issues of the period. The most prominent of these issues were British rule and their policies toward the Zionist movement. In response to Palestinian isolation and marginalization, the leadership of the Muslim population responded to local grievances.

In the north of Palestine, in the area around Haifa, Shaykh al-Qassām organized a populist response in the predominantly peasant community. He encouraged the peasants to reestablish the basic principles of Islamic faith and to resort to armed resistance against the British authorities and Jewish targets. Although al-Qassām was killed by British forces in November 1935, his followers continued their campaign and were key figures in the leadership of the Palestinian uprising (1936–1939). As an activist, rather than as a thinker, al-Qassām has influenced recent Islamic and nationalist groups, including Ḥamās, who named its military wing after al-Qassām, the Islamic Jihād in Palestine, and the Palestine Liberation Organization (PLO).

Al-Ḥājj Amīn al-Ḥusaynī played a pivotal role in the Palestinian uprising of 1936, and, as a consequence, was stripped of his religious authority and forced into exile by the British authorities. He is criticized for mishandling Palestinian aspirations for political self-determination because he acted as a moderating and appeasing influence during the uprising. Like al-Qassām, al-Ḥusaynī was not an Islamic savant, yet his influence on the politics of Islam in Palestine and on its relationship with nationalist and other forces has endured.

The points of view of these Islamic figures during the early twentieth century persist in the politics, culture, and social relations of the predominantly Muslim community of the West Bank and Gaza Strip. Regardless of political rule, that of the Jordanians and Egyptians from 1948 to 1967 and of the Israelis since 1967, the religious leadership of the Muslim population has reflected the pluralism of political viewpoints.

Since Israeli occupation in 1967 the traditional leadership, funded by Jordanian *awqāf* (sg., *waqf*), has sought to maintain the daily practice of Islamic religion and culture in a rapidly secularizing society. The Israeli authorities have confiscated Islamic lands, neglected Muslim shrines, arrested and deported preachers, censored sermons, and prevented worshipers from traveling to mosques to pray. These actions have radicalized sections of the Muslim clergy, who, following Shaykh al-Qassām's example, have formed independent political agendas and concentrated their work and activities among the poorer sections of the refugee community of the Gaza Strip and West Bank.

Preachers such as Shaykh ʿAbd al-ʿAzīz ʿAwdah, of the Islamic Jihād, and Shaykh Aḥmad Yāsīn, the leader of al-Mujtamaʿ al-Islāmī (the Islamic Assembly) and its *intifāḍah* offshoot Hamas, have built their own independently funded mosques, welfare, and health clinics. These radical Islamic leaders and their followers have distanced themselves from traditional figures like Shaykh ʿAbd al-Ḥamīd al-Saʾiḥ, president of the Palestine National Council, and the late Shaykh ʿIzz al-Dīn al-ʿAlamī, the *muftī* of Jerusalem, who support the Palestine Liberation Organization. Thus, rivalry within the Muslim leadership of the West Bank and Gaza Strip now exists between those who support the PLO and those who, like other Islamic radicals, resist the influences of nationalist-secularism and Western mores and values in favor of a return to the principles of Islam. These divergences have come to the fore during the Palestinian *intifāḍah* (uprising), which broke out in 1987 and has continued in the early 1990s. In the Gaza Strip the strength of Islamic forces has affected ideology, religious practice, and social relations within the community, leading to rivalry between supporters of the national movement and Islamic activists.

In the 1990s the Palestinian Islamic movement opposed the peace negotiations between Israel and the Palestinians and Arab states that were initiated under international auspices. In addition it denounced the signing of a "Declaration of Principles" for peace between Israel and the PLO in September 1993. The Islamic movement has stepped up armed attacks on Israeli targets. The Israeli government has outlawed Ḥamās and Islamic Jihād, it deported more than four hundred in 1992, and it has imprisoned the leaders of both organizations.

[*See also* Arab-Israeli Conflict; Ḥamās; Israel; Jihād Organizations; Palestine Liberation Organization; *and the biography of Ḥusaynī.*]

BIBLIOGRAPHY

Abū ʿAmr, Ziyād. *Al-ḥarakah al-Islāmīyah fīʾl-Ḍiffah al-Gharbīyah wa Qiṭāʿ Ghazzah* (The Islamic Movement in the West Bank and Gaza Strip). Acre, Israel, 1989. The best study to date of the Islamic *jihād* movement in the Israeli Occupied Territories.

Johnson, Nels. *Islam and the Politics of Meaning in Palestinian Nationalism.* London, 1982. Anthropological essay concentrating on the life of Shaykh ʿIzz al-Dīn al-Qassām.

Mattar, Philip. "The Mufti of Jerusalem and the Politics of Palestine." *Journal of Palestine Studies* 42 (Spring 1989): 227–240.

Milton-Edwards, Beverley. *Islamic Politics in Palestine.* London, 1995. Historical and contemporary examination of Islamic politics.

Porath, Yehoshua. *The Emergence of the Palestinian National Movement, 1918–1939.* London, 1974. Useful overview of Palestine under the British mandate.

Sahliyeh, Emile F. *In Search of Leadership: West Bank Politics since 1967.* Washington, D.C., 1988. Thoughtful account of issues of leadership, but like many other books, fails to address the Gaza Strip.

BEVERLEY MILTON-EDWARDS

WILĀYAH. In Shīʿī Islam, *wilāyah* or guardianship is the principle that a line of imams related to the prophet Muḥammad succeeded to spiritual and (ideally) to temporal authority in Islam after his death in 632 CE. Historically, only the Prophet's son-in-law ʿAlī ibn Abī Ṭālib actually achieved worldly power as caliph (656–661), but Twelver Shīʿīs believe that eleven of his lineal descendants retained a spiritual guardianship over believers and by all rights ought also to have ruled. In Shiism, believers owed the *walī* or guardian absolute obedience, and it was said that one who died without recognizing the imam of his age died an unbeliever.

The occultation of the twelfth imam late in the ninth century presented Twelver Shīʿīs with a major challenge. The hidden twelfth imam was thereafter permanently the imam of the age until his supernatural return, awaited at some point in the future. Some clergy of the Uṣūlī school began claiming for the Shīʿī clergy the position of general vicegerent *(nā'ib ʿāmm)* of the hidden imam; al-Muḥaqqiq al-Ḥillī, writing early in the thirteenth century, spoke of the clergy as having a guardianship of the imamate *(walā' al-imāmah).*

The vast majority of Shīʿī clerics in history were quietists and did not challenge the authority structures of their day. The shahs of the Shīʿī Ṣafavid dynasty (1501–1722) in Iran went so far as to claim to be the house of *wilāyah* or authority themselves. The great Imāmī jurisprudent Murtaḍā al-Anṣārī (d. 1864) rejected the notions that the clergy enjoyed the same authority *(wilāyah)* as the imam, or that no secular authority could exercise such authority. The doctrines of the absolute sovereignty or *wilāyah* of the imam, and the general vicegerency of the clergy on his behalf, however, provided a basis for some clerics to claim authority even over aspects of secular governance. The anticonstitutionalist cleric Shaykh Faẓlullāh Nūrī rejected the idea of modern parliamentary representation in 1907–1908 precisely on the grounds that it would intrude on the prerogative of the imam to *wilāyah.*

From being a relatively obscure term in Twelver Shīʿī theology and law, *wilāyah* was lifted by Ayatollah Ruhollah Khomeini to worldwide prominence. In his 1971 book *Islamic Government or the Wilāyah of the Jurisprudent,* he argued that the clergy as representatives of the hidden imam had a responsibility to take control of governmental authority *(wilāyah)* and *jihād,* enjoining good and forbidding evil—all functions of the state in most Muslim countries. For Khomeini, the guardianship of the jurisprudent *(wilāyah al-faqīh)* implied the end of any separation of religion and state. Whereas the general vicegerency of the clergy on behalf of the hidden imam had been exercised collectively, Khomeini envisaged a single clerical guardian as a sort of Platonic philosopher-ruler. He insisted that if any jurisprudent succeeded in founding such a government and ruled according to Shīʿī law, it would be incumbent on all other clerics and believers to follow him. After the Islamic revolution of 1978–1979, the principle of *wilāyah al-faqīh,* wherein ultimate authority in the Islamic state belongs to the supreme jurisprudent, was enshrined in article 5 of the constitution of the Islamic Republic of Iran. The supreme jurisprudent emerged with very broad and somewhat undefined powers; he is commander in chief of the armed forces and has the power to dismiss certain high officers of the state. Toward the end of his life Khomeini even suggested that the supreme jurisprudent could properly suspend laws of Islam, such as the commandment to perform the pilgrimage to Mecca. A somewhat less activist interpretation of the office has been offered since 1989 by Khomeini's successor, ʿAli Khamene'i.

[*See also* Imam; Ithnā ʿAsharīyah; Vicegerent; Wilāyat al-Faqīh; *for a discussion of the term's esoteric connotations as "devotion to ʿAlī," see* Walāyah.]

BIBLIOGRAPHY

Akhavi, Shahrough. *Religion and Politics in Contemporary Iran.* Albany, N.Y., 1980.

Arjomand, Said Amir, ed. *Authority and Political Culture in Shiʿism.* Albany, N.Y., 1988.

Bakhash, Shaul. *The Reign of the Ayatollahs.* Rev. ed. New York, 1990.

Calder, Norman. "The Structures of Authority in Imāmī Shiʿi Jurisprudence." Ph.D. diss., School of Oriental and African Studies, University of London, 1980.

Khomeini, Ruhollah. *Vilāyat-i faqīh: Ḥukūmat-i Islāmī.* Tehran, 1979.

Khomeini, Ruhollah. *Islam and Revolution.* Translated by Hamid Algar. Berkeley, 1980.

Sachedina, A. A. *The Just Ruler.* New York and Oxford, 1988.

JUAN R. I. COLE

WILĀYAT AL-FAQĪH. The term *wilāyat al-faqīh* in Arabic, or *vilāyat-i faqīh* in Persian, first gained wide currency in the Shīʿī world when it was used as the title for the published version of the lectures delivered by Ayatollah Ruhollah Khomeini (1902–1989) in 1969 to his students in Najaf. It means "the guardianship of the jurist"; and when the jurist Khomeini came to power in 1979 and became the supreme arbiter of all matters of government in Iran, it became clear to the Islamic world as a whole that such guardianship was one route to an ideal espoused by many contemporary Muslims, namely, Islamic government.

The term has immediate resonance in the example of the first imam, ʿAlī ibn Abī Ṭālib (d. 656), who is called by Shīʿīs: "Walī Allāh," which means both "the Friend of God" and "the Vicegerent of God." The phrase also has a kinship to the saying attributed by many Muslims, both Sunnī and Shīʿī, to the prophet Muḥammad: "The *ʿulamā'* [people of religious learning] are the heirs of the prophets." Some Muslims assume that this saying implies the inheritance by the *ʿulamā'* of direct government by the Prophet.

The specific background of the theory of *wilāyat al-faqīh,* however, is to be found in developments in eighteenth- and nineteenth-century Twelver Shīʿī thought. The Uṣūlī school of Twelver Shiism, which developed in the middle of the eighteenth century and achieved predominance by the middle of the nineteenth century, gave the exclusive right to interpret Islamic law to the *mujtahids,* experts who claim that their authority extends back in an unbroken chain of teacher-disciple recognition to the infallible imams. As the rank of *mujtahid* was passed on only to a very few pupils by existing *mujtahids*, it was seldom—if ever—held by as many as two hundred people. Among the *mujtahids*, a few of the most prominent put out manuals interpreting basic practice for ordinary believers, who are obliged by Uṣūlī theory to choose one of these few as a *marjaʿ al-taqlīd* ("source of emulation"). Shaykh Murtaḍa al-Anṣārī, thanks to his intellectual predominance, achieved wide recognition as the leading source of emulation before his death in 1864. He therefore received from all over the Twelver Shīʿī world the contributions payable to the Hidden Imam, which, according to Uṣūlī theory, went in his absence to the "sources of emulation." Another "source of emulation," Mirzā Ḥasan Shīrāzī (d. 1896), showed the political muscle of this office when, by his ruling of 1891, he forced Naṣīr al-Dīn Shāh (r. 1848–1896), the ruler of Iran, to cancel a tobacco concession to the British. However, it was only while Ayatollah Moḥammad Ḥosayn Borujerdi was the "source of emulation" from 1947 to 1962 that it became clear that one man could turn this office into authority over the overwhelming majority of Twelver Shīʿīs.

If this office in some sense represented the authority of the absent twelfth imam, who is, according to Twelver Shīʿīs, their infallible leader, this meant that the supreme "source of emulation" also had the worldly authority of the twelfth imam. Ḥājj Mullā Aḥmad Nirāqī (d. 1828 or 1829) drew this conclusion very early in the nineteenth century, and Khomeini often referred to Nirāqī. Shaykh Murtaḍa al-Anṣārī, who had studied with Nirāqī and was aware of the potential political implications of the newly expanded role of the "source of emulation" (called, for continuity with traditional Islamic legal sources, simply the *faqīh* or "jurist"), devoted a lengthy discussion in his masterwork, *Al-makāsib,* to refuting the theory of the guardianship of the jurist.

Since *al-makāsib* was a work on commercial law, it became a tradition to treat this subject in the context of discussions of the authority of the jurist-judge to have disposal over moneys. Khomeini, in a section of his *Book on Sale* (1970), opens the discussion with a direct quote from al-Anṣārī: "Among the guardians over the expenditure of money of the person who does not have independence in the expenditure of his or her money [e.g., a minor] is the judge. He is the jurist with all the qualifications to issue a *fatwā* [authoritative opinion]." To these words Khomeini adds: "It would not be wrong to turn one's attention to the guardianship of the jurist in general, in a summary way. A detailed discussion would require devoting an independent treatise to this subject, which the present scope of our work does not permit us to do." The lectures he delivered on this subject were published simultaneously in a somewhat more popular form in Najaf, first as fascicles as the lectures were completed, then in book form.

The resulting book, *Vilāyat-i faqīh,* which bears the subtitle *Islamic Government,* argues that it is incumbent on Muslims to establish such government, and that it is incumbent on jurists to assume all the tasks that the prophet Muḥammad had performed, including direct rule. In the version published in fascicles, Khomeini is said to have restated the traditional view of Uṣūlī Twelver Shīʿīs that every *mujtahid,* the exact equivalent for *faqīh* in this context, must follow his own judgment, which would imply that no *mujtahid* need defer to another in matters of government. The book version, however, states that if one *faqīh* possessing knowledge and moral integrity undertakes the task of government, "he will possess the same authority as the Most Noble Messenger [of God, Muḥammad], and it will be the duty of all people to obey him."

Uṣūlī theory ideally embodied leadership in a single

person, such as Ayatollah Borujerdi, who was called "the absolute source of emulation," and hence made it conceivable (if not necessary) that a *faqīh* be the final source of all authority. But Khomeini's assertion that all, even *mujtahids*, should submit to such a *faqih* continues to be a contested point among Shīʿī clergymen. The Iraqi clergyman Muḥammad Bāqir al-Ṣadr, in one of the lectures written shortly before his death in April 1980, developed a similar interpretation of the role of the *faqīh*, and Ṣadr's eloquent exposition of this theme, alongside the success of the Iranian Revolution of 1979, made the theory of the guardianship of the jurist known in the Sunnī world.

The Iranian Constitution of 1979, in articles 5 and 107 (which are not fully consonant with each other), treats the leadership of a single *faqīh* as the norm and says that "only in the event that no *faqīh* should be so recognized by the majority" should a "source of emulation possessing outstanding qualification" be chosen for this position. If such a candidate cannot be found, three or five "sources of emulation" would form a leadership council. When Khomeini found that his chosen successor as supreme *faqīh*, Ayatollah Ḥusayn ʿAlī Muntaẓirī, often opposed his policies, he got Muntaẓirī to withdraw from the succession. Such a withdrawal might imply that the *faqīh* recognized by so many as possessing qualities of knowledge and leadership suddenly no longer possessed these qualities. Khomeini, recognizing the strain that such change put on the clergy and ordinary believers, called for a revision of the constitution some months before his death in 1989. Khomeini also advised that the qualification that the religious leader be a "source of emulation" be dropped from the constitution.

The new constitution, presented to Iranians shortly after Khomeini's death, duly dropped this qualification. The circle around Khomeini reported that on his deathbed Khomeini recognized an important political figure, ʿAli Khamene'i (who had not completed the highest level of training as a theological student), as a *mujtahid*, now sole requirement for a national spiritual leader of Iran; Khamene'i assumed that position. The disjunction between the political theory of the guardianship of the jurist and the actual hierarchy among Shīʿī clergymen was emphasized by the Iranian government's attempt to persuade the public that they should accept Ayatollah Muḥamamd ʿAlī Arākī, a very pious *mujtahid* in his nineties, to be the leading "source of emulation," although Arākī had hitherto not aspired to be recognized as a "source of emulation" by even a minority of Shīʿīs. As a result, an interesting discussion of the meaning of the guardianship of the jurist has begun, in which some theorists have argued that the voice of the people is the voice of God and the true source of the authority of the *faqīh*.

[*See also* Faqīh; Ijtihād; Ithnā ʿAsharīyah; Marjaʿ al-Taqlīd; Uṣūlīyah; *and the biography of Khomeini.*]

BIBLIOGRAPHY

Anṣārī, Murtaḍā al-. *Kitāb al-Makāsib*. Vol. 2. Qom, 1991. Contains his refutation of the guardianship of the jurist (pp. 80–100).

Dabashi, Hamid. "Early Propagation of *Wilāyat-i Faqīh* and Mullā Aḥmad Narāqī." In *Expectation of the Millenium: Shīʿism in History*, edited by Seyyed Hossein Nasr et al., pp. 287–300. Presents the early history of the theory.

Khomeini, Ruhollah al-Musavi. *Islam and Revolution*. Translated and annotated by Hamid Algar. Berkeley, 1981. Contains a complete translation of Khomeini's treatise on government, which includes his assertion that *mujtahids* should defer to the jurist who holds actual leadership (p. 62).

Khomeini, Ruhollah al-Musavi. *Kitāb al-Bayʿ*. Vol. 2. Qom, n.d. See pages 459–539.

Maghnīyah, Muḥamamd Jawād al-. *Al-Khumaynī wa-al-dawlah al-Islāmīyah*. Beirut, 1979. Critiques the guardianship of the jurist from a traditional standpoint.

Mallat, Chibli. *The Renewal of Islamic Law: Muhammad Baqer as-Sadr, Najaf, and the Shiʿi International*. Cambridge, 1993. Compares the ideas of Ṣadr and Khomeini on Islamic government.

Modarressi, Hossein. "The Just Ruler." *Journal of the American Oriental Society* 111.3 (1991): 549–562.

Moussavi, A. "A New Interpretation of the Theory of Velayat-e Faqih." *Middle Eastern Studies* 28.1 (1992): 101–107. Revisionist approach to the concept.

Muntaẓirī, Ḥusayn ʿAlī. *Dirāsāt fī wilāyat al-faqīh*. Vol. 1. Qom, 1988. Revisionist treatment.

Muṭahharī, Murtaẓā. *Valā'hā va Vilayāt-hā*. Qom, 1983. Discusses the concept of *wilāyah* in Shiism.

Sachedina, A. A. *The Just Ruler (al-Sulṭan al-ʿĀdil) in Shīʿite Islam*. New York, 1988. Contains a discussion of the concept of *wilāyah* in Shiism; should be read in conjunction with Modarressi.

Tafṣīl va taḥlīl-i vilāyat al-faqīh. N.p., n.d. Anonymous text, usually ascribed to Mehdi Bāzargān, critiquing Khomeini's broader understanding of the guardianship of the jurist. Published by Nahẓat-i Āzādī.

ROY P. MOTTAHEDEH

WOMEN AND ISLAM. [*To consider the place of women in Islamic tradition, this entry comprises two articles. The first article examines the role and status of women in Islamic law and summarizing twentieth-century legal developments that have specifically affected women. The second article provides an overview of women's religious activi-*

ties in contemporary Muslim societies. For related discussions, see Women and Social Reform.]

Role and Status of Women

The Qur'ān, Islam's holy book, and the *sunnah* (traditions of the Prophet) considerably improved women's status by comparison to the pre-Islamic (Jāhilīyah) period. Before Islam, men treated women as their property, to be married or divorced at their pleasure. Women were subjected to polygynous practices and female children to infanticide. Women generally had no voice in the selection of spouses and, once married, lacked financial security, as the dower *(mahr)* was paid directly to their male guardians. However, apparently some pre-Islamic women practiced polyandry and also selected and divorced their own husbands. As a rule, these women were neither veiled nor secluded; some were poets and others even fought in wars alongside men.

Role and Status in the Qur'ān and Sunnah. Islamic holy law *(sharīʿah)* addressed some of the more flagrant gender inequities of the pre-Islamic period. For instance, Islamic regulation proscribed female infanticide; abolished women's status as chattel; emphasized the contractual, rather than the proprietary, nature of marriage; mandated that the wife, not her father, directly receive the dower; enjoined that a woman retain control and use of her property and maiden name after marriage; guaranteed her financial maintenance by her husband; accorded her the right to privacy; prohibited her husband from spying on or entrapping her; and prevented a woman's eviction from the house after divorce by requiring the husband to maintain his ex-wife for three menstrual cycles (until childbirth if she were pregnant).

To develop a clearer picture of the status and role of women in the Qur'ān and *sunnah,* one should distinguish between Islam as religion and Islam as culture. Islam as religion refers to regulations pertaining to piety, ethics, and belief. These spiritual aspects of Islam are considered duties of worship *(ʿibādāt)* and hence called "roots" or "foundations" *(uṣūl)* of the faith, for instance, Allāh's uniqueness, the final prophecy of Muḥammad, prayer, almsgiving, fasting, and the pilgrimage to Mecca. On this religious level, men and women are moral equals in the sight of God. Evidence for this is found in numerous Qur'ānic verses (2.187, 3.195, 4.1, 4.32, 9.71–72, 24.12, 30.21, 33.35–36, 40.40, 48.5, 57.12), which render the only distinction between women and men to be their piety, not their sex.

Islam as culture refers to the ideas and practices of Muslims in the context of changing social, economic, and political circumstances. People not only worship God but also interact in social relationships (called *muʿāmalāt,* or "transactions"). They make contracts, trade, fight, arbitrate disputes, collect taxes, and so on. Collectively, these constitute the *furūʿ* (the branches, or "superstructure").

On this cultural level, women have not been treated as men's equals. Such inequality has evolved largely as an artifact of the preferences and actions of patriarchal authorities (termed *scripturalists* here) after the Prophet's death, including certain rulers and administrators, most jurists, and some intellectuals. They justify this system of inequality by reference to certain verses of the Qur'ān and traditions of the Prophet. However, modernists, including a number of nineteenth- and twentieth-century political leaders, government bureaucrats, intellectuals, leaders of women's movements, and a minority of *ʿulamā'* (religious scholars), believe that many of these verses and traditions do not support such categorical claims.

Thus, the comprehensive veiling and seclusion of women would appear to have no warrant in the Qur'ān and the *sunnah.* However, Qur'ānic verses do assign women's testimony half the value of men's; permit men to unilaterally divorce their wives; deny women custody rights over their children after they reach a certain age; (seemingly) permit polygyny; and favor men over women respecting inheritance. But modernists hold that stipulations in the Qur'ān itself and existing legal principles adduced by jurists may be invoked to maintain that, since the social, cultural, and economic context of those verses has changed, the sanction for gender inequality is no longer legitimate.

Modernists support their argument by reference to holy law itself. First, in surah 3.7 the Qur'ān specifically distinguishes between two kinds of verse: (1) those that are unambiguous *(muḥkamāt),* and (2) those that are subject to interpretation *(mutashābihāt).* Hence, anti-scripturalists may claim that verses appearing to confer superiority upon men over women (for example, surahs 2.223 and 2.228) ought not be taken literally but, rather, allegorically. Second, the Qur'ān not only conditions polygyny on the requirement of equitable treatment for all wives (4.3), but explicitly asserts such treatment to be impossible (4.129). Third, Allāh says that He will not change a people's condition until they change what is in themselves (13.11). According to modernists, this verse calls upon Muslims to use their intrinsic endowment of reason to maximize their welfare. Fourth, a sound tradition ascribed to the Prophet maintains that "as for matters of your world, you know better." Modernists interpret this to mean that Muslims should use reason—repeatedly upheld in the Qur'ān as a meritorious human attribute—in pursuit of their welfare. Thus, it would be offensive to human reason to accept gender inequality when Allāh Himself enjoins spiritual equality of all Muslims. Finally, over the centuries reform-minded jurists have employed a number of legal devices that vindicate the use of reason in pursuing the welfare of Muslims, including: (1) public interest *(maṣlaḥah mursalah);* (2) the common expression, "necessities make permissible what are forbidden" *(al-ḍarūrāt tubīḥu al-maḥẓūrāt);* and (3) the application of discretion *(istiḥsān)* in reaching a ruling.

Scripturalists claim that the Qur'ān and *sunnah* mandate veiling and seclusion. However, modernists believe such arguments are tendentious. Of the seven Qur'ānic verses using the word "veil" *(ḥijāb),* six were revealed at Mecca (surahs 7.46, 17.45, 19.17, 38.32, 41.5, 42.51), and none of them refer to veiling Muslim women. The seventh verse (33.53), revealed at Medina, refers to the need for the Prophet's wives to be behind a *ḥijāb* when his male guests converse with them. Modernists hold that the verse does not pertain to Muslim women in general, while scripturalists, implicitly accepting this, argue that what applies to the Prophet's wives, exemplars of chastity, inheres all the more for Muslim women, since they are less chaste.

But modernists declare that the verse lacks the quality of obligation *(farḍ al-ʿayn* or *farḍ al-kifāyah),* since there is no textual stipulation *(naṣṣ)* which makes it obligatory *(wājib).* Indeed, al-Jāḥiẓ writes that women, with the knowledge of their kin, socialized freely and unveiled with men at the time of the early Islamic community. Furthermore, al-Wāḥidī, in his *Asbāb al-nuzūl,* and others maintain that the reference in surah 24.31 to scarves that should cover both head and bosom *(khumur;* in contrast to the full-length *ḥijāb)* was based on the need to differentiate among free women and slaves. The story is told of the caliph, ʿUmar ibn al-Khaṭṭāb, who slapped a female slave for wearing such a scarf. In the modernist view, if scarves were used to distinguish free women from slaves, then the abolition of slavery in the modern period has eliminated this reason for (partially) covering oneself.

Jurists differ as to the requirement of veiling and seclusion contained in the *sunnah.* References to veiling in the earlier, hence sounder, *ḥadīths* are vague and general; whereas the later, hence less reliable, *ḥadīths* are much more detailed. Historical evidence seems to indicate that veiling and seclusion were introduced after the Islamic conquests of Iran and Byzantium. As Muslims increasingly became urbanized, men veiled and secluded their women as a status marker of the family's wealth. Thus, in the modernist view, veiling had nothing to do with the requirements of the faith. [*See also* Ḥijāb.]

To modernists, the Qur'ān does not support or assert notions of inherent female inferiority, nor can women be judged less rational, more emotional, or less competent than men on the basis of holy law. Certain *ḥadīths* are sometimes cited to the effect that the Prophet regarded women as incapable of leadership. However, modernist scholars doubt the veracity of a number of these traditions and believe that they were invented by later generations to justify restrictions on the activities of women. It is clear from many *sunnah* that the Prophet consulted women and weighed their opinions seriously. According to Ibn Ḥanbal, founder of one of the four Sunnī schools of law, at least one woman, Umm Waraqah, was appointed as the imam of her household by the Prophet. Historical and other evidence indicates that women contributed significantly to the redaction of the Qur'ān and were entrusted with vital secrets affecting the Muslim community: women were first to learn of the revelation, they were told the location of the Prophet's hiding place prior to his escape to Medina, and they were vouchsafed with the Prophet's secret plans to attack Mecca. Upon the Prophet's death, the distinguished women of the community were consulted as to who should succeed him.

In spite of the claims of later traditions, then, modernists say that historical and canonical records demonstrate women's important and respected role in Muslim life, as reflected in the story of an older woman who corrected the authoritative ruling *(fatwā)* of Caliph ʿUmar ibn al-Khaṭṭāb on the dower *(mahr).* They cite the fact that women prayed in mosques unsegregated from men, and were involved in the transmittal of *ḥadīths* (Ibn Saʿd, the famous early biographer, records seven hundred cases of women who performed this important function). Women were known to give sanctuary *(jiwār)* to men. As an indication of their involvement in public matters, they owned and disposed of property and engaged in commercial transactions. Like men, they were encouraged to seek knowledge, which, indeed, they pursued in the Prophet's own home, and women were both instructors and pupils in the early Islamic period. The Prophet's favorite wife, ʿĀ'ishah, was a well-known authority in medicine, history, and rhetoric.

As to politics, the Qur'ān refers to women who, independently of their male kin, pledged the oath of allegiance *(bayʿah)* to the Prophet (surah 60.12). Additional examples of women making such pledges to the Prophet occurred at al-ʿAqabah, al-Riḍwān, and al-Shajarah. In a number of cases, distinguished women converted to Islam before their men did, again belying the traditional patriarchal view that women were incapable of independent action. As for public posts, Caliph ʿUmar appointed women to serve as officials (*muḥtasibs*) in the market of Medina, and Ḥanbalī jurisprudence upholds the qualifications of women to serve as judges.

In addition to all the foregoing, biographies of distinguished women, especially in the Prophet's household, show that women behaved autonomously in early Islam. These are the very women whom contemporary scripturalists invoke as models to justify women's seclusion and confinement today. The women about whom most data are available are Khadījah, the Prophet's first wife; ʿĀ'ishah, his favorite wife; Fāṭimah, his youngest daughter; Zaynab, his granddaughter; Sukaynah, his great-granddaughter; and ʿA'ishah bint Ṭalḥah, the niece of her namesake. These women—artists, poets, cultural patrons, soldiers—challenged the wisdom of men, insisted upon marital equality with their husbands, and took initiatives sometimes directly counter to patriarchal authority. Contemporary exhortations to restrict the activities of women in public arenas by reference to the examples of these women, therefore, are invalidated by the reality of their lives.

Role and Status in Various Muslim Lands. The seclusion and confinement of women in urban settings prevailed without significant change until the early twentieth century, but numerous attempts to modify personal status law have been made since then. These include the Ottoman Empire (1917), Algeria (1984), Egypt (1920, 1929, 1979, and 1985), India (1937, 1939, and 1976), Iran (1967, 1975, and 1979), Iraq (1959, 1963, and 1986), Jordan (1951 and 1976), Kuwait (1982), Morocco (1958), Pakistan (1961), South Yemen (1974), Sudan (1915, 1927, 1932, 1933, 1935, 1960, and 1969), Syria (1953 and 1975), Tunisia (1956, 1957, 1964, 1966, and 1981), and Turkey (1924).

Prior to the early twentieth century, the state left control over women and the family in the hands of patriarchal kinship groups. In contrast to its highly interventionist behavior in Islamic civil, commercial, and penal law, the state declined the very risky enterprise of tampering with personal status regulations, the very core of Muslim (masculine) identity. The patriarchal control of women's behavior and the family unit were central to the construction of this identity. Ultimately, however, the state's reluctance began to give way, not least because of the pressure brought to bear by women's groups under the leadership of prominent women in countries such as Egypt and throughout the Ottoman Empire.

In the past, inquiries into the role of women and the family often overemphasized the content of sacred texts, assuming these texts were the driving force behind people's behavior. In reaction to this "essentialist" approach, some scholars have stressed the relevance of conditions in "civil society" (for example, class differences) for understanding women's subordinate status. More recently, it has been suggested that neither the "sacred texts" nor the "civil society" approach are in themselves sufficient to explain the content of personal status legislation at any given time because they ignore the state's autonomy in pursuing its own agenda in this area.

For instance, the state has broadened its base of support by enfranchising women, in the process weaning them away from the kinship groups that traditionally have controlled them and redirecting their terminal loyalties to itself. Iran and Turkey at various times in this century exemplify this pattern. However, in doing this the state risks the growing disenchantment of the scripturalists, who generally view such developments to be "anti-Islamic." Thus, the state may attempt to conciliate such groups by enforcing modesty codes or curtailing women's public presence. Post-1979 Pakistan and Iran, and Egypt after 1985, provide relevant examples of such conduct.

In balancing the conflicting demands of women and traditionalists, the state has generally followed a cautious policy of reform. Such reforms have made polygynous marriages more difficult or abolished them outright (notably in Turkey, Tunisia, and Syria); permitted wives to sue for divorce by having recourse to religious courts *(sharʿ)*, especially in cases of cruelty, desertion, or dangerous contagious disease; provided women with the right to contract themselves in marriage; required husbands to find housing for a divorced wife during her custody over children; increased the minimum marital age of spouses; limited the ability of guardians to contract women in marriage against their wishes; provided opportunities for minor girls wed against their wishes to abrogate their marriage upon reaching majority; enhanced the rights of women in regard to child custody; and allowed women to write clauses into marriage contracts limiting their husbands' authority over them, for example, by his *ex ante* grant to his wife of the right to divorce him.

The following case study from Egypt captures the dilemma the modern state faces when intervening in this arena. The 1971 Egyptian constitution holds in Article 11 that the state "shall guarantee" a balance between women's "Islamic" duties and their right to employment and participation in public life. This language, attempting to reconcile women's "Islamic" obligations and their rights in the secular domain, was fraught with ambiguity because it left unclear how this reconciliation was to be achieved. In 1979, amendments were made to the 1929 personal status law that aligned the state to a modest attenuation of scripturalist positions by: (1) holding that polygyny automatically caused "harm" *(ḍarar)* to the first wife and thus *ipso facto* constituted grounds for divorce; (2) abolishing the forcible return of fleeing wives to the conjugal home *(bayt al-ṭāʿah);* and (3) granting a divorced wife with custody of minor children exclusive right to the couple's conjugal residence during the custody period.

Found unconstitutional on procedural grounds in 1985, the bill was quickly reintroduced and passed by parliament, but its provisions were now less liberal. It required the wife to demonstrate harm caused by her husband taking another wife, and granted the husband exclusive right to his residence (although he would still have to find housing for his divorced wife during the custody period).

Conclusion. The Qur'ān and *sunnah* markedly improved women's role and status relative to the pre-Islamic period by emphasizing the spiritual equality of women and men. Although certain social and economic regulations in the scripture seemingly favor men, the conditions prevailing at the time of the revelation, which seemed to justify such inequality, have lapsed. The Qur'ān, *sunnah,* and certain legal principles adduced by jurists provide mechanisms for reinterpreting, through the application of reason, those texts that putatively establish a categorical hierarchy favoring men over women. Twentieth-century reforms in personal status law, achieved through recourse to such instruments and arguments, have gradually moved in the direction of gender equality, but a certain degree of backsliding has occurred as a consequence of the rise of militant scripturalism—that is, scripturalism based on unyielding, even violent, confrontation with the state and modernist groups. It is not clear what the future will hold, but it is likely that the conflict between reformist and scripturalist outlooks on the role and status of women will continue.

BIBLIOGRAPHY

Arabic Sources

ʿAbd al-Raḥmān, ʿĀ'ishah [Bint al-Shāṭi']. *Tarājim Sayyidāt Bayt al-Nubūwah.* Beirut, 1967.

ʿAbduh, Muḥammad. "Ḥijāb al-nisā' min al-jihah al-dīnīyah." In *Fī qaḍāyā al-mar'ah.* Beirut, 1988.

Amin, Husayn Ahmad. "ʿAwdah al-nisā' ilá al-ḥijāb." In *Ḥawla al-Daʿwah ilá taṭbīq al-sharīʿah al-Islamīyah,* pp. 227–251. 2d ed. Cairo, 1987.

Amīn, Qāsim. *Al-mar'ah al-jadīdah* (1899). Cairo, 1987.

Amīn, Qāsim. *Taḥrīr al-mar'ah.* Al-Qahirah, 1984.

Darwazah, Muḥammad ʿIzzat. *Al-mar'ah fī al-Qur'ān wa-al-Sunnah.* Beirut, 1967.

Ghazālī, Abū Ḥāmid al-. *Iḥyā' ʿulūm al-dīn.* 5 vols. Beirut, 1991.

Iṣfahānī, Abū al-Faraj al-. *Kitāb al-aghānī.* 25 vols. Beirut, 1955–1964.

Wāḥidī, ʿAlī ibn Ahmad al-. *Asbāb al-nuzūl.* Cairo, 1968.

Wāqidī, Muḥammad ibn ʿUmar al-. *Kitāb al-Maghāzī lil-Wāqidī.* 3 vols. Edited by Marsden Jones. London, 1966.

English Sources

Ahmed, Leila. *Women and Gender in Islam.* New Haven, 1992.

Beck, Lois, and Nikki R. Keddie, eds. *Women in the Muslim World.* Cambridge, Mass., 1978.

Esposito, John L. *Women in Muslim Family Law.* Syracuse, N.Y., 1968.

Haddad, Yvonne Yazbeck. "Islam, Women, and Revolution in Twentieth-Century Arab Thought." *Muslim World* 74 (1984): 137–160.

Hoffman-Ladd, Valerie J. "Polemics on the Modesty and Segregation of Women in Contemporary Egypt." *International Journal of Middle East Studies* 19.1 (February 1987): 23–50.

Kandiyoti, Deniz, ed. *Women, Islam, and the State.* Philadelphia, 1991.

Sharīʿatī, ʿAlī. *Fatima Is Fatima.* Translated by Laleh Bakhtiar. Tehran, 1981.

Stern, Gertrude. "The First Women Converts in Early Islam." *Islamic Culture* 13.3 (1939): 290–305.

Stowasser, Barbara. "The Status of Women in Early Islam." In *Muslim Women,* edited by Freda Hussain, pp. 11–43. London, 1984.

Stowasser, Barbara. "Religious Ideology, Women, and the Family: The Islamic Paradigm." In *The Islamic Impulse*, edited by Barbara Stowasser, pp. 262–296. London, 1987.

Zuhur, Sherifa. *Revealing Reveiling: Islamist Gender Ideology in Contemporary Egypt*. Albany, N.Y., 1992.

SORAYA ALTORKI

Women's Religious Observances

Although women and men are assigned the same religious duties and promised the same spiritual rewards in the Qur'ān, social conventions, illiteracy, and Islamic requirements of ritual purity have all tended to restrict women's access to many aspects of Islamic religious life. These restrictions are not uniform across the Muslim world, and neither are women's responses to them. Regional variations in women's religious lives have not been sufficiently documented to make it possible to provide a truly balanced description of women's religious observances. Furthermore, social changes in this century have radically altered the situation of women in society, opening new opportunities for women in the religious domain as well.

Women and Basic Islamic Obligations. Although women are expected to perform the five daily prayers and the Ramaḍān fast, they may not pray, fast, or touch (or even, according to some interpretations, recite) the Qur'ān during menstruation or postpartum bleeding. According to *ḥadīth*, the exemption during menstruation denotes women's religious deficiency (just as the devaluation of their legal testimony, worth only half that of a man, denotes their mental deficiency). Women are rendered much more susceptible to ritual impurity than men, not only by menstruation and childbirth but also through their contact with young children, who may soil them. Although not required to fast while pregnant or nursing a baby, many women do observe the fast during these times, either totally or partially. Days of fasting that are missed because of these exemptions must be made up for later. Congregational prayer is said to be twenty-seven times more meritorious than prayer performed alone, and *ḥadīth*s from the Prophet enjoin men not to forbid women from praying in the mosque. Still, other *ḥadīth*s encourage women to pray in their homes. In the Prophet's own day women performed the dawn prayer in rows behind the men, and, according to *ḥadīth*, left the mosque before the men. Thus, theoretically, all contact between the sexes was avoided. During the caliphate of ʿUmar ibn al-Khaṭṭāb (634–644), women prayed in a separate room of the mosque with their own imam. Previously women had gathered for social purposes in the mosque as well, but ʿUmar forbade this activity and, according to al-Ghazālī (d. 1111), women were banned from the mosque altogether in the generation after the Prophet. Al-Ghazālī justified this reversal of the Prophet's edict by claiming that widespread moral deterioration made public spaces unsafe for any but elderly women, encouraging women not to leave their homes for any reason (*Marriage and Sexuality in Islam*, translated by Madelain Farah, Salt Lake City, 1984, pp. 100–101).

Ethnographic studies from a number of different Islamic countries indicate that women are commonly regarded as the initiators of illicit sexual relationships, and their presence in public is considered a source of temptation and social discord. The exclusion of women is thus considered necessary to preserve the holiness and dignity of religious ceremonies. For instance, the Friday noon prayer in the mosque is mandatory for men, but not for women, and according to Edward Lane (*The Manners and Customs of the Modern Egyptians*, London, 1836, p. 64), no women or young boys were allowed to be present in the mosque at any time of prayer. Although many mosques have segregated spaces for women, whether curtained areas, separate rooms, or balconies, until recently mosques have been considered male spaces to which a proper woman would not go. However, the Islamic resurgence that has swept the Muslim world since the 1970s, enlisting the active involvement of women, has helped change such attitudes. Most recently constructed mosques provide considerably more space for women than earlier ones. However, the actual spatial arrangement of the architecture reinforces women's marginality to life in the mosque, often isolating them in areas where they cannot see or hear the imam or preacher.

In the pilgrimage to Mecca, on the other hand, the sexes are not segregated, and Islamic law stipulates that women not veil their faces during the pilgrimage. This integration of the sexes also occurs during festivities at saints' shrines, indicating that at the loci of most intense holiness and access to God, one is in a liminal state where gender barriers collapse.

Religious Education for Women. Women have always played a role in the transmission of religious knowledge. The role of ʿĀ'ishah, Muḥammad's youngest wife, as a transmitter of *ḥadīth* was so important that Muḥammad is said to have told the Muslims they would receive half their religion from a woman. Muḥammad himself provided religious lessons for women, although later Muslims often complained that education would be used by women for unholy ends. Literacy was a rare achievement for women in later medieval Muslim society. Throughout Islamic history, some daughters of wealthy families have been favored with a private education in the home. More often, women were excluded from formal education, although women might serve as patrons or even supervisors of educational institutions. The Ḥanbalī jurist Ibn Taymīyah of Syria (d. 1328) lists two women among his teachers, and some female descendants of the Prophet, such as his granddaughter Zaynab and his great-great-great-great-granddaughter Nafīsah, are recognized as women of learning and wisdom, as well as piety. Although schools for girls in subjects such as midwifery, crafts, and housekeeping skills opened in the nineteenth century in many countries, and since independence secular education has been made available to girls as well as to boys throughout most of the Islamic world, religious education has lagged behind. Occasionally, women have become recognized as distinguished religious scholars through their writings alone, without attending institutions of higher Islamic education. ʿĀʾishah ʿAbd al-Raḥmān, the Egyptian Qurʾān exegete, and Khānum-i Amīn, the Iranian *mujtahid,* are examples. As part of Egyptian president Nasser's revamping of the Islamic University of al-Azhar, a College for Girls was opened in 1962, and graduates in the field of religion have been employed as teachers in religion classes in public schools. Al-Azhar began a limited program to train women as preachers in 1988. Women are not generally deemed fit to teach men, so it is assumed that these women are being trained only to serve women's religious needs. In Iran, religious schools in the holy city of Qom were opened to girls in 1976. However, private education and apprenticeship has produced innumerable women who serve as Qurʾān reciters in both Sunnī and Shīʿī communities, and as leaders of women's gatherings to commemorate the martyrdom of the imams among the Shīʿah. [*See also* Education, *article on* Religious Education; *and the biography of* ʿ*Abd al-Raḥmān.*]

Ṣūfī Orders. Mysticism is by definition a sphere that depends more on individual reputation for holiness and receptivity to spiritual impulses than on literacy and institutional certification. It is therefore not surprising to find that Sufism has been more open to women than the more legalistic and scholastic dimensions of Islamic religious life. The most famous Ṣūfī woman is Rābiʿah al-ʿAdawīyah (d. 801), credited with introducing the concept of selfless love into Sufism. Her poems of love for God have inspired mystics to the present day, and Ṣūfī tradition depicts her outwitting her male colleagues. She is listed alongside the men in Farīd al-Dīn ʿAṭṭār's (d. 1220) Ṣūfī biographical dictionary, because "when a woman becomes a 'man' in the path of God, she is a man and one cannot any more call her a woman" (*Muslim Saints and Mystics,* translated by A. J. Arberry, Oxford, 1966, p. 40). Rābiʿah is not unique in Ṣūfī tradition. Javād Nūrbakhsh has translated into English the brief biographies of some 124 Ṣūfī women (*Sufi Women,* New York, 1983), including Fāṭimah of Nisapur (d. 838), who was described by Dhū al-Nūn al-Miṣrī as the highest among the Ṣūfīs of his age. The great mystic Ibn ʿArabī (d. 1240) lists two women among his teachers (*Sufis of Andalusia,* translated by R. W. J. Austin, London, 1971), and claimed that the most perfect contemplation of God for a man is in woman.

In spite of its greater hospitality to female participants, Ṣūfī tradition is not uniform in its praise of women. Al-Ghazālī (d. 1111) scarcely speaks of women in the mystical path except as assets or obstacles to the spiritual life of men. Although Muslim tradition recommends marriage, in imitation of the example of the Prophet, the Ṣūfī al-Hujwīrī (d. about 1071) held celibacy to be the ideal, declaring that all the evils in the world had been caused by women (*The Kashf al-Maḥjūb,* translated by R. A. Nicholson, 2d ed., London, 1976, p. 364).

Celibacy and rigorous fasting were practiced by many early Ṣūfīs. In addition to aiding in the training of the soul and spiritual concentration, these may have been tools for women to avoid ritual impurity—refusing intercourse and childbirth through celibacy, preventing menstruation by fasting—and thereby guarantee uninterrupted access to God (Jamal Elias, "Female and Feminine in Islamic Mysticism," *Muslim World* 78 [1988]: 210–211).

Ṣūfī shaykhs were the most effective religious teachers in Muslim society and often served as popular counselors and healers, so it is not surprising that they touched the feminine world more than the mosque-centered sphere of religious scholars. Some Ṣūfī shaykhs in the Mamlūk and Ottoman periods admitted women into their orders, although their participation in the orders and in *dhikr,* the distinctive Ṣūfī ritual of chanting the names of God with special breath control and movement, was controversial. Women sometimes founded Ṣūfī retreat houses for men as a pious act. Annemarie Schimmel documents an Anatolian woman of the late fourteenth century who was head of a Ṣūfī retreat center with male disciples ("Women in Mystical Islam," *Women's Studies International Forum* 5 [1982]: 148). A Ṣūfī retreat house for women was established in Cairo in Mamlūk times in honor of a prominent woman Ṣūfī, Zaynab Fāṭimah bint ʿAbbās (late thirteenth–early fourteenth century), and according to Ibn Ḥajar al-ʿAsqalānī, there were women shaykhhs and scholars of the Law, most of them divorcees, who lived in extreme abstinence and worship in Ṣūfī hospices. In contrast to early Sufism, it seems that in the later medieval period only women who had already completed their duty of marriage were free to devote themselves to the mystical life.

Moroccan and Algerian orders frequently have women's auxiliaries with female leadership, and in many countries women's organizations with female leadership complement those of men. In contemporary Egypt, however, concerns with propriety in the face of reformist criticisms of Sufism have led to the official banning of female membership by the Supreme Council of Ṣūfī Orders, a government-sponsored body. Women nonetheless continue to participate in all aspects of life in many Egyptian Ṣūfī orders. Some women become recognized as "spiritual mothers" to both men and women, or as heirs of the "spiritual secrets" of their fathers who were shaykhs. In this latter case, the official position of shaykh is inherited by the deceased's eldest son, although actual spiritual leadership may be exercised by the daughter. In some Egyptian orders, women participate in *dhikr* on a par with men, but in many orders, and in society at large, it is considered improper for a woman to expose herself by rising to join a *dhikr*. Women who do so often shroud their faces, but more often women participate silently, sitting among the observers. When women do participate in *dhikr*, they are rarely as vocal as men, and use smaller, more contained movements. This is in marked contrast to Shīʿī commemorative assemblies in Iran, in which the women are said to be more emotionally expressive than the men (Anne H. Betteridge, "The Controversial Vows of Urban Muslim Women in Iran," in *Unspoken Worlds*, San Francisco, 1980, pp. 141–155). Women seem to be caught between competing social norms which say, on the one hand, that they are more emotional than men and, on the other hand, dictate that they suppress all public displays of emotion.

In Egypt, and probably in other places as well, some Ṣūfīs believe that once they have entered into the spirit, they may transcend the barriers of the flesh; "male" and "female" become meaningless categories. Ṣūfīs in such a state may exercise freedom in interpersonal relations between the sexes, a sanction considered shocking to the society at large. Ṣūfīs are sometimes criticized as immoral for the way in which men and women mingle at their ceremonies, and women sometimes avoid saints' day celebrations because of the dangers presented to their modesty by the dense crowds.

Saints and Spirits. Whereas ordinary mosques are usually regarded as male spaces, saints' shrines are traditionally open to women. Saints are men and women who are popularly recognized as *walīs* ("friends of God"). They are believed to be able to intercede with God on behalf of the faithful, and miracles occur at their hands. After their deaths, their tombs or alleged tombs become shrines and places of refuge for their devotees and other troubled individuals. Because they are, in some sense, champions of the downtrodden, and because the rituals surrounding their cult require no education, women are frequent visitors to their shrines, where they feel themselves able to plead with the saints on a par with men. Fatima Mernissi wrote that saints' shrines in Morocco are more like a social space for women than a religious space where prayers are made, and that male visitors may feel like intruders ("Women, Saints, and Sanctuaries," *Signs: Journal of Women in Society and Culture* 3 [1977]: 101–112). This is not the case in Egypt, where shrines are definitely sacred space in which it is considered appropriate to pray, and where women are seldom in the majority. Women are indeed very much in evidence (even in the small towns of Upper (southern) Egypt, where women are kept veiled and secluded, they might feel free to sit in the vicinity of the tomb, nursing their babies), but in some shrines special rooms are designated for women to prevent them from sitting by the tomb. The country's most important shrine of all, that of the Prophet's grandson Ḥusayn, does not allow women to enter after sunset.

Some shrines cater specifically to women's needs, such as fertility. In India, some Muslim saints' shrines are designated as women's shrines, while others are for men. In Iran and Iraq, Shīʿī women visiting the tombs of the martyred imams acquire a prestige similar to those performing the pilgrimage. The great saints' day festivals (*mawlids*) that commemorate particular saints, usually on the anniversary of their death, form the major focus of Ṣūfī devotion in Egypt, as Ṣūfīs travel from one such festival to another, setting up hospitality stations and performing *dhikr*. During the *mawlid* of Sayyid Aḥmad al-Badawī in Tanta, in the Egyptian Delta, the entire floor of the vast mosque associated with his shrine is transformed into a campground inhabited by a dense crowd of men, women, and children, without any segregation of the sexes. The activities at saints' shrines are a popular target of reformist criticism, and frequently the presence of women is deemed inappropriate, both for considerations of modesty and because the Prophet allegedly prohibited women from visiting tombs. The practice of saint shrine veneration has its defenders, however, who rely on the same type of scriptural sources used by its critics. Regardless of this criticism, the visitation of saints' shrines has formed an essential component of the religious lives of women all over the Muslim world. [*See also* Shrines; Mawlid.]

Women in many countries participate in spirit possession cults such as the *zār* of North and East Africa and the *bori* of West Africa. These cults are based on the assumption that both physical and emotional illness may be caused by spirits, whose anger must be appeased through the hosting of a feast and the performance of dances peculiar to the spirit in question. They often have both male and female functionaries, and the power and wealth of the "priestesses" may be considerable. While the cults are non-Islamic in origin, the scripturally endorsed belief in spirits and their effects on humans make Islam a hospitable environment for the introduction and spread of such cults. Public *zārs* in Egypt utilize male musical troupes singing praises to the Prophet in Ṣūfī style, and some of the spirits are those of great Muslim saints. Women *zār* musicians use a more African beat. Public criticism of the *zār* cult in Egypt has been vociferous enough that even illiterate women are aware of it.

Twentieth-century Developments. Religious reformers of all types have criticized the saint cult as idolatrous and the spirit cults as un-Islamic. The hue of illegitimacy has been cast over the very aspects of Islamic religious life that have traditionally been most open to women. In his book, *The Emancipation of Women* (1899), the Egyptian judge Qāsim Amīn (d. 1908) urged that women be educated in order to dispel the myths and superstitions they supposedly perpetuate among the young, and the Syrian-born writer Rashīd Riḍā (d. 1935) urged in his journal, *Al-manār*, that women be integrated into orthodox religious life, as they were in the days of the Prophet. Throughout the twentieth century, independently founded Islamic voluntary associations have assumed the task of providing religious education for women, in addition to offering courses in literacy and crafts. The Muslim Brotherhood, founded in 1928 by Ḥasan al-Bannā' in Egypt, had a women's auxiliary, the Muslim Sisters, which never succeeded on the level of its male counterpart. Zaynab al-Ghazālī founded the Muslim Women's Association in 1936 as an Islamic response to the Egyptian Feminist Union. [*See the biography of Ghazālī.*] Today there are approximately fourteen thousand Islamic voluntary associations in Egypt, and many of them offer religious classes for women. In addition, many government-operated mosques offer religious lessons to women. In many cases, the teachers are themselves women, although male instructors continue to predominate.

The university-centered Islamist movement that has swept the Muslim world since the 1970s has garnered the support of many women as participants and propagandists. Women in the movement wear Islamic dress, a loose-fitting garment that covers the entire body except the face and hands. Although Islamic dress was an anomaly when it appeared in the early 1970s, by 1980 it became the uniform of the aggressively religious woman. The women who wear this dress are usually well educated, often in the most prestigious university faculties of medicine, engineering, and the sciences, and their dress signifies that although they pursue an education and career in the public sphere, they are religious, moral women. Whereas other women are frequently harassed in public places, such women are honored and even feared. By the late 1980s, Islamic dress had become the norm for middle-class women who do not want to compromise their reputation by their public activities. Boutiques offer Parisian-style fashions adapted to Islamic modesty standards, thereby subverting somewhat the original intent of the movement. [*See* Dress.]

Despite the high visibility of female participation in the Islamist movement throughout the Muslim world, it espouses a conservative ideology regarding women's social roles, idealizing their importance as mothers and stressing allegedly innate gender differences that make work outside the home unsuitable for women. This rhetoric, both incorporatist and exclusionary, may appeal to women who are doubly burdened when they take on jobs outside the home, perhaps out of economic necessity, and feel degraded by their "public" conditions. The Islamic movement also encourages women to struggle on behalf of Islam as their counterparts did in early Islam. The contradictory rhetoric of the Islamic movement has been particularly effective in Iran, where women have been incorporated into a nationalist movement through symbolic appeals to female purity, while at the same time employment and educational opportunities for women have been somewhat curtailed since the Revolution and modesty norms have been strictly enforced. Although the rank-and-file of the Islamic movement includes many women, its leadership remains largely male. Zaynab al-Ghazālī of Egypt is one of the few women to attain prominence as an Islamic activist.

BIBLIOGRAPHY

Azari, Farah, ed. *Women of Iran: The Conflict with Fundamentalist Islam.* London, 1983. Provocative set of articles by Iranian Muslims critical of the Islamic regime as oppressive to women.

Bellhassen, Souhayr. "Femmes tunisiennes islamistes." *Annuaire de l'Afrique du Nord, 1979,* pp. 77–94. Paris, 1980. One of the few studies that includes interviews with ordinary women participating in an Islamic movement.

Berkey, Jonathan P. "Women and Islamic Education in the Mamluk Period." In *Women in Middle Eastern History: Shifting Boundaries in Sex and Gender,* edited by Nikki R. Keddie and Beth Baron, pp. 143–157. New Haven and London, 1991.

Clancy-Smith, Julia. "The House of Zainab: Female Authority and Saintly Succession." In *Women in Middle Eastern History: Shifting Boundaries in Sex and Gender,* edited by Nikki R. Keddie and Beth Baron, pp. 254–274. New Haven and London, 1991. On a woman who became a Ṣūfī shaykh in colonial Algeria.

Dwyer, Daisy Hilse. "Women, Sufism, and Decision-Making in Moroccan Islam." In *Women in the Muslim World,* edited by Lois Beck and Nikki R. Keddie, pp. 585–598. Cambridge, Mass., 1978. Information on women's auxiliaries in the Ṣūfī orders, and the influence wives have on the affiliation of their husbands with particular orders.

El Guindi, Fadwa. "The Emerging Islamic Order: The Case of Egypt's Contemporary Islamic Movement." *Journal of Arab Affairs* 1 (1981): 245–261. Reprinted in *Political Behavior in the Arab States,* edited by Tawfic E. Farah, pp. 55–66. Boulder, 1983.

Fernea, Elizabeth W., and Robert A. Fernea. "Variation in Religious Observance among Islamic Women." In *Scholars, Saints, and Sufis: Muslim Religious Institutions since 1500,* edited by Nikki R. Keddie, pp. 385–401. Berkeley, 1972.

Friedl, Erika. "Islam and Tribal Women in a Village in Iran." In *Unspoken Worlds: Women's Religious Lives in Non-Western Cultures,* edited by Nancy E. Auer Falk and Rita M. Gross, pp. 159–173. San Francisco, 1980.

Haeri, Shahla. "Obedience vs. Autonomy: Women and Fundamentalism in Iran and Pakistan." In *Fundamentalisms and Society: Reclaiming the Sciences, the Family, and Education,* edited by Martin E. Marty and R. Scott Appleby, pp. 181–213. Chicago, 1993. Rare comparative essay on the presentation of women by Islamic activists in two different countries, one Shīʿī and one Sunnī. Particularly good regarding the use of important early female figures as models of courage and heroism in Iran.

Hoffman-Ladd, Valerie J. "Polemics on the Modesty and Segregation of Women in Contemporary Egypt." *International Journal of Middle East Studies* 19.1 (February 1987): 23–50. Discussion of Islamist perspectives on women's participation in public life.

Hoffman-Ladd, Valerie J. "Mysticism and Sexuality in Sufi Thought and Life." *Mystics Quarterly* 18 (1992): 82–93. Women and sexuality in early and medieval Sufism, highlighting the writings of Ibn ʿArabī.

Hoffman-Ladd, Valerie J. *Sufism, Mystics, and Saints in Modern Egypt.* Columbia, S.C., forthcoming. Includes a chapter on women and sexuality in the Ṣūfī orders of Egypt.

Lewis, I. M. "The Past and Present in Islam: The Case of African 'Survivals.' " *Temenos* 19 (1983): 55–67. Study of the *zār* and *bori* spirit possession cults, making a good case for their compatibility with Islam.

Macleod, Arlene Elowe. *Accommodating Protest: Working Women, the New Veiling, and Change in Cairo.* New York, 1991. Excellent study of the social milieu of the lower middle class in Cairo that leads ordinary women to don Islamic dress.

Nelson, Cynthia. "Self, Spirit Possession, and World View: An Illustration from Egypt." *International Journal of Social Psychiatry* 17 (1971): 194–209. On the *zār* in Egypt.

Rosen, Lawrence. "The Negotiation of Reality: Male-Female Relations in Sefrou, Morocco." In *Women in the Muslim World,* edited by Lois Beck and Nikki R. Keddie, pp. 561–584. Cambridge, Mass., 1978.

Saunders, Lucie Wood. "Variants in *Zār* Experience in an Egyptian Village." In *Case Studies in Spirit Possession,* edited by Vincent Crapanzano and Vivian Garrison, pp. 177–193. New York, 1977.

Schimmel, Annemarie. *Mystical Dimensions of Islam.* Chapel Hill, N.C., 1975. See Appendix II, "The Feminine Element in Sufism."

Sharīʿatī, ʿAlī. *Fatima Is Fatima.* Translated by Laleh Bakhtiar. Tehran, 1981. Important revisionist interpretation of women's role in society, by the man who inspired many young Iranian intellectuals to seek an Islamically oriented society in the decade before the revolution.

Smith, Jane I., and Yvonne Yazbeck Haddad. "Women in the Afterlife: The Islamic View as Seen from Qur'an and Tradition." *Journal of the American Academy of Religion* 43 (1975): 39–50.

Tabari, Azar, and Nahid Yeganeh, eds. *In the Shadow of Islam: The Women's Movement in Iran.* London, 1982. Collection of translations from a variety of primary sources relevant to the status of women and feminism in the Islamic Republic of Iran.

Winter, Michael. *Society and Religion in Early Ottoman Egypt: Studies in the Writings of ʿAbd al-Wahhāb al-Shaʿrānī.* New Brunswick, N.J., 1982. Contains interesting information on the participation of women in the Ṣūfī orders in Mamlūk and Ottoman Egypt.

Zuhur, Sherifa. *Revealing Reveiling: Islamist Gender Ideology in Contemporary Egypt.* Albany, N.Y., 1992. Comparison of the opinions of women inside and outside the Islamic movement on the meaning of veiling and being religious, within the context both of Islamic paradigms and Egyptian feminism.

VALERIE J. HOFFMAN-LADD

WOMEN AND SOCIAL REFORM. [*This entry comprises five articles:*

An Overview
Social Reform in the Middle East
Social Reform in North Africa
Social Reform in South Asia
Social Reform in Southeast Asia

The introductory article provides an overview of modern legal and social reform in Muslim community life that has particularly affected women; the companion articles focus on social reform in four principal areas of the Islamic world. For related discussions, see Feminism; Women and Islam.]

An Overview

In Muslim countries, the role of women is central to three interrelated, unresolved issues: the search for identity in postcolonial societies, the role of religion in the modern state, and the role of the state itself. Consequently, with few exceptions, reforms since the nineteenth century have not radically altered women's legal status, although there have been some far-reaching changes in their social and economic status.

Postcolonialism and the Search for Identity. In seeking to forge a modern indigenous identity, Muslims generally fall into two camps: liberal reformers, who believe that combining Islamic tradition with European liberalism is the most effective way to challenge Western power; and conservatives, who contend that change will subvert social structures, thereby easing Western domination. Both camps view women as the key to reforming or conserving tradition, because of their roles in maintaining family size, continuity, and culture.

Both liberal and conservative positions were forged in response to early attempts at modernization in the Muslim world. The Ottoman administrative reforms, or Tanzimat, of 1839–1876, included some legislation redressing gender inequities, in particular, the 1858 Land Law, which covered women's inheritance rights. The legislation was crafted in the context of a debate about extending women's roles beyond home-based activity, and that same year the first secondary school for girls was opened.

The Tanzimat reforms were made by a seriously weakened empire under the influence of the British. Many Ottoman Turks, for example, the writers İbrahim Şinasi and Namık Kemal, criticized Western interference in the Tanzimat. At the same time, these critics, representing the burgeoning liberal camp, supported reform in women's conditions, and sought a synthesis of European notions of progress and Islam, rather than outright rejection of Western ideas (see Kandiyoti, 1991).

Similarly, in the Arab world, nineteenth-century reformers such as Rifāʿah al-Ṭahṭāwī argued that education and labor participation should be open to women, as did Muḥammad ʿAbduh, who served as *muftī* of Egypt. ʿAbduh's disciple Qāsim Amīn was the first Arab to publish a call for women's emancipation, in his book *Taḥrīr al-mar'ah* (The Liberation of Women). The book caused an uproar when it appeared in 1899, although the arguments were carefully phrased within the framework of Islam. Were he to visit the Muslim world today, Qāsim Amīn would be surprised to find many of the same debates still raging.

A forceful example of the conservative argument may be found in an article written by a Lebanese Muslim woman, Mona Fayyād Kawtharānī, in the 31 March 1985 edition of the newspaper *Al-safīr*. Noting that the Iranian Revolution of 1979 had been marked by the widespread participation of women using the veil, Kawtharānī argued that the veil constituted a weapon of resistance to the West. Highly critical of Western intrusions on indigenous cultures, she went on to claim that the West had found the "best way to control us was by destroying our cultural and religious beliefs, so that the believer came to be defined as a 'fanatic.' And this was done to enable the West to invade our lands and to penetrate with its consumer commodities, to transform our countries into markets. This led to political and economic dependency and to loss of cultural identity, which was replaced by 'modernisation.' The Easterner would not buy these diverse commodities—clothes, cars, electrical appliances, processed foods, furniture, etc.—unless he was convinced that he was in need of a culture other than his own, and that this culture represented 'modernity' whereas his own represented backwardness" (quoted in Hijab, 1988, p. 55).

The Iranian Revolution of 1979, which replaced a westernizing regime with one based on Islamic fundamentalist teaching, gave impetus to many explorations by Muslims, Sunnī and Shīʿī alike, into the question of what constitutes an "authentic" Islamic identity. In Iran, the two decades before the overthrow of Pahlavi rule were marked by the politicization of Islam as well as the islamization of secular politics. Afsaneh Najmabadi notes that a central theme in this process was that of *gharbzadah,* or "westoxication" (see Najmabadi, "Hazards of Modernity and Morality," in Kandiyoti, 1991). For both intellectuals and the masses, this process of "westoxication" was symbolized by the westernized woman, depicted as a consumer of Western goods and corrupt social morals. After the revolution, Iran was declared an Islamic republic, and its rulers decreed a very conservative interpretation of Islamic law and behavior. They imposed the veil, defined women's primary roles as wife and mother, and forbade women to serve as judges.

Although other Muslim countries did not carry the islamization of gender roles to such an extreme, their efforts to define a national identity have had profound repercussions on women's status. This is well illustrated by Algeria, where for 132 years French colonial rulers imposed extremely repressive measures against indigenous cultures. As part of their war of liberation, the Algerians adhered closely to Islam and Islam-based traditions to preserve their cultural identity. After liberation in 1962, all citizens, men and women, received full civil rights, including the right to vote and to run for political office. Algeria was defined as an Arab-Islamic country.

However, the question of the relation of Arab-Islamic identity to family structure and the role of women remained unresolved for over two decades. A conservative interpretation of Islamic law would make women perpetual legal minors needing the approval of a husband or other male guardian to work or travel. A liberal interpretation of Islamic law, as Tunisia had achieved, could threaten the "Arab-Islamic" identity that Algerians had fought to preserve.

In the early 1980s, women actively demonstrated against government attempts to settle the issue without their participation, prompting a debate in parliament and the press over the status and rights of women. Those supporting a liberal family code used the familiar arguments of the Ottoman Turks and Arabs. As the government newspaper *El moudjahid* put it in a 1983 editorial, "To want, in the name of Islam, to push an important part of the population out of the production process is to ignore the realities of today."

A family code was finally adopted by the National Assembly in May 1984, reflecting a very uneasy balance between liberalism and conservatism. The code's provisions are similar to those in many other Muslim countries. For instance, a marriage must be registered and both sides may insert any stipulations into the contract. A man may divorce at will, whereas a woman must apply for divorce by claiming nonmaintenance, infirmity, sexual neglect, imprisonment, absence, prejudice, or immorality on the part of the husband. Polygyny was restricted according to the limits of the *sharīʿah:* a husband must justify his desire or need for another wife, inform his first wife of his intentions, and ensure equal treatment for wives, while a woman was granted the right to divorce if she objected to the polygynous arrangement. Women may retain custody of children in case of divorce, keeping boys to age ten (which could be extended to sixteen) and girls until marriage.

Role of Religion in the Modern State. The debate on the laws affecting family life and the role of women within the family provides a rare opportunity for Muslim countries to examine the role of religion in the modern state. In most Muslim countries, Islam has been declared the state religion and the main, if not sole, source of law. In practice, this applies to personal status codes in most countries, since commercial or penal codes have been based directly on Western models. Separation of mosque and state is not widely discussed. Rather, most people strive to prove that European concepts of equality and citizenship can be achieved within the framework of Islam.

It was the status of women that led Turkey to embrace secularism. The founder of modern Turkey, Mustafa Kemal Atatürk, made a brief attempt to adapt Islamic law to the requirements of modernity, establishing a committee assigned with such a task in 1923. However, when the committee was unable to provide equal rights for women within the framework of Islamic law, Atatürk effected a complete break, and in 1926 Turkey's civil code was modeled on the Swiss civil code.

The major problem that faced this Turkish committee, as well as reformers before and since, has been that the Qur'ān has much to say about the roles of men and women in family and society, forcing the choice between a complete break, like Atatürk, or a compromise on women's equal rights. For example, when Egypt signed the United Nations Convention on the Elimination of All Forms of Discrimination Against Women in 1985, the government stated that "the equality of men and women in all matters relating to marriage and family relations during marriage and upon its dissolution . . . must be without prejudice to the Islamic Sharia provisions whereby women are accorded rights equivalent to those of their spouses so as to ensure a just balance between them. This is out of respect for the sanctity deriving from firm religious beliefs which govern marital relations in Egypt and which may not be called into question" (quoted in Hijab, pp. 4–5). Thus, while women have equal rights in the public sphere, they have "equivalent" rights in the private domain.

All Arab countries that have personal status codes base these on liberal or conservative interpretations of Islamic law. Of the Arab countries, Tunisia comes closest to achieving modern notions of equality within an Islamic framework, completely banning polygyny and allowing for equal rights in all spheres except inheritance, deferring here to the Qur'ān, which is specific on the share allotted each family member (sisters inherit half the share of brothers). Interestingly, while nationalism was at its height during the liberation struggle against the French Protectorate, Tunisian leader Habib Bourguiba refused even to consider such changes in women's status as removing the veil. At a nationalist meeting in 1929, he declared, "Is it in our interests to hasten, without caring for any transitions, the disappearance of our ways, of our customs, bad or good, and of all those little nothings which as a whole—whatever one might say—constitute our personality? My answer, given the very special circumstances in which we live, is categorical: NO!" (see Salem, "Islam and the Status of Women in Tunisia," in Hussain, 1984). Nonetheless, immediately after liberation in 1956, Bourguiba reversed his position and campaigned for a new code, giving among his reasons the need for a rational effort at adjustment to Islam.

The diversity of Muslim personal status codes reflects the continuous effort given over to interpreting and reinterpreting Islam, in effect seeking to shape the extent of its role in the modern state. Women have tried to capitalize on this diversity in arguing for more flexible interpretations of Islamic law and custom. For example, in 1982, when the Kuwaiti National Assembly was due to debate a personal status code, the Kuwaiti lawyer Badrīyah al-ʿAwaḍī published a comparative study of Arab and Islamic family law. She hoped that participants in the debate (all men) would review other, more liberal, laws before finalizing the Kuwaiti draft. However, when the law was passed in 1984, the amendments proposed by women's groups were largely ignored.

Bangladesh is one of the Muslim countries where the question of religion vis-à-vis secularism as the basis of the state has been most openly debated. Islam was the *raison d'être* behind the creation of the Pakistani state, partitioned from India in 1947. However, the attempts by the West Pakistanis to dominate the East Pakistanis politically and culturally led to war, and East Pakistan became Bangladesh in 1971. As a result, for Bangladesh, Islam was no longer the sole determining factor for the existence of the state, and secularism provided the basis for the 1972 constitution. Indeed, the East's resistance to West Pakistan had included emphasizing the Hindu part of their culture.

In the 1980s, there were moves toward islamization by Bangladeshi governments seeking support from fundamentalists, but the opposition was vocal in warning of the dangers of communal strife in a religiously based state. Women took the lead in opposing the government's Eighth Amendment in 1988, which declared Islam the state religion, brandishing the slogan "Religion is a personal choice. Keep politics out of religion" (see Kabeer, 1989). There were no sustained attempts to control women's behavior and dress.

Role of the State. In the postcolonial period, the governments of Muslim nation-states have been under notice to deliver economic growth and prosperity to their citizens. Although most constitutions declare citizens equal in rights, obligations, and opportunities, modern nation-building has centralized political power and economic decision making in governments headed by a small number of decision makers.

Although schools proliferated and education was accepted as a right and a necessity for girls as well as boys, success in building a skilled, literate population has eluded most developing countries. This has been particularly true for countries with large and rapidly growing populations such as Bangladesh and Pakistan, where illiteracy, especially among women, remains very high. In these two countries, the percentage of girls enrolled in primary and secondary schools stood at 29 percent and 17 percent respectively in the mid-1980s; the rates rise to 90 percent in countries with smaller populations, like Jordan (see United Nations, 1989).

The critical failure of most developing nations has been in creating sustainable economic growth. Concern for men's jobs gives added incentive to the conservative call for women to adhere to traditional roles as housewives and mothers. As the number of educated women working outside the home increases, the rhetoric of family preservationism intensifies. Moreover, the Muslim concept of society privileges the communal over the individualistic; society is not made up of individual men and women, but rather members of a community. Both sexes and different age groups are therefore expected to relinquish some rights and assume certain responsibilities to forge a coherent community.

Yet these concerns are overwhelmed by sheer economic necessity, which forces women to undertake whatever work they can find, usually low-paid unskilled labor. War and labor migration increase the number of female-headed households, now on the rise and ranging in the 1980s from around 16 percent of households in Bangladesh and Morocco to around 10 percent in Tunisia and Turkey. Among the middle classes, even in some of the oil-rich countries, the high cost of living necessitates a two-income family, regardless of the idealized image of women as wives and mothers.

In spite of their inability or unwillingness to legislate equal rights within the family, Muslim states are interventionist on family matters when the need arises. For example, Iran ignored its own rhetoric on women's roles during the war with Iraq, when it needed to mobilize women to replace men fighting on the front. States also intervene on such issues as family planning to avoid economic catastrophe. A liberal interpretation of Islam is drawn upon to demonstrate that family planning is not in conflict with religious values, and to combat the traditional preference for large families as a source of security and labor. On the other hand, states whose populations have been devastated by war have implemented pro-natalist policies, such as Iraq after its war first with Iran and then with Kuwait. In this case, the state reversed its policy of integrating women into economic development so as to rebuild the population base and reemploy men returning from the front.

The inability of Muslim nation-states to deliver goods and services to their citizens is a primary factor behind the present-day strength of fundamentalism throughout the Muslim world. Other equally potent factors are the extent to which the Muslim world still experiences de facto if not de jure forms of colonialization at the hands of an economically and culturally dominant West, and the state repression of secular and political opposition. In a sense, fundamentalist groups have coopted the high moral ground for independent development which formerly had been occupied by nationalists in their struggle against the colonizers.

The strength of fundamentalists, and the close links between nationalism, cultural identity, and religion, force liberals to articulate an agenda of political and social reform that includes equal rights for women within an Islamic framework, so as not to be accused of betraying their origins. Given the implications for their legal status, Muslim women may begin to call for a reexamination of this framework in order to achieve equality both within the family and as citizens of the nation-state. Education and employment opportunities outside the home-based subsistence economy have created an impressive and articulate community of women laying claim to such an endeavor.

BIBLIOGRAPHY

Abadan-Unat, Nermin, ed. *Women in Turkish Society*. Leiden, 1981.

Altorki, Soraya, and Camillia Fawzi El-Solh, eds. *Arab Women in the Field: Studying Your Own Society*. Syracuse, N.Y., 1988.

Atiya, Nayra. *Khul-Khaal: Five Egyptian Women Tell Their Stories*. London, 1988.

Beck, Lois, and Nikki R. Keddie, eds. *Women in the Muslim World*. Cambridge, Mass., 1978.

Fathi, Asghar, ed. *Women and the Family in Iran*. Leiden, 1985.

Fernea, Elizabeth W., ed. *Women and the Family in the Middle East: New Voices of Change*. Austin, 1985.

Fernea, Elizabeth W., and Basima Qattan Bezirgan, eds. *Middle Eastern Muslim Women Speak*. Austin, 1977.

Hijab, Nadia. *Womanpower: The Arab Debate on Women at Work*. Cambridge, 1988.

Hussain, Freda, ed. *Muslim Women*. London, 1984.

Kabeer, Naila. *The Quest for National Identity: Women, Islam, and the State in Bangladesh*. Sussex, 1989. See also Kabeer's essay in the Kandiyoti collection below.

Kandiyoti, Deniz, ed. *Women, Islam, and the State*. Philadelphia, 1991.

Mernissi, Fatima. *Beyond the Veil: Male-Female Dynamics in Modern Muslim Society*. Rev. ed. Bloomington, 1987.

Mernissi, Fatima. *Doing Daily Battle: Interviews with Moroccan Women*. Translated by Mary Jo Lakeland. New Brunswick, N.J., 1989.

Mumtaz, Khawar, and Farida Shaheed. *Women of Pakistan: Two Steps Forward, One Step Back?* London, 1987.

Saʿdāwī, Nawāl al-. *The Hidden Face of Eve: Women in the Arab World*. Translated by Sherif Hetata. London, 1980.

Shaʿrāwī, Hūdā. *Harem Years: The Memoirs of an Egyptian Feminist*. Translated and introduced by Margot Badran. London, 1986.

Smith, Jane I., ed. *Women in Contemporary Muslim Societies*. London, 1980.

Tabari, Azar, and Nahid Yeganeh, eds. *In the Shadow of Islam: The Women's Movement in Iran*. London, 1982.

World Survey on the Role of Women in Development, 1989. Vienna, 1990.

NADIA HIJAB

Social Reform in the Middle East

The general inability of the modern Arab nation-states to fulfill promises of political and economic progress, coupled with a widespread perception of deteriorating public morality, in recent decades have rekindled the historical conflict between the political and religious orders: between an Islamic state (presumably modeled after the original Islamic order) and a modern secular state (Riesebrodt, 1993), or between nationalism and utopian Islamic universalism (based on the concept of the *ummah*). The historical disputes over the legitimacy of the political order and the identity of an Islamic state became an apparently irreconcilable political and ideological conflict in the 1980s and early 1990s, exemplified by the Iranian Islamic revolution of 1979. The duel crises of legitimacy and identity underscore the fiercely competing religious and secular political discourses ("reformists," modernists," "traditionalists," and "Islamists") vying for power, political constituencies, and ultimately the sociomoral direction of society.

This essay briefly sketches some general patterns of legal reforms in family law and the status of Muslim Middle Eastern women in that context. The mounting friction between the state and religion has made many of the states politically unstable, thus rendering family legal reforms subject to periodic revision.

As part of the process of nation-building and secularization, most Middle Eastern states, with the exception of the Gulf states and Saudi Arabia, initiated legal reforms in the 1950s and 1960s timidly, only to come under strong criticism by Islamists in the late 1970s and 1980s. Central to the tension between the Islamists and the secularist states is the issue of women's status and family law. Taking a literal approach to Islamic law (*sharīʿah*), the Islamists believe its laws to be divine, unchanging, and fundamental to maintaining a distinctly Islamic way of life. They view family legal reforms as deviating from Islamic law and inspired by the West.

With the exception of Turkey, the secularist states maintained an Islamic rationale while attempting to reform family laws. The conflict over the proper Islamic approach to the role and status of women and family in the public and private domains has been particularly intense during the past two decades. Muslim women have gained access to education and employment, exercised their limited legal rights, and participated in the economic and political life of their countries.

Marriage. In Islam, marriage (*nikāḥ*) is an exchange contract (*ʿaqd*) between unequal partners, involving a complex set of marital rights and reciprocal obligations. On the basis of the currently controversial Qur'ānic verse 4.3, traditional Islamic law gives Muslim men the right to marry up to four wives simultaneously. Shīʿī men may further contract an unlimited number of temporary marriages (*mutʿah*), legitimated in their view by the Qur'ān (4.24) (following the second caliph's ban on temporary marriage in the seventh century, the Sunnīs reject this practice). The legal possibility of polygyny is an element of insecurity in Islamic marriage.

Conditions not contrary to the essence of Muslim marriage (e.g., that the husband divorce a former wife) may be added to the marriage contract to safeguard the rights of the wife. To reform Islamic marriage and divorce, Middle Eastern secular legislatures have adopted the form and rationale of a contract.

The overall objective of reforms in traditional Islamic family law has been to accommodate Muslim women within a religiously and culturally relevant context. Except for Turkey, Middle Eastern states have incorporated aspects of the *sharīʿah* in all the changes they have made in family law. Legal reforms affecting marriage are essentially variations on the same theme. They tend to restrict the husband's right to plural marriages by making that conditional not on the wife's consent but on the court's permission. The first wife's consent, though relevant, is not essential (Anderson, 1971, p. 24). Muslim women are faced with an unenviable choice: either to give their consent for a new marriage contract or to sue for divorce.

As an endemic problem in many Muslim societies, child marriage has been discouraged by raising the minimum age for marriage for both boys and girls. Generally it stands at eighteen for boys, but for girls it varies from fifteen in Kuwait to sixteen in Egypt, seventeen in Jordan and Syria, and eighteen in Iraq. Abolishing the Iranian Family Protection Law of 1975, the Islamic Republic of Iran returned to the Shīʿī minimum marriage age of fifteen for boys and nine for girls (New Civil Law, clause 1041). In all these cases, the age restrictions may be waived at the discretion of a judge.

In a few Middle Eastern states the reformers made minimal and conditional provisions for women's maintenance after divorce, while leaving the wrenching issue of custody of children—religiously and legally a father's prerogative—generally unchanged (Anderson, 1971, p. 25). Legal reforms in the Middle East share many similarities, but the success of their actual implementation has not been uniform. Depending on their sociopolitical strength, economic resources, and relationship with the clergy, states have pursued different strategies (Nasir 1990, pp. 119–136). On the whole, however, implementation has been impeded as much by the ineffectiveness of secular states as by the objections of the clergy.

Divorce. "Of all things permissible, divorce *(ṭalāq)* is the most reprehensible," states a popular saying attributed to prophet Muḥammad. Nonetheless, Islamic law does grant the unilateral right of divorce to the husband (Qur'ān, 2.226–237; 65.1). In attempting legal reforms, many Middle Eastern states have preserved unchallenged the right of the man to repudiate his wife, while allowing greater latitude for women seeking divorce in cases of cruelty, failure to be provided for, and abandonment (Anderson, 1971, p. 22). Potentially, the most threatening issues facing a married Muslim woman are a unilateral and capricious divorce and an absence of alimony beyond the three months' waiting period *(ʿiddah)* following divorce.

A divorce may take several forms; the most common is the revocable divorce. A revocable *(rajīʿ;* literally "returnable") divorce is semifinal: the bonds of marriage are not completely severed. Although the husband and wife may physically separate, he has the unilateral right to return to his wife during the three months of her waiting period and to resume his marital duties. The wife's consent is not bought, and she cannot remarry within the same period. Parallel to his right of return, she has the right to financial support (Schacht, 1964). Islamic law grants a repentant husband the right to return to his wife and revoke the divorce twice; but after the third divorce he can no longer do so, for this last divorce becomes irrevocable (Qur'ān, 2.229). Traditionally, Sunnī *sharīʿah* permitted the single pronouncement of a triple "I divorce thee," but in states such as Egypt, Syria, and Kuwait such triple divorce is null and is counted as only one (Nasir, 1990, p. 76). Shīʿī law prohibits the triple pronouncement of repudiation altogether (Anderson, 1971; Esposito, 1982).

An irrevocable *(bā'in)* divorce occurs when the dissolution of marriage is final from the moment of pronouncement. In this form of divorce the husband's right to return and the wife's right to maintenance are both curtailed. The woman, however, has to maintain her three months' sexual abstinence (Nasir, 1990, p. 77).

On specific grounds (e.g., absence of maintenance) Muslim women can apply for divorce, recognized as divorce of *khulʿ* (Qur'ān, 2.229). A fundamental difference, however, exists between *khulʿ* and divorce. Divorce is a unilateral *(īqāʿ)* act in which the wife's consent is not necessary, whereas *khulʿ* is a contract to which the husband must agree. If he refuses to cooperate, it is very difficult for a woman to use this option. Under this provision, women are obliged not only to forgo their brideprice and the three months' alimony, but also to pay some consideration to "ransom" their freedom (Nasir, 1990, pp. 78–81).

Legal Reforms. The rate of legal and political reforms accelerated in the 1950s, 1960s, and 1970s, when most of the Muslim states seem to have been at their reformist peak. The changes aimed at loosening the political, economic, and moral hold that the religious establishment had for centuries enjoyed over the domestic domain. The family legal reforms led to politicization and mobilization of the clergy in the 1970s and 1980s. Despite the clergy's opposition, with the exception of Iran these laws are still formally on the books.

The Ottoman Law of Family Rights of 1917 set into motion the earliest legal reform in a Muslim society, restricting the male privileges of plural marriage and divorce by permitting women to seek justice. The law, however, did not limit the husband's right to repudiate his wives without a cause (Kandiyoti, 1991, p. 11; White, 1978, p. 56). In 1926 the state adopted the Turkish Civil Code, severing all links with the *sharīʿah* It banned polygyny and gave marriage partners equal rights to divorce and child custody.

Egypt enacted a series of personal laws (1920–1929) that raised the marriage age for both girls and boys, prohibited marriage without the couple's consent, and restricted divorce by giving women the right to divorce on specified grounds (Coulson and Hinchcliffe, 1978, p. 49). The personal status laws have been amended several times since, most recently in June 1979, by presidential decree. The decree was declared unconstitutional in May 1985 but was legally adopted by the People's Assembly in July of the same year. While leaving unchanged the right of the husband to divorce and to marry more than one wife, it balanced the rights and privileges of spouses. Divorce must now be mediated by the court, registered, and witnessed, and the wife promptly and officially informed. Additionally, the divorced wife is to be provided one year's alimony and two years' maintenance. The age range for which the mother has automatic custody of children was raised to ten and twelve (from seven and nine) for boys and girls, respectively. A husband who desires to take a second wife must inform both the present wife and the wife-to-be of his intention.

In 1951 Jordan reformed the Law of Family Rights (amended in 1976), restricting polygamy and divorce and giving women the right to divorce on certain grounds. A "fair" alimony is provided for the wife if a judge determines that she has been divorced arbitrarily.

Syria enacted the Law of Personal Status in 1953 (amended in 1975), adding a right to financial support for a divorced wife of up to three years after arbitrary divorce. The law, though not banning polygyny or unilateral divorce, does restrict them.

In late 1967 Iran introduced the Family Protection Law, revised in 1975. It restricted polygyny and divorce and was the only case of reform to accord the wife an equal right to the custody of children. It also made provision for alimony for either partner, to be determined on the basis of income. The Family Protection Law was abolished after the Islamic Revolution of 1979, and Islamic precepts were reinstated, with no restriction on polygyny or temporary marriage and minimal conditional limitation on arbitrary and unilateral divorce.

In Iraq the Baʿth party amended the Personal Status Law in 1978 (adopted in 1959, and amended in 1963), which though limited in its objectives, aimed at reducing the control of the husband in plural marriages and unilateral divorce. A husband's desire for a second marriage has to be approved by a judge.

Lebanese ethnic heterogeneity has prompted the state to delegate family matters, divorce, and marriage to the control of each specific religious establishment. Consequently, the Lebanese state did not legislate a national family code.

Petrodollars brought about a significant change in women's position in the Gulf region (Kuwait, Bahrain, Saudi Arabia, the United Arab Emirate, Qatar, and Oman), particularly in education and employment, but little in terms of legal reform in family and personal status. Because of the similarity in the historical, cultural, social, religious, economic, and political conditions of women here, one may assume similarity in the status of women in the Gulf states (Allaghi and Almana, 1984, p. 17). They have remained very close to the letter of the *sharīʿah,* though in places such as Kuwait some attempts have been made to help women. Under the heading of "Compensation for Repudiation," Kuwaiti law states that in the case of a wife's arbitrary divorce, she is entitled to an amount "not in excess of a year's maintenance" above her three months' *ʿiddah* period. However, she is not entitled to any provision if the divorce is on the basis of the husband's insolvency or the the wife's injurious behavior or her consent, or is initiated by the wife. Variations of such conditions and reasoning form the basis of family reforms (or lack thereof) in the Gulf states, the Islamic Republic of Iran, and other Middle Eastern states. Adhering to a puritanical version of Islamic law known as Wahhābīyah, Saudi Arabia has resisted change and strictly enforces its version of Islamic law.

Heavy pressure from Islamists has forced many states in the region to reconsider family reforms periodically, to islamicize their rhetoric, or to reformulate them within an Islamic framework in order to placate these increasingly vocal challengers. The Islamists, unlike the "traditionalists," are not necessarily against certain legal reforms and women's participation in the political arena, provided that changes are legitimated within an Islamic framework, and that women uphold Islamic identity by observing Islamic conduct and veiling in public. Another notable trend is the emergence of politically aware religious and secular feminists who are questioning historical patriarchal assumptions and practices; they too are returning to the Qur'ān and giving it their own interpretation (Ahmed, 1992; Hassan, 1985; Mernissi, 1991).

[*See also* Family Law; Marriage and Divorce; Mutʿah; Polygyny; *and entries on specific countries.*]

BIBLIOGRAPHY

Ahmed, Leila. *Women and Gender in Islam.* New Haven, 1992.

Allaghi, Farida, and Aisha Almana. "Survey of Research on Women in the Arab Gulf Region." In *Women in the Arab World,* edited by Amal Rassam, pp. 14–40. London, 1984.

Anderson, J. N. D. "The Role of Personal Statutes in Social Development in Islamic Countries." *Comparative Studies in Society and History* 13.1 (1971): 16–31.

Coulson, Noel J., and Doreen Hinchcliffe. "Women and Law Reform in Contemporary Islam." In *Women in the Muslim World,* edited by Nikki R. Keddie and Lois Beck, pp. 37–51. Cambridge, Mass., 1978.

Esposito, John L. *Women in Muslim Family Law.* Syracuse, N.Y., 1982.

Haeri, Shahla. "Women, Law, and Social Change in Iran." In *Women in Contemporary Muslim Societies,* edited by Jane I. Smith, pp. 209–234. Lewisburg, Pa., 1980.

Haeri, Shahla. *Law of Desire: Temporary Marriage in Shi'i Iran.* Syracuse, N.Y., 1989.

Hassan, Riffat. "Made from Adam's Rib? The Woman's Creation Question." *Al-mushir* 27.3 (1985): 124–155.

Hinchcliffe, Doreen. "The Iranian Family Protection Act." *International and Comparative Law Quarterly* 17.2 (1968): 516–521.

Hussein, Aziza. "Recent Amendments to Egypt's Personal Status Law." In *Women and the Family in the Middle East,* edited by Elizabeth W. Fernea, pp. 229–232. Austin, 1985.

Joseph, Suad. "Elite Strategies for State Building: Women, Family, Religion and the State in Iraq and Lebanon." In *Women, Islam, and the State,* edited by Deniz Kandiyoti, pp. 176–200. Philadelphia, 1991.

Kandiyoti, Deniz, ed. *Women, Islam, and the State*. Philadelphia, 1991.

Mernissi, Fatima. *The Veil and the Male Elite: A Feminist Interpretation of Women's Rights in Islam*. Translated by Mary Jo Lakeland. Reading, Mass., 1991.

Nasir, Jamal J. *The Status of Women under Islamic Law and under Modern Islamic Legislation*. London, 1990.

Riesebrodt, Martin. *Pious Passion: The Emergence of Modern Fundamentalism in the United States and Iran*. Berkeley, 1993.

Schacht, Joseph. *Introduction to Islamic Law*. Oxford and New York, 1964.

Smith, Jane I. "The Experience of Muslim Women: Considerations of Power and Authority." In *The Islamic Impact*, edited by Yvonne Yazbeck Haddad, pp. 89–112. Syracuse, N.Y., 1986.

Stowasser, Barbara. "Women's Issues in Modern Islamic Thought." In *Arab Women*, edited by Judith E. Tucker, pp. 3–28. Bloomington, 1993.

White, E. H. "Legal Reforms as an Indicator of Women's Status in Muslim Nations." In *Women in the Muslim World*, edited by Nikki R. Keddie and Lois Beck, pp. 52–68. Cambridge, Mass., 1978.

SHAHLA HAERI

Social Reform in North Africa

Since the colonial period, North African women have been involved in social reform, but more often than not, they have been the object of social reform efforts, rather than participating actors. Although the pace of change was initially slow, it increased in the 1980s, as more women entered public life and created political discourses and organizations through which to transform their status. This change has not been uniform, and there are wide variations between and within countries, across social classes, and within political movements. Cross-cultural similarities do exist, however. For instance, in the past, change for women was usually pursued as part of a more universal reformist agenda, intended to benefit the entire society. Women and men often worked together for these reforms. Today, more women are promoting *woman*-specific reform.

Colonial Period. While the French controlled Algeria (1830–1962), Tunisia (1881–1956), and Morocco (1912–1956), few reforms were directed at the status of women. Instead, traditional female roles were often stressed as symbols of cultural authenticity. Early nationalist groups in all three countries favored secular reform, and education for women had limited support. In the 1950s, an Algerian political party recruited women, but they met separately. Some of the more popular religious reformists during the 1920s to 1950s, such as Algeria's Shaykh Ibn Bādīs, advocated primary school education for women, as well as a limited overlap of the separate gender spheres. For instance, he recommended that women and men participate in the market, learn, and teach together. A few Algerian and French women discussed women's veiling, education, and the conditions of marriage and divorce in newspapers or books. Tunisia had a French women's league chapter whose nearly all-male (French and Muslim) members debated women's rights. But Tunisia's *ʿulamāʾ* blocked secular reform and condemned its supporters, for example, attacking journalist al-Ṭāhir Ḥaddād's 1930 book, *Our Women in the Sharia and in Society*, in which Ḥaddād argued that the Qur'ān allowed for expanded roles for women. Few supported him.

As significant for postindependence reform was women's record of participation in all three anticolonial struggles. Their activities in Algeria's war of independence, from 1954 to 1962, have been most fully documented. Nearly eleven thousand women participated, and 20 percent were jailed or killed. The majority played traditional roles, providing food and shelter for resistance fighters. However, a few participated in combat and strategic actions, and were imprisoned and tortured, including Djamila Bouhired and Djamila Boupacha. Revolutionaries deferred the process of changing female roles until after independence (and later), but women's war heroism remains an important symbol of their potential. Their revolutionary roles are often most powerfully described in literary works, such as Moroccan Leila Abouzeid's semibiographical account, *Year of the Elephant* (Austin, 1989).

Postindependence Period. After independence (Morocco, 2 March 1956; Tunisia, 20 March 1956; and Algeria, 3 July 1962), each country carved its own path to social reform, including the establishment of a constitution, legal codes, and government agencies to promote change. In order to build viable national political constituencies, and to reconcile the competing interests of Islam and nationalism, however, reforms concerning women were limited. Yet while American women finally voted in 1920, 144 years after their "independence," Tunisian women voted in 1957, Algerian women in 1962, and Moroccan women in 1963.

Despite early constitutional reforms such as enfranchisement, Maghribi women are subject to contradictory legislation governing their status. While Maghribi constitutions support the principle of equal rights and duties of males and females, national codes actually legalize gender inequality as they are based on the Mālikī version of Islamic law. These personal status codes concern the regulation of individuals before, during, and after marriage, as well as the institution of marriage itself. Under Mālikī law, which has traditionally given male relatives control over key decisions in women's lives, the bride's consent to marriage is expressed via her father or male guardian. A man may marry up to four wives. Men may repudiate their wives at will, while women may request a divorce only under specific and limited conditions. Inheritance provisions overwhelmingly favor men.

The 1957 Moroccan Code of Personal Status essentially codified the provisions of Mālikī law, securing the status quo in gender relations. Likewise, under the 1984 Algerian Family Code, most legal prerogatives of men, including polygyny and preferential inheritance, remain intact. Divorce, replacing repudiation (a verbal dismissal of the wife by the husband), must now be conducted in the courts. A widowed mother becomes the children's guardian. Yet, as a woman, she legally remains a minor throughout her life, requiring a male tutor for any legal transaction. The 1956 Tunisian Code of Personal Status provides greater rights for women and reduces somewhat the authority of men over women. The bride's physical presence and verbal consent are required to make a valid marriage, and women are entitled to initiate divorce. Polygyny, repudiation, forced marriage, and the requirement that male tutors act on behalf of women have been banned. Despite these drastic legal changes, women, often ignorant of their legal rights, remain in a position of permanent dependency as daughters and wives, as men are always legally *chef de famille*.

"La femme en rondelles" ("a compartmentalized woman") accurately describes the Maghribi woman's dilemma (see Saadi, 1991). Legal constitutional changes have not altered social reality to any great extent. The real value of legislation stems from the way it is perceived and applied by those it addresses; in the Maghrib, traditional forces of the status quo tend to prevail.

Maghribi Women Today and in the Future. Advocates of social reform for Maghribi women include conservatives and liberals, secularists and scripturalists. Their reform agendas may be quite different, however. Some state-sponsored and some revolutionary groups call for the reinforcement of traditional roles, while women's organizations pursue social and legal equality. All of these groups present models for women's identities. But change for any individual woman has complex determinants, including local and global economic and political conditions; in other words, one cannot simply reduce the causes of gender inequality to "Islam."

Governments and "state feminism." On the state level, governments sponsor national women's unions focused on nation-building. These unions and also ministry programs often reinforce traditional sewing and embroidery skills. State-provided education has benefited women most. While few attended school before independence, in 1986 the primary school enrollment for girls was 62 percent in Morocco, 85 percent in Algeria, and nearly a hundred percent in Tunisia (see World Bank, *World Development Report*, 1989). Many state bureaucracies employ women, though not in highly influential positions. A number of political parties have affiliated women's groups or address women's issues, but with few results. Women may run for office and have won Moroccan municipal elections and two parliamentary seats (Fall 1993); women took 3 percent of the seats in Algeria's National Assembly.

Women's agendas. Women's own increasing public advocacy of their rights represents a new historical moment for reform in gender relations and women's status. Having paid employment increases women's leverage within the family, and often in society at large. Since 1988 nearly thirty Algerian women's associations have formed, most advocating change in the 1984 Family Code. As Moroccan feminist Fatima Mernissi says, women are now "designing a future instead of growing old" (*Beyond the Veil*, 1987, p. xii). A specifically North African feminist discourse is developing through scholarship like *The Veil and the Male Elite* (New York, 1991), in which Mernissi identifies the misogyny behind certain *ḥadīths* traditionally used to support male privilege and finds evidence for early Islam's egalitarianism.

Islamist women. Yet calls for reform among women are not univocal. An increasing number of Maghribi women, including many educated professionals, are electing to wear the *ḥijāb*. This modern-day version of the Muslim veil leaves the face uncovered and is worn with an ample gown. Islamists advocate separate public spheres for men and women, demanding segregated educational and public facilities. Their campaign has been only partially successful. But such a phenomenon cannot be solely ascribed to social pressure exercised by Islamists, particularly in countries where they lack an official power base. Women are defining their identity both as Muslims and as women within new social and economic realities, in which traditional boundaries of role and space are no longer clear-cut. Professional women are increasingly penetrating public space, hitherto reserved for men, while the boundaries between traditional public space and women's private sphere in the home are shifting. Against this current of change have emerged strong individual and social desires for permanence and stability.

Women adopt the *ḥijāb* for complex and manifold reasons, not simply as an acquiescence to male power. Although perceived by most Westerners as a symbol of female oppression, for many Maghribi women, wearing the *ḥijāb* represents a commitment to Islamic authenticity. The concept of authenticity is religious and cultural in nature, based essentially on indigenous cultural norms and a rejection of Western values. But the veil has taken on contemporary meanings and functions, to meet the demands of the new situations in which women find themselves. It allows women easier, less controversial access to public space, while at the same time reemphasizing their traditional primary role as dependent, domesticated keepers of the private sphere. The *ḥijāb*, novel in shape as well as meaning, meets the need for an overt expression of Islamic religious and cultural identity, while providing a solution to the spatial dilemma, accommodating women's expanded social presence within an Islamic framework. The veil ensures its wearer her private space (including freedom from male harassment), whatever the context.

For women wearing the *ḥijāb*, the societal rewards are twofold. First, through their overt statement of virtue and commitment to Islam, they gain the respect and consideration of traditional men. Second, the initiative taken by these women, deliberately choosing to wear the veil, is empowering for many, creating a strong self-image and providing unimpeded physical mobility in public space, previously unknown to all but a few privileged women. While for some the veil represents a retrograde mechanism of female oppression, for others it is psychologically liberating and facilitates access to a professional life. Paradoxically, then, the *ḥijāb*, advocated by the Islamists, has the potential for being a liberating device while at the same time strengthening constraints traditionally imposed on Maghribi women.

The end of the twentieth century is clearly a period of rapid and varied change for the women of North Africa.

[*See also* Ḥijāb *and the biography of Mernissi.*]

BIBLIOGRAPHY

Charrad, Mounira. "State and Gender in the Maghrib." *Middle East Report* 163 (March–April 1990): 19–23. Summarizes women's conditions and analyzes the reasons each Maghribi state has dealt differently with changes related to gender.

Fanon, Frantz. *A Dying Colonialism*. London, 1980. Contains lucid descriptions of the psychological importance of female veiling and traditional behavior in the maintenance of cultural authenticity.

Haddad, Yvonne Yazbeck, and Banks Findly Ellison, eds. *Women, Religion, and Social Change*. Albany, N.Y., 1985. See especially the introduction, "Islam, Women, and Twentieth-Century Arab Thought," and Haddad's discussion of how women are influenced by, or can influence, religion to accomplish social change.

Kandiyoti, Deniz, ed. *Women, Islam, and the State*. Philadelphia, 1991. Explores varied interrelationships between religion, family, politics, culture, and the state.

Knaus, Peter R. *The Persistence of Patriarchy: Class, Gender, and Ideology in Twentieth-Century Algeria*. New York and London, 1987. Stresses male domination, but includes a thorough examination of women's roles from precolonial times to the mid-1980s and an extensive bibliography.

Lazreg, Marnia. "Gender and Politics in Algeria: Unraveling the Religious Paradigm." 15.4 *Signs* (Summer 1990): 755–780. Well-documented discussion of Algerian women and their changing roles, from Algeria's independence to the present.

Mernissi, Fatima. *Beyond the Veil: Male-Female Dynamics in Modern Muslim Society*. Rev. ed. Bloomington, 1987. The introduction vividly portrays recent changes for women, as well as Mernissi's view of the bases and goals of Moroccan Islamist groups.

Micaud, Charles, et al. *Tunisia: The Politics of Modernization*. New York, 1964. Covers social change involving women during the protectorate and in the early years of independence.

See as well the volumes published by Editions le Fennec (Casablanca, 1991), which focus on legislation in three Maghribian countries as it pertains to men's and women's roles, status, rights, and duties: Alya Chérif Chamari, *La femme et la loi en Tunisie*, Moulay R'chid Abderrazak, *La femme et la loi au Maroc*, and Nouredine Saadi, *La femme et la loi en Algerie*.

Susan Schaefer Davis and Leila Hessini

Social Reform in South Asia

Various attempts at social and legal reform have provoked integral changes in Muslim women's lives in the subcontinent throughout the past century. Attention to Muslim women's status and ways of improving it began as an offshoot of two separate kinds of movements: the larger social reform movement in British India and the growing Muslim nationalist movement. In the postpartition era, the issue of social reform and Muslim women largely has been associated with the discourse of the role Islam can and/or should play in a modern state. Importantly, it addresses the extent to which the civil rights common in most Western democracies are appropriate in the South Asian Muslim context and whether they should override Islamic injunctions in the realm of family law, or vice versa. While this discourse is exemplified by events in Pakistan, it has also been important in Bangladesh and India.

Although Muslims in the nineteenth century did not have to contend with such social issues as abolishing *satī* or promoting widow remarriage as did Hindu reformers, they had an uphill struggle in introducing female education, easing some of the extreme restrictions on women's activities associated with *purdah,* restricting polygyny, and ensuring women's legal rights under Islamic law. Sir Sayyid Aḥmad Khān's Mohammedan Educational Conference, which began promoting modern education for Muslims in the 1870s, included many of the earliest proponents of female education and of raising women's social status in the wider society. As tended to be the case in many other parts of Asia at the time, these advocates for social reform were men. The intent was to advance girls' technical knowledge (evidenced in sewing and cooking classes) within a religious framework, and thereby reinforce Islamic values. A women's section of the Mohammedan Educational Conference was formed in 1896, followed three years later with the opening of the first teacher training school for girls. More Muslim girls' schools were opened in the first decade of this century, but the progress was slow: by 1921, only four out of every thousand Muslim females had enjoyed the benefits of education.

The promotion of female education was a first step in removing the bonds stipulated by traditional views of *purdah.* It contributed to transforming the very idea of *purdah,* of that symbolic curtain which separates the world of men from the world of women. Many writers and social groups emerged, ostensibly promoting female literacy but in effect advocating women's rights.

The nationalist struggle also tore at the threads in that curtain. Two important groups were soon established: the politically oriented All-India Muslim Ladies Conference, consisting of elite women, predominantly wives of leaders active in the Muslim League, and the social reform–oriented Anjuman-i Khavātīn-i Islām, the precursor to other social welfare–oriented women's groups. During the Khilāfat movement, Ābādī Begum (better known as Bī Ammān) began to tug at the *purdah* curtain further when she became the spokesperson for her imprisoned sons in 1917. She addressed all-male crowds as her brothers and sons, adroitly manipulating acceptable notions of kinship for a political cause. While remaining within the bounds of tradition, the precedent was set to challenge *purdah* itself.

In the gradual building up of support for a Muslim homeland, women's roles were being questioned and their empowerment linked to the larger issues of nationalism and independence. The demand for Muslim women to inherit property as well as other rights Muslims had lost with the anglicization of certain civil laws was rectified somewhat in 1937 with the enactment of the Muslim Personal Law.

After independence, elite Muslim women in Pakistan continued to advocate women's political empowerment through legal reforms. They mobilized support that eventually resulted in the passage of the Muslim Personal Law of Shariat (1948), which recognized a woman's right to inherit all forms of property, and were behind the futile attempt to include a Charter of Women's Rights in the 1956 Constitution. The most important sociolegal reform was the 1961 Family Laws Ordinance, regulating marriage and divorce, which is still widely regarded in Pakistan and Bangladesh as empowering to women.

Two issues—promoting women's political representation and finding some accommodation between Muslim family law and civil, democratic rights—came to define the discourse regarding women and sociolegal reform in Pakistan in the years following the 1971 war. The latter became particularly prominent during the era of the government of President Muhammad Zia ul-Haq (1977–1988), as women's groups emerged in urban areas in response to the promulgation of an islamization program that many feared would discriminate against women.

It was in the highly visible arena of law that women were able to articulate their objections to the islamization program initiated by the government in 1979. Protests against the 1979 "Enforcement of *Hudood* [Ar., *ḥudūd*] Ordinances" focused on its failure to distinguish between adultery *(zinā)* and rape *(zinā bi-al-jabr),* and that its enforcement was discriminatory to women: a man could only be convicted of *zinā* if he were actually observed committing the offense by other men, but a woman could be convicted more easily of adultery, as pregnancy became admissible evidence. This was followed by protests in 1983–1984 against the promulgation of the Qanoon-i Shahadat (Qānūn-i Shahādah; Law of Evidence), which many felt did not give equal weight to men's and women's legal testimony. They feared that women might be restricted from testifying in certain kinds of *ḥudūd* cases (such as when they were the sole witness to their father's or husband's murder), and that their testimony in other matters would be irrelevant unless corroborated by another woman. Importantly, the controversy surrounding the Qanoon-i Shahadat raised the issue as to whether or not women and men are equal economic actors and the extent to which parliamentary and civil rights, taken as givens in the West, are applicable in a modern Muslim context.

In 1984, women's groups launched a campaign against the promulgation of the proposed Qiṣāṣ and Diyat (Retaliation and Blood Money) Ordinance. Opponents of the ordinance were concerned with the interpretation being forwarded, that the amount of compensation given by the perpetrator of the crime to the victim or the victim's family for effecting injury or death would differ if the victim were a male or a female. In the latter case, the *diyat* would be about half of that compensated if the victim were a male. The bill was finally passed into law in 1990 without the gender-discriminatory clause.

The debate over the Shariat Bill and the Ninth Amendment—that all laws in Pakistan should be in conformity with *sharīʿah*—began in August 1986 and continues as of this writing. A range of organizations issued a joint statement opposing the Shariat Bill on the grounds that it negated principles of justice, democracy, and fundamental rights of citizens, and that it would give rise to sectarianism and divide the nation. They were concerned that *sharīʿah* would now come to be identified solely with the relatively conservative interpretation of Islam supported by Zia's government. They also felt the Shariat Bill and the Ninth Amendment could potentially reverse many of the rights women in Pakistan had already won. In April 1991, a compromise version of the Shariat Bill was promulgated, but the debate over the issue of which kind of law—civil or Islamic—should prevail remains unresolved.

Discourse about the position of women in Islam and women's roles in a modern Islamic state was sparked by the Pakistan government's attempts to formalize a specific interpretation of Islamic law and exposed the controversy surrounding its various interpretations and role in a modern state. While the issue of evidence became central to the concern for women's status, matters such as mandatory dress codes for women and whether females could compete in international sports competitions underscored the reality that Zia's islamization program was having a comprehensive effect on women's lives.

In the 1980s, Bangladesh also found itself in the grip of a similar debate: the extent to which Islamic law should be instituted as the supreme law in the country. While the rights granted women under the 1961 Family Laws Ordinance are still in force, they are being threatened by efforts to assert mandatory dress codes and conduct for women, and may be affected if legal changes are instituted.

Similar issues have been raised regarding Muslim women and social reform in postindependence India. As members of a minority community, Indian Muslims are caught in the dilemma of maintaining a communal identity and the need to adapt to the larger Indian society. A watershed event concerning sociolegal reform for Muslim women in India was the 1986 passage of the Muslim Women's Protection of the Right of Divorce Bill, which revoked Muslim women's rights to maintenance granted to Indian women under the state's civil laws. The bill was precipitated by the divorce case of Shāh Bāno, an elderly Muslim woman whose former husband claimed that, under Islamic law, he should not have to provide her with the maintenance determined by Indian civil laws. Demonstrations were held by women throughout the country as it was widely perceived that Rajiv Gandhi's government, for its own political ends, was allowing a conservative interpretation that would negate civil laws applying to all Indians, regardless of religion. This question remains pertinent today, as Indian Muslims continue to question the relationship between civil and religious laws.

[*See also* Ḥudūd; Islam, *article on* Islam in South Asia; Seclusion.]

BIBLIOGRAPHY

Chhachhi, Amrita. "The State, Religious Fundamentalism, and Women: Trends in South Asia." Institute of Social Studies, The Hague, Working Paper, Subseries on Women, History, and Development: Themes and Issues, no. 8, September 1988.

Government of India, Ministry of Education and Social Welfare, Committee on the Status of Women in India. *Towards Equality*. Delhi, 1974.

Government of Pakistan, Commission on the Status of Women. "Report of the Commission on the Status of Women in Pakistan." Islamabad, 1986. Controversial document produced by a commission appointed by President Zia ul-Haq, which condemns the conditions under which women in Pakistan live and the lack of government action to rectify them.

Government of Pakistan, Women's Division. *Women in Pakistan: A Statistical Profile*. Islamabad, July 1985. Composite based on the official census of Pakistan for the years 1951, 1961, 1972, and 1981.

Jayawardena, Kumari. *Feminism and Nationalism in the Third World*. London, 1986.

Lateef, Shahida. *Muslim Women in India: Political and Private Realities, 1890s–1980s*. London, 1990.

Metcalf, Barbara D. *Perfecting Women: Maulana Ashraf Ali Thanawi's*

Bihishti Zewar: A Partial Translation with Commentary. Berkeley, 1990.

Minault, Gail. "Political Change: Muslim Women in Conflict with Parda; Their Role in the Indian Nationalist Movement." In *Asian Women in Transition*, edited by Sylvia Chipp and Justin Green, pp. 194–203. College Park, Md., 1980.

Minault, Gail. "Shaikh Abdullah, Begum Abdullah, and Sharif Education for Girls at Aligharh." In *Modernization and Social Change among Muslims in India*, edited by Imtiaz Ahmad, pp. 207–236. Delhi, 1983.

Mirza, Sarfaraz Hussain. *Muslim Women's Role in the Pakistan Movement*. Lahore, 1969. Thorough account of the history of the Muslim women's reform movement in South Asia.

Mumtaz, Khawar, and Farida Shaheed. *Women of Pakistan: Two Steps Forward, One Step Back?* London, 1987.

Weiss, Anita M. "The Consequences of State Policy for Women in Pakistan." In *The Politics of Social Transformation in Afghanistan, Iran, and Pakistan*, edited by Myron Weiner and Ali Banuazizi, pp. 412–443. Syracuse, N.Y., 1994.

ANITA M. WEISS

Social Reform in Southeast Asia

Women's roles in Muslim societies in Southeast Asia have been largely defined by two interrelated factors. First, traditional Southeast Asian societies appear to have been based on bilateral kinship systems, in contrast to pre-Islamic Middle Eastern societies, which were largely patrilineal. Second, Southeast Asian societies at the time Islam was introduced had already been profoundly influenced by other world religious traditions, notably Hinduism and Buddhism. There was thus no tradition of the seclusion of women in Southeast Asian societies, and women enjoyed a relatively emancipated status; in peasant societies they were laborers and petty traders, and in court societies there are examples of women rulers.

Adherence to traditional customary law, or *adat*, is a vital part of the societal orientation of Southeast Asian Muslims. The relationship between *adat* and Islam has been an issue of considerable debate over the decades. Many scholars, for example, have been fascinated by how the Minangkabau, a matrilineal society reputed to be the most pious Muslim community in Indonesia, have managed to retain many elements of their matrilineal system, when it would appear to be in contradiction to the patrilineal nature of Islamic law and custom. Nikki Keddie (1987) interestingly argues that the answer may be found in the fact that the Minangkabau appear to stress matters of worship and individual ethics (*ʿibādāt*) while paying relatively little attention to the worldly aspects of *sharīʿah (muʿāmalāt)*, particularly questions of Islamic law and jurisprudence.

This insight is important to understanding Southeast Asian Islam, where there is indeed a preoccupation with *ʿibādāt*. Great stress is placed on acquiring an early familiarity with the Five Pillars of Islam, and the transmitters in this socialization process are women in their roles both as mothers and as *ustazah* (religious teachers).

Conversely, little attention has traditionally been paid to the exclusive implementation of Islamic law. In both Malaysia and Indonesia there are three basic legal systems upon which it is possible to draw: first, *adat* (customary) law; second, Western law (British in Malaysia and Dutch in Indonesia); and third, Islamic law. In both countries the sphere of Islamic law has been family law, governing such matters as marriage, divorce, child maintenance, and inheritance. The application of Muslim law in Singapore, Thailand, the Philippines has similarly been restricted to family law. [*See* Adat; Family Law.]

Colonial Period. Among Southeast Asian Muslims it was recognized that it was as important for women as for men to acquire a religious education. This emphasis on learning paved the way for some acceptance of secular education for women, particularly for upper-class women in the Dutch East Indies. Raden Kartini, born in 1879, was the Dutch-educated daughter of a Javanese *bupati* (regent) whose correspondence with a young Dutch woman has inspired generations of Indonesian women. Kartini argued that while there was much value in acquiring a progressive Western education, this must not supersede the religious education that provides a firm anchor in one's own traditional cultural heritage and value system. Kartini argued that there was a need for change and urged women to improve their lives, obtain their rights, and realize their duties. Education, both secular and religious, was the key to women's progress.

Kartini inspired a small circle of aristocratic Indonesian women to dedicate themselves to establishing educational opportunities for women. The first organization set up for this purpose was the Putri Mardika (Liberated Women) founded in Jakarta in 1912 as a sort of women's wing of the Budi Utomo. One of the most influential women's religious movements in Indonesia, Aisyiyah, was formed as the women's section of the Muhammadiyah, a reformist organization founded in 1912 in Jogjakarta by Kyai Haji Ahmad Dahlan; Aisyiyah was led by his wife, Nyai Ahmad Dahlan. Other groups in the Dutch East Indies included the women's wing of the Nahdatul Ulama, the Nahdatul Fatayat, and the Wanodya Utomo of the Sarekat Islam. [*See* Muhammadiyah; Nahdatul Ulama; Sarekat Islam.]

A pattern emerged for the foundation of women's organizations whether secular or religious. They were generally formed as counterpart organizations to exclusively male organizations, and the women directly involved in their formation were generally the wives of the founders of the male organizations. These women's organizations focused on the education of women as their primary mission; toward this end they published widely, establishing magazines and newsletters.

The emphasis on the education of women took on another dimension in the 1930s when Muslim women became actively involved in the nationalist movements in the Dutch East Indies and British Malaya. Given the prevailing attitude that women and men had an equal right to education (particularly Qur'ānic education), it followed that Islam served as a legitimating base for women's entry into political activity. In the 1930s young Malay women were sent to religious schools in Sumatra, where they imbibed nationalism along with their religious education. Two Malay women who later went on to become prominent Malaysian politicians, Aishah Ghani and Sakinah Junid, were both associated with one of the first women's movements in British Malaya, the Angkatan Wanita Sedar (AWAS or Progressive Women's Corps). AWAS was the women's section of the Malay Nationalist Party (MNP), a radical party dedicated to establishing an Indonesian republic that included Malaya.

Postindependence Period. The contributions of women in the independence movements of the 1930s in the Dutch East Indies and British Malaya helped to ensure them smooth entrance into the post-independence political arena. In British Malaya, both leading Malay political parties established women's wings. That of the United Malays National Organization (UMNO) was called Kaum Ibu (later Kaum Wanita), and that of the opposition Parti Islam Se-Malaysia (PAS), Dewan Muslimat (Women's Section). [*See* United Malays National Organization; Partai Islam Se-Malaysia.]

In Malaysia women's rights as citizens to participate in the political and administrative aspects of the nation have been recognized and safeguarded in the Federal Constitution. Similarly in Indonesia, the 1945 Constitution ensures rights and equal responsibilities for men and women.

Muslim women have continued to play an active role in Malaysian politics. In the 1990 elections Wanita UMNO fielded a total of twenty-two candidates at the federal and state levels. Although the PAS does not allow women to become candidates, members of the Dewan Muslimat are active campaigners. Women are also active in politics in Indonesia, and in 1992 there were two Muslim women cabinet ministers. They enjoy full membership and status in such nominally secular political organizations as GOLKAR.

The women's wings of religious reform movements have played active roles in advocating and implementing social and educational reforms. In Indonesia, Aisyiyah organizes religious courses, Qur'ān-reading groups, and kindergartens. It also runs orphanages, maternity clinics and hospitals, day-care centers, family planning units, and girls' dormitories. Its role as a catalyst for change is exemplified by its disseminating family-planning information and methods. When family planning was first introduced in Indonesia, Muslim response was generally negative. After the Muhammadiyah issued a *fatwā* in support of family planning in 1971, Aisyiyah began to recommend family planning in the context of total environmental welfare for families. [*See* Family Planning.]

Recent Developments. Since the early 1970s Islamic reformist movements have gained prominance in Southeast Asia. In Malaysia, the leading *dakwah* (from Arabic *daʿwah,* to respond to a call) organization has been the Malaysian Muslim Youth Movement (ABIM), which followed the pattern of other Malay organizations, by establishing a women's branch, HELWA. [*See* ABIM.]

Certainly the present reformist wave has had an impact on the status and role of women in Southeast Asia. In contrast to other earlier twentieth-century reform movements, there appears to be a greater preoccupation with elaborating a model for Islamic women that is distinctly different from the Western model. This is most visible in dress codes, where the most obvious indicator that a young women is a member of a *dakwah* organization is veiling. Veiling is commonly seen in secondary schools, colleges, and universities, although a majority of Muslim women remain unveiled in urban centers, and in villages very few women are veiled. Many women still prefer the traditional Southeast Asian Muslim head covering, the *selendang,* a long scarf wrapped loosely around the head, neck, and shoulders.

The expanded implementation of Islamic law, if successful, will affect the legal status of Muslim women as well as the social perception of their role. In Malaysia,

PAS, the Islamic party that controlled the state of Kelantan in 1993, has sought to expand the jurisdiction of the *sharīʿah* there; the most controversial element of this effort has been its call to introduce *ḥudūd* laws.

Some Muslim scholars in Indonesia have also advocated the expansion of the domain of Islamic law. In 1983 the Indonesian government introduced what came to be known as the "secular" marriage bill, which was unpopular with Muslims. In 1988 the Religious Court Bill, which establishes recognition of Islamic court jurisdiction over marriage, inheritance, and donations, received parliamentary approval.

True to their heritage, Southeast Asian Muslim women are taking an active role in current debates on the redefinition of women's social, cultural, legal, and economic roles in their modern societies. Groups of professional Muslim women are spearheading a reexamination of traditional Islamic sources for answers to these complex questions. Among these groups is the Malaysian organization Sisters-in-Islam, which has been active in publishing pamphlets, organizing seminars, and supporting books (e.g., Wadud-Muhsin, 1992), reinforcing the relevancy of Kartini's observation of a century ago that education is the key to progress for women.

[*See also* Women's Movements.]

BIBLIOGRAPHY

Anwar, Zainah. *Islamic Revivalism in Malaysia: Dakwah among the Students*. Kuala Lumpur, 1987. Provides interesting insights into the motivations of young women who join the *dakwah* movement.

Ariffin, Jamilah. *Women and Development in Malaysia*. Kuala Lumpur, 1992. Particularly strong with regard to the development of the political role of Muslim women in Malaysia.

Baried, Baroroh. "Islam and the Modernization of Indonesian Women." In *Islam and Society in Southeast Asia*, edited by Taufik Abdullah and Sharon Siddique, pp. 139–154. Singapore, 1987. Insider's view of the development of the Muslim women's movement in Indonesia.

Berninghausen, Jutta, and Birgit Kerstan. *Forging New Paths: Feminist Social Methodology and Rural Women in Java*. London, 1991. Western feminist view of social change in Muslim Java.

Karim, Wazir Jahan. *Women and Culture: Between Malay Adat and Islam*. Boulder, 1992. Balanced historical view of the role of Muslim women in Malay society.

Keddie, Nikki R. "Islam and Society in Minangkabau and in the Middle East." *Sojourn* 2.1 (February 1987). Seminal article on the relationship between culture and religion in this matrilineal society.

Wadud-Muhsin, Amina. *Qur'an and Woman*. Kuala Lumpur, 1992. Analysis of the concept of woman drawn directly from the Qur'ān.

SHARON SIDDIQUE

WOMEN'S ACTION FORUM. Formed in 1981 in response to the government of Pakistan's implementation of an Islamic penal code, the Women's Action Forum (WAF; Khavātīn Maḥāẕ-i ʿAmal) sought the strengthening of women's position in society. Members feared that many of the proposed laws being put forward by the martial law government of General Zia ul-Haq might be discriminatory against women and compromise their civil status, as they had seen with the promulgation of the Ḥudūd Ordinances in 1979 when women were indicted after having been raped. Women, most from elite families, banded together on the principal of collective leadership in the three major cities of Karachi, Lahore, and Islamabad to formulate policy statements and engage in political action to safeguard women's legal position.

In its charter, the WAF asserts that it is "committed to protecting and promoting the rights of women by countering all forms of oppression" by being a consciousness-raising group and acting as a lobby and pressure group, in order to create a heightened awareness of women's rights and mobilize support for promoting these rights and "counter adverse propaganda against women." The WAF has played a central role in the public exposure of the controversy regarding various interpretations of Islamic law, its role in a modern state, and ways in which women can play a more active role in political matters.

The WAF's first major political action was in early 1983 when members in Lahore and Karachi openly marched in protest against the Majlis-i Shūrā's (Consultative Assembly) recommendation to President Zia that he promulgate the Qānūn-i Shahādat (Law of Evidence). As initially proposed, the law would require oral testimony and attestation of either two male witnesses or that of one male and two females; the witness of two or more females without corroboration by a male would not be sufficient, and no testimony by a woman would be admissible in the most severe *ḥudūd* cases (cases that require mandatory punishments for crimes against Allāh) as stipulated in the *sunnah*. A revised evidence law, eventually promulgated in October 1984 following nearly two years of protests, modifies the one previously enacted during the British Raj.

WAF members used Islamic precepts as the basis of their protest. They argued that the proposed Qānūn-i Shahādat was not the only acceptable evidence law in Islam, and that there is only one instance in the Qur'ān (surah al-Baqr, 2.282) in which two women are called to testify in the place of one man. But, they contended, the latter was in regard to a specific financial matter and the role of the second woman was to remind the first about points that she may have forgotten. The intent (nīyah) of the law must be taken into consideration, as it was initially intended to help women and not discriminate against them. The protesters claimed that criteria for witnesses as stated in the Qur'ān are possession of sight, memory and the ability to communicate; as long as witnesses have these, testimony should be equally weighed regardless of gender. They also argued that the rigid interpretation of the Qur'ān that would support the Qānūn-i Shahādat (reading "male" for the generic word "man") would virtually exclude women from being members of the religion. Opponents of the evidence law also feared that women might be restricted from testifying in certain kinds of *ḥudūd* cases at all, such as when a woman is the sole witness to her father's or husband's murder.

The final adopted version restricts to financial cases the testimony of two women being equal to that of one man; in other instances, acceptance of a single woman's testimony has been left to the discretion of the judge. Even though the final evidence law was modified substantially from the initial proposal, the WAF held the position that the state's declaring a woman's evidence in financial cases unequal to that of a man's would constrain women's economic participation and was symbolic of an ideological perspective that could not perceive women as equal economic participants with men. They argued that for the first time in Pakistan's history, the laws regard men and women as having different legal rights, and, despite the rhetoric that such laws were being promulgated to protect women, they were indeed constraining women's power and participation in the larger society.

At protests in Lahore and Karachi in February 1983, women demonstrators were attacked by police, prompting much public outcry. The WAF's lawyers countered the martial law government's actions on Islamic grounds by claiming that the police, as unrelated men, had no right to physically touch the protesting women.

In fall 1983, the WAF and other women's groups organized demonstrations throughout the country to protest both the Qānūn-i Shahādat and the public flogging of women. The following year, in 1984, the now separate WAF groups mounted a campaign against the promulgation of the proposed Qiṣāṣ and Dīyat (Retaliation and Blood Money) Ordinance, which stated that the compensation to the family of a female victim be only half that given to the family of a male victim.

In the aftermath of the lifting of martial law in December 1985, the WAF became instrumental in organizing protests (which included nearly thirty other groups) in the wake of the debate over the Shariat Bill and the Ninth Amendment. WAF argued that in their proposed forms, both negated principles of justice, democracy, and fundamental rights of citizens, and that their passage would give rise to sectarianism and serve to divide the nation. The remaining years of the Zia regime (until fall 1988) found WAF members focussed on protesting against the Ninth Amendment, instituting legal aid cells for indigent women, opposing the gendered segregation of universities, and playing an active role in condemning the growing incidents of violence against women and bringing them to the attention of the public.

During the tenure of Benazir Bhutto's Pakistan People's Party's first government (December 1988–August 1990), the WAF was faced with the difficult task of transforming itself from a protest movement based on a collective moral conscience to an advocate, lobbying a more sympathetic government. With the displacement of that government, it then focussed its activities on three goals: to secure women's political representation in the parliament; to work to raise women's consciousness, particularly in the realm of family planning; and to counter suppression and raise public awareness by taking stands and issuing statements on events as they occur.

[*See also* Women and Social Reform, *article on* Social Reform in South Asia.]

BIBLIOGRAPHY

Carroll, Lucy. "Nizam-i-Islam: Processes and Conflicts in Pakistan's Programme of Islamisation, with Special Reference to the Position of Women." *Journal of Commonwealth and Comparative Politics* 20 (1982): 57–95.

Mumtaz, Khawar, and Farida Shaheed. *Women of Pakistan: Two Steps Forward, One Step Back?* London and Karachi, 1987. Thorough review of the history of the Pakistan women's movement, with a strong focus on the Women's Action Forum.

Pakistan Commission on the Status of Women. "Report of the Commission on the Status of Women in Pakistan." Islamabad, 1986. Controversial report by a commission appointed by President Zia ul-Haq that condemned the conditions under which women in Pakistan live and the lack of government action to rectify them.

Weiss, Anita M. "Implications of the Islamization Program for Women." In *Islamic Reassertion in Pakistan: The Application of Islamic Laws in a Modern State*, edited by Anita M. Weiss, pp. 97–110. Syracuse, N.Y., 1986.

Weiss, Anita M. "Benazir Bhutto and the Future of Women in Pakistan." *Asian Survey* 30. 5 (May 1990): 433–445.

Women's Action Forum. "Law of Evidence: WAF (National) Position Paper." Lahore, 1983.

Women's Action Forum. "Law of *Qisas* and *Diyat* as Proposed by the Council of Islamic Ideology: Position Paper of WAF (National)." Lahore, February 1984.

ANITA M. WEISS

WOMEN'S MOVEMENTS. Muslim women's participation in social movements and the emergence of women's associations, leagues, and organizations are closely related to the debates over women's status that emerged in the nineteenth century and continue today. These debates also fuel much of the discourse of the Islamist phenomenon, in which millions of Muslim women participate. Their involvement and articulation have varied greatly according to the challenges of the time, ranging from a general debate responding to the views and publications of reform-minded individuals to mobilized groups of women actively engaged in particular nationalist, feminist, conservative, or philanthropic activities.

From the mid-nineteenth century onward, women and men began to discuss societal reform and its appropriate direction within Islam. Conceptions of Islamic reform were responsive to Western colonialism, which influenced Muslim lands in differing degrees. Both women and men questioned the legal and social restrictions on women, especially in regard to women's rights to education, female seclusion (known as *purdah* in the Indian subcontinent), strict veiling of the face, polygamy, women's slavery and in some cases concubinage. Egyptian male reformers wrote on women's behalf, among them Aḥmad Fāris al-Shidyāq, author of *One Leg Crossed Over the Other* (1855); Rifāʿah Rāfiʿ al-Ṭahṭāwī (1801–1871); Muḥammad ʿAbduh (1849–1905), a founder of the Salafīyah (Islamic reform) movement; Qāsim Amīn, whose book *Women's Emancipation* (1899) unleashed furious discussion; and Luṭfī al-Sayyid, publisher of *Al-jarīdah*. Turkish counterparts included Namık Kemal and Ahmet Mithat.

Educated women, such as Wardah al-Yāzijī and Wardah al-Turk in Syria and ʿĀ'ishah al-Taymūrīyah in Egypt began writing to each other in the 1860s and 1870s, as women later did for women's publications regarding reform for women. As part of a growing women's press, Hind Nawfal (1860–1920), a Syrian immigrant to Alexandria, published and edited *Al-fatāh*, a women's Arabic monthly; Zaynab Fawwāz (1860–1914), who immigrated from Tibnin to the same city, founded the newspaper *Al-Nīl* in 1891.

In Turkey early feminists included the well-known Halide Edib Adıvar (1883–1964) and Fatma Âliye Hanım (b. 1862), who published *Nisvanı İslam* and *A Newspaper for Ladies*. In this period women in various Muslim countries were also involved in the establishment of schools for girls. Somewhat earlier, some Iranian women had participated in the Bābi movement, an offshoot of Shiism, whose leaders included Rustamah and the martyr Qurrat al-ʿAyn (1815–1851), who appeared unveiled and preached against polygamy and the veil. In Indonesia a famous advocate of women's education and emancipation was Raden Adjeng Kartini (1879–1904). She wrote and founded a school for daughters of Javanese officials, becoming most influential after her death.

Women also engaged in philanthropy and in nationalist movements. Both impulses instructed women in social mobilization and eventually gave rise to associations run for and by women. In Iran, women took part in the Tobacco Rebellion and subsequently in the Constitutional Revolution (1908) and its aftermath, when mainly upperclass women organized separate *anjumans* (political societies) seeking education and the right to vote.

Not all nationalist leaders or Muslim reformers supported female emancipation. Muṣṭafā Kāmil (1874–1908) and Ṭalʿat Ḥarb in Egypt opposed the end of veiling, and in 1882, Sayyid Aḥmad Khān of India felt that *purdah* should be maintained and female education postponed. Throughout the twentieth century some leaders characterized working women as a social drain and saw changes in women's status as attacks on the role of homemaker. Often the primacy of the national struggle forced feminist issues onto the back burner. Examples are Egyptian and Iranian women's quest for the vote, and during the Palestinian and Algerian national struggles.

Meanwhile, women's participation in nationalist movements eroded the preexisting custom of female seclusion, allowing women into various public forums. Upper-class women ventured to meetings in elite salons—Eugenie Le Brun's in Egypt, and later to the literary salon of May Ziada. Women's gatherings included lecture sessions, study groups, demonstrations, and formal associations. Individuals became well known; Hudā Shaʿrāwī (1879–1947), for example, became a symbol of feminist activism. [*See the biography of Shaʿrāwī.*]

Philanthropic activities of elite and middle-class women actually formed the basis for the Egyptian state's social services and demonstrated women's managerial expertise. In Palestine, after the dispersal of the Palestinian people in 1948, middleclass women conducted relief efforts until the establishment of UNRWA refugee camps and facilities. In exile and at home, charitable associations formed the major focus for Palestinian women's organized activities until the 1967 war. Women's interest in social services later translated into participation in developmental programs, such as the Bangladesh Jatiyo Mahila Sangshtha (National Women's Organization), which coordinated programs under official sponsorship.

Nationalist movements and the new states that emerged in the postwar period perceived women and gender issues as crucial to social development. Atatürk of Turkey, Reza Shah of Iran, and later Habib Bourguiba of Tunisia, leaders with unassailable nationalist credentials, initiated new policies to reform women's status and weaken the power base of the *ʿulamaʾ*. A state-advocated feminism emerged but was never fully articulated. Turkish and Iranian reforms from above attacked the veil (or head scarf). Later amendments in Iran, Tunisia, and Egypt addressed various areas of personal status, including divorce, child custody, women's rights to the family home, and alimony, as did the Family Law ordinance (1961) in West and East Pakistan. The modern states assumed control over education. State policies enabled groups of women to enter a male-dominated political sphere and professions previously closed to women, although the same policies may have caused a popular and religious aversion to state intervention in gender matters. [*See* Family Law.]

Muslim women who gained most from state advocated feminism mainly benefited as individuals. Many conformed to Muslim and cultural expectations of powerful women, postponing their careers until middle age and often succeeding through strong familial connections and influence. A small group of powerful older women have dominated official political life and associations in many Muslim countries. Family connections could heighten state control over women's associations, as in Iran, where Ashraf Pahlavi headed the Higher Council of Women's Organizations. Women in political life have been criticized for their elite origins, their patronizing attitude toward lowerclass women, and their inability to discard male-patterned modes of operation or to shed the influence of *sharīʿah*. This criticism is made for example in Pakistan, although small groups such as the WAF (Women's Action Forum) attempted unsuccessfully, to turn the tide (Ayesha Jalal, "The Convenience of Subservience," in Kandiyoti, 1991).

Egyptian women were accorded voting rights in 1956, in part as a consequence of advocacy by women's associations since the early twentieth century. Early activist women's groups included the Wafdist Women's Committee, the Egyptian Feminist Union, and the Bint al-Nīl association, founded in 1951 by Durrīyah Shafīq (Doria Shafik; d. 1975). Women also organized through a wing of Ḥasan al-Bannāʾs Muslim Brotherhood (founded in 1928) and in the Association of Muslim Women established by Zaynab al-Ghazālī. Those organized by the Islamic leadership wore the veil and eventually adopted a white *khimār* (head cover). They held that women must preserve their modesty, morals, and loyalty to their role in the home. The Muslim Brotherhood spread from Egypt to Syria, Jordan, the West Bank and Gaza, Libya, and after the suppression of the brotherhood, to the Gulf states. Their gender ideology originally opposed the female vote and coeducation, but it was moderate in comparison to that of the Takfīr wā al-Ḥijrah, the Jamāʿat al-Islāmīyah, or the Jihād, secessionist and radical groups that more actively opposed secular governments. [*See* Muslim Brotherhood; *and the biographies of Shafīq and Ghazālī.*]

Women were involved in the resistance movements of North Africa. In Algeria, the FLN (National Liberation Front) incorporated women in its rebellion against French authority. The Front's conception of Algerian identity linked religion and nationalism. Its leadership was male, but so many men were imprisoned or in hiding that women served as fighters, intelligence operatives, and liaison agents, as well as nursing and supplying fighters. Initially, the veil provided cover, as the French were reluctant to search women, who became increasingly involved in carrying bombs and arms. Later women were imprisoned and tortured, and in the process some became national heroines. However, the postrevolutionary government required the registration of their activities, and many lost benefits and recognition because they were illiterate or because they were designated "civilian" rather than "military" participants. After the revolution the linkage of *sharīʿah* with the constitution and suspicion of foreign influence meant that women were harassed in the streets, beaten or secluded, and legal reforms such as the minimum age for marriage were not enforced. With time Islamist parties gained large followings, including women who proposed a more conservative view of gender.

In another area of the Maghrib the Ṣaḥrāwīs, formerly subjects of Spanish colonialism, have lived since 1975 as refugees in the Western Desert. The Polisario, the chief party of the Ṣaḥrāwīs, has sought to diminish gender, race, and class barriers, and women participate in party activities, education, and their own associations, although they are not represented in equal numbers within the party leadership.

In the Omani resistance movement women were also empowered to a degree by the military nature of their engagement. In the former People's Democratic Republic of Yemen, after the revolution, various official agencies and associations were created for women, but their goal seemed to involve the economic wellbeing of the state more than a reform of gender inequities. Nonetheless, reforms were enacted that fostered women's education and increased their participation in the work force.

In Iraq, and Syria, women's associations are wings of the Baʿth party. A state feminism chiefly proposes liberation through education and is thus unable to translate its goals successfully or equally for all classes of society. In Syria, uniformed high school girls serve as clean-up crews in villages and participate in youth leagues, but they are still encouraged to marry early and to enter "female" professions such as teaching. Women have been important in religious opposition groups in Syria, including the outlawed Muslim Brotherhood. When Sunnī urban women adopted the *ḥijāb* (Islamic dress), some were met by officially organized demonstrations of ʿAlawī Baʿthī women, who unsuccessfully protested the wearing of *ḥijāb* in school and work settings. [*See* Dress; Ḥijāb.]

Women's participation in student movements has been a feature of Islamic revival in Malaysia, known generally as *dakwah* (Ar., *daʿwah*). Dissension has arisen over the increase in veiling, and in response to communal Muslim groups who hold spirituality high and reject traditional careers. Similarly, debate continues over the appropriate level of female participation in the public sphere, ranging from sermons emphasizing a strong Muslim family life to the complete segregation of female *dakwah* communal members. In Malaysia the gender discussion combines with that one concerning national identity, as the Malay majority coexists with other communities (Chinese, Indian, and aboriginal) who are legally free to observe their own faiths. The religious revival was propagated by several organizations including the Islamic Youth League of Malaysia, Dar ul Arqam, and the more traditional Jemaat Tabligh. Clusters of adherents to revivalist groups form same-sex "family" groups *(usrah)*, which create horizontal linkages, and solidarity.

In Indonesia the Muhammadiyah organization, begun in 1912, typifies apolitical educational and service activities. The Aisyiyah was the women's branch of this party, allowing for mobilization beyond the traditional teacher-peasant dynamic existing in Indonesia as well as Malaysia. [*See* Muhammadiyah.] After the Sukarno era, religious political parties were banned under Suharto, and the four existing Islamic parties combined into the PPP (Partai Persatuan Pembangunan). Nonetheless, religiosity has been on the rise in Indonesia, along with contemporary Islamic dress. Groups such as the Association of Islamic Students eschew militance but view gender issues as integrally tied to Muslim identity.

The most important locus of Islamist activity in Pakistan has been the Jamāʿat-i Islāmī and the Tablīghī Jamāʿat. Both propose countering secularization and Western gender identity with a Muslim notion of modesty and piety. With the growth of Islamist parties and persons in politics, disputes over gender issues have increased, including legal debates over whether rape victims can be prosecuted as adulteresses. Veiling and separation of the sexes have continued, though nuanced by the changing fortunes of the various political actors and parties. Many Muslim women's associations and publications exist, and growing numbers of Islamist or non-Islamist women are involved in politics.

The emergence of the Islamic Republic of Iran sparked new interest in women's role in the revolution and response to the Republic's legislation of gender. Many women, Islamist and non-Islamist, had been involved in opposition to Shah Muhammad Reza Pahlavi. However, when the government imposed Islamic dress and removed women from legal, judicial, and other offices, many Iranians fled. Nonetheless, women actively participated in the Mujāhidīn-i Khalq, an organization of Marxist-Islamic orientation not fully defeated in Iran until 1981–1982. A patrol and information division called the Zaynab Sisters and other women's associations began operating in Iran. Despite Ayatollah Ruhollah Khomeini's ideology of domesticity for women, they worked in higher numbers in the 1980s than ever before, probably owing to the impact of the Iran-Iraq war (Moghadam, 1988).

The islamization of Muslim society on both organized and informal planes heightened throughout the Muslim world in the 1980s. Women were fully involved in the process, whether because of familial loyalties, peer pressure—particularly in high schools and universities—or because they were recruited by Islamist groups. The tensions arising from young women's participation in Islamism were often related to a generational and ideological gap. For example, in the Sudan, where women were active in one of the strongest Communist parties in the region, reversals in the public sphere have been marked. Liberal Islamist groups such as the Republican Brothers and Sisters were repressed, and gender policies are now far more conservative.

In some areas, nationalist and Islamist goals interact and mobilize women, as among the Shīʿīs of southern and eastern Lebanon. Necessity impelled many women to make use of political networks in the absence of their imprisoned or fighting men. Women resisted the Israeli occupiers when possible and were harrassed, attacked, and arrested in return. Most adopted the *ḥijāb* and an actively anti-Western stance in reaction to the Israeli occupation and in order to assert communal identity.

Women were crucial to the waging of the *intifāḍah* in the occupied West Bank and the Gaza Strip. Their participation was both at the grassroots level and through the four women's committees of the PLO, founded in 1981, which have sponsored economic, health, and political projects. These committees and the General Union of Palestinian Women's Associations in diaspora include both Muslim and Christian women. Much tension has arisen between these activist women and supporters of Ḥamās and Islamic Jihād, with a virtual imposition of the *ḥijāb* in Gaza and campaigns attacking unveiled women elsewhere.

With global migration, large groups of Muslim women are now living outside historically Muslim lands. Some have begun to organize, as in the North American Association of Muslim Women (founded 1992). Certain secularist, feminist, and anti-Islamist organizations should also be mentioned: one is the Arab Women's Solidarity Association (dissolved in Egypt in 1992 in response to Islamist pressure); others based outside the region are the Women Against Fundamentalism in Britain, made up of Muslim, Hindu, and English women, which developed from the anti-racist movement, and the Network of Women Living under Muslim Laws, based in southern France.

[*See also* Feminism; Women and Islam; Women and Social Reform.]

BIBLIOGRAPHY

Afshar, Haleh. "Women, State, and Ideology in Iran." *Third World Quarterly*, no. 2 (1985).

Ahmed, Leila. *Women and Gender in Islam*. New Haven, 1992. Includes much information on social movements and women as part of a general survey on women and gender issues. The author considers first-wave feminism in Egypt to have been a handmaiden to colonialism.

Badran, Margot, and Miriam Cooke, eds. *Opening the Gates: A Century of Arab Feminist Writing*. Bloomington, Ind., 1990. Provides an introduction to the experience of Arab feminism and women's discourse, with translated selections of women's essays, poems, stories, memoirs, and interviews.

Beck, Lois, and Nikki R. Keddie, eds. *Women in the Muslim World*. Cambridge, 1978. Certain selections cover social movements while others concern women's status in particular settings.

Callaway, Barbara J. *Muslim Hausa Women in Nigeria: Tradition and Change*. Syracuse, N.Y., 1987.

Haddad, Yvonne Yazbeck. "Palestinian Women: Patterns of Legitimation and Domination." In *The Sociology of the Palestinians*, edited by Khalil Nakhleh and Elia Zureik. London, 1980.

Haddad, Yvonne Yazbeck, and Adair T. Lummis. *Islamic Values in the United States: A Comparative Study*. New York, 1987. Incorporates discussion of women's issues and roles among Muslim Americans.

Haeri, Shahla. "Obedience versus Autonomy: Women and Fundamentalism in Iran and Pakistan." In *Fundamentalisms and Society: Reclaiming the Sciences, the Family and Education*, edited by Martin E. Marty and R. Scott Appleby, pp. 181–213. Chicago, 1993.

Hamammi, Rema. "Women, the Hijab, and the Intifadhah." *Middle East Report*, nos. 164–165 (May–August 1990).

Hijab, Nadia. *Womanpower: The Arab Debate on Women at Work*. Cambridge, 1988. State-by-state coverage of the debates over family law and the workplace, including materials on the Gulf countries, Jordan, North Africa, and Egypt.

Hiltermann, Joost R. *Behind the Intifada: Labor and Women's Movements in the Occupied Territories*. Princeton, 1991. Because the "Muslim dimension" is not emphasized here, the reader is directed to Haddad, Hamammi, and Peteet.

Kandiyoti, Deniz, ed. *Women, Islam, and the State*. Philadelphia, 1991. Includes analyses of the interaction of nations, parties, and women's issues in Turkey, Iran, Pakistan, Bangladesh, India, Egypt, Iraq, Lebanon, and Yemen.

Keddie, Nikki R., and Beth Baron, eds. *Women in Middle Eastern History*. New Haven, 1992. See the introduction by Keddie and chapters by Nermin Abadan-Unat, Mary Hegland, Deniz Kandiyoti, Erika Friedl, and Cynthia Nelson.

Macleod, Arlene Elowe. *Accommodating Protest: Working Women, the New Veiling, and Change in Cairo*. New York, 1991.

Moghadam, Valentine M. *Modernizing Women: Gender and Social Change in the Middle East*. Boulder, 1993.

Mumtaz, Khawar, and Farida Shaheed. *Women of Pakistan: Two Steps Forward, One Step Back?* London, 1987.

Nagata, Judith. "Indices of the Islamic Resurgence in Malaysia: The Medium and the Message." In *Religious Resurgence: Contemporary Cases in Islam, Christianity, and Judaism,* edited by Richard Antoun and Mary Elaine Hegland, pp. 108–126. New York, 1987.

Peteet, Julie M. *Gender in Crisis: Women and the Palestinian Resistance Movement.* New York, 1991. Detailed account of the Palestinian movement in Lebanon.

Rugh, Andrea B. "Reshaping Personal Relations in Egypt." In *Fundamentalisms and Society: Reclaiming the Sciences, the Family and Education,* edited by Martin E. Marty and R. Scott Appleby, pp. 151–180. Chicago, 1993.

Shaʿrāwī, Hūdā. *Harem Years: The Memoirs of an Egyptian Feminist.* Translated by Margot Badran. London, 1986.

Tabari, Azar, and Nahid Yeganeh. *In the Shadow of Islam: The Women's Movement in Iran.* London, 1982.

Tucker, Judith E., ed. *Arab Women: Old Boundaries, New Frontiers.* Bloomington, Ind., 1993. See selections by Mervat Hatem, Margot Badran, Sondra Hale, Julie Peteet, Rosemary Sayigh, and Suad Dajani.

Utas, Bo, ed. *Women in Islamic Societies: Social Attitudes and Historical Perspectives.* London, 1983. Includes studies of women in Iran, Afghanistan, Albania, Malaysia, Indonesia, Palestine, Algeria, Turkey, and the western Sahel of Africa.

Zuhur, Sherifa. *Revealing Reveiling: Islamist Gender Ideology in Contemporary Egypt.* Albany, N.Y., 1992. Women and gender issues in and outside Islamist movements in Egypt, attributing the success of the ideology to a mixture of historical, political, religious, and socioeconomic factors. For a variant argument, see Macleod above.

SHERIFA ZUHUR

WORLD ASSEMBLY OF MUSLIM YOUTH. *See* International Islamic Federation of Student Organizations.

WORLD MUSLIM CONGRESS. *See* Congresses.

Y

YAN TATSINE. *See* Mai Tatsine.

YEMEN. For a number of reasons, the nineteenth century was a momentous period in modern Yemeni history: first, the Ottoman Empire decided to reassert its presence in both the lowlands (Tihama) and the highlands of the country; second, the British empire decided to take Aden in order to assert concretely its interest in the Red Sea and Indian Ocean arenas; and third, the Yemeni politicoreligious elite underwent significant changes that affected both state politics and certain aspects of Zaydī Islam. In the twentieth century, the aftereffects of these changes have produced the most dramatic and important alteration in the Zaydī community since its inception.

The establishment of the Zaydī sect in the mountains of Yemen in the ninth century CE is without doubt the most important political and religious event in Yemen after its conversion to Islam in 628. Although Zaydī Islam experienced vagaries under Yemen's various ruling dynasties (Ayyūbid, Rasūlid, Tahirid, and others) or in the regional ascendancy of families such as the Ṣulayḥids and the Yuʿfirids, it established itself as the dominant faith in the highland areas. Its views on matters of faith, morals, social organization, justice, taxation, and many other aspects of human behavior—many criminal acts, however, remained within the purview of tribal law (*ʿurf*)—had come to dominate the lives of most highland Yemenis; it spread into some lowland areas as well through the efforts of particularly ambitious or capable imams. Nevertheless, the predominantly Shāfiʿī population of the southern and lowland areas never fully accepted the legitimacy of Zaydī rule—a factor that was to play an important role in the dramatic political changes after World War II, including the creation of the Yemen Arab Republic in 1962.

A modern demographic survey of the population of Yemen was not undertaken until the 1970s, so there is considerable uncertainty concerning relative population strengths and percentages before that time. While it is generally conceded that the Zaydīs dominated the highland areas both demographically and politically, it is less certain exactly how much of the population consisted of Ismāʿīlīs and Shāfiʿīs, not to mention the Jews still found in Zaydī areas. Although some imams carried out policies designed to reduce or perhaps even eliminate the political, social, and most importantly the economic strength of the non-Zaydī population, we do not know how effective they were. Most writers, including Yemenis, accept that the Zaydīs made up more than 50 percent of the total population; if we divide the remainder among Shāfiʿīs, Ismāʿīlīs, and Jews, it is at least clear that no one of these three (least of all the latter) approached the proportion of the Zaydīs. The innumerable ways in which Zaydī thought has penetrated Yemeni social and political life (even in Shāfiʿī areas) provides additional if subjective evidence of Zaydī dominance.

Zaydī Islam is, at least in theory, exclusivist; that is, the leaders (imams) of the sect lay claim to the whole panoply of titles associated with leadership of the entire Islamic *ummah* (community)—*amīk al-mu'munīr* (commander of the faithful), and *khalīfah* (caliph, successor to Muḥammad as leader of the *ummah*). The attitudes of the imams to the other Islamic sects of Yemen varied considerably: some appear to have been quite dedicated to the conversion or eradication of non-Zaydī Muslims within the polity; others seem to have been rather liberal in their treatment of their Islamic brethren, to the extent of allocating at least some positions of authority (e.g., judgeships) to them. In fact, it may be argued that major factors in the eventual elimination of the imamate (1962) were the rather intolerant attitudes, policies, and activities—particularly with respect to the substantial economic role of the Shāfiʿīs—of the last two imams of the Ḥāmid al-Dīn clan, Yaḥyā (r. 1904–1948) and Aḥmad (1948–1962). Certainly the Shāfiʿī community was extraordinarily well represented in opposition parties and movements.

The most important office in the Zaydī structure is that of imam, at once a religious and political office. The fourteen requirements that must be fulfilled to claim legitimacy in the position effectively limited the field of candidates to a small fraction of the total Zaydī population; it was estimated in the 1950s that no more than 50,000 of the total estimated population of around 5.5 million were eligible. This group, who could demonstrate direct lineal descent from Muḥammad through his daughter Fāṭimah and her husband ʿAlī, were collectively known as the *sada* (the plural of *sayyid*) and constituted the pool from which the imam must be selected. However, in the past few centuries the imams were invariably selected from a much smaller group of families, among which some of the best-known are the Bayt al-Qāsim, Bayt Sharaf al-Dīn, Bayt al-Wazīr, and Bayt Ḥāmid al-Dīn.

In theory, the Zaydī community must have an imam for its continued legitimacy: his functions as religious leader of the community and chief policymaker cannot be assigned to others (though others may claim them). However, the last imam to exercise the authority associated with the position, Muḥammad al-Badr, today lives in exile in a suburb of London; he is barred from any leadership function whatsoever in the contemporary political system as part of the Compromise Agreement that ended the civil war of 1962–1970. In theory, this is an unacceptable situation for the Zaydī community.

Although Yemeni tradition does not condone succession within specific families to the imamate, this has often occurred. At the beginning of the nineteenth century, one of these dynasties was nearing the end of its tenure in the office of imam, and apparently its store of ability, effectiveness, dedication, and concern with the public weal: Bayt al-Qāsim had taken over the imamate in the late sixteenth century from Bayt Sharaf al-Dīn. By the mid-nineteenth century, however, conflicts among family members had become intense, and one member (ʿAlī Manṣūr) had served as imam on three separate occasions before being killed in 1849. For nearly fifty years thereafter, there was no effective leadership.

During this period, the various imams had to struggle with the new phenomenon on the Arabian Peninsula: the rise of the Wahhābī sect and the efforts of the Ottoman Empire and its putative agents, Muḥammad ʿAlī and the Egyptian army, to counter it, as well as the efforts of local shaykhs to assert their independence. The result was the occupation of the Tihama, the loss of Asir, and the temporary occupation of portions of Yemen by the contending forces. At the same time, Europeans were once again contesting control of the Red Sea trade after the opening of the Suez Canal in 1869.

The doctrines of the Wahhābīs had no theoretical impact on the characteristics of Zaydī Islam, but the Wahhābīs and their ideological campaigns had other effects on Yemen. First, the imams became embroiled in a number of campaigns in areas they perceived to be integral parts of Yemen, including Asir and the Tihama. Second, the imams asserted their right to decide, at a very minimum, matters of "faith and morals" for the Zaydī community, and opposed such matters being decided by Sunnī non-Yemenis, even if they were Arabs or lived in the peninsula. (This same logic applied later to the efforts of the [Sunnī] Ottoman Empire to impose its civil and criminal codes and conceptions upon the population of the highlands.) Third, the efforts of the sultan to diminish if not completely eliminate the Wahhābī threat brought another non-Zaydī and Sunnī influence to Yemen—that of the Egyptians. Perhaps the most important effect was the increased perception among Yemenis of their distinctiveness: the multitude of foreign presences and threats heightened the desire to maintain Zaydī culture and civilization.

The mid-nineteenth century was dominated by another of the frequent and prolonged disputes which have all too often characterized Yemeni history: conflicts between various imams and local notables who wished to retain their hold over specific areas, for example the Tihama, Asir, or such cities as Mokha. The length, scope, and ferocity of the battles eventually led the Ottoman Empire to conclude that it was an auspicious time to retake the Yemeni Tihama. This would give the empire leverage over the activities of the imam and his opponents in the highland regions; furthermore, the impact of the conflicts was beginning to spread into other areas of the empire, such as the Hejaz. The empire took the Tihama in short order and was soon able to persuade the imam to become its vassal in exchange for a contingent of troops to support his regime, a portion of revenues, and a monthly stipend. However, when Ottoman troops appeared in San'a, they were massacred; the imam's agreement with the empire was perceived as treacherous and traitorous by both tribal elements and the residents at San'a. The imam was deposed and shortly thereafter executed by his successor.

The aftermath of these developments appears to have

been anarchy in the highlands, including San'a, as various families and other factions competed for the imamate, for control of the city, and for whatever commercial activities were still viable. Within a period of less than six years, nine imams tried to gain control of the highlands. When developments in Yemen once again affected other areas, the Ottoman Turks decided to intervene, apparently with the support of an important segment of the San'ani commercial elite, who had concluded that Turkish rule would be an improvement on the existing anarchy.

Accordingly, in 1872 Ottoman troops entered San'a and added Yemen to the empire; there seems little doubt that the occupation was largely motivated by the increased importance of the Red Sea as a trade route after the opening of the Suez Canal, and by the fact that the British had already established themselves at the southern end of the Red Sea by taking Aden in 1839.

Ottoman rule, however, was not popular; both Zaydīs and Shāfiʿīs were offended by the Turkish administration (which was often corrupt as well as incompetent) as well as by the Turkish attitude toward Islam, which was perceived as too lax. Resentment and opposition grew; the selection of Muḥammad ibn Yaḥyā of the Ḥamīd al-Dīn clan as imam in 1891 was the occasion for a renewed outbreak of rebellion against the Ottomans. The empire sent a variety of administrators—some conciliatory and competent, some high-handed and corrupt—but none was successful in eliminating the basic grounds for Yemeni resentment and opposition.

The accession to the imamate of Muḥammad's son Yaḥyā in 1904 was the occasion for another outbreak against Ottoman rule; the next decade witnessed temporary agreements between the imam and the Ottoman authorities (e.g., the 1911 Treaty of Da'an) as well as renewed battles. The imam's primary motives and the bases for his success were essentially two: first, he was determined to see the Islamic legal code *(sharīʿah)* reinstated as the basis of both religious and civil life in Yemen; and second, he opposed the policies and presence of the Ottomans, especially their decision effectively to sign away parts of Yemen to its enemies, as in the 1904 border agreement delimiting a frontier between the Adeni possessions of Great Britain and the Ottoman *vilayet* of Yemen.

Yemen played only a minor role in World War I; in effect, the Ottoman and British authorities agreed to a stalemate truce on their mutual frontier. One fact concerning the imam's position is worthy of note: he refused to join the anti-Ottoman alliance developed among the Arabs by the British, because he considered it both inappropriate and inconceivable for Yemen to align itself with a Christian state against a Muslim one, no matter how atrocious the policies and actions of the latter. This commitment to Islam as a source of and a justification for public policy remains a consistent theme throughout Imam Yaḥyā's reign and appears to have been completely genuine.

The end of World War I brought the departure of the Ottomans and the de facto independence of Yemen under the leadership of Imam Yaḥyā. Despite his best efforts, however, international recognition of Yemen, and his role therein, was not forthcoming until about a decade after the war's end. Upon independence, the imam sought to implement a set of goals clearly influenced by his position as imam of the Zaydīs.

These may be briefly summarized. The first was to impose the *sharīʿah* over his entire realm. This was to prove far more difficult and contentious than one might suppose, since it amounted to a direct challenge to the power, influence, and position of the tribes, who from time immemorial had used tribal law to resolve many if not most of their disputes despite their nominal adherence to Zaydī Islam. Second, the imam wished to weaken the domestic political and military power of the tribes, if for no other reason than to make it difficult for them to challenge his authority in domestic matters. His third goal was to regain, by force if necessary, the territories that the imams saw as their legitimate patrimony, that is, parts of historic Yemen that had been alienated by the Ottomans or seized by the British, including Aden and its hinterland, Asir, and others. Finally, he sought to reduce the domestic power of other families that had historically held the imamate and could therefore legitimately challenge the Ḥāmid al-Dīns for power. This involved the assertion of Ḥāmid al-Dīn authority in all areas of the state, geographic, administrative, military, judicial, and elsewhere.

Imam Yaḥyā was resourceful, dedicated, strong-willed, and extraordinarily capable; it may be argued that he largely succeeded in all of his goals for the new state, of which he also declared himself king. It was, however, inevitable that his policies would produce domestic opposition; by the mid-1940s, they had generated an alliance of individuals and groups that were united primarily by their opposition to Imam Yaḥyā, but not in meaningful agreement on an alternative. Indeed, the opposition ran the gamut from progressives who saw the preceding three decades as a rearguard action for policies and goals completely out of touch with the twentieth century, to conservatives who wished to institute an alternative vision of Islam (e.g., the Muslim Brotherhood) or merely to place a different family in the imamate. They were briefly united in the movement, which assassinated Imam Yaḥyā in 1948.

Despite (or perhaps because of) the breadth of the coalition, it deteriorated immediately upon Yaḥyā's death in face of the determination of Imam Yaḥyā's son Aḥmad to reassert the role of the Ḥāmid al-Dīns and the political power of the Zaydī tribes. Within weeks Aḥmad was recognized as the new imam, and the political system largely reverted to the policies associated with his father. Over the next two decades a multifaceted opposition movement reappeared, including many of the same elements. This time, however, it had the support of significant elements of the military, as well as a much larger base among both the Zaydī and Shāfiʿī communities. When Imam Aḥmad died in September 1962 and was succeeded by his son Muḥammad al-Badr, the opposition decided to act. One week after Aḥmad's death, al-Badr was deposed and a Republic of Yemen was proclaimed.

Muḥammad al-Badr, however, was able to organize many of the northern Zaydī tribes in opposition to the new republic. The motivations of these tribal elements were complex and frequently involved non-Islamic and even non-Zaydī factors. Those seeking to return the imam to power became popularly known as "royalists," while those committed to the new government were known as "republicans." Unfortunately for Yemen, some countries viewed the dispute in terms of their regional and global interests and elected to intervene. For eight years the two groups of Yemenis and their respective allies fought for the right to determine the nature of the political system. Eventually, the two Yemeni antagonists decided to compromise, in no small measure to rid themselves of the foreign parties to the conflict. The two most important provisions of the Compromise were, first, that the new state would be a republic, but some prominent royalists would be integrated into the government; and second and probably more important in view of Yemen's history, the imam agreed to go into exile, thus ending more than one thousand years of the Zaydī imamate in Yemen.

It is probably too soon to declare permanently the end of the Zaydī imamate. First, although there has been relatively little public discussion of the issue, traditional Zaydī Islam does not really acknowledge or accept a state of affairs in which the community does not have an imam. Second, the contemporary political system is in a state of flux owing largely to the amalgamation in 1990 of the two formerly separate states of Yemen; some may see the reintroduction of the imamate as a possible integrating mechanism to provide the system with a measure of legitimacy that it has so far had difficulty in developing. Third, there is some support for those who seek to reinstate the imamate, although these individuals and their supporters usually cast their argument in terms of creating a "constitutional" imamate. Finally, the tendency in many other Islamic countries to reintroduce older, more traditional Islamic institutions to cope with the stresses of the modern secularized and westernized world suggests that it is premature to assert that Yemen is immune to such inclinations—though it is highly unlikely that the traditional imamate would be reinstalled.

[*See also* Imam; Zaydīyah.]

BIBLIOGRAPHY

Amin, S. H. *Law and Justice in Contemporary Yemen.* Glasgow, 1987. Survey of the contemporary legal system and the relevance of Islamic law to its development and current concepts.

Amri, Husayn b. Abdullah al-. *The Yemen in the 18th and 19th Centuries.* London, 1985. An essential work for this period, especially the life and works of Muḥammad al-Shawkānī, a key figure in modern Zaydī thought.

Daum, Werner, ed. *Yemen: 3000 Years of History.* Frankfurt 1988. Comprehensive survey of all aspects of Yemen, including Islam.

Dresch, Paul. *Tribes, Government, and History in Yemen.* Oxford, 1989. The most comprehensives survey and analysis of the role of the tribes in Yemen, and the relevance of Islamic concepts an principles to their politics and policies.

Gerholm, Tomas. *Market, Mosque, and Mafraj.* Stockholm, 1977. A description and analysis of the Yemeni social system, and the role that Zaydī Islam has played in its development.

Madelung, Wilferd. "Imāmā." In *Encyclopaedia of Islam,* new ed. vol. 3, pp. 1163–1169. Leiden, 1960–. Review and analysis of the Zaydī imamate.

Serjeant, R. B. "The Zaydis." In *Religion in the Middle East,* edited by A. J. Arberry. Vol. 2 Cambridge, 1969. Thorough survey of Zaydism in the context of Islam and the Middle East.

Serjeant, R. B. and Ronald Lewcock, eds. *Sana'a: An Arabian Islamic City.* London, 1983. Thorough, scholarly, and utterly fascinating survey of all aspects of Sana'a, including aspects of Islam and its impact on hygiene, diet, urban development, and so forth.

Strothmann, Rudolf. "al-Zaidiya." In *Encyclopaedia of Islam,* 1st ed., vol. 4, pp. 1196–1198. Leiden, 1934. One of the few articles in English by *the* scholar of Zaydī Islam.

Wenner, Manfred W. *Yemen Arab Republic.* Boulder, 1991. A survey of all aspects of Yemen that attempts to update the relevance of

Islam to contemporary politics after the abolishment of the imamate.

MANFRED W. WENNER

YOUNG OTTOMANS. The libertarian movement known as the Young Ottomans (Yeni Osmanlılar) developed the first constitutionalist ideology to appear in the Ottoman Empire; it was influential circa 1860–1876. In the first half of the nineteenth century Ottoman officials embarked on a policy of reforms that came to be known as the Tanzimat (Regulation). The first political expressions of this reform policy were contained in two documents: the Hatt-ı Hümayun of Gülhane (1839), a semiconstitutional charter that promised security of person and property to all Ottoman subjects, and the Reform Edict of 1856, which covered a more diverse catalog of rights and made a special point of guaranteeing protection to the non-Muslim population of the empire. The Reform Edict had extensive negative repercussions among Ottoman Muslims; one of its outcomes was the so-called Kuleli Conspiracy (1859). The leader of the conspiracy was a Naqshbandī (Tk., Nakşibendi) *shaykh*, and some younger officials took part in it. This alliance of disgruntled clerics and young officials shifted during the 1860s into a more clearly liberal-constitutionalist stance inspired by Western liberalism. At that time the religious component was relegated to a secondary role, possibly because the democratic ideals expressed in recently founded journals by the young officials could reach a wider audience through their use of demotic Turkish, although at least one newspaper represented the conservative strain.

In 1865 some young civil officials in Istanbul established a secret society, the Patriotic Alliance. With one foot in officialdom and another in journalism, these men began systematically to criticize the policy of the architects of the Tanzimat. Among their targets were two Ottoman officials, Âli Paşa and Fuad Paşa, who had shared the direction of Ottoman internal and foreign policy. These statesmen were accused of using westernization to establish the autocratic rule of a bureaucratic elite, of undermining Ottoman culture through their neglect of Islam as a guideline for social and political values, and of having failed to defend the interests of the Ottoman Empire against the encroachments of Western powers. Two leaders of the Young Ottoman movement, the poet Mehmet Namık Kemal and the administrator Ziya Bey (later Pasa), eventually had to flee from Istanbul into exile in 1867. They organized an opposition movement in Paris and London, funded by an Ottoman-Egyptian prince who expected to use the movement for his own narrower aims. The exiles were joined by the cleric Ali Suavi, who represented the earlier Islamic reaction to the Tanzimat and who seemed to support constitutionalism.

Kemal and Ziya soon perceived that Suavi's ideas of democracy had a very different foundation from theirs; Ziya himself was more conservative than Kemal. The newspaper they published, *Hürriyet* (Freedom), boldly expressed democratic ideals in Turkish, but it soon had to cease publication owing to conflicts among the movement's leaders. After 1870 the Young Ottoman leaders returned to Turkey and continued their defense of libertarian ideals, with repeated interruptions by censorship and exile. Their ideas were partially instrumental in inspiring civilian and military officials to dethrone Sultan Abdülaziz (r. 1861–1876), although the Young Ottomans themselves had never opposed the monarchic principle in theory.

The Young Ottomans were in part responsible for the elaboration of the first Ottoman Constitution (1876) and the short-lived Ottoman parliament it created. Namık Kemal's impassioned defense of liberty as well as his fiery patriotism—both strongly influenced by European Romanticism—continued to be an inspiration for the Young Turks who emerged in the 1890s.

[*See also* Ottoman Empire; Tanzimat; Young Turks; *and the biographies of Kemal and Suavi.*]

BIBLIOGRAPHY

Bilgegil, M. Kaya. *Yakın Çağ Türk Kültür ve Edebiyatı uzerinde Araştırmalar.* I: *Yeni Osmanlılar.* Ankara, 1976.

Mardin, Şerif. *The Genesis of Young Ottoman Thought.* Princeton, 1962.

Tansel, F. A. "Kemāl, Meḥmed Nāmıḳ." In *Encyclopaedia of Islam*, new ed., vol. 4, pp. 875–879. Leiden, 1960–.

Tevfik, Ebuzziya. *Yeni Osmanlılar Tarihi.* 3 vols. Edited by Zeyyat Ebuzziya. *Ankara, 1973–1974.*

ŞERIF MARDIN

YOUNG TURKS. Europe designated as the "Young Turks" the opposition to Sultan Abdülhamid II's regime (1876–1908) that restored the constitution on 23 July 1908 and ruled the Ottoman Empire until its destruction in 1918. This opposition movement was the successor to the "Young Ottomans" who had been responsible for the promulgation of the first constitution in December 1876. But after Abdülhamid shelved the constitution in February 1878 and dissolved the New Ottoman Association, the movement went underground or into exile.

In 1889 a new body was formed calling itself the Committee of Ottoman Union; it soon became famous as the Ottoman Committee of Union and Progress (CUP). It was active mainly in Europe and Egypt, and its members came from virtually every ethnic and religious community in the empire. Turks, Arabs, Kurds, Albanians, Armenians, and Greeks united under the umbrella of Ottomanism in opposition to Hamidian autocracy. In 1906 certain officials and military officers formed the secret Ottoman Freedom Society in the port city of Salonika. The following year, the two bodies merged under the established name of the CUP, but it was the Salonika group that led the revolution and forced the sultan to restore the 1876 constitution.

After July 1908, the Young Turks were divided into two broad groups, both determined to maintain the integrity of the Ottoman Empire, but by rather different methods. The Unionists emphasized unity and modernization under a centralized state as the way to progress. The liberals, who formed the Liberal Party (Ahrar Fırkası) in 1908 and the Liberal Union in 1911, favored a decentralized polity with substantial autonomy for the non-Turkish, non-Muslim communities. Both groups stayed away from religion as much as they could, a difficult task in an empire still organized on essentially religious lines in *millet*s or religious communities. In fact, the Young Turks had to undermine the traditional privileges enjoyed by the non-Muslim *millet*s in order to create a modern state. One such privilege permitted foreign states to act as protectors of particular *millet*s; thus Russia protected the Greek Orthodox community and France the Catholic, giving these nations power to interfere in Ottoman affairs and violating the state's sovereignty.

The goal of maintaining a multinational, multireligious empire forced the Young Turks to adopt a dynasty-based ideology of Ottomanism and to shun both nationalism and religion. There were, however, both nationalists and Islamists in their ranks: Said Halim Pasha was an Islamist and Ziya Gökalp a nationalist, and both were prominent in the CUP. Initially they were kept in the background, and Islam became the instrument of the conservative and reactionary opposition; yet even the liberals exploited it during the insurrection of April 1909 led by the İttihad-i Muhammadi Cemiyeti. [*See also* İttihad-i Muhammadi Cemiyeti *and the biographies of Said Halim and Gökalp.*] After this traumatic event, the Unionists became more cautious about fostering social reform that might alienate Islamist opinion influenced by such journals as *Sebilürreşad* and *Sirat-i müstakim*. Thus they emphasized the religious element in the ceremony of girding the sword of Osman when Sultan Mehmed V succeeded the deposed Abdülhamid. On 10 May 1909, Mehmed Reşad was taken to the mausoleum of his ancestor at Eyüb and, in the presence of civil and religious notables, Abdülhalim Efendi, the leader of the Mevlevî order who traced his line to Mevlana Jelâl ed-Din Rumi (Ar., Mawlānā Jalāl al-Dīn Rūmī), girded the sword on the new sultan.

After the abortive insurrection of 1909, the two factions of the Young Turks competed for political supremacy under the watchful eye of the military high command under Mahmud Şevket Pasha, the general who had crushed the rebellion. In July 1912, while Istanbul was at war with Italy over Libya, a military coup brought the liberals to power, and it seemed that the CUP's days were numbered. But the Unionists took advantage of the defeats suffered by Ottoman armies at the hands of the Balkan states (Serbia, Montenegro, Bulgaria, and Greece) in the war that broke out in October 1912. In the political chaos in the capital they seized power in January 1913 and consolidated it in June by destroying the liberal opposition.

The wars with Italy and the Balkan states weakened the multinational, multireligious character of Ottomanism while strengthening its Islamic and nationalist elements. Italy's attack and occupation of Libya, an Arab province, boosted Islamic solidarity. The loss of virtually all territories in the Balkans followed by the expulsions of much of their Muslim population left the empire with a predominantly Muslim/Turkish Anatolia and the Arab provinces. This trend continued during World War I with the massacre and deportation of the Armenians from eastern Anatolia as well as the arrival of Turks from the Caucasus.

In 1913, following the example of the Jacobins in the French Revolution, the nationalist faction of the CUP organized the Committees of National Defense and Public Safety to facilitate the conduct of war. To appease Arab opinion, Mahmud Şevket Pasha, who was born in Baghdad and claimed he was Arab, was appointed grand vizier in January 1913. Following his assassination in June 1913, the Egyptian prince Said Halim Pasha succeeded him and led the government until February

1917—the longest grand vizierate of the Young Turk period. Ottomanism strongly tinged with Islam had now become the ideology of the Young Turks.

The Islam of the Unionists, however, was ideologically different from that of the Islamists. This is apparent from articles that appeared in *Islam mecmuası* (Journal of Islam), first published in February 1914. Unlike the Islamists, the Unionists argued that nationalism was not contrary to Islam but complemented it. Moreover, religion had to conform to the needs of everyday life; this idea was summed up in the words on the journal's masthead, "A Religious Life and a Living Religion." Islam had to be interpreted in terms of the new conditions confronting Muslims in order to be of living significance. The writers in *Islam mecmuası* went so far as to propose the separation of religion from the state. Only this reform, they claimed, could make Islam a vital part of a Muslim's everyday life; religious reform required taking measures to make religion a matter of conscience while subordinating the legal aspects of Islam to secular legislation. The first step was the concern of religious leaders and institutions, while the second was the job of the state. Some of these ideas were put in action by the Unionist government during the war; they were adopted wholesale by Atatürk's republic and provided the foundations for its policy of secularization.

[*See also* Ottoman Empire; Young Ottomans.]

BIBLIOGRAPHY

Ahmad, Feroz. *The Young Turks*. Oxford, 1969. Useful for the politics of the period 1908–1914.

Arai, Masami. *Turkish Nationalism in the Young Turks Era*. Leiden and New York, 1992. Original analysis of nationalist thought with a most useful chapter on *Islam mecmuası*.

Berkes, Niyazi. *The Development of Secularism in Turkey*. Montreal, 1964. Superb study of Ottoman/Turkish intellectual history.

Lewis, Bernard. *The Emergence of Modern Turkey*. 2d ed. London and New York, 1968. Authoritative account of political and intellectual changes in post-Kemalist Turkey.

Ramsaur, Ernest Edmondson, Jr. *The Young Turks*. Princeton, 1957. Still the best account in English on the period before 1908.

Shaw, Stanford J., and Ezel Kural Shaw. *The History of the Ottoman Empire and Modern Turkey*, vol. 2, *Reform, Revolution, and Republic: The Rise of Modern Turkey, 1808–1975*. Cambridge, London, and New York, 1977. Useful survey of Ottoman and modern Turkish history, with an excellent bibliography.

FEROZ AHMAD

YOUTH MOVEMENTS.

Young people have played an increasingly active and important role in the unfolding of contemporary Islamic revivalism. They have provided Islamic revivalist movements with organizational muscle and foot soldiers, with workers, leaders, and ideologues. They have also exerted considerable control over the socialization of the population groups that will produce the next generation of bureaucrats, educators, and politicians. Islamic youth movements have thus extended the reach of Islamic revivalism and deepened its influence on society and politics. These young activists are significant in what they express and otherwise reveal about the goals of Islamic revivalism. The place of youth in various expressions of Islamic revivalism and their impact on their different societies is, however, far from uniform. Youth movements emerge at different stages in the development of general Islamic movements, and they play radically different roles in the development of revivalism across the Muslim world.

Youth movements can be categorized into three general types: Islamic student movements; Islamic revivalist movements that operate among and are largely composed of young people; and Islamic revivalist movements that are not aimed at youth, but because of the age structure of their societies have essentially become youth movements. The characteristics, modes of operation, and social impact of each will be considered here.

Islamic Student Movements.. Over the past four decades, Islamic student movements have mushroomed across the Muslim world and have even emerged in the West. They have organized university as well as *madrasah* students into important political entities in their respective societies. Some have been directly affiliated with an Islamic revivalist party, as is the case with the Islāmī Jamʿīyat-i Ṭulabā (Islamic Society of Students) of Pakistan, the official student wing of the Jamāʿat-i Islāmī party of that country. Others have not been so closely tied to a single revivalist party and have not operated as discrete entities, as has been the case with the Egyptian Jamāʿat al-Islāmīyah (Islamic Societies). The Jamāʿat are close to the Egyptian Muslim Brotherhood but also maintain ties with other Islamic parties and groups. The Jamaʿat, unlike the Islāmī Jamʿīyat-i Ṭulabā, are loosely structured and do not operate as a single formal organization. The third category consists of Islamic student movements that operate independent of any Islamic revivalist party. The clearest example is the Muslim Student Association of North America, centered in Indiana, which despite its ideological ties to Islamic revivalist parties of the Middle East or South Asia has operated as an autonomous unit. The Jamāʿat and Islāmī Jamʿīyat-i Ṭulabā models have been reproduced in several countries—the first mostly in the Arab world, and the second by other Pakistani Islamic national parties and in Bangladesh.

Despite the differences in their organizational models and origins, the three types of Islamic student movements have much in common. All three have evolved, to some extent, in debate and even confrontation with leftist student movements. The Jamāʿat in the 1970s and the Islāmī Jamʿīyat-i Ṭulabā in the 1950s, 1960s and 1980s even received encouragement from their governments in suppressing leftist activities on various campuses. In Pakistan in 1971, Islāmī Jamʿīyat-i Ṭulabā negotiated directly with the government to help the martial-law administration of East Pakistan launch counterinsurgency units against the left-of-center Bengali guerrilla forces.

All three types of Islamic student movement have produced a whole generation of the leaders and ideologues of Islamic revivalism. Many of Iran's revolutionary elite had been members of the Muslim Student Association during their student days in the United States. The Jamāʿat has produced many of the members of the Muslim Brotherhood as well as of other Egyptian revivalist groups since the 1970s; and one-third of the current leadership of the Jamāʿat-i Islāmī of Pakistan come from Islāmī Jamʿīyat-i Ṭulabā.

In the Muslim world, Islamic student movements also perform a direct social and political function. They generally work to spread the teachings of revivalist ideologues among students—through propaganda work and publications like Islāmī Jamʿīyat-i Ṭulabā's *ʿAzm* (Determination) newspaper and the Muslim Student Association's *Nasr* (Friend) magazine—and they enforce a strict code of ethics on campuses. The Egyptian students have sought to create a bastion of Islamicity on university campuses, a haven to defy the cultural hegemony of the "*jāhilīyah* society" outside. In contrast, in Pakistan and Bangladesh students have been more concerned to establish political control on campuses and to use student activism to mount effective challenges to government authority. Wherever student elections exist, Islamic student movements have participated in them, gearing their activities to wrest control of the universities through that means. They have been largely successful in this endeavor. In 1975–1976 the Egyptian Jamāʿat showed great success in the elections at Cairo University, and since 1971 the Islāmī Jamʿīyat-i Ṭulabā of Pakistan has dominated campus elections in that country.

These successes have encouraged other political forces, Islamic as well as secular, to compete for student support. Islamic student movements have thus intensified student politics and helped turn university campuses into political battlegrounds. As a result, they have also compelled governments to take an active interest in campus politics. Both President Anwar Sadat of Egypt and Prime Minister Zulfiqar ʿAli Bhutto of Pakistan interfered in student elections in their countries with the specific aim of blunting the momentum of the Jamāʿat and the Islāmī Jamʿīyat-i Ṭulabā respectively.

The two governments' concerns had to do with a characteristic all Islamic student movements share: their penchant for radical action. Student riots at Ayn Shams and Cairo universities in Egypt in the 1970s, and at the Punjab University and other campuses across Pakistan during the same time period, are cases in point. In Pakistan student activism reached such a scale that General Muhammad Zia ul-Haq, though sympathetic to Islamic revivalist parties, banned all student activities in 1984 with the specific aim of checking the activities of Islāmī Jamʿīyat-i Ṭulabā. Ideologically, too, student movements have tended to push for radical interpretations of Islamic revivalism. Islāmī Jamʿīyat-i Ṭulabā of Pakistan has been more outspoken than its parent party in demanding Islamic revolution, while the Jamāʿat members have at times favored the more extreme Takfīr wa al-Hijrah over the Muslim Brotherhood.

Islamic student movements, in many instances, were not established as political forces but rather as missionary movements. Politics, however, gradually came to dominate their agendas. As a result of this transformation, politics, and at times a proclivity for violence, have become endemic to these movements, producing an institutionalized mode of behavior that casts student politics in a particular mold.

The power of Islamic student movements emanates from their tightly knit organizational structure. The size of their following, however, reflects the problems that campus life and the urban environment present to Muslim students. Islamic student movements provide students—especially those from traditional families, small towns, and rural areas—with an embracing community. Given the anomie of life in a large metropolis and the myriad of immediate problems and anxieties about the future that surround the life of a student, this sense of community has great appeal. In the case of the Muslim Student Association in America, this community also shelters the student from the pressures of life in an alien culture.

Moreover, by exercising effective social control on campuses, Islamic student movements attract greater numbers, especially from the ranks of rural and small-town students who urgently need assistance. Student movements provide tutorials, help resolve academic and administrative problems, and often control the youth hostels where rural students live. In Pakistan, Islāmī Jamʿīyat-i Ṭulabā also exercises control over the admission process, which bolsters its position among high school students, urban as well as rural. As a result, the proportion of small-town and rural students in the membership of Islamic student groups has grown; student movements have thus extended the reach of Islamic revivalist movements into new social strata. This is especially evident in the case of Islāmī Jamʿīyat-i Ṭulabā of Pakistan, which through its *madrasah* students wing (Jamʿīyat-i Ṭulabā-i ʿArabīyah, Society of Arabic Students), its women's division (Islāmī Jamʿīyat-i Ṭālibāt), and its activity in high schools has significantly broadened the purview of the Jamāʿat-i Islāmī's activities.

Islamic student movements have most often surfaced where Islamic revivalism has developed into a recognized political force that has consciously sought to deepen its influence among various social groups.

Revivalist Movements Based in Youth. Young people have also played a direct role in Islamic revivalist parties. In fact, a number of prominent Islamic movements first emerged in the form of youth movements, and even after developing into political parties have continued to draw large numbers from among the young. The most notable cases are the Sāzmān-i Mujāhidīn-i Khalq-i Īrān (Organization of Iranian People's Mujāhidīn) and Anjuman-i Khayrīyah-i Mahdavīyah-i Ḥujjatīyah (Charitable Society of the Hidden Imam) of Iran, Hamas in the Occupied Territories, and the Sāzmān-i Javānān-i Musulmān (Muslim Youth Organization) of Afghanistan. The Mujāhidīn and the Ḥujjatīyah emerged in Iran in the late 1960s and grew in prominence in the 1970s. Since that time the Mujāhidīn has been an important protest movement, while the Ḥujjatīyah joined the revolutionary regime in 1979. Many Ḥujjatīyah members today occupy high offices in the Islamic Republic of Iran. Neither the Mujāhidīn nor the Ḥujjatīyah were student movements, but both recruited actively among high school and university students. The Mujāhidīn adhered to a left-of-center interpretation of Shiism in line with the ideas of ʿAlī Sharīʿatī, while the Ḥujjatīyah was essentially a missionary society aimed at limiting the appeal of the Bahā'ī faith. The Afghan Javānān and Hamas, on the other hand, advocated a puritanical reading of Islamic orthodoxy.

Unlike Islamic student movements, these youth movements have been less concerned with creating a veritable Islamic society on campuses or among youth more generally; rather, they from inception organized and operated as anti-government protest movements. Although some movements like the Iranian Mujāhidīn or the Afghan Javānān were first established by students, they were primarily concerned not with student affairs but with national politics; and as was the case with the Mujāhidīn, some resorted to radical activities.

These youth movements have not been bound by the perimeters of the university but have spread quickly out of the campuses into the society at large. Merchants, artisans, and bureaucrats were mobilized and recruited, diversifying the social and occupational composition of the movements. The Ḥujjatīyah, for instance, has a strong base of support in the bureaucracy, in the universities, in the armed forces, among the *ʿulamā'*, and in the bazaar. In addition, since these youth movements were not officially student organizations, they have enjoyed greater continuity in their leadership and membership. Leaders and members were not required to leave their offices or the movements upon the completion of their studies, so they have remained with the movement and moved up in its ranks. This has not only strengthened these movements but has also transformed them into parties with more diverse membership and thus broader concerns. The Iranian Mujāhidīn and the Ḥujjatīyah have developed into full-fledged Islamic movements, still recruiting among the youth but increasingly including a wider age group. Ḥamās has gained in strength to become a major actor in the Intifadah. The Afghan Javānān expanded in the 1970s, but eventually disappeared and gave place to the Jamʿīyat-i Islāmī (Islamic Society) and Ḥizb-i Islāmī (Islamic Party), both of which played prominent roles in the Afghan civil war of the 1980s. It should be noted that youth movements of this kind were more predominant during the early years of contemporary Islamic revivalism, when political and religious protest tended to emerge first among the youth. In time, they developed into Islamic movements with a national following and agenda.

Islamic Revivalism in Young Societies. The age structure of many Muslim societies has recently caused some forms of Islamic revivalism to become closely associated with youth. Iran in 1978–1979, Algeria in 1990–1991, Bangladesh in the 1980s, and the Amal and Ḥizbullāh in Lebanon since the 1970s best exemplify this trend [*see* Amal; Ḥizbullāh, *article on* Ḥizbullāh in Lebanon]. Since the 1970s, age distribution in the populations of many Muslim societies has changed so that youth now constitute a large and increasing share of the population. This development has had far-reaching social, economic, and political ramifications. It has placed an undue burden on the fragile economies of Muslim countries and has reduced the real rate of economic growth. As a result, the quality of social services has declined, and the economy has failed to absorb the increasing numbers of new entries into the job market. As the ruling establishment has failed to accommodate a large number of the youth in the formal economy, they have flocked to the ranks of opposition forces, the most important of which in recent years have been Islamic revivalist movements. As a result, the politics of Islamic revivalism in these societies reflects increasingly the frustrations and demands of the youth. Islamic revivalism has in such cases effectively become a youth movement.

Social Base of Youth Movements. Islamic revivalism has generally been associated with the urban lower middle classes. The same has been true of Islamic youth movements. It should be noted, however, that this social base has not been static over time. Youth movements have proven able to expand their reach into small towns and rural areas, gradually recruiting from among the rural middle classes and also the urban poor; Islāmī Jamʿīyat-i Ṭulabā of Pakistan is an example of the first trend, and the Amal and Ḥizbullāh in Lebanon of the second. The social composition of Islamic youth movements, and thus that of Islamic revivalism, has been diversifying in this process.

Some youth movements have also had an ethnic base. In Pakistan between 1947 and 1986, Islāmī Jamʿīyat-i Ṭulabā was strongest among the Muhājirs (the Urdu-speaking community that migrated in 1947 from northern India to settle in Pakistan). In Algeria, Islamic revivalism has had few followers among the sizable contingent of Berber youth and is essentially an Arab movement. Again, with the passage of time the ethnic base of a youth movement may change; for example, the ethnic background of Islāmī Jamʿīyat-i Ṭulabā today is closer to that of Pakistan as a whole, because the organization now includes many Punjabis and Pathans.

It is often argued that Islamic revivalism appeals to those youth who study the natural sciences or engineering. Although the educational background of the leaders and members of youth movements in several Muslim countries supports this assertion, there are important exceptions. In Pakistan, where several Islamic student movements are found, the background of the leaders and members does not show an inclination towards the sciences or engineering. In fact, no one field of study seems to predominate among the members of the various Islamic student movements. Therefore, a direct correlation between fields of study and membership in Islamic youth movements cannot be readily established.

In the end, it should be noted that despite their significant political role, the most important contribution of youth movements to contemporary Islamic revivalism is not political. It is rather manifested in their impact on the gradual islamization of social thought and practice. Youth movements are in a position to influence the socialization of Muslim youth at an impressionable period in their lives, thus laying the foundations for the continuing islamization of culture and society.

[*See also* Ḥamās; Ḥujjatīyah; International Islamic Federation of Student Organizations; Jamāʿat-i Islāmī; Mujāhidīn, *articles on* Mujāhidīn-i Khalq *and* Afghan Mujāhidīn.]

BIBLIOGRAPHY

Abrahamian, Ervand. *Radical Islam: The Iranian Mojahedin.* London, 1989. The most exhaustive source available on Iran's Mujāhidīn-i Khalq organization.

Abū ʿAmr, Ziyād. *Al-Ḥarakah al-Islāmīyah fī al-Ḍiffah al-Gharbīyah wa-Qiṭāʿ Ghazzah.* Akka, 1989. Good account of the Palestinian Islamic movement in the Occupied Territories.

Edwards, David B. "Summoning Muslims: Print, Politics, and Religious Ideology in Afghanistan." *Journal of Asian Studies* 53.3 (August 1993): 609–628. An account of the origins of Afghanistan's Ḥizb-i Islāmī and the role of students in it.

El-Effendi, Abdelwahab. *Turabi's Revolution: Islam and Power in Sudan.* London, 1991. Provides a thorough account of the unfolding of the Ikhwān al-Muslimūn's history.

Kepel, Gilles. *Muslim Extremism in Egypt: The Prophet and Pharaoh.* Berkeley, 1986. Provides a good account of Egyptian Islamic student movements.

Khālid, Salīm Manṣūr, ed. *Jab Vuh Nāẓim-i Aʿlā The!* (When They

Were Nāẓim-i Aʿlā!). 2 vols. Lahore, 1981. Compendium of interviews with the former leaders of the Islāmī Jamʿīyat-i Ṭalabā of Pakistan.

Khālid, Salīm Manṣūr, ed. *Ṭalabah Taḥrīkeṇ* (Student Movements). 2 vols. Lahore, 1989. Comprehensive history of Islāmī Jamʿīyat-i Ṭalabā and student activism in Pakistan, told by the organization's various leaders over the years.

Nasr, Seyyed Vali Reza. "Students, Islam, and Politics: Islami Jamiʿat-i Tulaba in Pakistan." *Middle East Journal* 46.1 (Winter 1992): 59–76. Examination of the history and politics of the student wing of the Jamāʿat-i Islāmī of Pakistan.

Norton, Augustus Richard. *Amal and the Shiʿa: Struggle for the Soul of Lebanon*. Austin, 1987. Provides a good account of the social base of the Amal organization in Lebanon.

Roy, Olivier. *Islam and Resistance in Afghanistan*. Cambridge, 1986. Provides an account of the importance of youth movements in the evolution of Islamic resistance in Afghanistan.

Seyyed Vali Reza Nasr

Z

ẒĀHIRĪ. *See* Law, *article on* Legal Thought and Jurisprudence.

ZAʿĪM. In modern usage the word *zaʿīm* (pl., *zuʿcal society signifying a "political boss." It is independent from the Ottoman usage, which signifies the holder of a zeamet* (a prefeudal territorially based leadership) or any of several other definitions. Derivatives of the word, such as "*zaʿīm*ship" or "*zaʿīm*ism," have been coined and are frequently used. The modern term may have come from Egypt, where it was an honorific title given to party leaders, such as Saʿd Zaghlūl, leader of the Egyptian Wafd party in the 1920s.

Arnold Hottinger (1966) defines the *zaʿīm* as a "political leader who possesses the support of a locally circumscribed community and who retains this support by fostering or appearing to foster the interests of as many as possible from amongst his clientele." The main distinction of this type of leadership is that it is personal and not party based in the modern sense of organizations with political or ideological grassroots. When they parade as such, "Their grass roots are the personal ties of socio-economic-political interest between the *zaʿīm* and his clients."

There is a traditional social dimension that dictates visits by the clients to the *zaʿīm* and by him on special occasions and the observance of *wājibāt* ("obligations") between them. The *zaʿīm* might have a religious or community base or transcend confessional boundaries by having a local or geographic base. He might also have a purely economic base as a large employer or landowner. His authority also has a moral dimension and involves a certain amount of reciprocity.

Albert Hourani (1976) distinguishes among three different types of *zuʿamā*, each referring to a different mode of political activity. First, there are feudal *zuʿamāʾ* who are based mainly in the countryside where large estates and traditional lordships exist and whose power rests on their position as landowners, often of ancient lineage, and their ability to give protection and patronage. Second, there are populist politicians of the mainly Christian regions in the northern half of Lebanon where smallholdings are common who maintain leadership on a less-solid base of socioeconomic power. Leadership is derived on the one hand from the use of powers of protection and patronage to maintain political clans and on the other from some kind of ideology or program of action. Third, there are Muslim leaders of the coastal cities who also obtain and retain leadership by ideological appeal and the exercise of patronage, but add to these a third source of power—the manipulation of the urban masses mobilized by strongarm men or *qabaḍāy*s.

In modern Lebanon *zaʿīm*ship is often linked to the attainment of high office, such as membership of parliament or a ministerial post. Political loyalty is also expressed by voting during elections. Relations among *zuʿamāʾ* ensure a wider availability of favors to the clients, and competition among them, especially in urban areas, provides a minimum of checks and balances to the otherwise absolute power that a *zaʿīm* may wield.

The holding of an office is also important because the *zaʿīm* provides two kinds of services: general services, such as the provision of electricity, roads, and other amenities to the region or community; or personal services, such as the provision of employment, *wāsṭaʾ* (mediation), and access to welfare services. Hence the *zaʿīm*'s power can be based on the loyalty of people in his district, the relationship he has with the state or central authorities, or both (Cubser, 1973). Both wealth and frequent return to high office, giving the *zaʿīm* access to state patronage, are important components in the legitimization of his powers.

*Zaʿīm*ship as a system can be described as the relations between *zuʿamāʾ* and their clients together with the relationship between local and national *zuʿamāʾ* in a continuous process of fine tuning of the provision of favors and services in exchange for political loyalty and power. In this system, every transaction is connected and dependent on the other. It is often referred to as the traditional political system as opposed to the modern one based on political parties and state institutions.

The final results of the process were not always seen as coinciding with the wider national interest, and the *zaʿīm* system was seen as a parallel or "backstage" system (Hottinger, 1961), which predominated over the "frontstage" of state institutions. The clash between the system and central government, when the latter impinged on the powerbase from which the authority of the former was derived, was seen as restrictive of state sovereignty and authority and as a hindrance to the development of a strong central government (Goria, 1985).

The decline and demise of the *zaʿīm* system has been often declared, but it endures and sometimes emerges stronger from crises and government reforms, for example, during the presidency of General Fuad Chehab (Fu'ād Shihāb, 1958–1964), who was particularly opposed to the system. It is also common to attack the system in political rhetoric, even by its very practitioners.

The civil war of 1975–1990 has, however, had consequences on the system which it is still too early to fully appreciate. The prolonged absence of state authority and institutions, the paralysis of the normal political process, the emergence of new powers in Lebanon, and the fragmentation of society must have taken their toll on the traditional system of *zuʿamā'*. Whether this involves a radical structural change or simply a change in the cast of characters, with the emergence of new and different types of *zuʿamā'*, remains to be seen.

[*See also* Lebanon.]

BIBLIOGRAPHY

Goria, Wade R. *Sovereignty and Leadership in Lebanon, 1943–1976*. London, 1985.

Gubser, Peter. "The *Zuʿamā'* of Zahlah: The Current Situation in a Lebanese Town." *Middle East Journal* 27 (Spring 1973): 173–189.

Hottinger, Arnold. "Zuʿamā' and Parties in the Lebanese Crisis of 1958." *Middle East Journal* 15 (1961): 127–140.

Hottinger, Arnold. "Zu'ama' in Historical Perspective." In *Politics in Lebanon*, edited by Leonard Binder, pp. 85–106. London, 1966.

Hourani, Albert. "Ideologies of the Mountain and the City." In *Essays on the Crisis in Lebanon*, edited by Roger Owen, pp. 33–41. London, 1976.

Johnson, Michael. *Class and Client in Beirut: The Sunni Muslim Community and the Lebanese State, 1840–1985*. London, 1986.

Khalaf, Samir. "Primordial Ties and Politics in Lebanon." *Middle Eastern Studies* 4 (April 1968): 243–269.

Khuri, Fuad Ishaq. *From Village to Suburb: Order and Change in Greater Beirut*. Chicago, 1975.

NADIM F. SHEHADI

ZAKĀT. The obligation known as *zakāt* constitutes one of the five pillars of Islam, the others being the Shahādah (declaration of faith), prayer, fasting, and the *ḥajj*. Muslims with the financial means (*niṣāb*) to do so are obliged to give a certain percentage of their wealth (2.5 percent of net worth, deducted annually) as *zakāt*. *Zakāt* was institutionalized as an obligatory edict of faith in both the Qur'ān and *sunnah*. The method by which an individual calculates his or her dues is outlined in the *ḥadīths*. To practicing Muslims, however, *zakāt* is more than merely a financial transaction. It connotes the path toward purity, the comprehension of material responsibility, and an enhanced sense of spirituality.

The concept of *zakāt* defies simple definition. Although it has commonly been defined as a form of charity, almsgiving, donation, or contribution, it differs from these activities primarily in that they are arbitrary actions. *Zakāt*, by contrast, is a formal duty not subject to choice. It compels believers to disburse a specific amount of their wealth; and it conditions their identity as Muslims on their willingness to adhere to this fundamental precept of Islam.

Origins. The Qur'ānic verses admonishing the faithful to impart portions of their wealth to the needy were revealed to the prophet Muḥammad during his years in Mecca. They urged Muslims to utilize their wealth for the assistance of the poor, the needy, and relatives: "That which you lay out for increase through the property of other people will have no increase with God; but that which you lay out for beneficence (*zakāt*), seeking the countenance of God [will increase]. It is these who will attain a recompense multiplied" (30.39).

It was in the Prophet's *ḥadīth*, however, that *zakāt* was formalized as an obligatory component of Islam's foundations: "On the authority of Abū ʿAbd al-Raḥman Abd Allāh, the son of ʿUmar ibn al-Khaṭṭāb, who said: 'I heard the Messenger of Allāh say: Islam has been built on five pillars: testifying that there is no God but Allāh and Muḥammad is His Messenger, performing prayers, paying *zakāt*, making the pilgrimage to the house [i.e., the Kaʿbah in Mecca], and fasting in Ramaḍān" (Imām Yaḥyā al-Nawawī, *Al-Nawawī's Forty Ḥadīth*, Beirut, 1976, p. 34).

Despite being a mandatory act of worship, *zakāt* was

not gathered or distributed via formal institutions during the early Meccan period because Muslims were still relatively few in number and lived in a society hostile to their beliefs. Muslims gave their *zakāt* privately to assist the poor and to buy the freedom of those in slavery. Yūsuf al-Qaraḍāwī, a scholar of Islamic jurisprudence, writes: "[*Zakāt*'s] practice in Mecca was general, without specificity or rules. It was left to the individual's conscience or his [sense of] hospitality and the feeling of duty towards [fellow] believers" (1986, p. 61).

Following the Prophet's *hijrah* to Medina, he received this revelation: "And be steadfast in prayer and regular beneficence *(zakāt);* and whatever good you send forth for your souls before you, you shall find it with God: For God sees well all that you do" (2.110). Unlike the earlier Qur'ānic reference, the task of *zakāt* is here expressed as a command, not merely advice.

Further testimony to *zakāt*'s prominence in Islam became evident when the Prophet dispatched numerous companions to invite tribal leaders to submit themselves to God:

> On the authority of Ibn ʿAbbās, the Prophet sent Muʿādh to Yemen, saying: "Invite the people to testify that none has the right to be worshipped but Allāh, and I am His apostle; and if they submit themselves, then teach them that Allāh has enjoined on them five prayers during each day and night. And if they submit to this, then tell them that Allāh has made it obligatory for them to pay *zakāt* from their property; it is to be taken from the wealthy among them and given to the poor (Ṣaḥiḥ al-Bukhārī, Ankara, 1979, vol. 2, pp. 271–272).

By the Hijrah's second year, the Prophet had defined the basic rules, the forms of wealth covered, and who should pay and receive *zakāt*. Thus *zakāt* had evolved from a voluntary practice to an institutionalized socioreligious duty expected of each Muslim who possessed the *niṣāb*, the minimum amount of wealth that may be subject to *zakāt*. Ibn Kathīr (d. 1373), a noted Islamic scholar, stated, "*Zakāt* was established in Medina during the second year of the Hijrah. Apparently the *zakāt* established in Medina was one with a specific values and amounts due, while the initial *zakāt* discussed in Mecca was merely a [personal] duty."

Al-Qaraḍāwī, a more contemporary Islamic jurist, concurs:

> The Muslims in Mecca were helpless individuals [unable to carry] their mission to others. Muslims in Medina, however, comprised a social majority owning land and property, as well as holding positions of power. The Islamic obligation [of *zakāt*] took on a new form to accomodate this new reality. *Zakāt* became specific . . . and legally binding. . . . The Medinan approach included legal institutions, predetermined percentages of wealth due . . . , the values and quantities that are "zakātable," eligible beneficiaries, and the state-run institutions empowered to administer, collect, and distribute *zakāt* (1986, p. 62).

In fact, neglecting to pay *zakāt* became an offense punishable by law. This was a precedent set by the first caliph, Abū Bakr, who fought against those who refused to fulfill their obligation of *zakāt*.

Socioreligious Role. *Zakāt* serves both a functional and a spiritual dimension. At a practical level, the system has three basic elements: those subject to *zakāt*, those eligible to receive it, and forms of "zakātable" wealth. Those subject to *zakāt* are the possessors of *niṣāb*, the more affluent Muslims. Those eligible to receive *zakāt* are predominantly the poor. According to the Qur'ān they fall into eight categories: the destitute *(al-fuqarā')*, the needy *(al-masākīn)*, the *zakāt* administrator *(al-ʿāmilīn ʿalayhā)*, those receptive to Islam *(al-mu'allafatah qulūbuhum)*, those who are to be freed from bondage *(fī al-riqāb)*, debtors *(al-gharīmīn)*, those in the way of God *(fī sabīl Allāh*, i.e., anything that enhances the religion), and the wayfarer *(ibn al-sabīl)*. The primary forms of wealth subject to *zakāt* dues include gold, silver, livestock, agricultural produce, articles of trade, currency, shares and bonds, and other liquid assets.

Zakāt's spiritual dimension cannot be underestimated, particularly since it holds a great deal of psychological as well as material importance to Muslims. Those who give and receive *zakāt* are bound together through this mutual love encouraged by the distribution of wealth. Fulfilling one's duty regarding *zakāt*, conscious that a pillar of Islam is being satisfied, instills in the believer a sense of completion and purity. In addition, setting aside a portion of one's wealth for eleemosynary purposes challenges the individual to face the selfishness, greed, and lust for material possession inherent in human nature. The poor also benefit spiritually from this transaction.

In the ideal Islamic society, the poor are admonished against begging. Therefore *zakāt* plays the important role of disbursing wealth while preserving the needy person's integrity. Receiving *zakāt* without the humiliation of begging evokes a sense of purity and allays feelings of envy, jealousy, and hatred toward the rich.

Ideally, *zakāt* creates a balance of wealth, freeing the individual to concentrate on spiritual advancement rather than material gratification. The Qur'ān, elucidating this point, warns against the concentration of wealth in the hands of the few: "What Allāh has bestowed on His Messenger (and taken away) from the people of the townships—belongs to Allāh—to His Messenger, and to the kindred and orphans, the needy and the wayfarer; in order that it may not (merely) make a circuit between the wealthy among you" (59.7).

Socioeconomic Function. *Zakāt* is an integral part of formal Islamic systems, affecting community development, society, and economy. By discouraging the hoarding of capital, *zakāt* stimulates investment. Since *zakāt* must be extracted from an individual's net wealth, whether or not the capital is utilized, Muslims are compelled to invest in productive ventures. As a result, the *zakāt* may be drawn from any profits, and channeling funds to investment will concomitantly prevent the erosion of the capital through *zakāt* deductions.

Moreover, *zakāt* according to Islamic scholars, does not include the means of production—equipment, factories, or tools—which provides an added incentive for investment. This exclusion of physical assets encourages trade and commerce, as opposed to such speculative investments as stocks, bond, and other monetary-oriented transactions.

Insofar as the disbursement of *zakāt* funds is concerned, it finances the consumption expenditure of the poorest groups in society. *Zakāt* constitutes a direct infusion of funds into a segment of society, increasing effective aggregate demand, that is, the ability of consumers to make viable transactions, with purchasing power. Eventually this leads to rising employment, and output, and consequently to economic development.

These contributions—based on both moral obligation and sound economic reasoning—play a major role in maintaining societal order and enhancing a cohesive social fabric among Muslims. Ideally, the productive bond created between the affluent and needy eliminates theft, vandalism, and other social ills. *Zakāt* is designed to build a cooperative environment throughout the community while directly combating feelings of resentment and rivalry.

Zakāt was formerly applied in all Muslim territories and respected as an Islamic obligation. Because the general populace viewed *zakāt* as a religious and moral duty, Muslim authorities had no problems in collecting it. With the advent of colonialism and the introduction of systems of government that excluded religious doctrine, authorities in most Muslim states largely abjured Islamic codes of law, including *zakāt*. As a result of the institutionalization of secular tax systems, *zakāt* has lost its once prominent position in Muslim life. In fact, writes al-Qaraḍāwī, "Were it not for the concern of some Muslim individuals and institutions, *zakāt* would have been completely eradicated from Muslim life" (1986, p. 1115).

Contemporary Application. Despite the external and internal obstacles that hinder the application of *sharīʿah* (Islamic law) in the Muslim states, some states have begun to do so. *Zakāt* is now applied in Jordan, Saudi Arabia, Malaysia, Pakistan, Kuwait, Libya, Iran, and Sudan. Needless to say, these are recent efforts that are considered as the beginning of a long road toward the ideal *zakāt* application. Experiences in two countries, Sudan and Pakistan, may serve as examples.

Sudan. After the period of Mahdist Islamic rule in Sudan (1885–1899), *zakāt* continued to be paid by individual Muslims on a personal basis as there were no voluntary or official institutions to carry on the duty of collection and distribution of *zakāt*. In 1980, twenty-four years after Sudan's independence, a voluntary *zakāt* chamber was established. Muslims were encourage to pay their *zakāt* voluntarily to this chamber so that it could disburse the funds on their behalf. Such procedures continued for four years.

In 1984, for the first time since Mahdist rule, *zakāt* became an official compulsory Islamic duty based on government legislation. The government of Sudan issued the 1984 taxation and *zakāt* law, which combined both taxes and *zakāt* and established a *zakāt* and taxation institution. To apply this legislation the institution appealed to the experiences of Pakistan, Libya, Kuwait, Jordan, and Saudi Arabia. The *zakāt* chamber continued to collect and distribute the *zakāt*, which became a compulsory and official state duty. In 1986 a new *zakāt* law was enacted by which a separate *zakāt* chamber was established. This law was an outcome of the Islamic laws of 1983 that were issued by the state as an attempt to apply the *sharīʿah* in Sudan. The 1986 law defined two specific goals. First, the state rather than individuals should take over the responsibility of collecting and distributing *zakāt*. The law left part of the *zakāt* to the individual payers to distribute themselves. Second, regional *zakāt* offices were to be established to work in collecting and distributing *zakāt* in addition to the central chamber in Khartoum.

Under the Islamic National Salvation government that came to power in 1989, the *zakāt* system entered a new phase. *Zakāt* became one of the prime focuses of the new government as part of its overall objective of fully applying *sharīʿah* as the source of public law. Immediately the National Salvation government issued the Zakāt Law of 1990. This law built on the previous experience but also added a much larger vision to the role of *zakāt* in the new Islamic society that the government was seeking to create. The principal elements of the 1990 law are as follows:

1. *Zakāt* became applicable to anything that could be called wealth if it reaches the *niṣāb* (the minimum required value that is subject to *zakāt*).

2. The expenditure areas were extended to go beyond the needs of individuals to those of society at large and the state.

3. To emphasize the popular dimension, the higher council of *zakāt* trustees and lower councils of *zakāt* trustees across the capital and other regions were established, and popular committees that would help in distributing *zakāt* were formed.

4. The law expanded the source of *zakāt* to include, beside the compulsory resources, the acceptance of *zakāt* from institutions and individuals throughout the Muslim world, alms, grants from inside and outside Sudan, and the returns of investment of the chamber resources.

5. *Zakāt* would be distributed in the areas of its collection.

6. The law established punishments for those who refused to pay *zakāt* or tried to avoid paying.

7. Twenty percent of the *zakāt* paid could be distributed by those who paid it to the eligible poor, relatives, and neighbors.

The Zakāt Law of 1990 addressed two important components of *zakāt,* its collection and its distribution. Regarding collection, the law defined six categories of wealth that would be subject to the *zakāt:* (1) agricultural production; (2) livestock production; (3) trade goods; (4) means of production, such as factories, real estate, modes of transportation, and so forth; (5) earned wealth (e.g., profits from investments); (6) salaries, benefits, awards, and profits. The Zakāt Law of 1990 established a clear definition for each of these categories and, based on the opinions of Muslim scholars, stated how the *zakāt* was to be collected.

As for the distribution of *zakāt,* in Sudan's fourteen years of experience administering *zakāt* the *zakāt* chamber developed a system that adheres clearly to the basic jurisprudence while taking into consideration Sudan's local circumstances. Hence, *zakāt* is divided according to the following rates: 50 percent of the *zakāt* goes to the needy—the poor, the destitute, and wayfarers; 30 percent is spent on the Islamic call (*daʿwah,* missionary activity); 12.5 percent is spent on the administration of *zakāt;* and 7.5 percent is reserved for the construction of facilities for *zakāt* collection and distribution.

Sudan's *zakāt* experience, short as it is, still requires great effort to solve the many problems that it faces. The relation between the *zakāt* and the secular tax system must be addressed. Some figures have questioned whether the *zakāt* should in fact be applied to the means of production. Scholars are attempting to determine which approach (to include the means of production or not) is more beneficial to the *zakāt* system and more likely to ensure its success.

Pakistan. Contemporary experience with *zakāt* in Pakistan began in 1979 with President Zia ul-Haq's islamization program. A *zakāt* fund was created in 1979 with substantial assistance from Saudi Arabia and the United Arab Emirates. Collection and distribution of *zakāt* was managed by a multitiered administrative system. The application of *zakāt* in Pakistan was based on the Zakāt and ʿUshr Ordinance of 1980, which took effect in 1981. According to this law, the collection and distribution of *zakāt* became a state duty instead of being left to individuals as before. Under the 1980 law, the *zakāt* or wealth tax of 2.5 percent is assessed annually on all income or assets in excess of 2,000 rupees (approximately $200) and deducted directly from bank accounts and other financial assets, such as investment shares, annuities, and insurance.

State collection and distribution of the *zakāt* drew some critics. They questioned government intervention and control of what they regarded as a personal obligation before God, not the state. The Shīʿī minority community, which has its own legal system, objected to the application of Sunnī law. In response, the government amended the *zakāt* ordinance to exempt those who believed that compulsory deduction of *zakāt* was against their school of law.

While in a number of Muslim nations *zakāt* as a state tax has become part of public law, questions have sometimes emerged from its application. It is believed that practical experience will solve those problems.

[*See also* Taxation.]

BIBLIOGRAPHY

Esposito, John L. *Islam and Politics.* 3d ed. Syracuse, N.Y., 1991.

Mayer, Ann E. "Islamization and Taxation in Pakistan." In *Islamic Reassertion in Pakistan,* edited by Anita M. Weiss, pp. 59–67. Syracuse, N.Y., 1986.

Qaraḍāwī, Yūsuf al-. *Fiqh al-zakāh* (The Jurisprudence of *Zakāt*). 2 vols. Beirut, 1986.

Zakāt Conference in Sudan. Held in Khartoum, 25–28 April 1994.

ABDALLAH AL-SHIEKH

ZAND DYNASTY. A line of Lakk (related to Lur) chieftains ruling western and southern Iran from 1751 to 1794 was known as the Zand dynasty. The founder, Karīm Khan (r. 1751–1779), was among the many tribal contingents impressed into Nādir Shah Afshār's army; he returned to his ancestral ranges near Hamadan after Nādir Shah's assassination in 1747. In alliance with other Zagros Mountain tribes and the magnates of Isfahan, the former capital, he enthroned a minor Ṣafavid prince as nominal shah (Ismāʿīl III), and by 1765, when he settled in Shiraz as the new capital, he had won mastery of all Iran except Khurasan [*see* Afshārid Dynasty]. He devoted the rest of his reign to restoring peace and prosperity to his realm. He made efforts to attract Jewish and Armenian merchants, who had fled Iran during the recent civil wars, and encouraged British and Indian merchants to trade at the Persian Gulf port of Bushire. His siege and occupation of Basra in Ottoman Iraq (1776–1779) was aimed chiefly at diverting trade to Iran.

Karīm Khan made a point of never styling himself shah; in a remarkable reversal of the conventional regent's title *vakīl al-dawlah* ("viceroy of the state"), he took the title *vakīl al-raʿāyā* ("deputy of the people"), which designated a provincial ombudsman charged with investigating administrative injustice. The many tales of Karīm Khan's redressing oppression testify that he took his title seriously. Through benign neglect, he was able to exorcize the tradition of support for the Ṣafavid dynasty, which Nādir Shah had failed to topple by direct confrontation; when Ismāʿīl III predeceased him in 1773, there was no outcry for a successor and no doubt that Karīm Khan was de facto monarch by popular consent.

A conventional Shīʿī, Karīm Khan issued coins in the name of the Hidden Imam and built a mosque in Shiraz, but he never sought clerical endorsement of his power. In fact, he is said to have refused stipends to sayyids and lesser *ʿulamā,* but to have granted them to Ṣūfī dervishes. During his reign, *ʿulamā'* who had fled from the Afghans or Nādir Shah to Najaf and Karbala, and Ṣūfīs who had taken refuge in India, were returning to Iran, and the two inevitably clashed. Two dervishes of the Niʿmatullāhī order were expelled from Shiraz during Karīm Khan's last years, and others sent elsewhere as missionaries were killed or mistreated by mobs incited by jealous *mujtahids* during the reigns of his successors. Popular dramatization of the rites commemorating the tragedy of Karbala evolved during the Zand period into the *taʿziyah* ("passion play") as seen in the following centuries.

On his death (probably from tuberculosis), Karīm Khan's kinsmen Zakī (r. 1779), Ṣādiq (1780–1782), ʿAlī Murād (1782–1785), Jaʿfar (1785–1789), Ṣayd Murād (1789), and Luṭf ʿAlī (1789–1794) fought each other over the succession more hotly than they fought off the encroaching Qājār tribe. Luṭf ʿAlī Khan, whose youth and courage have earned him some posthumous sympathy, was captured at Bam and tortured to death in Tehran by Āghā Muḥammad Khan, the future shah of the Qājār dynasty. The principal monuments of the Zand dynasty are Karīm Khan's fine buildings in Shiraz and his enduring reputation as the most humane Iranian ruler of the Islamic era.

[*See also* Iran.]

BIBLIOGRAPHY

Malcolm, John. *History of Persia,* vol. 2, chap. 16. London, 1815.

Perry, John R. *Karim Khan Zand: A History of Iran, 1747–1779.* Chicago, 1979.

Waring, Edward Scott. *A Tour to Sheeraz.* London, 1807.

JOHN R. PERRY

ZĀWIYAH. The development of the institution of the *zāwiyah* is closely linked to that of Ṣūfism, and so it is appropriate to situate it in relation to the latter. The word "Sufism" entered European usage with a book published in 1821 by the German Protestant pastor F. A. Deofidus Tholuck, *Ssufismus. Sive Theosophia Persarum Pantheistica. Ssufismus* here translates the Arabic concept of *taṣṣawwuf,* a word now generally believed to be derived from the Arabic root *ṣūf,* "wool," referring to the white woolen robe worn by the early mystics of Islam. In the first century of Islam *taṣṣawwuf* characterized the attitude of Muslims who were haunted by the Prophetic ideal of perfection and lived an ascetic and pious life similar to that of Christian monks.

With the emergence of early Ṣūfī circles (*ḥalqat*, pl., *ḥalaqāt*) at the beginning of the eighth century, when the Ṣūfī leaders (*shaykh*, pl., *shuyūkh*) began initiating disciples to the Ṣūfī path, Sufism began to assume a social dimension that was later reinforced with the appearance and the spread of *ṭarīqah*s ("paths")—that is, the path to be taken in order to achieve spiritual self-realization. The philosophy behind Sufism is that there is a conspicuous aspect of things (*ẓāhir*) and a hidden aspect (*bāṭin*). The *sharīʿah* belongs to the realm of the conspicuous. In order to gain access to knowledge of the hidden reality (*maʿrifah*), one has to follow *ṭarīqah* under the direction of a spiritual guide. This guide may be either the founder of a *ṭarīqah* or a disciple linked to the founder through a chain of transmission (*silsilah*) that symbolically goes back to the Prophet. The belief in the necessity of a spiritual leader to guide an aspirant toward fulfillment seems to have contributed immensely to the spread of the cult of saints in Islam.

In the West, Islamicists have used a variety of forms to render the idea of *ṭarīqah*, including religious order, religious congregation, religious association, religious brotherhood, and religious confraternity. From the thirteenth century onward the *ṭarīqah*s multiplied, split into branches, and spread over the Muslim world from the Maghrib to the Indian subcontinent and sub-Saharan Africa. Their spread was accompanied by the expansion of supererogatory practices and the cult of the saints as well as by the creation of institutions that supported these practices—mausoleums of venerated saints and places of worship and meditation, among which the *zāwiyah* is a prime example.

The origin of the term *zāwiyah* is obscure. Properly, *zāwiyah* means a corner of a building. There is not a single occurrence of this term in the Qur'ān. The Arabic etymological dictionary *Lisān al-ʿarab* refers to *zāwiyah* as a place situated in the Iraqi city of Basrah, where early Ṣūfī circles developed. The *Muʿjam al-wasīṭ*, another Arabic dictionary, defined *zāwiyah* as a place of refuge for Ṣūfīs and the poor; this definition indicates the sociology of the clientele of *zāwiyah*s. From these one can deduce two of their important functions—as a place of worship for Muslims who identify themselves as Ṣūfīs, and as a welfare institution.

In the Muslim world *zāwiyah*s are extremely diverse in form. For example, the *zāwiyah* may be identified with the mausoleum of a saint. Such structures may range from a wall several decimeters in height constructed in the tomb of a venerated saint, to a magnificent monument. The mausoleum of the Algerian saint Sīdī Bū Madyan in the village of Tlemcen is a good example of the latter, as are the mausoleum of Usuman Dan Fodio (1754–1816) in northern Nigeria. and that of Niẓāmuddīn Auliyā (1239–1325) in the Indian city of Delhi. With the expansion of *ṭarīqah*s in the Muslim world, the establishment of *zāwiyah*s became so widespread, that today in most Muslim countries there is hardly a remote village without one or more *zāwiyah*s.

Place of Worship. The *zāwiyah* is first of all a place of worship. It serves as a mosque where the five Islamic daily prayers are said, and equally as a lodge where the adherents of a *ṭarīqah* meet in order to recite litanies (*dhikr*s) specific to the *ṭarīqah*. Depending on the *ṭarīqah*, these litanies may be recited individually or collectively during religious gatherings; the latter type is known as *ḥaḍrah*. [*See* Dhikr.]

The *zāwiyah* is the designated place for the achievement of various spiritual states, notably *tarbiyah* and *khalwah*. *Tarbiyah* is the highest form of spiritual initiation. Under the direction of a spiritual guide, the aspirant isolates himself in the *zāwiyah*, eats minimally, and recites *dhikr*s in the hope that they will bring him to spiritual fulfillment. Several terms are used to refer to the end of this experience. The term *maʿrifah*, which conveys the idea of gnosis, is often employed. Also used are *wuṣūl*, realization of the pursued aim; *waṣl*, the union of the aspirant with God; *fanā'*, the extinction of the aspirant's being in divine totality, and *kashf*, "uncovering" or mystical revelation. During this period of ecstasy, the *murīd* or adept identifies himself with the divine and utters ecstatic phrases (*shaṭḥīyat*); a celebrated example is the Persian Ṣūfī al-Ḥusayn ibn Manṣūr al-Ḥallāj (858–922) who was executed for saying *anā al-ḥaqq* ("I am the truth," i.e., God). This state of ecstasy is not supposed to last forever. The aspirant, under the direction of a spiritual guide, must "put his feet back on earth," but he will live from then on strengthened by his spiritual experience.

Khalwah is another type of spiritual experience. It consists of isolation, lack of sleep, restriction of food, and the recitation of prayers for spiritual realization, but it also has a social dimension. By repeated *khalwah* practice, confirmed spiritual leaders reinforce their holy reputation and their influence in society, and aspirants can be raised to positions of leadership.

Many social activities that require religious blessing are conducted in *zāwiyahs*. Notable among these are funeral rituals, which proceed from the bathing of the dead to the last prayer after the shrouding.

Welfare Institution. Different types of socioreligious activities are organized in *zāwiyahs* at specific times of the year. Such activities as the anniversary of the birth of the prophet Muḥammad or of a local saint, often coincide with the harvest period. For this reason, *zāwiyahs* have become markets in the sense that participants not only come there to pray, but also to engage in economic activities.

As places to which people take offerings, *zāwiyahs* also contribute to the redistribution of social wealth. The handicapped and other persons who are incapable of meeting their needs are catered for and assured of food and lodging there. During periods of food shortage, *zāwiyahs* have constituted unique welfare institutions where those who were hungry have sought refuge in order to be fed, and, in the event of a poor harvest, where peasants could get seed to plant without having to pay for it.

Historically, another important function of the *zāwiyah* in the Maghrib was offering sanctuary to pursued fugitives. A fugitive who sought refuge in a *zāwiyah* had a greater chance of escaping trial, and thus, authorities seeking criminals often took the precaution of blocking access to *zāwiyahs*.

Political Role. The *zāwiyah* may also be a unit of politico-religious organization. The Sanūsīyah *ṭarīqah* founded by the Algerian Muḥammad al-Sanūsī (1792–1859) is an edifying example. After founding his *ṭarīqah,* al-Sanūsī chose as its seat the oasis of Jaghbūb in Cyrenaica, home to the second Islamic university of Africa after al-Azhar University and with a population of several hundred. The Sanusīyah eventually had a total of 146 *zāwiyahs* spread across Libya, Egypt, Chad, and Arabia.

Constructed on the sites of ancient Roman fortresses and at the crossroads of commercial routes, these *zāwiyahs* were complex organizations. Each *zāwiyah* had a mosque mainly for worship, a school to educate the inhabitants of the *zāwiyah* and the bedouin tribes living in the vicinity, accommodation for the leader of the *zāwiyah* and his family and students, and several hectares of land for agricultural purposes.

The Sanūsī *zāwiyahs* had heads nominated by the leader of the *ṭarīqah* and approved by the inhabitants of the area in which the *zāwiyah* was based. The leader was responsible for administering the properties of the *zāwiyah* and redistributing the resources these generated. Part of this wealth was sent to the central *zāwiyah* of Jaghbūb. The leaders of the Sanūsi *zāwiyahs* arbitrated conflicts among the bedouin tribes of Cyrenaica. The head of the *zāwiyah* was assisted by a deputy, an imam who led prayers and imparted religious knowledge, a teacher, and a *muʿadhdhin* (muezzin) who called parishioners to prayer. [*See* Sanūsīyah.]

Modern Developments. The *zāwiyah* today has arguably become less important in social life than it was up to the nineteenth century. The economic and social transformations in Muslim countries that have accompanied the emergence of centralized states, massive urbanization, the diffusion of oil wealth, and the expansion of communication systems has led to the emergence of competing institutions of socialization. Formal schools that award degrees have increasingly imposed themselves as places for the acquisition of knowledge, to the detriment of other, less formal institutions, particularly mosques and *zāwiyahs*. The emergence of a welfare state that caters for a large part of the needs of the population has also contributed to the weakening of traditional Muslim social institutions.

In Algeria, Morocco, Tunisia, and Libya, for example, the French colonial enterprise was accompanied by the confiscation of the religious endowments *(waqf;* pl., *awqāf)* attached to the *zāwiyahs*. These religious endowments had generated the necessary resources for running the *zāwiyahs*, thereby allowing them to perform their role of assisting the needy. Their confiscation by the French at the end of the nineteenth century and the beginning of the twentieth, contributed to the erosion of the social role of the *zāwiyahs*. In Libya, Italian colonization was followed by the dismantling of the powerful Sanūsī *zāwiyahs*, an exercise continued by the Qadhdhāfi regime.

The destruction of Ṣūfī institutions, including the *zāwiyahs*, was not always due to external forces. Various fundamentalist anti-Ṣūfī movements have appeared in the Muslim world, especially since the beginning of the eighteenth century. Some of them embarked on the destruction of Ṣūfī institutions, such as the mausoleums of saints and the *zāwiyahs*. Notable among these movements was the Wahhābī movement founded by the reformer Muḥammad Ibn ʿAbd al-Wahhāb (1703–1792). Adopted in 1744 by the family of Āl Saʿūd, Wahhābīyah became the official doctrine of Saudi Arabia. The disciples of ʿAbd al-Wahhāb, the Ikhwān, pursued with vigor the destruction of Ṣūfī institutions in Saudi Arabia. Another movement that confronted Sufism was the Association of Algerian ʿUlamāʾ founded in the 1930s by ʿAbd al-Ḥamīd ibn Bādīs, which had great impact in rolling back the frontiers of *ṭarīqah*s in Algeria. The Izālah movement in Nigeria, led by the late Shaykh Abubakar Gumi (1922–1992), and the Indian Ahl-i Ḥadīth movement founded at the end of the nineteenth century are further examples. [*See* Wahhābīyah; *and the biographies of Ibn ʿAbd al-Wahhāb and Ibn Bādīs.*]

Despite the erosion of its role as a welfare institution, one should perhaps not conclude that the *zāwiyah* has no social significance today. It still has some importance in the rural areas of the Muslim world, and in the cities it continues to perform a spiritual function. In European and American cities where Ṣūfī-oriented movements are devoted to proselytism, one can find some type of *zāwiyah*, which may be only the premises for worship, or a private house where adherents meet regularly to perform acts that closely resemble regular *ṭarīqah* religious meetings.

[*See also* Sufism, article on Ṣūfī Orders.]

BIBLIOGRAPHY

Abun-Nasr, Jamil M. *The Tijaniyya: A Sufi Order in the Modern World.* London, 1965. However biased against the Tijānīs, this work is the only comprehensive attempt to study a very popular *ṭarīqah* in North Africa and in Africa south of the Sahara.

Depont, Octave, and Xavier Coppolani. *Les confréries religieuses musulmanes.* Algiers, 1897. Pioneering work on the *ṭarīqah*s in the Middle East, compiled by French colonial officials.

Dermenghem, Émile. *Le culte des saints dans l'Islam maghrébin.* 4th ed. Paris, 1954. Excellent phenomenological study of rituals of the *ṭarīqah*s in North Africa.

Evans-Pritchard, E. E. *The Sanusi of Cyrenaica.* Oxford, 1949. Best analysis of the economic, political, social, and religious functions of the *zāwiyah*s of the Sanūsīyah in Cyrenaica.

Gilsenan, Michael. *Saint and Sufi in Modern Egypt.* Oxford, 1973. Insightful study of a modern Ṣūfī order in Egypt.

Lévi-Provençal, Évariste. "Zāwiya." In *Shorter Encyclopaedia of Islam,* edited by H. A. R. Gibb and J. H. Kramers, pp. 657–658. Leiden, 1974. Rather short article on the history of the *zāwiyah* in the Muslim world.

Triaud, Jean-Louis. "Khalwa and the Career of Sainthood: An Interpretative Essay." In *Charisma and Brotherhood in African Islam,* edited by Christian Coulon and Donal Cruise O'Brien, pp. 53–66. Oxford and New York, 1988. Interesting analysis of the *khalwah* practices.

Troll, Christian W., ed. *Muslim Shrines in India.* Delhi, 1989. Rich collection of essays on Indian Islam, with emphasis on the rites and festivals held in the shrines of Muslim saints in India.

OUSMANE KANE

ZAYDĪYAH. The Zaydīyah are a moderate branch of Shīʿī Islam that diverged from other Shīʿī denominations in a dispute over the succession to the imamate following the death of the fourth imam, ʿAlī Zayn al-ʿĀbidīn in 713. Rejecting the claims of Muḥammad al-Baqīr, the Zaydīs instead chose Zayd ibn ʿAlī (d. 740), a grandson of the martyr Ḥusayn, as the fifth imam (hence the common name for the Zaydīs, "Fivers"). One reason for their preference for Zayd was his activist revolutionary position against the Umayyad dynasty. Indeed, Zayd was the first of the descendants of Ḥusayn to openly rebel against the Umayyads, culminating in his violent death in 740.

Although the details of their early history are obscure, Zaydīs were active in ʿAlīd uprisings following the death of Zayd. As many as eight different Zaydī sects or movements are noted in early Islamic heresiographies. Some Zaydī scholars played important roles in the development of Islamic thought in the first two centuries AH. Independent Zaydī political power was first established when al-Ḥasan ibn Zayd (d. 844) founded a state in northern Iran. This imamate existed between 864 and 1126 among the Daylamīs and other groups of Tabaristan and the southern Caspian region. The most important intellectual figure of this dynasty was the imam al-Nāṣir al-Uṭrūsh (d. 917).

A more long-lasting state was established by al-Hādī ilā al-Ḥaqq al-Mubīn Yaḥyā ibn al-Ḥusayn (d. 911), grandson of a Hejazi Zaydī activist al-Qāsim al-Rassī. Al-Hādī was successful in uniting the feuding tribes of northern Yemen, converting them to Zaydī Islam, and establishing a Zaydī imamate around 893. He is noted in Zaydī tradition for his military prowess, statesmanship, and as a leading jurist of the Zaydī school. Thereafter, various imams of this Zaydī dynasty (893–1962) have remained a prominent force in Yemen, with their military power based on the allegiance of the warlike northern mountain tribespeople. Throughout these centuries, the power of the Zaydī imams was by no means absolute. They faced various internal feuds and revolts, as well as external invasions and competition from Fāṭimids (Ṣulayḥids), Ayyūbids, Rasūlids, and Ottomans. They nonetheless managed to hold onto their mountain strongholds until the Republican coup of 1962 ousted the last imam.

Although they have their own school of law based on the legal interpretations of Zayd and his successors, the Yemeni Zaydīs are otherwise the closest of all Shīʿī factions to the Sunnīs; this has often been interpreted by

Western scholars to mean that they are "moderate" or practical. The Zaydīs differ from other Shīʿī denominations in that they accept the legitimacy of the caliphates of Abū Bakr, ʿUmar, and, partially, ʿUthmān. In contrast to certain other Shīʿite groups, the Zaydīs do not view the imam as a quasidivine or supernaturally endowed person representing God on earth. In Zaydī belief, the qualifications for the imamate include: descent from ʿAlī and Fāṭimah, absence of physical imperfections, and personal piety. There can theoretically be several imams at the same time, or none. The imam must be able to take up the sword, either offensively or in defense, which rules out infants as well as "hidden imams" acknowledged by the Ismāʿīlīyah or Twelvers. The ultimate validity of an individual's claim to the imamate is demonstrated by his capacity to rule and his successful attainment of power. However, in addition to ʿAlid descent and the sheer ability to take and hold power, learning is required to confirm a claimant's right to the imamate. Such learning is acquired in the normal human fashion; the imam has no miraculous powers and no supernaturally conveyed knowledge. Zaydī imams have been prolific authors of works on jurisprudence and other important Islamic issues. The movement's theology was influenced considerably by the approach and doctrine of the Muʿtazilah. Historically, Zaydīs have tended to have puritanical moral teachings and to disapprove of Sufism. They reject Shīʿī practices of *taqīyah* (prudential concealment), and temporary marriage.

The Turkish occupation of various portions of Yemen from 1848 to 1918 provoked violent reaction among the Zaydīs. Rallying around their imam, Yaḥyā al-Mutawakkil (r. 1904–1948), the Zaydīs managed to retain control of much of northern Yemen. Following the expulsion of the Ottomans in 1918, Zaydī imams ruled most of Yemen until the revolution of 1962. Thereafter, armed conflict between the supporters of the Zaydī imam al-Badr and Republicans continued until 1972, when the Republicans were triumphant. Although the revolution of 1962 resulted in the collapse of the imamate and partial suppression of the sayyids (Zaydīs claiming descent from ʿAlī and Fāṭimah), Zaydīs continue as an important social and religious force in Yemen today.

[*See also* Shīʿī Islam, *historical overview article;* Yemen.]

BIBLIOGRAPHY

ʿAmrī, Ḥusayn ʿAbd Allāh al-. *The Yemen in the Eighteenth and Nineteenth Centuries: A Political and Intellectual History*. London, 1985. Basic survey of early modern Yemen, with discussions of the Zaydī role.

Arendonk, Cornelis van. *Les débuts de l'imāmat zaidite au Yemen*. Translated by Jacques Ryckmans. Leiden, 1960. Study of the origins of the Yemeni Zaydīyah.

Dresch, Paul. *Tribes, Government, and History in Yemen*. Oxford, 1989. Outstanding overview of Yemeni history, with numerous details on the Zaydīyah and a complete bibliography.

Madelung, Wilferd. *Der Imām al-Qāsim ibn Ibrāhīm und die Glaubenslehre der Zaiditen*. Berlin, 1965. Detailed account of Zaydī theology.

Serjeant, R. B. "The Zaydis." In *Religion in the Middle East*, edited by A. J. Arberry, vol. 2, pp. 285–301. Cambridge, 1969. The best short survey available.

Wenner, Manfred W. *Modern Yemen, 1918–1966*. Baltimore, 1967. Basic study of the rise and fall of the Yemeni Zaydī imamate in the twentieth century.

Wenner, Manfred W. *The Yemen Arab Republic: Development and Change in an Ancient Land*. Boulder, 1991. Continuation of the former study through the reunification.

WILLIAM J. HAMBLIN and DANIEL C. PETERSON

ZAYTŪNAH. One school of thought maintains that the Zaytūnah mosque was built in 734 by the governor of Ifrīqīyah (as Tunisia was called by the Arabs), ʿUbayd Allāh ibn al-Habhab; another asserts that it was built by Ḥassān ibn al-Nuʿmān al-Ghassānī, the Arab conqueror of Tunis and Carthage around 698. Whatever its origins it remained until the twelfth century primarily a place of worship, and the Kairouan (Qayrawān) mosque was the major center of Islamic thought and learning in North Africa. It is only when the Ḥafṣid dynasty (1207–1534) came to power, and made Tunis its capital, that Zaytūnah emerged as one of the most important Islamic institutions of higher learning at the time. Its famous library of al-Abdalīyah housed a very large collection of books and rare manuscripts that attracted Islamic scholars and men of learning from many nations. Students were taught the Qur'ān, jurisprudence, history, grammar, science, and medicine in its *madrasahs* (Islamic schools), and it also had a *kuttāb* (Islamic elementary school) to teach the youngest members to read and write and memorize holy texts. Among the historic figures who studied at the Zaytūnah was Ibn Khaldūn.

In 1534 the Ḥafṣid dynasty was ousted and the Spaniards occupied Tunis until 1574. They ransacked its libraries and mosques and burnt or removed many of the precious books and manuscripts of the Zaytūnah. That period was followed by the expansion of the Ottoman Empire into North Africa and the emergence of two local-Turkish dynasties: the Murādids and the Ḥusaynids, between 1631 and 1957. They restored and expanded the Zaytūnah mosque, its libraries, and *madrasahs* and made it once again a major center of Islamic culture in North Africa. A local family, the Bakrīs, took over the imamate and the care of the mosque from 1624 to 1812.

Administrative and curricular reforms began with Ahmed Bey in 1842 and continued in 1875 under the enlightened premiership of Khayr al-Dīn al-Tūnisī, who expanded al-Abdalīyah library and opened it to the public. New courses were introduced in 1896 including physics, political economy, and French as a foreign language, and in 1912 the reforms were extended beyond Tunis to the regional branches of the Zaytūnah in Kairouan, Sousse, Sfax, Tozen, and Gafsa, thoroughly modernizing the educational system.

Until the twentieth century students were recruited predominantly from the most notable and wealthiest families of Tunis, Sfax, Sousse, and Kairouan. These elites then became *muftīs* (official expounders of law), *qāḍīs* (judges), imams, teachers, and civil servants. In the twentieth century the Zaytūnah opened its doors to a much larger public as it became the fortress of Arab and Islamic culture, against French influence in the Maghrib. Among its students were ʿAbd al-Ḥamīd ibn Bādīs, Tawfīq Madanī, and Houari Boumédienne, who played very important roles in the nationalist movement of Algeria. In 1937 it had more than three thousand students, but by 1955 on the eve of independence, student enrollment had reached twenty-five thousand.

The reforms of 1958 that unified the educational system in independent Tunisia, and the creation of the University of Tunis in 1960, undermined the status of the Zaytūnah as a university. In 1965 its role as an independent educational institution was officially abolished, and it became the school of theology and Islamic studies of the University of Tunis with fewer than three hundred students.

[*See also* Tunisia.]

BIBLIOGRAPHY

Ibn ʿĀshūr, Muḥammad al-ʿAzīz. *Jāmiʿ al-Zaytūnah: Al-maʿlam wa-Rijālihi*. Tunis, 1991.

Montety, H. de. "La réforme moderniste à l'Université Ez-Zitouna." *L'Afrique et l'Asie*, no. 13 (1951).

Moula, Mahmoud Abdel. *L'Université Zaytounienne et la société Tunisienne*. Paris, 1971.

MARY-JANE DEEB

ZIKR. *See* Dhikr.

ZIYĀRAH. Literally, "visitation," *ziyārah* technically refers to visiting gravesites (*ziyārat al-qubūr*) for the purpose of praying for the dead and remembering death. According to well-documented practices in all Sunnī compilations, at some point in the period between 610 and 622, the Prophet had apparently forbidden visitation to gravesites because of the exaggerated importance attached to the practice. However, when Islam came he made it lawful and recommended it, because "it will remind you of the hereafter" (al-Sayyid Sābiq, *Fiqh al-sunnah*, Beirut, 1977, vol. 1, p. 477). In another tradition, such visits are recommended in order to remind oneself of death. The overall religious significance of *ziyārah*, as it emerges in several narratives, is remembrance of death and reflection over the hereafter. Therefore, some traditions even permit visitation of the graves of nonbelievers as reminders of the wrong that one commits against oneself by rejecting faith. It is also recommended to weep and to express one's need for God when passing through infidel graveyards.

The rituals connected with *ziyārah* require that, when reaching the grave, one should turn one's face toward the dead, offer a greeting and pray for that dead person. The Prophet used to visit the cemeteries and greet the dead saying: "Peace be upon you, o you the believers and the Muslims! We shall, God willing, join you. You have preceded us and we shall follow you. We pray to God for our and your well-being" (Sābiq, p. 477).

However, there was a problem with *ziyārah* by women. Again, the problem relates to pre-Islamic practice among the Arabs to which many narratives seem to be responding. The Mālikī and some Ḥanafī jurists deduced the permission of jurists on the basis of the narrative in which Āʿishah, the Prophet's wife, one day was returning from having visited her brother's grave. When reminded of the Prophet's prohibition by ʿAbd Allāh ibn Ubayy, she replied: "Yes he had forbidden the visitation of the graves [earlier], but had ordered [*amara bihi*] it afterwards" (Sābiq, p. 478). On the other hand, Ḥanbalīs, citing another tradition in which the Prophet cursed the women who visit graves, regard it as *makrūh* (reprehensible). They also argue that the reprehensibility is owed to the belief that women are less patient and excessively overcome by grief. The Wahhābīyah of Saudi Arabia, who also follow the Ḥanbalī school, extrapolate the same tradition to deduce absolute interdiction for women to visit the gravesite (ᶜAbd al-Raḥmān ibn Muḥammad ibn Qāsim al-ᶜĀṣimī al-Najdī al-Ḥanbalī, *Ḥāshiyat al-Rawḍ al-murbiᶜ sharḥ Zād al-mustaqniᶜ*, Riyadh, 1982, vol. 3, pp. 144–46). It is for this reason that they prohibit women from entering the historical Baqi cemetery in Medina where the Prophet's family, wives, and prominent companions are buried. In 1925 they leveled all the structures that marked these graves. Earlier, in 1801, they raided and destroyed the shrines at Karbala and Najaf. The Wahhābī belief, shared by no one else in the Sunnī community, regards the *ziyārah* in general as amounting to "saint veneration," which leads to the grave sin of *shirk*, associating divinity with these persons.

The Shāfiᶜī and the Shīᶜī jurists have no problem with the visitation by women to gravesites. The Shīᶜī jurists recommend that the visitor place his or her hand on the grave and read the Fātiḥah, the opening chapter of the Qur'ān (ᶜAmilī, *Wasā'il al-Shīᶜah*, vol. 2, p. 881ff). Several traditions regarding the prohibition of women from performing the *ziyārah* and expressing grief during the visitation must be regarded as a later reaction to the pre-Islamic funeral practices which included extravagant slapping of cheeks and tearing of clothes (Bukhārī, *Janā'iz, ḥadīth* 382). Otherwise there are traditions that explicitly establish that women did perform the *ziyārah*. In another tradition preserved by Bukhārī, the Prophet passed by a woman who was weeping beside a grave. He told her to fear God and be patient, without requiring her to leave the site or reminding her about the prohibition on her (Bukhārī, *Janā'iz, ḥadīth* 372).

The visitation to the tombs of the imams and their descendants (*imāmzādah;* formally extended only to male descendants, although female descendants are included as *sayyidah* or *bībī*) who were distinguished by special sanctity or by suffering martyrdom, and to the tombs of holy men and women, is treated as pilgrimage by both the Sunnīs and the Shīᶜīs. Hence the universal practice of *ziyārah* of Medina among all Muslims. Visitation includes the shrines of famous women in Islam, including those of Sayyidah Zaynab, daughter of ᶜAlī ibn Abī Ṭalīb, and Sayyidah Ruqayyah, daughter of Ḥusayn, in Damascus; Sayyidah Zaynab and Nafīsah in Cairo; Bībī Fāṭimah, daughter of Mūsā al-Kāẓim, the seventh imam, in Qom; Narjīs Khātūn, the twelfth imam's mother, and Ḥakīmah, the daughter of ᶜAlī al-Hādī, the tenth imam, in Samarra. It has always been common for both Shīᶜīs and Sunnīs to undertake pilgrimages to these mostly Shīᶜī shrines. Unlike the *ḥajj*, which is performed at a set time, *ziyārah* to these shrines can be undertaken at any time, although some particular days are recommended. In the case of some shrines, pilgrimage is associated with a special lunar month or season of the year. Thus, the *ziyārah* of Sayyidah Zaynab in Cairo is performed in the month of Rajab; whereas the *ziyārah* of Imam Riḍā in Mashhad is recommended in the month of Dhū al-Qaᶜdah. The *ziyārah* of *imāmzādah* Sultan ᶜAlī near Kashan is held on the seventh day of autumn. Only the *ziyārah* of Ḥusayn in Karbala is recommended every Thursday evening, in addition to the major occasion of ᶜĀshūrā' (the day of his martyrdom). That evening, the *mashhad* of Karbala is thronged with crowds of pilgrims from many lands. The performance of *ziyārah* is regarded by the pilgrims as an act of covenant renewal between the holy person and devotees. This is a covenant of love, sincere obedience, and devotion on the part of the believers. Through *ziyārah,* the person participates in the suffering and sorrows of the *ahl al-bayt* (the Prophet's family).

People who cannot undertake the arduous and expensive journey to the shrines of the imams can go into the wilderness, or onto a high roof of one's house, and then turn toward the *qiblah* (direction of Mecca) and pronounce the salutations. There are special *ziyāratnāmah* (salutations) for specific occasions. Although distinction is made between the *ziyārat* of the imams and other holy persons, Shīᶜī scholars have regarded it permissible to show them all honor and respect by addressing them in a prescribed way. Some of these salutations are taken from the words of the imams directly. However, the *ziyārah* of the imams is followed by two *rakᶜah* (units of prayer) as a gift to the imam whose *ziyārah* is being performed. The *ziyārah* is concluded with a petition for the intercession of the Prophet and his family and praise to God.

[*See also* Imāmzādah; Karbala; Mashhad; Najaf; Qom; Shrine.]

BIBLIOGRAPHY

Ayoub, Mahmoud M. *Redemptive Suffering in Islam: A Study of the Devotional Aspects of ᶜĀshūrā' in Twelver Shīᶜism*. The Hague, 1978. Discusses *ziyārah* and its prescribed rituals in Shīᶜī piety.

Lambton, Ann K. S. "Imāmzāda." In *Encyclopaedia of Islam*, new ed., vol. 3, pp. 1169–1170. Leiden, 1960–.

ABDULAZIZ SACHEDINA

ẒULM. The basic meaning of the Arabic word *ẓulm* is "putting something not in its proper place" (*Tāj al-*

ʿArūs); the word and its derivatives are found in more than 280 places in the Qur'ān. From this meaning is derived that of wrongdoing, which can be to God (surah 2.280), to others (42.42), or even to oneself; indeed, all wrongdoing is ultimately against oneself (11.101, *Tāj al-ʿArūs*). God, of course, wrongs no one to the slightest extent (4.40). Although the use of *ẓulm* to mean doing wrong to others is the least frequent in the Qur'ān, it has become over the years the predominant one; since the Middle Ages the word, in common usage, has come to mean oppression and tyranny, particularly by rulers over their subjects. Frequently used as the opposite of justice (*ʿadl*), it can also be translated as injustice. In these latter two senses it is often found in such Islamic literature as political treatises and books of counsel for princes and rulers. [*See* Justice, *article on* Concepts of Justice.] In jurisprudence, it refers to that which exceeds the legal limits of the *sharīʿah*.

The word *ẓulm* and its derivatives *ẓālim* (tyrant or oppressor) and *maẓlūm* (victim of oppression) sum up, perhaps better than any other words, the traditional ethos of Shiism. The whole of Shīʿī sacred history revolves around the oppression and tyranny which Shīʿīs consider was exercised by the Umayyad and ʿAbbāsid caliphs over the Shīʿī holy imams and, subsequently, by the Sunnī community over the Shīʿīs. To the Shiʿi imams is ascribed the quality of *maẓlūmīyat*, the patient and forbearing endurance of the suffering inflicted by the tyranny of rulers. The alternative attitude toward *ẓulm* is expressed by *qiyāmat* (the arising to oppose tyranny), the quality par excellence of the Imam Ḥusayn. Both attitudes to authority thus are paradigmatic for Shīʿīs. Until the Iranian Revolution, however, the *maẓlūmīyat* paradigm predominated. Perhaps Ayatollah Ruhollah Khomeini's most farreaching achievement was to shift the emphasis from the *maẓlūmīyat* paradigm toward the *qiyāmat* one.

Many elements in popular Shiism reflect this preoccupation with the theme of *ẓulm*. The stories of the tyranny of the caliphs and the *maẓlūmīyat* of the imams are told and retold countless times, particularly during the month of Muḥarram in narrations of the martyrdom of Ḥusayn at Karbala (the *rawẓah khvānī, majlis*, or *dhikrā*). It also figures in passion plays (the *taʿziyah* or *shabīh*) and in popular art (see Momen, 1984, pp. 240–244). In the Shīʿī worldview, heavily impregnated with the presence of *ẓulm*, suffering as a victim of tyranny and oppression is the hallmark of righteousness and legitimacy. [*See* Rawẓah Khvānī; Taʿziyah.]

It is not surprising, therefore, to find that *ẓulm* and its derivatives, with their highly political overtones, have found their way into modern political discourse. Most radical opposition groups, whether Sunnī or Shīʿī, at some time have accused the government of *ẓulm*. The word, however, was used most vividly and effectively in Shiism. Prior to the nineteenth century, the responsibility for the removal of *ẓulm* from society rested with the kings and rulers; by the beginning of the Qājār dynasty in Iran, the Shīʿī *ʿulamāʾ* began to see themselves as the protectors of the people against the tyranny of the rulers (Hamid Algar, *Religion and State in Iran, 1785–1906*, Berkeley, 1969, pp. 57–58, 117). Ayatollah Khomeini, while in exile (1964–1979), frequently referred to the shah's government as *ẓālim* and portrayed himself as the victim of its oppression. This self-identification was an important element in his propaganda as it placed him symbolically in the minds of the Shīʿī population of Iran in the role of the Shīʿī imams in their struggle against the caliphs. Correspondingly, the shah and his supporters were identified with Yazīd, Muʿāwiyah, and the other caliphs who had persecuted the Shīʿī imams and so were tainted with the loathing of these figures with which all Shīʿīs are indoctrinated from childhood through the Muḥarram commemorations. These identifications gave a powerful emotional impetus to the revolution by placing all those who came out into the street to demonstrate against the Shah in the ranks of the companions of the imams. A political struggle took on the proportions of a cosmic contest between good and evil. The combination of the shift from the *maẓlūmīyat* paradigm to the *qiyāmat* one and the successful casting of the Shah as a persecutor of the holy imams proved to be a powerful combination that overwhelmed the Pahlavi regime.

Khomeini's vision was of the *ʿulamāʾ* as the main social agents speaking out against and resisting *ẓulm* (Dahnavī, ed., *Majmūʿih-yiaz maktūbāt, sukhanrānī-hā, payām-hā va fatāwī-yi Imām Khumainī*, Tehran, 1981, pp. 50, 91). Upon the establishment of *vilāyat-i faqīh* (*wilāyat al-faqīh*, rule by a just cleric) with the inauguration of the Islamic Republic, Khomeini proclaimed the end of *ẓulm* by those in authority in Iran: "There is no injustice (*ẓulm*) in an Islamic republic" (Aneer, 1985, p. 74). After Khomeini's return to Iran, the principal oppressor was perceived to be the United States, which, accordingly, was accused of *ẓulm*. The term has also been used regularly of the present Islamic republic by its opponents.

BIBLIOGRAPHY

Aneer, Gudmar. *Imām Rūḥullāh Khumainī, Šah Muḥammad Riżā Pahlavī, and the Religious Traditions of Iran.* Uppsala, 1985. Contains a discussion of the use of the term *ẓulm*, particularly by Khomeini. See pages 73–75.

Khomeini, Ruhollah. *Writings and Declarations of Imām Khomeini.* Translated by Hamid Algar. Berkeley, 1981.

Momen, Moojan. *Introduction to Shīʿī Islam: The History and Doctrines of Twelver Shīʿism.* New Haven, 1984. For a traditional account of the lives of the holy imams and the persecutions they endured, see pages 23–45. On *maẓlūmīyat,* see page 236.

MOOJAN MOMEN

ZŪRKHĀNAH. Literally meaning "house of strength," the *zūrkhānah* is a traditional gymnasium exclusive to Iran, dedicated to the development of men's bodily strength, and ideally to spiritual guidance and the promotion of high ethical values of chivalry (*javānmardī*). The historical origins of the *zūrkhānah* cannot be established with certainty. One theory, based on architectural similarities, traces the *zūrkhānah* to the pre-Islamic Iranian temple. With the gradual islamization of Iranian society during the ninth and tenth centuries, this institution may have come to serve a more secular function. As recently as the early twentieth century, the *zūrkhānah* was considered a sanctuary where people went to seek healing. The survival of pre-Islamic military terminology for weight-lifting equipment and the practice of ancient rituals and customs also tend to support this theory. Like the Ṣūfī *khānqāh,* to which the *zūrkhānah* was closely tied and which offered an alternative to the normative religion of the mosque, the *zūrkhānah,* as the center for the *ayyārs* (the local urban militia) provided an alternative to the state military. [*See* Khānqāh.]

Substantial references to *zūrkhānahs* are found in sources of the Qājār period, when the court, especially under Nāṣir al-Dīn Shāh, patronized performing arts and sports. During this period the *zūrkhānah* was a gathering place for bazaar guilds and merchants as well as for *lūṭīs* (ruffians), who often engaged in factional and territorial fighting. This, along with charges of pedophilia, damaged the *zūrkhānah*'s reputation for purity and virtue; as a result, some merchants and other members of the elite started their own private *zūrkhānahs.*

The rise of the Pahlavis and of state-sponsored nationalism subscribing to an idealized image of the pre-Islamic era proposed the *zūrkhānah* as a symbol of ancient Iranians' love of sportsmanship. Limited efforts were taken for its promotion, but the *zūrkhānah* enjoyed little popularity among the modern middle class and was for a time merely a tourist attraction. Unlike the mosque, which during the 1970s underwent a revival by attracting rural migrants to the city, other traditional urban institutions such as the *zūrkhānah* continued to experience decline. The increased popularity of Western sports and the breakdown of the traditional bonds of loyalty in the urban community as cities grew rapidly contributed to this decline.

Structurally, the *zūrkhānah* consists of a square or hexagonal arena (*gawd*) with room for up to two dozen men to exercise. The arena is sunken below ground level and is surrounded by chambers used as dressing rooms and resting areas, where the local masseur (*mushtmālchī*) was stationed. A focal point of the *zūrkhānah* is the *sardam,* the decorated seat of the mentor or *murshid* (terms used in Ṣūfī processions), located above the arena, amid the spectators' seating area. Covered with a dome resembling the pre-Islamic Iranian temples, the arena itself is considered sacred. Customarily, the athletes kiss the arena as they enter it as a sign of humility, a practice that closely resembles the Ṣūfī's kissing the threshold of a saint's tomb or other shrine. Other signs of reverence for the *gawd* include prohibitions against the use of foul language and clownish behavior. Under the Islamic Republic, women are barred from the audience, as the athletes traditionally wear scanty attire.

The role of the *murshid* (a term also used for a Ṣūfī spiritual mentor) as the master of ceremonies is to introduce, inspire, and pay homage to athletes, particularly guests and those with seniority; to direct athletes in group and individual exercises; and to instill enthusiasm in athletes through rhythmic chanting of epic poetry accompanied by an oversized clay drum and a bell. In his capacity as moral mentor, the *murshid* would on occasion publicly admonish an athlete for a violation of the code of ethics. A hierarchical order based on seniority and descent from the family of the prophet Muḥammad is maintained through interaction between the *murshid* and the *miyāndār,* the person with most seniority inside the arena, who dictates the pace and the order of group exercises as well as the order of performances.

Membership in the *zūrkhānah* was traditionally informal, but was restricted to adult men and was usually drawn from the *maḥallah* (city quarter) where the *zūr-*

khānah was located. Membership dues were paid to the *murshid* on a voluntary basis. With the exception of a few government-sponsored *zūrkhānahs*, they were usually privately owned.

The exercises, which are usually conducted in the evening, are geared toward bodybuilding and involve variations on push-ups and weight-lifting exercises. Acrobatic jumping, rapid rotating of the body, and wrestling, the ultimate traditional sport, have a strong performance appeal. The solemn environment of the *zūrkhānah*, combined with the rhythm of the drum and chanting of epic verses, creates a remarkable spirit of elation and chivalry, which after many centuries continues to inspire athletes and lay individuals alike.

BIBLIOGRAPHY

Bayẓā'ī, Ḥusayn Partaw. *Tārīkh-i varzish-i bāstānī-i Īrān, Zūrkhānah.* Tehran, 1337/1958-1959.

Bernard, C. N., and Kazem Kazemaini. *The Zour Khaneh: Traditional Persian Gymnasium.* Tehran, 1970.

Kazemaini, Kazem. "Zūrkhānah." *Hunar va Mardum,* no. 55 (February 1967): 28–34; nos. 56-57 (June 1967): 55–62.

Shahrī, Ja'far. *Gūshah'ī az tārīkh-i ijtimā'ī-i Tihrān-i qadīm.* Tehran, 1357/1978–1979. See pages 82–93.

MEHRDAD AMANAT

DIRECTORY OF CONTRIBUTORS

Vemund Aarbakke
Doctoral Candidate in History, University of Bergen
Refugees

Mona Abaza
Temporary Researcher, Maison des Sciences de l'Homme, Paris
Madrasah

Mustafa Abdulhussein
Associate, al-Jāmiʿah al-Sayfīyah, Surat, India; Research Affiliate, Department of Middle Eastern Studies, University of Manchester, United Kingdom
Bohrās; Burhānuddīn, Sayyidnā Muḥammad; Jāmiʿah al-Sayfīyah, al-

Taufik Abdullah
Research Professor, Social Development, Centre for Social and Cultural Studies, Indonesian Institute for Sciences, Jakarta
Adat; Hamka

Shukri B. Abed
Senior Research Fellow, Center for International Development and Conflict Management, University of Maryland, College Park
Arab-Israeli Conflict

Saleha M. Abedin
Associate Professor of Sociology, King Abdulaziz University, Jeddah, Saudi Arabia
Institute of Muslim Minority Affairs; Minorities, *article on* Muslim Minorities in Non-Muslim Societies

Syed Z. Abedin *(deceased)*
Insititute of Muslim Minority Affairs, Jeddah, Saudi Arabia
Institute of Muslim Minority Affairs; Minorities, *article on* Muslim Minorities in Non-Muslim Societies

Sana Abed-Kotob
H. B. Earhart Postdoctoral Fellow in Government and Politics, University of Maryland, College Park
ʿIlm; Vicegerent

Khaled Abou El Fadl
Managing Editor, Princeton Papers In Near Eastern Studies, Princeton University
Diplomatic Immunity; Hostages

Ervand Abrahamian
Professor of History, Baruch College, City University of New York
Kasravi, Aḥmad; Mujāhidīn, *article on* Mujāhidīn-i Khalq

Mohamad Abu Bakar
Associate Professor of History, Universiti Malaya, Kuala Lumpur
Regional Islamic Daʿwah Council of Southeast Asia and the Pacific

Ḥibba Eltigani Abugideiri
Research Assistant, Center for Muslim-Christian Understanding, Georgetown University
Amīr

Asʿad AbuKhalil
Department of Politics and Public Administration, California State University, Stanislaus
Class, *article on* Concepts of Class; Ghazw; Iṣlāḥ; Jihād Organizations; Revival and Renewal

Baha Abu-Laban
Professor of Sociology, University of Alberta, Canada
Canada

Sharon McIrvin Abu-Laban
Professor of Sociology, University of Alberta, Canada
Canada

Ibrahim M. Abu-Rabiʿ
Professor of Islamic Studies and Christian-Muslim Relations, Hartford Seminary
Justice, *article on* Social Justice; Muslim-Jewish Dialogue; Ṣalāt

Hussein M. Adam
Associate Professor of Political Science, College of the Holy Cross
Somalia

Ludwig W. Adamec
Professor of Islamic and Middle Eastern Studies, University of Arizona
Constitution

Charles J. Adams
Professor of Islamic Studies, McGill University (Retired)
Kufr

Anis Ahmad
Professor of Religion and Dean, Faculty of Islamic Revealed Knowledge and Human Sciences, International Islamic University, Petaling Jaya, Malaysia
Ramaḍān

Feroz Ahmad
Professor of History and University Research Professor, University of Massachusetts, Boston
Anavatan Partisi; Demokrat Parti; Enver Pasha; İttihad-i Muhammadi Cemiyeti; Pan-Turanism; Said Halim Pasha, Mehmed; Turkey; Young Turks

Mumtaz Ahmad
Associate Professor of Political Science, Hampton University, Virginia
Pakistan; Tablīghī Jamāʿat

Akbar S. Ahmed
Fellow of Selwyn College and Member of the Centre of South Asian Studies, Cambridge
Education, *article on* The Islamization of Knowledge; Mosque, *article on* The Mosque in Politics; Popular Religion, *article on* Popular Religion in Europe and the Americas

Ishtiaq Ahmed
Associate Professor of Political Science, Stockholms Universitet
Hamdard Foundation

Rafiuddin Ahmed
Visiting Professor of History, Cornell University
Awami League; Popular Religion, *article on* Popular Religion in South Asia

Engin Deniz Akarlı
Associate Professor of History, Washington University, St. Louis
Abdülhamid II

Shahrough Akhavi
Professor of International Studies, University of South Carolina, Columbia
Dawlah; Iran; Quṭb, Sayyid; Revolution; Sharīʿatī, ʿAlī; ʿUlamāʾ, *article on* Shīʿī ʿUlamāʾ

Shirin Akiner
Director, Central Asia Research Forum, School of Oriental and African Studies, University of London
Khiva Khanate

Mohammad al-Asad
Assistant Professor of Architecture, University of Jordan, Amman
Architecture, *article on* Contemporary Forms

Syed Hussein Alatas
Petaling Jaya, Malaysia
Social Sciences

Michael W. Albin
Chief, Order Division, Library of Congress
Book Publishing

Hamid Algar
Professor of Islamic Studies, University of California, Berkeley
Akhbārīyah; ʿAtabāt; Bayramiye; Imam; Muṭahharī, Murtaẓā; Naqshbandīyah; Uṣūlīyah

Azizah Y. al-Hibri
Associate Professor of Law, T. C. Williams School of Law, University of Richmond
Marriage and Divorce, *article on* Legal Foundations; Modesty

Saleh Abdul-Rehman Al-Maniʾ
Associate Professor of Politics, King Saud University, Saudi Arabia
King Faisal Foundation

Nezar AlSayyad
Professor of Architecture, University of California, Berkeley
Urban Planning

Ahmed Al-Shahi
Lecturer in Social Anthropology, University of Newcastle upon Tyne
Khatmīyah

Abdallah al-Shiekh
Professor of Economics and Political Science, Omdurman Islamic University, Sudan
Zakāt

Soraya Altorki
Professor of Anthropology, American University in Cairo
Women and Islam, *article on* Role and Status of Women

Audrey L. Altstadt
Associate Professor of History, University of Massachusetts, Amherst
Azerbaijan

Sajida Sultana Alvi
Professor of Indo-Islamic History and Chairperson in Urdu Language and Culture, McGill University
ʿAbd al-ʿAzīz, Shāh

Ayman al-Yassini
Consultant, Chelsea, Canada
Ibn ʿAbd al-Wahhāb, Muḥammad; Wahhābīyah

Mehrdad Amanat
Doctoral Candidate in History, University of California, Los Angeles
Zūrkhānah

Hussein Y. Amin
Associate Professor of Journalism and Mass Communications, The American University in Cairo
Newspapers and Magazines

Tahir Amin
Associate Professor of International Relations, Quaid-i-Azam University, Islamabad, Pakistan
Kashmir

Hooshang Amirahmadi
Professor of Planning and International Development, Rutgers University
Bunyād

Biancamaria Scarcia Amoretti
Professor of Islamic Studies, Università degli Studi di Roma "La Sapienza"
Qadhdhāfī, Muʿammar al-; Ṣafavid Dynasty

Jon W. Anderson
Associate Professor of Anthropology, Catholic University of America
Honor; Loya Jirga; Shame

Munawar Ahmad Anees
Editor in Chief, Periodica Islamica, Kuala Lumpur
Periodical Literature

Sinan Antoon
Graduate Student, Center for Contemporary Arab Society, Georgetown University
Sharīf

Mohammed Arkoun
Professor Emeritus of Islamic Thought, Université de la Sorbonne Nouvelle, Paris
Islamic Studies, *article on* Methodologies

Roy Armes
Professor of Film, Middlesex University, London
Cinema

Guy Arnold
London, United Kingdom
Indian Ocean Societies

Ali S. Asani
Professor of the Practice of Indo-Muslim Languages and Culture, Harvard University
Urdu Literature

Syed Ali Ashraf
Director General, Islamic Academy, Cambridge, United Kingdom
Universities

Sarah G. Moment Atis
Associate Professor of Turkish and Chair, Middle East Studies Program, University of Wisconsin, Madison
Turkish Literature

Muriel Atkin
Associate Professor of History, George Washington University
Tajikistan

Gehad Auda
Director, Center for Political and International Development Studies, Cairo
Abdel Rahman, Omar

Peter Avery
Lecturer in Persian Studies, King's College, University of Cambridge
Monarchy

Mahmoud M. Ayoub
Professor of Islamic Studies, Temple University
Ḥusayn ibn ʿAlī; Pillars of Islam; Qurʾān, *article on* History of the Text

Nazih N. Ayubi
Reader in Politics and Director, Middle East Politics Programme, University of Exeter
Dūrī, ʿAbd al-ʿAzīz al-; Ghazālī, Muḥammad al-; Islamic State; Muslim Brotherhood, *overview article*

Mario J. Azevedo
Professor of African History and Chair, Department of African-American and African Studies, University of North Carolina, Charlotte
Cameroon

Fakhreddin Azimi
Assistant Professor of History, University of Connecticut
Pahlavi, Reza Shah

Fuad Baali
Professor of Sociology, Western Kentucky University, Bowling Green
ʿAṣabīyah; Ibn Khaldūn, ʿAbd al-Raḥmān

Gamal M. Badr
Adjunct Professor of Islamic Law, New York University
Commercial Law

Margot Badran
Visiting Fellow in Near Eastern Studies, Princeton University
Feminism; Mūsā, Nabawīyah; Nāṣif, Malak Ḥifnī; Shaʿrāwī, Hudā

Osman Bakar
Professor of Philosophy of Science, Universiti Malaya, Kuala Lumpur
Cosmology

Raymond Baker
Department of Political Science, Williams College
Egypt

Bahman Baktiari
Associate Professor of Political Science, University of Maine, Orono
Ākhūnd; Ḥujjatīyah

Julian Baldick
Lecturer in the Study of Religions, King's College, University of London
Chishtīyah

J. P. Bannerman *(deceased)*
Counsellor and Director, Middle East Section, Research and Analysis Department, Foreign and Commonwealth Office, London
Organization of the Islamic Conference, *article on* Structure and Activities

Amatzia Baram
Senior Lecturer in the Modern History of the Middle East and Deputy Director, Jewish-Arab Center and the Gustav Heinemann Institute for Middle Eastern Studies, University of Haifa, Israel
Ḥizb al-Daʿwah al-Islāmīyah

Nimat Hafez Barazangi
Visiting Fellow in Muslim Women's Education, Cornell University
Education, *articles on* Religious Education *and* Educational Reform

Iraj Bashiri
Associate Professor of Central Asian Studies, University of Minnesota, Minneapolis
Kyrgyzstan

Lois Beck
Professor of Anthropology, Washington University, St. Louis
Tribe

William O. Beeman
Associate Professor of Anthropology, Brown University
Iranian Revolution of 1979

M. A. J. Beg
Associate Professor of Middle Eastern History, University of Brunei Darussalam
Ḥaḍārah

Peter J. Bertocci
Professor of Anthropology, Oakland University, Rochester, Michigan
Bangladesh

Robert Brenton Betts
Visiting Associate Professor, Faculty of Arts and Sciences, American University of Beirut
Druze

Robert Bianchi
Litigating Intern, Edwin F. Mandel Clinic, The University of Chicago Law School
Capitalism and Islam; Ḥajj

Irene A. Bierman
Associate Professor of Islamic Architecture and Art, University of California, Los Angeles
Architecture, *article on* Traditional Forms; Textiles

Mehrzad Boroujerdi
Assistant Professor of Political Science, Syracuse University
Ḥizbullāh, *article on* Ḥizbullāh in Iran

Selma Botman
Associate Professor of Political Science, College of the Holy Cross
Socialism and Islam

Issa J. Boullata
Professor of Arabic Literature and Language, Institute of Islamic Studies, McGill University
Arabic; Ḥanafī, Ḥasan

Donna Lee Bowen
Professor of Political Science, Brigham Young University
Family Planning

John R. Bowen
Associate Professor of Anthropology, Washington University, St. Louis
Popular Religion, *article on* Popular Religion in Southeast Asia

Yuri Bregel
Professor of Central Eurasian Studies, Indiana University, Bloomington
Khoqand Khanate

Bert F. Breiner
New York, New York
Christianity and Islam

William M. Brinner
Professor Emeritus of Near Eastern Studies, University of California, Berkeley
Conversion

Edmund Burke, III
Professor of History, University of California, Santa Cruz
Abd el-Krim; Istiqlāl; Orientalism

Charles E. Butterworth
Professor of Government and Politics, University of Maryland, College Park
ʿIlm; Madīnah al Fāḍilah, al-; Vicegerent

Norman Calder
Lecturer in Arabic and Islamic Studies, University of Manchester
Ghaybah; Ḥillī, ʿAllāmah ibn al-Muṭahhar al-; Law, *article on* Legal Thought and Jurisprudence; Marjaʿ al-Taqlīd

Jean Calmard
Director of Research, Centre National de la Recherche Scientifique, Paris
Ayatollah

Juan Eduardo Campo
Associate Professor of the History of Religions, Islam, and Arabic Language, University of California, Santa Barbara
Dietary Rules; Houses; Mawlā; Mosque, *article on* Historical Development

Byron D. Cannon
Professor of History, University of Utah
Qāḍī; Qaramanlı Dynasty

Louis J. Cantori
Professor of Political Science, University of Maryland, Baltimore
Modernization and Development; Republic

Olivier Carré
Directeur de Recherche sur l'Orient Arabe et l'Islam, Fondation Nationale des Sciences Politiques, Centre d'Études et de Recherches Internationales, Paris
Bannāʾ, Ḥasan al-; Faḍlallāh, Muḥammad Ḥusayn

Jocelyne Cesari
Researcher, IREMAM, Aix-en-Provence
Union des Organisations Islamiques de France

H. E. Chehabi
Fellow, St. Antony's College, University of Oxford
Liberation Movement of Iran; Ṭāleqāni, Maḥmud

Peter Chelkowski
Professor of Near Eastern Studies, New York University
ʿĀshūrāʾ; Imāmzādah; Taʿziyah

W. K. Che Man
Senior Lecturer in History, Universiti Brunei Darussalam
Moro National Liberation Front

William C. Chittick
Associate Professor of Comparative Studies, State University of New York, Stony Brook
Miʿrāj; Sufism, *article on* Ṣūfī Thought and Practice

Golam W. Choudhury
Adjunct Professor, School of International and Public Affairs, Columbia University
Organization of the Islamic Conference, *article on* Origins

Youssef M. Choueiri
Lecturer in Arabic and Islamic Studies and Modern Middle Eastern History, University of Exeter
Majlis; Waṭan

Allan Christelow
Associate Professor of History, Idaho State University
Maḥkamah; Mai Tatsine

Julia Clancy-Smith
Associate Professor of Middle East and North African History, University of Virginia
ʿAlawī, Aḥmad al-; Barakah; Kabylia; Mawlāy

Lynda Clarke
Assistant Professor of Religion and Islam, Bard College
Sainthood; Ṣawm; Shahādah; Suicide

Juan R. I. Cole
Director, Center for Middle Eastern and North African Studies, and Associate Professor of History, University of Michigan, Ann Arbor
Khums; Wilāyah

David Commins
Associate Professor of History, Dickinson College, Carlisle, Pennsylvania
Modernism; Syria

Lawrence I. Conrad
Historian of Near Eastern Medicine, Wellcome Institute for the History of Medicine, London
Medicine, *article on* Traditional Practice

Miriam Cooke
Professor of Arabic Literature, Duke University
Arabic Literature, *article on* Gender in Arabic Literature

Vincent J. Cornell
Andrew W. Mellon Assistant Professor of Religion, Duke University
ʿAbd al-Qādir; Jizyah; Qurʾān, *article on* The Qurʾān as Scripture; Sultan

Kenneth Cragg
Professor of Arabic and Islamics, Hartford Seminary (Retired); Anglican Bishop in Jerusalem and the Middle East
ʿAbduh, Muḥammad

James Critchlow
Fellow, Russian Research Center, Harvard University
Uzbekistan

Harold Crouch
Senior Fellow, Research School of Pacific and Asian Studies, Australian National University
Masjumi

Alexander S. Cudsi
Assistant Professor of Middle East Politics, Panteion University, Athens
Ummah-Anṣār

Hamid Dabashi
Associate Professor of Middle Eastern and Asian Languages and Cultures, Columbia University
Mullah; Nūrī, Faẕlullāh; Persian Literature; Shīʿī Islam, *article on* Modern Shīʿī Thought

Ahmad S. Dallal
Assistant Professor of Arabic and Islamic Studies, Yale University
Fatwā, *article on* Modern Usage; Ummah; ʿUshr

Elton L. Daniel
Professor of History, University of Hawaiʾi at Manoa
Shah

Virginia Danielson
Curator, Archive of World Music, Harvard University
Devotional Music

Linda T. Darling
Assistant Professor of Middle East History, University of Arizona
Capitulations

Eric Davis
Associate Professor of Political Science, Rutgers University
ʿAbd al-Rāziq, ʿAlī

Susan Schaefer Davis
Independent Scholar, Haverford, Pennsylvania
Women and Social Reform, *article on* Social Reform in North Africa

Marius K. Deeb
Professorial Lecturer in Middle Eastern Politics, George Washington University
Ḥizb; Organization of the Islamic Jihād

Mary-Jane Deeb
Assistant Professor of Comparative Regional Studies, School of International Service, American University
Messali al-Ḥajj; Zaytūnah

R. Hrair Dekmejian
Professor of Political Science, University of Southern California
Sibāʿī, Muṣṭafā al-

Frederick Mathewson Denny
Professor of Religious Studies, University of Colorado, Boulder
Funerary Rites, *article on* Modern Practice; Islam, *article on* Islam in the Americas; Qurʾānic Recitation

Walter B. Denny
Professor of Art History, University of Massachusetts, Amherst
Aesthetic Theory; Carpets

Devin DeWeese
Associate Professor of Central Eurasian Studies, Indiana University, Bloomington
Bukhara Khanate

Moḥammad-Reza Djalili
Professor of International Relations, Institut Universitaire de Hautes Études Internationales, Geneva
Dār al-Ḥarb; International Law

Abdul Rahman I. Doi
Professor of Islamic Studies, Rand Afrikaans University, Melville, South Africa
Ḥisbah; Kharāj; Maṣlaḥah; Public Law

Manochehr Dorraj
Associate Professor of Political Science, Texas Christian University
Bāzargān, Mehdi; Borujerdi, Moḥammad Ḥosayn; Shadow of God

Eleanor Abdella Doumato
Lecturer in History, University of Rhode Island
Jāhilīyah; Marriage and Divorce, *article on* Modern Practice; Saudi Arabia; Seclusion; Shafīq, Durrīyah

Abul Fadl Mohsin Ebrahim
Senior Lecturer in Islamic Studies, University of Durban, South Africa
Abortion

David B. Edwards
Assistant Professor of Anthropology and Sociology, Williams College
Hekmatyar, Gulbuddin; Ḥizb-i Islāmī Afghānistān

Dale F. Eickelman
Ralph and Richard Lazarus Professor of Anthropology and Human Relations, Dartmouth College
Ethnicity; Ideology and Islam; Oman; Popular Religion, *article on* Popular Religion in the Middle East and North Africa; Shrine

Hermann Frederick Eilts
Professor Emeritus of International Relations, Boston University
Saʿūd, ʿAbd al-ʿAzīz ibn ʿAbd al-Raḥmān Āl

Fadwa El Guindi
Research Anthropologist, El Nil Research, Los Angeles, California
Ḥijāb; Mawlid

Jamal J. Elias
Assistant Professor of Religion, Amherst College
Mawlawīyah; Shaṭṭārīyah

Farid el-Khazen
Associate Professor of Political Studies, American University of Beirut
Jumblatt, Kamal

John P. Entelis
Professor of Political Science and Director, Middle East Studies Program, Fordham University
Tunisia

John L. Esposito
Director, Center for Muslim-Christian Understanding, and Professor of Religion and International Affairs, School of Foreign Service, Georgetown University
Fārūqī, Ismāʿīl Rājī al-; Islam, *overview article*

A. Sofia Esteves
Policy Consultant, The Vaden Group, Vienna, Virginia
Idrīsid Dynasty

Katherine P. Ewing
Assistant Professor of Cultural Anthropology, Duke University
Pir

Mohammad H. Faghfoory
Independent Scholar, Alexandria, Virginia
Kāshāni, Abol-Qāsem

Hani Fakhouri
Professor of Anthropology and Middle Eastern Studies, University of Michigan, Flint
Jordan

Farideh Farhi
Associate Professor of Political Science, University of Hawai'i at Manoa
Sipāh-i Pasdarān-i Inqilāb-i Islāmī

Asghar Fathi
Professor of Sociology, University of Calgary, Canada
Khuṭbah

Howard M. Federspiel
Professor of Political Science, Ohio State University, Newark
Pesantren

Elizabeth Warnock Fernea
Professor of English and Middle Eastern Studies, University of Texas at Austin
Family

Carter Vaughn Findley
Professor of History, Ohio State University
Mecelle

Michael M. J. Fischer
Professor of Anthropology and Science and Technology Studies, Massachusetts Institute of Technology
Bazaar; Qom

Alan Fisher
Professor of History, Michigan State University
Crimea Khanate

Willem Floor
Senior Energy Planner, The World Bank, Washington, D.C.
Ḥāʾirī Yazdī, ʿAbd al-Karīm; Nāʾīnī, Muḥammad Ḥusayn

Carolyn Fluehr-Lobban
Professor of Anthropology, Rhode Island College
Sudan

Yohanan Friedmann
Max Schloessinger Professor of Islamic Studies, The Hebrew University of Jerusalem
Aḥmadīyah; Jamʿīyatul ʿUlamāʾ-i Hind

Patrick D. Gaffney
Associate Professor of Anthropology, University of Notre Dame
Mosque, *article on* The Mosque in Society

Nancy E. Gallagher
Professor of History, University of California, Santa Barbara
Medicine, *article on* Contemporary Practice

Gene R. Garthwaite
Professor of History, Dartmouth College
Khan; Malkom Khān

Tomas Gerholm
Associate Professor of Social Anthropology, Stockholms Universitet
ʿUrf

David Gilmartin
Associate Professor of History, North Carolina State University, Raleigh
Anglo-Muhammadan Law

Dru C. Gladney
Associate Professor of Asian Studies, University of Hawai'i at Manoa; Research Fellow, Program for Cultural Studies, East-West Center
Islam, *article on* Islam in China

Alan A. Godlas
Assistant Professor of Religion, University of Georgia
Niʿmatullāhīyah; Rifāʿīyah

Ellis Goldberg
Associate Professor of Comparative Politics, University of Washington
Communism and Islam; Niqābah

Matthew S. Gordon
Assistant Professor of History, Miami University, Ohio
Amīr al-Muʾminīn; Jamʿīyat al-Shubbān al-Muslimīn; Shaykh al-Islām

William J. Griswold
Professor of History, Colorado State University
Janissaries

Marilyn Trent Grunkemeyer
Research Associate in Anthropology, University of North Carolina, Chapel Hill
Muhammadiyah

Bassam S. A. Haddad
Doctoral Candidate in Government, Georgetown University
Sharīf

Yvonne Yazbeck Haddad
Professor of Islamic History, University of Massachusetts, Amherst
Federation of Islamic Associations; United States of America

Shahla Haeri
Assistant Professor of Anthropology, Boston University
Mutʿah; Women and Social Reform, *article on* Social Reform in the Middle East

Wael B. Hallaq
Associate Professor of Islamic Studies, McGill University
Ahl al-Ḥall wa-al-ʿAqd; Consensus; Faqīh; Ijtihād

Fred Halliday
Professor of International Relations, London School of Economics
Class, *article on* Class Analysis

William J. Hamblin
Associate Professor of History, Brigham Young University
Eschatology; Zaydīyah

Earleen Helgelien Hanafy
Professor of Physical Education, St. Cloud State University, Minnesota
Games and Sport

S. Nomanul Haq
Assistant Professor of Religious Studies, Brown University
Alchemy; Astrology; Astronomy; Divination

John W. Harbeson
Professor of Political Science, City University of New York
Ethiopia

Muhammed Haron
Professor of Arabic Studies, University of the Western Cape, Bellville, South Africa
South Africa

Tawfiq Y. Hasou
Professor of Political Science, Applied Science University, Amman, Jordan
Arab League

M. Kamal Hassan
Professor of Islamic Studies, International Islamic University Malaysia, Petaling Jaya
International Islamic University at Kuala Lumpur; Malaysia

G. R. Hawting
Senior Lecturer in the History of the Near and Middle East, School of Oriental and African Studies, University of London
Rightly Guided Caliphs

Robert W. Hefner
Associate Professor of Anthropology, Boston University
Syncretism

Mary Elaine Hegland
Assistant Professor of Social-Cultural Anthropology, Santa Clara University, California
Ahl al-Bayt

Marcia K. Hermansen
Professor of Religious Studies, San Diego State University
Biography and Hagiography; Khānqāh; Walī Allāh, Shāh

Andrew C. Hess
Professor of Diplomacy, Fletcher School of Law and Diplomacy, Tufts University
Millet

Leila Hessini
International Overseas Consultant, Ford Foundation, Cairo
Women and Social Reform, *article on* Social Reform in North Africa

Elizabeth Hiel
Research Assistant, Center for Muslim-Christian Understanding, Georgetown University
Fez

Nadia Hijab
Senior Human Development Officer, United Nations Develpment Programme, New York
Women and Social Reform, *overview article*

Mervyn Hiskett
Professor of Hausa Studies, University of Sokoto, Nigeria (Retired)
African Languages and Literatures, *article on* West Africa; Dan Fodio, Usuman

Valerie J. Hoffman-Ladd
Associate Professor of Religion, University of Illinois, Urbana-Champaign
ʿAbd al-Raḥmān, ʿĀʾishah; Ghazālī, Zaynab al-; Ibn al-ʿArabī, Muḥyī al-Dīn; Women and Islam, *article on* Women's Religious Observances

Pervez Hoodbhoy
Professor of Physics, Quaid-i-Azam University, Islamabad, Pakistan
Science

M. B. Hooker
Formerly Professor of Comparative Law, University of Kent, Canterbury
Islam, *article on* Islam in Southeast Asia and the Pacific

Nicholas S. Hopkins
Professor of Anthropology, American University in Cairo
Land Tenure

Derek Hopwood
Director, Middle East Centre, St. Antony's College, University of Oxford
Nasser, Gamal Abdel

Michael Humphrey
Senior Lecturer in Sociology, University of New South Wales, Kensington, Australia
Ḥarakāt al-Tawḥīd al-Islāmī

R. Stephen Humphreys
Professor of History and King Abdul Aziz Al-Saud Professor of Islamic Studies, University of California, Santa Barbara
Historiography

Ibrahim Ibrahim
Research Professor of Arab Studies, Georgetown University
Jamāʿat al-Islāmīyah, al-

Khayrulla Ismatulla
Professor of Philology, Indiana University, Bloomington
Central Asian Literatures

Sherman A. Jackson
Assistant Professor of Arabic and Islamic Studies, Indiana University, Bloomington
Muḥtasib

Syed Husain M. Jafri
Professor of Islamic Studies and Director of Pakistan Study Centre, University of Karachi, Pakistan
Sayyid; Shīʿī Islam, *historical overview article*

Fadhlullah Jamil
School of Humanities, University of Science, Minden, Malaysia
Ibrahim, Anwar

Johannes J. G. Jansen
Lecturer in Arabic and Islam, Universiteit Leiden
Kishk, ʿAbd al-Ḥamīd; Takfīr wa al-Hijrah, Jamāʿat al-

J. E. A. Johansen
Cataloging and Imaging Projects Manager, al-Furqan Islamic Heritage Foundation, London
Shādhilīyah; Sufism and Politics

Cemal Kafadar
Associate Professor of History, Harvard University
Dīwān; Gökalp, Mehmet Ziya

Monzer Kahf
Research Economist, Islamic Development Bank, Jeddah, Saudi Arabia
Property; Waqf

Carolyn Kane
Lecturer, Cooper-Hewitt National Museum of Design and the New York School of Interior Design
Metalwork

Ousmane Kane
Professor of Political Science, Université de Saint-Louis, Senegal
Zāwiyah

Ibrahim A. Karawan
Professor of Political Science, University of Utah
Takfīr

Riva Kastoryano
Researcher, Centre d'Etudes et de Recherches Internationales, Fondation Nationale de Sciences Politiques, Centre National de le Recherche Scientifique, Paris
Groupement Islamique en France

Farhad Kazemi
Professor of Middle East Politics, New York University
Fidāʾīyān-i Islām

Joseph A. Kechichian
Senior Staff Member on International Policy, The Rand Corporation, Santa Monica, California
Saʿūd, Fayṣal ibn ʿAbd al-ʿAzīz Āl

Nikki R. Keddie
Professor of Middle Eastern History, University of California, Los Angeles
Afghānī, Jamāl al-Dīn al-; Constitutional Revolution; Qājār Dynasty

John Kelsay
Associate Professor of Religion, Florida State University
Ethics

Charles H. Kennedy
Professor of Politics, Wake Forest University
Jamʿīyatul ʿUlamāʾ-i Islām

Hugh Kennedy
Reader in Mediaeval History, University of St. Andrews, Scotland
ʿAbbāsid Caliphate

David A. Kerr
Professor of Islamic Studies and Director, Macdonald Center for the Study of Islam and Christian-Muslim Relations, Hartford Seminary
Prophethood; Waẓīfah

Rashid Khalidi
Associate Professor of Middle East History and Director, Center for Middle Eastern Studies, University of Chicago
Palestine Liberation Organization

Elaheh Kheirandish
Postdoctoral Fellow, Research Faculty of History and Philosophy of Science, Institute for Cultural Studies and Research, Harvard University
Mathematics

Philip S. Khoury
Professor of History and Dean of Humanities and Social Science, Massachusetts Institute of Technology
Muslim Brotherhood, *article on* Muslim Brotherhood in Syria

Charles A. Kimball
Associate Professor of Religion, Furman University, Greenville, South Carolina
Muslim-Christian Dialogue

Jan Knappert
Senior Fellow, School of Oriental and African Studies, University of London
African Languages and Literatures, *article on* East Africa

Omari H. Kokole
Associate Director, Institute of Global Cultural Studies, State University of New York, Binghamton
Uganda

Katherine C. Kolstad
Doctoral Candidate in Religious Studies, University of California, Santa Barbara
Puberty Rites

Bahgat Korany
Professor of International Relations and Comparative Politics, University of Montreal
Arab Nationalism

Gudrun Krämer
Professor of Islamic Studies, Rheinischen Friedrich-Wilhelms-Universität Bonn
Minorities, *article on* Minorities in Muslim Societies

Martin Kramer
Associate Director, Moshe Dayan Center for Middle Eastern and African Studies, Tel Aviv University
Congresses; Ḥizbullāh, *article on* Ḥizbullāh in Lebanon

Robert S. Kramer
Assistant Professor of History, St. Norbert College, De Pere, Wisconsin
Mahdi; Mahdīyah

Klaus Kreiser
Professor of Turkology, Otto-Friedrich-Universität Bamberg
Germany

Annie Krieger-Krynicki
Maître de Conférence (Public Law and Political Science), Université de Paris IX Dauphine
Conseil National des Français Musulmans; Fédération Nationale des Musulmans de France

Aptullah Kuran
Professor of Architectural History, Boğaziçi University, Istanbul
Mosque, *article on* Mosque Architecture

Timur Kuran
Professor of Economics and King Faisal Professor of Islamic Thought and Culture, University of Southern California
Economic Development; Economics, *article on* Economic Theory; Interest

Hamid R. Kusha
Assistant Professor of Sociology and Criminology, Maryville College, St. Louis
Polygyny

Ahmet Kuyaş
Assistant Professor of History, Mount Holyoke College
Gökalp, Mehmet Ziya

Jacob M. Landau
Gersten Professor of Political Science, The Hebrew University of Jerusalem
Pan-Islam

Bruce B. Lawrence
Professor of Islamic Studies and History of Religions, Duke University
Islam, *article on* Islam in South Asia

B. Todd Lawson
Assistant Professor of Islamic Studies, University of Toronto
Bahā' Allāh; Bahā'ī; Martyrdom; Nawrūz

Fred H. Lawson
Associate Professor of Government, Mills College
Gulf States

Edward J. Lazzerini
Professor of History, University of New Orleans
Gasprinskii, Ismail Bey; Jadīdism

David Leake, Jr.
Project Coordinator, Hawaii University Affiliated Program for Developmental Disabilities, University of Hawai'i at Manoa
Brunei

Jean-François Legrain
Researcher in Political Science, Centre National de la Recherche Scientifique, Amman
Ḥamās

David Lelyveld
Dean of Students, School of General Studies, Columbia University
Aligarh

René Lemarchand
Professor of Political Science, University of Florida
Chad

Ann Mosely Lesch
Professor of Political Science and Associate Director, Center for Arab and Islamic Studies, Villanova University
Ḥusaynī, al-Ḥājj Amīn al-

Nehemia Levtzion
Bamberger and Fuld Professor of the History of the Muslim Peoples, The Hebrew University of Jerusalem
Khalwatīyah; Tijānī, Aḥmad al-

Keith Lewinstein
Assistant Professor of History and Religion, Smith College
Ḥukūmah

David E. Long
Senior Associate, C & O Resources Incorporated, Washington, D.C.
Diplomatic Missions

Larry Luxner
Freelance Journalist, San Juan, Puerto Rico
Albania; Suriname; Trinidad and Tobago

Denis MacEoin
Honorary Fellow, Centre for Middle East and Islamic Studies, University of Durham, United Kingdom
Bāb; Bābism

Paul J. Magnarella
Professor of Anthropology and Law, University of Florida
Republican Brothers

Hendrik M. J. Maier
Professor of Malay and Indonesian Language and Literature, Rijksuniversiteit Leiden
Malay and Indonesian Literature

Cesar Adib Majul
Professor Emeritus, University of the Philippines
Philippines

Hafeez Malik
Professor of Political Science, Villanova University
Aḥmad Khān, Sayyid; Iqbal, Muhammad; Muslim League

Jamal Malik
Associate Professor of Islamic Studies, South Asia Institute, Universität Heidelberg
International Islamic University at Islamabad

Chibli Mallat
Director, Centre of Islamic and Middle Eastern Law, School of Oriental and African Studies, University of London
Contract Law; Iraq; Ṣadr, Muḥammad Bāqir al-

Fedwa Malti-Douglas
Director, Middle Eastern Studies Program, and Chairperson, Department of Near Eastern Languages and Cultures, Indiana University, Bloomington
Arabic Literature, *overview article*; Arkoun, Mohammed; Children's Books and Cartoons; Ḥusayn, Ṭāhā; Pamphlets and Tracts; Saʿdāwī, Nawāl al-

Lawrence H. Mamiya
Mattie M. and Norman H. Paschal Davis Professor of Religion and African Studies, Vassar College
Nation of Islam

Peter Mansfield
London, United Kingdom
Nasserism

Şerif Mardin
Chair, Islamic Studies, School of International Service, American University
Kemal, Mehmet Namık; Kısakürek, Necip Fazıl; Mevlevî; Nurculuk; Şinasi, İbrahim; Suavi, Ali; Tanzimat; Young Ottomans

Manuela Marín
Research Fellow in Arabic Studies, Consejo Superior de Investigaciones Científicas, Madrid
Córdoba, Caliphate of

Michael E. Marmura
Professor of Islamic Studies, University of Toronto
Sunnī Islam, *historical overview article*

Bradford G. Martin
Emeritus Professor of History, Indiana University, Bloomington
Qādirīyah

Richard C. Martin
Associate Professor of Religious Studies, Arizona State University
ʿĪd al-Aḍḥā; ʿĪd al-Fiṭr; Islamic Studies, *article on* History of the Field

Muhammad Khalid Masud
Professor of Islamic Studies, Islamic Research Institute, International Islamic University, Islamabad, Pakistan
Daʿwah, *article on* Modern Usage; Fatwā, *article on* Concepts of Fatwā; Tablīgh

Hanspeter Mattes
Senior Research Fellow, Deutsches Orient-Institut, Hamburg
Islamic Call Society

Diane K. Mauzy
Associate Professor of Political Science, University of British Columbia
Partai Islam Se-Malaysia; United Malays National Organization

Ann Elizabeth Mayer
Associate Professor of Legal Studies, Wharton School, University of Pennsylvania
Human Rights; Inheritance; Law, *article on* Modern Legal Reform

Ali A. Mazrui
Albert Schweitzer Professor in the Humanities, State University of New York, Binghamton
Islam, *article on* Islam in Sub-Saharan Africa

Michel M. Mazzaoui
Associate Professor of Middle East History, University of Utah
Majlisī, Muḥammad Bāqir al-; Mullabashi

Brinkley Messick
Associate Professor of Anthropology, University of Michigan, Ann Arbor
Fatwā, *article on* Process and Function

Barbara D. Metcalf
Professor of History, University of California, Davis
Barelwī, Sayyid Aḥmad; Deobandīs; India

Laurence O. Michalak
Vice Chair, Center for Middle Eastern Studies, University of California, Berkeley
Fāsī, Muḥammad ʿAllāl al-

Nancy Micklewright
Associate Professor of History in Art, University of Victoria, Canada
Painting

Mohsen M. Milani
Associate Professor of Comparative Politics, University of South Florida
Mustaḍʿafūn

Beverley Milton-Edwards
Lecturer in Middle Eastern Politics, Queen's University of Belfast
Muslim Brotherhood, *article on* Muslim Brotherhood in Jordan; West Bank and Gaza

Gail Minault
Associate Professor of History, University of Texas, Austin
Ameer Ali, Syed; Chirāgh ʿAlī; Khilāfat Movement

Mustansir Mir
Associate Professor of Islamic Studies, International Islamic University, Petaling Jaya, Malaysia
ʿAqīdah; Ghazālī, Abū Ḥāmid al-; Īmān; Qurʾān, *article on* The Qurʾān in Muslim Thought and Practice; Sin; Tafsīr

Mohd Anis Md Nor
Associate Professor of Southeast Asian Studies and Director, Cultural Center, University of Malaya, Kuala Lumpur
Dance

Baqer Moin
Head, Persian Service, British Broadcasting Corporation, London
Khomeini, Ruhollah al-Musavi

Moojan Momen
Director, Afnan Library, Biggleswade, Bedfordshire, United Kingdom
Ṭāghūt; Wakālah al-ʿĀmmah, al-; Wakālah al-Khāṣṣah, al-; Ẓulm

Yaḥyá Monastra
Librarian, International Islamic University, Petaling Jaya, Malaysia
Libraries

Ebrahim Moosa
Lecturer in Islamic Studies, University of Cape Town
Repentance; Sacrifice

Matti Moosa
Professor of Middle East History, Gannon University, Erie, Pennsylvania
ʿAlawīyah

Parviz Morewedge
Senior Research Fellow, Institute of Global Cultural Studies, State University, New York, Binghamton
Theology

D. O. Morgan
Reader in the History of the Middle East, School of Oriental and African Studies, University of London
Seljuk Dynasty

Soheir A. Morsy
Independent Scholar and United Nations Consultant, Washington, D.C.
Health Care

Roy P. Mottahedeh
Professor of History, Harvard University
Wilāyat al-Faqīh

Jeanne Moulierac
Institut du Monde Arabe, Paris, France
Pottery and Ceramics

Hamid Mowlana
Professor and Director of International Communication Studies, School of International Service, The American University
Communications Media; Radio and Television

Mehdi Mozaffari
Professor of Political Science, Aarhus University, Denmark
Rushdie Affair

Akbar Muḥammad
Associate Professor of Islamic and African History, State University of New York, Binghamton
Malcolm X

Muhammad Syukri Salleh
Chairman, Development Studies Section, School of Social Sciences, University of Science Malaysia
Dar ul Arqam

Henry Munson, Jr.
Professor of Anthropology, University of Maine, Orono
Morocco

Muhammad Muslih
Associate Professor of Political Science, C. W. Post College, Long Island University
Democracy

Hussin Mutalib
Senior Lecturer of Political Science, National University of Singapore
ABIM

Eden Naby
Associate, Center for Middle Eastern Studies, Harvard University
Islamic Renaissance Party

Hamid Naficy
Assistant Professor of Media Studies, Rice University
Cassettes

Judith Nagata
Professor of Anthropology, York University, North York, Canada
PERKIM

Nakamura Mitsuo
Professor of Anthropology, Chiba University, Japan
Abdurrahman Wahid; Nahdatul Ulama; Partai Persatuan Pembangunan

Emile A. Nakhleh
John L. Morrison Professor of International Studies, Mount Saint Mary's College, Emmitsburg, Maryland
Bayʿah

Azim A. Nanji
Professor of Religion and Chairperson, Department of Religion, University of Florida
Aga Khan; Aga Khan Foundation; Ḥalāl; Muftī; Sunnah

Guity Nashat
Associate Professor of History, University of Illinois, Chicago
Anjuman

Seyyed Hossein Nasr
Professor of Islamic Studies, George Washington University
Philosophy; Ṭabāṭabāʾī, Muḥammad Ḥusayn

Seyyed Vali Reza Nasr
Assistant Professor of Political Science, University of San Diego
Jamāʿat-i Islāmī; Jamʿīyatul ʿUlamāʾ-i Pākistān; Maryam Jameelah; Mawdūdī, Sayyid Abū al-Aʿlā; Youth Movements

Ronald L. Nettler
Fellow, Oxford Centre for Postgraduate Hebrew Studies; Hebrew Centre Lecturer in Oriental Studies, University of Oxford
Dhimmī; Ibn Taymīyah, Taqī al-Dīn Aḥmad; Judaism and Islam; People of the Book

Gordon D. Newby
Professor of Near Eastern Studies, Emory University
Angels; Muḥammad, *article on* Biographies; Satan

Jørgen S. Nielsen
Director, Centre for the Study of Islam and Christian-Muslim Relations, Selly Oak Colleges, Birmingham
Great Britain; Islamic Foundation; United Kingdom Islamic Mission

Ronald Niezen
Assistant Professor of Anthropology and Social Sciences, Harvard University
Mali

August H. Nimtz, Jr.
Associate Professor of Political Science, University of Minnesota, Minneapolis
Tanzania

David Nissman
Manassas, Virginia
Turkmenistan

Farhan Ahmad Nizami
Director, Oxford Centre for Islamic Studies, St. Cross College, University of Oxford
Fyzee, Asaf Ali Asghar

Augustus Richard Norton
Professor of International Relations, Boston University
Amal; Lebanon; Ṣadr, Mūsā al-; Terrorism

Jeffrey B. Nugent
Professor of Economics, University of Southern California
Economic Development

Sulayman S. Nyang
Professor of African Studies, Howard University
Elijah Muhammad; Gambia; Islamic Society of North America

R. S. O'Fahey
Professor of Middle Eastern History, University of Bergen, Norway
Ibn Idrīs, Aḥmad; Idrīsīyah

Kazuo Ohtsuka
Associate Professor of Social Anthropology, Tokyo Metropolitan University
Magic and Sorcery; Sufism, *article on* Ṣūfī Shrine Culture

Martha Brill Olcott
Professor of Political Science, Colgate Univesity; Senior Fellow, Foreign Policy Research Institute
Kazakhstan

David Owusu-Ansah
Associate Professor of African History, James Madison University
Ghana

John N. Paden
Clarence Robinson Professor of International Studies, George Mason University
Nigeria; Sokoto Caliphate

Misagh Parsa
Assistant Professor of Sociology, Dartmouth College
Komiteh

James L. Peacock
Kenan Professor of Anthropology, University of North Carolina, Chapel Hill
Muhammadiyah

David Stephen Pearl
Professor of Law, University of East Anglia
Family Law; Ḥudūd

Kenneth J. Perkins
Professor of History, University of South Carolina, Columbia
Bouhired, Djamila; Ḥusaynid Dynasty

Glenn E. Perry
Professor of Political Science, Indiana State University
Caliph

John R. Perry
Professor of Persian Language and Civilization, University of Chicago
Afshārid Dynasty; Zand Dynasty

F. E. Peters
Professor of Near Eastern Languages and Literatures, New York University
Allāh; Jerusalem; Mecca; Medina

Rudolph Peters
Professor of Islamic Law, Universiteit van Amsterdam
Dār al-Islām; Dār al-Ṣulḥ; Jihād

Daniel C. Peterson
Assistant Professor of Islamic Studies and Arabic, Brigham Young University
Eschatology; Ismāʿīlīyah; Zaydīyah

Carl F. Petry
Professor of History, Northwestern University
Mamlūk State

Elizabeth Picard
Chargée de Recherches (Monde Arabe), Fondation Nationale des Sciences Politiques, Paris
Baʿth Parties

James P. Piscatori
Professor of International Politics, University of Wales
International Relations and Diplomacy

Alexandre Popovic
Director of Research, Centre National de la Recherche Scientifique, Paris
Balkan States

Charlotte A. Quinn
First Secretary, U.S. State Department, Warsaw
Djibouti; Guinea

Mazhar Mahmood Qurashi
Principal Investigator, SATMU Project, Pakistan Academy of Sciences, Islamabad
Natural Sciences

Ali Jihad Racy
Professor of Ethnomusicology, University of California, Los Angeles
Music

Amal Rassam
Professor of Anthropology, Queens College, City University of New York
Mernissi, Fatima

André Raymond
Professor Emeritus, Université de Provence
Guilds

Howard A. Reed
Professor Emeritus of History, University of Connecticut, Storrs, and Consultant
Özal, Turgut

Donald Malcolm Reid
Professor of History, Georgia State University
Azhar, al-; Education, *article on* Educational Institutions; Ḥuṣrī, Abū Khaldūn Sāṭiʿ al-; Muḥammad ʿAlī Dynasty; Syndicates

A. Kevin Reinhart
Associate Professor of Religion, Dartmouth College
Birth Rites, *article on* Legal Foundations; Farḍ al-ʿAyn; Farḍ al-Kifāyah; Funerary Rites, *article on* Legal Foundations; Guardianship; Ḥarām

João José Reis
Professor of History, Universidade Federal Da Bahia, Brazil
Brazil

Elie Rekhess
Senior Research Fellow, Palestinian Affairs, The Moshe Dayan Center for Middle Eastern and African Studies, Tel Aviv University
Israel

Yann Richard
Professor of Iranian Studies, Université de la Sorbonne Nouvelle
Intiẓār; Shaykhīyah

D. S. Richards
Lecturer in Arabic and Fellow of St. Cross College, University of Oxford
Fāṭimid Dynasty

David Robinson
University Distinguished Professor of History and African Studies, Michigan State University
Murīdīyah; Senegal

Francis Robinson
Professor of the History of South Asia, University of London
Mughal Empire; Sirhindī, Aḥmad

Wilfrid J. Rollman
Adjunct Professor of History, Northeastern University
ʿAlawid Dynasty

Geoffrey Roper
Islamic Bibliographer, Cambridge University Library
Reference Books

Azade-Ayşe Rorlich
Associate Professor of Russian and Inner Asian History, University of Southern California
Bigi, Musa Yarullah; Fakhreddin, Rizaeddin; Ishaki, Ayaz

Lawrence Rosen
Professor of Anthropology, Princeton University
Justice, *article on* Concepts of Justice

Olivier Roy
Researcher in Political Sciences, Centre National de la Recherche Scientifique, Paris
Mujāhidīn, *article on* Afghan Mujāhidīn

D. Fairchild Ruggles
Ithaca, New York
Gardens and Landscaping, *article on* Traditional Forms

Dankwart A. Rustow
Professor of Political Science and Sociology, Graduate Center, City University of New York
Military Forces

Abdulaziz Sachedina
Professor of Religious Studies, University of Virginia
ʿAlī ibn Abī Ṭālib; Al-Khoei Benevolent Foundation; Imāmah; Ithnā ʿAsharīyah; Karbala; Khojas; Law, *article on* Shīʿī Schools of Law; Mashhad; Messianism; Najaf; Ziyārah

Yasir M. Sakr
Doctoral Candidate in Architecture, University of Pennsylvania
Fathy, Hassan

Eliz Sanasarian
Associate Professor of Political Science, University of Southern California
Islamic Republican Party

Paula Sanders
Associate Professor of Islamic History, Rice University
Clitoridectomy

Usha Sanyal
Lecturer in Islam, Rutgers University
Barelwīs

Emilie Savage-Smith
Research Associate, Wellcome Unit for the History of Medicine, University of Oxford
Geomancy

Asma Sayeed
East Windsor, New Jersey
Hostages

Uli Schamiloglu
Associate Professor of Central Asian Studies, University of Wisconsin, Madison
Kazan Khanate

Annemarie Schimmel
Professor Emerita of Indo-Muslim Culture, Harvard University
Calligraphy and Epigraphy; Devotional Poetry; Numerology

John S. Schoeberlein-Engel
Fellow, Russian Research Center, Central Asia Forum, Harvard University
Basmachis

Vernon James Schubel
Associate Professor of Religion, Kenyon College
Islamic Calendar; Muḥarram; Relics

Reinhard Schulze
Professor of Arabic and Islamic Studies, Institut für Orientalistik, Otto-Friedrich-Universität Bamburg
Daʿwah, *article on* Institutionalization; Muslim World League

Raymond Scupin
Professor of Anthropology, Lindenwood College, St. Charles, Missouri
Thailand

Aaron Segal
Professor of Political Science, University of Texas, El Paso
Technology and Applied Sciences

Michael A. Sells
Associate Professor of Islam and Comparative Religions and Chairperson, Department of Religion, Haverford College
Dhikr

Jack G. Shaheen
Professor of Mass Communications, Southern Illinois University
Stereotypes in Mass Media

Emad Eldin Shahin
Independent Researcher, Alexandria, Virginia
ʿAbd al-Razzāq al-Sanhūrī; Ghannūshī, Rāshid al-; Ibn Bādīs, ʿAbd al-Ḥamīd; Kawākibī, ʿAbd al-Raḥmān al-; Madanī, ʿAbbāsī; Rashīd Riḍā, Muḥammad; Salafīyah

M. Nazif Shahrani
Former Director, Middle Eastern Studies Program, and Professor of Anthropology, Indiana University, Bloomington
Afghanistan; Durrānī Dynasty

Stanford J. Shaw
Professor of Turkish and Judeo-Turkish History, University of California, Los Angeles
Ottoman Empire

Ahmad Shboul
Associate Professor of Arabic and Islamic Studies, University of Sydney
Ṣadr; Taqwā

Nadim F. Shehadi
Director, Centre for Lebanese Studies, Oxford
Zaʿīm

William E. Shepard
Senior Lecturer in Religious Studies, University of Canterbury, Christchurch, New Zealand
Australia and New Zealand; Khalafallāh, Muḥammad Aḥmad; Khālid, Khālid Muḥammad; Nahḍah

Andrew J. Shryock
Adjunct Lecturer in Anthropology, University of Michigan, Dearborn
Shaykh

Sharon Siddique
Director, Sreekumar-Siddique and Co., Pte. Ltd.; Formerly Acting Director, Institute of Southeast Asian Studies, Singapore
Singapore; Women and Social Reform, *article on* Social Reform in Southeast Asia

Peter Sluglett
Associate Professor of History and Director, Middle East Center, University of Utah
Arab Socialism

Charles D. Smith
Professor of Middle East History and Chair, Department of Near Eastern Studies, University of Arizona
Secularism

Jane I. Smith
Dean and Professor of History of Religions, Iliff School of Theology, Denver
Afterlife; Nasr, Seyyed Hossein; United States of America

Amira El Azhary Sonbol
Visiting Assistant Professor of History, Georgetown University
Futūwah; Kāmil, Muṣṭafā; Marāghī, Muṣṭafā al-; Shaltūt, Maḥmūd

Tamara Sonn
Director of International Studies and Associate Professor of Religions, St. John Fisher College, Rochester, New York
Rahman, Fazlur; Tawḥīd

Jay Spaulding
Associate Professor of History, Kean College of New Jersey
Funj Sultanate

R. Marston Speight
Adjunct Professor of Islamic Studies and Christian-Muslim Relations, Hartford Seminary
Ḥadīth

Charles C. Stewart
Professor of History, University of Illinois, Urbana-Champaign
Bakkā'ī al-Kuntī, Aḥmad al-; Mauritania; Popular Religion, *article on* Popular Religion in Sub-Saharan Africa

Astri Suhrke
Director of Research, Chr. Michelsen Institute, Bergen, Norway
Refugees

Denis J. Sullivan
Associate Professor of Political Science, Northeastern University
Maḥmūd, Muṣṭafā; Muslim Brotherhood, *article on* Muslim Brotherhood in Egypt; Muṣṭafā, Shukrī

Marie Lukens Swietochowski
Associate Curator of Islamic Art, Metropolitan Museum of Art, New York
Iconography

Sayyid Muhammad Syeed
Director of Academic Outreach, International Institute of Islamic Thought, Herndon, Virginia
International Islamic Federation of Student Organizations

Joseph S. Szyliowicz
Professor of Middle East Studies, Graduate School of International Studies, University of Denver
Education, *article on* Educational Methods

June Taboroff
Cultural Resource Specialist, Environment Department, The World Bank, Washington, D.C.
Gardens and Landscaping, *article on* Contemporary Forms

Suha Taji-Farouki
Lecturer in Modern Islam and Arabic, Centre for Middle Eastern and Islamic Studies, University of Durham, United Kingdom
Ḥizb al-Taḥrīr al-Islāmī

Seddik Taouti
Former Assistant to the President for Special Assignments in Charge of Assistance to Muslim Minorities, Islamic Development Bank, Jeddah, Saudi Arabia
Cambodia

David Taylor
Senior Lecturer in South Asian Politics, School of Oriental and African Studies, University of London
All-India Muslim League

R. H. Taylor
Pro-Director and Professor of Politics, School of Oriental and African Studies, University of London
Myanmar

Abdulkader I. Tayob
Senior Lecturer in Islamic Studies, University of Cape Town, South Africa
Abū Dharr al-Ghifārī; Muḥammad, *article on* Role of the Prophet in Muslim Thought and Practice; Purification

Joshua Teitelbaum
Research Associate, Moshe Dayan Center for Middle Eastern and African Studies, Tel Aviv University
Ḥusayn ibn ʿAlī

Gustav Thaiss
Associate Professor of Social Anthropology and Chairperson, Department of Anthropology, York University, North York, Canada
Ḥusaynīyah; Rawẓah Khvānī

M. Ladd Thomas
Professor of Political Science, Northern Illinois University
Patani United Liberation Organization

Hanns Thomä-Venske
Commissioner for Migrants and Refugees, Evangelische Kirche in Berlin–Brandenburg
Avrupa Millî Görüş Teşkilatı; Islamic Cultural Centers

Bassam Tibi
Director, Center of International Relations, Georg-August-Universität Göttingen
Authority and Legitimation

Binnaz Toprak
Professor of Political Science, Boğaziçi University, Istanbul
Erbakan, Necmettin; Refâh Partisi

Frances Trix
Assistant Professor of Anthropology, Wayne State University
Bektāshīyah

Christian W. Troll
Professor of Islamic Studies, Pontificio Istituto Orientale, Rome
Āzād, Abū al-Kalām; Christianity and Islam

Elias H. Tuma
Professor of Economics, University of California, Davis
Islamic Chamber of Commerce; Trade

Mete Tunçay
Formerly Associate Professor of Political Theory, Ankara University
Cumhuriyet Halk Partisi; Kemalism

M. Naim Turfan
Lecturer in Politics, IFCOS, School of Oriental and African Studies, University of London
Atatürk, Mustafa Kemal; Ersoy, Mehmed Âkif

A. Üner Turgay
Director, Institute of Islamic Studies, McGill University
Citizenship; Nation

Richard N. Tutwiler
Anthropologist, Farm Resource Management Program, International Center for Agricultural Research in the Dry Areas (ICARDA), Aleppo, Syria
Agriculture

Ahmad Ubaydli
Centre of Middle Eastern Studies, University of Cambridge
Ibāḍī Dynasty; Ibāḍīyah

Bjørn Olav Utvik
Research Fellow, Department of History, University of Oslo
Labor Party of Egypt

Michael K. Vaden
Policy Consultant, The Vaden Group, Vienna, Virginia
Idrīsid Dynasty

Dirk Vandewalle
Assistant Professor of Government, Dartmouth College
Libya

P. S. van Koningsveld
Professor of Islamic Studies, Universiteit Leiden
Islam, *article on* Islam in Europe

Knut S. Vikør
Director, Centre for Middle Eastern and Islamic Studies, University of Bergen, Norway
Mukhtār, ʿUmar al-; Sanūsīyah

John O. Voll
Professor of History, University of New Hampshire
Fundamentalism; Sufism, *article on* Ṣūfī Orders

Fred R. von der Mehden
Albert Thomas Professor of Political Science, Rice University
Indonesia; Sarekat Islam

Peter von Sivers
Associate Professor of Middle Eastern History, University of Utah
Algeria; Islam, *article on* Islam in the Middle East and North Africa; Islamic Salvation Front

Jacques Waardenburg
Professor of Science of Religion, Université de Lausanne
Mosque, *article on* The Mosque in Education; Sunnī Islam, *article on* Modern Sunnī Thought

Āmina Wadūd-Muḥsin
Assistant Professor of Religious Studies, Virginia Commonwealth University
Revelation; Walāyah

Paul E. Walker
Visiting Professor of Islamic Studies, University of Michigan, Ann Arbor
Daʿwah, *article on* Qurʾānic Concepts; Taqīyah

Susan Waltz
Associate Professor of International Relations, Florida International University
Destour; Ḥizb al-Nahḍah

Gabriel R. Warburg
Professor of Middle East History, University of Haifa, Israel
Anṣār; Mahdī, al-Ṣādiq al-; Muslim Brotherhood, *article on* Muslim Brotherhood in the Sudan

William Montgomery Watt
Professor Emeritus of Islamic Studies, University of Edinburgh
Umayyad Caliphate

Earle H. Waugh
Professor of Religious Studies, University of Alberta, Canada
Birth Rites, *article on* Modern Practice; Cirumcision; Names and Naming

Donald E. Weatherbee
Donald S. Russell Professor of Contemporary Foreign Policy, University of South Carolina, Columbia
Darul Islam

Nadine B. Weibel
Researcher, Anthropology of Islam, Société, Droit et Religion en Europe, Centre National de la Recherche Scientifique, Strasbourg
France

Gideon Weigert
Professor of History, Ben Gurion University of the Negev, Israel
Khalwatīyah

Anita M. Weiss
Associate Professor of International Studies, University of Oregon
Women and Social Reform, *article on* Social Reform in South Asia; Women's Action Forum

Bernard G. Weiss
Professor of Arabic and Islamic Studies, University of Utah
Taqlīd

Alford T. Welch
Professor of Religious Studies, Michigan State University
Muḥammad, *article on* Life of the Prophet

Manfred W. Wenner
Professor of Political Science, Northern Illinois University
Yemen

Catherine Wihtol de Wenden
Research Director, Centre d'Études et de Recherches Internationales, Centre National de la Recherche Scientifique, Paris
Union des Organisations Islamiques de France

Joyce N. Wiley
Lecturer in Political Science, University of South Carolina, Spartanburg
Ḥakīm, Muḥsin al-; Khoʾi, Abol-Qāsem

John Alden Williams
William R. Kenan Jr. Professor of Humanities in Religion, The College of William and Mary
Fitnah; Khawārij

John Ralph Willis
Professor of Near Eastern Studies, Princeton University
Tijānīyah; ʿUmar Tal

Rodney Wilson
Reader in the Economics of the Middle East, University of Durham, United Kingdom
Banks and Banking; Economics, *article on* Economic Institutions; Islamic Development Bank; Taxation

Wendy Wilson Fall
Director of Research and Development, Projet de Gestion des Ressources Naturels dans les Systemes Céréalières, Institut Sénégalais de Recherche Agricole, Dakar, Senegal
Niger

S. Enders Wimbush
Senior International Consultant, Runzheimer International, Rochester, Wisconsin
Islam, *article on* Islam in Central Asia and the Caucasus

Stanley Wolpert
Professor of South Asian History, University of California, Los Angeles
Jinnah, Mohammad Ali

Mark R. Woodward
Associate Professor of Religious Studies, Arizona State University
Natsir, Mohammad; Nurcholish Madjid; Popular Religion, *overview article*

Peter Woodward
Senior Lecturer in Politics, University of Reading
Turābī, Ḥasan al-

Imtiyaz Yusuf
Specialist in Islamic Studies, Center for Human Resources Development, Mahidol University, Bangkok, Thailand
Hijrah; Rites of Passage

Iftikhar Zaman
Lahore, Pakistan
Bidʿah; ʿUlamāʾ, *article on* Sunnī ʿUlamāʾ

Dror Ze'evi
Associate Professor of Middle East Studies, Ben Gurion University of the Negev, Israel
Slavery

Farhat J. Ziadeh
Professor Emeritus of Near Eastern Languages and Civilization, University of Washington
Criminal Law; Law, *article on* Sunnī Schools of Law; Uṣūl al-Fiqh

Madeline C. Zilfi
Associate Professor of Middle East History, University of Maryland, College Park
Vizier

Marvin Zonis
Center for Middle Eastern Studies, University of Chicago
Pahlavi, Muhammad Reza Shah

Sherifa Zuhur
Visiting Scholar of Middle Eastern Studies, University of California, Berkeley
Dress; Sexuality; Surrogate Motherhood; Women's Movements

SYNOPTIC OUTLINE OF CONTENTS

The outline presented on the following pages is intended to provide a general view of the conceptual scheme of this encyclopedia. Entries are arranged in the conceptual categories listed below. Because the headings for these categories are not necessarily mutually exclusive, some entries in the encyclopedia are listed more than once.

- History and Geography
- Schools of Thought
- Mysticism
  - Principal Articles
  - Ṣūfī Orders
  - Concepts and Terms
- Religious Belief
- Religious Practice, Devotionalism, Ritual
- Islamic Law
- Theology, Philosophy, Ideology
- Politics
  - Dynastic States
  - Political and Religious Roles
  - Poltical Concepts and Terms
- Economics
- Culture and Society
  - Personal Life
  - Community Life
  - Arts and Literature
  - Science and Medicine
  - Communications Media
  - Popular Religion
- Islamic Studies
- Institutions, Organizations, Movements
- Biographies

HISTORY AND GEOGRAPHY

General Overviews

- Islam
  - An Overview
- Shīʿī Islam
  - Historical Overview
  - Modern Shīʿī Thought
- Sunnī Islam
  - Historical Overview
  - Modern Sunnī Thought

Regional Overviews

- Islam
  - Islam in the Middle East and North Africa
  - Islam in Sub-Saharan Africa
  - Islam in Central Asia and the Caucasus
  - Islam in China
  - Islam in South Asia
  - Islam in Southeast Asia and the Pacific
  - Islam in Europe
  - Islam in the Americas

Middle East and North Africa

- Algeria
- Egypt
- Gulf States
- Iran
- Iraq
- Israel
- Jordan
- Lebanon
- Libya
- Morocco
- Oman
- Saudi Arabia
- Syria
- Tunisia
- Turkey
- West Bank and Gaza
- Yemen

Sub-Saharan Africa

- Cameroon
- Chad
- Djibouti
- Ethiopia
- Gambia
- Ghana
- Guinea
- Mali
- Mauritania
- Niger
- Nigeria
- Senegal
- Somalia
- South Africa
- Sudan
- Tanzania
- Uganda

Central Asia and the Caucasus

- Azerbaijan
- Kazakhstan
- Kyrgyzstan
- Tajikistan
- Turkmenistan
- Uzbekistan

South Asia

- Afghanistan
- Bangladesh
- India
- Indian Ocean Societies
- Kashmir
- Pakistan

Southeast Asia and the Pacific

- Australia and New Zealand
- Brunei
- Cambodia
- Indonesia
- Malaysia
- Myanmar
- Philippines
- Singapore
- Thailand

Europe

- Albania
- Balkan States
- France
- Germany
- Great Britain

Americas

- Brazil
- Canada
- Suriname
- Trinidad and Tobago
- United States of America

Regions and Sites

- Aligarh
- Fez
- Jerusalem
- Kabylia
- Karbala
- Mashhad
- Mecca
- Medina
- Najaf
- Qom

SCHOOLS OF THOUGHT

- Aḥmadīyah
- Akhbārīyah
- ʿAlawīyah
- Bābism
- Bahāʾī
- Barelwīs
- Bohrās
- Deobandīs
- Druze
- Ibāḍīyah
- Ismāʿīlīyah
- Ithnā ʿAsharīyah
- Khawārij
- Khojas
- Shaykhīyah
- Uṣūlīyah
- Wahhābīyah
- Zaydīyah

MYSTICISM

Principal Articles

- Sufism
  - Ṣūfī Thought and Practice
  - Ṣūfī Shrine Culture
  - Ṣūfī Orders

Ṣūfī Orders

- Bayramiye
- Bektāshīyah
- Chishtīyah
- Idrīsīyah
- Khalwatīyah
- Khatmīyah
- Mawlawīyah
- Mevlevî
- Murīdīyah
- Naqshbandīyah
- Niʿmatullāhīyah
- Nurculuk
- Qādirīyah
- Rifāʿīyah
- Sanūsīyah
- Shādhilīyah
- Shaṭṭārīyah
- Tijānīyah

Concepts and Terms
- Barakah
- Dhikr
- Khānqāh
- Mawlāy
- Pir
- Shaykh
- Walāyah
- Zāwiyah
- Ziyārah

RELIGIOUS BELIEF
- Afterlife
- Allāh
- Angels
- ʿAqīdah
- Conversion
- Cosmology
- Eschatology
- Hijrah
- Imāmah
- Īmān
- Jāhilīyah
- Jihād
- Kufr
- Martyrdom
- Messianism
- People of the Book
- Pillars of Islam
- Prophethood
- Qurʾān
  - The Qurʾān as Scripture
- Relics
- Repentance
- Revelation
- Revival and Renewal
- Sainthood
- Satan
- Shahādah
- Sin
- Suicide
- Sunnah
- Tafsīr
- Taqīyah
- Tawḥīd

RELIGIOUS PRACTICE, DEVOTIONALISM, RITUAL
- ʿĀshūrāʾ
- Birth Rites
  - Modern Practice
- Circumcision
- Daʿwah
  - Qurʾānic Concepts
  - Institutionalization
- Dietary Rules
- Dress
- Funerary Rites
  - Modern Practice
- Ḥajj
- Ḥalāl
- Ḥijāb
- Ḥusaynīyah
- ʿĪd al-Aḍḥā
- ʿĪd al-Fiṭr
- Imāmzādah
- Islamic Calendar
- Khuṭbah
- Mawlid
- Miʿrāj
- Mosque
  - Historical Development
- Muḥammad
  - Role of the Prophet in Muslim Thought and Practice
- Muḥarram
- Names and Naming
- Nawrūz
- Puberty Rites
- Purification
- Qurʾān
  - The Qurʾān in Muslim Thought and Practice
- Qurʾānic Recitation
- Ramaḍān
- Rites of Passage
- Sacrifice
- Ṣalāt
- Ṣawm
- Shrine
- Women and Islam
  - Women's Religious Observances
- Zakāt
- Zāwiyah
- Ziyārah

ISLAMIC LAW

Principal Articles
- Law
  - Legal Thought and Jurisprudence
  - Sunnī Schools of Law
  - Shīʿī Schools of Law
  - Modern Legal Reform

Supporting Articles
- Abortion
- Adat
- Ākhūnd
- Anglo-Muḥammadan Law
- Ayatollah
- Bidʿah
- Birth Rites
  - Legal Foundations
- Caliph
- Commercial Law
- Consensus
- Contract Law
- Criminal Law
- Dhimmī
- Family Law
- Faqīh
- Fatwā
  - Concepts of Fatwā
- Funerary Rites
  - Legal Foundations
- Ḥadīth
- Ḥalāl
- Ḥarām
- Ḥudūd
- Human Rights
- Ijtihād
- Imam
- Inheritance
- International Law
- Jihād
- Mahdi
- Maḥkamah
- Marjaʿ al-Taqlīd
- Marriage and Divorce
  - Legal Foundations
- Maṣlaḥah
- Mawlā
- Mecelle
- Muftī
- Mullabashi
- Mullah
- Mutʿah
- Polygyny
- Public Law
- Qāḍī
- Ṣadr
- Shaykh al-Islām
- Tanzimat
- Taqlīd
- ʿUlamāʾ
  - Sunnī ʿUlamāʾ
  - Shīʿī ʿUlamāʾ

BIOGRAPHIES *(cont.)*
ʿAbduh, Muḥammad
Afghānī, Jamāl al-Din al-
Bannāʾ, Ḥasan al-
Fathy, Hassan
Ghazālī, Muḥammad al-
Ghazālī, Zaynab al-
Ḥanafī, Ḥasan
Ḥusayn, Ṭāhā
Ḥuṣrī, Abū Khaldūn Sāṭiʿ al-
Kāmil, Muṣṭafā
Kawākibī, ʿAbd al-Raḥmān al-
Khalafallāh, Muḥammad Aḥmad
Khālid, Khālid Muḥammad
Kishk, ʿAbd al-Ḥamīd
Maḥmūd, Muṣṭafā
Marāghī, Muṣṭafā al-
Mūsā, Nabawīyah
Muṣṭafā, Shukrī
Nāṣif, Malak Ḥifnī
Nasser, Gamal Abdel
Quṭb, Sayyid
Rashīd Riḍa, Muḥammad
Saʿdāwī, Nawāl al-
Shafīq, Durrīyah
Shaltūt, Maḥmūd
Shaʿrāwī, Hudā

France
Arkoun, Mohammed

India
ʿAbd al-ʿAzīz, Shāh
Aḥmad Khān, Sayyid
Ameer Ali, Syed
Āzād, Abū al-Kalām
Barelwī, Sayyid Aḥmad
Burhānuddīn, Sayyidnā Muḥammad
Chirāgh ʿAlī
Fyzee, Asaf Ali Asghar
Iqbal, Muhammad
Mawdūdī, Sayyid Abū al-Aʿlā
Sirhindī, Aḥmad
Walī Allāh, Shāh

Indonesia
Abdurrahman Wahid
Hamka
Natsir, Mohammad
Nurcholish Madjid

Iran
Afghānī, Jamāl al-Din al-
Bāb
Bāzargān, Mehdi
Borujerdi, Moḥammad Ḥosayn
Ḥāʾirī Yazdī, ʿAbd al-Karīm
Kāshāni, Abol-Qāsem
Kasravi, Aḥmad
Khomeini, Ruhollah al-Musavi
Majlisi, Muhammad Baqir al-
Malkom Khān
Muṭahharī, Murtaẕā
Nāʾīnī, Muḥammad Ḥusayn
Nasr, Seyyed Hossein
Nūrī, Faẕlullāh
Pahlavi, Muhammad Reza Shah
Pahlavi, Reza Shah
Sharīʿatī, ʿAlī
Ṭabāṭabāʾī, Muḥammad Ḥusayn
Ṭāleqāni, Maḥmud

Iraq
Dūrī, ʿAbd al-ʿAzīz al-
Ḥakīm, Muḥsin al-
Ḥuṣrī, Abū Khaldūn Sāṭiʿ al-
Khoʾi, Abol-Qāsem
Ṣadr, Muḥammad Bāqir al-

Lebanon
Faḍlallāh, Muḥammad Ḥusayn
Jumblatt, Kamal
Ṣadr, Mūsā al-

Libya
Mukhtār, ʿUmar al-
Qadhdhāfī, Muʿammar al-

Malaysia
Ibrahim, Anwar

Mauritania
Bakkāʾī al-Kuntī, Aḥmad al-

Morocco
Abd el-Krim
Fāsī, Muḥammad ʿAllāl al-
Ibn Idrīs, Aḥmad
Mernissi, Fatima

Nigeria
Dan Fodio, Usuman
Mai Tatsine

Ottoman Empire
Abdülhamid II
Afghānī, Jamāl al-Din al-
Enver Pasha
Ersoy, Mehmed Âkif
Gökalp, Mehmet Ziya
Ḥusayn ibn ʿAlī (Sharif of Mecca)
Ḥuṣrī, Abū Khaldūn Sāṭiʿ al-
Kawākibī, ʿAbd al-Raḥmān al-
Kemal, Mehmet Namık
Said Halim Pasha, Mehmed
Şinasi, İbrahim
Suavi, Ali

Pakistan
Iqbal, Muhammad
Jinnah, Mohammad Ali
Mawdūdī, Sayyid Abū al-Aʿlā
Maryam Jameelah
Rahman, Fazlur

Palestine
Bahāʾ Allāh
Fārūqī, Ismāʿīl Rājī al-
Ḥusayni, al-Ḥājj Amīn al-

Saudi Arabia
Ibn ʿAbd al-Wahhāb, Muḥammad
Saʿūd, ʿAbd al-ʿAzīz ibn ʿAbd al-Raḥmān Āl
Saʿūd, Fayṣal ibn ʿAbd al-ʿAzīz Āl

Senegal
ʿUmar Tal

Sudan
Mahdī, al-Ṣādiq al-
Turābī, Ḥasan al-

Syria
Ḥuṣrī, Abū Khaldūn Sāṭiʿ al-
Rashīd Riḍa, Muḥammad
Sibāʿī, Muṣṭafā al-

Tunisia
Ghannūshī, Rāshid al-

Turkey
Atatürk, Mustafa Kemal
Erbakan, Necmettin
Kısakürek, Necip Fazıl
Özal, Turgut

United States of America
Elijah Muhammad
Fārūqī, Ismāʿīl Rājī al-
Malcolm X
Maryam Jameelah
Nasr, Seyyed Hossein
Rahman, Fazlur

INDEX

N.B.: Volume numbers are printed in boldface type, followed by a colon and relevant page numbers. Page numbers printed in boldface indicate a major discussion.

E

F

G

H

J

N

P

Q

S

T

Printed in the USA/Agawam, MA
November 9, 2012
570268.029